MW01445479

Praise for *The Handbook of Loan Syndications and Trading*

"This handbook is a wealth of important information for all who regularly navigate the U.S. loan market, compiled by some of the industry's leading experts. From the basics of market structure, to some of today's more complex topics, it's all in here."
—**Jeff Bakalar**, Senior Managing Director, Group Head and CIO of Voya Investment Management

"This is a fantastic resource that explains the intricacies of the growing U.S. corporate loan market—from the primary market where the loans are originated to the secondary market where they are actively traded. Everything is explained in one easy to use source."
—**Andrew Sveen**, Vice President of Eaton Vance Managing Director of Morgan Stanley, Director of Bank Loans

"This book captures all the loan market's developments since the Global Financial Crisis—it's an amazing resource for new entrants to the market, seasoned professionals, and investors!"
—**Scott Baskind**, Head of Global Senior Loans and Chief Investment Officer of Invesco

THE HANDBOOK OF LOAN SYNDICATIONS AND TRADING

Second Edition

Editors:

LEE M. SHAIMAN

BRIDGET K. MARSH

Mc Graw Hill

New York Chicago San Francisco Athens London
Madrid Mexico City Milan New Delhi
Singapore Sydney Toronto

Copyright © 2022 by McGraw Hill. All rights reserved. Printed in the United States of America. Except as permitted under the United States Copyright Act of 1976, no part of this publication may be reproduced or distributed in any form or by any means, or stored in a database or retrieval system, without the prior written permission of the publisher.

1 2 3 4 5 6 7 8 9   LCR   27 26 25 24 23 22

ISBN   978-1-264-25852-9
MHID   1-264-25852-6

e-ISBN   978-1-264-25853-6
e-MHID   1-264-25853-4

Library of Congress Cataloging-in-Publication Data

Names: Marsh, Bridget K., editor. | Shaiman, Lee M., editor.
Title: The handbook of loan syndications and trading / edited by Lee M. Shaiman and Bridget K. Marsh.
Other titles: Handbook of loan syndications and trading
Description: 2E [edition]. | New York : McGraw Hill, [2022] | Includes bibliographical references and index.
Identifiers: LCCN 2021033619 (print) | LCCN 2021033620 (ebook) | ISBN 9781264258529 (hardcover) | ISBN 9781264258536 (ebook)
Subjects: LCSH: Bank loans.
Classification: LCC HG1641 .H26 2022 (print) | LCC HG1641 (ebook) | DDC 332.1/753068—dc23
LC record available at https://lccn.loc.gov/2021033619
LC ebook record available at https://lccn.loc.gov/2021033620

McGraw Hill books are available at special quantity discounts to use as premiums and sales promotions or for use in corporate training programs. To contact a representative, please visit the Contact Us pages at www.mhprofessional.com.

McGraw Hill is committed to making our products accessible to all learners. To learn more about the available support and accommodations we offer, please contact us at accessibility@mheducation.com. We also participate in the Access Text Network (www.accesstext.org), and ATN members may submit requests through ATN.

CONTENTS

List of Contributors   ix
Acknowledgments   xiii
Preface   xvii

Chapter 1

An Introduction to the Loan Asset Class   1
Lee M. Shaiman

Chapter 2

The Primary Market   29
Ralph Hinckley, Robert Scheininger, Elizabeth Grzywacz, Jon Mooney, Ellen Hefferan, Steven Miller

Introduction to the Primary Market   31
Information in the Loan Market: Material Nonpublic Information and Confidential Information   59
Settling Primary Allocations   82
Bringing Benchmarks to the Complex Realm of Loan Covenants   100

Chapter 3

Understanding the Credit Agreement 103
Michael Bellucci, Jerome McCluskey

Chapter 4

The Seismic Transition: From LIBOR to a New Reference Rate 295
Meredith Coffey, Tess Virmani

Chapter 5

Loans Are Not Securities 313
Elliot Ganz, James A. Florack, Michael P. Kaplan, Jeong M. Lee, Yoon-Young Lee

Introduction 315
Effects of the Legal Characterization of Loans Under the Securities Laws 316
Some Practical Implications of Treating Loans as Securities 331

Chapter 6

Loan Structures 335
Marc Hanrahan, Benjamin Miles, Michael Price, Benjamin Sayagh, Charles Stern, Paul Forrester, Monique Mulcare

Second Lien Loans 337
Role of Commercial Banks in Project Finance 369

Chapter 7

Loan Trading 383
Fran Sutter, Bridget K. Marsh

Introduction to Loan Trading 385
How to Trade Loans and the Strategies to Use 388

Contents

Chapter 8

The Secondary Loan Market 405
Theodore Basta, Marina Lukatsky, Sheryl Fulton

Overview of the Secondary Loan Market 407
The U.S. Leveraged Loan Market Through the Lens of the S&P/LSTA Leveraged Loan Index 441
The Secondary Loan Market: Settling Loan Transactions 455

Chapter 9

Analytics and Performance 477
Andrew Hosford, Sean Kelley, David Keisman

Portfolio Engineering: Applying Quantitative Tools for Efficient CLO Investment Management 479
Lessons from More than a Trillion Dollars in Defaults 507

Chapter 10

Distressed Loan Investing 527
Jason Friedman, Jeff Jacob, Susan D. Golden, Joshua A. Sussberg, Saul E. Burian, Jessica Reiss

The History of the Distressed Corporate Loan Market 529
Overview of Chapter 11 of the Bankruptcy Code 555
Critical Financial Considerations in Distressed Situations 574
A Closer Look at Provisions Permitting Liability Management Transactions 601

Chapter 11

Overview of Loan Credit Default Swaps and Loan Total Return Swaps 619
John Clark, Jennifer Grady, Richard Lee

Overview of Loan Credit Default Swaps 621
Overview of Bank Loan Total Return Swaps 627

Chapter 12
Loan Fund Portfolio Management 639
Carly Wilson

Chapter 13
Collateralized Loan Obligations (CLOs): A Primer 659
Maggie Wang

Chapter 14
Public Policy and the Loan Market: How the Syndicated Loan Market Is Impacted by Legislation, Regulation, and the Judicial System 703
Meredith Coffey, Elliot Ganz

Chapter 15
The Globalization of the Loan Market 727
Bob Kricheff, Clare Dawson, Sadaf Khan

Non-U.S. Dollar (Non-USD) Syndicated Institutional Leveraged Loan Market 729
The Global Syndicated Loan Market–EMEA 745
The Evolving Asia Pacific Loan Market 753

Chapter 16
Middle Market Lending 767
Fran Beyers

Chapter 17
Private Credit 789
KKR & Co. Inc.

Chapter 18

ESG in the Loan Market   807
Tess Virmani, Swami Venkataraman, CFA, Amara Gossin, Robert Lewis, Maria Christina Dikeos

Introduction   809
ESG Considerations in Credit Analysis   811
Sustainable Lending: Where We Stand as We Enter 2021   828
The Evolution of Sustainability-Linked Lending: Watershed Moments and Expanding Investor Participation   849

Chapter 19

Accounting for Loans   859
Cara Brugel, Chase Hodges, Chris Rogers

Chapter 20

The Loan Market, Blockchain, and Smart Contracts: The Potential for Transformative Change   875
Josias Dewey, Bridget K. Marsh

Glossary of Terms   889
Index   913

LIST OF CONTRIBUTORS

Theodore Basta
Executive Vice President of Market Analytics and Investor Strategy
Loan Syndications and Trading Association

Michael Bellucci
Partner
Milbank LLP

Fran Beyers
Managing Director
Cliffwater, LLC

Cara Brugel
Audit & Assurance Manager
Deloitte & Touche LLP

Saul E. Burian
Managing Director
Houlihan Lokey

John Clark
Senior Counsel
Crowell & Moring LLP

Meredith Coffey
Executive Vice President of Research and Co-Head, Public Policy Group
Loan Syndications and Trading Association

Clare Dawson
Chief Executive
Loan Market Association

Josias Dewey
Partner
Holland & Knight LLP

Maria Christina Dikeos
Head of Global Loans Contributions
Refinitiv LPC

James A. Florack
Partner
Davis Polk & Wardwell LLP

Paul Forrester
Partner
Mayer Brown LLP

Jason Friedman
Partner
Marathon Asset Management LP

Sheryl Fulton
Associate Manager
IHS Markit

Elliot Ganz
General Counsel and Co-Head, Public Policy Group
Loan Syndications and Trading Association

Susan D. Golden
Partner
Kirkland & Ellis LLP

Amara Gossin
Vice President, Legal
Barclays

Jennifer Grady
Partner
Crowell & Moring LLP

Elizabeth Grzywacz
Senior Counsel
PNC Bank, National Association

Marc Hanrahan
Partner
Milbank LLP

Ellen Hefferan
Executive Vice President of Operations and Accounting
Loan Syndications and Trading Association

Ralph Hinckley
Vice President and Portfolio Manager
Eaton Vance Management

Chase Hodges
Senior Manager, Audit & Assurance
Deloitte & Touche LLP

Andrew Hosford
Vice President, Project Manager
U.S. Bank

Jeff Jacob
Partner
Marathon Asset Management LP

Michael P. Kaplan
Partner
Davis Polk & Wardwell LLP

David Keisman
Senior Vice President, Corporate Finance Corporate Defaults and Recoveries–U.S.
Moody's Investors Service

Sean Kelley
Senior Vice President, Head of CLO Data Analytics and Research
U.S. Bank

List of Contributors

Sadaf Khan
Consultant
Asia Pacific Loan Market Association

Bob Kricheff
Senior Vice President and Portfolio Manager
Shenkman Capital

Jeong M. Lee
Partner
Davis Polk & Wardwell LLP

Yoon-Young Lee
Partner
WilmerHale

Richard Lee
Partner
Crowell & Moring LLP

Robert Lewis
Partner
Sidley Austin LLP

Marina Lukatsky
Senior Director
S&P Global Market Intelligence Leveraged Commentary and Data

KKR & Co. Inc.

Bridget K. Marsh
Executive Vice President & Deputy General Counsel
Loan Syndications and Trading Association

Jerome McCluskey
Partner
Milbank LLP

Benjamin Miles
Partner
Milbank LLP

Steven Miller
Chief Executive Officer
Covenant Review, a Fitch Solutions Service

Jon Mooney
Managing Chief Counsel
PNC Bank, National Association

Monique Mulcare
Counsel
Mayer Brown LLP

Michael Price
Partner
Milbank LLP

Jessica Reiss
Head of U.S. Leveraged Loan Research
Covenant Review, a Fitch Solutions Service

Chris Rogers
Partner, Audit & Assurance
Deloitte & Touche LLP

Benjamin Sayagh
Partner
Milbank LLP

Robert Scheininger
Partner
Reed Smith LLP

Lee M. Shaiman
Executive Director
Loan Syndications and Trading Association

Charles Stern
Partner
Milbank LLP

Joshua A. Sussberg
Partner
Kirkland & Ellis LLP

Fran Sutter, CFA
Managing Director, Head of Loan Trading
Citi

Swami Venkataraman, CFA
Senior Vice President and Manager – ESG Analytics and Integration
Moody's Investors Service

Tess Virmani
Associate General Counsel and Executive Vice President, Public Policy Group
Loan Syndications and Trading Association

Maggie Wang
Managing Director, Global Head of CLO and CDO Research
Citi Global Markets

Carly Wilson
Portfolio Manager, Loan Strategies and Global Long/Short Credit Strategies
BlackRock

ACKNOWLEDGMENTS

Sixteen years ago, I helped the Loan Syndications and Trading Association (LSTA) by reviewing articles that had been submitted for the first edition of *The Handbook of Loan Syndications and Trading*. I learned a lot from that exercise. Until then, as a finance attorney, I had not fully appreciated the importance of certain provisions tucked away at the back of every credit agreement nor their significance to the growing loan market. Once I was in-house counsel to the LSTA, those provisions took on a much greater importance to me as I learned more about origination practices, secondary market trading, loan assignments, and the settlement of loan trades.

Perhaps I was an unusual choice—a lawyer—to be an editor of the second edition. Over the past year, I've had the pleasure of working with the book's authors, the majority of whom have not been lawyers, and through the editorial process, I have developed a deeper understanding for other loan market–related (nonlegal) topics such as loan trading strategies, ESG and the loan market, and portfolio management.

The book provides an overview and history of the U.S. loan market. It examines the primary market where loans are originated and the second loan trading market, which continues to break records for trading volumes. It provides insights on trading strategies, portfolio management techniques, and key provisions of credit agreements. It also tackles the latest trends, including the cessation of LIBOR, the emergence of ESG, and the globalization of the loan market.

The first edition was published shortly after the LSTA celebrated its 10th anniversary. The second edition will be published after the LSTA's 26th anniversary. During that time, the LSTA has grown enormously—membership is now close to 600 entities (which includes an impressive 25,000 individuals), although the LSTA, itself, remains streamlined with 16 full-time staff. Together the LSTA staff covers all disciplines within the loan market—the loan origination; trading and settlement of loans; the legal, regulatory, and advocacy side of the loan market; and the market's practices and operations—we cover it all while working to educate our membership on the market, its activities, and trends.

As the loan market has evolved, so too has the LSTA's profile and prominence. Our Executive Director, Lee Shaiman, our General Counsel and Co-Head Public Policy Group, Elliot Ganz, and EVP of Research and Co-Head Public Policy Group, Meredith Coffey, all work to promote the loan market in Washington, DC and may be found, from time to time, in the halls of Congress testifying, educating, and meeting staff there. Ted Basta, EVP of Market Analytics and Investor Strategy, is synonymous with the secondary loan market; he knows everyone and everything about it. My colleague and EVP of Public Policy and Associate General Counsel, Tess Virmani, has worked tirelessly for the past few years on the market's transition away from LIBOR, on the growth of ESG, and of course on her day job involving the LSTA legal work. Ellen Hefferan, EVP of Operations and Accounting, continues tirelessly to fight hard to move the ball forward in the tricky area of loan operations. Lisa Schneider, EVP of Membership, works hard both to grow our membership and keep in contact with our existing members. Together we are a formidable and talented team.

I would like to thank my colleagues for their valuable contributions to the book. Lee has updated the first chapter on the overview of the entire market. Meredith and Elliot have teamed up to write the regulatory chapter. Elliot has written the ever-important "loans are not securities" introduction. Tess has written the ESG introduction. Meredith and Tess together tackled the transition away from LIBOR chapter, and Meredith and Elliot wrote the regulatory chapter. Ted has updated the entire chapter on the secondary loan market and created many charts in this book. Ellen has written the primary market delayed compensation article and been incredibly helpful on the accounting chapter.

Acknowledgments

I would like to thank all my LSTA colleagues for their time, effort, and articles. They have all contributed immensely to the Handbook's successful completion. I would also like to thank all of the authors of the first edition of the Handbook. Some of the articles from that first edition have been used here but all of them have been incredibly useful. Finally, I would like to give a very special thank you to my colleague, Margarita Valdes, Administrative Assistant, who has worked tirelessly with me, the authors, and McGraw Hill to help pull this enormous project over the end line. She is a true professional who has done an excellent job.

Whether you are a newcomer to the market, a seasoned professional, or someone who is merely interested in learning more about the corporate loan market, I hope you find the book a useful guide. Take it, read it, and join us on our quest to continue to make the corporate loan market a fair, orderly, efficient, and growing market.

Bridget K. Marsh
EVP and Deputy General Counsel
Loan Syndications and Trading Association

PREFACE

The corporate syndicated loan market, indeed the entire leveraged finance marketplace, has changed and developed significantly since publication, in 2007, of the first edition of *The Handbook of Loan Syndications and Trading* (the "Handbook"). The syndicated loan market has more than quadrupled in size over nearly 15 years in spite of the Global Financial Crisis (GFC) and COVID-19 pandemic. Today's market is stronger and has more diverse ownership than it ever has had in its history. The investor base still includes the banks and mutual funds, who were early investors, but those early pioneers are overshadowed by collateralized loan obligations (CLOs) and other structured vehicles, pension funds, international banks, insurance companies, sovereign wealth funds, exchange traded funds (ETFs), and hedge funds.

Average leveraged loan issuance over the last 10 years, according to Refinitiv LPC, has been $864 billion, up significantly from the period prior to the GFC of 2008–2009. Recovery from the GFC demonstrated the resilience of the asset class, encouraging investors that the credit risks were reasonable, while low absolute level of interest rates provided further encouragement with significant returns. With overall growth in the market came improvements in trading and liquidity. Total trading volume for 2019 was $743 billion. The pandemic shadowed 2020, but the market still registered $772 billion of loans changing hands, with first quarter volume alone witnessing over $250 billion of trades, as some investors exited risk-based assets and others repositioned portfolios.

The first edition of the Handbook was written over 15 years ago, with the help of nearly 50 participants within the loan market. The Handbook has been a useful tool and reference for financial professionals and students, seeking to understand the many nuances of what was then a relatively new segment of the broader capital markets. Times change, markets develop, documentation evolves, and market practices are refined. The Handbook needed updating to reflect all those trends. With this second edition we are confident that readers will continue to rely on the Handbook as they consider the corporate loan market or look to negotiate its nuance.

THE LSTA

The Loan Syndications and Trading Association (LSTA) was founded by a group of market participants in 1995, over 25 years ago, to advance the interests of the marketplace and to promote the highest degree of confidence for investors in floating rate corporate loans. The LSTA's mission is to foster cooperation and coordination among all loan market participants, facilitating just and equitable market principles, and inspiring the highest degree of confidence among investors in the corporate loan asset class.

FULFILLMENT OF THE LSTA'S MISSION

Loans are not securities! As a result, no single regulatory authority oversees and sets standards on how loans are to be structured, sold, and traded among the various parties and counterparties. Following the GFC, Congress created, through the Dodd-Frank Wall Street Reform and Consumer Protection Act, the Financial Stability Oversight Council within the Treasury Department. The Federal Reserve System, the Office of the Comptroller of the Currency (OCC), and the Federal Deposit Insurance Corporation (FDIC) have regulatory oversight for the banking system. The Securities and Exchange Commission (SEC) has regulatory authority over markets, investment companies, and investment managers. Through joint rule making, these agencies have an ability to regulate the loan market, which, to this writing, has been limited. That said, the development of market standards and documentation has largely been left to the self-determination of the market. The LSTA has since its inception been focused on the consensus building necessary to solving problems, improving market practices, and developing efficiencies that have led to the market's growth.

Today the corporate loan market is well established as a large and mature market. While its growth has been gratifying to the many participants who have dedicated their careers to it, the loan market continues to present many challenges. Its virtue as a flexible provider of capital to help American companies grow is also a principal source of those challenges. Terms and conditions are dynamic, and documentation must accommodate that variability. The flexibility provides further stress on trading, settlement, and liquidity. Structuring, trading, and management of loans and loan portfolios is a specialized area of finance. The LSTA seeks to educate both new investors as well as veterans as we grow the market, streamline processes, improve documentation, and increase the transparency and competence of all market participants.

Lee M. Shaiman
Executive Director
Loan Syndications and Trading Association

CHAPTER 1

An Introduction to the Loan Asset Class

Lee M. Shaiman
Executive Director
Loan Syndications and Trading Association

An Introduction to the Loan Asset Class[1]

Lee M. Shaiman
Loan Syndications and Trading Association

The bank loan asset class has enjoyed significant growth, in issuance by borrowers, and broad acceptance by investors, achieving "core-plus" status within traditional fixed income allocations. In 2007, when the first edition of the *Handbook* was published, corporate bank loans were considered an exotic or alternative asset class, not quite in the mainstream. It is instructive to review the history and unique characteristics of the asset class as a way of explaining how these changes have taken place in the capital markets.

Historically, markets develop at the intersection of supply and demand. Acceptance of higher levels of financial leverage on corporate balance sheets, both by corporate managements and investors, converged with the needs of banks to distribute or syndicate credit risk as a tool to optimize use of bank capital. To meet these diverse requirements, a floating rate, term loan market developed, which, over time, has produced modest, though solid, risk-adjusted returns with lower correlations when compared to other major asset classes.

A SHORT HISTORY OF BANK CREDIT RISK SINCE THE 1980s

Commercial Bank Credit Culture

Pioneering loan market participants learned their craft in highly formalized training programs designed by large commercial banks. Such programs were conducted at great expense to develop hundreds of trainees who learned to evaluate creditworthiness from scores of dedicated instructors. Course materials included an intensive indoctrination in accounting, risk analysis, cash flow

---

[1] We would like to thank Scott Page and Payson Swaffield, authors of "An Introduction to the Loan Asset Class," which was in the first edition of this book. Portions of that article have been used here.

projections, legal ramifications, and many other topics that institutions deemed young analysts must know before being deployed in a lending department of a bank.

Each of these departments created commercial loans, the large majority of which were expected to be held to maturity or repayment by the lending bank. The loans were sometimes syndicated, usually to other banks, and typically through a corresponding banking unit. Such syndication was a laborious and rudimentary process compared to today's practices. Syndicate lenders had no expectation that the loans would trade or even be assigned a market-determined value. Corporate loans are now, and have always been, private, customized contracts between a lender (or lenders) and a borrower. Prior to the advent of a robust syndicated market, banks were expected to hold credit risks on the balance sheet, often with large undiversified exposures, driven by customer relationships, profit centers, excess capital, and other business considerations having nothing to do with portfolio management techniques associated with securities such as stocks and bonds. Despite the best efforts of credit-risk management departments and pedantic credit evaluation, relationship banking has been blamed for repetitive and noteworthy credit debacles in real estate, oil and gas, sovereign debt, and ill-conceived leveraged buyout (LBO) loans. The cumulative effect of such lapses on banking practices and capital created conditions that led to a significant restructuring of bank lending through mergers, consolidations, outright bank failures, and the development of nonbank institutional lending, along with repeal of the Glass-Steagall provisions of the Banking Act of 1933, which separated commercial and investment banking.

High-Yield Bonds Emerge as an Asset Class

Prior to the 1980s advent of the high-yield bond market, underwriting and trading of corporate credit was largely the purview of investment banks and focused on raising money for investment grade–rated transportation, utility, and a few financial corporations. The now defunct Drexel Burnham Lambert started a revolution by trading fallen angels, companies whose credit ratings had fallen from investment-grade to speculative ratings in the late 1970s and early 1980s. Seeing success in secondary trading of these risky credits, investment banks began underwriting new bond issues. The emergence of the high-yield market changed everything, filling a vacuum that had defied nature for far too long. There can be no doubt that the emergence of a robust high-yield market acted as a catalyst for change in corporate finance generally, and for the emergence and growth of the bank loan asset class. Although both asset classes began to grow dramatically into the turn of the next century, by 2013 institutional syndicated loan issuance was eclipsing high-yield bond issuance.

Prior to the formation of the high-yield bond market, credit risk was something to be avoided, not something to be managed. The banking system—investment or commercial—rarely created noninvestment-grade securities. In the case of commercial banks, loans were relationship-driven and held on balance sheets, and no one even considered external ratings profiles or other risk labels. In secondary markets, the noninvestment-grade bonds that did exist were mostly the unfortunate products of downgraded fallen angels to be shunned by the majority of banks and investors. With the growth of the high-yield market, skills learned and honed to avoid credit risk were employed to structure around and manage deep credit risk. Portfolio management tools such as diversification were implemented such that no single credit failure or industry distress would destroy returns.

The Credit Buy-Side Emerges

To our knowledge, the first explicit application of basic portfolio management techniques to credit-risk assets on any scale was performed by Drexel's investor clients: savings and loan institutions; insurance companies; and, most important, the mutual funds that came to dominate the market as consumers of high-yield bonds. Credit portfolio management principles require that credit selection be based on objective credit analysis, and portfolio construction considers diversification by both issuer and industry. High-yield bond investors founded credit-risk portfolio management, creating an investor base, to which the bank loan asset class also appealed. When Drexel unraveled in 1990, most of its competitors rushed, somewhat ironically, to fill the void. Commercial and investment banks recruited teams of former Drexel bankers, establishing or fortifying their own high-yield practices. After a few lean years in the early 1990s, the high-yield bond market recovered from the excesses of the 1980s, and leveraged finance conferences once again filled resort venues as investor interest grew stronger each year.

At many of these conferences, generally taking the form of one or two panels in a small conference room, a market began to gather and take form for *syndicated loans*, in addition to bonds.

LEVERAGED LOANS AS AN INVESTMENT ASSET CLASS

There is no clear history of what single loan, made to which individual borrower, and syndicated to what group of nonbank lenders can lay claim as being first in establishing the syndicated loan market. In truth, capital markets innovations rarely work that way. The spark that ignited today's institutional leverage loan market was generated because it fulfilled multiple aims and goals of its various participants. Borrowers sought flexible term financing for mergers, acquisitions, or general corporate purposes, whereas banks looked to meet their customers' needs while at the same time managing their own risks and the limits of their own capital. Institutional asset managers and their clients were comfortable evaluating and assuming the credit-risk transfer for a short-duration asset that could further limit risk through diversification. It was an idea whose time had come! Institutional investors looked at various investment vehicles and structures to best package loan portfolios in a manner that fit investors' risk appetite. Initially, two broad classes of investors emerged as lenders: structured vehicles, primarily in the form of collateralized loan obligations (CLOs), which are generally sold to institutions, and mutual funds, which were primarily sold to individual investors. By the early 2000s, foundations, endowments, and sovereign wealth funds began to allocate to separately managed accounts or unlisted funds, followed later by public and private pension funds. Managed funds could be structured with or without the use of financial leverage, which increased returns at the cost of some additional risk of loss.

In those early days, there were many challenges to developing and marketing these vehicles beyond the initial group of investors. A principal shortcoming was the limited data available on the risk-and-return profiles of bank loans; the components and structuring features that are taken for granted today were still under development, being tested through educated trial and error. There was no market pricing or pricing service; no standardized settlement procedures, or even documentation; and no agreed-upon procedures for structuring and capitalizing CLOs. Loan trading, when a loan did trade hands, was "by appointment." There were no ratings of bank loan instruments. Many banks that originated loans were wary of the developing market and were at times reluctant to show new investors any loans other than their riskiest, least attractive assets. Borrowers, accustomed to dealing with their bank, or banking relationships, were skeptical of this new class of lender.

As noted earlier, this market developed to serve many needs; the largest and most influential banks recognized the mutual benefit for many parties, not least of which the impact distribution of risk had on the banks' own balance sheets. Banks such as Manufacturers Hanover, Bankers Trust, Chemical Bank, Continental Bank, Chase Manhattan, Citibank, and a number of other important institutions, whose names are today unfamiliar, embraced the development of institutional investor-lenders such as mutual funds and CLOs that provided the balance sheet but did not have, or want, the borrower relationship. With time, new investor-lenders and larger capital pools invested in leveraged loans, and most large banks became confident and more competent, viewing leveraged loans as a capital markets' product, to be distributed to customers, not retained on the balance sheet.

Financial regulations served as another catalyst in the growth of the institutional loan market. In the wake of the 1987 stock market crash and the failure of several highly leveraged companies, Washington pushed regulations limiting the ability of banks to lend in highly leveraged transactions. The so-called HLT regulations of the early 1990s were a reaction by the Federal Reserve Bank to limit commercial bank involvement in the high-yield excesses of the time. The new rules made holding high-yield loans more expensive, in terms of regulatory capital, making it difficult for banks to make and hold such loans. In response, the B term loan was created, a crucial innovation favored by issuers that relaxed the high levels of amortization generally required by commercial banks. Many commercial banks would not, or could not, hold B term loans (due to capital requirements), despite their popularity with borrowers, and this void increased the market's further reliance on nonbank institutional investors, as lenders, to successfully syndicate transactions.

As the 1990s passed, each year saw the development and refinement of the numerous components required for a full institutional asset class. The Loan Syndications and Trading Association (LSTA) was formed as the forum in which important operational and structural issues regarding the loan market—documentation, pricing, trading standards, settlement, etc.—were debated and decided. With time, additional infrastructure developed. The Loan Pricing Corporation, which began providing rudimentary pricing for a select number of issues, refined and built its pricing model in conjunction with the LSTA. As CLOs became important structures for holding loans, rating agencies, agent banks, and issuers slowly embraced the concept of assigning ratings to single-name bank credit risk.

Major commercial banks and investment banks evolved under the forces of changing financial markets, regulations, and macroeconomic forces. The second half of the 1990s witnessed a winnowing of banks as major players merged: New York-based Chemical Bank merged with Manufacturers Hanover, and then with The Chase Manhattan Bank (and later with JP Morgan). Bankers Trust merged into Deutsche Bank. Los Angeles-based Security Pacific Bank and First Interstate Banks, respectively, merged into West Coast rivals, Bank of America and Wells Fargo. Charlotte-based NationsBank acquired Bank of America (changing its name to Bank of America), followed by the merger of its neighbors, First Union and Wachovia. The Global Financial Crisis (GFC) further changed the landscape as JP Morgan absorbed Bear Stearns, Bank of America took over Merrill Lynch, and Washington forced Goldman Sachs and Morgan Stanley to become banks under Federal Reserve control. Throughout this period the syndicated bank loan market sometimes survived, sometimes prospered, but ultimately grew to more than $1 trillion in par value outstanding by 2020.

Risk, Returns, and Bank Loans

Today, as at the beginning, investor and asset allocators have been attracted to leveraged loans based on three key features: seniority, security/collateral, and the floating rate nature of loan returns. The first two components mitigated credit risk, and the third virtually eliminated interest rate risk. Compared to high-yield bonds, another deep credit-risk asset class (instruments that are generally unsecured and that came with fixed interest rates), bank loans exhibit lower risk of loss given default and have virtually no interest rate duration. But the question today is the same as it was in the early days: How much lower risk? After all, leveraged bank loans are, like high-yield bonds, rated noninvestment grade, so how defensive could they be? In the early days, it was hard to say with any precision. Without data, institutional investors mostly shunned the asset class, causing a "chicken-and-the-egg" dilemma that is probably common to all new investment categories. But retail investors, stretching for yield most vigorously, pursued the opportunity through broker-sold mutual funds, not analysis-driven institutional investors, who were limited by lack of data. Twenty years on, several investment cycles have generated reams of data comparing the performance of loans to high-yield bonds and other asset classes. Although loans have generally underperformed high-yield bonds (63% of the time) since 1997 from an annual total return perspective, they have, in fact, been an outperformer during periods of rising interest rates, more of a worry than a fact over the past 20 years. With the growth of the asset class and armed with data supporting loans as a core-plus allocation to fixed income, institutional asset allocators are the dominate end-investor in leveraged loan strategies and through CLO tranches.

Default versus Recoveries

Credit-risk studies by rating agencies and academics primarily focus on one key event: default. Although credit risk can be categorized differently, most credit analysts focus on predictions and probabilities of loss given events of *default*—the inability of a company to meet the terms of its debt obligations. The bursting of the tele-technology investment bubble of the early 2000s and defaults experienced through the GFC provided both the impetus for serious predictive analysis and the data to support it. However, an analysis of recoveries is critical because of the simple equation that credit losses equal the incidence of default multiplied by one minus the recovery rate.

The treatment of the separate phenomena of default and recovery is an issue that rating agencies continue to wrestle with. Until CLOs, with their arcane collateral quality tests, became the dominant holder of senior secured bank loans, few investors really cared if a borrower defaulted as long as the investor recovered all principal and was paid full interest in the process. The degree of added safety, created by seniority and security, was the subject of debate as the asset class took full form. Data tracking recoveries today are generally better than they were for early investors in loans. What defines a recovery remains heavily reliant on investor experience and anecdotes, and definitions often are dictated by intervals or moments in time. The degree of defense offered by a bank loan's seniority, security, and other protective features relies heavily on the loan documentation—the credit agreement—that forms the essential contract between lenders and borrowers. And even then, outcomes are likely to vary based on actions taken and the timeliness of those actions. Early investors in the asset class were experienced in and optimistic about the advantages of seniority and security in default recoveries. Understanding of credit markets and default–recovery cycles has only improved from those early days, and investors have no less reason to remain optimistic about the performance of the loan asset class.

Enterprise Value, Hard Collateral, and Bankruptcy

One of the most significant questions investors in bank loans raise concerns the treatment of senior secured classes in bankruptcy and reorganization. Such treatment in bankruptcy weighs heavily on recovery values and, therefore, investment outcomes. Bankruptcies and out-of-court restructurings are a part of the normal functioning of companies and corporate financial outcomes. The growth in capital available for riskier credits and higher leveraged companies made the likelihood for an increased number of bankruptcies inevitable. The default cycle of the late 1980s produced little transparent information about bank loan default and recovery; nonbank institutional lenders were too few, and banking institutions controlled the workout process and had little reason to publicize discrete information on debt recoveries.

Leveraged lending differed from traditional bank lending in the determination of creditworthiness. Loans were structured as both senior and secured by all, or substantially all, of the borrower's assets, but the amount of credit extended was no longer limited to the value of hard assets—accounts receivable, inventory, property/plant/equipment—but to the more abstract assessment of enterprise value, such as capitalization of cash flow or earnings value. Enterprise value of firms in the growing service economy had never been tested on a large scale as collateral in the courts, particularly from the early 1990s through the first decade of the 2000s. The law gives bankruptcy judges considerable discretion in consideration of this form of collateral. The value of seniority and security in many loan agreements could have been greatly diminished, and the advantages of this asset class would have been diluted. But the law looks for outcomes that favor a way for the concern to reorganize and potentially prosper, setting the stage for enterprise value (or the value of a going concern) to be deemed highly significant in bankruptcy and restructuring situations. Such treatment resulted in better recoveries and greater investor confidence in spite of increased levels of price volatility through time.

RISK AND RETURN IN BANK LOANS: A HISTORICAL REVIEW OF THE NUMBERS

Conclusion: The bank loan asset class has earned its place among investors, serving a core-plus role in fixed income allocations. Its attributes are: modest but solid risk-adjusted yields, lower volatility than high-yield bonds or emerging market debt, and a lower loss-given-default rate when compared to high-yield bonds. Borrowers see virtue in the flexibility and bespoke nature of this privately placed capital source. See Exhibits 1.1 and 1.2.

EXHIBIT 1.1

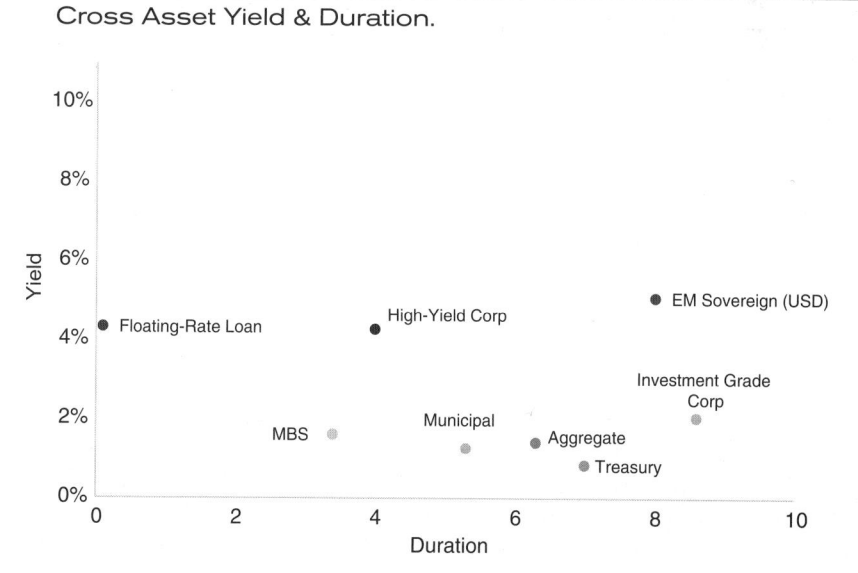

Cross Asset Yield & Duration.

Source: Eaton Vance.

EXHIBIT 1.2

Average 12-month Lagging Standard Deviation of Returns.

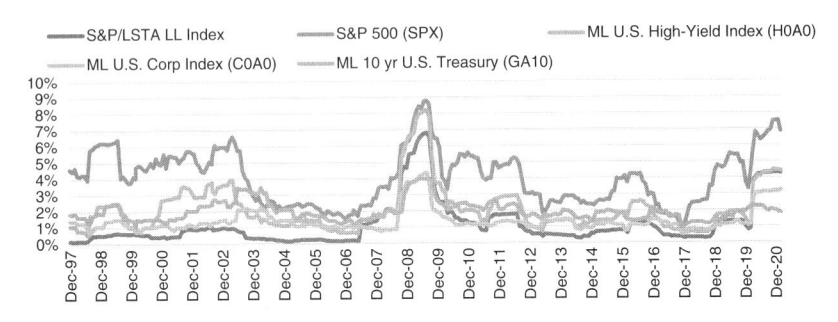

- S&P/LSTA LL Index
- S&P 500 (SPX)
- ML U.S. High-Yield Index (H0A0)
- ML U.S. Corp Index (C0A0)
- ML 10 yr U.S. Treasury (GA10)

Source: S&P Global Market Intelligence.

Conclusion: As an asset class, bank loans have lower correlations with most other major investment asset classes, creating a powerful instrument for dampening volatility in broader portfolios. See Exhibit 1.3.

EXHIBIT 1.3

Bank Loans: Correlation with Other Major Asset Class Indices. 1997—Feb-21

Asset Class	S&P/LSTA LL Index	High-Yield	10yr Treasury	S&P 500	High Grade Corp
S&P/LSTA Leveraged Loan Index	1.000	0.791	-0.358	0.491	0.426
Performing Loans Index		0.785	-0.360	0.489	0.422
ML U.S. High-Yield Index		1.000	-0.175	0.649	0.583
ML 10 yr U.S. Treasury Index			1.000	-0.283	0.555
S&P 500				1.000	0.275
ML U.S. Corp Index					1.000

Source: S&P Global Market Intelligence.

Conclusion: Defaults tend to occur in waves, concentrated with regard to both time and industry, because they usually follow a severe recession. Average default rates are not as meaningful as peak default rates. In general, the episodic nature of credit losses and recoveries wreaks havoc with investment statistics, numbers that require higher-than-normal caution when being interpreted. See Exhibits 1.4 and 1.5.

An Introduction to the Loan Asset Class

EXHIBIT 1.4

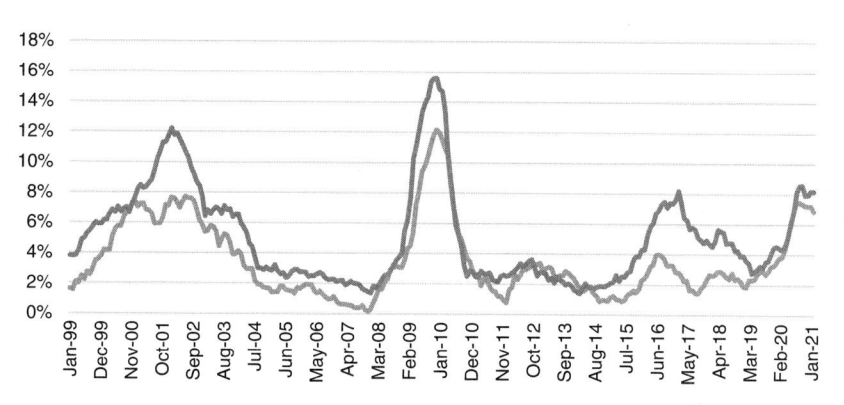

Speculative Grade Issuer Default Rates.

Source: Moody's.

EXHIBIT 1.5

S&P/LSTA Leveraged Loan Index Default Rates.

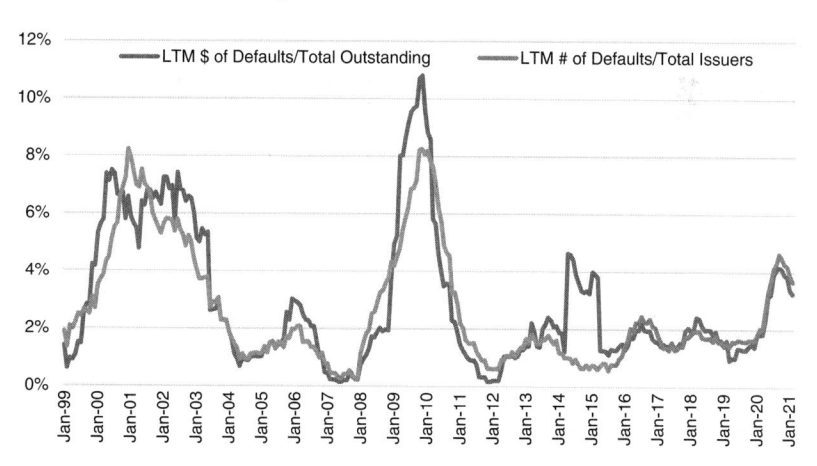

Source: S&P Global Market Intelligence.

Conclusion: Credit spreads in the bank loan market ebb and flow but vary within a much narrower range than spreads in the high-yield bond market. See Exhibit 1.6.

EXHIBIT 1.6

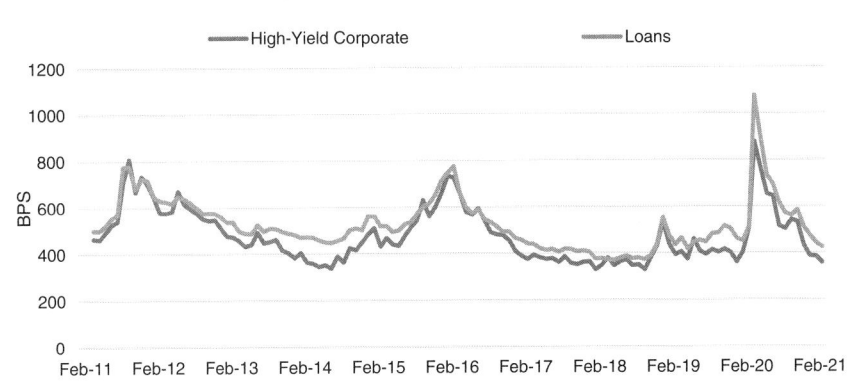

Bank Loan and High-Yield Bond Spreads.

Source: S&P Global Market Intelligence, JPM.

Conclusion: There are numerous ways of measuring and estimating annual credit losses in this asset class. The exact numbers depend on management style and skill, market entry and exit timing, and a number of other factors. When the actual credit experiences of a variety of public mutual fund managers, measured over various periods, are averaged into theoretical estimates from rating agency default/loss data and idealized loss studies, we believe that the best overall average estimate is approximately 60 basis points of annual credit loss. Variations from this point estimate can be considerable, driven most powerfully by market timing and investment style, but this estimate provides a starting point on which to base expectations. Of course, the future could be very different, but that's the basic experience so far.

Observation: The advantages of seniority and security are significant, but the statistics supporting this conclusion are weak. We have seen all kinds of numbers over the years, but reliability is difficult given measurement errors, apples and oranges-type data sets (e.g., senior secured securities, such as first mortgage bonds, versus senior secured bank loans), varying definitions of recovery, and other suspicious flaws in data. There may be clean numbers out there, but from what we have found thus far the results are inconclusive. We have seen some studies that claim that recoveries are 100% and others that claim 50%. Based on our experience, we believe that senior secured recoveries applicable for the relevant range of bank debt used in most mutual funds and CLOs vary between 60% and 80%, with the best estimate of recoveries through a full cycle being approximately 70%.

Observation: Default probabilities increase geometrically as ratings decline into B/B2 and B/B3 territory (or further), and generally there is not sufficient additional coupon to compensate for the much higher default risk *unless* (1) recoveries in the event of default are strong and/or (2) investors hang tight through a downturn to experience the rebound on the other side. Interpreting the data supporting this observation is complex, and this is perhaps the most central debate among investors in all high-yield instruments (both bonds and bank loans). It is beyond the scope of this section to resolve this debate, other than to point out our belief that in the bank loan universe, at the very least, enhancing stability achieves more than chasing yield. Most investors prefer the rolling, gentle, more predictable statistical topography of the more stable end of the bank loan asset class than the sudden, sharp peaks and valleys of the more aggressive end. But the debate is a worthy one, and in the end it remains a matter of investor preference. A talented credit manager or an investor with market-timing skills and some guts can do well in the riskiest loans, evidenced perhaps best by the very strong results experienced by distressed bank loan investors in 2009.

Observation: Various investment managers with public track records have approached this asset class quite differently, with results that vary widely. In the mutual fund arena, defensive managers who have moderate volatility relative to the index have better long-term results on a risk-adjusted basis. Mutual funds experience withdrawals during market declines, and aggressive funds that perform poorly in bear markets experience greater withdrawals. These withdrawals can negatively affect an investor's experience through the usual whipsaw of buy high and sell low. See Exhibits 1.7, 1.8, 1.9, and 1.10.

EXHIBIT 1.7

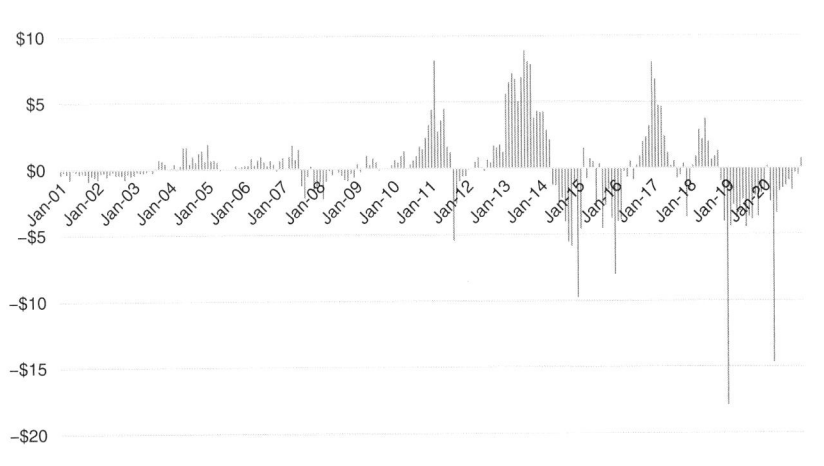

Loan Mutual Fund Flows ($ Billions).

Source: Refinitiv LPC, Lipper.

EXHIBIT 1.8

CLO Issuance ($ Billions).

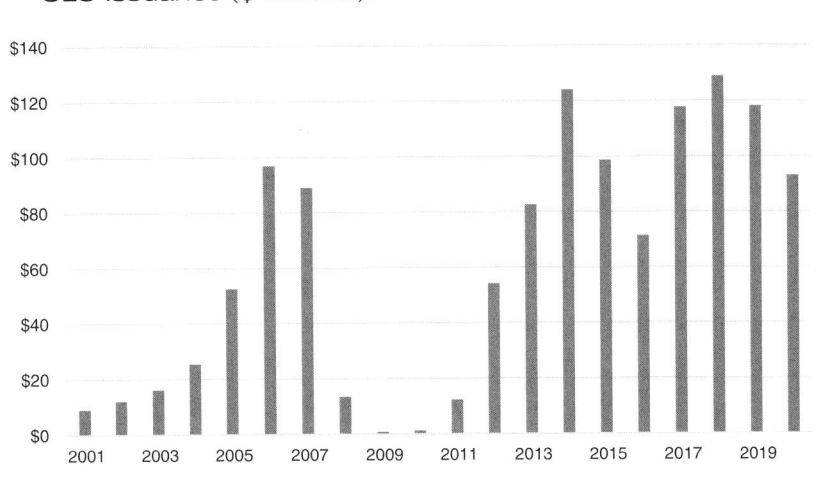

Source: LPC Collateral.

Observation: The measurement techniques used by Lipper and Morningstar in the mutual fund arena, which highlight returns more clearly than risk, may push managers into taking greater credit risks. The episodic nature of credit risk, with short but intense down cycles and declining mutual

An Introduction to the Loan Asset Class

EXHIBIT 1.9

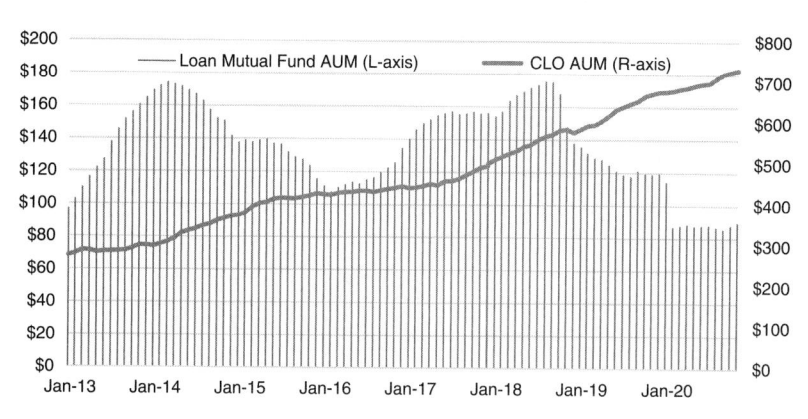

CLO & Loan Mutual Fund AUM ($ Billions).

Source: Refinitiv LPC.

EXHIBIT 1.10

S&P/LSTA Leveraged Loan Index Outstandings ($ Billions).

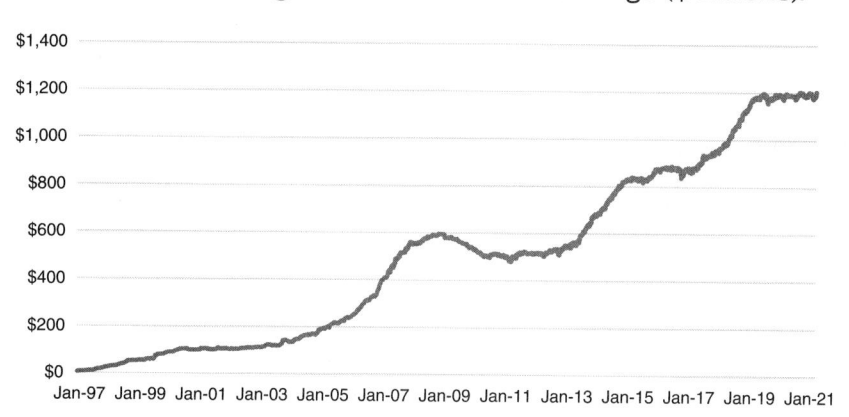

Source: S&P Global Market Intelligence.

fund net asset values (NAVs), combined with the usually much longer bull or calm portions of the credit cycle, has a tendency to tempt many risk managers to take on greater risks. In other words, credit conditions are typically stable most of the time, and a manager will seek to gain yield and total return by taking on more risk, even unreasonable risk, which will move the manager up in Lipper's quintile

EXHIBIT 1.11

Investor Share of Institutional Loan Outstandings.

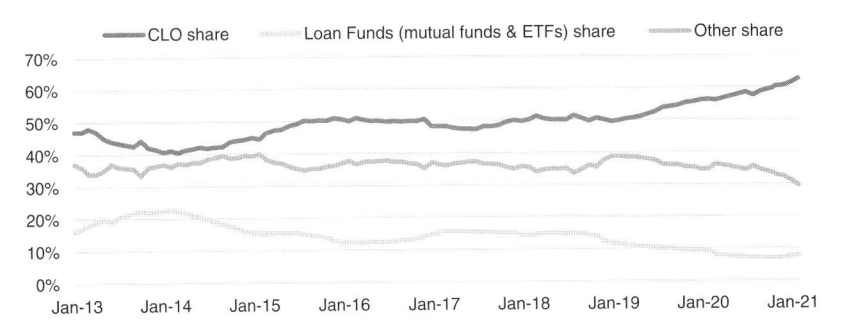

Source: LPC Collateral, Refinitiv LPC, Lipper.

rankings and gain Morningstar stars. These rankings will face sharp reversals during credit downturns, and some investors will suffer even more because of the whipsaw effect of fearfully withdrawing funds at market bottoms.

Observation: CLOs are generally structured to survive market declines, and most of them survived the sharp downturn in 2001 and 2002, as they did again following the GFC of 2008–2009 and the COVID-19–induced recession of 2020. Because investors cannot withdraw funds from CLOs during market declines unless structures are breached—a rare occurrence—and because CLOs are a significant and growing percentage of the asset class, the presence of CLOs is a stabilizing influence on the asset class, particularly during market declines. See Exhibit 1.11.

RISK AND RETURN IN BANK LOANS: THE NARRATIVE

The economic development of nearly every major civilization—east, west, north, or south—has depended on a form of lending practices to provide capital to business and agriculture. During the Renaissance era in Europe, informal practices developed into more complex banking systems, first in Italy as banks fueled the growth of the first mercantile societies of Western Europe. It is no surprise, then, that the advantages of seniority, security, flexible terms, and the floating rate interest profile proved attractive to borrowers and institutional lenders, whose end-investors are nonbank institutions and individuals. Although leveraged lending carries greater credit risk than lending to investment grade–rated borrowers, the asset class has proven to be attractive, especially when compared to high-yield bonds. The asset class has survived and thrived through several trials through the mid-1990s, several industry-specific downturns through the early 2000s, during the GFC of 2008–2009, and again during the early months of the COVID-19 pandemic in 2020.

The Timeline of Risk and Return in Bank Loans

The early 1990s were characterized by high interest rates and a number of lagging credit defaults resulting from credits weakened by the late 1980s LBO binge. Most of the ensuing credit losses were suffered by banks, the institutional market not yet having developed to hold significant exposures to those troubled companies. Subsequently, regulatory restrictions limiting exposure to HLT lending and other excesses having passed to history, credit defaults were extremely low, and the period proved an attractive one for nascent bank loan investors. The slow and relentless decline in interest rates, which progressed in fits and starts across the decade, although attractive to borrowers, made investing in loans somewhat unattractive when compared to fixed rate bonds. (Loan returns are a function of a base interest rate, initially a published bank prime rate, "Bank Prime" or "Prime," and later the London Interbank Offered Rate [LIBOR], plus a credit spread. In those early years the base rate comprised more than half the total return available from a loan.)

A global boom in new and capital-intensive telecommunications and technologies businesses intersected with yield-hungry investors, fueling a new bubble beginning in the late 1990s. Investors were willing to obtain large exposures to credits with great long-term promise but no available, or often negative, cash flow and overstated collateral valuations. Enthusiastic lending to fiber-optics and Internet strategies fueled overbuilding of infrastructure to the point of excess capacity, making debt service, let alone repayment, impossible. True to Murphy's law, which states that anything that can go wrong will go wrong, overextended emerging markets in Asia and Latin America began suffering large defaults. Soon easy credit terms were responsible for overcapacity in other capital-intensive sectors such as nursing homes and hospitals, adding to investor woes. By early 2001, overleveraged technology and telecommunications companies began defaulting in significant numbers on bonds and loans, creating a default–loss cycle larger than anything seen since the Great Depression. This difficult period was followed quickly by large fraud-related defaults, most of which were by investment-grade companies (Enron, WorldCom, and so on), that tested liquidity across debt markets and compounded the difficulties created by the technology and telecommunications defaults.

The First Credit Test

The technology crash of 2000 is mostly viewed as the bursting of a stock market bubble, which was true: the Nasdaq composite stock market index lost 78% of its peak valuation by October 2002. But, with increasing defaults, this period was also the first real test for the bank loan market, which this time was dominated by mutual funds and CLOs. Loan losses piled up and the loan mutual funds most aggressively positioned, particularly with tele-tech exposures, had the largest NAV declines and experienced the largest withdrawals. Still, even the most aggressively positioned bank loan funds suffered significantly lower losses than those experienced by high-yield bond funds. More conservatively managed funds weathered the downturn with positive total returns throughout.

CLO vehicles, though 8 to 12 times leveraged, are also required to be highly diversified, and so largely survived the downturn. Although market-value funds experienced some instability as the market struggled to find levels at which to price risk during the cycle, cash flow CLOs that did not have market-value tests survived the period. The strength of CLOs during this period stood in stark contrast to the experience of investors in collateralized bond obligations (CBOs), vehicles that invested primarily in high-yield bonds. CBOs were not structured to survive a severe credit downturn, and many did not. Those that survived did so with significant damage to investors. Similar experiences played out broadly during the GFC, where both market and corporate liquidity, or lack of it, played a broader role. Market-value CLOs became a victim of the extreme loan price volatility suffered through the GFC.

The Rebound of 2003

Following the downturn, 2003 was an extraordinary year in the bank loan market. Although many of the technology and telecommunication loans created realized losses that would never be recovered, the overall market, which had traded down in sympathy, did recover. Aggressively positioned bank loan mutual funds, many of which became even more aggressive as they met redemptions, snapped back and provided annual returns in 2003 that in some cases exceeded 20%. More conservatively positioned funds enjoyed less robust snapbacks, but they had not experienced as much of a decline in 2001 and 2002. Perhaps the most important development during the 2001–2003 period was the success of investors in distressed bank loans. Distressed loan investors, through dedicated private funds or general credit hedge funds, were aggressive buyers of senior secured bank loans during 2001 and 2002, and their investments provided a handsome return during 2003. These funds bet on the advantages of seniority and security, and these successful and often debt-financed bets were the cornerstone of many of the legendary hedge fund returns experienced in 2003. It was hoped that the success enjoyed by distressed investors coming out of the dotcom bust would be reflected in better secondary market support for bank loans during the next credit decline; it didn't work out that way the next time.

The Global Financial Crisis (GFC) of 2007–2008

The causes of the GFC of 2007–2008 have been well covered, and there is little debate that, once again, plentiful credit and relaxed lending standards, this time centered in housing markets, were the initiate of what became a multinational financial crisis and the deepest economic recession since the Great Depression of the 1930s.

By the summer of 2007 financial markets around the world were showing signs that a reckoning was in process. Less than a year later several major financial institutions had failed or were forced to merge with better capitalized institutions. What began as problems in housing and real estate finance quickly spread and began to choke credit across the global financial system. In leveraged finance markets, high-yield bond spreads widened, pulling loan credit spreads with them, and average bid prices of loans fell below 90. Daily liquid loan mutual funds experienced demands for redemptions as investors exited risk-based assets such as leveraged loans. Loan performance following the rebound from the tele-tech bust discussed earlier, encouraged hedge funds, using prime leverage to enhance returns, to become significant investors in loans, and they were forced to post additional collateral or sell-out positions against margin calls. Although most CLOs had long-term capital, a bull-market creation known as the market-value CLO failed leverage tests, and those CLOs were forced to sell into a collapsing market. This was the final straw for the market-value CLO. New CLO creation became impossible as structured finance investors, typical investors in the senior CLO tranches, were suffering losses in residential mortgage-backed securities (RMBS), commercial mortgage-backed securities (CMBS), and mortgage and other subprime collateralized debt obligations. At the center of this whirlwind were the banks, investment banks, insurance companies, and other systemically important financial institutions. Many of these banks had further extended already stressed balance sheets by originating firmly underwritten commitments to large leverage buy-out transactions. Loans backing these LBOs were intended to be distributed to the very mutual funds, hedge funds, and CLOs that were now net-sellers into a declining market. The financial crisis quickly turned into an economic crisis as job losses and foreclosures mounted. The Federal Reserve Bank had to step in, shoring up money markets as a liquidity crisis began to develop. Loan investors saw prices of par loans of performing credit trade into the low 60s as the once stable asset class suffered enormously from volatility and loss of investor confidence.

Economic Recovery and a Way Forward

The financial crisis and ensuing economic recession were so pervasive that central banks globally stepped in, expanding their own balance sheets to liquefy a frozen market. But the damage was so deep that central banks alone proved inadequate to the scope of the task and were joined by the full force of governments. In the United States the Federal Reserve Bank ("the Fed") responded beginning in early 2008 with a two-track effort to support market liquidity and function and pursue macroeconomic objectives through monetary policy. The Fed expanded its balance sheet through a number of programs, but neither leveraged loans nor CLO liability tranches were eligible for acquisition by any of those programs.

Loan markets continued to suffer through most of 2008, ending the year at an average bid price of 64 with a bid/offer spread of 315 basis points. Loans closed 2008 with the S&P/LSTA Leveraged Loan Index (LLI) declining a record 29.1% on the year, the first negative return year for the asset class. A recovery in the loan market was to be dependent on broader financial and economic recovery. The conventional view held that such recovery could not happen until governments intervened with stimulus and support. In the United States taxpayers stepped up in late 2008 with a $168-billion stimulus package in the form of the Economic Stimulus Act of 2008, and again with the Emergency Economic Stabilization Act of 2008, which included the $700 billion in funding for the Troubled Assets Relief Program (TARP). Further economic stimulus came in early 2009 with passage of a $787-billion package called the American Recovery and Reinvestment Act. The impact of all these programs began to take effect as the economic recession officially ended in the second quarter of 2009. By April, the secondary loan market broke through following on gains made earlier in the year. Distressed and opportunistic investors began to selectively buy loans, and secondary loan volumes increased by nearly 25% measured against trading volumes recorded in the first quarter. Importantly, bid/offer spreads, a measure of market liquidity, narrowed considerably.

The credit arms of several large private equity firms raised multibillion-dollar pools of capital among their base of mostly institutional limited partners (LPs) aimed at acquiring large pools of heavily discounted loans, particularly loans made as commitments to those large LBOs that remained on the balance sheets of many banks.

It has been well documented that the economic recovery was a long and shallow slog, likely the shallowest, in terms of gross domestic product (GDP) growth rates, on record. Recovery in terms of market prices, trading volumes, and ultimately the return of significant levels of primary issuance was reflective of general economic conditions. For the loan asset class, a number of specific challenges needed to be overcome for the market to return to prosperity. Among them were the steep decline of prices in the secondary market; the concomitant decline in net assets allocated to loan strategies; the volume of rating downgrades, bankruptcies, and financial restructurings, and the impact of those actions on CLOs in particular; and the overhang of loans held by banks and other opportunistic or nontraditional holders; to name a few.

The continuation of the Federal Reserve's low interest rate policy, called quantitative easing, served to reduce investor interest in loans through much of the period as interest rates remained near zero for much of the elongated recovery. Likewise, recovery in CLO issuance rates proceeded slowly in 2010 and 2011 as the Nationally Recognized Statistical Rating Organizations (NRSROs) revamped and reevaluated CLO structure and criteria into what became commonly referred to as CLO 2.0.

Regulation of the Syndicated Loan Market

As we will discuss in a later chapter, significant legislation directly affecting loans and the loan market was passed into law in the wake of the GFC. In 2010, as the economy generally and loan market returns and conditions were improving, Congress passed the Dodd-Frank Wall Street Reform and Consumer Protection Act (Dodd-Frank). Two parts of Dodd-Frank, Section 619, often referred to as the Volcker Rule, and Section 941, the Risk Retention Rule, weighed heavily on the loan market's continued recovery. Since the New Deal, Congress had increasingly delegated significant authority to federal regulatory agencies in interpreting laws. Few pieces of legislation have vested greater powers of interpretation and implementation of financial regulation than has Dodd-Frank. The banking agencies along with the Securities and Exchange Commission imposed significant restrictions and obligations on loan market participants that had very material implications for the syndicated loan market. The regulators released rules implementing Volcker that impacted CLOs, specifically dictating how they were to be organized and the composition of underlying assets, and at the same time issuing leveraged lending guidance that appeared to change lending standards. It is interesting to note that the most significant result of the 2013 guidance was to accelerate the growth of direct lending by institutions organized on an asset management model rather than on a banking model. Ultimately, the most restrictive provisions imposed on the loan market by the 2013 agency guidance were overturned by challenges from Congress itself. The Risk Retention Rules, which equated CLO management to sponsorship, thus requiring the manager/sponsor to hold a portion of the CLO risk (through ownership of a portion of its capitalization) was successfully challenged by the LSTA and overturned by the DC Circuit Court of Appeals. Congress rebuked the administrative branch for its overzealousness in attempting to enforce leverage lending guidance as a rule without properly seeking approval from the legislative branch; the agencies demurred, restating that guidance was guidance and would not be strictly enforced.

COVID-19 and the Pandemic Recession

By late 2019, the loan market was already experiencing a peaking bull market for loans. Performance of the S&P/LSTA LLI remained positive, having returned 3.12% for the full year with a market par value of $1.2 trillion. While macroeconomic trends were pointing to a cooling of the U.S. economy, and the Fed took a pause in recent moves to tighten monetary policy, the economy was still robust. By January 2020, interest rate expectations were flat to slightly lower, causing some investor interest in floating rate loans also to cool. News of the spread across Asia and some early reported cases of a "new strain" of SARs virus was causing ripples across global financial markets. Stock markets experienced reversals in mid-February, and by March the loan market, along with other risk assets, was in full retreat as mutual fund and exchange traded fund (ETF) investors liquidated positions for the "safety of cash." As the sell-off accelerated, dealers performed a yeoman's service in matching sellers with buyers, albeit at declining prices, but meeting the liquidity needs of panicked investors. Prior to the sell-off, loans were trading in a mid-97 context at the beginning of March, after suffering a 150-basis point decline during the last week of February. But by mid-March, the secondary loan market traded down to levels not seen since the height of the GFC. From March 16th through the 23rd, trade prices fell an additional 14 points, to a sub-78 context, before rallying back to the high 80s by the months end. Total secondary trading volume for March was a record $119 billion. Loan settlement times, always a point of contention in the loan market, actually compressed as operations groups, largely working remotely or from home, were the unsung heroes as the market cleared tens of thousands of individual trades, expeditiously providing settlement liquidity for redeeming funds.

The voluntary lockdown of the broad economy, globally, immediately moved the economy from prosperity to recession. The closing of national borders and curtailment of domestic travel quickly impacted airlines, tour, travel, and hospitality industries. As the virus spread, hospitals and healthcare facilities were cleared of profitable elective surgeries and other procedures to create capacity for gravely ill victims of the virus. Credit concerns dominated the market, accelerating selling and further depressing asset values. The NRSROs very quickly began to downgrade the credit ratings of hundreds of borrowers in the leveraged loan markets. These downgrades took an air of procyclicality in that they immediately impacted CLO collateral quality tests, increasing CCC-rated assets above threshold levels and causing collateral managers to reduce risk or deleverage structures by either selling low-rated assets at a loss or diverting income, expected to be distributed to tranche holders, to acquiring additional assets.

Both the Fed and Congress stepped in quickly, first to support market liquidity needs, and then to provide financial support to employees and businesses where revenues had dried up and payrolls could not be met. On March 27, 2020, then-President Trump signed the Coronavirus Aid, Relief, and Economic Security Act (CARES Act), injecting a historic $2.2 trillion of economic stimulus into the economy.

Through the CARES Act, Congress directed the U.S. Treasury to fund programs such as the Paycheck Protection Program (PPP) through the Small Business Administration and the Main Street Lending Program (MSLP) through the Fed to provide loans and grants to businesses in need of emergency capital. In most cases the programs created under the CARES Act were designed not to support large and mid-cap leveraged businesses. The immediate effect of the CARES Act was to provide a psychological salve to panicked financial markets, and the PPP program quickly provided cash to small businesses and select nonprofits sufficient to meet some payroll and other expenses. The $600-billion MSLP, like the PPP, was structured not to support the type of companies that were traditional borrowers in the leveraged loan market. Although some business types, such as some fast-food and casual-dining franchisees, were able to access PPP, most borrowers in the leveraged loan market were not directly assisted by the stimulus and support programs. Nonetheless, the CARES Act and other programs, such as the Term Asset Leverage Facility, stood up by the Fed provided a strong underpinning for financial markets that ultimately provided investor confidence, renewed liquidity, and prompted general price recovery that accelerated through the first quarter of 2021, even while the pandemic continued its disruptive effect on commerce.

The Current Market

Bank loans, as an investible asset class, survived both the GFC of 2007–2008 and the COVID-19 epidemic. Although the pandemic and the attendant societal restrictions on commerce have stressed corporate credit across most industries, economic stimulus and plentiful liquidity have both helped to keep borrowers solvent. These same forces have pushed yield-seeking investors to reconsider leveraged finance, concluding, based on fund flows, that risks and rewards are balanced. The S&P/LSTA LLI, as measured in par outstanding, was larger than the ICE BofA US High Yield Index. Even though we have witnessed several significant periods of price volatility and credit concerns, including increased bankruptcies and lower recoveries, investors continue to see loans as a core-plus asset serving a specialized supporting role in the fixed income portfolios of institutional and individual investors. Sharpe ratios after the GFC and COVID-19 are not as compelling as they once were, and correlations with other assets, particularly during periods of global panic, are far more correlated. Bank loans serve a useful role by driving risk-adjusted returns and reducing exposure to volatile interest rates. A broader number of institutions, particularly long-term investors such as pensions, endowments, and sovereign wealth funds, have taken notice, and have increased their exposure to this investment class through CLOs, other leveraged vehicles, and separately managed accounts. An increasing portion of that investor base is also making the trade-off between liquid credit strategies, choosing to allocate toward direct lending. Although retail investors, mostly investing through mutual funds and ETFs, have maintained their interest in this asset class, inflows and outflows have been more volatile. Daily liquid mutual funds, which dominated the nascent loan market, as of this writing, represent significantly less than 20% of all institutional investors.

Increased acceptance of bank loans has come at a cost, however. Spreads today have narrowed across the risk spectrum and are at historic lows. Although spreads now are only modestly below the levels experienced during the early and mid-1990s, they are significantly below the unusually wide spreads seen during earlier periods. Even more concerning has been the continued degradation of other terms and conditions or protective covenants in modern loan documentation. Although loans remain senior and secured, the relaxation of restrictions on the borrower as well as the reduction of remedies available to lenders have led to abuses and increased concerns over recoveries in the event of default. Although it may be difficult to distinguish the normal ebb and flow of both monetary and nonmonetary terms through a credit cycle from a potential secular decline in such terms caused by greater familiarity with and interest in the asset class, there is probably an element of the latter. Once again, investment managers' ability to draw the line on risk is likely to be tested, and those results and additional lessons will be learned in the next credit cycle.

CHAPTER 2
The Primary Market

Introduction to the Primary Market

Ralph Hinckley
Vice President and Portfolio Manager
Eaton Vance Management

Information in the Loan Market: Material Nonpublic Information and Confidential Information

Robert Scheininger
Partner
Reed Smith LLP

Elizabeth Grzywacz
Senior Counsel
PNC Bank, National Association

Jon Mooney
Managing Chief Counsel
PNC Bank, National Association

Settling Primary Allocations

Ellen Hefferan
Executive Vice President of Operations and Accounting
Loan Syndications and Trading Association

Bringing Benchmarks to the Complex Realm of Loan Covenants

Steven Miller
Chief Executive Officer
Covenant Review, a Fitch Solutions Service

Introduction to the Primary Market[1]

Ralph Hinckley
Eaton Vance Management

In the primary market for syndicated loans, issuers and investors come together to price, structure, and invest in one of the oldest of financial instruments—bank loans. Although parts of the loan market have evolved significantly over the past few decades and now resemble the markets for other fixed income products more closely, the primary market for syndicated loans retains some unique attributes that are distinct from those of other debt markets. Some of those distinguishing attributes are set forth here:

- *Flexible structuring.* Loans remain one of the most customized credit products in the capital markets, with highly negotiated packages of covenants and other structural elements. Arrangers compete by creating unique structures, and investors are willing to accept these unique structures as long as they believe that the structures represent an acceptable risk. The primary market for loans accommodates this structural flexibility with highly negotiated term sheets and documentation.
- *Revolving loans.* Unlike other fixed income markets, the loan market as a whole remains heavily weighted toward revolving loans. Nearly every company has at least some amount of unfunded revolving loan in its capital structure that allows it to manage the fluctuations in its cash levels caused by working capital and other needs. The need to accommodate requirements for revolving credit is a structural challenge that is unique to the loan market.
- *Floating rate/callable.* Loans are generally floating rate instruments, and as such do not have the interest rate and inflation risk inherent in fixed rate debt. In addition, because loans are priced on a floating rate basis, generally at a spread over the 30- to 90-day London Interbank Offered

---
[1] We would like to thank Barry Bobrow, Mercedes Tech, and Linda Redding who were the authors of this article as it appeared in the first edition. It has been updated here.

Rate (LIBOR) index, loans do not have the same prepayment breakage costs as fixed rate debt, where pricing is based on longer-term Treasury rate indices. For this reason, loans are generally callable at par at any time. Most loans feature soft call protection, which features the payment of a fee, typically 1%, if the loan is refinanced at a lower spread above LIBOR within the first 6 to 12 months of the life of the loan. This is still very different from the bond market, where the debt generally has a lengthy noncall period and prepayment penalties designed to discourage early termination.

- *Relationship underpinnings.* Much of the loan market is still made up of relationship-oriented banks making loans to their corporate clients and may or may not hold those loans on their balance sheets (in the leveraged loan market, the banks arrange but typically do not hold the loans on their own balance sheets). Because corporate issuers expect their core relationship banks to provide credit in order to be eligible to provide other products, banks are critical investors in the loan market. This is in contrast to other fixed income markets, where investment decisions are made purely on a risk-and-return basis, and issuers are not reliant on their investors for other financial services.

- *Public and private markets.* Investors may participate in the market on a public basis or a private basis, with an increasing number of institutional investors participating in the loan market on a public basis. Private-side investors in the loan market receive more information than is typically available for public securities, including detailed historical analysis and projections. Private investors are not permitted to actively trade other securities of the issuer while they are in possession of the private offering materials. In addition, the principal regulatory oversight comes from bank regulators such as the Office of the Comptroller of the Currency. There is no direct Securities and Exchange Commission (SEC) regulation, because bank loans are not securities.

LOANS: A BRIEF HISTORY

Until the mid-1980s, loans to corporate borrowers were made almost exclusively by banks. These loans held the first-priority position in the issuer's capital structure, and the credit exposure represented by the loans formed the cornerstone of the broader banking relationships between banks and their clients. These credit facilities were used for a wide range of corporate purposes, including the financing of working capital, capital expenditures, and acquisitions, and as backstops for commercial paper programs. Banks tended to hold the entire loan for their own account, and in those rare situations where they needed to limit their credit exposure to a particular borrower, they typically contacted other banks to share the loan with them. The process of forming a syndicate of lenders at that time was relatively informal and completely opaque to public view. Hold levels were high, trading was nonexistent, and loans were not viewed as a financial market instrument. There were none of the features typically associated with a primary market, such as information memoranda, a sales/marketing process, credit ratings, and secondary market trading. The clear delineation between arrangers and investors that we see today did not exist, because most banks played both roles, as necessary. Public data on the size of the loan market or the relative position of the various players were not available. Similarly, there was no publicly available analysis on the relative value of loans compared to other credit markets. In addition, because much of the large bank consolidation had not yet occurred, the market was much more fragmented than it is today, with many more banks active as lenders to the corporate arena than there are today.

The syndicated leveraged loan market is the market segment that has undergone the most change over the past three decades, and it is the primary focus of this book. Numerous events occurred over the past three decades to create the primary loan market as it exists today. Consolidation of banks created a small number of large banks that had long and deep relationships with their corporate clients. Hold levels became much more disciplined as part of the banks' portfolio management practices, and the consolidated banks were not willing to hold all of the loans on the balance sheets of their acquired banks. In addition, the substantial amount of financing needed to support the leveraged buyout business that emerged in the late 1980s required larger and more risky loans. The need to distribute loans reliably in order to permit the large banks to manage their balance sheets and act as arrangers for their corporate clients led to the creation of formal capital markets and loan sales functions.

As banks began acquiring securities capabilities during the mid-1990s, the leading investment banks also entered the loan business as arrangers, primarily as a defensive measure to protect their other capital-raising businesses from being taken from them by the better capitalized commercial banks.

Beginning in the early 1990s, banks and investment banks alike sought to broaden their distribution networks by actively marketing the merits of loans as a distinct asset class to a broad range of alternative investors, including offshore banks, insurance companies, and pension funds. They also created new types of loan buyers by helping to structure collateralized loan obligations (CLOs), mutual funds, and synthetic funds that could serve as outlets for the loans they originated and traded. With these new types of investors came an expanded need for public data on loans, including performance measurements and market quotes. By the late 1990s several entities had begun creating and publishing formal research on the loan asset class. Today the relative stability in the value of loans compared to other debt asset classes is well documented and understood by a wide range of parties. The research available on loans today includes the issuance by the major rating agencies of a category of ratings specific to bank loans. Throughout all of these changes, secondary market volumes have increased exponentially as the new investor classes have actively traded their portfolios through the rapidly growing ranks of traders and brokers.

MARKET SIZE AND SCOPE

There is no consistent definition of what the "loan market" encompasses, and because it includes both public and private companies it is impossible to know with complete certainty what the actual size and scope of the market are on an annual basis.

The Federal Reserve defines a *syndicated loan* as any loan in excess of $100 million that has two or more participants (i.e., investors). As part of its annual Shared National Credit Exam, which reviews the credit quality of all syndicated loans owned by member banks, the Federal Reserve publishes an estimate of the total amount of commitments and loans outstanding that it considers to be syndicated. According to its 2020 exam, the total syndicated loan market was $5.1 trillion in terms of commitments outstanding, with outstanding borrowings of $2.6 trillion.

The total market has many distinct submarkets, each of which has unique structuring characteristics as well as different arrangers and investors. As in the public bond markets, the loan market can be divided into two broad categories in terms of ratings quality. As shown in Exhibit 2.1, approximately 40% of the overall market was rated investment grade and 30% was below investment grade (the leveraged market), based on a trailing five-year average. The remaining 30% of the market included nonrated financings.

The investment-grade market consists largely of unfunded revolvers used by investment-grade companies to backstop their commercial paper programs and provide for working capital and other general corporate purposes. It is used less frequently for event-driven transactions such as acquisitions. This market is characterized by high dollar volume, and it is not unusual to see revolvers run into the billions of dollars for a single issuer. Transactions are more consistently structured than in other market sectors of the loan market in terms of financial covenants and borrowing mechanics. Banks are the primary investors in the investment-grade loan market, and their investment decisions are often driven by overall relationship considerations.

By comparison, the leveraged loan market is much more complex in terms of its structure and players. Transactions in this

EXHIBIT 2.1

U.S. Syndicated Loan Volume by Issuer Rating ($ billions).

Quarter	AAA	AA	A	BBB	BB	B	CCC	CC	D	NR
1Q16	$0.0	$16.8	$68.3	$79.0	$63.5	$23.4	$0.7	$0.0	$0.1	$104.6
2Q16	$1.3	$69.0	$91.1	$126.3	$97.3	$71.9	$11.4	$0.0	$0.5	$141.4
3Q16	$15.0	$4.0	$54.6	$83.1	$112.5	$35.4	$8.0	$1.0	$0.0	$126.6
4Q16	$0.2	$50.1	$88.5	$114.0	$77.1	$106.7	$8.1	$0.0	$0.0	$138.0
1Q17	$0.0	$6.1	$53.1	$84.1	$139.3	$130.9	$13.0	$0.0	$0.0	$177.8
2Q17	$0.0	$69.3	$53.9	$142.5	$93.1	$130.1	$22.5	$0.1	$0.0	$192.4
3Q17	$15.0	$0.4	$66.1	$99.8	$66.2	$101.3	$13.6	$0.0	$2.3	$173.9
4Q17	$0.0	$36.6	$67.9	$126.0	$131.6	$97.4	$13.1	$1.0	$0.0	$179.9
1Q18	$0.0	$5.4	$98.3	$110.6	$97.6	$105.3	$14.2	$0.0	$0.0	$190.6
2Q18	$0.8	$54.3	$109.3	$162.1	$151.0	$108.4	$32.1	$0.0	$0.0	$252.2
3Q18	$16.0	$9.3	$68.1	$105.1	$48.5	$74.8	$1.9	$0.5	$0.0	$164.2
4Q18	$0.0	$46.5	$104.0	$145.5	$91.6	$73.2	$8.3	$1.0	$1.2	$188.5
1Q19	$0.0	$9.2	$70.6	$137.0	$52.4	$35.8	$8.3	$0.0	$2.0	$131.7
2Q19	$0.4	$54.4	$133.8	$138.4	$58.0	$55.4	$3.3	$0.0	$0.4	$203.2
3Q19	$17.5	$17.0	$90.0	$91.2	$62.9	$48.7	$9.0	$0.0	$0.0	$166.2
4Q19	$0.0	$35.6	$79.2	$77.4	$103.4	$46.6	$6.7	$0.4	$0.0	$169.5
1Q20	$0.0	$17.8	$62.6	$117.3	$57.7	$98.2	$28.1	$0.1	$0.1	$168.4
2Q20	$0.4	$42.5	$42.6	$95.0	$67.1	$16.7	$4.1	$0.0	$0.1	$107.3
3Q20	$10.0	$21.5	$38.3	$19.0	$31.8	$31.0	$10.0	$0.0	$0.6	$82.7
4Q20	$0.0	$8.2	$70.8	$59.6	$14.2	$65.2	$6.0	$0.0	$1.2	$146.8

Source: Refinitiv LPC.

market sector are typically smaller than those in the investment-grade loan market, but activity is higher in terms of deal count. Deal activity is heavily influenced by event-driven transactions such as leveraged buyouts and corporate acquisition financing. Structurally, the leveraged loan market is more heavily reliant on funded term loans than on large revolving credit facilities, because many leveraged issuers have higher funded debt needs and/or less access to the public bond market. Leveraged loans tend to be much more structured than investment-grade loans, and generally include more comprehensive collateral packages, financial covenants, and borrowing/repayment mechanics owing to the higher credit risk. The investor base includes both bank and non-bank investors.

Leveraged new issue volume is driven primarily by mergers and acquisitions (M&A) and other transactional activity (see Exhibit 2.2). M&A accounted for 47% of total new-issue volume of leveraged loans denominated in U.S. dollars in 2020 not related to refinancing, and 43% in 2019.

Sponsor-related transactions have represented an increasing portion of leveraged volume. In 2020, new-issue sponsor volume represented 26% of total volume, and 34% in 2019.

Practitioners in the leveraged loan market typically draw a distinction between larger issuers and middle market issuers. The

EXHIBIT 2.2

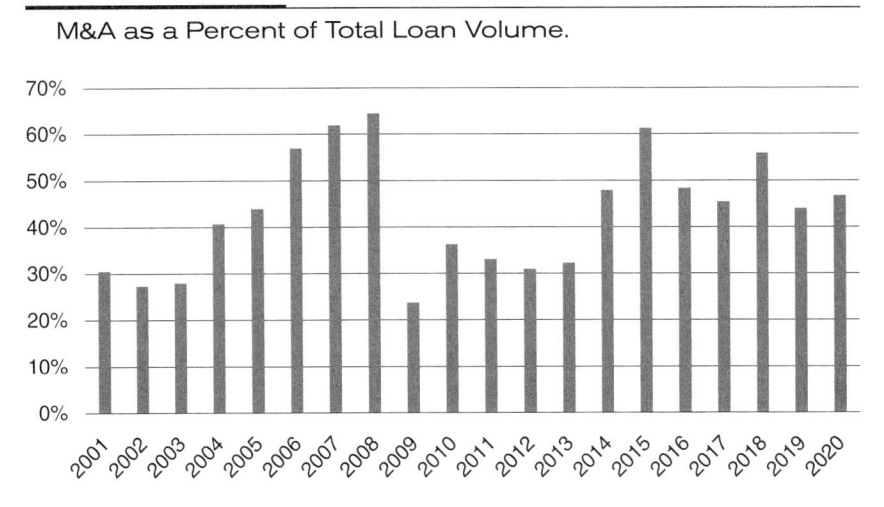

M&A as a Percent of Total Loan Volume.

Source: S&P Global Market Intelligence.

definition of *middle market* varies widely; it can be based on either the size of the issuer or the size of the transaction. Broadly speaking, middle market lending includes loans of up to $500 million that are made to companies with annual revenues of under $500 million. On a relative basis, middle market loans are more stringently structured than their higher-rated leveraged counterparts, and they often carry a pricing premium to compensate investors for the assumed higher risk associated with smaller issuers as well as the relative illiquidity of middle market transactions in secondary trading.

LOAN MARKET PLAYERS: ISSUERS, INVESTORS, AND LEAD ARRANGERS

Issuers

Companies seek syndicated loans to finance their working capital needs or to finance a wide variety of activities, including funding capital expenditures and financing acquisitions. Companies may also seek syndicated loans to construct new facilities or for stand-alone real estate development projects. Given the primary purpose of the loan market, which is to facilitate the distribution of loans among financial institutions, any loan that exceeds the desired hold level of the originating institution is a candidate for syndication.

Private equity funds are also prominent players in the loan market. These funds finance the acquisition of companies through a combination of debt and equity. The debt portion typically relies heavily on debt raised through the syndicated loan market. These transactions, known as *leveraged buyouts*, are a key driver of activity in the leveraged loan market.

Investors

There are many types of investors in the loan market today, ranging from traditional banks that participate in loans for relationship reasons, to highly sophisticated institutional investors, including hedge funds, that invest in the asset class for return and for diversification of their fixed income portfolios. Exhibit 2.3 shows the breakdown of the investor base for leveraged loans as of the end of 2020.

EXHIBIT 2.3

Investor Share of Institutional Loans Outstanding.

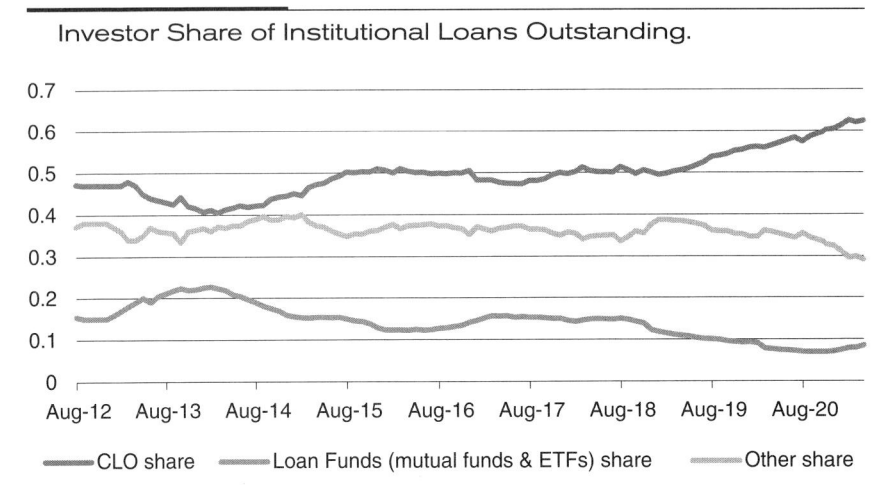

```
0.7
0.6
0.5
0.4
0.3
0.2
0.1
  0
    Aug-12  Aug-13  Aug-14  Aug-15  Aug-16  Aug-17  Aug-18  Aug-19  Aug-20
```
━━━ CLO share   ━━━ Loan Funds (mutual funds & ETFs) share   ━━━ Other share

Source: Refinitiv LPC. Data from LCD Interactive Volume Report.

Generally speaking, loan investors can be broadly classified into two distinct segments: pro rata investors and institutional investors. These segments are described in more detail below.

Pro Rata Investors

Bank investors, often referred to as *pro rata investors*, are the traditional investors in loans. This investor class includes commercial banks and investment banks. Historically, banks, including investment banks, participated in loans as a way to augment their banking relationships with issuers. Banks may also use syndicated loans as a way to boost loan outstandings, and therefore drive incremental interest income. Bank investors have become increasingly sophisticated in the way they manage their loan portfolios, and some banks will actively trade all or a portion of their loan portfolio to manage credit risk or portfolio return; however, because of issuer-relationship reasons, banks may still attempt to maintain positions in the loans of their important clients as a demonstration of support. Bank investors are able to invest in revolvers because they have the back office to support repeated advances and repayments, and they also invest in term loans. Banks have very flexible funding sources, consisting of the deposits and other core activities of the lending institution. These fund sources are generally very stable and not subject to significant fluctuations based on market conditions. The combination of a revolving loan and a term loan is referred to as a *pro rata commitment*.

Institutional Investors

The institutional, or nonbank, investor class is a diverse mix of investment vehicles, including structured funds such as CLOs, mutual funds, finance companies, insurance companies, hedge funds, distressed investors, and high-yield funds. This investor class invests in loans as a way to diversify fixed rate portfolios and generate returns on their own equity capital. These investors, described more fully below, typically have less flexible funding sources than banks, and therefore have a strong desire for fully funded loans with longer tenors, with limited need for amortization. Because of the great liquidity in the institutional lender segment, a typical leveraged loan structure will include a nonamortizing term loan designed to be sold to these investors. This is typically referred to as the *"institutional term loan"* or *"term loan B."*

From 2010 to 2020, loans have become an increasingly popular asset class for institutional investors. According to Standard & Poor's, in 2020 there were approximately 300 institutional investors participating in the leveraged loan market, versus 225 in 2010. As shown in Exhibit 2.4, the composition of the institutional segment of the leveraged loan market has changed markedly over time. In

EXHIBIT 2.4

Primary Investor Market: Institutional Market by Type—LTM 3/21.

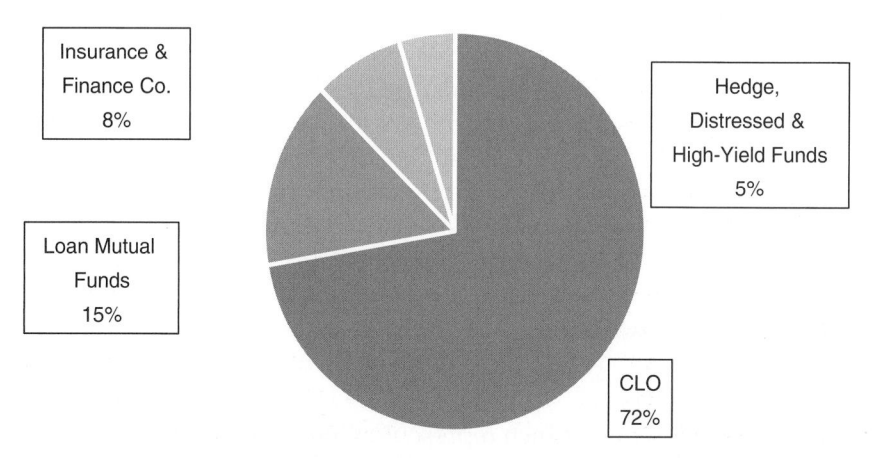

Segment	Share
Insurance & Finance Co.	8%
Loan Mutual Funds	15%
Hedge, Distressed & High-Yield Funds	5%
CLO	72%

Source: S&P Global Market Intelligence.

its initial phases the market was dominated by mutual funds. As it has grown, CLOs have become the dominant source of demand in the market. The major components of the institutional market are explained further below.

Collateralized Loan Obligations (CLOs)
CLOs are the largest segment of the institutional market, accounting for more than 70% of total market share in 2020, according to Standard & Poor's. CLOs are special-purpose vehicles that invest in leveraged loan portfolios. Like other types of institutional investors, CLOs generally have portfolio limits prescribed with respect to minimum ratings, diversification, and defaults through the indenture agreement with the structure's underlying investor base. CLOs are funded through a combination of debt and equity raised from third-party investors, and as such, are highly susceptible to market conditions. The CLO market has been the fastest growing portion of the nonbank investor base, growing from approximately 43% in 2010 to 70% in 2020.

Bank Loan Mutual Funds
Bank loan mutual funds, which represented 15% of the institutional market in 2020, are mutual funds that invest solely in bank loans or a combination of bank loans and high-yield bonds. Originally known as *loan participation funds* or *prime rate funds*, these vehicles were originally marketed as an alternative to money market funds to investors seeking returns that tracked the prime rate. Bank loan funds can be structured as open-ended, with daily redemption or periodic tender periods, or closed-ended, and are generally listed securities. The investment objectives and restrictions with respect to diversification and so on are included in the individual fund's prospectus, as for any other mutual fund. Bank loan mutual funds are funded by the investment activities of the underlying investors (generally individual investors), and therefore are subject to cash inflows and redemption activity. Most bank loan mutual funds offer daily redemptions. As a result of this, these funds are highly subject to fluctuations in market conditions and investor sentiment to drive inflows and outflows.

Insurance Companies
Insurance companies, which represented 6% of the institutional market in 2020, are among the oldest nonbank investor classes in the

loan market. As traditional investors in traditional privately placed bonds, insurance companies began investing in the loan asset class in the early 1990s as a way to supplement their fixed income portfolios. Insurance companies have traditionally invested in the loan market via their general investment accounts; however, they are increasingly investing in the loan market via self-structured CLOs as well.

Finance Companies

Finance companies, which represented approximately 1% of the institutional market in 2020, invest in both the pro rata market and the institutional market, often with a focus on smaller facilities.

Other Investors

A variety of niche investors are also active in the loan market, including hedge funds, high-yield funds, and other investors. Together, these investors represented approximately 5% of institutional loan volume in 2020. Each investor class has a different investment rationale. Investors in this category are generally seeking a higher level of income and are willing to take on more risk to achieve the return. This category of investors represented 37% of the primary market for institutional loans with rating of B/B2 or B/B3 or lower or unrated loans. High-yield funds will occasionally invest in a loan rather than investing in the bonds of a specific issuer for return, duration, or security reasons.

Institutional market participants currently provide approximately 85% of the liquidity in the leveraged loan market, compared with approximately 67% in 2005 (see Exhibit 2.5). This market share

EXHIBIT 2.5

Primary Investor Market: Specific Type.

	Asian Bank	Canadian Bank	European Bank **	U.S. Bank	Securities Firm	CLOs, Ins Comp. & Loan, Hedge & High-Yield Funds	Finance Co.
2010	2%	2%	5%	8%	2%	77%	5%
2011	2%	2%	5%	8%	1%	77%	4%
2012	1%	1%	3%	6%	1%	85%	2%
2013	1%	1%	3%	7%	2%	84%	2%
2014	1%	1%	3%	4%	2%	88%	2%
2015	2%	1%	3%	7%	2%	85%	1%
2016	1%	1%	3%	5%	2%	87%	1%
2017	1%	1%	2%	4%	1%	89%	1%
2018	1%	1%	3%	4%	1%	90%	1%
2019	2%	1%	3%	9%	1%	82%	2%
2020	1%	1%	2%	8%	1%	85%	1%

Source: S&P Global Market Intelligence.

has been taken primarily from domestic banks, which held 8.1% in 2020 compared with 12.3% in 2005 and European banks, which held 2.1% in 2020, compared to 8.5% in 2005.

Continued acceptance of leveraged loans as an asset class and the performance of these loans relative to that of comparable asset classes has encouraged increasing levels of institutional involvement.

CREDIT ANALYSIS

Credit analysis is a fundamental determinant of the structure and pricing of a syndicated bank loan. Credit analysis determines the probability that a borrower will make its scheduled interest payments and repay the debt at maturity. It includes an assessment of the relevant industry characteristics and trends; assessment of the borrower's business fundamentals, competitive position, and strength of management; and a thorough financial analysis.

The analysis of the relevant industry includes an assessment of industry strength and prospects for growth or decline as a result of economic cycles, product cycles, technological change, labor situation, and regulation, among other factors. In addition, the nature of the competitive environment, the number and relative position of existing competitors, barriers to entry for new competitors, and key success factors will be analyzed. The borrower's business fundamentals—its competitive position in the industry (which is often measured by market share but may also be assessed with respect to strength in a particular niche)—will also be analyzed. Competitive strengths can include price, product quality, service, and trademarks or branding. Although a company's size does not directly correlate with its competitive strength, size often affects a company's market advantage in terms of breadth of product line and extent of distribution capabilities. Furthermore, larger companies generally benefit from a greater degree of diversification, which can mitigate the effects of market volatility. Further business analysis will include the borrower's relative strength with respect to marketing and distribution, technological expertise, operating efficiency, and risk management.

Management's strength and track record of success are critical components of credit analysis, because management's financial plans and policies will directly affect a company's performance and credit quality. Breadth of management is an important factor because of the inherent risk of reliance on one or a small number of individuals.

A financial analysis of a potential borrower includes an analysis of certain financial statistics that are used to measure and compare credit risk—for example:

- Profitability measures (gross margin, earnings before interest, taxes, depreciation, and amortization [EBITDA] margin, return on capital)
- Leverage ratios (debt to capitalization, debt to EBITDA)
- Coverage ratios (EBITDA to interest, fixed charge coverage)
- Liquidity tests (working capital, current ratio)

Credit-risk standards for various financial statistics vary substantially across industries. Profitability and coverage measures indicate a company's ability to generate cash flow, withstand economic cycles, and obtain external capital. Leverage and liquidity measures are further evidence of financial flexibility. In addition, a financial analysis includes an assessment of accounting quality, including methodologies used for basis of consolidation, income recognition, capital expenditures and depreciation, and financing, especially off-balance-sheet obligations. Management's policies with respect to financial risk are also a critical factor. Finally, specific loan terms and conditions will be factored into a fundamental credit analysis. The quality of the collateral security provided for a syndicated loan improves the probability of repayment under a distressed scenario.

THE SYNDICATION PROCESS

Syndication effectively begins with an issuer selecting a lead arranger for a particular loan. The selection of a lead lender is based on a number of factors, including the proposed terms and conditions of the facility, the reputation and experience of the potential lead lender, the relationship between the issuer and the potential lead lender, and the ability of the lead lender to execute and support other types of capital markets products for the company. In the process of competing for a mandate, lending institutions evaluate the viability of taking the borrower into the loan market, and generally do this using their capital markets desks. The capital markets process involves an assessment of a potential borrower's financing requirements and credit quality to determine the optimal financing structure to meet the borrower's objectives.

Often, more than one institution is selected to play a leading role in a given transaction. Because of the rules established by the numerous league-table rankings, a fairly stratified title assortment is granted to these lead institutions. Titles will be discussed below.

Lead Arrangers and Agents

In most transactions, the lead arranger will also act as the Administrative Agent and be responsible for the ongoing administration of the loan. The titles *syndication agent* and *document agent* are often awarded in conjunction with large commitments, but the actual responsibilities that go with these roles may be shared or handled by the Administrative Agent or the lead arrangers.

Titles such as *co-agent* or *managing agent* may be awarded on a case-by-case basis, generally to bank loan investors with significant commitments; however, these titles have less significance for league-table purposes and no functional responsibilities.

League Tables

Market share in the syndicated loan market is quoted in league tables published by several companies, including Refinitiv and Bloomberg.

The lead arranger is essentially the middleman in the syndication process. Up to two institutions may receive league-table credit for acting as the lead arranger. In most transactions, the lead arranger structures the term sheet; interfaces with the client and with investors; prepares, negotiates, and closes documents; and manages the syndication process. Consequently, the lead arranger generally receives premium compensation; the title of *lead arranger* is the most coveted title from a league-table standpoint.

The title of *book runner*, which designates the lender or lenders who are managing the syndication sales process, is usually given to one or more of the lead arrangers or Agents.

Agent Titles

In most deals, there are up to five lenders given Agent titles that signify important roles in a syndicated loan financing: Administrative

Agent, syndication agent, and documentation agent. These titles may or may not correspond to actual roles performed with respect to a loan.

- *Administrative agent.* The Administrative Agent generally represents the bank and manages all funding of interest, principal, and other loan payments.
- *Syndication agent.* The syndication agent handles the syndication of the loan (up to two positions can be offered).
- *Documentation agent.* The document agent handles the documentation governing the loan, including security agreements (up to two positions can be offered).

Co-Agent Title

The titles of *managing agent, senior managing agent,* and *co-agent* often are used to give special treatment to lenders committing at a level just below the Agent tier, but above the untitled lenders in the syndicate. These less prestigious titles are not limited in number.

According to Refinitiv LPC, in 2020, the top three arrangers (Bank of America, JP Morgan, and Citigroup) represented 36% of the total market for syndicated loans (see Exhibit 2.6). However, concentration has decreased. The top three leads represented 65% of the total market in 2004. In the leveraged market, the top three arrangers represented less than 29% of total leveraged volume. Furthermore, competition is stronger than the league-table statistics might suggest. Beyond the top three lead arrangers, there is a significant number of other banks and securities firms that compete, often with particular expertise in specific niches. More than 40 arrangers led financings aggregating over $5 billion in 2020, maintaining strong competition.

Pricing

Loan pricing is defined as the interest rate charged on the loan, plus any associated fees required as part of the financing package. Loans in the domestic syndicated loan market are generally priced via a floating interest rate, such as LIBOR plus a percentage, or *spread*, that reflects the risk of the issuer relative to the market and to other issuers with a similar profile. Generally, the spread, also known as the

EXHIBIT 2.6

2020 Lead Arrangers League Table.

Rank	Lender Parent	Volume (USD)	Deal Count	Market Share (>1%)
1	BofA Securities	227,462,124,990.60	869	14.03%
2	JP Morgan	213,852,941,819.81	766	13.19%
3	Citi	145,821,227,152.02	384	8.99%
4	Wells Fargo & Co	126,941,054,443.75	547	7.83%
5	Barclays	60,373,901,960.71	261	3.72%
6	Goldman Sachs & Co	57,256,221,290.63	239	3.53%
7	Credit Suisse AG	50,465,887,612.04	187	3.11%
8	Morgan Stanley	46,951,049,769.07	153	2.90%
9	US Bancorp	44,404,932,675.20	301	2.74%
10	Mitsubishi UFJ Financial Group Inc	43,296,272,487.96	226	2.67%
11	Deutsche Bank AG	42,812,375,702.89	193	2.64%
12	BNP Paribas SA	35,636,613,151.37	156	2.20%
13	PNC Bank	35,058,220,863.55	248	2.16%
14	Truist Financial	34,545,536,180.59	249	2.13%
15	RBC Capital Markets	32,928,933,069.90	159	2.03%
16	Mizuho Financial Group Inc	32,042,779,786.99	150	1.98%
17	BMO Capital Markets Financing Inc	27,308,347,405.77	214	1.68%
18	HSBC Banking Group	21,011,795,851.73	103	1.30%
19	Jefferies	20,634,210,224.20	102	1.27%
20	Toronto Dominion Bank	19,808,801,521.54	105	1.22%
21	Sumitomo Mitsui Financial Group Inc	18,260,314,094.75	95	1.13%
22	Citizens Financial Group	17,298,177,350.95	162	1.07%

Source: Refinitiv LPC.

applicable margin, is shown either as a percentage (LIBOR + 3.50%) or, more commonly, in basis points (LIBOR + 350 basis points).

Most often, loan pricing is negotiated between the lead arranger(s) and the issuer during the initial negotiation of the loan, along with the other key structural and pricing issues, including fees, tenor, and covenants. These terms are summarized in a term sheet, which will be discussed in greater detail later. In situations where the loan is being underwritten by the arranger(s), the term sheet will be accompanied by a commitment letter and a fee letter, the execution of which affirms the mandate.

Loan pricing is influenced by a number of factors, including the following:

- Credit profile of the issuer
- Prevailing market conditions

- Comparable deals in the market
- Comparable prior transactions (i.e., similar industry, use of proceeds, size of company, and so on)
- Investor relationships
- Ancillary business opportunities
- Relative value
- Secondary market trends

Unlike other fixed income products, where the pricing is set for the life of the instrument, loan pricing may be expressed in a matrix or pricing grid, where the LIBOR spread will vary depending on certain post-closing conditions. These conditions are intended to capture changes in the relative risk or performance of the company and can include many different criteria. Several common examples of such criteria include public ratings, leverage ratios, and coverage ratios. An example of a performance-based grid is shown in Exhibit 2.7.

Pricing Flex

Historically, loans were priced by the arrangers at the time the mandate to lead the loan was granted and did not vary as they came to

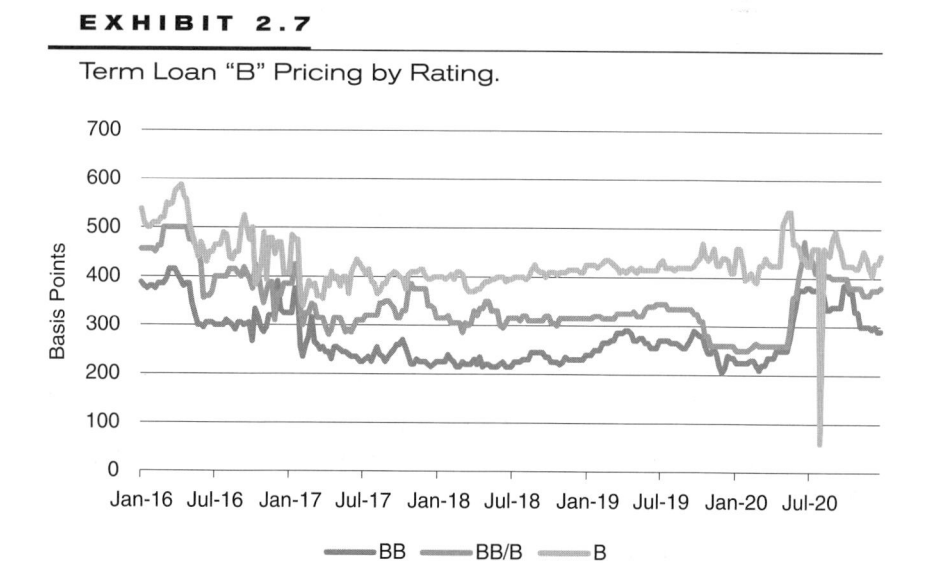

EXHIBIT 2.7

Term Loan "B" Pricing by Rating.

Source: Refinitiv LPC.

market. This is in contrast to bonds, which are typically priced at the time the offering is completed, based on the pricing required to "clear the market" and sell the entire issue. Over time, the pricing mechanism on loans has come to more closely resemble that of bonds through the inclusion of pricing "flex." Arrangers and issuers agree on a targeted and often a maximum price for the issue, but the actual pricing is determined through the loan marketing process. Loans are announced with a target price, but the price will either flex up or flex down depending on demand and general market conditions. Although the inclusion of price flex has limited the risk to the arrangers of pricing a deal incorrectly during the pitch and negotiation process, it has not eliminated the risk entirely. The degree of price flex permitted to the arrangers is often one of the most heavily negotiated elements of a commitment letter.

Different Types of Fees

A key part of the syndication strategy involves determining the fee payout structure to the investors that make up the loan syndicate. An *upfront fee* is a fee paid to investors to augment the return on their portion of the loan. The pro rata portion of a loan typically has an upfront fee associated with it. The fee will vary from transaction to transaction, and will frequently vary within the same transaction based on the level of commitment offered by an investor. In this case, investors will be paid a one-time fee based on the level of their commitment. In transactions where the loan is oversubscribed and investors' commitments are being reduced through allocation, the actual fee they receive will be based on their allocated amount. Most institutional loans come with an original issue discount (OID). The OID is provided to enhance the yield to the investor by offering the loan at a slight discount to par.

Non-use Fee

Revolving loans pay interest on the amount of the facility that is actually used. In order to compensate investors for making the unused commitment available at all times, they are typically paid a commitment, or non-use fee. This fee is payable either monthly or quarterly in arrears based on the daily amount of the commitment that is undrawn. Often these fees will vary based on the same criteria used in the loan-pricing grid.

SYNDICATION STRATEGY

By forming a syndicate of investors, the arrangers are fulfilling the objectives of the borrower—to raise the required amount of financing on the required timetable while also fulfilling their own objectives—maximizing the revenue from the transaction and further developing relationships with the investors. The strategy for meeting these objectives will vary widely from one transaction to another. In formulating the strategy, the arrangers take a wide range of factors into consideration, including the following:

- *Underwritten versus best efforts.* The borrower may decide to ask its lead bank either to underwrite a loan or to simply arrange it on a best efforts basis. In an underwritten loan, the arrangers are taking on themselves the risk that syndication will not be successful and that they may need to hold more of the loan than they had originally intended. In a best efforts arrangement, this syndication risk is taken on by the issuer. An underwriting is more expensive to the issuer, but when issuers do not have strict timetable requirements or when they feel that it is not worth paying for the certainty of receiving funds, they will opt for a best efforts arrangement.
- *Timing to close.* Syndication can take several weeks to complete, even after it is launched. If there is insufficient time to complete the syndication, the arranger can opt to close the transaction first and syndicate afterwards. Alternatively, a two-step syndication could be conducted, where a small group of relationship lenders closes the transaction and jointly syndicates afterwards. Issuers typically pay a premium to have their arrangers close a loan prior to completion of syndication.
- *Size of transaction.* Larger transactions require more investors and larger holding levels in order to complete.
- *Anticipated investor demand.* The assessment of how many investors may be interested is based on a wide variety of factors, including:
    - The number of existing lenders for this borrower typically considered to be attracted to this type of transaction

- The aggressiveness of the loan in terms of pricing and structure compared to other transactions currently in the market
- Leverage
- Ratings
- Complexity of the story and structure
- Current supply and demand factors in the market for similar transactions
- Desire of the borrower to have its bank loan held widely and trade well

After considering all of these factors, the arrangers will determine what they feel is the optimal strategy, including the timetable, titles, and requirements of potential participants in terms of fees and commitment levels.

RATINGS PROCESS

While banks still rely primarily on their internal credit analysis as the primary tool for determining their interest in making a particular loan, structured vehicles such as CLOs are required by their indentures to balance the levels of loans with various ratings within their portfolios. The rapid growth in CLO investors has therefore given rise to a need for loans to receive ratings (either public or private) from the major rating agencies. The agencies have, in turn, developed significant expertise in the loan asset class. As of 2020 year-end, bank loan ratings can be found on more than 98% of the 1,450 individual loans that are contained in the S&P/LSTA Leveraged Loan Index which holds roughly $1.2 trillion in loans outstanding.

The process for obtaining a rating for a loan is very similar to that for obtaining a rating for other debt instruments. The agencies undertake a multistep process. First, they evaluate the issuer's overall risk of default on its financial obligations and assign one of their traditional letter ratings (AAA, AA, A, BBB, and so on). This analysis can be done with or without a presentation from the company, but for leveraged loans, where ratings are thought to be critical in the syndication process, it generally involves a formal meeting between the company and the rating agency analyst and a presentation by the company. The analyst will then undertake a deal-specific analysis of the loan itself, which looks beyond the risk of default to factor in the likelihood of ultimate loss and recovery. This analysis considers not only the overall creditworthiness of the borrower, but also the unique features of the loan instrument, such as collateral, covenants, and other structural features that may determine how much loan investors are ultimately repaid in a post-default scenario. This may result in a loan rating that is "notched" up from the issuer's rating or from other debt of the same issuer.

Arrangers typically attempt to have the ratings available at the beginning of the syndication process to assist investors in making credit and pricing decisions. Frequently, the loan rating is obtained simultaneously with the rating for other layers of a firm's capital structure, including bonds and preferred stock. In addition to the actual ratings, the agencies will issue detailed commentary on their ratings and on the assumptions and expectations they formed during the ratings process. These commentaries are often of critical importance to potential investors.

As with other debt products, after an initial rating, investors generally want ongoing surveillance and updates from the rating agencies. For this reason, issuers may choose to meet regularly with their agency analysts to make sure that the analysts have the best available information when issuing their ratings and updates.

OFFERING MATERIAL AND PREPARATION

Once the transaction has been mandated, the lead arranger will begin working with the issuer to draft the offering materials that will be distributed to potential investors. The information provided for a leveraged loan can be extensive, and the drafting process can often be lengthy. Although the arrangers work extensively with the issuer on the preparation of the information memorandum, the finished product is considered to be delivered from the issuer to the investors. Generally, the final information memorandum will include a statement from the company that it has approved the information contained within the memorandum and that the information is accurate and complete. In addition, investors acknowledge that they have done their own independent credit analysis and are not relying on specific representations made by the arrangers.

Typical sections included in those materials are:

- *Executive summary*—a high-level summary of the transaction, the company, and the financial sponsor (if any)

- *Investment considerations*—selling points of the transaction
- *Terms and conditions*—a summary of the term sheet agreed to by the arranger(s) and the company
- *Business overview*—an in-depth review of the company's business
- *Management overview*—short biographies of the company's officers
- *Industry overview*—an overview of the company's industry
- *Historic financial overview*
- *Projected financial overview for private side investors*

As appropriate, the information memorandum may contain appendices with additional information on the issuer, including annual reports, SEC filings, product descriptions, and so on. In addition to this information, the information memorandum will contain a schedule of the syndication timing, including information regarding the investor meeting, commitment deadline, and scheduled closing. The information memorandum typically also includes housekeeping information, such as contacts for the arrangers and the issuer for questions and an administrative questionnaire for investors. Finally, the information memorandum will include a release letter or company authorization letter signed by the issuer and a confidentiality agreement. It is worth noting that in today's market the offering materials often also take the form of a shorter lender presentation in the form of a PowerPoint that includes many of the same elements typically found in the information memorandum.

Although much of the information in a typical information memorandum can be drawn from the public filings of a company, not all borrowers file public statements. In addition, many loan investors require information that is not public in order to make their credit decisions. For this reason, the primary market for loans includes processes whereby investors must declare themselves to be on either the public side or the private side prior to reviewing any information. If they choose to remain public and review only the public information provided by the company, they are entitled to continue trading in the other securities of the company throughout their review process. Private-side investors may receive information that is beyond the available public information, such as projections, but they are then restricted in their ability to trade the public securities of the company. Arrangers must prepare two sets of memoranda for these investors and make sure they have the opportunity to declare their preference before they receive information. Market practice is that investors must police themselves on their trading activities once they have made a public declaration.

INVESTOR MEETING

A key part of the syndication process is known as the *bank meeting* or the *investor meeting*, which may be in person or a virtual investor presentation over the phone or online. In both instances, a presentation slide deck is provided to the lenders in advance of the meeting. This meeting generally consists of a presentation by the issuer's management team to investors that are interested in participating in the transaction. The purpose of the meeting is to give investors the opportunity to meet the issuer's management.

Typically, an investor meeting agenda will include the following:

- Introduction and overview of the transaction (this is usually managed by the book runner)
- Management introduction
- Management presentation
- Business overview
- Strategy
- Industry
- Financial review
- Projected financial performance

There will also generally be a discussion of the merits of investing in the loan and an overview of the credit facility. These latter sections are generally conducted by the lead arrangers. In the event of a meeting with both public and private investors in attendance, the audience for the projected financial performance discussion will be limited to private investors. The bank meeting may also include facility tours, if applicable.

SALES PROCESS

The sales process is generally conducted by the sales desks of the arranging banks, which have divided up their coverage of the investor universe. Generally, the salespeople will receive a briefing on the loan from the origination side of the deal team prior to the actual launch. A determination will be made as to how many investors to invite and which investors are deemed to be most suitable or potentially interested in a particular loan offering. The sales process will be launched with calls from the sales team to investors inviting them to review the loan. The salesperson is responsible for making sure that investors' questions are addressed, and that the feedback he or she is getting from investors gets back to the origination and capital-markets teams.

FUNDING AND BREAKING INTO THE SECONDARY MARKET

When the sales process is complete, the arrangers will allocate the facility among the committed investors. The announcement of this allocation is the point at which the primary syndication is completed, and the loan will immediately break into a secondary market. The loan may then begin trading, even though it may not have actually closed. This preclosing trading is called *when-issued trading*.

FORMS USED

Commitment Letter

The commitment letter is used to document the agreement between the arrangers and the borrower with respect to the basis for and conditions of the arrangers' commitment. In addition to specifying the amount and tenor of the loan, the commitment letter will generally include a brief description of the purpose of the financing to set the basic understanding of the deal. The commitment letter will also specify conditions for the commitment, which may include:

- Completion of due diligence
- Absence of material adverse change in the business, financial condition, or prospects of the borrower
- No material adverse change in the loan syndication or capital market
- Negotiation of documentation by date certain
- Payment of fees and expenses

Furthermore, the commitment letter will define certain rights and responsibilities of the borrower and the arrangers with respect to the syndication process. For example, the commitment letter will specify the borrower's obligation to provide requested information for the bank book and to participate in meetings with potential bank loan participants. The commitment letter will also define certain legal protections for the benefit of each party, including indemnification, confidentiality provisions, jurisdiction, governing law, and so on.

Fee Letter

The fee letter will specifically identify the type and amount of fees payable in connection with a syndicated loan, including arrangement and structuring fees or underwriting fees, administrative agency fees, collateral Agent fees, and other amounts payable to the arrangers. As discussed previously, the fee letter will also generally include market flex language, which details certain provisions of the facility that may be subject to change if necessary to complete syndication (e.g., the structure of the facility and its terms or pricing).

Term Sheet

The term sheet provides a summary of the terms of the loan financing, which will be documented in more detail in the credit agreement, which provides the definitive documentation for the financing, as described in more detail in Chapter 3. The term sheet will generally include the following types of provisions:

- *Parties to the financing.* Definitions of the borrower(s) and guarantor(s) (if any), as well as the arrangers and lead Agents.
- *Terms and amounts of the facilities.* A description of the type (e.g., revolving credit, term loan, and so on), amount, currency, and tenor of the facility.
- *Payment provisions.* A description of the fees and interest rates, optional prepayment provisions, and mandatory amortization and prepayment requirements.
- *Collateral.* A description of any security interests to be provided to the lenders.
- *Conditions for availability.* A list of any actions to be taken by the borrower or items to be delivered by the borrower to the Administrative Agent and any other requirements

that must be satisfied in order for the credit to be available. This may include, for example, receipt of the executed loan documentation; compliance with covenants; satisfactory legal structure; perfection of security interests, if applicable; receipt of financial statements and other required information; receipt of all required government and third-party consents; and opinions of counsel.

- *Representations and warranties.* A description of the types of representations and warranties (with appropriate materiality and reasonableness standards) that will be included in the credit agreement, which may include accuracy of the financial statements, absence of undisclosed liabilities, no material adverse change, corporate existence, compliance with law, corporate power and authority, enforceability of credit documentation, no conflict with law or contractual obligations, no material litigation, no default, ownership of property, indebtedness, liens, intellectual property, taxes, government regulations, ERISA, purpose of loans, subsidiaries, environmental matters, solvency, investments, labor matters, accuracy of disclosure, leases, creation and perfection of security interests, and status of the credit facilities as senior debt.

- *Affirmative covenants.* A description of the covenants of the borrower; that is, covenants regarding the delivery of financial statements, reports, accountants' letters, projections, officers' certificates, and other information reasonably requested by the senior lenders; payment of other obligations; continuation of business and maintenance of existence and material rights and privileges; compliance with laws and material contractual obligations; maintenance of property and insurance; maintenance of books and records; right of the senior lenders to inspect property and books and records; notices of defaults, litigation, and other material events; compliance with environmental laws; further assurances (including, without limitation, assurances with respect to security interests in after-acquired property); terms of leases; and interest-rate protection to be agreed upon.

- *Financial covenants.* Details of the measures of credit quality that the borrower will be required to maintain for the tenor of the loan. Examples of financial covenants include minimum consolidated EBITDA/consolidated interest expense, minimum consolidated EBITDA/consolidated fixed charges, and maximum consolidated total debt/consolidated EBITDA, minimum net worth, and minimum current ratio.

It is worth noting here that traditionally credit agreements have included both financial maintenance and incurrence covenants, but in today's leveraged loan market credit agreements are "covenant lite," meaning that it is a loan that lacks financial maintenance covenants. A financial maintenance covenant requires the borrower to maintain a given level of financial performance. Although covenant-lite loans lack these financial maintenance covenants, they typically do include covenants constituting incurrence tests. An incurrence covenant requires the borrower *not* to take some action within its control, such as borrowing more money or paying dividends, unless a given financial ratio meets agreed parameters. Other than during the Global Financial Crisis, since 2005, the loan market has been heavily trending toward covenant-lite transactions (Exhibit 2.8).

EXHIBIT 2.8

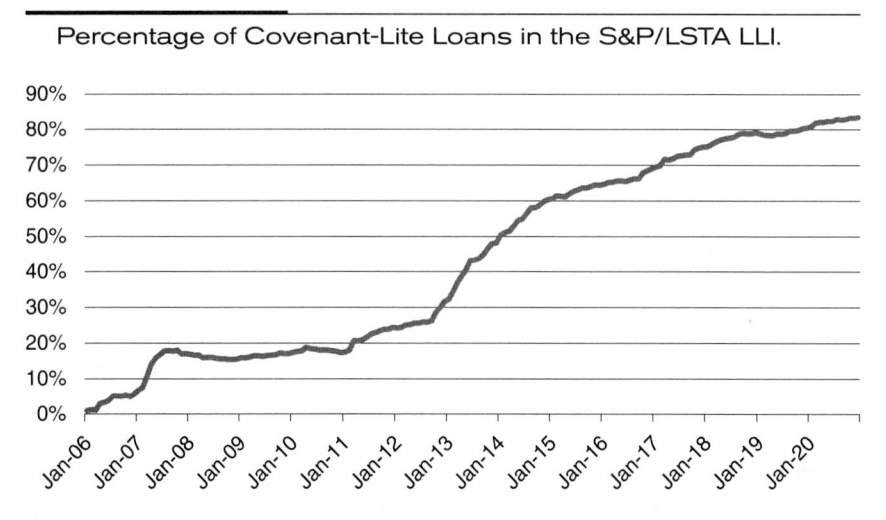

Percentage of Covenant-Lite Loans in the S&P/LSTA LLI.

Source: S&P/LSTA Leveraged Loan Index (LLI).

- *Negative covenants.* Negative covenants imposed on the borrower may include limitations on indebtedness; liens; guarantee obligations; mergers, consolidations, liquidations, and dissolutions; sales of assets; capital expenditures; dividends and other payments in respect of capital stock investments, loans and advances, optional payments, and modifications of subordinated and other debt instruments; amendments to material contractual obligations; transactions with affiliates; sale and leasebacks; changes in fiscal year and organizational documents; negative-pledge clauses; and changes in lines of business.
- *Events of default.* Generally, events of default will include nonpayment of principal when due; nonpayment of interest, fees, or other amounts after a grace period; material inaccuracy of representations and warranties; violation of covenants (subject, in the case of certain covenants, to certain grace or notice and cure periods); default under other credit documentation; bankruptcy events; cross-defaults with respect to outstanding indebtedness; material judgments; certain ERISA events; termination or amendment of certain material agreements if such termination or amendment could reasonably be expected to have a material adverse effect; actual or asserted invalidity of any guarantee or security document, subordination provisions, or security interest; and a change of control (the definition of which is to be agreed upon).
- *Other documentation matters.* The term sheet will also usually detail provisions with respect to voting requirements for amendments, assignments and participations, expenses and indemnification, yield protection, and governing law.

CONCLUSION

The primary market for bank loans has evolved significantly over the past 30 years and has become more and more similar to the markets for other types of fixed income debt. Most of the changes have been in the direction of increased liquidity and transparency of the market, and toward the development of a robust secondary market for loan assets. Importantly, the pace of change has accelerated over time, and shows no signs of slowing. The size of the market alone ensures that the market will continue to attract new entrants and new service providers, all of whom will push the pace of change. Despite all of these changes, though, the market retains many unique characteristics, rooted in issuers' need to reliably access revolving loans and the banks' need to cross-sell other products. The complex relationship between issuers and investors in the bank loan market, combined with the overall attractiveness of this market to new investors, ensures that this market will remain distinct from other fixed income markets, even as it continues to evolve.

Information in the Loan Market: Material Nonpublic Information and Confidential Information

Robert Scheininger
Reed Smith, LLP

Elizabeth Grzywacz
PNC Bank, National Association

Jon Mooney
PNC Bank, National Association

PART 1: INTRODUCTION AND SCOPE

This article focuses on key risks surrounding the receipt by lenders and other market participants of confidential information of a borrower in the syndicated loan market in the United States and describes the architecture for handling such information, including some suggested compliance mechanisms that could be put in place in order to address the inherent risks of handling such information.

Participants in the syndicated loan market in the United States include banks, broker-dealers, and other loan market participants (LMPs), such as funds, asset managers, and insurance companies (collectively, "Lenders") and agent banks and other arrangers (collectively, "Agents," and together with Lenders, LMPs). Loans are originated, maintained, and distributed on confidential information provided by borrowers to LMPs, on the basis of which each LMP makes its individual lending decision. Such information may include detailed disclosures about the borrower's financial results and prospects, internal borrower analyses, information about the borrower's suppliers and customers, and other highly sensitive business data, and may at times include material nonpublic information (MNPI). Lenders generally require this sort of private information regarding a borrower prior to extending credit and then require periodic reporting of private information once a loan has been made. Borrowers have a keen interest in protecting this confidential information.

Receiving or having access to any confidential information regarding a borrower imposes certain responsibilities upon an LMP and its employees from a relationship perspective, a legal and regulatory perspective, and often, contractually, through confidentiality undertakings. As a result, LMPs are advised to implement and enforce robust compliance policies and procedures to guide employees regarding the receipt, use, and dissemination of such information.

To address this and other legal considerations and concerns affecting the syndicated loan market, the Loan Syndications and Trading Association (LSTA) has from time to time issued various nonbinding guidance, which provides recommendations with respect to the receipt, use, and distribution of confidential information by and to LMPs. Such guidance includes the LSTA Code of Conduct dated as of December 14, 2020 (the "Code of Conduct"), Statement of Principles for the Communication and Use of Confidential Information by Loan Market Participants dated as of November 16, 2017 (the "Confidentiality Principles"), and the LSTA Guidance Note and Confidentiality Legends for Distribution of Syndicated Loan Marketing Materials dated April 26, 2021 (the "Guidance Note," and, together with the Code of Conduct and Confidentiality Principles, the "LSTA Guidance"). The LSTA Guidance will be updated from time to time, and the above dates are the most recent as of the date of publication of this article.

Although this article touches on several regulatory enforcement actions as a reference point, it is not intended to be a comprehensive regulatory overview. LMPs may be subject to various regulatory regimes both outside of the United States and within. Each LMP should consider the regulatory regimes applicable to such LMP as well as its own specific activities when developing compliance policies and procedures. Moreover, the scope of this article is limited to the trading of syndicated loans in the United

States and does not address any other assets or debt instruments or jurisdictions. In particular, transfers of debt and equity securities, which are governed by the SEC and the Securities Exchange Act of 1934 (among others), are explicitly excluded from this article and, when discussed herein, only for purposes of analogy to the syndicated loan market.

Finally, it should be noted that the material presented in this article presumes that loans are not "securities." This presumption is a fundamental tenet of syndicated lending in the United States that has been the subject of judicial scrutiny from time to time. A detailed discussion of this issue can be found in Chapter 5.

PART 2: CATEGORIES OF CONFIDENTIAL INFORMATION IN THE SYNDICATED LOAN MARKET

Issues around confidential information are complicated by the fact that many LMPs (including prospective Lenders) also participate in the securities markets. LMPs' participation in the securities markets requires the loan market to address certain information flow issues to ensure that LMPs can conduct ordinary course business and remain in compliance with applicable securities law. In short, in order to be able to trade securities issued by the borrower, the trading function of an LMP must not be in possession of (or be deemed to be in possession of) MNPI about the borrower or its securities. Because it is not uncommon for the information received by LMPs in connection with a particular loan to include MNPI, effective control of information flow is crucial to achieving a "clean" securities trading function.

Issues around confidential information are further complicated by definitional confusion. As a result, an important first step is understanding the "how" and "why" of information distribution is defining the types of information that will be discussed in this article.

Categories of Confidential Information

Table 2.1 provides key definitions that will be used throughout this article. These definitions are helpful in identifying the types of information that are in the market (and are consistent with definitions contained in the LSTA Guidance).

Term	Definition	Example	Confidential?
MNPI (material nonpublic information)	Information that is material with respect to a security or issuer and is not public information	Information regarding an unannounced merger or acquisition	Yes
Syndicate Information	Confidential information that a borrower provides or makes available (typically through an Agent) to all members and potential members of a lending syndicate[2]	Information regarding earnings before public disclosure	Yes; may include MNPI
Borrower Restricted Information (also called agent-only information)	Confidential information, which may include MNPI, that is made available by or on behalf of a borrower to some, but not all, members, and potential members of a lending syndicate in connection with the loan origination and periodic reporting obligations[3]	Information regarding a potential covenant breach in a loan agreement	Yes; may include MNPI
Bank Loan Nonrestricting Information	Information that does not include MNPI and is provided confidentially by or on behalf of a borrower to members and potential members of a lending syndicate. It is subject to standard confidentiality undertakings.[4]	Information contained in a Confidential Information Memorandum that is provided to LMPs that choose not to receive MNPI	Yes; does not include MNPI
Public Information	Information that has been broadly disseminated to, or is accessible by, the public[5]	Information contained in a press release	No

Public- and Private-Side LMPs

Whether an LMP is a *public-* or *private-side* LMP is essential to understanding the potential risks and liability related to receipt of and trading on information from the borrower. An LMP may be a private-side participant; a public-side participant; or, if the LMP creates an information barrier and assigns different personnel to each side, both. The key difference between a private-side LMP and a public-side LMP is that a private-side LMP receives MNPI, whereas

---
[2] Confidentiality Principles, p. 2.
[3] Confidentiality Principles, p. 2.
[4] Confidentiality Principles, p. 2.
[5] Confidentiality Principles, p. 3.

a public-side LMP has chosen not to receive MNPI. Whether information is known to the public should not be confused with whether an LMP is a public-side LMP. Public-side LMPs receive confidential information, but, as noted, do not receive MNPI.

What Is "Material" and Who Makes That Determination

The definition of the word *material* in the loan and securities contexts has been discussed for decades, and will undoubtedly continue to be discussed; however, there is general agreement that the so-called reasonable-investor test is at the root of the analysis. If there is a substantial likelihood that a reasonable investor would consider the relevant information to be important to their investment decision (i.e., to buy, sell, or hold a security), the information is likely material.[6]

In particular, the Confidentiality Principles provide that information is:

> deemed to be material where (i) there is a substantial likelihood that a reasonable investor would consider the information important in making an investment decision; (ii) there is a substantial likelihood that the disclosure of the information would be viewed by the reasonable investor as having significantly altered the total mix of information made available; or (iii) the disclosure of the information is reasonably certain to have a substantial effect on the market price.[7]

The reasonable investor test is a facts-and-circumstances analysis—what is material in one context may not be material in another. Moreover, the materiality of information is not perpetual, and information that is material one day may quickly become stale. The challenge that many LMPs face is that often the individuals who would be the reasonable investor in the best position to determine what is material in a particular situation are the same individuals who will be participating in trading activity on the

---

[6] TSC Industries v. Northway, 426 U.S. 438, 445 (1976). *TSC Industries* concerned information that a reasonable investor might consider important in how to *vote* their securities, but Justice Marshall's standard enunciated in *TSC Industries* has been applied more broadly to other actions with respect to a security.

[7] Confidentiality Principles, p. 3.

public side, and therefore may be restricted from receiving the information in the first place.

Ultimately the determination of what the reasonable investor would consider material is made in retrospect by securities regulators or the courts deciding securities class-action cases. As such, and because confidential information provided by a borrower to its LMPs may be material, it is prudent for LMPs to act cautiously and often err on the side of caution when determining whether certain information may be deemed MNPI.

Why It Matters

The financial services industry is concerned about corralling private information and the risks related to disclosure or improper use of such information for several important reasons.

- *Borrowers' desire to protect confidential information.* The cornerstone of how the industry handles a borrower's private information is the borrower's desire to zealously protect its confidential information. Dissemination of confidential information without careful controls and protections could result in unintended public disclosure of a borrower's confidential business practices, strategies, and trade secrets, which could have a negative economic impact on the borrower's business.
- *Breach of contract risk.* An LMP will generally be required to agree to certain confidentiality undertakings in connection with an original syndication or by becoming a Lender under a syndicated loan during the life of the loan. Improper use and/or disclosure of confidential information could, therefore, result in a breach by an LMP of its contractual obligations to the borrower, Agent, creditors' committee, or other parties to which it owes such contractual obligations. This particular issue would be relevant irrespective of whether such information contains MNPI.
- *Common law duty of confidence, fraud, and unfair dealing.* LMPs may have a common-law duty of confidence to their borrowers. If an LMP were to disseminate a borrower's confidential information to third parties without obtaining a confidentiality undertaking from those third parties, the

LMP would be at risk of breaching that duty and being held liable for such breach (including monetary damages). Furthermore, an LMP that disseminates a borrower's confidential information without careful controls could face severe reputational damage in the industry. Being seen as a poor steward of confidential information would almost certainly have a deleterious effect on an LMP's competitive position in the market.

In addition, the failure to disclose or offer to disclose confidential information to a trading counterparty in a secondary market loan trade could expose the nondisclosing LMP to fraud or unfair dealing common-law claims by the trading counterparty.

- *Regulatory risk.* For borrowers with tradable securities outstanding, Regulation FD ("Reg FD"; 17 C.F.R. 243.100–243.103) may be applicable. In essence, Reg FD is intended to help level the playing field between individual investors and large institutional investors,[8] the latter of which were accustomed to receiving information in advance of the broader public and either trading on the information, disclosing it to their brokerage customers, or both. Reg FD sought to end that practice by requiring information either (1) be made available substantially simultaneously to the market or (2) be distributed to certain classes of entities (including Lenders) under a confidentiality undertaking. Accordingly, even for Bank Loan Non-Restricting Information, many borrowers insist on a confidentiality undertaking because the absence of such an undertaking would require the borrower to determine whether the distribution of the information is compliant with Reg FD.

In addition, each LMP is subject to specific regulatory regimes that may have rules or regulations regarding receipt of confidential information by an LMP in the syndicated loan context or otherwise. In particular, although syndicated loans have typically not been considered "securities" for

---

[8] According to the Adopting Release for Regulation FD (17 C.F.R. 240, 243, and 249), FD stands for "Fair Disclosure" and is "designed to promote the full and fair disclosure of information by issuers."

these purposes,[9] a number of securities law issues should be considered, particularly for LMPs that also trade in the securities market:

- *Receipt of MNPI.* U.S. securities laws and regulations impose significant prohibitions on trading securities on the basis of MNPI. SEC Rule 10b-5 prohibits certain persons who are aware of MNPI regarding a company or its securities from trading in the securities without appropriate disclosures. LMPs will often be deemed to have actual or imputed confidential information regarding the underlying borrower absent proper controls, policies, and procedures. If such LMP also trades in the securities market and it receives the confidential information without the proper controls, policies, and procedures (whether advertently or inadvertently), such LMP may be required to immediately cease trading the public securities or risk violating securities insider trading laws.

- *Migration to a third party.* Tippers and tippees may also be liable under Rule 10b-5. A *tipper* is a person who, in violation of a duty and for his or her own direct or indirect benefit (including intangible benefit), discloses MNPI to another person with the expectation that that person might trade on the information, even if he or she does not trade. A *tippee* is the recipient of the MNPI and may violate Rule 10b-5 if he or she knew or should have known that the MNPI was provided by the tipper in violation of a duty owed to a third party.

- An LMP may be required contractually or otherwise to share confidential information regarding a borrower with a third party. If such confidential information contains MNPI and the recipient of such information trades the securities of the applicable borrower based on that information, the provider of the information could be considered a tipper under the securities laws and regulations absent adequate assurance by the recipient

---

[9] Although not free from doubt, the LSTA Guidance is written under the assumption that SEC Rule 10b-5 does not apply to the trading of syndicated loans. The same assumption has been applied in preparing this article, as noted above.

that such information will be handled by the recipient in compliance with applicable securities laws and regulations. Violations of securities laws can result in serious criminal and civil liability.

- *Maintenance of policies and procedures.* Under Rule 3110(d), the Financial Industry Regularity Authority (FINRA) requires a firm under the authority of FINRA to include in its supervisory procedures a process for reviewing securities transactions that is reasonably designed to identify trades that may violate the provisions of the Securities Exchange Act of 1934, its regulations, or FINRA rules. Under the Investment Advisers Act of 1940, regulated institutions are required to develop and maintain written policies and procedures to prevent the misuse of MNPI.[10] Most LMPs are subject to at least one of the foregoing regulatory regimes, and are therefore obligated to develop and maintain policies and procedures addressing the receipt and use of MNPI in the syndicated loan context. Failure to do so could draw the scrutiny of the applicable regulatory agencies as well as potential enforcement actions.
- *Violation of internal policies and procedures.* Most LMPs should and do have internal policies and procedures regarding the receipt and use of confidential information. Misuse of such information would likely result in a violation of those policies and procedures. It is therefore important for LMPs and their personnel to be aware of the fact that LMPs will often receive or have access to confidential information in order to ensure compliance with their own internal policies and procedures.
- *Reputational and relationship risk.* Improper use or dissemination of confidential information by an LMP could damage the relationship that the LMP has with the borrower and/or its trading counterparty (if applicable). Even an assertion of wrongdoing in this area could potentially severely damage the reputation of the LMP with its regulators and/or the general public.

---

[10] *See* Investment Advisors Act, Section 204A.

How Confidentiality Is Maintained in the Loan Market

The loan market attempts to ensure compliance with the matters described in the previous section (borrowers' expectations, Lenders' duties, Reg FD, and securities law issues) through three primary tools: (1) confidentiality undertakings, pursuant to which recipients of information agree to maintain the confidentiality of that information; (2) contractual provisions, pursuant to which recipients of information acknowledge that the information received may include MNPI and will be treated accordingly; and (3) explicit notices, pursuant to which recipients of information are warned that they may be receiving MNPI, and instructing (expressly or implicitly) that they should not receive the information if they are public-side personnel. These tools and market best practices will be discussed in more detail in Part 4.

PART 3: LSTA GUIDANCE AND RELEVANT PROVISIONS IN LSTA TRADING DOCUMENTS

The LSTA Guidance contains suggestions regarding best practices for the distribution of confidential information in the syndicated loan market. In addition, the form documentation published by the LSTA contains various provisions that deal with confidential information. The following is a summary of these resources. The tools and practices described in these resources will be applied to market practices in Part 4.

LSTA Guidance

- *Code of Conduct.* The Code of Conduct sets forth voluntary broad standards of conduct that apply to LMPs in connection with their activities in the loan market. These standards are designed to promote integrity, fairness, efficiency, and liquidity in the loan market. Although nonbinding, the general market convention is for LMPs to adhere to the extent possible. Many LMPs have adopted all or portions of the LSTA Guidance as part of their internal compliance policies and procedures.
- *Statement of Principles for the Communication and Use of Confidential Information by Loan Market Participants.* The

Confidentiality Principles provide guidance to LMPs on controls, policies, and procedures for receipt, use, and communication by their employees and Agents of different types of confidential information generally available in the loan market.

Specifically, the Confidentiality Principles, *inter alia*, (1) define the types of information in the loan market (similar to Table 2.1 above); (2) describe the types of information available to public- and private-side LMPs; (3) address the appropriate standards for trading on and disclosure of Syndicate Information and Borrower Restricted Information in loan transactions; (4) describe how confidentiality undertakings may be contained in a "splash page" (which is an electronic workspace set up by an arranger), in the evaluation materials provided to LMPs (e.g., the confidential information memorandum [CIM]), or in a bilateral confidentiality agreement; and (5) recommend tools such as information barriers, trading restrictions, restricted lists, and watch lists for LMPs to comply with applicable securities law.

- *Guidance Note and Confidentiality Legends for Distribution of Syndicated Loan Marketing Materials.* The Guidance Note provides guidance regarding distribution of confidential information and MNPI in the loan market.
    i. *Notice to and Undertaking by Recipients.* The Guidance Note contains a recommended form of Notice to and Undertaking by Recipients to be included in evaluation material (usually a CIM) pursuant to which an LMP is reminded of its confidentiality obligations and, by accepting the evaluation material, agrees to be bound by the confidentiality obligations set forth in the Notice to and Undertaking by Recipients.
    ii. *Company authorization letter.* In the syndicated loan market, it is standard for arrangers to obtain a Company Authorization Letter and rely on a borrower's determination of what information is confidential and what information may constitute MNPI. A Company Authorization Letter is a document provided by the borrower to the arranger that indicates the borrower has been involved in the preparation of the CIM, Lender Presentation (LP), or other

evaluation material, that the information contained in the evaluation material is true and accurate (with certain qualifiers), and whether the evaluation material contains either public information or confidential information. The Company Authorization Letter also authorizes the arranger to distribute the evaluation material. The Guidance Note provides recommended forms of Company Authorization Letters. One such form is for evaluation material that includes MNPI and another is for evaluation material that does not contain MNPI.

   iii. *Special notices—MNPI.* In the Guidance Note, the LSTA recommends that the cover of each CIM or LP clearly indicate whether MNPI may be included within. The Guidance Note contains two forms of Special Notice to be displayed on the cover of the CIM or LP, one that indicates that the CIM or LP may contain MNPI and one that indicates that the CIM or LP does not contain MNPI. If there are both private-side and public-side LMPs in a transaction, the arranger may create two separate versions of the CIM or LP, one that may contain MNPI and one that does not. The cover page of the CIM or LP that contains MNPI would utilize the LSTA form Special Notice Regarding Material Nonpublic Information and be distributed to private-side LMPs, and the cover page of the CIM or LP that does not contain MNPI would utilize the LSTA form Special Notice Regarding Publicly Available Information and be distributed to public-side LMPs.

- *Agency Splash Page Principles.* Finally, the LSTA Agency Splash Page Principles dated May 22, 2006, contain a basic list of recommendations of what should be included in an arranger's splash page. As noted earlier, a splash page is an electronic workspace set up by an arranger. The splash page is a pop-up page that precedes access to information on an Internet-based document delivery system such as SyndTrak. An LMP must click "accept" (and thereby enter into a binding contract to be bound by the splash page terms) before being granted access to the borrower information and deal documents posted on the website. Splash pages almost always contain a confidentiality undertaking and often contain a securities law compliance provision.

LSTA Guidance Regarding Trading Loans in the Secondary Market with Confidential Information

- *Trading syndicated loans on Syndicate Information.* Pursuant to the LSTA Guidance, LMPs may trade on Syndicate Information in a manner "consistent with appropriate standards of professional integrity and fair dealing," and so long as the following parameters are met: (1) it has disclosed the Syndicate Information to its counterparty in accordance with the applicable confidentiality provisions; (2) the counterparty has already received such Syndicate Information; or (3) the LMP has offered to provide such Syndicate Information, but the counterparty has declined such information and (a) the LMP reasonably believes that the counterparty is sophisticated and understands the nature and importance of Syndicate Information and (b) the counterparty has evidenced (or is expected to evidence) in writing that it is not relying on the LMP to provide the Syndicate Information or for investment advice.
- *Trading syndicated loans on Borrower Restricted Information.* The LSTA Guidance provides that LMPs should generally not trade while in possession of Borrower Restricted Information, except "(1) if the LMP has obtained the Borrower Restricted Information without a breach of any duty owed by the LMP to the borrower and (2) the LMP reasonably believes that the counterparty is in possession of or has access to such Borrower Restricted Information." LMPs are advised to depart from such guidance in limited circumstances only with the approval of internal legal and compliance and in accordance with the applicable LMP's internal policies and procedures and in a manner that is generally consistent with the Code of Conduct, which states that an LMP cannot intentionally mislead a trading partner with respect to information and that LMPs should act with professional integrity and fair dealing.

  Borrower Restricted Information may also be subject to confidentiality undertakings beyond those contained in the underlying credit agreement and should be treated accordingly. An LMP that receives Borrower Restricted Information as a result of its participation on a creditor's committee or steering committees could also be subject to additional restrictions (such as trading orders) imposed by the borrower, other members of the committee or a court. Generally, LMPs in receipt of Borrower Restricted Information should exercise caution with respect to any ongoing loan-trading activities and be mindful of the additional confidentiality or other restrictions that may be imposed as a result of such LMP receiving Borrower Restricted Information. In addition, recipients of Borrower Restricted Information may owe fiduciary duties to the borrower or other members of a particular group to which they belong. In each case, an LMP needs to consider its various fiduciary duties when dealing with confidential information of any kind.

LMPs that possess Borrower Restricted Information and wish to trade with other LMPs that do not possess such Borrower Restricted Information may consider using enhanced disclosure language.[11] Such a disclosure should be made in writing on the governing documents used in connection with the transaction and should be explicitly acknowledged in writing by the counterparty.

LSTA Form Documents

In addition to the published guidance described above, the LSTA has also published form trading documents and templates to be utilized in the syndicated loan market. The following LSTA documents are relevant to the distribution and use of confidential information in the syndicated loan market.

- *Form of Credit Agreement.* The LSTA Form of Credit Agreement dated November 1, 2021, provides a template credit agreement for use in syndicated loan transactions. This template includes an agreement by all Lenders to maintain the confidentiality of a borrower's confidential information. This direct confidentiality undertaking

---

[11] Enhanced disclosure language between sophisticated market participants historically has been called "super-big-boy" language. In an effort to move toward more inclusive and less gendered nomenclature, we will refer to such language as "super-sophisticated market participant" or "SSMP" language.

provides the borrower with the necessary assurance of each Lender's confidentiality obligation throughout the life of the credit facility. In addition, the template provides that confidential information by a Lender may be provided to a prospective assignee or participant in connection with a proposed transfer of the loan subject to the prospective assignee or participant agreeing to treat the confidential information in accordance with the applicable credit agreement or no less restrictive confidentiality provisions.

- *Master Confidentiality Agreement:* The LSTA has also issued a form of Master Confidentiality Agreement, effective July 8, 2020, for use in secondary sales and trading (i.e., sales of loans after the initial closing and syndication of the loan). This form can be used by a syndicator to share information with potential post-closing LMP purchasers regarding a variety of borrowers on an ongoing basis without the necessity of separate confidentiality undertakings for each specific transaction. After the Master Confidentiality Agreement is executed, specific transactions are included within the agreement via either (1) execution of a paper schedule identifying the specific borrower and particular transaction documents or (2) the recipient clicking an "Acceptance" button on an electronic workspace that contains information regarding the specific borrower and particular transaction documents. Use of a Master Confidentiality Agreement increases the ease and speed of sharing and accessing and evaluating information regarding loans for sale on the secondary market.

    In practice, some of the Master Confidentiality Agreements among frequent market participants may become outdated, as the parties to the agreement simply add additional schedules every time a new deal enters the market (often with several schedules in effect simultaneously). Although the majority of the market will update the agreements as the LSTA and other sources modify the form, it is good practice to inspect existing Master Confidentiality Agreements from time to time to ensure that the forms are up-to-date.

- *LSTA Trade Confirmation/Purchase and Sale Agreement:* Finally, the LSTA has produced the Trade Confirmation Standard

Terms and Conditions (the "Confirm STCs") form, which works together with its Trade Confirmation form (the "Trade Confirmation") and Purchase and Sale Agreement (PSA) form for distressed trades.[12] When a loan is sold in the secondary market, the verbal agreement (which is binding) is confirmed via the Trade Confirmation, which incorporates the Confirm STCs. For distressed credits, a PSA is also entered into in connection with consummation of the transaction referenced in the Trade Confirmation.

The Confirm STCs contain various acknowledgments and agreements by the buyer and/or seller regarding the nature and importance of Syndicate Information, whether Syndicate Information has been requested/obtained, and each party's responsibilities regarding diligence and providing Syndicate Information. In addition, the Confirm STCs and PSA contain confidentiality undertakings by the parties, an acknowledgment that the Syndicate Information may contain MNPI, and an agreement to handle all MNPI in accordance with applicable securities laws. By utilizing the Confirm STCs, the seller obtains the confidentiality undertakings and securities compliance acknowledgments that would be obtained via an LMP's acceptance of a CIM and splash page click through during the original syndication.

In addition, both the Confirm STCs (under each of the primary, par and distressed regimes) and PSA include a broad nonreliance provision designed to address the potential for information asymmetry in loan trades. Pursuant to this provision, each party to a trade represents and warrants to the other party that it is a sophisticated party with respect to the transaction, has access to the information it deems appropriate to enter into the transaction, and has independently made its own analysis and determination to enter into the transaction. This standard provision also includes an acknowledgment from the buyer that it has not relied upon the seller to furnish any documents or information regarding the borrower or any obligors. The parties can indicate in the specific

---

[12] LSTA trading documents are frequently updated. The most recent versions as of the date of this article were published and made effective on September 13, 2021.

Trade Confirmation whether the buyer has received the underlying credit documents, and if it has not, whether the buyer has agreed not to receive those documents (which is often done when the buyer wishes to remain public on a deal). Perhaps most important, the Confirm STCs contain a mutual acknowledgment that the other party may have and later may come into possession of information regarding the underlying loans and obligor that is not known to it and that may be material to a decision to enter into the transaction as well as a waiver of liability and release of claims in respect of the nondisclosure of such information.

PART 4: MARKET PRACTICE: OVERVIEW OF METHODS OF MANAGING THE RISK

Use of Nonreliance Acknowledgments and Waivers

Although the LSTA Guidance acknowledges that in certain circumstances enhanced disclosure language and explicit acknowledgment of nonreliance may be used,[13] it does not elaborate on the use of Super-Sophisticated Market Participant (SSMP) language or offer any specific guidance in that respect. As a result, analogy to court decisions regarding contractual disclaimers of reliance in connection with securities trading could be helpful in establishing reasonable guidelines and parameters for SSMP language in the syndicated loan context.

The enforceability and effectiveness of nonreliance provisions is highly contextual and depends on the specific facts of the case. However, LMPs should consider several relevant established principles when developing and evaluating their compliance practices and procedures in connection with SSMP provisions. These include an evaluation of the following:

- The sophistication of the parties
- The character of the transaction/trade
- The scope and terms of the disclosure and related acknowledgment
- The materiality of the information at issue

---
[13] Confidentiality Principles (August 2017), p. 5, fn. 12.

- The source of the information
- The intent of the parties
- The reliance of the parties
- The role of each party to the transaction
- Whether there are downstream transactions/trades
- The effect on other market participants
- The overall effect on the market in general

Courts in the securities context have looked for particular items in evaluating the enforceability of nonreliance provisions such as the disclaimer being a product of negotiation between sophisticated parties, the type and quality of the nondisclosed information being specifically described, both parties acknowledging that they voluntarily entered into the sale notwithstanding the nondisclosure, and each party expressly agreeing to do their own due diligence on the transaction and disclaim any reliance on the other party.

It should be noted that under New York law, the "peculiar knowledge" doctrine provides an exception to the enforceability of an exculpatory nonreliance clause and allows for a plaintiff to recover if certain material information is uniquely within the defendant's knowledge or if the plaintiff could have only discovered the truth with extraordinary effort or great difficulty. Agents, in particular, that are in possession of confidential information must be aware of this exception and understand the limitations that it imposes on them even if they enter into SSMP undertakings.

Information Barriers, Controls, Policies, and Procedures

LMPs with personnel or business units that trade on the basis of public information will typically employ information barriers and other controls to separate the public (i.e., traditional securities sales and trading) aspects of their business from their private syndicated lending activities. To remain on the public side, an LMP, or the relevant personnel or group within the LMP, should make sure that it cannot receive or have access to Syndicate Information or Borrower Restricted Information even though such information may be material to a decision whether to buy or sell a loan position. Where an LMP has established effective information barriers, information in the possession of LMP employees or units on the private side of the information barrier should not be imputed to or considered in possession of LMP employees or units on the public side of the information barrier.

A common issue among LMPs that choose to remain on the public side is that certain voting and other rights (often relating to credit agreement amendments, plan support agreements, and/or enforcement of forbearance agreements) are only available to private-side participants. By remaining on the public side, LMPs may be foregoing the right to take such actions and the associated fees that may be available. Public-side LMPs have sought to remedy this issue in a variety of ways, oftentimes appointing internal colleagues in legal, compliance, or operations who are not directly involved with the trading of the specific loan at issue to receive and act on such information (often with standing instructions) or outsourcing to external service providers.[14] In each case, those solutions are imperfect in that often the individuals empowered to make critical investment decisions are not always the individuals in the best position to make the necessary decisions.

The following are some common practices and conventions employed by LMPs that trade in loans and securities or otherwise have an interest in separating public and nonpublic information.

Lenders
- Set up clear policies and procedures to control access to MNPI, including procedures for communicating across functional areas and dealing with inadvertent receipt of MNPI and appropriate recordkeeping.
- Restrict trading in securities if securities traders inadvertently receive MNPI regarding the underlying borrower.
- Maintain lists of restricted securities that cannot be traded or that must be monitored for possible conflicts.
  - *Restricted lists* are internally maintained lists of issuers, some or all of whose securities and other traded instruments a firm has determined to restrict.
  - *Watch lists* are internally maintained lists of issuers whose securities are subject to scrutiny by the financial institution's legal or compliance department.

---

[14] Often personnel in legal, compliance, and operations will be "above the wall" and not subject to the restriction imposed by the information barrier.

- Create information barriers between business units that have access to MNPI and those that do not. These barriers can include the physical, functional, and/or technological separation of personnel, including, for example, (1) separate functional controls such as separate employees, reporting lines, recordkeeping and support groups, and ongoing compliance oversight; (2) physical separation such as separate floors or access areas; and (3) technological controls such as limiting access to files, information databases, or computers that contain nonpublic information.
- Ensure that information is distributed internally on a "need-to-know" basis only.
- Set up an independent compliance and monitoring and testing function.
- Develop and implement training programs for personnel.
- Designate nontrading personnel or outside service providers who can receive and act on Syndicate Information (that may contain MNPI), as necessary (such as voting on an amendment).
- Create an open line of communication among sales/trading, legal, and compliance.

Agents

- Require the borrower to assist in preparing a separate information memorandum and other syndication materials for prospective public-side Lenders that excludes MNPI.
- Distribute syndication materials and borrower information via Internet services that separate information (and access to such information) into separate workspaces for public-side Lenders and private-side Lenders.
- Include some form of confidentiality undertaking with syndication materials whereby recipients acknowledge their obligation to comply with securities laws and maintain confidentiality of the materials, including confidentiality splash pages on websites, legends on documents, cover letters for written materials, or confidentiality agreements.
- Hold two-part bank meetings with prospective Lenders that present only public information in the first half so

that public-side Lenders may be excused before MNPI is presented.
- Execute an agreement with borrowers that the Agent and Lenders can rely on the borrower's determination of whether information is deemed public or private without independent verification and that the Agent is authorized to disseminate any information identified by the borrower as public to the public-side Lenders.

Production and Distribution of Evaluation Materials

When structuring a syndicated loan, the Agent will often compile information about the borrower's business and operations for distribution into a confidential evaluation memorandum and other evaluation materials (collectively, "Evaluation Materials"), which are then made available to all prospective LMPs who are evaluating the loan. In addition, throughout the lifecycle of a syndicated loan, borrowers are typically required to provide ongoing reports, updates, and information to the lending syndicate (often through the Agent) that is also considered Evaluation Material. Because prospective LMPs may want certain business units or personnel to remain on the public side, the borrower will often provide the information necessary to compile separate Evaluation Materials that contain only public information and Bank Loan Non-Restricting Information that does not contain MNPI (i.e., "Non-Restricting Evaluation Materials"). Agents generally will not reevaluate the borrower's determination of what is included in Non-Restricting Evaluation Materials or independently analyze that information.

Per LSTA Guidance, Agents should consider using legends and undertakings (including, without limitation, splash pages) to remind all recipients of Evaluation Materials of their confidentiality obligations and their responsibility to use the information in such Evaluation Materials in a manner consistent with such confidentiality restrictions and in accordance with applicable securities laws. The LSTA Guidance further suggests that Agents should establish and implement procedures for working with borrowers to produce Non-Restricting Evaluation Materials for distribution to public-side LMPs. The procedures could include a requirement that borrowers provide appropriate assurances that the information to be included in the Non-Restricting Evaluation Materials does not contain MNPI.[15]

In connection with the distribution of Evaluation Materials, the LSTA Guidance suggests that Agents should require recipients thereof to provide certain representations and undertakings, including: (1) an agreement that such recipient will maintain the confidentiality of the Evaluation Materials in accordance with the terms of (a) the confidentiality provisions of the underlying credit agreement, (b) the confidentiality provisions set forth on the splash page itself, or (c) the confidentiality provisions included within the Evaluation Materials; (2) an acknowledgment that the Evaluation Materials may contain MNPI (unless information has been designated public or nonrestricting based on a borrower representation); (3) a representation that such recipient has developed compliance procedures regarding the use of MNPI; (4) an undertaking that such recipient will handle MNPI in accordance with applicable law; (5) an acknowledgment that the arranger makes no representation as to the designation of information as public or private but instead has relied on the borrower; and (6) an agreement that the underlying borrower may rely upon all the recipient's representations and undertakings.

With respect to distributions to public-side LMPs, Agents are advised to establish procedures that either (1) clearly mark or identify on the workspace the Evaluation Materials that have been determined to be Non-Restricting Evaluation Materials, or (2) automatically deny access to everything except Non-Restricting Evaluation Materials to public-side LMP declarants.

LMPs that conduct some or all of their loan activities as private-side LMPs often receive MNPI from borrowers. Although these firms may not need to be concerned with internal information controls (in the case that they do not have public side personnel or units), they should still have procedures in place to both identify MNPI they may receive and restrict the transmission of any MNPI to outside parties. This is often performed by technological identification, flagging of information, the use of legends, and other methods as described earlier. Each firm should implement one or more of these measures as appropriate, depending on the firm's size, the information it typically receives, and the type of information that it disseminates.

---

[15] Confidentiality Principles (October 2017), Section IV.C(3), pp. 9–10.

LMPs that conduct some or all of their loan activities as public-side LMPs should implement a more robust system of policies than their private-side counterparts to guard against any violations regarding the receipt of Evaluation Materials. The LSTA Guidance suggests the following: (1) a requirement that public-side employees be permitted to access and view only Non-Restricting Evaluation Materials, (2) compliance oversight and periodic audits designed to ensure that public-side employees' access is limited to Non-Restricting Evaluation Materials only, and (3) restricting trading in securities of a borrower in cases where MNPI inadvertently comes into the possession of public-side employees.[16] Labeling materials as public side or private side (as applicable) and restricting the review of such materials to appropriate personnel should provide further protection against misuse of information.

Public-side LMPs may be asked periodically to act upon Syndicate Information (such as amendment votes, covenant violation waivers, etc.). Because such LPMs will want to avoid receiving Syndicate Information that may contain MNPI, individuals within the institution or external service providers should be designated to receive the information with the authority to act on it. Public-side LMPs should provide such individuals or outside service providers with guidance on how to act in particular circumstances, such as standing instructions or a decision tree, if possible.

In addition, recipients of both Evaluation Materials and Non-Restricting Evaluation Materials are subject to confidentiality undertakings, whether due to the fact that the applicable LMP was part of the initial syndication or purchased the loan in a secondary market transaction. Accordingly, all lenders and prospective lenders, whether on the private side or public side, are subject to and bound by the applicable confidentiality undertakings irrespective of whether such information contains MNPI. Agents in particular may be in receipt of confidential information regarding the borrower that is not yet available to the lenders in the syndicate. Agents must evaluate their underlying confidentiality undertaking and fiduciary duties that may be owed to the borrower as well as the particulars of the information they have received in order to determine if and when such confidential information may be shared externally and internally.

---

[16] Confidentiality Principles (October 2017), Section IV.C(6), p. 11.

CONCLUSION

The syndicate loan market in the United States is unique in that members of a syndicate will often receive or have access to ongoing nonpublic information about the underlying borrower (which could include MNPI). There are inherent risks involved with the receipt of any such information. Establishing proper policies and procedures, together with ongoing compliance oversight, personnel education, and open communication regarding established policies and procedures, is essential to ensure that LMPs in the syndicated loan market mitigate these risks and promote an open and liquid market.

Settling Primary Allocations

Ellen Hefferan
Loan Syndications and Trading Association

INTRODUCTION

Most loans are structured and syndicated to accommodate two primary syndicated Lender constituencies: banks (domestic and foreign) and institutional investors (primarily CLOs, mutual funds, hedge funds, separately managed accounts, and insurance companies). Pro rata debt includes revolving credit and amortizing term loans, which are packaged together and usually syndicated to banks that typically sign the credit agreement. Institutional debt includes term loans structured specifically for institutional investors, though there are some banks that buy institutional term loans.

The arrangers will allocate a term loan facility to prospective committed Buyers during the syndication process. With the announcement that the facility has been fully allocated, the primary syndication is completed, and the loan will immediately break for trading in the secondary market. Because this trading may occur either before or shortly after the credit agreement (or Amendment Agreement) has been made effective, it is often referred to as *when-issued trading*. This article will describe the mechanics and nuances of settling primary allocations and when-issued trades. It will highlight important issues and identify certain pitfalls to avoid as a Seller and as a Buyer when closing these allocations and trades. It will also review the documentation used to settle primary allocations.

BACKGROUND

Until March of 2020 there was neither a standard confirmation nor a delayed compensation protocol applicable to purchasing and closing primary allocations, and, consequently, primary allocations often took weeks to settle. In March of 2020, the LSTA instituted the Primary Delayed Compensation Protocol (the "Protocol"), which was designed to: (1) increase liquidity, (2) expedite the settlement of primary allocations and secondary trades, and (3) comply with the mission of the LSTA, which is to promote a fair, orderly, efficient, and growing corporate loan market and provide leadership in advancing and balancing the interests of all market participants. Implementation of the Protocol resulted in two new legal documents: the LSTA Primary Allocation Confirmation and the LSTA Standard Terms and Conditions for Primary Allocations. To reflect that delayed compensation traveled with settlement risk, the LSTA Standard Terms and Conditions for Par/Near Par Trades was also revised to reflect two new types of secondary trades: Pre-Trigger Trades and Post-Trigger Trades, which are described later in this article.

It should be noted at the beginning of this discussion that the Protocol will not apply in the following circumstances:

- When the Seller and the Administrative Agent and any other entity (other than the borrower and any affiliate of the borrower) that must consent to the transfer of the Facility pursuant to an Assignment Agreement are neither the same Entity nor Affiliates.
- When the Buyer is not onboarded and approved as a counterparty by both the Seller and the Administrative Agent on the Ready Date (as defined below). In this case, the Buyer has not satisfied the know-your-customer (KYC) requirements or other diligence requirements, as determined in the sole discretion of the Seller and the Administrative Agent (each acting in good faith) pursuant to applicable regulatory requirements and each of their respective internal guidelines and procedures.
- If the Allocation is settling on an Electronic Settlement Platform (ESP) and the Buyer is not identified with a unique Markit Entity Identifier (MEI) by the Ready Date.
- If the Allocation settles by participation and not by assignment.

That said, let us assume for the remainder of this chapter that the Protocol does apply.

THE PRIMARY ALLOCATION

In the primary market, arrangers/syndicate desks allocate new or additional money commitments (whether funded or unfunded) to prospective Lenders (the *Allocation*). This takes place in connection with the syndication of either a facility under a new credit agreement or an incremental component of an existing facility or add-on facility under an Amendment Agreement. There are two types of Allocations. A Pre-Trigger Allocation refers to an Allocation that is made or communicated by the Seller (or its affiliate) to the Buyer on or before the Trigger Date. A Post-Trigger Allocation means any Allocation that is made and communicated by the Seller or its affiliate to the Buyer after the Trigger Date.

The *Trigger Date* is the date that the credit agreement or Amendment Agreement becomes effective (aka the Effective Date); provided, however, that if (1) there is no funding of any Facility on such date and that (2) prior to the Settlement Date any Facility subsequently funds, then the Trigger Date is deemed to be the first date on which any Facility subsequently funds. To avoid confusion, *Facility* means the specific facility and/or tranche name under the credit agreement related to the Debt, as specified in the Primary Allocation Confirmation. The *Allocation Date* refers to (1) the *Pre-Trigger Allocation Date* when a Pre-Trigger Allocation is made and communicated by the Seller (or an Affiliate of the Seller) to the Buyer on or before the Trigger Date or (2) the *Post-Trigger Allocation Date* when a Post-Trigger Allocation is made and communicated by the Seller (or an Affiliate of the Seller) to the Buyer after the Trigger Date.

SELLER'S RESPONSIBILITIES

In keeping with the Protocol, the Seller has certain responsibilities.

Delivery of Information to an ESP

To establish the deal and Facility on the ESP within 24 hours of receipt, the Seller must deliver the following to the platform by no later than either (1) the earlier of (a) the Pre-Trigger Allocation Date or (b) three business days before the Trigger Date for a Pre-Trigger Allocation or (2) three business days before the Post-Trigger Allocation Date for a Post-Trigger Allocation:

- (1) a draft of (a) the credit agreement and (b) if the Allocation is pursuant to an Amendment Agreement, the Amendment Agreement or (2) the description of (a) the credit agreement as set forth within the introductory paragraphs of the credit agreement and (b) if the Allocation is pursuant to an Amendment Agreement, the Amendment Agreement as set forth within the introductory paragraphs of the Amendment and,
- Each of the following:
  - Deal and Facility CUSIPs
  - Legal name of the Borrower
  - Legal name of the Facility
  - Legal name and MEI of the Seller
  - Legal name and MEI of the Administrative Agent

Submission of the Assignment Agreement to the ESP

Primary Allocations settle upon the execution of an Assignment Agreement in the form attached to the applicable credit agreement. Under an assignment, the Seller transfers all of its legal, beneficial, and economic rights in the loan to the Buyer. The Buyer becomes the Lender of record when the Administrative Agent updates the applicable register, at which time legal title passes from the Seller to the Buyer, and the Buyer assumes the obligations of the Seller. Agent transfer fees are not applicable to Primary Allocations. For this to be accomplished, the Seller must deliver a substantially final execution version of the Assignment Agreement to the ESP by no later than three business days before (1) the Trigger Date in connection with a Pre-Trigger Allocation or (2) the Post-Trigger Allocation Date in connection with a Post-Trigger Allocation.

The Seller shall review and approve the Assignment Agreement as programmed by the ESP, including additional changes, if any, as the Seller requests, in a timely manner so that the Assignment Agreement is available to the Buyer on the ESP by no later than (1) one business day following the Trigger Date in connection with a Pre-Trigger Allocation or (2) on the Post-Trigger Allocation Date in connection with a Post-Trigger Allocation.

Submission of Allocation Details to the ESP

The Seller must submit the agreed-upon terms of each Allocation, including, without limitation, the Allocation Date, the Facility, the Purchase Amount of the Debt, and the Purchase Rate (collectively, the "Allocation Details") to the ESP by no later than the Allocation Date plus one business day, at which time the allocation ticket must be made available to the Buyer on the ESP. If the Seller submits the details manually, rather than systemically via an automatic upload, such submission must be made by no later than 3:00 p.m. (New York time). Then the ESP will automatically generate an allocation ticket at a master-entity-name level for each Buyer; however, a Buyer that is an asset manager is required to suballocate its ticket into the funds (the actual Buyers) on behalf of which it is acting. The ESP will then generate the necessary closing documents (i.e., the Confirmation, the Assignment Agreement and the funding memo) and facilitate the electronic signature by the Seller, Buyer, and Administrative Agent, as needed. The borrower's signature is automatically populated onto the Assignment Agreement for a Primary Allocation.

Notification of Effective Date and the Funding Date

The Seller must (1) notify the ESP of the occurrence of the Effective Date by no later than 8:00 p.m. (New York time) on (a) the Effective Date in connection with a Pre-Trigger Allocation or (b) the Post-Trigger Allocation Date, in connection with a Post-Trigger Allocation and (2) instruct the ESP to provide a notification to the Buyer of such Effective Date by no later than 9:30 a.m. (New York time) on the next business day.

If there is no funding of any Facility in connection with an Allocation on the Effective Date, and after such date a Facility subsequently funds before the Settlement Date (such date being referred to as the *Funding Date*), the Seller must (1) notify the ESP by no later than 8:00 p.m. (New York time) of the occurrence of such funding on either (a) the Funding Date, in connection with a Pre-Trigger Allocation or (b) the Post-Trigger Allocation Date, in connection with a Post-Trigger Allocation (to the extent the Funding Date had not occurred as of the Post-Trigger Allocation Date) and (2) instruct the ESP to provide a notification to the Buyer of the Funding Date by no later than 9:30 a.m. (New York time) on the next business day.

It is very important for all parties to know the Effective Date and the Funding Date, because they determine the Trigger Date.

The Primary Allocation Confirmation

This confirmation is a two-page document that lists the deal-specific terms of the Allocation. Note that the standard LSTA confirmation incorporates by reference the detailed Standard Terms and Conditions (STCs) that set forth the market conventions and other terms that apply to all allocations.

The terms enumerated on the trade confirmation include the following:

- *Allocation Date*: The date on which an Allocation is made and communicated by the Seller (or an affiliate of Seller) to the Buyer.
- *Seller*: The legal name of the entity communicating the Allocation.
- *Buyer*: The legal name of the entity receiving the Allocation.
- *Credit Agreement*: A legal description of the credit agreement to which the Facility being allocated relates.
- *Purchase amount/type of debt*: The notional amount of debt being allocated, whether it is a term loan, revolver, letter of credit, or other; the relevant facility (tranche); and the CUSIP number.
- *Purchase rate*: Stated as a percentage of par.
- *Upfront fee*: Whether an upfront fee is payable, and, if so, when and by whom.
- *Trade-specific other terms of Allocation*: This is a catchall designed to pick up any mutually agreed upon deviations from the standard confirmation or the STCs.

The confirmation ends with signature blocks for both the Buyer and the Seller.

BUYER'S RESPONSIBILITIES

What Are the Buyer's Responsibilities with Respect to Allocations under the Protocol?

In order to receive Delayed Compensation, in connection with (1) a Pre-Trigger Allocation by no later than the Pre-Trigger Allocation Ready Date (Trigger Date plus three business days) or (2) a Post-Trigger Allocation by no later than the Post-Trigger Allocation Ready Date (Post Trigger Allocation Date plus three business days), the Buyer must:

- Be an entity that (a) maintains an accurate MEI on the ESP and (b) has been onboarded, including meeting the KYC requirements determined by the Administrative Agent/Seller.
- Sign the Trade Confirmation and the Assignment Agreement.
- Select a Proposed Settlement Date of no later than the respective Ready Date and Persist within the ESP.
- In addition, on the Settlement Date, the Buyer must pay the Purchase Price to the Seller.

Proposed Settlement Date means the date proposed and submitted by the Buyer to the ESP as the date the payment of the Purchase Price shall occur in connection with the settlement of the Transaction and the effectiveness of the Assignment Agreement.

Persisted means the election by the Buyer on an ESP whereby it represents that it is financially able to settle the Transaction on any business day from and including the applicable Commencement Date until and including the Delayed Settlement Date without interruption. The *Ready Date* means either a Pre-Trigger Allocation Ready Date or a Post-Trigger Allocation Ready Date, as the case may be.

In addition, if the Seller fails to make the Allocation Details available on the ESP by the Allocation Date plus one business day:

- The Buyer must notify the Seller by no later than the Allocation Date plus three business days that the Allocation Details are not available on the ESP.
- Upon such notification, the Seller must submit the Allocation Details into the ESP by no later than the Allocation Date plus four business days.

- If the details are not entered by this time, a Buyer that has met the Seller's and Administrative Agent's onboarding requirements shall receive Primary Delayed Compensation from the respective Commencement Date, provided, however, that the Buyer pays the Purchase Price on the Settlement Date in accordance with any applicable lead time.
- If the details are entered by the Allocation Date plus four business days, instead of satisfying the requirements by the Ready Date the Buyer must, by no later than six Business Days after the Trigger Date for Pre-Trigger Allocations or by no later than six Business Days after the Post-Trigger Allocation Date for Post-Trigger Allocations, execute the Primary Allocation confirmation and assignment agreement and select a proposed settlement date of no later than such date and persist within the ESP in order to receive delayed compensation from the Commencement Date. Again, the Buyer must have met the Seller's and Administrative Agent's onboarding requirements by the Ready Date and paid the Purchase Price on the Settlement Date in accordance with any applicable lead time.

When Does Delayed Compensation Begin?

Provided that all Buyer requirements have been met, delayed compensation will commence on the *Pre-Trigger Commencement Date* (Pre-Trigger Allocation Ready Date plus six Business Days) if a Pre-Trigger Allocation has not been settled by this date and on the *Post-Trigger Commencement Date* (Post-Trigger Allocation Ready Date plus six Business Days) if a Post-Trigger Allocation has not been settled by this date. The *Commencement Date* means either a Pre-Trigger Commencement Date or a Post-Trigger Commencement Date, as the case may be. Examples 2.1 and 2.2 are based on the timeline presented in Exhibit 2.9.

EXHIBIT 2.9

Pre-Trigger Allocation Model.

Pre-Trigger Allocation Date Mon Jan 25		Trigger Date (Funding Date) Wed Jan 27		Fri Jan 29		Tues Feb 2		Thurs Feb 4		Mon Feb 8	
	Tues Jan 26		Thurs Jan 28		Pre-Trigger Allocation Ready Date = (Trigger Date +3) Mon Feb 1		Wed Feb 3		Fri Feb 5		Commencement Date = (Pre-Trigger Allocation Ready Date +6) Tues Feb 9

When calculating the Purchase Price for this Pre-Trigger Allocation, multiply the funded amount of the loan on the Settlement Date by the Purchase Rate. This section describes the price being paid for the loan. All loan trade prices are expressed as a percentage of par.

Assuming the allocation of a term loan settles on or before the applicable Commencement Date (February 9), the Purchase Price for the Allocation would be the fully funded commitment amount multiplied by the Purchase Rate, as shown in Example 2.1.

EXAMPLE 2.1

Term Loan Pre-Trigger Allocation, Settlement on or before the Commencement Date (Pre-Trigger Allocation Ready Date +6 Business Days).

Pre-Trigger Allocation Date:	January 25th	
Trigger Date:	January 27th	
Settlement Date:	Any day from January 27th up to and including February 9th	
Term Loan Purchase Price:	$5,000,000 × 99.50%	$4,975,000.00

Although calculating the price of a funded loan is simple (notional amount × Purchase Rate), calculating the price for an unfunded revolver is trickier, because the Buyer will fund the loan at par no matter what the Purchase Rate under the trade may be. An example illustrates this concept: Assume that a Buyer purchases a $5,000,000 loan commitment at 98%, and assume that $4,000,000 is funded and $1,000,000 is unfunded but available to the borrower. At closing, the Buyer would pay the Seller $3,920,000 ($4,000,000 × 98%) minus a credit on the unfunded portion equal to $20,000 [$1,000,000 × (100% − 98%)], for a total purchase price of $3,900,000. This protects the Buyer if any portion of the $1,000,000 is drawn by the Borrower later.

Delayed Compensation and Cost-of-Carry Calculations

Solely for the purpose of determining the Commencement Date, a Business Day is any day that is not a Saturday, a Sunday, or some other day on which the Federal Reserve Bank of New York or the New York Stock Exchange is closed. If a primary allocation closes after the Commencement Date, it is considered a *delayed settlement*. To compensate for the delay, a credit to the Purchase Price shall be given by the Seller to the Buyer in an amount equal to Interest, that is, the *All-In-Rate*, which is the appropriate reference rate + margin + spread adjustment (if applicable) and the Accruing Fees accrued with respect to the Purchase Amount of the Debt and allocable from the Commencement Date through but not including the Settlement Date (the *Delay Period*). To further compensate for the Delay, the Buyer shall pay the Seller (or if the Seller is required to pay the Buyer the Purchase Price, the Seller shall pay the Buyer) on the Delayed Settlement Date an amount equal to interest that would accrue for each day during the Delay Period at the Cost of Carry Rate (as defined below) on an amount equal to the Purchase Price calculated as of the Commencement Date utilizing the loan and commitment amounts outstanding on the Commencement Date (but without adjustment for delayed compensation payable hereunder). If the Purchase Price (without adjustment for delayed compensation, Assignment Fees or Consent to Transfer Fees; i.e., the *Gross Purchase Price*) calculated on the Delayed Settlement Date has increased or decreased more than 25% from the Purchase Price calculated as of the Commencement Date, then the cost of carry shall be calculated based on the Gross Purchase Price so calculated on each day during the Delay Period.

For trades entered into prior to December 1, 2021, the Cost of Carry Rate for the Delay Period means:

- (i) If the debt references (a) a LIBOR or (b) an Alternate Base Rate (ABR) as defined in the credit agreement as the applicable benchmark rate of interest as of the last day of the Delay Period, (1) the sum of all the individual one-month LIBOR for each day in the period from (and including) the date two Business Days before the Commencement Date and to (but excluding) the date that is two Business Days before the Delayed Settlement Date (2) divided by the total number of days in such period.
- (ii) If the Debt references a risk-free rate (RFR) as the applicable benchmark rate of interest as of the last day of the Delay Period, (1) the sum of all the individual applicable RFRs for each day in the period from (and including) the date two Business Days before the Commencement Date and to (but excluding) the date that is two Business Days before the Delayed Settlement Date and (2) divided by the total number of days in such period.
- (iii) If the Debt references a benchmark rate other than one described in clause (i) or (ii) above (including, but not limited to, a Credit Sensitive Rate) as the applicable

benchmark rate of interest as of the last day of the Delay Period, (1) the sum of all of the individual RFRs applicable for the LIBOR Currency in which the Debt is denominated for each day in the period from (and including) the date two Business Days before the Commencement Date and to (but excluding) the date that is two Business Days before the Delayed Settlement Date and (2) divided by the total number of days in such period; and

- (iv) If the debt references both a LIBOR and one or more of any other benchmark rate described in clause (ii) or (iii) as applicable benchmark rates of interest as of the last day of the Delay Period, (1) the sum of all the individual applicable RFRs for each day in the period from (and including) the date two Business Days before the Commencement Date and to (but excluding) the date that is two Business Days before the Delayed Settlement Date and (2) divided by the total number of days in such period.
- With respect to a Multi-Currency Commitment, the applicable RFR shall be the RFR in the Master Currency.
- For trades entered into on or after December 1, 2021, regardless of the rate that the Debt references, the Cost of Carry Rate for the Delay Period will mean (1) the sum of all of the individual daily simple Secured Overnight Financing Rates (SOFR) for each day in the period from (and including) the date two Business Days before the Commencement Date and to (but excluding) the date that is two Business Days before the Delayed Settlement Date, (2) divided by the total number of days in such period (3) plus a spread. Adjustment equal to 11,448 basis points.

Based on the timeline presented in Exhibit 2.9, if you settle the same allocation after February 9th, for example, on February 16th, delayed compensation will be due to the Buyer by passing the All-in-Rate from February 9th through but not including February 16th. For purposes of delayed compensation, assume that the new Term Loan Facility is earning the daily SOFR determined on a lookback of two Business Days. Further assume that the daily SOFR, also determined on a lookback of two Business Days is utilized to calculate the Cost of Carry Rate. Note that February 15th is not a Business Day. The Facility is earning a margin of 4%.

EXAMPLE 2.2

Term Loan Pre-Trigger Allocation, Settlement after Commencement Date.

Pre-Trigger Allocation Date:	January 25th		
Trigger Date:	January 27th		
Commencement Date:	February 9th		
Settlement Date:	February 16th		
TL purchase price:	$5,000,000 × 99.50%		$4,975,000.00
Less: delayed compensation:			
	$5,000,000 ×		
February 9th	(.0002+.04/360)	$ 558.33	
February 10th	(.0002+.04/360)	$ 558.33	
February 11th	(.0005+.04/360)	$ 562.50	
February 12–15th	(.0006+.04/360) × 4	$ 2,255.56	−3,934.72
Plus:			
Seller's cost of carry:	$4.975,000 ×		
	((.0002+.0002+.0005+.0006)/ 4+.0011448) x 7/360		147.02
Delayed Settlement Purchase Price:			$4,971,212.30

EXHIBIT 2.10

Post-Trigger Allocation Model.

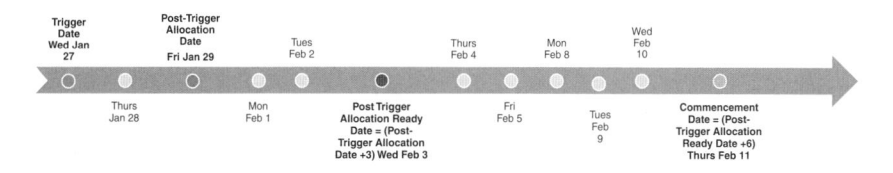

Examples 2.3 and 2.4 are based on the timeline presented in Exhibit 2.10. When calculating the Purchase Price for this Post-Trigger term loan Allocation, multiply the funded amount of the loan on the Settlement Date by the Purchase Rate. Assuming that the Allocation settles on or before the applicable Commencement Date (February 11), the Purchase Price for the Allocation would be the fully funded commitment amount multiplied by the Purchase Rate, as shown in Example 2.3.

EXAMPLE 2.3

Term Loan Post-Trigger Allocation, Settlement on or Before the Commencement Date (Post-Trigger Allocation Ready Date Plus Six Business Days).

Trigger Date:	January 27th	
Post-Trigger Allocation Date:	January 29th	
Settlement Date:	Any day from January 29th up to and including February 11th	
Term Loan Purchase Price:	$5,000,000 × 99.50%	$4,975,000.00

If the trade settles on February 16th, delayed compensation will be due to the Buyer by passing the All-in-Rate from February 11th through, but not including, February 16th.

EXAMPLE 2.4

Term Loan Post-Trigger Allocation, Settlement after Commencement Date.

Trigger Date:	January 27th		
Post-Trigger Allocation Date:	January 29th		
Commencement Date:	February 11th		
Settlement Date:	February 16th		
TL purchase price:	$5,000,000 × 99.50%		$4,975,000.00
Less: delayed compensation:			
	5,000,000 ×		
February 11th	(.0005 +.04)/360	$ 562.50	
February 12th–15th	(.0006 +.04/360) × 4	$ 2,255.56	−2,818.06
Plus:			
Seller's cost of carry:	$4,975,000 ×		
	((.0005 +.0006)/2+.0011448) × 5/360		117.11
Delayed Settlement Purchase Price:			$4,972,299.05

How Did the Protocol Change the Secondary Market?

The Protocol adds two new types of secondary trades, the Pre-Trigger Trade and the Post-Trigger Trade, while retaining, though amending, the Early Day Trade. When a Facility previously allocated by means of a Pre-Trigger Allocation is traded in the secondary market on or prior to the first business day following the Trigger Date for that Facility, this is defined as a *Pre-Trigger Trade*. When a Facility previously allocated by means of a Post-Trigger Allocation is traded in the secondary market on the Post-Trigger Allocation Date or the following Business Day, this is defined as a *Post-Trigger Trade*. Delayed compensation for the primary allocations will mirror the delayed compensation for the Pre-Trigger and Post-Trigger Trades. This is important because delayed compensation should pass with the risk.

The Protocol also revises the definition of an Early Day Trade. *Early Day Trade* will continue to mean a trade of a Facility in which the Trade Date is a date on or before the sixth Business Day following the Trigger Date for the Facility. The definition has been modified to clarify that an Early Day Trade relates to a Facility whose underlying Allocation did not meet the terms of the Protocol. The Buyer of such Allocation was not capable of receiving delayed compensation, and therefore delayed compensation with respect to an Early Day Trade continues to begin at the Trigger Date plus fourteen Business Days.

Any trade other than a Pre-Trigger Trade, a Post-Trigger Trade, or an Early Day Trade is defined as a Secondary Trade. The settlement of Secondary Trades is described in Chapter 6.

Note that a Pre-Trigger Trade or a Post-Trigger Trade is based upon whether the Facility was previously allocated to prospective Lenders by means of Pre-Trigger Allocations or Post-Trigger Allocations, in which case had the Allocations not settled by the Ready Date plus six Business Days the prospective Lenders would have been capable of receiving the economic benefit of interest and accruing ordinary course fees under the STCs of such Primary Allocation Confirmation. It is not based upon whether the actual Seller, party to the trade, received such Pre-Trigger or Post-Trigger Allocation.

What Are the Buyer's Responsibilities with Respect to Pre-Trigger and Post-Trigger Trades under the Protocol?

To receive delayed compensation in connection with (1) a Pre-Trigger Trade by no later than the Pre-Trigger Trade Ready Date

(Trigger Date plus five Business Days) or (2) a Post-Trigger Trade by no later than the Post-Trigger Trade Ready Date (Post-Trigger Allocation Date plus five Business Days), the Buyer must:

- Sign the Trade Confirmation and the Assignment Agreement.
- Select a Proposed Settlement Date of no later than the respective Commencement Date and Persist within the ESP.
- In addition, on the Settlement Date the Buyer must pay the Purchase Price to the Seller.

If the Buyer Fulfills the Requirements and the Allocation or Trade Has Not Previously Settled, When Does Delayed Compensation Begin?

In connection with a Pre-Trigger Allocation, delayed compensation begins on the *Pre-Trigger Commencement Date* (Pre-Trigger Allocation Ready Date plus six Business Days).

In connection with a Post-Trigger Allocation, delayed compensation begins on the *Post-Trigger Commencement Date* (Post-Trigger Allocation Ready Date plus six Business Days).

In connection with a Pre-Trigger Trade, delayed compensation begins on the *Pre-Trigger Commencement Date* (Pre-Trigger Trade Ready Date plus four Business Days).

In connection with a Post-Trigger Trade, delayed compensation begins on the *Post-Trigger Commencement Date* (Post-Trigger Trade Ready Date plus four Business Days).

When delayed compensation applies, the cost of carry simultaneously applies.

When calculating the Purchase Price for the Pre-Trigger Trade, set forth in Example 2.5, multiply the funded amount of the loan on the Settlement Date by the Purchase Rate. This section describes

EXHIBIT 2.11

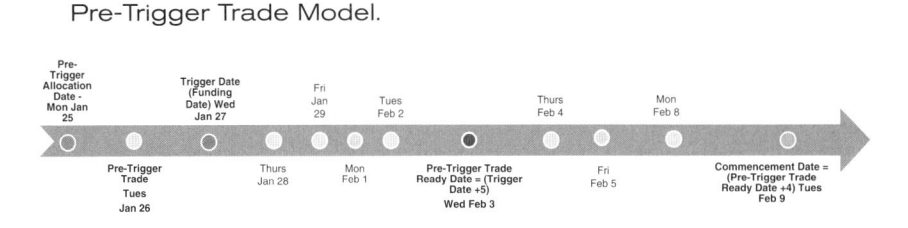

Pre-Trigger Trade Model.

Pre-Trigger Allocation Date - Mon Jan 25
Pre-Trigger Trade Tues Jan 26
Trigger Date (Funding Date) Wed Jan 27
Thurs Jan 28
Fri Jan 29
Mon Feb 1
Tues Feb 2
Pre-Trigger Trade Ready Date = (Trigger Date +5) Wed Feb 3
Thurs Feb 4
Fri Feb 5
Mon Feb 8
Commencement Date = (Pre-Trigger Trade Ready Date +4) Tues Feb 9

the Purchase Price being paid for the loan on any day up to and including the Commencement Date, February 9th.

Examples 2.5 and 2.6 are based on the timeline presented in Exhibit 2.11.

EXAMPLE 2.5

Term Loan Pre-Trigger Trade, Settlement on or before the Commencement Date (Pre-Trigger Trade Ready Date Plus Four Business Days).

Pre-Trigger Trade Date:	January 26th	
Trigger Date:	January 27th	
Settlement Date:	Any day from January 27th up to and including February 9th	
Term Loan Purchase Price:	$5,000,000 × 99.75%	$4,987,500.00

If the trade settles on February 16th, delayed compensation will be due to the Buyer by passing the All-in-Rate from February 9th through but not including February 16th.

EXAMPLE 2.6

Term Loan Pre-Trigger Trade, Settlement after Commencement Date.

Pre-Trigger Trade Date:	January 26th		
Trigger Date:	January 27th		
Commencement Date:	February 9th		
Settlement Date:	February 16th		
TL purchase price:	$5,000,000 × 99.75%		$4,987,500.00
Less: delayed compensation:			
	$5,000,000 ×		
February 9th	(.0002+.04)/360	$ 558.33	
February 10th	(.0002+.04)/360	$ 558.33	
February 11th	(.0005+.04)/360	$ 562.50	
February 12th–15th	(.0006+.04/360) × 4	$2,255.56	−3,934.72
Plus:			
Seller's cost of carry:	$4,987,500 ×		
	((.0002+.0002+.0006+.0002)/4 +.0011448) × 7/360		140.12
Delayed Settlement Purchase Price:			$4,983,705.40

EXHIBIT 2.12

Post-Trigger Trade Model.

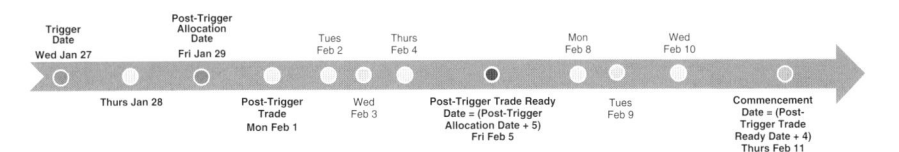

```
Trigger          Post-Trigger
Date             Allocation          Tues     Thurs                    Mon        Wed
Wed Jan 27       Date                Feb 2    Feb 4                    Feb 8      Feb 10
                 Fri Jan 29
───○──────●──────○──────●──────●──────●──────●──────●──────●──────●──────●──────────▶
      Thurs Jan 28    Post-Trigger    Wed     Post-Trigger Trade Ready    Tues    Commencement
                      Trade           Feb 3   Date = (Post-Trigger        Feb 9   Date = (Post-
                      Mon Feb 1               Allocation Date + 5)                Trigger Trade
                                              Fri Feb 5                           Ready Date + 4)
                                                                                  Thurs Feb 11
```

When calculating the Purchase Price for this Post-Trigger Trade, multiply the funded amount of the loan on the Settlement Date by the Purchase Rate. Example 2.7 describes the Purchase Price being paid for the loan on any day up to and including February 11th.

Examples 2.7 and 2.8 are based on the timeline presented in Exhibit 12.2.

EXAMPLE 2.7

Term Loan Post-Trigger Trade, Settlement on or before the Commencement Date (Post-Trigger Trade Ready Date +4 Business Days).

Trigger Date:	January 27th
Post-Trigger Allocation Date:	January 29th
Trade Date:	February 1st
Settlement Date:	Any day from January 29th up to and including February 11th
Term Loan Purchase Price:	$5,000,000 × 99.75% $4,987,500.00

The trade settles the same trade on February 16th, delayed compensation will be due to the Buyer by passing the All-in-Rate from February 11th, the Commencement Date, through but not including February 16th.

EXAMPLE 2.8

Term Loan Post-Trigger Trade, Settlement after Commencement Date.

Trigger Date:	January 27th
Post-Trigger Allocation Date:	January 29th
Trade Date:	February 1st
Commencement Date:	February 11th
Settlement Date:	February 16th

The Primary Market

Term Loan Purchase Price	$5,000,000 × 99.75%		$4,987,500.00
Less: delayed compensation:			
	$5,000,000 times:		
February 11th	(.0005+.04)/360	$ 562.50	
February 12th–15th	(.0006+.04)/360*4	$2,255.56	−2,818.06
Plus:			
Seller's cost of carry:	$4,987,500 times:		
	((.0005+.0006)/2+.0011448)*5/360		117.40
Delayed settlement purchase price:			$4,984,799.34

To navigate the new changes, please refer to Table 2.2.

Allocation/ Trade	Allocation Date/Trade Date	Ready Date	Commencement Date
Pre-Trigger Allocation	Pre-Trigger Allocation Date = on or before the Trigger Date	Trigger Date + 3 BDs	Pre-Trigger Allocation Ready Date + 6 BDs
Pre-Trigger Trade	On or before Trigger Date +1 BD	Trigger Date +5 BDs	Pre-Trigger Trade Ready Date +4 BDs
Secondary Trade	On or after Trigger Date +2 BDs	Trade Date + 5 BDs	Trade Date + 7 BDs
Post-Trigger Allocation	Post-Trigger Allocation Date = after the Trigger Date	Post-Trigger Allocation Date +3 BDs	Post-Trigger Allocation Ready Date + 6 BDs
Post-Trigger Trade	Post-Trigger Allocation Date or Post-Trigger Allocation Date +1 BD	Post-Trigger Allocation Date +5 BDs	Post-Trigger Trade Ready Date +4 BDs
Secondary Trade	On or after Post-Trigger Allocation Date +2 BDs	Trade Date + 5 BDs	Trade Date + 7 BDs
Allocation – Protocol does not apply	Not applicable	Not applicable	Not applicable
Early Day Trade	On or before Trigger Date +6 BDs	Trigger Date +10	Early Day Trade Ready Date +4 BDs
Secondary Trade	On or After Trigger Date +7 BDs	Trade Date +5 BDs	Trade Date +7 BDs

Note: BD refers to Business Days.

Bringing Benchmarks to the Complex Realm of Loan Covenants[17]

Steven Miller
Covenant Review, a Fitch Solutions Service

Peter Drucker is credited with the management aphorism: "If you can't measure it, you can't improve it." Over the past 30 years, the loan market has experienced the power of this idea as vendors have introduced a variety of quantitative tools—such as credit ratings, return indices, default rates, loan-loss statistics, leverage trends, new-issue-spread averages, secondary pricing services, portfolio management software and analytical tools, and the list goes on—that have allowed the market to blossom from a largely closed, bank-only financing segment to a trillion-dollar-plus asset class with a large and vibrant investor base. In recent years, covenant terms have joined the long list of topics that have drawn investor scrutiny, and thus merit a quantitative benchmark.

Since the Global Financial Crisis of 2008, deteriorating covenant protection is the most profound—and arguably least understood—loan market theme. Unlike spreads and credit statistics, which have long been subject to fundamental and technical conditions, tightly drawn covenants were an unwavering pillar of leveraged loans until the mid-2000s, when improved secondary liquidity and booming demand from CLO vehicles opened the door to more flexible terms. The first link in this chain, of course, was the advent of covenant-lite structures that replaced the traditional maintenance financial tests for looser, bondlike incurrence tests. Covenant lite has gone from the exception to the rule, now comprising more than 90% of such market-standard indices as the Credit Suisse Leveraged Loan Index and the S&P/LSTA Leveraged Loan Index.

---

[17] Covenant Review acknowledges Jonathan Blau for his critical intellectual contribution—conceptually, mathematically, and coding-wise—to the development and ongoing evolution of the documentation scores.

With covenant-lite structures now pervasive, saying a loan is covenant lite is now like calling a TV high-definition or a mobile phone a smartphone. The once-novel has now become standard. Thus, credit agreements require new metrics that look deeper to see how much, say, collateral leakage the agreement allows, or how much debt an issuer can pile onto its balance sheet without permission from lenders.

It was in this context that *Covenant Review*, a Fitch Solutions Service, developed Documentation Scores. The Scores run from 1 (highest) to 5 (lowest) for each first-lien syndicated U.S. loan we analyze. As of year-end 2020, the initial data set covered more than 95% of the par amount of first-lien loans in the U.S. and European Credit Suisse Leveraged Loan Index. The Documentation Scores and Sub-Scores are generated by a rigorous mathematical model based on a combination of empirical data, qualitative factors, and judgment grades from *Covenant Review*'s legal analysts.

Documentation Scores and Sub-Scores are each published in three phases:

- An Initial Score on Term Sheet is circulated with a loan's offering memo. *Covenant Review* projects a score using information available in the Term Sheet, supplemented with (1) averages for other fields over the prior three months to form an *Expected Average Score* and (2) the weakest data for the unavailable fields to form an *Expected Worst-Case Score*. *Covenant Review* also provides a completion factor to give participants a read on what percentage of the fields is based on actual data culled from the term sheet.
- Preliminary Scores on the draft credit agreement are circulated to potential lenders during syndication.
- Final Score information is based on the executed credit agreement.

In addition to a composite Documentation Score, *Covenant Review* provides Sub-Scores that reflect the document's efficacy in (1) limiting collateral leakage, (2) limiting the issuer's ability to put further stress on the balance sheet, and (3) allowing lenders to extract additional value in the form of wider spreads or fees if the borrower's financial condition deteriorates or it tries to amend the document. Understanding and measuring this final point, which often seems pro forma, was brought into stark relief by Serta, the bedding manufacturer. Serta, in fact, has become synonymous with the ways in which loans that are structured with a simple majority vote to approve priming debt to, as *Covenant Review* described in a note dated November 10, "subordinating their senior secured credit facility in right of payment and/or security to other permitted debt." Along with Serta, in 2020, lenders in TriMark and Board Riders exploited this loophole to subordinate claims of fellow first-lien lenders.

CHAPTER 3
Understanding the Credit Agreement

Michael Bellucci
Partner
Milbank LLP

Jerome McCluskey
Partner
Milbank LLP

INTRODUCTION

This chapter is intended to address some of the basic questions that a lender, borrower, or their respective counsel may confront in understanding a standard credit agreement. It is broken into 11 parts.

Some key assumptions should be kept in mind when reading this chapter. First, we address only syndicated credit agreements for nonbankrupt borrowers. We will not address the unique issues that arise in the context of debtor-in-possession financings, for example, or other forms of lending. Second, although we discuss some of the issues that arise with non-U.S. borrowers, the principal thrust of this chapter will be issues raised when lending to domestic companies. Third, we presume (unless indicated otherwise) that the credit agreement will be governed by New York law. We do not, in particular, address issues that would arise under an English-law credit agreement. Last, for ease of reading, we generally refer throughout this chapter to provisions applicable to "the borrower." Other than in the context of the making of loans, the term should nevertheless be understood to include subsidiaries of the borrower, and it should be noted that many provisions, including representations and warranties, covenants, and events of default, apply as well to other parties (guarantors, pledgors, and others) that support the credit.

This chapter is intended to be solely an overview of the most common provisions found in a credit agreement. It cannot encompass the tremendous variety of provisions found in credit agreements. Also what is typical practice today will certainly evolve over time as new pricing options are created, new covenants are devised, new court decisions are rendered, new tax structures evolve, and new regulations are implemented. We hope, nevertheless, that the reader will find the explanations here useful as a resource when reviewing or drafting the next credit agreement that comes across his or her desk. Lastly, for a more fulsome treatment of each of the topics covered in this chapter, we would suggest that the reader consider looking to the authors' book, *The LSTA's Complete Credit Agreement Guide, Second Edition* as another resource.

Part 1: Making the Loan: Commitments, Loans, and Letters of Credit

CREDIT VARIANTS

Loans

In its simplest form, a credit agreement will provide merely for loans; in its more complex forms, it may encompass letters of credit and deposit facilities as alternative ways of making credit available to borrowers. Over many decades, the financial markets have developed a number of loan variants, as well as other devices by which lenders can provide financing to borrowers. Here we discuss the following:

- *Revolving credit versus term loans.* Revolving credit loans, as their name implies, "revolve" within "commitments" established by the lenders. The borrower may borrow, repay, and reborrow the loans during the term of the commitments, so long as the applicable conditions to borrowing are satisfied. By contrast, term loans, once borrowed and repaid, may not be reborrowed. This is not to say that term loans cannot be made available under commitments that contemplate multiple drawdowns (a so-called delayed draw or standby term loan facility), but simply that once the loan has been repaid, the borrower has no ability to reborrow the amount repaid. An easy analogy is to equate revolving credit loans to credit card debt and term loans to a home mortgage.
- *A and B loan tranches.* Term loans have evolved over time into two types: a so-called A loan tranche and B loan tranche. A loans are generally understood to be term loans that are made by bank lenders (as opposed to funds or other institutional investors), have a tenor equal to the term of any revolving credit commitments in the credit agreement, and are entitled to the benefit of real amortization; that is, installments that over the term of the loan will represent sizeable (and not just nominal) paydowns of the principal amount of the facility. By contrast, B loans will have a

maturity longer than any related A loan (usually six months to a year longer), and have only nominal amortization until the last year (i.e., typically 0.25% per quarter and 1% per year until the last year or the very final installment). Revolving credit and A loans are often referred to as the *pro rata tranches*; B loans are referred to as the *B tranche*. The latter is true even though a credit agreement may have multiple series of B loans (Series B, Series C, Series D, and so forth).

- *Swingline loans.* Swingline loans are loans made available by a "swingline lender." They are an adjunct to and a sublimit within the revolving credit facility. One purpose is to give the borrower faster availability to loans than would otherwise be permitted under the notice periods prescribed in the credit agreement, which will typically require at least three business days' notice for London Interbank Offered Rate (LIBOR) loans and one business day's notice for base rate loans. Even in cases where same-day availability is allowed for base rate loans, a swingline facility will permit loans to be made later in the day. The reason swingline loans can be made on such short notice is that they are being advanced by only one lender, usually the lender serving as the administrative agent (though some agreements will contemplate more than one swingline lender). A second purpose is to give the borrower access to loans of lower minimum amounts than would otherwise be required for a syndicated borrowing from all the lenders participating in the revolving credit facility.

  Swingline facilities have several key features. First, the swingline lender will customarily be obligated to make swingline loans only within the limit of its revolving credit commitment. Second, a maximum amount of swingline loans will be specified. Third, swingline loans will normally be required to be repaid in a very short time, typically within five business days or two weeks and, sometimes, concurrently with the next regular borrowing under the credit agreement. Finally, in the event that for any reason the borrower does not repay the swingline loans within their prescribed maturity (including by reason of an intervening event of default or even bankruptcy), the other revolving credit lenders will be unconditionally obligated to purchase participations in the swingline loans so that the risk of the swingline loans is shared ratably among all revolving credit lenders.

Letters of Credit

Often a credit agreement will provide that the revolving credit facility is available not only for loans, but also for letters of credit, with the maximum for both loans and letters of credit not to exceed the amount of the revolving credit commitments. Typically, the aggregate amount of letters of credit must be within a sublimit of the revolving credit commitments.

The content of the letter of credit provisions in a credit agreement is driven in large part by the nature of letters of credit. A letter of credit is an undertaking by the issuer of the letter of credit (virtually always a bank, although legally it can be anyone) to pay the beneficiary of the letter of credit a specified sum upon delivery of documents during the term of the letter of credit. The issuer is *unconditionally* obligated to honor a drawing under the letter of credit if the proper documents are presented, without any requirement on the part of the issuer to verify the truth of statements in the documents. So long as the documents "strictly comply" with the terms of the letter of credit, the issuer is obligated to pay. The borrower (in letter of credit terminology, the *account party*) will, in turn, be unconditionally obligated to reimburse the issuer for the amount paid by the issuer as a result of any drawing under the letter of credit.

Letters of credit can be either commercial letters of credit (if they support the shipment of and payment for goods) or standby or performance letters of credit (if they support an obligation of the borrower to make payments to a third party under a separate contract). Standby or performance letters of credit may be issued to support, say, a borrower's obligation to an insurance company for workers' compensation payments or franchise obligations by a cable television company to a municipality or an infinite variety of other obligations.

Letters of credit issued under syndicated credit agreements will rarely have an expiration date more than one year after issuance, though market practice has adopted the concept of an "evergreen" letter of credit. In an evergreen letter of credit, the initial expiration date will automatically be extended for an additional year (or other period) unless the issuer notifies the beneficiary within, say, 30 days that the letter of credit will not be renewed. Commercial letters of credit are typically for shorter terms; standby letters of credit are of longer duration and will, if appropriate, employ the evergreen option. A credit agreement will normally not allow letters of credit to have an expiration date (taking into account evergreen renewals) beyond the termination date of the revolving credit commitments.

The credit agreement will commonly require the borrower to reimburse the issuer of a letter of credit on the day upon which a drawing under the letter of credit is honored by the issuer (or, at most, one business day later). Sometimes the credit agreement will state that the reimbursement claim automatically converts into revolving credit loans, with the lenders obligated to fund their portion of the loans so that the issuer obtains full reimbursement for the drawing.

To ensure that the exposure to the borrower associated with each letter of credit is shared by all of the revolving credit lenders ratably in accordance with their revolving credit commitments, the credit agreement will commonly provide that each revolving credit lender is deemed to have acquired a participation in the letter of credit upon its being issued. Payment for such participation is not required unless the borrower shall for any reason (including bankruptcy) fail to reimburse the issuer, at which point the revolving credit lenders will be unconditionally obligated to pay for their previously purchased participations in the related reimbursement claim.

A point that sometimes arises in negotiating letter of credit provisions is what happens if the issuer wrongfully honors (or dishonors) a drawing made under a letter of credit. The customary approach is to provide that the issuer may dishonor any drawing that does not "strictly comply" with the provisions of the letter of credit, but to require the borrower to reimburse the issuer for any drawing honored by the issuer that "substantially complies" with the requirements of the letter of credit. Letters of credit normally require that documents strictly comply, but to protect the issuer against close judgment calls in reviewing documents, the "substantially complies" standard is applicable as between the issuer and the borrower and the borrower's reimbursement obligation.

Letters of credit cannot be unilaterally paid off. If the borrower wishes to refinance the loans under a credit agreement, it can do so easily just by prepaying the outstanding principal with interest. However, because a letter of credit is an unconditional obligation of the issuer to the beneficiary, it cannot be cancelled by the issuer without the beneficiary's consent. The only way it can be "refinanced" is by causing a replacement letter of credit to be issued to the beneficiary and having the beneficiary consent to the termination of the letter of credit under the credit agreement. To coordinate this at a closing can be cumbersome, especially if there are many letters of credit outstanding at the time. An alternative custom that has developed is for the letters of credit under the credit agreement to continue even following a refinancing and for the borrower either to post cash collateral for its reimbursement obligation or to post a backup letter of credit from another institution to support the reimbursement obligation. In either event, the amount of cash posted or the face amount of the backup letter of credit will normally be 102% to 105% of the potential reimbursement obligation, in order to cover letter of credit fees and any default interest accruing on the reimbursement obligation. The borrower would then undertake to replace all backstopped letters of credit within some relatively short period.

COMMITMENTS
Several Liability

A commitment represents the obligation of a lender, at the request of the borrower, to make loans or issue letters of credit. In a syndicated credit facility, each lender undertakes a separate commitment to the borrower; its commitment may be part of a tranche in which a number of other lenders participate, but each lender is individually obligated (i.e., *severally* obligated) to make loans to the borrower. It is not, in other words, a condition to a lender's obligation to make a loan that other lenders are also making their loans; no lender is excused from making its loan if the conditions to lending are satisfied, even though one or more other lenders in the same tranche are refusing, or defaulting on their obligation, to lend.

Reducing Commitments

Just as term loans can amortize (i.e., have required installments for repayment), so also can a revolving credit commitment "amortize." Such a facility is a so-called reducing revolving credit facility. The installments will be phrased as reductions of the commitments coupled with a requirement that whenever the aggregate outstanding loans and letters of credit exceed the amount of the commitments, the borrower must prepay the excess. The borrower will also typically be allowed to reduce the commitments at any time, subject to giving prior notice (although it is customary to limit the ability of the borrower to reduce the commitments to the unutilized portion of the commitments).

Terminating Commitments

The credit agreement will virtually always give the borrower the option to terminate commitments for any tranche of loans at any time, and, of course, the remedies provisions of the agreement will provide that the commitments terminate (either automatically or at the election of the lenders) upon the occurrence of any event of default.

Increasing Commitments: Incremental Facilities and Accordion Features

Many credit agreements will accord the borrower the right to increase the amount of credit available under the agreement after the closing. No lender will at the outset commit to providing any increase (the credit agreement will be explicit on this point), but all of the lenders will in effect agree that, if the borrower is able to obtain the agreement of one or more lenders to step up for increased credit exposure, no further consent of the lenders is required to permit the *increasing* lenders to commit to the increase. The increase will thus be automatically entitled to the benefit of any guarantees or collateral security to which the closing date facilities are entitled.

Increases under a credit agreement can be offered in two forms, either as so-called incremental facilities or as accordion features. An accordion feature is the simpler of the two. It is normally available only for increases to revolving credit facilities and will contemplate that the amount of the revolving credit commitments may go up (usually up to some specified maximum) if the lenders are willing. The interest, maturity, and other terms of an increase will be identical to those applicable to the existing (and increased) revolving credit facility. The accordion mechanism will provide that, upon any increase, the borrower will adjust the loans (through appropriate borrowings and prepayments) so that the loans in the increased facility are held by the lenders ratably in accordance with their respective commitments (as increased), a requirement discussed in more detail under "Pro Rata Treatment" in Part 8, "Keeping Peace Among the Lenders."

Incremental facilities, in comparison, do not contemplate an increase in existing commitments, but rather contemplate that entirely new commitments or tranches can be established. The credit agreement may even allow for more than one incremental facility, although these are always capped at a dollar maximum. Based on the flexibility afforded to the borrower, the new tranches may be either revolving credit or term facilities. The terms of an incremental facility, unlike an increase pursuant to an accordion, do not necessarily need to be the same as those of any other tranche in the credit agreement. The upfront fees, interest rate, maturity, and amortization will be specified at the time the incremental facility is established. Accordingly, an incremental facility providing for term loans may result in either A or B loans. It is typical for the credit agreement to require that, relative to the existing tranches in the credit agreement, the incremental facility not have an earlier maturity or a shorter weighted average life-to-maturity and not share in mandatory prepayments on a greater-than-ratable basis. It is also typical for the credit agreement to require that the covenants and events of default applicable to the incremental facility not be more restrictive and that guarantees and collateral security supporting the incremental facility not be greater than those applicable to the existing tranches. The incremental commitments themselves may be set forth in a separate, usually very short, two- or three-page incremental facility agreement executed by the borrower, any guarantors, the administrative agent, and the lenders that are to provide the facility.

One concern that the initial lenders have with providing flexibility for incremental facilities to a borrower is the possibility that an incremental facility may have more favorable pricing than the existing loan tranches. As noted earlier, upfront fees, interest rate, and other terms will be specified at the time the incremental facility is established, and such terms do not need to be the same as such terms under any existing tranche. Having different and more favorable terms can have the immediate effect of depressing the trading value of the existing and relatively less favorably priced loan tranches. Therefore, many credit agreements that provide for an incremental facility option will also provide for a so-called most-favored-nation (MFN) clause where the existing loan tranche pricing will receive a concurrent increase in margin equal to the yield of the incremental facility (or at least an increase within, say, 50 basis points of the incremental facility yield). MFN provisions typically will take account of upfront fees payable to all lenders or original issue discount on the incremental facility, in addition to the interest rate margin, and equate those fees or discount to yield based upon an assumed life to maturity of the incremental facility.

In the case of increases under an accordion or an incremental facility, the lenders that provide the increase or incremental facility will not typically be limited to those that are already party to the credit agreement. Any institution that is willing to provide the increase or incremental facility will be allowed to step up. However, the identity of any new institution will be subject to the consent of the borrower, the administrative agent, and any issuer of letters of credit under the facility to the same extent that the consent of those parties would be required if the new institution were taking an assignment of loans.

The incremental facility and accordion clauses are rarely presented as separate provisions but rather appear in the same section of the credit agreement. It has become increasingly common for the credit agreement to permit the additional debt capacity afforded by the incremental financing provisions to be in the form of pari passu loans or secured notes, subordinated secured loans or notes, and/or unsecured loans or notes, in each case pursuant to a separate credit agreement, indenture, or note purchase agreement. These so-called sidecar facilities or incremental equivalent debt utilize the credit agreement's incremental financing capacity (e.g., a dollar of debt incurred under a sidecar facility will reduce availability under the incremental financing facility by a dollar) and are subject to the same limitations.

In terms of maximum size of incremental or accordion facilities, traditionally credit agreements provided that the maximum permitted amount would be capped at a fixed dollar amount with the availability of such amount being subject to pro forma compliance with the credit agreement's financial covenants. Nowadays, it is more common for credit agreements to cap incremental facilities at the sum of a fixed dollar amount (based on the borrower's earnings before interest, taxes, depreciation, and amortization

[EBITDA]) plus an additional unlimited amount subject to pro forma compliance with a ratio of the borrower's debt (or secured debt) to EBITDA.

Term-out of Revolving Credit Commitments

Sometimes a credit agreement will provide that at the commitment termination date for revolving credit commitments any outstanding revolving credit loans will convert into term loans (sometimes called a *term-out option*). This type of conversion is normally automatic (i.e., not subject to a bring-down of representations or the absence of a default), but in some agreements those conditions will be required to be satisfied.

MULTICURRENCY FACILITIES

Credit agreements will sometimes provide for loans to be made (or letters of credit to be issued) in currencies other than U.S. dollars. Normally, the available currencies will be specified at closing, with an option to add currencies later, subject to agreement of each relevant lender and the conditions that the currency be freely convertible and no central bank or other approval be necessary for the loans or letters of credit to be made or repaid.

Multicurrency facilities can be structured in a variety of ways, based on the needs of the borrower, the depth of the market for the currency, and tax and other considerations. The following are some common structures:

- *Ratable committed loans.* In the ratable committed loan structure, the relevant lenders in a tranche will ratably commit to make loans in dollars and in specified foreign currencies. Sometimes sublimits will be imposed on the amount of any particular foreign currency. This structure has the advantage of being easy to administer, but the disadvantage that each lender in the tranche must have access to each of the specified currencies. This may limit the universe of lenders to which the tranche can be syndicated. The size of any sublimit will also be subject to the depth of the market for the currency.
- *Nonratable committed loans.* In this structure, a subgroup of lenders in a dollar tranche will agree to make loans in the

currencies specified. Each subgroup may have different lenders. This structure enhances the number of foreign currencies that can be made available to the borrower, because not every lender is required to have access to all currencies, but it has the disadvantage of being difficult to administer, because loans end up being made on a nonratable basis. It also has the disadvantage of not spreading the credit exposure ratably among the lenders; the subgroup that holds exposure at any time is a function solely of which currencies were borrowed.

- *Local currency tranches.* In a local currency structure, a separate tranche is created for each foreign currency, with specified lenders making loans directly to the relevant borrower out of local offices in the relevant foreign country. This eliminates the administrative disadvantage of the nonratable committed loan structure, and has the advantage of increasing the number of currencies that may be made available. Given that the loans are made out of local offices, it may also have the advantage of eliminating any withholding taxes. It has the disadvantage of breaking the total credit available under the facility into discrete segments; thus, unused commitments in one currency cannot be accessed in other currencies. It also does not solve (and may, in fact, exacerbate) the problem of the credit risk not being spread ratably among the lenders. The latter risk is sometimes eliminated by having the local currency tranche be supported by a letter of credit issued under the credit agreement, but this can raise the cost to the borrower of accessing the foreign currency.

MINIMUMS, MULTIPLES, AND FREQUENCY

A borrower will sometimes push to have complete freedom to designate the amount of any loan, regardless of whether that results in an extremely small loan or a loan with an odd value. The borrower will want as much freedom to borrow $23.37 as to borrow $10,000,000. More frequently, a borrower will push to be able to have any number of separate LIBOR loans (i.e., separate LIBOR interest periods) outstanding at any time. Arguably, none of this should be an issue to administer for any administrative agent or lender. However, both administrative agents and lenders want to be spared the administrative nuisance of very small loans. In the context of LIBOR loans, a small principal amount is inconsistent with the principle of match-funding, discussed in "LIBOR" in Part 2, "Making Money off the Loan," because most deposits taken into the London interbank market are in minimums of $5,000,000. It also forces the administrative agent and the lenders to track a potentially very large number of LIBOR loans with distinct interest periods and distinct interest rates. Accordingly, most credit agreements will require that loans have relatively large minimums ($5,000,000 is typical for LIBOR loans, with somewhat smaller figures for base rate loans) and that the aggregate number of LIBOR loans be limited (10 is typically the maximum). Both of these constraints will operate to reduce the frequency of borrowings under the credit agreement.

MECHANICS OF FUNDING

In syndicated credit agreements, most remittances between the borrower and the lenders will pass through the administrative agent. Thus, when a loan is to be made, the lenders will be required to remit funds to the administrative agent, who will then disburse the funds to the borrower. This is usually not the case for swingline loans where the credit agreement may provide that the swingline lender remits proceeds directly to the borrower.

The administrative agent is the agent of the lenders, not the borrower; consequently, the loan is not made when funds are received by the administrative agent. Rather, the loan is made only when the administrative agent transfers funds to the borrower. The discussion in "The Clawback Clause" in Part 8, "Keeping Peace among the Lenders," addresses what happens if a lender does not provide the administrative agent with its portion of a loan, but the administrative agent, not being aware that the lender has failed to remit funds, nevertheless forwards to the borrower an amount representing that lender's loan.

The credit agreement will require that the borrower give advance notice of any borrowing to the administrative agent, who will then notify the relevant lenders. Except in rare cases, notices will be required to be delivered on business days, and in the case of LIBOR loans, will be required to be delivered at least three business days prior to the date the loan is to be made. Base rate loans, depending on the number of lenders in the facility, may require one business day's or same-day notice. The credit agreement will almost always specify a time of day by which notices are to be given and a time of day by which the lenders are to provide funds to the administrative agent. It will not ordinarily specify a time of day for the administrative agent to remit funds to the borrower, because the administrative agent does not have control over when it will receive funds. Notices will typically be irrevocable, because it will be presumed that the lenders will have allocated funds for the anticipated lending, and were the borrower to decline to take the loan, the lenders would not have an alternative for redeploying the funds that were to have been lent to the borrower.

In some cases, when the borrower requires loan proceeds to make an acquisition and needs funds in the morning of the closing day, the parties may enter into a "prefunding" agreement, under which the lenders will deposit funds with the administrative agent the business day preceding the anticipated closing date and the borrower will agree to pay interest on such funds until the closing date as if the loans had been made. If for any reason the closing does not occur on that day, the deposited funds would be returned to the lenders by the administrative agent. This mechanism enables the administrative agent to know at the opening of business on the closing date that it has been put in funds by all lenders.

Prefunding agreements are also sometimes used when a borrower wishes to take down LIBOR loans at closing and has not yet executed the credit agreement (this is normally the case, because most credit agreements are not in fact executed until the initial funding, even though the language of the credit agreement will invariably contemplate that the funding is to occur some days after execution). Because the credit agreement is not yet in effect, there is no agreement under which the borrower can give notice (and no agreement under which it is obligated to make "breakfunding" payments if for any reason the borrowing does not occur). See the discussion of breakfunding in "Breakfunding" in Part 2, "Making Money off the Loan." The prefunding agreement will bridge this gap by having the borrower undertake that, if the closing does not happen when expected, it will make breakfunding payments as if the lenders had received a valid notice of borrowing.

Part 2: Making Money Off the Loan: Loan Pricing and Fees

PRICING

Interest

Credit agreements provide more variability in pricing than bond indentures or private placements, where interest is calculated at a constant rate for the life of the deal. The interest rate on U.S. dollar–denominated loans under credit agreements is normally expressed as the sum of (1) a base component, usually either the base rate or LIBOR or other benchmark rate (explained more fully later), that is reset from time to time, plus (2) a margin that is either fixed for the life of the transaction or subject to change based upon pre-agreed criteria.

Typically, a borrower can elect to borrow either base rate loans or loans referencing an applicable benchmark rate, or both simultaneously, under a credit agreement, and the borrower can switch back and forth between the two types of loans. Switching from one type to another is referred to as *conversion*. By way of example, a company might initially borrow $100,000,000, consisting of $10,000,000 of base rate loans and $90,000,000 of LIBOR loans; three months later, convert all of the base rate loans, so that the full $100,000,000 is outstanding as LIBOR loans; and six months further on convert some or all of the LIBOR loans back into base rate loans. The key pricing options generally made available to borrowers are discussed here:

- *Base rate:* The base rate (sometimes referred to as the *alternate base rate*, or ABR) is typically defined as the higher of (1) a specified bank's (normally the administrative agent's) publicly announced benchmark base rate or prime rate, (2) 50 basis points over the federal funds rate, and (3) 100 basis points over one-month LIBOR. Some banks prefer calling their publicly announced rate their *base rate* and others prefer *prime rate*, but the two terms mean essentially the same thing. This is the primary benchmark rate publicly announced by the bank for interest on its loans.

    The base or prime rate is unilaterally determined by the bank based on its cost of funds, competitive pressures,

and other factors. Even though it can be changed at any time, banks are reluctant to change it to reflect seasonal or other short-term increases in their cost of funds because of its economic (and sometimes political) importance. Thus, the second component of the base rate, the market-based federal funds rate, serves to protect lenders at times when the base or prime rate is not adjusting quickly or frequently enough to reflect the increased cost of funds. (The addition of the 50 basis points is done to bring these two rates closer to parity.) The federal funds rate for any day is usually defined as the volume-weighted median rate on overnight federal funds transactions for the preceding business day, as published by the Federal Reserve Bank of New York. If that rate is not published, it will be determined by the administrative agent either based on actual quotes from federal funds brokers or the federal funds rate charged to the administrative agent. The third component of the base rate ensures that the base rate will never be lower than one-month LIBOR and protects lenders from the unusual circumstance (which occurred in the 2008 Global Financial Crisis [GFC]) where the base rate is lower than LIBOR (plus 100 basis points, which represents the typical amount by which the applicable margin for LIBOR loans exceeds that for base rate loans).
- *LIBOR.* Sometimes referred to as *LIBO Rate,* LIBOR is an acronym for London Interbank Offered Rate. It refers to the London-based wholesale market for jumbo U.S. dollar deposits between major banks. Because such deposits are often referred to as *Eurodollar deposits,* the terms *Eurodollar* and *LIBOR* are often used interchangeably; some credit agreements may refer to LIBOR (or *LIBO Rate*) *loans,* whereas others may refer to *Eurodollar loans.* The applicable LIBOR interest rate for a loan under a credit agreement is the prevailing interest rate offered by banks for a matching Eurodollar time deposit. This rate is usually determined by reference to a "screen quote" from Reuters.

As will be discussed further in the section "Breakfunding," the assumption underlying the pricing provisions for LIBOR loans is that each lender will fund its loan by accepting a Eurodollar time deposit on which it will have to pay interest at a certain rate, and that it will relend the funds to the borrower at the same rate (plus a margin representing profit). This is so-called match funding. This assumption drives many provisions of credit agreements, both substantive and mechanical, conforming LIBOR loans to the market practice for Eurodollar deposits.

Perhaps the most important mechanical feature is fixing the interest rate on LIBOR loans for specific periods, referred to as *interest periods*, that correspond to the tenor of the "matching" Eurodollar time deposits. The durations for interest periods are normally limited to the tenors for deposits commonly available in the Eurodollar market. The desired duration among these options is then selected by the borrower. The most common tenors, and therefore the most customary interest periods available to borrowers, are one, two, three, and six months. Other interest periods are also often available, but when they include tenors where the Eurodollar market is less liquid, such as 12 months, or shorter than one month, unanimous consent of the affected lenders is usually required because of the difficulty of finding matching deposits.

The beginning and end dates of interest periods are also subject to rules that may seem somewhat arcane, generally pertaining to what happens if the last day of an interest period would otherwise fall on a nonbusiness day or when the relevant months do not have corresponding days (e.g., is February 30 the three-month anniversary of November 30?). These rules are driven by the corresponding market conventions for Eurodollar deposits. At the borrower's election, it may have LIBOR loans with different interest periods outstanding simultaneously, with the maximum number of allowed interest periods limited as described in "Minimums, Multiples, and Frequency" in Part 1. Because by market convention the interest rate for a Eurodollar deposit is set two business days before the deposit is accepted (i.e., its value is two business days forward), the interest rate for a LIBOR loan is set two business days before the interest period begins. For the meaning of *business day*, see the discussion in "Business-Day Conventions" later in Part 2.

The interest rate for a LIBOR loan is fixed for the duration of its interest period, given that the interest rate for the matching Eurodollar deposit is also fixed for that period. If the borrower repays the LIBOR loan or converts it into a base rate loan in the middle of the interest period, the lenders are still obligated to maintain any matching Eurodollar deposit. They could therefore incur a funding loss if interest rates have declined since the beginning of the interest period and they are unable to cover the interest they are paying on the matching Eurodollar deposit by redeploying the proceeds of the repayment for the remainder of the interest period. Credit agreements require the borrower to indemnify the lenders for these losses (see the section "Breakfunding" later in Part 2). A few credit agreements prohibit voluntary repayments and conversions of LIBOR loans in the middle of interest periods. Borrowers are sometimes prohibited from selecting interest periods that would extend beyond the final maturity of the credit agreement or that would straddle scheduled amortization dates if the amortization could force a repayment of LIBOR loans in the middle of an interest period.

At the end of each interest period for a LIBOR loan, the borrower is required to elect whether that loan will be converted into a base rate loan or be continued (or "rolled over") as a LIBOR loan (and, if the latter, to specify the new interest period). If the borrower fails to do so, the credit agreement will normally provide one of two fail-safes: (1) either the LIBOR loan will be automatically converted into a base rate loan or (2) the LIBOR loan will be rolled over into another LIBOR loan with an interest period of one month. There are advantages to each fail-safe. The advantage to the borrower of an automatic conversion into a base rate loan is that its oversight may be corrected immediately without breakfunding, rather than waiting until the end of a one-month interest period. The advantage to the borrower of continuing the loan as a one-month LIBOR loan is that LIBOR is likely to be lower than the base rate and will therefore result in lower interest charges. Breakfunding is never an issue for base rate loans, because base rate loans do not have interest periods; they continue as base rate loans forever until they are repaid or converted into LIBOR loans.

When a base rate loan is converted into a LIBOR loan, or when a LIBOR loan is rolled over or converted into a base rate loan, it is normally *not* considered a new borrowing that requires the satisfaction of conditions precedent. It is treated merely as the resetting of interest on an outstanding loan, similar to the resetting of the interest rate from time to time on an adjustable-rate home mortgage loan.

Because the pricing of LIBOR loans is premised upon the assumption that lenders fund those loans with matching Eurodollar deposits, lenders consider this pricing to be "cost-plus." They require compensation for any direct or indirect costs of funding LIBOR loans above the interest they pay on the Eurodollar deposits. Most of these items are described in the section "Yield Protection" later in Part 2, but one, reserve requirements, merits special mention here. When a bank is required to maintain reserves against a deposit, it will not have the full amount of the deposit available to it to lend to its customers. By way of example, if a bank is required to maintain a reserve equal to 3% of a deposit, it would have only $9,700,000 available to lend from a $10,000,000 deposit. This means that in order to make a $10,000,000 LIBOR loan, it would have to fund itself with (and pay interest on) a larger Eurodollar deposit (in this example, a deposit of $10,000,000 *divided by* 0.97, or $10,309,000).

Lenders are generally compensated for the additional cost by one of two methods. The first method is for the definition of the interest calculation to include a *gross-up* for the reserve requirement. The definition (sometimes referred to as *adjusted LIBOR* or the *adjusted Eurodollar rate*, if the gross-up is not contained in the definition of LIBOR itself) is written arithmetically as follows:

Adjusted LIBOR = LIBOR/(1 − R)

The R in this definition means the maximum gross rate at which reserves are required to be maintained against Eurocurrency liabilities, as defined in Regulation D of the Federal Reserve Board. Because this method provides for recovery according to the maximum possible reserve rate, it is referred to as compensation for reserves on a "statutory maximum" basis. Lenders prefer this method because it is straightforward and easy to calculate, and because it implicitly assumes that the full amount of the matching Eurodollar deposit is a "Eurocurrency liability." In fact, the calculation of Eurocurrency liabilities for a bank under Regulation D is more complex and can change daily. Lenders that are not subject to any reserve requirements (or are subject to lower reserve requirements) will be overcompensated. For this reason, some borrowers insist on indemnifying lenders for reserve costs only on an "as incurred" basis. When calculated on an as incurred basis, the compensation would be based upon the individual position of each lender.

All of this notwithstanding, the reserve rate for Eurocurrency liabilities has been zero for more than 30 years. Nevertheless, negotiations continue to take place over these provisions in credit agreements because it is always possible that the reserve rate could be reset to a level higher than zero.

It should be apparent that the need for LIBOR loans to follow certain conventions of the Eurodollar market reduces the flexibility of this pricing option for borrowers. There are also other typical restrictions that further limit flexibility. For example, the fact that Eurodollar deposits are priced two London business days prior to the delivery of funds means that the typical credit agreement will require notices of borrowings, prepayments, and conversions for LIBOR loans at least three business days in advance. The question thus arises, why do borrowers elect LIBOR loans over base rate loans? The answer is easy: the interest on LIBOR loans is invariably lower. Indeed, the more apt question is, why do borrowers ever elect base rate loans? Here, the answer does go back to the need for flexibility in certain circumstances. For example, in the context of an acquisition with a moving closing date or another urgent need for financing without much advance notice, the three business days' requirement for borrowing LIBOR loans may not be practicable. Similarly, a borrower's cash management may result in frequent borrowings and repayments, and the advance notice requirements and restrictions on repayments of LIBOR loans in the middle of interest periods (or the requirements for breakfunding if such repayments do occur) may lead a borrower to maintain at least a portion of its loans as base rate loans.

- *Other pricing options.* Over the years, the bank loan markets have seen a variety of other pricing options tied to various indices. These have included pricing determined by reference to certificate of deposit rates and term federal funds rates. LIBOR has spawned HIBOR (Hong Kong), SIBOR (Singapore), and IBOR (indeterminate global markets). The pricing options explained here reflect the predominant preferences in today's markets. There will doubtless be other preferences that come in and out of vogue over time.
- *LIBOR discontinuation and replacement.* In 2012, European and American regulatory authorities uncovered a widespread LIBOR-fixing scheme. Major financial institutions on both sides of the Atlantic were accused of artificially manipulating LIBOR to their benefit, and ultimately paid fines in the billions of dollars to settle claims. Since then, banks have reduced their interbank funding (LIBOR) borrowings, which are the informational foundation of the LIBOR quotes submitted by banks that are, in turn, used to create the LIBOR curve. Due to potential legal liability and the small number of actual interbank trades, banks do not particularly like providing LIBOR submissions. In 2017, the U.K. Financial Conduct Authority announced that they would not compel banks to submit LIBOR after 2021. This resulted in a market expectation that LIBOR will be discontinued, or at best unreliable, after 2021. In March 2021, the end dates for LIBOR were confirmed with the most widely used USD LIBOR settings ending after June 30, 2023.

    In response, credit agreements since then have taken the approach of including provisions that contemplate replacement of LIBOR during the life of the loan facility with replacement benchmark provisions. These LIBOR replacement provisions come in two varieties: (1) an "amendment" approach, in which if certain trigger events occur, the borrower and administrative agent may amend the credit agreement to replace LIBOR with an alternative rate that is the then-prevailing benchmark and make various conforming changes, subject to the required lenders providing affirmative consent, or, more commonly, "negative consent" (i.e., failure to affirmatively object) or, occasionally, without any lender consent required; or (2) a "hardwired" approach, in which if certain trigger events occur LIBOR will be automatically replaced with a predetermined alternative rate, typically based on the Secured Overnight Financing Rate (SOFR), and various conforming changes will be implemented, without the requirement for an amendment.

Applicable Margins

As noted earlier, the interest rate on each base rate loan and each LIBOR loan includes an additional margin, sometimes also referred to as the *spread*. The applicable margin is in some cases a flat rate that is fixed for the life of the agreement, but in other instances it increases over time or is dependent on the credit ratings and/or a financial test (such as leverage) of the borrower. Whichever approach is taken, the applicable margin for LIBOR loans is always higher than the applicable margin for base rate loans in order to bring the two rates closer to parity. The difference is usually 100 basis points in today's market, although the applicable margin for base rate loans would not be less than zero even if the applicable margin for LIBOR loans were less than 1%.

A flat margin or one that increases over time is rather straightforward and requires no further explanation. When the applicable margin is dependent on the credit rating and/or a financial test of the borrower, the various rates are set forth in the credit agreement in the form of a grid that varies by type of loan (by tranche and by pricing option) and the relevant financial measure (hence the term *grid pricing*).

When grid pricing is based on credit ratings, the relevant parameters will include reference debt (sometimes referred to as the *index debt*), the identity of the credit rating agencies to be relied upon (Moody's, S&P, and Fitch are the most frequently used), and the treatment of split ratings (when the rating agencies assign different ratings to the same index debt). The index debt can be the loans under the credit agreement, a specific issue of debt securities of the borrower, or unspecified non-credit-enhanced, publicly issued debt of the borrower. Often, when there is a split rating, the higher of the two ratings will be used, but when the ratings differ by more than one level (with each movement from "-" to flat to "+" constituting a level), the most standard approach is to split the difference by using the level immediately above the lower of the two ratings. Typically, any change in the applicable margin takes place either when the borrower notifies the administrative agent of the change in the rating or simultaneously when the change in rating occurs. If the index debt is rated by only one of the rating agencies or ceases to be rated at all, the applicable margin reverts to the highest rate in the grid.

When grid pricing is based on leverage or other financial test, the relevant date on which to test leverage is the end of the borrower's most recent fiscal quarter, and changes therefore occur no more frequently than quarterly. The administrative agent is dependent upon receiving the pertinent information from the borrower, typically a certificate by the borrower showing the leverage calculation (usually the ratio of EBITDA to indebtedness) and the related financial statements of the borrower. The applicable margin customarily changes upon delivery of that information or within two or three business days thereafter. Any adjustment in the applicable margin based on leverage ceases to apply when either (1) the borrower furnishes information for its subsequent fiscal quarter, in which case the applicable margin is reset (or continues) based on the new information, or (2) the borrower fails to furnish that information for the next quarter on a timely basis, in which case the applicable margin reverts to the highest rate in the grid.

Regardless of the form of grid pricing, many credit agreements will provide that, during the existence of an event of default, the applicable margin will bump up to the highest level on the grid. This will be in addition to any default interest payable, described later.

Interest Payment Dates

The credit agreement will specify the dates on which interest is to be paid. In the case of base rate loans, most credit agreements will specify quarterly payment dates (often at the end of calendar quarters or on quarterly anniversaries of the closing date). In the case of LIBOR loans, interest will be payable on the last day of each interest period and, if any interest period is longer than three months, on each quarterly anniversary of the first day of the interest period. The result is that if the borrower has multiple LIBOR loans outstanding, it may be paying interest frequently during the course of a quarter as interest periods come and go. Most credit agreements will also provide that, for all loans, interest is payable on the date that the principal is paid or the loan is converted to a different type. In some cases, the latter rule will not apply to base rate loans, on which interest may be payable only at quarterly dates.

Default Interest

There are two principal approaches to default interest (an increased interest rate by reason of default) taken in credit agreements. One approach requires default interest to be paid only on amounts that are not paid when due. If the overdue amount is the principal of a loan, then the interest rate on that amount is increased to the default rate, described later. For example, if loans in the amount of $100,000,000 are outstanding and the borrower fails to pay an installment of $10,000,000, then the increased interest rate would apply only to the overdue amount of $10,000,000. (Of course, if all of the loans are accelerated because of the payment default, then all of the loans would be overdue and would therefore attract the higher interest rate.) When the overdue amount is something other than principal, say interest or fees, then interest is paid on that overdue amount at the default rate.

A second approach requires that interest be paid at the default rate on the entire amount of the loans whenever an event of default exists, regardless of whether the event of default involves nonpayment. Thus, using the previous example, if loans in the amount of $100,000,000 are outstanding and the borrower fails to pay an installment of $10,000,000 (or, indeed, if a financial covenant is breached), and such failure (or breach) constitutes an event of default, then the increased interest rate would apply to the full $100,000,000. Because it is not feasible to apply interest to accruing obligations like interest and fees until they are overdue, even when an event of default exists, the default interest rate would apply to the amount of these obligations only if they are not paid when due.

The default rate of interest for the principal amount of any loan under both approaches is usually 2% above the then-applicable rate for that loan. The default rate of interest for other amounts is usually 2% above the then-applicable rate for base rate loans. This increase of 2% is in addition to whatever applicable margin is in effect. It is customary that interest accruing at the default rate be payable on demand rather than on the regularly scheduled dates otherwise provided in the credit agreement.

Another aspect of interest in a default scenario is worth noting. When an event of default exists, it is possible that lenders may become concerned about the likelihood of repayment. They may consider accelerating the maturity of loans. They may be willing (indeed, eager) to accept repayments of LIBOR loans in the middle of an interest period rather than risk waiting until the end. However, in order to avoid the funding losses referred to earlier, they may prefer to structure the credit agreement to minimize the likelihood that interest periods for LIBOR loans are outstanding when these problems exist. Accordingly, when an event of default exists, credit agreements typically either require LIBOR interest periods to be short in duration (one month is typical) or limit the borrower's ability to request LIBOR loans. Some credit agreements provide that when an event of default exists, LIBOR loans automatically convert into base rate loans on the last days of their respective interest periods, and the borrower is precluded from having additional LIBOR loans. This approach may present difficulties for an administrative agent, who may or may not know of the existence of the event of default. Accordingly, the more common approach is for these limitations to apply only after notice that an event of default exists has been delivered to the borrower by the administrative agent.

Fees

Fees in credit agreements typically include some combination of the following: commitment fees, facility fees, utilization fees, and letter of credit fees. Administrative agency fees and upfront fees are not covered in this discussion because they are generally provided for in fee letters rather than in credit agreements.

- *Commitment fees.* Commitment fees are compensation for the lender's contractual commitment to make loans. Commitment fees accrue at an agreed per annum rate on the daily average unused commitments of the lenders. They are most often paid on the unused portion of revolving credit commitments. Whether they are paid on unused term loan commitments varies by transaction and may depend on the length of the period for which the term loan commitments are available. The rate at which commitment fees are payable is generally either flat for the duration of the credit agreement or subject to grid pricing.

    In calculating the unused amount of revolving credit commitments, all outstanding loans, undrawn letters of credit, and outstanding reimbursement obligations for

payments under letters of credit are considered utilizations of the revolving credit commitments. In credit agreements with swingline loans, the amount of outstanding swingline loans is generally not deducted for purposes of calculating commitment fees (even though it is considered a utilization of the revolving credit commitments for other purposes). This is because the lenders that have not advanced swingline loans nevertheless remain committed to extend credit to the borrower in the amount of those loans, whether by funding participations in the swingline loans or by making revolving credit loans for the purpose of repaying the swingline loans. Accrued commitment fees are generally payable quarterly in arrears.
- *Facility fees.* In contrast to commitment fees, which are computed on unused commitments, facility fees are computed on the total amount of revolving credit commitments, both used and unused. Facility fees generally do not apply to term loan facilities, and commitment fees and facility fees are mutually exclusive—the same revolving credit facility would not attract both. Facility fees are most often seen where the usage of a revolving credit facility is expected to be low. Like commitment fees, facility fees are either calculated at a flat rate or subject to grid pricing and are generally payable quarterly in arrears. Some credit agreements provide that facility fees are payable only until the revolving credit commitments terminate. Others, however, provide that facility fees are payable until the later of the termination of the revolving credit commitments or the repayment in full of the loans and termination of the other extensions of credit. This latter structure is designed to avoid a reduction in the aggregate cost of the facility when the commitments expire. After termination of the revolving credit commitments, the fee is payable on the total amount that would be considered utilization of the revolving credit commitments.
- *Utilization fees.* In transactions where the revolving credit commitments are not expected to be heavily utilized, the commitment fee or facility fee may be lower than in other comparable transactions. However, to address the possibility that utilization may in fact turn out to be high, the credit agreement may provide for an additional fee to be payable if utilization exceeds a certain percentage, say,

30% or 50%, of the commitments. On each day when this percentage is exceeded, the utilization fee is payable on all utilizations of the revolving credit facility (i.e., not merely on the portion in excess of the 30% or 50% threshold).

In contrast to the approach used to calculate the commitment fee, utilization for this purpose is more likely to be defined broadly, including not only outstanding revolving credit loans, letters of credit, and reimbursement obligations, but also swingline loans. Like commitment fees and facility fees, utilization fees are either calculated at a flat rate or subject to grid pricing. Approaches vary as to whether accrued utilization fees are payable quarterly in arrears or concurrently with payments of interest on the related loans, although quarterly payments are more common. Utilization fees are characterized under some credit agreements as additional interest on loans because interest may receive more favorable treatment than fees under the Bankruptcy Code.

- *Letter of credit fees.* As letters of credit are issued under a revolving credit facility, all of the revolving credit lenders share in the credit exposure because, even if they are not the issuer of the letters of credit, they have participations in the letters of credit. Accordingly, borrowers are obligated to pay to each revolving credit lender a letter of credit fee accruing at an agreed per annum rate on its participation in the undrawn amount of each outstanding letter of credit. In the case of the issuer of each letter of credit, its participation therein for purposes of this calculation is deemed to be its remaining credit exposure after subtracting the participations of the other revolving credit lenders. It is very common for the rate for the letter of credit fees to be the same as the applicable margin for LIBOR loans, taking into account the use of any applicable grid pricing.

    Even though all revolving credit lenders share in the credit exposure to the borrower, the letter of credit issuer bears an additional risk—the risk that one or more of the revolving credit lenders might not fund their participations in a letter of credit if the borrower fails to reimburse it. Letter of credit issuers are compensated by borrowers for this additional risk in the form of a fronting fee (so called because the issuer "fronts" the letter of credit for the other revolving credit lenders). The fronting fee accrues at a modest agreed per annum rate on the undrawn amount of each outstanding letter of credit, and the rate is generally flat rather than based on grid pricing.

These letter of credit fees and fronting fees are customarily payable quarterly in arrears, although they are often paid two or three business days after the quarterly period ends in order to give the administrative agent sufficient time to make the necessary calculations. In addition to these fees, the letter of credit issuer may impose administrative charges for issuing, amending, and making payments under letters of credit.

Computation of Interest and Fees

There are two generally used methods of calculating accruing interest and fees under a credit agreement. The first method calculates the accruing amount on the basis of a year of 360 days and actual days elapsed. For example, if the formula for determining interest on a LIBOR loan results in a rate of 6% per annum, then the effective interest rate would be 6% × 365/360 = 6.08% per annum. The second method calculates the accruing amount on the basis of a year of 365/366 days and actual days elapsed. This method does not result in any adjustment to per annum rates determined in accordance with the applicable formulae.

The first method just described is the one used in the market for Eurodollar deposits. It is universally used when calculating the interest on LIBOR loans. There is less uniformity in the method used for calculating interest on other types of loans and for calculating accruing fees, because policies are not consistent among lenders.

There is also a third method of calculating interest, although it is more prevalent in bond indentures than in credit agreements. This method calculates interest on the basis of a year consisting of twelve 30-day months. If the stated interest rate is 6% per annum, then the rate for any calendar month would be 6% × 1/12 = 0.5%, regardless of how many days there actually are in that month (28, 29, 30, or 31). This method results in the same amount of interest being payable over an entire year as would result from the application of the second method (i.e., a year of 365/366 days), but it results in a "distortion" for any individual month with other than 30 days.

Accrual Conventions

When calculating interest and fees, one final overarching principle should be borne in mind. If a loan is made on a Monday and repaid on Tuesday, for what day is interest payable? Stated another way, if the base rate is 6.00% on Monday and 6.25% on Tuesday, what is the interest rate on the loan? Market convention is that interest (with the exception of that on intraday loans, which are beyond the scope of this chapter) is charged for the day on which the loan is made and each day thereafter that it is outstanding, but *not* for the day on which it is repaid. In this example, therefore, interest would be payable at 6.00%. Fees are calculated on a similar basis.

BUSINESS-DAY CONVENTIONS

The definition of *business day* in any credit agreement will typically have two components. First, it will set out a general rule as to what constitutes a business day in the jurisdiction in which the administrative agent is located. Second, if LIBOR loans are to be available, it will lay out the rules applicable for determining LIBOR business days. The definition of *business day* will determine notice periods for borrowings and prepayments and other actions to be taken under the agreement and will also determine when loans are to be made available or payments to be made. Loans will, for example, be made and repaid only on business days.

In a New York-law agreement, the general rule will state that a business day is any day other than a day on which banks are required or authorized to close. Note that this is *not* equivalent to days on which the stock exchanges are open (the approach customarily seen in bond indentures), nor will it include Saturdays. Even though many banks may be open on Saturdays, they are in fact authorized to close, so Saturdays, under the definition, will not constitute business days. Days upon which banks are authorized to close may happen unexpectedly if, for example, there is a blackout or some other disaster and the governor issues an order that banks are authorized to close. Sometimes a borrower will push to have the business-day definition specify the jurisdiction in which it is located, so that, for example, the base definition will consist of New York and Kentucky business days. Administrative agents generally resist this approach because of the complications it creates when determining LIBOR business days.

If the credit agreement includes LIBOR borrowings, the second part of the definition will provide that, insofar as it relates to LIBOR, the term will refer to any New York business day (as determined in accordance with the general rule) that is *also* a day on which dealings in dollar deposits (or other relevant currency) are carried out in the London interbank market. Thus, the typical notice period for a LIBOR loan (three days) will need to allow for three full New York and London business days. Thus, a request for a LIBOR borrowing made on a Thursday where the Friday is a holiday in New York and the Monday is a holiday in London will result in the borrowing not being available until Thursday of the following week.

LENDING OFFICES

Lenders (at least bank lenders) have traditionally specified different "lending offices" for different classes of loans. When the LIBOR market first developed, banks almost uniformly specified a domestic office for base rate loans and nondomestic offices for LIBOR loans. Most credit agreements now give lenders the flexibility to use whatever lending offices they choose. Thus, a typical provision would allow each lender at its option to make a loan through any domestic or foreign branch or affiliate of the lender, as specified by the lender. Lenders have a variety of internal considerations (including income tax issues and internal regulatory concerns, among others) that may lead them to elect to fund LIBOR loans from offices outside of the United States.

YIELD PROTECTION

Yield protection clauses, as the name implies, are intended to protect the yield to the lender from making a loan to the borrower. With some exceptions (the taxes clause being the principal one), they are designed to address yield issues as they relate to LIBOR loans. Yield protection clauses do not protect base rate loans, the theory being that changes affecting the underlying cost of base rate loans can generally be passed on to borrowers immediately by the relevant institution changing its prime rate.

The focus of yield protection clauses on LIBOR borrowings is a product of how LIBOR loans are (nominally) funded. As described earlier, the theory underlying a LIBOR loan is that a bank takes in a deposit for a relatively short term (say, three or six months) in London and lends the proceeds of the deposit to its customer for a longer term (say, five or seven years). The interest rate on the loan will simply be the sum of the interest paid by the lender on its deposit *plus* an interest margin. LIBOR will be adjusted every three or six months as deposits are renewed or "rolled over" by the lender in London to maintain the loan outstanding to its customer, and any change in pricing (whether higher or lower) will be passed on to the customer. Hence, LIBOR loans are, in essence, a cost-plus loan product.

When the LIBOR market first developed, this practice was nearly universally employed by banks that made LIBOR loans. It is described as *match-funding*; that is, the funding for a loan is "matched" to a deposit. Today, with the LIBOR market having developed to the point where many tens of billions of deposits are traded each day, few banks will match-fund. Nonbank lenders will not in any event match-fund because they do not take deposits. Nevertheless, the principle of match-funding still lives in the yield protection clauses of credit agreements as a way of protecting the lenders against unexpected events during the term of a LIBOR deposit that would adversely affect their ability to make, maintain, and earn money from LIBOR loans.

In decades past, yield protection clauses were the source of long, agonizing negotiations between borrowers and lenders. In recent years, the language has become more settled. The Model Credit Agreement Provisions provided by the Loan Syndications and Trading Association (LSTA) include market-standard yield protection clauses. Although yield protection clauses can vary widely, they almost always consist of the following provisions and are included in credit agreements even though (apart from breakfunding) the number of times that lenders have invoked the clauses since the creation of the LIBOR market can probably be counted on one hand. Lenders remain convinced that the potential damage to them from omitting the clause far outweighs any detriment to requiring borrowers to cover lenders for unknown costs if a yield protection event were ever to occur.

Increased Costs

An early concern of lenders was that the cost of a deposit taken into their London branches to provide funds for a loan might change during the term of the deposit by reason of a change in law, such as through the imposition of a tax, a new reserve, or some other regulatory requirement. The increased costs clause of a credit agreement was therefore invented to protect the lender against this risk (again, consistent with the cost-plus assumptions of LIBOR loans) by allowing it to pass on those costs to the borrower in the event of a "regulatory change" or a "change in law." Those terms were defined broadly to pick up not only changes in law, rules, and regulations, but also requests, guidelines, or directives from a government authority "whether or not" these have the force of law. The latter was intended to address the approach taken by central banks (particularly the Bank of England) of using "persuasion" to induce banks to take action (such as maintaining reserves) rather than setting out the requirements in explicit published regulations. "Costs" for these purposes are not limited to out-of-pocket cash costs, but also include reductions in the return for a lender (as would be the case if it were required to maintain reserves against a deposit that funds the loan).

This clause generally provides that the amount of the cost incurred by a lender (and which it will therefore pass on to a borrower) is within the good faith determination of the lender (or, alternatively, that it will be conclusive "absent manifest error," or words of similar import). The clause may, in some cases, require the lender to deliver supporting calculations for its determination. However, given the difficulty for an institution with many hundreds of millions (or billions) of offshore deposits with different tenors, located in different legal jurisdictions and in different currencies and funding many different loans, the general consensus is that it is not appropriate to require a detailed analysis of the cost determined by the lender for reimbursement from a borrower. Reliance on the lender's acting in good faith is generally deemed sufficient.

Sometimes a borrower will attempt to limit a lender's ability to seek compensation from the borrower to situations in which the lender is seeking similar compensation in similar amounts from other customers "similarly situated." Apart from the difficulty of determining what "similarly situated" means, the general consensus is that requiring "equal" or "similar" or "comparable" treatment among customers is not appropriate. It is also nonstandard. If incorporated, it puts a lender in the difficult position when a yield protection event occurs of having to review potentially hundreds or thousands of agreements to determine whether there are individual variances that require different steps to be taken *vis-à-vis* different borrowers.

Another issue generally addressed in the clause will be the ability of a lender to seek retroactive reimbursement for increased costs. One concern that lenders have is that, because of the difficulty of working through the implications of regulatory changes for an institution with a loan portfolio in the billions, they may discover after the fact that an increased cost event has occurred. A common resolution is to allow the lender to seek recovery for costs for some retroactive period from, say, 90 to 180 days prior to the effectiveness of the regulatory change. Costs incurred prior to that period will be solely for the account of the lender.

Capital Costs

Capital costs are usually dealt with in a clause separate from the general increased costs clause (the LSTA Model Credit Agreement Provisions are consistent with this approach) because the provision seeks reimbursement for costs suffered not only by the lender, but also by the lender's holding company (capital adequacy rules often apply at the bank holding–company level). Capital costs are an example of costs that reduce the rate of return for a lender by requiring it to increase the amount of capital to be maintained by the lender or its holding company against its assets (including, of course, the loan). Capital costs are imposed on any class of loans made by the lender; they are not confined to LIBOR-based loans.

Eurodollar Market Disruption

Another concern when banks first started making LIBOR-based loans was the possibility that some "disaster" could occur in the LIBOR market that would result in the lenders being unable to obtain LIBOR quotes at the end of an interest period, or that, although they could obtain quotes, those quotes would not adequately reflect the cost to the lenders of making the loan. The solution was the Eurodollar market disruption clause, under which the borrower's ability to obtain LIBOR loans would be suspended until the disruption was over. The clause is normally triggered in one of two ways: *first*, if the administrative agent determines that rates are not available in the Eurodollar market in the relevant amounts or for the relevant maturities, and, *second*, if the required lenders of the relevant tranche make the determination that the rates quoted in the LIBOR market do not adequately cover the cost to the lenders of obtaining funds to make the loans. If the credit agreement contemplates both base rate and LIBOR pricing, the clause will simply require that any LIBOR loan requested by the borrower be made instead as a base rate loan. If the credit agreement does not provide for base rate pricing (as would normally be the case with offshore borrowers), then the clause will contain a detailed procedure for the borrower and the lender to negotiate a "substitute basis" upon which to price the loans. Absent agreement within a defined period of time, the borrower would be required to repay the loan.

Illegality

With some historical justification, when the LIBOR loan market first developed, lenders were concerned that making or continuing a loan based upon LIBOR could be made illegal. The fear was that a regulatory change could give rise to more than just increased costs; it might involve a flat prohibition against pricing loans based upon offshore deposit taking. One area of concern arose in the late 1960s when interest equalization regulations were issued by President Nixon. It was feared at the time that the newly developing LIBOR market would be perceived as circumventing these regulations, and thus that the U.S. government might prohibit U.S. banks from making LIBOR loans. Under the illegality clause, if a regulator outlaws pricing based on LIBOR, either interest will be shifted to a different interest rate (the base rate or a substitute basis as described in the section "Eurodollar Market Disruption"), or the borrower will be obligated to repay the loan immediately. Of course the illegality would probably still arise if the borrower were unable to repay, but at least the lender could argue that it had done everything possible to adhere to the law and that any violation by it was solely attributable to a pesky borrower in breach of its agreement.

Notwithstanding all this, there is an emerging consensus that, given the tremendous growth in international financial markets since LIBOR loans were first created, it is almost inconceivable that a government or regulator would declare LIBOR-based loans unlawful in the manner contemplated by the clause. As a consequence, some credit agreements today no longer include an illegality clause.

Breakfunding

Under the theory of match-funding, if a borrower repays a LIBOR loan in the middle of an interest period (which notionally corresponds to the term of a deposit taken in by the lender), the lender will be deprived of an interest stream (namely, the one on the loan) necessary to service the payments that the lender must make to its depositor at the end of the deposit term. Similarly, a borrower might request a LIBOR loan and then, for whatever reason, decline to take down the loan. The lender will have obtained a deposit in London two business days prior to the anticipated borrowing date and yet find itself in the position of having the deposit proceeds not being put to work. In either case, the lender would be forced to find an alternative use spanning the balance of the deposit term for the money repaid to it by the borrower. The alternative use might yield a lower interest coupon than the amount that was to be paid by the borrower.

The breakfunding clause is intended to address the possibility that the source of funds for interest on the deposit (namely, the anticipated interest payments to be made by the borrower on its loan) is "broken" in the middle of the deposit term. The breakfunding clause will, in essence, allow the lender to be compensated for any shortfall between the amount of interest that would have accrued on the loan (usually not including the margin) for the balance of the interest period and the amount of interest that the lender is able to earn by reinvesting the prepaid proceeds into alternative assets.

Breakfunding clauses take two basic forms. One form allows the lender in its good faith to specify the cost suffered by it through having to redeploy the repaid loan proceeds. This approach is consistent with that used in the increased costs clause in that no detailed mathematical calculation of the loss to the lender will be made. The clause will customarily permit the lender, in determining its loss, to assume that it funded each LIBOR loan by taking in a deposit in the London interbank market in an amount, and for a term, equal to the interest period for the LIBOR loan. In other words, the lender shall be deemed to have match-funded all of its LIBOR loans.

Another form of the clause simply sets out an arithmetical formula for calculating the minimum amount that should be payable to the lender as a result of the breakfunding event. The formula assumes match-funding, but because the math is explicit, a statement confirming the assumption is not express. The formula also assumes that the lender reinvests the funds in the LIBOR market. Sometimes the shortfall payable to the lender will include the interest margin, but in most cases the borrower is required to make up for the difference in LIBOR only for the two periods (i.e., the original interest period and the remaining portion of the interest period following the breakfunding event).

An illustration of the calculation may be useful. Assume that a $1,000,000 LIBOR loan has a six-month interest period and a rate of 6%, consisting of LIBOR for the interest period of 5% and an interest margin of 1%. Assume next that the borrower prepays the $1,000,000 in full at the fourth month. Finally, assume that at the time of the prepayment, LIBOR for a two-month interest period is 4.5%. The lender will be unable to reinvest the funds at a sufficient rate to cover the hypothetical six-month deposit that it took in to fund the loan. The borrower will, therefore, be required to pay breakfunding of $833, which represents 5% *minus* 4.5%, or the difference in LIBOR rates, *times* $1,000,000 (the amount prepaid) *times* 2/12 (the number of months of the original interest period remaining *divided by* the number of months in a year). If the lender were to be compensated for the loss of interest margin as well, the amount payable by the borrower would increase to $2,500, which represents (6% *minus* 4.5%) *times* $1,000,000 *times* 2/12.

Taxes

As noted previously, the taxes clause is not confined to compensating a lender for LIBOR-related costs. Rather, the clause is intended to protect the lender against taxes that would reduce its yield on the loan. Net income taxes (and comparable taxes, however denominated) imposed by the jurisdiction of the lender's organization, its principal office, or the lending office for the loan would be excluded. Certain other exclusions for taxes resulting from lender activities unrelated to the specific loan are sometimes also negotiated. The primary concern relates to taxes that the borrower would be required to withhold from the stated interest that it would otherwise pay to the lender. The typical approach of the taxes clause is to require the borrower to gross-up the interest payment so that the lender realizes an amount in cash that, after deduction for the withheld taxes (including further withholding taxes on the gross-up payments), is equal to the stated interest on the loan.

An illustration of this may be helpful. Assume that interest on a loan made by a bank located in the United States is equal to 6%. Assume also that the borrower is in a jurisdiction that imposes a withholding tax of 30% on interest payments made to the United States. Absent a gross-up, the lender will receive only 4.2% per annum on its loan, that is, (100% *minus* 30%) *times* 6%. The taxes clause will, accordingly, gross-up the interest payment to an amount equal to 8.571% (i.e., 6% *divided by* 0.70). When the 30% withholding is then applied to the 8.571%, the lender will receive 6% (i.e., 8.571% *times* 0.70 = 6.0%) in cash.

The lender in this situation may, of course, be entitled to claim a foreign tax credit on its U.S. tax return for the amount withheld from its grossed-up interest (the full amount of which, i.e., the 8.571%, is included in gross income). Typically, lenders resist agreeing to reimburse the borrower for the benefit derived from foreign tax credits because of practical and administrative difficulties in tracing credits to particular loans. There is also a certain rough justice to this because borrowers typically refuse to cover the lender's additional net income taxes resulting from the payment of the larger grossed-up amount (a so-called spiral gross-up or super gross-up), even when the lender cannot obtain benefit from the additional foreign tax credits (e.g., because the lender otherwise already has more credits than it can use, given the complex limitations that apply).

A lender may also in the future receive a refund from the foreign jurisdiction of the 2.571% paid to that jurisdiction if more than the amount required by law was withheld. The taxes clause may provide that if a refund is received from the foreign jurisdiction that, in the discretion of the lender, can be associated with the loan made to the borrower, then the borrower will be entitled to receive an amount equal to the proceeds of the refund (net of any related expenses incurred).

The taxes clause will protect both domestic lenders that make loans to foreign borrowers and foreign lenders that make loans to domestic borrowers. The rate of withholding by a country (the United States is no different on this score) is usually determined on a country-by-country basis and is dependent upon whether the payor country and the recipient country have a tax treaty. Thus, interest paid by a U.K. borrower to a U.S. lender is generally not subject to withholding. In contrast, interest payments by a Mexican borrower to a U.S. lender are subject (with some exceptions) to withholding at a rate of 35%.

If loans by a particular lender to a borrower are going to result in withholding, the borrower probably will not allow that lender into the syndicate. Most taxes clauses, therefore, provide that a lender is entitled to be grossed-up only if at the inception of the loan (i.e., closing or the date on which the lender acquired a loan by assignment), the lender is exempt from withholding. The clause thus becomes, in effect, merely a change in law provision, designed to address the circumstance of new taxes or changes in treaties. Of course, the borrower may sometimes have no choice if its jurisdiction does not have in place relevant tax treaties that reduce the withholding rate to zero. A borrower located in such a jurisdiction may have to gross-up lenders at inception (not merely based on a change in law) as a cost of obtaining financing.

INTEREST SAVINGS CLAUSES

Many credit agreements will contain a so-called interest savings clause. The provision addresses what happens if, for any reason, the stated rate of interest on the loans exceeds the maximum rate (the usury rate) allowed under applicable law. This could happen if the interest rate under a credit agreement were higher than the permitted usury limit in the borrower's jurisdictions. In many cases, for example, usury laws will treat upfront fees as "interest." In such a case, if on syndication the borrower paid a 1% upfront fee to each lender and the initial loan interest rate is 10%, the actual stated rate of interest should the loan be repaid in 30 days would be 22%.

Some usury laws, if violated, can have draconian effects on lenders. Lenders might, for example, be required to return *all* interest (not just the excess interest) or even a multiple of the interest paid. Fortunately none of this is a problem under New York law, which in essence provides that any loan of $2,500,000 or more, or any loan made under a facility providing for aggregate loans of $2,500,000 or more, is not subject to New York's usury limitations. A question may remain as to whether the New York rule applies (even for a New York-law credit agreement) if the borrower is not located in New York. Although interest limitations for banks that are federally regulated are determined by the jurisdiction from which a loan is made, this is not necessarily the case for nonbank lenders.

To deal with these concerns, an interest savings clause will provide that any interest paid on the loans in excess of that permitted under applicable law will be deemed to have been a prepayment of principal and not a payment of interest. There are few court decisions confirming that this approach works, but it has developed as the market-standard solution to the usury problem.

Part 3: Making the Borrower Repay the Loan: Amortization and Maturity

PAYMENTS GENERALLY

Immediately Available Funds

Credit agreements will almost universally require that payments be made (and loans advanced) in so-called immediately available funds. Immediately available funds are funds that are immediately available in the place of payment. Payment by check would generally not be in immediately available funds because, before the recipient can have access to the funds represented by the check, they must first be collected (which may take several business days, depending upon where the bank on which the check has been drawn is located). Advances of funds from lenders to the administrative agent through the Fedwire Funds Service, the Federal Reserve's wire transfer system (or in Europe, with respect to euro-denominated fundings, the Trans-European Automated Real-time Gross Settlement Express Transfer [TARGET2] payment system) are immediately available when received by the agent and are immediately available to be deposited into a borrower's account or remitted as the borrower directs. Payments made by the borrower directing that the administrative agent debit an account of the borrower at the administrative agent itself will be considered to be immediately available.

Time of Payment

Credit agreements generally require that payments be made at a particular time on the date of payment. Absent specification of a time, a borrower would be able to make payment at any time up to the close of business. Receiving funds so late in the day would probably make it impossible for the lenders to reinvest those funds. It would also probably be too late for investment by the administrative agent if, in reliance on the clawback clause, discussed in the section "The Clawback Clause" in Part 8, "Keeping Peace among the Lenders," it has forwarded funds to the lenders. Not designating a specific time may also confuse the setoff rights of the lenders by making it unclear when during the day the borrower first goes into default.

Extensions for Nonbusiness Days

Under New York law (General Construction Law, Article 2, §25), if a payment is due on a day that is not a business day (such as a Sunday or public holiday), the payment will automatically be extended to the next succeeding business day (i.e., Monday), but (unless the parties have otherwise agreed) no interest will be payable for the period of the extension. Credit agreements are almost universally structured so that payments are due on business days to avoid this rule. Nevertheless, because nonbusiness days can occur unexpectedly (see the discussion in the section "Business-Day Conventions" in Part 2, "Making Money off the Loan"), credit agreements will also state that if any extension should ever occur, interest will be payable during the extension.

SCHEDULED REPAYMENT

Lenders ultimately want their loans to be repaid, and the credit agreement will, accordingly, always include a maturity date. The exact date is determined by negotiation, and there is no general custom as to what the maturity should be, except that revolving credit and A loan tranches (discussed in the section "Credit Variants" in Part 1, "Making the Loan") will almost never extend beyond six years and B loan tranches will rarely extend beyond seven years. Additionally, B loan tranches will nearly always mature well after any revolving credit or A loan tranche set out in the same credit agreement.

Although revolving credit commitments can be repayable in installments by providing for reductions in accordance with a commitment reduction schedule, in most cases a revolving credit commitment will have a bullet maturity (i.e., the entire commitment will be available until maturity, and then the whole amount will terminate). By contrast, both A loan and B loan tranches will invariably provide for installments of principal to be paid prior to maturity. As noted earlier (see the section "Credit Variants" in Part 1, "Making the

Loan"), the installments for a B loan tranche will be nominal until the final year; the installments for an A loan tranche will be larger, so that the loan is substantially repaid by the time it matures.

ADVANCING THE MATURITY DATE

In the "Commitments" section in Part 1, "Making the Loan," we described the so-called accordion feature that allows commitments to be increased at the option of the borrower (assuming that it finds willing lenders). To confuse things, bankers also use the term *accordion* to describe a quite different feature whereby the maturity date for a loan will be advanced because of an intervening bond maturity or other event. An example might arise when a loan is made with, say, a seven-year maturity, while a large subordinated bond indenture, scheduled to mature in five years, is outstanding. As a credit matter, most lenders will find this situation unacceptable. Of course, the expectation of the borrower will be that it will refinance the bonds in advance of their maturity, so that no conflict between the lenders and the bondholders will ever occur. To ensure that the borrower in fact completes the refinancing in a timely fashion, the credit agreement may provide that, if the bonds are still outstanding on the date six months prior to their maturity, the maturity date for the loans will automatically be advanced to that date. Hence, the "accordion."

364-DAY FACILITIES

One very common category of credit agreement is the so-called 364-day facility. These facilities originate from Federal Reserve capital rules to the effect that banks are not required to hold capital against any commitment having a term of one year or less. A lender can, therefore, offer more advantageous financing to borrowers because the cost to the lender is lower. Although Federal Reserve rules stipulate that the zero-capital requirement applies for any facility of one year or less, the market practice is for these facilities always to expire one day earlier than a full year, that is, on the 364th day.

Note that 364-day facilities are made available primarily to investment-grade borrowers and will almost always provide a mechanism for extension of the facility at its expiration. The Federal Reserve has issued only very general guidance as to how such extensions must be affected in order that the facility not lose zero-capital treatment. Perhaps as a consequence, the market practice is to lay out in the credit agreement explicit extension procedures by which the lenders can extend their commitments. The Federal Reserve recognizes (and the customary extension procedures reflect) that from the standpoint of business practicality, a borrower will want to know prior to the expiration of the commitments whether or not they have been extended. The LSTA Model Credit Agreement Provisions include language that has been approved by the Federal Reserve for extensions of 364-day facilities. Under this language, lenders are allowed to commit to an extension as early as 30 days prior to the expiration date, even though the resulting commitment could have a term of 394 days. With certain exceptions, the Federal Reserve will also allow the borrower to request the extension as early as 45 days prior to the expiration date.

VOLUNTARY PREPAYMENTS

The general rule under New York law is that a loan may not be prepaid without the consent of the lender. The theory is that the lender has contracted for a loan of a particular term, and that it would constitute a breach of that contract were the borrower to be allowed to pay early. Credit agreements will nearly always expressly override this general rule and allow the borrower to prepay loans at any time at its option. There are exceptions, and of course any payment of a LIBOR loan prior to the expiration of its interest period will need to be accompanied by a breakfunding payment (described in the section "Yield Protection" in Part 2, "Making Money off the Loan"). In contrast, the typical bond indenture or private placement often will not allow prepayments for the first three or four years, and will allow them thereafter only if a premium is paid.

In the case of the prepayment of a loan that is otherwise payable in installments, the prepayment provision will address how the prepayment is to be applied to the installments. Absent specification, under New York law the borrower would be free to apply the prepayment to whichever installments it chose. Lenders will prefer to have prepayments applied to installments in inverse order (which is to say, starting with the last installment and then working forward), so that the credit exposure is shortened and the borrower remains subject to the discipline of having to make the regular agreed-upon installments of principal initially contemplated by the parties. Borrowers will prefer the opposite, namely, that prepayments be applied to installments in the direct order of maturity. Some agreements will compromise on the two extremes by stipulating that prepayments are applied to installments ratably. Other twists are also seen, such as applying prepayments first to the next four installments and then ratably or in inverse order. There are no limits here to what the parties can negotiate.

Another allocation issue that credit agreements may from time to time address is between loans within a particular tranche. This might occur, for example, if the loans outstanding under a tranche were broken into three classes, base rate loans, LIBOR loans with an interest period expiring in a week, and other LIBOR loans with an interest period expiring in four months. To minimize breakfunding costs, the borrower will of course want to prepay the base rate loans first and then the LIBOR loans with the interest period expiring in one week. Credit agreements will invariably allow the borrower to pick and choose among these loans to minimize its costs, because the lenders are essentially indifferent as to which loan is repaid. Sometimes, however, the credit agreement will lock in this type of allocation by an express statement that base rate loans are paid first and then LIBOR loans are paid in the order in which interest periods expire.

Voluntary prepayments may usually be made only upon notice given by the borrower to the administrative agent (who then advises the appropriate lenders). For a LIBOR loan, the notice period is typically three business days; for a base rate loan, the notice period will normally be one day in advance and in some cases on the day of the prepayment. A notice, once given, will be irrevocable, because it is presumed that the lenders, in reliance on the notice, will have committed to redeploy the funds to be repaid to an alternative asset (though a borrower will often be allowed to issue a revocable notice of prepayment in connection with an anticipated refinancing).

As with the making of loans, prepayments will be required to be in certain minimum amounts (and sometimes multiples in excess of those minimums) to ease the administrative burden of dealing with small funds transfers.

MANDATORY PREPAYMENTS

Mandatory prepayments, as the term indicates, *mandate* that the borrower prepay loans upon the occurrence of specified events.

Mandatory prepayments should be contrasted with the corresponding requirements in bond indentures, where a required prepayment (which is normally confined to asset sales and changes of control) will be structured as an "offer to prepay" made to all bondholders rather than as an obligation that bonds be prepaid or redeemed. There are at least two substantive differences between the credit agreement approach and the bond indenture approach. First, in a credit agreement, the prepayment is usually required to be made immediately (or virtually so). In a bond indenture, the process can take up to 90 or more days, with the issuer being given 30 or more days in which to make an offer, the bondholders being given another 30 or more days to accept the offer, and the issuer being granted yet more time in which to make payment. The second major difference is that in a credit agreement, the lenders (with the exception for B loan tranches, as described later in this part in "Prepayment Opt-Outs") will not be given the opportunity to opt out of a prepayment. In the bond indenture context, whether or not a particular bondholder is prepaid is purely a function of whether it elects to be prepaid by accepting the offer to prepay. What follows is an overview of the mandatory prepayment provisions most commonly included in credit agreements.

Revolving Clean-Downs

In a revolving credit facility, a clean-down requirement would force the borrower, typically for a period of 30 days during each calendar year, to have no outstandings under the revolving credit commitments. This type of mandatory prepayment would customarily be inserted for a seasonal business, where, if its business is successful, a borrower should not require any borrowings during a particular time of year (such as, in a retail business, during the months of January or February following a robust holiday sale season). The prepayment is in effect a control against adverse developments in the borrower's business.

Borrowing Base

Borrowing bases are typically found only in secured agreements with revolving credit facilities. If the credit agreement has a borrowing base, the availability of revolving credit loans will be tied to an agreed valuation (i.e., the "borrowing base") of the collateral security. Hence, if, giving effect to a borrowing, the amount of the loans and letters of credit exceeds the borrowing base, the lenders will not be obligated to honor the borrowing request. Similarly, if the amount of the borrowing base falls below the aggregate outstanding loans and letters of credit, the borrower would be required to immediately repay a sufficient amount of the loans to eliminate the shortfall.

Borrowing bases, which occur primarily in so-called asset-based deals, are usually structured around the value of easily liquidated collateral, such as accounts receivable and inventory. The percentage "advance rates" to be lent against each type of collateral will be determined by the lender after extensive analysis of the assets in the borrowing base. The typical borrowing base definition will apply the advance rates only to "eligible" accounts receivable and inventory to improve further the chances that the borrowing base, when liquidated, will be sufficient to repay the secured loans. The prepayment has an effect very similar to that of the cleandown prepayment described previously. Thus, in a seasonal business, when the borrower is flush with cash (and therefore when its receivables and inventory are relatively low), shrinkage in the borrowing base will force it to reduce its outstanding loan balance.

Asset Sales

The asset sale prepayment will force the borrower to prepay loans upon any sale of assets that is out of the ordinary course of business and, usually, is over an agreed-upon threshold. The asset sale prepayment is often redundant of the asset sale covenant in that a sale that requires a prepayment is frequently also a sale that must first be consented to by the lenders. As a consequence, lenders are almost always in a position to impose conditions on their consent to a sale (such as requiring prepayment), whether or not the credit agreement incorporates a mandatory prepayment. See the discussion in the "Fundamental Changes" section of Part 5, "Monitoring the Loan."

Typically, the asset sale prepayment will also allow the borrower a period within which to reinvest the proceeds before being required to make the prepayment. The reinvestment will normally be required to be made into replacement or equivalent assets, although the covenant will sometimes permit the reinvestment to be applied to "capital expenditures" generally. See the discussion regarding capital expenditures in the "Capital Expenditures" section in Part 5, "Monitoring the Loan." Lenders frequently grant the borrower up to a year to make a reinvestment. It has become increasingly common to allow an extended reinvestment period if the borrower commits to make the reinvestment within the initial period. This extended period may be helpful if the borrower is reinvesting in assets that will be acquired or constructed over time and where payment in full is not required to be made upfront. Only if a reinvestment does not occur within the specified time frame will the borrower be required to make a prepayment. In highly leveraged, fully secured deals, it is not uncommon for the borrower to be required to pledge the proceeds with the administrative agent (or collateral agent) pending reinvestment or to apply the proceeds to revolving credit loans until they are borrowed to make a reinvestment.

One of the things that lenders must address when drafting asset sale prepayment provisions is that the covenant not be inconsistent with the asset sale provisions of any outstanding bond indentures. For example, if the bond indenture specifies a reinvestment period of 180 days, the credit agreement will not want to specify a longer period; otherwise, the bonds would conceivably be paid before the loans. Similarly, if the bond indenture specifies dollar thresholds over which prepayments are to be made, the dollar thresholds in the credit agreement should not be higher. A borrower also wants to be alert to the problem that one dollar of asset sale proceeds does not result in two dollars of required prepayments. This could arise if a borrower has an asset sale prepayment in both a credit agreement and one or more bond indentures. The typical solution may already be incorporated into the bond indenture. The latter normally treats any prepayment of credit agreement debt as a deduction from the asset sale proceeds, and thus avoids any double count. However, if the borrower has other outstanding debt that is secured on a pari passu basis with the credit agreement, care should be taken to require that only the respective pro rata portions of the asset sale proceeds (rather than 100%) be required to make prepayments under the credit agreement and such other debt.

The asset sale prepayment will customarily be required to be in the amount of the net proceeds of the sale. *Net proceeds* will be defined as all cash proceeds received by the borrower net of transaction costs (including transfer taxes), and typically also net of income taxes that the borrower anticipates having to pay by reason of the sale. The borrower is normally allowed to estimate these taxes in "good faith," even though there may be potential for abuse in that regard. Net proceeds may also include promissory notes or deferred installments received in connection with a sale, as and when the cash realized on the notes or installments is actually remitted to the borrower. This is another instance in which the credit agreement will not want to be looser than any outstanding bond indentures.

Casualty Events

Somewhat akin to the asset sale prepayment, a casualty event prepayment will require the borrower to prepay the loans, generally out of insurance or condemnation proceeds, in the event that property (over a threshold value) is destroyed or is taken by a governmental entity. The prepayment will normally allow the borrower a period, again similar to that for the asset sale prepayment, in which to reinvest the proceeds of the casualty event into replacement assets.

Debt and Equity Issuances

In highly leveraged deals, or in transactions in which the credit agreement is in effect a bridge to a bond or equity offering, the agreement will include a debt or equity prepayment requirement in respect of cash proceeds of debt or equity raises. In agreements with both types of prepayments, the borrower will often be afforded greater flexibility to keep a portion of the proceeds of an equity issuance than of a debt issuance. It is thus not uncommon to see the borrower be obligated to apply to the prepayment of the loans 100% of the proceeds of a debt issuance, but only 50% of the proceeds of an equity issuance. Many credit agreements do not even include an equity issuance prepayment at all, particularly where the borrower is a public company or where it is owned by a private equity sponsor that wants the ability to make ongoing equity investments to finance the borrower's ongoing business operations or growth.

Excess Cash Flow

Lenders may ask to receive earlier repayment if a borrower is doing well. The cash flow prepayment is one device to accomplish this. It stipulates that some percentage (the number is strictly up for negotiation, although 50% and 75% are common, and it is not uncommon to see the percentage step down and ultimately fall away if a leverage or other ratio is reduced below an agreed-upon level) of the borrower's excess cash flow will be applied to prepay the loans. *Excess cash flow* will be defined in such a way as to capture the "excess" cash being thrown off by the borrower's business. Thus, the definition will typically start with EBITDA and then subtract interest, scheduled principal payments, capital expenditures, scheduled dividend payments, and taxes, to name a few items. It may also pick up changes in working capital, so that if working capital increases from the beginning to the end of the year, excess cash flow is reduced and, conversely, if working capital decreases, excess cash flow increases.

In some credit agreements, the excess cash flow formula starts with consolidated net income (CNI) rather than EBITDA, which can be advantageous for borrowers. By starting with CNI for both the EBITDA definition as well as the excess cash flow formula and adding numerous items to arrive at a larger amount for EBITDA while subtracting numerous items to arrive at a smaller amount for excess cash flow, the borrower can, in a way, have their cake and eat it too.

One of the issues that this kind of prepayment provision should address (not all credit agreements do) is how voluntary prepayments of term loans should be treated. Logically, if the borrower is flush with cash in July because the first six months have been strong, the lenders will want the borrower to prepay the term loans immediately (there may be no revolving credit loans outstanding at the time). The excess cash flow prepayment is not typically required to be made more than once a year, and then only when the audited financial statements are delivered. So, in this example, the borrower would not be obligated to make a prepayment until the end of March in the year following, nine months after July. The solution is to induce the borrower to prepay in July by giving it full dollar-for-dollar credit against the excess cash flow prepayment that would be required to be made in March of the year following. Thus, the borrower will not have a disincentive to make a prepayment in July because it knows that what it pays in July will reduce its March obligation on a dollar-for-dollar basis.

Change of Control

Credit agreements vary as to whether a change of control should be an event of default or a mandatory prepayment. Because the borrower may regard such an event as being outside its control, many borrowers prefer that it be a prepayment event rather than a default. By contrast, the near-uniform practice in bond indentures is to require the issuer to make an offer to prepay upon the occurrence of a change of control rather than have it trigger a default. The change of control prepayment (or default) derives from the fundamental principle that a lender wants to "know its customer," including who ultimately controls that customer. If the customer should change, or if control of the customer should devolve upon a new entity, the lenders may want the right to exit the facility.

In the case of a privately owned company, the lenders will typically require that all or a majority of the borrower's stock continue to be owned by the individuals, financial sponsors, or companies that own the borrower at the inception of the facility. The lenders will trust the current owners' integrity, competence, strategy, policies, and management style and will not want them replaced. In some cases, the change of control definition may simply require that voting power be retained; in other cases, the lenders may require that the existing owners continue to have sufficient "skin in the game," and thus also trigger the default upon a sale of nonvoting stock. (If the sponsor or investor has already realized its target return on the investment, it may have less incentive to support the borrower in the future.)

In the case of a public company, the definition will be triggered if any person or group obtains control by acquiring a percentage of the outstanding shares greater than a negotiated threshold (20% to 30% is typical). The assumption is that so long as the borrower's shares are widely held, its character will not change. A change of control in a public company may also be triggered by changes to the board of directors, such as if a majority of the board cease to be continuing directors (usually defined as new directors that have been approved by incumbent directors). This might occur if a competing shareholder or group were to attempt to take over the borrower through a proxy fight.

Although the concept of a change of control provision sounds entirely lender-favorable, certain classes of borrowers may actually want a change of control provision to be included in a credit agreement, viewing it as a form of "poison pill"—another hurdle that a potential acquiror of the borrower would need to overcome if it wanted to make a hostile bid for the borrower. Recent court decisions have, however, cast a skeptical eye on change of control provisions to the extent that they, contrary to board fiduciary obligations, simply entrench existing directors and managers.

Currency Adjustments in Multicurrency Deals

As with a purely U.S. dollar credit agreement, a credit agreement with a tranche available in both U.S. dollars and one or more other currencies will normally delineate the amount of credit available under the tranche by reference to a U.S. dollar commitment level. Thus, although loans may be available in euro, the credit agreement will typically state that the borrower can borrow euro only up to the U.S. dollar equivalent of, say, U.S. $100,000,000. The credit approvals obtained internally by each lender will then reflect this limit upon their exposure. Of course, if the euro equivalent of U.S. $100,000,000 is borrowed at closing and the euro subsequently increases in value against the U.S. dollar, then the aggregate exposure of the lenders will have effectively been increased. The same mismatch can occur if nondollar letters of credit are issued.

To address this risk, a credit agreement will customarily require a periodic calculation (typically quarterly, but sometimes more frequently or at every borrowing) of the aggregate amount of loans and letters of credit under a multicurrency credit agreement, taking into account any fluctuations in currency values. The normal approach is to require a prepayment down to an exposure level equal to 100% of the commitments to the extent that the aggregate exposure (the U.S. dollar equivalent of outstanding loans) exceeds 105% of the commitments.

In a credit agreement where the only currency available under a particular tranche is a designated foreign currency, these issues do not arise, because it is presumed that the initial credit approval of the lenders was couched in terms of the particular foreign currency.

APPLICATION OF PREPAYMENTS AMONG TRANCHES

In addition to specifying how mandatory prepayments are to be applied to loan installments, the credit agreement will specify how prepayments are to be applied among loan tranches (assuming that there are multiple tranches). The normal approach is to require that prepayments be applied first to the term loan tranches (which will typically be allocated ratably across tranches) and then to revolving credit tranches. This is driven by the borrower's desire not to lose the liquidity afforded by the revolving credit commitments until the term loans have been paid in full.

If the revolving credit commitments provide for letters of credit, the prepayment provisions will also typically specify that revolving credit loans are paid in full first before any prepayment proceeds are applied to provide cover for letters of credit (see the discussion in the next section, "Cover for Letters of Credit").

COVER FOR LETTERS OF CREDIT

As noted in the section "Letters of Credit" in Part 1, "Making the Loan," letters of credit cannot be unilaterally repaid. A letter of credit is an irrevocable undertaking on the part of the issuer owing to a third party, with the borrower being obligated to reimburse the issuer only in the event of a drawing. Because the reimbursement obligation is not payable until the drawing is made, it cannot be paid or prepaid prior to a drawing. To enable letters of credit nevertheless to be "repaid" (or "prepaid" upon a mandatory prepayment event), credit agreements will contemplate that the borrower "cover" its contingent reimbursement obligation by posting cash collateral with the administrative agent in an amount equal to the face amount of the letter of credit. If the facility is being repaid in full, this amount may be a higher percentage of the face amount (102% or 105%) in order to also cover future fees and costs. The agreement will typically provide that any posted cash be invested solely in very short-term Treasury securities (though many credit agreements are silent on investment). Because of the negative arbitrage implicit in posting cash in this manner, mandatory prepayment provisions will normally stipulate that all loans are paid in full before cover is posted for any letters of credit.

PREPAYMENT OPT-OUTS

As noted previously, one of the basic differences between the prepayment provisions of a credit agreement and those of a bond indenture is that, in the credit agreement, all lenders of a particular tranche will be prepaid, and there is no ability to elect or not elect a prepayment. B loan tranches are one exception to this general rule that has developed in the market. B loan lenders will sometimes be given the right to opt out of a mandatory prepayment (but not an optional prepayment) if there are A loans outstanding. The monies that would otherwise be applied to the B loans are instead applied to the A loans. More commonly, the opt-out is granted whether or not there are A loans outstanding and the borrower is permitted to retain those monies. Whether B loans are afforded this option is strictly a question for negotiation. Borrowers may resist the lack of flexibility that the opt-out entails for them.

PREPAYMENT PREMIUMS

In addition to any breakfunding payments that may need to be made upon a prepayment (see the discussion in "Breakfunding" in Part 2, "Making Money off the Loan"), in some cases the borrower will also be required to pay an additional fee (a prepayment premium) in a percentage equal to the amount of principal being prepaid. In a bond indenture or private placement, the premiums may start as high as 5% or 6% of the amount of the prepayment and descend to zero over a period of years. In a credit agreement, the prepayment premiums, if specified at all, will normally apply only to the B loans, will be in much lower amounts (2% descending to 1%), and will apply only to prepayments made in the first or second year following the closing. This type of prepayment premium is a so-called hard call and is more commonly seen in second lien credit agreements. In addition, some agreements provide that a premium is not payable at all unless the source of the prepayment is a refinancing by the borrower with cheaper debt—this approach is a so-called soft call. The theory behind the soft call is that if the borrower is prepaying B loans from the proceeds of an asset sale, earnings, or just cash on hand, it should be free to do so without paying the premium, and that only if the borrower is fleeing to cheaper financing should it be forced to pay a premium. Typically, the soft call provision is written broadly to pick up not only a true refinancing amendment, but also a forced assignment pursuant to the credit agreement's yank-a-bank provision resulting from a lender's refusal to consent to the repricing amendment.

MULTIPLE BORROWERS

Some credit agreements, rather than having loans made to a single borrower under the guarantee of one or more subsidiaries or parent entities, will provide instead that the loans are deemed to be made to multiple borrowers, with each borrower being jointly and severally obligated to repay all loans. This is sometimes referred to as a *co-borrower arrangement*. There is little practical legal difference between having a single borrower with guarantees and having a co-borrower structure, but some believe that the co-borrower structure may provide a slight advantage under fraudulent conveyance rules (see the section "Solvency" in Part 4, "Conditioning the Loan"), in that it may be easier to argue that each co-borrower received the full amount of the loan proceeds. It is unclear, however, whether a bankruptcy court would give much credence to this argument if it can be shown that the proceeds in fact went to a particular borrower or subsidiary.

There are also instances when a non-U.S. borrower is seeking to raise loan financing that lenders may require or prefer that there be a U.S. co-borrower. For example, an institutional lender may not be permitted under its organizational documents to own a loan of a Peruvian borrower but can own that same loan if jointly borrowed with a U.S. co-borrower. The use of a U.S. co-borrower in these circumstances makes a loan eligible for investment by the institutional lenders.

Part 4: Conditioning the Loan: Conditions Precedent and Representations

CONDITIONS PRECEDENT

The conditions precedent in a credit agreement are in essence a simplified closing list. They specify what the borrower must deliver to the lenders (or the administrative agent), what actions it must take, and what other circumstances must exist in order for credit to be available. Normally the conditions will be broken out into two types: (1) those to be satisfied at closing and (2) those to be satisfied at both closing and each borrowing thereafter (the latter are the so-called ongoing conditions).

Normally, a majority vote will be required to waive any of the conditions precedent, although some credit agreements will require unanimity for any changes to the closing-date conditions. However, unless the lenders have waived a condition by an appropriate vote, any lender that believes that a condition has not been satisfied is still free to take up a dispute with the borrower; a disagreement with the borrower by one lender will not affect the obligation of any other lender.

The particular conditions set out in a credit agreement are typically crafted (and negotiated) for the specific credit facility, though certain conditions are so basic that they are contained in nearly every credit agreement. The following are some of those conditions that are contained in basically every credit agreement.

Execution

The credit agreement (and other related agreements) must be executed by all parties. Perhaps the most basic of conditions precedent is therefore the requirement that the credit agreement and related contracts be fully executed by all parties before any money is lent. In rare cases, the parties may gather together in a conference room to sign all relevant documents, but most closings do not occur this way. In practice, most closings are accomplished by delivery of email signatures. See the discussion in the section "Electronic Execution" in Part 10, "Understanding the Boilerplate," of the issues raised by electronic signatures.

Lenders may not be identifiable and commitments may not be allocated until just prior to (or, in some cases, the day of) the closing. This problem is most common where the credit agreement includes a broadly syndicated tranche. A practice that has developed to address this situation is the use of *lender addenda*. Lender addenda allow a credit agreement to be executed between the borrower and the administrative agent, with each lender becoming a party to the credit agreement by signing a short lender addendum in which the add-on party agrees to be a "lender" under the credit agreement with a "commitment" in an amount specified in the lender addendum. Delivery of lender addenda is no different in legal concept from returning signed signature pages, except that lender addenda have the advantage of referring to a particular agreement (not always the case with a signature page) and also specifying the amount of the lenders' commitments.

Another practice that is more common at the time of this writing is for the lead arranger or its lending affiliate to fund the entire amount of (or "front") the syndicated loan tranche and then to sell the loans by post-closing assignments to the lenders. Such a fronting arrangement is typically documented under a fronting letter signed by the lead arranger and the other loan arrangers. Pursuant to a fronting letter, the other arrangers will be required to purchase from the lead arranger their pro rata shares of the syndicated loan tranche subject to any post-closing assignments not settling. The LSTA has promulgated a form of fronting letter that evidences the agreements of the arrangers to front loans and share the risk of primary allocation with trades that have not settled.

Corporate and Organizational Matters

The borrower must, of course, exist as a legal entity (corporation, limited liability company, partnership, or other creature), and the credit agreement must also be appropriately authorized and duly executed by the borrower. The president of a corporation (or the managing member of a limited liability company or the general partner of a partnership) probably has sufficient authority under general legal principles to bind the borrower, even for a very large financing. However, most credit agreements are not in fact signed by the president, managing member, or general partner, but rather by a treasurer or chief financial officer (CFO). In the case of a corporation, execution of an agreement that is "material" to the borrower normally requires board of directors' approval, so it is inadvisable in that context to rely just on the "apparent authority" of the president. Similar action may be necessary for execution by a limited liability company or limited partnership.

Accordingly, the conditions precedent should require evidence of authorization. That evidence will normally consist of a certificate by an officer of the borrower, attaching appropriate organizational documents (in the case of a corporation, these would be the certificate of incorporation and bylaws), attaching the relevant board or shareholder resolutions, and setting forth a certificate of incumbency and specimen signatures of the officers that will be executing the credit agreement. Delivery of a false certificate will typically be an event of default. In addition, delivery of a false certificate to a bank could violate the Federal Bank Fraud statute, which makes it a felony to knowingly obtain monies from a bank by means of "false or fraudulent" representations.

Government Approvals

In cases where the credit agreement, or borrowings thereunder, requires government approval, it is customary for the conditions to state expressly that evidence of approval has been delivered to the lenders (usually also supported by a legal opinion). Evidence will normally consist of a copy of the approval certified by an officer of the borrower. A requirement for government approval in the context of domestic credit agreements is infrequent, but it does occur from time to time, such as with respect to borrowings by certain public utilities. It is much more common in the context of non-U.S. borrowers. See the discussion in the later section "Special Conditions Applicable to Non-U.S. Borrowers."

Legal Opinions

It is customary for lenders to require, as a condition to closing, that formal written legal opinions, dated the closing date, be delivered affirming the legality, validity, binding effect, and enforceability (collectively, *enforceability*) of the credit agreement. One opinion is typically rendered by the borrower's legal counsel, addressed to the administrative agent and the lenders, and covering matters such as due organization of the borrower, its power to enter into the financing, its authorization of the transaction, and the like ("corporate" matters), as well as enforceability. Sometimes all or portions of the borrower opinion are given by the borrower's internal counsel. This may be acceptable to the lenders, given that the internal counsel is, in most cases, likely to be closer to the internal authorization process than outside counsel, although the independence of outside counsel is an important countervailing factor that tends to argue for an outside opinion.

A second opinion, if the conditions provide for one, is given by the firm that is identified as legal counsel to the administrative agent or the lead bank, and is typically limited to enforceability. Although the more frequent formulation is that the opinion is rendered by counsel for the administrative agent, stating that the firm is counsel for the lead bank may actually more accurately reflect the realities of the typical role of the counsel.

Legal opinions speak as of their date, and the opining firm has no obligation to update the opinion unless it otherwise agrees to do so.

The required opinions expand and multiply with the circumstances of particular financings. For example, if there are ancillary agreements such as guarantees and security agreements, the closing opinions will cover these as well, and if the parties are in multiple jurisdictions, counsel in each relevant jurisdiction will generally be required to deliver an opinion.

The language of the typical closing opinion is the product of many years of developing custom, and opinion-givers endeavor to ensure that the scope and language of their opinions are consistent with customary practice as well as with their internal policies (most law firms have opinion committees that establish what may be said in a closing opinion and what due diligence is required to say it). Among the principal sources of opinion practice today are published reports by New York's TriBar Committee, which began its existence as a group formed by three New York bar associations but today includes representatives from a number of states and Canada. Despite the emphasis on customary practice, however, there is still considerable divergence in approach from one law firm to another, and discussion of opinion forms for a particular transaction is often needed.

The proposed forms of legal opinion may be attached to the credit agreement as exhibits. This helps ensure that the lenders are aware of their content prior to signing, and provides certainty to the borrower that an opinion in the prescribed form will satisfy the conditions.

In a secured credit facility, an opinion may be required to confirm the creation of the relevant security interests (such a "creation" opinion is regarded as distinct from an opinion that the security agreement is enforceable), and sometimes to confirm the perfection of the security interests (although many firms are reluctant to give perfection opinions, and such opinions generally in any event require a number of exceptions and qualifications). The manner in which a security interest is perfected, and which law governs its perfection, will vary with the kind of collateral involved and various other factors, and the question of perfection of a security interest is not necessarily governed by the same law as determines the enforceability of the credit agreement or even of the security agreement. In general, law firms do not render legal opinions on the priority of a security interest, except in certain limited circumstances (e.g., an opinion may be given that the pledgee of certificated securities is, subject to certain assumptions, a "protected purchaser" as that term is defined in Article 8 of the Uniform Commercial Code (UCC), an opinion that is equivalent to a first-priority lien opinion).

In many transactions, the legal opinions will cover other specialized matters. For example, an opinion may be required to cover the status of the borrower under the Investment Company Act of 1940, matters relating to the Federal Communications Act, or issues arising under other regulatory statutes.

Legal opinions express legal conclusions and do not generally cover factual matters, such as the accuracy or completeness of financial statements. One exception is the so-called no-litigation opinion, in which the opinion-giver confirms that there is no pending or threatened litigation or proceedings against the client. However, recent litigation against law firms alleging negligent misrepresentation is making no-litigation opinions, at least by outside counsel, a rare phenomenon, and many firms will not give them under any circumstances. (So-called negative assurance in Rule 10b-5 opinions in connection with securities transactions and law firm responses to audit letters, each of which may address the question of material litigation, involve considerations that are not present in the typical loan financing, and are beyond the scope of this chapter.)

The rationale for obtaining legal opinions at a credit agreement closing goes beyond giving the lenders a law firm to sue in the event that the conclusions set out in the opinion are incorrect. Delivering an opinion forces the opinion-giver to go through a due diligence process that should have the beneficial result of making the conclusions accurate by, for example, forcing any corporate deficiencies to be fixed, clarifying board resolutions, obtaining necessary third-party consents, and the like. It is not enough, in other words, that the opinion-giver believes that a legal conclusion is correct; it is more important that the conclusion in fact be correct, and the due diligence required for an opinion helps ensure that. There are at least two other reasons for an opinion to be required at closing. First, bank regulators often expect to see an opinion in the loan file. Second, an opinion from the borrower's counsel can be valuable in the event that, at enforcement of the loan, the borrower tries to raise defenses that are addressed by the opinion. For example, a borrower might contend that the transaction had not been properly authorized or that it violated some law or contract; the opinion, in this context, could have significant estoppel value if it covered the same points.

Conditions Relating to Perfection of Collateral

The conditions precedent will require evidence that each security interest granted to the lenders has been perfected, which means in general terms that steps have been taken to give public notice of the security interest and to make it enforceable against other creditors of the borrower. If a security interest is not perfected, it may be set aside if the grantor files for bankruptcy. An unperfected security interest is often regarded as valueless.

Perfection may involve a number of different steps. Security interests in most kinds of personal property collateral (as distinct from real property) may be perfected by filing a simple "financing statement" under the UCC, normally at a designated central location in the state of organization of the grantor of the collateral. For some kinds of collateral, such as collateral consisting of instruments (such as promissory notes) or certificated securities (such as stock certificates), perfection may also be accomplished by taking possession of the collateral. For certain categories of collateral (such as deposit accounts and letter of credit rights), however, neither of these steps perfects the security interest, and the secured party must take *control*—a technically defined term—of the collateral. Some kinds of personal property collateral are sufficiently related to real estate that a filing in the real estate records is required in order to perfect the lien against competing interests in the real estate, and of course a mortgage (or, as the terminology has it in certain states, a *deed of trust*) on real estate must be duly recorded in the real estate records. Lastly, in the case of real estate collateral, title insurance is often obtained (basically, third-party insurance that the mortgage lien has been perfected and ensuring its priority).

The conditions precedent will require evidence that the relevant steps required for perfection have been taken. Even when a security interest has been perfected, the lenders will also concern themselves with the question of priority: a security interest, though perfected, may rank behind an earlier perfected security interest. The conditions precedent will therefore often require evidence that the relevant security interests are "subject to no equal or prior lien or security interest." With respect to collateral perfected by filing, this may be accomplished by conducting a search under the UCC of the filing records in the relevant jurisdiction or jurisdictions, with a view to determining whether any existing, perfected lien covers the collateral. There is no public record of a security interest perfected by control, so with respect to such security interests, it is necessary to rely upon representations and warranties and certificates of the grantor and third parties.

Promissory Notes

Historically, it was unthinkable for a bank to make a loan without obtaining a physical promissory note from the borrower. Times have changed. Most credit agreements today are so-called note option deals: promissory notes are not executed to evidence loans under the credit agreement unless a lender requests them. Few lenders actually do, although some banks have a policy that all loans must be evidenced by notes. Some fund investors may, under their organizational instruments, be required to obtain a note in order to pledge the loans as security for financing being provided to the fund. One potential advantage of obtaining promissory notes is that if they qualify as "instruments for the payment of money only," they entitle the holder to summary enforcement under Section 3213 of the New York Civil Practice Law and Rules (CPLR).

Promissory notes may be somewhat more common in cross-border deals because they may give the lenders an enhanced ability to enforce payment of the loan in the borrower's home jurisdiction. However, in other instances, a promissory note may attract stamp taxes, so whether to obtain a promissory note if the borrower is foreign is normally examined on a case-by-case basis.

In a revolving credit facility, the form of promissory note is typically a so-called grid note. In a grid note, the face of the note will specify a dollar amount that corresponds to the commitment of the lender, but the text of the note will provide that the real amount payable is the aggregate of all the loans actually advanced and outstanding. These are often set forth in a schedule (or grid) attached to the note. To deal with the possibility that a borrower may object to the amount entered on the grid, the credit agreement (and the note) will usually provide that the entries on the grid are "prima facie" accurate or accurate "absent manifest error." This has the effect of shifting to the borrower the burden of establishing that the notations were wrong.

The MAC Condition

The representations in a credit agreement will typically include a material adverse change (MAC) clause. Although there are many possible formulations of the MAC clause, a typical provision might read as follows:

> The Borrower hereby represents and warrants that since [specify date], there has been no material adverse change in the business, condition (financial or otherwise), assets, operations, or prospects of the Borrower and its subsidiaries, taken as a whole.

As noted in the section "Ongoing Conditions" later in this part, the continued accuracy of representations will generally be a condition precedent to new loans under a credit agreement. Thus, if a MAC has occurred, the MAC representation cannot be truthfully made, and the obligations of the lenders to make new loans would therefore be suspended for so long as the MAC continues (unless the condition is waived).

The typical MAC provision tests whether a material adverse change has occurred since a particular date. The date specified is generally the date of the most recent audited financial statements of the borrower delivered to the lenders prior to signing the credit agreement. The audited financials are, of course, the most reliable financial information, forming the basis of the lenders' credit decision to enter into the credit agreement. Audited financial statements, however, are not always available and in such cases unaudited or pro forma financial statements must be used. In any event, referencing a fixed date protects the lenders against both deterioration in the borrower's condition that becomes material over time as well as a single dramatic event that is material by itself. By way of example, if a borrower requests a loan in the fourth year of a five-year credit agreement, whether it could satisfy the material adverse change condition could be determined by comparing its condition at the time of the requested borrowing against its condition four years earlier or, as discussed below, against the last delivered audited financial statements.

The MAC clause removes some of the certainty that the borrower can access funds under the credit agreement. Borrowers may sometimes seek to reduce any uncertainty by changing the benchmark date against which a MAC is measured. For example, instead

Understanding the Credit Agreement

of specifying a fiscal date that occurred prior to the closing date, a MAC condition might look to whether a MAC has occurred "since the date of the latest financial statements delivered to the lenders under this agreement." Because financial statements are usually delivered quarterly, this would mean that the MAC clause would test whether there has been a MAC over a period of generally no more than 90 days before the borrowing. Changing the benchmark date in this manner may deprive the lenders of protection against a steady, incremental deterioration in the borrower's condition. It may also allow the borrower to wipe out a catastrophic adverse change simply by delivering a new set of financials. For example, if a category 5 hurricane were to destroy all of the borrower's manufacturing facilities, the borrower could arguably eliminate the resultant MAC by simply serving up financials that reflect a reduction in book value of fixed assets to zero.

Just as a borrower may seek to reduce its risk by changing the benchmark date for testing a material adverse change, it may alternatively request a cutoff date for the period over which a MAC is measured. It might, for example, request that the clause measure whether a MAC has occurred from a fiscal end date (prior to the closing date) to the closing date. Changing the standard MAC clause in this way can be even more detrimental to lenders, because it excludes from the MAC clause any MAC that occurs after the cutoff date (in this example, the closing date). This type of MAC clause will most often be found in a revolving credit facility used as a backup line for commercial paper or the like, because rating agencies may consider a more traditional MAC condition as rendering the facility too conditional to support a desired credit rating. The same result could be obtained by explicitly excluding the MAC clause from the list of representations that must be accurate as a condition precedent to each borrowing. This is often done in the case of strong investment-grade borrowers.

The litany of items to be tested for a MAC—in the previous example, "business, condition (financial or otherwise), assets, operations, or prospects"—is intentionally broad and overlapping. The term that is most often the subject of discussion is *prospects*. A MAC clause that includes prospects protects lenders against an MAC affecting a borrower's future performance (and therefore its ability to repay the loans) that has not yet resulted in measurable consequences. Examples might include the permanent loss of a material license or the borrower's pulling a principal product from the market, the consequences of which are the loss of future revenues only.

Borrowers occasionally request other exceptions to the MAC clause. A frequent plea is that the MAC provision exclude changes arising from general macroeconomic circumstances, or changes affecting the borrower's industry generally. Notwithstanding the fact that such events or circumstances are general in nature and not particular to the borrower, they could nevertheless have a material adverse impact on the borrower's ability to repay the loans. For this reason, lenders often resist these exclusions. Whether they (or any other exceptions) are included in any given transaction will depend on how the parties believe that these risks are most appropriately allocated.

The entities to be covered by a MAC clause are those companies whose creditworthiness is the basis of the lending decision. These companies are usually the borrower and its subsidiaries, and any guarantor and its subsidiaries, but in an acquisition financing, the target company and its subsidiaries may also be included. In the context of an acquisition, it is not uncommon for the language of the MAC clause to follow the corresponding language in the acquisition agreement, because a borrower will not want to be contractually bound to complete a purchase if lenders have suspended funding on the basis of a different MAC clause for the target.

Whether a MAC has occurred is generally a question of fact, and there can be no legal certainty as to whether any given set of circumstances constitutes a MAC. The few court decisions that exist tend to be in the acquisition or merger context. Courts have considered some common elements to decide whether a MAC has occurred. One is whether the event was something "unknown" to the lenders at the time of the closing (if the event is covered by a covenant or representation, it may not be considered unknown). A second is whether the event threatened the company's overall earnings potential in a "durationally significant" fashion (as opposed to representing a decline in earnings as a result of business or commodity price cycles). Courts also consider the plaintiff's presumed investment time horizon in making a call as to durational significance. Namely, to a short-term speculator, the failure of a company to meet projected earnings for a quarter could be highly material; for a longer-term investor (lenders under a multiyear credit agreement are likely to fall in this category) such a failure would be less significant. In the context of a credit agreement, "durationally significant" may therefore depend upon whether a court concludes that the lenders are taking a short-term or long-term view of their borrower.

Special Conditions Applicable to Non-U.S. Borrowers

In the case of a non-U.S. borrower, certain additional conditions precedent may be included. The most significant of these is the delivery to the lenders of evidence (in addition to the required legal opinions of non-U.S. counsel) that the borrower has obtained all necessary foreign exchange licenses and other governmental approvals in order that it (and any other non-U.S. party) is entitled to make necessary payments in the prescribed currencies. There can be serious legal risks in proceeding with a cross-border financing without assurance as to compliance with the governmental requirements of the relevant non-U.S. jurisdictions.

Repayment of Other Debt

The lenders will want any debt that does not fit within the permitted debt covenant to be repaid as a condition to the initial loans under the credit agreement. To repay debt is, in most instances, straightforward. The borrower simply remits the requisite funds to the lender or other debt holder and instructs that they be applied to outstanding principal and interest (and any breakfunding or premium or other payments). Sometimes, however, the other debt may not be prepayable, such as is often the case with bonds, which during their early years generally do not permit redemption. In this case, the borrower may need to resort to alternative strategies. One is to purchase the outstanding bonds in the open market. Another strategy is to defease the bonds, although this solution is not practical unless interest on the bonds is at a fixed rate. Another quasi-repayment option that is sometimes employed when a bond maturity follows relatively quickly after the credit agreement closing is to deposit into escrow with the bond trustee (or the credit agreement administrative agent or other third party) an amount equal to the outstanding principal, interest, and premium. When the bond maturity arrives, the escrow funds are then applied to repay the bonds.

When the target debt to be repaid includes letters of credit, either replacement letters of credit are issued (and the existing letters of credit are terminated) with the consent of the beneficiary or the existing letters of credit are left outstanding and the borrower posts cash collateral or a backup letter of credit to support reimbursement obligations in respect of the existing letters of credit.

Other Conditions

Other conditions that are from time to time inserted into credit agreements include the following.

- *Solvency.* A condition to deliver a certification of solvency from the borrower's chief financial officer or other senior financial officer (or even from an independent specialist or appraisal firm although these may be less common due to expense) might be inserted if the terms of the credit facility give rise to fraudulent conveyance or fraudulent transfer issues. Examples might include facilities where the proceeds of the loans are to pay a large dividend to shareholders or where upstream guarantees from subsidiaries are taken. Such a condition has also become common in acquisition finance credit agreements. These conditions would be intended to give the lenders confirmation that they could later show a court (if the borrower were to go bankrupt) to demonstrate the borrower's financial condition at the time of the loan closing and show that it was solvent. Whether any of this works is open to question. Nevertheless, having a certification from the borrower's CFO or senior financial officer should, at a minimum, make it more difficult to prove that the loan transaction gave rise to a fraudulent conveyance.
- *Appraisals.* Appraisals are typically required only in credit agreements that are secured and where a borrowing base (see the section "Mandatory Prepayments" in Part 3, "Making the Borrower Repay the Loan") measured by the value of inventory, receivables, or other assets is employed to limit the amount of credit available. The appraisal will frequently be undertaken by an affiliate of the lead bank. An appraisal may also be required if the loan is being made against the value of real estate. In this instance, the

Financial Institutions Reform, Recovery and Enforcement Act of 1989 (FIRREA) requires that any federally regulated bank obtain an appraisal of the real estate before making the loan. FIRREA appraisals are not required where real property is merely part of a lien on the overall assets of an operating company or is obtained out of an excess of caution.

- *Environmental due diligence.* Lenders often require an environmental due diligence report with respect to properties owned or leased by the borrower, particularly in situations where the nature of the business poses environmental risks or where there is real estate collateral. Such a report, which is generally undertaken by an engineer, can either be a so-called phase I report (where the engineer looks at public records and performs a physical inspection of the property) or a phase II report (where the engineer may conduct groundwater testing, take sample borings, and perform other investigations). Typically, unless a phase I report raises major concerns, a credit agreement will not require a phase II report. In many cases, the lenders will rely solely on a representation from the borrower as to environmental matters and will not conduct independent due diligence or request an engineer's report.
- *Insurance.* If the borrower is required under the insurance covenant to maintain insurance, the conditions in a credit agreement may require that the borrower deliver evidence of the insurance and that (if mandated by the covenant) the administrative agent has been designated as the loss payee and as an additional named insured party. Although evidence normally consists of a certificate issued by the borrower's insurance broker, in certain circumstances the credit agreement may require delivery of the actual policy and all endorsements.
- *USA PATRIOT Act.* In addition to the credit agreement notice referred to in the discussion of the USA PATRIOT Act in Part 10, "Understanding the Boilerplate," some credit agreements go further and throw in a condition precedent requiring that "know-your-customer" documentation and other information required by bank regulatory authorities be delivered in advance of closing.

No lender subject to the USA PATRIOT Act wants to sign a credit agreement until it has first completed its diligence on the borrower as required by the act and has determined that the borrower is not on the list of "Specially Designated Nationals." The condition is therefore less a condition to effectiveness or lending and more a condition to execution and, as such, is technically unnecessary. Nevertheless, it has become common to include such a provision in a syndicated credit agreement with any U.S.-based lender.

- *Catchall.* Credit agreements generally include a catchall condition that allows the administrative agent to request additional documents that it reasonably concludes are appropriate. Borrowers sometimes question the inclusion of this condition, but from the standpoint of the lenders, it provides a method to obtain satisfaction on matters discovered during the closing process. These might include issues raised as closing documents are being assembled, issues arising out of information set out on a disclosure schedule, and issues arising from an intervening change in law. In many closings, this condition is irrelevant, because the credit agreement will be signed and closed at the same time. However, when the credit agreement is signed in advance of the closing, the condition can provide substantial insurance against being required to close in the face of late-developing facts.

Effectiveness

Unless otherwise stated, the credit agreement becomes effective as a contract when all parties have executed and delivered counterparts. However, the effectiveness of the lenders' obligation to extend credit will be conditioned on the borrower's satisfying the conditions precedent. The administrative agent has an important role in confirming the satisfaction of the conditions, and will normally send out a confirmation, although the role of the administrative agent (and confirmations of effectiveness) will commonly be limited to the stated documentary conditions. The administrative agent will not be responsible for conditions that are nondocumentary, such as the standard condition that there is no actual or incipient event of default, that the representations of the borrower are correct, or that the lenders themselves are satisfied as to particular matters (the credit agreement will typically provide that the administrative agent may presume that each lender is satisfied in the absence of notice to the contrary).

Ongoing Conditions

The previous sections have described the conditions to be satisfied at the closing in order for the lending commitments to become effective. For each extension of credit (not just the initial one), the credit agreement will also require that all representations be true and that no actual or incipient event of default exist. These conditions become particularly important if the credit agreement allows for multiple drawdowns. Invariably, a senior officer (usually the CFO) of the borrower will be required to deliver a certificate to this effect (the truth of representations and the absence of defaults) on the closing date, but will not normally be required to deliver a certificate at later borrowings. Credit agreements do not normally allow the mere delivery of a certificate to satisfy the condition itself; rather, the condition will go to the underlying facts, so that if the lenders have reason to believe that the certificate is inaccurate, they are not barred from asserting that the condition has not been satisfied. Conversions of loans from one pricing option to another are not normally subject to a bring-down of ongoing conditions.

Some key principles should be borne in mind when reading the ongoing conditions provision of a credit agreement:

- *Representations.* The condition will generally require that all representations be true and complete on the date of a borrowing "as if made on and as of that date." In other words, if a borrowing is requested in July following a closing date in March, the representations must be true in July as if they were being made in July (being true in March is not sufficient). There is one exception to this general rule. It is customary for representations that refer to a specific date (such as a list of the subsidiaries of the borrower "on the [signing date]") to be true only as of that specific date. This allows borrowings to be made without updating those representations (e.g., a representation listing all subsidiaries of the borrower as of the signing of the agreement would not fail to be satisfied at a later date because of the establishment of new subsidiaries).

Some credit agreements will require that representations need be true and complete only "in all material respects." This can lead to potential interpretation issues and may be redundant when the representations themselves are already qualified by materiality, but it has become fairly standard in the market.

In credit agreements for investment-grade borrowers, and where the facility is to backstop commercial paper, this condition may expressly exempt the MAC clause and the litigation representation for any borrowing being made after the closing date. Thus, the borrower would be permitted to borrow even though a MAC or material adverse litigation has occurred.

- *Defaults.* The ongoing conditions will also include a requirement that no default or event of default exist at the time of or giving effect to a borrowing. The distinction between a default and an event of default is discussed in the section "Events of Default" in Part 7, "Enforcing the Loan." The basic rule is that, although the loans may be accelerated only if an event of default occurs, the lenders are entitled to not increase their exposure (i.e., by making additional loans) if a mere default exists.

Conditionality in Acquisition Financings

There are some unique conditionality practices that have developed for acquisition financings—a concept that has come to be known as *SunGard conditionality*, so-named for the 2005 financing for the acquisition of SunGard Data Systems, Inc. that first introduced them. Contrary to the customary practice described above, it is not a requirement that all of the credit agreement representations and warranties be true on the date of the borrowing that finances the acquisition. Rather, only so-called Specified Acquisition Agreement Representations and Specified Representations must be true. The Specified Acquisition Agreement Representations are those that relate to the target company and its business. The key consideration from the borrower's perspective is that the truth of these representations does not condition the availability of the financing unless the borrower has the right to terminate the acquisition agreement (or decline to close the acquisition) as a result. The Specified

Representations are a limited subset of the credit agreement representations that relate more to integrity of the financing structure than to the target company and its business.

In a typical secured financing outside of the acquisition context, collateral security must be in place and properly perfected before lenders are willing to fund. However, in acquisition financings the typical condition to funding is that the borrower must only perfect liens that can be perfected by simple UCC or intellectual property filings or by delivery of physical equity securities (typically the stock certificates acquired in the acquisition) and must use only commercially reasonable efforts to perfect the liens on other collateral. If the liens on that other collateral cannot be perfected at closing, the borrower will have a post-closing period (60 days is typical) to perfect those liens. Perfecting liens on other types of collateral may require more involvement of the target company (examples include negotiating a control agreement with the target company and the bank that maintains its accounts or obtaining a title insurance policy in connection with a mortgage over real property), which is harder to obtain before the buyer owns and controls it.

SunGard conditionality involves a few other concepts. First, the list of conditions precedent is typically limited and clearly defined. There is no catchall or otherwise an ability for the lenders to request additional items. Second, the condition requiring the absence of a material adverse change with respect to the target company (the "Target MAC") will either be defined in the commitment letter exactly as it is defined in the acquisition agreement (and accordingly will include all the carve-outs negotiated by the buyer and seller) or will simply cross-reference the definition in the acquisition agreement. Third, the customary absence of defaults condition will not be applicable. Fourth, the commitment letter will typically reference agreed "precedent" documentation that will be the fallback if the parties cannot agree on terms not detailed in the term sheet included as part of the commitment letter. Fifth, with the exception of the solvency representation included in the Specified Representations and the Target MAC, lenders must rely on the acquisition agreement for protections relating to the target company, and it is typically a condition to the availability of the loan facility that the acquisition must be completed in accordance with the terms of the acquisition agreement and that the acquisition agreement cannot be modified or waived in a manner materially adverse to the lenders without the consent of the lead arranger(s). Finally, even if the acquisition loan facility is syndicated to lenders prior to funding, the lender(s) that signed the commitment letter will be responsible to fund the loans on the closing date if the syndicate lenders fail to do so and retain sole voting control to grant waivers on the closing date.

Note that SunGard's special conditionality applies only on the closing date, when the loans that will finance the acquisition are funded. For a subsequent borrowing of revolving loans, all the representations and warranties in the credit agreement must be true, there must be no default, and the absence of a MAC will be determined by reference to the credit agreement definition of that term and not to the Target MAC.

REPRESENTATIONS

The representations in a credit agreement affirm the fundamental understandings upon which the lenders are extending credit. Although the items outlined in this section refer to the borrower, each credit party will normally provide appropriate representations as to itself and the ancillary documents that it signs. The representations address legal and financial issues, matters relating to the business and capital structure of the borrower and its subsidiaries, and various other matters of concern to the lenders. To the extent required to enable a borrower to make a particular representation, an appropriate qualification will be set out in a disclosure schedule. The disclosure schedules, when complete, end up being a very useful tool with which to understand the borrower's business.

Some representations, particularly those relating to legal condition, will also be covered by the opinion of the borrower's counsel. The representations and the legal opinion will to that extent provide double confirmation of the same underlying issues. There is a difference, though, between the two. If a legal opinion is inaccurate, the lender's remedy, if any, is against the counsel that delivered the opinion. If a representation is inaccurate, the lender's remedy is more powerful: it can demand payment of the loans. See the section "Inaccuracy of Representations" in Part 7, "Enforcing the Loan."

Certain representations are qualified by reference to materiality, eliciting whether a circumstance "could" or "would" or "could reasonably be expected to" or "would reasonably be expected to" result in a material adverse effect. Although credit agreement drafters will sometimes negotiate passionately over which of these approaches to take, there may in fact be little difference between the two. If there is any consensus as to what they mean, it is grounded in the distinction between *can* and *will*. *Could* asks whether there is any circumstance (regardless of how likely) in which a material adverse effect could occur. Thus a patently frivolous lawsuit for $1 trillion has the potential, if lost (i.e., *can*), result in a material adverse effect. The borrower would therefore be unable to represent that there is no litigation that *could* result in a material adverse effect. *Would* asks whether the suit is likely to be lost; that is, taking into account the strength of the case against the borrower, does it appear likely (i.e., *will*) it will be lost, and, if lost, will it result in a material adverse effect? "Could reasonably be expected to" or "would reasonably be expected to" probably just soften (or confuse) the distinction by requiring that any determination be "reasonable." This may cut both ways. It may prevent the borrower from being too carefree in making these determinations, but it also may allow the borrower to argue that a determination of likely materiality must be reasonable; that is, that the frivolous $1 trillion lawsuit should be ignored (even if the word *could* is used) because it is, well, frivolous.

Lenders will much prefer the *could* formulation because it allows them to make a credit judgment based on the worst-case scenario, that the outcome of all litigation will be adverse to the borrower. Borrowers naturally prefer the *would* formulation because it relieves them from listing litigation that they conclude will be decided favorably. Any related disclosure schedule thus becomes much shorter, although this approach may limit the usefulness of the representation as a disclosure device to enable the lenders to learn as much as possible about the borrower and its business.

Legal Matters Representations

The following representations address the legal status of the borrower and its subsidiaries:

- *Due organization.* The borrower, whether a corporation, limited liability company, partnership, or some other kind of entity, will affirm that it is duly organized under applicable law and has the power to enter into the credit agreement and to undertake the transactions contemplated by the credit agreement. It will also affirm that it is qualified to do business in all relevant jurisdictions. The latter point can be important, because many states will not allow an entity organized elsewhere to enforce contracts (such as accounts receivable) unless it is qualified to do business in the state and is in "good standing" (i.e., has made all necessary annual filings and paid all applicable taxes). The good standing representation will normally be qualified with reference to materiality.

- *Due authorization.* The borrower will confirm that it has taken all necessary action to authorize the credit agreement and the transactions that it contemplates. See the discussion in "Corporate and Organizational Matters" earlier in this part.
- *Due execution.* The borrower will affirm that it has duly executed and delivered the credit agreement and other relevant documents. Thus, the borrower will confirm to the lenders that the officers who have been granted authority by the resolutions are in fact the ones that executed the documents.
- *Enforceability.* The borrower will confirm that the credit agreement and other agreements are "legal, valid, binding, and enforceable." These words have achieved near religious status for both representations and legal opinions. The representation may include qualifications for bankruptcy and similar events (in a case under federal bankruptcy law, all enforcement becomes subject to bankruptcy court approval), as well as for "equitable remedies" (this refers to remedies such as ordering "specific performance," that are in a court's discretion).
- *No conflict.* This representation will cover three classes of potential conflicts. The first is legal conflicts, to the effect that the credit agreement does not violate any law (e.g., that it does not breach applicable usury laws or regulatory restrictions). The second is governance conflicts (e.g., that the credit agreement does not violate the organic documents of the borrower). The preferred stock provisions of a charter, for example, may prohibit secured debt in excess of a given percentage of the equity capital of the borrower; violation of such a restriction could affect the enforceability of the credit agreement and lead to other

adverse consequences for the borrower (such as a shift of board control to the holders of preferred stock). Lastly, the representation will address conflicts with other contracts to which the borrower is subject. It would, for example, have the borrower confirm that there is no debt limitation in a bond indenture or other agreement that would be violated by the borrowings contemplated by the credit agreement. The latter addresses the concern that the credit agreement could, for example, subject the lenders to a claim that they had interfered tortiously with holders of the borrower's bonds.

One risk arising from a breach of any of these representations is the potential impact on the borrower's credit profile. For example, breaching a debt covenant in a bond indenture or violating a government regulation could dramatically affect the borrower's ability to service the loans if the bonds are accelerated or a compliance proceeding is instituted by a regulatory agency against the borrower.

- *Government approvals.* The borrower will confirm that all necessary government filings and approvals have been obtained. In an acquisition context, this would include reference to any necessary Hart-Scott-Rodino approval by the Justice Department and, in a secured financing, would include reference to filings to perfect any security interests. In the case of a non-U.S. borrower, the representation would also list any central bank approvals or foreign exchange or other approvals.

- *Compliance with licenses.* This representation will affirm that the borrower has obtained all licenses necessary for it to operate its business (at least in all material respects). This representation is different from the governmental approvals representation described above. The former addresses approvals necessary for the credit agreement itself; the latter addresses approvals necessary for the borrower to operate its business.

- *Investment Company Act.* Here the borrower is asked to confirm that it is not an "investment company," or otherwise "affiliated with" an investment company, as those terms are defined in the Investment Company Act of 1940. If a borrower were an investment company or an

affiliate of an investment company, then a loan made in violation of the act would, with some exceptions, be void.
- *Anticorruption regulations.* The Foreign Corrupt Practices Act of 1977 (FCPA) prohibits issuers of U.S. securities, U.S. domestic concerns, and non-U.S. persons that take certain actions within the United States from "corruptly" offering or giving "anything of value" to a non-U.S. government official, directly or indirectly, in order to influence official action or otherwise obtain an improper business advantage. Analogous laws around the world, such as the U.K. Bribery Act 2010 in England, similarly regulate such behavior. Lenders are not required to guarantee that borrowers with whom they enter into financing relationships will not, in the future, violate antibribery provisions of the FCPA or analogous laws, and there is no basis for lender liability for planned or future FCPA violations by a borrower based merely on the financing relationship. However, as a practical matter, a lender will want to take reasonable steps to mitigate its FCPA risk such as conducting due diligence and including anticorruption provisions in a credit agreement in appropriate circumstances.
- *Foreign assets control regulations.* The Office of Foreign Assets Control (OFAC) of the U.S. Department of the Treasury is the primary federal agency tasked with administering and enforcing U.S. economic sanctions programs against countries, governments, entities, and individuals ("U.S. Sanctions"). Under regulations administered by OFAC, U.S. persons are generally prohibited from engaging in transactions, directly or indirectly, with persons and countries targeted by U.S. Sanctions, unless the transactions are exempt or licensed by OFAC. U.S. persons are also generally prohibited from "facilitating" actions of non-U.S. persons, which—although they may be entirely legal for a non-U.S. person to perform—may not be directly performed by U.S. persons due to prohibitions under U.S. Sanctions. Lenders that are U.S. persons must ensure that they do not run afoul of these regulations and avoid providing any benefit, directly or indirectly, to any person or country targeted by U.S. Sanctions by, for example,

making loans to such targeted persons or countries, or to borrowers that use proceeds from such loans to finance business with such targeted persons or countries.
- *USA PATRIOT Act.* Credit agreements may in rare instances require the borrower to represent that it is not identified as, or affiliated with, a terrorist or a terrorist organization on U.S. Department of Treasury lists. This is not common practice, however. The more typical approach in this regard is for the credit agreement to include the notice referred to in the section "USA PATRIOT Act" in Part 10, "Understanding the Boilerplate."
- *Margin regulations.* This representation will have the borrower confirm that the loans will not violate Regulations U and X of the Federal Reserve Board. Regulation U applies to banks and certain other lenders; Regulation X applies to borrowers. Sometimes the borrower will also make the same representation with respect to Regulation T (which applies to brokers and dealers). Typically the representation states that the loan proceeds will not be applied to "buy or carry" margin stock (the definition of which is discussed later in this section) and that the loans will not be secured "directly or indirectly" by margin stock. To *carry* margin stock basically means to refinance other debt originally incurred to purchase margin stock.

The basic rule of Regulation U is that no lender may make a loan to enable a borrower to buy or carry margin stock if the loan is "directly or indirectly" secured by margin stock, unless the amount of the security is twice the amount of the loan. Note that the loan must *both* be made to buy margin stock and be directly or indirectly secured by margin stock before it is required to satisfy the 2-to-1 collateral coverage ratio. Thus, neither borrowing against the shares of a public company to buy a new factory nor borrowing against a factory to buy the shares of a public company requires compliance with the ratio. If a loan violates the margin regulations, it may be void.

Margin stock is defined, with limited exceptions, as any equity security publicly traded on the domestic markets, including American depositary shares, warrants, and debt that are exercisable for publicly traded equity securities.

A loan is "directly or indirectly" secured by margin stock not only in the situation where the borrower grants a lien on margin stock to the lenders to secure the loans, but also where there is any restriction upon the borrower's ability to create liens on margin stock in favor of third parties or to sell margin stock to third parties. However, if not more than 25% of the assets of the borrower and its subsidiaries subject to the restriction consist of margin stock, the loan will not be deemed to be indirectly secured by margin stock by reason of such restrictions.

In the event that a loan is directly or indirectly secured by margin stock, the lender is required, under Regulation U, to obtain from the borrower an appropriately completed Form U–1.

Regulations U and X can be particularly constraining when a credit agreement is financing a tender for outstanding publicly traded shares of a target. In this instance, where the value of the margin stock will by definition be equal to the amount of the loans, it is necessary to resort to interpretive rulings issued under Regulation U that describe how the nonmargin assets of a borrower may supplement the margin stock collateral pool and allow the requirements of Regulations U and X to be satisfied.

Financial Condition Representations

The following representations address the financial or other business condition of the borrower and its subsidiaries:

- *Financial statements.* In preparing the credit agreement and obtaining the necessary internal credit approvals, the lenders will have examined recent financial statements of the borrower, typically the most recent annual audited statements and, if available, the most recent interim unaudited statements. All of these statements will almost certainly be included as part of any confidential informational memorandum. In many cases they will include "consolidating" as well as consolidated statements.

    The financial statements representation has the borrower affirm that all of these statements have been prepared in accordance with generally accepted accounting principles (GAAP), and that they are "complete and correct" (or, alternatively, that they "fairly present" the borrower's financial condition) in "all material respects." "Complete and correct" is perhaps more precise; "fairly present" is the phrase generally used by accountants when writing their audit report. For a discussion of GAAP, see the section "Definitions Generally: GAAP and IFRS" in Part 5, "Monitoring the Loan."

The financial statements representation will also generally include language to the effect that the statements and footnotes reflect all material liabilities or unusual forward or long-term commitments of the borrower. There is no uniform practice in respect of this regard, and some agreements simply rely upon the completeness of disclosure representation to protect the lenders. Including an express statement that there are no undisclosed material or unusual liabilities or commitments has one key purpose. This language is included because not all potential liabilities or commitments are required under GAAP to be disclosed in the financial statements or footnotes. For example, the fact that a borrower has agreed to supply oil to third parties at $20 a barrel when the cost of producing the oil has jumped to $40 a barrel and the market price is $60 a barrel probably will not appear anywhere in the financial statements or the footnotes. Sometimes borrowers will request that this language be qualified by reference to GAAP; that is, that the statements reflect all material liabilities and unusual commitments *required to be disclosed under GAAP*. This approach generally defeats the purpose of addressing these liabilities and commitments in the first place. The financial statement representation will typically include the MAC representation. See the section "The MAC Condition" earlier in this part regarding the material adverse change representation.

If the credit agreement is to finance an acquisition, the representation may cover pro forma financial statements (financial statements for a period, usually consistent with one of the periods covered by the financial statements referred to previously) prepared as if the acquisition had occurred at the beginning of the period.

- *Projections.* In some instances, projections will have been delivered to the lenders. Borrowers are normally reluctant to make the same kinds of representations with respect to projections as they make with respect to historical financial statements. The typical credit agreement will, accordingly, soften the representation by simply requiring the borrower to state that any projections have been prepared in good faith based upon assumptions that the borrower has deemed reasonable. There may also be a statement to the effect that no assurances can be given that the projections will accurately reflect future financial condition or performance.
- *Taxes.* The taxes representation will have the borrower confirm that all income, franchise, property, and other taxes (at least to the extent that a failure to pay the same would be material) have been paid. Property taxes, if not paid, raise concerns because unpaid property taxes give rise to a lien (in many cases senior to all other liens, including preexisting mortgages) on the particular property being taxed. Franchise taxes are of concern because failure to pay a franchise tax could result in the dissolution of a corporation or the failure of a company to qualify to do business (with the consequences described in the section "Due Organization" earlier in this part). Failure to pay income taxes can give rise to a lien in favor of the Internal Revenue Service (IRS) on all of the borrower's property. The IRS tax lien is not automatically senior to all other liens, but it may nevertheless capture property not covered by a lien in favor of the lenders and, certainly, in an unsecured deal will give the IRS the status of a lien creditor while the lenders are unsecured.
- *Pension and welfare plans.* Under the Employee Retirement Income Security Act of 1974 (ERISA), to the extent that a company is obligated to pay retired employees a defined pension benefit, the company will be required to pay into a trust an amount sufficient to cover future benefit obligations. ERISA establishes a government corporation (the Pension Benefit Guaranty Corporation [PBGC]) that ensures that retired employees will receive their pension payments. In turn, the PBGC is granted, under

ERISA, a lien equivalent to the tax lien granted in favor of the IRS described above. Thus, the lenders have an interest in knowing that the borrower is complying with the requirements of ERISA. In cases where the borrower has no employee benefit plans subject to ERISA, the representation may simply be a statement to this effect.
- *Solvency.* The solvency representation was originally intended for those situations in which a transaction gave rise to concerns under fraudulent conveyance or fraudulent transfer laws—for example, when the proceeds of the loans were to be applied to pay an extraordinary dividend or distribution to shareholders. Similarly, such a concern might exist if the loans were to be guaranteed by subsidiaries. However, many lenders now include solvency representations as a matter of course, regardless of these structural issues. Sometimes a credit agreement will go further and require the borrower to deliver a professional evaluation from an independent appraisal firm, known as a *solvency opinion*, that confirms that the borrower (or a guarantor) will not be rendered insolvent by the financing.

Fraudulent transfer laws originated by statute many centuries ago. They have been continued as legislation in every state and have also been incorporated into the Federal Bankruptcy Code. They are intended to capture a transaction in which (1) an entity undertakes an obligation or transfers property without receiving "reasonably equivalent" value and (2) the entity is insolvent at the time of, or would be rendered insolvent as a result of, the transaction. An illustration of the potential abuse that the fraudulent transfer laws prohibit might be the case of a penniless musician who sells his valuable Stradivarius to his brother for $1.00 and then declares bankruptcy. A fraudulent transfer will have occurred, because both tests of the law will have been met: first, $1.00 is probably not a "reasonably equivalent" value for the sale of a Stradivarius, and, second, the musician is insolvent at the time of the sale to his brother.

In the corporate lending context, these issues arise in a variety of ways. For example, if the proceeds of the loans will finance the payment of a dividend or distribution, the borrower is probably not receiving reasonably equivalent value for the payment; in fact, it is likely to be receiving no value at all. In the case of a guarantee of the loans by a subsidiary, unless the entire amount of the loan proceeds is being advanced to the subsidiary, the subsidiary also is not likely to be receiving reasonably equivalent value, because it will be guaranteeing the full amount of the loans but receiving only a portion (or none) of the proceeds. Restructuring a deal to eliminate the dividend or the upstream guarantees is not terribly practical.

The solution most often adopted in credit agreements is to attack the second prong of the fraudulent transfer test by having the borrower represent that it is "solvent." The term *solvent* will be defined as the obverse of the term *insolvency* as used in fraudulent transfer laws. A borrower is insolvent (1) when its liabilities (including contingent liabilities) exceed its assets, (2) when its property or capital is unreasonably small in relation to its business or the obligations being undertaken under the credit agreement, or (3) when it undertakes the obligations under the credit agreement with the intent to "hinder, delay or defraud" creditors. Occasionally the solvency representation will be further supported by a solvency opinion, as described earlier. Although this was common in leveraged acquisitions in the early 1990s, the more common practice today is for the lender to conduct its own independent analysis of the borrower's solvency.

Representations and Disclosures Regarding the Business

Whereas the financial condition representations address the financial or other business *condition* of the borrower, the representations set forth in this section address particular *facts* about its property or business. Not every credit agreement, of course, contains all of these representations, although in a highly leveraged transaction it would not be unusual to see them all.

- *Capitalization.* Here the borrower, usually by reference to a disclosure schedule, will represent to the lenders what its capital structure is, including the amounts and classes of capital stock and other equity that have been authorized and are outstanding; in the case of a privately held company, the identity of the owner; and in all cases whether or not any extraordinary equity rights (such as an obligation to buy in equity from a shareholder) are outstanding. The disclosure schedule can thus be used as a base to determine whether a change of control has occurred.

- *Subsidiaries.* The subsidiaries representation will normally make reference to a disclosure schedule. The disclosure schedule will typically set forth details regarding the various types of equity interests of each subsidiary that are outstanding, and which entity (the borrower or some other subsidiary or entity) owns those equity interests. The schedule will customarily have sufficient detail for the lenders to understand the ownership structure of the borrower and its subsidiaries, and thus determine whether, in structuring the agreement, they have taken the right guarantees from subsidiaries and the correct pledges of subsidiary equity. Some credit agreements will go further and require that the borrower attach an organizational chart displaying the ownership structures of all subsidiaries.
- *Existing debt and liens.* The borrower will be asked to affirm a disclosure schedule setting out any existing debt or existing liens. These items will then be "grandfathered" in the debt and liens covenants described in "Negative Covenants" in Part 5, "Monitoring the Loans." They will also enable the lenders to determine that they find acceptable the amount of other debt and other liens they will be competing with if the borrower sinks into financial difficulties.
- *Real property.* A disclosure schedule will list all real property owned or leased by the borrower. In a deal secured by mortgages, this list becomes a basis for confirming that mortgages on the relevant real property interests are being granted in favor of the lenders.
- *Litigation.* The purpose of the litigation representation is to force the borrower to identify any "material" litigation or threatened litigation (including arbitrations and regulatory proceedings) to which the borrower or any of its subsidiaries is subject. Once the disclosure schedule

is complete, the lenders can then make an independent judgment as to whether or not to proceed with the loan.

One of the problems that a borrower will confront in completing the disclosure schedule is determining whether an item of litigation needs to be listed, that is, whether it rises to the level of materiality. Some borrowers throw up their hands and just list all litigation to which they are party. This may not be particularly helpful to the borrower, because it may in effect be conceding that a $500 lawsuit is material. Borrowers may try to overcome this conundrum by stating expressly in the disclosure statement that the mere listing of an item of litigation does not concede that it is in fact material. This latter approach, of course, can produce a problem for the lenders. A lender, if informed of material litigation, may feel that it is compelled to investigate thoroughly the nature of the litigation and whether it might eventually impair the borrower's ability to satisfy its obligations under the credit agreement. Overinclusive listing by borrowers makes this task much more difficult.

- *Title to property.* In a sense, the title representation covers some of the same territory covered by the liens representation. The title representation, however, goes beyond the mere existence of liens and addresses additionally whether the borrower has taken the actions necessary to give it proper ownership of its properties. An example might include purchasing real property from an entity that did not have adequate title to sell (perhaps a Native American tribe asserts ultimate ownership of the underlying land). Another example might be a Federal Communications Commission (FCC) license purportedly issued to the borrower, but mistakenly issued to a subsidiary.
- *Labor matters.* This representation will typically have the borrower confirm that there is labor peace with its employees. To the extent that the borrower's employees are unionized, the representation may affirm that the borrower has made copies of all collective bargaining agreements available to the lenders.
- *Intellectual property.* Ultimately, every borrower has some important intellectual property (if nothing else, its name).

For a borrower such as a chemical company that is heavily dependent on patents or a wine and spirits company that is heavily dependent on trademarks, intellectual property can be vital. This representation, therefore, has the borrower affirm that it has all intellectual property (patents, trademarks, and copyrights) necessary for it to operate its business.

- *Environmental matters.* Lenders may be concerned that environmental problems (current or former) of the borrower may adversely affect its credit quality. Under federal superfund legislation, for example, any past or present contributor of hazardous materials to a superfund site is jointly and severally liable for the entire cleanup cost. As a practical matter, the so-called de minimis contributors are allowed off the hook with relatively small payments. Nevertheless, credit agreements routinely ask the borrower to identify on a disclosure schedule any environmental exposure it may have (including current and past noncompliance).

    When listing environmental matters on its disclosure schedules, the borrower (and lenders) may be faced with some of the same materiality questions that were discussed above with regard to litigation.

- *No burdensome restrictions.* This representation is intended to elicit from the borrower whether it is subject to agreements that materially constrain its business. Examples might be a contract that limits its ability to use a patent to compete against a new product on the market, or a contract requiring the borrower to purchase a product from a supplier at above-market rates.

Completeness of Disclosures

This representation, similar to a Rule 10b-5 representation in a securities underwriting agreement, makes the borrower confirm that the information supplied by it to the lenders in connection with the credit agreement (including all financial statements and other disclosures, and including any confidential information memorandum), when taken as a whole, is accurate and complete and does not omit any information necessary to be not misleading. This representation provides overarching comfort to the lenders that the borrower is not selectively supplying information that, individually, is perfectly accurate but that, in the aggregate, is deceptive.

Status as Senior Indebtedness

In transactions where the borrower may have outstanding subordinated indebtedness, it may be useful for the lenders to obtain an affirmation from the borrower that its obligations under the credit agreement constitute "senior indebtedness" for purposes of the subordinated debt. The same conclusions would normally also be confirmed in an opinion of counsel. Both the representation and the opinion may be stating the obvious (typically the status of the credit agreement under the definition of senior indebtedness will be apparent). They nevertheless give the lenders an argument (if any subordinated debtholder should assert otherwise) that they acted in good faith in believing that their loans are senior.

Perfection and Priority of Security

A security interest in property is created when an appropriate security agreement is signed, value is given by the lenders (the commitment to lend is "value" for this purpose), and the debtor has "rights in the collateral." Representations will typically be included in the credit agreement, or in the security agreement, to the effect that the relevant security agreement creates a valid security interest in the collateral, that such security interest has been perfected (depending on the nature of the collateral and other factors, a variety of steps may be required to perfect a security interest covering different kinds of collateral), and that such perfected security interest has first priority, subject to no equal or prior security interest (unless a different priority has been agreed). The priority representation may have to be qualified in some respects.

Representations for Foreign Borrowers

For a borrower that is not organized in the United States, the credit agreement may contain certain additional representations covering matters unique to nondomestic borrowers, including the following:

- *Immunity.* This is a representation that the borrower's participation in the transaction constitutes commercial

activity and is subject to civil and commercial law. As noted in the section "Waiver of Sovereign Immunity" in Part 10, "Understanding the Boilerplate," a "foreign state" under the U.S. Sovereign Immunity Act of 1976 is entitled to immunity from court jurisdiction, and its property from attachment and execution, in the United States. A foreign borrower that at closing is private would acquire immunity if it were later to be acquired by the government of its country. A "commercial activity" representation thus affords the lenders a basis upon which to defeat a claim of sovereign immunity being raised by a borrower (even one that starts out privately held).
- *Pari passu ranking.* This is a representation to the effect that the obligations of the borrower under the credit agreement rank at least pari passu with all other obligations of the borrower (this provides assurance that the laws of the borrower's country do not grant senior status to other claims that might trump the lenders' rights). An example of the latter was the legal rule in Argentina a number of years ago that non-Argentine creditors always ranked junior in priority to Argentine creditors in the insolvency of an Argentine borrower. Other countries have at times created special structural priorities, such as between notarized and nonnotarized documents.
- *Legal form.* This is a representation to the effect that the credit agreement and other relevant documents are in proper legal form for enforcement in the country in which the borrower is located. This will address, for example, whether the credit agreement is properly notarized and consularized, and whether it needs to be translated into a local language to be enforceable in a local court.
- *Taxes.* This is a representation to the effect that the loans and the credit agreement are not subject to tax by the borrower's country. In many cases, of course, the borrower's country will impose a withholding tax on payments of interest and on some other payments by the borrower, and may require payment of a stamp or other documentary tax in order for a creditor to enforce the documents in court; in such cases, the representations will be tailored so as to correctly reflect the tax position.

- *Sovereign borrowers.* In the case of a loan to a sovereign borrower (e.g., a government, central bank, or majority-owned government agency), this representation states that the borrowing country is a member in good standing of the International Monetary Fund (IMF) and is eligible to use the resources thereof (among other things, this confirms the ability of the country to access IMF funding in certain circumstances), and possibly includes similar representations as to other applicable multilateral organizations. If the borrower is the country itself, it is also customary to have the borrower represent that its obligations under the credit agreement are entitled to the "full faith and credit" of the country; that is, that the loan is not payable solely from a narrow source of funds, but rather is payable from the general revenue of the country.

Part 5: Monitoring the Loan: Financial, Affirmative, and Negative Covenants

SOME GENERAL PRINCIPLES

Covenants can be divided into three categories: financial covenants, affirmative covenants, and negative covenants. Many credit agreements will create a separate overarching section or article for each category, but frequently financial covenants are treated as negative covenants.

All covenants are independent of one another. Thus, a transaction that the borrower wishes to undertake that is captured by more than one covenant must be allowed under each covenant. Simply because the transaction is permitted under one covenant does not carry with it any claim or argument that it is ipso facto to be permitted under another covenant. An illustration of this might arise in the context of the borrower's wanting to guarantee the debt of a valued customer. Guarantees of this type are likely to be controlled by the debt covenant (because this is a guarantee of debt) and by the investments covenant (because guarantees of the debt of a third party are normally also treated as an investment in the third party). To issue the guarantee, the borrower would therefore need to find a basket or other exception in each of the debt and investments covenants.

CATEGORIZING SUBSIDIARIES

Subsidiaries Generally

Most credit agreements will apply not just to the borrower, but to the borrower and its subsidiaries, the theory being that the financial strength of the borrower is only as good as the strength of the entire group of entities of which the borrower is parent. A subsidiary will normally be defined as any entity that either is consolidated with the borrower in the preparation of financial statements or a majority of whose voting equity is owned or controlled by the borrower or another subsidiary. Thus, the term *subsidiary* will include a limited partnership where the sole general partner is wholly owned by the borrower, even though the limited partnership interest is held by an unrelated third party and constitutes 99% of the equity. A sole general partner will by definition control the partnership.

Restricted and Unrestricted Subsidiaries

Bond indentures and, in recent years, credit agreements frequently include a concept of "restricted" and "unrestricted" subsidiaries. In those agreements that incorporate the concept, the motivation is to create a class of subsidiary (unrestricted subsidiaries) that is free from the representations, covenants, and events of default to which subsidiaries would otherwise be subject. Thus, for example, the borrower can allow an unrestricted subsidiary to incur debt (and secure it, if desired), make acquisitions, and undertake riskier, even nonperforming business activities without having to worry about the impact upon financial tests and without using the negotiated, dollar-limited baskets in negative covenants. A distressed borrower can also use an unrestricted subsidiary to remove value entirely from the restricted credit group in order to consummate liability management transactions for the benefit of entirely new lenders and equity holders. Therefore, the unrestricted subsidiary concept has come under increased scrutiny from lenders.

In a credit agreement with both restricted and unrestricted subsidiaries, the restricted subsidiaries will be subject to all of the representations, covenants, and defaults, while unrestricted subsidiaries will typically be subject to none of these. An exception will be made, however, for those representations, covenants, or defaults where an event or condition at an unrestricted subsidiary could affect the consolidated group, such as a failure of an unrestricted subsidiary to pay tax or ERISA liabilities (which, as to subsidiaries organized in the United States that are 80% or more owned by a common parent, under federal law become the joint and several liability of every entity in the consolidated group). In these instances, unrestricted subsidiaries will not be treated differently from restricted subsidiaries.

The flip side for the borrower's having the greater flexibility of unrestricted subsidiaries is that unrestricted subsidiaries are treated essentially the same way as unrelated parties. Thus, for example, investments in unrestricted subsidiaries will be controlled and the EBITDA (positive or negative) of unrestricted subsidiaries will not be included in the EBITDA of the borrower and its restricted subsidiaries. Unrestricted subsidiaries will be treated as affiliates for purposes of the affiliate transactions covenant, forcing transactions with unrestricted subsidiaries to be on an arm's-length basis.

Designation of subsidiaries as restricted or unrestricted is usually at the discretion of the borrower or its board of directors. The mechanism for designation in credit agreements is typically less formal than that in bond indentures (a bond indenture will usually require a board resolution), but many of the other conditions for designation will be employed, such as the requirement that the investment in a subsidiary designated as unrestricted be within whatever limits are imposed in the agreement upon investments in third parties. Any designation of a restricted subsidiary as unrestricted (or vice versa) will typically be conditioned upon the absence of any default (and potentially the satisfaction of a financial performance test such as a leverage test) after giving effect to the designation. Subsidiaries of unrestricted subsidiaries will always be treated as unrestricted.

A further typical requirement to unrestricting a subsidiary is that neither a subsidiary nor any of its subsidiaries may have debt or other liabilities guaranteed in any way by the borrower or its restricted subsidiaries nor may such unrestricted subsidiary otherwise derive credit support from the credit group by being an equity holder in the borrower or any restricted subsidiary or owning property or liens in property of the credit group. Along the same lines, the unrestricted subsidiary may not have any outstanding debt or other liabilities that will be accelerated upon a default under the credit agreement.

The theory here is that an unrestricted subsidiary should, in all cases, behave as if it were a completely unrelated entity. Adverse events at an unrelated third party do not normally trigger potential defaults at the borrower, and the same should be the case for an unrestricted subsidiary.

Significant Subsidiaries

If the borrower is a large corporation with many subsidiaries, it will often push for a concept of "significant subsidiaries" and attempt to limit the application of the representations, covenants, and defaults solely to such significant subsidiaries. A significant subsidiary will typically be any subsidiary that meets the definition of a *significant subsidiary* under the SEC's Regulation S-X, although other definitions are possible. In general, this definition captures any subsidiary that has 10% or more of the assets or 10% or more of the income of the borrower's consolidated group. In its narrowest application, the definition of significant subsidiary will be used only in a bankruptcy default; that is, the insolvency of a subsidiary will give rise to an event of default only if the subsidiary is significant. Other agreements will expand the concept further to certain of the representations or, in its broadest application, to many of the affirmative covenants. The underlying theory is that the lenders should not be concerned with bad events or conditions at subsidiaries that do not rise to the level of being significant. The concept may not be appropriate if a borrower, though large, has many subsidiaries, none of which rise to the level of being significant under Regulation S-X.

An alternative to the significant subsidiary concept is the converse concept of an "immaterial subsidiary." While the former seeks to *include* the defined group under the scope of representations, covenants, and defaults, the latter seeks to *exclude* such defined group from covenants, defaults, and certain other provisions. In particular, a borrower seeking to carve out smaller subsidiaries from the requirement to become a guarantor or from triggering bankruptcy defaults will often seek to include an immaterial subsidiary concept. An *immaterial subsidiary* is commonly defined as any subsidiary that holds less than a minimal percentage of the group's consolidated total assets or consolidated revenues (often in the 3% to 5% range, but sometimes higher, and up to as high as 10%). Along with this individual subsidiary-level threshold, the concept will usually include an aggregate threshold prohibiting the total amount of assets and revenue that can potentially be carved out through the immaterial subsidiary concept.

COVENANT DEFINITIONS

Definitions Generally: GAAP and IFRS

In any agreement, definitions are the building blocks upon which all other provisions are based. This is particularly true when it comes to covenants. The operative principle to keep in mind (at least when reading definitions that are relevant for negative covenants) is that definitions are often worded to have sweeping effect. Verbosity is deliberate here, motivated, to a great extent, by bad court decisions, where a court (to illustrate) may have ruled that a reference to a *car* cannot have meant an SUV or a van or even a taxi or a limousine or a rental. Thus, the definition of *lien* will not just cover liens as they are normally understood, but will also include all charges, security interests, pledges, mortgages, encumbrances, assignments, and other similar arrangements and so forth, ad nauseam. Similarly, the definition of *dividend* will refer not just to dividends and distributions, but also to purchases of stock, sinking funds for that purpose, and even "phantom stock" arrangements.

Perhaps the most basic building block is the definition of *generally accepted accounting principles* (GAAP). Credit agreement covenants, when being set by the administrative agent and the borrower, are normally based upon the borrower's historical and projected financial statements. These will be required by the credit agreement to be prepared upon the basis of GAAP that have been "consistently applied." That is to say, if the borrower delivered financial statements for its two most recent fiscal years, the statements will not have employed one set of principles in one year and a different set of principles in the second year. To take an example, the statements will not calculate inventory on a first-in, first-out (FIFO) basis in the first year and on a last-in, first-out (LIFO) basis in the second.

Thus, the *historical* financial statements delivered to the lenders must be "consistent" and will be used as the basis for determining financial covenants and other levels. This then raises the question of what is to happen after the closing. Is the borrower to be free to change accounting principles from year to year—to switch from LIFO to FIFO, for example? Borrowers may want precisely this flexibility. They may also want to prepare statements based upon GAAP as applied from time to time, reflecting changes in principles required by the accounting profession. Conversely, the lenders will want the principles used in calculating covenants to remain stable and not to reflect changes if those changes would affect the outcome of covenant compliance.

The definition of GAAP in a credit agreement, therefore, will address either one or the other of these approaches. One variant (preferred by borrowers) is to have GAAP defined as generally accepted accounting principles "as in effect from time to time." The other variant (preferred by lenders) is to have GAAP frozen in time to those principles that were in effect at closing and were used in preparing the statements upon which financial covenants were determined. A borrower may object that this requires it to prepare two sets of financial statements. The solution often adopted is discussed in the section "Fiscal Periods and Accounting Changes" later in this part.

Foreign borrowers, U.S. subsidiary borrowers of foreign parents, or U.S. borrowers with substantial overseas operations may desire the flexibility to move from reporting under GAAP to reporting under International Financial Reporting Standards (IFRS). In those credit agreements that provide the right to switch between GAAP and IFRS, there are a few elements in common. First, all that is typically required to commence the conversion from GAAP to IFRS, for example, is a simple borrower election and notice to the administrative agent. Following such election and notice, the borrower may start reporting in IFRS. Second, following election and notice, a borrower cannot switch back to reporting under GAAP, and the decision becomes irrevocable. Third, financial reporting is required to subsequently conform to IFRS standards. Although it may be rare for a credit group to request a switch whole cloth from GAAP to IFRS, it is a reality that some part of a multinational credit group's operations may be reported under IFRS and credit agreements increasingly take that into account.

Key Financial Definitions

To state the obvious, financial definitions are in large part based on accounting and heavily negotiated. Nevertheless, in looking at definitions to decipher covenants, some twists should be kept in mind.

- *Debt.* Note that *debt* is not a GAAP concept, but rather a term created in finance documents for purposes of financial tests, covenants, and defaults. The intent is to capture all nonordinary course claims against the borrower. The definition of *debt* will invariably pick up balance sheet indebtedness, but will not normally pick up current accounts payable and accrued expenses. Obligations with respect to capital leases (but not operating leases) will thus be counted as debt. The definition will also encompass guarantees of other debt, even though guarantees are normally footnoted in financial statements and are not carried as a liability on a balance sheet. In a similar vein, it will include all letters of credit (although trade letters of credit will normally be excluded). Obligations of third parties secured by a lien on assets of the borrower will be treated as debt, even though the obligations have not been assumed by the borrower. Sometimes the amount of such obligations will be deemed to be limited to the value of the property subject to the claim. That may not, however, be the correct result given Section 1111 of the federal Bankruptcy Code, which in some circumstances will allow a creditor to submit a full claim against the borrower in a bankruptcy proceeding even if the borrower has not assumed the debt.

Finally, many credit agreements will state that debt includes obligations under hedging agreements, even though this may lead to time-consuming calculations for the borrower in determining leverage ratios. For example, to establish the amount of a hedging agreement, a borrower cannot simply look at an internal statement of account. Instead, it would need to ascertain from market quotes the hedge's termination liability. This could change daily. Many credit agreements avoid this problem by treating hedges as investments (see the discussion in the section "Investments" later in this part).

- *EBITDA.* Recall that EBITDA is an acronym for earnings before interest, taxes, depreciation, and amortization. The term is important for financial covenants, for interest margins (to the extent that margins are determined with reference to a debt ratio that incorporates EBITDA as one of its elements), and for excess cash flow and, when applicable, asset sale prepayment provisions contained in the credit agreement. Some agreements will use the term *cash flow* or *operating cash flow* in lieu of EBITDA, though substantively the terms will be the same.

The purpose of the term is to capture the amount of cash thrown off by the borrower's business before taking into account nonoperating cash expenses, such as interest and taxes. Depreciation and amortization are added back because, although they reduce earnings, they do not reduce the amount of cash generated during any calculation period. Beyond adding back interest, taxes, depreciation, and amortization to a borrower's net operating income, most credit agreements include numerous additional adjustments that must be made to net operating income to arrive at an EBITDA number. These adjustments, referred to as *add-backs*, are heavily negotiated and generate significant attention from borrowers and lenders alike because add-backs can meaningfully swing EBITDA to the benefit of the borrower and, in turn. weaken the effectiveness of covenants. It is beyond the scope of this chapter to spell out all of the add-backs that can go into a full-blown EBITDA definition.

EBITDA is intended to be a predictor of the ability of a borrower to pay interest and, ultimately, to repay principal. The debt ratio, interest coverage ratio, debt service coverage ratio, and fixed charges coverage ratio, discussed in greater detail later in this part, each of which has EBITDA as a component, test the amount of cash available to the borrower against its debt service needs.

FINANCIAL COVENANTS

Date-Specific versus Performance Covenants; Annualized and Rolling Periods

Financial covenants can be divided into three categories: (1) those that test the borrower's financial position at a particular date (such as a net worth or current ratio covenant), (2) those that test its performance over one or more fiscal periods (such as a fixed charges or interest coverage covenant), and (3) those that are a hybrid of the first two categories and that contain both date-specific and performance elements, such as a debt ratio covenant that tests the ratio of debt at a particular date to earnings for a specified fiscal period.

A performance-based covenant will in rare cases test performance on a quarter-by-quarter basis (i.e., measure earnings only for the most recent fiscal quarter). It is much more common for the relevant fiscal period to consist of the four most recent fiscal quarters, a so-called rolling four-quarter period. Thus, when testing the covenant at the end of December, the relevant test period would be the four quarters ending December 31. When testing again at the end of March, the relevant period would be the four quarters commencing on April 1 of the preceding year and ending on March 31 of the current year. The benefit of this approach (from the standpoint of both the borrower and the lenders) is that it avoids the borrower's falling into default because of seasonality issues, which might otherwise occur if only the most recent single fiscal quarter were tested. Retail businesses, for example, frequently have much lower earnings in the first fiscal quarter of the year than in the last fiscal quarter of the year.

Performance may also be "annualized." An example might be the case where a debt ratio is defined as the ratio of debt to earnings for the most recent fiscal quarter *times* four (or the two most recent fiscal quarters *times* two). This approach can be useful for a startup borrower, where earnings are expected to start low but grow quickly from quarter to quarter. Of course annualizing is technically not necessary—the lender could simply adjust the maximum permitted debt ratio—but cosmetically (and cosmetics often matter when crafting a credit agreement) it looks better to have a debt ratio maximum of 5 to 1 rather than 20 to 1.

Phase-in and Pro Forma Treatment

An issue that comes up in the context of credit agreements that finance acquisitions is how to deal with the impact of an acquisition upon performance-based covenants. For example, if an acquisition will double the borrower's business, it may make little sense to measure EBITDA on a strictly historical rolling four-quarter basis, because much of the rolling four quarters will reflect a lower preacquisition EBITDA. Similarly, testing interest expense only for that period will understate the borrower's future interest costs as a result of the increased acquisition borrowing. The solution typically adopted in credit agreements will be to calculate performance numbers (such as EBITDA, interest expense, capital expenditures, debt service, and taxes) on a hypothetical (or pro forma) basis as if the acquisition had occurred at the beginning of the rolling four-quarter period. Particularly in calculating EBITDA, this can lead to a tangled discussion between the parties. The lenders simply want to add the borrower's and target's *actual* EBITDA figures for the relevant periods to obtain the pro forma numbers. Borrowers, on the other hand, will want to take into account cost savings that they anticipate realizing once the acquisition occurs. The combined business will not have two finance or legal departments, or so the borrower will argue, so EBITDA should be appropriately adjusted upward to reflect the elimination of redundant personnel. And so the negotiation goes. The parties are usually left to themselves to find a middle ground. SEC pro forma rules that apply to public reporting companies provide one possible basis for scoping out a middle ground. Namely, Article 11 of Regulation S-X contains principle-based requirements for the presentation of pro forma financials. Under Article 11, pro forma adjustments, such as cost savings, must be (1) directly attributable to the subject transaction, (2) expected to have a continuing impact on the borrower, and (3) factually supportable. Even though Article 11 does not apply to loans or other nonsecurities, credit agreements still may refer to Article 11 or similar requirements for pro forma calculations. It is not only acquisitions but other material transactions, including dispositions, debt incurrences, and the making of investments or restricted payments that can trigger the use of pro forma calculations under a credit agreement.

One approach sometimes used to ameliorate the difficulty of running pro forma calculations is to annualize the relevant earnings and other numbers until a full four quarters (or other relevant roll-up period) have elapsed after the acquisition. Using this approach, at the end of the first fiscal quarter after the acquisition, EBITDA for that quarter would be multiplied by four. At the end of the second fiscal quarter, EBITDA would be calculated for two quarters and multiplied by two. At the end of the third fiscal quarter, EBITDA would be calculated for three quarters and multiplied by 4/3. Only after four full fiscal quarters have elapsed subsequent to the acquisition is the performance period rolled forward at the end of each fiscal quarter. Annualizing in this way may simplify (or eliminate) pro forma calculations, but it does not avoid the risks of a bad quarter or the cyclical nature of the combined business. For this reason, the pro forma calculation approach is used more often than annualization.

For interest expense, a variant that is frequently used is to take interest expense for the period from the closing to the test date and multiply it by an appropriate fraction to bring it up to a full 365-day year. Thus, if an acquisition occurs on February 17 of a year, interest expense for March 31 would be annualized by multiplying the actual interest for the 42-day period between February 17 and March 31 by a fraction, the numerator of which is 365 and the denominator of which is 42. A similar calculation would be run at the end of June 30 (the fraction being 365/133) and at the end of each quarter thereafter until four full quarters have elapsed subsequent to the acquisition.

Performance-Based Financial Covenants

The following are examples of covenants test performance over one or more fiscal periods.

- *Leverage ratio.* Typically, the leverage ratio (sometimes referred to as the *debt ratio* or *cash flow ratio*) will be defined as the ratio of debt (or in the case of a secured leverage ratio, secured debt) at a given date to EBITDA for the rolling four quarters most recently ended prior to that date. Sometimes credit agreements provide for the determination of the leverage ratios after netting out the borrower's cash and cash equivalents. This is the so-called net leverage ratio. Under the net leverage formulation, the numerator of the leverage ratio is reduced dollar-for-dollar by the amount of the borrower's unrestricted cash and cash equivalents (cash netting may be capped by a fixed dollar amount or otherwise, depending on what the parties negotiate). The debate in negotiating the credit agreement will be between whether the debt ratio is tested only at the end of a fiscal quarter (i.e., only at the end of the relevant rolling period) and whether the ratio is tested each day during the year. The former would allow the ratio during a fiscal quarter (i.e., between fiscal quarter ends) to exceed the maximum otherwise required at the end of the quarter. The latter would prevent this and certainly should be feasible from an accounting standpoint if you assume that a borrower can keep track of its outstanding debt at any

given day even while measuring EBITDA only at fiscal-period ends.
- *Interest coverage ratio.* The interest coverage covenant tests the ratio of EBITDA to interest expense during a fiscal period (typically the most recently ended rolling four quarters). *Interest expense* will normally be defined to include only cash interest. Thus pay-in-kind (PIK) interest and capitalized interest charges will be excluded. However, cash interest will not be literally confined to interest paid in cash during a particular period, but rather will include interest payable in cash during the particular period. To provide otherwise would potentially allow a borrower to manipulate interest expense by paying interest a day before the beginning (or a day after the end) of a fiscal period. Finally, interest expense will normally reflect payments made (or cash received) under interest hedging agreements.
- *Debt service coverage ratio.* The debt service coverage covenant is virtually identical to the interest coverage covenant except that it factors in payments of principal in addition to payments of interest. The covenant measures the ratio of EBITDA to debt service during a fiscal period (as with interest coverage, the period is typically the most recently ended rolling four quarters). *Debt service* will consist of interest expense and *scheduled* principal payments. The latter will not normally include mandatory prepayments (such as excess cash flow, disposition, or debt and equity issuance prepayments). It will also not include voluntary prepayments. It will, however, include scheduled reductions of revolving commitments if that requires a payment of debt.
- *Fixed charges coverage ratio.* The fixed charges coverage covenant builds upon the debt service coverage covenant and factors in other so-called fixed charges. This covenant measures the ratio of EBITDA to fixed charges during a fiscal period (again, as with interest coverage and debt service coverage, this is typically the most recently ended rolling four quarters). The purpose of the covenant is to test the ability of the borrower to generate sufficient cash during a period to service all of its nonoperating cash needs during that period (operating cash needs are

implicitly covered by the borrower's having a positive EBITDA). *Fixed charges* will start with debt service, but will go further by picking up capital expenditures and often (but not always) taxes and dividends (particularly regular, scheduled dividends).

- *Capital expenditures.* Although frequently included in the financial covenants section of a credit agreement, the capital expenditures covenant is perhaps more accurately characterized as a negative covenant than as a performance-based covenant. The restriction limits the aggregate capital expenditures that the borrower may make during a fiscal quarter or fiscal year. *Capital expenditures* will be defined as any expenditure in respect of a capital asset of the borrower (i.e., an expenditure that does not flow through the borrower's income statement). Repairing a building thus would probably not be a capital expenditure; erecting a new building probably would. The covenant is calculated for discrete fiscal periods (one quarter or one year), rather than on a rolling basis. Once the maximum levels are set, the debate between the borrower and the lender will revolve around carryovers: how much of one period's unused capital expenditure capacity may be carried forward into a future period. The borrower will, of course, push for unlimited carryforwards, whereas the lender will wish to limit carryovers to one or two years (or permit none at all).

- *Lease payments.* Credit agreements will sometimes limit the aggregate payments that may be made during a fiscal period with respect to operating leases (as distinct from capital leases, which will normally be captured by the definition of debt and thus included in the interest coverage, debt service coverage, or fixed charges coverage covenant). Sometimes the limit will be phrased in terms of an aggregate dollar cap. In other instances, the credit agreement will create a concept of "attributable debt," where, even for operating leases, the future rental stream is discounted to present value to produce an attributable dollar amount. The aggregate of such attributable debt will then be limited by the debt covenant.

Date-Specific Financial Covenants

The following are examples of financial covenants that measure performance at a specific date.

- *Net worth.* The net worth (or, more frequently, tangible net worth) covenant will test the balance sheet shareholders' equity of the borrower at a specific date (normally a fiscal quarter or fiscal year end). Tangible net worth will start with shareholders' equity as set out on the balance sheet, but will then adjust the figures to exclude intangibles (such as goodwill, research and development costs, and licenses) carried on the balance sheet. Tangible net worth will typically also exclude treasury shares.
- *Current ratio/working capital.* The current ratio covenant will test the ratio of current assets to current liabilities at a given date. The working capital covenant will measure the excess of current assets over current liabilities at a given date. Though these covenants have fallen out of favor and are used in relatively few credit agreements as lenders focus increasingly upon a borrower's cash flow rather than its assets, these covenants may still be seen in asset-based financing transactions.

AFFIRMATIVE COVENANTS

Disclosure Covenants

Once lenders have made (or purchased) loans under the credit agreement, they will want to monitor the performance of the borrower. Credit agreements will therefore require delivery of annual audited and quarterly unaudited financial statements. In the case of foreign borrowers, where quarterly financial statements may not be regularly prepared, the covenant may limit the required financial statements to semiannual or perhaps only annual statements. In specialized situations (such as highly leveraged or asset-based facilities), financial statements may be required to be delivered monthly.

Delivery has traditionally been made by the borrower's sending statements directly to lenders. However, in recent years, as the size of lending syndicates has expanded and Web-based posting services (such as Intralinks or Debtdomain) have become popular, financial statements are made available to lenders through posting on websites. These websites will normally contain a warning identifying those areas of the site that contain material nonpublic information, so that public-side investors can elect not to receive private-side information.

The financial statements to be delivered will normally be "consolidated" (i.e., they will consolidate the borrower with its subsidiaries), and in some cases will also be "consolidating" (i.e., they will show how the balance sheet and the results of operations for each entity in the consolidated group were added together to produce the consolidated statements). Consolidating statements are considered particularly useful because they show more clearly which entities in the consolidated group are responsible for the assets and earnings. It is thus another method by which the lenders can determine that they have guarantees and security from the proper entities in the consolidated group.

Annual financial statements will be required to be audited by the borrower's independent public accountants; interim financial statements need only be certified by an officer of the borrower. One issue that arises is whether delivery of financial statements with a "going concern" qualification can satisfy the covenant. Borrowers frequently resist the requirement that no such qualification exist, reasoning that, if a particular condition is not a default under the financial covenants or other provisions of the agreement, it should not become a default through the inability to deliver unqualified financial statements. In other words, they argue, whether the borrower is in default should be determined by reference to the negotiated tests incorporated in the credit agreement and not by whether the accountants have determined that a going concern qualification should be taken.

Concurrently with the delivery of quarterly or annual financial statements, the borrower will typically also be required to prepare a compliance calculation for financial and other number-based covenants. The credit agreement will normally require that all financial statements and any compliance calculations be certified by the CFO or a senior financial officer of the borrower. In some instances, the credit agreement may require that the certification be made by the borrower's public accountants. Accountants resist this approach and are normally unwilling to say anything about a covenant unless it relates to "accounting matters." They may also charge an additional fee to make the certification.

The disclosure covenant will almost always include a general catchall allowing the lenders to request additional financial or other information from the borrower. Sometimes the request can be made individually by any lender, although often it may be made only through the administrative agent. The right to request additional information from the borrower can be important if the lenders have reason to believe that the borrower's financial condition may have deteriorated.

The credit agreement will typically include a requirement that the borrower notify the lenders of any default and of other material events. Thus, the borrower would be required to notify the lenders of the institution of any litigation that, if lost, could result in a MAC, of any ERISA or environmental claim that exceeds a specified dollar threshold (or could result in a MAC), and of any other event that results or could be expected to result in a MAC. Borrowers often negotiate for this covenant not to be triggered unless a senior officer, or group of senior officers, has "actual knowledge" of the existence of the event requiring disclosure.

Visitation Rights

Potentially one of the most important rights granted by borrowers to lenders is the so-called visitation or inspection right. This right is important for two reasons. First, it affords the lenders the right to visit and inspect the borrower's properties and books. This right can potentially be very significant if there is reason to believe that the borrower may be in default, although borrowers often try to limit the inspection right to situations where a default is known to exist. Conditioning the right in this manner undercuts the purpose of an inspection right in the first place (i.e., to determine whether the borrower really is in default). Second, bank regulators consider the visitation or inspection right important and may look to see if the lenders have been accorded this right in the credit agreement.

Maintenance of Insurance

Almost every credit agreement (except perhaps for credit agreements with investment-grade borrowers) will include an insurance covenant. In its simplest form, the covenant will require the borrower to maintain insurance in a manner consistent with that maintained by other businesses in the same industry. The exact types of insurance, appropriate deductibles, limits on self-insurance, and covered risks will not be specified. In its more complex form, such as in highly leveraged secured transactions or project financings, the covenant will be detailed as to the risks to be covered and the deductibles or self-insurance to be permitted and will specify the qualifications for insurance carriers and that the lenders (or the administrative agent) must be named as "loss payees" or "additional named insureds." The covenant may also provide for the borrower to deliver an annual insurance compliance certificate to the administrative agent, demonstrating that all insurance required to be maintained under the covenant continues in effect and that all applicable premiums have been paid.

Sometimes credit agreements will also require that the borrower obtain key-man life insurance on one or more senior officers or key employees. The purpose of key-man life insurance is not to have a pot of money from which to pay the loan, but rather to ensure that the borrower has at hand a ready source of cash to pay an incentive bonus or the like to induce a replacement from another company to step in and take over for the officer or employee who has died.

Miscellaneous "Who-Can-Object" Covenants

A number of affirmative covenants in effect require the borrower to do nothing more than any right-minded borrower would do in the first place. The covenants are nevertheless included to guard against those situations in which a borrower is so abjectly sloppy or incompetent that it fails to run its business in the manner customarily expected of any good management team. The following are some examples of these covenants:

- *Books and records.* A credit agreement will normally expressly mandate that the borrower maintain appropriate books and records. Few borrowers fail to do this, but if, in exercising its inspection rights, a lender were to determine that inadequate books and records were being maintained, the lenders could obviously point to this covenant as a basis for taking remedial action.
- *Properties.* This covenant will require maintenance of all properties, subject invariably to a materiality qualifier.

It is hard to see how any borrower would ever trip this covenant, but in an egregious case, it could be important.
- *Existence and franchises.* This covenant will require the borrower to maintain franchises and licenses necessary for the conduct of its business, although there is usually a materiality qualifier. Of course, if the business is heavily dependent upon licenses (such as FCC licenses if the borrower is a television station or wireless company), the credit agreement will probably deal more explicitly, usually in the defaults, with what happens if any material licenses are revoked or not renewed.
- *Compliance with law.* This covenant will require the borrower to comply with laws, at least if failure to do so would materially adversely affect its business. Sometimes the covenant will explicitly state that the laws the borrower is to comply with include environmental laws (in case there were any doubt), but otherwise it simply obligates the borrower to do something that it should be doing already. Including the covenant in the credit agreement may give the lenders an argument that they acted in good faith in extending credit to the borrower and that they should not therefore be responsible if a government authority should seek to charge them with aiding and abetting the borrower's violation of law.
- *Payment of taxes and other obligations:* This covenant is much like the compliance with law covenant; that is, it merely obligates the borrower to do something that it should be doing already. It will normally be qualified by materiality. Absent that qualification, the covenant might be a backdoor cross-default without the customary thresholds and notice and grace periods. The covenant will typically allow the borrower not to pay its taxes and other obligations if it is contesting the payment "in good faith" and keeping "adequate reserves" against the obligation.

  In theory, the requirement that the borrower pay taxes has some marginal utility, given that defaulted taxes can result in a lien upon property; however, in practice, any such lien would be captured by the negative pledge covenant, and thus is already controlled. As with the compliance with law covenant, this covenant may help insulate the lenders against any claim by a taxing authority or party to a contract that the lenders were aiding and abetting the borrower's failure to pay taxes or breach of contract. The lenders will be able to point to the covenant and say that they have acted in good faith *vis-à-vis* the borrower.

- *Government approvals.* If the borrower is a non-U.S. entity, the credit agreement will frequently include a covenant requiring the borrower to maintain in force any government licenses and approvals necessary to permit it to pay the loans and perform its other obligations under the credit agreement.

Substantive Consolidation

Where loans under a credit agreement are being made to a borrower that is part of a larger consolidated group of companies, the lenders may be concerned with substantive consolidation in bankruptcy. "Substantive consolidation" arises out of a line of bankruptcy court cases that treats a group of affiliated entities as if they were a single company, so that the assets of each of the affiliated companies are deemed to be owned by one entity and the creditors of each of the affiliated companies are deemed to be creditors of one entity. If in making their original credit analysis, a group of lenders relied upon the borrower having particular assets and liabilities, substantive consolidation in a bankruptcy of the borrower and the other members of the affiliated group could run roughshod over the lenders' careful analysis. Credit agreements will, therefore, sometimes include a covenant requiring that the borrower take appropriate actions to minimize the risk of substantive consolidation. These include such things as (1) observing corporate formalities (in other words, keeping the borrower's assets identified and separate from affiliates' assets), (2) not commingling borrower cash with affiliates' cash (unless done pursuant to a cash management agreement that precisely lays out the rights and liabilities of each entity that is a party to the agreement), (3) dealing with customers under the borrower's name (and not using a common name for the group of companies as if they were all one entity), and (4) maintaining books and records separate from those of its affiliates.

A federal court decision (*In re Owens Corning*) emphasizes the desirability of lenders' performing a separate credit analysis of the borrower and each entity obligated on the loans as another tool to avoid substantive consolidation. The case suggests that assessing the strength of each support party and including in the credit agreement appropriate restrictions emphasizing their "stand-alone" value (such as those described in the preceding paragraph), and allowing lender visitation rights at the level of each support party, will make it less likely that a bankruptcy court will order substantive consolidation.

Use of Proceeds

The use of proceeds covenant ensures that the borrower will in fact use the loan proceeds for the purpose it specified at the time the credit agreement was entered into. Of course, if the credit agreement is providing funds for a major financing, the conditions themselves will control the actual disbursement of proceeds, so there is little likelihood that the borrower could stray. Most agreements will provide that the proceeds of term loans will be used only for one-time expenditures, such as acquisitions or capital expenditures, or to repay other debt, and that revolving credit facilities will be available for the working capital needs and general corporate purposes of the borrower. *General corporate purposes* is customarily construed broadly to allow the use of revolving loan proceeds to finance acquisitions, repay debt, or pay dividends, though the term may not permit transformational acquisitions or extraordinary dividends of a substantial portion of a borrower's capital. The term may, as a result, have little practical effect in constraining the borrower's use of the loans.

The use of proceeds covenant may also require that loan proceeds be used in accordance with applicable law (including Regulations T and U, discussed in the section "Representations" in Part 4, "Conditioning the Loan"). This language, as with the compliance with law covenant, may help give the lenders an argument that they were not, in making the loans, assisting the borrower to use the proceeds for an unlawful scheme or other purpose.

Hedging Transactions

The credit agreement will frequently restrict the borrower from entering into hedging transactions for "speculative" purposes. At the same time, the credit agreement may compel the borrower to undertake a certain minimum amount of interest hedging in order to guard against swings in interest rates that could jeopardize the borrower's ability to service interest on the loans. The normal approach will be to require that a percentage of the borrower's overall debt (including loans under the credit agreement) be hedged so that the aggregate portion of its floating-rate debt (taking into account the hedge) does not exceed a percentage (usually somewhere around 50% or 60%) of its total debt. Note that this gives the borrower credit for fixed-rate bond or private placement debt, because that will be treated as "hedged" for these purposes.

Hedging covenants are typically phrased fairly loosely: they will obligate the borrower only to enter into the appropriate hedges within some period (commonly three months or so) of the closing and set out only general parameters as to the manner of the hedge (though the administrative agent or the required lenders will sometimes have approval rights over final terms). The borrower will also typically not be required to maintain the hedge for more than two or three years after the closing.

Further Assurances

This covenant is most often seen in security documents as an undertaking on the part of the borrower to execute additional agreements and take other action in order that the lenders have good liens on collateral. In that context, the covenant will apply only to the property that is specified as "collateral" in the relevant security document. When a further assurances covenant is contained in a credit agreement, it will be more expansive, setting out overarching rules that govern what entities are to guarantee the loans and what types of property are to constitute collateral. This covenant is where any negotiated exceptions or thresholds will be specified, such as which subsidiaries will be deemed sufficiently immaterial to escape becoming guarantors and which real properties will be deemed too low in value to be subjected to a mortgage. The covenant may also prescribe mini-closing conditions that must be satisfied whenever any new subsidiary becomes a guarantor, requiring that the lenders be provided the same corporate assurances (resolutions and opinions, for example) as were provided on the closing date by the borrower and the initial guarantors.

NEGATIVE COVENANTS
Lien Covenant

The lien covenant (sometimes referred to as a *negative pledge*) restricts the borrower's granting of security interests and other encumbrances over its assets. The term *liens* will be defined expansively to include all manner of liens, charges, encumbrances, pledges, security interests, and the like and will also typically include the interest of a lessor under a lease and of a vendor in a conditional sale. The term may also refer to "any other type of preferential arrangement"; this is intended to capture the circumstance in which, without granting a lien, the borrower agrees to set aside or designate certain revenues for the benefit of a lender (a practice that is not infrequent in international trade or project financings). Lastly, the term may, in the case of securities, pick up purchase and call options and other similar third-party rights. The purpose of the covenant is to limit the number of creditors that will enjoy a preferential status in a bankruptcy or insolvency of the borrower. Secured creditors normally vote as a separate class in a bankruptcy, and thus can have significant bargaining leverage in addition to their right to be paid the entire proceeds or value of the property in which they have a lien.

The previous paragraph describes the lien covenant normally seen in credit agreements; that is, a covenant that prohibits liens except to the extent that they fall into one or more exclusions. In the context of most bond indentures and some credit agreements, the lien covenant may take a different approach: rather than prohibiting liens directly, it will simply provide that, if liens (other than "permitted encumbrances") are granted by the borrower to a third party, the lenders must be "equally and ratably" secured. This is the so-called equal and ratable sharing clause.

There is basically no law and only very little lore concerning what an equal and ratable sharing clause means. The general consensus seems to be that, at least prior to acceleration or insolvency, "sharing" requires only sharing of the lien and does not require sharing control over the collateral. Thus, the tag-along debt (the debt that contains the equal and ratable sharing clause, and that therefore is entitled to be equally and ratably secured by reason of liens being granted to a third party) would have no right to consent to a release of collateral; that right would reside exclusively with the lenders triggering the clause. Further, there would be no requirement (again, absent acceleration or foreclosure) that the tag-along debt be entitled to approve a sale of collateral or share in the proceeds of a sale. In fact, there may not even be a requirement that the tag-along debt be entitled to initiate foreclosure, that right again residing solely with the debt whose lien triggers the clause. In effect, an equal and ratable sharing clause requires only the sharing of proceeds when and if they arise. The clause thus affords much less protection than a straight lien covenant, and consequently is not normally seen in credit agreements.

With liens being defined so broadly, it naturally follows that the lien covenant will contain numerous exceptions. Customary exclusions include, among others:

- *Lender liens*: Liens in favor of the lenders. In most cases, this exception will automatically include liens securing increases under the credit agreement as well as refinancings of credit agreement debt.
- *Grandfathered liens*: Liens that were in existence on the closing date (normally listed in a disclosure schedule if they exceed a dollar threshold). The agreement may permit these liens to be "extended, renewed, or refinanced," though it typically bars the affected lien from spreading to new property.
- *Permitted encumbrances:* Permitted encumbrances are usually defined to sweep up a wide variety of liens that any business enterprise cannot avoid incurring in the ordinary course of business, such as easements and rights of way, warehouse liens, workers' compensation liens, mechanics' liens, utility pledges, rights of offset, and the like. Inchoate tax liens may also be permitted if the tax is not yet due or is being contested in good faith by the borrower.
- *Purchase money liens*: Liens covering property that secure financing for the purchase price of the property. The lien could thus be in favor of the seller of the property or in favor of a bank that supplied funds to enable the property to be purchased. Typically, the lien will not be allowed to exceed the cost of the property (or sometimes a percentage of the cost) and must be incurred within some short period (say 90 days) of the property being acquired. In addition, to qualify as a purchase money lien, the underlying

obligation may not be secured by any other property of the borrower. Purchase money liens would not include liens in existence on the property at the time it was acquired; those liens would need to fit into the acquisition lien basket, discussed next.

- *Acquisition liens*: Liens that were in existence on property (or on property of a subsidiary) at the time the property (or subsidiary) was acquired. Liens created in anticipation of the acquisition will not qualify.
- *General lien basket*: Additional liens permitted without restriction up to a negotiated dollar threshold or some other negotiated limitation. The general lien basket is included in many, though not all, credit agreements.

Negative Negative Pledge or Burdensome Agreements

A negative pledge limits the ability of the borrower to grant liens on its assets. A *negative negative pledge*, or what is frequently referred to as a *burdensome agreements* or *limitation on burdensome agreements* provision, takes this one step further and limits the ability of a borrower to enter into negative pledges with third parties. Thus, if an agreement has a negative negative pledge, the borrower would be prohibited from agreeing with a third party that its ability to grant liens is constrained (an equal and ratable sharing clause, discussed in the section "Negative Pledge," may count as a negative negative pledge for these purposes). The principal reason why a lender would want a negative negative pledge is to ensure that the borrower is free to grant security to the lender in the future without having to obtain consent from any third party.

Because a borrower can be expected to be subject to many lien restrictions in the ordinary course of its business, a negative negative pledge covenant will normally contemplate a long list of exclusions. Thus, for example, there will be exclusions for preexisting limitations and exclusions for contracts to which the borrower is a party that cannot be assigned or pledged without the consent of the counterparty. Similarly, there will be exclusions for property subject to permitted liens in favor of third parties and for leases (lessors customarily limit the ability of a lessee to grant liens on the leased property). Exclusions also may be permitted for contracts of sale where, pending a closing, the prospective purchaser of an item of property or division will want to limit the borrower's ability to grant liens on the property or division.

Debt

The debt covenant restricts the incurrence by the borrower and its subsidiaries of "debt." As with many definitions used in negative covenants, the term *debt* is defined expansively. The objective of the covenant is to ensure that the borrower does not take on more debt than it can service, given the cash being thrown off by its business. Customary exceptions include:

- *Lender debt*: Loans and letters of credit under the credit agreement. As with liens, this will automatically include any increases under the credit agreement as well as refinancings of like amounts of lender debt with new debt incurred under the credit agreement.
- *Grandfathered debt*: Debt in existence on the closing date that is permitted after the closing date will often be grandfathered by being listed in a disclosure schedule. One issue that will frequently be addressed is whether grandfathered debt includes extensions, renewals, and refinancings. Generally, to the extent that these are allowed, the credit agreement will state that the principal amount of the debt that is extended, renewed, or refinanced not be increased (other than for accrued interest and premiums). Any increase would, therefore, force usage of another basket.
- *Purchase money debt*: Debt that finances the purchase price of property, whether in favor of the seller or in favor of a bank that supplies funds to enable the property to be purchased. Because this debt is normally secured by the underlying property, the exception may cross-reference to the purchase money basket in the lien covenant.
- *Working capital debt*: Debt that provides working capital (at least in cases where the credit agreement does not have a revolving credit facility and is not supplying all necessary working capital liquidity to the borrower). Because working capital debt can often be short term or even payable on demand, the credit agreement will typically

impose limitations on the amount of such debt and the institutions from which it may be incurred. It may also limit the basket to particular subsidiaries, such as foreign subsidiaries.
- *Acquisition debt*: Debt that exists at the time an entity becomes a subsidiary. As with acquisition liens, debt created in anticipation of the purchase will not qualify.
- *Intercompany debt*: Debt between and among the borrower and its subsidiaries. In some instances, the credit agreement will provide that debt of the borrower to subsidiaries (as distinct from debt of subsidiaries to the borrower and intersubsidiary debt) must be subordinated to the claims of the lenders under the credit agreement. This is to prevent the subsidiaries (or, more important, creditors of a subsidiary that becomes insolvent) from competing with the lenders in obtaining payment of claims against the borrower.
- *Subsidiary debt*: Third-party debt of subsidiaries, although sometimes the credit agreement will limit the aggregate amount of this debt to avoid "structural subordination." The term structural subordination derives from the fact that all claims against a subsidiary must be paid in full before any money may flow up to a shareholder (i.e., the borrower). If the credit agreement permits a subsidiary to have a large amount of debt, then (unless the subsidiary is also a guarantor of the loans) all debt of the subsidiary must be paid in full before any cash can be upstreamed to the borrower to service the loans. The lenders would, therefore, be effectively subordinated to the debt of the subsidiary.
- *Additional debt*: Additional public or quasi-public debt, such as a senior or subordinated high-yield bond. Normally debt of this type will be subject to constraints as to aggregate amount, tenor (typically not earlier than 90 days after the maturity of the loans under the credit agreement), weighted average life to maturity (not earlier than that for the loans under the credit agreement), and redemption requirements and covenants. Sometimes the latter will be required to be approved by the required lenders, but more frequently the credit agreement will simply mandate that they satisfy the market standard in effect at the time the debt is issued.

- *Debt basket and ratio debt basket*: As with the lien basket, a basket for debt that does not fit into any of the other listed exceptions. Sometimes the portion of the basket debt that may be utilized by subsidiaries is limited because of the structural subordination issues described previously.

Ratio debt baskets historically appeared in bond indentures and not credit agreements, but as bond-style and credit agreement covenants have converged, ratio baskets are now commonly seen in credit agreements. The typical covenant is styled as an incurrence test requiring the pro forma satisfaction of a certain credit ratio as a condition to incurring debt under the ratio basket.

Disqualified Stock

Although this is not normally a separate covenant, some credit agreements will control the issuance of "disqualified stock." The concept, which is very common in the bond indenture context, restricts the amount of debtlike equity, such as preferred stock that is entitled to mandatory redemption at a future specified date. Generally, if that date is within a defined period (typically 90 days or a year) *after* the maturity date for loans under the credit agreement, the lenders will want to treat the preferred stock as equivalent to debt. It will thus be controlled by the debt covenant and will be included in leverage tests.

Fundamental Changes, Asset Sales, and Acquisitions

Fundamental changes covenants, asset sale covenants, and permitted acquisition covenants all have the same objective of preventing transactions that would change the business or assets of the borrower upon which the lenders' initial credit decisions were made in some fundamental way.

- *Mergers.* The limitation on mergers will restrict the ability of the borrower to merge or consolidate with other entities. There will be exceptions. Almost universally, a credit agreement will permit mergers and consolidations of subsidiaries into the borrower if the borrower is the surviving or continuing corporation. Less frequently, a credit agreement will permit nonsubsidiaries to merge with the borrower if the borrower is the surviving entity *and* if the merger itself would be permitted under the acquisition limitation. The requirement that the borrower always survive contrasts with the approach typically found in bond indentures, where mergers are permitted even in cases where the issuer is not the survivor. A bond indenture will nevertheless still constrain the issuer by requiring that the surviving entity assume the issuer's obligations under the indenture and that the survivor satisfy certain other tests, such as being organized in the United States, not having a reduced net worth, and being able to incur at least $1.00 of additional debt.

- *Acquisitions.* A limitation on acquisitions will control the ability of the borrower to acquire another business. It will thus control not just acquisitions of the equity of another company, but also acquisitions of a business or division of another company. As with the limitation on mergers, an exclusion will be made for "acquisitions" that are transfers of assets between and among subsidiaries or by subsidiaries to the borrower.
- *Dispositions.* A covenant limiting dispositions will usually be in one of two forms: either it will limit sales by the borrower of "all or substantially all" assets or it will limit sales of "any assets."

   The "all or substantially all" restriction, of course, is considerably more flexible from the viewpoint of the borrower than an "any assets" covenant. The latter will need (and will customarily incorporate) exclusions for sales of inventory in the ordinary course of business and for sales of worn-out or obsolete property or equipment (the latter usually being capped at a dollar maximum).

Credit agreements will regularly require prepayments from the proceeds of nonordinary course asset sales. Borrowers will frequently push for the flexibility to keep the sale proceeds in the business by negotiating for reinvestment rights in lieu of forced debt repayment.

Sale-Leasebacks

Very common in bond indentures, sale-leaseback covenants are sometimes also incorporated into credit agreements. The basic purpose is to control a transaction in which the borrower sells an asset and then immediately leases it back under a capital or operating lease arrangement. It restricts, in sum, a form of secured financing. Of course, in the context of a credit agreement (but perhaps not in the context of a bond indenture), each of the elements of a sale-leaseback transaction should already be controlled by other covenants (among them the lien, debt, and fundamental changes or asset sales covenants) and mandatory prepayment requirements, and so, from a technical standpoint, the restriction may be unnecessary. Nevertheless, it is sometimes inserted into credit agreements to set minimum standards for how sale-leaseback transactions otherwise permitted within an applicable debt, lien, or dispositions basket are to be structured.

Investments

From the standpoint of a lender, the objective of an investments covenant is much like that of the fundamental changes covenant: to control material changes to the business or assets of the borrower upon which the lender's initial credit decision was made. There is considerable overlap between the two covenants (a purchase of 100% of the stock of a corporation would, for example, constitute both an investment and an acquisition, and therefore any such purchase would need to satisfy the conditions of both covenants).

The definition of the term *investments* will, like other definitions, be perhaps overexpansive and encompass not just the acquisition of securities, but also extensions of credit, issuance of guarantees, and, sometimes, entering into hedging agreements. The term will normally not include extensions of credit by the borrower to customers in the ordinary course of business (i.e., the customary credit terms given by a borrower for payment of inventory or services, though sometimes credit terms longer than 90 or 180 days will be treated as investments). Expansiveness leads, in turn, to a variety of exceptions, including:

- *Grandfathered investments.* Grandfathered investments include those investments in existence on the closing date (usually listed on a disclosure schedule if they exceed a dollar threshold). Grandfathered investments will not normally need to cover subsidiaries or cash equivalents, because each is customarily covered by other exceptions.

- *Cash and cash equivalents.* The term *cash* incorporates all cash on hand, held by the borrower and its subsidiaries, including amounts held in deposit accounts. *Cash equivalents* is a more expansive term and is normally defined to mean a variety of liquid investments of high credit quality, such as commercial paper with high ratings from Moody's and Standard & Poor's (S&P), short-term Treasuries (or short-term repos on Treasuries), short-term certificates of deposit, and money market funds that primarily invest in other securities fitting within the definition of cash equivalents. The term is intended to capture investments that can be treated essentially as equivalent to cash. Accordingly, equity securities are not included because of the potential for market volatility. Longer-term bonds (even if given the highest rating by Moody's and S&P) and longer-term Treasury securities are normally not included because interest rate volatility can adversely affect their market value.
- *Subsidiaries.* In cases where the credit analysis of the borrower is based upon its being an operating entity with operating assets, the lender may want to control the movement of assets from the borrower into subsidiaries, and will therefore impose a dollar cap. The concern for the lender is allowing itself to be structurally subordinated to creditors of a subsidiary, which are entitled to be paid in full from the assets of the subsidiary before any money flows up to the borrower. Allowing the borrower to put money into subsidiaries may simply be supporting creditors of the subsidiaries. Sometimes this concern can be dealt with by having the subsidiaries guarantee the loans under the credit agreement. Another possible solution is to require that investments in subsidiaries be in the form of debt rather than equity. Claims by the borrower as a creditor with respect to the intercompany debt should then compete (in theory) with the other creditors of a subsidiary (though in some cases in a bankruptcy, the claims of a borrower against a subsidiary will be equitably subordinated). See the discussion of structural subordination in the section "Debt" earlier in this part.
- *Ordinary course items.* These are investments that any company cannot avoid in the ordinary course of business, such as operating deposit accounts with banks

(sometimes subject to a requirement concerning the size or creditworthiness of the deposit institution) and security deposits with utilities in the ordinary course of business.
- *Acquisitions.* Investments constituting acquisitions that are permitted under the fundamental changes covenant.
- *General investment basket.* Investments that are not allowed under the other exceptions, usually up to some agreed dollar threshold or subject to an incurrence-based financial ratio, "grower basket" or "builder basket."

Lines of Business

Consistent with the concerns described in the section "Fundamental Changes" earlier in this part, lenders make a credit analysis of the borrower based upon the nature of its current business. To take an example, the lenders will not want to see a cable television company enter the fast-food business. Not only may the borrower's management be unfamiliar with the operation of a fast-food business, but the financial covenants may no longer appropriately measure how the company is performing. As a result, many credit agreements will contain a line of business covenant that will require that a borrower not enter in any material respect into lines of business different from those in which the borrower is engaged at the closing of the credit agreement.

Derivatives

As discussed in the section "Affirmative Covenants" earlier in this part, lenders will often require a borrower to enter into hedging agreements (particularly interest hedges) in connection with the execution of the credit agreement. At the same time, however, the lenders may be concerned that the borrower could "overhedge" (speculate) in currencies, commodities, interest indices, or any of the numerous other products available in the derivatives markets. Accordingly, credit agreements will frequently control the hedging transactions into which the borrower may wish to enter beyond those required by the lenders in the affirmative covenants. These limitations can be found in a number of places. Sometimes hedges are deemed to be debt, and thus are limited by the debt covenant. A second approach is to treat hedges as investments. A third approach is simply to deal with hedges in a stand-alone covenant.

Regardless of how hedges are controlled, it is often not terribly practical to limit hedge exposures to a dollar cap, because that would require daily recalculation of the exposure under a hedge as interest and other indicators change. The more customary approach, therefore, is to avoid dollar caps and allow hedges so long as they are entered in the ordinary course of the borrower's financial planning and not for speculative purposes.

Guarantees or Contingent Liabilities

Guarantees are frequently controlled by both the debt covenant (by treating guarantees of debt of a third party as debt of the guarantor) and the investments covenant (by treating guarantees of obligations of a third party as an investment in the third party). Some credit agreements will also control guarantees and other contingent liabilities with a separate covenant as well. "Guarantees" for these purposes, as in the debt and investments covenants, will be defined very broadly to pick up not just a simple guarantee, but also a broad variety of other arrangements, such as the borrower's causing a bank to issue a letter of credit to support the obligations of a third party or the borrower's agreeing to protect a third party against loss arising out of a commercial transaction. So-called take or pay agreements would also be captured, where, for the benefit of a creditor of a third party, the borrower agrees to purchase products (such as oil or processed chemicals) from the third party whether or not the third party is able to deliver the products to the borrower. Similarly, support arrangements where the borrower agrees with the creditor of a subsidiary to maintain the net worth of the subsidiary regardless of adverse events would be treated as a guarantee. If the net worth must always be positive, the borrower has in effect guaranteed the indebtedness of the subsidiary. The breadth of the definition stems from the expectation that borrowers will have an infinite capacity to be creative in structuring deals, and so the broader (and more verbose) the guarantee concept, the better.

The amount of a guarantee will be deemed to be equal to the amount of the stated limit. The amount of the guarantee will not be reduced by the fact that other parties are jointly and severally obligated with the borrower and that, therefore, the borrower can seek reimbursement from other parties for any payment by it in excess of its pro rata share.

Dividends and Equity Repurchases

The dividend covenant in a credit agreement will limit dividends and distributions by the borrower. It will not, as is typically the case in bond indentures, be part of a broader category of "restricted payments" that limits both investments and dividends. A credit agreement will customarily control dividends and investments in separate covenants.

As with other definitions employed in other negative covenants, the term *dividend* or *dividend payment* will be defined expansively. It will not only pick up the layman's understanding of periodic dividends declared by the borrower's board, but also capture any other device by which money could leave the borrower and be paid to equity holders. Thus, it will include distributions, sinking fund payments, purchases of stock, and even "phantom stock" payments (i.e., where a creditor or employee is entitled to an equity-like return as if it held stock without actually owning any equity). It will include those actions if they are undertaken by the borrower; it will also include those actions if they are undertaken by subsidiaries (the theory being that a repurchase of *borrower* stock by a subsidiary is still money out of the consolidated group). Customary exceptions include:

- *Employee stock plans*: Dividend payments arising when the borrower repurchases stock from employees upon their death or retirement. The aggregate repurchases in any single year are usually subject to a dollar cap.
- *Intercompany dividends*: Dividend payments by subsidiaries of the borrower to the borrower and to other subsidiaries. In the case where a subsidiary is not wholly owned, the exception will simply require that dividend payments be made ratably by the subsidiary to all of its shareholders.
- *Stock dividends*: Dividends paid through the issuance of additional shares of stock (other than disqualified stock; see the discussion in "Disqualified Stock" earlier in this part). Stock dividends will almost always be permitted without limit (frequently by carving out stock dividends from the definition entirely), because they do not represent money leaving the borrower's consolidated group.
- *Preferred dividends*: Dividends on preferred stock. Normally the exclusion will permit dividends only at the level in

effect at the closing date and will not provide for dividends on future issuances of preferred. Normally, this type of dividend will be blocked during an event of default.
- *Parent company debt*: If the parent of the borrower has outstanding debt, dividend payments to the extent necessary to pay interest on such debt, so long as no event of default exists. As with preferred dividends, the amount of dividends permitted will normally be locked in at the closing date and will not be increased if additional parent debt is issued.
- *Dividend basket*: Dividend payment baskets are based on a simple per annum dollar amount; a "grower" basket that is sized on a percentage of total assets, cash flow, or some other figure negotiated among the parties; or a "builder" basket that is sized on cumulative retained excess cash flow, cumulative net income, equity contributions, and other amounts that may aggregate over time. The basket may also be a combination of the foregoing. Sometimes also there may be a requirement that the borrower deliver an officer's certificate with a supporting calculation demonstrating that the borrower is in compliance at the time of the dividend and will continue to be in compliance after payment of the dividend.

Tax-Sharing Payments and Permitted Tax Distributions

If the borrower is a domestic corporation that is more than 80% owned by another domestic corporation, under the U.S. Internal Revenue Code, it will be consolidated with its ultimate parent for tax purposes. This means that the ultimate parent will be the entity that actually pays taxes to the government. Of course the parent will look to its subsidiaries (including, in this case, the borrower and its subsidiaries) for funds to make the tax payments. Credit agreements sometimes limit the aggregate amount of payments that may be made to a borrower's parent to an amount deemed to be "fair" from the standpoint of the borrower. The parent might, for example, have other subsidiaries that are generating substantially more current income than the borrower; in these circumstances, it would not be appropriate (arguably) for the borrower to pay more to its parent than the amount it would have been required to pay had it been an independent taxpayer. The restriction on tax-sharing payments is typically not a separate covenant, but is incorporated into either the dividend or the affiliate transactions covenant. The typical permitted tax distribution basket will be sized to permit the borrower to distribute cash, often whether or not a default exists, to the tax-paying parent in an aggregate amount required to pay U.S. federal, state, local, and/or non-U.S. income or similar taxes imposed on such parent company but only to the extent such income or similar taxes are attributable to the income of the borrower.

Dividend Blockers

A dividend blocker relates to a dividend covenant in the same way that a negative negative pledge relates to a negative pledge covenant. In other words, a dividend blocker will prohibit the borrower from agreeing with third parties that dividends and distributions by subsidiaries to the borrower are constrained. The covenant will also typically restrict other kinds of limitations on money or property going "upstream," such as through sales or mergers or other transfers. Lenders are concerned in this context that the borrower's access to funds may be dependent upon money flowing upstream from subsidiaries. Restricting that flow could impair the borrower's ability to pay the scheduled principal and interest on the loans.

As with the negative negative pledge, there are a number of customary exceptions that will be incorporated into the dividend blocker covenant, including exclusions for preexisting limitations and exclusions for contracts of sale of a subsidiary where, pending a closing, the prospective purchaser of the subsidiary will want to freeze dissipation of the assets of the subsidiary by means of upstream transfers.

Modification and Prepayment of Other Debt

Loans under the credit agreement are often not the borrower's only debt. Subordinated debt and other senior debt may be outstanding, whether in the form of a private placement, a bond indenture, or other debt issuance. The credit analysis of the borrower by the lenders will, of course, have taken into account the borrower's closing date capital structure, including the maturity of any other debt and the terms and conditions applicable to the other debt. Changes in the other debt, such as to shorten the maturity, tighten covenants, increase interest rates, or the like, may adversely affect the credit profile of the borrower.

Credit agreements deal with these issues by controlling amendments to other debt and by limiting the ability of the borrower to prepay other debt. Sometimes the restriction on amendments will apply only to "nonmaterial" modifications. However, this approach can lead to difficulty in determining whether a change rises to the level of materiality that requires lender consent. One issue that will often be addressed is whether debt may be refinanced. When this is permitted, the credit agreement will typically set out a detailed set of criteria, including criteria with respect to amortization and maturity, interest rate, covenants, and redemption or repurchase events that will be applicable to any refinancing indebtedness.

The prepayments limitation will apply only to voluntary prepayments of other debt; it will not apply to scheduled principal or interest payments or to mandatory prepayments. The reason for this latter approach is the doctrine of "tortious interference." Courts will generally not permit parties to enter into an agreement if compliance with that agreement would require a breach of another agreement by which one of them is bound. Thus, a court would probably not allow a borrower to enter into a credit agreement with a group of lenders if compliance with the credit agreement would constitute a breach of a covenant in another debt agreement (such as by restricting the borrower's ability to make required debt payments). If the lenders did not carve out required payments or mandatory prepayments, they could expose themselves to liability to the holders of the other debt.

Affiliate Transactions

The affiliate transactions covenant restricts transactions between the borrower and its affiliates. *Affiliates* will typically be defined with reference to the SEC standard (i.e., whether an entity is "controlled" by voting power, contract, or otherwise). Anyone controlling the borrower or under common control with the borrower will be an affiliate. The definition may in some cases deem a percentage ownership (5% or 10%) to constitute control. If the borrower is closely held, the term may also sometimes expressly include family members of controlling parties.

The rationale for the covenant is the fear that an entity or individual controlling the borrower may be able to unduly influence the terms of transactions with that entity or individual (or with other entities that it or the individual controls). In a sense, the affiliate transactions covenant is another leg of the dividend covenant, in that it controls money going out of the system to equity holders. Thus, while a dividend covenant might prohibit the payment of dividends to the owner of a privately held company, absent a restriction on affiliate transactions, there would be nothing to prevent that company from purchasing pencils at a price of $1,000 each from the owner or from the owner's wife or son. Of course, in a public company, the securities laws will provide a measure of legal protection that may make this kind of abuse less likely.

Normally a credit agreement will allow transactions between the borrower and affiliates for the purchase or sale of property in the ordinary course of business if the transaction takes place on terms not less favorable to the borrower than terms that would be applicable to a transaction between two disinterested parties. This is the so-called arm's-length exception. Credit agreements will rarely adopt the approach taken in bond indentures, which will apply the arm's-length exception to any transaction (not just for the purchase and sale of property) and determine compliance with the arm's-length standard based upon either a board resolution or, if the transaction exceeds a dollar threshold, upon a third-party appraisal.

An affiliate transactions covenant will also normally contain exceptions for transactions otherwise expressly permitted under the credit agreement, such as the payment of dividends, and, because directors and senior officers may be deemed to be affiliates, for compensation to directors and officers, loans and advances to officers, and stock and bonus plans.

Amendments to Organic Documents and Other Agreements

Credit agreements may sometimes limit amendments to the borrower's charter, bylaws, or other organic documents. The fear is that the borrower might amend these instruments in a manner adverse to the lenders, such as by authorizing the issuance of preferred stock that benefits from mandatory dividends or redemption provisions. In most agreements, these concerns will be addressed by other covenants (in this example, the debt and dividend covenants), so including a limitation on amendments to organic documents is relatively rare.

Credit agreements may also sometimes limit amendments to material agreements. Modifications to other debt documents is one example and is discussed in "Modification and Prepayment of Other Debt" earlier in this part. Other examples might include a purchase and sale contract pursuant to which a major acquisition financed by the proceeds of the loans was consummated. In this case, the lenders may limit the ability of the borrower to waive rights it may have under the indemnification provisions of the contract. Similarly, if a supply contract is an important source of raw materials for the borrower, or if sales under a requirements contract provide funds critical to servicing the loans, modifications to those contracts could be restricted by the covenant.

One qualification that is frequently inserted into the covenant, as applied to either organic documents or other material agreements, allows the borrower to effect modifications without the consent of the lenders if the modification is "not adverse" or "not materially adverse" to the lenders, or if the modification will not adversely affect the rights of the borrower under the contract. From the borrower's perspective, this allows it to effect de minimis changes (such as modifications to the notice provisions or other routine matters) without having to obtain the consent of the lenders. There is considerable logic to this type of exclusion (especially because agents and lending syndicates typically do not want to be bothered with nonmaterial modifications), so many credit agreements carve out nonmaterial changes. This is so despite the difficulty of determining what is material in any particular circumstance (though some agreements will permit the administrative agent to decide whether a change is material, and only if it is material will a vote of the required lenders be taken).

Fiscal Periods and Accounting Changes

Financial covenants are often prepared with a view to step-ups or step-downs occurring at times of the year corresponding to fiscal quarter or fiscal year end dates. This makes determining compliance with the covenants straightforward for both the borrower and the lenders. To permit the borrower to change fiscal end dates would either require the lenders to guess whether the borrower is in compliance or force the borrower to prepare one-off, less reliable financial statements at a date that does not correspond to a fiscal period end. Credit agreements, accordingly, frequently restrict the ability of a borrower to change fiscal end days.

As noted earlier in the discussion of GAAP, the financial covenants set forth in a credit agreement are usually prepared on a base set of "generally accepted accounting principles" that have been "consistently applied." Changes in the application of those principles to the financial statements of the borrower, whether at the borrower's own initiative or as a result of changes in GAAP, could mean that the financial covenants no longer adequately measure business performance. The lenders, of course, fear that a change might make compliance too easy; the borrower fears that compliance will become too difficult. Credit agreements will thus often include a requirement that all financial covenants be calculated in a manner consistent with GAAP used when the lenders made their initial credit analysis leading up to the closing. To minimize the expense of the borrower having to prepare two sets of financial statements, the agreement will contemplate that, in the event of a change in GAAP, the parties will negotiate appropriate changes to the financial covenants so that the required covenant levels reflect the changed GAAP. Absent agreement, the financial covenants will be calculated in accordance with original closing date GAAP.

INCORPORATION BY REFERENCE

From time to time, a credit agreement will incorporate covenants from another agreement. When necessary, these provisions will also incorporate related definitions and specify any necessary changes in terminology. For example, if the covenants being incorporated are set out in a bond indenture, the incorporation will need to stipulate that references in the covenants to "notes" and "noteholders" will be deemed to refer to "loans" and "lenders."

One key question that the incorporation provision will address is whether covenants are to be incorporated "as amended from time to time" or "as in effect" on the date of incorporation. The former removes the ability of the lenders to consent to changes to the incorporated covenants. The latter gives the lenders an independent consent right. Of course, even if incorporated "as amended from time to time," the covenant will still need to address what happens if, say, the bond indenture from which the covenants are incorporated is terminated. In that instance, the incorporation provision will normally provide that the indenture covenants are incorporated "as last in effect."

COVENANT-LITE

Covenants in credit agreements have historically been different from those usually found in bond indentures. For several reasons, covenants found in indentures have tended to be somewhat looser. To begin with, the duration of covenants in an indenture is usually longer, corresponding to the generally longer tenors of bonds as compared with loans. The longer the duration of covenants, the more flexibility the issuer wants to accommodate its planning needs, its growth projections, and unforeseen circumstances that may affect its business. In addition, bonds tend to be more widely held than loans, which makes it more difficult to obtain waivers and amendments for indenture provisions. Also, the cost of issuing bonds is generally higher than the borrowing cost for loans, and issuers often have the view that a looser covenant package is one of the advantages they are "buying" with the higher-priced alternative. Finally, although bank lenders have historically been focused on deleveraging and amortization, the typical bond investor has been less focused on paydown during the term of the instrument and content with keeping its money "at work" and accruing interest. Therefore, bonds in the past were viewed as more liberal than loans in terms of forcing principal repayment prior to maturity.

Notwithstanding the past differences, at the time of this writing there has been a steady trend of convergence of bond and loan covenants over the last decade or so. First in the late 1990s, when the two markets began to mix and match maturities, interest rates (fixed versus variable) and covenant packages. Starting in about 2005 and ending at the beginning of the financial crises in mid-2007 and then again commencing in the post-crisis period circa 2011, the loan market could be described as heavily trending toward so-called covenant-lite transactions, in which credit agreements incorporated many of the looser covenants from typical high-yield securities in place of the more restrictive covenants typical of leveraged loan transactions.

The hallmark of covenant-lite transactions is the replacement of financial covenants that constitute "maintenance" tests with covenants constituting "incurrence" tests. Whereas the former requires the borrower to maintain a given level of financial performance (with a default occurring if that level is not continually satisfied for any reason), the latter simply requires the borrower not to take some action within its control such as issuing additional debt or paying dividends, unless a given financial ratio meets agreed parameters (with a default occurring only if the borrower nevertheless takes the voluntary action in breach of the parameters).

Regardless of one's view of covenants, the advent of the covenant-lite structure has been profound and, at the time of this writing, may be the most identifiable hallmark of the current institutional term loan market.

Part 6: Securing and Guaranteeing the Loan: Collateral Packages

GUARANTEES AND SECURITY GENERALLY

The obligations of a borrower under a credit agreement are frequently guaranteed, either by its parent or by its subsidiaries or other affiliates. The obligations of the borrower and guarantors are also frequently secured. Whether guarantee and security provisions are set forth in the credit agreement or in a separate agreement varies. Guarantees are often set out in the credit agreement (primarily for ease of reading); security provisions, except perhaps in the asset-based lending context, are rarely set forth in the credit agreement.

GUARANTEES

Guarantees Generally

A guarantee is a secondary obligation, meaning that the guarantor generally becomes obligated to make payment only if the primary obligor (the borrower) fails to do so. Guarantees are governed by common law decisions of the courts of the various U.S. states. At common law, guarantors were favored. As a result, court decisions have established a number of qualifications to the obligations of guarantors that, unless waived in the guarantee itself, can present pitfalls and traps for the lender. These qualifications drive much of the language that is seen in the typical guarantee.

Guarantee of Payment versus Guarantee of Collection

Guarantees are almost always structured as guarantees of payment rather than guarantees of collection. A guarantee of collection would require the lender to exhaust all remedies against the borrower before making a claim under the guarantee (and then only for the ultimate shortfall not paid by the borrower). By contrast, a guarantee of payment obligates the guarantor to pay the lender immediately upon the default of the borrower, regardless of whether the borrower has been notified of the default, whether a demand has been made on the borrower, or whether the lender has taken any other action against the borrower. This can be a very important right if, for example, the borrower is in bankruptcy and the guarantor is not. If a lender were required to take action against the borrower as a precursor to making a demand on a guarantor, it would be in a hopeless situation, because taking action against the borrower would violate the Bankruptcy Code's automatic stay. Accordingly, the typical guarantee will very explicitly have the guarantor waive any requirement that the lender first take any action against the borrower so that the lenders receive a guarantee of payment.

Waivers

At common law, the granting of extra time to the borrower, waiver or amendment of its obligations, the release of security, the release of other guarantors, and a host of other actions by a lender could have the effect of releasing a guarantee. Guarantees, therefore, routinely state that they are "absolute and unconditional" and include waivers of these common law defenses. Case law in California counsels that these waivers be as explicit as possible, resulting in detailed waiver provisions; in New York, it is common for guarantee waivers to refer specifically to only a few of the circumstances that could release the guarantor at common law, and to rely otherwise on a "sweep-up" phrase waiving "any other circumstance whatsoever that might otherwise constitute a legal or equitable discharge or defense of a guarantor or surety."

Subrogation

If a guarantor makes payment, it may at common law be "subrogated" to the rights of the payee to the extent of the payment. In other words, the guarantor would step into the shoes of the lender with respect to the loan paid by the guarantors. Customary guarantee provisions allow such subrogation, but require that any exercise of subrogation rights by the guarantor (which, at that point, would make the guarantor a competing creditor of the borrower) be postponed until the lenders have received full payment of their claims.

Reinstatement

If a borrower were to make payment on a loan within 90 days of filing for bankruptcy, the payment could potentially be recovered from the lenders as a "preference" under Section 547 of the Bankruptcy Code. To avoid the lenders' having to argue with the guarantor as to whether the borrower's original payment (now reversed) discharged the guarantee, guarantees generally include an express "reinstatement" clause, to the effect that a guarantee is automatically revived if a payment by the borrower is reversed or recaptured. The reinstatement clause will typically also require the guarantor to indemnify the lenders for any costs that they may incur in resisting the preference claim, the theory being that the lenders' fight in this regard is, in substance, a fight for the account of the guarantor.

Insolvency of Borrower

Lenders may make a demand on a guarantor only for amounts that have not been paid by the borrower when due. What happens if the borrower declares bankruptcy and the automatic stay operates to prevent an acceleration of the loans or if any other court order prevents acceleration? (See the discussion of the automatic stay in the section "Insolvency" in Part 7, "Enforcing the Loans.") To prevent the guarantee's being rendered worthless because there is nothing payable by the borrower that can be demanded from the guarantor, guarantees will include a provision that, if an event of default occurs and for any reason the lenders are prevented from accelerating the loans, the loans are nevertheless deemed to be due and payable for purposes of any claims on the guarantor. Thus, even though the loans are not accelerated as against the borrower, the loans are accelerated as against the guarantor.

Continuing Guarantee

A guarantee will typically specify that it is "continuing"; that is, that it covers not only obligations outstanding at the time the guarantee is issued, but also future obligations of the borrower incurred from time to time. Absent this language, the guarantee arguably would not cover future advances, for example, loans and letters of credit made under the revolving credit facility after the closing.

Summary Procedure

Sometimes a guarantee that is stated to be governed by New York law includes a provision that the guarantee is "an instrument for the payment of money only" within the meaning of Section 3213 of New York's Civil Practice Law and Rules. An instrument that so qualifies may be enforced by expedited (or summary) procedure under Section 3213. It is not clear that saying that a guarantee is such an instrument makes it so (many guarantees include a variety of undertakings beyond the obligation to pay money), but there is some authority in New York that an express consent by the parties to enforcement under Section 3213 will be given effect.

Downstream, Cross-Stream, and Upstream Guarantees

Guarantees can be "upstream" (a subsidiary guaranteeing the debt of its parent); "cross-stream" (a subsidiary guaranteeing the debt of a "sister" company, where both are ultimately owned by the same parent); or "downstream" (a parent guaranteeing the debt of a subsidiary). An upstream or cross-stream guarantee may be vulnerable to attack under federal and state insolvency laws because, except to the extent that the guarantor received the proceeds of the guaranteed loans or other "reasonably equivalent value," one of the two requirements for a "fraudulent conveyance" or "fraudulent transfer" will have been established. If, after giving effect to the guarantee, the guarantor is "insolvent," then both requirements will have been established. See the discussion in the section "Solvency" in Part 4, "Conditioning the Loan."

Credit agreements deal with this risk in two ways. Some will incorporate a so-called solvency cap or savings clause, where the agreement will limit or cap the guarantee at the maximum amount (but not one penny more) that would allow it to be enforced without resulting in a fraudulent conveyance. To take a simplified example, if a subsidiary has an excess of assets over liabilities of $10,000,000, and it guarantees debt in a face amount of $10,000,000, the aggregate amount of the guarantee would be limited automatically to $9,999,999 (leaving an excess of assets over liabilities of $1.00). Thus, even though the subsidiary may not receive any of the proceeds of the loans, it would not be rendered insolvent by reason of the guarantee, and so no fraudulent conveyance will arise. One weakness of the solvency cap is that it makes the amount of the guarantee unclear.

Other credit agreements will insert a so-called cross-contribution concept, where the borrower and each of the other guarantors agree that if any guarantor makes payment under a guarantee greater than the excess of its assets over its liabilities, it will be entitled to be reimbursed by the borrower and each other guarantor for the amount of the excess. The effect of this structure is to give the guarantor an additional asset (namely, the contingent reimbursement claim against the borrower and any other guarantors), which is designed to make the guarantor solvent at the time the guarantee is undertaken. The solvency representation (discussed in the section "Solvency" in Part 4, "Conditioning the Loan") will verify that the borrower and guarantors (together with their subsidiaries) as a whole are solvent (and thereby confirm that the contingent reimbursement claims are in fact money good).

Neither of these solutions may work if an upstream or cross-stream guarantee is being given by an entity organized outside of the United States. Many countries have so-called financial assistance rules that carry much more severe consequences than the fraudulent conveyance and fraudulent transfer doctrines in the United States. If a guarantee would render a guarantor insolvent, violation of these rules can result in personal liability (and even, in some cases, criminal liability) for managers or directors. Often, savings and cross-contribution clauses such as those described previously will be ineffective. As a result, even in situations where the tax problem described in the section "Deemed Dividends" later in this part does not exist, guarantees from foreign subsidiaries may become a patchwork of full guarantees, dollar-capped guarantees, and no guarantees—altogether a confused structure when compared to guarantees from U.S. subsidiaries.

COLLATERAL PACKAGES

Whole treatises have been written about the legal intricacies of collateral security. This chapter will not do so, but will focus briefly only on how collateral security affects the drafting of a credit agreement. In some cases, the parties may set forth the full set of security provisions in the credit agreement rather than placing them in a separate security agreement. As noted previously, this approach is quite rare. In most cases, therefore, taking collateral security affects only a few discrete provisions of a credit agreement, including the following:

- *Conditions.* The conditions precedent will typically include a requirement that the liens be perfected and that evidence (such as UCC or title search results) of the priority of the liens be delivered to the administrative agent. In the case of a mortgage on real property, the conditions may also include the delivery of title insurance and surveys. If other particular kinds of collateral are to be included, such as collateral located outside of the United States, the conditions may be explicit as to the action that must be taken under relevant local law.
- *Representations.* The credit agreement may include a representation that all action to perfect the liens has been taken (though, more frequently, this representation will be incorporated into the security documents).
  In some cases, credit agreements will adopt an approach used in secured bond indentures of requiring the borrower to deliver an annual certificate (sometimes accompanied by an opinion of counsel) to the administrative agent confirming that all actions necessary to continue the perfection of liens has been taken. The agreement may also include similar annual confirmations that all insurance required to cover collateral is being maintained.
- *Affirmative covenants.* The further assurances covenant will typically be more expansive, including a description of

action to be taken with respect to future acquired property (particularly real estate).
- *Defaults.* The defaults clause may provide that an event of default will occur if the underlying security documents shall for any reason be unenforceable or if the lien on the collateral shall for any reason fail to be perfected.
- *Voting.* The voting provisions will address the votes required to release collateral (usually, only releases of all or substantially all of the collateral require unanimous consent; otherwise consent of the required lenders is sufficient).
- *Expenses.* The expenses provision may include an express statement that the borrower is obligated to pay the costs of perfecting liens (including recording taxes and the cost of title insurance).

SPRINGING LIENS

In some cases, the lenders will not take security at closing, but will enter into an understanding with the borrower that, upon specified adverse events occurring in the future, the borrower will grant security to the lenders. Often the adverse event is the occurrence of an event of default, but in other instances it is an adverse development in a financial ratio short of an event of default. The future contingent lien that this structure contemplates is a so-called springing lien.

Springing liens are relatively rare; if collateral security is important, the parties normally create and perfect it at closing. Lenders, in particular, do not want something as significant as security to be dependent upon the future cooperation of the borrower. If the adverse event that is to trigger the springing lien is an event of default, the borrower may see little advantage in granting the liens at the time required unless the default is concurrently being cured (most springing lien clauses do not so provide). Of course, assuming that the borrower cooperates and grants the relevant liens, the lenders are still not home free. A lien that "springs" will necessarily secure an antecedent (preexisting) debt, and thus the lenders benefiting from such a lien will not be fully secured until the Bankruptcy Code preference period (90 days for noninsiders) has passed. If the borrower commences a bankruptcy case prior to the 90th day, the liens may well be undone by the Bankruptcy Code. (See the discussion in "Reinstatement" earlier in this part.)

TRUE-UP MECHANISM

In certain circumstances, it is not possible to secure all tranches equally and ratably. For example, if a credit agreement has a revolving credit commitment provided to the borrower in the United States and a term loan commitment provided to a subsidiary in Europe, collateral security granted by the European subsidiary may be able to secure only the term loan because of either the financial assistance rules described in "Downstream, Cross-Stream, and Upstream Guarantees" earlier in this part or the tax issue to be discussed in the next section, "Deemed Dividends." Another example is sometimes confronted in New York, where there is a very severe mortgage recording tax for liens on real property. In New York, if a term loan is secured by real property, the recording tax need be paid only once. If a revolving credit loan is secured by real property, the tax is payable on each drawing (at least, that is the uniform position of New York State recording offices). To minimize taxes, the parties would want to stipulate that only the term loans are secured by the mortgage.

Notwithstanding these dynamics, a successful syndication may be dependent upon the credit agreement's being structured to allow all lenders to share equally in all collateral. The mechanism that is often used is the so-called true-up. In a true-up, taking the first example, each tranche, upon realizing on the collateral for its loans, would purchase participations in the other tranche. Thus, the lenders that have made term loans in Europe would purchase participations in the revolving credit loans made in the United States, and the revolving credit lenders would, similarly, purchase participations in the term loans. The net result is that the risks and benefits of the collateral security for both tranches of loans will be shared equally among all lenders. In the second example, the term loan lenders would purchase participations in the revolving credit loans so that the proceeds of any foreclosure on mortgaged property in New York would be shared equally among all lenders.

DEEMED DIVIDENDS

Historically, a loan to a U.S. borrower that was guaranteed by a non-U.S. subsidiary would raise the so-called deemed dividend problem. Under Section 956 of the U.S. Internal Revenue Code, a guarantee of this type was generally deemed to be a dividend by the subsidiary to its U.S. parent (up to the amount of the guarantee) of the earnings and profits of the subsidiary. Although it is not something that affects the enforceability of the guarantee, a deemed dividend can have potentially terrible tax consequences for the U.S. parent, because the parent will have to include the subsidiary's earnings and profits as taxable income without receiving any cash to pay the associated taxes. As a consequence, most guarantees of debt of a U.S. borrower were restricted to U.S. subsidiaries.

The deemed dividend problem can also surface if a U.S. borrower pledges the equity of a non-U.S. subsidiary. Historically under the U.S. Internal Revenue Code, a pledge of more than 66⅔% of the total combined voting power of the non-U.S. subsidiary was deemed to be a dividend to the same degree as a guarantee by the subsidiary. To avoid this result, security agreements customarily limited the percentage of equity pledged to 65% (though 66⅔% is the number actually set out in the tax rules). Customarily also, the carve-out above 65% applied to all equity capital of the non-U.S. subsidiary, although the tax rule referred only to voting stock.

As the result of changes in U.S. tax laws that became effective in 2018, the impact of Section 956 on many groups has been mitigated because historic untaxed earnings sitting in foreign subsidiaries at the end of 2017 were generally taxed at the time and, as previously taxed earnings, will now not be taxed again whether as a result of a deemed or an actual dividend. These new U.S. tax rules will limit (but not eliminate) the future buildup of untaxed foreign earnings that could be swept up by Section 956.

Part 7: Enforcing the Loan: Events of Default and Remedies

EVENTS OF DEFAULT

Events of default are events or circumstances that suggest a decreased likelihood that the borrower will be able to pay its obligations under the credit agreement and that may lead the lenders to want to terminate the credit. Although some events of default, such as the commencement of a bankruptcy proceeding, constitute serious and urgent problems, events of default are more often signs of incipient difficulties. Credit agreements include the event of default concept to give the lenders a hammer over the borrower should it breach the agreement or if certain other specified events occur.

Some breaches or events will result in immediate events of default; others ripen into events of default only after notice is given or time has elapsed (or in some cases both notice is given and time has elapsed). Prior to the point that a breach or event ripens into an event of default, it is commonly referred to as a *default* or *unmatured default*. As will be discussed in greater detail in the section "Remedies" later in this part, lenders may accelerate the loans only once an actual event of default occurs; they may not do so upon the occurrence of a mere default. The lenders' remedy during the period when a breach or event is merely a default is to decline to make additional loans or issue additional letters of credit (and, perhaps, to sue the borrower or make a demand on the guarantors).

A breach or event should be a default or event of default only so long as it is continuing (though some credit agreements are not written clearly on this point). For example, if a borrower fails to pay an installment of principal when due, that will constitute (at least in most credit agreements) an immediate event of default. If the lenders take no action to accelerate the loans and the borrower later pays the defaulted principal, the event of default is cured, and the lenders may no longer accelerate the loans. See the discussion in the section "Remedies" later in this part for what happens if the lenders accelerate the loans prior to the payment of the defaulted principal.

Not all events of default are within the control of the borrower. For example, a borrower will typically have no control over its shareholders' selling their stock in the borrower, and thus will have no ability to prevent a change of control. Similarly, a non-U.S. borrower probably will not have any ability to prevent nationalization of its property, or a moratorium affecting outstanding debt of its home country, both of which are common events of default for borrowers that are not in Organisation for Economic Co-operation and Development (OECD) countries.

If the borrower is a reporting company under the Securities Exchange Act of 1934 and the credit agreement is deemed "material," it is required to disclose any acceleration and may be required to disclose the occurrence of a default or event of default even if it does not result in acceleration.

The events and circumstances that are normally listed in the events of default clauses under credit agreements include the following.

Default in Payment

Generally, the failure to pay when due the principal of a loan or the reimbursement obligation that arises upon a drawing under a letter of credit is an immediate event of default. A default in the payment of interest, fees, and other amounts will typically enjoy a grace period of from two to five business days (with two or three business days being the most common) before ripening into an event of default. A short grace period avoids an event of default based on wire transfer difficulties or administrative error. In contrast, the typical grace period for a payment default in a bond indenture is 30 days, whether for principal or interest. The longer grace period for bonds reflects the practical reality (at least historically) that, if a default occurs, there is greater difficulty in first locating and then obtaining waivers from a disparate and anonymous bondholder group than from lenders under a credit agreement. A similar rationale may explain the longer grace periods for covenant breaches under a bond indenture.

Inaccuracy of Representations

An event of default will arise if a representation is incorrect in any material respect when it is made or deemed to be made. The default will typically extend not only to the representations in the credit agreement, but also to those in related agreements, such as security agreements, intercreditor agreements, guarantee agreements, and the like. The default will also typically include statements made "in connection with" the credit agreement, which will sweep in representations made in amendments and in certificates and other documents furnished under the credit agreement (including preclosing commitment letters). Inaccuracies in closing certificates will therefore, if material, give rise to events of default.

The default is normally predicated upon the relevant representation being inaccurate *when made* (or when deemed made, such as upon the making of a loan). It is not a default if a representation that was initially correct later becomes incorrect. Thus, if at the closing of a single-draw term loan, the borrower is not a defendant in any material litigation, but subsequently is sued for a material amount, no default based upon a misrepresentation will arise, inasmuch as the representation was true when made.

The default is also predicated upon the inaccuracy's being *material*. Thus, an inadvertent failure to list an inactive subsidiary with no assets, no liabilities, and no operations is probably not a default. A failure to list an active subsidiary that has significant assets and liabilities and is also the holding company for a number of other listed subsidiaries probably would be material. Sometimes borrowers will push for an added "materiality" qualification by requesting that the default arise only if *material* representations are *materially* inaccurate. This approach is problematic, although it may be seen in rare cases. The difficulty is that it implies that some representations are not material. Taken to its logical conclusion, the qualifier could just as easily be inserted into the covenant default (i.e., that an event of default will occur only if a *material* covenant is breached) or even into the payment default (providing that an event of default occurs only if a *material* payment is not made).

Borrowers occasionally request that they be afforded a grace period to cure an inaccurate representation. It is unusual to see this concept incorporated into a credit agreement. However, if it is included, it will normally afford a grace period only for representations that are curable; most are not. The qualifier is in any event largely unnecessary. A borrower is much more likely than the lenders to know that a representation is inaccurate and, if it is so easily curable, can fix the problem itself even before being required to notify the lenders.

Breach of Covenants

Events of default based upon covenant breaches generally fall into two categories: those that are immediate and those that first require a grace period to run or notice to be given. As to who must give the notice, agreements differ. Some require that it be given by any lender; others prescribe that only the administrative agent or the required lenders are permitted to do so.

Commonly, breaches of negative covenants, financial covenants, and certain affirmative covenants (such as the agreement to maintain corporate existence and the undertaking that all subsidiaries shall be guarantors) will be immediate; others will require notice, lapse of time, or both. There is, however, no completely uniform approach for all credit agreements. In many instances the parties will negotiate to include or exclude a grace period for particular covenants. Factors that are weighed in determining what is appropriately an immediate event of default include (1) whether a breach, if it occurs, is susceptible of cure; (2) whether the covenant is so important that the lenders should have the right to act without delay; and (3) whether a breach, if it occurs, will be the result of intentional action of the borrower. One seemingly benign covenant—the borrower's obligation to notify the lenders promptly after obtaining knowledge of a default—is generally an immediate event of default, even if the underlying event or circumstance would not constitute an event of default until after notice or a grace period. The reason is simple: if the lenders do not know that a breach or other event has occurred, they are unable to deliver a notice or monitor the lapse of any grace period.

Bond indentures (in contrast to credit agreements) usually have longer grace periods (30 or 60 days is customary) and will require that notice be given before the grace period commences; in other words, there are no immediate events of default based on covenant breaches. As noted in the section "Default in Payment" earlier in this part, this more borrower-favorable approach is probably a function of the greater difficulty (historically) in locating and then obtaining waivers from a group of bondholders.

Cross-Default; Cross-Acceleration

The cross-default clause in a credit agreement is one of the most misunderstood provisions; it is also one of the most powerful tools that the lenders have to avoid being disadvantaged as against other creditors. Certain key principles need to be kept in mind when analyzing cross-default clauses:

- *Why a cross-default?* When a borrower defaults on indebtedness owed to other creditors, lenders may have at least three separate concerns. First, the default may indicate that the borrower is having credit-related problems that may also affect the borrower's ability to repay the loans. Second, the borrower is at risk of the other indebtedness being accelerated. Acceleration might not only jeopardize its ability to repay the lenders, but also subject it to other remedial actions, such as foreclosure on collateral (if the other creditors are secured) or a bankruptcy filing. Third, the borrower may enter into negotiations with the other creditors for a waiver or amendment that would eliminate the default or forestall the exercise of remedies. These negotiations could involve the restructuring of the other indebtedness by the borrower in a way that provides advantages to the other creditors over the lenders, such as the granting of collateral security, changing the average life of the other indebtedness, increasing compensation, or other concessions. As a result, the default in respect of other indebtedness may create intercreditor issues.

- *What indebtedness is crossed?* In most credit agreements, the cross-default will be triggered if debt or hedging and other derivative obligations under another agreement go into default. Sometimes the definition is narrower, covering only indebtedness for borrowed money. Frequently, a term such as *material indebtedness* is used, which will set forth thresholds that the other debt must exceed to trigger the cross-default. The threshold for hedges and other derivatives is typically measured by reference to the amount payable by the borrower if the arrangement were terminated, rather than by reference to the amount overdue or to the notional amount, and is negotiated based upon the size of the borrower and the amount of other debt outstanding or permitted to be outstanding.

- *Meaning of cross-default and cross-acceleration:* The term *cross-default* is often used loosely to describe both cross-default and cross-acceleration clauses. *Cross-default* refers more accurately to a provision that allows the credit agreement to be accelerated whenever a default occurs in another instrument, *whether or not* the debt under that other instrument may be accelerated. *Cross-acceleration* refers to a provision that allows the credit agreement to be accelerated only when the other debt has actually been accelerated. Some agreements will contemplate a third, in-between category that is perhaps best described as *cross-accelerability* or *cross-event of default*; that is, a provision allowing the credit agreement to be accelerated when the other debt may be accelerated immediately without any further notice (other than mere demand) or lapse of time.

Using this terminology, the cross-default clause is more protective of the lenders than the cross-acceleration clause. However, from the perspective of the borrower, the cross-default may have the effect of wiping out grace periods, and thus prevent it from being able to cure a default or to work out a problem with other creditors. Thus, if the credit agreement and another debt instrument each have a cross-default clause, when a default (but not yet an event of default) occurs under one instrument, an event of default will immediately occur under the other. By reason of the cross-default in the first instrument, this means that an event of default will now exist there as well. Thus, the borrower suffers events of default under both agreements for a breach that was, under each, intended to have a grace period.

Conversely, a cross-acceleration is viewed by lenders as very weak. It arguably defeats the whole purpose of the clause, because it is triggered only when other creditors *actually* accelerate their indebtedness, rather than merely being entitled to do so. The cross-acceleration clause allows those other creditors to threaten and cajole and obtain additional favorable terms without according the lenders any matching bargaining power unless an acceleration actually takes place. Because indebtedness is rarely accelerated, this provides substantially less protection to lenders and is usually seen only in credit agreements for the most highly rated borrowers. It is also the approach taken in virtually all public debt indentures.

The cross–event of default clause may strike a middle ground between the two extremes of the cross-default clause and the cross-acceleration clause. By not triggering an event of default until all grace periods have run on the other debt instrument, it avoids the borrower's concern of losing its grace periods, and it avoids the lenders' losing leverage in a workout. The clause should, however, provide that clemency be available only for the original grace period in the other debt instrument and not for any extensions. In other words, once the original grace periods have run, a default should arise; "grace" should not include lengthy

periods of repeated deferrals designed precisely to keep the lenders away from the negotiating table.
- *Cross-payment defaults.* Because of their obvious importance, credit agreements frequently deal with payment defaults separately from other defaults. A typical clause, often called a *cross-payment default*, reads as follows:

> The Borrower or any of its subsidiaries shall fail to make any payment (whether of principal or interest and regardless of amount) in respect of any Material Indebtedness, when and as the same shall become due and payable.

The reference to "regardless of amount" in this language is intended to make clear that it is *not* the amount of the payment default, but rather the principal amount of the debt *in respect of which* the payment default occurs, that determines whether the cross-payment default is triggered. The seriousness of the default is best measured by the amount of indebtedness that can be accelerated rather than by the amount needed to effect a cure.

- *Mandatory prepayments.* A cross-default clause will often carve out secured debt that becomes due prematurely as a result of the permitted sale or transfer of property or assets securing that debt. This is intended to exclude normal mandatory prepayment events that do not reflect adversely on the borrower.

Insolvency

The insolvency default is generally phrased broadly to pick up not merely bankruptcy proceedings against the borrower, but a host of other insolvency-related events (liquidation, reorganization, the appointment of a custodian or receiver, and the like) that have an effect similar to that of a bankruptcy filing. If the borrower or any of its subsidiaries is a bank or an insurance company, the default will also be triggered by a receivership or conservatorship (the equivalent terms for those entities). The default is normally divided into three categories: those based on actions by the borrower (the voluntary default), those based on actions of third parties (the involuntary default), and those based upon an admission of insolvency by the borrower (the admissions default):

- *Voluntary.* The voluntary default will be triggered when the borrower commences a voluntary bankruptcy or insolvency proceeding (including applying for a custodian or receiver for its property). It will also be triggered if the borrower rolls over and plays dead when any of these actions are instituted by third parties. In most cases, the default will include the borrower's taking action (such as a board or shareholder meeting) to effect any of the listed items. Because all of these actions are voluntary, they constitute immediate events of default, and the borrower does not benefit from any grace period. As will be more fully discussed in the section "Remedies" later in this part, they also result in an automatic termination of commitments and automatic acceleration of the loans.
- *Involuntary.* The involuntary default normally encompasses all of the actions listed in the voluntary default, if instituted by a third party against the borrower or its property. Because these actions may be without merit, the borrower is allowed a grace period, typically 60 days, to have the action dismissed. If dismissal has not been obtained upon expiration of the grace period, the involuntary filing would ripen into an event of default. As with the voluntary default, if an involuntary default becomes an event of default, commitments will be automatically terminated and the loans will be automatically accelerated.
- *Admission.* The third category of insolvency default is triggered if the borrower "becomes unable, admits in writing its inability or fails generally to pay its debts as they become due." This language is an element of proof required for an involuntary bankruptcy proceeding to succeed, and so an admission of this type by a borrower may place it in immediate jeopardy of a bankruptcy case being commenced. Also, from a purely practical standpoint, if a borrower makes this type of admission, it is probable that payment and other defaults are imminent. It constitutes an immediate event of default, with no grace period, but will customarily not result in automatic termination of commitments or acceleration of loans.

Judgment Default

The litigation representation addresses whether any material suit or proceeding is pending against the borrower. The judgment default addresses what happens after the suit or proceeding has been lost and converted into a judgment. The default is triggered by an *unpaid* and *unappealed* judgment; the mere loss of a lawsuit and resulting obligation to pay monetary damages is not itself an event of default. There is typically a grace period of 30 or more days to allow the borrower to pay the judgment or to obtain a stay of enforcement by appealing. Failure to pay a judgment gives rise to concerns similar to those that arise when a cross-default occurs. It may indicate that the borrower is unable to meet its financial obligations and that the judgment creditor may be on the verge of exercising remedies such as obtaining and enforcing a judgment lien or instituting bankruptcy proceedings.

Like the cross-default, the judgment default also generally has a minimum dollar threshold. Because the credit considerations in this context are similar to those for the cross-default, it is quite common for the two thresholds to be the same. However, in the case of the judgment default the amount covered by insurance is sometimes excluded on the theory that the borrower will not actually need to go out-of-pocket in the event that the judgment ultimately must be paid. Judgment defaults that exclude portions covered by insurance may sometimes require that the insurer be creditworthy and have first accepted responsibility for the judgment.

ERISA Events

As discussed in the section "Pension and Welfare Plans" in Part 4, "Conditioning the Loan," to the extent that a company is obligated to pay retired employees a defined pension benefit, the company will be required under the Employee Retirement Income Security Act of 1974 (ERISA) to pay into a trust an amount sufficient to cover future benefit obligations. If a business fails to meet this obligation, the Pension Benefit Guaranty Corporation (PBGC) may be entitled to a statutory lien on the assets of the company. This lien would cover not just the borrower, but subsidiaries that are 80% or more owned. In addition, ERISA provides that, in certain circumstances, any funding deficiency of the plan can become immediately due and payable, rather than being paid over a period of years. Acceleration of the deficiency could result in a sudden, unanticipated burden on a company's resources.

The typical ERISA event of default is triggered if any of these events occurs *and* if the result would be material. Materiality is often measured by reference to a dollar threshold or to a percentage of the borrower's net worth (or some other balance sheet item). In other instances, materiality is determined by a more subjective standard, such as whether the event would result in a "material adverse effect." In this latter case, many credit agreements will allow the required lenders to determine whether the event can be expected to produce a "material adverse effect."

Environmental Events

An event of default tied to possible environmental liabilities will typically be inserted in agreements for a company engaged in manufacturing or processing. It is normally triggered upon the assertion of liabilities against the borrower under environmental laws, including fines, penalties, remediation costs, and damage claims by private persons, that could have a material adverse effect upon the borrower or its business. An obvious example would be an assertion that the borrower either owns a superfund site or has contributed hazardous materials to a superfund site. As noted in the section "Environmental Matters" in Part 4, "Conditioning the Loan," under federal superfund legislation, any past or present contributor of hazardous materials to a superfund site is jointly and severally liable for the entire cleanup cost.

In the typical credit agreement, the assertion of an environmental liability will not be an event of default unless it can be expected to have a material adverse impact on the borrower, taking into account the likelihood of the claim's being successful. Given the subjective nature of this test, some credit agreements will provide that the required lenders determine whether the materiality standard has been met, rather than leaving it to dispute between the parties.

Change of Control

As noted earlier, a change of control may be treated as either a prepayment event or an event of default. Probably more credit agreements treat a change of control as a default than treat it as a mandatory prepayment. For a more complete discussion of change of control, see the section "Change of Control" in Part 3, "Making the Borrower Repay the Loan."

Invalidity of Guarantees or Liens

If the loans either have been guaranteed by subsidiaries or other parties or are secured by liens on property of the borrower or guarantors, the credit agreement will frequently include an event of default triggered by the failure of the guarantees or liens to be enforceable. In the case of liens, the event of default may also be triggered by the lien's not being perfected or entitled to the agreed-upon priority. In some instances, the mere assertion by the borrower or a guarantor of any infirmity will result in an event of default.

With one exception, it is difficult to conceive how this event of default could be triggered in the absence of deliberate acts by the borrower or a guarantor. The exception would be a failure to perfect a lien. This could happen with particular items of property if the parties simply do not bother to take cumbersome additional steps (such as noting the lien on certificates of title for motor vehicles, or implementing control agreements with respect to the borrower's deposit accounts). Recognizing this, borrowers will sometimes request a carve out for collateral not having a material value in relation to their property as a whole. Sometimes also, borrowers will request a carve-out for a failure to perfect based upon actions by the administrative agent (such as its losing possessory collateral). The latter point is infrequently conceded, though, on the theory that it is the responsibility of *both* the borrower and the administrative agent to maintain perfection.

Foreign Borrowers

Loans made to a non-U.S. borrower or guaranteed by a non-U.S. guarantor carry greater political risk than comparable transactions with purely domestic companies. The risk is thought to be less if the borrower or guarantor is located in an OECD country. For borrowers located in emerging markets, lenders will be concerned with the possibility of (1) expropriation (the taking by a foreign government of property of the borrower or guarantor), (2) moratorium (the prohibition by a foreign government of local companies servicing external debt), (3) loss of any necessary local licenses or approvals (such as foreign exchange approvals) necessary to perform obligations under the credit agreement, and (4) the home country's inability to access the resources of the International Monetary Fund if foreign exchange reserves are depleted. Borrowers frequently argue that such events of default are unnecessary because, if the covered events are truly problematic, the lenders would be protected by their eventual manifestation as payment defaults. Lenders, on the other hand, consistent with their views on other events of default, wish to be able to take action at the earliest reasonable time to mitigate adverse consequences.

Specialized Events of Default

Credit agreements often include additional events of default that are specific to the borrower. For example, if a borrower is in a regulated industry (such as wireless telecommunications), it may be appropriate to include an event of default based upon the loss of a material portion of the governmental licenses necessary for its business. Similarly, if the borrower's success is dependent on one or more specific contracts remaining in effect, the credit agreement may contain an event of default triggered by the termination of any of those contracts or the default by one of the parties.

Material Adverse Change (MAC)

In rare cases, particularly in asset-based lending transactions or in cross-border loans, a credit agreement will include an event of default based upon a MAC. (See the section "The MAC Condition" in Part 4, "Conditioning the Loan," for a discussion of the meaning of material adverse change.) Domestic borrowers strenuously resist a MAC default. It is arguably inconsistent with the principle that the financial covenants test the performance of the borrower. It may cause the borrower's accountants to classify the loans as short-term. It may also produce an element of business uncertainty akin to the loans being payable on demand. If the borrower is located outside the United States, however, the MAC clause may supplement the specialized events of default for non-U.S. borrowers discussed in the section "Foreign Borrowers" earlier in this part and is more frequently seen.

REMEDIES

When an event of default occurs, the lenders may be entitled to exercise a range of remedies against the borrower under both the credit agreement and any related security agreements. We will discuss here the remedies available under the credit agreement; the rights of the lenders *vis-à-vis* collateral security are beyond the scope of this chapter.

Whether to exercise remedies upon the occurrence of an event of default is not always an easy determination. To begin with, before taking any action, the lenders should be absolutely certain that an event of default has in fact occurred, and that it is of sufficient materiality to justify the proposed remedies. Other considerations come into play as well. Accelerating loans, for example, rarely results in the loans being immediately repaid by the borrower; if it were that simple, the borrower would presumably have retired the loans before the default ever occurred. Acceleration can also have adverse effects on the borrower, the lenders, and other creditors. It typically results in an immediate filing by the borrower for protection under the Bankruptcy Code and is likely to result in significant legal and other costs. Bankruptcy may also shunt the borrower into a long period of uncertainty as the case progresses and will subject many nonordinary course decisions to cumbersome court approval. As a consequence, absent evidence of fraud or rank incompetence on the part of the borrower's management, it is almost always better for the parties to agree to an out-of-court restructuring of the loans.

The remedies afforded to the lenders under a typical credit agreement are discussed next, in ascending order of severity.

Stop Lending

As discussed in the section "Ongoing Conditions" in Part 4, "Conditioning the Loan," it is a condition to the making of any loan (or the issuance of any letter of credit) that no default or event of default exist. Any individual lender therefore has the right, absent waiver of the event of default, to refuse to make additional loans under the credit agreement; exercising this right is not dependent upon a determination by the required lenders to stop lending. Of course, once the default or event of default is cured or waived, assuming that all other conditions are satisfied, the lenders again become obligated to lend.

Terminate Commitments

Upon an event of default, the lenders may at their option terminate any outstanding commitments. This remedy is not typically exercisable by a lender alone, but is a right available only to the required lenders. In some credit agreements, the administrative agent will also be given the authority to terminate commitments on its own initiative (though only in the most extreme circumstances would an administrative agent want to do this without authorization from the required lenders). Most credit agreements will allow the lenders to terminate the commitments independent of accelerating the loans, thus affording a remedy short of a "nuclear option" to send a signal to the borrower. Most credit agreements will also provide that, if the event of default is based upon an insolvency, the commitments will automatically terminate without action by any party. See the following section, "Accelerate," for the rationale for this.

Accelerate

Upon an event of default, the lenders have the right to declare the loans due and payable. As with the termination of commitments, this right is almost never exercisable by an individual lender, but requires action by the required lenders. By way of contrast, bond indentures and private placements will frequently permit acceleration to be affected by a vote of less than a majority of the noteholders (25% is a figure that is often seen). In some credit agreements, the administrative agent will be permitted to accelerate the loans on its own (though, as with the termination of commitments, only in extreme circumstances would an administrative agent exercise this right). Granting this power to an administrative agent can nevertheless be important. Acceleration by the administrative agent is much speedier than acceleration by the required lenders, and thus can enable setoff rights to be quickly exercised or other protective actions rapidly taken.

Most credit agreements will provide that an event of default based upon the borrower's insolvency results in an automatic acceleration of all loans. This is intended to avoid the automatic stay under Section 362 of the Bankruptcy Code, which decrees that a filing of a voluntary or involuntary petition against a debtor results in an automatic injunction against anyone in the world taking action against the debtor. Among other things, the stay may bar sending a notice of acceleration or other demand to a borrower. By having the acceleration occur automatically, the theory goes, no violation of the stay occurs, because no notice or other action is being taken by the lenders. Whether lenders would be in any less advantageous position in a bankruptcy proceeding if their loans were not accelerated is questionable, but when the Bankruptcy Code was originally enacted, it was deemed important that lenders have an already-liquidated claim at the start of a proceeding. Another (arguably more persuasive) justification is that automatic acceleration allows a full claim to be made against a guarantor (assuming that the guarantor is not itself in bankruptcy). The typical guarantee will of course also include language to the effect that if acceleration is for any reason prohibited, a full claim may nevertheless be made on the guarantor. See the discussion in the section "Insolvency of Borrower" in Part 6, "Securing and Guaranteeing the Loan."

Sometimes lenders will ask that automatic acceleration be expanded beyond insolvency defaults to all events of default. This might seem superficially appealing. It would avoid any vote by the lenders or initiative by the administrative agent, and it might serve as an added incentive for the borrower's not breaching the credit agreement in the first place. However, such an approach would have the disadvantage of removing control from the lenders. The lenders would no longer have the option of ignoring a default (which they might choose to do, even though they decline to waive the default, because the default is not sufficiently serious). It might also trigger cross-default or cross-acceleration clauses contained in other debt instruments. Except in rare cases, credit agreements will as a consequence provide for automatic acceleration only in the context of insolvency.

Demand Cover for Letters of Credit

If there are letters of credit outstanding at the time that an event of default occurs, the lenders can demand that the borrower provide "cover" (cash collateral) for any future reimbursement obligations that will arise upon drawings under the letters of credit. Demanding cover overcomes the structural difficulty that a letter of credit may not be accelerated or repaid in the same sense that loans can be accelerated and repaid. Nothing is due to the issuer until a drawing is made by the beneficiary. See the discussion in the section "Cover for Letters of Credit" in Part 3, "Making the Borrower Repay the Loan." Therefore, to create an obligation that can become due and payable upon an event of default, credit agreements routinely provide that the lenders have the right to demand that cash collateral be posted by the borrower in an amount equal to the future reimbursement obligations that will be payable upon drawings under the letter of credit. If the borrower does not immediately post the cash, the lenders then have a claim to which they can apply the proceeds of any collateral or that they can demand be paid by the guarantors.

Institute Suit

If a borrower defaults in the payment of any amount under the credit agreement, the lenders can institute suit against the borrower to compel payment. Suit can be an alternative to accelerating the loans, and thus avoid the risk of precipitating a protective bankruptcy filing by the borrower (though once a judgment is issued and the lender starts taking action to collect money, a bankruptcy filing becomes more likely). Suing for a past-due payment is a remedy available to individual lenders; a credit agreement will not normally require that approval of the required lenders be obtained.

Demand Payment from Guarantors

To the extent that the credit agreement is guaranteed or secured by collateral provided by third parties, a payment default (or acceleration) will permit the lenders to demand payment of the guarantor or commence the exercise of lien remedies. Making a demand upon a guarantor is normally a right exercisable by each lender. Because liens are normally granted to the administrative agent (or a collateral agent), exercising remedies against collateral requires either the initiative of the administrative agent (or collateral agent) or the instruction of the required lenders; an individual lender would not normally have the right to start this process.

RESCISSION

The remedies clause of a credit agreement will sometimes give the required lenders the right to rescind an acceleration after it has occurred. This right will normally be subject to a number of conditions, including requirements that the borrower has cured the original event of default upon which the acceleration was based, there being no other intervening default or event of default, any default interest accrued on the accelerated principal during the period of acceleration having been paid, and (in some cases) the lenders not having commenced the exercise of judicial remedies. A rescission right is routinely included in bond indentures and private placements; it is rarely included in credit agreements.

WATERFALLS

The "waterfall" refers to the provision found in some credit agreements that specifies how monies are to be applied to obligations when the borrower pays an amount that is less than the full amount owing. Traditionally waterfalls were inserted only into mortgages, security agreements, and the like, but with the increase in credit agreements with multiple tranches, waterfalls have become more common. The typical structure provides for the fees and expenses of the administrative agent (or any collateral agent) to be paid before any other claims, for interest (and breakfunding payments) to be paid before principal, for term loans to be paid before revolving credit loans, and for revolving credit loans to be paid before cover for any outstanding letters of credit (except that during a default, the waterfall will require all principal and cover among all tranches of loans and letters of credit to be paid ratably).

SETOFF

A lender that has a monetary obligation to a borrower, such as a deposit liability or an obligation under a derivative contract, may be able to effect payment on the loan by canceling, on a dollar-for-dollar basis, the lender's obligation to the borrower against the borrower's loan obligation to the lender. The right to do this is referred to as the *right of setoff*.

The right of setoff arises under common law, as created by court decisions in each state. The key requirement is that the two obligations be "mutual." Among other things, this means that the two parties must be in the same legal capacity. There would, for example, be no mutuality in the case of an obligation of the borrower to a bank, on the one hand, and an obligation owed by the bank *in a fiduciary capacity*, on the other. In addition, common law restricts the right of setoff in a variety of ways; for example, common law setoff requires that both obligations be matured, and perhaps that they be in the same currency. There may be questions as to whether an obligation payable at one branch of an international bank may be set off against a loan booked at a different branch.

For these reasons, credit agreements generally include an express contractual right of setoff. Such a contractual right may validly extend setoff rights beyond the rights provided by common law (although it is not clear that a clause purporting to depart from the rule of mutuality would be given effect by a court).

Although lenders are customarily afforded the right of setoff, the borrower itself is normally denied setoff rights through a credit agreement clause requiring that all payments by the borrower be made "without deduction, setoff, or counterclaim."

In addition to common law and contractual rights of setoff, a lender may, in some jurisdictions, benefit from statutory setoff rights. Such a statute is Section 151 of the New York Debtor and Creditor Law, which creates a powerful right of setoff by a bank, and permits such setoff even after the bank is served with an attachment or garnishment order.

Exercise by a lender of its right of setoff in a syndicated credit agreement will typically trigger an obligation on its part to share the proceeds of the setoff with other lenders. See the discussion in the section "Sharing of Setoffs and Other Claims" in Part 8, "Keeping Peace among the Lenders."

Part 8: Keeping Peace Among the Lenders: Interlender, Voting, and Agency Issues

AGENCY PROVISIONS

Some Basic Principles

A syndicated credit agreement will, with rare exceptions, have an administrative agent. The role of the administrative agent is to interface between the borrower and the lenders, and among the lenders themselves. Thus, the administrative agent will receive financial and other reports from the borrower and ensure that they are made available to the lenders (typically by posting them on a website). It will take delivery of and forward notices. The administrative agent will also receive and disburse between the borrower and the lenders the proceeds of loans and payments of principal, interest, and fees.

Except for purposes of maintaining the loan register (see the discussion in the section "Loan Register" in Part 9, "Selling the Loan"), the administrative agent is the agent of the lenders and *not* of the borrower. Thus, the borrower has no right to instruct the administrative agent to take, or refrain from taking, any particular action. The administrative agent is also solely an agent—it is not a trustee or fiduciary for the lenders. The duties of the administrative agent should not be confused with the leadership role often assumed by the lead bank (though that is normally the same institution as the administrative agent). Recommendations made by the lead bank to a syndicate are just that: recommendations of the bank, not of the administrative agent. Stated another way, the job of the administrative agent is ministerial only. Although it may have the authority to take actions on its own initiative to accelerate the loans, to commence enforcement actions, or to realize on collateral, it would not normally be obligated under the credit agreement to undertake any of these (as would be the case with a trustee for a bond indenture).

Remembering these basic principles will help in understanding the agency provisions set forth in the typical credit agreement. For reference, the LSTA Model Credit Agreement Provisions include market-standard agency language.

Appointment

The lenders that are parties to the credit agreement will appoint an institution (as noted, this will normally be the lead bank) as the administrative agent. Any lender that joins the credit agreement at a later date by post-closing assignment will, through operation of the clause, also be appointing that institution as administrative agent. The appointment will be stated to be irrevocable, even though later provisions in the agency clause will allow the administrative agent to resign. The appointment is made irrevocable so that no lender in the future will question the administrative agent's continuing authority. The credit agreement will also explicitly state that the institution functioning as administrative agent has in its individual capacity all of the same rights as any other lender.

In most cases, if the credit agreement is secured, the administrative agent will hold the liens for the benefit of the lenders. In some cases, however, it may be useful for there to be a distinct collateral agent role (this might be the case if the collateral security is being granted by the borrower equally for the benefit of the lenders and a separate group of creditors). In those cases, all of the same rights and privileges set forth in the agency provisions will apply to the collateral agent as well.

No Fiduciary Duty; Exculpation

As noted earlier, an administrative agent is not a fiduciary for any lender. The agency provisions will normally state that the administrative agent is not required to do anything under the credit agreement unless other provisions of the agreement expressly require it to act. Furthermore, the agency provisions will free the administrative agent from any liability for action taken by it at the instruction of the appropriate group of lenders (either the required lenders or each lender).

The exculpation will also make clear that the administrative agent is not under any duty to ascertain whether or not the borrower is complying with the provisions of the credit agreement. Nor will the administrative agent be responsible for determining whether the representations are true, whether documents delivered at the closing are accurate, whether the credit agreement is enforceable and (in most agreements), nor whether any of the conditions have been satisfied.

The one limitation to the exculpation will cover instances in which the administrative agent is grossly negligent or commits willful misconduct. The argument for not requiring the administrative agent to be liable for mere negligence but rather only for gross (really bad) negligence is that a court or jury presented with an error as a result of a confused set of facts can too easily be persuaded that the administrative agent is somehow responsible. A similar fear underpins other uses of the "gross negligence and willful misconduct" standard in the credit agreement (see, for example, the discussion in the section "Borrower Indemnification; Consequential Damages" in Part 10, "Understanding the Boilerplate").

In the same vein, no lender will be entitled to rely upon the administrative agent in any respect for matters relating to the credit agreement. The customary approach is to affirm that each lender takes full responsibility for its own credit decisions with respect to the borrower and for obtaining such information as the lender deems appropriate in extending credit to the borrower and monitoring the loan. The administrative agent will not be under any duty to disclose any information relating to the borrower or any of its affiliates that it obtains in any capacity. The administrative agent will not be deemed to have notice of any default (even payment defaults) unless it has been delivered notice to such effect by the borrower or a lender. Some agency provisions will require that any such notice, to be effective against the administrative agent, be prominently identified as a "NOTICE OF DEFAULT."

Reliance

The administrative agent will be permitted to rely upon notices, certificates, and other documents that it believes to be genuine and sent by the proper, authorized person. The ability to so rely extends to oral communications as well as written communications. The administrative agent will be permitted to consult with counsel (which can include the borrower's counsel), and is typically exculpated from any action it takes in reliance upon advice from counsel. Most agency provisions will also allow the administrative agent to assume that a lender believes that conditions to the making of a loan have been satisfied unless the administrative agent has received notice to the contrary prior to making funds available to the borrower. See the further discussion on this topic in the section "The Clawback Clause" later in this part.

Delegation

Because the administrative agent may be required to act through its own agents (such as employees or, if collateral security is involved, local trustees or subagents), the agency provisions will make clear that the administrative agent may in fact carry out its responsibilities in this manner. Some agency provisions will also make explicit that the administrative agent shall not be liable for the actions or omissions of subagents so long as they were selected by the administrative agent in good faith.

Filing Proofs of Claim

Although the authority granted to administrative agents in standard agency provisions is certainly expansive enough to include filing proofs of claim on behalf of the syndicate, some credit agreements will include an express statement to this effect. From the standpoint of all parties (the borrower, the lenders, and the administrative agent), it is in any event preferable that the administrative agent file claims arising out of the credit agreement; it ensures accuracy, minimizes legal costs, and is normally insisted upon by bankrupt debtors. Even though it may be inadvisable for an individual lender to opt out of agent filing, the agency provisions will not normally require that all proofs of claim be submitted by the administrative agent. The Bankruptcy Court, though, may insist on this.

Successor Agents

One of the key concerns of an administrative agent is that it be able to exit its job as an administrative agent if it determines that this is appropriate. Standard agency provisions will, therefore, include a right of resignation, allowing the administrative agent to notify the borrower and the lenders that it no longer wishes to continue in this capacity. The resignation will typically be contingent upon a successor agent's having been appointed by the required lenders and having accepted the role as administrative agent. If no qualified institution is willing to serve as a successor, the administrative agent is given the authority to appoint a successor. This latter right may be more illusory than real for an agent that truly wants to resign. Simply having the right to appoint a successor does not mean that any successor that is willing to serve can be found. Credit agreements try to deal with this provision either by allowing the administrative agent to resign anyway and devolve its responsibilities upon the lenders individually (not always terribly practical) or by stipulating that the borrower pay whatever agency fee the market requires in order to find a willing successor.

Often borrowers will request that they be given approval rights over a successor administrative agent. Although superficially there is some logic to this, it is somewhat inconsistent with the concept that the administrative agent is an agent of the lenders and not of the borrower. Accordingly, most agency provisions (including the LSTA Model Credit Agreement Provisions) will require only consultation with the borrower. If a consent right is granted to the borrower, it will normally only apply so long as no default or event of default exists.

Removal rights (the ability of the required lenders at their option to remove an administrative agent) have largely disappeared in recent years as a result of resistance by administrative agents.

Syndication and Other Agents

It is of course typical for a larger syndicated credit agreement to have many agency roles in addition to that of administrative agent. These other agency roles (syndication agent, documentation agent, managing agent, and the like) are frequently identified on the cover page of the credit agreement, and, in some cases, the respective agents will sign the credit agreement in those capacities. Whether or not other agents execute the credit agreement, it has become customary in recent years that the agency provisions set out an express statement that none of these other agents has any duties or responsibilities under the credit agreement. It is a means of affirming that their role is for naming purposes only.

LENDER INDEMNIFICATION

The general rule in a credit agreement is that the borrower is obligated to indemnify the other parties against any loss, liability, or other cost. However, in the case of the administrative agent and, if there is one, the issuer of letters of credit, it is customary also for the lenders to provide similar indemnification. In the case of a letter of credit, this indemnification will generally come only from the lenders participating in the letter of credit itself (i.e., solely the revolving credit lenders). The indemnification will typically be on the same terms as that provided by the borrower: it will not indemnify either the administrative agent or a letter of credit issuer for its gross negligence or willful misconduct.

VOTING

Basic Rule

The voting provisions of a credit agreement are superficially very simple. They mask, however, considerable market custom (and some law).

The basic rule is that the "majority" or "required" lenders must approve any modification, waiver, or supplement to any provision of the credit agreement. "Majority" or "required" will normally mean lenders holding more than 50% of the aggregate credit exposure (i.e., unused commitments and outstanding loans and letters of credit). In some agreements the percentage will be higher (66⅔% is typical), but this is generally resisted by borrowers, because obtaining consents to changes may become more difficult. Sometimes the credit agreement will break out particular issues and require a so-called supermajority vote for changes. Borrowing base issues are an example of this. In so-called club deals (a credit agreement with only a very small number of lenders), the definition of *required lenders* may include a concept that a minimum *number* of lenders, as well as a minimum *percentage* of loans, vote in favor of a change.

Multitranche Agreements

In a multitranche agreement, one issue that will be addressed is whether the lenders vote as a single pool, or whether each tranche votes separately. The nearly universal practice that has developed in recent years is that all lenders vote together as a pool. This approach can, however, pose a potential risk to revolving credit lenders. For example, if the term loan lenders constitute a majority of the pool, there is nothing to prevent them from agreeing to delete the material adverse change clause if that would remove from the revolving credit lenders a basis upon which to refuse to lend. The solution that addresses this in the typical credit agreement is a clause that requires a separate majority vote of a tranche if a change would adversely affect that tranche without equally affecting all other tranches. Other, more explicit, language seen in many agreements states that no tranche can be required to make loans as a result of an amendment without the consent of a majority of that tranche. In this case, the waiver is still effective to eliminate an event of default, but is not effective for purposes of the conditions precedent.

The "Affected Lender" Concept

Although the general rule in all agreements is that no modification, supplement, or waiver can be effective unless it is approved by the required lenders, the typical voting provision will go on to lay out some exceptions where the consent of additional lenders is required. Thus, for example, changes to money terms (interest rate, amortization, amount of commitments, and the like) also require the consent of any "Affected Lender." An "Affected Lender" does not mean each lender in the particular tranche, but only those lenders affected by the change in terms. Thus, an extension of a subset of revolving credit commitments can be affected through consent of the required lenders and those particular revolving credit lenders whose commitments are being extended. Lenders whose commitments are not being extended have no consent right (other than to participate in the required lender vote).

Other changes require the consent of *all* lenders. Examples include changes to the pro rata provisions of the credit agreement and certain changes to the voting provisions. Lastly, any modification that will affect the rights or obligations of the administrative agent (or of any swingline lender or letter of credit issuer) will require the consent of that party.

Collateral Security

Matters relating to collateral security and guarantees will usually be separately addressed in voting provisions. As to security, the most common approach requires the consent of each lender (except in the circumstances described in the next paragraph) to release all or substantially all of the collateral security or all or substantially all of the subsidiary guarantees. (See the previous discussion in the "Fundamental Changes" section of Part 5, "Monitoring the Loan," for the meaning of "all or substantially all.") Unanimous consent may also be required if the borrower wants the collateral to secure additional obligations, unless the additional obligations have a lower lien priority (in which case the general rule, that is, the consent of only the required lenders, would apply). Absent language to the contrary, "additional obligations" in this context will not normally include increased credit under the credit agreement itself (which will normally be allowed to be secured pari passu with other loans so long as the increased credit is otherwise permitted under the credit agreement, or consented to by the lenders).

Voting provisions will also address releases of collateral in the context of asset sales that are permitted under the dispositions covenant, or to which the appropriate lenders have consented. Most credit agreements will authorize the administrative agent (or the collateral agent, if there is one) to release collateral in this context without any separate consent from any lender. In other words, the fact that a sale is permitted under the fundamental changes covenant or has been consented to by the required lenders (or other percentage) is deemed to carry with it full authorization to the administrative agent to release on its own any liens on the assets to be sold.

PRO RATA TREATMENT

A general principle in virtually all credit agreements is that the lenders are treated on a "ratable" basis. Thus, lenders in a tranche make loans of that tranche "ratably" in accordance with their commitments. Similarly, principal and interest are paid and prepaid "ratably" in accordance with the outstanding amounts of the relevant tranche. Commitments are reduced, and commitment and facility fees are paid, "ratably" in accordance with the commitments of the particular tranche. Much of this is self-operative, because payments are almost always made directly to the administrative agent, and it is the administrative agent that keeps track of the status of outstanding commitments and that will remit funds paid by the borrower to the lenders. If a lender should in any circumstance receive more than its pro rata share of any payment, the provisions of the sharing clause discussed in the next section may be triggered.

SHARING OF SETOFFS AND OTHER CLAIMS

As noted in the preceding section, all payments to lenders of principal and interest of a particular tranche are to be made ratably within the tranche. An individual lender may nevertheless receive a payment without the other lenders receiving their ratable share. This could happen if a payment were made by the borrower directly to a lender (perhaps by mistake, or perhaps to prefer one lender over other lenders), if a lender exercises a right of setoff with respect to deposit accounts of the borrower maintained with a lender, or if a lender receives proceeds from an exercise of other remedies. The sharing clause is designed to ensure that the lender receiving the nonratable payment share the proceeds with the other lenders, either through the purchase of participations or through the acquisition of assignments from the other lenders, so that all lenders receive the benefits of the proceeds on a ratable basis.

The borrower will be required to consent that any lender that acquires a participation or other interest in this manner may in turn exercise a right of setoff with respect to the participation interest. This concept is sometimes referred to as the "black hole" provision. An illustration of the way it works may be useful. Assume that a lender has $1,000,000 in loans in a $5,000,000 syndicate (i.e., it has 20% of the total loans). Assume also that it holds $1,500,000 of deposits from the borrower. After exercising its right of setoff against the deposits and before purchasing participations from the other lenders, it will have $0 in loans and $500,000 of deposits. However, when it purchases participations from the other lenders so that everyone receives the benefit of the setoff ratably, it will have $800,000 of loans ($800,000 representing 20% of $4,000,000). Under the black hole clause, it will then be entitled to set off the remaining $500,000 of deposits, leaving it before the second round of participations with $300,000 in loans and $0 in deposits. Following the second round of participations, it would hold $700,000 of loans ($700,000 representing 20% of $3,500,000). In practice, if the black hole clause is ever employed, the various stages of setoff and purchases of participations would be affected in one single action, though they would be deemed to have occurred in separate stages as described here.

THE CLAWBACK CLAUSE

As noted in the section "Mechanics of Funding" in Part 1, "Making the Loan," in syndicated credit agreements, all funding passes through the administrative agent. The clawback clause addresses what happens if a lender does not provide its portion of a loan to the administrative agent, but the administrative agent nevertheless forwards to the borrower the full amount of the loan (including the portion that was to have been provided by the defaulting lender). The concern is an everyday issue because of the near impossibility of an administrative agent's ascertaining whether it has actually received funds from lenders before forwarding them on to a borrower. The funds transfer system does not operate in real time; in many cases it takes hours for a transfer to wend its way through the payments system, and then further hours before the administrative agent is able to confirm receipt. If administrative agents always waited until they knew with certainty that funds had arrived, most loans would not be made until either very late in the day (probably too late for the borrower to use them) or on the next business day.

Under the clawback clause, an administrative agent will be entitled to presume that a lender is remitting funds to the administrative agent, unless that lender has otherwise informed the administrative agent (customarily at least one business day prior to the date of the borrowing). If the lender fails to so inform the administrative agent and the administrative agent remits that lender's portion of the loan to the borrower, then the lender is unconditionally obligated to pay such funds immediately to the administrative agent. The clawback clause will also require the borrower to return those funds to the administrative agent on demand, although expressly reserving any rights that the borrower may have against the lender for having defaulted on its obligation to make the loan.

Most clawback clauses will also address the obverse situation; that is, what happens if the borrower is to make a payment to the lenders but does not in fact remit appropriate funds to the administrative agent. Again, because of delays in the payments system, the administrative agent probably will not know whether the borrower has in fact made payment. The clawback clause will allow the administrative agent to presume that, unless the borrower advises it otherwise, the borrower has remitted the appropriate amount to the administrative agent. Further, the lenders will be obligated to return to the administrative agent any funds that the lenders are sent without the administrative agent's having received monies from the borrower.

Note that in either of these cases the administrative agent is *not required* to remit funds to the borrower or to the lenders; sending on money to either is completely within its sole discretion. Sometimes lenders will push the administrative agent to agree that it will not remit funds to the borrower unless it can confirm that all conditions have been satisfied. Consistent with the discussion in the section "Ongoing Conditions" in Part 4, "Conditioning the Loan," administrative agents resist this (and, accordingly, it will not be written into the credit agreement) because it in effect places the administrative agent in the position of watching the credit for the benefit of the lenders. Such a responsibility would be inconsistent with the concept (discussed in the section "Agency Provisions" earlier in this part) that the administrative agent's duties are ministerial only and that each lender takes full responsibility for monitoring the borrower and the agreement.

In all cases, for each day that a lender or the borrower has failed to remit relevant funds to the administrative agent, the credit agreement will specify an appropriate interest rate to be payable to the administrative agent on the defaulted amount.

ACCESS TO THE LOAN REGISTER

Pursuant to the assignments clause of a credit agreement (discussed in detail in the section "Assignments" in Part 9, "Selling the Loan"), the administrative agent may be required to maintain a register of loans identifying the names and addresses of the lenders and the amounts of their respective commitments and loan balances. See the LSTA Model Credit Agreement Provisions for an example of this provision. Although there may be exceptions, most of these clauses (the LSTA provisions included) will provide that the administrative agent make the register available for inspection by the borrower and any lender (usually at "reasonable" times and upon "reasonable" notice). This can be an important right for both borrowers and lenders in workout situations, even though, as a practical matter (because loan participations will not be logged in the register), it will not be a complete list of all interested parties if participation interests have been sold.

Part 9: Selling the Loan: The Assignments Clause

DISTINGUISHING ASSIGNMENTS AND PARTICIPATIONS

Credit agreements will typically control both assignments and participations. Understanding the legal distinction between the two is important. *Assignments* create direct contractual rights between the borrower and the assignee. That means that if the borrower defaults in payment of the loan, the assignee can sue the borrower. If the assignment is of a revolving credit commitment and the assignee breaches its obligation to make a loan, the borrower can sue the assignee. The assignee becomes a "lender" under the credit agreement, with full voting and other rights. If a lender transfers a portion of its commitment to an assignee, the lender will be relieved of its obligation *vis-à-vis* the borrower with respect to the portion sold, and the purchaser will become obligated with respect to that portion.

A *participation* does not create direct contractual rights between the borrower and the participant. Rather, the participant's rights and obligations *vis-à-vis* the borrower are derivative of the rights and obligations of the seller of the participation. The participant will not become a "lender" under the credit agreement, will not have voting rights, and will not be obligated directly to the borrower to make loans. The seller of the participation will remain fully obligated to the borrower for the full amount of its commitment and will not be relieved of the portion of its commitment sold to the participant. The borrower has no right to sue the participant directly. The participant will be entitled to receive only its applicable proportion of monies paid to the seller of the participation by the borrower. If the participant wants to sue the borrower, it must do so by persuading the seller of the participation to institute suit.

Because of the greater rights of an assignee as compared to a participant, assignments are normally subject to borrower consent (discussed in more detail in later sections), while participations generally may be made without consent.

ASSIGNMENTS

Most contracts (credit agreements are no different) specify that the agreement is binding upon the "successors and assigns" of the parties. A "successor" arises when a party merges with another entity; the survivor will be the successor. An "assign" arises when a party sells or assigns its interest to a third party. Assignments are, technically speaking, assignments only of rights and not of obligations, though many agreements will refer to an "assignment" of obligations. What this language really means is that rights have been *assigned* to a new party and that obligations have been *assumed* by the new party.

Consent Rights

From the standpoint of a lender, the ability to assign or participate interests in loans under a credit agreement is essential to preserving its access to liquidity and manage its loan portfolio. Consequently, lenders will press for credit agreements to stipulate, subject to limited and negotiated exceptions, that the lenders are free to assign their rights and transfer their obligations under the credit agreement without the consent of any other party. The general rule will be subject to some exclusions that will dictate limited circumstances in which the borrower, the administrative agent, any swingline lender, and the issuer of letters of credit will have a consent right. Some general principles are that:

- The borrower will lose whatever consent rights it has after the occurrence of any (or certain specified) event of default.
- The borrower will have no consent rights if an assignment is to another lender or an affiliate (including, in the case of a fund, other commonly managed funds).
- The administrative agent, each issuer of letters of credit, and each swingline lender will have a consent right over any assignment of a revolving credit commitment.
- The administrative agent will have a consent right over any assignment of term loans.
- Each of these consent rights will be qualified by a requirement that the consent not be unreasonably withheld or delayed.

Sometimes the consent right granted to the issuer of letters of credit and swingline lenders is absolute (i.e., not subject to the requirement that the consent not be unreasonably withheld or delayed). The theory is that, because a letter of credit issuer or swingline lender is taking the direct credit risk of other lenders who participate in the issuer's or swingline lender's exposure, the issuer or swingline lender should not have to debate in front of a court whether a credit decision made by it with respect to the assignee was "unreasonable" or "delayed."

Although there is constant pressure from the market to remove borrowers' and administrative agents' consent rights, their removal may raise other legal issues. For example, borrowers and lenders both have an interest in loans continuing to be treated as a commercial debt relationship and not as securities under federal and state securities laws. Borrowers' and administrative agents' consent rights can, in this context, be a significant factor in determining whether loans are covered by the securities laws. See the discussion in the section "Are Loans Covered by the Securities Laws?" later in this part.

Eligible Assignees and Disqualified Lenders

Some credit agreements will introduce a concept of "eligible assignees"—entities that are not "eligible" may not (even during a default) acquire loans under the credit agreement without the consent of the borrower. The definition of what entities are "eligible" will normally include banks, financial institutions, and funds (and thus pick up all of the usual suspects that will want to hold loans, including B loans). Nevertheless, incorporating a definition of eligible assignee has become less frequent. The LSTA Model Credit Agreement Provisions, for example, leave who can become a lender to the determination of the borrower and the administrative agent, without defining an underlying class of entities that are permissible holders of loans and commitments.

Another approach is to define who is ineligible to hold any loan interest. Enter the "disqualified institution" or "disqualified lender" concept that is the preferred approach in the U.S. loan market. Among other benefits, the precision of blacklisting particularly controversial entities from holding its loans is helpful to a borrower but must be carefully balanced with the need to maintain liquidity in the loan market. Disqualified lenders will typically include a borrower's competitors and their affiliates as well as financial institutions that have been determined by the borrower to be sufficiently antagonistic for whatever reason (e.g., activist funds that have displayed a loan-to-own investment strategy).

The disqualified lender concept is a powerful tool for borrowers because even during a default the borrower's specified disfavored institutions are prohibited from owning its loans. The borrower does not have to rely on any express consent rights, which consent rights can fall away during a default, when it has the disqualified lender concept as its shield.

Minimums

The assignments clause will almost always specify some minimum amount for an assignment, typically $5,000,000 or more for revolving credit loans and A loans and $1,000,000 or more for B loans. One of the issues that arises is whether the $1,000,000 figure applies to each individual fund in a family of funds that may be buying into the credit agreement, or whether it applies to the family as a whole. The market standard appears to be moving toward lumping together family funds for purposes of determining whether the minimum has been met.

Transfer Fees

A credit agreement will normally provide for a transfer fee to be paid to the administrative agent upon the occasion of each assignment of a loan. Who pays the fee will be left to negotiation between the assignor and assignee and will be specified in the assignment agreement.

Loan Register

Under the typical assignments provision, the administrative agent will be required to maintain a register of loans identifying the name and address of each lender and the amounts of their respective commitments and loan balances. The credit agreement will normally state that the loan register is conclusive and thus is the definitive determinant of who must consent to modifications to the agreement and who are the required lenders.

Are Loans Covered by the Securities Laws?

As noted previously, borrowers and lenders both have an interest in loans continuing to be classified as obligations that arise in a commercial debt relationship, and not as securities under federal and state securities laws. For example, treating loans as "securities" could trigger higher capital requirements for investment banks and could also impose formalities that increase execution time without meaningfully improving the basis upon which a sound credit judgment is made. Ultimately, such treatment could blur the distinction between the loan syndication market and the bond market and thus remove flexibility from the credit system.

The Securities Act of 1933 and the Securities Exchange Act of 1934 define *security* in slightly different ways, although courts have interpreted the definitions similarly. The Securities Act of 1933 defines a security, in addition to stock, bonds, debentures, and a long list of other instruments, as including "a note." Superficially, the definition could be read to include loans under a typical credit agreement because the term *note* is read broadly to include any evidence of indebtedness (including, therefore, noteless loans).

The courts have developed a number of tests to determine whether "notes" are securities. The latest word, adopted in 1990 by the Supreme Court (in the *Reves* case), is the so-called family resemblance test. Under this test, a note is presumed to be a security unless it looks like a nonsecurity. More precisely, a note is presumed to be a security unless, examining it against the four factors described in the next paragraph, shows a "strong resemblance" to one of the types of nonsecurities on a list that has been judicially created over the years. The list of nonsecurities includes (1) a note with a maturity of less than nine months, (2) a note delivered in consumer financing, (3) a note secured by a mortgage on a home, (4) a short-term note secured by a lien on a small business or some of its assets, (5) a note evidencing a "character" loan to a bank customer, (6) a short-term note secured by an assignment of accounts receivable, (7) a note that simply formalizes open-account debt incurred in the ordinary course of business, and (8) a note evidencing a loan made by a commercial bank to finance current operations.

If a note that is not on the list of nonsecurities comes before a court, the court will look at four factors to determine if it is a security. *First* is the motivation for the parties to enter into the transaction. If the purpose of the issuer/borrower is to raise money for the general use of a business enterprise or to finance substantial investments, and if the purchaser/lender is primarily interested in the profit that the note will generate, the instrument is likely to be considered a security. If, however, the note advances a commercial or consumer purpose (such as facilitating the purchase and sale of a minor asset or to correct for the cash flow difficulties of the issuer/borrower), the note is probably not a security. *Second* is the plan of distribution. Is the note an instrument in which there is "common trading for speculation or investment"? *Third* is the reasonable expectations of the investing public. A court will consider instruments to be securities on the basis of public expectations, even when an economic analysis might suggest that the instrument is not a "security" in a particular transaction. *Fourth* is whether there is some element, such as the existence of another regulatory scheme, that significantly reduces the risk of the instrument, thereby rendering the application of the securities laws unnecessary.

In the context of a credit agreement, the second and third of these factors are most important (i.e., the plan of distribution and the expectations of the trading public). Helpfully, there are a number of provisions in a typical credit agreement that are not compatible with a plan of distribution for "common trading for speculation or investment." These include (1) reliance by the borrower on the credit and liquidity of the lender to make advances; (2) reliance by the administrative agent on indemnities and clawbacks from lenders; (3) lenders having the right to receive periodic information that goes beyond public information, including computations of covenant compliance; (4) lenders having visitation rights to obtain information; (5) lenders having the right (subject to confidentiality undertakings) to furnish nonpublic information to potential purchasers; (6) assignments being subject to administrative agent and, absent certain defaults, borrower consent; and (7) purchasers being required to be financial institutions or otherwise familiar with the credit judgments required in the commercial loan market. While not every commercial loan has all these provisions, most commercial loans have some combination of many of them.

As to the expectations of the investing public, credit agreements are quite different from private placements and bond indentures, where the issuers and the purchasers clearly expect and intend that the notes or bonds will be securities. Those instruments will typically use securities-like terminology. Most credit agreements, however, are carefully constructed to use loanlike terminology and avoid language such as "accredited investors," "qualified institutional buyers," "purchase without a view to distribution," and other securities law buzzwords. Use of the latter, by building in provisions designed to create securities law exemptions, could create the expectation that the agreement gives rise to securities in the first place. Accordingly, unless done very carefully, exemption wording can have an effect exactly opposite to the desires of the borrower and the lenders. For a more complete discussion of this topic please see Chapter 5.

PARTICIPATIONS

As noted previously, participations (unlike assignments) do not give the participant any direct rights against the borrower, nor do they give the borrower any direct rights against the participant. The seller of the participation remains fully obligated on its commitment (including the portion sold). As a consequence, participations can generally be sold without the consent of any party.

Because a participant does not become a "lender" under the credit agreement, it is not directly entitled to voting rights, nor will the borrower typically want the participant to have voting rights. A participant could, of course, easily circumvent this by contractually restricting the seller of the participation from consenting to amendments or waivers without authorization from the participant. Participation provisions of credit agreements will, as a consequence, commonly limit the ability of a participant to control the seller's voting rights to matters that would adversely affect money terms (such as reductions of interest or principal, maturity, and the like) or terms where changes require unanimous lender consent. These limitations may, however, be more of a mirage than real. Given the development of loan trading in today's market, sellers and buyers of participations are in continual contact on both the buy and sell side of trading activity. They will naturally consult upon modifications and, although a participant may not have a legal right to force its seller to vote in a particular way, as a practical matter the seller will give great weight to the views of its participant.

One frequent exception to the rule that participants do not have direct rights against the borrower is with respect to yield protection and taxes. In this instance, the typical participations clause will permit a participant to make claims directly against the borrower (usually capped by the amount of the claim that the seller could have made had the participation not been sold).

LOAN PLEDGES

Many lenders will want to have the flexibility to pledge loans to support their own funding needs. Banks may want to pledge loans to the Federal Reserve under Regulation A to obtain short-term or emergency credit, and B loan lenders may need to pledge the loans held by them to secure financing provided to the lender. A restriction on the assignment of loans could be construed as a restriction on a pledge of loans. Although the UCC as enacted in all 50 states should override any such restriction, the conventional assignments clause will still expressly allow a lender to pledge any loans held by it, with the qualification that no pledge will relieve the pledgor of any obligations under the credit agreement. One of the issues that these provisions leave open is what happens if the pledgee forecloses on the pledge and seeks to take title to the loan. In this instance, any necessary consents otherwise required in the assignments clause would arguably need to be obtained.

Part 10: Understanding the Boilerplate: All the Stuff at the End that No One Ever Reads

NOTICE PROVISIONS

The notice provisions set out the contact information for each party to the credit agreement, though, with respect to lenders, current practice is for the information to be specified in administrative questionnaires collected by the administrative agent during the syndication process or when a lender joins the credit agreement by assignment. Administrative questionnaires avoid the hassle of completing a notice schedule to be appended to the credit agreement in the last minutes prior to the closing.

Notification provisions routinely address the treatment of electronic communications such as email, Internet, or extranet-based communication and settlement platforms and the like. In recognition also that Internet and Web-based technology is changing continuously, most agreements do not lock in detailed procedures for electronic notification. The LSTA Model Credit Agreement Provisions, for example, contemplate that the administrative agent will independently prescribe procedures for the delivery of electronic communications, which it can change as technology and market practice develop.

NO DEEMED WAIVERS

One concern of lenders is that acquiescence in a breach by the borrower will, if continued, establish a course of conduct that might be viewed by the borrower or a court as an implied waiver. Lenders also fear that the act of making the loan might itself constitute a waiver if a borrower could charge them with knowledge of a breach at the time a loan is made (by, for example, asserting that the lenders are aware of facts that should lead to a recognition of the breach).

The "no deemed waivers" provision of the credit agreement attempts to address these issues by having the borrower agree at inception that no waivers will be deemed to arise in any circumstance unless they are expressly agreed in writing by the requisite lenders. Of course, there is no legal certainty that the provision will have the desired effect if it is ever presented to a court, so the closing date legal opinions will typically take a qualification for the clause. In addition, whenever lenders are aware of a breach that they are neither waiving nor using as a basis to exercise remedies, the borrower will often receive a "friendly" reminder from the administrative agent that acquiescence does not constitute waiver.

CUMULATIVE REMEDIES

The typical credit agreement will state expressly that the lenders are entitled to exercise remedies "cumulatively"—that if a medley of actions is available to the lenders, taking one action now does not preclude taking other actions later. Thus, setting off against deposit accounts immediately following acceleration should not preclude later suit or foreclosure; commencing suit against the borrower in New York does not preclude later suit against a guarantor in Canada.

Some states will not recognize a cumulative remedies provision. California's so-called One Form of Action Rule is an example. The One Form of Action Rule provides that, if a lender is secured by real property, it must foreclose on the property before or at the same time as bringing any other type of legal action to recover a debt. The rule also requires that any judicial action brought by a secured creditor to collect on its debt must include all real property security. If a lender does not include all real property in the action, any lien on nonincluded real property may be waived. The One Form of Action Rule may not be waived in advance of a default.

EXPENSES

The expenses provision will obligate the borrower to bear several different categories of costs. First, the borrower will agree to reimburse the administrative agent for costs incurred in connection with negotiating and closing the credit agreement or amendments. Second, in a secured deal, the borrower will agree to pick up costs, such as recording taxes, title insurance, and the like, that must be paid in order for the liens in favor of the lenders to be perfected and enforceable. Third, the borrower will undertake to pay costs and expenses associated with enforcement actions.

Credit agreements tend to be wordy on this latter point because of concern that the term *enforcement* has not been universally interpreted to include negotiations in connection with a workout or restructuring, or in connection with litigation over the expenses clause itself.

As to who is entitled to reimbursement in the context of enforcement, credit agreements take two approaches. Some credit agreements, in response to pressure from borrowers, permit only enforcement expenses of the administrative agent to be reimbursed; other agreements cover the expenses of any lender (the LSTA Model Credit Agreement Provisions take this approach). Regardless of the language in any particular credit agreement, there may be little practical difference between these two approaches. In the context of a workout, the borrower will invariably request a consent of some form, and thus the lenders will be free to insist that their legal costs be covered as a condition to granting their consent.

BORROWER INDEMNIFICATION: CONSEQUENTIAL DAMAGES

It is customary for lenders to obtain from the borrower a general indemnification against loss or liability suffered by the lenders in connection with the credit agreement. This indemnification is separate from the borrower's agreement (discussed in the section "Expenses" earlier in this part) to reimburse costs and expenses incurred directly in connection with the credit agreement. Reflecting the tendency of courts to construe indemnities narrowly, it will contain a long list of items for which the borrower is to indemnify the lenders: "losses, claims, damages, liabilities and related expenses" is the litany in the LSTA Model Credit Agreement Provisions. The indemnity will also expressly cover any of those items arising out of a claim by the borrower itself. The latter is intended to override a 1989 New York case (*Hooper*) that held that, unless an indemnification is explicit, it does not cover disputes between the parties to the contract itself, but covers only claims asserted by third parties.

Traditionally, credit agreements did not include a general indemnification from the borrower. However, when the practice of banks financing hostile acquisitions became widespread, and targets began suing lenders providing funds to the hostile bidder, indemnification clauses began to appear. No good idea goes unpunished, and the clauses soon became routine, to the point where their inclusion is now the market standard.

The borrower indemnity is deliberately broad and will cover not only the lenders, but affiliates of the lenders (such as securities affiliates that may have acted as arrangers of the credit facility) and their officers, directors, professional advisors, and others. The indemnity will also cover a broad range of events that might give rise to losses, including costs of investigations and litigation, regardless of origin. Normally, the clause will explicitly cover any environmental claims that might be asserted against the lenders in the event that they take over property from the borrower. However, it will typically exclude liability based upon "gross negligence" or "willful misconduct," as finally determined by a court of competent jurisdiction. Some borrowers may additionally seek to exclude liability for breach of contract by the lenders. The latter can be a sensitive point, because it is most likely to arise in a crisis situation, such as where the lenders refuse to honor a borrowing request because they believe that a "material adverse change" has occurred. The LSTA Model Credit Agreement Provisions provide that the indemnification is lost in this context only if there is a breach "in bad faith" by the indemnified party of its obligations under the credit agreement. Thus, if a lender determines that a MAC has occurred and a court later holds that it was wrong, the indemnity is not lost so long as the determination was made in good faith.

Because of concerns arising out of court cases involving "lender liability," it is common for an indemnity to state that the lenders shall have no liability for any "indirect, consequential or punitive damages." The words *indirect* and *consequential* are alternative ways of referring to damages that were not reasonably in the contemplation of the parties when the contract was made. For example, if the failure of a lender to make a loan results in the borrower's not being able to consummate an acquisition, consequential damages might be the resulting loss of future profits for the borrower from not owning the business it sought to acquire. Punitive damages are damages of unpredictable amount, beyond any actual damages, that are awarded by juries to punish what they see as a party's wrongful behavior. One New York court has said that punitive damages are appropriate only where necessary to deter parties from engaging in conduct that may be characterized as "gross" and "morally reprehensible" and of such "wanton dishonesty" as to imply a criminal indifference to civil obligations. It is difficult to see how such behavior could arise in the context of a credit agreement, or that a waiver of punitive damages could even be enforceable, but it is customary nevertheless to address the issue in credit agreements. The LSTA Model Credit Agreement Provisions take this approach.

GOVERNING LAW

A credit agreement—indeed, virtually every contract—will include a "choice of law" provision, by which the parties agree as to the jurisdiction whose law will be applied to determine the validity of the contract and its interpretation. The contractually chosen law will not govern such matters as the borrower's existence and its power to enter into the financing (which are matters that are governed by the law of its jurisdiction of organization). It will also not govern issues such as perfection or priority of security interests (here the relevant governing law is determined by statute). It will, however, determine which jurisdiction's contract law applies as well as various other matters, including such issues as applicable usury limitations.

A provision choosing the law governing a contract is different from a "submission to jurisdiction" clause (see the discussion in the next section). The latter relates to the possible locale for litigation, while the former relates to which state's substantive law will be applied in whatever locale is used. Courts are accustomed to applying the law of other jurisdictions where required.

As a general principle, the law chosen by the parties to govern a contract must, if it is to be applied, bear a reasonable relation to the transaction. What constitutes a "reasonable relation" is not well defined, but the choice of New York law in a financing where the loans will be disbursed, and payments made, in New York and where the administrative agent or lead lenders are in New York, probably satisfies the reasonable relation standard. However, for any transaction of $250,000 or more, a New York statute (Section 5–1401 of New York's General Obligations Law) allows the parties to choose New York law regardless of whether there is a reasonable relation to New York.

New York law is extensive, stable, and relatively "creditor-friendly," and this fact, coupled with the enactment of Section 5–1401 of the General Obligations Law, makes it a favored choice as the governing law of credit agreements. Nevertheless, some agreements may choose other jurisdictions. For example, transactions led and managed outside the United States are often governed by English law, for many of the same reasons that New York law is considered attractive. It is *not*, however, considered advisable in cross-border lending to provide that the credit agreement be governed by the law of the borrower's jurisdiction. Selecting the borrower's jurisdiction forces the lenders into the difficult position of having to understand how a different legal regime would construe the standard provisions of a credit agreement, and perhaps subject the lenders to increased risk of changes in the applicable substantive law. It may also be against many lenders' internal credit policies.

A typical choice of law clause provides that the agreement "shall be governed by and construed in accordance with the law of the State of New York." Sometimes the clause goes on to exclude "conflicts of law" rules out of concern that the chosen jurisdiction's choice of law rules may direct the court to a different law (e.g., the law of the borrower's jurisdiction). This is both unnecessary and undesirable. The better view is that the reference to "the law" of the chosen jurisdiction means that jurisdiction's *internal* law. Excluding conflicts of law principles could exclude the doctrine that the intentions of the parties should be given effect, not to mention (in the New York context) Section 5–1401 of New York's General Obligations Law. Some credit agreements adopt an alternative and better, though wordier, approach, excluding those conflict of law rules "that would otherwise direct application of the law of another jurisdiction."

ENFORCEMENT PROVISIONS

Submission to Jurisdiction; Process Agents

Lenders always prefer to enforce a credit agreement, should it come to that, in New York or some other "home" jurisdiction. Commencing litigation in the borrower's jurisdiction can entail incremental travel and other expenses, be less certain of a proper outcome, and of course eat up more lender officer time. This is particularly true when the borrower is organized outside of the United States, where additional factors come into play, such as the difficulty of communication with local counsel and the possibility that a local court would favor a local company and perhaps misconstrue New York law.

Court jurisdiction comes in two shapes and sizes: subject matter and personal. *Subject-matter jurisdiction* refers to the power of a particular court to hear a particular kind of case. *Personal jurisdiction* refers to the power of a court over a particular entity.

For the most part, subject-matter jurisdiction cannot be created by agreement among the parties, and thus a submission to jurisdiction clause will not to this extent be enforceable. Parties cannot by agreement, for example, force a tax or customs court to hear a landlord–tenant dispute. Parties to a credit agreement could not require the New York Family Court to pass judgment on an interest rate provision. The subject-matter jurisdiction of a federal court in the context of a commercial loan generally depends on the circumstance of "diversity of citizenship," a concept in the U.S. Constitution that requires that, in any litigation, the plaintiffs and defendants be from different jurisdictions (and that there not be "aliens" on both sides of the controversy). There are other sources of federal subject-matter jurisdiction, including where the borrower is a "foreign state" (see the discussion in the section "Waiver of Sovereign Immunity" later in this part) and where litigation involves a U.S. national bank or other entity organized under U.S. federal law (12 U.S.C. §632).

State courts (except for specialized courts, such as family courts, traffic courts, and landlord–tenant courts) have far fewer limitations on their subject-matter jurisdiction. As a result, even though a particular dispute cannot be heard in a federal court, it may nevertheless be heard in a state court. Thus, a dispute under a credit agreement where the borrower is a non-U.S. corporation and there are many foreign banks in the lending syndicate can nevertheless be heard in New York State courts even though there are "aliens" on both sides of the dispute. However, even state courts of general jurisdiction may have limitations. For example, a so-called door-closing statute in New York precludes an action in a New York State court by one non–New York entity against another unless, among other exceptions, the contract is performable in New York (loans payable in New York probably satisfy this requirement).

Personal jurisdiction, which as noted previously refers to the power of a court over a particular defendant, consists of two components, each of which can be established by contract. First, there must be a "basis" for jurisdiction; second, notice must have been given to the defendant. A basis for personal jurisdiction over a borrower may be created simply by having the borrower consent (or "submit") to the court's jurisdiction. Most credit agreements will, therefore, include a formal submission to jurisdiction by the borrower. The submission will customarily be "nonexclusive"; that is, the parties will not be forced to litigate in the selected jurisdiction, but will be free to commence suit before any other court having the proper subject-matter and personal jurisdiction. This preserves for the lenders the right to sue the borrower in its home jurisdiction.

Notice can be affected in any manner agreed to by the borrower. For a borrower in the United States, the typical approach is simply to have the borrower consent to being advised of a suit by mail delivered to its "address for notices" specified in the credit agreement. For non-U.S. borrowers, credit agreements usually adopt a more formal approach of having the borrower appoint an agent in New York to which notice can be given (referred to in legal jargon as *service of process*). The agent will then be defined as a *process agent*. This more formal approach for non-U.S. borrowers is designed to avoid a foreign court's refusing to enforce a New York judgment on the grounds that notice was inadequate.

Venue and Forum Non Conveniens

In addition to the concept of subject-matter jurisdiction, federal and state courts are typically also subject to "venue" requirements. Thus, although a federal court might have subject-matter jurisdiction to hear a suit, the venue statute might stipulate that only a court where one of the parties has a place of business may take on the suit. Venue requirements are generally waivable, and so it is customary in credit agreements for there to be a waiver of venue on the part of the borrower.

Even if a court has subject-matter jurisdiction and venue is proper (or has been waived), the court may still have the discretion not to hear a case if it thinks there is a more convenient forum for the suit. This is the so-called forum non conveniens doctrine. A court might thus force transfer of the case if that would be more convenient for the parties, taking into account such factors as the location of documents and witnesses, the place where relevant events occurred, and the like. It is customary to require the borrower to waive objection on forum non conveniens grounds, although the court is still free to transfer the case despite a waiver. A New York court, however, is precluded from granting a transfer (Section 327 of the New York Civil Practice Law and Rules) if the credit agreement provides for loans of $1,000,000 or more and contains both a choice of New York law and a submission to New York court jurisdiction.

Waiver of Sovereign Immunity

Sovereign immunity refers to the special status that a borrower has if it is a "foreign state" under the U.S. Foreign Sovereign Immunity Act of 1976, namely, immunity from court jurisdiction and immunity of its property from attachment or execution. Thus, a foreign state cannot be forced to appear in a U.S. court (federal or state) and cannot have its property in the United States seized to pay a judgment. The act permits sovereign immunity to be waived. Accordingly, credit agreements with foreign states almost universally have the borrower relinquish whatever rights it has under the act.

The term *foreign state* is defined broadly. It includes not only a foreign government, but any agency of a foreign government. It also sweeps in any entity that is majority-owned by a foreign country (if it is organized under the laws of that country). Because even a private company becomes entitled to sovereign immunity if a majority of its shares are acquired by its home country after the closing, sovereign immunity waivers are standard in all cross-border credit agreements, whether or not the borrower starts out governmental.

Waiver of Jury Trial

Unpredictable jury awards in "lender liability" cases have led lenders for many years to require borrowers to waive the right to trial by jury, so that any litigation will be before a presumably more sophisticated judge. The right is set out in the U.S. Constitution as well as in many state constitutions and statutes. Insofar as federal law is concerned, a waiver that is "knowing" will generally be enforceable. A waiver will almost certainly be knowing in the context of commercial credit agreements where the borrowers are sophisticated and represented by counsel. It is also more likely to be enforceable if the waiver is mutual, that is, if *both* the borrower and the lenders waive their right to a jury trial. The LSTA Model Credit Agreement Provisions adopt the mutuality approach. In a few states, a waiver of the state constitutional jury right may not be enforceable even if it is knowing and mutual (California is an example).

Judgment Currency

A judgment currency clause will be inserted either when the credit agreement provides for nondollar loans or when it provides for dollar loans and the borrower is located outside the United States. It addresses the problem of transporting a judgment rendered by a court in one country to a second country that has a different currency. An example might arise if a borrower that is organized and has all of its assets in Germany is obligated on a loan denominated in U.S. dollars made available in New York by a group of U.S. lenders. If a judgment for U.S. $1,000,000 is rendered against the borrower in New York, the lenders will probably need to present the New York judgment to a German court and request that it order the borrower to pay. A German court, however, will probably render its own judgment in euro in an amount equal to the equivalent of U.S. $1,000,000. Between the time that the German court issues a judgment and the borrower actually pays the stipulated euro, the value of the euro may fall, and thus when the lenders convert those euro into U.S. dollars, they may end up short. The judgment currency clause allows the lenders to go back to the New York court and request a new judgment in the amount of the shortfall, which could then be similarly enforced in Germany against the borrower.

As of this writing, no court in New York has yet upheld the concept (as contemplated in the judgment currency clause) that a lender can go back to court to obtain a supplemental judgment if currency fluctuations render the initial judgment amount insufficient. Accordingly, legal opinions delivered at closing will normally include an exception as to the enforceability of the clause.

SEVERABILITY; COUNTERPARTS; INTEGRATION; CAPTIONS

Severability

Some court decisions have ruled that, if the illegality of one provision "destroys" an agreement, the whole agreement will be nullified. If, however, the illegality does not destroy the agreement, the illegal provision can be severed and the balance of the agreement enforced. This concern can be particularly acute in cases where the borrower is located in a jurisdiction other than the governing law of the agreement. Would, for example, an entire New York law credit agreement fail because, say, the indemnification clause might be unenforceable in Arizona? Severability clauses are thus inserted into agreements as an expression of intent that the parties do not want the normal rule described above to apply.

Counterparts

The counterparts clause is one of those provisions that is frequently overlooked, but that has great practical significance. It permits a credit agreement to be executed by each party signing a different copy, or an individual signature page, and then assembling all of the respective copies or signature pages into one, single agreement. This practice is quite different from the method used in many foreign jurisdictions, where a contract, to be enforceable, must include the signatures of all parties on a single document that is executed at a single time.

Integration

The integration clause will stipulate that the credit agreement reflects the entire understanding between the parties and that it supersedes all prior agreements (including commitment or engagement letters or any "side letters," and including also oral understandings) executed between the parties. Frequently fee letters will be excluded, since not all fees are incorporated into the credit agreement. The LSTA Model Credit Agreement Provisions take this approach.

Superseding oral conversations can be particularly important. For example, when a deal goes sour, a borrower might allege that there were prior understandings as to whether and when remedies might be invoked. A borrower may even want to bring a lender liability claim against the lenders for breach of alleged prior conversations. The integration clause can be a shield against the borrower's raising these types of arguments.

Captions

The table of contents and the section and paragraph headings of a credit agreement can be extraordinarily useful in moving around and finding relevant provisions in the document. However, because captions could potentially be used by a borrower to help a court misconstrue the meaning of the words of a credit agreement, the captions clause provides that captions and the table of contents are not to have interpretive effect and are inserted for "convenience of reference" only.

ELECTRONIC EXECUTION

Lawyers may worry whether receipt of a fax, photocopy, PDF by email, or other electronically delivered signature page of an agreement is sufficient for enforcement purposes against the party that submits the signature page. For more than a century, a legal doctrine, the so-called best evidence rule, has required that if a party wishes to enforce a contract, it must produce an original of the contract or the "best evidence" of the execution by all parties of the contract. Revisions to the best evidence rule in both New York and federal courts now treat a telecopy or photocopy as equivalent to the original, so this concern has largely disappeared. Nevertheless, a photocopy, PDF, or other electronically delivered signature page may still be challenged if genuine questions are raised as to the authenticity of the original.

Modern federal and state statutes now at least support standard market practice for the exchange of signature pages by fax and email. At the federal level, the United States enacted the Electronic Signatures in Global and National Commerce Act (the "E-Sign Act") which provides that a signature may not be objected to "solely because it is in electronic form." The E-Sign Act though expressly permits states to preempt the federal statute with alternative procedures and requirements that are nonetheless consistent with the federal act and that are "technologically neutral." For example, New York has adopted the Electronic Signatures and Records Act, and other states have enacted their own versions of the Uniform Electronic Transaction Act. As a consequence, essentially all states allow electronically delivered signature pages and provide that a signature, contract or other record may not be denied legal effect, validity or enforceability solely because it is in electronic form.

SURVIVAL

Under traditional legal doctrine, once a closing occurs the representations and warranties set forth in a contract lapse and cease to have any continuing force. The purpose of the survival clause is to overcome this traditional rule by providing that all representations survive throughout the entire term of the credit agreement. It is consistent with the principle underlying the no deemed waivers provision (see the section "No Deemed Waivers" earlier in this part) that simply because a lender may be aware of a breach when making a loan does not mean that the lender has waived the breach.

The survival clause will also explicitly state that indemnification and yield protection provisions will survive the repayment of the loans and termination of the credit agreement. Such survival is important, given that a lender will not necessarily know at the time of payoff whether it may suffer future claims or losses with respect to matters that the borrower has agreed to cover. The survival clause will not restore security or guarantees that the lenders have released, but it will at least preserve for the lenders a claim against the borrower for indemnification and the like that arise after payoff.

USA PATRIOT ACT

Shortly following the attacks of September 11, 2001, the United States enacted the so-called USA PATRIOT Act. The term abbreviates the rather meandering full title of the act: Uniting and Strengthening America by Providing Appropriate Tools Required to Intercept and Obstruct Terrorism Act of 2001. Under the act, the Treasury Department is required to prescribe regulations setting out procedures for financial institutions to verify the identity of customers, maintain records relating to customers, and consult lists of known or suspected terrorists or terrorist organizations to determine whether customers appear on the list. The regulations issued by the Treasury Department require that customers be advised that the financial institution will be collecting this information. The term *customer* does not include a public company or any existing customer of a bank, so notice is in fact not legally required in most cases. Nevertheless, for simplicity's sake it has become common for credit agreements to include a USA PATRIOT Act notice for all borrowers.

Part 11: The Borrower Can Have Rights, Too

THE RIGHT THAT LENDERS MAKE LOANS

As was discussed earlier (see the section "Several Liability" in Part 1, "Making the Loan"), when a group of lenders undertakes to make loans to a borrower, each lender is individually obligated, assuming all relevant conditions are satisfied, to extend credit up to the full amount of its commitment. These obligations are "several"; that is, the failure of one lender to make its loan does not relieve any other lender of its obligation.

Any lender that fails to make a loan requested by the borrower when all conditions precedent are satisfied will be in breach of its commitment under the credit agreement. The borrower may, as a consequence, suffer damages and may seek to recover those from the defaulting lender. Although the standard indemnification provisions in a credit agreement (see the discussion in the section "Borrower Indemnification; Consequential Damages" in Part 10, "Understanding the Boilerplate") will normally constrain the borrower's ability to assert consequential damages against the lenders for any breach, the borrower may still claim *actual* damages. In this context, actual damages might include the costs (higher interest, upfront fees, and other costs) of the borrower's procuring alternative financing.

In addition to any damage claims it may be exposed to, a defaulting lender will also be subject to so-called defaulting lender provisions of a credit agreement. Defaulting lender provisions of a credit agreement address what happens if a lender defaults in performing its obligations under the credit agreement. Any defaulting lender includes any lender that (1) has failed (after a grace period) to comply with its obligations to fund a loan or a swingline or letter of credit participation; (2) has become the subject of a bankruptcy or insolvency proceeding or has had a receiver, trustee, or similar entity appointed in respect of its assets; (3) given notice or made a public declaration that it will not comply with those obligations (either under said credit agreement or under another similar credit agreement to which it is party); (4) failed to confirm to the administrative agent or borrower (in response to a specific request) that it will comply with those obligations; or (5) has a parent company in respect of which any of the foregoing events have occurred. The consequences of being tagged a defaulting lender (which determination is most often the purview of the administrative agent) include disenfranchisement from lender votes, forfeiture of fees and risking replacement under the "yank-a-bank" provisions described below.

THE RIGHT THAT LENDERS MITIGATE COSTS

Credit agreements will normally require that any lender requesting compensation under the increased costs or taxes clauses use "reasonable" efforts to book loans at a different branch or transfer loans to an affiliate if either action would reduce or eliminate these costs. The purpose, of course, is to minimize what costs are passed on to the borrower. The obligation to use "reasonable efforts" typically provides that any action taken not be "otherwise disadvantageous" to the lender. This is intended, among other things, to override any requirement that the lender book a loan in a particular jurisdiction if that would violate an internal lender policy. Some lenders, for example, have a policy that all LIBOR loans be booked in offshore offices and thus would not want to move those loans to a domestic office.

THE "YANK-A-BANK" PROVISION

If mitigation by a lender (as described in the preceding section) is not feasible, the so-called yank-a-bank provision (usually captioned "replacement lenders") will permit a borrower to replace a lender that requests reimbursement for increased costs or taxes. As normally written, the borrower will be responsible for finding a replacement lender and also for paying any associated transfer fees; the new lender will take an assignment of loans and commitments from the lender being replaced. Typically, replacement must result in a reduction of costs that the borrower would otherwise be required to pay. The replaced lender will be entitled to the full amount of its principal, interest, and any related breakfunding costs or fees (or, if applicable, premium).

Sometimes the yank-a-bank provision will allow a borrower to replace a defaulting lender, as noted above, as well as any lender that has declined to consent to a proposed amendment. With a yank-a-bank provision, if an amendment needs unanimous approval, no small group of lenders will be in a position to extract a higher amendment fee or other concession, because the borrower could always replace those lenders with more compliant institutions. It used to be that, in some cases, the aggregate percentage of the lenders that may be so replaced was limited (5% was frequently seen), but the market has moved to greater flexibility and there is typically no express cap on the percentage of lenders that can be replaced.

While historically lender replacement was allowed only for issues that required unanimous consent, it is now common to see the yank-a-bank provision apply to consents that require affected lenders as well as those that require unanimous lender consent. In both cases of unanimous or affected lender votes, required majority lenders (or the required class lenders if applicable) must have provided their consents before the yank-a-bank right is triggered.

THE RIGHT THAT LENDERS ACT IN GOOD FAITH

It is a general principle of New York law that every contract contains an implied covenant of "good faith and fair dealing." No party to an agreement may do anything that will have the effect of destroying or injuring the right of the other parties "to receive the fruits of the contract." In the context of credit agreements, some worry that lenders might not be acting in good faith if they accelerate loans based upon a technical or nonmaterial default. Breach by a lender of the implied covenant of good faith could potentially expose a lender to liability to the borrower (or, at a minimum, make a court reluctant to allow a lender to exercise remedies).

THE RIGHT TO DESIGNATE ADDITIONAL BORROWERS

Credit agreements sometimes permit the borrower to designate subsidiaries as additional borrowers. This right is most often granted with respect to foreign subsidiaries, where for tax or other reasons the subsidiary needs direct access to funds. Typically, the obligations of the subsidiary borrowers will be guaranteed by the borrower; absent such a guarantee, any such designation would normally require an independent credit approval (and hence consent) by each affected lender.

CURE RIGHTS

As discussed in the section "Events of Default" in Part 7, "Enforcing the Loan," a breach of the credit agreement will constitute an event of default only so long as the breach continues. By way of example, if a borrower fails to pay an installment of principal and then 10 days later (before the lenders have accelerated the loans) pays the full amount that is past due, the event of default that originally arose upon failure to pay no longer continues, since it has been cured.

Certain types of breaches cannot be cured. If a borrower defaults on an interest coverage or leverage covenant at the end of a fiscal quarter, no cure is possible absent going back in time. However, a credit agreement that contains an equity cure right provision expressly allows a borrower to wipe out a financial covenant default after the fact, even though it is otherwise incurable.

How does an equity cure provision work? An equity cure provision grants a borrower and its equity owners a finite cure period (e.g., 10 to 15 days after a financial statement delivery due date, but cure periods are often negotiated) to cure the default by injecting a sufficient amount of additional cash equity capital or even subordinated debt that, after the proceeds are applied to repay debt or increase the amount of cash netting where applicable, can put the borrower back in compliance after recalculating the financial covenant after giving effect to the debt repayment or cash netting. Another approach for equity cure provisions allows the borrower to treat the infusion of capital dollar-for-dollar as additional EBITDA for the relevant test period. The "additional EBITDA" approach requires a smaller infusion of capital compared to the approach requiring debt repayment and therefore is favored by borrowers.

Lenders are barred from exercising remedies during the cure period. Because a continuing event of default does in fact exist, borrowers are also subject to consequences. Namely, borrowers are usually prohibited from drawing on revolving credit facilities under the credit agreement during the cure period and prior to a cure being effected.

Lenders are normally reluctant to agree to cure rights in a credit agreement because they disrupt the benchmarks that the covenants are designed to measure. Curing a financial covenant breach by allowing an infusion of equity or subordinated debt to reduce senior debt or bump up EBITDA may do nothing to solve the underlying problem of low earnings. Because an equity cure may represent a short-gap remedy, equity cure rights, if granted at all, are subject to additional limits. In addition to having a short finite cure period, the frequency and number of times equity cures may be exercised are often limited, for example, by not being exercisable in consecutive fiscal quarters or limiting the number of equity cures in any period of four fiscal quarters. Total caps on the number of equity cures that may be exercised overall during the life of the credit agreement are also common and typically capped at up to five in today's market syndicated credit agreements.

CONFIDENTIALITY

Confidentiality

Credit agreements require borrowers to deliver a substantial amount of financial and other sensitive information to lenders. Much of this may not be publicly available. Examples of such nonpublic information include projections, consolidating financial statements, product-line and divisional detail, and information delivered to the lenders in response to lender inquiries. Borrowers will want this information kept confidential. Disclosure could adversely affect their position with customers, competitors, and employees. For public companies, there is the added concern of the SEC's Regulation FD, which prohibits selective disclosure of material nonpublic information. Although revealing information to lenders without disclosing it publicly could be deemed "selective," Regulation FD contains an exemption for information delivered pursuant to a confidentiality agreement. The confidentiality provision serves that purpose.

The standard confidentiality provision customarily requires that the lenders and administrative agent maintain the confidentiality of all "information" (usually being a defined term) supplied by the borrower. Information will generally encompass any information that relates to the borrower or its business and that (although credit agreements are not uniform on this) is identified as confidential by the borrower at the time it is delivered to the lenders. Information that prior to the borrower's disclosure is already available to any lender or the administrative agent on a non-confidential or even public basis should not be deemed to constitute "information" and is often carved out of the definition.

There will, of course be exceptions that allow, among other things, disclosure to agents, accountants, and counsel; disclosure to other lenders and to prospective lenders (but only if they also agree to maintain the confidentiality of any information received by them); disclosure to regulators; disclosure to ratings agencies; disclosure in response to a proceeding or in connection with enforcement; and disclosure of information that becomes public other than through a breach by a lender.

The LSTA Model Credit Agreement Provisions set out a confidentiality clause that incorporates these basic principles.

Use Restrictions

Sometimes, as part of a confidentiality provision, borrowers will request that lenders agree to a so-called use restriction, that is, that information disclosed to lenders be used only "in connection with" the loans or the credit agreement. This can be problematic. Most banks have a single internal credit review function for all business dealings with a borrower, including loans, derivatives transactions, cash management services, letters of credit, deposit services, and the like. Revealing information to a credit officer in connection with a credit agreement will necessarily mean the information is being used for other purposes as well. In addition, lenders will use all information available to them in their overall portfolio management, arguably a use that is not "in connection with" a specific agreement. Thus, from the standpoint of the lenders, use restrictions are not terribly practical, and so they are rarely seen in credit agreements. To the extent that it is included at all, a use restriction may simply have the lenders affirm that they are aware of their responsibilities under applicable securities laws and will not use any information "in contravention of" the securities laws.

CONCLUSION

The discussion of the credit agreement set out in this Chapter 3 is intended to be solely an overview of the most common provisions found in a syndicated credit agreement governed by New York law. It does not encompass the tremendous variety of provisions that will be found in credit agreements since borrowers and arrangers each have an infinite capacity for creativity and negotiation. What is typical practice today will certainly evolve over time as new covenants are invented, new court decisions are rendered and new tax and other structures evolve. We hope, nevertheless, that the reader will find the discussion here useful as a resource when reviewing or drafting the next credit agreement that comes across his or her desk.

CHAPTER 4

The Seismic Transition: From LIBOR to a New Reference Rate

Meredith Coffey
Executive Vice President of Research and Co-Head, Public Policy
Loan Syndications and Trading Association

Tess Virmani
Associate General Counsel and Executive Vice President, Public Policy
Loan Syndications and Trading Association

For decades, the U.S. syndicated loan market largely used LIBOR, the London Interbank Offered Rate, as the reference rate on syndicated loans. Lenders and borrowers never really thought about what LIBOR was; it was simply the reference rate over which leveraged and investment-grade loans were priced. However, following allegations of manipulation during the Global Financial Crisis and a subsequent decline in interbank lending, LIBOR became a diminished and potentially unreliable reference rate. Finally, in 2017, the U.K.'s Financial Conduct Authority (FCA)—the de facto regulator of LIBOR—announced that it could no longer compel banks to make LIBOR submissions past the end of 2021. Thus began LIBOR's formal demise. LIBOR is scheduled to have ceased entirely for pound sterling, Swiss franc, euro, and Japanese yen by year-end 2021. For the U.S. dollar it will be a longer fade: U.S. banking regulators have said that LIBOR originations based on U.S. dollar LIBOR (USD LIBOR) must end by year-end 2021, but legacy USD LIBOR products have until mid-2023 to fully transition to a replacement rate. In this chapter, we discuss the transition process as it stood in Summer 2021, including the potential replacement rates for USD LIBOR and the documentation, systems, and convention implications those rates bring with them.

TRANSITION PROCESS

In July 2017, Andrew Bailey, the then-CEO of the FCA, announced that the FCA would not compel banks to make LIBOR submissions after year-end 2021. Because the banks generally disliked providing LIBOR submissions, it was widely expected that LIBOR rates would end shortly thereafter. Of course, the FCA announcement did not simply affect U.K. banks; at the time, there was an estimated $300 trillion of contracts globally—mostly in the form of derivatives—that referenced LIBOR in different currencies. It would be a mammoth undertaking to shift the world's markets away from LIBOR in a bit more than four years.

In the United States, that task fell to the Alternative Reference Rates Committee (ARRC). In 2014, the Federal Reserve Board convened the ARRC and tasked the group with identifying an alternative rate to USD LIBOR that was robust, compliant or aligned with the International Organization of Securities Commissions

(IOSCO) Principles,[1] and derived from a deep and liquid market. In 2017, the ARRC fulfilled this mandate by selecting the Secured Overnight Financing Rate (SOFR), a rate built on the deep overnight Treasury repurchase agreement market. However, this work had been undertaken primarily in conjunction with the derivatives market, not the cash markets. In 2018, the ARRC was reconstituted by the Federal Reserve Board and the New York Fed to represent derivatives *and* cash market participants and was tasked with an expanded mandate—to help ensure a successful transition from LIBOR to SOFR. In this reconstitution, the Loan Syndications and Trading Association (LSTA) joined the ARRC and became the co-chair of the ARRC's Business Loans Working Group (BLWG) and an active member of its Securitization Working Group (SWG). The BLWG immediately began to develop workable "fallback" language; that is, contractual language that explained the rate to which LIBOR loans would fall back once LIBOR ended. Simultaneously, the BLWG worked to (1) scope the differences between LIBOR and SOFR; (2) identify all the variants of SOFR, their characteristics and requirements; and (3) determine how the SOFR variants could be implemented in the loan market. Ultimately the LSTA, in both its BLWG co-chair role and its trade association role, concluded that instead of arbitrating the "right" replacement rate, it was critical to ensure that *all* replacement rate architectures could be implemented. This meant that all potential replacement rates had workable conventions, were operationalized (e.g., loan systems could consume them), and had practicable loan documentation. And it all needed to be done in a few short years.

LIBOR versus SOFR

To determine how changing reference rates would change the loan world, it was first imperative to understand the critical components of LIBOR. LIBOR offers two key characteristics for the loan market. First, it is a forward-looking term rate, meaning that it is quoted on a forward-looking basis for one-month and three-month periods.[2]

---

[1] The International Organization of Securities Commissions published "Principles for Financial Benchmarks" in July 2013, available at https://www.iosco.org/library/pubdocs/pdf/IOSCOPD415.pdf.

[2] LIBOR has many more tenor settings, but one-month and three-month are the settings most frequently used in syndicated loans.

Because LIBOR is known (and locked) two days before the interest period, at the start of the interest period the borrower knows what it will pay and the lender knows what it will receive at the end of the interest period. Because of this interest rate certainty, borrowers can easily forecast their cash flows. In addition, technology vendors built loan systems that generally used one rate that was input into the system at the beginning of the period and that calculated daily accruals based on that one initial rate. Likewise, technology vendors made similar assumptions when building software to administer collateralized loan obligations (CLOs). This "known-in-advance" aspect of LIBOR was a fundamental tenet upon which the loan and CLO markets were built.

The second critical characteristic of LIBOR is that it is an estimate of where banks would lend to each other in the interbank market. Thus, it takes into consideration banks' credit risk (i.e., it is a "credit-risky rate"), and it is considered to be banks' cost of funds. Because LIBOR contains bank credit risk, in periods of financial market uncertainty it tends to widen, and thus allows banks to continuously lend above their cost of funds.

SOFR, in contrast, is an overnight, nearly risk-free rate. SOFR is based on overnight transactions in the U.S. dollar Treasury repo market, the largest rates market—often with more than $1 trillion of transactions daily—at a given maturity in the world. Because the Treasury repo market is so large, it would be nearly impossible for a bank to manipulate it, as LIBOR allegedly was. However, although SOFR may be sturdy, it is very different from LIBOR, and thus molding it into a workable rate for loans was challenging. Because SOFR is a risk-free rate, a spread adjustment must be added to the rate to make it economically comparable to LIBOR. Adding a static spread adjustment to compensate for the lack of credit risk is a conceptually straightforward, if sometimes contentious, issue for legacy products. However, fixing the second difference—transforming an "overnight" SOFR rate into one that offers terms or tenors—proved to be far more challenging.

The ARRC ultimately determined that there were two main ways to build a one-month or three-month interest period from an overnight SOFR rate. First, a one-month or three-month tenor could be developed by averaging the daily rates either *before* the interest period (i.e., Daily SOFR in Advance) or *during* the interest period (i.e., Daily SOFR in Arrears). Alternatively, a forward-looking Term SOFR curve could be developed from SOFR futures trading (i.e., Term SOFR). The LSTA and the BLWG spent several years converting these potential replacement rates, along with credit-sensitive rates (CSRs), a latecomer, into rate architectures that could be operationalized and that could be reflected in loan documentation. See Exhibit 4.1 for an economic comparison of LIBOR, the Bloomberg Short-Term Bank Yield Index (BSBY; one of the CSRs), and two versions of SOFR.

EXHIBIT 4.1

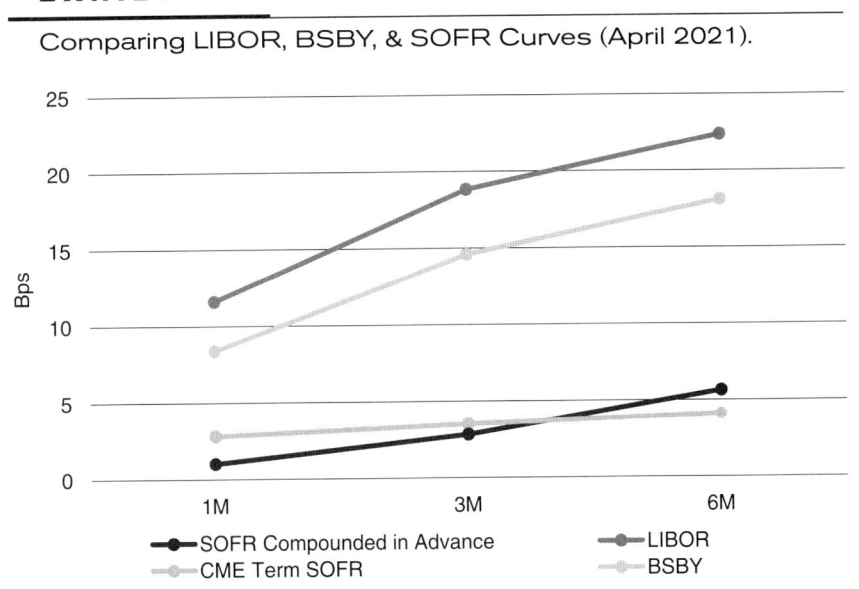

Comparing LIBOR, BSBY, & SOFR Curves (April 2021).

Source: St. Louis Fed, CME, Bloomberg.

RATE ARCHITECTURES

The LSTA and BLWG identified major characteristics of reference rates that would determine how borrowers and lenders would use the rates, and how loan systems would consume the rates (see Exhibit 4.2). These characteristics define a rate's *architecture*; the architecture, in turn, specifies how a rate would be implemented in loans. Reference rate characteristics include the following:

- *Is the replacement rate credit sensitive?* If a rate has a credit-sensitive component (like LIBOR), then there is no need to add a credit-sensitive spread adjustment or to adjust the loan margin to keep it consistent with all-in rates in preexisting LIBOR loans. CSRs are, by definition, credit sensitive.

EXHIBIT 4.2

Comparison of LIBOR and Potential USD Replacement Rates.

Rate/Characteristic	Known in Advance of Interest Period?	Significant Calculation Required?	Credit Sensitivity?	Strengths/ Weaknesses
LIBOR	Y	N	Y	Fragile; LIBOR loan origination ends at 12/31/21.
Credit Sensitive Rates	Y	N	Y	Nearly seamlessly substitute for LIBOR; may be less robust than SOFR; may be impacted by Money Market Reforms.
Forward Looking Term SOFR	Y	N	N	Easily substitutes for LIBOR in loan systems; official sector questioned whether it is as robust as daily SOFRs.
SOFR Compounded in Advance	Y	N	N	Robust and easily substitutes for LIBOR in loan systems; viewed as stale and arbitragable by loan borrowers.
Daily Simple SOFR	N	N	N	Robust and relatively easily hedged. Does not substitute easily for LIBOR in loan systems and conventions, but is more implementable than Daily Compounded SOFR.
Daily Compounded SOFR	N	Y	N	Robust, very hedgeable. Challenging substitute for LIBOR in loan systems and conventions.

Source: LSTA.

- *Is the replacement rate known in advance of the interest period?* If the rate is known in advance of the interest period, then the loan conventions and the operationalization and documentation of the rate would be straightforward and would behave much like LIBOR. The known-in-advance replacement rates are Term SOFR, SOFR Compounded in Advance, and most CSRs.
- *Is the replacement rate captured daily (and thus not known in advance),*[3] *but does not require calculations to be built on top of the daily rate?* Although there are no complicated calculations on these rates to introduce complexities into loan systems, nonetheless their "daily" aspect requires

---

[3] Loans use a daily rate to calculate daily interest accruals. In contrast, some other floating-rate instruments are able to use SOFR averages published near/at the end of the interest period to more easily calculate that period's interest amount.

loan conventions, systems, and documentation to change materially. Daily Simple SOFR is an example of this rate.
- *Is the replacement rate captured daily (and not known in advance), and also requires calculations to be built on top of the daily rate?* Because it is a daily rate *and* there are additional calculations, this type of rate requires loan systems, documentation, and conventions to change dramatically. Daily Compounded SOFR is an example of this rate.

STRENGTHS AND WEAKNESSES OF THE REPLACEMENT RATE ALTERNATIVES

Rates Known in Advance

The rates known in advance were by far the easiest to implement for the loan market. Because their architecture was very similar to LIBOR, there was little need to change loan systems or alter documentation or conventions. Borrowers could easily forecast their cash flows, lenders could easily accrue daily interest, loan documentation would be quite similar, and reconciliation processes would not change. However, as Exhibit 4.2 demonstrates, each of these potential replacement rates have weaknesses as well:

- *Term SOFR.* Because SOFR is an overnight rate, a Term SOFR would need to be built from SOFR futures trading, not from SOFR itself. Thus, the existence of Term SOFR was predicated on the existence of a deep and robust SOFR derivatives market. Some ARRC participants worried that if a Term SOFR developed too quickly or was used too widely, a daily SOFR derivatives market would not be robust enough to support a sturdy Term SOFR. For this reason, the ARRC was reluctant to recommend a Term SOFR too early in the development of replacement rates. However, by Summer 2021, the ARRC recognized that many business loans would need to use Term SOFR and subsequently included business loans in the scope of use of Term SOFR. Importantly, Term SOFR is a credit-risk-free rate, and therefore a spread adjustment would be necessary for loans that fall back to SOFR upon LIBOR's cessation. In addition, a spread adjustment might also need to be added to new SOFR loans or the interest margin on new SOFR loans might need to increase to maintain approximately the same economic profile between LIBOR loans and SOFR loans.

- *SOFR Compounded in Advance.* This rate can easily be calculated by compounding the rate for the previous period and then locking the rate at the beginning of the interest period and using that one rate the entirety of the interest period. As an example, a 90-day loan beginning on April 1st would use the 90-Day SOFR Average (published by the Federal Reserve Bank of New York) from January 1 through March 31. Because the rate is known in advance of the interest period, the rate would be operationalized and documented similarly to LIBOR. However, because the rate looks to the *previous* period, it does not reflect the current period's interest rate; thus, it can become stale in periods of changing interest rates, and banks have said it can introduce asset-liability management issues, particularly when used for longer interest periods. Like all the SOFRs, SOFR Compounded in Advance is a credit-risk-free rate, and therefore a spread adjustment would be necessary for loans that fall back to SOFR upon LIBOR's cessation. In addition, a spread adjustment might also need to be added to new SOFR loans or the interest margin on new SOFR loans might need to increase to maintain approximately the same economic profile between LIBOR loans and SOFR loans.

- *Credit-sensitive rates.* CSRs developed much later than the SOFR alternatives, and largely were created to address the concern that SOFR did not contain a bank credit risk element (whereas CSRs did) and/or the fear that a "Term SOFR" might not be recommended by the ARRC for loan products. CSRs typically use market instruments to estimate what banks must pay for funding. These underlying instruments generally included certificates of deposits, bank commercial paper, bank deposits, and bank bonds. As of May 2021, CSRs such as Bloomberg's BSBY, the ICE Benchmark Administration's (IBA) Bank Yield Index, IHS Markit's USD Credit Inclusive Term Rate, the American Financial Exchange's (AFX) Ameribor, and SOFR Academy's Across-the-Curve Credit Spread Index (AXI) were widely discussed in the loan market. CSRs generally are highly correlated with LIBOR because their underlying transactions are very similar to the market data that LIBOR panel banks consider when making their submissions. For this reason, CSRs substitute easily for LIBOR in loan systems and documentation; very little change is needed to implement the rates. However, they may be less robust than the SOFR rates, and the use of CSRs could lead to loans diverging from other asset classes that may be more likely to reference SOFR. CLOs, in particular, could face increased basis risk if liabilities were priced off of SOFR and assets were priced off of CSRs.

Daily Simple SOFR

Daily Simple SOFR relies on rates that are pulled from a screen and consumed every day; consequently, it is more operationally complex than known-in-advance rates and requires a new set of documentation and conventions. However, it is much less operationally complex than Daily Compounded SOFR. A strength of Daily Simple SOFR is that it does fit into a "Daily LIBOR" or "Daily Prime" architecture, and thus is not entirely unfamiliar to the loan market. It also is economically very similar to Daily Compounded SOFR, which means it can be effectively hedged using a standard "compounded in arrears" hedging agreement. However, because the rate is pulled daily, significantly more information needs to be consumed by already-overburdened loan systems. In addition, because the full rate is not known until near the end of the interest period, conventions must develop to communicate the full-period interest rate to the borrower with enough time that the borrower can pay interest when due. The ARRC recommended that business loans use a *lookback*, which effectively means that the rate observation period begins and ends a set amount of time before the beginning and end of the interest period itself. As an example, a SOFR loan might have a "five-business day lookback," which means that the interest observation period begins and ends five business days before the interest period itself. Thus, an interest period beginning on April 1st would use the SOFR rate from May 25th, the rate for April 2nd would be the SOFR rate for May 26th, and so on for the entire interest period. Although these complexities can be solved, they are not intuitive, and they need to be built into loan systems, documents, and norms. In addition, Daily Simple SOFR is a credit-risk-free rate, and therefore a spread adjustment would be necessary for loans that fall back to SOFR upon LIBOR's cessation. Finally, a spread adjustment might also need to be added to new SOFR loans or the interest margin on new SOFR loans might need to increase to maintain approximately the same economic profile between LIBOR loans and SOFR loans.

Daily Compounded SOFR

Daily Compounded SOFR is the most complex of the SOFR alternatives for loans. SOFR must be pulled daily, and then each day's SOFR rate is compounded on the previous day's cumulative compounded rate to ultimately calculate the interest for the interest period.[4] This process requires both a daily rate and a complex calculation atop the daily rate. The benefit of this approach is that it is very similar to what is being adopted for derivatives (which lead to nearly "perfect" hedges), floating rate notes, and sterling loans. However, it requires the changes enumerated above for Daily Simple SOFR *and* the compounding calculation is quite complex for a product that trades without accrued interest and that can be prepaid intraperiod. In addition, reconciliation of mistakes could be very difficult because a complex calculation must be unpicked to determine where mistakes were made. Because of these complexities, the ARRC ultimately recommended that, if Term SOFR did not exist, Daily Simple SOFR should be used in ARRC's hardwired LIBOR fallback language for business loans. In addition, Daily Compounded SOFR is a credit-risk-free rate, and therefore a spread adjustment would be necessary for loans that fall back to SOFR upon LIBOR's cessation. Finally, a spread adjustment might also need to be added to new SOFR loans or the interest margin on new SOFR loans might need to increase to maintain approximately the same economic profile between LIBOR loans and SOFR loans.

The architectures of the potential replacement rates defined how the conventions and systems would change. Although none of the rates were perfect replacements for LIBOR, the loan market had to prepare for all rates because it was not clear which one—or

---

[4] This description of Daily Compounded SOFR uses the Compound the Rate methodology. Compound the Balance is an alternative, simpler calculation, but was not broadly endorsed by the syndicated loan market.

ones—would be widely adopted. Of course, it was not simply a matter of developing conventions and systems. Loan documentation needed to evolve and, in some cases, change quite materially.

DRAFTING IN A POST-LIBOR WORLD[5]

As noted above, not all replacement rates are created equal, and the level of change in new documentation varies greatly across the replacement rate options. Understanding that the in-advance rates represented the most minimal, straightforward changes to existing credit agreements, the LSTA's focus first centered on the daily, in arrears rates: Daily Simple SOFR and Daily Compounded SOFR. Once the ARRC included business loans in the scope of use of Term SOFR, however, momentum swiftly shifted to Term SOFR. At the time that this chapter was going to print, focus was heavily on "in advance" rates, namely Term SOFR and the CSRs, and it seemed that more than one benchmark rate would replace USD LIBOR—for a short time or perhaps indefinitely.

IN ARREARS RATES

In many ways, these daily rate loans are akin to Alternate Base Rate (ABR)/Prime loans, which also accrue interest daily. (A principal difference being that ABR/Prime loans are rarely elected by borrowers!) In a Daily Simple SOFR loan, the SOFR rate published each day or the negotiated floor, if applicable, is applied daily to outstanding principal, and then those daily amounts are added together to calculate the interest payment for the period. A key difference between referencing LIBOR-/term-based benchmarks and referencing simple, daily interest is that the concept of an "Interest Period" is no longer relevant, because in a daily, in arrears loan the borrower does not lock in a rate for a set period. Moreover, because the loan accrues interest on a simple basis, it is economically irrelevant whether the payment period is of a one-month or three-month duration; it is simply a question of paying interest monthly or quarterly. Therefore, it is anticipated that these daily, in arrears loans would not permit the borrower to elect different "interest periods" as was permitted in LIBOR-referenced loans. Instead, a single payment period would

---

[5] This section highlights only the key credit agreement features of each of the loan types and is not intended as a comprehensive summary of those agreements.

be set forth in the credit agreement, which could provide for interest to be due on the same date as interest payments based upon ABR (i.e., scheduled payment dates) or due in regularly scheduled intervals (i.e., every one or three months) after borrowing. Importantly, because interest is accruing in arrears (or in real time) some convention is needed to build in a cushion between when the borrower knows the interest amount due and the interest payment date. To accomplish this, as described fully above, the ARRC recommended a business day lookback with no observation shift, and that lookback is set forth in the definition of Daily Simple SOFR.

Although most of the changes are to interest rate mechanics, certain other provisions are implicated as well. For instance, breakage indemnities, ubiquitous in LIBOR-referenced syndicated loans, may no longer make sense in a daily, in arrears loan. As this chapter was going to print, whether the borrower should be responsible for breakage costs is an open question. The genesis of break funding is linked to the assumption that drives many other LIBOR-related credit agreement provisions, which is that lenders historically match-funded, meaning that a lender would take a Eurodollar deposit for the same period and same rate as that for which they would make the LIBOR loan. If the borrower prepays, the lender would lose a portion of the interest cash stream but still be responsible for making the full interest payment on the deposit it took. To compensate lenders, the borrower is responsible for any shortfall that occurs from their intraperiod prepayment. Although it is not expected that lenders will match-fund their daily SOFR loans, they will of course incur a funding cost. At the time this chapter was going to print, where a break-funding provision was included, the drafting followed the approach of some LIBOR loans where the lenders certify the costs incurred by having to redeploy the repayment. The borrower is then responsible for those costs. It is too early to know whether breakage indemnities will be a common feature of daily SOFR loans. Relatedly, another difference is found in the market-disruption provision. Whereas, in LIBOR loans, lenders comprising Required Lenders are permitted to notify the Administrative Agent that LIBOR for a given interest period will not adequately and fairly reflect the lenders' cost and the borrower's ability to request, continue, or convert LIBOR loans is then suspended, such a provision may not be appropriate for daily SOFR loans. Lenders rarely, if ever, took advantage of this provision even in LIBOR loans and, given the departure from match-funding, in daily SOFR loans such a suspension may only occur if the Administrative Agent determines that Daily Simple SOFR cannot be determined.

Looking at Daily Compounded SOFR in arrears, many of the features described above are applicable; however, the calculation of the interest rate and the requirement of "interest periods" are unique to Daily Compounded SOFR loans. As described above, this interest convention uses the daily SOFR rates but apply those rates to a two-step compounding formula that is set forth in the credit agreement.[6] The complexity introduced by compounding per the formula also requires the use of "interest periods," the repayment of unpaid, accrued interest together with any principal payment, and that no prepayments are made on non–U.S. Government Securities business days (the relevant "business day" for SOFR loans). Like Daily Simple SOFR loans, it is expected that Daily Compounded SOFR loans would also follow a set interest payment schedule without the ability for the borrower to toggle between monthly and quarterly payment frequencies.

IN ADVANCE RATES

Unlike the changes to current LIBOR mechanics required by daily, in arrears rates (a few of which were discussed above), all three versions of in advance rates are largely "plug and play" with LIBOR-referenced credit agreements. This is perhaps self-evident for the CSRs, which are designed to be highly correlated to USD LIBOR, but it is also true for the SOFR-based in advance rates. One notable difference between the CSRs (and LIBOR) and the SOFR-based in advance rates is the tenor offerings. CME Group's Term SOFR, the term SOFR rate recommended by the ARRC, is published in one-month, three-month, and six-month tenors, with CME having indicated it would look to offer a 12-month tenor in the future. SOFR Compounded in Advance which utilizes the Federal Reserve Bank of New York's published SOFR Averages, is available in 30-day, 90-day, and 180-day tenors. However, in practice, there is little appetite to offer a 180-day SOFR Average loan because, as a backward-looking rate, staleness concerns are more acute.

---

[6] A detailed examination of that formula is outside of the scope of this chapter.

FUTURE-PROOFING FALLBACK LANGUAGE

If any lesson was learned by market participants during this marathon transition process it was that we do not want history to repeat itself. Therefore, much more focus is being paid to ensuring that there are robust fallback provisions in the event of benchmark unavailability or discontinuance. For CSRs, it is expected that the credit agreement will provide that after certain trigger events (e.g., a statement that the benchmark is or will cease), the replacement benchmark will be determined by the Administrative Agent in accordance with a predefined waterfall of rates—in fact the same or similar waterfall set forth in ARRC's recommended fallback language for LIBOR-referenced loans: (1) Term SOFR, (2) Daily Simple SOFR, and (3) a benchmark selected by the borrower and Administrative Agent subject to the objection of Required Lenders. For SOFR-based loans, it remains to be seen if Term SOFR-referenced credit agreements will also adopt a predetermined waterfall (i.e., Daily Simple SOFR, if determinable, otherwise a streamlined amendment process), or rather will only include the streamlined amendment process.

Likewise, the daily SOFR in arrears loans, although based on an incredibly robust benchmark, include the streamlined amendment process to select a replacement rate after a trigger event. It looks like the comprehensive amendment-style fallback language that has become so familiar to market participants over the last several years will be here to stay.

WINDING DOWN LEGACY LIBOR LOANS

The ability to originate new LIBOR-referenced loans generally ended in 2021. Therefore, an examination of the fallback language odyssey that the loan market had endured for years is no longer germane. Solely for legacy loans, the widely used tenors of USD LIBOR will continue as reference rates through the end of June 2023. It is expected that the vast majority of outstanding loans with no fallback language or amendment-style fallback language will be repaid, refinanced, or amended to adopt a replacement benchmark. However, 2021 has seen most new LIBOR-referenced loans include the ARRC's recommended fallback language, which "hardwires" a replacement rate and adjustment that is determined by the Administrative Agent in accordance with the waterfall described above together with the appropriate spread adjustment. A significant minority of institutional loans include an additional feature which allows for an opt-in to an alternative benchmark that is not set forth in the waterfall, which would be selected by the borrower and Administrative Agent subject to the objection of Required Lenders. Whether many of these hardwired loans remain outstanding over the next two years remains to be seen, however, if they do, they will potentially introduce a new dynamic into the then-existing syndicated loan market. If that market is largely referencing SOFR, these legacy loans will include set spread adjustments and those adjustments may differ from the market negotiated adjustments included in new SOFR loans. If that market is largely referencing CSRs, a pool of SOFR-based loans may also exist alongside for some time. Of course, it could also be that the loan market of 2023 has long learned to thrive in a multirate environment.

CONFUSION AT THE CONCLUSION?

As this chapter was going to print, lenders were attempting to figure out which (or whether a single) LIBOR replacement rate would likely be LIBOR's successor. Market participants had built the conventions, systems, and documentation to support all the rate architectures. In that process, many lenders and borrowers determined that they strongly wanted most loans to use a rate known in advance, because the costs of the Daily SOFRs—primarily in the form of operational risk—might not be worth the benefit of being *nearly* perfectly aligned with derivatives.

The known-in-advance rates included SOFR Compounded in Advance, Forward-Looking Term SOFR, and CSRs. Banks appeared reluctant to adopt SOFR Compounded in Advance for business loans because it looked backwards, and thus the observation period did not align with the interest period and gave borrowers an option to select out-of-date (but favorable) rates. As an example, in a period of rapid interest rate increases, a borrower could select 180-day SOFR Average, which would lock in the average SOFR rate for the previous six months, and which could be materially lower than the actual interest rate in the actual interest period. Although other products, such as mortgages and mortgage-backed securities, used SOFR Compounded in Advance, most loan market participants did not support SOFR Compounded in Advance for business loans for the reasons described above.

With SOFR Compounded in Advance largely spurned by banks, this left Term SOFR and CSRs as the known-in-advance alternatives. For several years, regional banks had argued that a CSR was important because they needed to lend over their cost of funds; meanwhile, most money center banks were largely indifferent to the credit-sensitivity argument, viewing the better liquidity that was expected to exist in SOFR as more important than credit sensitivity. However, in early 2021, banks became increasingly concerned that the ARRC might not recommend a Forward-Looking Term SOFR before the end of 2021—when LIBOR loan originations must end—and might actually publish restrictive use cases for Term SOFR. As that concern deepened, money center banks began considering CSRs more for the fact that they offered a known-in-advance rate than for their credit sensitivity. Ultimately, the ARRC determined that it could responsibly recommend a Term SOFR for cash products. As this chapter goes to print, it is not clear whether the loan market would ultimately settle on a CSR, a Term SOFR, or a combination of replacement rates. Of course, the reader—with the benefit of many more months of observation—likely knows which of the contending rates won the day.

CHAPTER 5
Loans Are Not Securities

Introduction
Elliot Ganz
General Counsel and Co-Head, Public Policy Group
Loan Syndications and Trading Association

Effects of the Legal Characterization of Loans Under the Securities Laws
James A. Florack
Partner
Davis Polk & Wardwell LLP

Michael P. Kaplan
Partner
Davis Polk & Wardwell LLP

Jeong M. Lee
Partner
Davis Polk & Wardwell LLP

Some Practical Implications of Treating Loans as Securities
Yoon-Young Lee
Partner
WilmerHale

Introduction

Elliot Ganz
Loan Syndications and Trading Association

This chapter focuses on one of the most fundamental principles underlying the syndicated loan market: loans are *not* securities and are *not* subject to federal and state securities laws. Why is this even an issue? Over the past 30 years, the loan market has morphed from a bank-only market to one whose primary class of lenders is institutions such as mutual funds, collateralized loan obligations (CLOs), insurance companies, and other fund managers. During this time, the loan market has also transformed to a much more liquid one, with trading volumes steadily rising over the years. Some observers suggest that the loan market has, in certain ways, taken on characteristics of the bond market, and others have raised the question of whether loans *should be* considered securities subject to state and federal securities laws. Although there are no reported cases in the United States that have ruled that loans are securities, the issue is currently being challenged again. Most important, the consequences of loans becoming securities would be profound. The first part of this chapter describes the main advantages of the current legal categorization of loans, identifies some of the changes that would need to be made if loans were considered securities subject to the laws applicable to securities, and provides practical suggestions for loan market participants if the legal climate changes. The second part of the chapter addresses some practical implications of treating loans as securities, such as how origination, trading, and settlement practices would be affected, and how such changes would impact the market, the "public–private" nature of the loan market, and regulations such as the Volcker Rule.

Effects of the Legal Characterization of Loans Under the Securities Laws

James A. Florack

Michael P. Kaplan

Jeong M. Lee
Davis Polk & Wardwell LLP

A foundational principle of practice in the U.S. syndicated loan market is that loans are not "securities" under federal or state securities laws, and that therefore the underwriting, syndication, and trading of loans are not regulated by such laws. This assumption sustains a trillion-dollar market in syndicated loans and, although it has recently been challenged, there has been no reported judicial decision to the contrary.[1] What are the main advantages of the current legal categorization of loans? What changes would need to be made to the underwriting, syndication, and trading practices of loan market participants if loans were considered securities subject to the laws applicable to securities? This article analyzes these questions and provides practical suggestions for loan market participants to consider if the legal climate changes.

LEGAL BACKGROUND

To appreciate the significance of loans not being characterized as securities for purposes of the securities laws, one must first have some appreciation of those laws and their application to capital market transactions involving the offer and sale of securities.

Regulation under the Federal Securities Laws

The public and private sale of "securities" is governed by the Securities Act of 1933 (as amended, the "'33 Act") and the Securities

---

[1] *See* Kirschner as Tr. Of Millennium Lender Claim Tr. v. JPMorgan Chase Bank, N.A., No. 17 CIV. 6334 (PGG) (S.D.N.Y. 2020) ("Plaintiff has cited no case in which a court has held that a syndicated term loan is a "security," and this Court has found no such case in its review of *Reves* and its progeny.").

Exchange Act of 1934 (as amended, the "'34 Act," and, together with the '33 Act, the "Acts"), together with, in each case, the rules and regulations thereunder. The Acts regulate the process by which securities may be issued and sold by *issuers, underwriters,* and *dealers* (as these terms are defined in the '33 Act) and subject each of them to the antifraud provisions of the '34 Act.

The '33 Act focuses on the initial distribution of securities by issuers and underwriters, not secondary trading (other than by underwriters), and its primary purpose is to ensure that investors are given full and fair disclosure about the issuer and the securities offered before making an investment decision. The '34 Act, on the other hand, provides protection to buyers and sellers in the secondary markets by requiring issuers to keep their information current through periodic reporting requirements and regulates the activities of various intermediaries, such as brokers and dealers.

As a general matter, the sale of a security by an issuer or an underwriter may be made only if the Securities and Exchange Commission (SEC) has declared a registration statement relating to the sale effective or if either the security itself or the transaction in which the security is being sold is exempt from the registration requirements. Exemption from registration does not, with limited exceptions, exempt the sale of a security from the relevant antifraud provisions of the '34 Act. The exemptions from registration that are most relevant to the discussion in this chapter are the Section 4(a)(2) private placement exemption and the safe harbor provided by Rule 144A.

Section 4(a)(2) Exemption

Section 4(a)(2) of the 1933 Act provides an exemption from the registration and other requirements of the 1933 Act for any issuance of securities by an issuer "not involving a public offering." Although the cases are varied, from the first Supreme Court case on the issue (*SEC v. Ralston Purina*), the key to the exemption has been whether the offering is made solely to those who are able to fend for themselves, and therefore do not need the protection that registration would afford to investors. In addition, buyers cannot purchase with a view to broad distribution. As a result, transactions relying solely on Section 4(a)(2) for an exemption from registration are generally limited to offerings to very large institutional investors. In these transactions (often referred to as "old-style" private placements), each purchaser enters into a contract directly with the issuer to acquire the securities.[2] If an investment bank is involved, it agrees only to use its best efforts to identify purchasers as a placement agent for the issuer and does not take any underwriting risk. The placement agent generally restricts contacts to customers with which the agent has a preexisting relationship, keeps records on the number of offerees contacted, and limits the number of offerees. Because of the sophistication and bargaining power of the potential purchasers, each purchaser undertakes its own due diligence of the issuer, and the only "disclosure" document may be a term sheet for the securities offered and, depending on the issuer, whatever information is publicly available.

Both the terms of the offering and the terms of the purchase agreement are the subject of significant negotiation among the issuer, its placement agent, and the potential purchasers. If the group of institutions is large, those making smaller purchases typically rely on the one or two largest purchasers to take the lead in negotiations. Counsel to the issuer is expected to deliver an opinion at closing that no registration of the offered securities is required under the Securities Act, but a Rule 10b-5 disclosure letter is rarely provided.

The purchasers in these old-style private placements generally expect to hold the securities they acquire for a substantial period of time. Because Section 4(a)(2) is a transaction exemption that exempts only the initial sale of securities by the issuer to the initial purchasers, these purchasers acquire what are commonly referred to as *restricted securities*. These purchasers then must establish a separate exemption for any resale of the securities, as long as the securities they hold remain restricted. Any resale that is not pursuant to an exemption could retroactively vitiate the exemption of the initial placement. One such exemption for resale is Section 4(a)(7), which was introduced under the Fixing America's Surface Transportation Act in 2015. Section 4(a)(7) allows for private resale of securities by persons other than the issuer if certain conditions are met, including that there shall not have been any general solicitation or general advertising or that the securities must have been outstanding for at least 90 days prior to resale. Although not as flexible as Rule 144A,

---

[2] Note that many investors in the syndicated loan market are constrained by tax or other considerations in their governing documents from directly originating loans and rely on arranger entities to streamline access to diligence and other borrower information and structure and negotiate terms so that the investors can participate through secondary market transactions.

as discussed below, the Section 4(a)(7) exemption could be used by investors to transfer securities on a private basis after the initial placement of securities pursuant to Section 4(a)(2).

Rule 144A Exemption

Rule 144A supplements the statutory private placement exemption with an exception for resales of restricted securities, and by doing so has created a highly liquid market for privately placed securities.

Rule 144A accommodates important variations from the old-style private placements just described. First, it permits investment banks to perform their customary underwriting function without requiring them to register the sale of securities. Second, the rule facilitates secondary trading of securities after the initial placement of securities to the syndicate by permitting resales to sophisticated institutional investors without limitations on time or volume. It is important to note that Rule 144A provides an exemption for the resale of the securities, not the original purchase from the issuer. Thus, in an underwritten offering of debt securities, investment banks rely on the Section 4(a)(2) exemption for the initial sale of the securities by the issuer to them, and rely on Rule 144A for their resale of the securities (as well as for resales by investors).

Rule 144A clarifies that an investment bank that acquired securities from an issuer in a private placement and resells those securities under Rule 144A will not be deemed a dealer under Section 4(a)(3) of the '33 Act or an underwriter under Section 2(11) of the '33 Act, thus permitting investment banks to perform the functional role of underwriter without causing them to become "underwriters" or "dealers," which would make their purchase of securities subject to the '33 Act. The rule also permits resales of securities, without limitation of time, to persons whom the seller reasonably believes are "qualified institutional buyers," so long as reasonable steps are taken to ensure that the potential purchasers are aware that the seller may rely on the rule for an exemption from registration.

Practice under Rule 144A

A Rule 144A offering typically involves (1) business and legal due diligence by the investment bank and its outside counsel, in order to enable counsel to provide a Rule 10b-5 disclosure letter; (2) preparation of an offering document (typically referred to as an offering memorandum or circular) with input from counsel and auditors; (3) preparation and negotiation of the underwriting papers (typically referred to as a purchase agreement) and related documents; and (4) negotiation with auditors and counsel regarding the contents of comfort letters and legal Rule 10b-5 disclosure letters. With respect to the contents of the offering document for a Rule 144A offering, although such an offering does not have to comply with the strict letter of the SEC's extensive requirements for a registration statement, the antifraud provisions of the federal securities laws, as well as the common law of fraud, apply to disclosures made in connection with the marketing of unregistered securities. As a result, Rule 144A offering documents tend to include (or incorporate by reference from the issuer's SEC filings, if eligible) disclosure that is substantially similar to what would have been required if the offering were registered under the '33 Act.[3]

Advantages of Loan Characterization

The fact that loans currently are not characterized as securities for purposes of the securities laws affords both borrowers and arrangers of syndicated loan facilities greater flexibility in accessing sources of debt capital. This flexibility results from two related legal considerations: first, the absence of any requirement either to go through the registration process with the SEC or to ensure that the transaction satisfies all technical requirements for an exemption from the registration requirements of the securities laws; and second, the absence of exposure to antifraud liability under the securities laws, which is discussed in more detail in the next section of this chapter. These legal considerations translate into important practical benefits: there is no need, either as a legal matter or as a matter of market practice, to create a prospectus or similar offering document that satisfies detailed SEC disclosure requirements, and there is no need for some of the traditional due diligence elements of a securities offering—accountants' comfort letters and lawyers' Rule 10b-5 disclosure letters—that can add both time and expense to the transaction and in certain cases make it impossible to consummate a securities offering within a particular time frame.

---

[3] At a minimum, Rule 144A requires availability of current basic financial information about the issuer upon request by an investor.

IF LOANS WERE SECURITIES

If loans were to be considered securities for purposes of the securities laws, the impact on syndicated loan market participants would be twofold. First, loan market participants would have to satisfy themselves that the origination, syndication, and trading of loans were effected in a manner that did not contravene the registration requirements of the '33 Act. Second, loan market participants would need to reassess their approach to disclosure and due diligence issues in light of the potentially greater risk of liability under the antifraud provisions of the securities laws. Finally, certain other regulatory regimes, including state securities laws and regulations by the Financial Industry Regulatory Authority (FINRA), would impose additional compliance burdens.

Compliance with Registration Requirements

Under current market practice, the initial underwriting and placement of a syndicated "term loan B" facility, considered apart from secondary trading, would probably qualify for an exemption from registration requirements under Section 4(a)(2) of the 1933 Act. The transaction does not involve a public offering because the purchasers of these syndicated loan facilities—including both the arrangers that may serve as initial purchasers and the syndicate of longer-term lenders—are very large and/or sophisticated investors. The range of institutions that invest in syndicated loans has broadened since the early days, when loan market participants were almost exclusively commercial banks, to entities such as CLOs and other institutional investors, but such institutions are nevertheless sophisticated investors of the type that can (and do) fend for themselves. These facilities, by their terms, generally restrict assignment of the loans, including by prohibiting assignments to natural persons and, with certain exceptions, requiring consent of the borrower, who, in turn, has an interest in ensuring that only sophisticated institutions hold its loans.[4] The problem with relying on Section 4(a)(2) by itself, however, is that the legal analysis of the initial purchase cannot be considered apart from secondary trading in the loans, which is an integral part of the syndicated loan

---

[4] See the assignment provision in the LSTA Form of Credit Agreement available at: https://www.lsta.org/content/form-of-credit-agreement.

market; as noted earlier, Section 4(a)(2) does not provide an exemption from registration requirements for resale of restricted securities (and indeed, resales can retroactively taint the exemption afforded for the initial purchase). Therefore, loan market participants would have to turn to Rule 144A or Rule 4(a)(7).

To establish the availability of the Rule 144A exemption, loan market participants would need to consider adoption of the following procedures:

- The participants would need to confirm that the issuer/borrower is eligible for the Rule 144A exemption. Investment companies are not eligible, and if an issuer is not a reporting company under the '34 Act or a foreign private issuer that voluntarily furnishes certain information to the SEC pursuant to Rule 12g3-2(b) under the '34 Act, the issuer must agree to provide certain current information to potential investors who request the information.[5]
- The participants would need to screen potential investors that would be solicited during the syndication process to ensure that all investors are qualified institutional buyers (QIBs) as defined in Rule 144A or that the participants reasonably believe such investors are QIBs. (In general, QIBs are institutions that have $100,000,000 or more invested in securities of unaffiliated issuers.) Reasonable belief may be established by certification from potential buyers, but the certification does not have to relate to a specific transaction. Reasonable belief may also be established through recent publicly available information about the prospective purchaser. Certain professional services publish lists of investors that have been identified as QIBs, and most investment banks have solicited certifications from their clients as to their status, on which they rely.
- The arranger should notify the potential syndicate members that the seller may be relying on the exemption from '33 Act registration requirements provided by Rule

---

[5] To ensure compliance with the informational requirement of Rule 144A, members could include in the bank book for any borrower that is not a reporting company three years of financial statements and a brief business description. The financial statements need not be audited (or include footnotes) to the extent that an audit is not reasonably available.

144A. The following language could be included in the bank book or other applicable marketing documentation and the definitive documentation for the loan:

The Borrower and the Arranger intend that the term loans should not and each lender hereby acknowledges and agrees that the term loans do not constitute "securities" for purposes of U.S. securities laws. If notwithstanding the foregoing the loans are deemed to be securities, potential lenders are hereby notified that the Borrower and the Arranger may be relying on the exemption from registration under the Securities Act provided by Rule 144A thereunder in connection with the loans.[6]

- The participants should ensure that the borrower makes a representation in the credit agreement that the execution and delivery of the credit agreement and the notes (if any are issued) do not violate applicable laws and that no consents are required in connection therewith. If members wish, they could add an explicit reference to the securities laws and Rule 144A in the representation. With respect to trading, the credit documentation could require that lenders certify in the assignment documentation that any assignment of a loan is done in compliance with applicable law.[7]

---

[6] This legend is drafted on the assumption that a change in the law in this area will be evolutionary; a case or two will decide on its facts that the loans in question are securities, with the consequence that loan market participants will as a matter of prudence alter their practices on the assumption that loans may be held to be securities without necessarily wishing to concede the issue if litigation later arises on a particular transaction. The decision in *Kirschner v. JPMorgan Chase* (S.D.N.Y. 2020), where the court ruled that the term loan B loans of Millennium Laboratories did not constitute securities, has reduced somewhat the risk that syndicated loans would be characterized by a court as securities subject to the registration requirements of the Securities Act.

[7] Technically, the arranger or initial purchaser of an initially valid Rule 144A placement does not need to police secondary market resales to maintain the validity of the initial placement, but it is customary in securities offerings to restrict further resales to QIBs. Similarly, an arranger of a syndicated loan facility who initially makes the loan and then assigns portions to other lenders would not necessarily need to restrict further resales to maintain any relevant private placement exemption for the initial transaction and resale. However, any subsequent lender that wishes to assign its loan (including the arranger if it intends to make a market in the loans) will need to make sure that its resales comply with applicable law. If the loans are deemed to be securities, then lenders would need to resell using Rule 144A, Rule 4(a)(7), or another exemption. This suggestion is a middle ground between ignoring resales altogether and adding securities-type transfer restrictions, which would appear unusual in a credit agreement.

- Finally, although Section 201(a) of the Jumpstart Our Business Startups Act removed the prohibition against "general solicitation" in offerings under Rule 144A, market practice is to avoid general solicitation. If this practice is to be followed, the parties involved—the borrower, the members arranging the syndicate, and the members acting as agents for the syndicate—should avoid talking publicly, including to the press, about the loans prior to the completion of syndication. Disclosure in a press release is also often limited to what is permitted under Rule 135c of the Securities Act (which permits a brief announcement of the transaction and the use of proceeds, without naming any arranger or agent bank).

Rule 4(a)(7) provides an alternative to Rule 144A to permit resales after an initial placement pursuant to Section 4(a)(2). However, one of the requirements of the Rule 4(a)(7) exemption is that the security has been outstanding for at least 90 days prior to the resale, and this requirement alone might make this an unattractive option for the loan market participants because they may have to hold loans for as long as 90 days prior to resale.[8]

Antifraud Liability Considerations

The more difficult question, and potentially the greater change in current market practice, concerns the approach to disclosure and due diligence issues if loans are held to be securities for purposes of the antifraud provisions of the securities laws.

Under the current legal regime, regardless of whether loans are securities, loan market participants are liable for common law fraud for material misrepresentations in connection with the syndication of loans. Although the specific elements of common law

---

[8] The Rule 4(a)(7) exemption requires that the following conditions are met: (1) each purchaser is an accredited investor as defined under Rule 501; (2) there is no general solicitation or general advertising; (3) the seller and a prospective purchaser are able to obtain from the issuer (borrower) certain basic information relating to the issuer; (4) the transaction is not by the issuer or a subsidiary of the issuer; (5) the seller or anyone who will be paid remuneration or a commission for the resale is not subject to an event that would disqualify the issuer under the bad actor rules under Rule 506(d)(1); (6) the issuer is engaged in business and not a blank check or shell company; (7) the securities are not part of an unsold allotment to a broker or dealer; and (8) the securities have been outstanding for at least 90 days prior to the date of the transaction.

fraud may vary among jurisdictions, generally, a plaintiff will need to establish that (1) the defendant made a material false representation; (2) the defendant knew that the representation was false, and made it with the intent to defraud (*scienter*); (3) the plaintiff reasonably and justifiably relied on the false representation; and (4) the plaintiff suffered damage as a result of such reliance. The exposure of a loan market participant arranging a syndicate (the arranger) to liability for material misstatements may be mitigated by representations from other loan market participants that they have done their own due diligence with respect to the borrower and are not relying on the arranger with respect to credit decisions, which have been upheld by some courts as evidence of lack of justifiable reliance.[9] However, courts have not always respected such representations and disclaimers. For example, when loan market participants do not have sufficient access to the borrower and its records to complete their own due diligence, or when the arranger has made independent oral representations to the loan market participants that are not specifically covered by the mitigating representations or disclaimers, courts have found that such mitigating representations or disclaimers are not sufficient to render the reliance of the loan market participants on the misstatements made by the arranger unjustified.[10]

If loans were considered securities, loan market participants would be subject to the antifraud provisions of Rule 10b-5 under the '34 Act, in addition to the common law fraud liability for material misrepresentations described previously. Rule 10b-5 generally prohibits the use of a materially misleading statement or omission in connection with the purchase or sale of a security. Courts have long recognized an implied private cause of action for violations of Rule 10b-5 and have imposed liability based on material misstatements and omissions in connection with purchases and sales of securities in contexts where a statutory remedy is not permitted under Sections 11 and 12 of the '33 Act (which impose liability for material misstatements or omissions in connection with registration

---

[9] *See, e.g.*, Banque Arabe et Internationale d'Investissement v. Maryland Nat'l Bank, 57 F.3d 146 (2d Cir. 1995); UniCredito Italiano SPA v. JPMorgan Chase Bank, 288 F. Supp. 2d 485 (S.D.N.Y. 2003); Purchase Partners, LLC v. Carver Fed. Sav. Bank, 914 F. Supp. 2d 480 (S.D.N.Y. 2012); Kirschner as Tr. Of Millennium Lender Claim Tr. v. JPMorgan Chase Bank, N.A., No. 17 CIV. 6334 (PGG) (S.D.N.Y. 2020).

[10] *See, e.g.*, Hitachi Credit America Corp. v. Signet Bank, 166 F.3d 614 (4th Cir. 1999).

statements and prospectuses in a registered offering). As civil liability under Rule 10b-5 is judicially inferred, courts have generally required the same elements as under common law fraud to establish liability. However, with respect to scienter, courts have relaxed the requirement, so that affirmative intent to deceive may not be necessary. Instead, reckless disregard for the truth or falsity of the statements in question may be sufficient, although a strong inference of fraudulent intent needs to be alleged. Moreover, in most jurisdictions common law fraud must be proven by "clear and convincing evidence" rather than by a "preponderance of the evidence," which is the standard for Rule 10b-5 liability.[11] Therefore, Rule 10b-5 violations may be easier to prove than common law fraud. In addition, the effectiveness of representations and disclaimers in syndicated loan documents to limit the liability of the arranger for misstatements in the common law fraud context previously discussed may be diminished or called into question by Section 29(a) of the '34 Act in the Rule 10b-5 context. Section 29(a) voids any "condition, stipulation or provision binding any person to waive compliance with any provision" of the '34 Act. Although some courts have held that nonreliance clauses do not violate Section 29(a), other courts have reached the opposite conclusion.[12] Although nonreliance clauses in agreements between sophisticated parties may be evidence of nonreliance, the nonreliance clause is but one factor to be considered in determining whether reliance is justified. Rule 10b-5 also contemplates civil liability in enforcement actions brought by the SEC or even, in extreme cases, criminal sanctions in cases brought by the U.S. Department of Justice, and the government need not prove reliance at all in bringing such suits. Therefore, in Rule 10b-5 cases, especially if brought by the government, the ability to rely on contractual representations and disclaimers to rebut claims of

---

[11] *See, e.g.,* Herman & MacLean v. Huddleston, 459 U.S. 375, 388-90 (1983).

[12] Compare *AES Corp. v. Dow Chemical Co.*, 325 F.3d 174 (3rd Cir. 2003) and *Rogen v. Ilikon Corp.*, 361 F.2d 260 (1st Cir. 1966) [use of nonreliance clause to bar fraud claims was inconsistent with Section 29(a)] with *Harsco Corp. v. Segui*, 91 F.3d 337 (2d Cir. 1996) [nonreliance clause did not run afoul of Section 29(a)]. See also, *In re Nat'l Century Fin. Enterprises, Inc., Inv. Litig.*, 541 F. Supp. 2d 986 (S.D. Ohio 2007) [nonreliance disclaimers did not preclude showing of reliance because other contradictory clauses stated that investors should only rely on information contained in the offering materials]; *San Diego Cty. Employees Ret. Ass'n v. Maounis*, 749 F. Supp. 2d 104 (S.D.N.Y. 2010) [use of nonreliance disclaimer combined with the fact that the investor was a sophisticated fund barred showing of reliance].

justifiable reliance would be even more limited than in common law fraud cases.

The central question, then, is whether, in light of the potential increase in liability exposure, the current practice with respect to offerings of debt securities under Rule 144A would be imported wholesale into the syndicated loan market, or whether instead the syndicated loan market would continue to follow a different and less rigorous path. The addition of an SEC-style disclosure document to the loan syndication process, coupled with due diligence backups in the form of auditors' comfort letters and outside counsel's disclosure letters, would represent a significant change from current market practice and would decrease flexibility and add transaction costs to the loan syndication process. Whether this will in fact happen is difficult to say, because it will ultimately reflect a judgment as to the degree of legal risk and the cost of mitigating that legal risk as opposed to compliance with any particular requirement of statute or regulation. As noted earlier, the Section 4(a)(2) private placement market has traditionally operated without these features. On the other hand, the dynamic of the loan market seems more analogous to the Rule 144A market, and it would be hazardous to predict that the prevailing practices in the latter would not ultimately be adopted in the former if loan market participants could no longer rely on the legal underpinning for the current difference in practice—the conclusion that loans are not securities.

Regulation under State Blue-Sky Laws and the FINRA Rules

If loans were considered securities, then, in addition to the regulation under the Securities Acts, they would be subject to other regulatory regimes applicable to offers and sales of securities, including state securities or blue-sky laws and the rules and regulations of FINRA.

Under the state securities, or blue-sky, laws, it is unlawful to offer or sell securities unless the securities are either registered or exempt from registration. As a general matter, there are self-executing exemptions (i.e., no filings are necessary) for (1) securities listed on U.S. stock exchanges (e.g., the New York Stock Exchange and Nasdaq) and securities that rank senior or equal to securities so listed (Section 18 of the '33 Act also preempts the blue-sky laws with respect to these securities) and (2) sales to certain classes of institutional purchasers ("institutional sale exemptions"). The institutional sale exemption of every state exempts offers and sales to banks, insurance companies, pension funds, and registered investment companies. However, there is no uniformity in the state securities laws with respect to exemptions for sales to other classes of institutions (e.g., large corporations, hedge funds, investment partnerships, and so on). Certain states also have limited offering exemptions, but some of these exemptions require a preoffer or presale filing. Therefore, securities (and correspondingly, loans if they were considered securities) of publicly listed companies would be exempt from state blue-sky laws. In addition, sales to traditional institutional purchasers of loans would probably fall within the institutional sale exemptions. In Rule 144A offerings, underwriters typically have internal procedures in place to ensure that securities are distributed in a manner that complies with the institutional sale exemptions. Loan market participants may consider adopting similar internal procedures in connection with loan syndications.

FINRA is a self-regulatory member organization of broker-dealers that is subject to oversight by the SEC. FINRA (1) proposes rules and regulations on how member firms conduct their business, including as underwriters and broker-dealers; (2) sets qualifications and administers testing for persons seeking to become registered representatives; (3) has the power to institute disciplinary proceedings against member firms and registered representatives; and (4) conducts arbitrations of disputes between member firms and their representatives and customers.[13]

In general, FINRA Rule 5110 requires a broker-dealer to file all SEC-registered and other public offerings of securities with the

---

[13] Note that the FINRA rules and regulations apply only to activities of registered broker-dealers, which are generally required to maintain FINRA membership. Even if loans were considered securities, trading of loans by regulated commercial banks as principal for their own account is unlikely to require registration of such banks as broker-dealers under the '34 Act, because even under the current regime trading of debt securities by a bank (or any other person) for its own account would generally not require registration as a dealer. In addition, there are exceptions to the definitions of *Broker* and *Dealer* with respect to purchases and sales by a bank of "identified banking products," which include loans, and loan participations that are sold to certain "qualified investors" or other investors that have access to material information and are capable of evaluating such information (based on their financial sophistication, net worth, and knowledge and experience in financial matters). Therefore, trading of loans (if they were considered securities) by banks is unlikely to be affected by the FINRA rules and regulations.

Corporate Financing Department and prohibits unfair or unreasonable underwriting or other terms or arrangements in connection therewith. FINRA Rule 5121 imposes restrictions on a broker-dealer's participation in an offering if it is deemed to be an affiliate of the issuer or is deemed to have a conflict of interest with respect to the issuer. However, securities exempt from registration with the SEC pursuant to Section 4(a)(1) or 4(a)(2) of the '33 Act are also exempt from FINRA Rules 5110 and 5121. Therefore, generally, loans, even if they were considered securities, would be exempt from FINRA Rules 5110 and 5121 to the extent that they fell within the Section 4(a)(1) or 4(a)(2) exemption (including through compliance with Rule 144A).

However, if loans were securities, various other FINRA and SEC rules would still apply to the conduct of broker-dealers in connection with their secondary trading even if the initial syndication of the loans fell within the Section 4(a)(1) or 4(a)(2) exemption. For example, Rule 10b-10 under the '34 Act and FINRA Rule 2232 require a broker-dealer to give its customer, at or prior to the completion of a transaction, a written confirmation that discloses (1) whether the broker-dealer is acting as an agent for such customer, as agent for some other person, as agent for both such customer and some other person, or as principal for its own account; and (2) if the broker-dealer is acting as agent for such customer, for some other person, or for both such customer and some other person, either the name of the person from whom the security is purchased or to whom it is sold or the fact that such information will be furnished upon request, and the amount of any remuneration received or to be received by the member in connection therewith. FINRA Rule 2111 prohibits a broker-dealer from making recommendations to a customer unless the broker-dealer has a "reasonable basis" to believe that a recommended transaction is suitable for the customer, based on information obtained through reasonable diligence, although this obligation is somewhat reduced with respect to certain institutional investors.

FINRA Rule 2121 (the "markup rule") provides that in over-the-counter transactions, a broker-dealer must sell or buy a security to or from its customers at a fair price, in the case of a principal transaction, or charge a fair commission, in the case of an agency transaction, taking into consideration all relevant circumstances, including market conditions with respect to such security at the time of the transaction, the expense involved, the fact that the broker-dealer is entitled to a profit in the case of a principal transaction, and the value of any service rendered by reason of the broker-dealer's experience and knowledge of such security and market in the case of an agency transaction. FINRA has adopted a general policy that markups in excess of 5% of the prevailing market price of a security are prohibited. However, each transaction must be examined based on its own facts and circumstances, and markups or commissions of 5% or less may still in certain circumstances be considered unfair. The relevant factors include (1) the type of security involved; (2) the availability of the security in the market; (3) the price of the security; (4) the amount of money involved in the transaction; (5) disclosure; (6) the pattern of markups; and (7) the nature of the broker-dealer's business. In the absence of other bona fide evidence of the prevailing market, a broker-dealer's own contemporaneous cost is the best indication of the prevailing market price of a security.

To the extent that loans are considered securities, a broker-dealer who trades loans in the over-the-counter market would therefore be required to comply with the markup rule. Generally, the broker-dealer should not charge a markup or commission of more than 5% over the prevailing market price in selling loans (or a markdown in the case of a purchase of loans), which would generally be deemed to be unfair. However, a broker-dealer must also consider each trade based on the factors listed previously in determining a fair markup (or markdown) or commission. For instance, thinly traded loans that require additional effort or cost to buy or sell may justify a higher markup than more actively traded loans. A loan with a high prevailing market price may require a lower markup, whereas a transaction involving a small loan principal amount may justify a higher markup. To the extent possible, the broker-dealer should look to its own contemporaneous cost for the type of loans being traded in determining the prevailing market price. Generally, in connection with sales of loans by a broker-dealer from its inventory, the broker-dealer should not consider its historical basis in such loans in determining the prevailing market price. If the broker-dealer is engaging in a "riskless" transaction (e.g., buying a loan in order to fill a previously received order to buy the same from a customer), the broker-dealer should ensure that the markups and/or markdowns charged in both transactions are reasonable in relation to each other.

Some Practical Implications of Treating Loans as Securities

Yoon-Young Lee
WilmerHale

THE ORIGINATION/SYNDICATION PROCESS

As detailed in the preceding article, if loans were to be considered securities, loan market participants would have to take steps to qualify the initial underwriting and placement of a syndicated loan under Section 4(a)(2) of the '33 Act and to make loans eligible for resales under the Rule 144A exemption. Although the universe of borrowers and eligible lenders would remain largely the same, the process would be more extensive and expensive because of the disclosures and due diligence that likely would be required. For example, obtaining auditors' comfort letters and opinions from counsel would impose additional costs and constraints on the borrower.

In addition, certain terms and arrangements that are common in syndicated loan documents are generally less common in bond indentures. For example, borrowers and lenders expect syndicated loans to be amended more frequently than bond indentures, and consents and waivers are routinely requested and obtained. Syndicated loan documents give borrowers the right to approve or reject the sale or assignment of a loan to a lender who is not already part of the lending syndicate. Accordingly, borrowers have wide latitude to reject prospective lenders who they believe may be unreasonable with respect to future consents and waivers. If loans trade in the secondary market in reliance on Rule 144A, which permits sales of securities to any person that the seller, or any person acting for the seller, reasonably believes to be a QIB, the borrower will likely lose the ability to control the composition of the lender group in the secondary market.

PUBLIC–PRIVATE NATURE OF THE PRIMARY AND SECONDARY LOAN MARKET

In the loan market, borrowers regularly provide lenders and prospective lenders with access, subject to a nondisclosure agreement

(NDA), to confidential financial and other corporate information (*Syndicate Information*) during the syndication process and through the life of the loan. Because Syndicate Information may at times contain material nonpublic information that would restrict a recipient from engaging in public securities transactions, the loan market has long operated under a public–private model. This model allows borrowers to share Syndicate Information on a confidential basis with its lenders, while allowing some lenders to avoid receiving information that could trigger restrictions on their securities trading activities. Loan market participants who elect to be public-side participants prefer to rely on their own research and analysis of publicly available information rather than signing an NDA and receiving confidential information that could restrict their activities. When trading with private-side participants who do have access to syndicate information, public-side participants typically provide their private-side counterparties with "big boy" letters acknowledging that there is a disparity of information, that the private-side participant may have material nonpublic information, but that the public-side participant is relying on its own due diligence and choosing to enter into the transaction.

This bifurcated model may not be tenable if syndicated loans are deemed to be securities. Because Section 29(a) of the '34 Act voids any "condition, stipulation, or provision binding any person to waive compliance with any provision of the federal securities laws," private-side loan market participants may no longer be comfortable relying on big boy language to protect them from Rule 10b-5 liability when trading with a public-side counterparty that does not have the same information that the private-side loan participant has. This change would disrupt both the primary and secondary loan markets. The loan market would likely become a public-only market, and borrowers who want to provide financial information to lenders on a confidential basis would have to seek financing from other markets, such as direct lending.

SECONDARY TRADING

If loans were considered securities, the trading of such loans would be subject to the federal securities laws, state securities laws, and the rules and regulations of FINRA. As discussed above, the application of these regulatory regimes has numerous implications for secondary loan trading, including with respect to confirmations and markups. Loan transactions would also be subject to rules regarding trade settlement, best execution, net capital, recordkeeping, and trade settlements.

Unlike securities transactions, secondary trades in loans often take 10 or more days to settle, and such extended settlements would implicate margin, net capital, and other rules. For example, Rule 15c6-1 requires T + 2 settlement for securities transactions, unless the parties agree on a trade-by-trade basis to extend the settlement period. Under Regulation T, a broker-dealer must receive full cash payment in a cash account within T + 4.[14] Loans in a cash account settled beyond T + 4 would likely be considered an extension of credit subject to margin regulation, and broker-dealers may have to take a charge against net capital as a result of delayed settlements if the client fails to post margin or fails to deliver within five business days. Delayed settlements may also trigger buy-in and closeout requirements under Rule 15c3-3.

VOLCKER RULE

Section 13 of the Bank Holding Company Act, also known as the Volcker Rule, and implementing regulations prohibit a banking entity from engaging in proprietary trading activities and certain activities involving covered funds.[15,16] The implementing regulations define *proprietary trading* to mean engaging as principal for the trading account of the banking entity in any purchase or sale of one or more financial instruments.[17] Although the implementing regulations make clear that a *financial instrument* does not include, among other things, a loan,[18] *loan* is defined to mean "any loan, lease, extension of credit, or secured or unsecured receivable *that is not a security* or derivative."[19]

If loans were deemed to be securities, banking entities would be required to treat syndicated loans as financial instruments subject to the Volcker Rule. A banking entity would need to analyze

---

[14] 12 C.F.R. § 220.2 (defining payment period as the standard settlement cycle under Rule 15c6-1 plus two days).
[15] A banking entity subject to the Volcker Rule generally includes an insured depository institution (IDI) and any affiliate or subsidiary of an IDI. 12 U.S.C. 1851(h)(1).
[16] See 12 U.S.C. 1851(a)(1); 12 CFR 248.
[17] 12 CFR 248.3(a).
[18] 12 CFR 248.3(c)(2).
[19] 12 CFR 248.2(t) (emphasis added).

whether its loan trading activities constitute prohibited proprietary trading activity and to incorporate its loan trading activities in its Volcker compliance program. Because CLOs would be "covered funds" under the Volcker Rule if syndicated loans were considered to be securities, CLO managers would have to review their indentures to determine if such loans are instruments that are eligible assets; amending indentures to permit holdings of loans would be time-consuming and cumbersome.

CHAPTER 6
Loan Structures

Second Lien Loans

    Marc Hanrahan
    Partner
    Milbank LLP

    Benjamin Miles
    Partner
    Milbank LLP

    Michael Price
    Partner
    Milbank LLP

    Benjamin Sayagh
    Partner
    Milbank LLP

    Charles Stern
    Partner
    Milbank LLP

Role of Commercial Banks in Project Finance

    Paul Forrester
    Partner
    Mayer Brown LLP

    Monique Mulcare
    Counsel
    Mayer Brown LLP

Second Lien Loans

Marc Hanrahan
Milbank LLP

Benjamin Miles
Milbank LLP

Michael Price
Milbank LLP

Benjamin Sayagh
Milbank LLP

Charles Stern
Milbank LLP

Loans are structured to reflect the negotiated interests of the two primary constituencies in any loan origination: (1) the borrower of the loan (and often its shareholders, particularly where the borrower is controlled by a private equity sponsor) and (2) the entity or entities providing the loan. The second constituency in syndicated loan transactions will be the loan arrangers as well as the institutional investors to which the arrangers will syndicate the loan; in direct lending transactions, it will be the direct lenders and debt funds providing the loan.

There are three broad categories of leveraged loan facilities:

1. *Pro rata loan facilities* consist of revolving credit facilities and amortizing term loan facilities.
2. *Institutional loan facilities* consist of institutional term loans.
3. *Direct lending facilities* consist of debt financing provided directly to the borrower by certain debt funds without the use of an investment bank, arranger, or other intermediary. These funds also provide large orders called *anchor orders* for syndicated institutional debt, junior lien or mezzanine financings, and unitranche facilities.

TYPES OF SYNDICATED LOAN FACILITIES

The four main types of syndicated loan facilities are revolving credit facilities (within which are swingline, multicurrency-line, competitive-bid option, term-out, and evergreen structures), term loans, letters of credit, and acquisition lines (delayed-draw term loans).

1. A *revolving credit facility* allows borrowers to draw down, repay, and reborrow. The facility acts much like a corporate credit card, except that borrowers are charged an annual commitment fee on unused amounts (i.e., the *commitment fee*), which drives up the overall cost of borrowing. Revolvers to noninvestment-grade issuers are sometimes tied to borrowing-base lending formulas; these are referred to as *asset-based revolving facilities*. Asset-based revolving facilities limit borrowings to a percentage of certain collateral, most often accounts receivables and inventory. Revolving credit facilities for noninvestment-grade issuers typically mature within five years or less from the initial closing date (and, most often, no later than 91 days prior to the maturity of any first lien term loans).

   There are a number of options that can be offered within a revolving credit facility:

   - A *swingline* is a small, overnight borrowing line, typically provided by the Agent and often available to be drawn on a same-day basis.
   - A *multicurrency line* allows the borrower to borrow in currencies other than U.S. dollars. Traditionally, these had sublimits on non-U.S.-dollar currencies. Often, credit agreements allow borrowers to request additional currencies so long as each revolving lender agrees to provide them and the Agent can administer the flow of funds.
   - A *competitive-bid option* (CBO) allows borrowers to solicit the best bids from its syndicate group. The Agent will conduct what amounts to an auction to raise funds for the borrower, and the best bids are accepted. CBOs are typically available only to large investment-grade borrowers.
   - A *term-out* allows the borrower to convert revolving borrowings into a term loan at a given conversion date.

This, again, is usually a feature of investment-grade loans. Under the option, borrowers may take what is outstanding under the facility and pay it off according to a predetermined repayment schedule. Often the spreads ratchet up if the term-out option is exercised.
- An *evergreen* is an option allowing the borrower—with the consent of the syndicate group—to extend the facility each year for an additional year.

2. A *term loan* is simply an installment loan, like the loan one would use to buy a car. The borrower may draw on the loan during a short commitment period and repay it either through a scheduled series of repayments (amortization payments) or in a one-time lump-sum payment at maturity (bullet payment).

    There are two principal types of syndicated term loans:
    - A pro rata term loan or amortizing term loan (term loan A, or TLA) is a term loan with a progressive repayment schedule that typically runs six years or less. These loans are normally syndicated to banks along with revolving credits as part of a larger syndication. The banks hold TLAs pro rata with their revolving commitments. Starting in 2000, TLAs became increasingly rare, as issuers bypassed the less accommodating bank market and tapped institutional investors for all or most of their funded loans. Pricing on a TLA is often lower than on a term loan B because the institutions offering TLAs may take into consideration other fee-driven business an investment bank can generate from its relationships with TLA borrowers.
    - An institutional term loan (term loan B) is a term loan facility carved out for nonbank institutional investors and syndicated by a third-party arranger or investment bank. These loans came into broad usage during the mid-1990s as the institutional loan investor base grew. Institutional investors that provide institutional term loans include structured finance vehicles or collateralized loan obligations (CLOs), hedge funds, private equity funds, business development companies, pension funds, mutual funds, and insurance companies. In making their decision to invest in institutional term loans, these

investors generally consider the credit ratings applicable to the institutional term loan and the borrower (typically from two major rating agencies), the borrower's historical and projected cash flow, the borrower's geographic and industry profile, disclosures included in any relevant materials provided to prospective investors in connection with the syndication, the reputation of the borrower, and, if applicable, that of its private equity sponsor, as well as their own due diligence.

3. *Letters of credit* (LOCs) differ in nature, but, simply put, they are guarantees provided by the bank group to pay off debt or obligations if the borrower cannot. There are traditionally two kinds of LOCs: standby and trade. Standby LOCs are a backup for a counterparty's obligation to pay and are used as a second recourse if the primary obligor does not pay. Trade LOCs, in contrast, are intended as the primary source of payment and often are used to facilitate foreign trade of goods or services. Trade LOCs are intended to be issued and drawn upon on a more frequent basis than standby LOCs. In syndicated revolving credit facilities, there is often one "fronting" LOC issuer performing this role for a fronting fee. Any drawings under the LOCs are backstopped by the lenders under the revolving credit facility (to the extent not paid by the borrower).

4. *Acquisition lines*, or *delayed-draw term loans*, are credits that may be drawn down for a given period to purchase specified types of assets or equipment or to make acquisitions. The issuer pays a fee during (or for some agreed portion of) the commitment period (a ticking fee). The lines are then repaid over a specified period (the term-out period). Repaid amounts may not be reborrowed. The drawn term loans are usually structured to have the same risk profile (so that they can trade without distinction) as any term loans issued by the same borrower and having the same credit support.

ASSET-BASED LENDING

Asset-based lending is a distinct segment of the loan market. Asset-based loans are secured by specific assets and usually governed by a borrowing formula (or a *borrowing base*). The most common type of asset-based loans is backed by receivables and/or inventory lines. These are revolving credits that have a maximum borrowing limit, say $100 million, but also have a fluctuating cap based on the monthly (or in times of distress, weekly) value of an issuer's pledged receivables and inventories. Usually, the receivables are pledged as collateral, and the issuer may borrow against an agreed percentage of the value thereof (e.g., 80% of value, give or take). Inventories are also often pledged to secure borrowings. However, because they are obviously less liquid than receivables, lenders are less generous in their formula. Indeed, the borrowing base for inventories is typically lower—sometimes as low as 50% to 70%, taking into account the liquidation value thereof. In addition, the borrowing base may be further divided into subcategories—for instance, 50% of work-in-process inventory and 65% of finished goods inventory or in-transit inventory—and also subject to "concentration" limits for receivables from the same counterparty or with respect to inventory of a specific type (e.g., in-transit inventory may be capped at a certain amount of the borrowing base at any time).

In many receivables-based facilities, issuers are required to place receivables in a "lock box." That means that the bank lends against the receivables in their borrowing base, takes possession of them, and then collects them to pay down the loan.

In addition, asset-based lending is often based on specific equipment, real estate, car fleets, and an unlimited number of other assets.

DIRECT LENDING

Direct lending, as market participants use the term, is debt financing provided directly to a borrower without the use of an investment bank, arranger, or other intermediary. From that description, direct lending seems to be a return to the early days of the loan market when it consisted primarily of large commercial banks making loans directly to a borrower. However, although direct lending does bear similarities to commercial lending (such as the "buy and hold" nature of direct lending), there are several significant distinctions. Importantly, the providers of direct lending financing (or *direct lenders*) are generally not commercial banks. Rather, they are generally funds formed primarily for the purpose of investing in debt (i.e., *private debt funds*), pension funds, insurance companies, and business development companies (BDCs). In addition, whereas commercial loans are generally first lien loans that are conservatively structured to incentivize repayment, the debt financing provided by direct lenders can take many different forms (e.g., second lien, unsecured, pay in kind) and can be structured to meet the bespoke needs of the particular borrower and the particular direct lenders and take into account the direct lender's own investment fund requirements and guidelines.

DEBTOR-IN-POSSESSION FINANCING

Debtor-in-possession (DIP) financing is financing arranged by a company that is (or is anticipated to become) a debtor in a Chapter 11 bankruptcy case. DIP financing is unique among financing methods in that it usually has priority over existing debt and other claims. (Chapter 11 can give the debtor a fresh start, subject to the debtor's fulfillment of certain obligations and confirmation of a plan of reorganization.) DIP financings are usually secured by the debtor's assets; however, secured creditors of the debtor (whose liens may be "primed" by the DIP financing liens) have a right to "adequate protection" against the diminution of the value of their collateral. This means that the DIP financing is often provided by the existing senior secured creditors of the debtor, unless the existing secured creditors are overcollateralized (i.e., the value of their collateral exceeds the value of their claims) or there are alternative unencumbered assets available on which "adequate protection liens" could be granted to provide those existing secured creditors protection against diminution in value of their interest in the existing collateral.

INTRODUCTION TO SECOND LIEN TERM LOANS

What Is a Second Lien Term Loan?

A typical second lien loan is a term loan B secured by a lien on substantially all of the borrower's assets on the same assets as a first lien tranche of loans or bonds. Second lien term lenders will almost certainly be sharing the capital structure with at least one other credit facility of a more traditional variety—possibly just a revolver, or possibly a term loan and revolver—secured by a first lien on substantially the same collateral.[1] The second lien term loan is denominated "second" because the two classes of creditors agree that, in the event that any of their shared collateral is ever sold in a foreclosure or other enforcement action, either before or during a bankruptcy proceeding, the first lien debt (and all other first lien obligations, if any, that are then outstanding) will be entitled to be paid in full from the proceeds of the shared collateral before any of the proceeds from the shared collateral are distributed to the second lien term lenders. As discussed later in this article, second lien loans are not contractually subordinated in the traditional sense (i.e., holders are not subordinated in terms of payment), but are subordinated only in their claim to the proceeds of the shared collateral.

Second lien loans are a widely used financial instrument for junior capital in lieu of unsecured high-yield debt or mezzanine financing. Typically, there is a pricing difference (traditionally approximately 400 basis points) between first lien and second lien loan spreads above the applicable reference rate, though this can vary based on demand and makeup of the second lien market.

Note that there are often significant differences between second lien loans that are structured as "club deals," which are privately placed by a handful (or even a single) direct lender and second lien loans sold to a broader range of investors. Club deals and deals involving a single direct lender tend to be more "hand sewn" and can contain varying provisions that usually result from more extensive negotiations among the smaller number of lenders involved, though there is a relatively settled universe of terms that direct lenders negotiate for that would otherwise deviate from a syndicated second lien term loan. In contrast, broadly syndicated second lien loans tend to follow the terms of the first lien credit facilities, subject to an agreed "cushion" applicable to the dollar-based (and often the ratio-based) exceptions to the negative covenants in the second lien documentation that makes them "wider" (or more permissive for the borrower) than those set forth in the first lien documentation.

---

[1] According to Standard & Poor (S&P), first lien debt in a capital structure consists predominantly of first lien bank debt.

What Are the Pros and Cons of a Second Lien Loan for a Borrower?

Second lien loans are attractive to borrowers for a number of reasons. Because of the benefits of secured creditor status, a borrower should get better pricing on second lien loan financing than it would if it incurred unsecured debt on substantially the same terms. In addition, a borrower may get broader access to the debt markets because of the tremendous interest in second lien loans across a range of institutional investors, including financial institutions, insurance companies, mutual funds, collateralized debt obligation (CDO) and collateralized loan obligation (CLO) funds,[2] and hedge funds. Loan documents also tend to impose fewer disclosure obligations for a company than a high-yield bond, making them more accessible to less mature or middle market companies. For some borrowers, this deeper level of market interest can make the difference between being able to complete a financing package and not having requisite access to the capital markets. Some borrowers may also perceive second lien lenders to be potentially less volatile in a distress scenario than unsecured creditors to the extent that the holders of second lien loans believe that they are sufficiently secured to successfully weather a period of poor financial performance. To the degree that a borrower's alternative to a second lien loan is a high-yield bond or mezzanine debt, the borrower may also be attracted to the relatively modest call protection typically found in the second lien loan market.[3]

---

[2] CDOs and CLOs are structured vehicles that issue asset-backed securities, generally secured by debt obligations that may include term loans. These vehicles are major players in the secondary debt markets and play an important role in developing a liquid secondary market for term loans and high-yield bonds. For tax reasons, these vehicles do not invest in the primary debt offering, but they often acquire debt in the secondary market within a few days after the initial offering. Since 2003, CDOs and CLOs have been incorporating second lien term loans in their portfolios. As investors, rating agencies, and other market players have become more familiar with second lien financings, their treatment in CDOs and CLOs has been evolving and continues to evolve. Nevertheless, second lien term loans are, and are expected to continue to be, a part of the portfolios of many CDOs and CLOs.

[3] Second lien loans distributed in the broadly syndicated market are often subject to prepayment premiums during the first two or three years after funding at relatively modest levels (e.g., 102/101 or 103/102/101). By comparison, high-yield bonds are typically subject to "noncall" provisions for the first three to five years, with higher call premiums thereafter. A borrower anticipating a refinancing or seeking a material corporate event (e.g., IPO or sale, acquisition or disposition) in a short period of time may find the difference to be of major significance in choosing a second lien loan rather than alternative financing such as a high-yield bond.

However, there are also costs to the borrower associated with providing collateral to second lien lenders. First, depending on the value of the collateral and the cash flow of the enterprise, the borrower's ability to obtain additional first lien financing in the future may be impaired by the presence of a significant tranche of second lien secured debt on its balance sheet. Further, the total amount of additional second lien loans that may be incurred in the future will probably be capped, usually based on a maximum leverage ratio or other limitations. The existence of a second lien loan in its capital structure may also make it harder for a borrower to obtain unsecured debt in the future because future unsecured creditors of the borrower would be effectively subordinated to the second lien loan. Finally, there may be some incremental costs associated with providing collateral to second lien lenders (e.g., filing fees, title insurance costs, and local counsel opinions), although these costs alone rarely result in borrowers deciding against a second lien loan.

Why Would a First Lien Lender Want to Permit a Second Lien Loan Deal?

In the early days of the syndicated loan market, first lien lenders were not generally inclined to allow their collateral to be encumbered by junior liens securing other debt facilities. The concern was that the existence of other secured creditors and their rights in collateral could result in complications for first lien lenders in the event of a workout or bankruptcy. However, as the loan market has evolved and as second lien debt financing has become more commonplace, first lien lenders have largely abandoned this pushback and now readily accept the existence of junior liens on their collateral so long as their first lien position is protected. First lien lenders protect their interests through intercreditor arrangements that limit or control the secured creditors' rights that second lien lenders might otherwise exercise to the detriment of the first lien lenders. Such an arrangement leaves the second lien lenders with what is sometimes referred to as a *silent second lien*. The term *silent second* refers to the concept that, under the applicable intercreditor arrangements, the second lien lenders will not interfere in any way with the exercise of secured creditors' rights by the first lien lenders (i.e., they will remain truly silent while the first lien lenders exercise their rights as to shared collateral). However, as discussed later in this article, the evolution of the second lien loan market and the resulting requirements of second lien lenders have made the term *quiet* or *well-behaved second lien* more applicable in certain cases than *silent second lien*.

Why Would a Junior Creditor Be Willing to Accept a Second Lien?

A second priority lien, even a silent second, gives a second lien lender effective priority over trade creditors and other unsecured creditors, to the extent of the value of its interest in the collateral. In terms of payment priority, second lien status does not affect the value of being secured; a second lien lender is nearly always better off in this regard than it would be if it were unsecured (as further discussed later in this article). In addition, under applicable intercreditor arrangements in most deals the second lien lenders expressly reserve many, if not all, of the rights of an unsecured creditor, subject to some important exceptions discussed later.

SOME IMPORTANT BACKGROUND INFORMATION

So far, we have established that second lien lenders get paid second when it comes to the proceeds of collateral. We have also said that second lien loans are usually silent seconds (or at least quiet or well-behaved seconds). So where's the controversy? Well, the key question is, "How silent is silent?" How well behaved must second lien lenders be *vis-à-vis* first lien lenders? Market participants from the old school of senior lending believe that second lien lenders should speak only when they are spoken to. The new school of players in the second lien loan market today is not as demure as the old school lenders would like. In today's market, second lien lenders are willing to defer to first lien holders on various matters up to a point or for a limited period of time, but no more than that. This shift from the old school to the new school has been, and continues to be, fueled to a large degree by the emergence of direct lenders in the second lien market. While direct lenders in the second lien market accept the general premise of lien subordination and of being silent (or at least quiet or well behaved), they, as "buy and hold" lenders who will directly bear the consequences of subordination, tend to negotiate for broader rights for (and fewer restrictions on) their second lien position.

Loan Structures

The action in the structuring and negotiating of second lien deals revolves around the determination of the relationship between the rights of first lien lenders and second lien lenders under what are commonly referred to as *intercreditor arrangements*. In order to address the critical questions of how and why those intercreditor arrangements are being sorted out in the loan market today, we need to explore some background information about what it means to be a secured creditor in the first place. We will then discuss which of these rights second lien lenders may be willing to part with.

What Is the Difference Between Debt Subordination and Lien Subordination?

- *Basics.* In traditional debt subordination, the debt claim itself is subordinated. If holders of subordinated debt obtain any payment or distribution in a bankruptcy, they agree to turn it over to the holders of senior debt until the senior debt is paid in full in cash. In the case of second lien debt, only the liens are subordinated; the underlying debt claim is not. This means that holders of second lien debt agree only to turn over proceeds of shared collateral from an enforcement or in a bankruptcy to the first lien lenders. The holders of second lien debt are not required to turn over to the first lien lenders payments or distributions to them that do not constitute proceeds of shared collateral.
- *Priority vis-à-vis the trade.* In its simplest terms, debt subordination places the subordinated debt behind the senior debt, but does not place it ahead of any other debt of the borrower or the guarantors (unless the holders of that other debt agree, in turn, to subordinate their debt to the subordinated debt). By contrast, although lien subordination does place the second lien debt behind the first lien loans to the extent of the value of the first lien lender's security interest in the collateral, it also places the second lien debt ahead of trade and other unsecured creditors to the extent of the value of its security interest in the collateral. This is the key benefit for the holders of second lien debt.
- *Payment blockage issues.* Unlike traditional subordinated debt, second lien debt is not typically subject to payment blockage provisions of any kind with respect to scheduled payments

of principal and interest. However, voluntary prepayments of second lien debt are often (but not always) treated as restricted payments under the negative covenants of the first lien documentation, and the intercreditor agreement would typically restrict the rights of holders of second lien debt to seek post-petition interest in a bankruptcy.

- *Remedy standstill provisions.* The remedy bars in second lien deals typically apply only to remedies associated with the collateral. Most second lien deals specifically preserve all or almost all of the remedies that would be available to an unsecured creditor, with a few exceptions (as we will discuss later).

In a Bankruptcy, What Rights Do Secured Creditors Gain?

In a bankruptcy proceeding, secured creditors have a variety of meaningful rights that unsecured creditors do not have. As a result, secured creditors typically enjoy significantly higher recovery rates in bankruptcies and other reorganizations than unsecured creditors.

- *Priority vis-à-vis trade and other unsecured creditors.* Under the Bankruptcy Code, prepetition (i.e., prebankruptcy) creditors' claims can generally be divided into three basic classes: (1) secured claims, (2) priority unsecured claims, and (3) general unsecured claims.[4] A second lien lender's claim is treated as a secured claim to the extent of the value of its security interest in the collateral. For example, assume that the company in bankruptcy owes $50 to a

---

[4] Under the Bankruptcy Code, unsecured claims are not all treated equally. Certain unsecured claims, called *priority unsecured claims*, have the right to be paid in full before any of the residual unsecured claims, called *general unsecured claims*, are paid. Priority unsecured claims include:
- Post-petition administrative expenses needed to operate the bankrupt company (such as employees' wages and other ordinary course operating expenses) or to pay lawyers, accountants, and other professionals hired by the bankrupt company or certain types of creditors
- In an involuntary bankruptcy, *gap claims*, which are ordinary course unsecured claims incurred between the bankruptcy filing date and the entry of an order for relief
- Certain prepetition employees' wages
- Certain contributions to employee benefit plans
- Certain types of tax claims

first lien lender and $200 to a second lien lender and that both the first lien and second lien loans are secured solely by liens on an asset worth $150. In this case, the first lien lender will have a $50 secured claim and no unsecured claim. The second lien lender, in turn, will have a secured claim of $100. The second lien lender's residual $100 claim will be treated as a general unsecured claim. As a result, an undersecured creditor will hold both secured and unsecured claims. Under the Bankruptcy Code, secured claims are entitled to receive value equal to the full value of their interest in the collateral before any value is given to holders of unsecured claims, and any priority unsecured claims are entitled to receive the full value of their claims before any unsecured claims receive any value. To the extent that a secured creditor is undersecured (i.e., the value of its collateral is less than the amount of its prepetition claim), that undersecured creditor will share pro rata with other general unsecured creditors (including trade creditors) in the amount, if any, remaining after repayment in full of both secured claims and priority unsecured claims.

- *Post-petition interest.* A secured creditor is entitled to post-petition interest under the Bankruptcy Code to the extent that the value of its interest in the collateral securing its claim is greater than the amount of its prebankruptcy claim. An undersecured creditor is generally not entitled to post-petition interest. As a result, in the example discussed previously, the first lien lender's $50 secured claim could increase during the pendency of the bankruptcy proceeding to the extent of any accrued interest that is not paid currently, thereby reducing the likely recovery by the second lien lender.
- *Adequate protection rights.* Under the Bankruptcy Code, a secured creditor has the right to be protected against declines in the value of its interest in the collateral following the date of the bankruptcy filing. This is a very broad right and entitles a secured creditor to a voice in any actions taken in a bankruptcy proceeding that could affect the value of its collateral (including the use of cash collateral, sales of collateral, substitutions of collateral, or the grant of a priming lien on collateral to secure a DIP financing). Upon request, a secured creditor is entitled to

assurance that its interest in its collateral is adequately protected if there is a serious risk of the value of its interest diminishing. This "adequate protection" may take the form of a court-ordered grant of additional or substitute collateral or the provision of periodic cash payments to the secured creditor or any other form providing the secured creditor with the "indubitable equivalent" of its interest. The Bankruptcy Court has broad discretion in fashioning an appropriate remedy in this regard.

- *Right to object to use of cash collateral.* The Bankruptcy Code defines the term *cash collateral* to include cash, negotiable instruments, securities, deposit accounts, and other cash equivalents in which a prepetition creditor has a security interest. Under the Bankruptcy Code, a company in bankruptcy is not permitted to use cash collateral unless each creditor that has a security interest in the cash collateral consents to its use or the Bankruptcy Court authorizes its use, after notice and a hearing. This gives each secured creditor a say on the use of cash collateral, unless the Bankruptcy Court orders otherwise.
- *Right to approve asset sales.* Under the Bankruptcy Code, a company in bankruptcy can sell assets, free and clear of all liens, in various circumstances. However, under certain circumstances, the consent of a secured creditor to a sale of its collateral may be required. If more than one party has a lien on the collateral, each of the secured creditors may be required to consent to the sale.
- *Right to approve secured DIP financings.* A company in bankruptcy needs funds with which to operate during the pendency of the case. Not surprisingly, many bankrupt companies have negative or marginal cash flow, which prompts the need for DIP financing arrangements. DIP financings can be secured or unsecured, but they are typically secured on a first-priority basis (because most lenders are unwilling to lend to the bankrupt borrower on an unsecured or junior basis). The Bankruptcy Code authorizes the Bankruptcy Court to provide for a DIP loan to be secured by a lien that is senior (i.e., a "priming lien") or equal to the liens held by other secured creditors, as long as those other secured creditors are given adequate protection or consent to the senior or equal liens. As a result,

creditors whose claims are secured by all or substantially all of the bankrupt company's assets will have a strong say as to the company's ability to obtain a priming DIP loan.
- *Harder to be "crammed down."* In a bankruptcy, the creditors in each class of impaired claims have the right to vote on any proposed plan of reorganization. However, in certain circumstances a plan of reorganization can be confirmed over the objections of a particular class of creditors. A class of creditors that is forced to accept the terms of a plan that it voted against is said to be "crammed down." It is generally much harder for a class of secured creditors to be "crammed down" in a bankruptcy than a class of unsecured creditors. Under the Bankruptcy Code, a class of creditors can be crammed down only if the plan of reorganization is "fair and equitable" to that class. The standard for what is fair and equitable is higher for secured creditors than it is for unsecured creditors, which gives secured creditors greater leverage at the bargaining table in bankruptcy plan negotiations.[5]
- *More leverage in plan negotiations.* The combined effect of these various rights of secured creditors is to give secured creditors far more leverage than unsecured creditors in negotiating and shaping the plan of reorganization.

What Rights Do Unsecured Creditors Have outside of Bankruptcy?

Unsecured creditors (as well as secured creditors) have several important rights outside of bankruptcy, including the following:

- The right of any three unsecured or undersecured creditors to put a company into an involuntary bankruptcy[6]

---

[5] Under the Bankruptcy Code, a plan of reorganization is "fair and equitable" to a class of secured creditors if each secured creditor in that class either (1) retains the lien securing its claim and receives deferred cash payments totaling at least the allowed amount of its secured claim; (2) receives the "indubitable equivalent" of the value of its claim; or (3) receives a lien on the proceeds of a sale of its collateral (free and clear of its lien) subject to its right to purchase the property by credit bidding its secured claim against the purchase price.

[6] Any three unsecured or undersecured creditors can commence an involuntary bankruptcy case against a company if the total value of their claims against the company is at least $16,750 more than the total value of their interests in assets of the company pledged to secure those claims.

- The right to accelerate their debt and sue for payment
- The right to challenge the validity, enforceability, or priority of any liens on the company's assets

What Rights Do Unsecured Creditors Have in a Bankruptcy?

Unsecured creditors (as well as secured creditors) have other meaningful rights during a bankruptcy, including the following:

- The right to request the appointment of a trustee in bankruptcy (e.g., because they believe the bankrupt company is mismanaging the business)
- The right to propose a plan of reorganization, but only at the end of the 120-day (or longer) time period in which the bankrupt company has the exclusive right to propose a plan
- The right to seek termination of the period in which the bankrupt company has the exclusive right to propose a plan
- The right to vote on a plan of reorganization
- The right to seek to challenge the validity, enforceability, or priority of any liens on the bankrupt company's assets
- The right to challenge or dispute any other actions taken or not taken, or any motions made, by the bankrupt company, any secured creditor, or any other interested party

Although, generally, the rights of an unsecured creditor in bankruptcy are significantly less than those of a secured creditor, they are enough to give unsecured creditors (often through an "official committee" of unsecured creditors) a seat at the table in the plan negotiations.

What Are the Relationships between Multiple Secured Creditors at Law Absent an Intercreditor Agreement?

- *Order of priority.* The general rule is first in time, first in line. Under that general rule, as between two secured creditors, unless otherwise agreed by those creditors, the first to "perfect" its security interest in an asset gets the first-priority lien on that asset. The second in time is second in line.[7] Priority is important because it determines the order of repayment when the collateral is sold or otherwise disposed of and the party with the earlier perfected security interest has a right to be paid in full from the proceeds of assets over other secured creditors before a second priority creditor can recover anything.

- *Control over enforcement actions.* If two creditors are secured by liens on a particular asset, the general rule under the Uniform Commercial Code (UCC) and other applicable laws is that either creditor has the right to foreclose on the asset. If the first lien lender forecloses on the asset, the second lien lender is not entitled to any of the foreclosure proceeds until the first lien lender has received the full value of its claim. If the second lien lender forecloses on the asset, the first lien remains in place on the sold asset, and the second lien lender is entitled to the foreclosure proceeds. However, as a practical matter, few buyers in a foreclosure sale are willing to buy an asset subject to a first lien, and few first lien lenders are willing to release their first liens unless their debt has been repaid in full. As a result, it is common for the agreements between creditors to provide that the first lien lenders have the right to control the disposition of collateral (possibly subject to time or other limitations).
- *Restrictions on dispositions of collateral.* A secured creditor does not have an unfettered right to dispose of collateral. The interests of the debtor and other secured creditors are protected by a variety of rules designed to protect those interests in the value of the collateral, if any, remaining after repayment in full of the claims of the secured creditor that forecloses on the collateral. As discussed below, any party enforcing their rights on collateral must

---

[7] There are numerous exceptions to this general rule, including liens securing purchase money debt and certain tax, ERISA, and other statutory liens. In addition, with respect to many types of collateral, certain methods of perfection, such as possession or control, may be entitled to priority over an earlier security interest that is perfected solely by the filing of a financing statement.

also proceed in a commercially reasonable manner to obtain commercially reasonable value for any sale or disposal of assets, irrespective of the value of the secured creditor's claim. Most of these rules can't be waived by a debtor or other pledgor or may be waived by a debtor or other pledgor only under an agreement entered into after a default has occurred. In addition, in certain cases, particularly where the first lien lender has agreed to serve as Agent for the second lien lender, a first lien lender may owe fiduciary duties to the second lien lender.[8] These rules effectively limit the ability of a secured creditor to conduct collateral "fire sales."

- *Rules governing foreclosure on UCC collateral.* The UCC contains a variety of substantive and procedural requirements governing foreclosure on personal property collateral that is subject to the UCC.[9] Most important, under the UCC, every aspect of a disposition of collateral must be "commercially reasonable." A secured party is liable to the debtor and other parties with a security interest in the same collateral if it fails to comply with this standard or if it fails to comply with any of the notice or other requirements surrounding foreclosure imposed by the UCC. These UCC requirements also effectively limit the ability of any secured creditor to sell collateral at a fire sale.

- *Rules governing foreclosure on real property collateral.* The substantive and procedural requirements that govern foreclosure on real property collateral vary from state to state. In most states, a secured creditor can foreclose on real property through a judicial foreclosure, supervised by a state court. In some states, a secured creditor can also enforce remedies against real property outside of the court system through a nonjudicial foreclosure in which a trustee or referee conducts the sale. If the

---

[8] We are not aware of a general fiduciary duty owed by a senior secured creditor to a junior secured creditor simply by virtue of having a senior lien on common collateral.
[9] The UCC covers most types of tangible and intangible personal property. Some of the significant categories of property that are not covered by the UCC include:
- Real estate (other than fixtures)
- Some types of intellectual property (namely federally registered copyrights)
- In most states, insurance policies and any claims under those policies (other than as proceeds of other collateral)

sale is conducted through a judicial foreclosure, the secured party will typically have to satisfy procedural requirements intended to ensure that the sale is conducted in a public forum to protect against a sale of the real property below fair market value.
- *Bankruptcy Code restrictions.* The Bankruptcy Code imposes its own set of restrictions on asset sales. During a bankruptcy, with limited exceptions, a secured creditor generally does not have a right to compel sales of collateral. As a general matter, the company in bankruptcy decides which assets to sell (albeit, in practice, following discussions with its secured creditors). Asset sales are governed by Section 363 of the Bankruptcy Code. These *363 sales*, as they are commonly known, are subject to overbidding and Bankruptcy Court scrutiny and approval, with a view to achieving the best available sale price.

STRUCTURING SECOND LIEN LOANS

With that background discussion behind us, we will now turn to a series of specific issues relating to the structure of second lien loans financings in the broadly syndicated loan market today.

What Makes a Second Lien Loan Silent/Quiet/Well Behaved?

The terms *silent*, *quiet*, and *well behaved* all refer to degrees to which the second lien lenders agree not to exercise (or restrict the exercise of) some or all of the special rights that they would otherwise enjoy by virtue of their secured creditor status. The arrangements to forgo or restrict their rights are usually set out in an agreement entered into by the representatives of the various classes of creditors (typically an intercreditor agreement or, in some cases, a collateral trust agreement). Although the degree to which second lien lenders agree to give up their rights may vary from deal to deal, the categories of restrictions at play may be summarized as follows:

- Prohibitions (or limitations) on the right of the second lien holders to take enforcement actions with respect to their liens (possibly subject to time or other limitations)

- Agreements by the second lien lenders not to challenge enforcement or foreclosure actions taken by the holders of the first liens (possibly subject to time or other limitations)
- Prohibitions on the right of the second lien holders to challenge the validity or priority of the first liens
- Waivers of (or limitations on) other secured creditor rights by the holders of second liens loan in and outside of bankruptcy
- Acknowledgments by the second lien lenders of the first lien lenders' entitlement to first proceeds of the shared collateral.

What Restrictions Do the Second Lien Lenders Typically Agree to with Respect to the Period before a Bankruptcy Filing?

The answer to this question depends on the nature of the second lien debt and its holders. In the case of truly silent second lien debt, the first lien lenders generally control all decisions regarding the enforcement of remedies against the collateral as long as any first lien loans are outstanding. As a result, following a default on the first lien loans, subject to the UCC, the Bankruptcy Code, and other legal limitations discussed previously, the first lien lenders typically decide, among other things:

- Whether and when to exercise remedies against the collateral
- Which items of collateral to proceed against, and in which order
- Whether the sale should be a public or a private sale
- To whom collateral should be sold, and at what price
- Releases of the security interests of both the first and second lien lenders on any collateral that is sold

However, in the current leveraged finance market, even holders of broadly syndicated second lien loans would not typically agree to remain truly silent. Generally, in both syndicated and privately placed second lien deals, holders of second lien debt will agree to refrain from exercising their secured creditor rights only for a limited period of time, typically 90 to 180 days. This period of time is referred to as a *standstill period*, and standstill periods in intercreditor agreements for privately placed second lien deals tend to be shorter than those for syndicated deals. At the end of the standstill period, unless the first lien lenders have commenced and are diligently pursuing the exercise of secured creditor remedies (or, of course, the borrower or any guarantor has filed for bankruptcy), the first lien lenders lose their exclusive right to exercise secured creditor remedies.

In addition, under most intercreditor arrangements, second lien lenders typically waive their right to challenge the validity, enforceability, or priority of the first liens and acknowledge the first lien lenders' entitlement to receive the proceeds of the collateral until all first lien obligations are repaid in full. In a privately placed second lien deal, the second lien lenders will often negotiate for the first lien lenders to provide a reciprocal waiver of their right to challenge the second liens.

Intercreditor agreements also typically restrict certain amendments and other modifications (including through refinancing) of the second lien debt (in many cases, with corresponding restrictions on the first lien debt). These restrictions might include restrictions on increasing the second lien debt above a specified cap, increasing the interest rate margin on the second lien debt above a threshold or accelerating the final maturity date, or decreasing the weighted average life to maturity of the second lien debt (in each case, with corresponding restrictions on the first lien debt). However, the extent to which an intercreditor agreement will contain these restrictions will depend on a variety of factors, including the leverage of the borrower in the context of the intercreditor negotiations and whether the first lien debt and/or the second lien debt is broadly syndicated or closely held. Where they have the leverage to do so, borrowers resist the inclusion in the intercreditor agreement of robust restrictions on amendments, out of concern that such restrictions could complicate future amendments to their underlying loan documents. In the context of a syndicated first lien deal, the first lien lenders tend to be less focused on restricting amendments to the second lien debt. And, in the context of a privately placed second lien deal, direct lenders tend to push for these types of restrictions in an effort to protect against amendments to the first lien debt that could erode or jeopardize their security position.

What Restrictions Do the Second Lien Lenders Typically Agree to in a Bankruptcy Proceeding?

The short answer is all of the rights that they waive before bankruptcy (as discussed earlier), plus some others. The longer answer depends, again, on the nature of the second lien debt and its holders. The following waivers and consents (to varying degrees) are commonly seen in intercreditor agreements in the second lien loan market:

- Adequate protection waivers
- Advance consents to use of cash collateral
- Advance consents to sales of collateral
- Advance consents to DIP financings (including some level of "priming")

Waiver of the Right to Seek Adequate Protection

Second lien lenders will typically reserve their adequate protection right to ask for a junior lien on any property on which the Bankruptcy Court grants a lien to secure first lien loans, as long as the new junior lien is subject to the same lien subordination arrangements as the original second lien. This right is critical to avoid erosion of the second lien lenders' bargained-for collateral. Most security agreements contain an "after-acquired collateral" clause that grants the secured creditor a lien on all then-owned collateral and on any collateral acquired in the future. However, under the Bankruptcy Code, liens created prior to a bankruptcy generally do not attach, or apply, to assets acquired or arising after the commencement of the bankruptcy proceeding. As a result, it is customary for secured creditors to agree to permit uses of the cash proceeds from sales of their collateral consisting of inventory, accounts receivable, or other similar classes of "quick assets" only if the court permits them to obtain a lien on quick assets created or acquired after the commencement of the bankruptcy. In general, the first lien lenders can be counted on to make this request (typically in connection with the debtor's request for authority to use cash collateral to obtain DIP financing, or it may be phrased as an adequate protection motion). However, the second lien lenders need to be able to tag along in order to preserve their second liens on quick assets acquired after the commencement of the bankruptcy, or they will lose the benefit of their bargain.

The practical significance of these adequate protection waivers depends on the facts of the case. Excluding the ability to have a say in the use of cash collateral and DIP financings, the principal benefit of adequate protection is the right of a secured creditor to ask for additional or substitute collateral to protect against declines in the value of its interest in the collateral after the date on which the bankruptcy commenced. This right is of critical importance to a holder of liens on quick assets (as discussed earlier), and it is also meaningful if the company in bankruptcy has valuable unencumbered or partially encumbered assets on which additional or replacement liens can be granted to protect the value of the original liens. The remedy is of more limited utility to a second lien lender that already has a lien on all of the borrower's assets.

In most cases, the borrower will have some unencumbered assets, and the grant of a lien on those assets to compensate for deterioration in the value of the second lien holder's original collateral may materially enhance the second lien lender's ultimate recovery. The value of the second lien lender's interest in any additional or substitute collateral obtained to secure its obligations protects, dollar for dollar, against erosion of the value of second lien lenders' interest in their collateral. As a result, giving up the opportunity to obtain additional or substitute collateral in the name of adequate protection could have a real-world cost. On balance, however, if the second lien lenders preserve their right to obtain a second lien on any new collateral provided to the first lien lenders in the name of adequate protection, their waiver of the right to seek other forms of adequate protection on their own will not prove to be an imprudent concession in most real-world circumstances.

Waiver of the Right to Oppose Adequate Protection for the First Lien Loans

Second lien lenders typically waive any right to dispute actions taken by the first lien lenders to seek adequate protection with respect to the collateral securing the first lien loans. This waiver is not particularly controversial and is not usually subject to any time limitation.

Advance Consent to the Use of Cash Collateral

Second lien lenders typically give an advance consent to any use of cash collateral approved by the first lien loans (effectively waiving their right to oppose the company's proposed use of cash collateral on adequate protection grounds). Under the Bankruptcy Code, a debtor may use cash collateral with the secured lender's consent. Absent such consent, the debtor may obtain an order of the Bankruptcy Court authorizing the use of cash collateral. To obtain the order, the debtor must demonstrate that the secured creditor is adequately protected. The primary benefit to a secured creditor of the right to consent to the use of cash collateral is that it allows the secured creditor to leverage how the company uses its cash. Because a borrower in bankruptcy invariably cannot operate without access to cash and other cash collateral, secured creditors can, and frequently do, condition their consent to the use of these funds on adoption by the company in bankruptcy of a satisfactory operating budget. As a result of this advance consent, the second lien lenders will almost certainly be required to rely on the first lien lenders to handle these budget negotiations.[10]

Advance Consent to Sales of Collateral

Second lien lenders often agree to not object to any court-approved asset sale that is also approved by the first lien lenders as long as liens attach to the proceeds of the sale in accordance with the lien priorities agreed to in the intercreditor agreement. In the context of privately placed second lien deals, second lien lenders often require that all or a specified portion of the sale proceeds must be used to permanently reduce the first lien loans. In agreeing to this waiver, second lien lenders rely on the protection that the sale must be approved by the Bankruptcy Court and must be conducted

---

[10] In the early stages of a case, a debtor may have no source of liquidity for operations other than cash collateral. As a result, if the debtor is denied the use of cash collateral, it may be required to cease operations and liquidate. As a practical matter, if a Bankruptcy Court is faced with either permitting the use of cash collateral over a secured creditor's objection or causing the debtor to liquidate, the Bankruptcy Court will routinely permit the use of cash collateral. Thus, as discussed in the text, first lien lenders tend to concentrate their efforts not on seeking to prevent such use, but rather on requiring that such use be conditioned on the debtor's adherence to a tight operating budget.

through an auction process. In addition, second lien lenders will also be focused on preserving their rights to "credit bid"[11] in connection with any such asset sale. First lien lenders will typically agree to expressly permit second lien lenders to credit bid, so long as any credit bid provides for the payment in full in cash of the first lien debt.

Advance Consent to DIP Financing Approved by the First Lien Lenders

Second lien lenders typically agree to some form of agreement not to object to DIP financings consented to by first lien lenders. This agreement by second lien lenders appears in various permutations, including:

- Unconditional agreement not to object to any DIP financing approved by the first lien lenders
- Conditional agreement to any DIP financing approved by the first lien lenders, subject to a dollar cap (which may include a cushion to allow "protective advances") on the amount of the DIP financing (referred to as a *DIP cap*) and, potentially, certain other restrictions on the terms of the DIP financing (such as the DIP financing not compelling the borrower to seek confirmation of a specific plan of reorganization, referred to as a *sub rosa plan*, and not requiring the liquidation of shared collateral prior to a default under the DIP financing)

Very often (but not always), regardless of whether an intercreditor agreement includes a DIP cap or the other restrictions on

---

[11] Unless the court orders otherwise, at the auction, the second lien lenders can "credit bid" (i.e., reduce dollar for dollar the cash price payable by the second lien lenders for the auctioned asset by an amount equal to) the value of their interest in the collateral in excess of the value of the first lien lenders' interest in the collateral. For example, assume that the bankrupt company owes $50 to the first lien lenders and $200 to the second lien lenders. Both the first and second lien loans are secured solely by liens on an asset worth $150. If a third party makes a cash bid of $120 for one of the bankrupt company's crown jewels, and there are no other bidders, the first lien lenders are likely to favor the sale because they will get paid off in full. With credit bidding, the second lien lenders are required to cash bid only $50 (the value of the first lien lenders' interest in the collateral) and can credit bid up to the full amount of their $200 debt. Credit bidding allows second lien lenders to lower the cash component of their bid, which gives them a competitive advantage over other bidders without credit bid rights.

DIP financing described above, the intercreditor agreement will require the liens securing the DIP financing to rank prior or equal to the liens securing the first lien loans. This requirement is important to second lien lenders because it requires the first lien lenders to "share the pain" and thereby reduces the chances of an overly generous DIP, and it is generally acceptable to first lien lenders and borrowers because it is consistent with their expectations as to the seniority of the DIP financing. In addition, some second lien lenders require certain quid pro quos in exchange for an agreement of this type, including the reservation of a right to propose a competing DIP financing or a DIP financing secured by liens on the collateral that are equal to those of the second lien lenders and junior to those of the first lien lenders (a so-called junior DIP).

Are Intercreditor Agreements Enforceable?

Courts are generally willing to enforce intercreditor agreements between a debtor's creditors, even when the borrower is in bankruptcy. The Bankruptcy Code specifically provides that a subordination agreement is as enforceable in a bankruptcy as it is outside of bankruptcy. As a general matter, an agreement containing the types of intercreditor provisions discussed here should be enforceable under state law, both before and during a bankruptcy. As a court of equity, a Bankruptcy Court may allow the second lien lenders to assert rights that they agreed to waive in the intercreditor agreement, leaving the first lien lenders to sue the second lien lenders in state court for breach of contract damages. In practice, that course will probably not be appealing to the first lien lenders absent repeated and flagrant disregard of the original bargain by the second lien lenders.

Does a Second Lien Lender Ever End up Worse off than an Unsecured Creditor?

Typically, an intercreditor agreement expressly states that, both before and during a bankruptcy, the second lien lenders can take any actions and exercise any rights that they would have had if they were unsecured creditors, except any rights that they expressly waive in (or that would be inconsistent with the terms of) the intercreditor agreement, such as with respect to challenges to sales of collateral, DIP financings, and the lien priority of the first lien loans.

In some cases, first lien lenders request advance agreements by the second lien lenders regarding how they will vote on a plan of reorganization. Most commonly, such a voting agreement would provide that second lien lenders may not support or vote in favor of a plan unless the first lien lenders vote in favor of the plan or the plan meets certain conditions (e.g., that the first lien loans get repaid in full in cash). This provision came into particular focus in the wake of the *Momentive* bankruptcy,[12] in which the first lien lenders were crammed down (and received replacement debt at below-market interest) in a plan of reorganization that was supported by the second lien lenders.

The right to vote on a plan of reorganization provides significant protections for a secured creditor. First and second lien lenders have very different interests, and they frequently (and often strongly) disagree on the merits of a proposed plan. Furthermore, unsecured creditors almost never agree to limit their voting rights in a plan, and including such a provision in an intercreditor agreement could cause the second lien lender to have significantly less bargaining power than an unsecured creditor in plan negotiations.

Do Second Lien Lenders Have the Right to Purchase the First Lien Loans?

In many second lien financings, the first lien lenders give second lien lenders an option to purchase the first lien obligations. The exercise price in such arrangements is generally the par value of the outstanding first lien loans plus accrued interest and other amounts due. Usually, the option can be exercised during an agreed-upon time period starting on the date on which a material event of default arises under the second lien debt documentation that is notified to the first lien Agent. First lien lenders generally view the purchase option as acceptable, because, if it is exercised, it allows them to exit from a troubled credit at par. However, where a prepayment of the first lien loans would trigger the payment of a significant prepayment premium (and where the first lien lenders have negotiated to have that prepayment premium payable in connection with a bankruptcy filing by the borrower), the first lien lenders may not

---

[12] Momentive Performance Materials Inc. v. BOKF, NA *(In re MPM Silicones, L.L.C.)*, 874 F.3d 787 (2d Cir. 2017), *cert. denied*, 138 S. Ct. 2653 (2018).

be willing to give the second lien lenders the right to buy them out at only par plus accrued interest.

The purchase option has some value for the second lien lenders, because, once it is exercised, the second lien lender will no longer be subject to any of the intercreditor arrangements discussed earlier and will be free to exercise all the rights of a secured creditor. As a result, the second lien lenders will have increased leverage in the plan or out-of-court restructuring negotiations, which may translate into a higher net recovery for the second lien lenders. However, in any restructuring where the second lien lenders are sufficiently organized and are able and willing to buy out the first lien position at par, an amicable arrangement is likely to be within easy reach. As a result, many market participants do not attribute significant value to including this option in the original documentation.

Do We Need Two Sets of Security Documents?

There is some debate as to whether the first and second liens can be granted in a single set of security documents (containing separate grants of security interests for the first and second liens) rather than in separate sets of security documents. Some first lien lenders are concerned that they may prejudice their right to post-petition interest unless the first and second liens have completely separate security documents.[13] We believe that, if properly prepared, a single

---

[13] This concern stems from a decision in *In re Ionosphere Clubs, Inc.*, 134 B.R. 528 (Bankr. S.D.N.Y. 1991), in which three series (series A, B, and C) of creditors had a security interest in the same assets of the bankrupt company. The security interest for each of the series A, B, and C creditors was granted in the same security agreement. The security agreement contained a single "granting clause" that granted one security interest in favor of the series A, B, and C creditors. The issue at stake in the case was whether the series A, B, and C creditors held three separate secured claims or were co-owners of a single combined claim. The answer would determine whether the series A creditors were entitled to post-petition interest. In bankruptcy, only an oversecured creditor is entitled to post-petition interest. A creditor is oversecured if the value of its interest in its collateral exceeds the amount of its claim. If the series A, B, and C creditors each held a separate secured claim, the series A creditors would be oversecured and the series B and C creditors would be undersecured. However, if the series A, B, and C creditors were co-owners of a single combined secured claim, the entire class, including the class A creditors, would be undersecured.

The Bankruptcy Court held that the series A, B, and C creditors were co-owners of a single secured claim because the series A, B, and C creditors were secured by a single security interest. The court stated that, if the three series had been secured by three separate liens on the collateral, there would have been three separate secured claims.

set of security documents should work to ensure that the first and second lien lenders hold separate secured claims. Each security document should contain two separate granting clauses and a clear statement of an intention to create two separate classes of secured creditors.

How Do Various Classes of Creditors Vote?

As we discussed earlier, the first lien lenders generally control (at least for some period of time) many of the key decisions relating to the collateral. Typically, the collateral Agents are authorized to take action only if instructed to do so by first lien lenders holding more than 50% of the total amount of the outstanding first lien loans, outstanding LOCs, and unfunded commitments.

If there is more than one tranche of first lien loans outstanding, the first lien lenders need to decide among themselves how the various tranches of first lien loans will vote together as a single class. There are two general approaches to this conundrum, although the first one described below is the overwhelming market approach.

The first approach is the *controlling agent system*, under which one of the representatives of a debt facility is appointed as the controlling Agent at the outset of the intercreditor relationship—most often, this is the Agent or trustee representing the debt facility holding the largest quantum of debt outstanding; however, in a capital structure where there are first lien bank facilities and first lien notes, the borrower and structuring parties often have a preference to allow the bank facility Agent to control the class on the assumption, right or wrong, that bank lenders and bank Administrative Agents will be more nimble and quicker to react and organize a lender group than will a notes trustee. The controlling representative will take instruction from a majority (or supermajority) of the holders of that particular facility (with the voting percentages required for instructing the Agent dependent on the voting mechanics of the underlying debt facility). Only where the controlling class fails to act for a period of time (called a *standstill period*), will another class gain control of the class. Note that this approach creates a disincentive to enter into sidecar or separate tranches of debt that are not part of the largest tranche in a class.

The second approach is the *popular vote system*, which is more rarely seen, in which all of the debt in a class (regardless of tranche) votes together as a single class. The popular vote system tends to be less attractive because it does not address the situation in which different tranches of debt have different voting requirements to approve a particular action. One tranche of debt may require majority approval for a particular action, whereas another tranche of debt may require supermajority approval for the same action. By lumping all the tranches of debt into a single voting group, the voting requirements for the various tranches of debt may be effectively replaced with a single uniform voting standard that is not consistent with the parties' bargained-for intent.

Are There Any Limits on the Amount of Future First Lien Loans?

Yes. In order to protect the second lien lenders from losing the value of their accrued claims, the typical covenant package in a second lien deal will fix the maximum principal amount of first lien loans that may be incurred, and second lien lenders will often seek to replicate this cap in the intercreditor agreement (with any first lien debt in excess of the first lien cap being subordinated to the second lien loans). The cap is typically fixed at the maximum amount of first lien debt permitted to be incurred in the future under the first lien debt documents as they exist at the outset of a transaction (which is often subject to a "cushion" to permit some additional flexibility without running afoul of the second lien lenders). This maximum amount may include amounts that can be incurred based on a leverage ratio or other financial test. Strong issuers have often prevailed to remove any cap on first lien loans within bounds of an intercreditor agreement, in which case second lien lenders may only rely on their debt agreement's covenant protections to ensure that they are not subordinated beyond their expectations. The lack of a cap in the intercreditor agreement creates some ambiguity as to whether the cap under the second lien debt agreement can be enforced against a first lien creditor group.

Are There Any Limits on the Amount of Future Second Lien Loans?

Yes. In order to protect the second lien lenders from being diluted, the typical second lien covenant package will cap the borrower's ability to incur additional second lien loans.

Can Second Lien Loans Be Voluntarily Prepaid Prior to First Lien Loans?

Generally, yes, subject to limitations that are agreed to in first lien loan agreements. In most first lien loan agreements, the borrower is contractually prohibited from voluntarily prepaying second lien loans prior to repayment of first lien loans in full, but there are exceptions that have become customary in the term loan market, including allowing refinancings with replacement junior or unsecured debt, fall-aways upon achieving certain leverage ratios, "builder" baskets, and other dollar-based baskets.

What Sorts of Mandatory Prepayments Typically Apply to Second Lien Loans?

Generally, the same categories of mandatory prepayments that are applicable to the first lien loans (e.g., asset sales, equity proceeds, and excess cash flow) apply to second lien loans. However, almost all second lien deals provide that such mandatory prepayments of second lien loans are not required to the extent that the relevant proceeds are required, under the terms of the first-lien loan documentation, to be used to repay first lien loans.

Are There Any Unique Restrictions on the Assignability of Second Lien Loans?

No. In typical second lien loan documents, the assignment provisions are the same as those found in first lien term loan documentation. The point to be aware of is that in any given first lien or second lien loan transaction the same investors may own both the first lien loans and the second lien loans. It is possible that a group of investors could control decisions and the exercise of remedies for both the first lien loans and the second lien loans and often there are cross-over holders.

Are the Second Lien Loans Cross-Defaulted to the First Lien Loans?

In most transactions, in the event of a covenant default under the first lien loan agreement, a default under the second lien loan agreement is not immediately triggered through a cross-default provision. To do so would deprive the first lien lenders of the earlier triggers they receive by virtue of their tighter covenant package, described earlier. However, in many second lien loan agreements the second lien loans are cross-defaulted to a first lien loan default if the default is a payment default (sometimes limited to a payment default at maturity) or if the first lien lenders have accelerated their loans and declared all amounts due and payable (a so-called cross-acceleration).

SUMMARY

Second lien loan financings have become a fixture of the institutional loan market in the last 20 years. These financings can provide some companies with access to the syndicated loan market where they would otherwise not have access at all, and their popularity with a range of institutional investors from CLOs/CDOs to hedge funds continues to fuel their growth. Regulatory restrictions on highly levered structures have created opportunities for new entrants to the leveraged loan market—direct lenders—to expand access to second lien loans. Although these new entrants have created greater variety in the types of second lien loan terms and intercreditor provisions seen in the market, second lien loan and first lien/second lien intercreditor agreements have largely coalesced around a consensus on key structuring points.

Role of Commercial Banks in Project Finance[14]

J. Paul Forrester

Monique Mulcare
Mayer Brown LLP

INTRODUCTION

Beyond their traditional lending role in project finance transactions, many commercial banks also provide one or more of the following related services: advisory services; construction financing; intermediate to permanent long-term fixed rate financing; commodity, currency, and interest rate risk management; foreign tax absorption; and working capital financing and arranging permanent capital markets funding for projects throughout the world. Looked at separately, the development of these roles was in response to increasing competition among commercial banks, other institutional lenders, and intermediaries to meet the worldwide demand for project finance, which has increased steadily since the 1990s. Today, commercial banks still differ considerably in both their focus and ability to provide such services.

WHAT IS PROJECT FINANCE?

Project finance allows the assets of a project to be (1) separated from the other assets of the sponsor and (2) financed on the basis of the cash flow from those assets alone. It allows a sponsor to undertake a project with more risk than the sponsor is willing to underwrite independently.

Project finance is generally regarded as having begun in the 1930s when a Dallas bank made a nonrecourse loan to develop an oil and gas property. Project finance, in which commercial banks played an integral role, "came of age" in the 1970s and 1980s with

---

[14] A similar version of this article was originally published in *The Financier*, Vol. 2, No. 2 (1995). The views expressed are those of the authors and should not be attributed to Mayer Brown LLP.

the successful financing of North Sea oil and gas projects, Australia's Northwest Shelf gas project, and independent nonutility power generation in the United States, and continues to be an important source of funding for capital-intensive projects, especially with relatively long construction periods, involving complex equipment, and in emerging markets.

Project finance is now employed in almost all capital-intensive industries, particularly in transportation (aircraft, rail, and shipping), in mineral and other natural resource exploration and development (including oil and gas), and in independent power projects. Project finance is also commonly used in developing countries and long-established industrialized countries whose domestic capital markets are small relative to their project development requirements.

TRADITIONAL ROLE

Commercial banks are well-suited to provide project financing because they are able to (1) evaluate complex project financing transactions and (2) assess and, within limits, assume the construction and performance risks often involved in such financings. However, although commercial banks are able to closely monitor their project finance assets in the same manner as they do their other long-term assets, largely because of the short-term nature of a commercial bank's liabilities (i.e., its deposits), participation by banks in such financings is usually limited in amount due to asset–liability mismatch concerns.

A project's sponsor typically requests commitments from its commercial banks for both construction financing and then the permanent long-term financing of the related project. A commitment for construction financing is often for two or more years, and permanent financing is usually a commitment that ranges between 10 to 15 years after the completion of the project and the commencement of its commercial operation. In rarer cases, commercial banks have provided permanent financing commitments of 20 years or more. Most permanent financing commitments by commercial banks include specified increases in the applicable interest rate ("step ups" in the applicable margin or spread over the bank's cost of funds) to provide economic incentives to encourage refinancing of the commercial bank's investment before its scheduled maturity in a permanent capital markets financing.

Accordingly, because project sponsors frequently seek financing through a request for proposal (RFP) process, commercial banks are likely to form separate syndicates or "clubs" to respond to an RFP. The division of work within a syndicate is often highly functional, and has become quite efficient, with individual banks designated (and with related roles) such as technical agent, documentation agent, syndication agent, and variations thereof.[15]

The successful commercial bank syndicate for a project financing usually seeks to "sell down" its underwritten commitments through a further coordinated syndication to a larger bank group. This subsequent syndication may occur before financial closing (i.e., the execution and delivery of definitive financing documents) or after, depending on (1) the confidence of the original syndicate banks in the "marketability" of their transaction in the commercial bank project finance markets, and their willingness to assume the risk of adverse change in such markets; (2) the timing constraints of the project; (3) the project sponsor's preferences in this regard, or the original banks' desire to reduce their levels of commitment; or (4) all or any combination of these circumstances.

The project's construction financing, which normally bears interest at a floating rate, usually requires interest rate risk to be hedged through an interest rate swap, cap, or collar.[16] Upon completion of construction and demonstration of the project's acceptable performance, most sponsors will seek to refinance the project with permanent, long-term, and fixed rate financing. This refinancing is usually on terms that allow the project more operational flexibility because (1) the construction risk has been eliminated from the project and (2) obtaining waivers from public holders is quite difficult and time-consuming.

This traditional model has proven very successful over a considerable period of time and in a wide variety of industries and specific applications. It has historically provided and will likely

---

[15] Some cynical observers suggest that the division of project finance responsibilities has less to do with efficient teamwork than with agency "league tables" kept on commercial banks. See, for example, *Q3 2019 Infrastructure and Project Finance League Table Report*, published by IJ Global, September 20, 2019, at https://ijglobal.com/uploads/Q3%20 2019%20IJGlobal%20League%20Tables.pdf. The authors are of the view that the division of tasks is primarily a matter of experiential efficiency.

[16] A drawback to hedging through swaps and collars is that payments in this type of arrangement may be due from the project. If there is a default, these swap or collar providers may become creditors of the project, and project collateral will have to be shared with them.

continue in the foreseeable future to provide substantial capital to qualifying projects throughout the world.

INTERNATIONAL OPPORTUNITIES: THE IMPACT OF COVID-19 PANDEMIC AND ENERGY TRANSITION

The COVID-19 pandemic and some extreme weather events (e.g., the 2020 Australian and California wildfires and the more recent Storm Uri affecting Texas) have highlighted the material vulnerabilities in critical infrastructure. Even in developed countries there is evidence that prolonged underspending on building and maintenance of required infrastructure has led to significant consequences. For example, in the United States, real infrastructure spending nationally has fallen over the past decade, from $450.4 billion in 2007 to $440.5 billion in 2017.[17] This has resulted in a "C" grade in the quadrennial 2021 report card by the American Society of Civil Engineers,[18] which concluded in the accompanying report that the United States is still just paying about half of its infrastructure bill,[19] and the total investment gap has risen from $2.1 trillion over 10 years to nearly $2.59 trillion over 10 years.

Climate change has also made energy transition to cleaner sources more urgent, and it will not be cheap. Estimates vary but are often very large and in the range of $1 to $2 trillion per year until 2050. For example, the International Renewable Energy Agency, in a 2018 report on Global Energy Transition,[20] estimated that additional costs of a comprehensive, long-term energy transition would amount to $1.7 trillion annually in 2050, but noted that this cost would be offset (and possibly even exceeded) by cost savings from reduced air pollution, better health, and lower environmental damage. Of course, the various pathways to the Paris Agreement target of less than a 2 degree Celsius rise in temperature can make estimation of costs (and benefits) more complex, but there is little doubt that significant

---

[17] See Joseph W. Kane and Adie Tomer, "Shifting into an Era of Repair: US Infrastructure Spending Trends," Brookings, May 10, 2019, at https://www.brookings.edu/research/shifting-into-an-era-of-repair-us-infrastructure-spending-trends/.
[18] Available at https://infrastructurereportcard.org.
[19] Available at https://infrastructurereportcard.org/wp-content/uploads/2020/12/National_IRC_2021-report.pdf, with an executive summary at https://infrastructurereportcard.org/wp-content/uploads/2020/12/2021-IRC-Executive-Summary.pdf.
[20] Available at https://www.irena.org/-/media/Files/IRENA/Agency/Publication/2018/Apr/IRENA_Report_GET_2018.pdf.

related investment will be required, and it is likely that higher levels of investment will be required earlier to obtain later benefits.

However, according to the World Bank, participation by private sponsors and financiers decreased 56% in the first half of 2020 to $21.9 billion.[21] The sharpest decreases occurred in two regions—East Asia and Pacific (which saw a 79% decrease to just $4 billion) and Europe and Central Asia (which saw a 72% decrease to $1.3 billion).[22] Not only were the investments smaller, but the size of the projects that were able to obtain financing also markedly dropped. In 2020, the average size of a project was $173 million. In 2019, over the same period of time, the average size of a project was $244 million.[23] Yet, of the projects that retained their financing and continued to work despite the COVID-19 pandemic, projects in the energy sector attracted $15.1 billion of financing. In fact, energy-generating projects accounted for 69% of the global private participation in infrastructure (PPI).[24] Importantly, 28 of the 73 projects that were closed in the first half of 2020 received support from either multilateral institutions and bilateral agencies that have development mandates or export credit agencies (collectively, "Development and Export Finance Institutions," or DEFIs).[25] In terms of impact, 22% of all PPI projects had support from DEFIs.

All available evidence indicates that, once there is a saturation of vaccines that have a sustained efficacy against COVID-19 and its variants throughout the world that allows for the return of public resources to infrastructure, private infrastructure investment (as opposed to public investment) will continue to grow steadily throughout the world, especially in the developing countries in Asia, Latin America, and the former Eastern bloc.[26]

---

[21] World Bank's "Private Participation in Infrastructure (PPI) 2020 Half Year Report," pp. 2 and 6 at https://ppi.worldbank.org/content/dam/PPI/documents/PPI_2020_Half-Year_Update.pdf.

[22] Ibid.

[23] Ibid., 7.

[24] Ibid., 3.

[25] Ibid., 18.

[26] This assessment is borne out by the published statistics of Raynor de Best of Statista, which showed China, followed by Georgia, Greece, Belarus, and Hungary, leading the way in deploying the highest percentage of GDP in 2018 in construction and maintenance of infrastructure. In fact, de Best found that "[a]s a percentage of the country's GDP, China's average infrastructure spending in 2018 was 10 times higher than that of the United States." See Raynor de Best, "Infrastructure spending as share of GDP in 48 OECD countries 2018," December 10, 2020, at https://www.statista.com/statistics/566787/average-yearly-expenditure-on-economic-infrastructure-as-percent-of-gdp-worldwide-by-country/.

In fact, even though developing countries have passed the trillion-dollar-a-year mark on infrastructure development, infrastructure projects in these countries are still primarily financed by governments.[27] This level of government spending, which experts agree needs to be markedly increased in scope and size to meet the needs of each country's citizens, places an enormous burden on public finances. Obtaining long-term institutional debt and equity financing in sufficient amounts remains a challenge even for financially sound, well-structured projects.

CONSTRAINING FACTORS

Several factors have historically constrained the participation of commercial banks in the project financing for international infrastructure projects and several of these factors remain intransigent:

- Finding "bankable" projects; that is, finding projects that have the "right" risk profile, because during the "conceptualization" phase, the responsible government agency or ministry has structured the entire project or key achievable portions of the project to attract capital.[28]

---

[27] The authors of "Hitting The Trillion Mark—A Look at How Much Countries Are Spending on Infrastructure" estimated total infrastructure spending to range between $0.8 trillion and $1.2 trillion across the low- and middle-income world, with significant regional variations. In absolute terms, the East Asia and Pacific [region] was found to account for more than half (54%) of total infrastructure investment by low- and middle-income countries, followed by Latin America and the Caribbean as a distant second (about 15%). The vast majority (87% to 91%) of low- and middle-income countries' investment in infrastructure[was] undertaken by the public sector. See Marianne Fayl Hyoung Il Lee, Massimo Mastruzzil, Sungmin Han, and Moonkyoung Cho, Policy Research Working Paper 8730, "Hitting The Trillion Mark—A Look At How Much Countries Are Spending On Infrastructure," 2019, at 46, at http://documents1.worldbank.org/curated/en/970571549037261080/pdf/WPS8730.pdf.

[28] See Fida Rana, "Preparing Bankable Infrastructure Projects," September 26, 2017, at https://blogs.worldbank.org/ppps/preparing-bankable-infrastructure-projects. See also François Laurens, "Avoiding Financial Distress in Project Finance: A Case for Implementation of Improved Capital Structure Frameworks," October 12, 2012, p. 4, at https://www.researchgate.net/publication/256036994_Avoiding_Financial_Distress_in_Project_Finance_A_Case_for_Implementation_of_Improved_Capital_Structure_Frameworks ("According to a study of seventeen projects . . ., cash flow issues occurred in 71 percent of the projects, completion delays occurred in 59 percent of the projects, inaccurate cash flow projections in 35 percent of the projects and nine of the projects experienced 'severe trouble'"). Laurens concisely encapsulates the issue of bankability, when he states in his introduction:

- Continued direct investment in projects by the largest and most creditworthy commercial bank customers who can access the capital markets directly as well as specialized financial services (e.g., advisory, commodity/currency/rate hedging), and are therefore less dependent on commercial bank financing and other financial intermediation.
- In a long sustained low interest rate environment, competition for deposits from money market mutual funds (money invested in money market mutual funds exceeds commercial bank deposits) and investment banks (cash management accounts).[29]

> The viability of project financings is predicated on the merits of projects rather than the creditworthiness and history of the sponsors/borrowers because project financings are generally structured on a nonrecourse or limited recourse basis, and collateral is typically limited to project assets (which are often insufficient in value to cover the debt). . . . Therefore, before embarking on a project, participants to the project need to establish whether the project will be economically viable . . ., and lenders and investors need to be convinced of the financial feasibility of the project, i.e., that the returns will be adequate to compensate them for the risks they undertake. . . .
>
> *Ibid.*, 3.

Therefore, to avoid having the "bankability" issues that Laurens has encapsulated, being obscured by the execution issues that will inevitably arise during the project, a combination of the following factors will prove to be critical in determining whether a project is able to attract commercial bank participation:

1. Project mapping that will allow for an early and frank assessment of the project's viability (i.e., a conservative rather than hopeful assessment of whether the project, once completed, will generate cash flows that will cover both (1) future operating costs, and (2) debt service.)
2. Documentation that incorporates clear early marker/triggers that will blunt issues and prevent project failure
3. Government commitments that are not at risk upon changes in administration
4. Reliable and robust restructuring laws

> While the first two factors are rightfully focused on the project itself, the last two factors, which are an assessment of government "predictability," are arguably more important. Countries that do not have a proven track record of stability—that is, maintaining their financial commitments to infrastructure projects and an even-handed and predictable application of law (particularly, restructuring schemes)—will continue to find obtaining capital commitments for even small critical projects challenging. In sum, predictability fosters bankability.

[29] Statista notes that in 2019 the total global net assets of mutual funds registered in the United States amounted to approximately $21.29 trillion at https://www.statista.com/statistics/255518/mutual-fund-assets-held-by-investment-companies-in-the-united-states. Compare, the Economic Research division of the Federal Reserve Bank of St. Louis, which reported that, as of March 10, 2021, deposits at all commercial banks aggregated to $16,615.1828 billion at https://fred.stlouisfed.org/series/DPSACBW027SBOG. Please note that this page is updated regularly.

- Continued competition from financial services companies and the remaining stand-alone investment banks that have focused on infrastructure projects as well as arranging and syndicating commercial loans.
- The imposition of minimum risk-based capital requirements (which require that the activities of commercial banks be internally measured against return on risk-adjusted capital, and which have driven commercial banks to maximize fee income opportunities).
- The relatively more recent liquidity regulatory requirements (that is the Net Stable Funding Ratio under Basel III) that further constrain longer-term bank funding of projects.

Although a complete analysis of the responses by commercial banks to the above factors is beyond the scope of this article, the expanded roles that affected banks occupy in the area of project finance are both illustrative and instructive.[30]

EXPANDED PROJECT FINANCE ROLES

Commercial banks continue to expand their offerings to generate fee income by "unbundling" their financial services. Many have well-established project finance advisory groups, and some have operated with considerable success. These groups offer advisory services that capitalize on the commercial bank's experience in feasibility assessment and financial analysis, trade credit, and international finance (especially the bank's experience with the multi- and bilateral institutions, which are the critical participants in most international infrastructure projects), and their overall project development and management skills (including the negotiation and documentation of increasingly complex transactions). In addition, some commercial banks have used their project finance experience to market corporate trust services in international capital market financings for projects. These banks can sell the value to sponsors and investors of having an experienced trustee or fiscal Agent involved in complex project financing transactions.

---

[30] *See generally*, Barry N. Machlin and Brigette A. Rummel, "The Plus and Minus of Project Finance," November 5, 2020, at https://www.mayerbrown.com/en/perspectives-events/publications/2020/11/the-plus-and-minus-of-project-finance.

Either through direct capital investment or acquisition of investment banks, most of the larger commercial banks have well-developed syndication, private placement, and other similar debt distribution groups. These banks now hold the top places in overall private placement activity.

In a related development, commercial banks continue to "team up" with their competitors, insurance companies, and other institutional investors to provide longer-term or permanent financing for projects. An insurance company may provide a separate commitment for permanent financing (to "take out" the commercial bank's construction financing) that the commercial bank can rely on in extending its construction financing commitment. More often, an insurance company and the commercial bank together provide commitments for both construction and permanent financing. The insurance company typically holds the longer maturities of the permanent financing (thus allowing the commercial bank to hold earlier maturities to minimize its asset–liability mismatch).

A prime asset in any role is the commercial bank's trade credit and international finance experience with the multi- and bilateral agencies, including the World Bank and its agencies, such as the International Finance Corporation (IFC) and Multilateral Investment Guarantee Agency; the Export Import Bank of the United States (U.S. Ex-Im); the U.S. International Development Finance Corporation (DFC); and other regional development banks and export credit agencies. These entities are critical participants in providing and arranging financing and political risk insurance cover for international infrastructure projects.

The technical requirements of the international agencies and the terms of their financing and risk cover vary in important respects, so it is an advantage to have an advisor who is familiar with such requirements and terms to facilitate the analysis of their relative values. Several of these entities (e.g., U.S. Ex-Im and DFC) have expanded and redefined their own project finance lending groups, however, and some even have their own project advisory groups (e.g., the IFC).

Commercial banks have been major participants in the creation and development of interest rate, currency exchange, and commodity risk management markets. In these generally mature and efficient markets, many commercial banks offer risk management services as separate financial products. The risks commercial banks efficiently manage include:

- Interest rate risk is present during the construction period of almost every project. Occasionally, it is present when the permanent financing or some portion of it bears interest at a floating rate.
- Currency exchange risks arise frequently in international projects because, in such projects, the currency in which the cash flow is generated is often different from (and at some point must be converted into) the currency in which all or some portion of the project's financing is denominated.
- Commodity risks also arise frequently in natural resource projects (even when the financing currency and cash flow currency are the same). The creativity that commercial banks have developed in this area can be the difference between a successful or a failed project. For example, a commercial bank will swap volumes of crude oil or gas over time into dollars (a series of forward sales), so that a development project can be financed on the basis of the bank's swap. The bank thus essentially takes the commodity risk from the project and "substitutes" its own credit under the swap.

Several commercial banks or their affiliates have also provided development or mezzanine financing for projects. Some have even made equity investments in projects. Others have made equity commitments to, or equity investments in, pooled investment vehicles specifically targeted for project and other infrastructure investments.

When a commercial bank is already engaged in local activity in a project's jurisdiction, it may provide tax absorption. That is, the bank will not require a full gross-up for applicable withholding or similar deductions from interest payments under a project financing but will agree to absorb some portion of this tax burden. The bank can do this usually because its local activity does not generate taxable income, so tax losses are available from such activity to shelter some portion of this tax burden. If a commercial bank provides this service, it will agree to do so only for a limited period (one or two years) and will probably limit the maximum amount of tax burden absorbed.

Commercial banks that have local banking presence can also provide working capital financing for a project. Although such financings are usually small when compared with the size of the permanent financing, almost all projects require working capital financing.

COMPETITION FROM CAPITAL MARKETS

Many have suggested that the international capital markets, especially the U.S. Rule 144A market,[31] might provide an alternative source of project financing to commercial banks. Yet, the impact of COVID-19 on the market demonstrates the volatility of the capital markets as a source of project finance. From a project sponsor's viewpoint, the devaluation of the currency in the top countries that the World Bank has identified as having the most projects in the pipeline, in particular, is evidence that capital markets cannot be relied upon as an alternative to project financing by commercial banks. Events that have a global impact (e.g., COVID-19) or a regional impact (e.g., a catastrophic event or government instability) also adversely affect projects in emerging markets and have even resulted in the abandonment of capital market financings for such projects at the eleventh hour.[32]

In addition, the capital markets are not particularly receptive to project financing during construction of a project for three principal reasons:

1. The investors cannot price the construction risk that they would assume.
2. The project will incur negative arbitrage on funds raised in anticipation of construction costs not yet incurred. This can represent a substantial financial penalty, depending on the construction timetable, scheduled project draws, and the applicable spread between interest paid to investors and interest earned on funds invested.
3. As a technical matter, it is difficult to balance appropriate investor protections during the construction period while at the same time providing the project sponsor with the necessary flexibility to deal with unexpected events

---

[31] Including one of the authors, *see* https://www.mayerbrown.com/-/media/files/news/2011/10/the-future-of-infra-funding-playing-cassandra/files/11747pdf/fileattachment/11747.pdf.
[32] *See supra* n. 4–8 and the accompanying text.

(e.g., crafting construction draw provisions that create well-tempered achievable markers).

Nevertheless, for completed projects that have demonstrated satisfactory performance (i.e., generate projected cash flows), the international capital markets are an attractive source of permanent long-term fixed rate financing. While such capital markets financing would allow for the replacement of the commercial bank's financing, it may or may not affect some of the other services that commercial banks provide for the project, such as commodity or currency exchange hedges.

Moreover, it may be a commercial bank that undertakes the capital markets financing for the project's sponsor. There are several reasons for this to be the case because the commercial bank:

1. If it has previously provided financial services to the project, is uniquely positioned because of its familiarity with the project and risks to identify and control for potential investors.
2. Can advise the project's sponsor as to the most attractive financing plan for the project, given investor risk profiles, particular capital market volatility, and the like.
3. Can negotiate documentation for such financing that balances the lenders' need for investor protections and the sponsor's need for project flexibility.

Investment by institutional investors in infrastructure debt has been growing steadily for several years, and the largest infrastructure debt fund managers are routinely raising successive multibillion-dollar funds. However, one important constraint on the ability of institutional investors to invest in such debt is the application of risk-based capital requirements to investments that will include exposure to less than investment-grade borrowers and issuers. A potential solution to this issue is to use structured finance techniques to provide such investors with more risk/reward choices and more capital-efficient investments.[33] Of course, commercial banks have decades of experience in such structured

---

[33] *See* "Springtime for Project Finance CLOs" in *Power Risk & Finance* at http://www.powerfinancerisk.com/Article/3830329/Industry-Current-Springtime-for-Project-Finance-CLOs.html.

finance arrangements and in the distribution of the resulting securities into the capital markets.

CONCLUSION

The commercial banks that have already differentiated themselves from their competitors by their ability to offer "unbundled" financial expertise and services in the area of project finance will be well-positioned to capitalize on the new opportunities in the explosion of worldwide project finance needs.

CHAPTER 7
Loan Trading

Introduction to Loan Trading

Fran Sutter
MD, Head of Loan Trading
Citi

How to Trade Loans and the Strategies to Use

Bridget K. Marsh
Executive Vice President & Deputy General Counsel
Loan Syndications and Trading Association

Introduction to Loan Trading

Fran Sutter
Citi

The leveraged loan market has shown amazing growth and development over the last 30 years. What originally started as just a bank-dominated investor base that focused on holding loans to maturity has transformed into a dynamic market where billions of dollars of loans trade every day. Of course, this has come with growth in the asset class as well, as the loan market is over 10 times the size of what it was at the turn of the century. In fact, despite enormous volatility, 2020 marked the highest annual trading volume ever in the history of the loan market. The loan market has offered companies the ability to finance different projects and pursue growth opportunities, and the investor base that it has drawn to fund these new initiatives has expanded as well. These accounts have utilized numerous types of loan trading and investment strategies that have allowed the loan market to develop into the liquid, vibrant market it is today.

Many new players have entered the market, making movements in levels remarkably more efficient. Although the market is dominated by *collateralized loan obligations* (CLOs), changes in macro environment can cause money managers, insurance companies, hedge funds, high-yield funds, and banks to take varying levels of involvement in the market. Factors that can drive participation rates from these counterparties can be changes in interest rate expectations, idiosyncratic company headlines, and relative value of loans to other fixed income asset classes. Although there may be times where multiple types of accounts may be directionally going the same way, there have been many instances where liquidity in the market is improved by these different types of accounts trading amongst themselves, each meeting their own investment goals. Fortunately for the loan market, there has been a consistency with the number of different investors over the last 10 to 15 years which has allowed the asset class to grow, and liquidity has improved as a result.

Secondary trading can be driven by changes of macro or micro factors in the market. This can be centered upon a change in the overall investment environment where the loans can have varying levels of appeal given current yield characteristics relative to other asset classes. It may also have to do with levels of primary market issuance that can cause broader portfolio turnover or company specific events can cause investors to reposition risk. CLOs work within their own individual credit strategies to use the current primary and secondary landscape to optimize their portfolio metrics around spread, rating, and maturity. CLOs are especially cognizant of dollar price, and trading to "build par" is a popular strategy. In this situation, a CLO may look to sell a basket of loans then replace it with a subset of loans with superior credit metrics at lower dollar prices. This can revolve around primary issuance or secondary market dislocations that may cause these price variances to appear. Some retail-based funds may trade to manage their directional flows in and out of their funds. Depending on the size of these inflows or outflows, retail funds may have varying levels of impact to secondary trading levels as they attempt to meet their liquidity needs. High-yield based funds may look to trade loans as their yield changes relative to other bonds or derivatives in the capital structure. Hedge funds may also look to employ this strategy or would even look to set outright long positions in a loan depending on the dollar price and yield for a company's credit risk. So clearly, there are many different players, all with different trading strategies depending on the landscape of the market.

As investors try to quantify movements that drive trading, one would need to look into the characteristics of a loan to make an informed decision. Given that most leveraged loans are floating rate, have shorter average lives than a fixed rate bond, and are typically secured at the top of a capital structure, volatility in the loan asset class is oftentimes a fraction of what is exhibited in other markets. This is especially true as loans trade around par or above. Given limited call protection on loans (usually loans only get 6 to 12 months of call protection), loans trading around par have limited upside. For a given upside catalyst on a credit, loans will underperform other instruments due to their negative convexity and enhanced probability of a refinancing.

When trading at discounted dollar prices, although loans will still be exposed to the same downside risks, loans will exhibit more volatility given that their negative convexity will not restrain upward movement. As more of the market has moved to covenant lite structures (now 85% of the market versus less than 10% pre crisis), the loan market has begun to function more like a floating rate high-yield bond, so fluctuations at times can be volatile but still usually less so than other instruments. However, given that the market is long only, and investors cannot settle a short position, everyone in the market is either long or flat, which can make market moves one-directional at times. It is assumed that the dealer would be the first party to help find and define that clearing level so risk can change hands. In these cases, prices will eventually need to be reset to a level to get a new counterparty involved to help absorb some of the risk.

Loans are not a security; they are a nonTRACE instrument where one cannot look to an exchange to find the last transaction levels in a loan. As dealers look to find the appropriate level to price a loan, the first place that one would look would be other securities in the capital structure of the company itself, either in the company's bonds or the equity if it is publicly traded. If it is a private loan only company, then one would need to use the price of a company with similar credit metrics in the sector to determine a suitable trading level. Oftentimes, technicals in the market can cause variations around these strategies but usually they are a good starting point. As a sell-side trader, having frequent and constant conversations with all the various types of accounts in the market is important to determine their respective interpretations of a headline. This network will help make the appropriate assessment of the move in secondary levels and will also help to create an efficient risk exchange between buyers and sellers.

However there are times when buyers and sellers cannot be matched at exactly the same time, and in this situation, it is important for a sell-side trader to provide liquidity to the market. In constructing the levels where trades should occur, the dealer oftentimes has to take risk on the trade to facilitate the customer's agenda. As the dealer looks to unwind the risk, one has to make use of any of the other players in the market to find an outlet for the other side of the risk. Usually, this leads to a transfer of risk across different account types. Understanding these motivations for trading across different investors will allow a dealer's markets to be competitive and helpful to all those involved.

Even in times of extreme stress, these various players in the market have allowed trading to function properly so it is not merely a one directional flow. Using the COVID-19 pandemic as a case study, accounts were able to raise cash quickly, and although levels had to move dramatically to find clearing levels, the market was able to price the risk. Over time, this market has been able to withstand numerous shocks to the system because of the various types of players in the market that allow risk to change hands. As a dealer, helping these funds accomplish their goals quickly and effectively on both sides of every trade is paramount. When this occurs, capital can move freely across the system, and each player's objective will be accomplished. For a more in-depth discussion of trading strategies and motivations for loan market participants, please see the article below which details the nuances of trading loans.

How to Trade Loans and the Strategies to Use

Bridget K. Marsh
Loan Syndications and Trading Association

The original article, "How to Trade Loans and the Strategies to Use," that appeared in this book's first edition was written by Robert Milam. To update the article, I interviewed several traders in the loan market. I would like to thank those traders for sharing their insights so that this article could be updated and their teachings included and passed on to the next generation of loan market participants.

INTERVIEWEES

- Maegan Gallagher of Octagon Credit Investors, LLC
- Michael Schechter of Ares Management, LLC
- Patrick Wallace of Antares Capital

INTRODUCTION

The most important step in loan trading, as in any other form of trading in the capital markets, is to know and understand the basics of the product in question and the conventions of the market. At first glance, it might seem that loans trade much like high-yield bonds. After all, they are cash instruments, and they trade on a dollar price as a percentage of par. As in the high-yield market, sell-side dealers in the loan market show prices for bids and offers, which could be either indications or firm prices at which the dealer will buy or sell the particular loan referenced. There are, of course, significant differences between loans and high-yield bonds, and these come into play in the trading of these instruments.

LOANS VERSUS BONDS

Loans are typically structured with very different maturities, average lives, and interest rates from bonds, and this impacts the way they trade compared to bonds. High-yield bonds will often be issued with an 8- to 10-year maturity, no amortization schedule, and a fixed rate coupon. By contrast, an institutional term loan will often have a 5- to 7-year maturity and will typically mature before a bond. Most loans feature London Interbank Offered Rate (LIBOR)–based, floating rate interest rates rather than the predominantly fixed rate coupons of bonds. Loans, therefore, have much lower interest rate durations than bonds, and, as a result, will be much less sensitive to changes in price caused by rising or falling interest rates. Fundamentally, loan prices should be affected only by interest rate moves that are large enough to affect interest expense and therefore credit quality in a meaningful way.

Another major difference between loans and bonds lies in their respective collateral and security. Leveraged loans are typically senior secured, whereas bonds issued by the same companies are senior unsecured and senior subordinated. In the event of a default, this means that the loans will have first priority on any recovery available to the debtholders. As a result, the implied recovery rate of the loans is higher than that of the bonds, and therefore the risk to principal is lower for loans. The additional risk to principal embedded in the bonds explains in large part why an unsecured bond will generally be issued with a higher coupon, or interest rate, than a senior secured loan for the same borrower, and also why, on the trading side, the bonds will have more downside risk than loans.

Additionally, bonds are commonly issued with strong call protection and may be noncallable for half of their terms and then step down each year from a price as high as 110 or 115. By contrast, in today's loan market, loans often have little call protection, with six months being standard and callable at 101 typical (in the past, call protection of one year was commonly seen in deals). Lenders seeking to invest in a loan will, of course, try to get call protection in periods of uncertainty where, for example, the execution of a new loan origination may be 25 to 50 basis points wider than a short time earlier. Ultimately, of course, the amount of call protection on any given loan deal is often a sign of how strong the demand for the loan was in the primary market, and is also dependent upon general primary market conditions (greater call protection reflects a deal that was a harder sell to the market, and vice versa for lighter call protection).

LOAN TRADE SETTLEMENT ISSUES

When trading loans, there are also a few settlement issues that are important to note. First, par loans typically trade on a "settled without accrued interest" basis, as opposed to bonds, which trade on a "settle with accrued interest" basis. When an interest payment on a loan is made, the administrative agent distributes to each lender the interest accrued in its name over the course of the accrual period for the length of time it was a lender of record. This differs from bonds, where the trustee under the indenture pays the bondholder the entire coupon as of the record date. It also means that, from the perspective of the lender, there is rarely a reason to calculate a "clean" or "dirty" price as is done in the bond market, and figuring accrued interest is not part of the settlement process. In distressed situations, if the borrower is making interest payments or adequate protection payments in the same amount and as frequently as required to be paid under the terms of the credit agreement, and thus keeping interest payments on the loan current, the loan will continue to trade on a settled without accrued interest basis. If the borrower is no longer paying interest on the loan, the market typically then flips and trades that loan on a "trades flat" basis, which requires that all interest if and when paid by the borrower will be for the buyer's account. This is similar to the terminology used when trading distressed or defaulted bonds: if a coupon is paid at some point in the future, the entire sum is for the benefit of the buyer.

Another important settlement issue to be aware of at the time of the trade is the documentation that will be used. Loans may trade on either par or distressed documents, and the documentation type selected generally depends on the financial condition of the borrower and must be specified by the traders at the time of trade (although in many instances it will be assumed that the parties are trading on par). Since the Global Financial Crisis (GFC), a trend has emerged in the loan market where dealers do not begin to trade loans on distressed documents until the borrower has filed for bankruptcy. Previously, loan traders may have decided to switch from trading on par documents to distressed documents if, for example, (1) the trading price fell below 90, (2) there was a general market belief that a restructuring of the credit was imminent, or (3) the industry in which the borrower operated was encountering problems. The type of document chosen at the time of trade will determine how the loan settles. If a trade is done on distressed documents then the parties settle not only on the assignment agreement in the form attached to the relevant credit agreement (as they do in a par trade), but they will also complete the Loan Syndications and Trading Association's (LSTA) Form of Purchase and Sale Agreement in which the seller and buyer give additional representations and warranties about themselves and the loan being traded. Practically speaking, however, from the perspective of the loan market participant, settlement documentation is particularly relevant with regard to settlement timing, because the current market convention is T + 7 for par and T + 20 for distressed loans (7 and 20 business days past the trade date, respectively), and overall closing costs, because distressed documents generally require additional legal expenses to be incurred.

The overall settlement process and back-office requirements for loan trading continue to be more cumbersome than those for bonds and other securities. Loan trade settlement requires multiple documents to be signed, some by multiple parties (including the borrower, agent, swingline lender, issuing bank, etc.), thereby requiring more paperwork and time. Although the vast majority of loan market participants use ClearPar, an electronic settlement platform that has helped enormously in streamlining the settlement process over the years, settlement times remain an issue in the market. For a loan trade to close, both counterparties must sign the trade confirmation, and then also an assignment agreement, and eventually the funding memo that details the purchase price calculations. It is worth noting that average settlement times in the broadly syndicated market exceed these target dates by a number of days, but administrative agents in the middle market typically manage to settle loan trades within this target.

TRADES ARE BINDING CONTRACTS

When completing a trade, both counterparties should know the name of the borrower; the name, type, and amount of the debt being traded; the price; whether the loan is trading on par or distressed (in most instances, it will be assumed to be par); the treatment of accrued interest (it will often be assumed by the parties that the trading convention is settled without accrued interest when the credit is performing); and any other details that are unique or relevant to the particular transaction. Some examples of the latter include nonstandard representations or warranties being made in the case of a distressed trade, specific terms for participations, and any negotiation of potential voting rights. Some dealers still adhere to the trading practice of reciting a full verbal confirmation of those items at the time of the trade, and often a "trade recap" will be sent by the dealer to its counterparty shortly after they have agreed upon the material terms of the trade.[1] Take the following statement by way of example: "[Name of Dealer] sells $5 million of Serta term loan B at 45, distressed documents, assignment fees waived." The complete statement is important because verbal trades are legally binding contracts under New York law, and the statement gives both counterparties one more chance to be clear with each other as to the exact details of the trade, which can be important for both preventing and potentially resolving future disputes resulting from a disagreement concerning the original trade terms. The use of Bloomberg IB has become even more popular as traders worked remotely during the COVID-19 pandemic and will likely continue to be the favored means of communication between trading desks.

---

[1] Generally, parties will have entered into a binding trade (an oral trade, since 2002 under New York law, may be legally binding) once they have agreed the following five material terms of a trade: (1) the name of the borrower; (2) the name, (3) type, and (4) amount of the debt being traded; and (5) the price. Parties can, of course, raise other terms to the level of being material, but if they do not state that at the time of trade then they will typically have entered a legally binding trade once they agree on those terms.

LOAN TRADING AND VOLATILITY

For those loan market participants that are actively managing loan portfolios, and therefore frequently trading in the secondary market, measuring the volatility of this asset class, both alone and relative to other securities, is an important challenge and can sometimes be a helpful predictor of market moves. Understanding the impact of price movements of a company's equity or bonds (if any) is important to loan trading. Since the GFC, data illustrate that loan prices, on average, are far less volatile than high-yield bonds in the same capital structure, as loan price changes have consistently stayed in a range of 20% to 25% of the high-yield bond price change. Practically speaking, this means that if a company's high-yield bond price changes by a point, the price of the company's bank loan will usually move about a quarter of a point in the same direction. As shown in Exhibit 7.1, which shows the 12-month-lagging standard deviation of return (which incorporates changes in market values), loan return volatility has averaged 1.6% since 2008, as compared to 2.3% for high-yield bonds. However, this relationship will most likely fail in two instances. First, when both the loan and the bond are trading at a premium, increases in bond prices will be less and less likely to be accompanied by a corresponding loan price movement because of differences in call protection and the shorter average life of the loans. Second, when bond prices move as a result of movements in interest rates, loan prices may not move because of the floating rate coupons and low interest rate duration of the asset. Furthermore, in some cases, for deeply distressed issuers whose bonds are expected to have little to no recovery, the absolute (not percentage) price movements in the loan can actually be greater than in the bond. This is due to the fact that the major driver of distressed prices is the rate of return provided by the expected recovery of the loan or security, factoring in the embedded risks of the investment, rather than a yield to an expected maturity at par.

As a loan (or bond for that matter) becomes distressed, the volatility of the loan price will typically increase, thus driving the standard deviation of return higher. We can see this trend in Exhibit 7.1 from an overall market perspective. During the height of the GFC in early 2009, the 12-month-lagging standard deviation of return for the loan market peaked at a record 6.8%. This figure compared

EXHIBIT 7.1

Average 12-Month Lagging Standard Deviation of Returns.

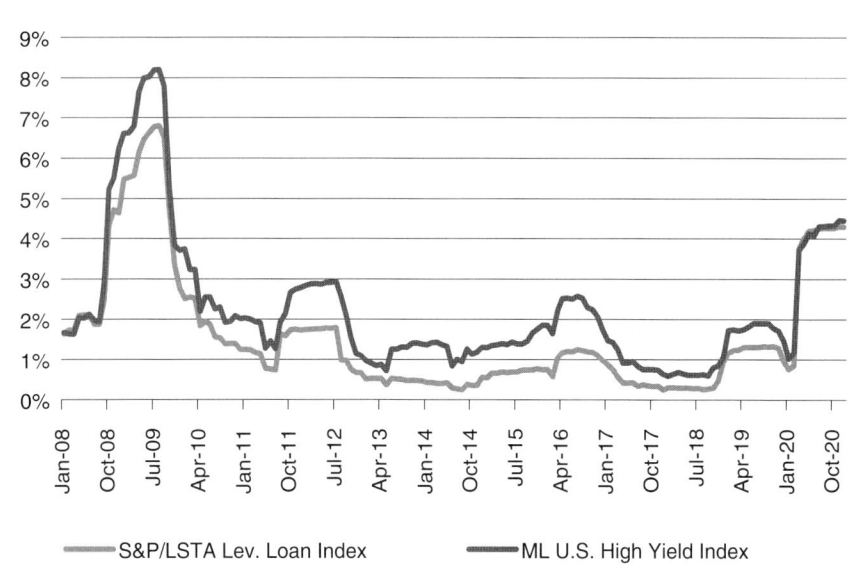

Source: S&P Global.

to the sub 0.5% figure that was reported across 2018 when price volatility was nearly nonexistent as the overwhelming majority of loans was trading at or near par value.

There is generally less volatility in middle market loans, and most managers committing significant funds to a middle market loan will view their investment as a "buy and hold" position and may only look to trade "around the edges." Where managers do seek to trade out of larger positions, middle market dealers will typically help do this over several weeks so as not to disrupt secondary levels. There is typically enough liquidity in the bank group and with the dealer's own trading book to execute that type of order in the middle market.

INFORMATION DISPARITY IN THE LOAN MARKET

A major difference between loans and other capital market instruments that is important for trading purposes is the recognition that not all investors have the same information. Traditionally, lenders have access to a borrower's Material Non-public Information

(MNPI), such as company projections of future earnings, before making a loan; will receive such information on an ongoing basis; and are bound by a confidentiality agreement that restricts the sharing and use of such information. Since the GFC, a trend has emerged where dealers and many institutional investors have chosen to be on the public side only, and thus do not want access to MNPI so that they can continue to trade in the borrower's securities. If they were in receipt of MNPI, it would be illegal for them to trade in those securities. The advantage to public-side lenders is the ability to trade and manage positions in other securities, such as hedging a loan position with a short sale of a bond or credit derivative. When a loan is in bankruptcy, many lenders who are on creditors' committees will add "big boy" language to the trade confirmation that augments the LSTA's big boy language in the standard terms and conditions of the LSTA trade confirmation. Although initially only dealers were including this language, certain institutional investors are now opting to include it in their trade confirmations as well. The language alerts counterparties to the discrepancy of the type of information the parties each may have available to it. Dealers will typically want to ensure that they only receive syndicate information when the rest of the syndicate receives it, and thus are walled off from their originations, risk, and capital markets teams so that they do not get tainted with information that might restrict them from trading a loan.

There are, however, many borrowers that are entirely private, with no publicly traded securities in their capital structure. In these cases, all lenders may be on the private side, but it is possible that there will be both a public-side and private-side group of lenders if, for example, the borrower is anticipating issuing bonds in the near future.

LOAN VERSUS BOND TRADING: NAKED SHORT SALES

Another significant difference between trading loans and bonds is that because loan investors can be positioned only on the long side, there is a finite amount of loans that can possibly trade. With no ability to be naked short (and then borrow to settle in a timely manner) in the loan market, the only practical way for a market participant to sell a loan is if the market participant owns it. Although attempts have been made to create a short-selling capability in the loan market in the past, there remains no method of borrowing loans to deliver into a short sale, as can be done in most bond markets or with equities. Technically, a loan market participant can short a loan simply by selling a loan that it does not yet own (a naked short sale), but the net effect is similar to that of shorting a bond without a borrow, and the practice is generally frowned upon, because it can lead to failed trades, delayed settlement times, buy-ins, and other general inconveniences, especially from the perspective of the buyer. Having said that, many loan market participants sell loans for which they have open buys to cover the sale. Although, strictly speaking, they are short because the trade under which they are buying the loan has not yet settled, it is not a naked short, and the loan market has adapted to the somewhat longer settlement times caused by this practice and other loan settlement issues in the market, especially when compared with other asset classes.

In any case, the inability to cover a naked short sale with a borrowing mechanism changes the personality of the way the loan market trades relative to the other asset classes. From a risk perspective, a loan market participant is either long or flat a loan. In particular, with no ability to short loans, what may happen in a down market is that bids drop but offerings may remain relatively unchanged, leading to a wider bid-offer spread and a lack of activity. Sellers who own the paper may wait for an uptick in price before selling, as they attempt to minimize their losses and often trade with their original cost basis in mind, whereas a short seller of a bond does not yet have a cost basis to be concerned with and might be more willing to set a position by making a sale at a lower level. However, in today's market, the more liquid names are so widely owned that even in a down market there will typically be investors that own the paper looking to sell their positions. Without the naked shorts, the loan market also avoids many of the technical-related trading events observed in bond markets, such as short squeezes and buy-ins.

Generally, most lenders, if not forced to sell their positions, would prefer to wait for an increase in the loan price. Depending on the length or severity of a market decline, however, certain lenders may need to sell to meet fund redemptions or to help manage certain tests within their own particular structured vehicles, especially if there are ratings downgrades.

MARKET TECHNICALS

A common perception of the secondary loan market is that the technical indicators can make it seem as if all market participants are attempting to transact in the same direction at the same time—that the market has only buyers or only sellers at any given point. Of course, that is not an accurate statement, or loans would never trade, and generally speaking, the number of narrow bid-ask, two-sided markets that dealers will make is substantial, and liquidity can actually rival or exceed that of the high-yield bond market on any given day. Nonetheless, the added liquidity for both the bid and the offer that is provided by the short seller or short-covering bid can help alleviate the perception of one-sidedness for the bond or equity markets and makes it easier for dealers to show two-sided markets. Additionally, there will always be certain borrowers whose loans will have more buyers than sellers, and other loans that rarely trade because of the lack of a bid for the loan. In these cases, it is also up to the market as a whole and the dealer community in particular to attempt to find the price where the marginal buyers and sellers meet to define the correct trading level. In recent years, there has been more demand than supply in the loan market, and this abundance of cash being invested in the market has given rise to more borrower-friendly credit agreement terms (aggressive credit agreement terms from the lenders' perspective), and the market may feel entirely "bid" with no real offers. The opposite has happened when offerings have swamped buy-side interest and subsequently forced trading levels lower. Both types of markets again lead to a generalization of one-sidedness in the technical indicators. In these cases, if the entire market appears to be characterized as either a buyer or seller, a prepared trader should have his or her analysis as complete as possible so that if the other side of the trade appears, the trader can quickly make a decision to buy or sell at the given price.

LOAN MARKET CHARACTERISTICS

The loan market has seen a huge growth in trading volumes, with secondary trading volumes rising in 2020 to a record $772 billion. During the height of the COVID-19 pandemic in March 2020, monthly secondary trading volume hit a record $119 billion. Liquidity levels have improved in recent years as a result of several factors. The overall size of the market, in terms of both the amount of cash to be invested and the number of market players buying or selling loans, has increased substantially in the past decade, as evidenced by the $1.2 trillion of leveraged loans outstanding in 2020. The number of market participants has expanded dramatically as well, with the largest single constituency, CLOs, representing approximately 70% of the demand for loans. The average facility size has also seen a commensurate rise with loans of nearly $1 billion now regularly being allocated and actively traded.

The increased number of loan market participants in the market has impacted the trading characteristics of the loan market. The growth of the number of new entrants has, of course, added competition for primary issuance, but the growth has also significantly deepened the secondary market liquidity. In the early years of the nascent loan market, if a deal became stressed or distressed, a fund investing primarily in par loans would have difficulty finding a bid until the asset reached the long-term internal rate of return sought by long-only distressed investors, which was sometimes upwards of 20% to 30%. In practical terms, that meant that there might be very little liquidity from prices in the mid-90s until the prices broke below 80. Today, distressed hedge funds, which might not be investing from a long-only perspective, will often purchase loans as part of a strategy across the larger corporate capital structure; therefore, they are a major liquidity provider in the once very illiquid distressed trading space. Since the GFC, the average size of funds in the middle market has grown significantly, and their hold size has also increased dramatically over the past decade, giving rise to the impression that their appetite for loans is nearly limitless.

Although overall trading volumes as well as the growth in the number and size of funds has been a huge driver for the syndicated loan market, the growth in the volume of CLOs participating in this market has had even more of an impact. The U.S. CLO market has more than doubled in size since the GFC to reach $760 billion at the end of March 2021. With its expansion in the past decade, the U.S. CLO market has been the most dominant buyer of the U.S. leveraged loan market, accounting for over 70% of primary market purchases in 2020, compared to 13% by mutual funds and less than 20% by other loan investors.

Loan trading continues to take place at a faster and faster pace, with dealers making two-sided markets, rapid trading happening after the allocations for new deals or news events, and prices immediately moving to reflect updated perceptions of risk and returns. The days of the secondary loan market as a sleepy backwater market with low trading volumes and even lower volatility are long gone. Indeed, a large dealer in the loan market several years ago launched the first electronic trading platform for loans. The platform is designed to bring together loan market participants in the secondary trading of loans. On the platform, the "trading desk sets fixed, mid-market prices and then hosts simple matching sessions. During the sessions, clients bid or offer against the mids for a low, flat commission. When two participants match, they automatically, immediately and discretely trade."[2]

SPECIFICS OF LOAN TRADING STRATEGIES

Loan market participants invest in and trade loans using a large number of strategies, especially considering, as discussed above, that there is no way to short the product. Loan market participants can employ loan-only trading strategies, including relative value between loans to different borrowers, between different tranches of the same borrower, or between the primary and secondary markets. They can use leverage to increase returns. They may also trade into various positions to get information or to control or have a voice in various corporate negotiations, such as amendments or restructurings.

For the long-only community, they look at relative value across loans and bonds in the same capital structure and exploit inefficiencies driven by market technicals. Loans can also be combined as the long side of capital structure relative value trades, such as buying loans versus buying protection, shorting bonds, or defending a position in bonds or the stock.

Secondary Market

From the long-only side, active portfolio managers use the secondary market in several ways to generate excess returns. The old trading adage of "buy low, sell high" aside, traders look to buy

---
[2] *See* https://www.bofaml.com/en-us/content/instinct-loans.html.

loans that will provide above-average returns based on fundamental credit analysis, are cheap relative to the return implied in the trading price of a loan to another borrower, or are cheap relative to another tranche of the same borrower. Of course, traders will sell loans that look likely to trade lower, either for technical reasons or because of fundamental credit analysis, or are expensive relative to other options. Some examples include buying a "risky" distressed loan for which credit analysis suggests an expected yield of 20% and selling a par loan that looks headed for trouble or a negative credit event. An investor may also look to sell a loan yielding L + 200 to buy another yielding L + 300 when the borrowers are in similar industries and are similarly rated. Additionally, a market participant might sell a loan to buy another if the dollar price of the loan purchased is significantly lower, even if the yield to maturity of each is the same, especially in cases where there is little or no call protection, since, as discussed earlier, loans are often refinanced early as well as having average lives that are much shorter than their stated maturities.

During the pandemic in 2020, loan traders were more focused on credit risk trading and less so on relative value trading, and during that period liquidity in the top 100 loans remained strong, but it decreased sharply for other smaller loans.

Primary Market versus Secondary Market

Another common trade is to look at value in the primary market versus the secondary market. In times of strong demand for loans, often referred to as a "hot" market, secondary market prices may average north of par, and in many cases north of 101. In these times, a popular strategy is to purchase almost every loan available in the primary market, which traditionally offers loans at par or a discount, and then make room in the portfolio by selling older positions in the secondary market. This strategy may not work for investors that are heavy in cash, because the struggle to stay invested prevents giving up coupon-paying assets, regardless of price. For CLOs looking to ramp up, often they are unable to ramp up fully in today's market through the primary market only and will need to turn to opportunities in the secondary market. In these cases, it's "buy, buy, buy" in both the primary and secondary markets, with little or no selling at all. Fund flows for CLOs will, of course, significantly impact their motivation for trading a loan. When there is sufficient new issue in the primary market and decent primary allocations are more common, investors can afford to be a little pickier.

Using Leverage

Loan market participants may also use leverage to generate excess returns. Banks do offer total return swaps or similar financing vehicles, allowing a loan buyer to borrow money in an amount anywhere from say 2 to 10 times the required collateral at a range of rates. Using leverage in this way to generate excess returns is much less common today than it was before the GFC.

Getting in the Information Flow

When building a new position in a loan, a loan market participant might choose from among a few strategies. The most conservative is to buy a very small position to "get in the information flow" (most credit agreements specify a minimum amount of $1 million of a term loan may be assigned). A small position will encourage the participant to follow the markets in the name and allow access to information distributed to the syndicate as well as the borrower's management team, both of which can be particularly important if the participant intends to trade the name from the private side. From there, a study of market technical indicators and the completion of credit analysis helps in determining additional entry points for more buys. For large deals, it is easy to be patient, because the likelihood of more paper being available is high; it is a matter of measuring out events that will drive secondary pricing and trading accordingly. For small situations, the buyer will need to be more aggressive in terms of lifting offers in the desired price context, because only a limited amount of paper may be offered, and competition among buyers could become fierce.

Control Positions

Depending on the size of the deal and the capital available to the buyer, the buyer may ultimately seek to take a control position. For companies going through the Chapter 11 bankruptcy process, this will be two-thirds of a voting class for control or one-third for a blocking position. For performing loans undergoing an amendment, approvals usually require a greater than 50% majority, but require 100% for changes in money terms that are unfavorable to lenders, such as a reduction in collateral or an extension of maturity. A control position allows the participant to drive negotiations with the borrower, and this strategy is particularly common during bankruptcies or restructurings. It is also one of the strategies at the core of traditional distressed loan investing. Buyers accumulate a majority stake in the loan in a fundamentally good but overlevered or soon-to-be-bankrupt company, convert all or a large portion of the loans to equity, possibly wiping out other stakeholders such as the prepetition equity or bonds, and allow the now delevered company to improve and grow its business. This allows the new equity to increase in value and the original distressed buyer to sell the equity or the entire company at a future date. Indeed, the energy crisis of 2015 saw the loans of C&J Energy Services trading at about 130 as it emerged from bankruptcy because traders saw incredible value in the "post reorg equity." The unique characteristics of distressed loans require thoughtful attention, and the possibility of an investor getting reorganized equity as proceeds for their loans can be incredibly valuable.

Capital Structure Trades

Loans are also used in a variety of capital structure trades. Traders may buy loans against a short in the equity, bond, or credit derivatives market. The longer-term view of the credit determines the weighting of the long and short ratios. For instance, an even notional amount of long loans versus short bonds or long credit protection is an implicitly bearish trade. As discussed earlier, bonds historically fall much further than loans in a negative credit event, so while the loan might fall a point, the bond might fall five; thus, the participant would be ahead four points on that particular trade. The loan will underperform on the upside as well, though, so the participant putting this trade on is taking the view that the borrower is going to have a negative credit event. Additionally, recall that bonds tend to have higher coupons than loans, so an even-dollar long/short is likely to have negative carry. This being the case, a trade could also be constructed as carry neutral, which means that the loan investor could weight the trade such that the carry generated by the long was roughly equivalent to that required to be paid on the short, allowing more patience, because there is no cost of carry in the trade. In both of these trades with a negative bias, the loan is effectively financing the short.

Hedging

For those looking to hedge a bond or loan position rather than to express a strong view, the historical bond versus loan volatility discussed above suggests that a relatively market-neutral hedge is a 4-to-1 ratio of loans to bonds for high-yield borrowers, and closer to half that ratio for distressed borrowers, though fundamental credit analysis and predictions for potential trading levels will ultimately dictate the ideal ratios.

Macroeconomic Factors

Macroeconomic factors are followed in portfolio management and then that leads to trading. Traders will watch equities, rates, and where the exchange traded funds (ETFs) are trading (at a discount or a premium) on a daily basis. For example, in today's market a trader may be monitoring the possibility of wage inflation and where that may be a negative factor and a material risk for certain loans.

Hedging loans against a potential default, rather than just against market moves, using credit derivatives can be complicated as well, because the trader needs to have a view on recovery rates for both loans and bonds, and weighting the trade properly can again be difficult. Hedging loans on a single name can be particularly difficult.

As a final strategy, traders may weight a trade overwhelmingly to the long side, so that the bond provides only a partial hedge against any downside scenario for the loan trading levels, for instance, using an 8- or 10-to-1 ratio of loans to bonds.

In general, though, none of these trades should be put on without looking past the models and historical numbers and taking a view on future news and credit events that may affect the borrower and the related outcomes and impacts on trading levels.

CONCLUSION

A loan trader will have different motivations for trading a loan. Perhaps they are ramping up a new structure and need to buy assets, perhaps they need to diversify their portfolios, or perhaps they want or need to sell out of distressed credits. No matter the trader's motivation, the increasing complexities of the loan market mean that the trader will need to monitor a host of factors to be successful. Fortunately, the sophistication of the market, the continued growth of the number of loan market participants, and the market liquidity will enable them to accomplish their goals quickly and effectively.

CHAPTER 8
The Secondary Loan Market

Overview of the Secondary Loan Market

Theodore Basta
Executive Vice President of Market Analytics and Investor Strategy
Loan Syndications and Trading Association

The U.S. Leveraged Loan Market Through the Lens of the S&P/LSTA Leveraged Loan Index

Marina Lukatsky
Senior Director
S&P Global Market Intelligence
Leveraged Commentary and Data

The Secondary Loan Market: Settling Loan Transactions

Sheryl Fulton
Associate Manager
IHS Markit

Overview of the Secondary Loan Market

Theodore Basta
Loan Syndications and Trading Association

TERMINOLOGY AND BACKGROUND

For the purposes of this chapter, this review of the origin and subsequent expansion of the U.S. corporate secondary loan market will center on leveraged loan transactions. Leveraged loans, those made to noninvestment-grade borrowers, offer higher returns for their increased level of risk as compared to investment grade loans. The term *leveraged* is normally defined by a bank loan rating of BB+ and below, or a loan with an interest rate spread over LIBOR (London Interbank Offered Rate) that is greater than 125 basis points. Although investment-grade loans, or nonleveraged loans, constitute quite a large portion of the primary syndicated loan market, broadly syndicated leveraged loans represent the overwhelming majority of secondary market trading activity, and hence are the cornerstone of the discussion in this chapter. Furthermore, this chapter will focus on the institutional term loan portion (commonly referred to as a *term loan B*) of leveraged loan credit agreements, which along with a revolving credit facility and a noninstitutional term loan (commonly referred to as a *term loan A*) comprise the majority of all broadly syndicated leveraged loan agreements between the borrower and lender group. The term *institutional loan* is normally defined as a term loan that is carved out for nonbank or institutional lenders, such as collateralized loan obligations (CLOs) and mutual funds. Such loans generally have a longer maturity and a more aggressive amortization schedule, and thus offer a higher interest rate than that of noninstitutional term loans, which have historically been marketed to banks and other risk-adverse lenders. Along with a revolving credit facility, the noninstitutional term loan comprises what industry participants refer to as the *pro rata* portion of the loan agreement. Pro rata loans generally trade far less actively than institutional loans, primarily due to their accompanying risk–return profile and the subsequent composition of their lender group.

THE ORIGINS OF THE SECONDARY LOAN MARKET

The U.S. syndicated corporate loan market has become one of the most innovative and expanding sections of the U.S. capital markets over the past three decades. Today's corporate loan market consists of an efficient primary market, where agent banks originate and syndicate loan transactions, and a liquid, transparent secondary trading market, where traders can efficiently buy and sell pieces of such loans (following the original syndication process). But it was not always that way. There was a time when banks lent to their corporate borrowers and simply kept those loans on their books, never contemplating that loans would be actively managed and traded just like stocks and bonds.

The story of the syndicated corporate loan market began in the United States during the late 1980s, with the first wave of growth being driven by corporate mergers and acquisitions (M&A) activity, and in particular leveraged buyouts (LBOs). This type of financing required loans to be not only larger but to also offer lenders higher interest rates, given the increased level of risk associated with such larger leveraged transactions. This phenomenon led to significant changes to the structure and composition of leveraged loan transactions. Because banks found it difficult to underwrite very large loans on their own, they formed groups of lenders, or *syndicates*, which are responsible for sharing the risk associated with funding such large transactions. Syndication enabled the banks to satisfy borrower demand while limiting their risk exposure to any single borrower. The changing role of banks greatly facilitated the development of the secondary market. Back in the 1980s, banks focused almost exclusively on their role as originators because they were reluctant, or even forbidden, to take the principal risk required for trading loans. Instead, any secondary trading was brokered; it was a negotiated transfer between a buyer and a seller and did not require the broker to carry inventory or take principal risk. Moreover, beginning in the early 1990s banks began to realize the benefits of freeing up capital by selling portions of their leveraged loan holdings to both traditional (bank) and nontraditional (nonbank) institutions in a secondary market, instead of holding such investments to maturity as they had done historically. About this time, banks began to establish trading desks, designed to hold inventory, take positions, and provide liquidity to market participants, thereby creating a significantly more active secondary market for loans. Although brokers remain active in today's secondary loan market, traders are the dominant players. Today, more than 35 sell-side institutions have full-time resources dedicated to secondary loan trading activity.

Another key driver in the matriculation of the secondary loan trading market was the highly leveraged transaction (HLT) regulations of the early 1990s. The regulations were a reaction by the Federal Reserve Bank to commercial bank involvement in the high-yield excesses of the 1980s. The HLT regulations made holding leveraged loans more expensive for banks, and effectively became the catalyst for the further development of the institutional loan market and lender class. By design, the higher interest rates associated with larger syndicated leveraged loans attracted nonbank lenders to the market, including traditional bond and equity investors, thus creating a new demand stream for this emerging asset class. Insurance companies and retail mutual funds were the first adopters. It is here that fund managers would begin to create funds for the sole purpose of investing in leveraged loans. These loans were generally senior secured by real assets and sat atop the capital structure. As a result, loans would get paid out first in the event of default, which led to much higher levels of recovery as compared to bonds. The interest rates paid by the borrowers would consist of a fixed coupon rate plus a floating interest rate, commonly three-month LIBOR. This floating rate would offer lenders a natural hedge against rising interest rates, unlike fixed rate bonds, which generally underperform in rising rate environments. The resultant senior secured, floating rate asset class had a favorable risk-adjusted return profile, which would also offer a lower level of correlation to other asset classes. In time, institutional lenders became drawn to the attractive features of such loans. Again, unlike bonds, loans were senior secured debt obligations with a floating rate of return, which allowed fixed income investors a new and unique way to obtain exposure to corporate credit. As a result, an institutional asset class emerged, which would go on to redefine leveraged lending and secondary trading in the years to come.

Although banks continued to dominate both the primary and secondary markets, the influx of new institutional lender groups in the mid-1990s saw an inevitable change in market dynamics within the syndicated loan market. In response to the demands of this new institutional lender class, originating banks began structuring traditional credit agreements with an eye toward developing the features that define today's institutional loan portion of the deal, or the term loan B. First, the size of these tranches was increased to meet (or create) demand. Second, their maturity dates were extended and their amortization schedules were back-weighted, which meant that much, or all, of the loan principal would not need to be paid back until the final year of the agreement, when a large bullet payment was to be made by the borrower. In return, term loan B lenders were paid a higher rate of interest. All these structural changes contributed to a more aggressive risk–return profile, which was necessary to build out an even more diverse institutional lender base and create liquidity in the secondary loan market. Indeed, nonbank appetite for syndicated leveraged loans would be the primary driver of demand that helped propel the loan market's growth and the emergence of a liquid secondary trading market. Further development of this secondary market injected liquidity into the corporate loan market, which attracted a growing institutional investor base, which further fueled increased market liquidity into the next decade.

BY THE TURN OF THE CENTURY

The emergence of a true secondary loan trading market would go down as one of the most influential changes in the history of the syndicated loan market. Its development went on to attract and support the emergence of the nonbank, institutional lender community, which needed to rely upon the secondary market to manage their loan exposures and credit risk. It is here that banks would now begin their metamorphosis from simply loan originators to loan arrangers and traders. This process engineered the flight to liquidity that ensued at the turn of the century and gave rise to active loan portfolio management. Historically, holders of loans would carry performing loans at par or face value, whereas valuations (expected sale prices) were internally assigned to defaulted loans. By the early 1990s, banks such as BT Alex Brown, Bear Stearns, Citibank, and Goldman Sachs began to create loan trading desks that acted more as brokers than traders, simply matching up buyers and sellers. In these early years, trade activity was relatively scarce, growing to roughly $40 billion by the mid-1990s, according to Refinitiv LPC. At that time, banks remained the dominant funding source as institutional lenders were funding less than one-third of primary market leveraged lending activity. For that reason, most trades in the secondary market occurred on the distressed side, as banks looked to clear their books of loans that had declined in value since their initial syndication. But the market was clearly changing, and in 1995 the Loan Syndications and Trading Association (LSTA) was formed, with a mandate to promote the orderly development of a fair, efficient, liquid, and professional trading market for corporate loans. In those early years, standardized documentation was the most significant contributor to the rise in liquidity in the leveraged loan market. Because loans are not securities, no single authority regulates their sale and trading. As the LSTA began delivering on its mandate to create and improve loan trading documentation and standard market practices, the availability of secondary market pricing information became of the utmost importance.

By the mid-1990s, a growing class of asset managers were recognizing bank loans as a relatively stable, senior secured asset class. However, many of these nonbank lenders wanted (or needed) to value their loan investments on a regular (often daily) basis. In the early days of loan trading, there was no service that provided valuations. Initially, originating banks (which came to be thought of as primary dealers, or brokers, as in the bond market) were increasingly asked by their nonbank clients to provide "indicative quotes," known as the indicative "bid" (the level at which the dealer might buy the loan) and the indicative "ask" (the level at which the dealer might sell the loan). This process was typically accomplished by faxing individual "ax sheets" containing indicative prices back and forth between clients and dealers. Clients would then need to manually aggregate prices from several dealers to value their portfolio holdings. Because this was clearly a cumbersome and inefficient process, pricing services developed to meet the market's need for a reliable, independent source of secondary loan prices. At the same time, auditors and comptrollers of the many banks that were participating in secondary trading demanded an independent third-party provider of secondary market prices to validate the levels at which loan traders were marking their loan positions "to market." In early 1996, the LSTA established a dealer quote–based secondary mark-to-market (MTM) process to value loans at a price indicative of where they would presumably trade, providing the broker-dealer community with a standard pricing methodology. The LSTA began collecting monthly dealer quotes (indicative bid and ask values reflective of where a loan would be expected to trade) on roughly

155 loan facilities from 12 broker-dealers. By the late 1990s, the need to properly mark-to-market loan positions on a more frequent basis grew precipitously, as secondary trading volume reached $80 billion a year. With more than 20 banks involved in both brokering and trading bank loans, banks were increasingly selling off pieces of loans to mutual funds and other institutional investors that were entering the marketplace.

Continuing its effort to facilitate liquidity and transparency in the secondary market, the LSTA, along with Refinitiv LPC, created the LSTA/LPC Secondary Mark-to-Market Pricing Service (SMPS) in 1999, the first independent third-party provider of daily U.S. secondary loan prices. Although this service was initially developed with a view toward providing net asset values (NAVs) for nonbank lenders, they ended up serving more than that purpose, aiding greatly in creating transparency in the secondary market. As the institutional lender base grew and the number of deals in the market continued to expand, an ever-increasing number of loans were being priced in the secondary market, and the terms and conditions on these loans were beginning to be readily available. Thanks to the pricing service and an overall increase in information transparency, asset managers could now easily research and evaluate loans while finding buying opportunities through techniques such as relative value analysis. They could also use these prices for risk management purposes, to validate past actions, to track the performance of investment vehicles, and to keep watch lists of possible trading opportunities. The increased transparency into the market facilitated the rapid development of active portfolio management through secondary trading. Another extremely important driver in the continued evolution of the secondary market was the widespread availability of bank loan ratings during the late 1990s, through companies such as Standard & Poor's (S&P), Moody's, and Fitch Ratings (formerly Fitch IBCA). According to S&P, the agency rated 56% of the leveraged loan universe in 1998 (today that figure exceeds 98%).

By the year 2000, the LSTA was clearly having a profound influence on the development of secondary market liquidity through successful initiatives such as the creation of standardized trading documents and market practices, the partnership with Refinitiv LPC in forming the pricing service, and a partnership with S&P in the creation of the S&P/LSTA Leveraged Loan Index (S&P/LSTA LLI), which went on to become the standard benchmarking tool of the industry. At the same time, technology was advancing, and sell-side broker-dealer trading desks were now providing daily "runs" to their bank loan clients, where they offered secondary trade information on the loans that they were making active markets in, including transactable bid and offer levels at lot sizes. And these "runs" were no longer being emailed out to clients, but instead were updated and sent out in real time via Bloomberg instant messaging.

Despite the daily secondary market price fluctuations that were a product of increased trading volume and the new daily valuation process, many lenders, particularly those running loan mutual funds, were still valuing most of their loan positions at face value until the Securities and Exchange Commission (SEC) issued an interpretive letter in the year 2000. The SEC ordered funds to change their valuation methodology, mandating that bank loan fund managers use a MTM price (recording the market price or value of a security daily) rather than a fair value price (a rational and unbiased estimate of the potential market price) to determine the price of bank loans for NAV calculations. Loans that traded or were available to trade in the secondary market now needed to be priced as they traded, or "marked to market," like stocks and corporate bonds. Although this policy increased day-to-day market volatility, it had a dramatic positive effect on trade activity and liquidity. This growth in secondary market activity was particularly notable because loans are not securities, but rather private placement instruments, which were generally extremely awkward to trade efficiently in a secondary market. For institutional lenders, however, Rule 144a of the Securities Act broke down many of the barriers to efficient secondary market activity and greatly facilitated resale activity among that class of lenders. As a result, these lenders could enhance liquidity, which, in turn, also increased the appeal of leveraged loans as a viable investment option.

By the turn of the century, the scales began to tip in favor of institutional lenders who were now funding more than 50% of new issue leveraged loan transactions in the primary market. At the same time, diversification within the institutional lender base was expanding and now included finance and insurance companies; hedge, high-yield, and distressed funds; loan mutual funds; and structured vehicles, namely CLOs. By the year 2000, CLOs had already become the dominant lender within the nonbank, institutional lender group. Between 1995 and 2000, several data points illustrate the transformation of the market, all of which created the foundation for the flight to liquidity that would ensue in the 2000s:

- The number of loan investor groups managing bank loans grew by approximately 130% to 74 manager groups.
- Institutional lenders accounted for more than 54% of new deal allocations in leveraged lending (Exhibit 8.1).
- The number of sell-side loan trading desks that were actively taking positions and trading loans increased 150% to 30 institutions.
- Daily MTM pricing coverage doubled to 1,514 loans (between 1999 and 2000).
- Secondary trading volume tripled to $102 billion (Exhibit 8.2).

Taken all in, the advancements that occurred during the 1990s had a profound effect on increasing investor confidence in the syndicated loan market. Loans were no longer considered an esoteric asset class but were now becoming a part of core fixed income investing. And just as the market's viability was on the rise, so was its visibility. The *Wall Street Journal* began weekly coverage of the syndicated loan market in 2000 by publishing LSTA/Refinitiv LPC secondary market prices on the most widely quoted and volatile

EXHIBIT 8.1

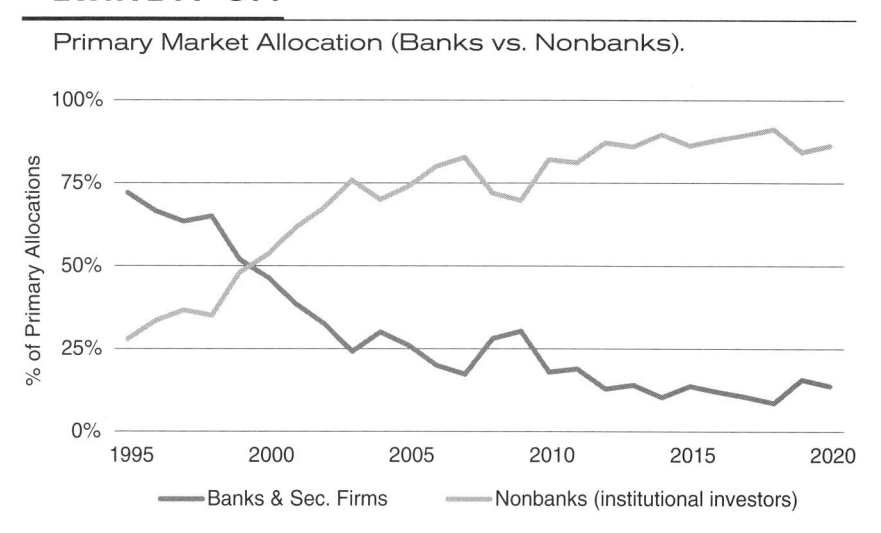

Primary Market Allocation (Banks vs. Nonbanks).

Source: S&P Global Market Intelligence.

EXHIBIT 8.2

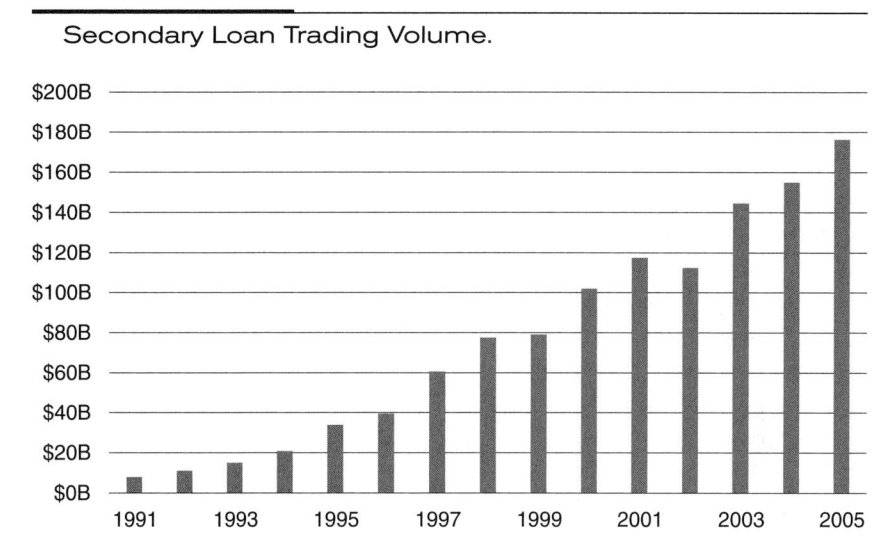

Secondary Loan Trading Volume.

Source: Refinitiv LPC.

loans, a true testament to how the secondary market had evolved over the preceding decade. The market was now poised to experience a period of rapid growth and expansion in both the primary lending and secondary trading markets, which would last until the Global Financial Crisis (GFC) of 2008.

LEADING UP TO THE GLOBAL FINANCIAL CRISIS

The rapid development of the secondary market for syndicated loans would continue on into the twenty-first century, but growth did not come easy during the early 2000s as the U.S. economy entered into recession in 2001, and not to mention the tragedy of September 11th. Although the eight-month economic downturn ended in November of that year, its impact lingered in the credit markets well beyond 2001. Actually, the credit default cycle started in late 1999 and resulted in a torrent of distressed loans from companies in default and bankruptcy—particularly in the tele-technology sector. By year-end 1999, the 12-month lagging default rate on the S&P/LSTA LLI had already risen above 4%, before increasing above 6% across 2000 and 2002. But despite the recession, which hampered growth, and a historic default cycle, which did not normalize until

2003 (the default rate fell back to just 2.25%), both the primary and the secondary loan markets would begin to expand exponentially through 2007. As the primary market came back online in 2003, institutional loan issuance breached the $100 billion barrier for the first time (Exhibit 8.3). By 2007, that figure had increased 260% to a record north of $425 billion. As a result, the par dollar amount of loans that the S&P/LSTA LLI was tracking increased from just $112 billion at the end of 2002 to $554 billion by the end of 2007—a rise of almost 400% (Exhibit 8.4). By that time, institutional lenders, or nonbanks, had already become the dominant funding source of leveraged loans, by purchasing more than 80% of new loans. The widespread use of securitization through CLOs was fueling much of that growth, as CLO issuance totaled $280 billion through the five-year period ended 2007, with $186 billion worth of new vehicles coming online between 2006 and 2007 (Exhibit 8.5). Loan mutual fund assets under management (AUM) was also increasing—growing from just $9.7 billion in 2002 to its mid-2000s peak of $47 billion established in 2006 (Exhibit 8.6). This new wave of investors was demanding higher levels of transparency into the secondary loan market. Prior to 2006, the only real transparency into the secondary loan trading market was an annual survey conducted by Refinitiv LPC that provided an annual estimate of secondary trading volume. According

EXHIBIT 8.3

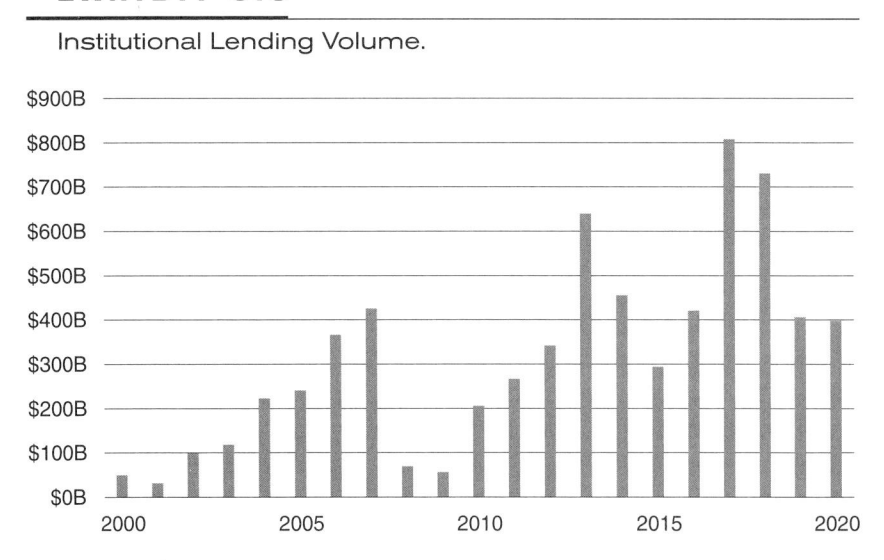

Institutional Lending Volume.

Source: Refinitiv LPC.

EXHIBIT 8.4

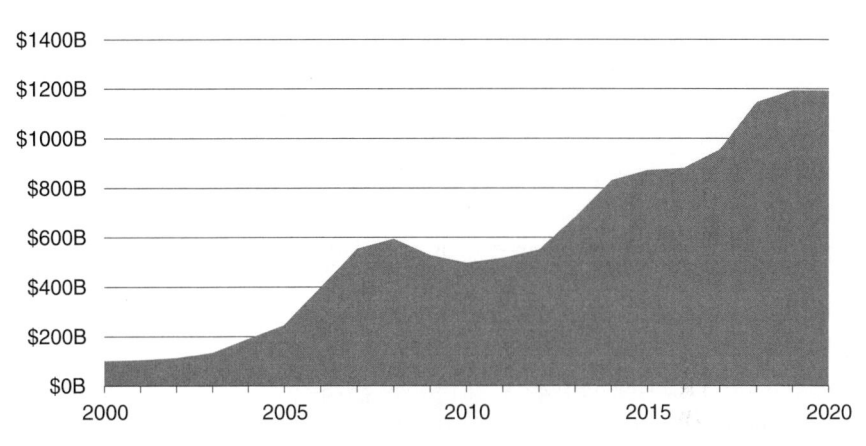

S&P/LSTA LLI Outstandings.

Source: S&P/LSTA Leveraged Loan index.

EXHIBIT 8.5

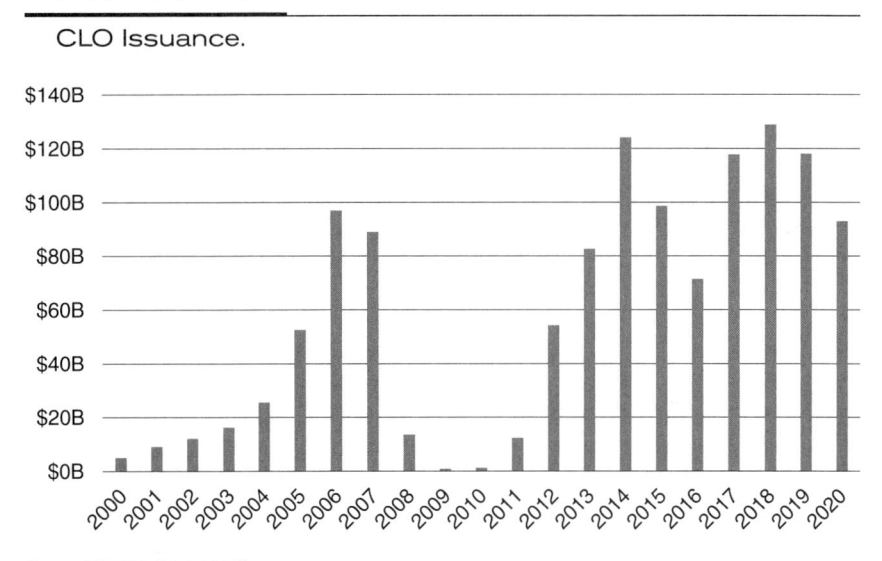

CLO Issuance.

Source: S&P Global Market Intelligence.

to survey results, secondary loan trading volume had increased from just over $100 billion in 2000 to $176 billion by 2005. But investors demanded a much deeper dive into the secondary trading market, so in 2006 the LSTA board of directors approved the quarterly collection of secondary trade data from buy- and sell-side institutions

EXHIBIT 8.6

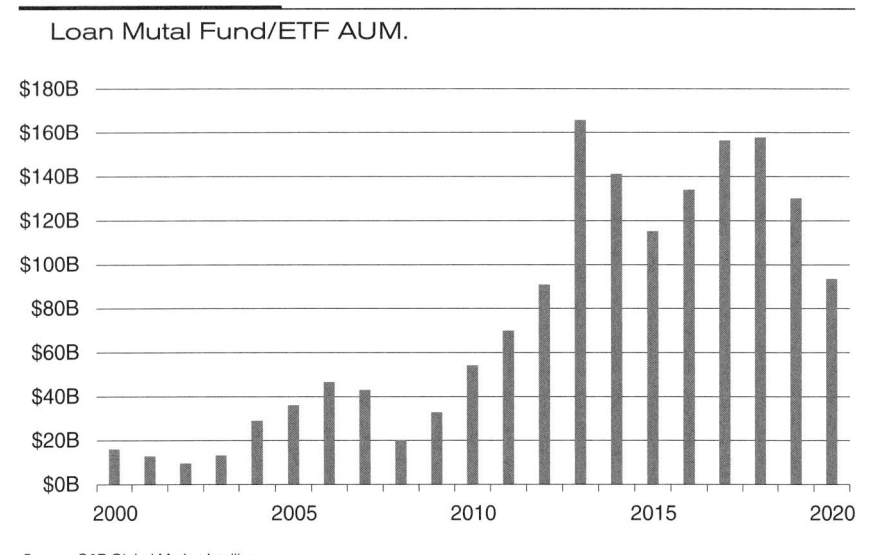

Loan Mutal Fund/ETF AUM.

[Bar chart showing values from 2000 to 2020, ranging from near $0B in early 2000s to peaks around $160B in 2017-2018]

Source: S&P Global Market Intelligence.

that sat on the LSTA board. The trade data collection process was quickly moved to monthly in 2007 and the reporting mandate was expanded. The LSTA was now equipped to offer its member base an unprecedented level of transparency into the syndicated loan trading market—remembering that loans are not securities, not traded on a public exchange, and up to that point any trade-level information was restricted to the parties of a particular loan trade. The matriculation of the analytics offered by the LSTA would become what loan market participants refer to today as the LSTA's Trade Data Study (the "Study"). The Study would go on to be yet another important driver of the sequential growth and acceptance of the asset class by end-investors, regulators, and the like. Although the original mandate of the Study was to confirm secondary MTM price accuracy levels by comparing individual trade prices to the MTM prices that were supplied by the pricing service, the LSTA began reporting official trade price and bid-ask spread levels; trade volume statistics; and general liquidity metrics, such as market breadth/depth and turnover ratio. The Study would also go on to produce the first official secondary market settlement times, because, unlike other asset classes, loan settlement times are not based on a market standard, although the LSTA has instituted several market practices (delayed compensation protocols) that dictate how and when interest passes to the buyer post-trade date in both the primary and secondary markets. For the remainder of this chapter, we will source the LSTA's Trade Data Study results to define the flight to liquidity that ensued in the secondary market over the next 15 years and to also illustrate the growth and performance of the secondary market through the crisis of 2020 induced by COVID-19.

2007 AND THE GLOBAL FINANCIAL CRISIS OF 2008

According to the LSTA's full-year review of 2007, annual secondary loan trading volume increased a staggering 85% to $521 billion that year, after rising 60% in 2016 to $283 billion. Although most of the gains in 2006 trading volume were a natural by-product of a larger market, an increase in CLO issuance, and the new LSTA trade data collection process, 2007's growth rate was driven by a sizeable increase in secondary market price volatility. Prior to the second half of 2007, the secondary market, as we knew it then, had not traded through the level of volatility that would ensue during the next 18 months. That is because between the years 2004 and 2006 (when trade activity became meaningful), traders were unwittingly bidding up large portions of the secondary market above 100 cents on the dollar (or par value), because demand for loans was seemingly unquenchable. One of the more daunting realities of trading loans is that, unlike other markets, where capital price appreciation is, to a certain extent, unlimited, there is little upside potential on loans that are trading at or around par. That is unless one is in the business of buying distressed loans that are trading at a huge discount to par value. In normal market conditions, loans are purchased at or near 100 cents on the dollar, and thus contain limited upside potential, given that a performing loan's price does not normally move above the 101 to 102 range in the secondary market. This is true because performing loans generally will be refinanced at a lower coupon level once they trade meaningfully above 100 cents on the dollar or par value.

During the first half of 2007, the average trade price was still reported north of 100 or par value, while the average bid-ask spread level on the traded universe of loans sat at just 50 basis points. During those first six months of 2007, monthly secondary trading volume averaged less than $40 billion, with an average of 1,150 distinct loan tranches trading in the secondary per month. At this time, the credit environment continued to appear benign, risk-aversion had long gone missing, and volatility levels suggested compliance across the capital markets. As a natural result of the bull market backdrop, institutional lending volume was tracking to an all-time high, as was overall deal and term loan B tranche sizes. After that bullish first half though, the leveraged credit markets seized up abruptly—and suddenly a record pipeline of new loan deals were stuck and unable to move, even at sizable discounts. By July of 2007, credit concerns, supply pressures, and contagion from other asset classes would begin to challenge the lender community across all fixed income products and pummel prices in the secondary loan market. But while price volatility spiked across the second half of 2007, liquidity surged to record levels. From June through December, the average trade price fell roughly 5% in the secondary market, to 95 cents on the dollar, while the average bid-ask spread level widened out more than twofold, to 100 basis points (as credit risk increases, prices grind lower while bid-ask spreads widen). During those last six months of 2007, monthly secondary trading volume increased 20% to an average north of $47 billion.

While the year 2007 will be remembered for the subprime mortgage meltdown that fueled the subsequent credit crunch of the second half of the year, it also marked the beginning of a new era for the secondary loan market. Liquidity levels would be tested like never before as secondary loan prices became even more volatile and performance became increasingly correlated to other asset classes. Clearly, there was much more at stake for the loan market than maintaining its explosive growth rates of the years prior. Up to this point, loan managers had pitched the asset class as a low volatility, low correlation investment option that delivered a high Sharpe ratio relative to other fixed income asset classes. While volatility would eventually normalize post-crisis, the asset class would no longer be shielded from the market dynamics that dictate performance in other asset classes, such as high-yield bonds and equities. This would have a lasting effect on the risk–return profile of leveraged loans. Exhibit 8.7 demonstrates loans' historical return behavior (the 12-month lagging standard deviation of return), as well as their dramatic departure from this behavior in the second half of 2007 and beyond. While historically loans had barely flinched in times when bond prices gyrated, 2007–2008 was different. Loans would now sport a higher level of correlation to other asset classes (Exhibit 8.8), a natural product of the higher

EXHIBIT 8.7

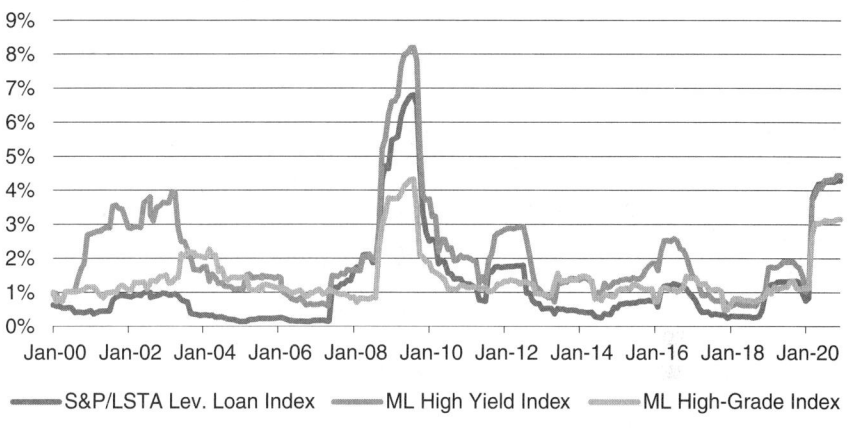

Average 12-Month Lagging Standard Deviation of Returns.

— S&P/LSTA Lev. Loan Index — ML High Yield Index — ML High-Grade Index

Source: S&P Global Market Intelligence.

EXHIBIT 8.8

Correlation to Other Asset Classes.

Asset Class	S&P/LSTA LL Index	High-Yield	10yr Treasury	S&P 500	High Grade Corp
S&P/LSTA Leveraged Loan Index (LLI)	1.00	0.79	–0.36	0.49	0.43
ML U.S. High Yield Index	0.79	1.00	–0.17	0.65	0.58

Source: S&P Global Market Intelligence.

levels of price volatility in the secondary market that a larger, more liquid trading environment would necessitate. And that brings us to the shift in lender base, where a migration from low volatility, long-term money structures (namely CLOs) to faster money complexes such as hedge, distressed, and high-yield funds (which were attracted to the higher loan yields available during the crisis). These funds would help bridge the liquidity gap until the next phase of market expansion, which would be led by the reemergence of CLOs, several years later (Exhibit 8.9).

Thus, 2008 will be remembered as the year the U.S. economy was sent spiraling into a recession. Within the leveraged loan market, 2008 will be more closely remembered as the year of the negative return—the S&P/LSTA LLI recorded an annual return of negative 29.1%, the loan market's first annual loss after 11 years in the black. While returns plummeted to historical lows in 2008,

EXHIBIT 8.9

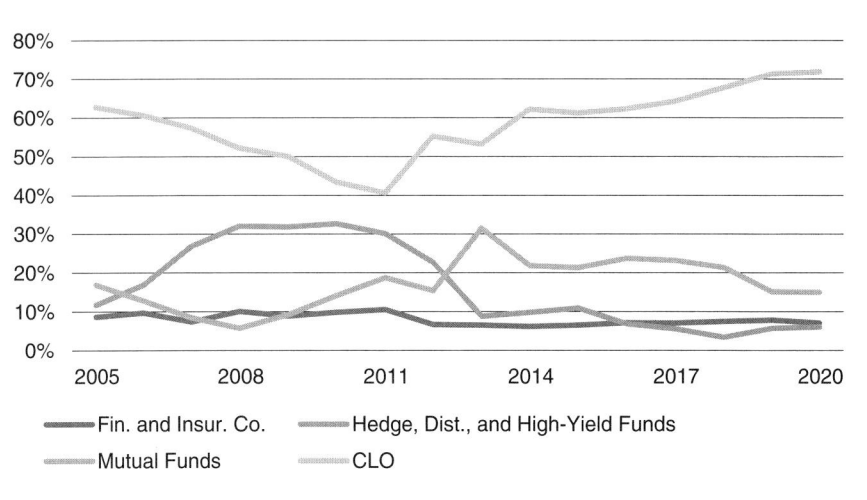

Primary Institutional Market Share by Lender Type (Ex-Banks).

- Fin. and Insur. Co.
- Hedge, Dist., and High-Yield Funds
- Mutual Funds
- CLO

Source: S&P Global Market Intelligence.

volatility reached all-time highs as secondary trading volume remained above $500 billion, despite a primary market that all but seized up. The year 2008 would go on to be the first of several liquidity tests that the secondary loan market would have to pass. By the end of first quarter 2008, conditions across the credit markets deteriorated meaningfully, while the economy teetered around recession. Prices in the secondary loan market fell hard and fast as total return swap (TRS) transactions began to face potential forced unwinds while hedge funds confronted similar margin calls. By the end of March, the secondary market was trading in a sub-90 range. At the same time, bid-ask spreads widened out to a 150–basis point context. Furthermore, 50% of loans were trading below 90. But despite the unprecedented downturn, market participants traded through the volatility during the first quarter at a historic rate. Secondary trade volume totaled a then-record high for a quarter at more than $158 billion. Following what was then considered its worst performance ever, the secondary market rallied back from perceived oversold territory in the second quarter amid the GFC. As nontraditional lenders (hedge, distressed, and high-yield accounts) scooped up the advantageous yields available in the secondary market, loan prices improved off their first quarter lows. Despite a late June sell-off, trade prices still rallied to a 92 level, as bid-ask spreads tightened back to a 100–basis point context by the end of second quarter 2008. During the brief rally, quarterly trading volume remained elevated, but fell to $142 billion.

Taking a cue from the last week of June, trading levels in the secondary weakened during each month of the third quarter; falling precipitously at the tail-end of September. By quarter's end, the average trade price fell back to a sub-90 range. As bids fell across the secondary market, the percentage of loans priced below 90 reached a then-record high of 69%. By the end of September, previous sources of demand, such as hedge funds, faced redemptions, while some market-value CLOs and TRS lines were forced to unwind. This process flooded an already slumping secondary market with still more supply. This caused a systemic strain on liquidity as secondary trading volume fell 24% to a six-quarter low of just $107 billion.

The secondary loan market's price declines of the third quarter paled in comparison to the metamorphic losses that reverberated through the secondary during October. At this point, the lagging 12-month default rate was already approaching 4%, a seismic rise from 2007's year-end figure of 0.24%. Unsurprisingly, the trend of force selling in the secondary market was accelerating as lenders who faced price triggers and margin calls needed to raise even more cash through "Bids Wanted In Competition" (BWIC)—a fast and efficient way to raise capital by offering portions of a loan portfolio for sale through an auction process. According to S&P Global, year-to-date BWIC volume had already totaled a record $10 billion, with more than one-third of that amount occurring in the month of October alone. Price levels were clearly being further pressured by this influx of additional supply into the secondary market as the process of price discovery was becoming extremely difficult. In turn, average trade prices plummeted into the high 70 bid range, and bid-ask spreads gapped out a full point to 233 basis points by month-end. October's loan return unceremoniously tumbled to the worst monthly point to date—a record-shattering negative 13%— which led to the worst quarterly performance ever at negative 23%. All told, the secondary market traded down 23 points across the fourth quarter (29 points on the year) to a sub-70 bid range as bid-ask spreads gapped out another 123 basis points to 256 basis points by the end of 2008 (Exhibits 8.10 and 8.11). Fourth-quarter trade volume fell $7 billion to a two-year low of just $101 billion, with an astounding two-thirds of trades occurring at a price point below 80. Furthermore, 57% of loans traded at a price point below 70, up drastically from the third quarter's 10% reading. By the end of 2008, the secondary market was trading at an average bid level of 68, roughly 10 points lower than the market's historical recovery rate, which at that time sat at 78 cents on the dollar. This would be

EXHIBIT 8.10

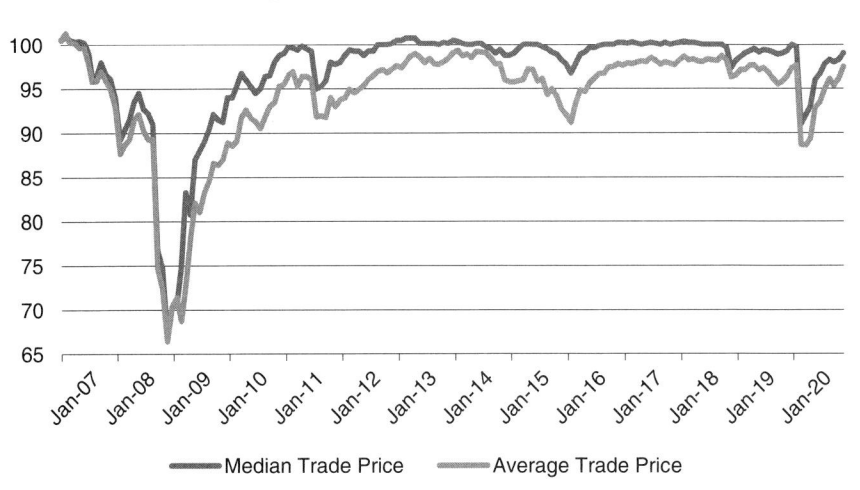

Secondary Trading Levels.

Source: LSTA Trade Data Study.

EXHIBIT 8.11

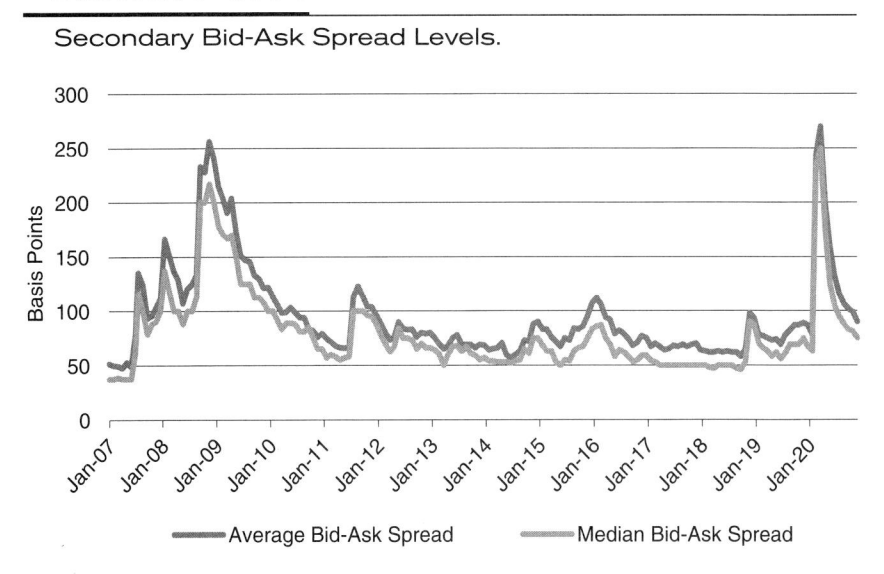

Secondary Bid-Ask Spread Levels.

Source: LSTA Trade Data Study.

the last time that the secondary loan market would trade below its average recovery value. If there was another positive to point to during the height of the crisis, it was a confirmation that the establishment of a transparent and liquid secondary loan trading market would enable managers to trade through historic levels of price volatility and withstand the rigors of the worst financial crisis in a generation.

THE RECOVERY PERIOD AND SUBSEQUENT LIQUIDITY TEST OF 2011

If 2008 is remembered for the leveraged loan market's first negative return, with the S&P/LSTA LLI recording a 29% loss, then 2009 will be remembered as the year the S&P/LSTA LLI posted a record-setting 51.6% gain. Across the entirety of 2009, secondary trading levels rallied off their lows as the market ended the year trading in a high-80s context. As important, bid-ask spreads came in substantially, to roughly 100 basis points, after tightening more than 50% from 2008's historical wides. The secondary market would continue to rally through 2010 and produced a total return just north of 10% on the year. By year-end, the default rate finally normalized, (Exhibit 8.12), while the secondary was once again trading at close

EXHIBIT 8.12

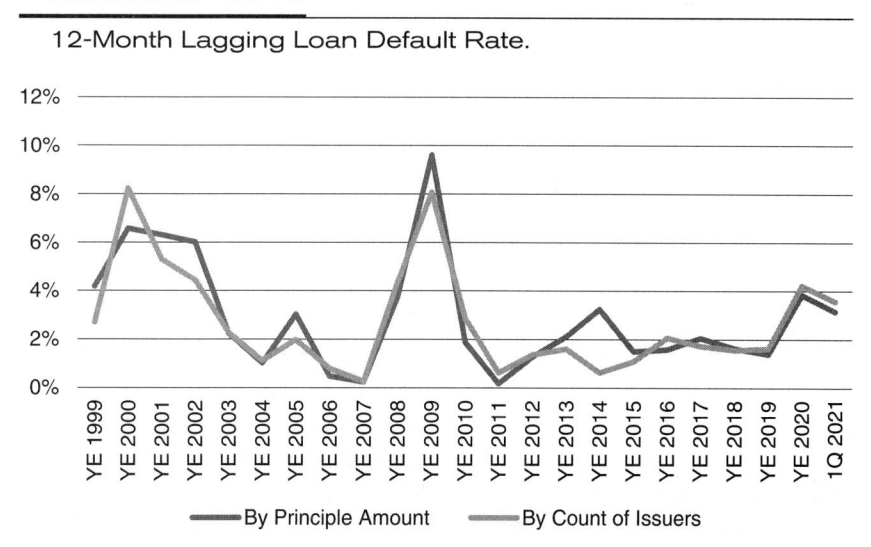

12-Month Lagging Loan Default Rate.

Source: S&P Global Market Intelligence.

to par value while bid-ask spreads tightened back into to a 60–basis point context. As price volatility normalized, traders would now concentrate on individual borrower fundamentals and shifts in technical conditions (supply and demand dynamics) as they did prior to the crisis. Little did they realize the technical dislocation that would ensue during the summer of 2011. While that became the major story line of 2011, another major event would redefine how regular way investors could access exposure to the leveraged loan market—both on the long and short side of the trade. In March 2011, Invesco launched the first ever loan exchange traded fund (ETF), the Invesco Senior Loan ETF (ticker BKLN), which tracks the market's 100 largest and most liquid term loans that comprise the S&P/LSTA Leveraged Loan 100 Index. This was a landmark event for the loan market because it signified not only the loan market's flight to liquidity that had already taken place, but also the broad-based acceptance of the asset class by not just institutional investors, but also by regular investors like you and me. As of early 2021, BKLN had more than $6 billion in AUM and remained by far the largest of the nine ETF loan strategies that exist in today's market, which when combined represent north of $11.5 billion in total AUM. Although this historic event defined the first quarter of 2011, the summer of 2011 would go down as the next liquidity event for the loan market—but this time it was predicated on a technical dislocation as opposed to a credit-induced sell-off. Furthermore, it was not just trade liquidity that came into question, it was a test of settlement liquidity as well, because loans do not have a standard settlement time—such as those in the security markets. Since the LSTA began collecting settlement data back in 2007, the median settlement time to close a secondary trade (on par documentation) averaged 11 business days—that is, 11 business days post trade date that cash is received by the seller. However, the LSTA Settlement Data Study has proven over time that during times of heightened volatility and subsequent selling pressures, the street settles buy-side sales much faster than the headline numbers would suggest, particularly during times where loan mutual funds need cash to meet investor redemptions. Furthermore, LSTA analysis of loan mutual funds has suggested that raising cash through selling assets is just one aspect of a fund's much broader liquidity risk management procedures. Other technics include a funds mandate to hold a minimum level of cash and liquid assets in the portfolio, as well as the continuous access to dedicated liquidity lines that were put in place for precisely such instances.

In this next section is an excerpt from the LSTA's Executive Summary of 2011, which highlights the loan mutual fund market's ability to settle loan trades efficiently while meeting redemptions during an unprecedented level of outflows. The LSTA would go on to engage on this topic again in greater detail during the market sell-off of 2018, which will be covered later in this chapter.

Leveraged loans were hit hard by a trifecta of debilitating news during mid-third quarter 2011: the U.S. downgrade/risk of a double-dip, Europe's debt crisis, and finally and most important to this conversation, the Federal Reserve revised its interest rate expectations stating that they now expect short-term rates to stay close to zero "at least through late 2014." These events, particularly the Federal Reserve Bank's action (or inaction), put the brakes on the loan market's "technical" imbalance. This technical imbalance, driven by minimal net new lending activity and excessive demand, was credited with driving up prices in the secondary market during the first half of the year when loan mutual fund inflows totaled a record $26 billion. But in August, the cash spigot abruptly ran dry on the aforementioned Federal Reserve Bank announcement, as outflows from loan mutual funds totaled a monthly record $5.5 billion (which would not be surpassed until late 2014). The subsequent selling pressure was severe; an astonishing 92% of the secondary traded down that month, with 31% of decliners reporting losses in the secondary market of 5% or worse. And this all occurred despite near-record low default rates and stronger corporate earnings.

In what proved to be the fourth worst month in the history of the loan market (only to be outdone by the three months following Lehman's collapse), August 2011 represented the market's first true liquidity test since the ill-fated fourth quarter of 2008. With the secondary finding itself in a massive August sell-off, the market suffered considerable losses—and a subsequent negative 4.4% return on the S&P/LSTA LLI. These losses were exacerbated by certain retail mutual funds needing to raise fast cash by selling liquid assets to quickly meet redemptions in the wake of the then-record $5.5 billion of August outflows (Exhibit 8.13). While many pundits spoke of market illiquidity during this time, the LSTA's Study offered presumably illuminating statistics. According to August trade data submissions, secondary trade volumes rose above $43 billion for only the second time in more than two years. (The last time was January of 2011 when the market took in a record $5 billion of mutual fund inflows.) August's $43.9 billion

EXHIBIT 8.13

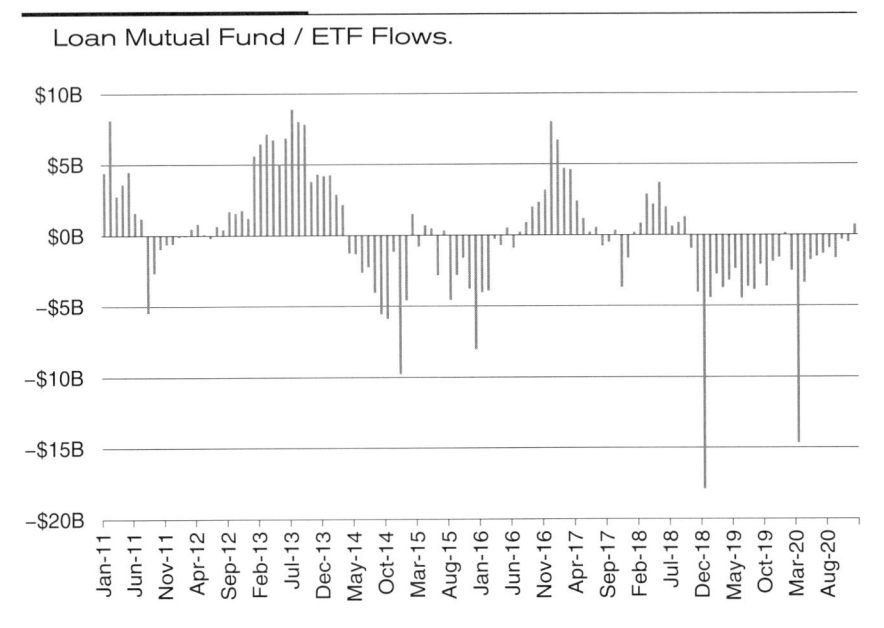

Loan Mutual Fund / ETF Flows.

Source: Refinitiv LPC.

of trade activity was spread among 1,242 individual loan facilities—a 20% increase over 2011's monthly average. If volumes and market breadth are the definition of liquidity, then the market proved to be in a very liquid state. But that obviously isn't the whole story; as liquidity is also measured by price movement, best execution, and bid-ask spreads. Here, the results were not as rosy in August. The average loan traded down 5.3%, to a 91-handle, while the average bid-ask spread on the traded universe gapped out 70%, to 115 basis points. (Let us not forget that during the same period the S&P 500 fell 5.4%, as heavy losses were realized across all risk assets). Regarding secondary loan settlements, the market did a remarkable job of closing par trades in an expedited fashion; despite higher trading volumes that supported the record level of redemptions which spawned an even greater level of price volatility. Case in point, the average and median par settlement times each tightened month-over-month in August by five days to T + 15 and T + 9, respectively. Even more impressive, the percentage of loan trades that settled within the LSTA guideline of T + 7 climbed to 40%—an all-time high that would not be witnessed again until the COVID-19 induced sell-off of March 2020. As the market would teach us over the next 10 years, the secondary loan market reacts well to heightened levels of volatility, in terms of both trade and settlement liquidity. Time and time again, as volatility levels spiked, secondary trade activity swelled while settlement times contracted.

THE NEXT PHASE OF MARKET EXPANSION

Since the leveraged loan market's emergence in the 1990s, the selling points of the asset class consisted of senior security, floating rates, low volatility, low correlation to other asset classes, and relatively high risk-adjusted returns, which increase during rising rate environments. By the late 2000s, ample liquidity levels were added to the list. But it took several years after the crisis before leveraged lending activity in the primary and trading volume in the secondary markets was restored to precrisis levels. During the years from 2009 through 2012, the growth rate on the S&P/LSTA LLI (a proxy for total institutional loans outstanding) averaged negative 2%. In turn, secondary trading volume fell from more than $500 billion in 2008 to just $400 billion in 2012. As the primary market reopened for business in a meaningful way across 2013 and 2014, the market's annual growth rate in outstandings surged to an average of 23%, which lifted S&P/LSTA LLI outstandings to a fresh record $831 billion by year-end 2014. In turn, secondary trading volume surpassed the $500 billion barrier in 2013, for the first time since 2008, and then hit a fresh record $628 billion in 2014 (Exhibit 8.14).

EXHIBIT 8.14

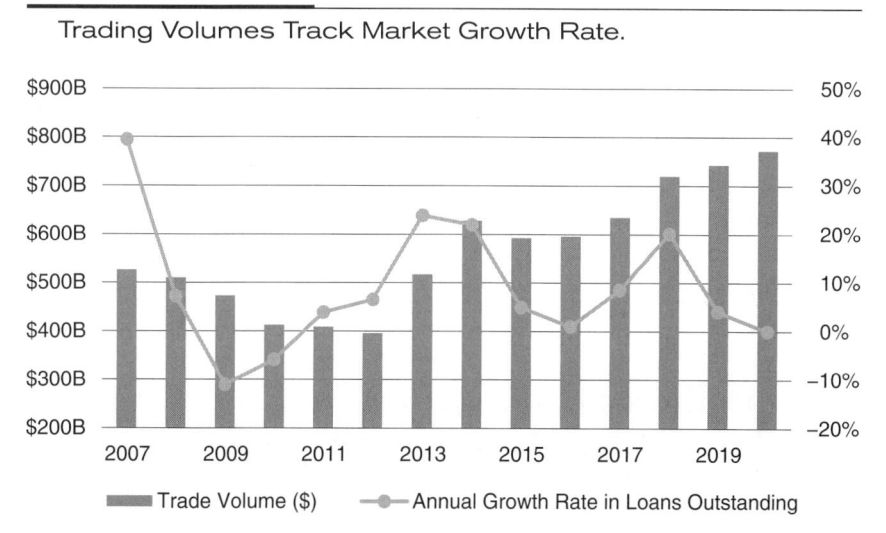

Trading Volumes Track Market Growth Rate.

Source: LSTA Trade Data Study.

On a percentage basis, loans outstanding grew at the same rate as secondary trading volume across 2013 and 2014—23%. Fueling that growth was a resurgent CLO market, where CLO issuance over the two-year period totaled a record $206 billion—surpassing the 2006–2007 previous record of $186 billion. CLO AUM would now approach $400 billion as CLOs were responsible for funding more than 60% of new institutional terms loans in the primary market. In comparison, the next largest buyer of new institutional terms loans were loan mutual funds, at a 21% market share.

The exuberance of 2013 and 2014 quickly faded during the second half of 2015 as market sentiment (and returns) would remain negative for the remainder of the year. While the secondary market's median trade price dropped 50 basis points during the third quarter, it still stood at a very healthy 99.5-handle. Little did investors anticipate the contagion that would spread to the loan market as the price of oil plummeted and global economies weakened. December 2015 would mark the seventh consecutive month of red ink for the S&P/LSTA LLI. December's negative 1.05% return would lead to the market's only other annual loss (−0.7%) besides that of the GFC (Exhibit 8.15). All in all, liquidity trends offered a mixed bag of results in 2015. While trade volumes were only off

EXHIBIT 8.15

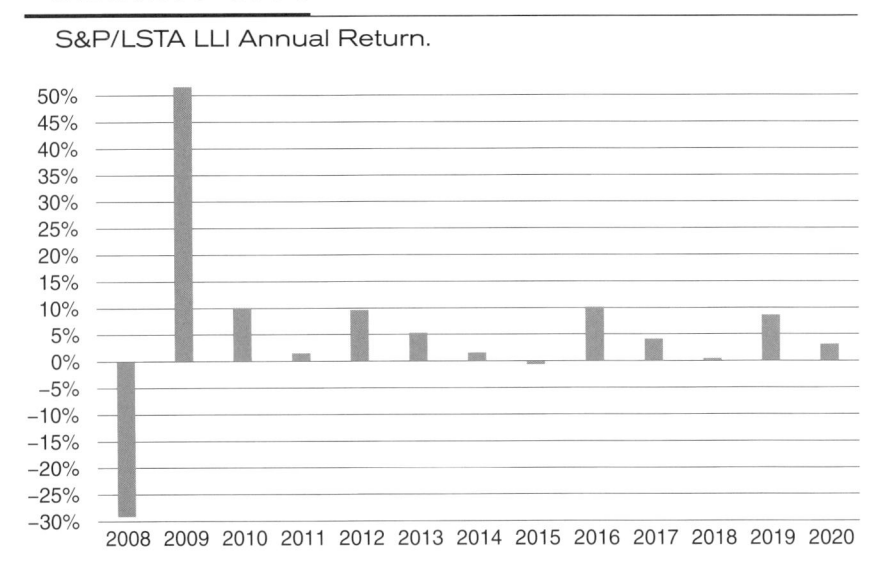

S&P/LSTA LLI Annual Return.

Source: S&P/LSTA Leveraged Loan Index.

minimally (6%), the market's annual turnover ratio (as defined by the average annual size of the S&P/LSTA LLI divided by annual trade volumes) suffered a pretty severe drop-off—falling from 83% in 2014 to only 71% in 2015. Simply put, the S&P/LSTA LLI reached a record $872 billion in outstandings by year-end 2015 as compared to trading volumes, which reached their record of $628 billion in 2014 (Exhibit 8.16).

Fortunately, disappointment with the market's performance was short-lived. In 2016, risk assets and commodities rallied, lifting loan returns above 10% for only the third time in the past 20 years. Beginning in March 2016, the market entered into a storied recovery period where loan prices in the secondary market ran higher through December. By year's end, the secondary market's V-shaped recovery was complete as the median trade price pushed back above par after hitting a post-recession low of 96.75 in February. This "risk-on" recovery was the product of both favorable technicals and stronger fundamentals.

While secondary trading volumes barely budged in 2016, rising just $4 billion to $596 billion, a noteworthy technological development took place that year—the introduction to electronic trading in the loan market. In June 2016, Bank of America, one of

EXHIBIT 8.16

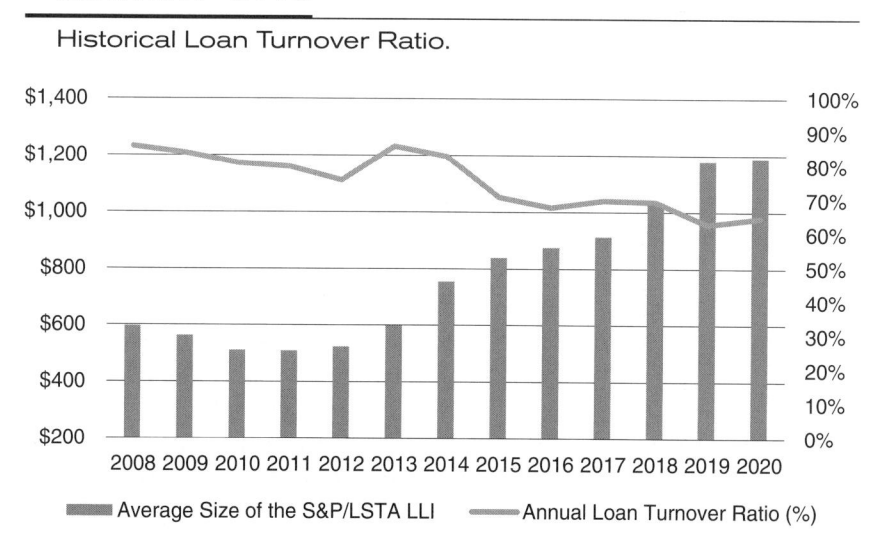

Historical Loan Turnover Ratio.

Source: LSTA Trade Data Study.

the largest syndicated agents in the loan market, launched an electronic syndicated loan trading platform under the name, Instinct Loans. The platform, which allowed for multiple clients to bid on particular loans during two daily trading sessions, began by mainly targeting loans of $1 billion or more in outstandings. Later the same year, MarketAxess Holdings Inc., the operator of a leading electronic trading platform for fixed income securities announced that it had launched the industry's first client-to-multidealer electronic trading platform for leveraged loans. While both systems were said to benefit liquidity levels, the overwhelming majority of loans still trade the old fashion way, through the telephone or via the Bloomberg terminal. That trend though might change in the 2020s as Bank America and Citibank are working together to build a new industry-led independent data and execution platform for the fixed income markets, including loans and CLOs. This new multidealer platform has the opportunity to create greater efficiency and transparency into secondary loan trading, while decreasing the cost of execution and enhancing liquidity and market participation.

The trend of favorable technical conditions, stronger fundamentals, and rising prices in the secondary market would continue across 2017 and into late 2018. Loan prices proved to be quite stable in the secondary market over this period, with most loans trading within a very tight band around par value. While the average trade price fluctuated (a bit), the median price remained at or above 100 since September 2016, a trend that would continue until November 2018. Back in 2017, secondary trading volumes increased 7% to $635 billion while S&P/LSTA LLI outstandings grew 8% to $880 billion. Once again, CLO issuance was driving market growth. At $118 billion, 2017 CLO issuance came in north of $100 billion for just the second time in the history of the market. Those figures though would pale in comparison to the 20% growth rate in loans outstanding in 2018—although the year did not end well from a performance perspective. That said, S&P/LSTA LLI outstandings went on to finally breach the $1 trillion barrier, ending 2018 at $1.15 trillion. That same year, CLO issuance came in at a record $129 billion, with total CLO AUM approaching $600 billion, or 51% of total loans outstanding (Exhibit 8.17). In comparison, loan mutual funds held just 15% of total outstandings at that time.

EXHIBIT 8.17

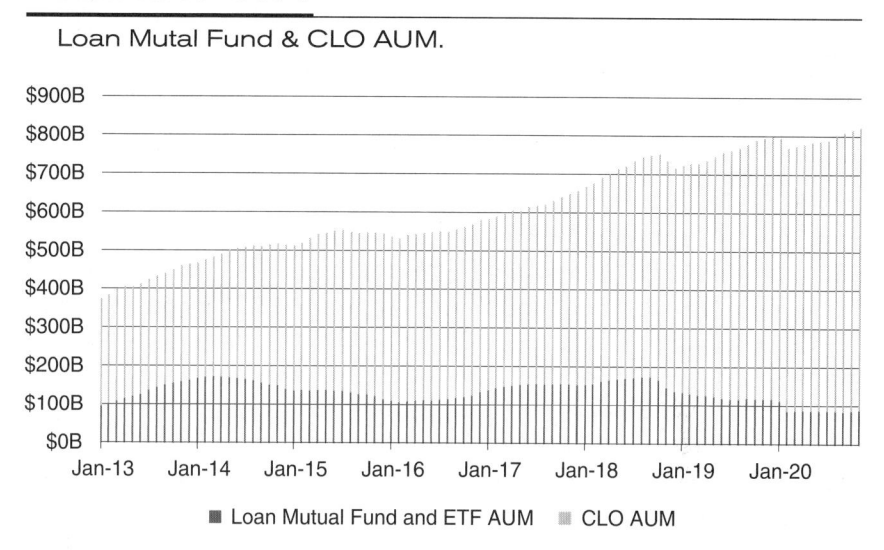

Loan Mutal Fund & CLO AUM.

[Bar chart showing Loan Mutual Fund and ETF AUM and CLO AUM from Jan-13 to Jan-20, with values ranging from $0B to approximately $800B+]

■ Loan Mutual Fund and ETF AUM   ■ CLO AUM

Source: Refinitiv LPC.

LOAN LIQUIDITY RISK MANAGEMENT TESTED AGAIN IN 2018

In fourth quarter 2018, loan mutual funds and ETFs underwent yet another "natural experiment" as loan prices declined 5 points in the secondary market and funds experienced nearly $20 billion of redemptions in short order. Loan mutual funds successfully navigated that turbulent market, selling assets and managing their liquidity and redemption needs. Importantly, this experience reaffirmed the efficacy of funds' Liquidity Risk Management plans and their "Highly Liquid Investment Minimums," or the amount of highly liquid investments they must keep on hand. Both of these safeguards had been developed in conjunction with the SEC's 2016 Liquidity Risk Management Rule. Historically, observers questioned whether leveraged loans, which often take longer than three days to settle, belong in open-end mutual funds that permit daily redemptions by investors. The concern, which was the subject of debate in 2016 when the SEC issued its open-end fund Liquidity Risk Management Rule ("the Rule"), was that loan funds may not be able to meet redemptions due to settlement delays. Ultimately, the Rule created a category of assets—"Less Liquid Assets"—that could be sold relatively quickly but took longer than three days to settle. Leveraged loans typically fall into this category, and thus are permissible assets for open-end mutual funds. Still, questions continued about whether loans were sufficiently liquid for an open-end structure. December 2018 allowed the LSTA to test that question yet again.

Loans—like all risk asset classes—suffered a period of significant volatility and declining prices in fourth quarter 2018. All told, the average price of institutional term loans dropped from 98.6 at the end of September to 93.8 at the end of December. At the same time, loan mutual funds experienced redemptions totaling $20 billion during the fourth quarter and $15 billion in December alone. This created another natural experiment that allowed the LSTA to analyze once again loan mutual funds in a period of significant stress. At the same time that loan prices dropped 5 points, loan trading activity increased from $54 billion in September 2018 to $70 billion in December. Many members of the LSTA noted that loans actually remained more liquid than high-yield bonds in December. The LSTA tested this thesis, particularly in the context of open-end mutual funds. The LSTA compared the *absolute* level of flows (e.g., inflows or redemptions) in loan and high-yield bond mutual funds. High-yield bond funds experienced more consistent outflows across the year, which is unsurprising considering the rising rate environment for much of the year and the risk-off mentality in the fourth quarter. In contrast, loan mutual funds enjoyed moderate inflows most of the year. However, the combination of negative loan headlines, market-wide risk aversion, and a shift in interest rate views created sudden and sharp redemptions in loan mutual funds. In December alone, there were $15 billion in redemptions, far above the absolute outflows in the high-yield bond market. However, it is important to remember that high-yield bond mutual funds are larger than loan mutual funds. In turn, the LSTA weighted the size of outflows by the original size of loan and high-yield bond mutual funds. In December 2019, loan mutual funds suffered redemptions equivalent to 9% of their AUM; high-yield bonds suffered redemptions of "only" 3.3%. Thus, loan mutual funds needed to sell a much larger share of their assets to meet redemptions. Next, the LSTA compared the impact of this selling pressure on loan prices versus high-yield bond prices. In December, the price of loans dropped 2.9 points, as compared to a 2.6-point decline for high-yield bonds. In other words, even though loan mutual funds had relative outflows of 9% versus

3.3% for high-yield bonds, loan prices dropped just slightly more. The LSTA viewed this as an indication that loan trading liquidity was superior. One reason the loan market was able to hold up well in the face of such large redemptions was that mutual funds were a relatively small part of the lender base. At their high point in September 2018, open-end loan mutual funds comprised just 14% of loan market assets. (By March 2019, this had dropped to 10%.) Almost all other vehicles, including cash flow CLOs and Separately Managed Accounts—are long-term investors with no or limited redemption rights. In fact, while loan mutual funds were selling in December 2018, many other investors saw it as an opportunity to buy (and thus stabilize the market).

THE COVID-19-INDUCED PRICE VOLATILITY OF 2020

At the close of 2019, many loan portfolio managers were calling for a slow but certain deterioration in credit quality, which would lead to a coupon-level return in 2020. After all, loan returns hit almost 9% in 2019 as loans rallied in the secondary market off of their 2018 lows. Turns out, those managers were not off by that much— and let us not forget that those calls were made pre-COVID-19. All told, the S&P/LSTA LLI returned 3.12% in 2020 as the market value component of return came in at negative 1.77%. And while the downgrades were nothing short of brutal during the second quarter (the 12-month trailing downgrade/upgrade ratio peaked at 43:1 in May), rating actions normalized during the second half of 2020 with the ratio reported at just short of even in December. But defaults did increase in 2020 as the default rate (by amount) increased 245 basis points to a five-year high of 3.83%.

So, what were the other noteworthy takeaways for the 2020 loan market? On the demand side, loan mutual fund outflows totaled more than $26 billion, $16 billion of which occurred during first quarter 2020. This was an actual improvement over the $38 billion in outflows reported a year earlier. As a result, loan fund AUM ended 2020 at less than $90 billion, or just 8% of total loan outstandings. In contrast, the CLO market, which continued to drive most of the loan demand in 2020, saw $90 billion in issuance, which elevated total CLO outstandings to a fresh record $731 billion, or 61% of total loan outstandings. On the supply side, S&P/LSTA LLI outstandings barely budged, growing less than 1%, its lowest growth rate in 10 years. Net-net, visible loan demand alone outpaced new loan supply by more than $63 billion—a stat that speaks volumes to the 2020 supply–demand imbalance that ultimately drove a continuation in borrower-friendly deal terms and loose credit agreement provisions.

In terms of the 2020 secondary loan market, the epic COVID-19 induced March sell-off culminated in a negative 12.4% monthly return (only October 2008 was worse) as bids plummeted to 10-year lows. Clearly though, the market proved to be extremely oversold and so, the storied rally began. It took the market eight months for returns to get back firmly into the black, despite flirting with positive territory in September and October. Risk assets went on to stage impressive rallies across November and December on hopes of a successful rollout of the COVID-19 vaccine. In the loan market, bids surged market wide while reporting an extremely bullish advancer/decliner ratio of 15:1 since month-end October—a trend that continued through the first quarter of 2021. As of the time of this writing (April 2021), the V-shaped recovery in the secondary loan market was more than complete as trading levels not only retraced but surpassed their previous highs, roughly 12 months later (Exhibit 8.18). This last section of the chapter will focus on

EXHIBIT 8.18

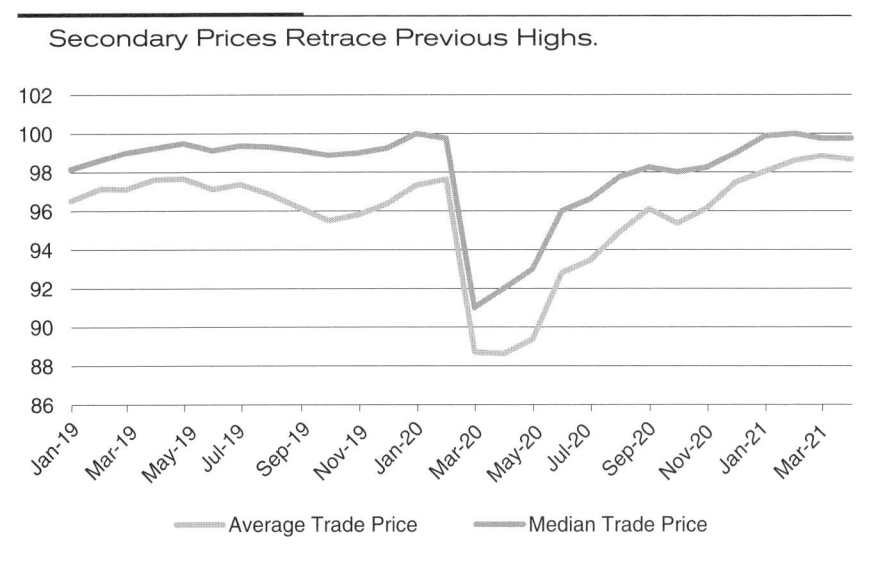

Secondary Prices Retrace Previous Highs.

Source: LSTA Trade Data Study.

the LSTA's 2020 Trade Data Study, which will provide an in-depth review of secondary trade activity during the height of the crisis and the recovery period that quickly followed. Its results are a true testament to the level of liquidity available in today's market, and even as important, its continued resiliency during times of severe duress.

Secondary loan trading volume increased 4% to a record $721 billion in 2020 (Exhibit 8.19). The COVID-19–induced price volatility of March went on to set the groundwork for a record year in trade activity and the storied V-shaped recovery in secondary market prices that followed. According to the LSTA's 2020 Study, loans were trading in a mid-97 context at the beginning of March while $76 billion (January 2019) stood as the high-water mark for monthly secondary trade activity. By March 23rd, the secondary market traded down to levels not seen since the height of the financial crisis—the daily average trade price plummeted roughly 20 points to a 78 context, as bid-ask spreads, on the traded universe of loans, gapped out an unprecedented 275 basis points—to an average of 375 basis points. But the market quickly found its bottom, partly thanks to the Federal Reserve Bank, as loans caught an immediate bid following the liquidity-fueled sell-off—particularly in the BB space where credit had clearly been oversold.

EXHIBIT 8.19

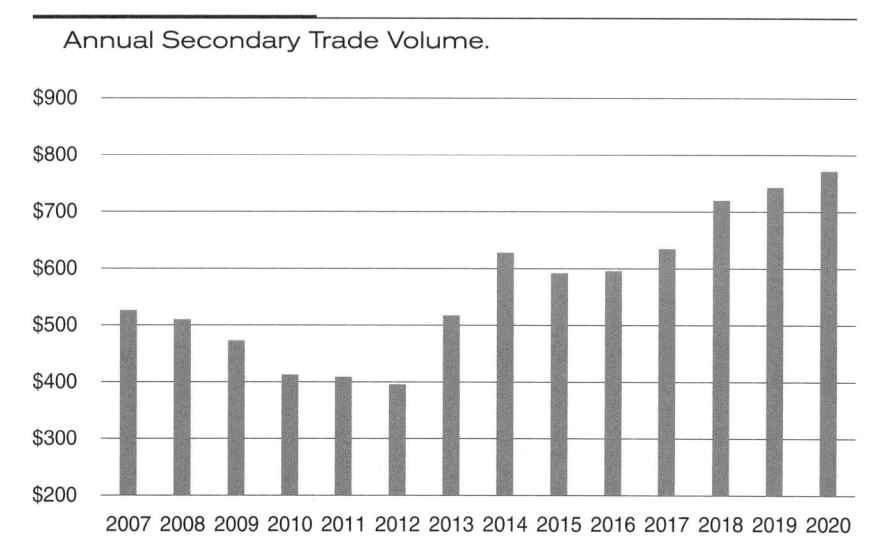

Annual Secondary Trade Volume.

Source: LSTA Trade Data Study.

From March 24 through month-end, a span of just six trading sessions, prices rebounded 11 points as the average trade price rallied back into an 89 context. Prices had never fallen so fast, nor had they ever rebounded in such fashion over such a short period of time. In turn, secondary trading volumes totaled a staggering $119.3 billion across March (Exhibit 8.20), 57% higher than January 2019's previous high and a staggering 100% higher than 2020's monthly average (less March activity) which came in just shy of $60 billion. For this reason, the market's annual turnover ratio improved by 2 percentage points in 2020—to 67% or its third sub-70% reading across the past five years.

From a historical standpoint, the only other period where the secondary market traded in a sub-90 range was between August 2008 and March 2010—a span of 20 months. That is because loan prices continued to rise off their lows in April 2020 as the average trade price crossed the 90 bid-level barrier on heavy trading volume ($75.2 billion). Secondary price levels continued their march back to fair value across the entirety of the second quarter of 2020 with the average trade price improving another 410 basis points, to a 93-handle. Turns out, the market was not deterred by rising defaults and declining credit quality. Even still, volatility and trading activity were simultaneously normalizing. Monthly trade

EXHIBIT 8.20

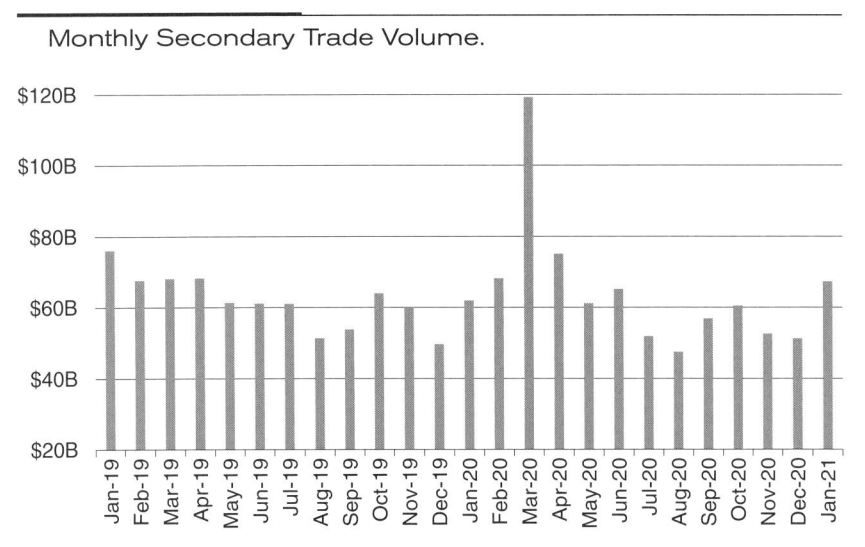

Monthly Secondary Trade Volume.

Source: LSTA Trade Data Study.

volume fell to an average of $67.2 billion across the second quarter, while the average bid-ask spread tightened an impressive 85 basis points to 160.

Trading volumes finally improved toward the backend of the third quarter with September's total increasing 19%, to a three-month high of $57 billion, which stood in contrast to August's 33-month low reading. September's uptick in activity was closely tied to several factors (including stronger CLO demand and new issuance volume) that signified some semblance of a return to normalcy. But despite the increase in September activity, third quarter trading volume plummeted 23% to just $156.2 billion—the market's first sub-$160 billion quarter since fourth quarter 2017. The price rally though, remained well intact as strong market breadth continued to drive trading levels higher across most of the third quarter. The average trade price increased 320 basis points, to a 96-handle, while the average MTM bid-ask spread tightened another 53 basis points, to 107 basis points. While aggregate trading volumes had declined for the better part of the past six months, distressed trading activity surged. This is hardly surprising given that the default rate had more than doubled to 4.3% since the end of the first quarter 2020. Since the end of March, quarterly distressed volumes increased 29% to $9.5 billion, or 6% of total activity. The last time that statistic was that high was back in the first quarter of 2017 (when the default rate was falling back below 1.5% after the energy crisis of 2016 that drove the oil/gas sector default rate to 30%).

To begin the fourth quarter, monthly trading volumes increased yet again, this time by 6% in October, to a four-month high of $60.4 billion. October marked the first time volumes increased in back-to-back months since March—a trend that was closely tied to improving technicals (supply and demand conditions). First, CLO issuance ran above $11 billion during consecutive months for the first time since April 2019. Better yet, CLO activity averaged $12.1 billion over September and October, a stat which comes in $6.3 billion higher than the previous six-month trailing average of $5.8 billion. Second, institutional loan volume totaled an impressive $76 billion over the same period. This two-month total was higher than the previous five months combined. But as new-issue primary volumes surged in October, prices in the secondary market softened, thus ending the market's storied price rally at six months. Although loan returns on the S&P/LSTA LLI remained positive in October, at just 0.2%, it marked the first time since March where

(1) the market's advancer/decliner ratio fell below 1:1 and (2) market values ran negative, albeit slightly at negative 0.17%. The trading market though, revealed a deeper decline in prices (−0.8%) as an increase in "off the run" activity drove aggregate price levels lower but volumes higher. In turn, the number of individual loans that changed hands in the secondary market, or market breadth, hit a two-year high of 1,550 loans in October (the S&P/LSTA LLI holds 1,440 loans). While trade activity fell 15% in November and another 3% in December (to a four-month low of $51.2 billion), loan prices staged yet another massive rally (on the hopes of a successful rollout of the COVID-19 vaccine) where 87% of the secondary market traded higher. All told, the average trade price increased 212 basis points, to a nine-month high of 97.5 over the last two months of the year—ending December just 15 basis points off its pre-COVID-19 high. The median trade price, which seems to be a better indicator of where the secondary is currently trading, improved 200 basis points to a 99-handle across November and December. The median level ended the year 800 basis points richer than its March low but 100 basis points lower than its January high. At the same time, bid-ask spreads on the traded universe of loans tightened marginally across the last two months of 2020 as roughly 15 basis points were shaved from both the average and median levels. These ended December at 90 and 75 basis points, respectively. Both figures are now in earshot of their February tights, which were reported at 78 and 63 basis points, respectively. While the secondary trading market has retraced its pre-COVID-19 highs from various statistical viewpoints, the one metric that still fell well short was the percentage of trading activity at a price point above par. While the metric improved markedly across the fourth quarter (rising from 4% to 13% of trading activity), traders remained generally hesitant to pay above par in the secondary during December as compared to January 2020 when the percentage sat north of 40%.

In conclusion, the matriculation of the secondary trading market for corporate loans during the 1990s went on to attract and support the emergence of the nonbank, institutional lender community that now funds more than $1.2 trillion of institutional loans outstanding. The flight to liquidity that ensued enabled an ever-growing class of asset managers and investors to acknowledge bank loans as a relatively stable and liquid, floating rate senior secured asset class. Loans were no longer considered an esoteric asset class but a part of core fixed income investing. Today, a diverse set of market participants rely upon the secondary market to efficiently and effectively manage their loan exposures and credit risk. As we look ahead, advancements in technology will certainly lead to greater efficiency and transparency into secondary loan trading, while decreasing the cost of execution and enhancing liquidity and market participation.

The U.S. Leveraged Loan Market Through the Lens of the S&P/LSTA Leveraged Loan Index

Marina Lukatsky
S&P Global Market Intelligence
Leveraged Commentary and Data

It has been over a decade since the GFC brought an abrupt end to a booming credit cycle. The global loan markets rebounded, of course, setting off the next long-running cycle marked by soaring issuance, record-low yields, and sustained investor demand for loan paper, ever-looser covenants, and a stubbornly low default rate. Of course, the longest economic expansion in U.S. history came to an even more screeching halt in March 2020, amid the global COVID-19 pandemic, upending a record run for the U.S. leveraged loan asset class during which it doubled in size and became a dominant player in the capital markets (see Exhibit 8.21).

In this analysis, Leveraged Commentary and Data (LCD), an offering of S&P Global Market Intelligence, looks at how the U.S. leveraged loan market has evolved and performed in the last 20 years through the lens of S&P/LSTA Leveraged Loan Index (S&P/LSTA LLI).

The S&P/LSTA LLI is a market value–weighted index designed to measure the performance of the U.S. leveraged loan market based upon market weightings, spreads, and interest payments. The S&P/LSTA LLI was rolled out in 2000; it was back-loaded with four years of data dating to 1997. Term loans from syndicated credits must meet the following criteria at issuance in order to be eligible for inclusion in the S&P/LSTA LLI: senior secured; minimum initial term of one year; U.S. dollar denominated; minimum initial spread of LIBOR + 125 basis points; and $50 million in initially funded loans.

EXHIBIT 8.21

Growth of $1.00 in the S&P/LSTA Loan Index.

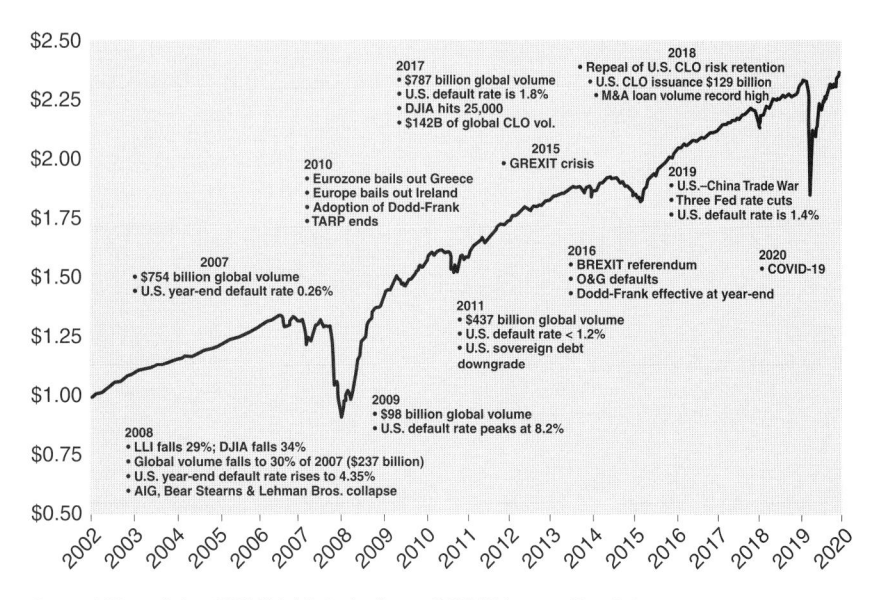

Sources: LCD, an offering of S&P Global Market Intelligence; S&P/LSTA Leveraged Loan Index.

$1.2 TRILLION ASSET CLASS

In the last 20 years, the U.S. institutional loan market has grown into a $1.2 trillion asset class, expanding by more than 10 times from just $100.5 billion at the end of 2000, based on the par amount outstanding in the S&P/LSTA LLI. During the peak growth years leading up to the GFC—between 2004 and 2007—the index expanded by an average of 43% per year, to $554 billion by the end of 2007. The S&P/LSTA LLI reached its pre-GFC peak in November 2008 at $595 billion of loans from 826 issuers, as seen in Exhibit 8.22.

The surging pace of buyouts and other acquisition-related lending supported the extraordinary growth rate of the loan market leading up to the GFC. Indeed, at $160 billion, 2007's buyout-related loan volume set a record that remains unbroken today. Close to 60% of all loans issued in 2006 and 2007 funded either a buyout, an acquisition, a merger, or a spin-off. These transactions typically represent new supply to loan investors, as opposed to refinancings and recaps in which a new loan replaces an existing one (see Exhibit 8.23).

EXHIBIT 8.22

S&P/LSTA LL Index: Par Amount Outstanding and the Growth Rate.

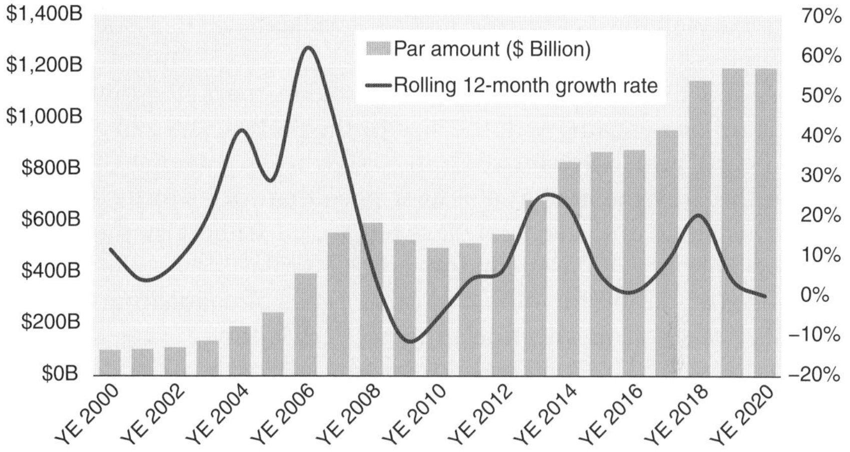

Data through Dec. 31, 2020.
Sources: LCD, an offering of S&P Global Market Intelligence; S&P/LSTA Leveraged Loan Index.

EXHIBIT 8.23

Institutional New-Issue Loan Volume.

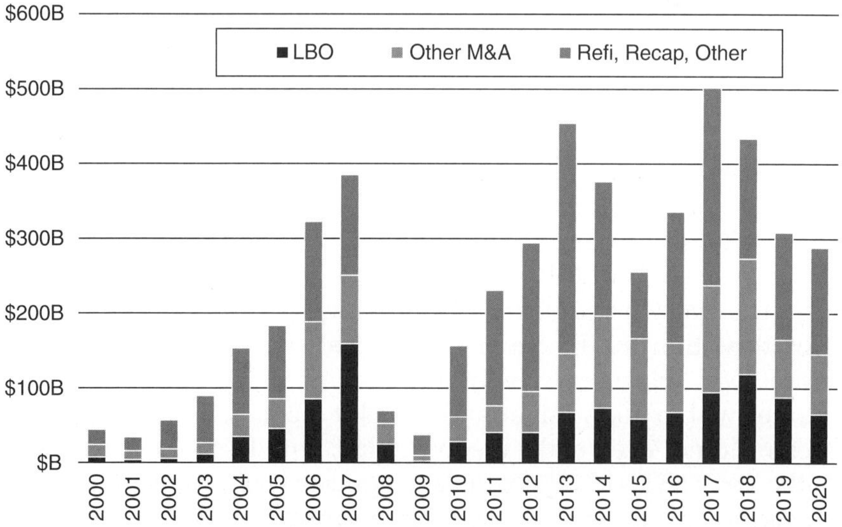

Source: LCD, an offering of S&P Global Market Intelligence.

As the GFC gripped the capital markets, new-issue loan activity plummeted, and as a result the par amount outstanding tracked by the S&P/LSTA LLI shrank by roughly $100 billion between the end of 2008 and the end of 2010. Roughly 150 issuers exited the leveraged loan market during that period, leaving the issuer count at around 670.

Aided by renewed M&A activity, loan market growth then picked up once again, with the size of the S&P/LSTA LLI expanding in each year between 2011 and 2019 by an average of 10.5%. While the growth came at a slower pace than prior to the GFC, it was consistent, and the asset class topped $1 trillion by the end of 2018, via about 1,100 issuers. Indeed, 2018 total M&A-related loan issuance (including buyouts and other types of acquisition-related activity) reached an all-time high of $275 billion, exceeding the 2007 tally of $252 billion and boosting the size of the leveraged loan market by 20%.

However, since reaching that peak, M&A borrowing has declined and the onset of the COVID-19 pandemic in the first quarter of 2020 further suppressed activity in this space of the loan market. As a result, new-issue institutional loan volume to fund these types of transactions fell to the lowest level in eight years, to $142 billion in 2020. Consequently, the growth of the S&P/LSTA LLI stalled, with the total par amount outstanding hovering around $1.2 trillion throughout 2020—the first year since the GFC when it did not expand.

TECH BOOM

In terms of issuer sector differentiation, the market is more concentrated around the biggest sectors now than 10 years ago. The top three industries in the S&P/LSTA LLI accounted for 34% of all par amount outstanding in 2020, up from 26% in 2010. Similarly, the five biggest sectors accounted for 43% of the S&P/LSTA LLI in 2020, versus 37% in 2010.

The most drastic shift over the last decade came from the growth within the Electronics/Electrical sector, LCD's proxy for technology, which now holds the dominant position in the loan market with a 15.5% share (see Exhibit 8.24). Ten years ago, this sector did not even make the top 10 list, with less than a 4% share of the S&P/LSTA LLI. Looking at it another way—outstanding leveraged loans to technology-related borrowers rose from less than $20 billion to $183 billion in the last 10 years.

EXHIBIT 8.24

S&P/LSTA Leveraged Loan Index, Breakdown by Sector (at par, in $ billions).

	YE 2010 share	YE 2020 share	YE 2010 amount	YE 2020 amount
Electronics/electric	3.39%	15.48%	16.85	184.72
Health care	9.52%	9.68%	47.37	115.52
Business equipment and services	7.45%	9.49%	37.04	113.22
Leisure	3.63%	4.08%	18.07	48.71
Telecommunications	5.19%	4.08%	25.82	48.70
Chemical/Plastics	3.51%	4.04%	17.47	48.23
Insurance	0.83%	3.79%	4.15	45.23
Cable television	4.78%	3.64%	23.75	43.43
Hotels/motels/inns and casinos	3.84%	3.59%	19.09	42.80
Industrial equipment	1.43%	3.56%	7.10	42.50
Retailers (other than food/drug)	4.62%	3.18%	22.99	37.89
Oil and gas	2.05%	3.06%	10.21	36.54
Building and Development	3.06%	2.92%	15.25	34.82
Automotive	3.73%	2.98%	18.55	35.59
Utilities	6.41%	2.74%	31.87	32.73
Food service	2.69%	2.67%	13.37	31.87
Containers and glass products	1.98%	2.38%	9.84	28.36
Drugs	0.93%	2.39%	4.61	28.52
Broadcast radio and television	4.28%	2.24%	21.30	26.77
Food products	2.16%	1.91%	10.73	22.77
Financial Intermediaries	5.42%	1.82%	26.97	21.74
Aerospace and Defense	1.82%	1.49%	9.06	17.78
Air transport	0.91%	1.46%	4.52	17.38
Publishing	7.74%	1.35%	38.52	16.13
Other	8.64%	5.97%	42.97	71.18

Sources: LCD, an offering of S&P Global Market Intelligence; S&P/LSTA Leveraged Loan Index.

Health care has retained its position as one of the top three biggest sectors for the loan market with around 9.6% share in 2020 and 2010. In contrast, publishing, the second largest industry within the S&P/LSTA LLI in 2010 with an 8% share, became one of the smallest sectors in 2020, with just over 1% share.

Looking beyond sector differentiation, while much of the loan market expansion has been homegrown, globalization of the markets is evident. Roughly 10% of outstanding loans now are courtesy of companies domiciled in Europe, versus just 3%

before the GFC. The surge in Yankee supply has largely stemmed from companies expanding operations—and having a greater need to match dollar cash flows—and from increased global M&A activity.

SINGLE B DOMINATION

The credit quality of the loan market began to shift toward riskier credits prior to the onset of the COVID-19 pandemic, but the massive wave of downgrades in the second quarter of 2020 hastened the deterioration in credit quality. By the end of June 2020, a record 34% of par amount outstanding tracked by the S&P/LSTA LLI had an issuer rating of B– or within the CCC/CC/C range from S&P Global Ratings, up from 22% a year earlier or 25% at the end of 2019. For reference, these prepandemic readings are more than double the post-GFC low of 9% at the end of 2014 (see Exhibit 8.25).

In absolute terms, $398 billion of outstanding leveraged loans carried an issuer rating of B– or CCC/CC/C at the end of December

EXHIBIT 8.25

Loan Outstandings by Issuer Rating.

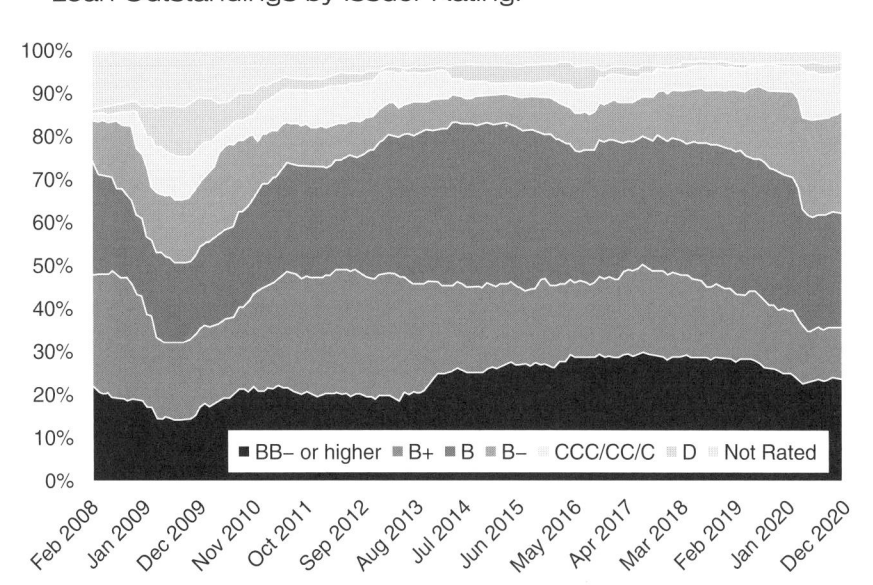

Sources: LCD, an offering of S&P Global Market Intelligence; S&P/LSTA Leveraged Loan Index.

2020, a record high, more than tripling over a 5-year period (it was $106 billion at the end of 2015) and quadrupling from 10 years earlier ($96 billion in 2010).

Downgrades contributed to the increase of riskiest loans in the S&P/LSTA LLI, but they were not the only culprit. New-issue market trends reveal a risk-on sentiment over the last decade as the share of U.S. leveraged loans issued from borrowers with at least one B– or B3 rating has consistently crept up. In 2007, these borrowers accounted for 16% of new-issue volume, and in 2010, as the market reopened following the GFC, this share fell to just 5% (see Exhibit 8.26). In 2013, the B– share topped 20%, and by 2018 it crossed over 30%, reaching an all-time high of 36% in 2020.

Data also shows that volume from the B– rating category has exceeded that of the B/B+ category, at $104 billion versus $99 billion, respectively. Prior to 2020, there has never been a year in which B– issuance topped B/B+ issuance, although the gap between the two ratings classes has narrowed in recent years. For the five years through year-end 2014, B/B+ issuance was on average $91.4 billion higher than B– issuance, but in the five-year period ended December 31, 2019, that average difference winnowed to $50.5 billion.

EXHIBIT 8.26

U.S. Leveraged Loan Issuance by Borrower Rating, Share.

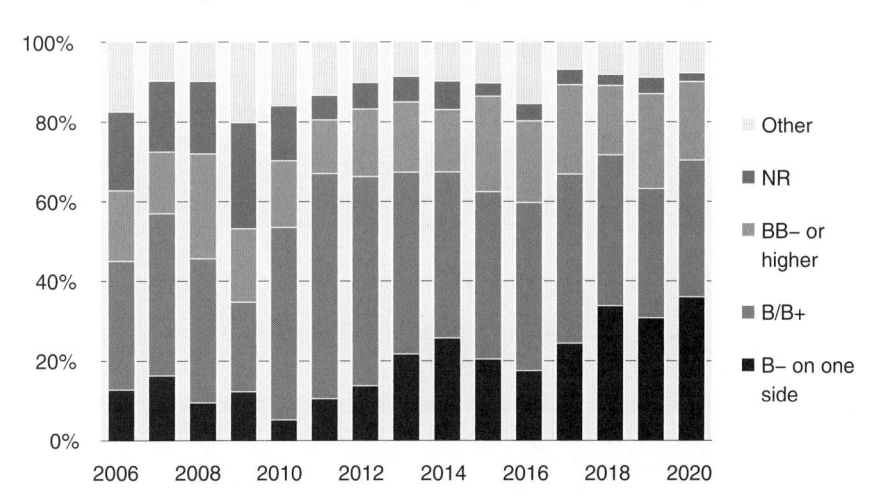

Legend:
- Other
- NR
- BB– or higher
- B/B+
- B– on one side

Data through Dec. 31, 2020.
Source: LCD, an offering of S&P Global Market Intelligence.

COVENANT-LITE BECOMES THE NORM

The story of the loan market evolution cannot be complete without mentioning the rise of the covenant-lite loan structure. Traditionally, loans included multiple financial maintenance covenants such as maximum leverage ratio or minimum interest coverage. At the end of 2006, 93% of outstanding loans tracked by the S&P/LSTA LLI included such maintenance covenants. By the end of 2007, this share declined to 81% and has remained around low to mid-80% mark through the end of 2010. However, as the loan market recovered from the GFC, covenant protection began to erode, and by the end of 2013 half of outstanding loans were covenant-lite (see Exhibit 8.27).

In the years that followed, covenant-lite became mainstream, and by the end of 2020 the vast majority (86% by volume) of the $1.2 trillion loan asset class lacked financial maintenance covenants. In absolute terms, that is a staggering $1 trillion, versus $602 billion five years earlier and just $96 billion 10 years earlier.

It is worth mentioning that the investor base for leveraged loans has shifted significantly since LCD began tracking this information 20 years ago. In 2000, banks and securities firms, as opposed to institutional investors, accounted for 46% of the new-issue market for leveraged loans. Loans syndicated to this group of investors

EXHIBIT 8.27

Covenant-lite Loans: Par Amount Outstanding and Share of All Loans.

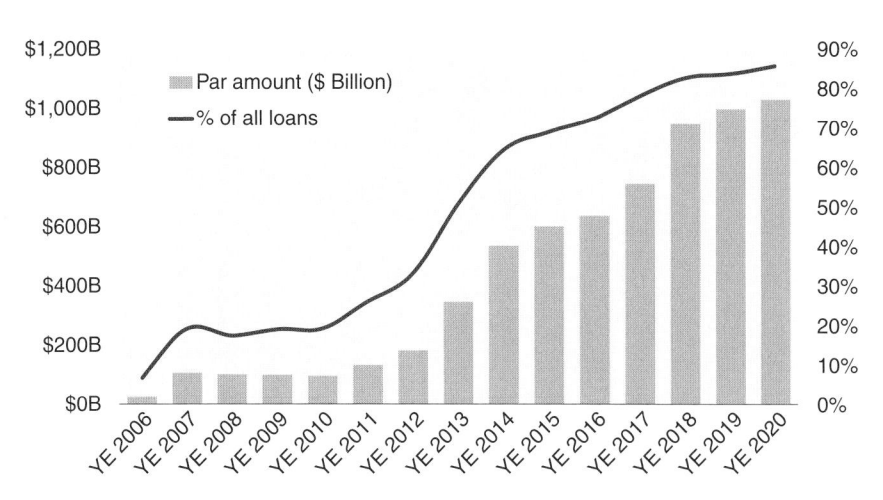

Data through Dec. 31, 2020.
Sources: LCD, an offering of S&P Global Market Intelligence; S&P/LSTA Leveraged Loan Index.

typically require financial maintenance covenants. By 2006, this share had dropped to 26%, and then hovered in the 20% to 30% area for the next five years and then 10% to 14% between 2012 and 2017. By 2018, banks' share had dropped to just 9%.

Institutional investors use primarily structured vehicles such as CLOs and some form of a pooled loan fund, either a mutual/prime fund or a privately managed credit fund. CLOs, specifically, have become the dominant player in the loan market, accounting for roughly 70% of the institutional new-issue market in 2019, versus 43% in 2010, according to LCD. As demand from CLOs and other types of investors grew, documentation shifted away from traditional covenant-heavy loans.

In addition, the credit quality of covenant-lite paper has moved toward riskier credits in recent years. By the end of 2020, issuers rated B– by S&P Global accounted for 25% of outstanding loans lacking maintenance covenants, up from 12% three years earlier and just 9% five years earlier (see Exhibit 8.28). In absolute terms, the 25% share translates into $250 billion of loans, a record high, up from less than $100 billion in 2017 and just $56 billion in 2015.

EXHIBIT 8.28

Outstanding Covenant-lite Loans by Issuer Rating.

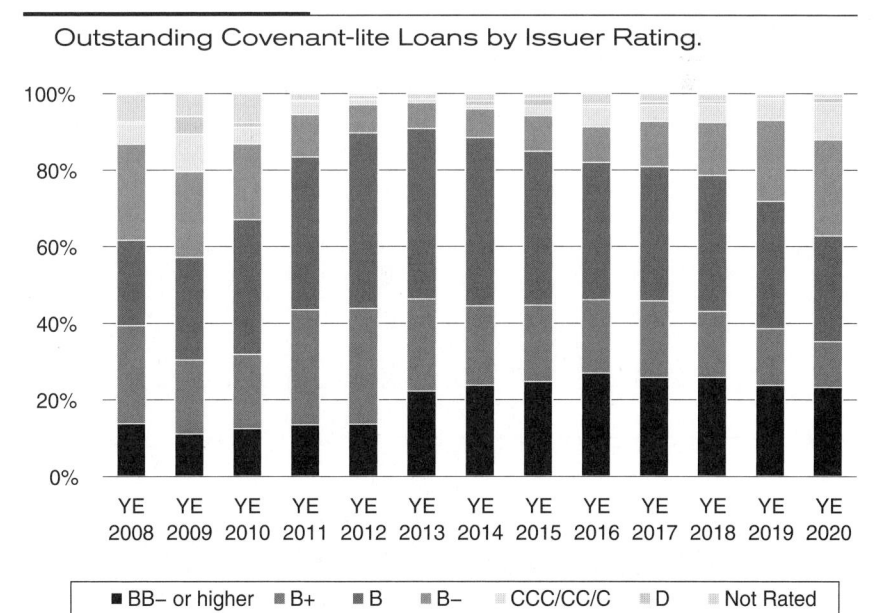

Sources: LCD, an offering of S&P Global Market Intelligence; S&P/LSTA Leveraged Loan Index.

PERFORMANCE

The U.S. loan market has provided a steady stream of positive returns over the 24 years since the inception of the S&P/LSTA LLI, averaging around 5.5% per year. The index posted an annual loss on total return basis just twice—down a devastating 29.10% in 2008 and a milder 0.69% in 2015 (see Exhibit 8.29). In March 2020, following the onset of the COVID-19 pandemic, the index plunged by 12.37%, its second steepest monthly decline in its 24-year history. As a result, it appeared likely that 2020 would be the third year ever with a negative annual total return, but positive news around a COVID-19 vaccine lifted all capital markets in November, raising the 2020 return for the asset class to positive 3.12%.

Compared with other asset classes, namely high-yield bonds and equities, loan returns have historically been lower but far less volatile (see Exhibit 8.30). In fact, in the 24 years since the inception of the S&P/LSTA LLI, loans outperformed both high-yield bonds and equities only four times, and only one of those years, 2018, was since the end of the GFC.

EXHIBIT 8.29

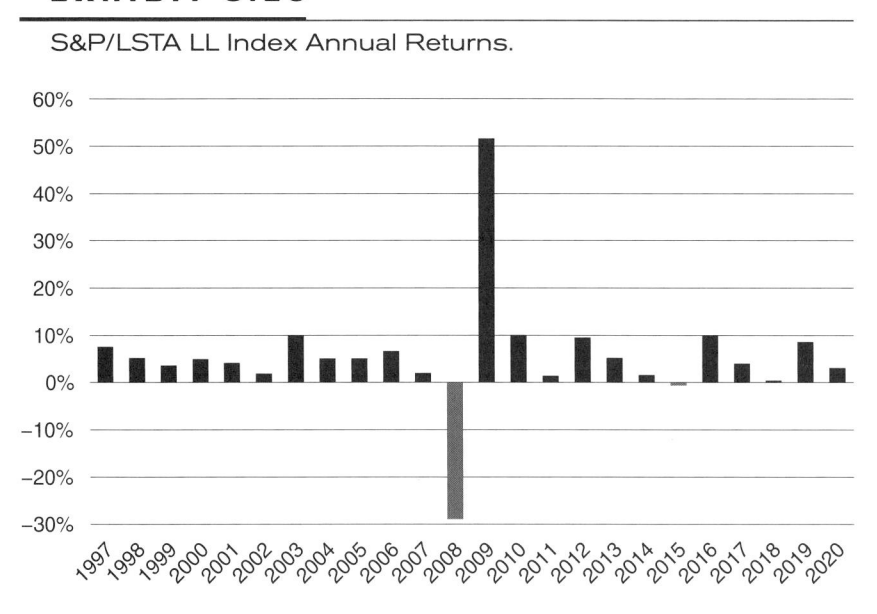

S&P/LSTA LL Index Annual Returns.

Data through Dec. 31, 2020.
Sources: LCD, an offering of S&P Global Market Intelligence; S&P/LSTA Leveraged Loan Index.

EXHIBIT 8.30

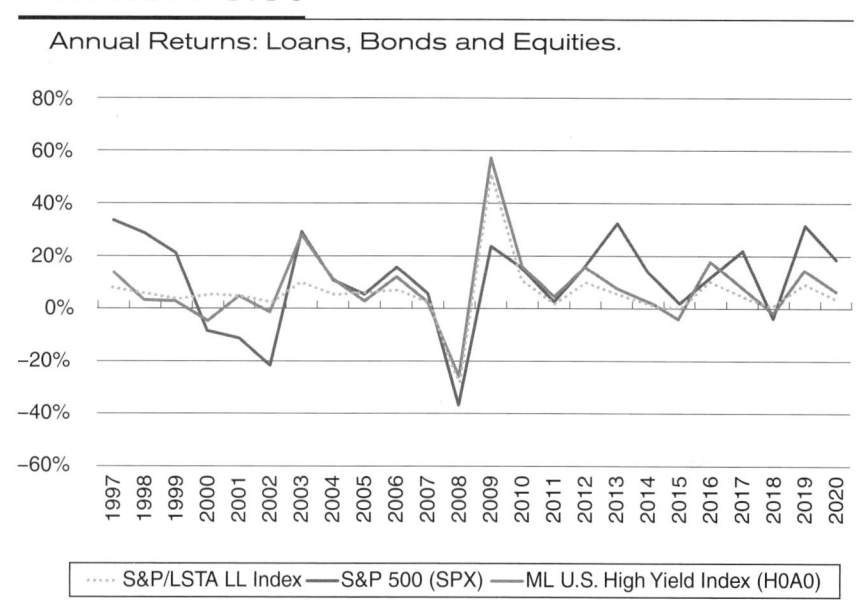

Annual Returns: Loans, Bonds and Equities.

S&P/LSTA LL Index — S&P 500 (SPX) — ML U.S. High Yield Index (H0A0)

Sources: LCD, an offering of S&P Global Market Intelligence; Bank of America Merrill Lynch.

However, secondary market volatility—as measured by the average 12-month-lagging standard deviation of returns—has consistently been lower for loans than for bonds and equities. Looking at the period between 2011 and 2019, the standard deviation of monthly returns averaged 0.82% for the S&P/LSTA LLI, with the median at 0.69% (see Exhibit 8.31). For bonds, the average was 1.54% and median 1.41%, while for the S&P 500, the average was 3.38% and median 3.04%.

For reference, the trailing 12-month standard deviation peaked during the GFC for all three asset classes compared here in August 2009, at 6.8% for loans, 8.20% for bonds, and 8.78% for equities. In 2020, the upheaval caused by the COVID-19 pandemic pushed secondary market volatility to the highest levels since those 2009 peaks. In addition, the difference between the loan market and high-yield bond market volatility virtually evaporated. By the end of 2020, the standard deviation of monthly returns rose to 4.29% for the S&P/LSTA LLI, more than four times the 0.96% reading from the end of 2019. The same measure for high-yield bonds closed out 2020 at 4.45%, roughly three times higher than the end of 2019, at 1.47%.

EXHIBIT 8.31

Average 12-Month Lagging Standard Deviation of Returns.

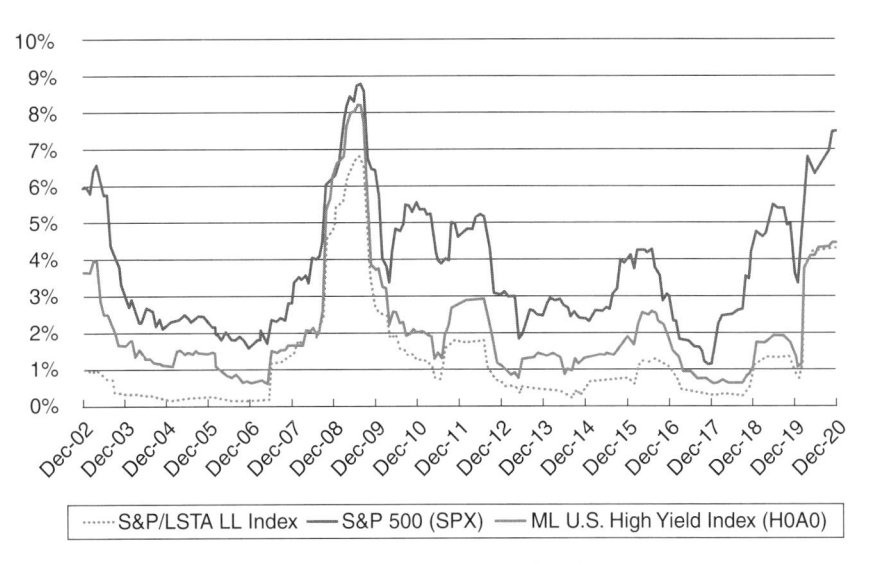

······ S&P/LSTA LL Index ——— S&P 500 (SPX) ——— ML U.S. High Yield Index (H0A0)

Sources: LCD, an offering of S&P Global Market Intelligence; Bank of America Merrill Lynch.

SPREAD TO MATURITY

Leading up to the start of the GFC, loans carried an average nominal spread of roughly L + 250. The discounted spread to maturity, which takes into account the secondary price, stood at around the same level, with the average bid near or over par through 2006 and the first half of 2007 (see Exhibit 8.32 and Exhibit 8.33). In fact, 75% of performing loans in the S&P/LSTA LLI were priced at par or higher at the end of 2006.

As the GFC took root, both the nominal spread and the discounted spread to maturity climbed, albeit at very different paces. The latter measure peaked at a whopping L + 1,699 in December 2008, as the weighted average bid of performing loans plummeted to 62.01, a record low. Moreover, yield to maturity, which includes the three-month LIBOR, exceeded 21% at its peak at the end of 2008. At the same time, the average nominal spread rose less than 20 basis points between the end of 2006 and the end of 2008, to L + 268.

Following the end of the GFC, the average nominal spread continued to increase, reaching its all-time high of L + 467 at the start of 2013. Of course, more than 80% of outstanding credits at that time

The Secondary Loan Market

EXHIBIT 8.32

S&P/LSTA LL Index: Spread-to-Maturity and Nominal Spread.

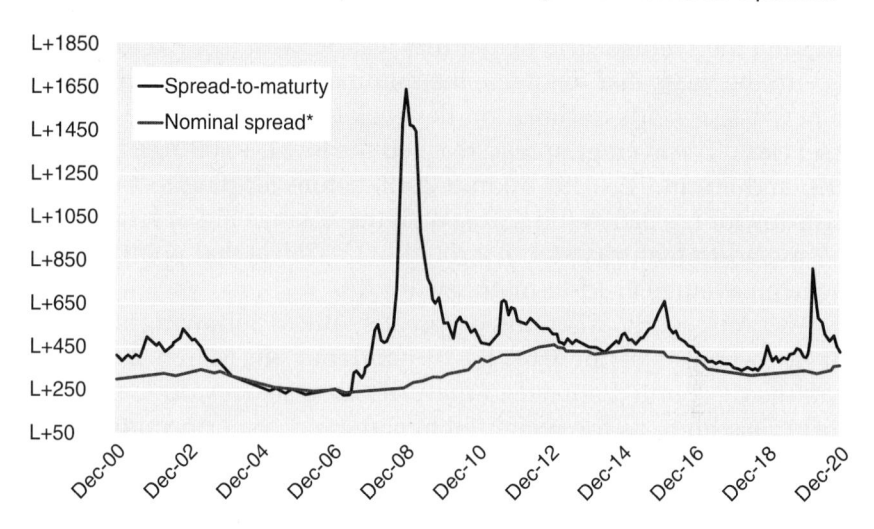

Data through Dec. 31, 2020.
*Nominal spread is adjusted with LIBOR floor benefit.
Sources: LCD, an offering of S&P Global Market Intelligence; S&P/LSTA Leveraged Loan Index.

EXHIBIT 8.33

S&P/LSTA LL Index Weighted Average Bid Price.

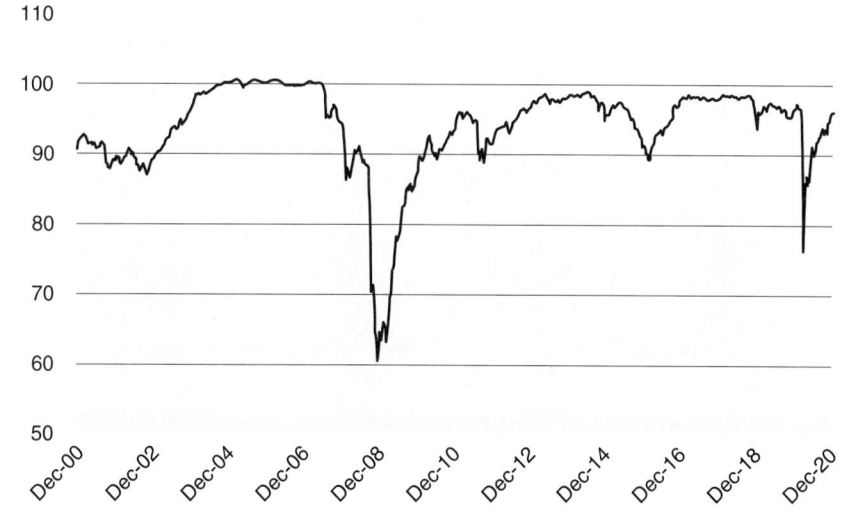

Data through Dec. 31, 2020.
Sources: LCD, an offering of S&P Global Market Intelligence; S&P/LSTA Leveraged Loan Index.

were issued post-crisis, between 2010 and 2012, amid a rising new-issue spread environment. However, with the average loan price around 98, the discounted spread to maturity stood at L + 515 in early 2013 and the average yield to maturity was at 5.45% (see Exhibit 8.34).

In the years that followed, the nominal spread reversed course as new-issue yields declined on the back of strong demand for the asset class. The average spread reached the low L + 400 area by mid-2016 and around L + 350 by mid-2017, before dipping to the post-crisis low of L + 328 in July 2018. With the average bid at around 98, the spread-to-maturity stood at roughly L + 360 at that point, resulting in an average yield-to-maturity of 5.8%.

More recently, discounted spreads spiked following the sell-off at the onset of the COVID-19 pandemic. In March 2020, the average discounted spread-to-maturity rose sharply, to L + 980, a post-crisis high, as the weighted average bid of performing loans tumbled to 78.87. As a result, the yield-to-maturity rose to 11.9%. However, as secondary prices recovered by end of December, to just over 96, the discounted spread-to-maturity retreated to L + 443 (yield of 4.70%). Although this is roughly in line with levels seen just before the late February rout, these spread levels are wider than

EXHIBIT 8.34

S&P/LSTA LL Index Yield-to-Maturity.

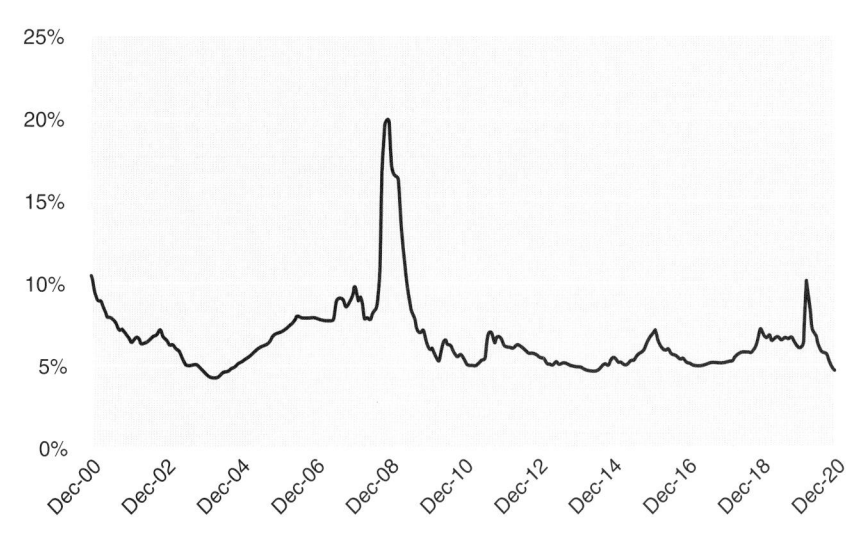

Data through Dec. 31, 2020.
Sources: LCD, an offering of S&P Global Market Intelligence; S&P/LSTA Leveraged Loan Index.

the L + 423 reading at the end of 2019, although the yield is lower (the yield was 6.13% in December 2019 due to a higher LIBOR).

CREDIT WHERE IT'S DUE

In summary, the evolution of leveraged loans into a mature asset class has established the market in accordance with (the historically more developed) high-yield bond market as an important tool for investors and speculative-rated borrowers alike.

Presenting investors with a solid history for returns, on the flip side, leveraged loans typically offer companies a lower average cost of senior secured debt with an added benefit of prepayment optionality. The growth of the past 20 years that went hand-in-hand with a growing investor base has provided better liquidity for investors, but this growing demand that facilitated a post-GFC boon of highly leveraged buyouts has eroded the overall quality mix of the market—a risk proposition that is still being met by strong debt servicing metrics and lower historical default rates and higher recovery rates in comparison to high-yield bonds.

The Secondary Loan Market: Settling Loan Transactions[1]

Sheryl Fulton
IHS Markit

INTRODUCTION

Perhaps the greatest difference between loan trades and trades in virtually every other tradable asset is how loan trades settle. Whereas stocks, bonds, and most other tradable assets settle electronically over computerized systems, loans, because of their complexity, close on the basis of the exchange of documents that may be negotiated by the parties. Distressed trades, in particular, present even greater challenges than par trades. Although the LSTA has

---

[1] We would like to thank the authors of this article which appeared in the First Edition: Laura Torrado and Michele B. Piorkowski. The article has been updated to reflect developments in the loan market and the LSTA Trade Confirmations as of September 13, 2021.

made great strides in shortening the settlement process and making loans more transparent, loan market participants still struggle to close many loan trades on a timely basis and in an efficient manner.

This article will describe the mechanics and nuances of settling loan trades. It will highlight important issues, identify certain pitfalls to be avoided when closing trades, and review some of the documentation that is used to settle loan trades.

BACKGROUND

Before the organization of the LSTA in 1995, there was no standard documentation for purchasing, selling, or closing loans. Consequently, simple par trades could take weeks to close. The situation for distressed loans was far worse.

The LSTA's initial goal was to bring some standards to bear in the market, first by developing standard confirmations for both par and distressed trades, then by developing widely accepted market standards, and finally by developing and constantly improving additional standard trading documentation, a process that continues to this day. As a result of the efforts of the LSTA and interested market participants, the settlement of loan trades has indeed become more efficient and transparent, and settlement times have improved over the years. The trading and settlement structure described in this article is based on the market standards developed over the years by the LSTA and its members.

PRETRADE ISSUES

Although the trade confirmation is the first step in closing a trade, it is not the first step in making a trade. The trade is actually entered into between two loan market participants representing a seller and a buyer when they agree the material terms of the trade either on the phone or by email or some other electronic means or a combination of all of them. Since October 2002, with an amendment to the New York State Statute of Frauds, loan trades entered into orally are binding contracts, so long as the material terms of the contract have been agreed upon.

Because a trade is binding as soon as the parties agree to the material terms, it is crucial that traders be prepared and have a good handle on exactly what they are selling or purchasing. In addition, it is important that they make clear at the time of the trade whether the trade is a par or distressed trade. This issue will be discussed in detail later in this article. Because most credit agreements have numerous tranches and many borrowers have more than one credit agreement, this can be confusing, so it is important for traders to ensure that they are trading the same asset. In addition, there are many other important terms that can affect the economics of a loan trade. Understanding these issues is crucial to avoiding mistakes. The next step after a trade is agreed upon is the completion by each trader of a trade ticket that memorializes the economic terms of the trade. The trade ticket is then typically entered into the party's operational system. Traditionally, the trade confirmation would be sent to the counterparty for its review and signature. In trades between dealers and buy-side loan market participants, the confirmation is usually prepared by the dealer; in trades between dealers, the seller typically prepares the confirmation.

Although the manual exchange of trade confirmations is still followed for some middle market trades, the vast majority of loan trades are now settled on an electric settlement platform called ClearPar. The trade details will be entered into the ClearPar system, either manually or by automatic upload, depending on a counterparty's selection. Generally, this is done by the seller. The ClearPar system is used by most loan market participants because it automatically generates the necessary closing documents and facilitates electronic signature by each counterparty. Although rare in today's market, certain counterparties may still choose to download the applicable confirmation and assignment agreement and manually sign off of the electric settlement platform and then send their signatures, which will be posted to the trade.

THE CONFIRMATION: THE FIRST STEP IN CLOSING A TRADE

The face of a confirmation is a short document that sets out the deal-specific terms of a trade. Importantly, the standard LSTA confirmation incorporates by reference the detailed Standard Terms and Conditions (STCs) that set forth the market conventions and other terms that apply to all trades.[2]

---

[2] There are different STCs for par/near par confirmations and distressed confirmations.

The terms enumerated on the trade confirmation include the following:

1. *Trade date*: The date on which the parties entered into the trade.
2. *Seller*: The legal name of the entity selling the loan and whether it is acting as agent or principal.
3. *Buyer*: The legal name of the entity purchasing the loan and whether it is acting as agent or principal.
4. *Credit agreement*: A legal description of the credit agreement to which the loans being traded relate.
5. *Form of purchase*: Whether the loans are being sold via assignment, participation, or otherwise.
6. *Purchase amount/type of debt*: The notional amount of debt being purchased, whether it is a term loan, revolver, litigation claim, letter of credit, or other; the relevant facility (tranche); and the CUSIP number.
7. *Purchase rate:* Stated as a percentage of par.
8. *Upfront fee (for par trades)*: Whether and when an upfront fee is payable, and, if so, by whom.
9. *Accrued interest (for distressed trades)*: Whether interest settles on a "trades flat" basis or with accrued interest.
10. *Credit documentation to be provided by seller*: Whether the seller is responsible for delivering the underlying credit documentation.[3]
11. *Collateral Annex applicable*: The seller may require the buyer to post collateral for any unfunded portion of a revolving loan/commitment in which the buyer participates, unless parties agree otherwise.
12. *Collateral account institution:* If the Collateral Annex is applicable, the parties must decide if the relevant account will be established with the seller or if the collateral account will be held in accordance with the collateral segregation provisions set forth in the Collateral Annex or with a third-party custodian.

---

[3] This is applicable only if the buyer is not already a party to the credit agreement and made its request on or prior to the trade date.

13. *LSTA standard other terms of trade (for distressed trades)*: These include whether the trade is subject to the buyer's or seller's first completing a third-party purchase or sale of the underlying loan asset or whether flip representations apply.
14. *Trade-specific other terms of trade*: Parties should set out any other terms of the transaction. They may consider specifying the required collateral percentage if it is determined at the time of trade and the Collateral Annex is applicable.

The confirmation ends with signature blocks for both the buyer and the seller.

COMMON SETTLEMENT ISSUES

The STCs address a number of deal-specific issues. These issues are discussed below.

Principal–Agency Issue

The buyer and the seller indicate whether they are acting as principal, agent, or riskless principal:

- A *principal* is directly liable for the consummation of the transaction.
- An *agent* has arranged for another party to enter into the transaction but has no direct liability if the transaction is not completed and is usually paid a fee for arranging the transaction.
- A party acts as a *riskless principal* if on or prior to the trade date the parties have agreed that the other party's obligation to complete the trade is contingent on the successful completion of the purchase or sale of the underlying loan to a third party.

Allocation

Buyers and sellers who are asset managers also need to designate the funds on behalf of which they are acting, if applicable. The LSTA has set the standard that by trade date plus one day (T + 1) the parties should designate any specific funds involved in the transaction.

FORMS OF PURCHASE

Assignments

There are a number of different ways in which a transfer can be affected. The most common is through an assignment. Under an assignment, the seller transfers all of its legal, beneficial, and economic rights in the loan to the buyer. Legal title passes from the seller to the buyer; the buyer assumes the obligations of the seller; and, with certain limited exceptions, the seller is released from its obligations under the relevant credit agreement. In effect, the buyer replaces the seller.

Participations

Another form of purchase is a participation. Under a participation, the seller transfers to the buyer an undivided interest in its right, title, and interest in a loan. Effectively, the seller transfers to the buyer the beneficial and economic interests but not the legal title of the loan.

Unlike assignments, most credit agreements limit the voting rights that can be passed on to participants. These rights typically include the right to vote on (1) an extension of the maturity date, (2) an increase in the commitment, (3) the release of collateral, and (4) a change in the rate of terms of repayment.

Notwithstanding the provisions of the credit agreements, some sellers prefer not to grant any voting rights to participants or prefer to limit their rights in other ways, generally by imposing a majority vote concept. Sellers seek to further limit the voting rights of participants in order to protect their own proprietary interests in the same loans or to protect important relationships with borrowers.[4] The LSTA has published a Form of Par/Near Par Participation Agreement and a Form of Distressed Participation Agreement which have been adopted by loan market participants.

---

[4] Because voting rights of a lender are typically not divisible under the terms of the credit agreement in the broadly syndicated loan market, a seller of a loan participation that retains an interest in the loan cannot bifurcate its vote to accommodate its loan participant(s). Consequently, in order to protect its interests, it may refuse to grant any voting rights or, at a minimum, require a majority vote among all its participants. Conversely, even though credit agreements limit the voting rights of participants, sellers may consult with participants even on votes that are beyond the scope of the participants' rights.

Assignment or Participation?

For many reasons, assignments are generally preferred over participations. Nevertheless, buyers purchase participations rather than assignments for a number of reasons. A primary reason for purchasing a participation is that a buyer cannot meet certain requirements of the credit agreement. For example, many credit agreements have minimum size requirements, and the buyer could be trying to purchase an interest in the loan that is below this threshold.[5] Alternatively, certain buyers might not meet the criteria necessary to become assignees under the credit agreement. Another reason why a buyer might prefer to purchase a participation is to accumulate a significant position in a loan without the borrower (or other loan market participants) knowing.

Other Forms

When an assignment is not possible but a buyer has indicated on its confirmation that it will accept assignments only, a trade—a binding contractual obligation—*still* exists. This is a fundamental principle in the loan market and is often referred to as "a trade is a trade." The parties are entitled to the benefit of their bargain and must settle the trade on the basis of a mutually agreeable alternative structure or other arrangement that affords the buyer and seller the economic equivalent of the agreed-upon trade.[6]

Purchase Amount/Type of Debt

This section of the confirmation describes the amount of the loans and the tranches that are being traded. Parties need to be diligent in accurately describing the tranches to ensure that the confirmation reflects their original agreement. Because different tranches are likely to have different values, the economics of a transaction rely on the accuracy of the confirmation and the description of what is being purchased and sold.

---

[5] Or, the buyer could be suballocating its interest among a number of funds, none of which is purchasing an interest large enough to make the threshold.

[6] One way to resolve the trade is to cash settle, where the parties determine the cash value of the loan and the "out of the money" party agrees to pay the economic benefit to the other.

Purchase Rate

This section describes the price being paid for the loan. All loan trade prices are expressed as a percentage of par.[7]

Interest Treatment

For any trade that is entered into on the LSTA Par/Near Par Trade Confirmation ("Par Confirm"), any interest and accruing ordinary course fees (such as commitment, facility, and letter of credit fees) payable in connection with the loan under the credit agreement from and after the trade date (except for any paid-in-kind [PIK] interest) shall be treated in accordance with the "settled without accrued interest" convention described later (unless otherwise specified in trade-specific other terms of trade). Any amendment, consent waiver, and other similar nonrecurring fees payable from and after the trade date are for the benefit of the buyer.

All PIK interest is for the benefit of the buyer (at no cost) for any amount that has not been capitalized before the trade date. PIK interest is noncash interest that is "paid" as an increase to the principal amount of the loan that is owed to the lender.

Under the LSTA's Distressed Trade Confirmation ("Distressed Confirm"), the parties choose the interest convention. *Trades flat* means that any interest or other amounts in connection therewith that accrue on or before the trade date but are paid after the trade date are for the account of the buyer. All payments made from and after the trade date are for the benefit of the buyer.

Alternatively, parties may choose to trade on a "settled without accrued interest basis." Section 5 of the Distressed Confirm defines this as follows:

> *If "Settled Without Accrued Interest" is specified in the Confirmation, subject to the application* of [delayed compensation] . . . *all Interest and Accruing Fees accrued but*

---

[7] Although calculating the price of a funded loan is simple (notional amount × purchase rate), calculating the price for an unfunded revolver is trickier, because the buyer will actually fund the loan at par no matter what the purchase rate under the trade may be. An example that illustrates this concept: assume that a buyer purchases a $5,000,000 loan commitment at 68%, and assume that $4,000,000 is funded and $1,000,000 is unfunded but available to the borrower. At closing, the buyer would pay the seller $2,720,000 ($4,000,000 × 68%) *minus* a credit on the unfunded portion equal to $320,000 [$1,000,000 × (100% − 68%)], for a total purchase price of $2,400,000. This protects the buyer in the event that any portion of the $1,000,000 is drawn by the borrower at a later time.

unpaid before the Settlement Date shall be for the account of Seller. Buyer shall pay to Seller any such Interest and Accruing Fees promptly upon any receipt thereof by Buyer; so long as such amounts are received by Buyer (a) on or before the due date thereof or the expiration of any applicable grace period, each as specified in the Credit Documents as in effect on the Trade Date (or, if no such grace period exists (other than due to any acceleration of the Debt pursuant to the Credit Documents following the Filing Date (as defined below)), the expiration of thirty (30) days from such due date), and (b) before a default by any obligor(s) in connection with any other payment obligations of the obligor(s) under the Credit Documents. Otherwise, (i) such Interest and Accruing Fees (if and when paid, whether to Seller or Buyer) and any other accrued amounts due from and after the Settlement Date shall be for the account of Buyer, and Seller shall not be entitled to any part thereof and (ii) if applicable as of the Settlement Date, notwithstanding the "Settled Without Accrued Interest" specification in the Confirmation and in the applicable Transfer Documentation (as defined below), "Trades Flat" shall be deemed to have been specified in the Confirmation solely for the purpose of clarifying that the crediting provisions of subsection (b) of Section 6, "Compensation for Delayed Settlement," . . . do not apply with respect to Interest and Accruing Fees accrued and unpaid as of the Delayed Settlement Date (as defined below). The foregoing notwithstanding, if Buyer and Seller agree that the treatment of Interest and Accruing Fees shall be on a "Settled Without Accrued Interest" basis and (x) (i) the Trade Date is prior to the Filing Date and (ii) during the period from the Filing Date through the Settlement Date, any obligor(s) is (are) making Adequate Protection Payments as and when due under the applicable Adequate Protection Order no less frequently than as required for payments of Interest and Accruing Fees under the Credit Agreement as in effect immediately prior to the Filing Date or (y) (i) the Trade Date is on or after the Filing Date and (ii) during the period from the Trade Date through the Settlement Date, any obligor(s) is (are) making Adequate Protection Payments as and when due under the applicable Adequate Protection Order no less frequently than as required for payments of Interest and Accruing Fees under the Credit Agreement as in effect immediately prior to the Filing Date, then any such Adequate Protection Payments shall, subject to Section 6, "Compensation for Delayed Settlement," . . . be allocated on a

> "Settled Without Accrued Interest" basis and treated as if such payments were Interest and Accruing Fees, without giving effect to the deemed "Trades Flat" election provisions described above . . . Otherwise, such Adequate Protection Payments (if and when paid, whether to Seller or Buyer) and any other accrued amounts due from and after the Settlement Date shall be for the account of Buyer, and Seller shall not be entitled to any part thereof or obligated pursuant to subsection (b) of Section 6, "Compensation for Delayed Settlement," . . . to credit Buyer with respect to such Adequate Protection Payments accrued during the Delay Period and unpaid as of the Delayed Settlement Date.

Finally, parties may choose the convention "paid on settlement date" but this is rarely selected. Where parties do make this election, the buyer agrees to pay the seller up front for any accrued interest owed to the seller up to the settlement date (subject also to the terms for delayed compensation). If the obligor fails to pay all or a portion of that amount on or prior to the scheduled due date thereof, then the seller shall be required to promptly reimburse the buyer, upon demand by the buyer, that amount *plus* interest that would accrue for each day on such amounts at the Federal Funds Rate, and that amount that had not been paid shall be for the account of the buyer, and the seller shall not be entitled to any part thereof.

Trade-Specific Other Terms of Trade

Two common LSTA trade-specific terms of trade that are added to distressed confirmations are (1) that the seller's obligation to sell is subject to the successful completion of the purchase of the asset by the seller ("subject to buy-in") and (2) whether a seller can provide "flip" representation on its sale to the buyer.

Subject to the Buy-In

If this condition is agreed to, the selling broker does not have to deliver the loans to the buyer if it cannot purchase the loans from its counterparty.[8]

---

[8] Distressed loan transactions may be highly negotiated, and usually the buyer knows that the broker is working to acquire the loans for the purpose of selling such loans to

Flip Representations

"Flip representations" are chosen when the seller is a broker that is purchasing the loan on the same day on which it is selling it or on the previous day. Because the broker is making only a small commission, it is reluctant to assume the additional risks associated with distressed document representations. To qualify to make flip representations, the seller must indicate on the confirmation that it is acting as a riskless principal, and the seller must be prepared to settle the loan no later than one business day after the settlement of its purchase of the loans.

Under flip representations, the seller limits the scope of its representations with respect to title, outstanding principal amount/commitment, and proof of claim filing (if applicable) by assuming the truth and accuracy of the representations and warranties on such matters made to the seller by the immediate prior seller(s).[9]

Reasonably Acceptable Documents

Finally, with respect to the Distressed Confirm and trading terms, each distressed transaction is subject to the negotiation, execution, and delivery of reasonably acceptable contracts and instruments of transfer. This section means that the parties will agree to negotiate a document, usually in the form of the LSTA's Purchase and Sale Agreement (PSA), to complete the transfer of the loan. This language is standard in every distressed loan transaction and binds the parties to work in good faith to agree to an acceptable transfer agreement to transfer the loans.

At this point, whether par or distressed, the transaction moves into the closing phase, and the closing documentation is drafted.

---

the buyer. The buyer knows that it will be paying a small spread or markup to the selling broker for its work in acquiring the loans. If this provision is not included in the trade confirmation from the broker to the buyer, and if the broker is not able to acquire the loans, the broker would be naked short the loans to the buyer. If the value of the loans were to increase, the broker could be at risk for a significant sum on a transaction for which it would be receiving minimal compensation. Buyers understand this risk and consider agreeing to the "subject to" provision on a transaction-by-transaction basis.

[9] If the seller has met the conditions necessary to settle on the basis of flip representations, the buyer cannot avoid receiving the flip representations merely by delaying the closing.

Buy-in/Sell-out (BISO)

Under the Par Confirm, if the buyer and seller are unable to effect settlement on or prior to the BISO Trigger Date, 15 business days after the Trade Date, due to the failure of either the buyer or seller to perform certain obligations relating to settlement that are set forth in the Par Confirm, then the performing party (the party that did meet its settlement requirements) may require the nonperforming party (the party that did not meet its settlement requirements) to take steps outlined in the Par Confirm to move toward a settlement. A similar concept is included in the Distressed Confirm, but the timeline is extended (the BISO Trigger Date is 50 business days after the Trade Date) to reflect the complexities of distressed trading.

Amendments/Restructures

There are various types of actions that the borrower may take to restructure the credit agreement while a trade is open. These actions will be communicated via an agent notice and typically include notification of a change, a voluntary election that allows but does not require the lender to take a specific action, or a proposal from the borrower that will be decided by a vote from its lenders. Depending on how the applicable credit agreement was structured, the administrative agent would send the lenders in the syndicate a notice setting out the details of the proposal. The notice would advise the deadline for lenders' responses and if there are any amendment/consent fees attached to the election.

Market practice has evolved and sellers will typically reach out to any counterparties with which they have open trades to advise of the agent notice and seek direction from the buyer as to how they would like them to vote on their behalf. Importantly, the Confirms expressly state that the seller need not solicit a vote from the buyer with respect to any such amendment or waiver.

LOAN CLOSING DOCUMENTATION
Par Loans

Par trades settle upon the execution of an assignment agreement in the form attached to the applicable credit agreement (or on the LSTA's form of Par Participation Agreement) and a funding memo, and the buyer becomes a lender of record when the agent updates the applicable register. There is usually no involvement of counsel for the settlement of par trades, and the attendant costs are low. Agent transfer fees (often in the range of $3,500 per trade), to the extent that they are not waived, are usually split between the buyer and the seller. Settlements involving assignments are also subject, in most cases, to consents by the borrower and/or the agent, which typically are not to be unreasonably withheld. The standard period for settlement of a par trade is T + 7, after which delayed compensation (calculations to be discussed later) begins to accrue.

The LSTA published new delayed compensation rules in 2016 to address when a buyer must be ready to close par trades and the steps to be taken to be entitled to delayed compensation. By no later than T + 5, the buyer must (1) execute online or submit via electronic mail its signature pages to both the Par Confirm and the assignment agreement to the electronic settlement platform, (2) select a proposed settlement date of no later than T + 7 and "persist" (meaning that it represents that it is financially able to settle the transaction on any business day from and including T + 7) until the delayed settlement date without interruption, and (3) pay the purchase price to the seller (to the extent that the purchase price is a positive number) on the delayed settlement date, in accordance with any applicable lead times. Failure to meet the requirements results in the buyer's forfeiture of delayed compensation. A buyer may request that a seller reinstitute such compensation, but it is in the seller's sole discretion to accommodate such a request.[10]

Distressed Loans

Distressed loan trades settle upon the execution of an assignment agreement also in the form attached to the applicable credit agreement (or, sometimes, on the LSTA's Distressed Participation Agreement), the LSTA's PSA, a pricing letter, and sometimes a funding memo. Virtually all distressed loan trades are reviewed by lawyers. In the same way as par trades, agent transfer fees (often in the range of $3,500), to the extent that they are not waived, are usually split between the buyer and the seller. Settlements involving assignments are typically subject to the agent's consent (but, typically not the borrower's consent if the borrower has filed for bankruptcy).

---

[10] Please see Ellen Hefferan's discussion of primary delayed compensation in Chapter 2.

The standard settlement period is 20 days, after which delayed compensation kicks in.

LSTA's Form of Purchase and Sale Agreement

The most important of the distressed settlement documents is the LSTA's Purchase and Sale Agreement (PSA). The PSA is divided into two sections, transaction-specific terms (TSTs) and Standard Terms and Conditions (PSA STCs). The TSTs set forth all the salient points that are specific to a particular trade and is the only part of the PSA that is completed by the parties to the trade. The TSTs identify the asset being traded, the trade date, the agreement date, the names of the buyer and seller, the purchase amount, the name of the borrower, and whether credit documentation is to be provided. It is also the section that identifies any changes to the provisions of the PSA STCs.

The major representations that are contained in a PSA pertain to the assigned rights and are not limited to the loans. The seller represents to the buyer that it is indeed transferring the entire bundle of rights, including claims and ancillary rights derived from ownership of the loans. The seller also represents the principal amount of the loans being transferred and that no other funding obligations related thereto exist (except as set forth in the TSTs). It also represents that it owns the assigned rights free and clear of any encumbrance, including any pledge, lien, security interest, charge, or other adverse claim. The seller also represents that it is not a party to any documents that could adversely affect the assigned rights, not just the loans. Perhaps most important, the seller represents that it has not engaged in any "bad acts" or conduct or made any omissions that would result in the buyer's receiving less favorable treatment than any other lender holding the same type of loans. This representation protects the buyer from anything the seller may have done that would not be detected by a review of the credit documentation.

One of the more recent updates to the LSTA suite of distressed documents is the LSTA Form of Proceeds letter ("Proceeds Letter"). The Proceeds Letter is a bilateral agreement between the parties of a secondary loan trade where the loan has been converted in connection with a Chapter 11 restructuring plan of the applicable borrower. The Proceeds Letter provides for certain representations, warranties, and other provisions relating to the loan proceeds as well as mechanics for the transfer of the proceeds from the seller to the buyer.

The Proceeds Letter is used to settle a trade only if (1) the trade was confirmed using an LSTA Distressed Confirm and (2) (a) the applicable borrower is a debtor under Chapter 11 of the Bankruptcy Code, (b) the class in which the loan is placed under the plan of reorganization is "impaired" (as that term is used in Section 1124 of the Bankruptcy Code), (c) the plan has been confirmed, and (d) the plan's effective date has occurred. The LSTA strongly recommends using the form only after the record date for distributions under the plan has occurred and distributions under the plan have been begun.

A Proceeds Letter is premised on the accepted principle in secondary market loan trading that a "trade is a trade." As set forth in the Distressed Confirm, a buyer assumes the obligation to purchase the debt as it may be "reorganized, restructured, converted, or otherwise modified." Often debt is reorganized in connection with a Chapter 11 plan, and the Proceeds Letter is intended to document the transfer of such reorganized debt.

Upstream Due Diligence

Another costly element of distressed loan trading is the buyer's practice of conducting due diligence on the seller's "upstream" chain of documentation. If the buyer finds a deficient document anywhere in the chain, the buyer is likely to demand "step-up" representations from the seller to the extent that the upstream documents are not "market standard." Step-up representations are discussed below.

Par or Distressed Documents: How to Decide?

Whether to trade on par or distressed documents is a question for the parties to decide at the time of trade. Although there are no hard-and-fast rules, there are a number of issues to consider:

- Has the borrower filed for bankruptcy? Loans of borrowers in bankruptcy typically trade on distressed documents regardless of the price.[11] (Debtor in possession loans typically trade on par documentation.)

---

[11] Many secured loans in bankruptcy trade above par, reflecting the expectation that unpaid accrued interest will be paid as part of a reorganization plan.

- What are the ratings of the borrower, its loans, and its other funded debt? What is the *trend* of its ratings?
- What is the *market* doing at the time the trade is done? If the market has shifted to distressed documents, a buyer will expect (and want) distressed documents.
- Is there significant litigation risk associated with the borrower? Does the borrower have public image problems?
- Are there negative prospects for the borrower and/or its industry?

These factors must be weighed against the increased cost and time necessary to close a loan trade on distressed documents. Are the protections that come with distressed documents worth the added cost? Since the GFC, dealers have increasingly kept trading on par documents until the borrower has filed for bankruptcy. It will be interesting to see if this continues, or if the trend reverses.

Step-up Representations

It is also important to note that the seller shall provide to the buyer customary step-up provisions with respect to those prior sellers, if any, that transferred the loan on par documents on or after such date as is determined by the LSTA to be the date on which market convention for transferring the loan shifted from par documentation to distressed documentation. By giving "step-up" representations in this way, any deficiencies in the documents of the prior sellers are covered. Before the implementation of the LSTA Shift Date Rules in 2011, the LSTA had adhered to a regime whereby it merely polled dealers asking when they thought a loan had shifted from trading on par documents to trading on distressed documents. Under the polling process, the LSTA often received only a couple of responses to the polling requests and would then share those responses with the market, leaving it to the parties to agree on a date. This process contributed to settlement delays, and thus in 2011 the LSTA moved to a review of trading data that it had begun to receive from dealers on a monthly basis (the data includes every loan trade entered into by that dealer and lists the document type—par or distressed—for each such trade), and the LSTA then published the date after reviewing the data. The revised procedures were designed to promote efficiency in the loan market.

Finishing the Closing: Pricing and Payment

After the relevant documentation is completed, the parties are ready to close. Both parties will review the funding memorandum that was automatically generated on the electronic settlement platform to confirm there are no discrepancies in the calculations.

On the settlement date, the buyer pays the seller a purchase price for the amount of the loan being transferred (or, if the calculation produces a negative number, the seller pays the buyer). Purchase price calculations based on various trade scenarios are described step by step. These calculations are based on the LSTA Par Confirm as of September 13, 2021, at the time of this writing. The sample scenarios contemplate par trades, performing loans, unfunded commitments, and par settlement times of T + 7. The examples also include delayed settlement scenarios that describe cost of carry calculations, as well as interest and fee allocation. To simulate reality, additional variables such as paydowns and commitment reductions before settlement have been included.

There are basic questions that need to be asked before beginning the calculation for each trade, and they are highlighted below:

1. Is the trade a par trade or a distressed trade?
2. Is the loan a term loan, which is fully funded debt with no future funding obligation, or is it, for example, a revolving credit facility, which may have future funding obligations?
3. What was the loan amount on the trade date?
4. What was the loan amount on the settlement date?
5. Is the loan denominated in U.S. dollars, or is it a multicurrency loan that is subject to one or more borrowings in one or more currencies other than the master currency?
6. What was the agreed-upon purchase rate for the loan?
7. Has the commitment amount of the loan changed since the trade date? Have there been any commitment reductions or principal repayments?
8. What was the agreed-upon treatment of interest?
   - Trade flat?
   - Settled without accrued interest?
   - Paid on settlement date?

9. Have any ordinary course fees (such as commitment, facility, and letter of credit fees) or nonrecurring fees (amendment, consent, waiver, and so on) been received by the seller since the trade date?
10. Is the settlement date a "delayed settlement date," occurring after the T + 7 date for par trades or after the T + 20 date for distressed trades?
11. Is there an agent fee?

Par Trades

Most loans trading on par documents are generally considered "healthy" loans, where the borrower is making regularly scheduled interest and fee payments, which further categorizes them as "performing loans." As noted above, par loans, unless otherwise specified in the trade confirmation, are usually traded using the settled without accrued interest treatment. This trading convention directs that all interest and recurring fees accrued up to, but not including, T + 7 or the settlement date, whichever is sooner, are for the account of the seller (i.e., the seller gets to keep these amounts). The only exception is for nonrecurring fees, which are for the buyer's account.

The following examples illustrate various purchase price and delayed settlement compensation calculations. To simplify matters, all examples will be based on the following repeating parameters, with a calendar provided for reference as seen in Exhibit 8.35.

Term Loans

When calculating the purchase price for a term loan, you begin by multiplying the funded amount of the loan on the settlement date

EXHIBIT 8.35

Sample Term Loan Trade Constants	
Commitment amount:	$5,000,000
Trade date	March 24 (Thursday)
T + 7	April 5 (Monday)*
Purchase price	98.00%

* April 2 is a holiday and not counted as a business day.

EXHIBIT 8.36

Basic Term Loan Trade, Settlement within T + 7.

| Term loan purchase price: | $5,000,000 × 98.00% | $4,900,000.00 |

EXHIBIT 8.37

Term Loan Trade with Commitment Reduction before T + 7.

Term loan purchase price:	$4,500,000 × 98.00%	= $4,410,000.00
Commitment reduction credit:	$500,000 × 2.00%	= ($10,000.00)
Net term loan purchase price:		$4,400,000.00

by the purchase rate. Assuming that the trade settles within T + 7, the purchase price for our sample trade would be the fully funded commitment amount multiplied by the purchase price, as shown in Exhibit 8.36.

Now let's add a twist: assume that there is a permanent repayment of principal (a "permanent reduction" as it is referred to in the Confirms) between the trade date and the settlement date. Because the buyer "owns" the loan from the trade date, it is entitled to capture the 2.00% discount on the permanent reduction. This discount will be credited to the buyer at settlement. For example, using our sample trade, if the borrower repaid $500,000 on March 26 and the trade was settled on April 5, the buyer would pay 98% on the *settlement date* balance of $4,500,000 and receive a credit for the 2% discount on the $500,000 commitment reduction, as shown in Exhibit 8.37.

Settled without Accrued Interest Treatment

If the loan is a performing loan, the seller is entitled to keep all of the accrued but unpaid interest and fees up to the settlement date. These amounts are not reflected in the purchase price. If the buyer receives such amounts after the settlement date, the buyer shall pay them to the seller. Nonrecurring fees (e.g., amendment fees, consent fees, and waiver fees) are treated differently. If the seller receives any nonrecurring fees from and after the trade date, they are for the benefit of the buyer and are subtracted from the purchase price. For

EXHIBIT 8.38

Term Loan Trade within T + 7 with Nonrecurring Fee Allocation.

Term loan purchase:	$5,000,000 × 98.00	= $4,900,000
Amendment fee credit:	$5,000,000 × 50 bps	= ($25,000)
Net term loan purchase price:		$4,875,000

instance, in the above exhibit, if the borrower paid an amendment fee of 50 basis points after the trade date, the buyer would be entitled to a credit of $25,000, as shown in Exhibit 8.38.

Delayed Settlement Compensation Calculations for Par Loans

Par trades are expected to close on or before seven business days after the trade date. A business day is any day that is not a Saturday, a Sunday, or some other day on which the Federal Reserve Bank of New York *or* the New York Stock Exchange is closed. If a par trade closes after T + 7, it is considered a "delayed settlement." In order to compensate for the delay, the seller pays the buyer a delayed compensation interest credit and the buyer pays the seller the cost of carry.

For example, using our sample trade, if you settle on April 12, delayed compensation will be due to the buyer. If the borrower has two outstanding interest contracts, each with an all-in rate (base contract + margin) of 2%, you would calculate the delayed compensation interest credit by multiplying the funded amount of the loan by the all-in rate and then dividing that amount by 360 to determine the per diem interest amount. This amount is then multiplied by the number of days from and including T + 7, up to but not including the settlement date (April 5 through, not including, April 12 = 7 days). The delayed compensation interest credit amount is then subtracted from the purchase price as a credit for the buyer, as shown in Exhibit 8.39.

If the borrower has two outstanding interest contracts with differing applicable margins, delayed compensation would be calculated on each contract separately. In the following table, we assume

EXHIBIT 8.39

Term Loan (TL) Trade with Delayed Compensation.

Term loan purchase price:	$5,000,000 × 98.00%	= $4,900,000.00
Delayed compensation for contracts:	$5,000,000 × 2.00% × 7/360	= ($1,944.44)
Cost of carry:	$4,900,000 × 2.92% × 7/360	= $2,782.11
Total delayed settlement purchase price:		$4,900,837.67

EXHIBIT 8.40

TL with Multiple Interest Contracts and Delayed Compensation.

Term loan purchase price:	$5,000,000 × 98.00%	= $4,900,000.00
Delayed compensation for contract 1:	$2,000,000 × 2.50% × 7/360	= ($972.22)
Delayed compensation for contract 2:	$3,000,000 × 2.00% × 7/360	= ($1,166.66)
Cost of carry:	$4,900,000 × 2.92% × 7/360	= $2,782.11
Total delayed settlement purchase price:		$4,900,643.23

that one contract is for $2,000,000 with an all-in rate of 2.50% and the other is for $3,000,000 with an all-in rate of 2% and calculate the purchase price, as shown in Exhibit 8.40.

ASSIGNMENT FEES

Although not discussed in detail above, assignment fees have traditionally been an added cost of most loan trades. Assignment fees reimburse the agent for its administrative efforts and are due whether a loan is traded on par documents or distressed documents. These fees are usually in the area of $3,500. Under the most common practice, the seller remits the entire assignment fee to the agent and is reimbursed for half of the fee by the buyer as an increase in the purchase price. Recently, in an effort to enhance liquidity, many agent banks have discontinued charging assignment fees, which have been a drag on loan returns.

CONCLUSION

The loan trading business can be very lucrative. Like any lucrative business, it is fraught with risk. However, unlike the situation in the markets for most other tradable instruments, the process for settling loans, particularly in the market for distressed loans, can itself present risks. The analytics, trading, and settlement all work hand-in-hand in loan trading. These risks can largely be mitigated if care is taken prior to trading and in the settlement process.

CHAPTER 9

Analytics and Performance

Portfolio Engineering: Applying Quantitative Tools for Efficient CLO Investment Management

Andrew Hosford
Vice President, Project Manager
U.S. Bank

Sean Kelley
Senior Vice President, Head of CLO Data Analytics and Research
U.S. Bank

Lessons from More than a Trillion Dollars in Defaults

David Keisman
Senior Vice President, Corporate Finance
Corporate Defaults and Recoveries–U.S.
Moody's Investors Service

Portfolio Engineering: Applying Quantitative Tools for Efficient CLO Investment Management

Andrew Hosford

Sean Kelley
U.S. Bank

Leveraged loan portfolio managers can outperform their peers by embracing quantitative techniques to help efficiently execute their investment strategies. Such an approach does not mean that managers abandon their fundamental credit research and market experiences in favor of statistical filters. Rather, a thoughtful quantitative framework includes both portfolio management inputs and strategy converted into numeric values by the investment team, as well as other portfolio constraints, such as compliance tests. A constrained optimization problem jointly considers manager assessments and asset attributes when evaluating how each loan advances the management objective compared with every other loan in the investment universe, while respecting management and compliance requirements.

Successful leveraged loan portfolio management depends upon robust credit research. Like most debt instruments purchased at par, leveraged loans have an asymmetric return distribution. The lender earns an income stream defined by the loan credit agreement but faces the possibility that the borrower stumbles when executing its business plan and cannot repay the full principal balance. Credit losses from leveraged loan defaults have averaged approximately 20% since the asset class became a syndicated liquid market in the mid-1990s.[1] This downside experience compares with a current average coupon of 4.65% for the par loan held to maturity.[2] Disproportionate

---

[1] "The average discounted recovery rate for all bank loans issued between 2004 and now [December 31, 2019] is 80%." Marina Lukatsky, "LossStats: As Credit Cycle Ends, Data Point to Lower Recoveries," S&P Leverage Commentary & Data Recovery Study 2020, p. 7.

[2] Marina Lukatsky et al, "LCD's Quarterly Leveraged Lending Review," S&P Global Market Intelligence, 3Q 2020, p. 51.

losses can feel like the old investment adage "picking up nickels in front of a steamroller" during the tough phase of the credit cycle when leveraged loan annual default rates can approach 10%.[3] Because these default peaks do not occur often, however, leveraged loan portfolio management mostly involves preparing for these bad times and picking up as many nickels as possible until the cycle turns.

In its most basic form, a leveraged loan portfolio manager evaluates which companies will most likely repay their obligations in full along with the periodic coupon (that stream of nickels). A small community bank might approach this problem in binary terms. The loan officer posts lending rates on a board in the bank lobby and evaluates each loan application on whether the borrowing entity meets certain criteria. Either the bank makes a loan or not, and loans that the bank does extend do not have price differentiation. The leveraged loan portfolio manager, in contrast, must consider many more strategy dimensions. Adding a loan to the portfolio depends upon relative creditworthiness and pricing. Some companies may not deserve a loan for a stream of nickels, but may look attractive, to extend the metaphor, if the coupon resembles a stream of quarters. Unlike the community banker who serves an individual market, the leveraged loan portfolio manager can construct the portfolio across industries and geographies. Finally, the leveraged loan portfolio manager can look beyond primary loan underwriting for opportunities in the secondary market. Loans that the portfolio manager declined in the primary market for poor relative value (a coupon of nickels when the credit profile suggested quarters) may have a place in the portfolio at a lower price.

A leveraged loan portfolio manager today can make these broad investment choices through many different mandates and structures. Banks and insurance companies have purchased leveraged loans since the early syndications of the mid-1980s. The first prime funds for individual investors were launched in the late 1980s. For decades, leveraged loans have been managed in separate accounts and as allocations in high-yield and hedge funds. By far the most dominant leveraged loan investment vehicle today,

---

[3] Issuers in default or bankruptcy as a percentage of the S&P/LSTA Leveraged Loan Index peaked during the 2001–2003 credit cycle at 8.9% (2001) and during the 2008–2009 credit cycle at 9.6% (2009). *Ibid.*, p. 173.

however, is the cash flow collateralized loan obligation (CLO). Early CLOs were balance sheet transactions that provided banks with capital relief for the leveraged portion of their loan portfolio. Soon, third-party sponsors began proactively purchasing loan collateral pools so that investment banks could structure arbitrage CLOs that provide investors with leveraged loan exposure at their desired tranche risk profile. As arbitrage CLO structures have evolved since the early 1990s, the market has grown from an esoteric asset class to among the largest ABS categories with $116 billion annual issuance and commanding more than 60% of the leveraged loan funding base.[4,5]

Beyond their outsized importance to the leveraged loan market, the CLO life cycle and management style lends itself particularly well to quantitative techniques. CLO sponsors raise capital by purchasing a collateral pool and then issuing a full debt stack against it. The notes typically receive ratings from AAA to BB based upon their relative priority and attachment points. Coverage tests value the collateral pool relative to the note balances with collateral haircuts following loan defaults, excess Caa/CCC rated loans and trading losses. Violations of coverage tests result in deleveraging from the highest priority notes down, a dynamic that supports the rating differentiation. Deal note rating stability also depends upon the loan portfolio metrics. A series of collateral quality tests measure relative portfolio health, with most tests requiring a maintain-or-improve standard upon violation, acknowledging that some loan attributes, such as ratings, can change after purchase. Finally, several concentration limitation tests further define the collateral pool and capture key investor risk preferences.[6]

---

[4] Charlie Dinning, "US CLO League Tables," CreditFlux, January 8, 2020, at https://www.creditflux.com/CLOs/2020-01-08/US-CLO-league-tables-CSAM-makes-it-three-in-a-row-as-Citi-completes-a-clean-sweep.

[5] Lukatsky et al., pp. 108, 113. During the last 12 months ending September 30, 2020, institutional investors comprised 85% of the leveraged loan market and CLOs had a 72% share among those institutional investors.

[6] We focus on the Moody's CLO rating methodology that disaggregates the collateral pool attributes. For the most recent methodology, see Jun Kim and Ramon O. Torres, "Moody's Global Approach to Rating Collateralized Loan Obligations," *Moody's Investor Service*, August 14, 2020. Standard & Poor's (S&P) CLO rating methodology has some nuanced differences but leads to similar ratings conclusions. S&P, however, combines many loan attributes in a single loss model, thereby eliminating the discrete constraints that make the Moody's approach so interesting for this discussion.

The extensive CLO tests undoubtedly constrain the feasible region in which a portfolio manager can invest. Curiously, the CLO compliance normative differs greatly from other investment mandates. An Investment Company Act of 1940 (40-Act) mutual fund manager, for example, considers compliance rules quite differently. Take a large cap equity fund manager with a 10% emerging market domicile limit. If that manager favored emerging market companies and the portfolio concentration approached 10%, the manager's compliance officer would call throughout the day for status updates about how investment activity affects that limit. CLO constituents, in contrast, expect compliance violations throughout the life cycle of each deal. The maintain-or-improve standard for many failing tests makes the consequence less severe. Moreover, because investors and the rating agencies model rating deterioration and credit losses, they take portfolio developments in stride. In contrast, a mutual fund compliance failure can result in board reporting; restitution; and, if it is a serious enough breach, notification to the Securities and Exchange Commission (SEC). A CLO test failure appears on the monthly trustee report, but its consequence depends on the test importance and remedy. It also depends on relative test performance compared with other CLOs, particularly those issued around the same time.[7]

CLO portfolio managers explicitly incorporate compliance tests in their investment decisions. Consider the objective of the CLO mandate. The portfolio manager strives to achieve the highest possible return to the CLO equity tranche by constructing a collateral pool with the greatest possible net cash flow. For each loan, the spread over a base rate, the London Interbank Offered Rate (LIBOR),[8] approximates its cash flow contribution so, in aggregate, the portfolio weighted average spread over cost of funding represents equity return potential. We can express the CLO mandate then as an objective function: maximize the portfolio weighted average spread. Without compliance tests or any risk program, the maximum spread portfolio would include many aggressive loans

---

[7] CLO performance generally involves comparison to similar deals (broadly syndicated vs. middle market) issued during the same period. Although deals are most often grouped by vintage year, quarterly cohorts arguably provide a better balance between meaningful membership and similar issuance environment.

[8] At the time of writing, LIBOR was the most common base rate applied to leveraged loans. This chapter will reference LIBOR in place of a generic base rate.

from the second lien and Caa/CCC-rated cohorts. We can think about compliance tests and manager prudence as constraints on the objective function. Given that portfolio managers often take compliance tests to their limits when executing the CLO mandate, the test boundaries together define an investment feasible region.

A simple everyday trading example illustrates how a CLO portfolio manager considers her investment options: the CLO currently fails its Weighted Average Rating Factor Test (WARF) as well as its junior overcollateralization test. As such, investments must satisfy a maintain-or-improve standard on both ratings and trade price. The portfolio manager has the trader execute a $1 million sale of a B2-rated loan at a price of 95 and spread of LIBOR + 350. She now must identify replacement collateral that best advances her objective function, maximizing the Weighted Average Spread (WAS). During the morning trading meeting, her investment team identified two assets trading at attractive levels. First, the Web.com second lien term loan (WEB) has an offer price of 87.5, a rating of B3, and a spread of LIBOR + 775. Second, the Jaguar Holdings II term loan (PPD) has an offer price of 99.625, a rating of Ba3, and a spread of LIBOR + 250. The portfolio manager wants to calculate what par balances of each loan she can purchase with the sale proceeds while achieving the ratings and price values of the sold asset and maximizing the blended spread over LIBOR.

We can solve the problem intuitively using high school algebra and graph paper. As displayed in Exhibit 9.1, we set the two axes to the par purchase amount. With no other considerations, the portfolio manager could purchase up to $0.950 million/0.875 = $1.086 million of WEB or $0.950 million/0.99625 = $0.954 million of PPD; these points are the intercepts of the x- and y-axes, respectively. Along this par amount line are feasibility functions for WAS, WARF, and weighted average price (WAP). The functions follow the par amount line before dropping in a straight line to the axis that corresponds to the constraint of that test. For example, we know that 0.875 * WEB + 0.99625 * PPD ≤ 0.95. We must purchase a certain amount of the lower-priced WEB to satisfy the price constraint, and if we do not purchase WEB, we purchase PPD. Replacing PPD with (1 − WEB), we can calculate the minimum par amount of WEB as $0.381 million, where the WAP constraint line drops to the WEB par value on the x-axis. Following this logic for the other constraints, we identify the feasible region for the solution between the constraint functions and can

EXHIBIT 9.1

Simple Portfolio Optimization Problem.

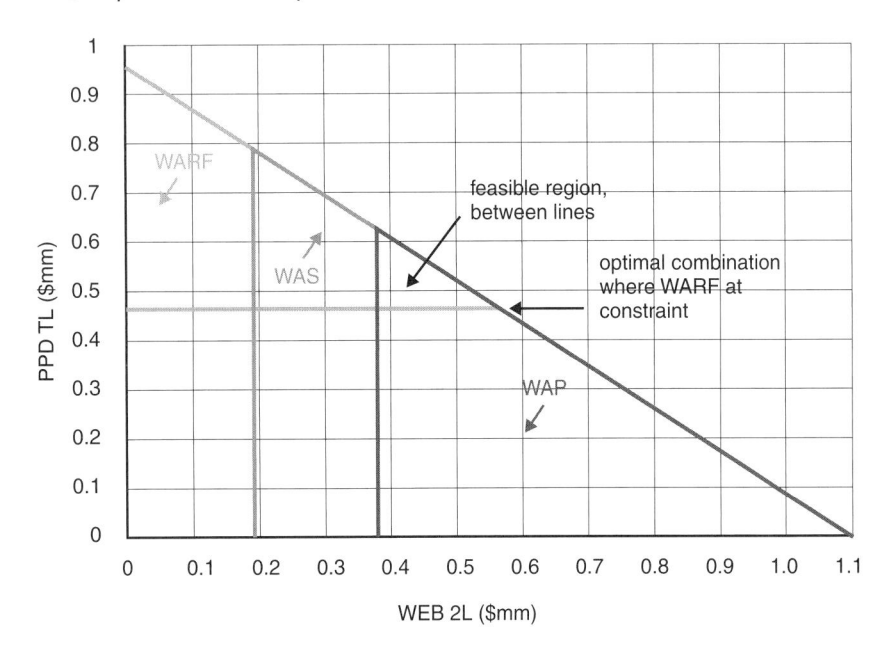

[Graph: X-axis "WEB 2L ($mm)" from 0 to 1.1; Y-axis "PPD TL ($mm)" from 0 to 1. Lines labeled WARF, WAS, WAP. Annotations: "feasible region, between lines", "optimal combination where WARF at constraint".]

quickly find the optimal solution at the outer boundary of the WARF constraint.

This solution utilizes the basic concepts from a field of mathematics and computer science called mathematical programming, with the setup classified as a constrained optimization problem. During and after World War II, the U.S. military funded research on planning processes for troop deployments and supply lines. The need to optimize the deployment of limited (constrained) resources led to major mathematical advances, notably by George Dantzig, Richard Bellman, and others at the RAND Corporation during the late 1940s.[9] When combined with early computers, mathematical programming suddenly enabled scientists to study problems previously considered unsolvable. The previous example shows a graphical solution to a constrained optimization problem where the objective is to maximize WAS by choosing different values for

---

[9] For more background on early developments in linear programming, see George B. Dantzig, "Linear Programming," *Operations Research*, 50, no. 1 (January–February 2002): 42–47, and Richard Bellman, "Eye of the Hurricane" (Singapore: World Scientific Press, 1984).

our portfolio weights of WEB 2L and PPD TL. The possible values for these two variables are constrained by linear functions that are the weighted average of some other attribute, such as WARF. Because the objective and constraint functions are all linear, this example falls into the subset of constrained optimization known as linear programming.

The combined effects of exponential growth in computing power and advancements in algorithms for solving linear equations simultaneously means that we can now solve linear problems with tens of thousands of variables in seconds, rather than hours or days. The techniques have broad application across many operational and economic problems but all with consistent form: a linear objective function that describes the variable to maximize or minimize within a linear constraint set that bounds the feasible solution region. Further advancements in solving mixed integer problems allow us to extend the linear framework to include discontinuous variables, while sacrificing a small amount of solution speed. This important advancement allows the practitioner to include "decision" variables in otherwise continuous problems.

Graphical interpretation of linear programs becomes abstract when the number of variables increases beyond two or three. Therefore, we will look at an example that introduces many of the mathematical principals required to develop a performant linear program, where nonlinearities exist. The linear programming approach for CLO portfolio management resembles a classic blending problem.[10] Because the authors reside in Chicago, we can think about the setup through the lens of hot dog production. Although most people "don't want to know how the sausage is made," reviewing constituent selection in relatively simple context can provide insight into the CLO portfolio construction process.

For this example, we assume that the manufacturer is mandated to produce hot dogs with at least 31% protein by weight, at least 51% water by weight, and cost no more than $2.36 per pound for the blend. The manufacturer identifies demand for a "low fat"

---

[10] The authors acknowledge that performant algorithms exist to quickly solve convex optimization problems, of which linear programs are a subset. For brevity, the authors focus on the linear subset of these problems, but the framework can be extended to the full set of convex problems. For a full explanation of convex programming and deeper dive into linear programming, please reference the following text: Vandenberghe Boyd, *Convex Optimization* (Cambridge, United Kingdom: Cambridge University Press, 2004).

product and wishes to minimize the fat content of the hot dog. Note the close relationship between the objective function and various constraints. Perhaps the manufacturer later realizes that low-fat hot dogs are not a popular product and wishes to simply reduce the cost of the blend. In that case, minimizing cost can be substituted for the objective function, and fat content will be specified as another constraint (e.g., fat content cannot exceed 20%).

This problem is completely linear as the objective function and constraints are all linear combinations of the percent by weight of each constituent in the blend. Such problems can readily become nonlinear, however, when we introduce common variations of the original conditions. To extend this example, let us assume that if the percent by weight of pork in our hot dog is greater than or equal to 15%, our order size will be large enough that our pork supplier will discount the entire order by 5 cents per pound. While the logic is relatively simple, the problem violates linearity since the price attribute is no longer constant.

Thankfully, we can deploy a technique to reform this seemingly nonlinear problem into what is known as a Mixed Integer Linear Program (MILP). It should be noted that MILP is less efficient than pure linear programs but still solves much faster than nonlinear programs. Unfortunately, many nonlinear complications cannot be reformed to provide linearity nor mixed integer linearity. In these cases, we must balance accuracy and calculation speed.

To resolve this complication, we can consider pork as two separate inputs, distinguished by price. We can then use a decision variable ρ, that can take the value of 0 or 1, to control which pork product to include in our blend. This variable ρ is controlled by the computer during the optimization process and will also be constrained so that it behaves according to our pricing relationship. The following equations define attributes of the optimized blend:

$$Total\_Weight = W_c + W_{p_1} + W_{p_2} + W_b \qquad (Eq\ 9.1)$$

$$Total\_Protein = P_c * W_c + P_p * (W_{p_1} + W_{p_2}) + P_b * W_b \qquad (Eq\ 9.2)$$

$$Total\_Fat = F_c * W_c + F_p * (W_{p_1} + W_{p_2}) + F_b * W_b \qquad (Eq\ 9.3)$$

$$Total\_Water = Wa_c * W_c + Wa_p * (W_{p_1} + W_{p_2}) + Wa_b * W_b \qquad (Eq\ 9.4)$$

$$Total\_Cost = C_c * W_c + C_{p_1} * W_{p_1} + C_{p_2} * W_{p_2} + C_b * W_b \qquad (Eq\ 9.5)$$

Where the *Total_Weight* of our final product is the sum of the individual weights of each constituent ingredient. W_c and W_b represent the final blended weights of chicken and pork, respectively. W_{p_1} and W_{p_2} represent the final blended weights of pork with and without the volume discount, respectively. *Total_Protein*, *Total_Fat*, and *Total_Water* are linear combinations of the individual protein (P_c, P_p, P_b), fat (F_c, F_p, F_b), and water (Wa_c, Wa_p, Wa_b) content of each constituent meat product.

Next, we constrain these equations to enforce the manufacturer's mandate:

$Total\_Weight = 1$ (Eq 9.6)

$Total\_Protein \geq 0.31$ (Eq 9.7)

$Total\_Water \geq 0.51$ (Eq 9.8)

$Total\_Cost \leq 2.36$ (Eq 9.9)

We need to add a few more constraints to ensure positive-value weights. Unlike shorting a stock, for example, we cannot have negative amounts of chicken, pork, or beef:

$W_c \geq 0$ (Eq 9.10)

$W_{p_1} \geq 0$ (Eq 9.11)

$W_{p_2} \geq 0$ (Eq 9.12)

$W_b \geq 0$ (Eq 9.13)

Next, we add constraints that control how our decision variable ρ will interact with our other pork variables, W_{p_1} and W_{p_2}:

$W_{p_1} \leq (0.15 - \epsilon) * \rho$ (Eq 9.14)

$W_{p_2} \geq 0.15 * (1 - \rho)$ (Eq 9.15)

$W_{p_2} - (1 - \rho) * 999 \leq 0$ (Eq 9.16)

Equation 9.14 states that the percent by weight of pork, corresponding to the first price condition, C_{p_1}, must always be less than 15% if $\rho = 1$; however, if $\rho = 0$ then W_{p_1} must equal 0. ϵ is a small tolerance value (e.g., 0.000000000001) that is required because strict inequalities are incompatible with linear programming constraints.

Equation 9.15 states that the percent by weight of pork, corresponding to the second price condition, C_{p_2}, must always be greater than or equal to 15% if $\rho = 0$; since this equation does not constrain W_{p_2} if $\rho = 1$, we require Equation 9.16 to complete the constraints.

Equation 9.16 states that the percent by weight of pork, corresponding to the second price condition, C_{p_2}, must always be equal to 0 if $\rho = 1$, but is not constrained if $\rho = 0$. We know W_{p_2} is bound between 0 to 1, inclusive, by Equation 9.6, Equation 9.11, and Equation 9.12.

Finally, we define our objective. In this case, we wish to minimize fat content:

Objective = Minimize(Total_Fat) (Eq 9.17)

This system of equations fully constrains the optimization problem and accounts for the nonlinear step function inherent in the tiered pricing complication. Should the practitioner wish to explore this example further, we have provided additional guidance in the Appendix of this chapter including the Python code to replicate and solve the "hot dog" example.

Similar to the hot dog blending problem, the portfolio manager blends asset attributes such as credit rating, price, and industry concentration with the objective of producing the highest WAS. Whatever the objective function, the setup resembles hot dog production, but with considerably more factors to evaluate simultaneously.

Through experience, many CLO portfolio managers can weigh choices efficiently on several dimensions. Consider an example expanded from the single sale and two purchases that we originally considered. Our slightly larger portfolio has two dozen assets with various coupon, ratings, prices, and other attributes. We assign equal initial weights to eight assets and define three constraints: maximum WARF, minimum weighted average recovery rating (WARR), and maximum second lien. As before, we want to maximize the portfolio WAS. Applying linear programming on a laptop computer, we get an initial solution in seconds, summarized in Exhibit 9.2. The WAS jump from 297 to 421 pleases the portfolio manager, but she decides not to push the WARF to the limit, so she updates that test threshold to a more conservative credit level 50 points higher. She reruns the optimization and a few seconds later reviews the results in the next column that shows a

EXHIBIT 9.2

Expanded Portfolio Optimization Problem.

Test	Threshold	Current Results	2700 Optimized Results	2650 Optimized Results	2600 Optimized Results
WAS	MAX	2.97	4.21	4.20	4.18
WARF	2700.00	2434.5	2700.00	2650.00	2600.00
WARR	48.25%	45.00%	49.56%	49.47%	49.32%
2nd Lien %	5.00%	12.50%	5.00%	5.00%	5.00%

Issuer	Facility	Current Position	2700 Optimized Position	2650 Optimized Position	2600 Optimized Position	Spread	WARF	S&P Recovery Rating	Bid	Offer	2nd Lien
Delta Air Lines, Inc.	Term Loan B	0.0%	12.5%	12.5%	12.5%	4.75	610	50%	99.375	100.000	N
Western Digital Corporation	Term Loan B-4	0.0%	0.0%	0.0%	0.0%	1.75	610	50%	98.000	99.500	N
Citadel Securities LP	Term Loan	0.0%	0.0%	0.0%	0.0%	2.75	940	45%	98.000	99.000	N
Dell International LLC	Term Loan B-1	0.0%	0.0%	0.0%	0.0%	2.00	940	50%	98.125	98.750	N
Reynolds Consumer Products LLC	Term Loan	12.5%	0.0%	0.0%	0.0%	1.75	940	45%	97.625	98.000	N
Stars Group Holdings B.V.	Term Loan	0.0%	0.0%	0.0%	0.0%	3.50	1350	50%	99.250	100.500	N
Brookfield Property REIT Inc.	Term Loan B	0.0%	0.0%	0.3%	1.8%	2.50	1350	40%	84.000	86.000	N
Gardner Denver, Inc.	Term Loan B	12.5%	0.0%	0.0%	0.0%	1.75	1350	45%	96.000	97.000	N
Neilsen Finance LLC	Term Loan B5	0.0%	12.5%	12.5%	12.5%	3.75	1766	60%	99.375	100.125	N
Arch Coal, Inc.	Term Loan B	0.0%	11.2%	12.5%	12.5%	2.75	1766	45%	84.500	87.500	N
Sabre GLBL, Inc.	Term Loan B	12.5%	0.0%	0.0%	0.0%	2.00	1766	45%	93.500	95.125	N
Asurion, LLC	Second Lien TL B-2	12.5%	12.5%	0.0%	0.0%	6.50	2220	15%	99.750	100.625	Y
Aria Energy Operating LLC	Initial Term Loan	0.0%	0.0%	12.5%	12.5%	4.50	2220	45%	93.000	96.000	N
Foundation Building Materials Holdings	Term Loan B	12.5%	0.0%	0.0%	0.0%	3.00	2220	40%	97.250	98.250	N
NeuStar, Inc.	Second Lien TL B	0.0%	5.0%	5.0%	5.0%	8.00	2220	15%	75.500	81.500	Y
Aldevron, LLC	Term Loan B	12.5%	0.0%	0.0%	0.0%	4.25	2720	50%	99.438	100.063	N
American Airlines, Inc.	Term Loan B	0.0%	12.5%	12.5%	12.5%	2.00	2720	60%	81.500	85.000	Y
Web.Com Group, Inc.	Second Lien TL	0.0%	0.0%	0.0%	0.0%	7.75	3490	15%	84.000	87.500	Y
Advantage Sales & Marketing Inc.	Second Lien TL	0.0%	0.0%	0.0%	0.0%	6.50	3490	15%	81.500	85.500	Y
AHP Health Partners, Inc.	Term Loan	12.5%	12.5%	12.5%	12.5%	4.50	3490	60%	98.625	99.375	N
Radiology Partners, Inc.	Term Loan	0.0%	9.4%	8.7%	8.1%	4.25	4770	50%	93.875	94.875	N
Learfield Communications LLC	Initial Term Loan	0.0%	11.9%	11.0%	10.1%	3.25	4770	15%	76.000	81.000	Y
Coty Inc.	Term Loan B	12.5%	0.0%	0.0%	0.0%	2.25	4770	50%	90.000	92.500	N
Gateway Casinos Entertainment Inc.	Term Loan B	0.0%	0.0%	0.0%	0.0%	3.00	6500	60%	82.000	83.000	N

489

WAS penalty of only 1 basis point. Encouraged, she runs the optimization yet again with a further improved WARF. Given a pencil and paper, a calculator or Excel, and, importantly, time, some portfolio managers could solve this problem themselves. Few would however, beat the computer at clock speed, nor would they have the patience to quickly explore other more lucrative portfolio combinations.

This example approaches the boundary of how much information a CLO portfolio manager can jointly evaluate. Consider that a typical broadly syndicated loan CLO holds nearly 300 issuers, and assume that any given manager monitors several hundred additional companies.[11] Each loan in this investment universe has variables that map to more than 25 constraints. On a problem of this scale, the human brain cannot compete with a computer on the raw calculation requirements.

Typical modern general-purpose desktop CPUs can process upward of 200 billion floating-point operations per second (FLOPS), with robust error correction.[12] This means that computers are excellent calculators, but unlocking this brute force requires skilled programming to define a problem in such a manner that a desired solution can be found by executing a set of deterministic instructions. Advances in artificial neural networks that mimic the activation of neurons in a brain have given classical computers the ability to perform rudimentary pattern recognition. However, these skills are still considered narrow in scope, and a discussion of advancements in general-purpose artificial intelligence (such as IBM's Watson, Alphabet's DeepMind, Tesla's Autopilot) is beyond the scope of this chapter. Furthermore, the nondeterministic nature of machine learning means that different training data, model construction, and training epochs will produce different outcomes when presented with novel inputs. In our case, we are interested in finding a stable global solution

---

[11] Data from U.S. Bank, December 29, 2020. Data comprised broadly syndicated loan CLOs in their reinvestment period where U.S. Bank serves as the trustee. In this data set, the average CLO holds 285 issuers. As a proxy for each collateral manager coverage universe, we consider the union of issuers across CLOs for each collateral manager. By this measure, the average collateral manager invests in 332 issuers with a wide range between 123 and 810 issuers.

[12] High Performance Computing, *High Performance Computing Explained* [White paper], May 2019, Advanced Micro Devices, Inc., available at https://www.amd.com/system/files/documents/hpc-explained.pdf.

given a rigid set of rules and parameters. Therefore, linear programming is better suited to this task.

In contrast, the human brain is exceptionally well evolved to learn and recognize patterns by activating and reinforcing the connection between tens of billions of neurons. However, we struggle with the brute force calculations required to perform the floating-point arithmetic necessary to solve complex optimization problems. Humans are simply not wired to efficiently encode and process this type of data. Rather than compete with the computer on basic calculations, the portfolio manager should play to the strength of her brain by reflecting, connecting events, and formulating investment strategy. She then can encode this information in a manner digestible by the computer to perform the mathematical optimization required to solve her asset allocation problem.

Critics of quantitative investment tools observe that the output often does not make sense; nobody would ever follow the unrealistic trades and put on the risky portfolio positions suggested by a poorly designed tool. The computer will only calculate a solution to the problem as we define it. If we have not designed the tool to account for manager style, the tool will produce results upon which the manager may not be able to act. In the 24-asset example, a portfolio manager might argue that the WAS improved from LIBOR + 297 to LIBOR + 421 by purchasing loans that are much more risky than their ratings suggest.

When calibrating the portfolio optimization constraints, we should constantly ask whether the model captures the investment strategy and, if not, what adjustments will make the output more relevant and actionable. This portfolio manager, then, should include an internal rating test that penalizes loans that are "downgrades waiting to happen" according to the internal credit research staff. With this additional constraint, the portfolio must satisfy both the official WARF test that Moody's dictates as well as the internal WARF constraint that reflects the portfolio manager's opinion.

So far, we have examined the construction of a constrained optimization problem using simple weighted average tests that translate easily into linear functions, thereby allowing us to use linear solvers. However, this is not the case for all CLO tests. Special attention must be paid when including nonlinear tests because the practitioner will be forced to make trade-offs between speed and accuracy. We will explore this process in depth through two related

CLO topics: issuer concentration (Diversity Score) and trade size (manager-dependent constraint).

The compliance tests that measure diversity in CLO collateral pools perform poorly in our portfolio optimization both in construct and function. The Moody's CLO rating criteria incorporates issuer concentration through absolute single-issuer limits as well as the Diversity Score, a value derived from several calculation steps and table references. The Diversity Score approximates the number of independent default paths in the portfolio under Moody's binomial expansion method.[13] The test has foundational importance but unfortunately gums up the portfolio optimization calculations given its nonlinear construct.

A linear function for our optimization purposes has four important properties:[14]

1. *Proportionality*: The contribution from each variable scales consistently. If we purchase $2 million of a loan rather than $1 million, that loan will have twice the impact on each constraint and the objective function.
2. *Additivity*: The impact from each constraint follows from summing the contributions to that constraint. In a CLO, the WARF represents the sum product of the rating factor and percentage weight of each position.
3. *Continuity*: Variables must be continuous and may be infinite or bounded.[15]
4. *Certainty*: Perhaps obvious, but we must know the impact of each parameter.

The Diversity Score violates proportionality, and therefore negatively affects our model's linearity. It does so because increasing the size of an asset's position does not necessarily increase the asset's marginal contribution to the Diversity Score at a constant rate.

A single nonlinear function can significantly increase calculation run times when optimizing a CLO against a typical investment

---

[13] Kim and Torres, *Moody's Investor Service*, 7, (see chap. 9, n. 6).
[14] Wayne Winston, *Operations Research: Applications and Algorithms, Fourth Edition* (Belmont, CA: Brooks/Cole–Thomson Learning, 2004), pp. 54–55.
[15] As previously mentioned, we extend the basic linear programming with discontinuous integer variables. This means our final program will be of the Mixed Integer Linear Program (MILP) type.

universe. As illustrated in Exhibit 9.3, we can revisit our original two-asset blend and convert one constraint to a nonlinear function on our graphical depiction of the problem.

Unlike the linear function that has one clear solution, the oscillating curve crosses the other constraint lines several times for multiple potential solutions. Mathematically, this constraint is said to be *nonconvex*, meaning that two or more local minima (maxima) exist. Without exploring all optimal points, you cannot be certain you have found a globally optimal point.

Some advanced optimization techniques exist that can quickly find approximate solutions to complex nonlinear (nonconvex) problems. Their basic principal is to explore many locations within the feasible solution set and find local minima (maxima) in those regions. The practitioner calibrates the exhaustiveness of the search. She can specify a certain number of search iterations or a tolerance that is some percentage (or absolute value) of a theoretical optimal solution for a given region, precalculated by the optimization engine. By whatever method the search is terminated, the best

EXHIBIT 9.3

Simple Portfolio Optimization Problem with Nonlinear Constraint.

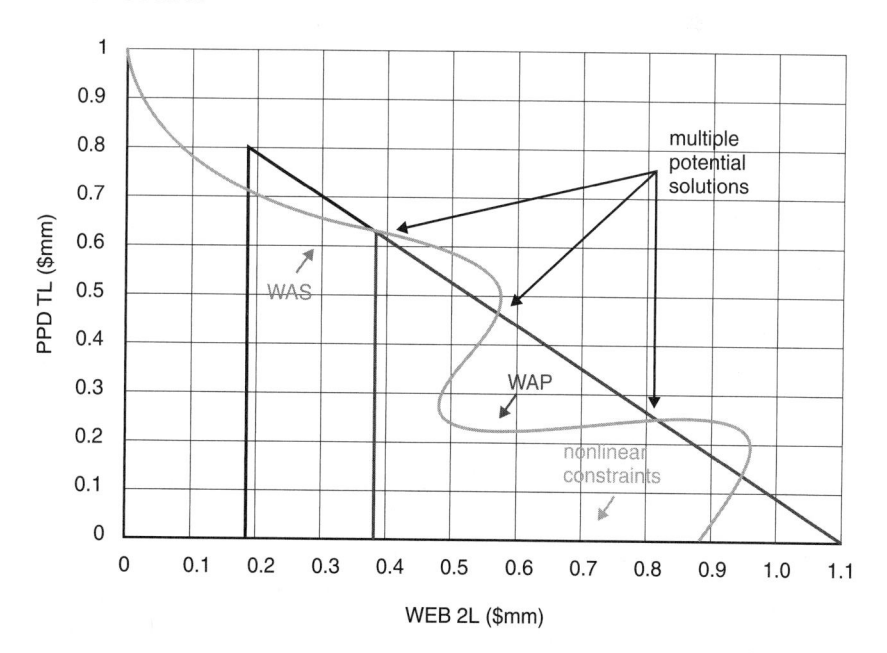

solution found so far is returned as the optimized solution, even if many areas of the solution set are never searched.

This means that the practitioner must accept a level of ambiguity in exchange for finite solve times. If the program is terminated prior to searching all possible convex regions of a problem, there is no guarantee that the solution to a complex nonlinear program will be globally optimal. As we increase the degrees of freedom, the solution surface increases exponentially and makes the calculation speed untenable. A great deal of research has been dedicated to solving these problems, but they all rely on a trade-off between precision and run time. Our solution to the Diversity Score nonlinearity, described below, also makes this trade-off, but we do so through dimensionality reduction.[16]

Realistically, most portfolio managers are unwilling to wait eons, or even minutes, for a globally optimal solution. In fact, investment decisions require a tool that can be run iteratively so the practitioner can evaluate the output, make adjustments, and rerun until a satisfactory solution is found. Because we have intuition into the structure of the nonlinear Diversity Score constraint, we can replace it with a small number of linear proxy constraints that are adjusted in a hierarchical manner, outside our main MILP. We then provide the user with a set of "proxy variables" that control the construction of the proxy constraint.

We confirm that this proxy constraint properly estimates the Diversity Score by calculating the actual Diversity Score of the optimized portfolio and then compare that value to the actual Diversity Score threshold. If the proxy constraint value does not lead to an optimized portfolio with a passing Diversity Score value, we adjust the proxy variables and rerun the optimization tool; we call this process *convergence*. This process can be thought of as a black box optimization (the main mixed-integer optimization) within a nonlinear optimizer. However, because we have reduced the number of dimensions the nonlinear optimizer can control from several hundred asset weights to a few proxy variables controlling a proxy constraint, the nonlinear optimizer has a much smaller solution surface in which it needs to explore, and the user has control over how that exploration occurs, which is explained in the next section. This strategy has a simple thesis: running a linear model through

---

[16] The act of reducing the nonlinear variables from several hundred to a few variables that can be iterated over in predetermined step sizes.

several cycles at 10 to 20 seconds per cycle will generally have a much faster cumulative calculation time than the nonlinear formulation. It allows us to find an acceptable answer relatively quickly and gives the user the ability to control how the nonlinear optimization searches the solution surface.

For the proxy constraint to effectively replace the original nonlinear constraint, the proxy constraint must replicate how the original constraint bounds the investment universe or, in general linear programming terms, how the original constraint defines the feasible region. For our purposes, we must choose the proxy constraint thoughtfully, minding both mathematical and portfolio management context. For a good starting point, we examine what variables contribute to the Diversity Score. As previously noted, the Diversity Score involves several calculation steps and table references that effectively penalize heterogenous position and industry size. Conversely, the highest Diversity Score for a given number of issuers occurs when the portfolio has identical weights for every issuer and industry.

Because portfolio managers understand this relationship, we can assume that they will consider it when constructing their portfolios and will generally migrate toward equal issuer and industry weights when possible. We take a leap of faith and assume equal issuer and industry weights. These assumptions simplify the Diversity Score to a piecewise linear function of the number of issuers in the portfolio, depicted in Exhibit 9.4.

This analysis suggests that we replace the nonlinear Diversity Score with a proxy constraint based upon the number of issuers. The number of issuers constraint can take linear form given its proportionality. Importantly, we have also established a clear relationship between its value and the actual Diversity Score, so we can set the proxy constraint value strategically based upon the true Diversity Score threshold.

Testing of this proxy constraint reveals unintended consequence. Recall our trivial observation that the computer will only solve the problem as we present it, nothing more and nothing less. Given individual issuer limits of 2% to 2.5% and an objective function to maximize the WAS, we should not be surprised that the optimal portfolio includes many positions sized at the 2% to 2.5% limit. We have told the computer to identify the issuer weights that correspond to the maximum WAS portfolio and have only limited issuer weight size directly by the individual issuer limit and

EXHIBIT 9.4

Relationship between Diversity Score and Number of Issuers.

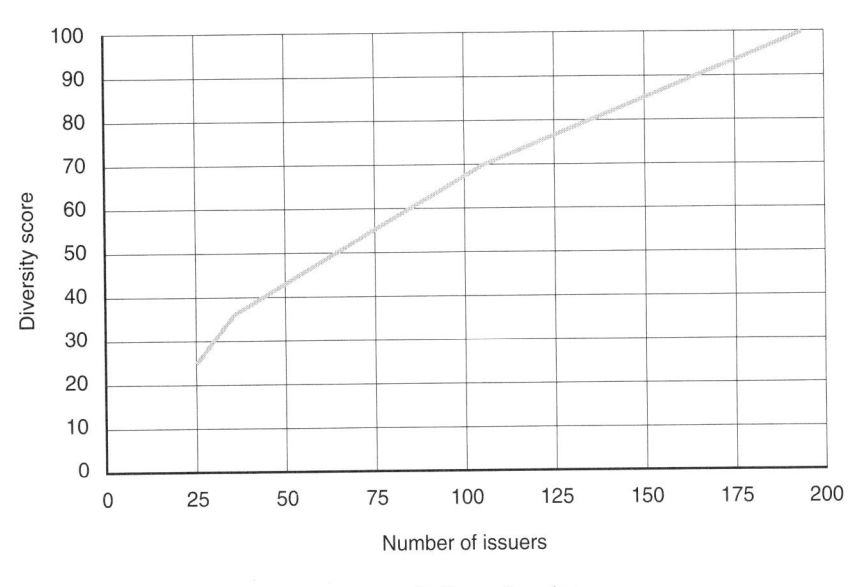

[Line chart: x-axis "Number of issuers" from 0 to 200; y-axis "Diversity score" from 0 to 100. Curve rises from ~25 at 25 issuers to ~100 at 200 issuers. Legend: Uniform allocation.]

indirectly by other constraints. Of course, the maximum WAS portfolio will contain the largest weight to the highest spread assets that we allow. Moreover, the "number of issuers" constraint alone does not materially change the optimized portfolio composition. We have told the computer nothing about minimum position size requirements, so it does not know that we prefer more homogenous issuer weights. Instead, the computer merely covers the number of issuers constraint through technicality. Maximum-sized issuers still dominate the optimal portfolio, and the computer suggests achieving the number of issuers requirement by purchasing de minimus positions in less accretive loans, illustrated in Exhibit 9.5. This strategy fails on both impracticality, because the portfolio manager will not ask the trader to execute hundreds of tiny trades, and perception, given how such trades clearly game the Diversity Score.

The optimization tool requires additional constraints to guide the computer away from de minimus positions. We could consider a minimum position size, but such an approach requires logic to allow for weights of zero. In addition, we may want to retain smaller positions currently in the portfolio where the sizing resulted from

EXHIBIT 9.5

Issuer Distribution with Minimum Number of Issuers Constraint.

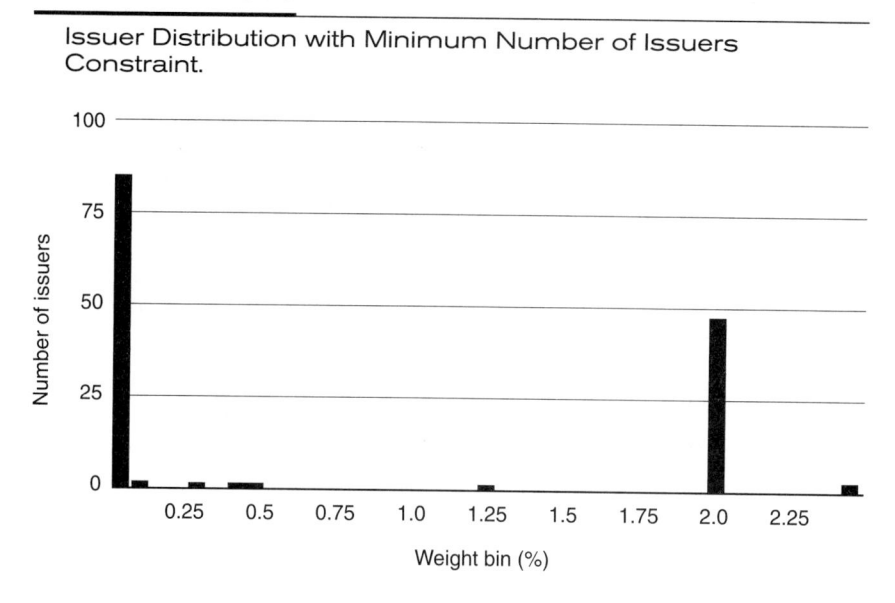

principal paydowns. Instead of an absolute lower size limit, we add a "trade size constraint." This approach has the added benefit that it makes the optimization output more actionable. The portfolio manager sets the minimum trade size constraint at the amount just above where she would hesitate to send the trading desk an order. She could think about the statement, "My trader does not get out of bed for trades less than X size" and set the constraint accordingly. Exhibit 9.6 displays issuer concentration results after adding a minimum trade size constraint set at 0.10% portfolio par.

A visual comparison of the first issuer distribution and the result after adding the trade size constraint does not suggest any discernable change. To better understand how the computer gets from the original portfolio to the optimized state, we sort the optimized portfolio by weight and review the trades associated with the smallest positions. The computer stubbornly favors the high-coupon positions and still covers the number of issuers constraint with de minimus positions. Rather than small purchases that we have disallowed, the computer generates stub positions after sales (tiny positions designed solely to satisfy the minimum number of issuers constraint). For example, the current portfolio includes a position for $2 million that does not advance the objective function. The computer identifies it as a sale candidate except a small portion.

EXHIBIT 9.6

Issuer Distribution after Adding Trade Size Constraint.

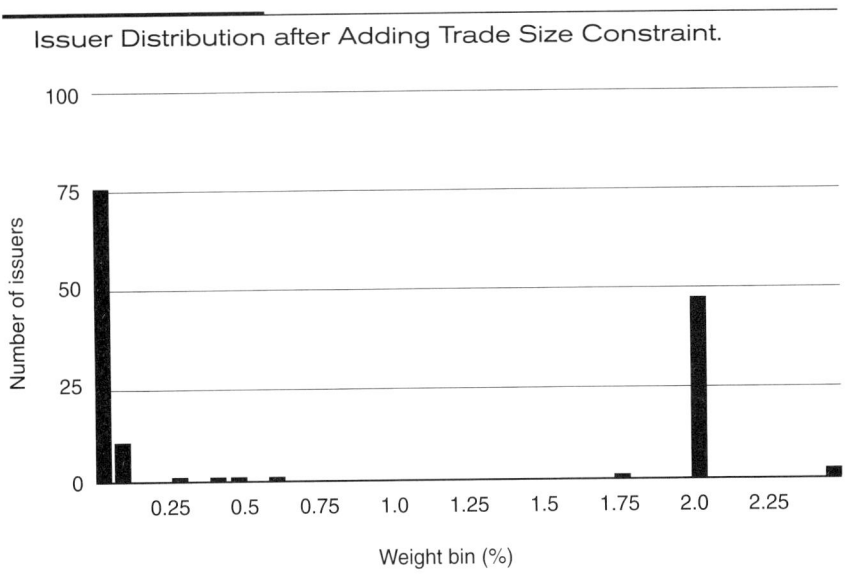

In practice, this stub could be as small as the smallest floating-point number the system can create. For a single-precision floating-point number, this would be approximately 1.175×10^{-38}. For simplicity, let us assume that $1,000 is the smallest number our system can assign to a single asset. If the sale of all but a stub is repeated many times, the computer will be able to satisfy the minimum number of issuers constraint, but the remaining position sizes will be completely unrealistic. Given the proportionality characteristic of linear programming, a small position has negligible impact on the objective function, so the optimized portfolio includes a $1,000 position after a $1,999,000 sale. We must add an additional constraint to prohibit such activity. Our "post-trade balance constraint" has nuanced logic but basically provides for (1) sales of entire positions and (2) sales of partial positions if the ending position exceeds the post-trade balance value. Exhibit 9.7 summarizes issuer concentrations after adding the post-trade balance constraint, set at 0.10% portfolio par.

Despite the improvements, many portfolio managers would still observe that they do not manage barbell portfolios suggested by this issuer histogram. Our current construct has a fundamental limitation in that the optimized portfolio will always involve maximum positions in the most accretive loans and the smallest

EXHIBIT 9.7

Issuer Distribution after Adding Minimum Post-Trade Balance Constraint.

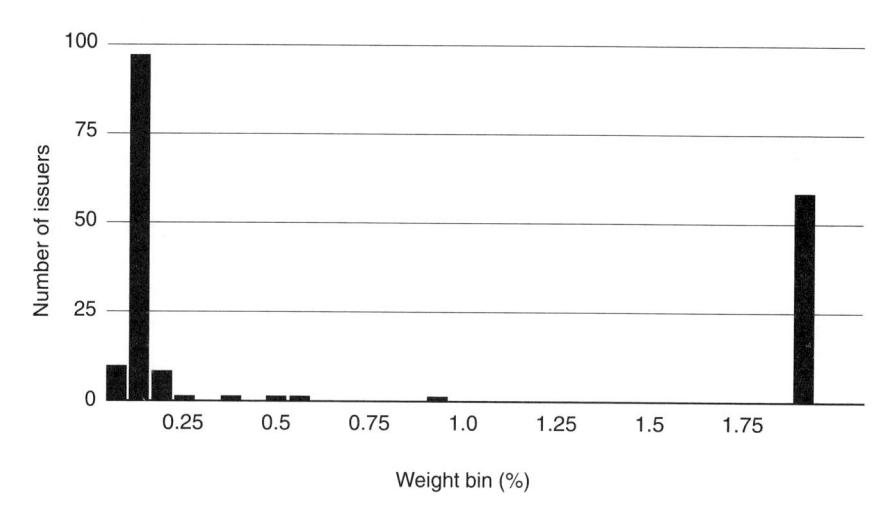

[Histogram: x-axis "Weight bin (%)" with values 0.25, 0.5, 0.75, 1.0, 1.25, 1.5, 1.75; y-axis "Number of issuers" from 0 to 100. Tall bar near 0.25 reaching ~95, smaller bar at ~0.5, and a bar near 1.75 reaching ~55.]

possible size in what amount to filler loans. The portfolio manager would state that she understands why the computer overweights the accretive loans but that she would never actually take on those positions. The next question should be, "What position sizes make sense to you?" and then we create a framework around that answer.

We introduce an issuer concentration constraint set based upon the beta distribution from statistics. The mathematical description of the beta distribution includes some attractive properties for our purpose. First, the beta distribution is defined on the interval [0, 1]. Unlike other commonly used distributions such as the normal distribution and Student's t-distribution, we can scale and confine our analysis to the true problem boundaries and not worry about long tails. We only concern ourselves with issuer concentrations between [0, 2.5%] and nothing outside those boundaries. Second, the beta distribution is parameterized by two variables, α and β, that have a distinct relationship at the mean μ:

$$\mu = \frac{\alpha}{\alpha + \beta}$$

Most portfolio managers can articulate a target issuer size for their CLO strategy. If we set this value as the mean and hold it constant, we can control the distribution shape by altering one variable β

in our setup. The larger the value, the tighter that the issuer distribution clusters around the mean.

We implement the beta distribution into the portfolio optimization tool through several steps. First, we define the interval as the range between the post-trade balance constraint and the maximum issuer size. Second, we scale the beta distribution to this range. Third, we have the user set the distribution granularity by selecting the number of histogram buckets into which we will convert the beta distribution values. Fourth, we calculate the target number of issuers as 100 divided by the target issuer size. Finally, we assign the target number of issuers to each histogram bucket based upon the beta distribution probability associated with each bucket. Each histogram bucket functions as an individual constraint in the optimization tool. For efficient calculation, we allow for some slack in the problem.

We prioritize strictness on the right-hand side buckets and allow any slack to accumulate in buckets to the left. For example, if the optimizer cannot fill the right-most bucket with enough issuers to meet its maximum number of issuers, the bucket to the left is allowed to overfill. This relaxation is cumulative from right to left. The reason that we permit this behavior is because lumpiness in the right-hand side buckets will necessarily lead to a lower Diversity Score. We know that issuer sizes greater than the mean do not continue to contribute to the Diversity Score as they get further from the mean. Therefore, a bucket may overfill so long as it has gained some slack from a bucket to its right. Compared with the original distribution the optimizer was trying to fill, the Diversity Score will not be negatively impacted by this structured relaxation of the distribution constraints.

Example: t_1 theoretically allows two issuers to have a concentration between 1.3% and 1.5%. However, the optimizer only wants to allocate one issuer to this bucket. t_2 allows four issuers to fill the 1.1% to 1.3% bucket, whereas the optimizer only fills this bucket with three issuers. Theoretically, only nine issuers should have concentrations between 0.9% and 1.1%, but we allow this bucket to be overfilled by the number of issuers not allocated to the buckets right of t_3. This means that the optimizer may fill this bucket with 11 issuers, rather than 9. This process continues from right to left. t_4 is again underfilled, so O_5 is allowed one additional issuer.

This construct satisfies our initial objective of replacing the nonlinear Diversity Score with a meaningful proxy constraint.

After using these features in practice, it quickly becomes apparent that two variables affect portfolio diversity rather directly: beta shape and average issuer size. Minimum post-trade balance and maximum issuer size have secondary importance, and other portfolio characteristics in the pre-optimization portfolio have third-order impact. Recall our strategy to calculate the Diversity Score post-optimization, compare the result with the Diversity Score threshold, and rerun the model, if necessary, after adjusting the proxy constraint threshold. For our setup (Exhibit 9.8), we allow the user to select convergence on one or both of beta shape and average issuer size. However, we would rather that the optimization results satisfy the actual Diversity Score constraint on the initial run with no

EXHIBIT 9.8

Distribution Fill Hierarchy.

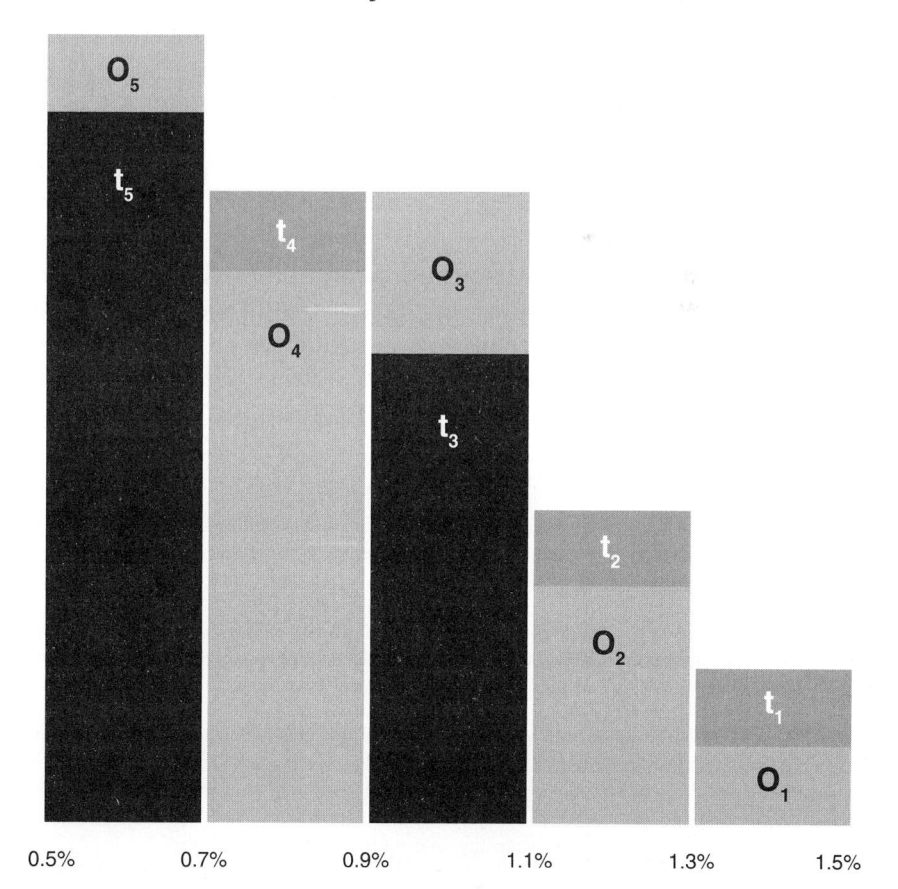

convergence required. To advance this possibility, we use machine learning to establish a relationship between certain constraints and portfolio characteristics to estimate the likely Diversity Score result and the number of potential convergence runs. With this functionality, the user can adjust the constraint settings to make the initial run more likely to satisfy the Diversity Score constraint.

Finally, we cannot overstate how much this diversity construct improves the optimization output for users when compared with canned CLO compliance constraints. The portfolio manager will disregard an optimized portfolio bounded by de minimus position sizes for the smallest positions and indenture maximum concentrations for the largest positions. She views those barbell weights as inconsistent with her strategy, and therefore not useful. The beta distribution functionality, in contrast, enables her to calibrate her diversity strategy in the optimization tool. She still allows the computer to overweight assets that best advance the objective function, but within a distribution that matches her risk tolerance. In addition, the trade size and post-trade balance constraints eliminate unrealistic trade size. Taken together, these optimization tool settings enable the portfolio manager to very efficiently source investment ideas that satisfy both the indenture requirements and the management strategy constraints.

Good CLO managers formulate investment decisions through strong credit research and deep understanding of the CLO structural features, with execution through a capable secondary trading desk. Credit research involves considerable skill and remains more elusive to computer modeling techniques than most other investment management disciplines.[17] Accordingly, we advocate that portfolio managers should structure portfolios around this

---

[17] Improved machine-learning modeling techniques still predict defaults with only approximately 66% success. In their analysis of modeling shortcomings, Moody's Analytics describes some of the "connecting the dots" capabilities that good credit analysts possess: "to improve default prediction accuracy and to expand the field of credit risk modeling in general, efforts should focus on the data dimension. Besides financial statement and loan payment behavioral data, additional information such as transactional data, social media data, geographical information, and other data can potentially add a tremendous amount of insight. We must gather more varied, nonconventional data to further refine and improve our approaches to assessing risk." Dinesh Bacham and Janet Zhao, *Machine Leaning: Challenges, Lessons, and Opportunities in Credit Risk Modeling*, July 2017, available at https://www.moodysanalytics.com/risk-perspectives-magazine/managing-disruption/spotlight/machine-learning-challenges-lessons-and-opportunities-in-credit-risk-modeling.

core competency. As long as the credit research team can express their views in a numeric scale, quantitative tools can systematically and exhaustively incorporate those opinions into actionable investment decisions.

The human brain is not wired to identify the optimal portfolio, whereas computers, in contrast, excel at the required brute force calculations. To effectively harness this capacity, we recognize that the CLO investment mandate resembles a classic linear programming blending problem. We employ linear programming calculation algorithms with some constraints utilizing integer formulation. Finally, we transform the few nonlinear functions among the CLO compliance tests into linear form by replacing the actual constraints with linear proxies. When done thoughtfully, this strategy maintains quick calculation speed while also providing the portfolio manager with more control over constraint settings.

Although complicated and dependent upon more qualitative inputs derived from credit research, CLO portfolio management can benefit tremendously from carefully designed quantitative tools. Given well-maintained inputs, our proposed framework provides a comprehensive survey of market opportunities, so that the portfolio manager has confidence that she has left no stone unturned.

APPENDIX

The following example code provides a demonstration of the use of open-source software to solve the "hot dog" example previously described in the chapter. These examples use Python 3 for the main scripting language and a convex modeling language called CVXPY. These are not required, as there are many open-source and third-party programming languages that can be used to solve linear and nonlinear equations such as R, Matlab, and Excel.

Python and CVXPY were chosen to detail our example because both are open-source and free to use. CVXPY also allows the practitioner to select many different solvers from its library as well as several supported commercial solvers. This flexibility matters when a practitioner starts with a relatively simple problem that eventually evolves beyond the capabilities of open-source solutions.

For the hot dog problem, we assume our suppliers provide the following data for each constituent type of meat:

Meat type	Protein Content (% by weight)	Fat Content (% by weight)	Water Content (% by weight)	Cost ($/lb)
Chicken	28%	15%	57%	$ 2.25
Pork (w/o vol disc)	31%	18%	51%	$ 2.30
Pork (with vol disc)	31%	18%	51%	$ 2.25
Beef	35%	17%	48%	$ 2.60

Example code:

import cvxpy **as** cp

 # Define Variables (% by weight of final blend)
W_c = cp.Variable() *# % content of chicken*
W_p_1 = cp.Variable() *# % content of pork at price 1*
W_p_2 = cp.Variable() *# % content of pork at price 2*
W_b = cp.Variable() *# % content of beef*

 # Decision variable for pork price
rho = cp.Variable(boolean=**True**) *# Set boolean= True so variable can only take value of 0 or 1*

 # Constants
Chicken content
P_c = 0.28 *# chicken protein content*
F_c = 0.15 *# chicken fat content*
Wa_c = 0.57 *# chicken water content*
C_c = 2.25 *# cost of chicken $/lb*

Pork
P_p = 0.31 *# pork protein content*
F_p = 0.18 *# pork fat content*
Wa_p = 0.51 *# pork water content*

C_p_1 = 2.30 # cost of pork $/lb - standard price
C_p_2 = 2.25 # cost of pork $/lb - volume discount price

Beef
P_b = 0.35 # beef protein content
F_b = 0.17 # beef fat content
Wa_b = 0.48 # beef water content
C_b = 2.60 # cost of beef $/lb

# Equations
Total_Weight = W_c + W_p_1 + W_p_2 + W_b # (Eq 9.1)
Total_Protein = P_c * W_c + P_p * (W_p_1 + W_p_2) + P_b * W_b # (Eq 9.2)
Total_Fat = F_c * W_c + F_p * (W_p_1 + W_p_2) + F_b * W_b # (Eq 9.3)
Total_Water = Wa_c * W_c + Wa_p * (W_p_1 + W_p_2) + Wa_b * W_b # (Eq 9.4)
Total_Cost = C_c * W_c + C_p_1 * W_p_1 + W_p_2 * C_p_2 + C_b * W_b # (Eq 9.5)

# Constraints
e = 0.000000000001 # define feasibility tolerance
constraints = [

Total_Weight == 1, # (Eq 9.6)
Total_Protein >= 0.31, # (Eq 9.7)
Total_Water >= 0.51, # (Eq 9.8)
Total_Cost <= 2.36, # (Eq 9.9)

W_c >= 0, # (Eq 9.10)
W_p_1 >= 0, # (Eq 9.11)
W_p_2 >= 0, # (Eq 9.12)
W_b >= 0, # (Eq 9.13)

use decision variable to control what price to use based on the price threshold
W_p_1 <= (0.15 - e) * rho, # (Eq 9.14)
W_p_2 >= 0.15 * (1 - rho), # (Eq 9.15)
W_p_2 - (1 - rho) * 999 <= 0 # (Eq 9.16)
]

```
# Define the objective - minimize the total fat
content of the final product
objective = cp.Minimize(Total_Fat) # (Eq 9.17)

# Define the problem
problem = cp.Problem(objective, constraints)

# Solve the problem
problem.solve(solver=cp.CBC)

# Print results to console
print('')
print('-------------- EXAMPLE -----------')
print('-------------- RESULTS -------------')
print('Chicken content: ', W_c.value * 100, '%')
print('Pork content WITHOUT vol discount: ', W_p_1.value * 100, '%')
print('Pork content WITH vol discount: ', W_p_2.value * 100, '%')
print('Beef content: ', W_b.value * 100, '%')
print('----------------------------------')
print('Total Cost: ', Total_Cost.value, ' $/lb')
print('Total Protein: ', Total_Protein.value * 100, '% of final blend')
print('Total Fat: ', Total_Fat.value * 100, '% of final blend')
print('Total Water: ', Total_Water.value * 100, '% of final blend')
```

Executing the Example code will produce the following results:

```
------------- EXAMPLE -----------
------------- RESULTS -------------
Chicken content: 41.905 %
Pork content WITHOUT vol discount: 0.0 %
Pork content WITH vol discount: 26.667 %
Beef content: 31.429 %
----------------------------------
```

Total Cost: 2.360 $/lb
Total Protein: 31.0 % of final blend
Total Fat: 16.429 % of final blend
Total Water: 52.571 % of final blend

This result shows that the optimized blend has a Total Fat content of 16.429%, which is the minimum fat content achievable while maintaining or beating the cost, protein, and water constraints. The blend was also able to take advantage of the pork price discount: "Pork content WITH vol discount" = 26.667%, and as expected no pork purchase was made at the higher price, "Pork content WITHOUT vol discount" = 0%, because these were constrained to be mutually exclusive.

Lessons from More than a Trillion Dollars in Defaults[18]

David Keisman
Moody's Investors Service

Our Ultimate Recovery Database encompasses over 5,900 debt instruments from more than 1,200 nonfinancial companies that defaulted between 1987 and 2020. When we reviewed this data in 2017, it covered around $1 trillion in defaults, but since then defaulted companies' funded debt grew more than $400 billion and now exceeds $1.4 trillion. The trends we can tease out of this cache of data—among others, how recoveries vary based on position in the debt structure, how default types evolve and whether private-equity ownership alters the equation—provide valuable insights for downturn scenarios.

Firm-wide recovery rates are widely dispersed, with a mean recovery rate of 54% and standard deviation of 28%. The average discounted ultimate recovery rate on term loans included in the

---

[18] We would like to thank Moody's for giving us permission to reprint this article. We were not permitted to make any changes; therefore, references to "our" should be read to refer to Moody's.

database is 72%, while the median is 100%. For revolvers the average is 86% and the median is 100%. Bonds average and median recoveries are 45% and 35%, respectively.

Recoveries for specific debt instruments are significantly influenced by their rank in the defaulted company's liability structure and the associated percentage of total debt both above and below. For instance, second-lien debt recoveries are higher in complex structures, where there is debt above and below it, than in simple structures, where there is no cushion below.

The timing of default cycles also influence firm-wide recovery rates, with measured correlation based on the US speculative-grade default rate at the time of resolution. Higher ranked loan recovery rates are less cyclical than firm-wide recoveries, while bond recovery rates are more cyclical. By contrast, over the long-term there is no relationship between ultimate firm-wide recovery rates and industries. Therefore, there is no observable relationship between recovery rates and asset-heavy or asset-light industries.

Private-equity ownership also has little influence on firm-wide recovery rates, but does affect the type of default and the recoveries on certain types of debt. Companies sponsored by the largest PE firms are much more likely to pursue distressed exchanges (DEs) as a restructuring tool, because it helps them to retain at least some ownership and postpone/avoid a bankruptcy filing. Prevalence of DEs, prepackaged bankruptcies and bank debt comprising a majority of the debt structure among PE defaulters, in general, result in higher losses for junior creditors.

ULTIMATE RECOVERY DATABASE HITS A NEW MILESTONE AND TEACHES A FEW LESSONS

Our Ultimate Recovery Database (URD) hit a new milestone of more than $1.4 trillion from more than 1,200 non-financial corporate defaults spanning from 1987 through year-end 2020. That means another more than $400 billion in defaulted debt for us to examine than when we did a broad review on this data in 2017. The database includes both rated and unrated US corporate borrowers with over $50 million in total funded debt at the time of default. As of January 2021, it contains detailed information on nominal and discounted ultimate recoveries for over 5,900 debt facilities (over 2,430 term loans/revolvers and over 3,470 bonds.)

"Ultimate recovery," in contrast to 30-day post-default trading prices that are often used to measure creditors' recovery rates, refers to the settlement value creditors received when the default was resolved. The annual distribution by year of emergence from default, which further divides the defaults into bankruptcies and other types of non-bankruptcy, out-of-court debt restructuring, mostly distressed exchanges (DEs), can be seen in Exhibit 9.9.

EXHIBIT 9.9

Default Distribution by Year of Default Resolution, URD (1987–2020).

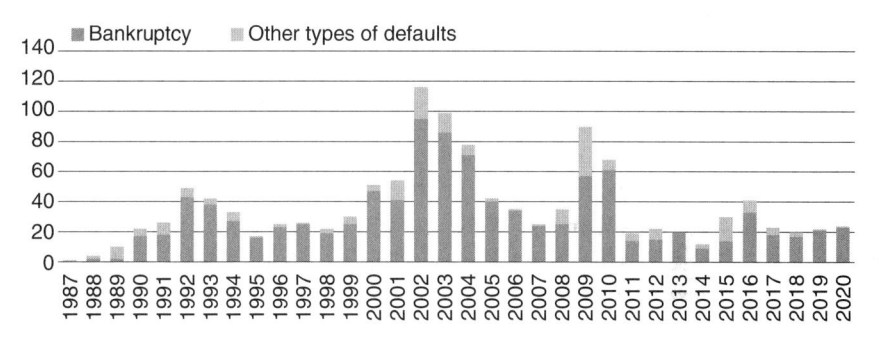

Data as of January 2021; database is updated each month with new resolved defaults as public recovery data becomes available
Source: Moody's Ultimate Recovery Database

The default cycle associated with the Global Financial Crisis (GFC) highlighted a major change in default behavior, with distressed exchanges increasing significantly, as seen in Exhibit 9.10, and that trend has continued through the pandemic-driven default cycle. Distressed exchanges rose from about 16% of rated defaults before 2009 to about 46% of defaults during the 2008–09 downturn, and peaked at 48% during the 2015 energy downturn. For 2009 through the end of 2020, these out-of-court debt restructurings constituted 42% of rated defaults.

EXHIBIT 9.10

Share of DEs Surged in 2008–2009, Remain Elevated.

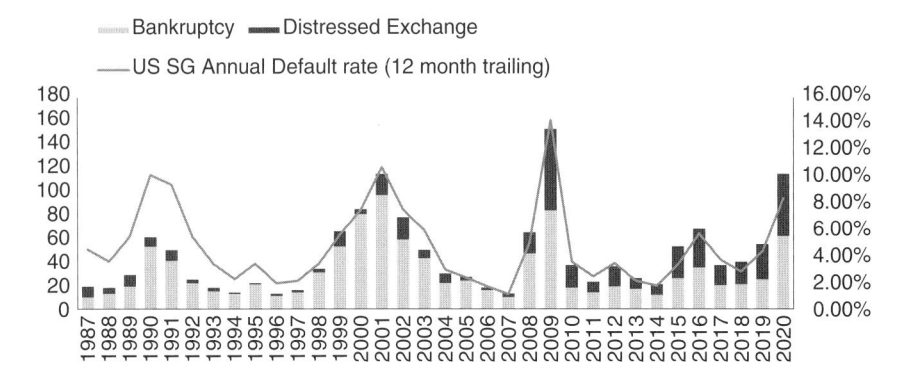

Counts of corporate family level-defaults
Source: Moody's Investors Service

Records of resolved defaults, both DEs and bankruptcies, across industries (as defined by Moody's) are shown in Exhibit 9.11 with, Distribution (mainly Retail), Oil & Gas, Consumer Products, being the top three default contributors. For example, in 2020 Oil & Gas contributed the most defaults on an absolute and dollar volume basis.[19] In the US, our Credit Transition Model (CTM) now expects the speculative-grade default rate to fall to 5.4% by the end of 2021, down from the current level of 8.3%—still somewhat higher than the 4.7% long-term average.

LESSON 1: DEBT STRUCTURE MATTERS, CERTAINLY MORE THAN WHAT YOU CALL THE DEBT

As would be expected, senior debtholders realize higher recovery rates than those lower in payment priority. Our data in Exhibit 9.12, which breaks down the mix of debt types across over 5,900 debt facilities, shows average ultimate recovery rates demonstrate a positive correlation with the priority of claims in the

---

[19] For more details, please see defaults will continue to ease in 2021 following fourth quarter slowdown.

EXHIBIT 9.11

Distribution, Oil & Gas, Consumer Products Dominate Other Industries with Recorded Default Resolutions.

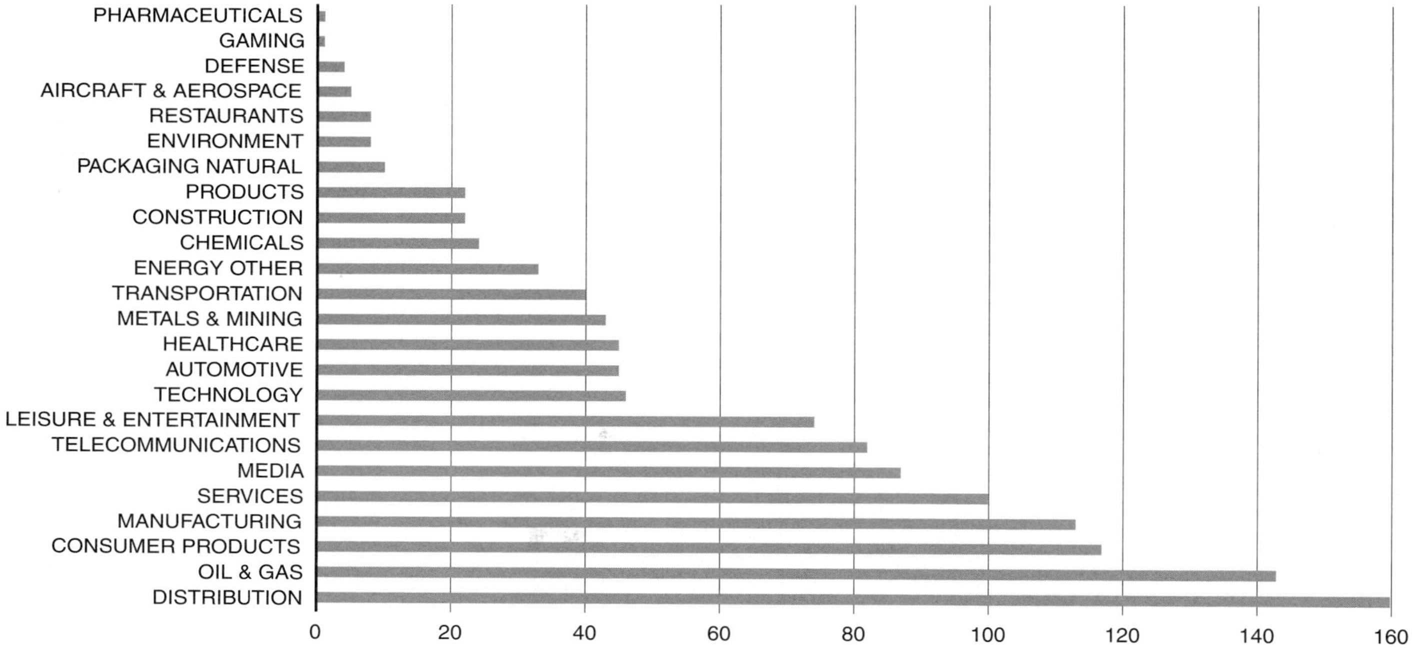

Industry	Value
PHARMACEUTICALS	~2
GAMING	~3
DEFENSE	~7
AIRCRAFT & AEROSPACE	~9
RESTAURANTS	~12
ENVIRONMENT	~12
PACKAGING NATURAL PRODUCTS	~15
CONSTRUCTION	~22
CHEMICALS	~22
ENERGY OTHER	~27
TRANSPORTATION	~40
METALS & MINING	~42
HEALTHCARE	~45
AUTOMOTIVE	~45
TECHNOLOGY	~47
LEISURE & ENTERTAINMENT	~74
TELECOMMUNICATIONS	~82
MEDIA	~87
SERVICES	~100
MANUFACTURING	~114
CONSUMER PRODUCTS	~117
OIL & GAS	~145
DISTRIBUTION	~160

Distribution industry includes mainly stores, distribution centers; Energy:Other includes utilities, coal companies
Source: Moody's Ultimate Recovery Database

capital structure. The average discounted ultimate recovery rate on revolvers included in the database is 86%, while the median is 100%, as for term loans, the average and median recovery rates are 72% and 100%, respectively. Bonds' average and median recovery rates are 45% and 35%, respectively. As discussed, default type influences debt's recovery rate for instance, the data in Exhibit 9.12 includes both bankruptcies and DEs. With only bankruptcies in the mix, an average recovery on Senior Unsecured Bonds drops, from 47% to 39%.

According to our records through January 2021, firm-wide recovery rates of 1,233 resolved defaults between 1987–2020, which measure the enterprise value of the corporate family relative to its total liabilities at default resolution, are widely dispersed with a mean recovery rate of 54% and a standard deviation of 28%.

EXHIBIT 9.12

Average Discounted Ultimate Recovery Rates by Debt Type, 1987–2020.

Debt Instrument	Avg Recovery Rate	Counts
Revolver	86%	1214
Term Loan	72%	1203
Senior Secured Bonds	61%	792
Senior Unsecured Bonds	47%	1672
Senior Subordinated Bonds	28%	540
Subordinated Bonds	29%	389
Junior Subordinated Bonds	20%	80
Firm-wide recovery	**54%**	**1233**

Source: Moody's Ultimate Recovery Database

What the instrument is called does not matter much, but its relative position in the liability waterfall does. Our data reinforce the significance of a debt instrument's place in a company's capital structure and the amount of debt cushion beneath it. For instance, second-lien debt recoveries are higher in complex structures, where there is debt above and below it, than in simple structures, where there is no cushion below. There is a high positive correlation of debt cushion with ultimate recovery rates, as shown in Exhibit 9.13.

Analytics and Performance

EXHIBIT 9.13

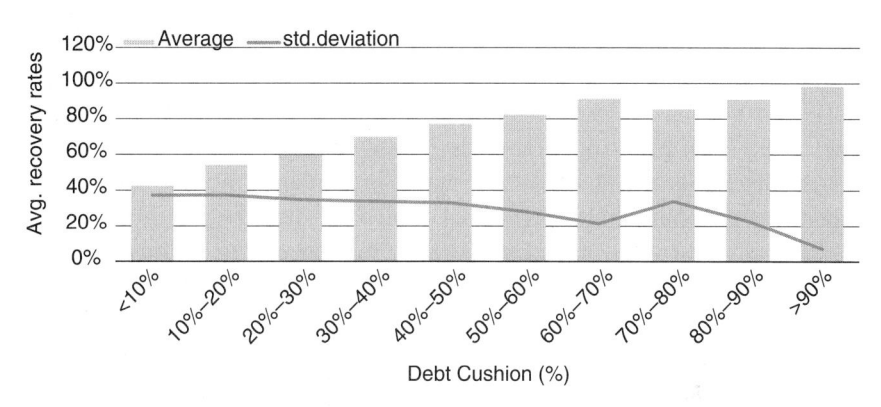

Debt Cushion Enhances Recoveries.

[Bar chart with line overlay: x-axis "Debt Cushion (%)" with bins <10%, 10%-20%, 20%-30%, 30%-40%, 40%-50%, 50%-60%, 60%-70%, 70%-80%, 80%-90%, >90%; y-axis "Avg. recovery rates" 0%–120%; series: Average, std.deviation]

Source: Moody's Ultimate Recovery Database

A debt tranche's position on the balance sheet and the overall firm-wide recovery rate, rather than how it is described, are the key factors. For example, Exhibit 9.14 shows variation in historical recoveries for different types of revolvers and term loans as opposed to other debt instruments.

EXHIBIT 9.14

Recovery Rates of Better-Structured Bank Debt Show Less Volatility over the Years.
Discounted ultimate recovery rates of defaulted debt instruments are plotted by year of emergence from default

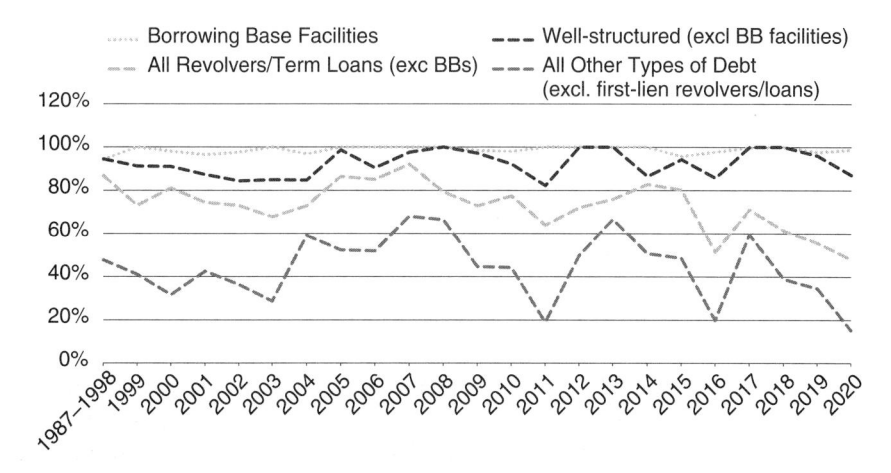

[Line chart, y-axis 0%–120%, x-axis years 1987–1998 through 2020; series: Borrowing Base Facilities; Well-structured (excl BB facilities); All Revolvers/Term Loans (exc BBs); All Other Types of Debt (excl. first-lien revolvers/loans)]

"All other Types of Debt" include sub bank debt (such as second-lien, unsecured loans, etc) and all types of bonds. BBs—borrowing base facilities
Source: Moody's Ultimate Recovery Database

Borrowing-base facilities consistently performed well, exhibiting low volatility in recoveries between 1987 and 2020, as did well-structured bank debt (which we defined as term loans and revolvers secured by a first lien on all assets and a debt cushion equal to or greater than 40%, excluding borrowing base facilities). When lower-ranked and less heavily secured loans are added into the bank–debt mix and borrowing base facilities are excluded, the variation of average recovery rates increases, and overall average recoveries are below those of well-structured counterparts (as demonstrated by the gray dotted line in the middle of the chart).

Revolver Recoveries Remain High, While Recoveries on Term Loans Diminish

In the quaint old days, "bank debt" usually meant debt that was senior, secured and top-ranked in the debt structure. Previously, research produced from the Ultimate Recovery Database would often combine the two instrument types together under the heading of "bank debt." The cumulative average recovery rates for revolvers (R/Cs) and term loans (T/Ls) were roughly similar until around 1995. Since then, revolver cumulative average recovery rates have remained in the mid-to-upper 80s, while that of T/Ls has steadily decreased to as low as mid-70s, an average 14% difference, see Exhibit 9.15. For example, the single year recovery average in 2020 alone for T/Ls were in the low-50s, compared to mid-80% for revolvers.

EXHIBIT 9.15

Cumulative Average Recovery Rates of Revolvers and Term Loans.

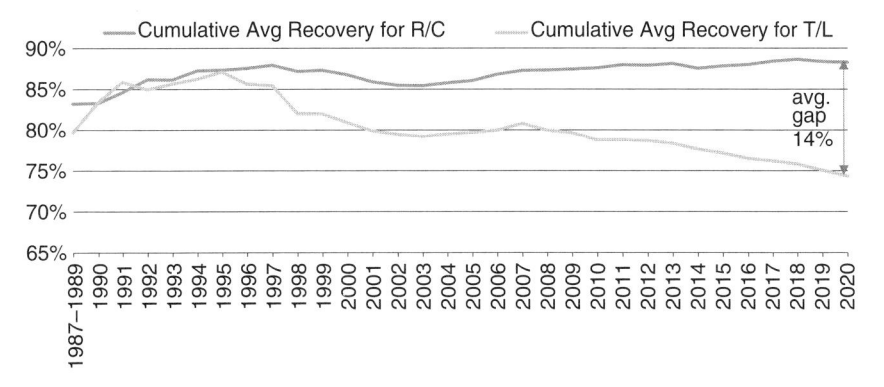

Source: Moody's Ultimate Recovery Database

What is the cause for this? How often an R/C or a T/L was the top-ranked debt in the debt structure of a defaulted company in the URD has an influence, see Exhibit 9.16. While the R/Cs almost always remained at the top, the percentage of T/Ls that were top-ranked debt in a defaulted company declined steadily from the 90s to the mid-70s.

EXHIBIT 9.16

Shares of Top-Ranked Revolvers and Term Loans on the Balance Sheets of Defaulters.

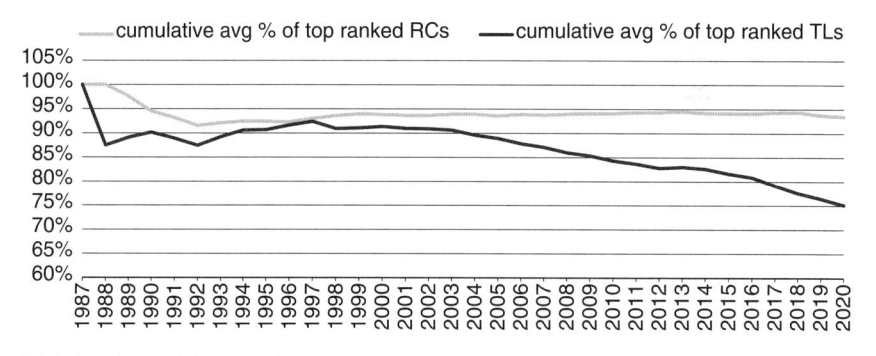

Data is shown in a cumulative average format
Source: Moody's Ultimate Recovery Database

Considering this divergence in structuring and recoveries of revolvers and term loans, it does not make sense to lump all R/Cs and T/Ls together under a generic heading of "bank debt" when attempting to do loss-given-default (LGD) analysis. As a result, most of our research evolved into analysis that segregates first-lien bank debt, subordinated or junior bank debt, etc. It makes us long for the days when analyzing just the "bank debt" was enough.

LESSON 2: RECOVERIES ARE NEGATIVELY INFLUENCED BY DEFAULT RATES, BUT INDUSTRY RARELY MATTERS

Firm-wide recovery rates of defaulted debt issuers have long shown a negative correlation with the US speculative-grade default rate. Losses are exacerbated during default peaks and less pronounced during more benign credit cycles, see Exhibit 9.17.

EXHIBIT 9.17

Losses Climb When the Default Rate Is Peaking Firm-Wide LGD of Bankruptcies.

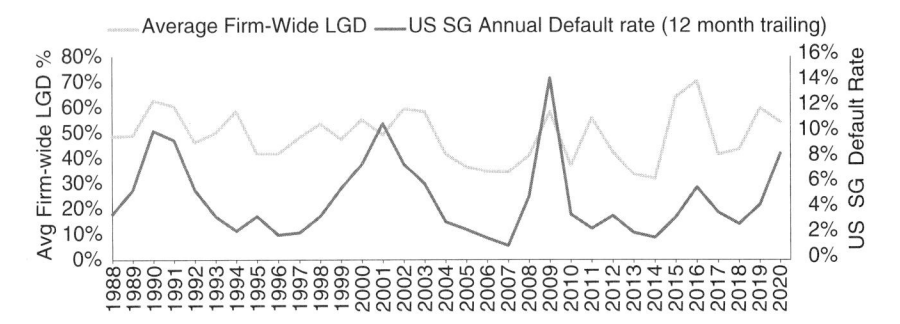

US SG Default Rate is issuer-weighted 12-month-trailing as of Dec 31 for each given year
Source: Moody's Ultimate Recovery Database

On the other hand, there is relatively little variation in firm-wide recovery rates among the industries, as shown in Exhibit 9.18. Fifteen industries with at least 20 or more bankruptcies (out of 23 tracked) have average firm-wide recovery rates that fall between 32% and 62%, with a standard deviation of 7%—and industries with less than 10 defaulters have firm-wide recovery rates in the range between 31% and 81% but with a much higher standard deviation

EXHIBIT 9.18

Firm-Wide Recovery Rates of Bankrupt Companies by Industry.

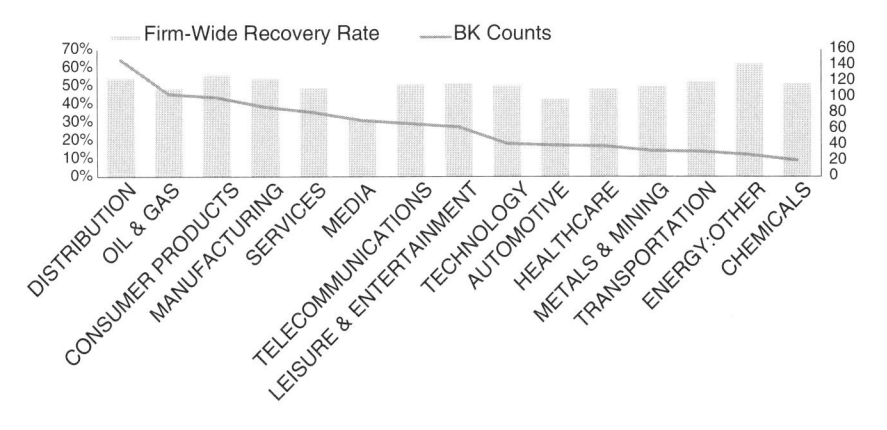

Distribution industry includes mainly stores, distribution centers; BK Counts—number of resolved bankruptcies
Source: Moody's Ultimate Recovery Database

of 17%. (This noise can be explained by small sample sizes with some industries featuring only one resolved bankruptcy, such as Pharmaceuticals.)

Further evidence that industry is unimportant in determining firm-wide ultimate recovery rates is shown in Exhibit 9.19, which shows very little difference in firm-wide recovery rates for asset-heavy and asset-light industries.

EXHIBIT 9.19

Asset-Light or Asset-Heavy Has Little Bearing on Firm-wide Recoveries.

	Bankruptcies	Population size	Other forms of restructurings	Population size
Asset Heavy	48%	470	75%	122
Asset Light	52%	550	70%	91

All types of defaults were included
Source: Moody's Ultimate Recovery Database

A high level of defaults in a particular industry, such as what occurred in the oil and gas sector in 2015, and in telecom in 2002, can lead to extraordinarily low firm-wide recovery rates for defaulted companies emerging during those years, as we have discussed in previous research. The 12-month trailing speculative-grade default rates for those years and industry groups were 14.1% and 14.4% and the corresponding firm-wide recovery rates in the database were 37.5% and 30.2%, respectively.

LESSON 3: FIRM-WIDE RECOVERIES VARY LITTLE BASED ON PE SPONSORSHIP, BECAUSE OF THEIR TACTICS

Because of different strategies, average firm-wide recoveries of companies with private-equity sponsors are about the same as those with no PE presence. The 54% average firm-wide recovery rate for creditors of companies with a private-equity sponsor was on par with 54% recoveries of those without PE backing, see Exhibit 9.20.

However, our review of 261 PE-sponsored deals in Moody's URD (1987–2020) confirmed the presence of a PE sponsor resulted in junior creditors suffering greater losses. Differences in debt instrument-level recoveries in bankruptcies were clearer, with junior debtholders bearing the brunt of losses. Senior unsecured bonds on the balance sheets of PE defaulters recovered 22 cents on a dollar—about half of 41% recovered by their counterparts.

EXHIBIT 9.20

Defaults That Had PE Sponsor(s) Hurt Junior Debtholders Most Bankruptcies, DE (including non-defaulted debt tranches).

Defaulted Companies with PE Sponsors			Defaulted Companies without PE Sponsors		
Debt Instrument	Average Recovery Rate	No. of debt instruments	Debt Instrument	Average Recovery Rate	No. of debt instruments
First-Lien Revolver	86%	272	First-Lien Revolver	89%	829
First-Lien Term Loan	78%	320	First-Lien Term Loan	80%	645
Sub Bank Debt	38%	112	Sub Bank Debt	59%	239
Senior Unsecured Bonds	39%	253	Senior Unsecured Bonds	48%	1423
Subordinated Bonds	23%	182	Subordinated Bonds	29%	815
Family recovery	54%	261	Family recovery	54%	972

Bankruptcies only (excluding non-defaulted debt tranches)

Defaulted Companies with PE Sponsors			Defaulted Companies without PE Sponsors		
Debt Instrument	Average Recovery Rate	No. of debt instruments	Debt Instrument	Average Recovery Rate	No. of debt instruments
First-Lien Revolver	83%	212	First-Lien Revolver	87%	689
First-Lien Term Loan	73%	262	First-Lien Term Loan	78%	553
Sub Bank Debt	30%	89	Sub Bank Debt	55%	215
Senior Unsecured Bonds	22%	157	Senior Unsecured Bonds	41%	1113
Subordinated Bonds	16%	148	Subordinated Bonds	20%	682
Family recovery	49%	210	Family recovery	51%	810

Source: Moody's Ultimate Recovery Database

That occurred because PE-sponsored defaulters had a significant amount of senior debt above senior unsecured bonds, on average, twice as much by percentage as companies without any sponsor. This means senior-secured creditors were ahead of subordinated debt to receive bankruptcy settlements/repayments, and there was little left for those at the bottom of the debt waterfall when the bankruptcy was resolved.

In general, PE-sponsored companies have a higher percentage of bank debt (R/Cs and T/Ls) in their debt structure compared with non-sponsored companies. Bank debt usually has a higher recovery rate than that of other debt instruments. The difference in bank debt as the percentage of total debt at default, and its higher recovery rate, has led to the interesting "optical illusion" where

PE-sponsored companies have lower recovery rates for almost each type of debt instrument compared with non-sponsored companies and yet produce substantially similar firm-wide recovery rates.

Another reason firm-wide recoveries of defaulted, PE-sponsored companies were close to those of non-PE defaulters, was the high proportion of DEs and prepackaged bankruptcies in the PE default mix, see Exhibit 9.21. The largest PE firms tend to favor distressed exchanges, which historically produced the highest average recovery for any type of default, as a restructuring tool because DEs help them to retain at least some ownership position.

EXHIBIT 9.21

Default Type Drives Recoveries of PE-Sponsored Deals Large PE firms favor DEs as a restructuring tool.

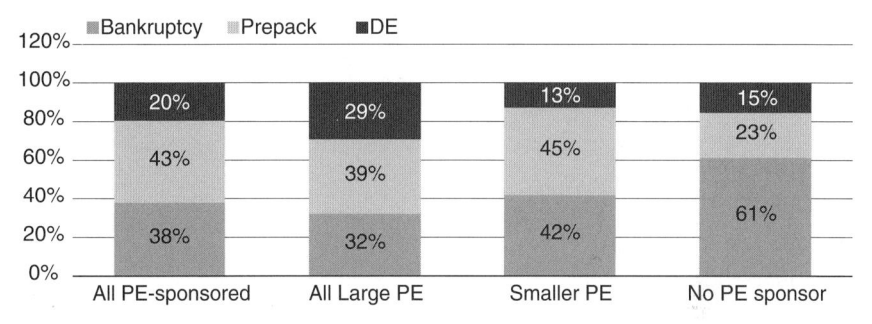

	Bankruptcy	Prepack	DE
All PE-sponsored	38%	43%	20%
All Large PE	32%	39%	29%
Smaller PE	42%	45%	13%
No PE sponsor	61%	23%	15%

Distributions of default types for various types of defaulters; Large/Top PE Firms include firms such as Apollo, Bain, Blackstone, Carlyle, Cerberus, Goldman Sachs, KKR & Co, Madison Dearborn, Providence Equity, TH Lee, TPG, Warburg Pincus, Welsh Carson
Source: Moody's Ultimate Recovery Database

Around 30% of the top PE-owned leveraged buyout defaults in our database were DEs. That is more than twice the number executed by companies with a smaller PE sponsor and around two times more DEs consummated by companies that had no PE backing.

The overwhelming majority of the latter companies, or 61% of all the examples in our review, filed for a court-supervised bankruptcy protection, at almost twice the rate of companies sponsored by the large PE sponsors and significantly higher [sic] those filed by companies with a smaller PE sponsor (with an additional 23% entering bankruptcy with a prepackaged plan in place, the instances of prepacks were more common among PE-owned companies).

The average family recovery data shows DEs historically produced the highest average recoveries, regardless of the presence of a PE sponsor. In the case of DEs, in our database, we allocate a full recovery for the debt instruments that were not part of debt restructuring. Hence, firm-wide recovery rates were high among DEs, even though the defaulted debt that was subject to the exchange incurred large losses.

APPENDIX

EXHIBIT 22

Asset Heavy Industries	Bankruptcies	Other forms of restructurings
AIRCRAFT & AEROSPACE	4	1
AUTOMOTIVE	39	6
CHEMICALS	21	3
CONSTRUCTION	17	5
DEFENSE	1	3
ENERGY:OTHER	28	5
ENVIRONMENT	8	0
MANUFACTURING	88	25
METALS & MINING	32	11
NATURAL PRODUCTS	18	4
OIL & GAS	104	39
RESTAURANTS	6	2
TELECOMMUNICATIONS	71	11
TRANSPORTATION	33	7

Asset Light Industries	Bankruptcies	Other forms of restructurings
CONSUMER PRODUCTS	100	17
DISTRIBUTION	147	13
HEALTHCARE	42	3
LEISURE & ENTERTAINMENT	63	12
MEDIA	67	20
PACKAGING	9	1
SERVICES	81	19
TECHNOLOGY	40	6
PHARMACEUTICALS	1	0

Distribution industry includes mainly stores, distribution centers; En ergy:Other includes utilities, coal c-ompanies
Source: Moody's Ultimate Recovery Dotobose

MOODY'S RELATED PUBLICATIONS

- Corporate Defaults and Recoveries—US: Lessons from a Trillion Dollars in Defaults, April 2017
- Corporate Defaults & Recoveries—US: Recoveries in a pandemic-driven default cycle, May 2020
- Leveraged finance: Corporates—US and EMEA: Show me the money: liquidity access will dictate survival or default from pandemic, July 2020
- Corporate Defaults and Recoveries—US: Cov-lite 2.0 loans take over market, bring structural deterioration, lower recoveries, March 2020
- Corporate Defaults and Recoveries—US: Lessons from the 2019 energy default cycle: Liquidity is not recovery, January 2020
- US Corporate Default Monitor—Fourth Quarter: Defaults will continue to ease in 2021 following fourth quarter slowdown, January 2021
- Default Trends—Global: Corporate defaults fell in January, February 2021

Note that these references are current as of the date of publication of this report and that more recent reports may be available. All researc may not be available to all clients.

© 2021 Moody's Corporation, Moody's Investors Service, Inc., Moody's Analytics, Inc. and/or their licensors and affiliates (collectively, "MOODY'S"). All rights reserved.

CREDIT RATINGS ISSUED BY MOODY'S CREDIT RATINGS AFFILIATES ARE THEIR CURRENT OPINIONS OF THE RELATIVE FUTURE CREDIT RISK OF ENTITIES, CREDIT COMMITMENTS, OR DEBT OR DEBT-LIKE SECURITIES, AND MATERIALS, PRODUCTS, SERVICES AND INFORMATION PUBLISHED BY MOODY'S (COLLECTIVELY, "PUBLICATIONS") MAY INCLUDE SUCH CURRENT OPINIONS. MOODY'S DEFINES CREDIT RISK AS THE RISK THAT AN ENTITY MAY NOT MEET ITS CONTRACTUAL FINANCIAL OBLIGATIONS AS THEY COME DUE AND ANY ESTIMATED FINANCIAL LOSS IN THE EVENT OF DEFAULT OR IMPAIRMENT. SEE APPLICABLE MOODY'S RATING SYMBOLS AND DEFINITIONS PUBLICATION FOR INFORMATION ON THE TYPES OF CONTRACTUAL FINANCIAL OBLIGATIONS ADDRESSED BY MOODY'S CREDIT RATINGS. CREDIT RATINGS DO NOT ADDRESS ANY OTHER RISK, INCLUDING BUT NOT LIMITED TO: LIQUIDITY RISK, MARKET VALUE RISK, OR

PRICE VOLATILITY. CREDIT RATINGS, NON-CREDIT ASSESSMENTS ("ASSESSMENTS"), AND OTHER OPINIONS INCLUDED IN MOODY'S PUBLICATIONS ARE NOT STATEMENTS OF CURRENT OR HISTORICAL FACT. MOODY'S PUBLICATIONS MAY ALSO INCLUDE QUANTITATIVE MODEL-BASED ESTIMATES OF CREDIT RISK AND RELATED OPINIONS OR COMMENTARY PUBLISHED BY MOODY'S ANALYTICS, INC. AND/OR ITS AFFILIATES. MOODY'S CREDIT RATINGS, ASSESSMENTS, OTHER OPINIONS AND PUBLICATIONS DO NOT CONSTITUTE OR PROVIDE INVESTMENT OR FINANCIAL ADVICE, AND MOODY'S CREDIT RATINGS, ASSESSMENTS, OTHER OPINIONS AND PUBLICATIONS ARE NOT AND DO NOT PROVIDE RECOMMENDATIONS TO PURCHASE, SELL, OR HOLD PARTICULAR SECURITIES. MOODY'S CREDIT RATINGS, ASSESSMENTS, OTHER OPINIONS AND PUBLICATIONS DO NOT COMMENT ON THE SUITABILITY OF AN INVESTMENT FOR ANY PARTICULAR INVESTOR. MOODY'S ISSUES ITS CREDIT RATINGS, ASSESSMENTS AND OTHER OPINIONS AND PUBLISHES ITS PUBLICATIONS WITH THE EXPECTATION AND UNDERSTANDING THAT EACH INVESTOR WILL, WITH DUE CARE, MAKE ITS OWN STUDY AND EVALUATION OF EACH SECURITY THAT IS UNDER CONSIDERATION FOR PURCHASE, HOLDING, OR SALE.

MOODY'S CREDIT RATINGS, ASSESSMENTS, OTHER OPINIONS, AND PUBLICATIONS ARE NOT INTENDED FOR USE BY RETAIL INVESTORS AND IT WOULD BE RECKLESS AND INAPPROPRIATE FOR RETAIL INVESTORS TO USE MOODY'S CREDIT RATINGS, ASSESSMENTS, OTHER OPINIONS OR PUBLICATIONS WHEN MAKING AN INVESTMENT DECISION. IF IN DOUBT YOU SHOULD CONTACT YOUR FINANCIAL OR OTHER PROFESSIONAL ADVISER.

ALL INFORMATION CONTAINED HEREIN IS PROTECTED BY LAW, INCLUDING BUT NOT LIMITED TO, COPYRIGHT LAW, AND NONE OF SUCH INFORMATION MAY BE COPIED OR OTHERWISE REPRODUCED, REPACKAGED, FURTHER TRANSMITTED, TRANSFERRED, DISSEMINATED, REDISTRIBUTED OR RESOLD, OR STORED FOR SUBSEQUENT USE FOR ANY SUCH PURPOSE, IN WHOLE OR IN PART, IN ANY FORM OR MANNER OR BY ANY MEANS WHATSOEVER, BY ANY PERSON WITHOUT MOODY'S PRIOR WRITTEN CONSENT.

MOODY'S CREDIT RATINGS, ASSESSMENTS, OTHER OPINIONS AND PUBLICATIONS ARE NOT INTENDED FOR USE BY ANY PERSON AS A BENCHMARK AS THAT TERM IS DEFINED FOR REGULATORY PURPOSES AND MUST NOT BE USED IN ANY WAY THAT COULD RESULT IN THEM BEING CONSIDERED A BENCHMARK.

All information contained herein is obtained by MOODY'S from sources believed by it to be accurate and reliable. Because of the possibility of human or mechanical error as well as other factors, however, all information contained herein is provided "AS IS" without warranty of any kind. MOODY'S adopts all necessary measures so that the information it uses in assigning a credit rating is of sufficient quality and from sources MOODY'S considers to be reliable including, when appropriate, independent third-party sources. However, MOODY'S is not an auditor and cannot in every instance independently verify or validate information received in the rating process or in preparing its Publications.

To the extent permitted by law, MOODY'S and its directors, officers, employees, agents, representatives, licensors and suppliers disclaim liability to any person or entity for any indirect, special, consequential, or incidental losses or damages whatsoever arising from or in connection with the information contained herein or the use of or inability to use any such information, even if MOODY'S or any of its directors, officers, employees, agents, representatives, licensors or suppliers is advised in advance of the possibility of such losses or damages, including but not limited to: (a) any loss of present or prospective profits or (b) any loss or damage arising where the relevant financial instrument is not the subject of a particular credit rating assigned by MOODY'S.

To the extent permitted by law, MOODY'S and its directors, officers, employees, agents, representatives, licensors and suppliers disclaim liability for any direct or compensatory losses or damages caused to any person or entity, including but not limited to by any negligence (but excluding fraud, willful misconduct or any other type of liability that, for the avoidance of doubt, by law cannot be excluded) on the part of, or any contingency within or beyond the control of, MOODY'S or any of its directors, officers, employees, agents, representatives, licensors or suppliers, arising from or in connection with the information contained herein or the use of or inability to use any such information.

NO WARRANTY, EXPRESS OR IMPLIED, AS TO THE ACCURACY, TIMELINESS, COMPLETENESS, MERCHANTABILITY OR FITNESS FOR ANY PARTICULAR PURPOSE OF ANY CREDIT RATING, ASSESSMENT, OTHER OPINION OR INFORMATION IS GIVEN OR MADE BY MOODY'S IN ANY FORM OR MANNER WHATSOEVER.

Moody's Investors Service, Inc., a wholly-owned credit rating agency subsidiary of Moody's Corporation ("MCO"), hereby discloses that most issuers of debt securities (including corporate and municipal bonds, debentures, notes and commercial paper) and preferred stock rated by Moody's Investors Service, Inc. have, prior to assignment of any credit rating, agreed to pay to Moody's Investors Service, Inc. for credit ratings opinions and services rendered by it fees ranging from $1,000 to approximately $5,000,000. MCO and Moody's Investors Service also maintain policies and procedures to address the independence of Moody's Investors Service credit ratings and credit rating processes. Information regarding certain affiliations that may exist between directors of MCO and rated entities, and between entities who hold credit ratings from Moody's Investors Service and have also publicly reported to the SEC an ownership interest in MCO of more than 5%, is posted annually at www.moodys.com under the heading "Investor Relations — Corporate Governance — Director and Shareholder Affiliation Policy."

Additional terms for Australia only: Any publication into Australia of this document is pursuant to the Australian Financial Services License of MOODY'S affiliate, Moody's Investors Service Pty Limited ABN 61 003 399 657AFSL 336969 and/or Moody's Analytics Australia Pty Ltd ABN 94 105 136 972 AFSL 383569 (as applicable). This document is intended to be provided only to "wholesale clients" within the meaning of section 761G of the Corporations Act 2001. By continuing to access this document from within Australia, you represent to MOODY'S that you are, or are accessing the document as a representative of, a "wholesale client" and that neither you nor the entity you represent will directly or indirectly disseminate this document or its contents to "retail clients" within the meaning of section 761G of the Corporations Act 2001. MOODY'S credit rating is an opinion as to the creditworthiness of a debt obligation of the issuer, not on the equity securities of the issuer or any form of security that is available to retail investors.

Additional terms for Japan only: Moody's Japan K.K. ("MJKK") is a wholly-owned credit rating agency subsidiary of Moody's Group Japan G.K., which is wholly-owned by Moody's Overseas Holdings Inc., a wholly-owned subsidiary of MCO. Moody's SF Japan K.K. ("MSFJ") is a wholly-owned credit rating agency subsidiary of MJKK. MSFJ is not a Nationally Recognized Statistical Rating Organization ("NRSRO"). Therefore, credit ratings assigned by MSFJ are Non-NRSRO Credit Ratings. Non-NRSRO Credit Ratings are assigned by an entity that is not a NRSRO and, consequently, the rated obligation will not qualify for certain types of treatment under U.S. laws. MJKK and MSFJ are credit rating agencies registered with the Japan Financial Services Agency and their registration numbers are FSA Commissioner (Ratings) No. 2 and 3 respectively.

MJKK or MSFJ (as applicable) hereby disclose that most issuers of debt securities (including corporate and municipal bonds, debentures, notes and commercial paper) and preferred stock rated by MJKK or MSFJ (as applicable) have, prior to assignment of any credit rating, agreed to pay to MJKK or MSFJ (as applicable) for credit ratings opinions and services rendered by it fees ranging from JPY125,000 to approximately JPY550,000,000.

MJKK and MSFJ also maintain policies and procedures to address Japanese regulatory requirements.

CHAPTER 10

Distressed Loan Investing[1]

The History of the Distressed Corporate Loan Market

Jason Friedman
Partner
Marathon Asset Management LP

Jeff Jacob
Partner
Marathon Asset Management LP

Overview of Chapter 11 of the Bankruptcy Code

Susan D. Golden
Partner
Kirkland & Ellis LLP

Joshua A. Sussberg
Partner
Kirkland & Ellis LLP

Critical Financial Considerations in Distressed Situations

Saul E. Burian
Managing Director
Houlihan Lokey

A Closer Look at Provisions Permitting Liability Management Transactions

Jessica Reiss
Head of U.S. Leveraged Loan Research
Covenant Review, a Fitch Solutions Service

---

[1] We would like to thank the authors of Chapter 9 of the first edition of this Handbook, Peter Santry, Joe Lamport, David Isenberg, Gregory Bray, and William Wagner. Portions of that chapter have been used in this chapter.

The History of the Distressed Corporate Loan Market[2]

Jason Friedman

Jeff Jacob
Marathon Asset Management LP

Distressed corporate loans have evolved from a little-known esoteric corner of the fixed income market to an asset class drawing a wide variety of investors and specialized investment strategies. Once considered solely the problems or mistakes of banks, they have evolved into an asset class sought after by investors at certain points in the credit cycle to enhance portfolio returns and by investors focused exclusively on distressed investment strategies. Distressed companies create significant analytical complexities and risk management challenges for loan portfolio managers, but they can also provide opportunities to earn outsized returns for knowledgeable and experienced investors. At times of economic weakness and heightened corporate defaults, distressed loans can account for as much as 10% of a well-diversified loan portfolio. During the Global Financial Crisis (GFC), at the peak of corporate defaults, 66% of the syndicated loan market traded at distressed levels (bid below 80 cents on the dollar), and roughly 20% of the syndicated loan market ultimately suffered a default from 2008-2010.

Distressed loans offer attractive investment opportunities for several reasons. First, they are highly risky. We have seen distressed loan recoveries significantly below par in situations where the company does not fully recover or survive a restructuring process (see later section "Factors Affecting Recovery Rates"). In situations in which companies require significantly more capital to stabilize their business, priming debt can layer and subordinate existing loans, also reducing their ultimate recoveries. Second, analyzing companies experiencing cyclical or secular decline can be extremely challenging and can result in a broad range of outcomes. Third, many

---

[2] The authors would like to thank Jordan Bryk and Randy Raisman for their assistance with and contribution to the article.

investors cannot own distressed debt due to noneconomic reasons, such as rating downgrades, inability to own certain types of securities such as equity, portfolio cash flow needs requiring the sale of nonperforming loans, and lack of resources required to navigate a restructuring process. For these reasons, when a company becomes distressed, forced selling often causes the prices of distressed loans to trade significantly below fundamental value. Taking advantage of these technical pressures is the cornerstone of distressed investing.

Before the leveraged buyout boom of the 1980s spawned what we now recognize as distressed investing, bankruptcy proceedings were usually attended by the debtor and traditional lending institutions such as banks. Today, with the complexity of capital structures and their evolution as a borrower becomes distressed, there are more diverse constituents involved than ever before. The varied potential outcomes in a distressed corporate situation often attract a much wider variety of investors than performing par loans. Value investors, direct lenders, high-yield funds, loan funds, hedge funds, and private equity investors can be attracted to the many different types of investments available in distressed situations. Investors can invest with the objective of lending fresh capital with the expectation of a return on, as well as a return of, capital. Others invest with the strategy of participating in a full bankruptcy restructuring through which a borrower utilizes the Chapter 11 bankruptcy process to delever its balance sheet, converting debt to equity and new debt instruments.

Widespread distressed opportunities, driven by heightened corporate defaults, typically follow periods of increased volumes of leveraged loan issuance, increased corporate leverage, and relaxed lending standards. Peak defaults in 1992 followed record high-yield and leveraged loan issuance to finance the buyout boom of the late 1980s (see Exhibits 10.1 and 10.2). Defaults spiked again in 2000 and 2001 following years of record new issuance in the 1990s to finance the growth of technology and Internet companies, many of which generated years of negative free cash flow. As seen in Exhibit 10.3, the rise in defaults that began in 2020 occurred after an 11-year economic expansion that culminated with record issuance and the creation of new multilayered and covenant-lite debt capital structures driven by insatiable investor demand for yield and relaxed lending standards.

Because of the size of the distressed and defaulted loan market, it cannot be ignored by managers actively investing in corporate

Distressed Loan Investing

EXHIBIT 10.1

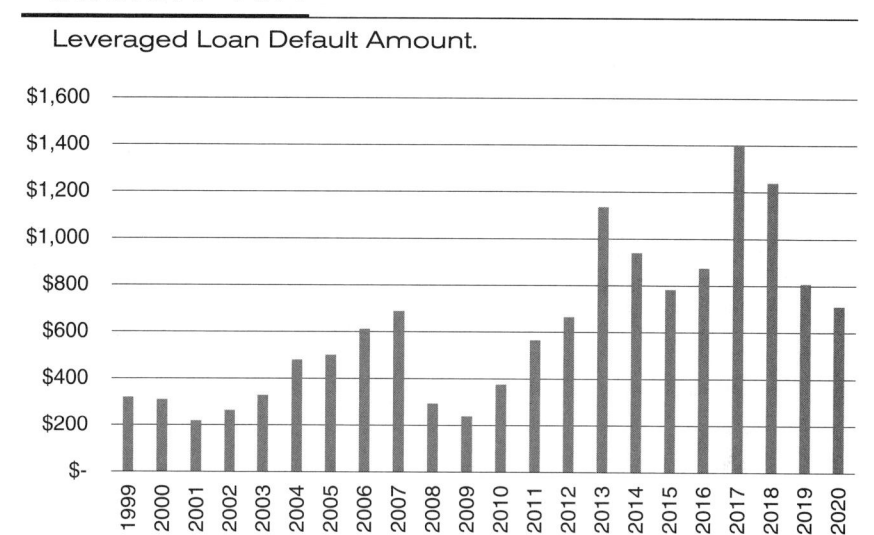

Leveraged Loan Default Amount.

Source: Refinitiv LPC.

EXHIBIT 10.2

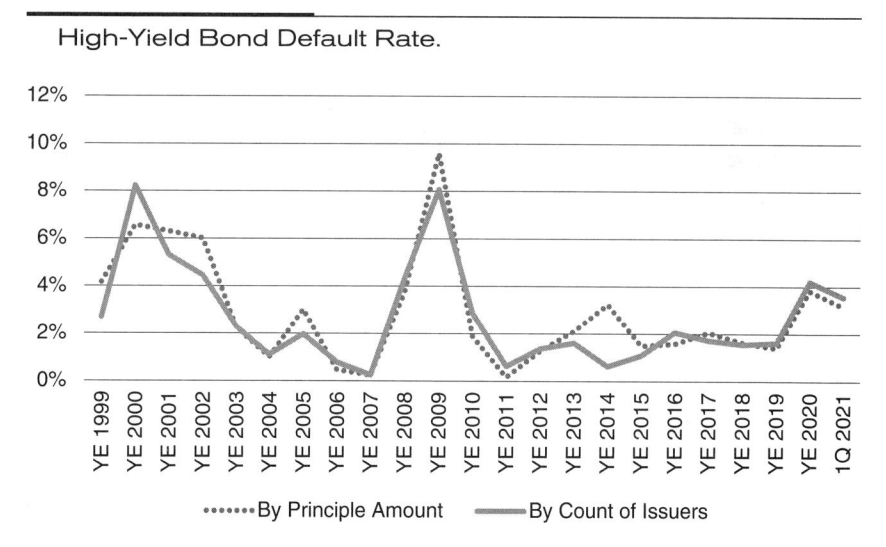

High-Yield Bond Default Rate.

······ By Principle Amount ——— By Count of Issuers

Source: S&P Global Market Intelligence.

loan instruments. At times of peak corporate default rates, distressed debt can amount to more than 50% of the leveraged loan market. Even a well-diversified loan fund can at these times have over 10% of its holdings in distressed loans (see Exhibit 10.3).

EXHIBIT 10.3

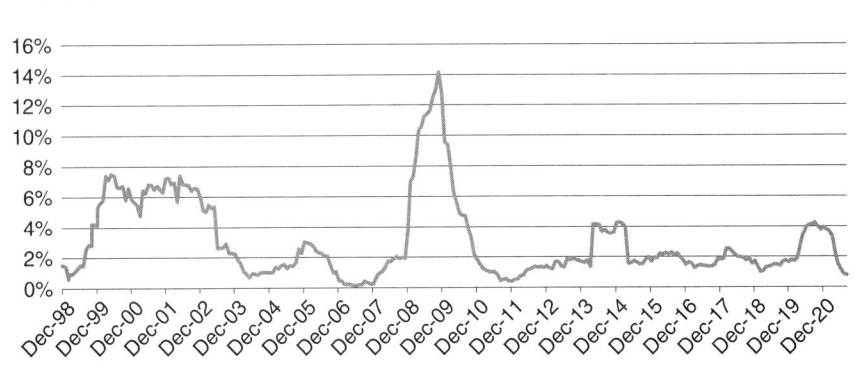

Percent of Loans Defaulted.

Source: JPMorgan Research.

The complexity associated with a restructuring process, the ability of borrowers to shift value outside the reach of creditors, the issues in valuing companies in financial decline, and the various constituents with sometimes conflicting interests all contribute to the decision to invest in, and subsequent challenges and opportunities of, distressed loans.

In this chapter we will discuss how companies become distressed, the tools available to companies in financial distress, the strategies for investors seeking to generate outsized returns by actively investing in distressed loans, and the legal and analysis factors portfolio managers must consider in order to maximize recoveries on loans that become distressed. We will discuss the multidisciplined approach required to succeed in distressed investing, factors that affect recoveries, the special analytical considerations that have emerged recently as the market has evolved, as well as the many types of players involved in this asset class.

WHAT OPTIONS EXIST FOR A DISTRESSED COMPANY?

Having examined the background of the distressed loan market, we will now consider the range of alternatives available to a company to manage through its challenges. As we will see, the path selected depends on many factors, including the nature and extent of the underlying problem facing the company (e.g., liquidity issues, approaching maturities, covenant violations or other credit document defaults, overleverage, and litigation), the amount of time, or "runway," to address the issue, the complexity of the capital structure, the parties involved, and the state of the capital markets. For more detailed discussion on strategies for operating distressed companies, see the section later in this chapter "Developing a Strategy and a Business Plan."

The alternatives available to a distressed firm generally fall into two broad buckets, liability management and comprehensive restructuring. *Liability management* is the industry term that refers to targeted adjustments to a company's capital structure to address or achieve a narrow purpose. A *comprehensive restructuring*, in contrast, refers to a major overhaul of the company's capital structure, often implemented using the powers of Chapter 11 of the Bankruptcy Code. Such transactions typically have the effect of significantly deleveraging the balance sheet in a manner that results in a change of control, and accordingly are only pursued once it becomes clear that liability management is insufficient to address the magnitude of the challenge facing the company.

LIABILITY MANAGEMENT TRANSACTIONS

As an alternative to a complete in-court or out-of-court restructuring, many distressed companies now work with their creditors to resolve capital structure issues with other types of actions. These alternative actions, broadly referred to as *liability management transactions*, attempt to address the same problems that a bankruptcy would, including technical defaults, liquidity issues, and overleverage, but do so in a less disruptive and less drastic ways. For debtors, these transactions present several advantages. First, companies can avoid the cost and negative publicity of a bankruptcy or complete restructuring. Second, it is much easier with liability transactions to leave equity in place; in a bankruptcy, in particular, equity will generally be mostly or fully impaired if all debtors do not recover in full. Third, if a debtor faces a particular problem that could be solved by, but would not fully justify, a complete restructuring (e.g., the company is fully solvent, but has breached a financial covenant), liability management transactions may provide a more targeted solution. Finally, liability management transactions often will give a debtor more time for the business to recover without drastic changes.

For creditors, liability management transactions can be attractive for similar reasons, including less cost, complexity, and publicity and a more targeted approach relative to a bankruptcy or complete restructuring. In the context of COVID-19 (and possibly other recession-like events), creditors generally also view giving debtors time to recover as mutually beneficial. These creditors presumably view forcing a comprehensive restructuring as short-sighted if an organic recovery is still possible, because a comprehensive restructuring might lock in impairment of their investment, cause significant operational and structural changes to the business, or force sales of assets in a weak market. Still, such preferences may vary by creditor types or even particular creditors; for example, bank participants in a syndicated loan, which would need to write down their investment in the event of a full restructuring and also prefer not to take equity, would presumably have more patience than a distressed private equity fund attempting to execute a loan-to-own strategy. Further, during periods of normal economic growth (rather than a recession), creditors might be less patient, especially if other attractive investments are available. Finally, in exchange for agreeing to liability management transactions, creditors generally receive some sort of concession from debtors (and, in fact, some liability management transaction types are primarily concessions to debtors).

The most common types of liability management transactions currently present in the market include "kick the can" transactions (including maturity extensions and covenant holidays), uptier exchanges, dropdowns of assets, injections of capital, and debt repurchases (often at a discount). Although each of these transaction types addresses a different need or issue, debtors and creditors often combine these various types of deals into single or serial transactions. As a result, liability management transactions are as diverse as they are now prevalent.

"KICK THE CAN" TRANSACTIONS

Kick the can transactions include several types of transactions that delay a likely issue relating to a debtor's viability or solvency, in the hopes that conditions for the debtor will improve, avoiding the need for additional action. The most common of these transactions types, particularly in the context of COVID, is covenant relief.[3] Even in the current covenant-lite credit environment, struggling companies often come close to or do violate their financial covenants. In the event that a company violates its covenant, creditor remedies typically include calling due the loan, declaring a technical default (in many cases, a technical default occurs automatically unless creditors affirmatively waive it), implementing additional restrictions on the debtor, or the option not to extend a loan. A covenant-relief transaction could be the simple waiver of an event of default (typically requiring the vote of a certain percentage of creditors) or a covenant holiday, a negotiated suspension or weakening of existing financial covenants for some predetermined period of time. Often, companies pay some consent fee to creditors to entice them to agree to a covenant modification, and may grant creditors other concessions. These covenant modifications allow a debtor to continue to operate normally, even as they fail to meet past performance benchmarks. Covenant modifications may be appealing to creditors when an unanticipated event significantly disrupts performance, but the creditors expect the company will be able to recover. As a result, they have been particularly common in the context of COVID-19, as many previously healthy businesses have been forced to shut down partially or completely.

A recent example of a covenant holiday involved Topgolf, a sports entertainment company that operates golf driving ranges that experienced significant disruption during COVID-19. Specifically, the company closed many locations entirely between March and August of 2020 and had to operate some locations at reduced capacity for months after due to local regulations. In September 2020, Topgolf reached an agreement with its term lenders to suspend the maximum leverage covenant (5.5 times) applicable to its $350 million term loan due 2026 and its $175 million senior secured revolver due 2024 through the first quarter of 2022. As part of the agreement, Topgolf paid its lenders a 37.5 basis points consent fee and increased the coupons on its debt by 75 basis points. Additionally, the company's financial sponsors agreed to equitize some of their debt and to make an additional equity contribution of $180 million. As part of the agreement, the company agreed to provide its creditors with call protection and enhanced reporting, and further restricted certain

---

[3] Leveraged Commentary & Data, an offering of S&P Global, tracks covenant relief transactions, and identified over 180 in 2020, compared to around 40 in 2019.

payments. This covenant holiday provides an example of creditors giving more time to a company that failed to hit performance benchmarks due to circumstances beyond its control, but also extracting significant concessions in doing so.

Another type of kick the can transaction is the maturity extension (sometimes referred to as an *amend and extend*). Typically, when a company's debt comes due, if the company does not intend to pay down the debt, it will attempt to refinance the debt on similar terms. Distressed companies typically are not able to fully refinance their debt on reasonable terms, and an upcoming maturity is often the impetus for a comprehensive restructuring. However, if a debtor and its creditors both believe that refinancing will not be possible at maturity, but that the company may recover enough to eventually refinance its debt, it could make sense for both parties to extend the debt instead of restructuring. Here again, the debtor avoids impairment of equity, the creditors avoid an immediate impairment of their debt, and everyone avoids potential lost value and business disruption from a comprehensive restructuring.

A maturity extension is typically executed either through a true amendment to a current credit agreement or through an exchange offer. An actual amendment would make sense for a debtor with a single creditor or a small group of creditors who are all willing to grant the extension, because an amendment that extends the term of a credit agreement would typically require unanimous consent. Simply amending the current agreement limits the effort of revising or creating a new contract and maintains contract terms with which both sides are familiar. However, for debt that is more widely held or where the creditors and debtors want to significantly modify the terms of the debt, an exchange offer is likely a better way to extend the debt. In an exchange offer, a debtor offers its creditors the option of exchanging existing debt for a new debt instrument. In the case of maturity extensions, the new paper has a later maturity debt, and often includes other features favorable to creditors, such as higher interest rates, partial repayment in cash, and uptiering. Debtors also typically offer some sort of consent fees. Prior to announcing an exchange offer, a debtor will often negotiate with its larger creditors to ensure there is interest in the terms of the exchange, and may announce initial support of the exchange offer along with the offer. Typically, a debtor will require that a certain percentage of debtholders opt into the exchange for the exchange to actually take place (often around 90%). Because the exchange is not binding on any creditors that do not consent, this provides certainty to both the debtor and the creditors.[4]

Sequa Corporation, an industrials company that provides metal coating and aftermarket aerospace and airline services, provides an example of a successful maturity extension through an exchange offer. Sequa, which is owned by The Carlyle Group, had three primary debt instruments: a $135 million secured revolver and an $892 million first lien term loan, both due in 2021, and a $350 million second lien term loan due 2022. Following initial COVID-19 shutdowns, which severely impacted airlines, Sequa's debt quality, which was already below investment grade, fell further. Moody's, for example, downgraded the ratings of Sequa's debt in April 2020, decreasing the company's family rating from Caa1 to Caa3, the first lien from B3 to Caa2, and the second lien term loan from Caa2 to Ca.[5] These ratings would typically make a normal refinancing difficult if not improbable. Facing over $1 billion in maturities in 2021, Sequa initiated an exchange offer to extend the maturity of all three debt facilities by two years. In exchange for this extension, Sequa offered a 50-basis point cash consent fee, a 175-basis point increase in coupon rate of extending debt, first-out priority for extending debt over nonextending lenders, and either up to $100 million of pro rata cash paydown or an additional 2.5% paid-in-kind (PIK) fee. In connection with this exchange offer, Sequa also reached an agreement with certain existing lenders to provide $200 million as part of a new first lien term loan (which would be pari passu to extending debt) and received a commitment from The Carlyle Group to provide an additional $56 million in preferred equity funding. The exchange was a success, as over 99% of existing debt opted in, with 80% selecting the PIK option rather than the cash paydown.

---

[4] If the debtor does not reach its threshold, they may modify the offer or explore other options. For creditors, the threshold ensures that consenting parties will not see a significant portion of nonconsenting debt paid out in cash in the short term. Additionally, debtors may offer uptiering of debt as part of a maturity extension exchange to discourage holdouts; although holdouts would still get paid first in theory, the debt would be subordinated if a bankruptcy occurs prior to the original maturity date.

[5] https://www.moodys.com/research/Moodys-downgrades-Sequa-ratings-CFR-to-Caa3-outlook-negative–PR_423499

The final type of kick the can transaction is conversion of cash interest to PIK interest. PIK interest is interest that is not paid in cash on coupon dates, but instead accumulates and compounds on these dates as part of the principal of the debt.[6] Like a maturity extension, a debtor might effect a conversion to PIK interest through either an amendment to a debt document or an exchange offer. A debtor generally would want to convert cash interest to PIK interest in the event that its cash interest payments have become restrictively large or if it has other short- or medium-term liquidity issues. Typically, a conversion to PIK interest is accompanied by an increase in coupon rate (often around 200 basis points); in some cases, a debtor may negotiate the option to either pay cash or PIK interest, with the PIK interest rate being higher, providing the debtor future flexibility as its liquidity situation changes. Conversions to PIK interest often accompany other liability management transactions, such as debt extensions. Because PIK debt will still eventually come due, creditors generally need to be convinced that there is some chance of recovery in order to give up the relative certainty of immediate cash payments from a distressed debtor.

UPTIER EXCHANGES AND DROP-DOWN TRANSACTIONS

An uptier exchange is the exchange of one type of more junior debt instrument for another more senior debt instrument. For example, unsecured debt could be exchanged for secured debt, or secured debt could be exchanged for more senior secured debt or debt secured by additional assets or entities. The purpose of an uptier is to give a creditor class additional rights, including in some cases security interests. Because uptier transactions favor creditors that participate in them, they are typically paired with other changes to debt that favors the debtor, such as a principal reduction, an injection of new capital, or a maturity extension. Although an uptier exchange may be used simply to limit the ability of a debtor to accumulate further debt senior to an existing debt instrument, very

---

[6] For example, for a $1 million term loan with semiannual coupons and a 5% annual interest rate, cash interest would result in two $25,000 cash payments over the course of the first year, whereas PIK interest would result in the principal amount of the loan first increasing to $1.025 million after six months and then to $1.051 million after a year.

often in distressed situations they primarily function to favor one class of existing creditors over another.

For example, in August 2020, Boardriders, a sports apparel company owned by Oaktree, required additional capital. At the time, its primary debt instrument was a $450 million first lien term loan due 2024. To get this capital, it reached an agreement with Oaktree, some of its existing first lien lenders, and the French government, another creditor of the company. The first lien lenders invested $45 million of new capital into a new superpriority A term loan tranche and had their $286 million in first lien term loan debt rolled up into a new superpriority B2 term loan tranche. Oaktree also invested $45 million of new capital and had $35 million of its existing first lien debt rolled up with this new capital into a new superpriority B1 term loan tranche. Finally, the French government invested $45 million of new capital and had this new capital and its existing $14 million in junior debt rolled up into a new secured facility that was senior to all old debt, but junior to all other new debt. As a result of the transaction, the $119 million that remained under the old senior secured term loan became junior to $470 million in new superpriority debt.

Because uptier exchanges often subordinate one class of debt to another, they can add a coercive element to an otherwise consensual exchange. In a public exchange, a debtor may use the implied threat of debt subordination through an uptier exchange to pressure creditors to accept changes such as principal reductions or maturity extensions. Any holdout would then be less well positioned in the event of a bankruptcy or comprehensive restructuring.[7] Uptiering may be limited by existing debt documents or intercreditor agreements, which often restrict the amount of additional debt that a debtor can accrue or which assets can be pledged as collateral. As with maturity extensions, uptier transactions can be executed through an amendment to existing debt documents or a debt exchange. However, modifying debt restrictions and baskets often requires a consent threshold less than unanimity (which

---

[7] In some cases, the benefit of an uptier transaction can largely be illusory if all or most creditors opt in. In the case of an uptiering of already secured debt, the creditors may not receive any new rights other than priority over creditors invested in the same debt facility that do not opt in. To derive actual benefit from the uptiering of existing secured debt, creditors may require the debtor to securitize additional unpledged assets (to the extent there are any) or tighten debt baskets relative to the old document.

would generally be required, for example, to extend or reduce debt outright). Therefore, a typical uptier exchange might ask creditors both to consent to necessary amendments to the existing debt document (and possibly an intercreditor document) and to pledge their debt to the exchange.

While the mechanics differ, drop-down transactions are executed for similar reasons to and often in conjunction with uptier exchanges. In a drop-down transaction, a debtor will move certain assets controlled by a subsidiary encumbered with debt into an unrestricted subsidiary. This may allow the debtor to effectively uptier certain debt through structural subordination (i.e., by moving the debt to the unrestricted subsidiary or granting a lien on the otherwise now unencumbered assets of that subsidiary) or to raise new debt at the level of the unrestricted subsidiary, where a refinancing would not otherwise be possible. Modern credit agreements tend to restrict the ability of debtors to move assets between subsidiaries without reasonable compensation to do such dropdowns, and such moves may face the threat of litigation. Some debt in the market still lacks such restrictions, so pure dropdowns, though rare, do occur. It is more common, however, for debt to allow creditors to waive dropdown restrictions with limited consent from creditors (e.g., a simple majority). In such a case, a debtor could agree with creditors to allow a dropdown of assets while granting consenting creditors debt at the unrestricted subsidiary, as part of an exchange that effectively results in an uptiering.

Party City, a publicly traded retailer of party supplies, presents a recent example of a dropdown with the consent of existing creditors. In May 2020, Party City entered into a transaction support agreement with an ad hoc group of holders of the company's $350 million in senior notes due in 2023 and $500 million in senior notes due 2026. The agreement involved moving Party City's foil balloon business to an unrestricted subsidiary, known as Anagram. As part of the significantly discounted exchange, existing noteholders had the opportunity to exchange the 2023 and 2026 senior notes for $100 million in second lien notes issued by Anagram (issued at $117.65 per $1,000 exchanged), up to $185 million in first lien notes at the corporate entity (issued at $217.65 per $1,000 exchanged), and up to 19.9% of Party City's common equity. The company also offered consenting creditors the opportunity to fund up to $50 million in new first lien notes at the unrestricted subsidiary. Given the combination of uptiering and dropping down, Party City was able to secure the participation of nearly 85% of its senior noteholders, despite the significant discount in debt value.

INJECTION OF CAPITAL

Although third parties tend to be reluctant to lend to distressed companies, these companies often face the need for additional capital to meet basic liquidity and investment needs, or even to pay for other liability management transactions.[8] Often, a distressed company seeking capital will turn to existing creditors or equity for its financing needs. Typically, an existing creditor will invest additional capital as new debt at par. In order to entice creditors to invest, a debtor may offer a new, higher tier of securitization and may also offer to uptier the existing debt of a creditor offering additional capital (as was the case in the Boardriders transaction summarized earlier). A debtor may also offer some equity upside to creditors offering additional capital. Where a distressed company is owned by a financial sponsor or by a separate nondistressed holding entity, the equity holder may also contribute new capital as either debt or equity. Debt contributions by equity operate in much the same way as debt contributions by existing creditors (consider again Boardriders). In the case of an equity contribution, a financial sponsor or holding company generally simply injects additional capital into the business without significant change to its position in the capital structure. With such an investment, an equity holder may seem to be giving money for nothing on the surface, an action that one might expect private equity groups and hedge funds being particularly opposed to. However, realistic equity holders may realize that injecting equity capital into the business is the only way to either entice creditors to take desirable action (e.g., covenant holidays, maturity extensions, or debt capital injections) or to avoid a comprehensive restructuring or bankruptcy, either of which could wipe out equity in part or entirely.[9]

---

[8] Consider, for example, the prevalence of DIP financing in Chapter 11 bankruptcy proceedings.
[9] The Sequa transaction provides a kind of in-between example. There, the company's financial sponsor, The Carlyle Group, provided preferred equity funding, which does technically modify the company's capital structure and perhaps also The Carlyle Group's rights to dividends; however, the capital structure remains effectively similar so long as The Carlyle Group owns all or most of both the preferred and the common equity.

A recent example of an equity sponsor providing an equity injection involved CSM Bakery Solutions, a manufacturer and distributor of bakery products that is based in the United States but earns most of its revenue in Europe. Prior to June 2020, CSM had two primary credit facilities coming due soon, a $448 million first lien term loan due in July 2020 and a $210 million second lien term loan due 2021. In order to entice creditors to extend the first lien term loan by 18 months and the second lien term loan by 7 months, CSM's financial sponsor, Rhone Capital, agreed to provide the company with €50 million of new equity capital. In addition to the equity contribution, the creditors also received as concessions increased interest rates (though most of the second lien interest was converted to PIK interest), consent fees, and tightened financial and reporting covenants. However, Rhone Capital remained the primary equity holder.

DISCOUNTED DEBT REPURCHASES AND EXCHANGES

In some cases, a distressed debtor may seek to retire debt at a discount without a comprehensive restructuring. Of the liability management transactions discussed, this transaction type generally reflects the least optimism among creditors about the debtor's prospects. In contrast to kick the can transactions, where creditors provide the debtor with the opportunity to recover, in discounted debt transactions, creditors come to terms with the inability of the debtor to pay down its debt in full. In the case of discounted debt repurchases, creditors agree to sell their debt back to the debtor at a discounted price. In this case, creditors accept the discount and loss of coupon payments in exchange for the certainty of immediate partial repayment in cash, while debtors are able to deleverage their capital structure at a discount. Often debtors will pursue a debt repurchase through a public Dutch auction, where the debtor offers a bidding range and a creditor can opt to bid or not participate. Typically, in a debt repurchase, the debtor limits the repurchase based either on an amount of principal tendered or a total amount of cash distributed. This format allows creditors to self-sort based on how they value the company's debt and ensure that the distressed debtor, which often has limited access to capital and cash, makes the best use of its available funds. Alternatively, a debtor may offer a single price (or a single price with an additional early tender payment) to its creditors, seek to surreptitiously repurchase its own debt in the open market, or negotiate with creditors to repurchase debt on an individual basis. Common sources of capital for use in a debt repurchase might include a capital injection from equity, an asset sale, or a drawdown of a revolver commitment (typically where the revolver is above the repurchased debt in the capital structure).

A recent example of a discounted debt repurchase involved Tupperware, a publicly traded multilevel marketing company known for selling food containers. In May 2020, Tupperware initially offered to repurchase up to $175 million in aggregate principal of its $600 million in senior notes due 2021 at a discount of $420 ($450 for early tenders) per $1,000 of notes tendered. After negative feedback from creditors, Tupperware increased the offer to $575 per $1,000 of notes tendered. Ultimately, Tupperware was able to repurchase $97.6 million of principal of its senior notes, completing the repurchase in early July 2020.

Debtors and creditors may also agree to a discount in principal amount as part of a debt exchange. Typically, the exchange will need to otherwise be attractive to creditors (e.g., an uptier or an increase in interest rate) in order to convince the creditors to accept a discount without a paydown. Alternatively, a debtor and its creditors may also agree to an exchange that involves both debt-for-debt at a discount and some amount of cash paydown. Regardless of the process, the debtor's offer must still be competitive with or above the market and attractive to potential participants, because creditors can generally trade debt with each other or with other market participants or attempt to force a bankruptcy or comprehensive restructuring, in which case the creditors may end up with the company's equity.

COMPREHENSIVE RESTRUCTURING

In general, the most attractive restructuring alternative available to borrowers and lenders alike in a "perfect" restructuring world would be the collective negotiation and implementation of a consensual restructuring scheme without the need to resort to court supervision. The fundamental reasons are clear: out-of-court workouts provide an opportunity to restructure more rapidly and at far less expense than would typically be expected in a traditional Chapter 11 bankruptcy proceeding.

Unfortunately, not all borrowers and creditor groups can avail themselves of the opportunity to restructure without a formal proceeding. For example, if amendments to a credit agreement contemplate an extension of the maturity date, a postponement of regularly scheduled payments, or a sale of assets representing substantial collateral, a creditor group may not be able to muster the unanimous consent that is generally required to give effect to such amendments and their underlying strategic and financial objectives. Additionally, participants in a consensual restructuring process may not be able to carry out their plans without the assistance of the Bankruptcy Court. A company that is in financial distress, for example, may wish to sell certain of its assets on a selective basis in order to pay down debt, generate working capital, or eliminate the costs associated with maintaining or operating the assets to be sold. At the same time, an otherwise willing buyer may be reluctant to proceed in the absence of a court order declaring that the sale is final and is free and clear of any liens or claims of other creditors.

Prearranged and prepackaged plans help to overcome these issues while still avoiding some of the costs associated with a traditional Chapter 11 proceeding. The need for unanimous consent is also avoided, as the Bankruptcy Code requires the approval of only "two thirds in amount and one half in number" of each class of creditors. Please see the "Voting and Confirmation" section later in this chapter for a further discussion of voting on plan confirmation. In each case, the plan is negotiated prior to the borrower's filing a petition with the Bankruptcy Court and becoming subject to the protections of the Bankruptcy Code. Prearranged plans are negotiated and agreed to by the borrower—as a prospective debtor—and the requisite creditors, and the terms are set forth in an agreement that is often referred to as a *lock-up agreement* or *restructuring support agreement*. Under that agreement, the creditors agree to vote in favor of a plan of reorganization that conforms to the agreed-upon terms when such a plan is filed with the Bankruptcy Court in a formal Chapter 11 proceeding. A prepackaged plan is not only negotiated prior to the filing but also approved by a vote of the requisite creditors. As a result, a prepackaged plan approved by the requisite creditors may be presented to the Bankruptcy Court at the time of the filing.

Finally, many cases simply require the supervision of the Bankruptcy Court and the structure of a traditional Chapter 11 proceeding in order to restructure the debtor's business and financial affairs. The Bankruptcy Court can provide a central forum for the settlement of outstanding litigation issues or disputes among creditors. In addition, the certainty of a Bankruptcy Court order will underscore restructuring efforts with far greater finality than would be enjoyed by the parties to a consensual agreement in an out-of-court restructuring.

At the same time, a traditional Chapter 11 proceeding has certain drawbacks. The first and perhaps most obvious is cost. A restructuring process that is conducted from start to finish under the supervision of the Bankruptcy Court can be far more costly than out-of-court alternatives and can take considerably longer to complete. In an out-of-court restructuring, control of the process is generally concentrated in the borrower and the lender group. In a formal Chapter 11 proceeding, that control is significantly diluted, as the restructuring process falls under the supervision of the Bankruptcy Court, and third parties (including the U.S. trustee and creditors' committees) join in the negotiation and development of a plan of reorganization.

WHO ARE THE PARTIES IN DISTRESSED SITUATIONS?

The complexity of the workout process is in large part a function of the many different players involved, each of whom brings their own set of motivations and perspectives. Broadly speaking, these players can be categorized into the *debtor*, the *creditors*, and the *judge*.

The Debtor

The *debtor* or *debtor in possession* (in Chapter 11 bankruptcies) is the commonly used term to refer to the company. The company's decision-making ultimately resides with its board of directors, whose fiduciary duties in the context of distress expand to include the company's creditors. Private company boards are typically controlled by the private equity owners, whereas public equity boards are often more diverse. Private equity firms have generally become more aggressive in recent years to explore creative *liability management* alternatives that extend their equity option before handing control of the company to its creditors. As a result, independent directors are frequently appointed as a company approaches a restructuring in order to mitigate conflicts of interest.

The management team will continue to exert day-to-day control of the business and is answerable to the board. However, in the context of Chapter 11 bankruptcy, business decisions that are outside of the ordinary course of business require court approval.

Debtors will lean very heavily on its slate of advisors because it is often the case that the board and management team have little to no experience in distress or a restructuring. The company's legal advisors will, among other things, advise the board on its fiduciary duties, the range of alternatives, and shepherd the company through Chapter 11 bankruptcy (if necessary) and negotiate and draft all transaction documentation.

The company's financial advisor will similarly be deeply involved in the evaluation of transaction alternatives, help the company assess its business and value-maximization strategies, prepare financial forecasts and valuation analyses, and coordinate with the various creditor classes to provide the requisite diligence information. The company may also hire an operational consultant to help manage near-term cash flows and liquidity.

The Creditors

Today's capital structures are increasingly complex. As a result, restructuring negotiations are often multifaceted, requiring the consent of several different tranches in order to reach an agreement. Moreover, the types of creditors involved within a given tranche are diverse. These intercreditor and intracreditor dynamics are far from static because stakeholders may trade loans and securities throughout the case (unless restricted), resulting in holder turnover.

Different creditor types bring very different priorities. *Long-only* investors, the broad label which includes collateralized loan obligations (CLOs) and other high-yield performing credit funds, are often par buyers of the underlying loans or securities. When they initially made the investment, their expectation was for the business to perform and to be paid principal and interest on time. Their participation in a restructuring is not by design; rather, something unexpected and disappointing occurred. Their overarching goal is return *of* capital, not return *on* capital. As a result, they prioritize cash payouts or takeback paper, or some combination thereof. However, they may ultimately have to equitize some or all of their claim, but it is generally a less desirable outcome. In fact, they have structural issues that limit their ability to participate in new equity transactions and that ascribe little or no value to equity interests.

Distressed investors, on the other hand, seek to buy loans or securities at a discount. They generally buy them with an eye toward becoming an active participant in the restructuring process in order to influence the structure, the timing, and the form of consideration distributed. Investors of this type typically have a long-term view and are comfortable using bankruptcy to gain control of the borrower's equity upon exit. They are achieving the same end result as a private equity fund that purchases a company in a more traditional manner and are seeking similar returns. Finally, these lenders are more inclined to put up new money when needed, especially if it takes the form of an equity rights offering.

Depending upon the scope and complexity of a particular restructuring, lenders (and borrowers) may need to engage professional advisors and consultants in addition to existing legal counsel. Restructuring advisors can provide industry expertise and can assist greatly in the analysis of the borrower's financial distress as well as in the evaluation of strategic alternatives and the development of a restructured business plan.

WHAT INVESTMENT OPPORTUNITIES EXIST IN DISTRESSED SITUATIONS?

Distressed borrowers provide several types of opportunities for investors. These opportunities include "value" investments in discounted senior secured loans, bonds, or other securities of distressed companies, rescue loans to companies going through distress, debtor-in-possession (DIP) loans to companies in bankruptcy, fulcrum security investments in companies going through bankruptcy, or holdup value strategies. Additionally, distressed investors can invest in situations that lead to debt exchanges, so that a distressed company can avoid bankruptcy and fix its balance sheet out of court. Finally, distressed investors at times make equity investments in companies that are either overleveraged or choosing to use bankruptcy as a means to address liabilities due to litigation or other cataclysmic events.

Distressed investing is one form of value investing. This type of opportunity is presented in distressed loans and securities all the time. The simplest form of a distressed value investment occurs when a borrower is going through fundamental changes in its business, which leaves its existing lenders feeling uneasy about the immediate future prospects for the borrower. This fear creates natural sellers of debt, which generally leads to an imbalance of supply and demand in the credit market, which is where the price for debt is ultimately set. An investor in these cases often purchases a distressed loan upon the announcement of a restructuring or the filing of a disclosure statement, looking for "value" early in a distressed case, and exits once the market recognizes that value. This type of investment was first practiced by hedge funds with backgrounds in the risk arbitrage business; many of the early distressed investors viewed distressed investing as a countercyclical business to their core deal-driven risk arbitrage efforts. Sometimes these situations create minor dislocations in debt trading prices, whereas in other more extreme situations there are major pricing dislocations.

In its simplest form, the investor buys the loan at a discount to the value of the consideration he or she will receive upon exiting the restructuring or bankruptcy. The discount often exists because the lender is getting paid to deal with all the issues and complexities surrounding a company's emergence from Chapter 11 bankruptcy. Given the substantial holdings in the loan market by CLOs, which are meaningfully penalized for holding defaulted or distressed loans, there often exists a substantial discount to value during the bankruptcy or reorganization period. Potential delays and last-minute changes to the plan and complex operational issues involved in the distribution out of the bankruptcy also can help to create the arbitrage opportunity. Usually, the consideration received once the company exits from bankruptcy (cash, new bank loans and/or notes, and sometimes equity or equity-like instruments) will exceed the value of the prepetition debt, creating the arbitrage opportunity.

In less extreme cases the market-clearing exercise will be orderly, which will result in a less severe change in trading prices. In the example of a pharmaceutical company that was expecting a drug or other product to receive FDA approval, and the approval was not obtained, lenders or other debtholders may be nervous about the company's business prospects going forward and will look to sell their holdings. If the regulatory news is not devastating to the company's ability to survive, its debt will trade at lower prices but not at levels that would reflect an ultimate restructuring of the company's balance sheet. This does create value-investing opportunities for debt investors. This is particularly attractive for sophisticated investors who have well-informed views on other products that the company may have in its pipeline, or on other sources of growth for the company that some of the company's existing lenders are not aware of. This is no different from classic value loan investing, and oftentimes creates tremendous opportunities for well-prepared investors.

Another form of distressed investing is rescue lending. Here a company may be going through an operational hiccup or a fundamental business change that is presenting the company with financial headwinds. This is particularly troubling for leveraged companies that have large fixed interest and principal payments. To avoid having to go into bankruptcy, troubled companies often seek rescue financing. These types of financings typically come in the form of loans and are oftentimes lent by the company's existing lenders. Because these loans are essentially rescuing the company from a bad situation and they are inherently very risky, the loans are often very expensive. The loans also usually benefit from enhanced protections for lenders, including strict covenants that bar the company from incurring any additional debt, paying any dividends, or making any acquisitions. Rescue loans sometimes rank senior to all other debt in the troubled company's capital structure, so that parties lending the money to the troubled company can minimize their risk of impairment by being the very first lenders to be repaid from the company's assets. Additionally, rescue loans typically have very high interest rates to compensate the rescue lenders for the risk being taken, and the loans typically offer call protection, which ensures that the debt will remain outstanding even if the troubled company's prospects have improved, which allows the rescue lender to continue to earn its high rate of interest even if the company is on sounder financial footing. Finally, rescue loans sometimes provide that the rescue lender is given board representation at the troubled company, because the rescue lender is taking significant risk and should be able to have a voice in the future direction of the troubled company.

Another form of senior secured loans that distressed investors make are debtor in possession, or DIP, loans. These are loans that are made to companies that have filed for bankruptcy and they typically benefit from special protections that are mandated by the Bankruptcy Court. Most DIP loans are characterized as priming loans, which means that they prime, or rank senior to, all of the company's existing debt. This requires court approval because the

DIP lenders will have a claim that attaches on a priority basis to the collateral pledged in favor of the company's existing lenders. For this reason, the company's existing lenders are typically the parties providing the DIP loan. These loans also benefit from being granted an administrative claim by the Bankruptcy Court. Administrative claims are required to be repaid in full before a company can emerge from bankruptcy. This is an added protection that DIP lenders receive in bankruptcy, because it ensures that the DIP loan will be repaid because the company cannot get out of bankruptcy without paying off all of its administrative claims. Apart from the priority position in the capital structure and the administrative claim status afforded to DIP lenders, DIP loans also benefit from high interest rates that are supposed to compensate lenders for making a loan to a company in bankruptcy, and they typically benefit from covenants or other milestones that give the DIP lenders control over the company in bankruptcy. These covenants usually include minimum liquidity tests and milestones that are set to encourage the company to use the bankruptcy process to the fullest extent possible. Finally, DIP loans are designed to ensure that if the company does not successfully restructure in bankruptcy, then there is an additional mechanism that DIP lenders can use to ensure repayment of their loan. In the case of retailers, which typically carry large inventory balances, DIP lenders will use a liquidation and going-out-of-business sale process as an alternative to a restructuring as a means for getting repaid. Recall that DIP lenders typically have liens on all of the assets of the company and that DIP lenders will use their liens to ensure repayment. Requiring a retailer to close stores and liquidate inventory is a good example of this. Another way that DIP lenders are often repaid is through sale processes where companies sell off some of their assets. Again, with an all-asset pledge, DIP lenders will benefit from asset sales, because the proceeds from the sale will be used to repay the DIP loan.

Fulcrum security investing is the most classic form of distressed investing. Distressed investors, in their quest for value, often will buy the security in a company's capital structure where they believe the last dollar of value exists. This security is often referred to as the *fulcrum*, because it will be partially addressed with new debt issued when the company emerges from bankruptcy and partially addressed through the issuance of new equity in the company. These are often considered to be "distressed-for-control" investments given the post restructuring equity ownership of the participants. Fulcrum security investing is incredibly attractive to distressed investors because the investor is able to receive equity in the company at a time when the company is healing from the issues that led to its distress and can present a tremendous upside. This is because the valuation for the company is struck at a point in time before the company is able to benefit from improvements in its industry or cost structure, depending on the nature of the issues that led it to restructure. The distressed-for-control investor will usually sit on creditors' committees and will look to maximize the return by influencing the structure, the timing, and the form of consideration distributed to the creditors when the company is restructured. As a result of their entry during the riskiest point in a bankruptcy and their activist role in the process, distress-for-control investors demand the highest compensation for their investment. While historically the fulcrum security was often at a level below the senior secured loan, with the advent of higher-levered as well as loan-only structures, the fulcrum security has in certain cases migrated into the secured loan asset class.

The most classic examples of fulcrum security investing in recent history occurred in the airline and automotive industries. In both situations, the large corporations in those industries used bankruptcy to address expensive labor contracts that were plaguing their cost structures. Because of the uncertainty associated with bankruptcy filings, traditional holders of airline and automotive company loans looked to sell their holdings, and distressed investors were often the only buyers of this debt. Airline loans and bonds traded for pennies on the dollar because of this dynamic and were actively purchased by distressed investors. During bankruptcy, the airlines were able to eliminate unneeded employees and renegotiate aircraft lease terms and exorbitant labor compensation packages. The distressed investors converted their debt into equity in the airlines, and once the airlines emerged from bankruptcy the prospects for their business looked so strong that the new equity traded to very rich valuations. Similar dynamics played out in the financial services industry when large banks, insurance companies, and other financial players were forced into bankruptcy as a result of the GFC. There are several examples of distressed investors earning many multiples on their initial investment in the fulcrum securities of the banks and insurance companies that restructured due to the GFC.

Distressed investors also get involved in debt exchange transactions. These typically occur out of court but have the same intention of deleveraging an overlevered, heavily indebted borrower's balance sheet. Out-of-court debt exchanges are a quicker and less costly way for a company to clean up its balance sheet. Sometimes company's look to complete debt exchanges when they have upcoming debt maturities that may not be currently refinanceable. If a company is able to organize its lenders and offer the lenders a new loan with a longer maturity, some lenders may be willing to exchange their existing debt for this new debt and enable the company to get more time to fix its business so that it ultimately can complete a traditional debt refinancing. Debt exchanges are more typical for distressed borrowers, because their debt generally trades at discounts to par, and distressed investors that have purchased the debt at discounted prices are willing to exchange their debt for new debt with better covenants and/or better interest rates in exchange for more time before the ultimate debt maturity. Debt exchanges are also an attractive opportunity for a distressed borrower to eliminate some of its debts. If a distressed borrower's debt is trading at distressed prices, but the company management believes that the prospects for the business will be improving, the company could launch a debt exchange where it offers the market new debt but at a discount to par. The simplest example of this would be a company that had debt trading at 50% of par and the company offers the holders a new loan at 75% of the original principal balance. This is attractive to the distressed investors holding the debt trading at 50% of par, and it is attractive to the company because it is able to eliminate 25% of its debt. These types of transactions occur all the time because they are efficient and do not require all of the costs and negative stigma associated with a bankruptcy filing. However, companies that use debt exchanges to address their overleveraged balance sheets miss out on all of the operation improvements that can be achieved in bankruptcy. These include cost savings associated with contract renegotiations and access to new capital on attractive terms because of the added protections that lenders obtain in DIP loans.

The holdup value investor, or nuisance investor, typically invests based upon documentation or structural clauses that allow the investor to "hold up" the process to extract value from distressed or bankrupt entities. Although typically viewed unfavorably by a large part of the market as well as by the corporations themselves, these investors typically insert themselves into situations whereby they can purchase deeply distressed loans or securities and establish a class or blocking position that can stall or slow the restructuring until the investor received incremental value.

FACTORS AFFECTING RECOVERY RATES

Now that we have discussed the types of investors focused on distressed senior loans and the types of investments in distressed companies' debt, we need to look at loan recovery rates (loss given default) to understand how a portfolio of senior secured loans will fare over time. Note that there have been significant changes over time in the loan market as it has evolved from a highly protected, senior-most security in the capital structure with strong covenants and restrictive clauses to a more flexible market and structure whereby investors have the ability at times to insert incremental capital at a pari passu (equal in seniority) or even senior position in the structure in distressed situations. These changes have altered the recovery rates over time, as seen in Exhibit 10.4, as well as the paths to potential monetization of distressed loans.

EXHIBIT 10.4

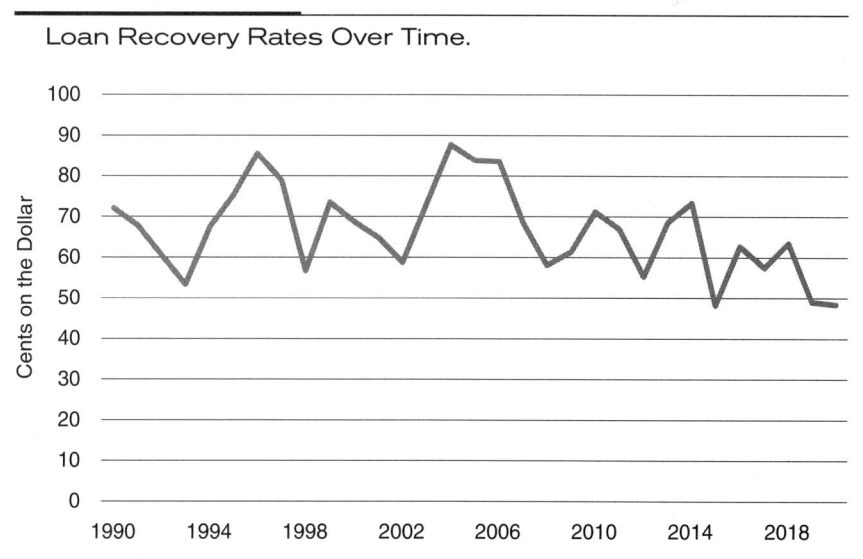

Loan Recovery Rates Over Time.

Source: JP Morgan.

Leveraged loans historically saw a strong benefit from their position at the top of the capital structure and from the collateral that is usually pledged as security only for the loans. As a result, corporate loans for over three decades have enjoyed the highest recovery rates among corporate debt obligations. While that relationship still holds true today as seen in Exhibit 10.5 by the relatively higher recovery rate for loans versus other obligations, the risks and paths to monetization have meaningfully changed over time and have decreased the overall recoveries over time.

EXHIBIT 10.5

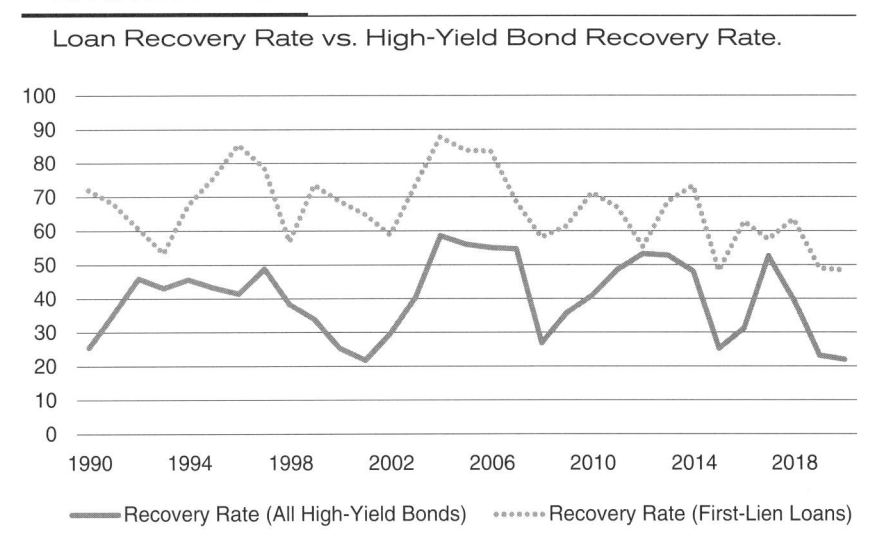

Loan Recovery Rate vs. High-Yield Bond Recovery Rate.

―― Recovery Rate (All High-Yield Bonds)   ······ Recovery Rate (First-Lien Loans)

Source: JP Morgan.

SUMMARY

While distressed loans were initially a by-product of the corporate syndicated market for leveraged loans, especially during recessions following prolonged periods of relaxed credit standards, they have become a more institutional and broadly traded asset class over time. These loans have continued to perform well versus other corporate debt instruments throughout the history of the leveraged credit markets and continue to attract a diverse group of investors with varied strategies and action plans. Distressed loans have become an accepted asset class more broadly over the past decade and a core holding across a broad group of asset managers.

We began this section by discussing the history of the distressed market and the attractiveness of distressed loan investing as an asset class. We then described how the investors and the available options for companies with distressed loans have evolved over time while exploring many of the strategies investors in distressed loans may utilize. We closed this section attempting to measure the performance over time of distressed loans and bonds by looking at the default rate history and recovery rate information over time. Comprehending this asset class and its market is a necessity for all credit managers, as distressed loans will make up a significant portion of their holdings at some point during an economic cycle, and have become a core asset class in and of itself for many managers. In the next article, we will explore Chapter 11 proceedings in detail.

Overview of Chapter 11 of the Bankruptcy Code[10]

Susan D. Golden

Joshua A. Sussberg
Kirkland & Ellis LLP

THE BANKRUPTCY CODE

Like much of the rest of Article I, Section 8 of the U.S. Constitution, which gave Congress certain authorities, such as the power to coin money, raise an army, and establish uniform rules of naturalization, the Bankruptcy Clause was constructed to remedy a persistent problem under the Articles of Confederation. Prior to 1787, insolvent debtors had little trouble escaping their financial obligations by fleeing across state lines and seeking protection from courts, which tended to have little compunction canceling the claims of out-of-state creditors. To address the issue, the Framers gave Congress the power to create "uniform Laws on the subject

---

[10] The authors would like to thank the following associates for their assistance with and contribution to the article: Spencer Caldwell-McMillan, Debbie A. Farmer, Ross Fiedler, Kyle Ferrier, Gabriela Zamfir Hensley, Richard Kenny, Alexander Lazar, Michael Lemm, Oliver Pare, Noah Z. Sosnick, Evan Swager, and Claire Terry.

of Bankruptcies throughout the United States."[11] Congress passed the first Bankruptcy Act of 1800 pursuant to this power, and United States bankruptcy law has been exclusively federal ever since.

After several iterations throughout the nineteenth and twentieth centuries, the modern "Bankruptcy Code" was established through the Bankruptcy Reform Act of 1978. The Bankruptcy Code draws heavily upon prior bankruptcy principles, statutes, and case law but supersedes all prior bankruptcy enactments and has been the subject of significant reforms and amendments. The most recent amendment, the Bankruptcy Abuse Prevention and Consumer Protection Act of 2005 (BAPCA), went into effect on October 17, 2006, for all cases filed on or after that date.

The Bankruptcy Code is divided into Chapters that govern different types of bankruptcies and the procedural standards relevant to each. Administrative and procedural matters are covered in Chapters 1, 3, and 5. Chapters 1 and 3 contain definitions, general provisions, and the applicable guidelines for case administration, and Chapter 5 addresses the rights and claims of debtors and creditors. The remaining Chapters address different types of bankruptcy cases, including the two most prominent procedures, Chapter 7 liquidations and Chapter 11 reorganizations. Chapters 9, 12, and 13 are specially tailored to the bankruptcies of municipalities, family farms and fisherman, and wage earners, respectively. Finally, Chapter 15, which was enacted as part of BAPCA, covers cross-border insolvencies.

GOALS OF CHAPTER 11

When a debtor defaults on an agreement to pay a single loan, the disgruntled lender can seek relief in state court without any systemic implications, but when a debtor on the verge of collapse defaults on agreements to pay many lenders at once, special concerns arise. Absent a sophisticated legal scheme to organize the affairs of an insolvent debtor, each creditor, knowing that fellow lenders are likely to pounce on the distressed debtor to save their investments, is incentivized to demand payment as soon as possible. This collective action problem risks creating a proverbial race to the courthouse, hastening the collapse of insolvent debtors even if their defaults arise due only to temporary cash flow constraints.

---

[11] *See* Todd J. Zywicki, "The Past, Present, and Future of Bankruptcy Law in America," 101 *Mich. L. Rev.* 2016, 2017–18 (2003).

The debtor might have perverse incentives as well. Recognizing that it has sufficient funds to pay only some of its creditors, an insolvent debtor might elect to pay a creditor with whom it shares a close business relationship irrespective of any promises to pay other creditors first.[12] The same debtor might also be tempted to capitalize on its impending collapse and take an unwise gamble with its assets knowing that failure would not leave it any worse off.[13]

Layered on top of the creditors' and debtor's incentives are the costs that failure imposes on other constituencies: the debtor's employees, suppliers, customers, and other vendors are all likely to be damaged if the debtor collapses. Without some mechanism to help an insolvent debtor reorganize its affairs and start anew, these constituencies might suffer irreparable harm even if the insolvent company is still valuable despite its balance sheet dilemmas.

The Bankruptcy Code exists to solve this collective action problem and to help profitable but overburdened debtors reorganize existing business and financial affairs and emerge from bankruptcy with a "fresh start." To facilitate this process, the Bankruptcy Code imposes an "automatic stay" to hold creditors at bay and offers the debtor a "breathing spell" to operate its business while negotiating a resolution—a plan of reorganization—with its creditors. The Bankruptcy Code also arms debtors with additional tools like the power to reject or assume executory contracts and special abilities to take on new debt to assist in the reorganization process.

COMMENCEMENT, FIRST-DAY ORDERS, AND THE AUTOMATIC STAY

All bankruptcy cases commence with the filing of a petition for relief with the Bankruptcy Court. The petition may be voluntarily filed by the debtor or involuntarily filed against the debtor by three or more of its creditors if they meet certain criteria.

The impact of a bankruptcy filing is felt immediately by the debtor and its creditors. At the "first-day" hearing—which is a hearing that generally happens within the three days following the filing—the Bankruptcy Court hears a series of motions to facilitate the transition into the bankruptcy process. These so-called first-day motions are necessary because, once a debtor files for bankruptcy

---

[12] *See* Warrant, *supra* note 1, at 790.
[13] *Ibid.*

relief, a debtor's ability to act without the Bankruptcy Court's consent is limited in several respects, including the payment of prepetition debts. First-day motions are generally not controversial and are intended to assist the debtor in the ongoing management and operation of its business. Some of the matters addressed by first-day orders include the use of cash collateral, the payment of certain prepetition obligations to employees (i.e., salary) and critical vendors, the preservation of existing bank accounts, the payment of taxes and utilities, and the extension of certain deadlines.

The most significant impact of the filing, however, is that *all* parties are automatically and immediately prohibited from taking any action against the debtor or its property to enforce or collect on the debtor's prepetition obligations. This "automatic stay" enjoins any and all judicial or administrative proceedings or any other enforcement actions available to creditors, whether or not such proceedings or actions were initiated prepetition. For the debtor, the automatic stay, in essence, provides a breathing spell during which it can manage its operations and begin the bankruptcy process in an orderly manner. Although the automatic stay may be lifted in certain circumstances, it generally prevents creditors from foreclosing upon or otherwise seizing assets that may be employed by the debtor in the restructuring process or distributed among the creditors according to an equitable scheme.

THE ESTATE AND THE DEBTOR IN POSSESSION

The filing of a bankruptcy petition creates an estate that consists of substantially all of the assets that were owned by the debtor at the time of the filing. With a few limited exceptions, the Bankruptcy Code takes a very broad and inclusive view of what constitutes assets of the estate. Although a trustee may be appointed in certain cases, the debtor generally remains in possession of its assets and manages its affairs subject to the oversight of the Bankruptcy Court.

U.S. TRUSTEE AND CREDITORS' COMMITTEE

The U.S. Trustee Program is the component of the U.S. Department of Justice vested with primary responsibility for monitoring and supervising the administration of Chapter 11 cases under the Bankruptcy Code. The U.S. Trustee Program operates nationwide out of 92 field offices, and, among other things, monitors the debtor's ongoing business operations; reviews the retention and reimbursement of all legal and financial professionals; reviews reports, plans, and disclosure statements filed in Chapter 11 cases; and appoints official committees, including the official committee of unsecured creditors (i.e., the creditors' committee).

The creditors' committee appointed by the U.S. trustee generally consists of a group of unsecured creditors holding the largest unsecured claims against the debtor, although it may also include a representative cross-section of other significant, but smaller, groups of unsecured creditors. The creditors committee is an estate fiduciary and serves to represent the interests of all unsecured creditors in the bankruptcy case. Among other things, the creditors' committee monitors the debtor's ongoing business operations and actively participates in the negotiations and process leading to the development of a plan of reorganization or other distribution of the debtor's assets.

AVOIDANCE POWERS

Chapter 11 provides the debtor in possession (or the trustee, as the case may be) with effective tools to void certain transactions and to recover assets that were transferred by the debtor during specified periods prior to the filing of the bankruptcy petition. Among the most significant of these tools is the ability to void certain transfers that are deemed to be "preferential" or "fraudulent." Within the meaning of the Bankruptcy Code, the subject of a "transfer" may include virtually any interest in the property of the debtor—Section 101(54) of the Bankruptcy Code defines the term *transfer* broadly to include, among other things, the payment of cash, the creation of a lien, and other direct or indirect dispositions of property or an interest in property. In effect, transactions meeting the criteria prescribed by the Bankruptcy Code may be nullified and the underlying assets returned to the debtor. Any assets that are recovered in this manner automatically become part of the bankruptcy estate. Although avoidance actions are assets of the bankruptcy estate, a creditor (or creditors' committee) may seek to obtain standing from the court to bring an avoidance action on behalf of the estate if it can show that (1) a colorable claim exists, (2) the debtor unjustifiably failed to pursue the claim; and (3) prevailing in the avoidance action is likely to benefit the estate. Third-party standing, however, is difficult to obtain, and avoidance actions typically remain the debtor's to pursue.

Preferential Transfer

One of the primary categories of avoidable transfers are "preferences." Section 547 of the Bankruptcy Code defines a preferential transfer to be one: (1) made to or for the benefit of a creditor; (2) for or on account of an "antecedent debt" owed by the debtor before such transfer was made; (3) made while the debtor was insolvent; (4) made on or within 90 days prior to the petition date (the "preference period"); and (5) that enables such creditor to receive more than such creditor would receive if (a) the case were a case under Chapter 7 of the Bankruptcy Code, (b) the transfer had not been made, and (c) such creditor received payment of such debt to the extent provided by the provisions of the Bankruptcy Code. All elements of a preference must be present for a trustee to avoid a transfer. Insolvency is presumed within the preference period. Note that, for insiders, the period for which a transfer is avoidable is one year prior to the petition date.

The Bankruptcy Code also identifies a number of defenses to a preference action. Of the enumerated defenses, the "new value" defense and the "ordinary course of business" defense are most frequently used in preference action proceedings. The new value defense is found in Section 547(c)(1). A successful new value defense requires the transferee to prove three elements: (1) the transfer was on account of new value given to the debtor, (2) the transfer was intended to be a contemporaneous exchange, and (3) the transfer was in fact a substantially contemporaneous exchange. The party asserting the new value defense bears the burden of establishing these elements by a preponderance of the evidence. *New value* is defined in Section 547(a)(2) of the Bankruptcy Code to mean "money or money's worth in goods, services or new credit but does not include an obligation substituted for an existing obligation." To determine whether a transfer was intended to be contemporaneous, courts examine evidence of the parties' mutual understanding of the payment arrangement and evidence of how payments were reflected on the parties' books. Whether a contemporaneous exchange actually occurred depends on the test employed by the court, with some courts applying a bright-line 30-day time period and others employing a more holistic examination of the circumstances surrounding the transfer.

The ordinary course of business defense is found in Section 547(c)(2). A trustee cannot avoid a transfer if the transfer was in payment of a debt incurred by the debtor in the ordinary course of business or financial affairs of the debtor and the transferee and such transfer was (1) made in the ordinary course of business or financial affairs of the debtor and the transferee or (2) made according to ordinary business terms. Courts in certain jurisdictions, however, will allow an ordinary course defense even if the parties did not have prior agreements. Factors that a court may consider include (1) whether the transaction between the parties is typical in the industry, (2) whether the debtor complied with the terms of the parties' contractual arrangement, (3) the general conduct of the parties, and (4) the parties' ordinary course of dealing in other similar business transactions.

Fraudulent Transfers

Fraudulent transfer law appears in both state law and in the Bankruptcy Code. Generally, prepetition transfers of a debtor's property are avoidable if they are intentionally or constructively fraudulent within the applicable lookback period. In bankruptcy cases, the debtor or trustee may invoke state fraudulent transfer laws through Section 544(b) of the Bankruptcy Code, which permits the trustee to avoid any transfer that an actual unsecured creditor could have avoided outside of bankruptcy, or Section 548 of the Bankruptcy Code, which provides the trustee with avoidance powers independent of applicable state law.

The elements of the Bankruptcy Code and state constructive fraudulent transfer statutes are very similar and the analysis by the courts is typically comparable. The primary difference is the applicable statute of limitations: the statute of limitations for fraudulent transfers is two years prior to the petition date under the Bankruptcy Code and four to six years from the date of the transfer or incurrence of the obligation under state law.

Constructive Fraud

A debtor may attempt to avoid the prepayment under a theory of constructive fraudulent transfer. To establish a constructively fraudulent transfer, the plaintiff must show that: (1) the debtor received less than the "reasonably equivalent value" for the assets transferred and (2) the debtor either (a) was insolvent at the time of, or became insolvent as a result of, the transfer; (b) was engaged in a business or transaction, or was about to engage in a business or transaction, for which its assets remaining after the transfer were unreasonably small; or (c) intended to, or believed that it would, incur debts after the transfer beyond its ability to pay as they matured.

Constructive fraudulent transfer disputes often center on whether the debtor received "reasonably equivalent value" for the transfer. Although the Bankruptcy Code does not explicitly define reasonably equivalent value, Section 548 defines "value" as "property, or satisfaction or securing of a present or antecedent debt of the debtor, but does not include an unperformed promise to furnish support to the debtor or to a relative of the debtor." To determine whether the debtor received reasonably equivalent value for a transfer, courts may consider, among other factors: (1) the good faith of the parties, (2) the difference between the amount paid and the fair market value, (3) the situation of the parties, and/or (4) whether the transaction was at arm's length. Key issues in the reasonably equivalent value analysis include: (1) whether each individual transfer, or the transaction as a whole, should be reviewed; (2) what indirect benefits, if any, should be considered; and (3) how to account for contingencies with guarantee obligations.

Regarding the insolvency factor, courts generally apply one of three different tests either on a consolidated or on an individual entity basis:

1. *Balance sheet test.* This test examines whether, at fair value, the debtor's assets exceeded its liabilities at the time of transfer, with assets typically valued on a going-concern basis.
2. *Capital adequacy test.* This test evaluates whether the debtor was able to generate sufficient profits or capital to sustain operations over a reasonable period of time. A company lacks adequate capital if its assets are "unreasonably small" in relation to its business.
3. *Cash flow test.* This test focuses on whether the debtor intended to incur or believed it would incur debts that it could not pay as they matured.

Actual Fraud

Section 548(a)(1)(A) of the Bankruptcy Code provides that the trustee may avoid any transfer of the debtor's property (or any obligation incurred by the debtor) if the debtor made such transfer or incurred such obligation with actual intent to hinder, delay, or defraud any entity to which the debtor was or became indebted, on or after the date that such transfer was made or such obligation was incurred. As set forth under the Federal Rules of Civil Procedure, fraud must be pled with particularity.

Given that a debtor will rarely plainly state its fraudulent intent, courts often look to see whether any of the following nonexclusive "badges of fraud" are present: (1) inadequate consideration; (2) transfers to insiders; (3) the retention of possession, benefit, or use of the property in question; (4) the financial condition of the party sought to be charged both before and after the transaction in question (i.e., whether the party was insolvent); (5) the existence or cumulative effect of the pattern or series of transactions or course of conduct after the incurring of debt, onset of financial difficulties, or pendency or threat of suits by creditors; and (6) the general chronology of events and transactions under inquiry.

PRIORITY OF CLAIMS

Section 507 of the Bankruptcy Code dictates the order that claims are paid pursuant to a plan of reorganization. Each type of claim must be paid in full before a claim with a lower priority receives a distribution under a plan of reorganization. Generally, claims are paid in the following order: secured claims, priority and administrative claims, general unsecured claims, and equity interests. The priority of claims and interests is important because the Bankruptcy Code outlines rules regarding distributions that depend on the relative priority of claims.

Secured Claims

Secured claims are claims with a valid and perfected security interest in property of the estate. The Bankruptcy Code does not explicitly provide that secured claims are indeed "first in line," but courts in every circuit have interpreted other provisions of the Bankruptcy Code and the intent of the Bankruptcy Code's priority structure to establish that secured creditors must be paid first.

Priority Claims and Administrative Claims

Section 507 provides 10 types of unsecured claims that are given statutory priority. Of the enumerated priority claims, priority tax claims, priority wage claims, and priority claims under employee plans are often important claims under a Chapter 11 plan of reorganization. One type of priority claim that is important in nearly every Chapter 11 case is administrative expense claims, or claims that are "the actual, necessary costs and expenses of preserving the estate." To qualify as an administrative expense: (1) the claim must arise from the debtor's operations, not the prepetition company's operations, and (2) the debtor must receive a benefit. All fees for professionals who represent the estate are administrative expense claims and are subject to court approval.

Unsecured Claims and Equity Claims

Unsecured claims and equity interests sit at the bottom of the claims "waterfall" and often receive little to no recovery. However, in certain circumstances, unsecured claimants or equity holders may receive a distribution under a plan even if the class above them does not receive payment in full. If all classes under a plan vote to accept the plan, junior creditors can be paid a recovery even if senior creditors are not paid in full. This satisfies the "absolute priority rule" of the Bankruptcy Code, which requires that a Chapter 11 plan provide any nonaccepting, impaired class of creditors with full payment prior to any junior class of claims or interests receiving a recovery.

Junior claimants may also receive a distribution under the doctrine of gifting. Gifting, when permissible, avoids the application of the absolute priority rule because recoveries to junior classes consist of gifts from recoveries already received by senior creditor classes—instead of receiving a distribution under a Chapter 11 plan, the junior class recovery comes directly from the senior class. A typical gifting scenario is one in which an undersecured creditor with a first priority lien negotiates with unsecured creditors to gift them a portion of its recovery in exchange for cooperation on the plan. Whether gifting is permissible depends on the circuit the Bankruptcy Court is located in.

Superpriority Claims

The Bankruptcy Code also provides certain situations where "superpriority" claims are granted to claimants. Parties who provide post-petition financing under Section 364(c) are granted superpriority claims that have priority over other administrative claims. Similarly, Section 507(b) grants superpriority administrative expense claims to claimants who are deemed to have adequate protection that subsequently failed. Occasionally, courts will grant superpriority status to claims even if not explicitly provided for in the Bankruptcy Code.

Certain superpriority claims can even supersede secured claims. Section 506(c) permits the trustee to surcharge a secured creditor's collateral, that is, to recover from the collateral the reasonable, necessary costs and expenses of preserving, or disposing of, such property to the extent of any benefit to the holder of such claim. Some "priorities" can also have the effect of trumping secured claims, including a "priming lien" for post-petition financing under Section 364(d) of the Bankruptcy Code and carve-outs often agreed to by secured lenders to cover professional fees for debtor and committee professionals.

ASSUMPTION AND REJECTION OF EXECUTORY CONTRACTS AND UNEXPIRED LEASES

Section 365 of the Bankruptcy Code governs "executory contracts and unexpired leases." This section of the Bankruptcy Code permits the debtor, with the approval of the Bankruptcy Court, to assume or reject certain leases and other agreements that are in effect on the date of the filing. As a result, the debtor is able to free itself from certain economically undesirable contractual obligations or agreements that would otherwise impair its ability to implement a restructured business model.

More specifically, a debtor may assume or reject any of its executory contracts. An executory contract is an agreement under which the debtor and its counterparty both have material performance obligations such that either party's breach would constitute a material breach. Similarly, the debtor may reject unexpired leases of real or personal property. In each case, the debtor must make its election within specified periods dating from the filing of the petition.

Notably, loan documents and certain other financial accommodation contracts are excepted from Section 365's assumption and rejection powers.[14]

USE OF CASH COLLATERAL

As the debtor in possession moves through each phase of a Chapter 11 case, it also continues with the day-to-day operation of its enterprise. In the course of managing its business, as a supplement or alternative to DIP financing, the debtor may seek to use cash collateral to fund its liquidity needs.

Section 363 of the Bankruptcy Code, which governs the use of cash collateral, broadly defines *cash collateral* as "cash, negotiable instruments, documents of title, securities, deposit accounts, or other cash equivalents, whenever acquired, in which the estate and an entity other than the estate have an interest" and includes the proceeds; products; or offspring, rents, or profits of property, such as the cash proceeds resulting from a sale of property of the estate. Practically, and in more simple terms, cash collateral is the debtor's existing cash and cash generated from continued operations that is subject to a secured creditor's perfected security interest. A debtor may only use cash collateral during the pendency of its case if the affected creditors consent or if the Bankruptcy Court permits use by court order. Even if secured creditors consent to the use of cash collateral, debtors typically seek interim and final orders from the Bankruptcy Court approving the use of cash collateral, affirmatively authorizing the debtors to provide the creditors sufficient "adequate protection."

ADEQUATE PROTECTION

A debtor may only use cash collateral with the consent of its affected secured creditors or by order of the Bankruptcy Court. To receive court approval for the use of cash collateral over the objection of

---

[14] Trades already entered into to acquire loans before the counterparty files for bankruptcy are, however, considered to be executory contracts.

a secured creditor, or as a condition for secured creditor consent to use cash collateral, a debtor must provide sufficient "adequate protection" to each creditor having an interest in the cash collateral. The Bankruptcy Court determines what constitutes sufficient adequate protection on a case-by-case basis, though Section 361 provides some guidance, permitting provision of adequate protection in the form of (1) periodic cash payments ("adequate protection payments"), (2) additional or replacement liens, or (3) "other such relief" as will result in a creditor receiving the "indubitable equivalent" of its interest in collateral. Adequate protection is a flexible concept, and common forms of adequate protection include: (1) an equity cushion, (2) payment of professional fees and expenses for creditors' legal and financial advisors, (3) maintenance of insurance on collateral, and (4) regular reporting of financial or operational results (including cash use), among others.

In addition to requiring that a debtor provide adequate protection to secured creditors before using cash collateral, the Bankruptcy Code also requires a debtor to provide adequate protection upon a showing from a creditor that adequate protection is necessary to protect the creditor's interest in collateral through the duration of the automatic stay, or when post-petition DIP financing includes grants of pari passu or priming liens. In evaluating adequate protection in both of these situations, as well as where a debtor intends to use cash collateral, the Bankruptcy Court focuses on whether the proposed measures sufficiently compensate a creditor for any diminution in the value of its interest.

The Bankruptcy Code's adequate protection requirements are an important form of leverage for secured creditors early in a Chapter 11 case. Through asserting adequate protection rights, secured creditors can exercise significant control over the terms of post-petition DIP financings and the restructuring process generally.

ASSET SALES

A Chapter 11 debtor has the power to sell all or part of its assets either pursuant to a plan of reorganization or Section 363 of the Bankruptcy Code.

In a sale under a Chapter 11 plan of reorganization, the court must confirm the plan, which requires full compliance with Section 1129 of the Bankruptcy Code, including longer notice periods, approval of a disclosure statement, and creditor voting requirements. Pursuing a sale under a plan rather than under Section 363 can be more attractive to the debtor because it offers the possibility of a comprehensive resolution to its restructuring. A plan sale may also allow a purchaser greater flexibility in the deal structure and provide for more favorable tax treatment. The purchaser under a plan sale, however, may be required to participate substantially in the Bankruptcy Court processes related to confirmation of the plan after creditor voting.

Under a Section 363 sale, the Bankruptcy Code's requirements are less stringent. The debtor generally must show a good business purpose for the sale and that fair value is being paid for the assets. Although courts typically defer to the debtor's business judgment regarding Section 363 asset sales, sales to insiders, such as existing equity owners, may be more closely scrutinized, and if a sale is for a substantial portion of the debtor's assets, it may be challenged as a sub rosa plan that is seeking to evade Section 1129's confirmation requirements. Section 363 offers attractive benefits to purchasers, such as protections for good-faith purchasers (Section 363(m)) and the ability to sell an asset free and clear of liens, claims, and encumbrances under certain circumstances (Section 363(f)).

Courts and creditors typically require a public marketing or auction process to show that a proposed sale will maximize value for the debtor's estate irrespective of whether it is structured as a plan sale or a Section 363 sale. Often, a debtor will present a sale for approval with a "stalking-horse" bidder to set a minimum purchase price and other baseline transaction terms against which other potential purchasers will bid pursuant to court-approved bidding procedures. "Naked" sales, or sales without a stalking-horse bid, are possible but less common. Under certain circumstances, courts may approve sales that result from private sale processes, but such sales generally garner greater scrutiny.

PLAN OF REORGANIZATION AND DISCLOSURE

Chapter 11 gives the debtor an exclusive right to propose and file a plan of reorganization during the 120-day period immediately following the petition date. During this "exclusivity period," no other creditor or party in interest may propose and file a plan. Chapter 11 also gives the debtor a 180-day period (a "solicitation exclusivity period") during which it may solicit and obtain the acceptance of its plan. Upon the expiration of the exclusivity period, however, a creditor may file and seek the approval of its own plan, which may compete with any plan previously proposed by the debtor.

On request of the debtor or a party in interest and after notice and a hearing, the court may for cause increase or reduce the exclusivity period or the solicitation exclusivity period, but the 120-day exclusivity period may not be extended beyond 18 months after the petition date, and the 180-day solicitation period may not be extended beyond 20 months after the petition date.

In tandem with the plan proposal, the debtor must also file a written disclosure statement with the Bankruptcy Court. The goal of the disclosure statement is to provide to creditors sufficiently detailed information ("adequate information") about the debtor and its business to enable creditors to make an informed decision as to whether to accept or reject the proposed plan. As a general rule, Bankruptcy Court approval of the disclosure statement is a prerequisite to plan approval.

VOTING AND CONFIRMATION

Sections 1129(a) and 1129(b) of the Bankruptcy Code set forth the elements required for the confirmation of a plan of reorganization depending upon the level of "acceptance" by all creditors who are entitled to vote.

Pursuant to Section 1123(a) of the Bankruptcy Code, a plan of reorganization must classify creditors according to their separate claims and interests and specify whether each class is "impaired" or "unimpaired." The designation of classes may be based, for example, on whether the creditor and its interest is secured or unsecured, priority or nonpriority, or otherwise distinguishable based upon its claim. A class of creditors is impaired if the plan offers less than payment in full to that class or otherwise modifies or limits the rights of that class.

The voting process to obtain plan approval is conducted by class. If at least two-thirds in amount and one-half in number of the holders of allowed claims or interests within a class vote to accept the plan, the plan is binding upon and is deemed to have been accepted by the entire class. Note, however, that only impaired classes are entitled to vote, because the unimpaired classes expect to be paid in full and, under Section 1126 of the Bankruptcy Code, are presumed to have accepted the plan.

A hearing must be held before the Bankruptcy Court to confirm a plan of reorganization. If the proposed plan satisfies all of the elements set forth in Section 1129(a) and the requisite lenders in each impaired class have voted to accept the plan, the plan may be confirmed by the Bankruptcy Court. In the event that an impaired class rejects the proposed plan of reorganization, Section 1129(b) of the Bankruptcy Code provides that the plan may still be confirmed if the plan (1) satisfies all of the elements of Section 1129(a), other than the requirement that each unimpaired class of claims or interests shall have accepted the plan; (2) has been accepted by at least one other impaired class; and (3) does not "discriminate unfairly" and is "fair and equitable" to the impaired class that has rejected the plan.

ALTERNATIVE PATHS

In general, the most attractive restructuring alternative available to borrowers and lenders alike in a "perfect" restructuring world would be the collective negotiation and implementation of a consensual restructuring scheme without the need to resort to court supervision. The fundamental reasons are clear: out-of-court workouts provide an opportunity to restructure more rapidly and at far less expense than would typically be expected in a traditional Chapter 11 case.

Unfortunately, not all borrowers and creditor groups can avail themselves of the opportunity to restructure without a formal proceeding. For example, if amendments to a credit agreement contemplate an extension of the maturity date, a postponement of regularly scheduled payments, or a sale of assets representing substantial collateral, a creditor group may not be able to muster the unanimous consent that is generally required to give effect to such amendments and their underlying strategic and financial objectives. Additionally, participants in a consensual restructuring process may not be able to carry out their plans without the assistance of the Bankruptcy Court. A company that is in financial distress, for example, may wish to sell certain of its assets on a selective basis in order to pay down debt, generate working capital, or eliminate the costs associated with maintaining or operating the assets to be sold. At the same time, an otherwise willing buyer may be reluctant to proceed in the absence of a court order declaring that the sale is final and is free and clear of any liens or claims of other creditors.

Prearranged and prepackaged plans help to overcome these issues while still avoiding some of the costs associated with a traditional Chapter 11 proceeding. The need for unanimous consent is also avoided, because the Bankruptcy Code requires the approval of only "two thirds in amount and one half in number" of each class of creditors. (See "Voting and Confirmation" above, for the discussion of voting on plan confirmation.) In each case, the plan is negotiated prior to the borrower's filing a petition with the Bankruptcy Court and becoming subject to the protections of the Bankruptcy Code. Prearranged plans are negotiated and agreed to by the borrower—as a prospective debtor—and the requisite creditors, and the terms are set forth in an agreement that is often referred to as a *restructuring support agreement* or *lock-up agreement*. Under the lock-up arrangement, the creditors agree to vote in favor of a plan of reorganization that conforms to the agreed-upon terms when such a plan is filed with the Bankruptcy Court in a formal Chapter 11 proceeding. A prepackaged plan is not only negotiated prior to the filing but also approved by a vote of the requisite creditors. As a result, a prepackaged plan approved by the requisite creditors may be presented to the Bankruptcy Court at the time of the filing.

Finally, many cases simply require the supervision of the Bankruptcy Court and the structure of a traditional Chapter 11 case in order to restructure the debtor's business and financial affairs. The Bankruptcy Court can provide a central forum for the settlement of outstanding litigation issues or disputes among creditors. In addition, the certainty of a Bankruptcy Court order will underscore restructuring efforts with far greater finality than would be enjoyed by the parties to a consensual agreement in an out-of-court restructuring.

At the same time, a traditional Chapter 11 proceeding has certain drawbacks. The first, and perhaps most obvious, is cost. A restructuring process that is conducted from start to finish under the supervision of the Bankruptcy Court can be far more costly than out-of-court alternatives and can take considerably longer to complete. In an out-of-court restructuring, control of the process is generally concentrated in the borrower and the lender group. In a formal Chapter 11 proceeding, that control is significantly diluted, as the restructuring process falls under the supervision of the Bankruptcy Court, and third parties (including the U.S. trustee and creditors' committees) join in the negotiation and development of a plan of reorganization.

PRENEGOTIATED AND PREPACKAGED PLANS

While a traditional bankruptcy involves a "freefall" into Chapter 11 without a plan or creditor support, prepackaged and prenegotiated plans allow debtors to move quickly through Chapter 11 to the confirmation of the plan. A prenegotiated, or prearranged, plan refers to a plan that already has key creditor consensus prior to the debtor filing the petition. This consensus often takes the form of a restructuring support agreement (RSA). The RSA is an out-of-court contract that binds the creditor to support the proposed Chapter 11 plan and, in turn, binds the debtor to key terms of the reorganization. A key difference between a prepackaged plan and a prenegotiated plan is that under a prenegotiated plan no solicitation occurs prior to the Chapter 11 filing.

Prepackaged plans allow for the solicitation of a plan prior to the filing of a Chapter 11 petition. A debtor can confirm a prepackaged plan in approximately 30 to 60 days after filing, although some courts have confirmed prepackaged plans in less than 24 hours after filing. In a typical prepackaged plan, the debtor solicits all or some of the plan votes prior to filing the petition. This is permitted pursuant to Section 1126(b), which allows for the prepetition acceptance and rejection of a plan to be used post-petition so long as the solicitation is in compliance with applicable nonbankruptcy rules and laws (e.g., federal securities laws or blue sky laws). The key advantage of a prepackaged plan is that the debtor moves more quickly through Chapter 11, which reduces the costs of the Chapter 11 case and the operational risk of remaining in bankruptcy. Prepackaged plans can be useful to drag along a holdout creditor (no unanimity is required to confirm a Chapter 11 plan). However, due to the speed of the bankruptcy case and the solicitation required before filing, it is difficult for the debtor to use a prepackaged plan to restructure trade debt, reject unfavorable vendor contracts, or seek other operational and cash flow advantages. These drawbacks need to be balanced against the other benefits that a more streamlined Chapter 11 case could provide.

EXCHANGES

One common form of an out-of-court restructuring transaction is the exchange offer, which involves the acquisition by an existing debtholder of a newly issued loan or security of an issuer using the existing loan or security as the purchase consideration through an exchange. Exchange offers can be divided into two main categories: (1) debt-for-equity exchanges and (2) debt-for-debt exchanges. In a debt-for-equity exchange, a company offers to exchange certain debt for equity in the form of either common or preferred stock. In a debt-for-debt exchange, a company offers to exchange certain debt for another type of debt—either loans or securities with, for example, a longer maturity date. Exchanges in out-of-court restructurings may be advantageous as compared to Chapter 11 proceedings, because they allow continuity in the management of the company, and such transactions may be consummated more quickly than they would under the Chapter 11 process.

One drawback to consider is that exchange offers involving public securities must be registered, and they are subject to review by the Securities and Exchange Commission (SEC). However, there are several exemptions under the securities law that may apply. Under 15 U.S.C. § 7c(a)(9), a transaction is exempt from the registration requirements if (1) the company exchanges securities with existing security holders, (2) the security holders do not pay any cash or additional consideration in exchange for the new securities, and (3) no fees are paid to any party for soliciting the exchange. Under 15 U.S.C. § 77(d)(a)(2), transactions involving private issuance of securities solicited exclusively to informed sophisticated investors are exempted from the registration requirements. Finally, under 17 C.F.R. § 230.504–.506, certain companies that are not investment companies and not subject to the Securities Exchange Act of 1934 are exempted from the registration requirements.

CONCLUSION

Most companies that are in financial crisis, if given the opportunity, would prefer to undertake a consensual restructuring process with their creditors. Restructuring without court supervision is generally less expensive and less time-consuming. Not all workouts, however, can be effectively implemented without the tools and safeguards afforded by Chapter 11. Prearranged and prepackaged plans mitigate some of the difficulties encountered by companies trying to affect a consensual restructuring, such as avoiding the need for unanimous consent. If, however, a company is not able to reach an agreement with its creditors in a consensual environment, a formal Chapter 11 proceeding may provide the only avenue for an effective financial restructuring of a borrower in distress.

Critical Financial Considerations in Distressed Situations[15]

Saul E. Burian
Houlihan Lokey

LIQUIDITY IS KING

Just as an army marches on its stomach, a bankruptcy runs on its liquidity.

Although there are a number of causes of financial insolvency, the preponderance of bankruptcies and restructurings involve some sort of liquidity crunch. Very often, the number one concern in a bankruptcy is liquidity, and this is especially true at the beginning of a bankruptcy case. Given the natural tendency to procrastinate, companies often wait too long before kicking off a restructuring or commencing a bankruptcy, and it is the lack of liquidity that ultimately forces the process. And, even in the best of circumstances, a bankruptcy or a comprehensive restructuring has the potential to cause operational and working capital disruptions to a business (e.g., customers and suppliers "protecting themselves" by limiting exposure to a distressed business), leaving management with less time and energy to focus on normal business operations. Nothing brings a business to a halt, and forecloses reasonable, value-maximizing options, like the inability to at least pay post-petition bills as they come due. The automatic stay of the Bankruptcy Code provides protection to debtors for most prepetition obligations. However, to stay in business, a debtor in possession will need to timely pay its liabilities accrued post-filing.

USE OF CASH COLLATERAL

The Bankruptcy Code balances the protections afforded to a debtor under Chapter 11 with significant restrictions on the ability of a debtor to manage its business while it is the subject of a bankruptcy

---

[15] The authors would like to thank Joseph A. Ebb and Zev Litwin for their assistance with and contribution to this article.

proceeding. Often, the most immediate and critical restriction is that a debtor is not permitted to use cash collateral (even in the ordinary course of business) without permission of the relevant creditor(s) who have a lien on such cash or as otherwise ordered by the court.[16] In most circumstances, a debtor will immediately request that the Bankruptcy Court approve its use of cash collateral in order to minimize disruption to the business, and most secured creditors readily agree in advance, subject to negotiated budgets, expense reimbursements, and other protections commonly found in a "cash collateral order." While most parties take for granted that bankruptcy courts will allow the debtor to use cash collateral for its liquidity needs, Section 361 of the Bankruptcy Code requires that the debtor provide "adequate protection" to each creditor having an interest in the cash collateral to be used.[17] Generally, a debtor will need to demonstrate that use of cash for funding the business will not significantly impair claims of current creditors. In other words, the debtor must demonstrate that it is not simply wasting valuable, distributable assets of the company in continuing to operate. However, in practice, a Bankruptcy Court will rarely disallow the use of cash collateral, due to the presumption that a business maximizes its value as a going concern and the risk of immediate and severe disruption if the business cannot pay its bills.

LIQUIDITY ANALYSES

With so much focus on liquidity in a bankruptcy, one of the important tasks for a financial advisor is to assess the adequacy of the business's liquidity. These analyses typically take two forms: 13-week liquidity forecasts and long-term liquidity projections as part

---

[16] Under Section 363 of the Bankruptcy Code, cash collateral includes "cash, negotiable instruments, documents of title, securities, deposit accounts, or other cash equivalents, whenever acquired, in which the estate and an entity other than the estate have an interest" and includes the proceeds; products; or offspring, rents, or profits of property.

[17] 11 U.S.C. § 361: "When adequate protection is required . . . of an interest of an entity in property, such adequate protection may be provided by—(1) requiring the trustee to make a cash payment or periodic cash payments to such entity to the extent that [a stay, use, sale, lease, or granting of a lien] . . . results in a decrease in the value of such entity's interest in such property; (2) providing to such entity an additional or replacement lien . . .; or (3) granting such other relief, other than entitling such entity to compensation allowable . . . as an administrative expense, as will result in the realization by such entity of the indubitable equivalent of such entity's interest in such property."

of the broader projections for the debtor. As the name suggests, the 13-week liquidity forecast is a current projection of the sources and uses of liquidity for a debtor over the next 13 weeks, taking into account the variety of impacts, both positive and negative, of the bankruptcy filing and related economic distress. Typically, the forecast shows fairly detailed estimates of cash receipts and disbursements (e.g., payroll, insurance payments, rent, healthcare insurance and other benefits, etc.) on a week-by-week basis for this period, with the expectation that ordinary course of business collections and cash expenditures over such an immediate time horizon are fairly predictable. The advisor will also consider any anticipated fees related to the restructuring (especially professional fees), debt service (if any), scheduled purchases and sales of assets, and any additional borrowing or repayment necessary or planned for the period. Given the granularity of the 13-week liquidity forecast, a financial advisor or management may need to work more closely with business line and operational employees to develop these projections than would be required for other projections. Based on all inflows and outflows of cash, the forecast will calculate ending balances from beginning balances for each week in the forecast, identifying any significant liquidity needs or shortfalls. This forecast is especially helpful in calculating compliance with asset-based lending and other covenants and keeping track of the short-term changes in current assets (inventory and account receivable) and related liabilities. When properly prepared prepetition, the 13-week liquidity forecast is useful in identifying a need for emergency financing (such as a bridge loan or DIP financing), determining when a bankruptcy filing may be necessary or opportune and identifying trends or other changes to the business. Given these uses, the 13-week liquidity forecast may be updated many times leading up to and during a restructuring, often weekly and usually no less often than monthly.

In addition to the short-term 13-week liquidity forecast, financial advisors will also typically perform long-term liquidity analyses as part of a broader set of financial projections. These projections are typically quarterly, are integrated with and dependent on the three-statement projections for a company, and are not quite as granular as the 13-week forecast, given the uncertainty associated with a longer time horizon. Long-term liquidity analysis generally looks at (and similarly treats) both projected cash and cash equivalents held by the debtor and any undrawn funds under letters of credit or revolving credit facilities, and, if done correctly, also accounts for seasonality of cash needs, "trapped" cash at domestic and foreign subsidiaries, deposits, escrows, capital needs, and appropriate levels of working capital. Because distressed companies tend to be experiencing liquidity deficits, these liquidity forecasts are very important and need to take into account both the positive and negative liquidity ramifications of an exit from bankruptcy or restructuring. These liquidity forecasts are often the most critical analyses used to "size" and price the take back or new debt burdening the restructured business and to assess the long-term adequacy and likelihood of success of a restructuring plan. Liquidity forecasts are of extreme interest to all creditors, including vendors, customers, and other counterparties that will continue to do business with the restructured company and will often be used to set significant financial covenants in the relevant new loan agreements.

DIP FINANCING

In many bankruptcies, the debtors' available cash collateral is insufficient to maintain the business operations through the bankruptcy process and to fund the often very expensive bankruptcy process itself. In such cases, the debtors will generally seek DIP financing. DIP financing is additional debt provided to a debtor in a Chapter 11 proceeding, usually shortly after filing.[18] While there are no specific limitations on the type of facility that a DIP financing takes, the Bankruptcy Code does mandate that the debtor first seek unsecured debt, then debt that is secured only by previously unencumbered assets or secured by encumbered assets with a lien junior to existing lien holders. If, as is often the case, none of the above is available, the Bankruptcy Code permits the granting of priming liens on existing collateral senior even to existing secured claims and with priority over administrative claims in the bankruptcy. While such priority may seem unfair on its face and may contradict the contractual terms of credit agreements contracted prior to bankruptcy, such favorable treatment is often viewed as necessary to ensure that the business can acquire the financing it needs to continue as a going concern (i.e., in order to avoid a forced cessation of business and liquidation).

---

[18] Often, a debtor will work with existing creditors or other parties to secure DIP financing prior to filing for bankruptcy, pending Bankruptcy Court approval.

DIP financing, especially DIP financing that enjoys a "priming lien," can have a significant impact on existing creditors, and therefore requires Bankruptcy Court approval before it is allowed. In addition, if the debtor is seeking to grant a priming lien in connection with the DIP financing, the Bankruptcy Court must specifically conclude that the existing lenders enjoying liens on the relevant assets are "adequately protected" notwithstanding the new financing, or that they have consented to the granting of the priming lien(s). The approval of DIP financing can be contentious as creditors may contest the need and/or the terms of the financing and may compete to provide what can often be quite desirable financing, both for its financial terms and the control over the process that DIP lenders enjoy through the covenants in the relevant documentation. Existing secured lenders often have the inside track to provide priming DIP financing because they are the parties whose consent is necessary to alleviate the debtor of the burden of proving adequate protection. Because prepetition liens are often granted for the benefit of large, multiparty syndicated loans or publicly issued or privately placed debentures, creditors (or groups of creditors) that control the consent rights with regard to the priming liens often have a significant advantage in the competition to provide DIP financing and have recently used that advantage to not only gain favorable terms from the debtor but to also better their position *vis-à-vis* other heretofore pari passu creditors within their own facilities.

Generally, the debtor must demonstrate a need for the additional capital that a DIP loan would provide, presumably through liquidity forecasting. Further, courts tend to require the debtor to disclose planned uses of the proposed funds, and may closely track the actual use of these funds through the bankruptcy process. A court will also require that the debtor demonstrate a lack of other viable alternatives to DIP financing (the Bankruptcy Code specifically requires that the court consider whether financing is possible through raising unsecured or junior secured debt),[19] and may allow existing creditors to present evidence to the contrary. Additionally, as noted above, given the priming lien generally granted to DIP facilities, a debtor must either receive consent from existing secured creditors or demonstrate to the court that the prefiling secured

---

[19] 11 U.S. Code 364.

creditors would remain adequately protected if the court grants the DIP facility. In other words, the debtor needs to demonstrate that secured creditors will be in a similar position in terms of ultimate recovery despite the additional debt and priming lien. This may be easier to demonstrate for some situations and certain types of assets than for others, such as where the value of existing secured assets depends heavily on the continued operations of the business (e.g., equipment and inventory) and where the secured debt is currently oversecured. On the other hand, a debtor may have trouble showing adequate protection where collateral value, net of the DIP financing, is expected to decrease. Finally, even if a Bankruptcy Court agrees that there is a need for DIP financing and that other secured interests are adequately protected, it may further consider whether the requested amount of DIP financing is appropriate; if the court does not agree with the amount, it may approve a smaller amount of DIP financing.

Often, however, prefiling secured creditors will recognize the need for DIP financing to protect the value of the business and will support or even seek to participate in the DIP loan. In fact, if proposed lending terms are otherwise similar, a Bankruptcy Court will generally favor an existing secured creditor's provision of DIP financing over a provision by a third party or more junior creditor (though it is worth noting that the provision of DIP financing should still be a competitive process). An existing lender may be motivated to provide the DIP financing because such financing can provide a favorable return with limited risk (given that DIP financing is often at the top of the capital stack). However, as the distressed debt market has evolved, DIP financing has become more competitive, and prepetition creditors may consider providing DIP financing for other reasons, even sometimes at or below market. Often, a prepetition creditor will look to become the DIP lender as a defensive measure, in order to prevent another creditor from priming its security interest (and instead priming its own interest, but remaining fully in control of the collateral). Additionally, provision of DIP financing will often provide the lender with additional control over the bankruptcy, particularly if the terms of the DIP financing allow the lender to restrict certain actions of the business, require the debtor to take specified actions (e.g., a sale of particular assets), or otherwise mandate the timetable of the restructuring. Finally, in some cases, a prepetition creditor that provides DIP financing may be able to obtain favorable treatment of its existing prepetition debt through either a roll-up or cross-collateralization.

Most DIP financings are supposed to be paid in full, in cash, on or prior to the conclusion of the bankruptcy proceeding. However, some companies may not project the ability to repay their DIP facilities by or upon emergence from bankruptcy. Typically, the company would rely on its ability to obtain exit financing to repay the DIP loans at exit. However, especially in prearranged or prepackaged bankruptcies where the debtor commences a case with a plan in hand for a successful exit, it is becoming more common for the DIP facility to include an option to "roll" into the post-bankruptcy exit financing. While the option can be expensive, it provides the debtor and all creditors with the confidence that the company will be able to exit bankruptcy without having to worry about obtaining new financing when it consummates its plan of reorganization and emerges. In some cases, these options may include valuable stock or warrants in the new reorganized business, in addition to the typical fees associated with financing.

DEVELOPING A STRATEGY AND A BUSINESS PLAN

Every restructuring is different, but the goal is always the same—to maximize the value of the relevant debtor and allocate that value fairly to the relevant creditor and equity constituencies. Once stability has been achieved by obtaining liquidity for the business, the debtor and its constituencies can focus on the broader strategic issues of how to maximize value, including changes to its business plan, operating all or only portions of its business, sales of discrete assets or business lines, and/or the disposition of all of the debtor's business. Restructurings and bankruptcies present an opportunity to reset the relevant business without regard to many of the mistakes (high leverage, bad contracts, onerous leases, indemnity, and other liabilities, etc.) that caused the distress to begin with and that would be impossible, or very difficult, to deal with out of court.

Most restructurings follow similar steps in developing a go-forward business plan and utilize similar strategies to implement these plans. As part of a restructuring, a business must evaluate existing business lines and locations and decide what to continue to operate and what to sell or liquidate. Although some businesses can continue to operate largely unchanged, many distressed companies need to consolidate their operations or shed noncore business lines or underperforming locations in order to return to financial health. Two bankruptcy provisions facilitate the excising of portions of a business: Section 363, which allows for the free and clear sale of assets during a bankruptcy (see the section "Asset Sales" in the previous Kirkland & Ellis LLP article for further discussion), and Section 365, which allows for the assumption or rejection of executory contracts and unexpired leases and can facilitate store closures and exits from onerous long-term obligations.

A restructuring company should also evaluate its management team. While in some cases management may have created the need for a restructuring through poor performance and should be supplemented or replaced, often a distressed company can benefit from management continuity during the turbulence of a restructuring. In fact, restructuring companies often incentivize management to stay during the difficult process. In other cases, a restructuring company may want to install experts in managing distressed companies into key positions to either replace or support existing managers.

In addition to decisions regarding operations and management, a restructuring company must assess its need for new money and what sort of capital structure it can support going forward. Restructuring companies with liquidity issues must determine how much new money is necessary and how to raise the additional capital both during the restructuring (often through DIP financing) and upon exit. Companies and creditors must also determine how much total debt a company is able to support (a company's debt capacity) and what the ideal capital structure for the company is post-restructuring. Where a company is unable to support all of its existing obligations as debt, obligations that are not repaid in cash or with new debt may be converted to equity, with control of the business often going to the fulcrum security as discussed in the initial section (see "What Investment Opportunities Exist in Distressed Situations?").

Although the debtor is often in the driver's seat when restructuring, creditors will frequently exert influence over the process and help determine what a company looks like upon emergence. Creditors, of course, often have views about and exert pressure on decisions related to business continuity, management, and capital structure. Additionally, creditors may force a restructuring company to accept restrictions on spending and future asset dispositions to reduce or manage risk, insert creditor representatives into key decision-making processes, and force additional austerity measures, and they can also threaten a default if the company fails to meet performance measures or otherwise comply. In sum, a restructuring presents possibilities and optionality for a debtor, but it also forces trade-offs, flexibility, and difficult decisions. When navigating through a restructuring, a debtor must weigh all of its decisions against the broader context of what it is trying to achieve, with laser focus on the optimal post-restructuring business plan and capital structure.

EXECUTORY CONTRACTS AND LEASES

One of the major advantages of filing for bankruptcy is the ability of the debtor to reject executory contracts and unexpired leases.[20] This tool is particularly useful for companies that have entered into bad contracts or that need to downsize or shut down certain parts of their businesses. Under normal nonbankruptcy circumstances, an attempt to terminate a contract or lease would constitute a breach and would allow the nonbreaching party to recover damages or seek specific performance. Typically, damages would be the expected value that complete performance of the contract or lease would have for the nonbreaching party less any costs avoided by the breach or expectation damages. In bankruptcy, a debtor's rejection of an executory contract or unexpired lease only results in an unsecured prepetition bankruptcy claim that is subject to compromise along with all other unsecured claims in the case. In addition, the unsecured claim arising from the rejection of an unexpired lease is capped as provided in Section 502(b)(6) of the Bankruptcy Code.[21] This has been especially helpful recently in the myriad of retail store bankruptcies that have followed the rise of online

---

[20] While the U.S. Bankruptcy Code does not explicitly define what an executory contract is, many courts utilize a definition from Professor Vern Countryman: "a contract under which the obligation of both the bankrupt and the other party to the contract are so far unperformed that the failure of either to complete performance would constitute a material breach excusing the performance of the other."Vern Countryman, "Executory Contracts in Bankruptcy: Part I," 57 *Minn. L. Rev.* 439, 469 (1973).

[21] Under 11 U.S.C. § 502(6), a lease claim is limited to the greater of one year's rent or 15% of the remaining rent due on the lease for a term of up to three years. Lessors may also have a duty to attempt to mitigate damages by re-leasing the property, if possible.

shopping and the impact of the COVID-19 pandemic. Rejections have also been particularly helpful when companies are saddled with long-term commodity contracts.[22]

There are some limitations to a debtor's ability to reject executory contracts and unexpired leases, including a narrow time frame for making a decision with respect to unexpired leases and the obligation to reject all or none of the applicable contract and limitations applicable to specific categories of leases or contracts (e.g., intellectual property licenses).

RETENTION OF MANAGEMENT

As part of a restructuring, a company also has to decide whether to retain or replace management. While intuitively it may seem that a management team that leads their company into financial distress should be terminated, there are actually a number of factors that make retaining management an attractive option for a distressed company. First, it may be difficult to hire qualified managers to take over a company in bankruptcy or severe financial distress. Potential hires may view the company as weak, the bankruptcy process as daunting and arduous, and the financial and reputational upside as limited. Further, the process of hiring new managers can be time-consuming, disruptive, and expensive.

Additionally, there is an agency problem: during a comprehensive restructuring, it is often unclear who will own the company going forward.[23] Often, equity is likely to be wiped out and some class of creditors will receive the company's new equity as part of the restructuring. In some cases, it may be unclear which class of creditors will receive the equity, and even if this is evident, it may be unclear which members of the class intend to keep the equity. As a result, a company may not have certainty regarding who should choose new managers, in which case retaining the current management team can be the simplest and most sensible

---

[22] Oil prices, for example, fell significantly after 2014 from around $100 a barrel to around $40 in 2020, reaching troughs of around $30 in January 2016 and $16 in April 2020. A company that is highly dependent on oil and entered into a long-term purchase agreement in 2014 to lock in oil prices at $100 a barrel likely could have saved significantly by rejecting such an agreement in a bankruptcy proceeding at any time between 2015 and 2020.

[23] This is less true in prepackaged bankruptcies.

approach.[24] During this period of uncertainty, decision makers may be risk averse and allow the future owners and future board to assess management and decide on changes, if any. Finally, it is not unusual for the management team that was responsible for any poor decisions that led to the distress to have already been replaced prior to the commencement of the reorganization process, in which case the current team may be a significant part of the solution and not part of the problem.

In any event, notwithstanding the ultimate treatment of management, it is not unusual for professionals to be added to the management team during the reorganization process to supplement the exiting team in dealing with the myriad of additional reporting and other obligations imposed by the process, to focus on a particularly difficult issue that requires specialized expertise, or to provide creditors with an additional level of confidence in the decision-making of the company.[25] Sometimes, such a new manager may be granted the title of chief restructuring officer to focus specifically on restructuring issues and to take pressure off the rest of the management team.

Often, upper management of a company is compensated largely through incentive-based pay and stock or stock options. In the case of a restructuring company, stock and stock options may be worthless, and management may not hit their short-term incentives. Therefore, at the onset of a bankruptcy, management may have limited financial incentive to take on the difficult work of saving a struggling company. Management incentive plans recognize this and provide new financial incentives to encourage management to stay. Because equity is not available during the case to incentivize management, incentive plans in the restructuring context typically consist of fairly shorter-term cash incentives and guaranteed payments.

DEBT CAPACITY

One of the key questions that a debtor and its creditors must answer during a restructuring is how much debt the debtor should carry post-restructuring. Most often, a debtor will emerge with less debt

---

[24] Even if the eventual equity holders may plan to replace management later, the company can generally save itself trouble by avoiding multiple changes of management in succession.

[25] In some cases, these managers may come from professional service firms specializing in turnaround management that are already working with the distressed company on a consulting basis.

or, at the very least, less cash interest than it had prior to the restructuring. A primary factor that creditors and debtors typically consider in determining a post-restructuring capital structure is the company's debt capacity, or how much debt the operations (and cash flows) of a business can support. Debt capacity can be measured and determined in a number of ways, and, in the restructuring context, is generally considered on a pro forma basis. One of the most common measures is the ratio of debt to EBITDA (earnings before interest, taxes, depreciation, and amortization), which looks at how much debt a company has (or will have post-restructuring) relative to the cash that the company earns (for which EBITDA is considered a reasonable proxy).[26] Parties in a restructuring may also consider the ratio of debt to the total asset or enterprise value of the company, which demonstrates what portion of the enterprise value of a company is in the form of debt and how much cushion there may be in the event of negative variations in the value of the company over time. Finally, debtors and creditors often consider interest coverage (generally EBITDA divided by interest expense) or cash interest coverage (EBITDA divided by cash interest expense) ratios. Interest coverage ratios demonstrate a company's ability to service its debt in the short term and also are indicative of potential liquidity issues. Given that these measures all depend on the pro forma valuation of, and projections for, the reorganized debtor, debt capacity is highly dependent on the work of financial advisors.

While debtors and creditors may consider all of these measures when determining how much debt is appropriate for a debtor post-restructuring, there are no hard and fast rules. The expertise of financial advisors can be particularly helpful here, as different benchmarks apply to different industries and types of companies in light of their earnings volatility, growth expectations, industry, size, and age of the company.[27] Typically, parties will also consider other similar restructurings and will look to credit markets to see at what debt levels a company might eventually be able to refinance. That being said, who a company's creditors are may have a

---

[26] Restructuring companies often have significantly depressed financial performance, including EBITDA. Often debtors and creditors will consider a stabilized or recovered EBITDA when valuing and determining debt capacity for a distressed company, though different parties often disagree regarding what an appropriate stabilized EBITDA value is.

[27] That being said, it is generally not a good idea to restructure a company such that it will have an interest coverage ratio below one or a debt to enterprise value ratio above one at emergence.

very material impact on the reorganized company's capital structure. For instance, certain creditors (CLOs in particular) may favor tradeable debt over equity, even when a more conservative capital structure (e.g., less debt and more equity) may maximize value or be more prudent under the circumstances.

EQUITIZATION OF DEBT

In most bankruptcies and many out-of-court restructurings, it is necessary for the company to reduce the total amount of debt without being able to fully compensate its creditors for this drop in value in the form of new debt or cash. Another way to think about this is that a debtor often comes into a restructuring with more debt than its debt capacity plus available cash. Where creditors are impaired in this way, a common solution is to redistribute the equity of the company to otherwise impaired creditors or bankruptcy claimants. This process is known as the equitization of debt; essentially, if a debtor is unable to pay off claims in cash or with new debt, the remaining claims will be compensated with the equity of the company.[28]

Because creditors are not entitled to recover more than their claims, the total valuation of the company becomes very important insofar as it impacts the presumed value of the company's equity (i.e., the value that remains available for distribution after new debt is determined). The holder of a fulcrum claim (or a potential fulcrum claim) must carefully consider his own incentives in arguing for a particular valuation, because different valuations can result in significantly different recoveries. Consider, for example, a debtor that files for bankruptcy with $100 million in senior debt, $30 million in junior debt, and $20 million in mezzanine debt with a reasonable asset value range of between $100 and $140 million. If the company plans to emerge with $90 million in reinstated senior debt, the senior creditor would be incentivized to argue that the company is only worth $100 million (or slightly less), so that it would be granted effectively all of the new equity of the company based on its debt deficiency of $10 million. In this case, the junior and mezzanine debt would receive no recovery. The mezzanine

---

[28] Some classes of claimants, such as trade creditors, often prefer cash in respect of their claims and are willing to accept cash at a discount in lieu of equity.

creditor would have incentive to argue that the company is valued right around $130 million, in which case both it and the senior debt would share in the equity and the junior debt would have no recovery. In this case, however, the mezzanine debt would be entitled to 75% of the new equity (reflecting its $30 million deficiency) and the senior debt would be entitled to only 25% of the new equity (reflecting its $10 million deficiency). The junior debt would have incentive to argue that the value of the company is as high as possible (e.g., greater than $130 million), so that the senior and mezzanine debt are paid in full, and the junior debt can recover some of the new equity (at a $140 million valuation, $10 million of $50 million in total equity, or 20%, with the senior debt also receiving 20% and the mezzanine debt receiving 60%). It is worth noting that these incentivized valuations, which result in significantly different recoveries and holdings of new equity, are independent of the true value of the company. If the court confirms a plan based on a $140 million valuation, the senior debt would receive only 20% of equity even if the company ends up being worth only $100 million (whereas at a $100 million valuation, the senior debt receives all of the equity, even if the company ends up being worth more).[29]

CREDITOR PROTECTIONS AND CORPORATE GOVERNANCE

Although a restructuring provides a debtor with a fresh start of sorts, creditors may use the restructuring as an opportunity to implement new protections for their investments or to modify the corporate governance of the debtor in a way that provides former debtholders with additional control, both as a protection against actions of the company but also as a bulwark against actions of their fellow creditors who are now co-equity owners. These protections take the form of financial and negative covenants in the relevant new debt instruments (e.g., minimum liquidity requirements, maximum debt to EBITDA ratios, and minimum coverage ratios), as well as in shareholders agreements, by-laws, and certificates of incorporation. In essence, a bankruptcy often gives birth to a new

---

[29] Note that this example is for illustrative purposes only and somewhat oversimplifies the process. It does not reflect a number of potential variables, such as administrative expenses and negotiated partial recoveries.

corporate entity and, at least lately, there has been an intense focus on majority/minority rights with respect to election of directors and corporate governance.

Market experts often describe the current credit market environment as covenant-lite, with creditors generally requiring very limited financial covenants (and no financial maintenance covenants) in standard credit agreements. However, creditors of a distressed company may use a restructuring as an opportunity to implement new financial covenants or to tighten existing ones. In the event that a debtor violates a financial covenant, the debtor may be subject to additional austerity measures, cash sweeps, or additional creditor controls, or the violation may be an event of default under the credit agreement. In the case of events of default, creditors can use the default resulting from a financial covenant violation (or even the likelihood of a future default) to bring the debtor back to the negotiating table post-restructuring.

Additional contractual controls may give creditors more direct control over the operations of a business, taking power away from the board and management. Following a restructuring, creditors may insist upon credit document terms that limit the debtor's ability to raise additional debt and to sell or move certain assets, and often will restrict spending on acquisitions and even capital expenditures. Of course, the terms of revised agreements will allow creditors to waive these restrictions on a case-by-case with a particular level of creditor consent, essentially giving creditors an approval right over the debtor's major financial and operational decisions. In some cases, creditors may take even more restrictive actions, such as requiring the debtor to submit a periodic business plan to them for approval. Additionally, it is fairly common for creditors to require the debtor to submit to its creditors more frequent or more detailed financial reporting. While equity owners continue to control the board, management, and day-to-day business decisions, creditors can implement post-restructuring corporate governance controls that give them a say in and insight into all major business decisions.

COMPETING MOTIVATIONS OF PARTIES

While it is a given that each party in a bankruptcy will try to maximize its own share of a limited pie, it is important for each party to consider the strategic motivations of other constituencies and the benefit and detriment of alliances or settlements of all or any of them. In some cases, parties with different perspectives own the same debt instruments going into a restructuring or are grouped together as a class in a bankruptcy, effectively tying their recoveries. For example, certain creditors may prefer to receive the equity of and actively manage a business (e.g., distressed private equity and hedge funds and current equity), whereas others may have absolutely no interest in holding equity (e.g., CLOs and trade creditors). Such differences may create opportunities for creative solutions but can also result in bitter, prolonged, and expensive fights about the direction of a restructuring. An obvious example of potential compromise may be an option plan where similarly situated creditors may choose the type of the consideration they may prefer, with those who want less risk through a distribution in new notes accepting less "value" than those willing to take a more risky equity recovery, but with greater upside.

VALUATION OVERVIEW

Valuation is one of the primary functions of a financial advisor in a restructuring transaction and plays a key role in the restructuring process. Although valuation is key to many financial transactions, given the uncertain nature of distressed companies and the intricacies of the bankruptcy system, valuation in the restructuring context can be both particularly contentious and consequential. In a bankruptcy (or an out-of-court restructuring), value is generally distributed based on priority (see "Unsecured Claims and Equity Claims" for a description of the absolute priority rule), so recoveries of a given class are highly dependent on valuations determined by relevant parties and, in a Chapter 11 context, the valuation accepted by the court. Differences in valuation can be the difference between a creditor class recovering fully, receiving debt back at a significant discount, having their debt equitized (which, in some cases and for some parties may be a desirable outcome), or being deemed out of the money. Therefore, even though different creditors and the debtor likely use similar valuation methodologies, they may come to significantly different conclusions about valuation based on their views of the business and their interests.

Further, as described in the section "What Investment Opportunities Exist in Distressed Situations?," the fulcrum security or securities play a special and central role among creditors in a

Chapter 11 bankruptcy proceeding: confirming the plan. Parties that are unimpaired (that are not impacted by the bankruptcy) and parties that are fully out of the money and receiving no distribution do not vote on whether or not to confirm a plan.[30] Although creditors in most situations will prefer a full recovery, there are some situations where a technically unimpaired class may prefer a say in the restructuring process, even if offered what looks like a 100% recovery (such as when they do not believe that the plan will truly leave them unimpaired). In these cases, a creditor or creditor class higher up in the capital structure may actually fight for a lower valuation that will leave them technically impaired.

Additionally, for investors, creditors, and the debtor, valuation is an important consideration in the decision-making process. Current creditors leverage valuation in determining what sort of plan they may be willing to accept (including how much remaining debt the debtor should emerge with) and whether they may want to exit a distressed investment. Investors consider valuation in determining whether they want to invest in or expand their investment in a distressed debtor. Finally, debtors should utilize valuations in determining whether to initiate a restructuring in the first place, proposing and negotiating a restructuring plan, and considering whether to sell off assets or portions of the business.

The broad methodologies used to value distressed and restructuring companies—discounted cash flow, comparable company analysis, and comparable transaction analysis—should be at least generally familiar to most financiers. However, distressed companies create challenges for each methodology, as described further in this section. Additionally, when considering the restructuring of a company, the debtor and creditors must at least consider liquidating the assets of the company rather than allowing the debtor to continue as a going concern. Finally, developing projections for a restructuring or distressed company presents unique challenges due to the additional considerations (e.g., future recovery/waterfall analysis, liquidity, and covenants), the unpredictable nature of businesses with significant disruption or in decline, and the significant changes to a business that often accompany a restructuring.

---

[30] Technically, under 11 U.S.C. § 1126(g), "a class is deemed not to have accepted a plan if such plan provides that the claims or interests of such class do not entitle" it to any recovery. In other words, the class is assumed to vote no, but the plan can still be confirmed.

DEVELOPING PROJECTIONS

As with valuation and financial analyses of a healthy company, financial projections of a distressed or restructuring company serve as the foundation of the valuation and other financial analyses for the company. In the case of a restructuring company, additional analyses that rely on financial projections include projection of the adequacy of liquidity going forward, assumptions about future recovery of various securities, sizing of and likelihood of breaching financial covenants, determination of debt capacity, and assessment of capital needs. The process for developing projections is largely similar to the projections process in a nondistressed context: a financial advisor generally builds out a three-statement model (balance sheet, income statement, and cash flow statement) based on past results and extends these statements into future periods. The financial advisor builds into the model a number of variables to drive the future financial projections and develops reasonable assumptions about these drivers. In determining these assumptions, the advisor likely considers factors such as past company performance, industry and company trends (including relevant equity research from industry experts), known business plans, management projections and guidance, and macroeconomic drivers. More granular considerations may include customer performance and preferences, supplier availability and negotiating power, competitor performance, and potential impacts of government regulation and market participation.

Typically, a financial advisor works to fine-tune his or her assumptions with the client (generally creditors or management) and any other stakeholders. Given the number of factors considered, different sets of projections may vary significantly among different parties. When working with and on the opposite side of stakeholders, it is important for the financial advisor to consider the motivations of these stakeholders. For both healthy and distressed companies, for example, members of management will generally have both the inclination and the incentive to optimistically project the prospects of their company.[31] Although this temptation is usually moderated in the normal course of business by the

---

[31] In other words, management is generally financially incentivized to have strong financial results and psychologically incentivized to think they are doing well. Additionally, management will tend to believe in their company and its business plan; otherwise, they would presumably work somewhere or do something else.

need to be viewed by investors as honest and reliable, the incentive to project optimistically increases significantly in the context of a potential transaction or distress. Companies that become distressed generally either underperformed past results or past expectations, and it may be very tempting for management to project the business to get back on track. However, financial advisors must be realistic and extremely cautious about projecting a full business recovery and, if they do, must be thoughtful about the timing of the recovery. A full recovery may be unlikely, for example, in a declining industry, where a key competitive advantage has been lost, or if the company has already lost significant market share to a competitor.[32]

Beyond ensuring that financial projections are thoughtful and conservative, a financial advisor projecting the performance of a restructuring company must also be sure to consider the financial impact of the restructuring. A bankruptcy typically has significant tangible and intangible costs that the debtor, which is often light on capital, must cover. Generally, the most recognizable tangible costs are those associated with the services provided by legal and financial professionals, as well as by consultants and other expert advisors who may be engaged to assist with the process. Intangible costs, by comparison, are not directly and immediately recognizable, but may have a substantial impact on a borrower's operations as well as on the efforts of lenders. Intangible costs include, for example, the time, energy, and commitment invested by management in coordinating the restructuring process and the time, energy, and commitment invested by the lenders' internal workout professionals in the same effort. Intangible costs also include the negative impact of the "stigma" attached to the financial distress experienced by a borrower, which may result in a lack of customer confidence, less favorable relationships with trade vendors, retention issues with key senior managers, and a generally reduced ability to focus on the long-term needs of the company, because the company is required to devote its energy and resources to the crisis at hand.

As bankruptcies have become more common, customers and suppliers in certain industries have become more comfortable working with companies going through a bankruptcy, allowing such businesses to limit operational disruption from a restructuring.

---

[32] It might be useful for a financial advisor to consider the likelihood of recovery in the context of a business competitiveness framework such as Michael Porter's five forces.

However, this is not true in all cases. For example, businesses that rely on a scarce supply of critical parts, those that provide their customers with promises of long-term maintenance or extended warranties, and government contractors with security clearance may be particularly impacted by a restructuring and reluctant to continue to work with a distressed company. Even in industries and sectors where operational disruption from a restructuring is limited, a financial advisor should still anticipate that the company will face difficulties in accessing capital and managing its net working capital going forward, because the company's long-term credit worthiness is called into question. As a result, it is often reasonable to project less access to liquidity and limited ability to take advantage of attractive investments than in the company's past.

Of note, the Bankruptcy Code provides certain advantages to debtors that financial advisors should also consider in projections. The ability of a bankrupt company to reject executory contracts and leases may have significant impact on the financial performance of some companies post-filing, as discussed in the section "Assumption and Rejection of Executory Contracts and Unexpired Leases."[33] The automatic stay (i.e., the ability to delay payments to creditors, including trade creditors) may provide the company with additional short- and medium-term liquidity. However, financial advisors should also consider the potential post-emergence impact of taking advantage of rejection of contracts and delay of payments to trade creditors, as should debtors when considering whether to take advantage of these options. While they provide short term relief, these options can impact relationships with suppliers and trade creditors going forward.

DISCOUNTED CASH FLOW ANALYSIS

Discounted cash flow (DCF) analysis is a process for valuing a company based on future expected cash flows of the company and is often considered to be the most complete form of corporate valuation, including for distressed companies. Although DCF analysis is simple in concept, it can often be very complex in execution.

---

[33] In fact, restructuring companies will often task financial advisors with projecting the impact of rejecting an executory contract or lease in deciding whether to accept or reject the contract or even as part of the decision of whether to file. In this way, consideration of executory contracts in projections can be an iterative process.

Typically, a financial professional builds a three-statement model for and projects future cash flows of a business, ignoring interest payments (i.e., calculating an unlevered free cash flow), and discounts cash flows from each period by a discount rate. The discount rate is often a weighted average cost of capital (WACC),[34] which considers the current return on debt of a company, the current expected return on equity of a company (generally based on the beta or volatility of a stock relative to the market), and the relative proportion of the firm's market equity and debt values.

At some period in the projections, the financial professional will determine that future operational assumptions for that period and all future periods are too uncertain, too imprecise, or generally unchanged. Instead of trying to project the company's financials after this point, the financial professional determines a future growth rate (often similar to the rate of inflation) and uses that and the discount rate to calculate a terminal value of the company.[35] Once an enterprise value is established, that value may then be split between debt, preferred equity, minority interest, and common equity.[36]

A distressed or restructuring company presents several issues for the execution of a DCF analysis. First, as discussed above, projecting the future performance of a distressed company involves unique challenges, making the cash flows portion of the DCF of a distressed company particularly difficult and contentious. Second, the determination of a discount rate of a distressed company typically requires some certainty of the value of debt and equity of a company. For a healthy company, debt is generally valued at or near par, the market capitalization provides a reasonable (if not always accurate) value of equity, and interest rates negotiated for current debt are considered to be good proxies for return on (or cost of) debt. For a restructuring

---

[34] $WACC = \dfrac{Market\ Equity\ Value}{V} * Return\ on\ Equity + \dfrac{Market\ Value\ of\ Debt}{V}$
*$Return\ on\ Debt * (1 - Tax\ Rate)$ where V is total market value of the firm's financing; the equation may also be modified to include preferred equity and minority interest, where necessary.

[35] Typically, a formula such as the following will be used:
$Terminal\ Value = \dfrac{Free\ Cash\ Flow_{final\ period} * (1 + Growth\ Rate)}{Discount\ Rate - Growth\ Rate}$

[36] *Enterprise Value = Market Capitalization + Preferred Equity + Debt + Minority Interest − Cash*
This formula is sometimes simplified and restated as *Equity Value = Enterprise Value + Cash − Debt.*

or heavily distressed company, the market will likely suggest a zero or near-zero equity value for the company, though the company can also face rapid and significant changes in the market value of equity. Further, debt, rather than being valued at par, will have a very uncertain value (and, in fact, in a restructuring, determining the value of each debt instrument is one of the main purposes of performing a valuation). Finally, interest rates on the debt of a distressed company almost certainly do not represent the cost of debt that the company would face in the market (and, in many cases, these companies would not be able to refinance their debt at all). As a result of the unavailability of numerators, denominators, and multipliers in the WACC equation, it is often not possible to perform a normal WACC calculation for a distressed company.

Instead, financial advisors will generally look to past experience and the market to determine a discount rate. Because there are no standard discount rates for distressed companies, an advisor could look at rates used in or implied by comparable distressed situations, considering factors including industry, company size, degree and type of financial distress, and market conditions when determining appropriate comparable rates or "comps." Another option would be for a financial advisor to find comparable healthy companies, determine the discount rates for these companies, and then apply a premium to the discount rate for the company's distress. In either case, it may be difficult to find good or even serviceable comps, so financial advisors must leverage significantly their judgment, expertise, and experience in this process. Finally, given the relative uncertainty about discount rates, it may be appropriate for a financial advisor valuing a distressed company to consider a wider range of discount rates when performing sensitivity analysis on its DCF than would be normal for a healthy company with more direct comparable companies. Still, given all of the uncertainty in a distressed DCF, parties may rely more on other valuation methods in a distressed scenario than they would otherwise.

COMPARABLE COMPANY ANALYSIS

Whereas a DCF analysis determines the intrinsic value of a company based on the present value of future cash flows, a comparable company analysis aims to determine the relative value of a company based on a comparison to similar public companies. The underlying assumption of the comparable company analysis is that similar companies should be valued at similar multiples of key operating metrics, such as EBIT or EBITDA. For companies with negative earnings, including early stage companies or severely distressed companies, a multiple of revenue will be used. Thus, a critical part of this analysis is selecting an appropriate operating metric of the subject company to capitalize. Typically, comparable company analysis uses historical metrics such as last fiscal year (LFY) or last 12 months (LTM). The first step in this analysis is "screening for comps"—selecting an appropriate group of comparable companies based on key characteristics such as industry, size, growth, and profitability. After selecting this group, the financial advisor will then "spread the comps"—compile a data set of relevant trading metrics for each company such as enterprise value (EV), market value of equity, and key multiples that can include EV/Revenue or EV/EBITDA. In addition to the individual metrics for each company, the advisor will typically look at the summary statistics for the comp set like the mean and median figures of the trading metrics. Finally, the last step in the comparable company analysis is to select an appropriate multiple to be applied to the subject company based on the observed trading multiples of the comparable public companies.

Performing a comparable company analysis for a distressed company presents certain challenges that advisors must address. First, although the performance metric used in a comparable companies' analysis will typically be a historical figure, this may not be appropriate for a distressed company as recent performance may not be representative of run-rate or normalized performance. Therefore, in a distressed context, the comparable company analysis will often be performed based on normalized or projected metrics rather than historical metrics. Additionally, as noted above, many distressed companies can have negative earnings, in which case a revenue figure would be more appropriate to capitalize than earnings metrics like EBIT or EBITDA. Lastly, there may be situations in which both historical and projected performance must be considered in the comparable company analysis. Under these circumstances, the financial advisor may incorporate a risk-weighting into the analysis in which a certain weighting is applied to each enterprise value indication, with the sum of all applied weightings equal to 100%. The concluded enterprise value from the analysis will be calculated by taking the weighted-average indication from all historical and projected metrics.

COMPARABLE TRANSACTION ANALYSIS

Similar to the comparable company analysis, the comparable transaction analysis is a relative value methodology that determines the value of a subject company based on a comparison to others. However, the main difference between the two methodologies is the data set that is used as the basis of comparison. Whereas the comparable company analysis is based on the implied multiples of similar publicly traded companies, the comparable transaction analysis looks at the actual multiples from completed mergers and acquisitions (M&A) transactions of similar companies (or, for distressed companies, a completed restructuring). Other than this critical difference, the process of the analysis is nearly identical to that described above for the comparable company analysis—select an appropriate group of comparable transactions; compile the data for the selected transactions, including relevant multiples; and select a proper multiple for the subject company based on a comparison to the companies in the selected transactions. Additionally, the distressed-specific issues discussed in the section "Comparable Company Analysis" apply equally to the comparable transaction analysis and can be addressed as explained above.

ADDITIONAL VALUATION CONSIDERATIONS FOR DISTRESSED COMPANIES

In addition to the projections and valuation methodologies above, financial advisors typically perform a number of other distressed-specific financial analyses to support a distressed or restructuring company and to ensure that any proposed plan can be successful. As discussed above, a financial advisor uses the projections that it develops to estimate the debtor's liquidity going forward and identify any potential shortfalls. Similarly, a financial advisor will typically project figures for and determine compliance and buffers for any financial covenants that a company has. Both liquidity analysis and covenant analysis are more essential for restructuring companies than for healthy companies because restructuring companies are more likely to become illiquid and violate covenants in downside scenarios. These projections are used not only to anticipate potential issues, but also to avoid them, as covenant sizing and capital at exit often depend on these analyses.

Additionally, financial advisors typically use projections for the debtor to determine the debt capacity of the company post-restructuring and establish what the company would need to do to eventually refinance its debt. Again, this is an important step in not simply anticipating issues but in avoiding them.

Finally, financial advisors perform recovery analysis for a restructuring company to determine where the value of the company would be distributed among current creditors, claimants, and equity holders. At its simplest, this analysis involves creating a waterfall, where value flows first from the most secured and senior creditors, to more junior creditors and unsecured claims, and eventually (if any value remains) to equity holders. However, a number of factors may complicate this analysis, such as structural subordination of claims, over- and undersecuritization, and plans to allow higher recoveries for employees and trade creditors. Financial advisors typically also use the waterfall to model and demonstrate the recovery types by creditor and claimant (combined with other projections and analyses, including debt capacity and liquidity). These analyses tend to be the basis for determining what sort of plan is feasible and ideal for debtors and creditors, because different parties will present different plans and projections, resulting in recoveries differing in both amount and type.

LIQUIDATION ANALYSIS

Liquidation analysis is a key component of the analysis that a financial advisor will conduct in a restructuring scenario, particularly in the context of a Chapter 11 bankruptcy. As opposed to the valuation methodologies discussed in the prior section, which are all based on the assumption that the company will continue to operate as a going concern, a liquidation analysis estimates a range of recovery values for each class of claims based upon a hypothetical disposition of all assets under Chapter 7 of the Bankruptcy Code. A liquidation analysis is most commonly prepared in the context of a Chapter 11 bankruptcy in order to fulfill the "best interests" requirement for the confirmation of a plan of reorganization, which stipulates that the plan may only be confirmed if no creditor will receive less in a reorganization than it would have in a complete liquidation of the business. Although the results of most liquidation analyses indicate that a company is more valuable as a going concern than it is under liquidation, there may be situations in which this does not hold true and therefore a liquidation of the company would maximize the recoveries to claimants and interest holders.

PERFORMING A LIQUIDATION ANALYSIS

As discussed above, a liquidation analysis examines and estimates the recovery values of all claimants based upon a theoretical liquidation of the debtor's assets under Chapter 7 of the Bankruptcy Code. The first step in this analysis is to estimate the recoverable value of all assets on the balance sheet, usually expressed as a percentage of the book value. Although there is some level of subjectivity in the assignment of recovery values based on the particulars of each individual case, there is a general rule that the level of recovery is often related to the relative liquidity of the asset. For example, a recovery of 90% to 100% may be assumed for assets such as cash, marketable securities, or accounts receivable (assuming a good history of collection and no ongoing disputes), whereas tangible assets such as buildings or vehicles may only be expected to recover closer to 50% of their book value, and intangible assets may have even lower recovery. In estimating these values, a financial advisor may dig deeper into what assets the company actually possesses, consult with operational and business line employees of the company, and, in some cases, engage third-party assessors. Financial advisors may also consider the timing of potential disposition of assets and the potential market for the assets that the company holds. Although a financial advisor may dig deeper, particularly where there is a question of whether the company can continue as a going concern, the advisor will typically present recovery range values at an asset class level (e.g., cash, accounts receivable, property, plant and equipment, etc.). After assigning recovery value ranges to all asset classes, the liquidation value of the company is calculated as the sum range of all asset recoveries less all administrative claims that would be expected to be incurred as part of a Chapter 7 liquidation.

DECIDING BETWEEN GOING CONCERN AND LIQUIDATION

In addition to the key role that going concern valuation plays in determining the fulcrum security in a Chapter 11 restructuring, comparing going concern value to a liquidation analysis helps determine whether the appropriate strategic decision is to continue operating as a going concern or to wind down the business through a complete liquidation. The main factor in arriving at this decision is value maximization—selecting the option that will maximize recovery values for creditors and other claimants. In a majority of situations, a going concern analysis will yield a higher value than a liquidation analysis, due to the difficulty of winding down and selling off a business with limited time and the ability of a stabilized business to efficiently combine human capital, fixed capital, and institutional knowledge to create financial capital (i.e., cash flows). In fact, in the past, liquidation analysis was a mere formality—it was generally accepted that a business is almost always more valuable as a going concern than in a liquidation, especially since the Bankruptcy Code grants debtors the ability to reject and terminate unfavorable executory contracts. However, there has been a recent trend to more seriously consider liquidation of a business as a viable option in bankruptcy proceedings. In particular, there have been recent liquidations of bankrupt companies in the retail and exploration and production sectors.

In addition to the binary decision of going concern versus liquidation, it is important to consider the varying motivations of different parties involved in the restructuring process. For example, senior creditors that would be fully unimpaired under a liquidation analysis and do not participate in the upside of the going concern business may prefer liquidation as an opportunity to recoup their investment quickly and with a relatively low level of risk. On the other hand, a largely impaired creditor, which stands to receive primarily equity in a bankruptcy proceeding (and might have limited or no recovery under a liquidation), would prefer that the business continue to operate as a going concern, even if this option might require additional investment or could jeopardize the interests of senior creditors. Similarly, company management, which would lose employment, sweat equity, and the possibility of a management incentive plan in a liquidation, might push to continue to operate a company, even if a liquidation would maximize value on a risk-adjusted basis.

A Closer Look at Provisions Permitting Liability Management Transactions

Jessica Reiss
Covenant Review, a Fitch Solutions Service

INTRODUCTION

The year 2020 saw the institutional loan market in upheaval due to COVID-19 and other macroeconomic considerations. As a result, a number of borrowers engaged in what have euphemistically been referred to as "liability management" transactions. These transactions took advantage of loosely drafted restrictions in credit agreements and other debt documentation to extend maturities or otherwise address liquidity concerns, but often left loan investors scratching their heads as to how they were conducted. This should come as no surprise; credit agreements are very carefully negotiated and drafted agreements that are filled with detailed provisions and concepts that can be difficult to decipher at first glance. Some of these provisions, which have existed in leveraged loan credit agreements for years, have become increasingly important of late as borrowers have begun to utilize available capacity to live to fight another day. This article explores some of these provisions and the underlying concepts behind them, in order to provide borrowers and lenders with a better understanding of these complex provisions.

Concerns around Value Leakage

In order to understand how borrowers and sponsor-backed issuers are able to weave together various credit agreement provisions to enter into advantageous transactions, let's first start with a breakdown of how a borrower's subsidiaries are treated under the loan documents.

The negative covenants in a typical leveraged loan credit agreement generally restrict the company and certain of its subsidiaries from engaging in a myriad of actions, including incurring debt, incurring liens, making dividends or distributions to equity, making investments, and selling assets, among other things. These prohibitions are usually subject to a lengthy list of exceptions and exclusions, which allow the company to complete these actions, subject to certain conditions and limitations. In order to successfully complete a liability management transaction, which may implicate one or several covenant provisions, a borrower must "find" sufficient capacity under the impacted covenants to permit the transaction.

In turn, credit agreements typically divide the borrower's subsidiaries into two main groups: a restricted group and an unrestricted group. The restricted group is further divided into the guarantor group and the nonguarantor group.

All members of the restricted group, regardless of whether they are guarantors or nonguarantors, are (together with the borrower) subject to the terms of the credit agreement; hence, they are "restricted" by the covenants. Guarantor restricted subsidiaries are also liable for the payment of obligations under the credit agreement, and guarantors also normally will pledge "substantially all" of their assets as collateral in support of such obligations. As a general rule, because of this universal credit support structure, transactions among the borrower and the guarantors (collectively known as the *loan parties* or *credit parties*) are relatively unfettered by the credit agreement.

As the name suggests, nonguarantor restricted subsidiaries are restricted subsidiaries that are not obligated to pay the debt of the borrower. However, even though they are not directly obligated to pay the credit agreement obligations, they still have to abide by the rules of the restrictive covenants. As such, in order for a nonguarantor restricted subsidiary to take certain actions or engage in certain types of transactions, it will need to make sure that sufficient capacity exists under the restrictive provisions of the credit agreement.

Unrestricted subsidiaries are almost never obligated to pay the debt of the borrower, but they are also generally not subject to the restrictive covenants of the credit agreement. Consequently, in contrast to the nonguarantor restricted subsidiaries, unrestricted subsidiaries do not need to find capacity under the credit agreement to engage in particular transactions.

A DEEPER DIVE INTO COLLATERAL-STRIPPING (DROP-DOWN) TRANSACTIONS

Having set the stage, let's walk through in more detail how a company can utilize specific credit agreement provisions to enter into a collateral-stripping, or drop-down, transaction. In a collateral-stripping transaction, a borrower strips out some assets (often material intellectual property) that were previously pledged as collateral for existing lenders. This is usually followed by another type of dilutive transaction, which can be the incurrence of debt backed by those same assets, a disposition of those assets, or another value-leaking transaction. The upshot of a collateral-stripping transaction is that assets that initially provided credit support for the loans will no longer be available to benefit the lender group in a default scenario, and (as mentioned briefly above) the existing lenders may be structurally or effectively subordinated to new lenders in respect of the transferred assets. Collateral-stripping transactions may be effected through use of either nonguarantor restricted subsidiaries or unrestricted subsidiaries. Companies may, however, prefer to use unrestricted subsidiaries to consummate these transactions, because, as noted above, nonguarantor restricted subsidiaries are still subject to the covenants under the credit agreement, whereas unrestricted subsidiaries are not.[37]

In order to determine whether a borrower has the ability to conduct a collateral-stripping transaction, lenders should carefully review the following credit agreement provisions:

1. *Can the borrower actually designate an unrestricted subsidiary, or does the borrower already have an unrestricted subsidiary that it can use?* A threshold consideration that must be satisfied is whether an unrestricted subsidiary already exists or if the company is able to designate an existing restricted subsidiary as unrestricted or create a new unrestricted subsidiary. Designation of an existing restricted subsidiary as an unrestricted subsidiary is typically subject to certain conditions, including the following:
    - *Investments covenant capacity.* Most credit agreements require that the designation of a restricted subsidiary as unrestricted be permitted under the investments covenant.[38] Although the value of investments held in such subsidiary may be determined in different ways (most commonly, as the fair market value of such

---

[37] For example, if a nonguarantor restricted subsidiary were to receive valuable assets through an intercompany investment, in order to monetize those assets through a debt incurrence it must still be permitted to incur the debt under the debt covenant of the relevant credit agreement.

[38] This is the negative covenant that limits various types of "investments," including equity investments, capital contributions, and extensions of debt.

investments at the time of designation),[39] the company must have sufficient capacity under the investments covenant carve-outs to transfer the underlying value out of the restricted group.

- *Default stopper.* Designation of an unrestricted subsidiary will not be permitted to the extent a "default," "event of default," or payment/bankruptcy "event of default" has occurred and is continuing.[40]
- *Ratio condition.* More traditional credit agreements require the company to be in pro forma compliance with either a specified ratio test or with financial maintenance covenants (if one exists). This condition has been watered down or dropped altogether in recent years.
- *Recourse debt condition.* Most credit agreements require that a subsidiary being designated as unrestricted may not hold debt that is recourse to the borrower or another member of the restricted group.
- *Material intellectual property blocker.*[41] In response to other collateral-stripping transactions, some credit agreements include "J. Crew blocker" provisions that prohibit a subsidiary that holds "material" intellectual property from being designated as unrestricted. These blockers may also prohibit the transfer of "material" intellectual property by a loan party to an unrestricted subsidiary or even to a nonguarantor restricted subsidiary. Note that J. Crew blockers do not *have* to be in respect of material intellectual property; they can function to block the transfer of any class of asset to which the drafting parties may agree.

---

[39] More aggressive credit agreements may measure value as the fair market value of the "net assets" of the subsidiary at the time of designation, proportionate to the company's equity interest in such subsidiary.

[40] Note that although credit agreements generally include some form of default stopper for designation of an unrestricted subsidiary, the level varies. The absence of any "default" is the most conservative, but more aggressive credit agreements may only require the absence of a payment or bankruptcy "event of default," allowing the borrower a greater degree of leeway.

[41] In most cases, this provision is tied to intellectual property and not to transfers of other collateral assets. Query how helpful these blockers are in credit agreements for companies with very limited intellectual property.

- *Minimum attribution condition.* In some more-conservative loans, upon designation of any subsidiary as unrestricted, the total value of certain financial metrics (e.g., total assets or EBITDA) attributable to that unrestricted subsidiary (or all unrestricted subsidiaries) cannot exceed a negotiated cap.

  As noted, these conditions are typically tested only upon designation and not for any subsequent transfer or investment of value. Some credit agreements may, however, include more robust versions of one or more of these conditions that might also apply in the case of subsequent transfers to unrestricted subsidiaries (the most common of these being the J. Crew blocker).

  Additionally, some borrowers may be able to bypass certain conditions (e.g., the ratio condition or the minimum attribution condition) by designating so-called empty box subsidiaries—newly formed restricted subsidiaries that have no assets and generate no EBITDA (the designation of which would not be expected to have any pro forma effect on the company's financial status).

  Assuming there either is an existing unrestricted subsidiary or the borrower can designate a subsidiary as unrestricted, the next portion of the analysis will be the lien and guarantee release provisions.

2. *Are the liens and guarantees automatically released?* It wouldn't be much use to designate or transfer assets to unrestricted subsidiaries if the liens on those assets weren't automatically released. As alluded to above, most sponsor credit agreements will specify that any guarantees previously provided by a subsidiary that is later designated as an unrestricted subsidiary will be released, either automatically or, in some cases, by request of the borrower, without the consent of the lenders. Similarly, liens on specific assets transferred to an unrestricted subsidiary will often be automatically released, or the administrative agent for the loan will be expressly authorized to execute any necessary release documentation in the case of assets that cannot be automatically released (e.g., real property or certain intangible assets) if the underlying transfer is permitted by the covenants.

3. *Is there sufficient investments capacity*? A company's ability to engage in a collateral-stripping transaction will ultimately depend upon capacity under the investments covenant baskets. Investments covenants, after all, almost never limit the types of assets that may be invested (unless there is a robust blocker as described above or another atypical prohibition on the transfer of certain assets). Typical baskets that could support any such investments include the following:
    - The "available amount"/"cumulative credit"/builder basket, which typically will build from either retained "excess cash flow" or a percentage (often 50%) of "consolidated net income."
    - Any dedicated basket(s) for investments in unrestricted subsidiaries.
    - Any general-purpose investments basket(s).
    - Any baskets for investments in "similar businesses."
    - Any other fixed or shared investments/restricted payments/junior debt prepayments capacity.
    - Any ratio investments carve-out.
    - An intercompany investments basket; note that this is normally limited to investments made within the restricted group but can potentially be "converted" into unrestricted subsidiary investments capacity if a "trapdoor" basket is present.[42]

    Of course, whether these baskets exist and whether there is any capacity available under these baskets is a complicated question that requires the review of the specific covenants in question and an analysis of whether any capacity has been generated or previously utilized, as well as a review for the presence of any blockers or other similar provisions.[43]

---

[42] The "trapdoor" is the basket infamously used by J. Crew to transfer its intellectual property to an unrestricted subsidiary, leading to the creation of the J. Crew blocker described above. Other examples of (mis)uses of intercompany investments capacity have included use of a basket for investments in "nonguarantor subsidiaries," where "nonguarantor subsidiary" is defined to include *any* subsidiary, not just restricted subsidiaries.

[43] Additional concerns may arise, for example, if a "trapdoor" basket is coupled with an uncapped basket for intercompany investments (a so-called "black hole"), which would potentially allow for unlimited transfers of assets from a loan party to a nonloan party restricted subsidiary and then by such nonloan party restricted subsidiary to an unrestricted subsidiary.

4. *Are there other miscellaneous concerns?* In addition to those threshold considerations, it may be necessary to also look at other provisions of the credit agreement to ensure that the drop-down transaction would still be permitted. A thorough analysis may also include review of the financial maintenance covenants (if any), as well as amendments, sale-leaseback, affiliate transactions, and asset sales provisions. Further, drop-down transactions may trigger fraudulent conveyance concerns.

5. *What options does the borrower have once it has successfully transferred assets into an unrestricted subsidiary?* As a baseline matter, all or some of the covenants will typically be subject to a prohibition on the restricted group entities engaging in any "direct or indirect transactions." This is most prevalent in the restricted payments covenant, but sometimes the lead-in to the covenants will broadly restrict the transactions prohibited by the covenants that are entered into directly or indirectly. In those cases, this prohibition might provide nonparticipating lenders with the ability to challenge a collateral-stripping transaction on the grounds that it is essentially occurring "indirectly" through the artifice of an unrestricted subsidiary.[44] This would essentially be an attack on any subsequent transaction that the unrestricted subsidiary in question might take after the transfer of assets (as the legitimacy of the transfer of assets itself will be determined based solely on investments and asset sales capacity).[45] In addition, there are a small number of deals, usually the most aggressive ones, which explicitly override the "direct or indirect" prohibition on this point. In those agreements, there is a separate clause at the end

---

[44] The argument would be that essentially this is an indirect incurrence of indebtedness, and therefore it should be prohibited by the debt covenant even though it is technically occurring through an unrestricted subsidiary.

[45] There is likely to be a temporal component to any argument that actions through an unrestricted subsidiary constitute an "indirect" prohibited transaction. If the subsequent transaction occurs substantially simultaneously with the collateral-stripping transaction, one could theorize that the two transactions are merely two steps of the same transaction. On the other hand, if the subsequent transaction occurs at a later date (say, two years), it becomes harder to argue that the subsequent unrestricted subsidiary transaction is a prohibited "indirect" transaction of the restricted group (and not merely a transaction conducted by the unrestricted subsidiary in conjunction with its own ordinary course of business).

of the investments and restricted payments provisions that essentially states that the borrower can use unrestricted subsidiaries as a conduit to return value to shareholders through restricted payments.

Assuming that the borrower can pass this (admittedly uncertain) bar, it will have many options based, of course, on the specific credit agreement provisions at issue. Some potential transactions include the following:

- *Spin-offs of the unrestricted subsidiary to equity holders.* Sponsor credit agreements will often provide flexibility to spin off unrestricted subsidiaries.[46]
- *Selling the unrestricted subsidiary.* The borrower may also seek to sell the unrestricted subsidiary; this would generate proceeds that will often not be subject to the asset sale sweep and as such will be free for the borrower to utilize for any other permitted purpose.
- *Raising debt at the unrestricted subsidiary.* The borrower can also raise debt at the unrestricted subsidiary. Given that the subsidiary is not subject to the negative covenants, the amount of any such debt is realistically only limited by what the market is willing to lend against the value of the assets contributed to that entity. The proceeds of that debt may be utilized either by the unrestricted subsidiary or, if distributed to the restricted group, for liquidity or any other permitted purpose.
- *Reloading the investments baskets.* The borrower can also argue that any proceeds that the restricted group receives as distributions from the unrestricted subsidiary (however generated) will refresh certain investments baskets, thereby freeing up capacity for future use.

ANOTHER BRAND OF VALUE DIMINUTION: UPTIERING TRANSACTIONS

Collateral-stripping transactions are only one means that borrowers may have under the terms of their credit agreements to effectuate

---

[46] The restricted payments covenant may expressly permit the distribution of unrestricted subsidiary equity interests without regard to other restricted payments basket capacity, though this may be limited to subsidiaries with primarily noncash assets.

a liability management transaction. If the drop-down avenue is unavailable to a borrower, it may instead look to its syndicate or an outside group of creditors and engage in an uptiering transaction. In an uptiering transaction, existing lenders are shunted behind priming debt under the same credit agreement (where one class of lenders is divided into two classes, with one class favored relative to the other) or separately documented credit agreements (where, in some cases, creditors under the existing credit agreement enter into a priming credit agreement, leaving former co-syndicate members behind).

This can be a major issue for lenders for obvious reasons. Investors in syndicated leveraged loans typically expect that the deal they are signing on to preserves their place at the top of the capital structure—for example, that they will be first in lien priority with respect to "substantially all" of the borrower's assets and senior (or at least pari passu) in right of payment with respect to other series of debt.[47]

However, this is not always the case, and lenders under existing first lien credit facilities may find themselves second in line behind new priming, superpriority credit facilities.

These types of transactions are often made possible as a result of weak consent requirements that allow for payment and/or lien subordination by a vote of only majority lenders.[48, 49] Distressed

---

[47] Of course, if there is a bankruptcy, the company may incur priming debt in the form of a DIP facility (subject to the strictures of the Bankruptcy Code), but senior secured lenders should be protected as long as the company is performing, even if it's distressed.

[48] Debt that is contractually subordinated in right of payment specifically states that the holder of such debt will only be paid after repayment in full of other designated senior debt. There is typically a period of time (a "standstill") after a default before the holders of the subordinated debt can take action to recover on their claims. If debt is subordinated in terms of security, the holders have expressly agreed that their liens on shared collateral will rank lower than the liens in favor of holders of the more senior secured debt with respect to those assets.

[49] Note that this article is not concerned with transactions that are purposely structured, from the outset, to include a superpriority facility (e.g., a so-called split-collateral deal, where there is a term loan facility and a separate asset-based lending facility). In such deals, the related intercreditor agreement provides that (1) the asset-based lending facility has a first lien on the shared current-asset collateral and a second lien on the other shared collateral and (2) the term loan facility has a second lien on the shared current-asset collateral and a first lien on the other shared collateral. Although less common, another example is a credit agreement that includes a first-out revolver and a last-out term loan (which typically arises under the so-called waterfall provision included in the credit agreement).

borrowers seeking liquidity or contractual relief may offer economic carrots to cooperative (or activist) lenders who agree to make company-favorable changes, leaving minority lenders behind.

UPTIERING WITHIN THE SAME CREDIT AGREEMENT: MODIFICATIONS OF PRO RATA SHARING PROVISIONS

A basic tenet of all syndicated loans is that each member of the syndicate should receive its *pro rata share* (or *ratable share*—we'll be using the terms interchangeably) of payments obtained from a borrower. Ratable share or pro rata share refers to the percentage of a lender's exposure in any given loan relative to the total exposure (i.e., outstanding amount) of that loan.[50] Borrowers, in other words, are not allowed to play favorites with individual lenders.[51]

In recent years, however, the pro rata sharing principle (or, more accurately, attempts to modify or work around it) has become the source of significant worry for the buy side, as borrowers have capitalized on flexibility under credit agreements to work with certain groups of lenders to the detriment of others. For example, lenders who cooperate with an out-of-court restructuring may receive a super-senior position in a waterfall—essentially subordinating those lenders who do not (or are not invited to) participate. These kinds of economic changes to the status quo are almost certainly at odds with one or more of the pro rata sharing provisions contained in the loan documents. This, in turn, puts an enormous amount of pressure on the provisions in a credit

---

[50] Pro rata sharing can be applied on an intraclass basis (i.e., the borrower must treat all lenders of a single class of debt equally with each other lender in that class) or on an interclass basis (i.e., the borrower must treat lenders of multiple classes equally as between those two classes). Further, the pro rata sharing principle dictates only the relationship of lenders under a single credit agreement.

[51] There are a number of customary exceptions to the pro rata sharing principle, which, even if they must be offered ratably to all lenders in a particular class, may be accepted or rejected by individual lenders, including: (1) discounted buybacks or prepayments, (2) incremental incurrence under the accordion, and (3) incurrence of credit agreement refinancing debt (including amend-to-extend transactions). There may also be blanket exceptions for other provisions that are expressly provided for elsewhere in the credit agreement.

agreement that allow ratable sharing mechanics to be modified or bypassed.[52]

1. *What do the "pro rata sharing" provisions encompass?* It is not uncommon for pro rata sharing provisions to be combined, split across sections, or even completely absent. Indeed, there isn't even a standardized approach as to where these provisions should be located within any particular credit agreement. There is simply no one-size-fits-all approach. That said, when market participants discuss "pro rata sharing," they are generally referring to some subset of the following key sections of a credit agreement:

    - *Collateral proceeds waterfall.* The waterfall provisions govern how proceeds of collateral (or other amounts received) will be applied following an event of default or other acceleration event.[53]
    - *Pro rata treatment provision.* The pro rata treatment provision generally provides that payments of interest or principal should be made to each lender based on such lender's ratable percentage of overall loans and commitments.
    - *Specific payment provisions.* Some credit agreements require ratable treatment in individual payment scenarios. Such an approach may provide (within the given provision) that the borrower will apply each payment to the lenders of the class being prepaid on a pro rata basis.
    - *Sharing of payments provision.* The sharing of payments provision provides that if any single lender obtains proceeds from a borrower in an amount that is greater than its ratable share, then such lender will purchase a

---

[52] Note that changing pro rata sharing potentially may also implicate other contractual/legal issues (e.g., "effective" releases of collateral or guarantee values, principles of commercial reasonableness, breaches of implied covenants of good faith and fair dealing, and fraudulent transfer regimes, just to name a few). However, these issues are beyond the scope of this article.

[53] Although the collateral proceeds waterfall is often found in the credit agreement, it may, in some transactions, be documented in a separate security, guaranty, and/or pledge agreement.

participation or subparticipation from each other lender such that the pro rata application of proceeds is restored.
- *Pro rata percentage definition.* This is the definition that sets forth exactly what *pro rata* actually means. The specific term can vary from deal to deal (*pro rata share, ratable share,* or *applicable share* being other common examples of the same idea).
- *Other relevant provisions.* The principle of pro rata sharing may also appear in commitment reduction provisions, the accordion, the insufficient/partial payments waterfall, and the Dutch auction provision, among others.

2. *Using (and abusing) consent rights to modify the pro rata sharing provisions.* A borrower's ability to manipulate the pro rata sharing provisions in a credit agreement is dependent, in large part, on the level of consent required to modify such provisions. Just as there is no one-size-fits-all approach to where and how the pro rata provisions appear in credit agreements, there are also a variety of approaches to what threshold of consent is required to amend such provisions. The degree of flexibility to change pro rata provisions will dictate a company's capacity to enter into uptiering transactions within its credit agreement.

Generally speaking, an amendment provision that broadly requires a higher consent threshold for changes to any provision that affects pro rata sharing or treatment among lenders provides a greater degree of protection than amendment provisions that enumerate only specific provisions. However, the omission of any threshold for consent is the most problematic.

- *Changes require only majority lender consent.* The most concerning variation on the ability to amend pro rata sharing provisions permits modifications solely with majority lender consent. As a general rule, if a credit agreement's amendment provision is silent in regards to pro rata sharing provisions, then it means that any change to those provisions can be effected with the consent of required lenders only. This approach is both the simplest from a drafting standpoint (merely omit to mention the pro rata sharing provisions from the list of enumerated exceptions) and the one that is probably easiest to overlook (because one is searching for the absence of language when assessing this risk).

- Under this approach, any provision that requires ratable treatment or sharing among lenders can be modified to benefit the majority consenting lenders at the expense of the minority nonconsenting lenders.[54]
- *Changes require consent of a majority of the affected class.* Some deals take the approach that changes to pro rata sharing provisions require the consent of lenders that hold a majority in interest of the affected "class" of debt. Majority class voting mechanics are subject to a number of material weaknesses (from the lenders' perspective). First, a majority class vote does not necessarily give an adversely affected lender a blocking position, and second, class voting theoretically provides no protection for lenders against intraclass changes. Consider the following scenario: a borrower has a single term loan facility and is seeking covenant relief. A majority of lenders agree to consent to such relief but only if they can take a superpriority position in a waterfall (relative to the nonconsenting lenders). In such a scenario, it is not clear whether the class voting mechanic would even be implicated, because one could argue that the "class" that is affected is the entirety of the existing term loan lenders (a majority of whom have consented to the modification).

On the flip side, class voting does tend to protect against interclass manipulations. For example, imagine a scenario where revolving lenders and term loan lenders are pari passu secured with one another, but revolving lenders account for a majority of all lenders. Without class voting, the revolving lenders could

---

[54] And keep in mind that leveraged loan credit agreements rarely prescribe specific amendment procedure; that is, there is usually no express requirement to offer the amendment to all lenders if the borrower has already negotiated the consent from a majority of lenders behind the scenes. That said, borrowers are usually incentivized to act in as transparent a manner as possible, given that at least some judges have suggested that keeping parts of the syndicate in the dark during amendment negotiations is fundamentally unfair.

potentially bootstrap their way into a superpriority position (relative to the term loan lenders, because in this hypothetical the revolving lenders account for the "required lenders"). With a class voting provision in place, however, such a change to the waterfall would require the consent of a majority of the term loan lenders as the adversely affected class (a consent that those lenders likely have no incentive to provide).

- *Changes require 100% or "affected" lender consent.* The most lender-friendly approach is to require the consent of either 100% of all lenders or 100% of all of the lenders that are directly (or directly and adversely) affected by the proposed modification.[55] Requiring this higher consent threshold makes the task of changing the specified sections of the agreement difficult—if not impossible—to accomplish, and gives those lenders most at risk of being damaged the opportunity to block the amendment (or at least it gives these lenders the ability to force a borrower to exercise a yank-a-bank to take them out).

- *Changes require other higher threshold of lender consent.* An alternative approach is to require supermajority lender consent for changes to pro rata sharing provisions (where *supermajority* is usually defined as the lenders holding two-thirds of the total outstanding loans/commitments). This approach provides less protection than the 100% lender consent threshold (though it is, of course, possible that it may provide more protection than an affected lender threshold, if the number of affected lenders is less than two-thirds of the total lenders).

    A supermajority vote is fairly unorthodox in the leveraged loan market, however, and is rarely utilized in credit agreements with a syndicated term loan (at least in the United States).

---

[55] From a practical perspective, whether an amendment requires 100% lender consent or only affected lender consent is a distinction without a difference. The two approaches are essentially the same—the key point being that lenders should be able to block any change that is against their economic interests.

As is the case with so many other provisions in credit agreements, however, the devil is in the details. Even if the market has accepted that changes to pro rata sharing require an affected or 100% voting threshold, the strength of the protection to lenders afforded thereby will ultimately depend on the scope and number of provisions covered by such higher threshold.

In many cases, only changes to specified pro rata sharing provisions will require a heightened level of consent. The risk of nonratable modifications therefore depends on (1) what exactly the borrower is seeking to do and (2) which pro rata sharing provisions are captured by the higher consent threshold. Attempting to consider every possible iteration of these two factors is impossible for purposes of this section. However, one could argue that the omission of any pro rata sharing provision will expose lenders to the risk that the ratable treatment prescribed in that provision will be undermined.

UPTIERING UNDER A SEPARATE FACILITY: SUBORDINATION BY MAJORITY CONSENT

Along similar lines, the confluence of certain provisions in credit agreements may also provide borrowers with the ability to incur priming debt and liens under separate agreements, with the result that lenders under the existing facilities must take a backseat in terms of payment priority, lien priority, or both. As noted above, the pro rata sharing provisions typically govern the relative treatment of lenders in the same class or different classes under the same credit agreement and do not extend to creditors under a different debt instrument. As such, the analysis above regarding treatment of various classes of lenders under the credit agreement does not apply to the treatment of creditors under separate debt instruments, but there are many parallels.

- *Changes require only majority lender consent.* As discussed above, in the absence of explicit provisions requiring heightened consent, the default is that only majority consent is required to amend any provision in the credit agreement. However, unlike the pro rata sharing provisions, one would be hard-pressed to find any language governing heightened consent requirements to amend provisions relating to subordination (either in terms of payment priority or lien priority) in most credit agreements. Very few credit agreements currently include a voting provision requiring all or affected lender approval to subordinate the credit facility in right of payment and/or security to other permitted debt incurred under a separate credit agreement or other debt instrument. Instead, there tends to be only a requirement for unanimous lender approval to "release" (as opposed to "subordinate") all or substantially all of the value of the guarantees or collateral. This leaves the door open for majority lenders to approve subordination of the credit facilities to outside debt.

- *Changes require 100% or "affected" lender consent.* Although the distinct minority, some credit agreements do require heightened consent thresholds for amendments that would subordinate the obligations thereunder either in right of payment or in terms of lien priority to an outside debt instrument. Lenders should take caution, however, because affected lender consent may only be required to the extent subordination relates to "all or substantially all of the collateral" or only applies to certain enumerated third-party obligations (e.g., debt for borrowed money).
- *Open market purchases.* An additional wrinkle posed by contractual subordination to an outside series of debt is that consenting lenders are exchanging their loans for debt in the new priming facility and will no longer be bound by the terms of the existing credit agreement.

Credit agreements generally permit the company to repurchase term loans on the open market, with any loans purchased by the company automatically deemed repaid and no longer outstanding under the credit agreement. As noted above, there is no requirement that this be done ratably, which gives the company the opportunity to repurchase only term loans held by the lenders consenting to (and providing) the superpriority debt.[56] Further, many

---

[56] This is different from the auction buyback provisions, which require that an offer be made to all lenders or all lenders in the relevant class. As noted above, these provisions are exceptions to the pro rata sharing provisions, because each individual lender has the option to accept or reject the offer, but the offer must be made ratably to all applicable lenders.

credit agreements do not define "open market purchase" or specify that such purchases must be made for cash consideration and may not include privately negotiated debt exchanges.

The provisions governing open market purchases are found in the assignments section of the credit agreement.[57]

- *Negative covenants and covenant-stripping.* As a general rule, only majority lender consent is required to amend or modify the negative covenants—in particular, for purposes of incurring priming debt, the debt and liens covenants. For example, a majority of lenders could agree to amend the credit agreement for the specific purpose of adding a basket for superpriority debt and/or liens, potentially creating an end-run around amendment provisions (depending on how loosely such provisions are drafted).

  However, this flexibility may also result in consenting lenders stripping other affirmative and negative covenants applicable to the existing credit agreement, among other provisions, leaving the nonmajority/consenting lenders with a much weaker credit agreement. Although this concept has been mostly foreign to the leveraged loan world until recently, and as such there has been no reasonably foreseen need to protect against this, it has been common in the high-yield bond universe for quite some time. Further, the credit agreement universe does not generally include a bond-style "payments for consent" covenant, which would require exit consent consideration to be offered to all lenders in a particular tranche.

CONCLUSION

Credit agreements have long provided borrowers with avenues that they can use to maneuver through tough times, often by weaving together capacity under various covenants and provisions.

---

[57] Interestingly, restrictions on sponsor buybacks were only added to the credit agreement fairly recently, in order to try to prevent some of these liability management transactions. Sponsors were buying back loans at a discount, without retiring or cancelling the amounts repurchased, and without a cap on amounts that were permitted to be repurchased. In some cases, sponsors held a majority of the outstanding loans and were able to utilize the majority voting provisions to effect amendments and strip covenants, giving the borrower more flexibility under the loan documents.

In recent transactions, the unifying principle among the different situations has been borrowers taking advantage of loose or incomplete credit documentation in order to prioritize one set of debt claimants at the expense of others. Although the provisions described above are not the only mechanics available to borrowers, having a better understanding of how these concepts work can give lenders insight into the potential for future liability management transactions.

CHAPTER 11
Overview of Loan Credit Default Swaps and Loan Total Return Swaps

Overview of Loan Credit Default Swaps

John Clark
Senior Counsel
Crowell & Moring LLP

Jennifer Grady
Partner
Crowell & Moring LLP

Richard Lee
Partner
Crowell & Moring LLP

Overview of Bank Loan Total Return Swaps

John Clark
Senior Counsel
Crowell & Moring LLP

Jennifer Grady
Partner
Crowell & Moring LLP

Richard Lee
Partner
Crowell & Moring LLP

Overview of Loan Credit Default Swaps

John Clark

Jennifer Grady

Richard Lee
Crowell & Moring LLP

INTRODUCTION

In 2006, the International Swaps and Derivatives Association (ISDA) and the Loan Syndications and Trading Association (LSTA) developed a unique credit default swap product tailored for loans—the loan credit default swap (LCDS). Although LCDS no longer trades in the current market, it remains a potential hedging strategy for the future, and the story of its development is both interesting and instructive.

LCDS—A DERIVATIVE PRODUCT

An LCDS is a derivative product designed to allow loan market participants to isolate and trade the credit risk underlying a single bank loan or a portfolio of loans. The use of LCDS in the loan market was preceded by the development of a robust trading market for vanilla credit default swaps (CDS), which facilitated the exchange of credit risk underlying the senior unsecured bond market. LCDS mirrors the structure of a standard CDS trade but is tailored to address the risks underlying the syndicated secured loan market and the unique settlement features of loans. Whereas CDS was used on a bespoke basis in the early 2000s to structure hedges in the loan market, a more standardized form of LCDS was developed in 2006 through a partnership between ISDA and the LSTA in order to encourage the development of a liquid tradable derivative product. For a number of years after its launch, standardized LCDS, along with the related LCDX index product, was offered by multiple loan market dealers and was used widely by loan market participants seeking to hedge their risk of loan ownership and by those seeking synthetic access to the credit risk underlying the loan market. Although the trading market for these products has been greatly diminished in recent years, LCDS structured on a bespoke basis remains an important method of hedging credit risk of borrowers in the loan market.

INTRODUCTION AND STRUCTURE OF LCDS

Under a single-name LCDS trade, much like a standard CDS trade, the seller of protection ("Protection Seller") sells, and the buyer of protection ("Protection Buyer") buys, a notional amount of protection against the default of a third party (the "Reference Entity") specified in the confirmation. During the term of the transaction, Protection Buyer makes "premium" payments to the Protection Seller in exchange for the promise of protection against the occurrence of specified defaults by the Reference Entity ("Credit Events"). (See Exhibit 11.1.) The Protection Buyer typically looks to hedge a long position in the Reference Entity's loans, whereas the

EXHIBIT 11.1

Loan Credit Default Swap.

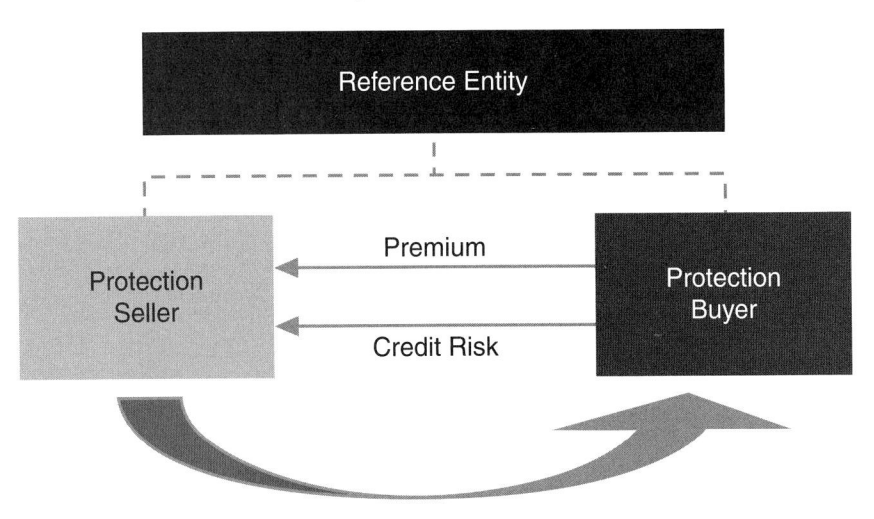

Protection Seller seeks synthetic exposure to the credit risk of the Reference Entity.

If a Credit Event occurs during the term of the transaction, the parties settle their obligations either through cash settlement or physical settlement. Cash settlement, which is required by the current standardized version of LCDS in the United States, provides that the Protection Seller will make a cash payment to the Protection Buyer equal to the par value of a syndicated secured loan of the Reference Entity minus the current market value of that loan. If physical settlement applies to a transaction, which may happen either at the election of the parties or as a fallback settlement method where the market value of a loan cannot be determined, then the Protection Buyer will physically deliver the loan of the Reference Entity to the Protection Seller in exchange for a cash payment equal to the par value of that loan.

Both settlement methods, therefore, achieve the same economic effect, but cash settlement enables the parties to settle in the most efficient manner possible by avoiding the logistical challenges involved in the physical settlement of loans. If no Credit Event occurs during the term of the transaction, then the transaction terminates without any further obligations on the part of either party.

EVOLUTION OF LCDS AND LCDX

Prior to 2006, LCDS was intermittently used on a bespoke basis and was therefore illiquid and provided inefficient and costly protection for Protection Buyers. An industry group convened in 2006 with the goal of designing a standardized LCDS product that would facilitate the development of a liquid trading market, and the initial version of the standardized product was launched to great fanfare by ISDA and the LSTA. After its initial launch, the LCDS product developed rapidly, and its structure evolved to reflect multiple significant design modifications:

- *June 2006: Initial product launch.* The initial LCDS product featured (1) mandatory physical settlement and (2) a no-cost cancellation provision, exercisable by either party, upon any refinancing that left the borrower without syndicated secured loans for a period of 30 business days.

- *May 2007: Version 2 of LCDS launch and initial launch of LCDX.* LCDS was redesigned in May of 2007 in order to hard-wire cash settlement pursuant to an ISDA-sponsored auction, which was intended to improve the efficiency of the product by eliminating the logistical challenges involved in physical settlement of loans. In addition, the first version of LCDX, the LCDS index product, was launched simultaneously with the second version of LCDS. An LCDX transaction represented a portfolio of 100 equally weighted LCDS transactions referencing the 100 most liquidly traded syndicated secured loans at the time of the trade. LCDX enabled loan market participants to go long or short on the loan market generally without selecting specific loans or borrowers. However, according to IHS Markit, the original administrator of the LCDX index, the last series of LCDX matured in June 2018, and the product has not been priced since February 2016.
- *April 2010: Version 3 of LCDS launched: Bullet LCDS.* The current version of LCDS, launched in 2010, is referred to as "Bullet LCDS" because it reflects the removal of the cancellation provision feature in legacy LCDS and features instead a single "bullet" maturity date. The cancellation feature had been included in the original LCDS product at the insistence of Protection Buyers concerned about "orphan contracts"—swap transactions where no deliverable obligations are available for delivery upon the occurrence of a Credit Event but nevertheless require continued premium payments by Protection Buyers. Orphan contracts occur in CDS transactions but were expected to occur more frequently in LCDS because loans are refinanced more frequently than bonds. However, the cancellation feature made it difficult for LCDS dealers to value an LCDS contract because of the difficulty predicting the likelihood and timing of a loan refinancing event. Market participants decided to forgo the cancellation option in order to provide the market with more certainty on term and pricing. Bullet LCDS was therefore designed to improve the liquidity and tradability of LCDS.

STANDARD LCDS TERMS AND DISTINCTIONS FROM CDS

The following is a summary of the key terms of LCDS transactions, including terms distinguishing LCDS from the more widely traded CDS product:

- *Credit Events.* In standard LCDS trades, two separate Credit Events are specified. If the Reference Entity (1) fails to make a scheduled payment of $1 million or more of "borrowed money" (including loans and bonds) after the expiration of any grace period applicable to such payment, or (2) enters bankruptcy proceedings, then the parties may trigger settlement of the relevant contract. Like standard CDS contracts on North American corporates, the LCDS Standard Terms do not include "restructuring" as a Credit Event.
- *Deliverable Obligations: Syndicated secured loans.* Although a payment default on bonds may trigger a Credit Event under LCDS transactions, only syndicated secured loans can be delivered to effect physical settlement, or used to determine the recovery value for purposes of cash settlement, following a Credit Event. In order to be eligible for delivery under an LCDS transaction in the case of physical settlement, an obligation must (1) be an obligation of the Reference Entity (either as a borrower or, in certain cases, as a guarantor) and (2) meet various "Deliverable Obligation Characteristics" specified in the confirmation. Most important, under LCDS, a Deliverable Obligation must be a "syndicated secured" loan of the Reference Entity, based on a market trading standard, rather than a legal definition. Lastly, unlike standard CDS, unfunded revolver or letter of credit commitments are eligible Deliverable Obligations and may be delivered after a Credit Event.
- *Successor/refinancing events.* LCDS updates the "successor" provisions applicable to standard CDS trades in order to incorporate the structure of standard refinancings in the loan market. In order to reduce the likelihood of orphan contracts in connection with the removal of the cancellation feature, LCDS trades provide that if a Reference Obligation is refinanced by a new loan borrowed by an entity other than the Reference Entity, then the transaction will migrate

to the new Reference Entity in order to increase the likelihood that a Deliverable Obligation is available.
- *Settlement and Physical Settlement Rider.* Although LCDS transactions are subject to mandatory cash settlement pursuant to an ISDA-sponsored auction, physical settlement may still apply in certain circumstances. Although physical settlement in the high-yield bond market is effected electronically and is subject to mandated settlement timelines, physical settlement of loans can present challenges and is often subject to delays as a result of the unique features of the loan market, including third-party consent requirements and lengthy upstream review. The market participants who designed the LCDS product were concerned that long and uncertain settlement timelines for loan trades resulting from an LCDS auction could hamper liquidity in the LCDS market. To mitigate these concerns, the LSTA developed the "Physical Settlement Rider" to the LCDS standard terms, which requires parties to physically settle using nonnegotiable settlement procedures and documentation based upon modified LSTA documentation and settlement standards.

DERIVATIVES REGULATION

As described below in the context of loan total return swaps, regulations promulgated in the United States and the European Union following the Global Financial Crisis of 2008 (GFC), including regulations promulgated under the U.S. Dodd-Frank Wall Street Reform and Consumer Protection Act ("Dodd-Frank") regulations in the United States, created a new system of regulatory oversight of the derivatives markets. Single-name loan credit default swaps, like loan total return swaps, are deemed to be "security-based swaps" in the United States, and thus subject to oversight by the Securities and Exchange Commission (SEC). One of the primary challenges for loan market participants of compliance with the applicable regulations, especially with respect to security-based swaps, relates to information asymmetry issues. Although security-based swaps are "securities" for purposes of Dodd-Frank regulations, and are therefore subject to SEC Rule 10b-5 and its restrictions on insider trading, loans are not deemed to be securities subject to SEC oversight, and loan market participants often have access to material nonpublic information provided by borrowers to their lending syndicate. The inconsistency in the treatment of information in the loan and swap markets creates a challenge, particularly for Protection Buyers looking to hedge long loan exposure.

LCDS IN THE CURRENT MARKET

LCDS and LCDX were first standardized in the mid-2000s, and both products enjoyed robust trading volumes for a few years following their initial launch. However, the liquidity of these products has been repeatedly challenged due to valuation concerns and market forces (including the GFC) which discouraged the use of derivatives generally. In addition, though CDS is an imperfect hedge for long loan exposure, some loan market participants have gravitated toward the CDS market for default protection given the superior liquidity of that more well established market. Today, LCDS is not widely used as a tradeable product, and LCDX is no longer rolled on a regular basis to populate the index with new liquid loans, suggesting that the product is essentially dormant. However, LCDS is still utilized on a bespoke basis by Protection Buyers seeking to establish positions on loans or loan portfolios subject to increased credit risk, particularly where relationships with the borrowers prevent the sale of those loans. Though standardized LCDS has suffered a bruising series of setbacks, the LCDS structure still provides a valuable hedging tool especially where tailored to the Protection Buyer's needs.

Overview of Bank Loan Total Return Swaps

John Clark

Jennifer Grady

Richard Lee
Crowell & Moring LLP

Bank loan total return swaps (LTRS) have contributed to the growth of the loan market over recent decades and remain widely deployed by market participants. LTRS were first utilized in the

1990s by investors seeking to amplify debt portfolio returns and were developed in part due to the lack of a robust "repo" market for bank loans. LTRS use declined after the GFC as investors reduced portfolio leverage and trading in complex derivative products. More recently, however, the initial dislocation of the U.S. syndicated loan market following the outbreak of COVID-19 spurred interest in LTRS among distressed debt investors, who sought to use the product to take advantage of temporarily depressed asset prices with a reduced cash outlay. Since its inception, LTRS has proven to be a flexible product that can be applied broadly by bank loan investors seeking leveraged economic exposure to bank loans and is a valuable tool for market participants who understand its unique structure and features.

INTRODUCTION AND OVERVIEW OF STRUCTURE

LTRS is a bilateral over-the-counter (OTC) derivative instrument that enables hedge funds, collateralized loan obligation (CLO) issuers, and other institutional investors to gain synthetic leveraged access to bank loans. The transaction is typically entered into between a buy-side investor (the "LTRS Buyer" or "Total Return Receiver") and a bank (the "LTRS dealer" or "Total Return Payer") and references a third-party borrower's syndicated loan (the "Reference Entity" and "Reference Obligation," respectively). During the term of an LTRS, the LTRS Buyer pays a periodic (typically monthly or quarterly) floating charge to the LTRS dealer, based on a benchmark interest rate plus a spread. In exchange, the LTRS dealer agrees to pay to the LTRS Buyer all interest, fees, and other economic benefits that a lender of the underlying Reference Obligation would receive during the same period. (See Exhibit 11.2.)

The LTRS dealer typically endeavors to be market risk neutral with respect to an LTRS transaction by entering into a back-to-back LTRS with another market participant, by purchasing the underlying Reference Obligation, or by structuring other hedges. If the LTRS dealer elects to hedge the LTRS transaction, the LTRS Buyer often may arrange the purchase of the underlying bank loans by entering into a bank loan trade and directing settlement of the trade to the LTRS dealer or a special purpose vehicle managed by the LTRS dealer to hold the underlying bank loans.

EXHIBIT 11.2

Loan Total Return Swap.

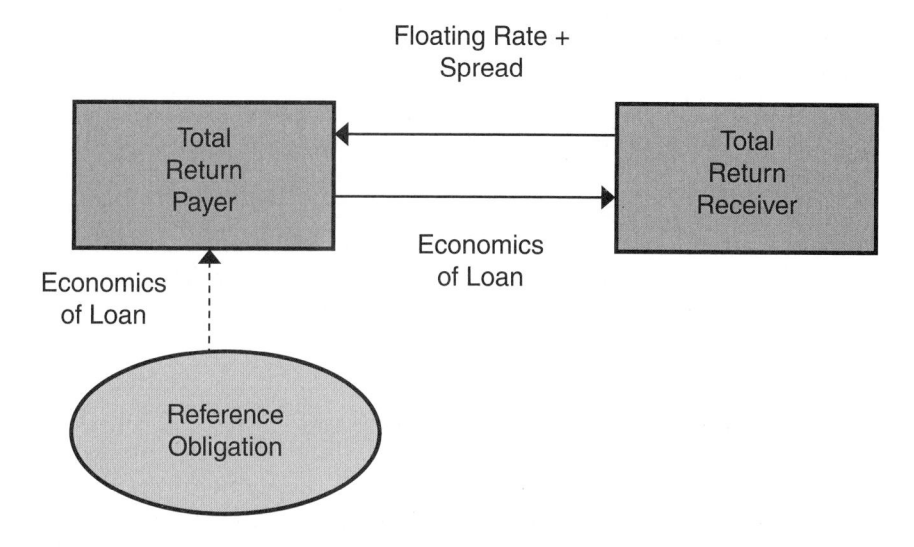

```
                    Floating Rate +
                        Spread
    ┌──────────┐ ◄──────────────── ┌──────────┐
    │  Total   │                    │  Total   │
    │  Return  │ ────────────────►  │  Return  │
    │  Payer   │                    │ Receiver │
    └──────────┘     Economics      └──────────┘
         ▲            of Loan
  Economics
    of Loan
         │
    ( Reference )
    ( Obligation )
```

CASH FLOWS AND COLLATERAL REQUIREMENTS

Cash flows under an LTRS transaction generally occur at trade initiation, at the end of monthly or quarterly periods thereafter, and finally upon termination of the transaction. At trade initiation, the LTRS Buyer pays the LTRS dealer "initial margin," calculated as an agreed percentage of the initial value of the underlying bank loan, which serves as collateral for the LTRS Buyer's obligations under the swap. Each period following the trade date, the LTRS dealer calculates the financing charge payable by the LTRS Buyer, which is based on a pre-agreed benchmark floating rate plus a spread. The LTRS dealer also periodically pays to the LTRS Buyer all interest, fees, and the amount of any whole or partial principal repayments exceeding the initial market value (as of the time of the LTRS trade) of the corresponding outstanding loan balance. Upon termination of the swap, the LTRS Buyer is obligated to pay any amount of capital depreciation in the value of the Reference Obligation since the trade date to the LTRS dealer, and the dealer must pay any capital appreciation if the value of the loan has increased. The dealer also must return any excess collateral to the buyer.

The cash flows under the LTRS illustrate that a fully hedged LTRS dealer should be risk neutral with respect to the transaction: although the dealer (or its affiliate) may hold the loan or an alternative hedge position on its books, all economic gains and losses under the loan are for the account of the LTRS Buyer. (See Exhibit 11.3.) The LTRS dealer profits by charging the LTRS Buyer a rate spread applied to the initial value of the loan, but otherwise it does not realize any gain from any appreciation in the value of the loan. Conversely, the LTRS Buyer, in seeking leveraged access to the loan, has agreed to accept the market risk on the loan, to absorb any potential decline in the value of the loan in exchange for receiving any increased value, and typically reimburses the LTRS dealer for certain hedging costs.

The primary risk faced by the LTRS dealer is the credit risk of its counterparty. To mitigate counterparty default risk, the LTRS dealer will collect from the LTRS Buyer daily "variation margin" to support any mark-to-market declines in the value of the Reference Obligation during the term of the LTRS. The initial margin (also referred to as *independent amount* or *haircut*) paid by the LTRS Buyer to the LTRS dealer at swap execution is intended to cover the risk of unexpected large declines in market value (i.e., "jump-to-default" risk) and operational delays, including during any period following an LTRS Buyer's contractual default but before settlement and liquidation of the underlying LTRS and hedge position. Since the implementation of regulatory requirements following the GFC, LTRS dealers must comply with various jurisdictional

EXHIBIT 11.3

LTRS Cash Flows and Margin.

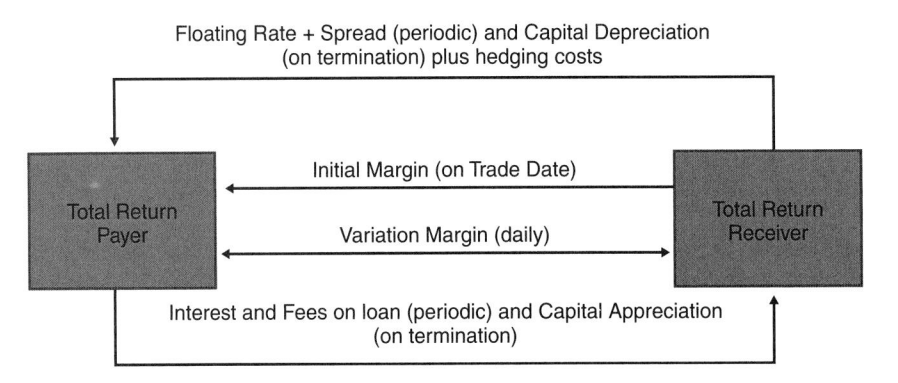

margin regulations which in some cases mandate the amount and frequency of the exchange of margin. Nevertheless, this posted margin is typically a fraction of the amount of cash that would be required to purchase a syndicated loan outright, thus enabling an LTRS Buyer to obtain leveraged exposure to a loan's economics.

LEVERAGE, RETURN, AND YIELD

As an example of the leverage that can be achieved by an LTRS Buyer, Exhibit 11.4 provides a simplified illustration of the different economic outcomes for a bank loan market participant seeking to invest in a $10,000,000 outstanding principal amount loan that is priced in the market at 90%. The investor can either purchase the loan outright or enter into an LTRS providing synthetic economic exposure to that loan where the LTRS dealer charges initial margin—in this example, 30%.

The initial margin requirement imposed by the LTRS dealer or, if applicable, by margin regulations, determines the extent of the leverage achieved by the LTRS Buyer and reflects the primary economic distinction between the two alternative investment

EXHIBIT 11.4

	Purchase of loan	LTRS transaction
Initial cash payment by Investor	**$9,000,000** purchase price (90% purchase rate × outstanding principal amount of loan)	**$2,700,000** initial margin requirement (30% initial margin rate × $9,000,000 initial market value of loan)
Impact of decline in the price of the loan to 80%	No immediate cash flow impact.	Investor must post variation margin of $1,000,000 ((90%−80%) × face amount of loan)
Sale of loan/termination of swap at a price of 80%	*Investor realizes $1,000,000 net loss.* $8,000,000 sale proceeds (80% purchase rate × outstanding principal amount) − $9,000,000 initial purchase price	*Investor realizes $1,000,000 net loss.* • LTRS Buyer owes capital depreciation on reference loan obligation of $1,000,000 to LTRS dealer • LTRS dealer returns collateral of $3,700,000 to LTRS Buyer

structures. In this example, the LTRS Buyer will free up $6,300,000 of capital at the time of its trade to deploy to other investments, and thus has achieved 3.33 times initial leverage by accessing a loan via LTRS rather than purchasing the loan outright. This investor will need to maintain liquidity for purposes of satisfying margin calls and will be responsible for the payment of a periodic floating payment to the LTRS dealer for use of the dealer's balance sheet.

The economics of the LTRS transaction mirror the economics of loan ownership, but the addition of leverage results in the amplification of the risk–return profile and an increase in the cash yield on the loan transaction. The example (see Exhibit 11.5), again showing a $10,000,000 loan priced at 90% but assuming a 10% increase in the price of the loan over the term of the swap, provides a simplified illustration of how the LTRS structure can increase the expected return on a loan investment. The higher expected return is of course accompanied by the risk of amplified loss from taking a leveraged position. In this example, a 10% change in price results in an increase of expected return (or loss) from 11.11% to 37.04%.

EXHIBIT 11.5

Face Amount at Par (Outstanding Principal Amount):	$10,000,000
Initial Loan Market Value:	90% of face amount = $9,000,000
Initial Margin:	30% of Initial Loan Market Value = $2,700,000
Change in Loan Market Value:	+10% of face amount = $1,000,000
Expected Return: Cash Trade	= Change in Loan Market Value / Initial Purchase Price = $1,000,000 / $9,000,000 = **11.11%**
Expected Return: LTRS	= Change in Loan Market Value / Initial Margin = $1,000,000 / $2,700,000 = **37.04%**

To build on the example presented in Exhibit 11.5, an LTRS can increase the annual yield as compared to a cash loan purchase. In the following example (see Exhibit 11.6), the LTRS Buyer has increased its annual yield from 5.83% to 15.38% by utilizing LTRS rather than purchasing the loan in a cash trade.

EXHIBIT 11.6

Face Amount at Par (Outstanding Principal Amount):	$10,000,000
Initial Loan Market Value:	90% of face amount = $9,000,000
Initial Margin:	30% of Initial Loan Value = $2,700,000
Loan Coupon:	Floating Rate + 5.00% = 5.25%
Floating Rate:	3-month USD LIBOR = .25%
LTRS Financing Charge:	Floating Rate + 1.00% = 1.25%
Interest Rate on Collateral:	Federal Funds (Effective) = 0.10%
Annual Yield: Cash Trade	= Interest from Loan (i.e., Outstanding Principal Amount × Loan Coupon)/Initial Loan Value = $525,000/$9,000,000 = **5.83%**
Annual Yield: LTRS	= (Interest from Loan (i.e., Outstanding Principal Amount × Loan Coupon) − LTRS Financing Payments (i.e., Initial Loan Market Value × LTRS Financing Charge) + Interest on Initial Margin (i.e., Initial Margin × Interest Rate on Collateral)/Initial Margin = ($525,000 − $112,500 + $2,700)/$2,700,000 = **15.38%**

PRIMARY USES AND TYPES OF LTRS

The flexibility of LTRS enables loan market participants both to achieve various investment strategies synthetically and to resolve certain settlement issues on cash trades.

- The majority of current LTRS Buyers are investment funds seeking to gain leveraged access to the loan asset class to increase target returns and preserve capital for other investments. As an example, in the spring of 2020, investors who believed loans were mispriced due to a short-term market dislocation sought to use LTRS to take long positions in temporarily underpriced loans with little upfront capital and unwind those positions after a subsequent market recovery.
- LTRS also has achieved widespread use as a warehouse product in the context of a CLO launch. A CLO manager may use LTRS to finance positions in an underlying CLO loan portfolio with minimal capital outlays prior to notes issuance. Upon the launch of the CLO, the proceeds of the notes issuance can be used either to convert the

LTRS positions into physically settled loan transfers to the CLO issuer or, if the LTRS dealer has purchased loan hedge positions into a special purpose vehicle (SPV), as consideration for the equity of that SPV, which is subsequently merged into the CLO issuer.
- Because loan assignments settle by physical transfers of record ownership, they are subject to potential lengthy settlement delays as a result of third-party consent requirements, unsettled upstream trades, and other logistical challenges arising from credit facility terms. Investors seeking access to a large loan portfolio, or those seeking relatively short-term access to loan positions, may be served well by using LTRS to achieve synthetic exposure to loans while side-stepping the operational challenges of direct loan ownership. LTRS dealers have a robust internal loan settlement, administration, and payment operations infrastructure so it may be more efficient for investors to access this infrastructure rather than administering loan positions, especially on a large scale or short-term basis, internally.
- Similarly, LTRS can be used by loan market participants as an alternative method for closing loan trades where settlement by assignment or participation may be impossible or impracticable.

Depending on the investment strategy, LTRS can be structured either as a single-name or a portfolio transaction. Single-name LTRS allows investment funds to gain leveraged access to a single loan where the economic terms relating to such loan, including the applicable spread and haircut charged by the LTRS dealer, will be agreed between the parties on a loan-by-loan basis. Single-name LTRS provides the most flexibility for both parties in terms of tenor and Reference Obligation eligibility requirements.

A portfolio-style LTRS may be more appropriate for an LTRS Buyer desiring access to a fixed portfolio of loans or a standing facility for financing a dynamic portfolio, whether for purposes of loan warehousing or as a stand-alone investment strategy. Portfolio LTRS transactions typically have a tenor of one to five years and are often extended by amendment. Under a portfolio LTRS, the parties agree on certain eligibility criteria and concentration limits that give the LTRS Buyer clarity on what types of loans will be permitted to be placed on swap, and in exchange the LTRS Buyer commits to maintain a certain minimum notional amount of loans on swap to guarantee the dealer a minimum profit generated. Portfolio LTRS structures often include (1) pre-agreed independent amounts for various categories of loans based on their underlying risk structures (e.g., first vs. second lien, term loan vs. revolver) and credit ratings, (2) ramp-up periods to allow the LTRS Buyer time to build up its portfolio before minimum trade requirements apply, and (3) portfolio concentration limits and obligation criteria in order to enable the LTRS dealer to limit and diversify its risk.

DOCUMENTATION AND ISSUES

LTRS documentation is not standardized, and its terms often can be heavily negotiated. LTRS transactions typically require the parties to establish the following contractual agreements:

- *ISDA Master Agreement.* LTRS trades are documented under confirmations incorporating the terms of a negotiated ISDA Master Agreement. This agreement governs payment mechanics, allocates various risks, and is tailored to parties' local insolvency laws and derivatives regulatory regimes. As a practical matter, parties should bear in mind that execution of this document can become surprisingly time-intensive without business focus and counsel sensitive to prevailing market standards and commercial risks.
- *ISDA Credit Support Annex.* The ISDA Credit Support Annex is a supplement to the ISDA Master Agreement that governs the posting of collateral and related mechanics between the parties, such as timing of collateral delivery, holding and use of collateral, and valuation dispute resolution procedures. This document must be tailored to comply with any applicable jurisdictional margin requirements.
- *Master Confirmation Agreement and supplemental confirmations.* Whereas the ISDA Master Agreement and Credit Support Annex are industry standard forms, each LTRS dealer typically has its own bespoke Master Confirmation Agreement (MCA). This agreement contains the terms and provisions governing all LTRS transactions entered into between the parties. The economic and loan-specific terms

relating to each individual transaction may be reflected in supplemental confirmations to the MCA documenting each individual transaction.

The MCA will generally provide for the calculation and timing of payments owed by each party under any LTRS transaction, any applicable eligibility and portfolio criteria in the context of a portfolio LTRS, voting and information rights of the LTRS Buyer with respect to the underlying loans, and termination rights of both parties. The following are examples of key provisions in the MCA, including some that are frequently negotiated:

- *Termination rights.* An LTRS Buyer typically has optional early termination (OET) rights, giving it the ability to close out its synthetic position just as if it sold out of an actual loan position. LTRS dealers typically do not have unfettered OET rights but will attempt to build in rights to unwind the swap in various situations posing increased risk to the dealer, including with respect to the credit quality or liquidity of the underlying Reference Obligation. These provisions are typically heavily negotiated and require an understanding of market conventions.
- *Information issues.* In the United States, a syndicated loan is not a security in the view of federal regulators, but an LTRS referencing such a loan is considered to be a security for purposes of certain provisions of the securities laws and regulations. This means both LTRS dealers and LTRS Buyers must understand how to comply with antifraud securities laws, including Section 10(b) of the Securities and Exchange Act. Concerns relating to trading while in possession of material nonpublic information can be especially acute for credit funds given the close relationships that naturally develop among lenders, agents, and borrowers over the course of lending relationships. In addition, the LTRS dealer may agree to forward to the LTRS Buyer information delivered to lenders in respect of an underlying syndicated loan, which may be subject to confidentiality restrictions.
- *Voting and control.* Although the purpose of the LTRS product is to replicate the economics of loan ownership, an LTRS typically does not extend voting and control rights

to the underlying loan to the buyer. There are a variety of practical, contractual, and bankruptcy law reasons why a dealer generally will not agree to act as the buyer's proxy for questions put to the lenders. That said, dealers typically try to accommodate their clients' needs, and creative negotiation during a trade can often allay buyer concerns regarding control. LTRS dealers will often agree to provide "consultation rights" with respect to consent requests or other significant votes put to lenders.

TAX AND BANKRUPTCY CONCERNS

LTRS market participants should be aware of certain tax and bankruptcy concerns that may arise under a transaction. Withholding tax may be applied to an LTRS transaction depending on the jurisdiction of the borrower as compared to the jurisdiction of the holder (or deemed holder) of the underlying loan in the event the dealer has elected to establish a hedge position. The LTRS dealer will typically attempt to shift the risk of the application of withholding tax to its counterparty so LTRS Buyers should analyze the tax provisions and jurisdictional issues carefully before entering into a new transaction. From a bankruptcy perspective, if the LTRS dealer has particular concerns about the credit risk of the LTRS Buyer, it will be focused on structuring the LTRS documentation to ensure the transaction is viewed as a "swap agreement" under the U.S. Bankruptcy Code. Among other things, the dealer, as a creditor under a safe harbor swap agreement, is entitled to relief from the automatic stay in order to terminate the transaction upon any bankruptcy of the counterparty buyer. The parties will structure the LTRS documentation in a way that minimizes the risk that the transaction might be recharacterized as a secured financing subject to the automatic stay and not otherwise benefiting from safe harbor provisions.

DERIVATIVES REGULATIONS

Since the GFC, the United States and the European Union (among other jurisdictions) have implemented extensive regulatory requirements applicable to derivatives products such as LTRS. Regulations promulgated under the U.S. Dodd-Frank Wall Street Reform and Consumer Protection Act and European Market Infrastructure

Regulation, respectively, govern the conduct of dealers' business, trade reconciliation, and reporting; central clearing of transactions; posting and holding of margin; fraud and market manipulation; and many other aspects of trading in derivatives. Which rules apply, and when, will depend on a variety of factors—including the parties' respective jurisdictions, size and type of financial enterprise, and the derivative product being traded. In all cases, parties must determine which jurisdictions' rules will govern their trade and understand mandatory variation margin collection requirements and applicable minimum initial margin requirements. Although this handbook discusses regulations applicable to the loan market, we note briefly here that market participants should pay particular attention to the potential securities law and regulatory implications of entry into an LTRS. This product began as a bilateral transaction subject to little regulation but has since been swept into a universe of OTC swaps that are subject to oversight by multiple regulatory agencies in domestic and foreign jurisdictions.

CONCLUSION

Although LTRS is a complex product, it provides investors with a flexible structure to access the loan market while retaining capital to pursue alternative investments. Because it is a derivative product subject to institutional and regulatory margin requirements, end-users must carefully analyze potential capital demands throughout the life cycle of their trades. However, for loan market participants with reliable sources of liquidity available to respond to margin calls, LTRS remains the most efficient method to leverage desired exposure to bank loans. Notwithstanding its complexity and recent challenges adjusting to new worldwide derivatives regulatory regimes, we expect interest in LTRS as an investment tool to continue to broaden with the growth of the loan market.

CHAPTER 12
Loan Fund Portfolio Management

Carly Wilson
Portfolio Manager, Loan Strategies and Global
Long/Short Credit Strategies
BlackRock

Loan portfolio management is often said to be "unique" or "too different" to compare to equity portfolio management or high-yield portfolio management. Certainly, the loan asset class has its nuances and idiosyncrasies, and these are critical to understand. Yet, so, too, are the best practices learned from other asset classes that can guide loan portfolio managers to best outcomes.

The loan market has evolved significantly over the past 20 to 30 years. With this market maturation has come a significant portfolio management evolution—from buy and hold investing to active portfolio management. Years back, loan portfolio management could hardly be called portfolio management at all. It was really about picking credits and then holding those positions to maturity. The old joke went something like: "I'd own the loan, it's a par piece of paper at the end of the day."

But now, given the market growth, broader ownership base, and the significant changes in market structure and liquidity, loan portfolio management has become much more sophisticated and is something to analyze and optimize.

WHO INVESTS IN LOANS?

The subinvestment-grade loan market has grown to approximately $1.2 trillion in total size and attracts a variety of investor types. The most significant source of demand comes from collateralized loan obligation (CLO) vehicles, representing approximately 60% of the demand base. Given the risk-based tranching of CLO liabilities, here, too, there is a wide variety of investors—from U.S. and foreign banks at the top of the capital structure (AAA rated), to hedge funds and asset managers for BBs and equity.

Loans are also owned in separately managed accounts (SMAs), with the end-investors most often being insurance funds and pension funds, though they can attract other buyers as well. The SMA investor base oftentimes slants up in quality and is typically focused on ratings as a proxy for risk.

In addition, loans are owned in retail mutual funds. Here the investment approach is more unconstrained, and performance is considered versus the peer group. Exhibit 12.1 provides a summary look at considerations for managing different types of loan mandates.

EXHIBIT 12.1

Types of Loan Investors.

Source of Demand	% of Market	Risk/Return Goals
CLOs	~60% to 70%	CLO equity returns; must optimize vs. various constraints across ratings, asset spread, diversification, and other considerations
SMAs	~15%***	Total return + return vs. benchmark; focused on higher rated assets and lower volatility experience
Mutual Funds	~10% to 20%	Total return, return vs. benchmark AND return vs. peers; most unconstrained demand base

There are different market participants across the risk spectrum, and fund structures vary widely. Yet, the key reasons for owning loans have significant overlap:

- To remove duration risk from an asset allocation, while staying long credit spread risk
- To maintain competitive income in an asset allocation, while reducing volatility
- To maximize total return

Analyzing the historical return and volatility experience of loans proves out these ideas: adding a loan allocation improves aggregate portfolio outcomes.

Notably, loan allocations often increase, particularly for retail players, when investors are expecting rates to sell-off. In Exhibit 12.2, we illustrate just how pronounced is this theme.

Because loans are floating rate, and most other risk assets are long-duration assets, loans compare favorably in these market scenarios. In addition, historical loan returns have proven consistently competitive with other asset allocations choices—in total return, excess return, and risk adjusted. Exhibit 12.3 shows historical excess returns and annualized volatility for the loan asset class, as compared to High Yield, Investment Grade, and TIPS.

In the following sections, we'll analyze how to most effectively construct loan portfolios, focusing on more unconstrained approaches. CLO portfolio management is a separate topic; although there are many overlapping principles, there are also significant CLO-specific considerations.

EXHIBIT 12.2

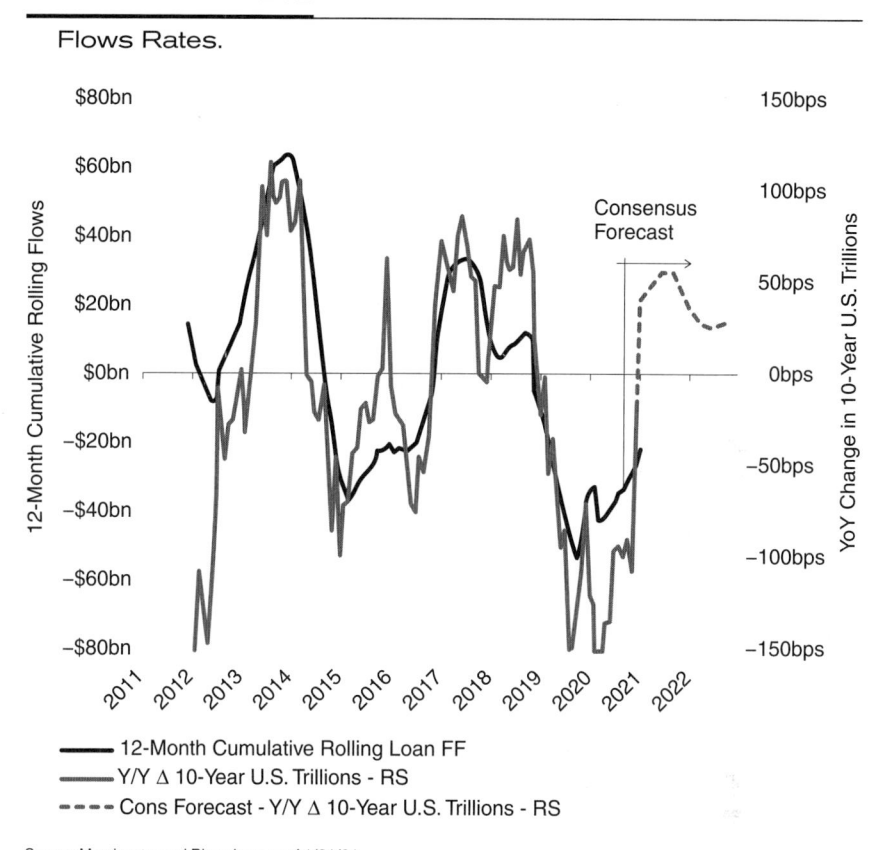

Flows Rates.

[Chart showing 12-Month Cumulative Rolling Loan FF and Y/Y Δ 10-Year U.S. Trillions from 2011 to 2022, with Consensus Forecast indicated]

— 12-Month Cumulative Rolling Loan FF
— Y/Y Δ 10-Year U.S. Trillions - RS
- - - Cons Forecast - Y/Y Δ 10-Year U.S. Trillions - RS

Source: Morningstar and Bloomberg as of 1/31/21.

HOW TO CONSTRUCT A LOAN PORTFOLIO

Thus, we have determined who invests in loans and why. Once this allocation decision has been made, a loan portfolio manager must establish the return and volatility goals for the client and for the portfolio. Some common goals include:

- To achieve positive active return versus a benchmark
- To outperform peers
- To maximize total return
- To optimize the Sharpe ratio
- To limit drawdown/volatility

After considering the client's goals, it is critically important to establish a risk benchmark and a performance benchmark for

EXHIBIT 12.3

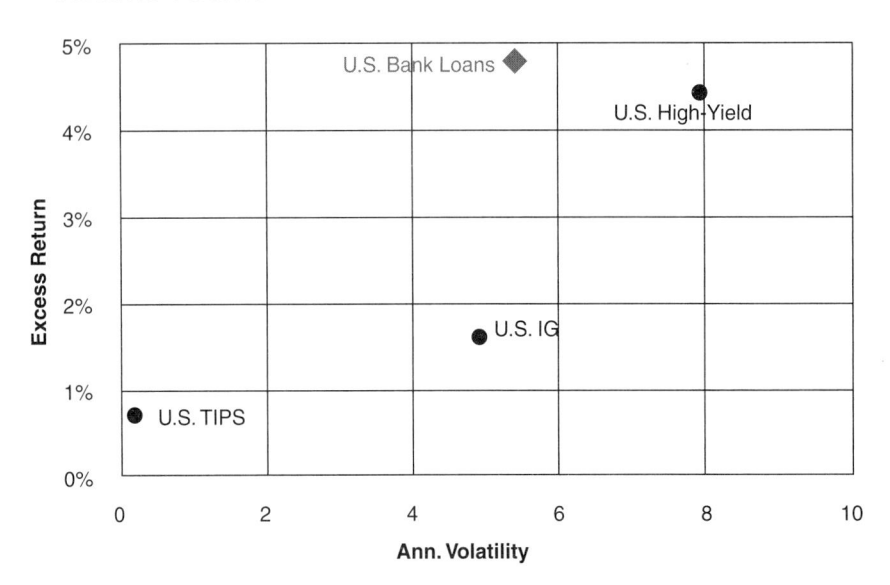

Returns Volume.

[Scatter plot with x-axis "Ann. Volatility" (0 to 10) and y-axis "Excess Return" (0% to 5%). Data points: U.S. TIPS (~0.5, ~1%); U.S. Bank Loans (~4, ~4.5%); U.S. IG (~5, ~1.5%); U.S. High-Yield (~8, ~4.5%).]

the portfolio. There must be clear goals, clear boundaries, and clear definitions of performance success. The following are example benchmarks for loan portfolios:

- The most common benchmark for loan portfolios is the S&P/LSTA Leveraged Loan Index (S&P/LSTA LLI).
- Up-in-quality mandates may utilize a double-B/single-B benchmark, which is a subset of the S&P/LSTA LLI.
- Some funds may have maximum volatility limits, either outright or versus another market (e.g., maximum volatility vs. the Bloomberg Barclays Aggregate Bond Index).
- Total return funds may be benchmarked off the London Interbank Offered Rate (LIBOR).
- Other total return funds may have specific performance hurdles; for example, the fund performance may be compared to a representative index consisting of one-third loans, one-third high-yield bonds, and one-third investment-grade issue.

Once the objectives are clearly defined, how does one craft the "right" portfolio? No matter the fund type or the client's goals, effective loan portfolio management can be boiled down to three factors, albeit three major factors:

1. Overall portfolio risk
2. Individual credit selection
3. Portfolio construction

This may sound simple, but all three are hard to do well! Let's dive into each of the three in more detail.

TOTAL PORTFOLIO RISK

Loans are often considered a niche asset class. It is also often said that loan portfolio management is all about single-name credit selection, with fewer macro inputs necessary.

However, I take the other side of that debate. It is critically important to have a macro component to your investment process, rather than purely relying on single-name selection. The best returns are created when macro and micro are considered together.

It is difficult to define all the macro inputs one should analyze, given the scope and scale of information available, but here are a few to highlight:

- Financial conditions indices
- Equity market valuations versus history
- Credit market valuations versus history
- Equity volatility
- Rate volatility
- Forward expectations in the rates market
- Company earnings growth
- Federal Reserve policy

The goal of these macro inputs is to, in effect, set the stage for your portfolio. What is the market backdrop? What is the current risk regime? Is the forward risk regime meaningfully different? How should these inputs influence your portfolio positioning?

There are also loan market specific macro factors to analyze:

- Loan market technicals
  - Is the new issue market busy?
  - Is CLO creation, plus other market inflows, outstripping supply?

- Are paydowns significant?
- Is the pace of mergers and acquisitions (M&A) notably fast or slow compared to history?
- Do private equity funds have significant dry powder?
- Loan market valuations
  - Are loan spreads wider than historical relationships, as compared to high-yield bonds, investment-grade issue, or CLO liabilities?
  - Are pari loan spreads wide to secured high-yield bonds?
  - Are loan spreads versus high-yield bond unsecured spreads unusually wide?

These are among a long list of macro factors that help portfolio managers analyze the state of the rate markets, the risk markets, and the loan market more specifically, which should guide the decision on how much total risk should be in a portfolio. (Later in the chapter we will discuss how to define aggregate risk in a portfolio.)

The amount of risk in a portfolio at any point in time should be a dynamic decision, not a consistent stance. Too often in loan portfolio management, there are portfolios/managers that stick with one style, all the time—either always positioned risk on or always positioned underweight risk. Sure, this eliminates the need to analyze complex and perhaps even opposing macro factors. However, it also eliminates significant opportunities to generate outperformance versus benchmark.

CREDIT SELECTION

After analysis of the various macro factors, we turn to credit selection. Fundamental credit analysis is the backbone of all credit portfolios, including loan portfolios. This is another topic that sounds simple but is in fact quite complex.

There are three main prongs to fundamental research/credit selection:

1. Understand the company's core business, competitive position, and the expected forward growth trajectory.
2. Analyze the credit agreement/term sheet.
3. Compare the relative value of this investment opportunity versus others in the market.

Step 1: Understand the Company

Here the research analyst takes over, diving into company-specific analysis. This involves performing due diligence on all deal materials and quarterly financials, speaking with management, and researching competitors, among other work. To oversimplify, the goals of this process are:

- To develop a deep understanding of the state of the business today, both qualitatively and quantitatively
- To have a strong grasp of what could go wrong with the business and that downside case
- To have strong conviction on the forward trajectory of the business

To answer these key questions, there are many smaller questions to answer first, including:

- What is the company's core business? Is there a real competitive advantage? How does the company make money (i.e., per unit, per subscriber, or per project)? Is this revenue recurring in nature?
- What is the company's cost structure? What percentage of costs are fixed versus variable? How have margins trended over time?
- What is the historical top- and bottom-line growth of the company, and is that run rate sustainable?
- What is the company's ability to generate free cash flow, across a variety of scenarios?
- What is management's track record? Is there a salient forward plan?
- What does the company's current balance sheet look like? Do current leverage and interest costs allow for sufficient free cash flow generation?
- What is the estimated future balance sheet? How much can the company deleverage over time? Can it deleverage via free cash flow or deleveraging acquisitions?
- What is the equity owners' exit plan? IPO? Asset sales? Roll-up strategy? Dividends?
- What is a "fair" multiple for this business? Are there relevant public equity market comparables?

It is also worth noting that in the loan market there is some nuance to how company-specific information is disseminated to market participants. Although this does not change key principles, it can impact the diligence process.

Only a minority of borrowers in the loan market are companies with public equity (historically about 25% to 30%). The balance is private equity owned or closely held. For these private companies, it is typical for financials to be posted to "lender only" via a password-protected data-sharing site (e.g., Debtdomain, Intralinks, and SyndTrak). This is largely a technicality, but it can have implications on liquidity, given the limited distribution of information.

Step 2: Analyze the Credit Agreement and Your Collateral

Once you have a deep understanding of the business and the financials (past, current, and estimated future), you must then analyze the loan covenants. Too often this topic is glossed over, or you may hear comments like "a 'good' doc is better than a 'weak' doc." Or, better yet, "I'd only buy that loan if you tighten the doc."

Of course, these sorts of comments gloss over the key issues. In analyzing covenants, what are the most important considerations? The following are some areas of recommended focus:

- What collateral is pledged to loan investors? Is there a transparent way to value this collateral (e.g., recent market transactions)?
- Is the collateral composed of tangible hard assets? Intangible assets? Is there a logical buyer?
- Are there financial maintenance covenants?
- Can the equity owner take dividends of significant size?
- Can assets be sold without paying down the term loan?
- How much pari passu incremental debt can be added to the balance sheet? Is there most favored nation (MFN) language to protect you?
- Do "sacred rights" require a unanimous vote, or a simple majority?
- Is the debt "portable" (i.e., if the company is sold, can the debt remain outstanding)?
- What is the LIBOR replacement language?

These are just some examples; a fulsome covenant review requires a full analysis, perhaps alongside a legal expert. In addition, it is worth noting that there are also third-party research providers that specialize in credit agreement analysis, which can be a helpful addition to the analysis.

The goal here is to further think through the downside investment case. Based on the deep dive into the business, and considering a bear case scenario, what is permissible in the credit agreement that would cause that bear case to result in even worse investor outcomes?

In isolation, a very restrictive document is certainly preferable to one with flexibility for the equity. But investors must also be practical and price the risk, not avoid the risk.

Step 3: Compare Relative Value

After analyzing the business, its historical financials, its future growth prospects, and the credit agreement, the question remains—what is the fair spread, yield, and dollar price for this loan investment? It is surely not as simple as buying "good" companies with "good" documents. The importance of this relative value analysis cannot be overemphasized.

Traditional relative value comparisons look within one sector. For example, is this software loan investment better or worse than another loan within the software sector? And, what is a reasonable spread differential between the two?

This question is perfectly reasonable and perfectly relevant. And, better yet, can be answered by a sector analyst. However, this approach has its shortcomings. It does not help the portfolio manager answer the more important question of whether this particular software investment at spread x is more or less attractive than his or her current healthcare investment at spread y or business services investment at spread z. Nor does it inform the portfolio manager as to what the relative sizing should be.

Investors take three main approaches in analyzing relative value across disparate sectors: (1) loan to value, (2) spread per unit of leverage, and (3) spread for the rating. A fourth method, though it can hardly be called a method, is direct leverage comparisons.

While I'm skeptical of these methods, to varying degrees, it is important to acknowledge them and their potential influence on market pricing. A brief description of each of the four methods follows:

- *Loan to value.* Asset A is 4x levered, paying a 350 spread. Public comparables trade for 8x, so Asset A has a 50% loan to value. Asset B is 5x levered, paying a 350 spread. Public comparables trade for 12x, so Asset B has a loan to value of approximately 40%. Therefore, Asset B is more attractive.
- *Spread per unit of leverage.* Compare Asset A paying a 350 spread, 3.5x first lien leverage to Asset B paying a 400 spread, 5x levered. This analysis would conclude that Asset A is better, paying 100 basis points of spread per unit of first lien leverage.[1]
- *Spread for the rating.* Asset A is rated B1, paying a 300 spread, Asset B is rated B2, paying a 300 spread. Therefore, Asset A is "better."[2]
- *Direct leverage comparisons.* To compare the relative value of two possible loan investments, look at first lien leverage. Asset A paying spread x is preferable to Asset B paying spread x if Asset A has 3.5x first lien leverage and Asset B is 4.5x levered through the first lien.[3]

Of these four methodologies, the loan-to-value method is by far the most analytically sound. However, I do not advocate using this method, or the other three listed.

Sure, all four of these methods can be helpful inputs to your investment process. But to me, these methods will only help you arrive at fair market pricing today, which is important, but not the goal. The goal is to pick the investments where the market is mispricing the risk.

So, the best approach focuses on future expected top- and bottom-line growth, future leverage, future free cash flow generation, and anticipated future valuation.

The market is fairly efficient at pricing today's known risks. The alpha is in uncovering tomorrow's winners and tomorrow's losers—today.

---

[1] Here, too, I do not agree because we cannot judge on this information alone.
[2] Again, I disagree with the approach, but ratings certainly factor into market pricing.
[3] I do not agree with this, but it is an approach you will encounter.

PORTFOLIO CONSTRUCTION

Once you have identified the top-down risk targets and picked your individual credit winners (and avoided the losers), it is time to move on to portfolio construction. But first, what is portfolio construction? Portfolio construction is all about analyzing how the building blocks of your portfolio come together. A portfolio is not a set of disjointed line items, but rather a cohesive set of investments that come together to create the best performance outcomes in portfolios.

One of the most critical aspects of portfolio construction is how to size a position. Although there is no one way to size a position, it is a topic that deserves significant page space but often receives limited focus.

Let's boil it down. How should we at least start to think about ideal sizing, name by name?

- *Conviction.* How large are your highest conviction credits? This should be considered in terms of outright percentage exposure, active percentage exposure, percentage contribution to overall risk, and expected performance (outright and compared to benchmark). What is the expected performance of this position? Additionally, a portfolio manager should ask, "The top 10 names in the portfolio represent what portion of my risk?" "20% of my risk?" "30 percent of my risk?" and so on.
- *Diversification.* A balance needs to be struck between sizing your conviction bets to "move the needle" while maintaining the benefits of diversification.

But how many line items should you have in a portfolio? What is the "perfect" number of credits to achieve the proper balance between conviction and diversification? Most managers in the loan space have 300 to 500 names in an unconstrained portfolio versus an index with about 1,200.

To me, the sizing question has many answers, and it depends on your credit-picking skills and investment style, but an honest historical analysis can be illuminating. Look at your portfolio over time. Where have you had the best selection? Is it your large overweights that have outperformed the market? Then your conviction bets should likely be larger! Or is it the names you do not own that are performing poorly? Do you have a tail of names with positions of 15 basis points or less? Did they drag down your performance? Then you have too many line items!

Each portfolio manager may arrive at a different answer here, but again it is critical that this is an active, dynamic decision, and *not* a passive byproduct.

I am a big believer that the path of returns matters just as much as the outcome, especially in loans. This is far from a consensus view, because most will say things like, "at the end of the day, this is a par piece of paper." But, to me, this does not give one a free pass. Assume the same spread on two assets. Would you rather own one with 10% volatility or 4% volatility? When crafting the optimal portfolio, you must do your best to project forward volatility of each single name line item.

Above and beyond these three core principles for sizing a single-name position—conviction, diversification, and expected volatility—there are many more portfolio-level considerations.

I believe that the more you analyze a portfolio—the more you dissect it, the more you slice and dice it—the better your understanding of the portfolio's risk, and in turn, the better the portfolio's performance.

Critical portfolio metrics include:

- Weighted average coupon of the portfolio (outright and compared to benchmark)
- Weighted average dollar price of the portfolio (outright and compared to benchmark)
- LIBOR floor analysis (What percentage have LIBOR floors? Are they in the money?)
- Beta of the portfolio
- Exposure by rating
- Call protection remaining
- Name count, CUSIP count
- Maximum single-name concentration
- Percentage of risk from top 10 names and top 20 names
- Percentage exposure by vintage
- Percentage exposure by sponsor
- Percentage loan-only capital structures
- Percentage exposure by sector

- Percentage exposure to off-benchmark asset classes (i.e., high-yield bonds, CLOs, investment grade, equities)
- Percentage exposure to unfunded commitments (e.g., delayed draws, new issue with ticking fee structure)
- Cash balance in the portfolio (see further discussion at the end of this chapter)
- Environmental, social, and governance (ESG) considerations/ratings (see further discussion at the end of this chapter)

Single-name sizing relies upon conviction, diversification, and volatility. Consider the whole portfolio when making investment decisions. Think, what does this new line item do for the portfolio?

But, don't stop there. A portfolio is not just a set of single-name line items. It is all about the credit selection, the sizing, and how the portfolio comes together on the whole. Remember, portfolio-level risk metrics and analytics are just as critical as single-name risk.

RISK ANALYTICS

Risk management is key to successful portfolio management, and loan portfolios are no exception. If we try to distill risk management into its simplest form, there are three guiding principles:

1. How much risk is in the portfolio?
2. Are realized returns in line with risk model predicted returns?
3. How much risk is in the portfolio if I shock the macroenvironment?

This seems simple enough. But, how should you define risk? There are many ways to think about risk in a loan portfolio. Some common risk metrics include:

- Value at risk (VAR)
- Stand-alone risk (SAR)
- Beta versus benchmark
- Tracking error
- Spread 10%, taking into account call protection

These metrics will give you a strong grasp on portfolio risk, as well as help perform historical risk comparisons. Also, these are not loan market–specific risk metrics, they apply to other credit portfolios, and thus enable comparisons across asset classes and portfolios.

However, these metrics are not always intuitive, especially in loan funds. I find that oftentimes the most effective tool is one of the simplest—scenario analysis. I prefer to use actual historical scenarios, coupled with estimated risk-on and risk-off scenarios. That way, you can frame portfolio risk in performance terms.

For example, if the S&P is up 10%, high-yield bonds are up 4%, and loans are up 2%, assuming each individual loan trades with its historical beta, how will my portfolio perform? How will it perform against the benchmark? Against its peers? Or, you can frame it a different way. What if single-B loans exhibit more than their historical beta? Or, to provide a third example, what if low dollar–price assets outperform by more than their beta would suggest?

There are countless iterations. All the analysis contributes to a fulsome feedback loop, and, in turn, the best performance outcomes.

PERFORMANCE ATTRIBUTION

The other critical piece of risk analysis is performance attribution, with two main prongs:

- Did my portfolio perform with its expected risk and volatility?
  - For instance, in a 2% index drawdown, the model expected my portfolio to be down 1.5%. Is this what occurred?
- If the portfolio did not perform as expected, why is this the case?
  - Did the model inaccurately estimate the risk?
  - Did historical risk relationships break down?
  - Did my single names perform materially better or materially worse than expected?

Risk management in loans can and should be sophisticated, detailed, and dynamic. However, there is no better risk management tool than realized performance! Although past performance does not predict forward returns, a deep understanding of historical performance will guide you toward more successful portfolio management.

CASH AND LIQUIDITY MANAGEMENT

A chapter on loan portfolio management would not be complete without a discussion of liquidity. Although many areas of loan portfolio management share principles with those of high-yield bonds or investment-grade issue, liquidity management is meaningfully different.

The following are a few areas of liquidity in the loan market to consider:

- Trading liquidity
- Settlement liquidity
- Fund structure/liquidity (e.g., daily or monthly liquidity; locked-up vehicle)

Trading Liquidity

As discussed earlier, trading liquidity has dramatically improved over the last several years. Whereas previously loan managers would simply buy and hold, today trading liquidity and active portfolio management are key. To put things in perspective, see Exhibit 12.4 for annual trading volumes.

EXHIBIT 12.4

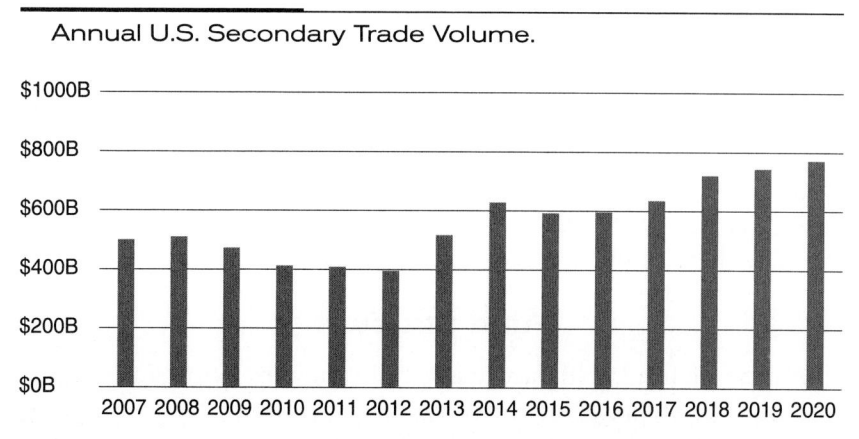

Annual U.S. Secondary Trade Volume.

Source: LSTA.

EXHIBIT 12.5

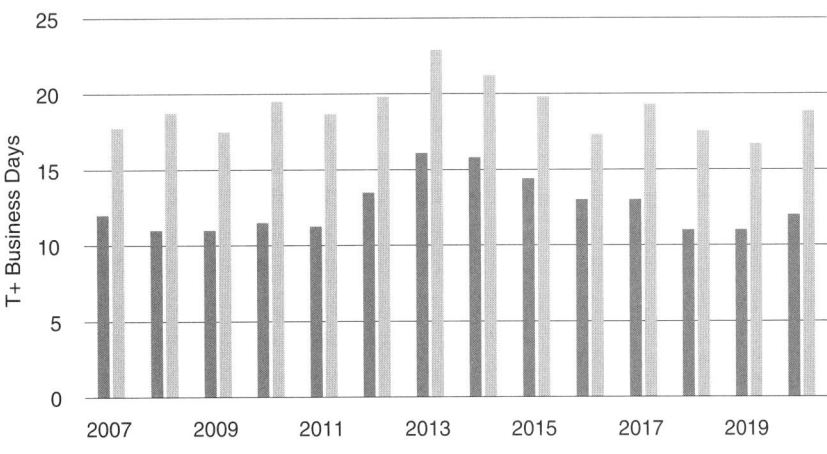

Annual U.S. Par Settlement Time.

Source: LSTA.

Settlement Liquidity

Although trading liquidity has meaningfully improved and was a necessary precursor to active portfolio management, settlement liquidity has remained one of the most challenging aspects of loan portfolio management.

Unlike other asset classes, loans do not have a standardized settlement time. Rather, loans settle over the counter. There are best practices, spearheaded by the Loan Syndications and Trading Association (LSTA), and settlement times have shown improvement. However, the mechanics of the settlement process are such that timelines are somewhat unpredictable and average settlement times can still be counted in the double digits. Exhibit 12.5 provides detail on U.S. Par Settlement Time.

Why does this matter? A loan fund portfolio manager needs to understand this potential timing mismatch to navigate liquidity needs. This is particularly acute for those portfolio managers who manage daily liquidity funds.

Fund Structure

The type of fund structure will guide the best approach to cash and liquidity management in loan funds. Exhibit 12.6 details some important considerations for daily liquidity funds, separately managed accounts, and CLOs:

EXHIBIT 12.6

Fund Liquidity Considerations.

Fund Type	Investor Liquidity Offered	Best Practices
Daily Liquidity Mutual Fund	T + 1 to T + 3	• Do not invest in illiquid loans • Hold liquid investments that settle T + 1, including cash, cash bonds, liquidity products (ETFs, index products) • Have a liquidity line in place for U.S. daily liquidity mutual funds, establish and track the funds "Highly Liquid Investment Minimum," per regulations
SMA	Varies by client	• Establish clear boundaries and goals
CLOs	Capital is locked up	• Vehicle can comfortably invest in illiquid loans • The spread and yield pick-up from illiquid loans may be beneficial to the vehicle • However, there may be opportunity costs to consider, particularly over the investment life • Track total aggregate exposure to illiquids

ESG CONSIDERATIONS

Loan portfolio management has become more sophisticated and analytical, following the growth and maturation of the loan market. As in other markets, ESG criteria are increasingly a focus for investors.

For the loan market, the biggest focus is on company disclosure of ESG data. As previously noted, the majority of borrowers in the loan market are private companies, and financial disclosure is typically on a password-protected website. Therefore, seemingly simple obstacles such as ESG disclosure present significant challenges.

In addition, third-party ESG ratings for loan borrowers are still limited, with only about 30% of the market rated. Thus, current ESG efforts in the loan market are focused upon tackling disclosure and determining the right approach to balance customization by sector with the ability to aggregate ESG information at the portfolio level.

The LSTA has been instrumental in these efforts; the LSTA rolled out an ESG questionnaire that helps on multiple fronts. The LSTA questionnaire:

- Adds consistency to disclosure for loan borrowers.
- Lays the groundwork for eventual quantitative scoring.

- Maintains the ability for companies to customize responses based on business- and sector-specific issues.

The future of ESG investing in the loan market will likely bring third-party ESG scores, similar to credit ratings, as well as green loans (there have been a few issued already) in greater scale.

CONCLUSION

To conclude this chapter on loan portfolio management, let's review what has been discussed:

- Loan portfolio managers should start the investment process by establishing client goals and determining the appropriate risk and performance benchmarks.
- Creation of the best actively managed loan portfolio involves three prongs: total portfolio risk, single-name credit selection, and portfolio construction. Getting all three right is key to optimizing alpha generation versus the benchmark.
- Risk management and performance attribution provide real-time feedback so that the portfolio can be repositioned, as needed.
- Cash management is particularly critical for effectively managing loan funds (especially mutual funds), with many loan market–specific considerations.
- ESG is a growing focus for the loan market, but there is more work to do.

Invest well and keep your approach dynamic—the market is always changing!

CHAPTER 13

Collateralized Loan Obligations (CLOs): A Primer

Maggie Wang
Managing Director, Global Head of CLO and CDO Research
Citi Global Markets

INTRODUCTION[1]

In this collateralized loan obligation (CLO) primer, we provide investors a detailed product and market overview, as well as a guide on how to read a CLO indenture, as highlighted below:

- *Robust growth.* The U.S. CLO market has more than doubled in size since the Global Financial Crisis (GFC), reaching $760 billion as of the end of March 2021, and is on track to potentially reach $850 billion by the end of 2021.
- *Why invest in CLOs?* CLOs allow investors to gain leveraged, diversified exposure to the loan market, capitalize on market price inefficiencies, and access a broad range of asset managers.
- *CLO structure.* The structure of CLOs has proved to be dynamic and resilient through various periods of market distress. The post-GFC CLO structure has evolved to be more conservative and offers better protection for CLO debt investors.
- *How to read a CLO indenture.* We provide a detailed summary of commonly asked questions and commonly negotiated documentation points for CLO investors.

Related

CLO MARKET BASICS

CLO Market Background

A collateralized loan obligation (CLO) is a securitized product backed by a diversified pool of leveraged loans that issues various tranches of CLO debt and equity. CLOs are comparable to finance companies that (1) borrow money by issuing CLO debt tranches/liabilities, (2) invest in collateral (loan assets), and (3) have residual value that represents an ownership stake and a first-loss position (CLO Equity). Unlike most other securitized products, CLOs are actively managed structures whereas the underlying loan collateral can be reinvested.

---

[1] The author would like to thank Lijing Wang and Kenneth Sang for their contributions to this article.

The U.S. CLO market started to develop in 1990 and has since grown tremendously. Since the GFC, the U.S. CLO market outstanding has more than doubled in size to reach $823 billion as of the end of September 2021 (Exhibits 13.1 and 13.2). The annual growth rate in the U.S. CLO market has averaged approximately 12.5% since 2012, consistently higher than the growth rate in the underlying loan market. With its expansion in the past decade, the U.S. CLO market has been the most dominant buyer of the U.S. leveraged loan market, accounting for more than 70% of primary loan purchases in 2020, compared to 13% by mutual funds and

EXHIBIT 13.1

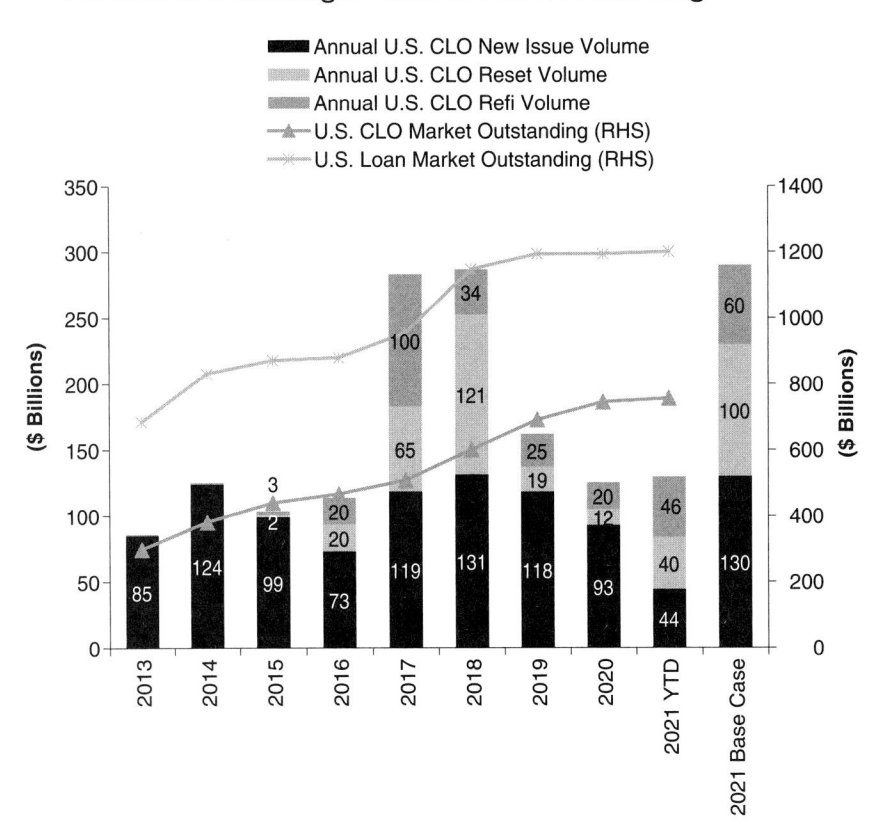

U.S. CLO and Leveraged Loan Market Outstanding.

Source: Citi Research, as of October 8, 2021. CLO Market Outstanding data is as of the end of September 2021 and represents the combined 1.0 and 2.0 universe. Issuance and Outstanding Volume includes both BSL and MM CLOs and excludes CBO.

Collateralized Loan Obligations (CLOs): A Primer

EXHIBIT 13.2

U.S. Leveraged Loan Investor Base.

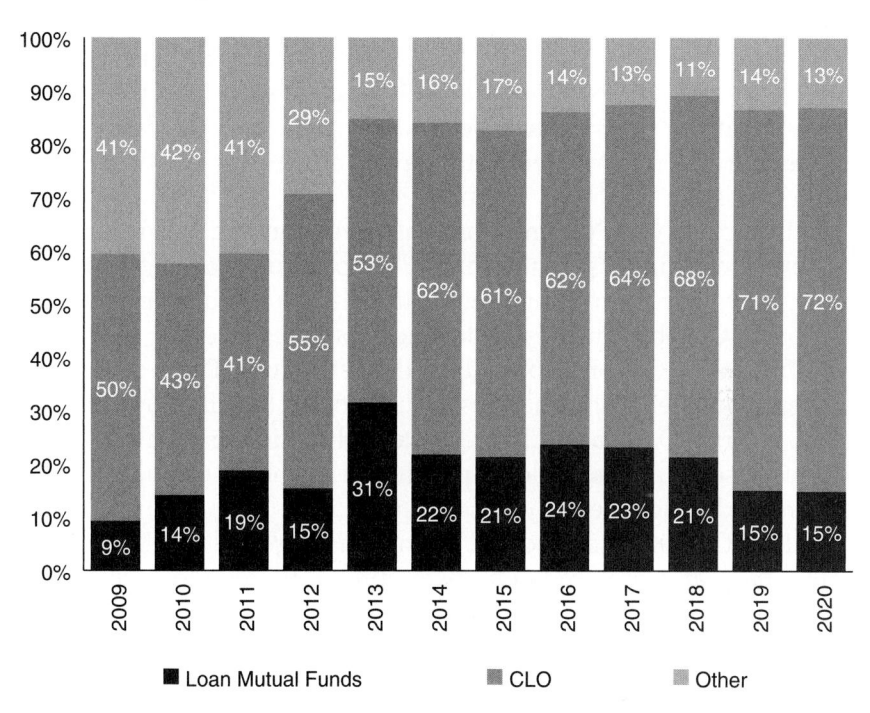

Year	Loan Mutual Funds	CLO	Other
2009	9%	50%	41%
2010	14%	43%	42%
2011	19%	41%	41%
2012	15%	55%	29%
2013	31%	53%	15%
2014	22%	62%	16%
2015	21%	61%	17%
2016	24%	62%	14%
2017	23%	64%	13%
2018	21%	68%	11%
2019	15%	71%	14%
2020	15%	72%	13%

Source: Citi Research, S&P LCD as of December 31, 2020. Other loan investors include finance/insurance companies, and hedge/distressed/high-yield.

less than 20% by other loan investors (finance and insurance companies and hedge funds) (see Exhibits 13.3 and 13.4).

The $823 billion outstanding U.S. CLO market includes approximately $738 billion in broadly syndicated loans (BSLs) and $85 billion in middle market (MM) CLOs. The collateral pool of BSL CLOs is composed of broadly syndicated leveraged loans, which are senior secured corporate credits that are structured, arranged, and administered by commercial/investment banks, sold/syndicated to banks and institutional investors, and rated BB or lower. In comparison, MM CLOs are composed of middle market loans or loans to issuers typically with less than or equal to $50 million EBITDA (earnings before interest, taxes, depreciation, and amortization) and/or less than or equal to $350 million in loan size.

The CLO Primary Market

The CLO primary market supplies three different types of CLO issuance: new issue, refinancing (refi), or reset.

New issue CLO is a brand-new type of CLO that is typically priced out of an existing warehouse and sources underlying loans from the primary and secondary loan markets. New issue CLOs are often considered to have "cleaner" portfolios than older deals.

In recent years, the mechanisms of refinancing and reset have become increasingly popular in the CLO primary market, with CLO Equity investors exercising their optionality to call back previously issued CLO debt tranches and issue new ones in order to reduce funding costs and/or to extend the deal structure. There could also be deal documentation changes in the process of full refinancing or reset. Both CLO refi and CLO reset keep the existing collateral pool, although some assets could be purchased or sold in cleaning up the collateral during reset.

In a *CLO refi*, some or all of the existing deal's liabilities are called back and replaced at a lower spread, thereby lowering debt cost and improving CLO arbitrage for the CLO Equity tranche holders. However, the deal structure typically remains unchanged (e.g., reinvestment period length, deal maturity date) and the collateral pool remains the same. Some minor changes may be made to the terms of the indenture during refi.

In a *CLO reset*, in comparison, the entire CLO is essentially called and reissued at current market spreads, which will have new terms, including the noncall period/reinvestment period/maturity date, thereby extending the CLO's deal life and the manager's fee stream.

We predict that 2021 will see $160 billion in new issue CLOs and $220 billion in refi/reset supply.[2] In total, we expect U.S. CLO issuance to reach $380 billion in fiscal year 2021, which would surpass the record issuance volume of 2018.

---

[2] Available at: https://www.citivelocity.com/rendition/eppublic/akpublic/reactui/current/registration.html?originURL=aHR0cHM6Ly93d3cuY2l0aXZlbG9jaXR5LmNvbS9yZW5kaXRpb24vZXBwdWJsaWMvZ9jdW1lbnRRTZXJ2aWNlL1pHOWpYMmxrUFRFd05UazBPRFltY0d4aGMTA1TVRrbVkyaGhibTVsYkQxamFYUnBbkJvVZzYjJOcGRIa21jM1ZpTFdOb1lXNXVaV3c5Yj0WMGJHOXZhdz09&locale=EN_US&deviceCookieName=cv_device_id&ts=1631907208387#/

The CLO Secondary Market

CLO tranches often trade on bid wanted in competitions (BWIC), a secondary auction in which a CLO account offers up a portfolio of CLO bonds via an investment bank that subsequently asks potential buyers to submit requests for individual names or the entire portfolio and awards each facility to the highest bidder. BWIC activity provides indicative market liquidity, and we track the percentage of bonds that failed to trade (aka do not trade, or DNT). The DNT ratio of investment-grade CLO tranches has consistently remained below 15% during different periods of market stress, while up to 30% of noninvestment-grade tranches did not trade last year during the COVID-19 pandemic (Exhibits 13.3 and 13.4).

EXHIBIT 13.3

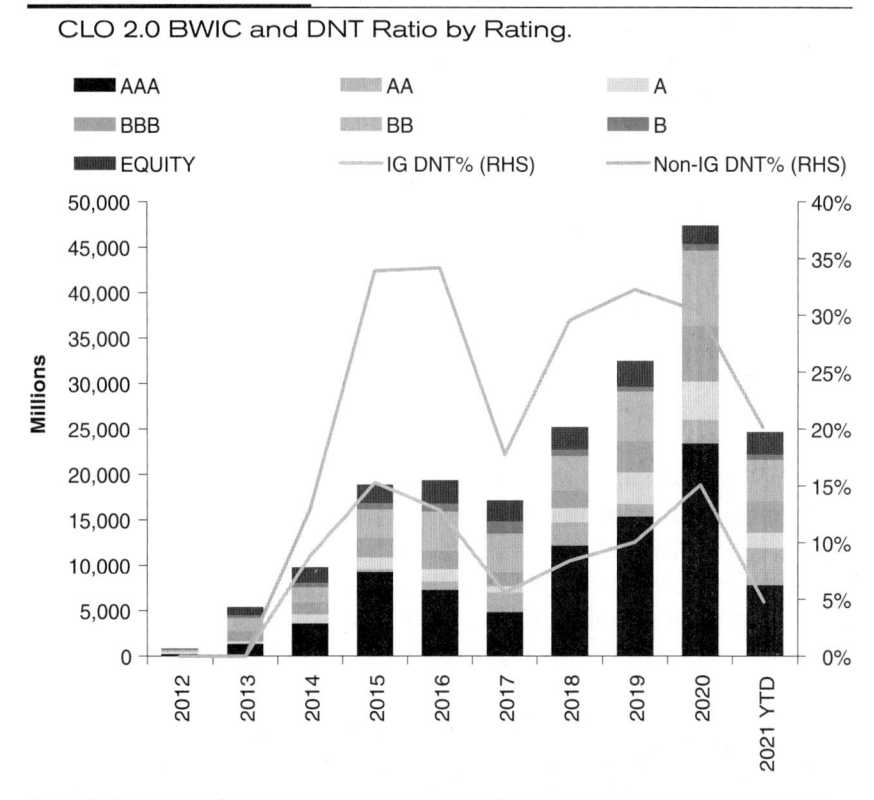

CLO 2.0 BWIC and DNT Ratio by Rating.

Source: Citi Research, as of October 12, 2021. DNT Ratio equals total CLO value that did not trade divided by total BWIC activity (DNT + Traded). Most CLO trades settle T + 2. Typically, 25% to 30% of CLO secondary trading happens on BWIC and the rest is trading off the list.

EXHIBIT 13.4

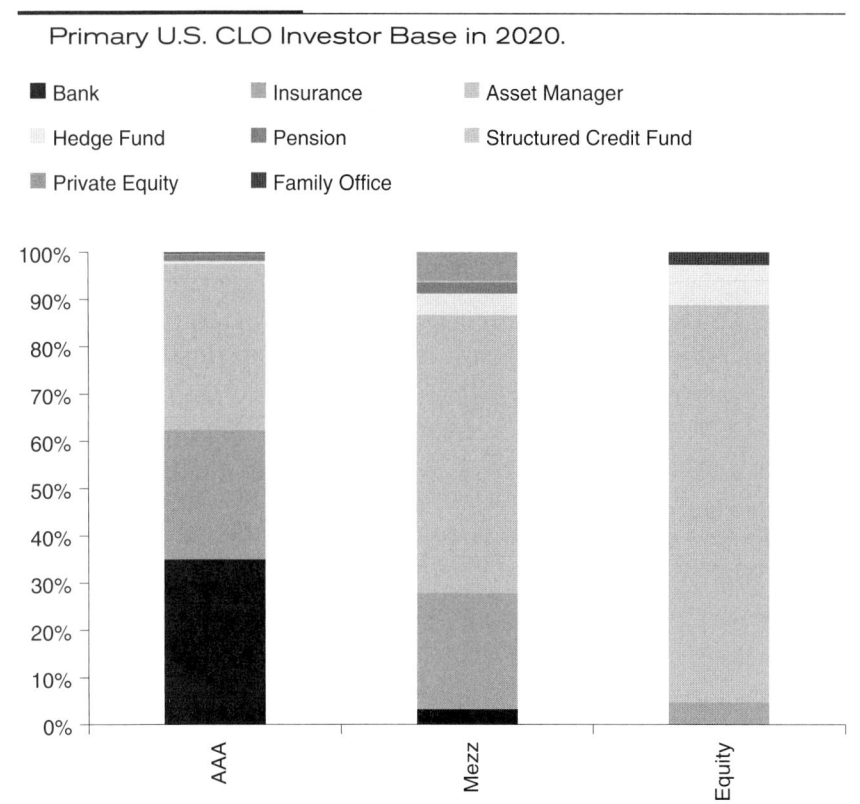

Primary U.S. CLO Investor Base in 2020.

- Bank
- Insurance
- Asset Manager
- Hedge Fund
- Pension
- Structured Credit Fund
- Private Equity
- Family Office

Source: Citi Research, as of December 31, 2020. Based on the dollar amount of new issue CLO deals priced by Citi.

Secondary turnover rate in the CLO market continued to improve despite the market stresses seen in 2020, thanks to an expanding market size and investor base. We estimate that 26% of the entire U.S. CLO market changed hands in 2020, up from 17% in 2019. The CLO turnover rate is catching up with other securitized products such as nonagency residential mortgage-backed securities (RMBS) (29%), asset-backed securities (ABS) (29%), and commercial mortgage-backed securities (CMBS) (27%), but remains well below credit products such as U.S. investment-grade (81%) and U.S. high-yield (192%).

Why Invest in CLOs?

A CLO allows investors to gain leveraged, diversified, and customized exposure to the loan market; capitalize on market inefficiencies; and access a broad range of asset managers. Compared to leveraged loan and bond markets, the CLO market has largely been a buy and hold market, especially for the top of the capital stack. Also, unlike the CLO 1.0 era, CLO investors now very rarely use leverage to buy CLO tranches, which provides more stability in times of market volatility.

CLO AAA tranche offers relatively wide spreads for their high ratings and are thus in high demand by domestic and foreign banks attempting to optimize various requirements such as margin (need for spreads), capital (need for highly rated assets), and regulation-defined liquid assets (CLOs do not comply, unlike more expensive assets). Japanese banks in particular desire AAA CLOs because their domestic low-yield environment drives pursuit of attractive global yield, and their mandate limits available investments to historically high-rated/robustly performing products. Global bank demand in CLOs, as a whole, has seen some pull-back in 2020 given market volatility but has come back strongly so far in 2021 (Exhibit 13.4).

Insurance companies have a similar need for margin but may have larger yield and total return considerations and a need for longer-dated assets for asset–liability matching purposes. Therefore, they account for a significant portion of demand in CLO mezzanine issuance (AA to single-B rated tranches). In 2020, insurance demand accounted for 25% of primary CLO mezzanine issuance, declining slightly by 4 percentage points year-over-year. Concurrently, insurance companies also added CLO AAA by 3 percentage points in 2020.

Asset managers participate more actively in CLO mezzanine and CLO Equity tranches for better yield and total return, and their demand has increased continuously since 2017. In recent years, many CLO managers would also hold some portion of their own deal's first-loss CLO Equity piece, although risk retention is no longer required for U.S. CLOs (see more in the "Regulatory Impact" section).

As an asset class, CLOs provide the following benefits for potential investors:

- Higher spreads offered by debt tranches compared to similarly rated corporate and structured investments (Exhibits 13.5 and 13.6).
- Strong and leveraged risk–return exposure to the senior secured loan asset class that is actively managed.
- Diversification benefits with exposure to a diverse pool of assets across more than 30 different industry sectors.

EXHIBIT 13.5

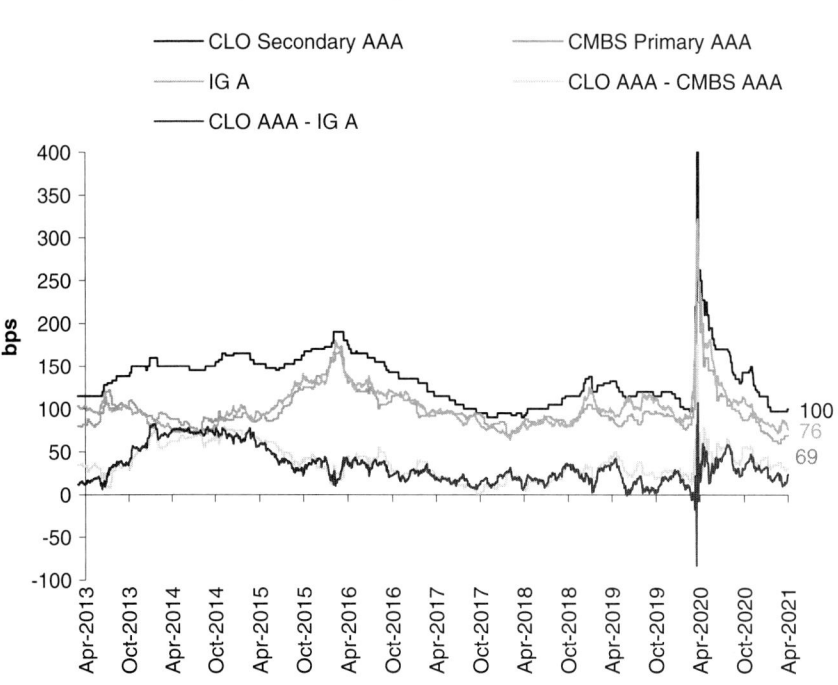

U.S. CLO AAA Spread Pickup.

Source: Citi Research, as of April 2, 2021.

- Structural protection that has led to extremely low CLO tranche principal loss due to embedded credit enhancement and built-in covenants, concentration limits, and portfolio quality criteria. According to Moody's, U.S. CLO investment-grade tranches have significantly lower loss rates over a 10-year horizon (0.3%) compared to ABS (2.9%), CMBS (14.2%), and RMBS (28.6%) (Exhibit 13.7). Previous CLO 1.0 deal losses were caused by exposure to high-yield bonds that saw lower recovery and higher defaults in collateral.
- Smoothed accounting from non-marked-to-market (MTM) vehicles.
- Access to premier and talented loan managers with the expertise and resources to capitalize on loan price inefficiencies.

EXHIBIT 13.6

CLO Mezzanine Spread Pickup.

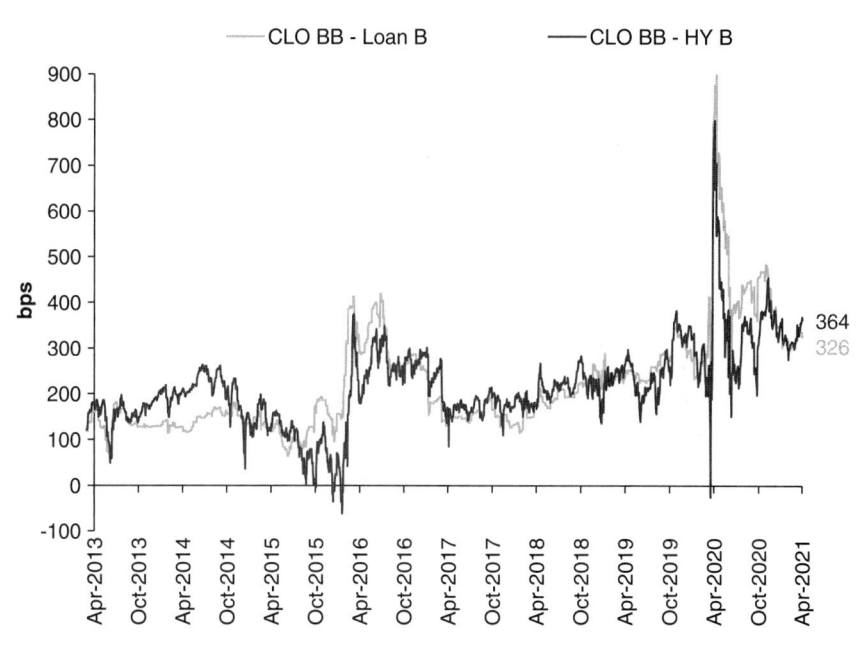

Source: Citi Research, as of April 2, 2021.

Why Issue a CLO?

The U.S. CLO market had 135 outstanding managers as of April 16, 2021, with a good mix of long-standing, well-established, and small CLO managers that have recently entered the market. We count 17 (or 13%) of outstanding U.S. CLO managers having above $10 billion CLO assets under management (AUM) and historically represented approximately ~30% to 35% of the primary CLO market supply. In contrast, U.S. CLO managers with $2 billion or less CLO AUM take up about 38% of the manager universe by count, but only 8% of the issuance in 2020 (see Exhibit 13.8).

A wide range of financial institutions have chosen to issue CLOs to expand their fee-generating AUM, including insurance companies, banks, private equity firms, hedge funds, and asset managers, many of which are CLO investors themselves. Through issuing in the primary CLO market, CLO managers aim to grow

EXHIBIT 13.7

Historical CLO and Structured Product Loss Rates.

	Cohort Size	5 Years	10 Years
U.S. CLO Aaa	4,148	0.0%	0.0%
U.S. CLO Aa	2,114	0.0%	0.0%
U.S. CLO A	1,936	0.0%	0.0%
U.S. CLO Baa	1,920	0.3%	1.2%
U.S. CLO Ba	1,622	0.7%	3.9%
U.S. CLO B	373	1.4%	4.3%
U.S. CLO Investment Grade	10,118	0.1%	0.3%
U.S. CLO Speculative Grade	1,996	0.8%	4.1%
U.S. ABS (IG)	20,671	1.3%	2.9%
U.S. ABS (SG)	430	13.4%	32.3%
U.S. RMBS/HEL (IG)	82,068	25.7%	28.6%
U.S. RMBS/HEL (SG)	3,629	58.3%	64.7%
U.S. CMBS (IG)	12,505	7.7%	14.2%
U.S. CMBS (SG)	2,834	30.8%	53.5%

Source: Citi Research, Moody's as of December 31, 2019.
"Impairment & Loss Rates of U.S. and European CLOs: 1993–2019" by Moody's, "Structured Finance—Global: Impairment and Loss Rates of Structured Finance Securities: 1993–2019" by Moody's. "Annual Default Study: Corporate Default and Recovery Rates, 1920–2019" by Moody's.

their fee-generating AUM in a highly scalable way and gain access to a global, diversified investor base (see Exhibit 13.9).

CLO PRODUCT BASICS

What Is a CLO?

A CLO is a securitized product backed by a diversified pool of leveraged loans that issues various tranches of debt and CLO Equity. CLOs are actively managed structures, whereas the underlying collateral (assets) can be sold and purchased by CLO managers. The CLO manager's incentives and competence and the CLO structure are important features affecting performance of various tranches.

Broadly Syndicated Loan (aka BSL) CLOs are comparable to a finance company that (1) borrows money (CLO liabilities), (2) invests in collateral (loan assets), and (3) has residual value (CLO Equity) that represents an ownership stake and a first-loss position.

EXHIBIT 13.8

Outstanding CLO Manager Count by Outstanding CLO AUM Bucket.

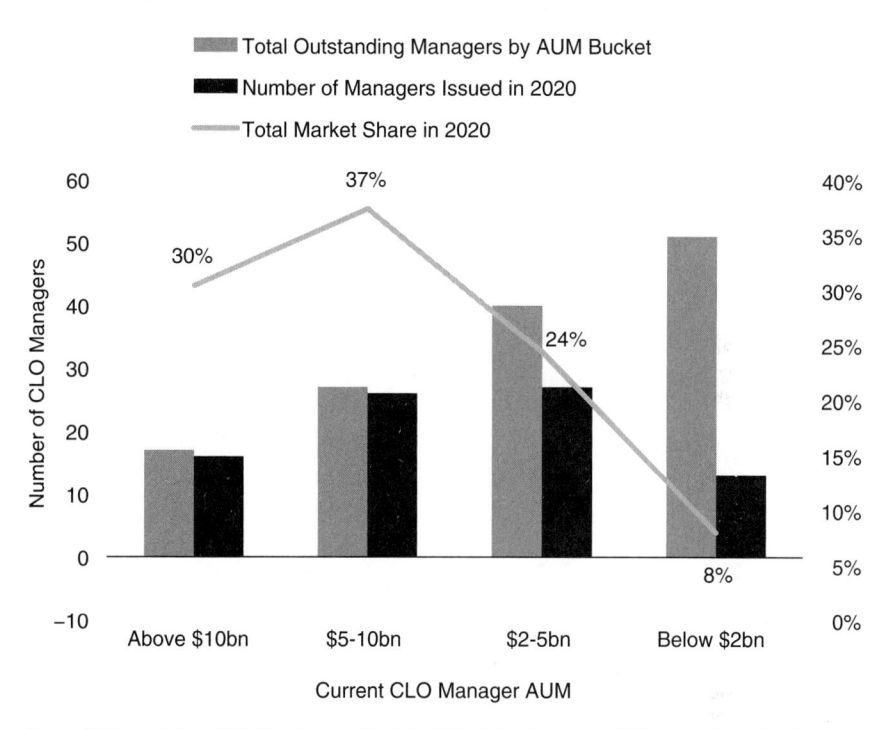

[Chart: Bar and line chart showing Total Outstanding Managers by AUM Bucket, Number of Managers Issued in 2020, and Total Market Share in 2020 across AUM buckets: Above $10bn, $5-10bn, $2-5bn, Below $2bn. Market share values: 30%, 37%, 24%, 8%.]

Source: Citi Research, Intex, LCD, Bloomberg as of April 15, 2021. Market share of each CLO manager is calculated based on their issuance as a percentage of total issuance volume in 2020.

BSL CLOs are by definition "arbitrage" CLOs that aim to capture the excess spread between the underlying loan portfolio and CLO debt tranches, with the CLO Equity investor receiving any excess cash flows after CLO debt investors are paid.

In comparison, "balance sheet" CLOs are structured primarily as a funding source for the issuer. With balance sheet CLOs, the issuer securitizes the bank loans off its balance sheet into a special-purpose vehicle (SPV), for the purpose of raising capital, and it typically retains the CLO Equity tranche.

The life cycle for new issue CLO varies by deal but follows a general timeline as described below (Exhibit 13.10):

- *Planning and marketing (3 months).* The CLO manager and arranger (investment bank) discuss deal creation, potential pricing terms, prospective CLO debt investors, and CLO

EXHIBIT 13.9

Dispersion of Market-Value–Based Par Build Among CLOs Issued in Different Quarters.

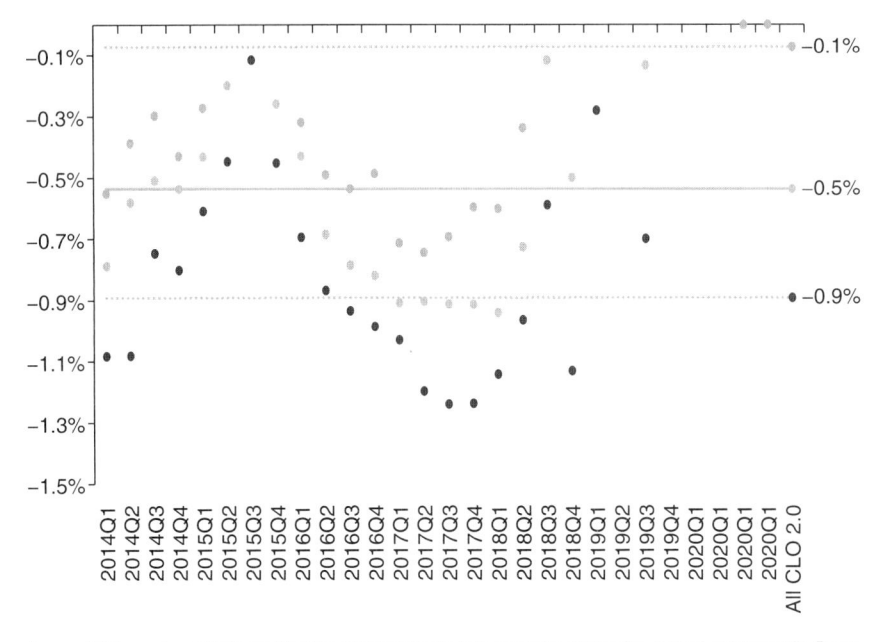

Source: Citi Research as of February 28. 2021. Green stands for 25th percentile, gray median, and red 75th percentile. Reset deals are kept in the original vintage.

Equity holders. At marketing launch, the arranger circulates CLO deal terms to potential investors, gauges interest, and communicates feedback to the CLO manager until the price date.

- *Warehousing period (6 to 12 months).* The CLO manager typically opens a warehouse line of credit with an investment bank to opportunistically purchase assets before the deal closing date and to construct the investment portfolio over time.
- *Price date.* CLO tranche orders and terms are finalized, the arranger allocates liabilities to investors that commit to an investment amount and specified floating spread/fixed coupon, and preliminary ratings are assigned to tranches.
- *Closing date.* The CLO transaction is legally finalized, and management fees and notes interest begin to accrue.

EXHIBIT 13.10

CLO Life Cycle.

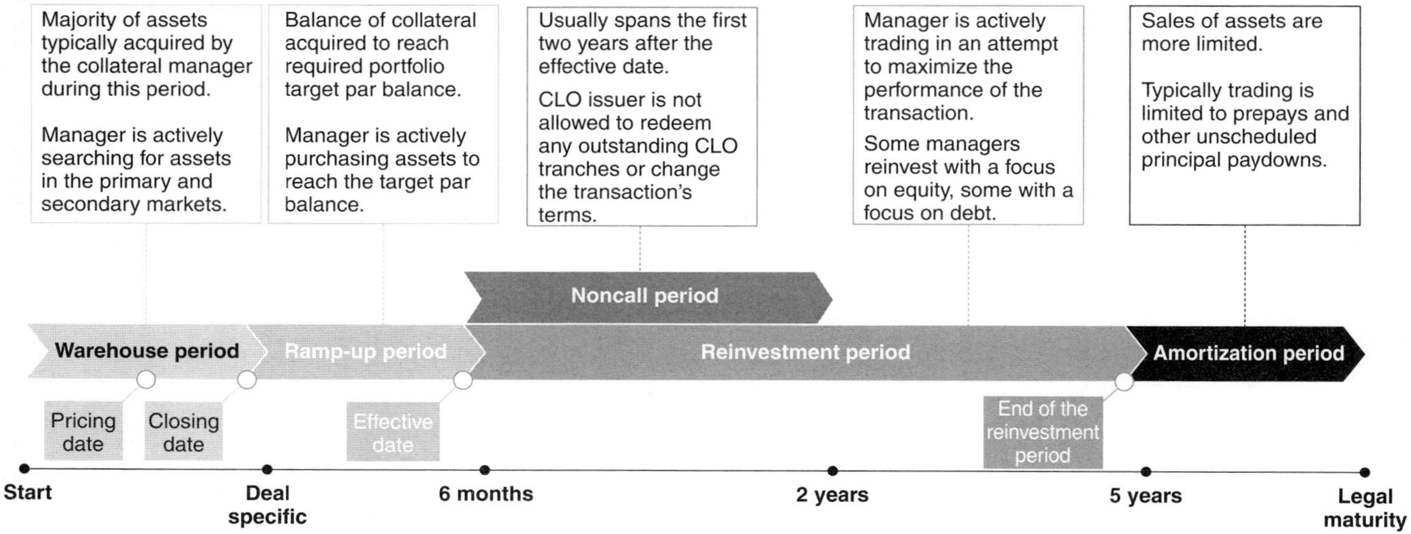

Warehouse period	Majority of assets typically acquired by the collateral manager during this period. Manager is actively searching for assets in the primary and secondary markets.
Ramp-up period	Balance of collateral acquired to reach required portfolio target par balance. Manager is actively purchasing assets to reach the target par balance.
Noncall period	Usually spans the first two years after the effective date. CLO issuer is not allowed to redeem any outstanding CLO tranches or change the transaction's terms.
Reinvestment period	Manager is actively trading in an attempt to maximize the performance of the transaction. Some managers reinvest with a focus on equity, some with a focus on debt.
Amortization period	Sales of assets are more limited. Typically trading is limited to prepays and other unscheduled principal paydowns.

Timeline milestones:
- Start → Pricing date → Closing date (Deal specific) → Effective date (6 months) → End of the reinvestment period (2 years / 5 years) → Legal maturity

Source: S&P Capital IQ.

- *Ramp-up period (0 to 6 months).* After the deal closes, the CLO manager has additional time to purchase and assemble additional collateral until the CLO becomes fully invested. The CLO transaction utilizes tranche (liability) sale proceeds to buy assets from the warehouse. At the ramp-up period end (effective date), the portfolio is fully constructed, the manager shifts to asset management, and the deal's coverage/quality tests initiate.
- *First payment date.* The CLO pays its first coupon to debt investors, and distributes excess cash flows to CLO Equity holders.
- *Noncall period (1 to 2 years).* As the ramp-up period ends, the CLO enters a period in which the tranche notes (liabilities) cannot be called/redeemed or refinanced/reset. When noncall ends, CLO Equity tranche holders may call these notes, refinance deal liabilities to reduce spreads paid, or reset to extend the deal life (and also reduce spreads). Alternatively, the deal may be amortized down after the end of the reinvestment period, which would see all the liabilities/notes redeemed at par by a set priority of payments.
- *Reinvestment period (3 to 5 years).* Simultaneously, after the ramp-up period ends, the CLO manager is now permitted to reinvest principal proceeds of loan collateral to purchase new collateral and focus on effective trading and building of par through maintenance of portfolio credit quality to maximize CLO debt/equity returns. Interest from loan collateral is used to pay CLO tranche holders their assigned spread over the benchmark. Most deals allow for limited reinvestment after the reinvestment period concludes, impacting the Weighted Average Life (WAL) of liabilities.
- *Amortization period (post-reinvestment period to legal maturity).* In the final phase of the CLO life cycle and post-reinvestment period, the CLO manager typically ceases to replace prepaying or maturing collateral (cannot reinvest further) and uses redemption cash flows to amortize tranches sequentially in class rating order until all have been fully repaid. Some CLO documentation may allow partial reinvestment even post-reinvestment period, which is document dependent. When the CLO reaches its maturity

date, if tranches have not been fully paid down, the manager sells all collateral and investors are paid with the proceeds.
- *Deals being called.* In some cases the majority CLO Equity holder may decide to call the deal (i.e., redeem all outstanding tranches in full), and payments will be made to CLO debtholders following the set priority of payments. There could be various incentives to call the deal, including targeted yield achieved, less satisfactory performance, rotating capital to other investments, etc.

Structuring a CLO

CLOs are typically structured as an SPV. During issuance of a CLO, the manager utilizes proceeds from sales of tranches (liabilities) to primarily purchase loan collateral (assets) of approximately the same amount, pay for underwriting, legal, and rating agency fees, and fund the interest reserve account (Exhibit 13.11). In addition to the loan assets that have been purchased through a CLO warehouse, the rest of loan assets are mostly purchased on the CLO closing date, and the remainder during a pre-agreed time window called a ramp-up period after closing. The cost of loan collateral typically does not affect the amount of debt that can be issued, and a higher percentage of collateral purchased preemptively signifies higher deal certainty.

CLO tranches are priced at par (in which case sales proceeds equal par value of the tranche) or at a discount after negotiation with debt investors. The larger the tranche liability discount, the more CLO Equity proceeds are needed.

The total par amount of CLO debt that can be issued for a given par amount of the loan portfolio is primarily driven by rating agency analysis of the CLO deal, through examining key portfolio metrics such as the Weighted Average Rating Factor (WARF), Diversity Score, Recovery Rate, Weighted Average Spread (WAS), and Weighted Average Life (WAL).

CLO Tranches

The CLO debt tranches are usually floating rate tranches benchmarked to three-month USD LIBOR for U.S. dollar deals and six-month Euro Interbank Offered Rate (EURIBOR) for Euro deals. Occasionally, fixed rated CLO tranches are issued to accommodate particular investor demand.

EXHIBIT 13.11

Sources and Uses of CLO Issuance Proceeds of a Sample New Issue CLO.

Sources

Tranche Type	Notes	Rating	Par	Sell Price	Proceeds (Par x Price)
Debt	Class A-1 Notes	AAA	385,000,000	100.0%	385,000,000
	Class A-2 Notes	AA	65,000,000	100.0%	65,000,000
	Class B Notes	A	34,500,000	100.0%	34,500,000
	Class C Notes	BBB	34,500,000	95.8%	33,035,820
	Class D Notes	BB	32,000,000	91.8%	29,362,880
	Class E Notes	B	6,500,000	89.2%	5,797,870
Equity	Subordinated Notes	NA	54,600,000	100.0%	54,600,000
	Total Sources				607,296,570

Uses

	Par	Buy Price	Proceeds (Par x Price)
Asset Cost	600,000,000	99.4%	596,460,000
Interest Reserve			1,000,000
Upfront Deal Expenses & Underwriting Fees			9,864,554
Total Sources			607,296,570

Source: Citi Research

Given that LIBOR is deemed to retire sometime after 2021 in the primary market, CLO deals have started adopting some type of LIBOR fallback language in the indenture in recent years. The detailed language remains customized, but the recommended fallback waterfall has been more widely adopted since last year. Starting January 1, 2022 all new issue U.S. CLOs need to use Secured Overnight Financing Rate (SOFR) as a reference rate. By June 30, 2023, USD LIBOR will cease to exist, meaning that legacy CLOs will need to transition to their replacement rates by this date.

CLO tranche ratings are achieved through subordination and credit enhancement. Similar to other securitized product, the process of tranching provides credit support to senior classes. All principal and interest payments flow from the top to the bottom of the structure. Losses flow in reverse sequential order, hitting the bottom tranches first, and thereby protecting the senior notes. Rating agencies take into account the credit support provided to various tranches while evaluating ratings for these tranches.

The most senior tranche in a CLO has first claims to principal and interest payments and last to take a loss and is usually rated AAA. The most senior AAA tranche is not deferrable and is the controlling class with privileges to negotiate the CLO indenture.

Next in line are the CLO mezzanine tranches (rated between AA and B) that pay progressively higher coupons and still offer protection against collateral defaults but carry lower ratings and are riskier.

The most junior tranche, the CLO Equity tranche (first-loss piece), receives only excess cash after paying the debt tranches. It is the first tranche to experience collateral losses and is the last tranche to be repaid. CLO Equity is long volatility, because holders obtain the residual cash flow and trading gains from a loan portfolio net of financing costs and management fees.

CLO Equity Sample Return

CLO Equity investors have leveraged exposure to loan portfolios, which can provide more front-loaded cash than junior mezzanine in normal markets. They could also participate in the deal structuring process and negotiate terms. In addition, CLO Equity owns the option to refinance, reset, and call the deal after the noncall period.

CLO Equity does not have a designated coupon paid at each quarterly payment date or a fixed principal amount paid at the

EXHIBIT 13.12

Sample CLO Capital Structure of Deals Issued in 2021.

Tranche	Size (%)	Spread to LIBOR (bps)
AAA	62%	118
AA	13%	153
A	5%	198
BBB	7%	309
BB	4%	636
Equity	9%	
	100%	~150 bps

Source: Citi Research, as of February 28, 2021. This data represents the February 2021 CLO BSL 2.0 new issuance deal sample. Debt financing cost is calculated as the weighted average coupon of all rated CLO tranches as shown in the exhibit. Spread to LIBOR is calculated assuming a mix of BB- and B-rated primary and secondary loans.

termination of the deal. The CLO Equity tranche receives the excess spread after costs have been paid and the residual principal value after all the debt tranches as well as any fees and expenses are fully paid. Therefore, numerous factors affect the income profile of a CLO Equity investment, such as CLO debt financing cost, loan default, loan recovery, loan prepayment rate, reinvestment spreads, CLO structural leverage, manager performance, and manager fees. In the current market, LIBOR floor benefit adds portfolio spread and therefore improves CLO Equity cash flow return. Current CLO debt financing cost has also reached the lowest level last seen in mid-2018, which improves CLO Equity modeled return as well, all else equal.

Exhibit 13.12 provides a sample calculation of U.S. CLO debt financing cost. Exhibit 13.13 provides a back-of-the-envelope CLO Equity return calculation.

The CLO Equity tranche bears the first-loss position. Therefore, CLO Equity investors are the most exposed to the downside risk and variable distribution but also have potential upside. Looking at historical CLO Equity performance, CLO 1.0 Equity benefited from having cheap funding costs and opportunities to buy discounted loans during the GFC, ultimately achieving over 20% internal rate of return (IRR).

CLO 2.0 Equity's returns have been running lower so far. However, we note top-quartile U.S. CLO Equity were able to deliver

EXHIBIT 13.13

Sample CLO Equity Return Calculation.

Spread to LIBOR	345 bps
LIBOR Floor Benefit	30 bps
Costs	
Credit Losses	−50 bps
Fees and Expenses	−60 bps
Debt Financing	−150 bps
Excess Spread	115 bps
Leverage Factor	10x
Expected Spread Return	11.5%
LIBOR Return	0.5%
Expected CLO Equity Return	12.0%

Source: Citi Research, as of February 28, 2021. This data represents the February 2021 CLO BSL 2.0 new issuance deal sample. LIBOR floor benefit is estimated given ~40% of CLO collateral has LIBOR floor of 90 bps on average.

low-to-mid-teens' returns, regardless of market timing. It is also worth noting that CLO Equity's deal-level and manager-level performance dispersion is evident across different vintages and even more pronounced today than before the GFC as the number of U.S. CLO managers grew from 100 managers before the GFC to more than 130 today.

CLO Structure Evolution

CLOs have proved to be a dynamic and resilient asset class through various periods of market distress. Compared to CLO 1.0 deals, U.S. CLO 2.0 deals are structured more conservatively and have evolved in the following main areas (Exhibit 13.14):

- *Better credit enhancement.* CLO AAA par subordination has increased by about 13% to 37% in U.S. CLO 2.0 deals compared to the CLO 1.0 era. Par subordination in mezzanine tranches have also grown by 1% to 6%. Strengthened credit support has led to limited principal loss in CLO 2.0 tranches. So far, we count only a dozen or

EXHIBIT 13.14

CLO Tranche Spread and Par Subordination.

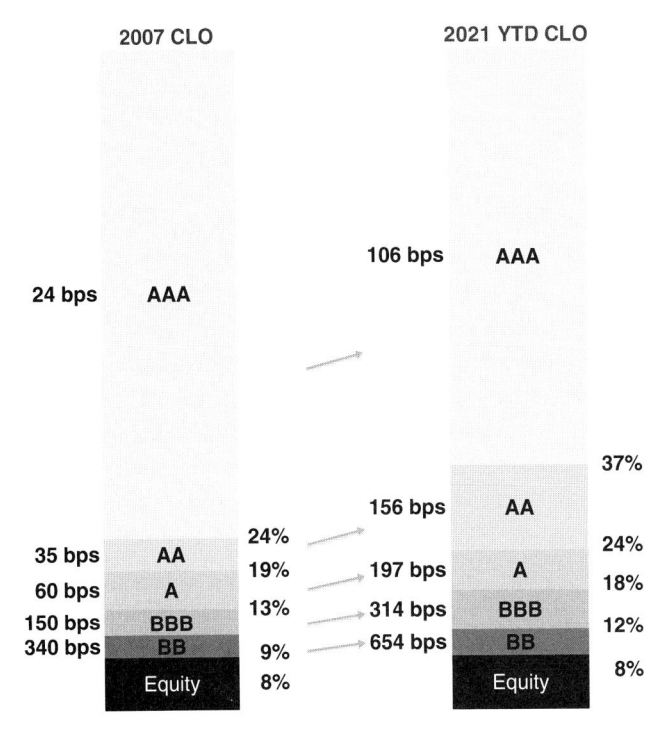

2007 CLO				2021 YTD CLO		
24 bps	AAA		106 bps	AAA		
						37%
		24%	156 bps	AA		24%
35 bps	AA	19%	197 bps	A		18%
60 bps	A	13%	314 bps	BBB		12%
150 bps	BBB	9%	654 bps	BB		8%
340 bps	BB					
	Equity	8%		Equity		

Source: Citi Research, as of April 16, 2021.

so CLO 2.0 tranches have experienced unrealized principal write-downs.

- *Shorter reinvestment period.* The typical length of the reinvestment period in U.S. CLO 2.0 deals has decreased to three to five years from six to seven years in 1.0 deals.
- *Shorter noncall period.* The noncall period has also been reduced by one to two years and is currently one to two years in U.S. CLO 2.0 deals.
- *More conservative portfolio construction.* Investment in structured products is no longer allowed in CLO 2.0 deals. The limit of the CCC bucket has been reduced from 10% or 15% in 1.0 deals to 7.5% in current deals. Non-first-lien assets are limited to below 10%, down from 10% to 20% in 1.0 deals (see Exhibit 13.16).

CLO Cash Flows Waterflow

The rules of distributing cash from collateral collection to the liabilities (notes) of the CLO are known as a waterfall. The rank of CLO debt tranches in the capital structure determines its priority with respect to interest and principal cash flows and its ratings (Exhibit 13.15).

CLOs have different sets of rules, one for allocating interest and another for allocating principal payments from the collateral. These are called the interest and principal waterfalls, respectively. On each payment date, interest is allocated according to the interest waterfall, which we illustrate using an illustrative CLO Senior → Mezzanine → Equity tranche structure. Proceeding down the CLO waterfall, portfolio tests are applied that must be passed for cash flow to flow further down the capital structure.

Cash flow is paid sequentially from the top, starting with the most senior CLO classes (Exhibit 13.15). Losses erode subordination and excess spread from the bottom, and possibly redirect cash flows toward senior classes. Again, the desired tranche ratings are achieved through diversification and leverage, and by employing a cash flow waterfall designed to protect the debt tranches.

Interest Waterfall

The typical CLO interest waterfall is as follows:

- *Senior expenses.* Expenses such as taxes, trustee and administrative fees, and hedge payments have the most senior rank in the interest waterfall. Next, senior management fees are paid for the CLO manager.
- *Senior note interest.* Once senior expenses are paid, interest flows to the senior-most class. The overcollateralization (OC) and interest coverage (IC) tests follow the senior interest payments. These tests must be satisfied if interest is to flow down the structure. If these tests fail, then the leftover interest is used to amortize the notes sequentially. These tests are designed such that they are cured (in the current or subsequent payment periods) when enough of the senior notes are paid down provided the performance of the deal does not deteriorate further.
- *Mezzanine note interest and subordinate management fees.* If the OC and IC tests are satisfied, then cash is used to pay

EXHIBIT 13.15

Sample CLO Waterfall.

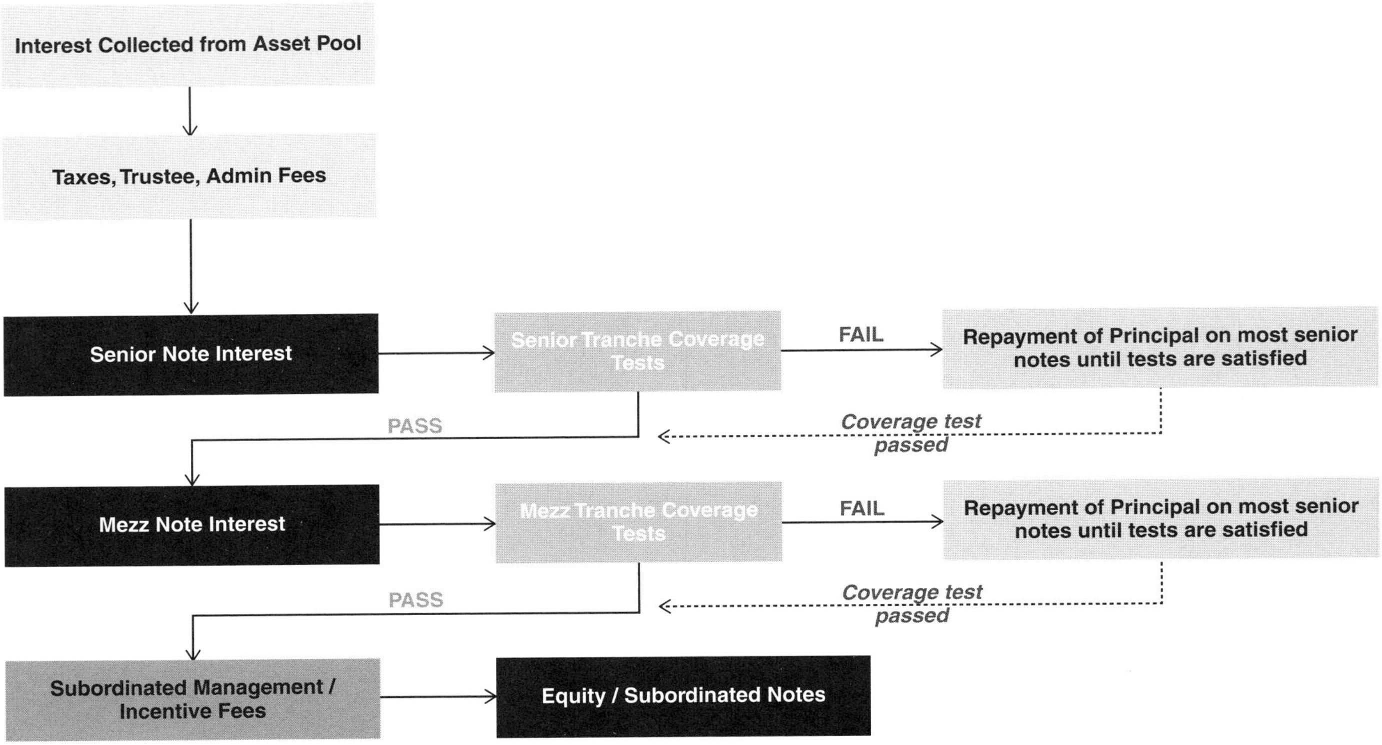

Source: Citi Research.

EXHIBIT 13.16

CLO Structure Evolution.

Deal Term / Feature	Then (1H07)	2016	2021
AAA Subordination (par basis)	23%	34% to 38%	35% to 40%
AAA par coverage	130%	151% to 161%	155% to 174%
AAA pricing	LIBOR + 22 to 25bps	LIBOR + 140 to 165bps	LIBOR + 80 to 150bps
Mezz/Sub tranches	Distributed via capital markets; little manager retention	Portion of Equity tranche likely retained by manager	Portion of Equity tranche likely retained by manager
Reinvestment period	6 to 7 years	4 to 5 years	3 to 5 years
Noncall period	3 years	2 to 3 years	1 to 2 years
Min. 1st lien assets	80% to 85%	90%	90%
Max. non 1st lien assets	10% to 20%	<10%	<10%
Caa/CCC assets	10% to 15%	7.5%	7.5%
High-Yield Bonds	10% to 20%	0%	5%
Structured Products	35%	0%	0%

Source: Citi Research.

the mezzanine notes' current and deferred (if any) interest. Post-payment of interest to the mezzanine notes, another set of OC and IC tests is encountered. If these tests are passed then a subordinated management fee is paid to the CLO manager. This subordinated management fee is senior to CLO Equity payments.

- *CLO Equity payments and incentive performance fee.* Any residual cash left post-payment of senior expenses, management fees, note interest, and subordinated management fees is allocated to the CLO Equity tranche. Some CLO structures have incentive management fees equal to about 15% to 20% of residual cash flows if the CLO Equity IRR surpasses a predetermined hurdle rate.

Principal Waterfall

There are two sets of rules (waterfalls) to allocate principal, one applicable during the reinvestment period and the other during the amortization period. As mentioned above, any principal proceeds during the reinvestment period are invested into new collateral to maintain the deal's par balance.

During the amortization period, principal proceeds are used to first pay taxes and fees and then to make whole any unpaid interest on the notes. After these obligations are met, principal proceeds amortize the notes sequentially. It should be noted that some structures allow certain reinvestment activity post-reinvestment period. This is a nuance that we discuss in detail in sections below.

CLO Coverage Tests

Unique features of CLOs include the over-collateralization (OC) and interest coverage (IC) tests that help protect senior tranche holders by diverting interest and principal upon test failures:

- *Over-collateralization (OC) test.* CLO indentures contain various clauses limiting the manager's ability to take uncalculated risk in the portfolio and their trading activities. The OC ratio is one of the most important. The OC ratio ensures that the deal has enough assets to pay back the full principal on the debt tranches if the deal gets liquidated. If the OC tests are not in compliance, interest is diverted from subordinated notes and used to reduce the balance of more senior notes, starting from the most senior tranche.
- *OC ratio.* The OC test is based on the OC ratio. The OC ratio is essentially an asset liability ratio and is defined for each class of notes. In a simple three-tranche CLO (i.e., senior, mezzanine, equity), there would be two OC ratios, one each for the senior and mezzanine debt tranches. The denominator is CLO tranche par, which includes the current par amount of outstanding principal for the respective CLO tranche and all tranches above it in seniority.

Adjusted Collateral Principal Amount

To calculate the OC ratio, as the numerator we need to add the cash available in the deal to the collateral par balance, adjusted for defaulted assets, excess CCC-rated assets, and discounted purchase assets. We detail these adjustments in Exhibit 13.17 and below:

- *Aggregate principal balance of assets*: Principal balance of loan assets, excluding defaulted and discount obligations.
- *Defaulted asset with adjustment*: Defaulted assets are carried at lower of market value and rating agency recovery value. For the purposes of defaulted assets adjustment, the defaulted balance is subtracted from the principal balance of assets and is added back at lower of market value and rating agency recovery value.
- *Discount purchase asset with adjustment*: The CLO manager could increase the total par amount of the collateral by purchasing heavily discounted loans. The noteholders wish to limit purchases of such collateral, and hence, for heavily discounted collateral, defined as loans purchased for a price below $80 to $85 pts, only the purchase value (instead of par value) is used while calculating the OC ratio's numerator.
- *Excess CCC adjustment*: The CCC adjustment penalizes the purchase of excessive amount of cheap CCC-rated assets above the limit. The most common way to calculate the adjustment is that all loans that are rated CCC and below by any agency in the deal are included, and a market value haircut is imposed for the excess over a threshold (typically 7.5%) instead of carrying all at par value.

In calculating the excess CCC haircut, the lowest market value is used among the loans in the CCC pool. In some deals, if the market price is lower than a rating agency recovery value, the recovery value will be used to calculate the CCC haircut. However, not all deals are the same. A few allow the use of an average price for a CCC pool for the haircut. Others allow investors to set the CCC bucket based on which agency has the lower CCC bucket. These situations are of great benefit to CLO Equity (which stands to lose the most from CCC haircuts) when there is little overlap among the downgrades of different agencies and using all CCCs would create a large bucket.

EXHIBIT 13.17
CLO Over-Collateralization Ratio Adjustment.

Over-Collateralization Ratio = $\dfrac{\text{Adjusted Collateral Principal Amount}}{\text{CLO Tranche Par}}$

A) Adjusted Collateral Principal Amount =
- C) Aggregate Principal Balance of Assets
- Plus D) Defaulted Assets
- Plus E) Discount Purchase Assets
- Minus F) Excess CCC Adjustment at predetermined haircuts.

B) CLO Tranche Par = Current par value amount of outstanding principal for the respective CLO tranche and all tranches above it in seniority.

where:
- C) Aggregate Principal Balance of Assets = Par value of assets. This excludes defaulted and discount obligations.
- D) Defaulted Assets = Defaulted assets are carried at the lower of Market Value or Rating Agency Recovery Value.
- E) Discount Purchase Assets = Asset bought below a specified price (Example: Bought at 80%).
- F) Excess CCC Adjustment = Difference between Par and the Market Value of any CCC assets that typically exceed 7.5% of the Collateral Principal Amount. This includes lower-rated assets as well.

Source: Citi Research.

All else equal, deals with more excess CCC assets will have a higher likelihood of failing their OC test, which would result in a diversion of interest payments from the CLO Equity tranche in order to amortize debt tranches. The impact on performance may be significant. Active management focused on keeping CCC exposure within reasonable bounds is key.

Exhibit 13.18 details a sample OC ratio calculation.

The interest diversion (ID) test is another OC ratio–based test and is designed to protect senior note holders. This test is performed after all the debt tranches have received interest and has a lower value than the junior-most OC test trigger. If the ID test is failing, the leftover interest (or a part of it) is used to purchase new collateral instead of paying the CLO Equity tranche and subordinated management fees.

The interest coverage (IC) test measures the available excess spread and is designed to ensure that the interest cash flows from the underlying collateral are sufficient to service the outstanding debt (notes). The IC ratio takes the sum of interest payments received from the CLO collateral portfolio and divides it by the sum of required interest payments due to the respective CLO tranche and all tranches above it in seniority (Exhibit 13.19).

If the test is tripped for a class, cash is diverted until the note passes the test, with that class and subsequent classes below it not receiving interest to pay off the most senior class outstanding.

CLO PORTFOLIO CRITERIA

A typical CLO is backed by a pool of bank loans diversified across 100 to 200 distinct obligors in 20 to 30 industries. CLO managers must constantly comply with collateral quality tests and concentration limitations on the invested loan collateral pool. Investors have the comfort of knowing that there are restrictions on the portfolio and substitutions can be made only when tests are passed.

Collateral Quality Tests

The different collateral quality tests are discussed below:

- *Weighted Average Rating Factor (WARF) test:* Fitch and Moody's define average portfolio rating differently, but

EXHIBIT 13.18

CLO Cash Flow Waterfall—Over-Collateralization Example.

Test	Outstanding Balance	Numerator	Denominator	Current	Trigger	Pass / Fail
Class A OC	366	430.8	366	117.7%	115.0%	Pass
Class B OC	47	430.8	413	104.3%	104.0%	Pass
Class C OC	10	430.8	423	101.8%	101.9%	Fail
Equity	41	N/A	N/A			

Numerator

		Aggregate Principal Balance of Assets	445
	Plus	Cash & Eligible Investments	5
Adjusted Collateral	Minus	Defaulted Assets Haircut	16
Principal Amount	Minus	Excess CCC Adjustment Haircut	3
	Minus	Discount Obligations Haircut	0.2
		Total	**430.8**

Denominator

		Denominator	
CLO Tranche Par		Class B Par	47
	Plus	Class A Par	366
		Total	**413**

Class B OC Ratio = $\dfrac{\text{Adjusted Collateral Principal Amount}}{\text{CLO Tranche Par (CLO Class A and Class B Par)}}$ = $\dfrac{430.8}{413}$ = 104.3%

Source: Citi Research, value in $ millions.

EXHIBIT 13.19

Interest Coverage Ratio.

$$\text{IC ratio} = \frac{\text{Interest from assets (net of senior expenses)}}{\text{Interest due on tranches/liabilities ranking equally or higher}}$$

Source: Citi Research.

both calculate a WARF. Each loan is assigned a numerical equivalent of its respective rating, which is then averaged over the collateral portfolio. A higher WARF number indicates lower average rating of the portfolio and can mean increased portfolio risk.
- *Weighted Average Recovery Rate (WARR) test:* Likewise, agencies have their own recovery assumptions for loans, and managers are expected to maintain a level above the minimum threshold.
- *Weighted Average Floating Spread (WAS) test:* Each CLO portfolio needs to satisfy the minimum floating spread test to ensure that the portfolio assets can generate sufficient cash flow to pay fees and CLO debt tranche interests.
- *Weighted Average Life (WAL) test:* The weighted average life of all collateral except for defaulted obligations cannot exceed a certain limit, to limit portfolio extension risk.

Failure of CLO portfolio criteria will mean that the manager has restrictions in the assets CLO managers can buy (if they can at all). Typically, any purchase or sale needs to maintain or improve the collateral quality tests if any of them are failing.

Concentration Limitations

Each CLO has a list of concentration limits that it needs to satisfy in order to ensure that the portfolio quality is managed by CLO managers properly. Failure to comply with any of the concentration limits would mean that any purchase made by CLO managers needs to either maintain or improve the concentration metrics.

For example, all agencies require the portfolio to maintain diversity by putting a cap on obligor and sector sizes. In addition, Moody's has its Diversity Score. The Diversity Score is used to measure the industry and issuer concentration of the CLO collateral portfolio, which is a shorthand for calculating, using their framework, an equivalent number of loans that would have a similar loss distribution that the actual portfolio of correlated assets has. The higher the Diversity Score, the higher the portfolio diversity.

Details of the portfolio criteria and concentration limitations between U.S. and European CLOs can be found in Exhibit 13.20. Many deals have a requirement of 90% or greater senior secured loan obligations, which provide significant reassurance on recoveries (historic loan recovery rates are around 70%).

EXHIBIT 13.20

Sample Terms of U.S. versus European CLOs.

Selected Deal Parameters	USD CLOs	EUR CLOs
Ramp-up Period Covenants	6 months	6 months
Target Par	$450,000,000	€400,000,000
Reinvestment Period	3–5 years	4.5 years
Non-call Period	1–2 years	1.5–2 years
Payment Frequency	3 months	3 months
Trustee Fee & Other Senior Expenses	$200,000	€300,000
Other Senior Fee Cap	0.02%	0.025%
Senior Management Fees	0.15%	0.15%
Subordinated Management Fees	0.35%	0.35%
Asset Purchase Price	99.75%	99.70%
Incentive Management Fees	0.125%	NA
Incentive Fee Distribution Share (Accruing from Closing Date)	0.10%	0.10%
Incentive Fee Distribution Cap per Payment Date	20%	30%
Incentive Fee Sub Notes IRR Hurdle	12%	12%
Selected Portfolio Concentration Limits & Collateral Quality Tests		
Max Obligors from Below-AAA Countries Maximum	10%	10%
CCC Assets Maximum	7.5%	7.5%
Senior Secured Debt Minimum	90%	90%
Unsecured Bond, 2nd Lien, Mezzanine Maximum	10%	10%
Fixed Rate Assets Maximum	5%	10%
Average Life Covenant Maximum	7 Years	8.5 Years
Top 10 Obligors Maximum	NA	20%
Cov-lite Loans Maximum	60%	30%
Weighted Average Spread Minimum	4%	4%
Weighted Coupon Minimum	6.5%	5.75%
Fitch / Moody's WARF Maximum	NA/3300	34/2750
Fitch Recovery Rate Minimum	NA	65.5%
Moody's Diversity Score Minimum	40%	34%
Non-USD/EUR Obligations Maximum	NA	25%
Corporate Rescue Loans Maximum	NA	5%
Any Single Obligor	2%	2.5%
Any Single Industry	10%	10% to 15%

CONSTRUCTING AND NEGOTIATING CLO TERMS

We provide a detailed guide on commonly asked questions and commonly negotiated documentation points for CLO investors.

Commonly Asked Questions and Issues for New Issue CLOs

- Warehouse/ramp-up
  - How much is the deal ramped? What is the expected time frame and strategy for remaining purchases?
  - What is the warehousing arrangement? Will assets be transferred to the CLO at cost or market value?
  - Explanation of the ability to achieve the portfolio metrics marketed in the "model portfolio"
- Manager due diligence
  - Historical track record in CLOs and other loan investments
  - Size of firm and CLO business/ability to dedicate resources toward CLO management
  - Experience of management team
- Par subordination/breakeven analysis
  - What is the "par subordination" of each debt tranche (i.e., how much loan portfolio par can be eroded before that tranche experiences loss)?
  - Breakeven analysis: Annual and/or cumulative default/loss rate that the portfolio can withstand before that tranche experiences loss.
- Issue price
  - How much OID will each debt tranche be issued with?

Commonly Negotiated Documentation Points

CLO structures differ across deals in multiple ways. Though all parts of transaction documents need to be understood, there are some parts that are more critical than others as far as the economic risks of a deal are concerned. These sections are usually cases where considerable effort is spent on negotiations. A summary is shown in Exhibit 13.21, with our comments below.

1. *Call/refinancing optionality*:
   - *Length of noncall period.* After the noncall period, most deals allow (1) assets to be liquidated with the proceeds used to repay CLO noteholders or (2) individual debt tranches or all debt as a whole to be refinanced or reset.
   - *Repricing.* Same concept as refinancing but CUSIPs stay the same.
   - *Payment dates.* Most CLOs have the ability to redeem/refinance/reset liabilities on any business day, but some transactions remain limited to payment dates only.
2. *Make-whole after refinancing and/or repricing notes.* The deal can be refinanced at the end of the noncall period. In many cases, the classes of notes can also be repriced, with no requirement that all classes be repriced. There may be conditions where a make-whole is paid if a deal is redeemed optionally.
3. *Ability to amend deal terms:* There may be situations where the manager or investors want to amend deal terms. The deal trustee needs to determine—with the assistance of counsel—if the amendment is material to investors. In some cases, rating agency confirmation would also be needed to ensure that the changes do not affect ratings. Investors might also need to consent—typically amendments deemed to have a material adverse effect (MAE) on any tranche or tranches need consent from a majority of the holders of that tranche. Some documents allow for a "raise your hand" right if an investor disagrees with the MAE determination.
4. *OC test definition.* The OC test adjusts the value of the collateral par amount by a number of factors. In addition to the value of the test triggers and how much cushion there is initially, discussions will likely include (1) whether CCC assets above the threshold will be carried at market value versus par, (2) whether multiple ratings are considered when defining CCC assets, (3) whether multiple rating agency-based haircuts are included for defaulted loans, (4) whether defaults are carried at lower of rating agency recovery rates or just one of the rating agencies, and (5) the deal's ability to carry certain discounted purchases at par in the OC calculation.

EXHIBIT 13.21

Important Sections in Deal Indenture.

Section	What does it contain?	Why does it matter?
Section 5: Event of Default	– The conditions that can cause a deal to enter Default (Downgrades, CCC Buckets, OC Breach, etc.) – Consequences and control rights – The EOD Waterfall	– This is a crucial section for distressed deals and determines the consequences if a deal deteriorates. Acceleration preserves collateral, liquidation wipes out Jnr note holders.
Section 8: Supplemental Indentures	– Amendments with consent – Amendments without consent – Execution procedure	– Volckerization – Relaxing reinvestment language – "Materially and adversely affected" – Negative consent/Positive consent
Section 9: Redemption of Notes	– Mandatory redemptions (OC test failure) – Optional Redemptions – Refinancings – Repricings – Reset Amendments	– CLO equity investors long these options – 1.0 Equity investors can call a deal more easily if only a simple majority needed – 2.0 Equity investors should know mechanics of the reset/refinancing options
Section 11: Application of Monies (Deal Waterfall)	– Principal waterfall (descriptions of OC test diversions, etc.).	– Order of cash flows – How can cash flows be diverted? – When interest is deferred how is it paid back? – Can principal be used to pay interest/can it be flushed to equity holder?
Section 12: Sales and Purchases of Collateral (Reinvestment Language)	– Restrictions around sales and purchases – Collateral quality tests – Reinvestment Periods	– Typically most important for POST reinvestment language – What can the manager buy and when? – Helps define the WAL of a deal

Source: Citi Research.

Discount "swaps" include the ability to carry certain discounted purchases at par in the OC calculation when swapping out of currently held discounted positions.
5. *Collateral value determination.* Although CLOs are not market value structure, market value becomes important when assets are distressed because they affect OC ratios. CLOs usually require the manager to determine market value of the underlying collateral using a recognized pricing service or three independent broker dealers. However, some managers have the flexibility to change these prices (marks) depending on whether they deem the prices to be incorrect. There are restrictions on the amount of collateral that can be marked by the manager. CLOs with less liquid underlying collateral are more likely to have CLO manager determined market value for a larger proportion of the collateral pool.
6. *Event of default.* CLO indentures detail the events that constitute an event of default (EOD). An EOD accelerates the deal (all cash flows are used to amortize senior notes) or sometimes enforces collateral liquidation. EOD triggers include missing senior note interest or principal payments and the senior OC ratio falling below a threshold (typically 102.5%).

Investors will need to understand the conditions that it takes to trigger an EOD in the CLO and the remedies for a breach. Once an EOD occurs, investors that are part of the "controlling class" (i.e., the senior-most class at that time) can typically declare an "acceleration," whereby interest and principal received from the loan assets are applied to pay down the debt in order of seniority. The controlling class may take certain remedial actions to correct an event of default, depending on the deal. The remedial actions can include rescinding the EOD or changing the manager. In certain circumstances, the controlling class investors have the ability to liquidate the loan assets. However, most CLOs have conditions in place to protect junior note holders when liquidations are being considered as a remedy. These protective features include restricting liquidation unless all tranches are redeemed in full and allowing the junior note holders to vote on liquidation.

What does it take to trigger an EOD in the CLO? Typical triggers include missed interest or principal payments on the AAA or AA rated debt classes and failure of the ratio of assets to AAA rated liabilities to exceed 102.5%. Once an EOD occurs, AAA investors can typically declare an acceleration, where interest and principal received from the loan assets are applied to pay down the debt in order of seniority.

In certain circumstances, AAA investors control the ability to liquidate the loan assets. Investors throughout the capital structure focused on maximizing recovery value in these scenarios. Language typically can be found in Section 5 of the CLO indenture.

7. *Classification of trading gains.* The CLO manager usually trades collateral on a regular basis, which results in trading gains that can either be classified as interest or principal proceeds. This classification has consequences for each set of notes; for example, classification as interest proceeds benefits the CLO Equity tranche, whereas principal gets paid to the most senior tranche. In some deals, trading gains might be classified as interest proceeds under certain conditions. The indenture governs this classification and should be consulted before an investment is considered.

8. *Post-downgrade trading restrictions.* CLOs usually restrict discretionary trading by the manager following note downgrades. The restrictions usually apply if junior notes are downgraded by two or more notches or senior notes are downgraded by even one notch. Some CLOs might not have these restrictions, and others might allow the controlling class to waive these restrictions.

9. *Trading flexibility before and after reinvestment period end.* In general, the ability of the manager to buy and sell assets in and out of the CLO is governed by what is usually defined as the "investment criteria" or "reinvestment criteria." Typically after giving effect to any new asset bought by the CLO, each test (OC and IC, collateral quality, concentration limitations, etc.) either need to be (1) satisfied or (2) maintained or improved.

However, the length of the reinvestment period in CLOs is not as straightforward as one might expect. Most CLOs have provisions in the indenture that allow reinvestment post-reinvestment period subject to certain conditions. These conditions vary from deal to deal and are of great consequence for the various classes of notes.

Depending on the deal, CLO managers may be allowed to reinvest prepayments or proceeds from sales of credit-risk loans after the reinvestment period. There is usually a stipulation that the deal's OC tests must be passing and reinvestment is barred if an EOD of restricted trading period has occurred. There could be other tests the deal has to pass before it is allowed to reinvest after the reinvestment period. A limitation is also usually placed on the size of the CCC bucket, and the reinvestment is usually only allowed if the purchased security maintains or improves collateral quality tests such as the average rating, spread, and average life.

Requests for loan maturity amendments may also face differing restrictions. In most deals, the manager may not agree to an "amend to extend" if the WAL test is failing, which may be counterproductive if the amendment prevents a loan default.

10. *Credit-risk criteria and sales.* Securities in the collateral pool designated as "credit-risk" securities are treated specially by CLO indentures. Managers are usually allowed to reinvest proceeds from sales of credit-risk assets even post-reinvestment period. Even if note downgrades enforce trading restrictions, some CLOs allow credit-risk securities trading. Various criteria can be used to test if a particular security is a credit-risk security; these include rating downgrades or watches, spread increases by threshold amounts, and/or market value decreases. How a manager deals with a credit-risk security has less to do with structure and more to do with the manager's skills. A sale at discount will deteriorate the OC cushion. If the minimum OC trigger is tripped, collections will be used to pay down the senior notes. Investors will view credit-risk sales favorably if the asset ultimately defaults and is sold at a price that is higher than the asset's ultimate recovery.

11. *Credit-improved criteria and sales.* As with credit risk, this is a combination of structure and manager skills. Credit-improved sales can benefit both rated notes and CLO Equity holders. The issue hinges upon how the premium from the sale is treated in the waterfall. The premium generated from a credit-improved sale may be treated as interest collections and used to enhance returns to the CLO

Equity or it can be used to grow OC through the purchase of additional assets. Clearly, the latter method benefits all note holders. When a manager sells an asset that has improved in credit quality, the rated note holders lose the benefit of upward credit migration. However, if the sale proceeds (including premium) are reinvested in additional assets, the manager may be able to maintain or increase OC.

12. *Workouts and restructurings.* Prior to 2019, the recovery packages that followed loan defaults typically included an offering of post-reorganization Equity. CLOs cannot purchase Equity securities outright, but they generally have been able to receive Equity securities in lieu of debts previously held. Beginning in 2019, sponsors and distressed investors began to take advantage of the tight restrictions in CLO indentures with respect to participating in workouts. Instead of just offering Equity securities, recovery packages now often require a purchase of new securities. If a recovery requires a payment, there are tighter restrictions for CLOs to be able to participate. In certain circumstances, CLOs were not allowed to participate in the recovery packages because of these restrictions, thereby enhancing the recovery rate of junior creditors. CLO documents now include provisions that grant additional flexibility to use proceeds in order to participate in these types of recoveries. Given that there is inherent risk in diverting CLO proceeds to acquire securities from a defaulted issuer, this flexibility has been highly negotiated between CLO managers, debt investors, CLO Equity investors, and rating agencies. These features vary heavily from deal to deal, and will continue to evolve. The crucial aspects of these negotiations have been the following:

- Are the proceeds that are used to acquire such securities limited to interest proceeds, or can the CLO also use principal proceeds?
- What conditions must be satisfied in order to use proceeds for a purchase (typically OC tests must be passing and/or deal must have built par since inception in certain occasions)?
- Does the acquired security get included in OC test calculations and other CLO tests?

- How are the proceeds received from the acquired security treated (typically expected that all proceeds received are treated as principal, until a certain recovery threshold is realized)?

13. *Discretionary sales.* Depending on the structure, a CLO manager also has the discretion to trade the portfolio within limits. Not surprisingly, rated CLO debtholders have a bearish view of large portfolio turnover; they prefer managers with strong credit fundamentals to execute a long-term investment strategy. Any problematic credits can be traded under the credit-risk trading rules. In contrast, income note holders favor discretionary trading provisions, because these allow the manager to continually search for assets with the best risk-adjusted returns and build up the par value of the portfolio.

14. *Collateral quality tests such as covenants, spreads, and maturity.* Even though the collateral quality tests appear straightforward, there are nuances in how they are defined in the indenture. Covenant definitions can often be linked to debt tranches that are not in the CLO but issued by the same loan borrower. Likewise, spread covenants can include the benefit of LIBOR floors in some deals but not in others. In some cases, WAL tests can be adjusted to exclude the longest maturity assets if the deal has built par.

15. *Portfolio criteria.* There could be also difference in limitations on the percentage of the portfolio that can be comprised of non–first lien loans, second lien loans, bond bucket, and covenant-lite loans, etc.

16. *LIBOR fallback language.* LIBOR fallback language is another item in CLO indentures that have been heavily negotiated by CLO Debt and CLO Equity investors in recent years. Although the fallback language has not become quite standardized yet, the fallback waterfall language recommended by the Alternative Reference Rates Committee (ARRC) has been more widely adopted.

    Some key negotiation points related to LIBOR fallback language have centered on what form of SOFR to use as an alternative rate and an appropriate asset trigger threshold (i.e., what percentage of underlying loans in CLOs or CLO deals that have transitioned to SOFR or another alternative rate will trigger CLO tranches to transition).

REGULATORY IMPACT

The CLO market has seen significant advancement in regulatory oversight since the start of the 2.0 era. Key regulations in the past are summarized below:

- *FDIC Surcharge (since April 2013).* Large U.S. banks pay a greater insurance assessment if their balance sheets carry "higher-risk" commercial and industrial (C&I) loan exposure (including securitization like CLOs). The rule "looks through" a securitization to the underlying assets and ignores the tranche rating, subordination, or credit enhancement in the securitization.
- *Volcker Rule (since April 1, 2014, and revised in October 2020).* The Volcker Rule was first implemented on April 1, 2014, and it prevented banks from having ownership interests in covered funds. Essentially, the Volker Rule prevented banks holding CLO AAA tranches in all but loan-only CLOs. As a result, regular CLOs issued post-2014 eliminated bond buckets in their portfolios, which are often referred as CLO 3.0s.

    Since October 2020, the Volcker Rule has been revised and bond buckets are allowed back again in U.S. CLOs. Under more aggressive interpretation of some market participants, CLOs are no longer deemed "covered funds," and therefore may be allowed to include more bond assets or other types of securities.

    In April 2021, the Loan Syndications and Trading Association (LSTA) concluded that the regulatory changes to the Volcker Rule that permit CLOs to hold nonloan assets are no longer subject to voidance under the Congressional Review Act.
- *U.S. Risk Retention (between January 1, 2017, and May 2018).* The U.S. Risk Retention regulation was officially implemented to U.S. CLOs in January 2017 to help the "alignment" of interest in new securitization transactions between managers and investors. The retention tranche could be a 5% junior-most horizontal slice (which is most

of the CLO Equity in a typical CLO) or a vertical slice of 5% of each tranche across the capital stack, held through maturity.

This rule was later revoked in May 2018 for U.S. CLOs with the court ruling that the Risk Retention Rule should not be applied to open-market BSL CLOs.[3] However, the risk retention funds raised during this period have continued to support the growth in U.S. CLO issuance in the last few years.

- *NAIC Risk-Based Capital Charge Revision (ongoing).* Insurance companies that invest in CLOs need to adhere to the risk-based capital charge (RBC) grid implemented by the National Association of Insurance Commissioners (NAIC). Starting in January 2021, the NAIC implemented the updated and more granular NAIC designation category that changed the way CLO tranches of different ratings will be treated in RBC calculations. There is an ongoing discussion around the updated set of bond factors to be used in the RBC calculation.[4]

- *LIBOR Transition (ongoing).* The Federal Reserve has been evaluating banks' LIBOR exposure, transition plans, and fallback provisions, and in March 2021 the end dates for LIBOR were confirmed with the most widely used USD LIBOR settings ending after June 30, 2023. By that time, remaining legacy products are required to switch to a valid replacement rate. The Federal Reserve had also warned that on November 2020 that failure to cease LIBOR deals would potentially lead to significant risks for banks, and a lack of transition preparation to SOFR could undermine financial stability.

    CLOs issued recently have increasingly incorporated the standard fallback waterfall language suggested by the ARRC. The key risk remains the potential basis risk between the benchmark rate used by CLO tranches and underlying loans after transition.

---

[3] Maggie Wang, "The Future without Risk Retention," Citi Velocity, February 20, 2018, available at https://www.citivelocity.com/t/r/eppublic/24jr3.
[4] "Life Risk-Based Capital (E) Working Group," Financial Condition (E) Committee, NAIC, accessed September 20, 2021, https://content.naic.org/cmte_e_lrbc.htm.

CONCLUSION

The CLO 2.0 era has seen many positive developments for investors, including better structural protections, more conservative reinvestment guidelines, a growing investor base, and better secondary liquidity.

Although the asset class experienced ups and downs over the past decade, the CLO structure proved to be resilient, with rare losses and superior performance in comparison to global spread products. As the market has matured, the CLO manager landscape,[5] regulatory environment, rating agency framework, and investor focus on sustainability (ESG) have all evolved concurrently, supporting the CLO asset class to continue growing as an asset class and essential component of the global market.[6]

---

[5] Maggie Wang, "Evolving CLO Manager Landscape & Primary AAA Spread Premium," Citi Velocity, September 9, 2020, available at https://www.citivelocity.com/t/r/eppublic/1tsJh.

[6] For additional information on CLOs see:
- Maggie Wang, "Finding Value in CLO Mezz with Moody's Proposed CLO Rating Methodology Change," Citi Velocity, September 18, 2020, available at https://www.citivelocity.com/t/r/eppublic/1uRlV.
- Maggie Wang, "US CLO Q4'20 Outlook & Deep Dive into CLO Equity," Citi Velocity, October 5, 2020, available at https://www.citivelocity.com/t/r/eppublic/1uoIv.
- Maggie Wang, "Citi US CLO Scorecard: March 2021," Citi Velocity, April 1, 2021, available at https://www.citivelocity.com/t/r/eppublic/23qRH.
- Maggie Wang, "What to Expect for CLO Equity IRR," Citi Velocity, February 23, 2021, available at https://www.citivelocity.com/t/r/eppublic/21pDy.
- Maggie Wang, "ESG: The Next Frontier for CLOs and Loans," Citi Velocity, February 5, 2021, available at https://www.citivelocity.com/t/r/eppublic/20sLa.
- NAIC, "Life Risk-Based Capital (E) Working Group," available at https://content.naic.org/cmte_e_lrbc.htm.
- Ratul Roy, "Loan Retention Vehicle (and CLO) Investment Primer," Citi Velocity, September 1, 2015, available at https://www.citivelocity.com/t/r/eppublic/21Yir.
- Ratul Roy, "A EUR CLO 2019 Primer: A Decade Since GFC, Two Decades Since First Euro CLO," Citi Velocity, April 16, 2019, available at https://www.citivelocity.com/t/r/eppublic/1biS2/.
- J. W. Ruslan Bikbov, "North America Multi-Asset Focus: Lost in Transition: A Cross-Asset Guide to LIBOR and SOFR," Citi Velocity, July 16, 2020, available at https://www.citivelocity.com/t/r/eppublic/24noK.
- Maggie Wang. (2016, February 10). Collateralized Loan Obligations: A Simple Guide for Investors. Retrieved from https://www.citivelocity.com/t/r/eppublic/22c6a
- Maggie Wang. (2017, March 10). Four Reasons Why CLO Premium to CMBS Should Compress. Retrieved from https://www.citivelocity.com/t/r/eppublic/12vXN
- Maggie Wang. (2018, October 12).

CHAPTER 14

Public Policy and the Loan Market: How the Syndicated Loan Market Is Impacted by Legislation, Regulation, and the Judicial System

Meredith Coffey
Executive Vice President of Research and Co-Head,
Public Policy Group
Loan Syndications and Trading Association

Elliot Ganz
General Counsel and Co-Head, Public Policy Group
Loan Syndications and Trading Association

INTRODUCTION

Syndicated loans and the institutions that participate in the syndicated loan market are directly or indirectly subject to a series of laws and regulations that develop along three interrelated streams: legislative, regulatory, and judicial. While Congress considers and passes laws that impact the loan market, it typically delegates to federal regulatory agencies a significant amount of authority to interpret and implement those laws.[1,2] Importantly, the regulatory interpretation of these laws can be challenged and overturned under the Administrative Procedure Act (APA).[3,4] Loan market participants are also subject to rules, regulations, and guidance that originate from the inherent and broad supervisory and rulemaking powers of federal regulators.[5] Many of these rules are also subject to administrative law challenges under the APA as well as legislative review under the Congressional Review Act.[6] Other laws that do not specifically target loans, such as Chapter 11 of the U.S. Bankruptcy Code,[7] nevertheless have important implications for their performance and pricing. These laws are subject to interpretation by federal and state courts through judicial rulings, and the effects of these rulings can be profound.[8] It is clear that financial services

---

[1] The federal regulatory agencies that supervise various aspects of the loan market and/or loan market participants include the Federal Reserve Board, the Federal Depository Insurance Company (FDIC), and the Office of the Comptroller of the Currency (OCC); with the Federal Reserve, the FDIC, and the OCC being collectively referred to as the "Banking Agencies," as well as the Securities and Exchange Commission (SEC). Occasionally, the Commodity Futures Trading Commission (CFTC) is involved, most recently with respect to the Volcker Rule.

[2] For example, whereas Section 941 of the Dodd-Frank Act broadly imposed "risk retention" with respect to certain types of securitization vehicles, it was up to the Banking Agencies and the SEC to develop the rules and regulations implementing the legislation. The final Risk Retention Rule ran 684 pages (available at https://www.sec.gov/rules/final/2014/34-73407.pdf).

[3] *Loan Syndications and Trading Association v. Securities and Exchange Commission*, available at https://www.cadc.uscourts.gov/internet/opinions.nsf/871D769D4527442A8525822F0052E1E9/$file/17-5004-1717230.pdf.

[4] Administrative Procedure Act, available at https://open.defense.gov/Portals/23/Documents/Regulatory/apa.pdf.

[5] For example, the Shared National Credit program and the Leveraged Lending Guidance, which are covered in depth below.

[6] See Part 3 for a discussion of how the CRA was raised in the context of the Leveraged Lending Guidance.

[7] Available at https://www.law.cornell.edu/uscode/text/11.

[8] See, for example, *RadLAX Gateway Hotel, LLC v. Amalgamated Bank*, available at https://www.supremecourt.gov/opinions/11pdf/11-166.pdf. (*RadLAX* will be discussed in Part 4.)

legislation, regulation, and litigation are all deeply interrelated and can only be understood through a holistic lens that fully takes into account those relationships.

The remainder of this chapter will rely on a series of case studies to better understand the interrelationship among legislation, regulation, and the judicial system and how it impacts the loan market as well as the role played by the Loan Syndication and Trading Association (LSTA) in this regard. Part 1 of this chapter will briefly review the history of legislation and regulation of the loan market. Part 2 will examine how laws passed by Congress, implemented by federal regulators, and, in one case litigated by loan market participants, have impacted the loan market. Part 3 will focus on how rules and regulations initiated by federal agencies have impacted the loan market and how they can, under certain circumstances, become subject to voidance by Congress. Part 4 will look at how judicial rulings can profoundly impact loan market performance and expectations. Part 5 will discuss how the LSTA, as the trade association for the loan market, has attempted to navigate the interrelated world of financial services regulation through advocacy and direct and amicus litigation. Part 6 will conclude.

PART 1: A BRIEF HISTORY OF REGULATION OF THE SYNDICATED LOAN MARKET

Until relatively recently, syndicated loans and many syndicated loan market participants were lightly regulated, mainly through the Banking Agencies' supervisory powers that focused on the loans that banks held on their balance sheets.[9] This was understandable in the early days of the syndicated loan market when loan market participants overwhelmingly consisted of banks. But, because syndicated loans were not (and still are not) considered securities, even when nonbank institutional lenders began to enter the syndicated loan market in the late 1980s they were not subject to federal or state securities laws.[10] To be sure, as an increasing

---
[9] See Part 3 for a deeper discussion of Banking Agencies' supervisory powers.
[10] See Banco Espanol v. Security Pacific, 763 F. Supp. 36 (S.D.N.Y. 1991), available at https://law.justia.com/cases/federal/district-courts/FSupp/763/36/1586392/, and Kirschner v. JPMorgan, available at https://www.courtlistener.com/docket/7133066/119/kirschner-v-jp-morgan-chase-bank-na/.

percentage of loan market participants such as collateralized loan obligation (CLO) and loan mutual fund managers were required to register as "registered advisors" under the Investment Advisors Act of 1940,[11] the conduct of participants in the syndicated loan market, if not the underlying assets, became subject to regulatory scrutiny. It is also worth noting that, as an asset class that overwhelmingly consists of loans that are senior in priority and secured by collateral, Chapter 11 of the U.S. Bankruptcy Code, which impacts the recovery of loans in the event of bankruptcy, has always been a major driver of performance and expectations in the syndicated loan market. (A case study involving Chapter 11 will be addressed in Part 4.)

It was not until the wake of the Global Financial Crisis (GFC) that significant legislation directly affecting loans was passed into law. In 2010, Congress passed the Dodd-Frank Wall Street Reform and Consumer Protection Act (the "Dodd-Frank Act").[12] Among the passages that affected the loan market, those on the Volcker Rule and risk retention were the most storied and impactful and, as such, are worthy case studies. Section 619 of the Dodd-Frank Act, commonly known as the "Volcker Rule," limited the ability of banks to invest in equity securities of certain securitizations, and Section 941 (the "Risk Retention Rules") required certain "securitizers" to retain at least 5% of the credit risk of any securitization they initiated and to which they sold assets. As discussed in Part 2, the regulatory agencies responsible for implementing these sections imposed significant restrictions and obligations on various loan market participants which had material implications for the syndicated loan market.

PART 2: LAWS ORIGINATING FROM CONGRESS: RISK RETENTION AND THE VOLCKER RULE

In July 2010, Congress passed the Dodd-Frank Act, representing sweeping financial regulatory reform. While the Dodd-Frank Act

---

[11] Available at https://www.govinfo.gov/content/pkg/COMPS-1879/pdf/COMPS-1879.pdf.
[12] Available at https://www.govinfo.gov/content/pkg/PLAW-111publ203/html/PLAW-111publ203.htm.

had an effect on many aspects of the syndicated loan market,[13] the two most impactful were the Risk Retention Rule and the Volcker Rule.

Risk Retention

Section 941 of Dodd-Frank Act required any "securitizer" to retain and hold 5% of the credit risk associated with any such securitization, commonly known as *risk retention*. Section 941 delegated to the SEC and the Banking Agencies the joint responsibility of issuing rules implementing risk retention. In October 2014, after a three-year rulemaking process, the agencies issued a Final Rule that concluded that CLO managers were the "securitizers" in respect of CLOs and required each manager to purchase and retain 5% of the fair value of any securitization it originates.[14] Thus, for example, a manager that originates a $500 million CLO would be required to retain $25 million.[15] Throughout the rulemaking process the LSTA argued that the statute did not give the agencies the authority to impose risk retention on CLO managers because the plain language of the statute did not include them within the definition of "securitizer."[16] All told, the LSTA filed six comment letters and met with the agencies numerous times, all to no avail.

Because CLO managers are generally not well capitalized, the cost of complying with the Risk Retention Rule was burdensome.

---

[13] For example, under the Dodd-Frank Act derivatives tied to loans fell under the definition of "security-based swaps" even though the underlying assets are not securities. For a time, it was not clear whether loan participations would also be considered security-based swaps, but ultimately the agencies agreed that they would not. See Final Rule on Definition of Swap and Security Based Swap, available at https://www.federalregister.gov/documents/2012/08/13/2012-18003/further-definition-of-swap-security-based-swap-and-security-based-swap-agreement-mixed-swaps.

[14] Final Credit Risk Retention Rule under Section 941 of the Dodd-Frank Act, available at https://www.federalregister.gov/documents/2014/12/24/2014-29256/credit-risk-retention.

[15] Retention could be in the form of a vertical strip of 5% of all liabilities, a horizontal, first-loss strip of the equity, or an "L-shaped" combination of vertical and horizontal strips adding up to 5% of the fair value. The retained piece could not be sold or hedged but could be held by a "majority-owned affiliate" and financed with recourse.

[16] The LSTA also argued that, as a matter of policy, the agencies should not impose risk retention even if they had the authority so to do because (1) CLOs performed very well through the GFC and (2) the structure of CLOs already builds in the types of "skin-in-the-game" features that the rules were meant to enforce.

A number of managers, particularly smaller ones, were unable to raise the capital necessary to purchase and hold 5% of the fair value of the CLOs they managed. Given the negative consequences of the Final Rule to the CLO and loan markets, in November 2014 the LSTA filed a lawsuit against the Securities and Exchange Commission (SEC) and the Federal Reserve Board under the APA, almost immediately after the agencies approved the Final Rule. The complaint asserted that the agencies lacked statutory authority to impose risk retention on CLO managers because they do not initiate CLOs by *selling* assets to the CLO as the statute, which targets "originate-to-distribute securitizations," requires. Instead, like other loan fund managers who are not subject to risk retention, CLO managers act on behalf of the CLOs by facilitating the purchase of the loans, and never actually originate or own any loans that they could sell or transfer. After a setback at the District Court in the District of Columbia, the LSTA appealed to the U.S. Court of Appeals for the District of Columbia Circuit, and on February 9, 2018 the Circuit Court ruled in favor of the LSTA holding that the Risk Retention Rules promulgated under Section 941 of the Dodd-Frank Act cannot be applied to open market CLO managers.[17]

The Circuit Court closely analyzed the statutory language and agreed with the LSTA's position that to be a securitizer for purposes of Section 941 "a party must actually be a transferor, relinquishing ownership or control of assets to an issuer" of the securitization notes. It also observed that the statute requires securitizers to "retain" credit risk and pointed out that one cannot retain that which it has never owned or controlled. After dismissing the agencies' statutory arguments the Circuit Court also dismissed its policy arguments and noted that no matter the policy arguments, the agencies "cannot compel us to redraft the statutory boundaries set by Congress. Our commentary on those concerns only reinforces the reasoning that the ordinary meaning of § 941 does not extend to CLO managers." The SEC and the Federal Reserve Board chose not to appeal the Circuit Court's decision, and the Risk Retention Rule was voided as to CLO managers.

---

[17] Loan Syndications and Trading Association v. Securities and Exchange Commission and Board of Governors of the Federal Reserve Board, available at https://www.cadc.uscourts.gov/internet/opinions.nsf/871D769D4527442A8525822F0052E1E9/$file/17-5004-1717230.pdf.

The Volcker Rule

Section 631 of the Dodd-Frank Act is commonly known as the Volcker Rule (named after its main proponent, former Federal Reserve Chairman Paul Volcker). The Volcker Rule limits proprietary trading by banks and also limits their ability to own or invest in equity-like securities ("ownership interests") of certain types of funds ("covered funds"). As with much of the Dodd-Frank Act, the statute delegated to the federal regulatory agencies the responsibility for interpreting and implementing the law.[18]

Under the original rules implementing the Volcker Rule (the "2013 Rules"),[19] securitizations, including CLOs, were considered covered funds. Oddly, the agencies interpreted the term *ownership interest* to include debt securities of CLOs because they usually allow the holder to remove and replace a manager "for cause" (which rights, they reasoned, are characteristic of ownership). Thus, banks were prohibited from purchasing or holding the notes of any CLO that held any assets other than loans and cash equivalents. Worse, already existing CLO notes (approximately $90 billion of which were owned at that time by U.S. banks) were not grandfathered so they, too, would become prohibited to banks on the effective date of the Volcker Rule. Fortunately, the 2013 Rules also included a carve-out from the definition of *covered fund* for "Loan Securitizations," which the agencies determined were securitizations that invested only in loans and cash equivalents. While CLO managers disagreed with the agencies' expansive interpretation of ownership interest, they quickly pivoted and, following the publication of the 2013 Rules, the CLO market evolved to meet the loan securitization model, that is, issuing new CLOs that hold loans and cash equivalents only and laboriously "Volckerizing" preexisting CLOs by dispensing with the right to purchase and hold assets other than loans.

In July 2018 the agencies published a revised proposal of all aspects of the Volcker Rule,[20] and on July 31, 2020, the agencies published a final rule on the "Covered Funds" portion of the Volcker Rule.[21] The most important and broadest change was the agencies'

---

[18] The Banking Agencies, the SEC, and the CFTC were jointly responsible for the implementation of the Volcker Rule.

[19] Available at https://www.govinfo.gov/content/pkg/FR-2014-01-31/pdf/2013-31511.pdf.

[20] Available at https://www.federalregister.gov/documents/2018/07/17/2018-13502/proposed-revisions-to-prohibitions-and-restrictions-on-proprietary-trading-and-certain-interests-in.

[21] Available at https://www.fdic.gov/news/board/2020/2020-06-25-notice-dis-a-fr.pdf.

revised interpretation of ownership interest. The agencies clarified that they would no longer consider a debt security to be an ownership interest solely because it contains the right to remove and replace a manager for cause, irrespective of whether that right is triggered by an event of default. As a result, banks were no longer prohibited from buying CLO debt securities, whether or not the CLOs own nonloan assets. Following this revision, many new CLOs were structured to permit the purchase of a limited amount of nonloan assets.

CONCLUSION

We live in an era where lawmakers typically delegate to regulatory agencies a significant amount of discretion to interpret and implement financial services legislation. Accordingly, in analyzing how a law may impact the loan market, it is important to consider how the responsible agencies might view that law and to be prepared to advocate on behalf of sensible views that support the loan market. As a last resort, it may also be necessary to resort to the courts to push back against regulatory overreach.

The CLO risk retention and the Volcker Rule sagas are good examples of these dynamics. In the case of risk retention, Congress passed a law to address a particular concern ("originate-to-distribute securitizations"), yet the federal agencies incorrectly applied the statute to a structure not addressed by Congress. The LSTA, on behalf of loan market participants, used the judicial system to reverse the regulatory overreach. In Volcker, the agencies, once again going beyond the Congressional mandate, initially prohibited banks from owning certain CLO securities. Rather than resorting to litigation, the market adjusted until the agencies, of their own volition, pulled back and realigned their regulatory approach closer to the clear congressional intent.

PART 3: RULES AND GUIDANCE ORIGINATING FROM THE REGULATORS: LEVERAGED LENDING GUIDANCE

While the 2010 Dodd-Frank Act introduced reams of legislation that affected loans—often inadvertently—the most targeted forms of bank loan regulation came from the regulators themselves. Although regulation developed by Banking Agencies may be the best fit for loans, it still can create unexpected or undesirable outcomes. Importantly, rules that come from regulators still are subject to congressional oversight—a fact that regulators forget at their own peril.

Leveraged Lending Guidance is a relevant case study for this form of regulation. While the 2013 Leveraged Lending Guidance (the "2013 Guidance")[22] was detailed, nuanced, and reflected a deep understanding of the leveraged loan market, it nonetheless created unexpected consequences for the leveraged loan market. It also demonstrated that the legislative branch would strike back if it saw mission creep from the administrative state.

Leveraged Lending Guidance through the Ages

The Banking Agencies have been focused on leveraged lending for more than 30 years. In 1989, the Banking Agencies categorized a group of loans as "highly leveraged transactions," or HLTs. Loan performance and concerns about increased regulatory oversight of HLTs caused some banks to retrench from the leveraged loan market;[23] this retrenchment was reputed to create an opening for the rise of the institutional loan market. Bank retrenchment notwithstanding, the leveraged loan market continued to grow during the 1990s (Exhibit 14.1), and the Banking Agencies continued to warily observe this growth.

In 1998 and 1999, the Federal Reserve Board and the Office of the Comptroller of the Currency (OCC) issued statements commenting on the relaxation of sound lending standards "for certain types of loans."

By 2001, following a rise in problem assets, the Banking Agencies were ready to act and, together with Office of Thrift Supervision, released the 2001 Leveraged Lending Guidance (the "2001 Guidance").[24] While the subsequent 2013 Guidance would be detailed and specific, the 2001 Guidance clocked in at a slim 11 pages and was limited to general definitions and

---

[22] Available at https://www.govinfo.gov/content/pkg/FR-2013-03-22/pdf/2013-06567.pdf.
[23] The Federal Reserve described banks' retreat from HLT lending in its Greenbook files from March 27, 1990, available at https://www.federalreserve.gov/monetarypolicy/files/fomc19900327gbpt119900321.pdf.
[24] Available at https://www.federalreserve.gov/boarddocs/press/general/2001/20010409/attachment.pdf.

EXHIBIT 14.1

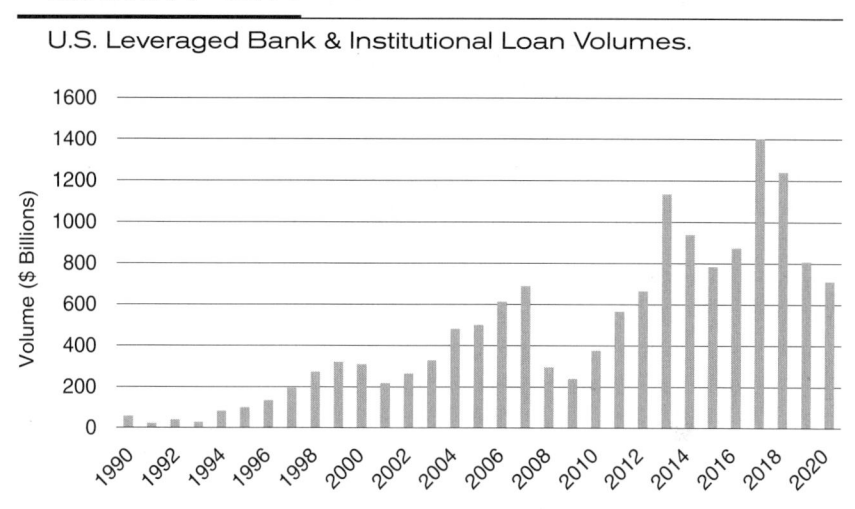

U.S. Leveraged Bank & Institutional Loan Volumes.

Source: Refinitiv LPC.

recommendations. The 2001 Guidance "addressed expectations for the content of credit policies, the need for well-defined underwriting standards, the importance of defining an institution's risk appetite for leveraged transactions, and the importance of stress-testing exposures and portfolios."[25]

While the 2001 Guidance flagged key areas of focus, it did not prescribe *how* a bank should measure its leveraged loan portfolio, nor did it focus on distributed deals or risks to the financial system. These omissions would be addressed in the 2013 Guidance. The expansion—and the reportedly prescriptive implementation—of the 2013 Guidance changed lending standards, probably accelerated the rise of direct lending, and ultimately led to a backlash in Congress and the retreat of the Banking Agencies.

2013 Guidance: The Rules . . . and the Market Response

The 2013 Guidance tackled a number of areas, but several are worth particular focus as they (1) socialized the idea that leveraged loans might generate risks to the financial *system*; (2) expanded the scope

---

[25] Description available in the 2013 Guidance, available at https://www.govinfo.gov/content/pkg/FR-2013-03-22/pdf/2013-06567.pdf.

of guidance from loans held by banks to loans originated and distributed by banks; and (3) seemed to lay out bright lines for acceptable underwriting standards. By appearing to expand regulators' scope, the 2013 Guidance changed the loan market—temporarily in some areas and permanently in others.

The 2013 Guidance socialized the idea that leveraged lending could create systemic risk, warning that "a poorly underwritten leveraged loan that is pooled with other loans or is participated with other institutions *may generate risks for the financial system*" (emphasis added). The 2013 Guidance also marked a shift in focus from the safety and soundness of individual institutions to the safety of the financial system when it clarified that its recommendations were intended for loans "underwritten to hold or distribute."[26] After 2013, the idea that leveraged lending could create systemic risk increasingly entered the regulatory and congressional dialogue, influencing lawmakers, regulators, and the academic literature.[27]

While the discussion of systemic risk may have changed the leveraged lending debate, it was the perception of "bright line" tests in the 2013 Guidance that shifted the loan market. Two critical bright lines grabbed the market's attention. First, the Banking Agencies stated that a loan that creates leverage "in excess of 6X Total Debt/EBITDA raises concerns for most industries." Second, in risk rating companies "supervisors commonly assume that the ability to fully amortize senior secured debt or the ability to repay at least 50 percent of total debt over a five-to-seven year period provides evidence of adequate repayment capacity ... when leveraged loan transactions have no reasonable or realistic prospects to de-lever, a substandard rating is likely." These two bright(ish) lines transformed the market—eventually. Banks initially thought

---

[26] See the 2013 Guidance commentary on delevering capability (*Federal Register* Vol. 78, No. 56, p. 17771), underwriting standards (*Federal Register* Vol. 78, No. 56, p. 17772), and stress testing (*Federal Register* Vol. 78, No 56, p. 17776).

[27] In December 2020, the General Accounting Office (GAO) released a report investigating whether leveraged lending could threaten financial stability. The GAO undertook this study after "[s]ome observers and regulators have drawn comparisons to the pre-2008 subprime mortgage market, noting that loan origination and securitization may similarly spread risks to the financial system." The GAO report found that, despite increased downgrades and defaults during the COVID-19 pandemic, regulators, while still cautious, "had not found that leveraged lending presented significant threats to financial stability." See the report at https://www.gao.gov/products/GAO-21-167.

EXHIBIT 14.2

Share of Loans to Companies with Debt/EBITDA ≥ 6X.

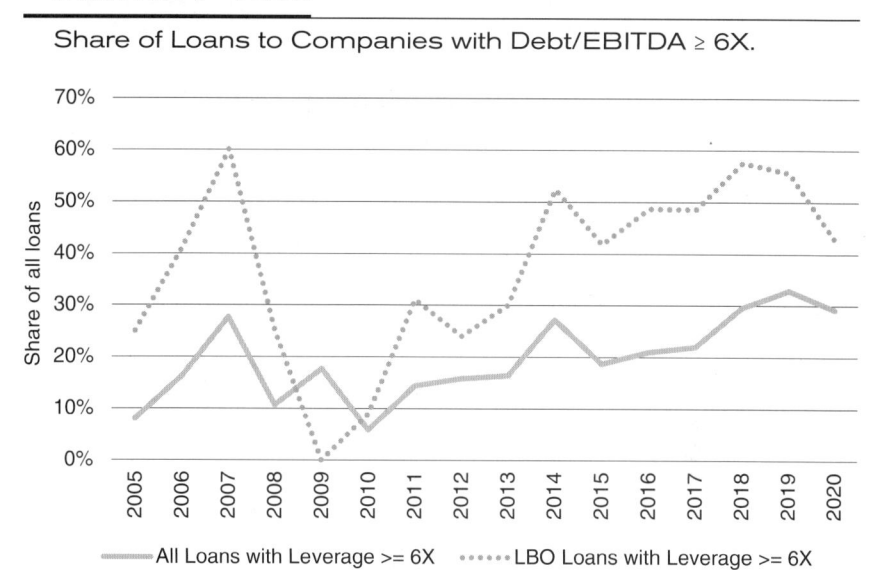

[Chart showing Share of all loans (y-axis, 0% to 70%) from 2005 to 2020, with two series: "All Loans with Leverage >= 6X" and "LBO Loans with Leverage >= 6X"]

Source: S&P/LCD.

the guidance was simply guidance or that they had the ability to underwrite a certain number of "criticized" loans.[28] After several Matters Requiring Attention (MRAs)[29] were issued to banks, they realized that the Guidance was meant to be applied more strictly—and, as can be seen in Exhibit 14.2, this began to affect lending standards.

Exhibit 14.2 measures the share of leveraged loans and leveraged buyout (LBO) loans with a total debt-to-EBITDA (earnings before interest, taxes, depreciation, and amortization) ratio of 6X or higher. In 2013, 30% of LBO loans were levered at 6X or more. With strong market demand for loans, this share of highly leveraged

---

[28] Criticized loans are those risk rated "special mention," "substandard," "doubtful," or "loss." Thus, when the Guidance observed that an inability to delever from base cash flows could create a "substandard" rating, and the Banking Agencies exhorted banks not to underwrite criticized loans, it was ultimately interpreted as banks should not underwrite loans that could not demonstrate the ability to amortize.

[29] The Federal Reserve defines MRAs as "matters that are important and that the Federal Reserve is expecting a banking organization to address over a reasonable period of time, but when the timing need not be 'immediate.'" More information on MRAs is available at https://www.federalreserve.gov/supervisionreg/srletters/sr1313a1.pdf.

loans climbed to 50% by the end of 2014. However, during 2014, the Banking Agencies handed out several highly publicized MRAs and banks pulled back from underwriting such highly leveraged loans. In 2015, the share of LBO loans and leveraged loans with leverage of 6X or higher fell by 10.6 and 8.5 percentage points, respectively.[30] Many bankers believe that the hardening of the Leveraged Lending "Rules" constrained the increase in leverage in the leveraged loan market.

But borrowers wanted higher leverage multiples—and there were less regulated lenders that were happy to give it to them. In this way, the Leveraged Lending Guidance may have accelerated the rise of private direct lending.[31] While the 2013 Guidance constrained regulated banks, direct lenders were not subject to the 2013 Guidance and could underwrite loans that did not demonstrate the delevering capability that the Banking Agencies required from supervised institutions. While definitive data are difficult to find, Refinitiv's "Sponsored Middle Market League Tables"[32] suggest a disintermediation of regulated arrangers. In 2013, lenders that were not regulated by the Banking Agencies held a combined 14% bookrunner market share (Exhibit 14.3). By 2019, their bookrunner market share topped 41%.

Although the rise of nonbank lenders is not due solely to the imposition of Leveraged Lending Guidance, many lenders believe that the 2013 Guidance widened the door to broader nonbank participation in the loan market.

Thus, the introduction of the Leveraged Lending Guidance by the Banking Agencies appeared to have had two market-changing effects: First, at least for a period of time, it constrained the level of leverage in loans. Second, it may have facilitated the rise of direct lenders. But the story didn't end there; in 2017, the legislative branch came into play.

---

[30] In the coming years, it became clear that the Banking Agencies were more focused on companies' delevering capabilities than on debt-to-EBITDA ratios. Thus, while the debt-to-EBITDA ratio may be an indication of ability to delever, banks were permitted to underwrite loans with a higher ratio, but were discouraged from underwriting loans where companies could not demonstrate the ability to delever in five to seven years.

[31] See Chapter 17 for details on private credit and direct lending.

[32] Loans to sponsored companies are likely to be the most leveraged in the market. In addition, the "nonbank lender" disintermediation of banks has been the most pronounced in the middle market.

EXHIBIT 14.3

Non-Regulated Bookrunner Market Share (Middle Market Sponsor League Table).

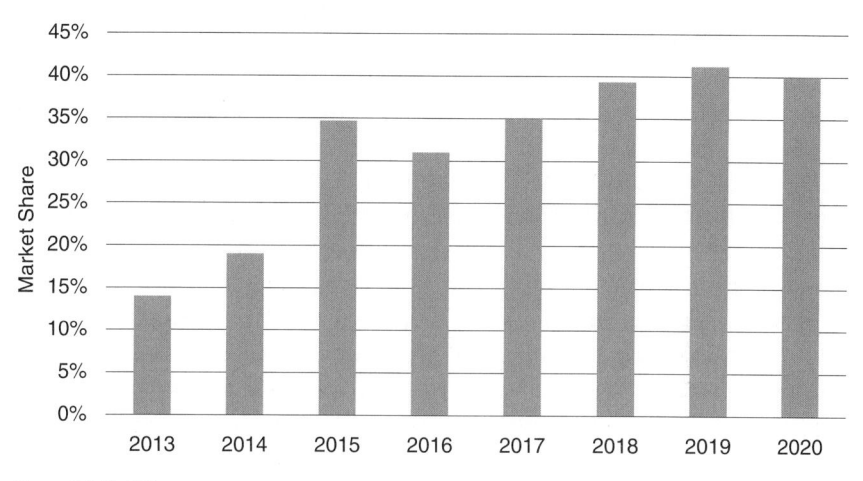

[Bar chart showing Market Share by year: 2013 ≈14%, 2014 ≈19%, 2015 ≈35%, 2016 ≈31%, 2017 ≈35%, 2018 ≈39%, 2019 ≈41%, 2020 ≈40%]

Source: Refinitiv LPC.

Congressional Review Act and Leveraged Lending Guidance

By 2017, regulated U.S. banks had largely conformed to the 2013 Guidance,[33] an indication that the Banking Agencies actually had changed the loan market. But then the legislative branch got involved. On March 31, 2017, Senator Pat Toomey (R. PA) sent a letter to the U.S. General Accountability Office (GAO) asking whether the 2013 Guidance constituted a rule under the Congressional Review Act (CRA).[34] The CRA requires that any rule promulgated by a federal agency be submitted to Congress for its review and provides Congress with the opportunity to disapprove the rule within a certain period of time. While the Banking Agencies argued that the 2013 Guidance was not a rule (but simply guidance), the definition

---

[33] The 2017 SNC Review noted that "[a]s a result of underwriting improvements, non-pass loan originations are at a de minimis level." Available at https://www.federalreserve.gov/newsevents/pressreleases/bcreg20170802a.htm.

[34] Available at https://uscode.house.gov/view.xhtml?req=granuleid%3AUSC-prelim-title5-chapter 8&edition=prelim.

of a rule under the CRA is very broad,[35] and, in October 2017, the GAO concluded that the 2013 Guidance was a general statement of policy and, as such, was a rule under the CRA.[36] Because the 2013 Guidance had never been introduced by the Banking Agencies to Congress, it could not be treated as an effective rule, and thus could not be defined by bright line tests. In November 2017, the Banking Agencies sent letters to Representative Blaine Luetkemeyer (R. MO) indicating that they might solicit additional comments and revise and reissue the Guidance.[37] In September 2018, the Banking Agencies, together with the National Credit Union Administration and the Bureau of Consumer Financial Protection, released an "Interagency Statement Clarifying the Role of Supervisory Guidance."[38] In that statement, the Banking Agencies explained that "[u]nlike a law or regulation, supervisory guidance does not have the force and effect of law, and the agencies do not take enforcement actions based on supervisory guidance." The Banking Agencies added that they "intend to limit the use of numerical thresholds or other 'bright lines' in describing expectations in supervisory guidance" and that "[e]xaminers will not criticize a supervised financial institution for a 'violation' of supervisory guidance."[39]

While the regulators appeared to have introduced "regulation" in the guise of the 2013 Guidance, after encroaching on the territory of the legislative branch that regulation was pared back again into guidance. This regulatory retrenchment again influenced

---

[35] Whether something is a rule for the purposes of the CRA is determined by Section 551(4) of the Administrative Procedure Act: *"'rule' means the whole or a part of an agency statement of general or particular applicability and future effect designed to implement, interpret, or prescribe law or policy or describing the organization, procedure, or practice requirements of an agency and includes the approval or prescription for the future of rates, wages, corporate or financial structures or reorganizations thereof, prices, facilities, appliances, services or allowances therefore or of valuations, costs, or accounting, or practices bearing on any of the foregoing."* Available at https://www.archives.gov/federal-register/laws/administrative-procedure/551.html.

[36] See GAO report on "Applicability of the Congressional Review Act to Interagency Guidance on Leveraged Lending," available at https://www.gao.gov/products/D17915.

[37] Tracy Ryan, "U.S. Regulators Consider Revising Leveraged-Lending Guidelines," *Wall Street Journal*, December 8, 2017. Available at https://www.wsj.com/articles/u-s-regulators-consider-revising-leveraged-lending-guidelines-1512764173.

[38] Available at https://www.federalreserve.gov/supervisionreg/srletters/sr1805a1.pdf.

[39] Although the Banking Agencies published a Notice of Proposed Rulemaking (NPR) in October 2020 that would formally establish that regulatory guidance is nonbinding and cannot form the basis of an MRA letter, no additional action on the NPR had been taken as of the date of publication of this book and most observers do not expect the rule to be finalized.

market standards. As Exhibit 14.2 demonstrates, although the share of loans with a debt-to-EBITDA ratio of 6X or more was flat in 2016 and 2017, it began rising materially in 2018 and 2019.

But while bright line tests could no longer be applied and debt-to-EBITDA levels were climbing again, it did not mean the Banking Agencies had become toothless. On the contrary, the Shared National Credit (SNC) Reviews that emerged after the GAO's decision made it clear that they were still supervising the banks under their "safety and soundness" mandates.[40] Although the SNC could no longer test debt-to-EBITDA multiples or delevering ability, the 2019 SNC Review still clearly states supervisors' expectations:

> Banks engaged in originating and participating in leveraged lending should ensure their risk management processes remain effective in changing market conditions. Controls should ensure that financial analysis, completed during underwriting and to monitor performance, is based on appropriate revenue, growth, and cost savings assumptions and considers the impact of incremental facilities. All banks should ensure that portfolio management and stress testing processes consider that recovery rates may differ from historical experience. Banks also should consider how potential risks from a downturn in the leveraged lending market may affect other customers and borrowers. The agencies expect identified risks to be measured against their potential impact on earnings and capital.

In other words, Leveraged Lending Guidance was not killed by the 2017 CRA kerfuffle; it just became guidance once again.

CONCLUSION

Regulation that impacts the loan market can emerge directly from the Banking Agencies. Because the Banking Agencies are closer to the loan market than the courts or Congress, their regulation may more effectively address perceived imbalances in the market. However, even detailed and nuanced rules like Leveraged Lending Guidance can create unintended consequences (the rise of direct

---

[40] The Shared National Credit (SNC) Program is an interagency review and assessment of risk in the largest and most complex credits shared by multiple regulated financial institutions. The 2019 SNC Review is available at https://www.federalreserve.gov/newsevents/pressreleases/files/bcreg20200131a1.pdf.

lenders), along with the intended ones (a reduction in the growth of leverage multiples). And, finally, however nuanced the Banking Agencies' regulations might be, the case of Leveraged Lending Guidance also demonstrates that when the regulation comes from the supervisory entity it still is not above the law.

PART 4: JUDICIAL RULINGS AND THEIR IMPACT ON THE LOAN MARKET

The judicial system plays an important role in the loan market in two distinct ways. First, as discussed in Part 2, direct litigation (or the threat thereof) under the Administrative Procedure Act can be a useful tool in pushing back against regulatory overreach. Second, litigation among third parties in connection with market-related disputes can lead to judicial decisions that change fundamental and long-held market norms, expectations, and principles. The remainder of Part 4 will focus on three lawsuits that challenged critical loan market norms. In each of the cases the LSTA filed briefs as amicus curiae (friend of the court) supporting the party that (successfully) sought to preserve long-held norms. The first, *RadLAX v. Amalgamated Bank*,[41] is a U.S. Supreme Court case that resolved an important bankruptcy question; that is, whether secured creditors can "credit bid" their loans in an auction for their own collateral. The second, *Stonehill Capital Management v. Bank of the West*,[42] is a case decided by New York State's highest court that resolved whether an agreement to make a loan trade subject to documentation constitutes an enforceable contract. The third, *Kirschner v. JPMorgan*,[43] is a U.S. District Court case that considered whether a broadly syndicated loan is subject to state (and, effectively, federal) securities laws.

RadLAX v. Amalgamated Bank: *Credit Bidding Is Sacrosanct*

On May 29, 2012, the U.S. Supreme Court emphatically put to rest a question that had been troubling secured creditors for years when

---
[41] Available at https://www.supremecourt.gov/opinions/11pdf/11-166.pdf.
[42] Available at https://www.nycourts.gov/ctapps/Decisions/2016/Dec16/191opn16-Decision.pdf.
[43] Available at https://cases.justia.com/federal/district-courts/new-york/nysdce/1:2017cv06334/479377/119/0.pdf?ts=1590223546.

it published a decisive opinion on "credit bidding." In *RadLAX Gateway Hotel, LLC v. Amalgamated Bank*,[44] the Court ruled unanimously that a Chapter 11 reorganization that provides for the sale of a creditor's collateral must offer the secured creditor the right to credit bid. Credit bidding is described in § 363(k) of the Bankruptcy Code and permits holders of secured claims to use the face amount of their claims as "currency" at the sale of the underlying collateral and offset such claims against the purchase price. The ability to credit bid protects secured creditors from "lowball" bids for their collateral; if they are unhappy with the amount bid by outsiders, they can obtain the collateral for themselves by bidding in their claims.

The decision resolved a split in the federal circuit courts and represented an important victory for loan market participants. It confirmed the right of a secured creditor to protect the benefit of its bargain to either be repaid in full or take possession of its collateral by preventing the debtor from stripping the creditor's lien for an amount less than the creditor thinks the property is worth. Because of the importance of this principle to secured creditors in the loan market, the LSTA filed an amicus brief in support of the secured creditor in this case and previously filed amicus briefs in two earlier U.S. Circuit Court cases,[45] one of which ruled that creditors had no absolute right to credit bid and one of which ruled that they did.

Stonehill v. Bank of the West: *"A Trade Is a Trade"*

In *Stonehill Capital Management v. Bank of the West*,[46] the New York State Court of Appeals (New York's highest court) unanimously upheld a long-held and fundamental principle of the loan market, that is, that "a trade is a trade." The court ruled on December 20, 2015, that (1) a seller at auction *cannot* withdraw a loan *after* it has accepted a winning bid for that loan, and (2) an oral loan trade, even if it is subject to documentation, *is* enforceable so long as it

---

[44] Available at https://www.supremecourt.gov/opinions/11pdf/11-166.pdf.
[45] Available at https://www.theclearinghouse.org/-/media/files/association-documents-2/20120309-tch-amicus-in-radlax-v-amalgamated.pdf. The LSTA also filed an amicus brief urging the Supreme Court to grant certiorari review of the case, available at http://sblog.s3.amazonaws.com/wp-content/uploads/2011/11/RadLAX-Amicus-Brief-of-Loan-Syndications-and-Trading-Association.pdf.
[46] Available at https://iapps.courts.state.ny.us/nyscef/ViewDocument?docIndex=42iOdxUV5lZAS8bfNnSOPw==.

identifies the material terms of the trade. The LSTA filed an amicus brief in that case (to which the court referred favorably during oral arguments) because a bad decision could have had serious negative ramifications for the viability of the loan trading market.[47]

In March 2012, Bank of the West (BOTW) engaged a broker to conduct an auction to sell a loan portfolio including the loan at issue. The auction offering memo set out the terms for bidding and stated that final bids would be "non-contingent offers (the acceptance of which by seller will require immediate execution of a pre-negotiated Asset Sales Agreement)." The parties agreed on the day that Stonehill submitted its bid to use standard LSTA documentation. Two days later, the broker informed Stonehill that its bid had been accepted, and followed up a week later with an email noting the material terms of the trade, including a description of the loan asset, the purchase price, the closing date, and the manner of payment. Subsequently, BOTW informed Stonehill that it would not proceed with the sale; internal documents from the bank appear to show that it withdrew the loan because it determined that it would make more money holding the loan.

Stonehill sued for breach of contract, and the trial court judge ruled that the seller could *not* withdraw the loan asset once a bid had been accepted and that an oral trade is, indeed, binding. While a panel of the Appellate Division, New York's interim appeals court, reversed that decision, the Court of Appeals recognized that Stonehill and BOTW formed a binding and enforceable oral contract, the material terms of which had been agreed, and that the fact that the agreement was "subject to final documentation" did not express a reservation of rights not to be bound. The ruling in *Stonehill* once and for all put to bed any notion that an oral loan trade is not binding and cemented the ability of traders and other loan market participants to freely trade without worrying that their trades can be undone at a later date when market circumstances change.

Kirschner v. JPMorgan: *Loans Are NOT Securities*

In *Kirschner v. JPMorgan*, a case brought by a litigation trust that arose from the bankruptcy of a lab company called Millennium, the plaintiff alleged that banks that underwrote a term loan B to

---

[47] Available at https://www.nycourts.gov/ctapps/Decisions/2016/Dec16/191opn16-Decision.pdf

Millennium violated state blue-sky laws, which are the state equivalent of the federal securities laws. The banks brought a motion to dismiss on several grounds, including that the loans in question are not "securities" under state or federal law, and are therefore not subject to state blue-sky laws. The LSTA weighed in with an amicus brief supporting the banks' contention that the loan was not a security and, in an enormously important decision published in May 2020, a judge in the Southern District of New York agreed.[48,49]

Why was this so important? The syndicated term loan at issue in *Kirschner* was a typical term loan B, with no clear characteristics to distinguish it from most other term loan Bs. Thus, a determination that it is a security would have suggested that most, if not all, institutional term loans would be so characterized. As laid out in detail in Chapter 5 of this book, a loan recharacterized as a security would immediately be subject to federal and state securities laws and liability for underwriting, syndication, and trading. Standard practices and the code of conduct developed by the industry for syndicated loans would have to be discarded, and the current public–private nature of loan markets would be untenable. Moreover, all syndication, distribution and trading activity would likely have to be conducted through broker-dealers. The syndication process itself would have to change, likely resembling that of a Rule 144A offering. This would require more extensive disclosures and due diligence and a slower and more expensive process. Secondary trading would also have to change and settlement would be subject to trade reporting, margin, net capital, trade clearance, recordkeeping, and other rules applicable to bonds. Some borrowers would not be able to access this market (because they cannot access the high-yield bond market), and those that could would lose control over the composition of the lender group and have less flexibility with waivers, consents, and amendments. From a lender's perspective, there would be less flexibility relating to bespoke terms and, perhaps most crucially, it would not be clear what happens to CLOs that own more than half the term loan Bs but are not structured to purchase securities.

---

[48] https://bpi.com/wp-content/uploads/2020/05/Notice-of-Motion-of-the-Loan-Syndications-and-Trading-Assocation-and-BPI-Amici-Curiae-2019.04.30.pdf.

[49] https://docs.justia.com/cases/federal/district-courts/new-york/nysdce/1:2017cv06334/479377/119.

The plaintiffs in Kirschner moved to amend their original complaint but, just before this book went to press, the court denied their motion. Consequently, the plaintiffs are likely to appeal the court's dismissal of their claims to the Federal Circuit Court for the Second Circuit, which would be asked to rule on the lower court's determination that the term loans in question are not securities. While the Kirschner decision was well reasoned, it is only the view of one district court judge and is not binding precedent. Thus, Kirschner is an important case, but not necessarily the end of the "loans as securities" story.

CONCLUSION

All three cases cited above illustrate how litigation involving third parties threatened to undermine long-standing, fundamental principles on which the loan market has relied. Although market norms were supported and even reinforced in all three cases, the examples demonstrate the risks inherent in this type of litigation and the need to be diligent in opposing these efforts.

PART 5: THE ROLE OF THE LSTA IN PUBLIC POLICY

The mission of the LSTA's Public Policy Group is consistent with its overall mission: to "promote a fair, orderly, efficient, and growing corporate loan market and provide leadership in advancing and balancing the interests of all market participants." The case studies highlighted in this chapter illustrate some of the ways in which the Public Policy Group advocates in Congress, among the Banking Agencies, and through the judicial system on behalf of its many diverse stakeholders. The LSTA closely monitors proposed legislation, regulation, and judicial cases that could impact the syndicated market and engages as appropriate for the benefit of the market and its stakeholders. Accordingly, the LSTA was heavily involved in each of these case studies (and countless others), sometimes as a direct principal and other times as an industry leader and representative. In connection with the legislative and regulatory matters, the LSTA testified at several congressional hearings, submitted a large number of comment letters, and held more than 100 meetings with members of Congress and federal regulators. On the judicial front the LSTA has filed more than 25 amicus briefs, including those filed by the LSTA in the cases described in Part 4, in each situation weighing in on cases where fundamental loan market principles were at stake.

PART 6: CONCLUSION

The syndicated loan market has grown dramatically over the past decades, evolving from a smallish bank-only market to an institutional market that has become a key component of the U.S. capital markets. It is no surprise that with such growth and development it has attracted the attention of members of Congress and regulators and that an increasing number of lawsuits are filed seeking to adjudicate issues that can profoundly impact the loan market. As we have demonstrated in this chapter, in order to understand public policy in this evolving market, it is not enough to focus on each of these factors separately. Instead, one must understand how Congress and regulatory agencies interact and how the judicial system can impact legislation, regulation, and legal principles.

CHAPTER 15
The Globalization of the Loan Market

Non-U.S. Dollar (NON-USD) Syndicated Institutional Leveraged Loan Market

    Bob Kricheff
    Senior Vice President and Portfolio Manager
    Shenkman Capital

The Global Syndicated Loan Market–EMEA

    Clare Dawson
    Chief Executive
    Loan Market Association

The Evolving Asia Pacific Loan Market

    Sadaf Khan
    Consultant
    Asia Pacific Loan Market Association

Non-U.S. Dollar (Non-USD) Syndicated Institutional Leveraged Loan Market

Bob Kricheff
Shenkman Capital

INTRODUCTION

This article looks at the non-USD syndicated institutional leveraged loan market and term loan B (also referred to as *TLBs* or *B loans*) issued by borrowers in that market. The focus is primarily on the European market, because this region has a more developed institutional loan market than other areas.

The growth of the U.S. B loan market has benefited from having a strong banking system, as well as a well-developed market-based financial system that has the structures in place for nonbank investment vehicles to develop and flourish. The U.S. market has also benefited from being a large market with a consistent set of regulations and well-established contract and bankruptcy laws. In the United States, much of the growth in this market has come from private equity–sponsored leveraged buyouts (LBOs) on the issuer side, and collateralized loan obligations (CLOs) on the lending (or buyer) side. These issuer and lender characteristics have also driven the expansion of the institutional loan market in Europe, and to some extent, in Asia.

Increasing comfort levels with market-focused financial systems as well as greater consistency in regulations and bankruptcy laws across the various European and Asian jurisdictions could lead to a larger and more diverse market for institutional loans. Changes in the ownership of banks in some markets may also accelerate growth in the TLB market. This could involve European bank mergers and less government ownership of banks in Asia. A developed institutional loan market can add to a region's private sector financial flexibility and be a valuable tool for the bank systems to diversify its balance sheet and distribute risk across multiple parties with varied capitalization structures.

BANK-CENTRIC VERSUS MARKET-CENTRIC MARKETS

One of the long running economic discussions has been the difference between bank- and market-centric economies. The United States and the United Kingdom are often viewed as major market-centric economies, whereas countries such as Germany and Japan have historically been viewed as bank-centric markets.[1] For an active institutional loan market to develop there must be at least some of the characteristics of market-centric economies.

There have been several theories of why certain economies favor one model over the other. One theory is that economies with more physical businesses (e.g., manufacturing) favor banking because of the ease of securitization, whereas technology- and service-driven economies are a better fit for market-based economies.[2] Another theory emphasizes the differences in legal systems, citing that countries that allow closer corporate interrelationships favor bank-centric systems. Japan is often cited as an example of this close relationship structure, where banks provide the bulk of funding, and there are often integrated business networks known as a *keiretsu* that sometimes include minority equity stakes among the firms.

Information sharing and flow is critical for market economies and the functioning of an institutional market. In a system like the keiretsu, networks help create an environment where the lenders will have access to the financial information necessary to gain a comfort level to make a loan, but information does not need to be shared more widely. The relationship can also be a form of enforcement of the terms of the loan, because a borrower may not have many other options. There must be a higher level of public financial disclosure and easy access to a larger group of investors in a market-oriented economy. Because the ultimate lender and borrower may have no interconnecting equity stakes and have little interaction, there also needs to be clear, strict structures for contract enforcement.

Both types of systems offer unique advantages. Bank-centric systems often benefit from closer relationships between lender and borrower, and a level of trust and understanding can be developed

---

[1] F. Allen and D. Gale, *Comparing Financial Systems* (MIT Press: Cambridge, MA, 2000).
[2] R. G. Raghuram and L. Zingales, "Financial Systems, Industrial Structure, and Growth," *Oxford Review of Economic Policy* Vol. 17, No. 4 (2001): 467–482.

over time, which can help in times of financial struggles. In market-centric systems lenders can benefit from market signals about the borrowers' financial health and performance and often can more easily exit an investment if they are unhappy with a company's performance. Borrowers in a market system usually have a broader array of financing options.[3]

It has been argued that the diversity of a market-based system helped allow a country like the United States to recover more quickly after the Global Financial Crisis (GFC) than more bank-centric regions. Liquidity at traditional financial institutions was very limited after the GFC, due, in part, to the concentration of assets in large real estate–related investments. This caused a liquidity squeeze that bled over to other markets initially. As the economy stabilized, corporations were able to raise capital much more quickly in equity and bond markets than in the bank market because they called on a diverse group of investors, even though the liquidity at banks was still suffering. Counterbalancing this argument is that many northern European countries felt that their banking system offered more stability through the GFC because their portfolios were more diverse and some of their holdings were not as sensitive as mark-to-market securities.[4,5]

The type of financing market that a country has can also impact how effectively monetary and fiscal policies can influence the economy. The European Central Bank (ECB) leadership has stated that the Eurozone's capital markets are smaller than those in the United States and that this has limited some of the effectiveness of its policies, such as quantitative easing,[6] because banks did not transmit this liquidity into the economy as quickly as market-centric systems did. On the other side, the argument can be made that in bank-centric systems there is greater ability for regulators to directly control the financial systems.

Additionally, there should, theoretically, be a more rigorous process of credit approval when it is done by "professional"

---

[3] R. Aggarwal and J. W. Goodell, "National Preferences for Bank or Market Financing,"Economic Commentary Number 2016-04, Federal Reserve Bank of Cleveland, May 11, 2016.

[4] Knowledge@Wharton, "A Decade after the Great Recession, Is the Global Financial System Safer," Wharton University of Pennsylvania, September 11, 2018.

[5] International Monetary Fund, "Systemic Liquidity Risk: Improving the Resilience of Financial Institutions and Markets," October 2010.

[6] Clair Jones, "Mario Draghi: Europe Has Too Many Banks," *Financial Times*, September 22, 2016.

lenders, which can limit malinvestment and keep financial liquidity in the system.

An economy that has too much dependence on traditional banking is less likely to see a syndicated institutional loan market develop. Having this B loan market can be a significant benefit to an economy because it can help the banking system diversify risk and give the economy a more diverse pool of capital from which to fund corporate growth and job creation.

In order for a meaningful syndicated institutional loan market to develop there needs to be elements of both a bank- and a market-centric economy present. A strong banking regime generates relationships and a construct for structuring and issuing loans. Loans are not securities, and contract construction is critical to a successful market developing. A strong bank environment should help to create thoughtful and useful loan documentation. Because the institutional loan market typically increases the number of participants in a loan and involves many lenders that are more removed from a relationship with the borrower, it is important for them to be comfortable that there is a very strong structure of contract enforcement and recourse, as well as good information flow.

The institutional market expects these investments to have a secondary trading market, and this requires a level of access to issuer financial information for both holders of the loan and potential buyers. This requires banks to have trading operations set up within their organizations.

Europe is still considered to be much more based on a bank-centric model than the United States, with strong relationships between lenders and borrowers. This may have limited some of the expansion of the development of the institutional market when compared to the United States. This relationship framework appears even stronger in major Asian markets, such as Japan and Korea and in areas in Asia where the banks are either owned or partially owned by the governments. A report by the European Systemic Risk Board (ESRB) showed that Europe and, to a lesser extent, Japan, both have had a historically higher ratio of bank debt as a portion of gross domestic product (GDP) than in the United States.[7] In Northern Asia (China, South Korea, and Japan) the relationships with the banks and corporations are so close that it is difficult to see

---

[7] M. Pagano and S. Langfield, "Is Europe Overbanked," European Systemic Risk Board, Reports of the Advisory Scientific Committee, No. 4, June 2014.

a significant institutional market for syndicated loans. In China significant amounts of lending activity are concentrated in real estate, and much of it is controlled by the banks, which are either owned or closely aligned with the government, although these markets have seen some growth in direct lending. There has also been more growth in leveraged buyouts (LBOs) in the region. The Association of Southeast Asian Nations (ASEAN)[8] region has also experienced high growth and has made efforts to have an integrated banking system. The region has also seen LBO and leveraged financing develop.

Regulatory Environment

The Eurozone is often talked about as one market, but it does not take any practitioner in the loan market to realize that this is not a fully integrated seamless market. There are differences in bankruptcy law as well as competition and collusion rules. There are also very different views of acceptable levels of financial risk across different boarders.

In a recent report on the European syndicated loan market released by the European Commission, the complexity of regulations within Europe was highlighted. The different competition rules in seven different countries were noted, highlighting how Europe continues to struggle to operate as one cohesive market.[9]

There have been many steps in trying to create a continent-wide unified banking system. The European Economic Area (EEA), originally included European Union (EU) countries plus Iceland, Liechtenstein, and Norway. They agreed to a common supervisory framework in 1992, implementing a "single passport" the following year to try to foster banking integration.[10] One of the problems with the original plan was a lack of a region-wide supervision system. This issue became apparent during the GFC from 2008 through 2011. Other issues that arose during this time were the lack of a cross-border tool for resolution of troubled banks or bailouts and

---

[8] The Association of Southeast Asian Nations (ASEAN) includes Brunei, Cambodia, Indonesia, Lao PDR, Malaysia, Myanmar, the Philippines, Singapore, Thailand, and Vietnam.

[9] "EU Loan Syndication and Its Impact on Competition in Credit Markets," Final Report published by the EU Commission, April 2019.

[10] E. Remolona and I. Shim, "The Rise of Regional Banking in Asia and the Pacific," *BIS Quarterly Review*, September 2015.

the always controversial concept of European-wide protection of depositors. Notable bank problems arose in Iceland as well as Italy. Since that time the EU has dramatically stepped up cross-border methods of troubled bank resolution as well as enhanced regulatory regimes with reviews of balance sheets and capital adequacy, including the Basel III agreements.

Some of this history may have created an environment in Europe that has more layers of regulations and a very tight monitoring regime on its bank system than in the United States. There have been studies that have indicated the European regulatory regime may have some impact on making debt financing more costly for borrowers on a relative basis.[11] Theoretically, one could argue this should encourage an expansion of the institutional loan market by the borrowers if it has the potential to lower costs.

Regulators in Europe have periodically examined the syndicated loan markets. There has been focus on competition and examining if collusion existed. Recent studies have summarized that there is typically reasonable competition before syndicate groups are formed and reasonable sharing of information after the mandate is signed. The most recent larger report also cited that there did not appear to be collusion in pricing in the secondary markets for these loans. However, these findings made it clear that the agencies were willing to step in and enforce actions and penalties if it found cases of collusion.[12]

Regulators in Europe appear to have a much more wary approach to increasing LBO financing activity in the market. Reports have raised concerns about risk frameworks being used by banks when undertaking financing in leveraged transactions. Concerns have been cited about increases in leverage and increases in the use of "covenant-lite" structures. The European Central Bank regulators are particularly focused on these risk factors around financings for LBOs where competition is very high to win the bank underwriting, and private equity sponsors behind the issuing companies push very hard for more aggressive terms. Regulators

---

[11] T. Berg, A. Saunders, et al., "Mind the Gap: The Difference between U.S. and European Loan Rates," *The Review of Financial Studies* Vol. 30, No. 3 (March 2017): 948–987. B. Becker and V. Ivashina, "Covenant-Light Contracts and Creditor Coordination," Sverges Riksbank Working Paper Series, No. 32 (2016).

[12] Ross Dawkins and D. Drury, "EU Loan Syndication on Competition and Its Impact in Credit Markets," European Commission, May 2019.

have been said to discuss adding capital requirement "add-ons" if they deem that risks have become too high in these transactions. The regulators are very sensitive to risk and appear likely to try to aggressively reign in leverage in the bank loan market even if banks are not holding significant portions of the loans after they are syndicated to nonbanks.[13] With large publicly held banks dominating the underwriting of syndicated institutional loans in Europe, regulatory concerns about credit risk in Europe could limit expansion of the leveraged syndicated loan market.

In a country such as China with a central government financial system, there has been major growth in bank lending, especially in real estate. However, as a report from the International Monetary Fund (IMF) has pointed out, the government-controlled financial system allows the government to recapitalize and/or merge Chinese banks as they see fit, which the government has done during financial stress.[14]

TYPES OF ISSUANCE AND ISSUERS

The leveraged lending market in Europe can be divided into three major categories—loans for LBOs, project finance, and infrastructure. Project finance and infrastructure loans tend to be club deals with smaller lender groups. In some cases, private and direct lending funds have become involved in some of these clublike transactions. In many cases, when banks are involved in project finance and infrastructure loans, they adhere to a "take and hold" strategy. The LBO loans are usually much more broadly syndicated and sold into the institutional investor market in Europe.

Commitments for LBO bank financing often happen prior to syndication so that the private equity firms behind the buyout can have certainty of financing when making the bid for an asset.

In the corporate loan market in Europe, LBOs tend to dominate issuance. The ability to syndicate these loans to nonbank institutions can help address one of the regulators' concerns about the syndicated bank loan market. This concentration of LBO-backed loans can have risks for these portfolios but also can develop some

---

[13] S. Morris and R. Smith, "ECB Threatens Banks with Capital 'Add-ons' over Leveraged Loans Risks," *Financial Times*, January 17, 2021.

[14] Monetary and Capital Markets Department, International Monetary Fund, "Peoples Republic of China, Financial System and Stability Assessment," October 24, 2017.

of the benefits of relationship banking. Because the private equity sponsors are repeat issuers, the lenders in a syndicated loan market can begin to build a relationship with the sponsors, and as repeat issuers in the market, the sponsors can develop a reputation for successful or unsuccessful transactions. A sign of how important these financing relationships are for private equity firms is how many of them have established their own capital markets teams that are in regular dialogue with the underwriters as well as the buyers of the syndicated loans.

Private equity sponsors will balance how they fund an acquisition depending on the after-tax funding costs and issuance by currency depending in which currencies their acquired asset generates cash flow. Therefore, leveraged loan issuance in the European market could include:

- A European currency loan only issuance
- A European currency loan and bond issuance
- A U.S. and European currency issuance of bank loans
- An issuance of U.S. and European currency mix of bonds and loans

Exhibit 15.1 shows what preliminary terms might be for a cross-currency funding of an LBO that also uses loans, secured bonds, and unsecured bond issuance.

The leveraged bond market in Europe has a substantial amount of issuance from companies that are not LBOs. However, there appears to be many fewer non-LBO corporate issuers of institutional leveraged loans in the market. Some of this is probably due to many of the large issuers in the European high-yield bond market having been fallen angels from investment grade. Other large corporate issuers in the bond market operate in traditional leveraged industries and are providers of cable television and mobile communications. Due to the bank-centric nature of the market, many midcap companies have long-standing relationships with local banks and utilize them for liquidity and for longer-term financing. Anecdotally, it is said that although many of these companies would be rated below investment grade if they entered the public markets, their management and ownership do not view themselves as below investment grade and do not get pricing at below investment grade levels from their historic banking relationships. Some conversations with bankers in Europe highlight that there still seems to be more

EXHIBIT 15.1

Indicative Preliminary Terms of a Cross-Currency LBO Funding in Bonds and Loans.

	USD	EURO
Term Loan		
Size (millions)	2,000	1,000
Maturity	7 Years	7 Years
Margin	L + 425	E + 425
Floor	0%	0%
OID	TBD	TBD
Call Protection	101 soft call 12 Million	101 soft call 12 Million
Ratings	B1/B	B1/B
Senior Secured Notes		
Ranking	Senior Secured	Senior Secured
Size (millions)	900	700
Maturity	7 Years	7 Years
Coupon	5.5% area	4.50% to 4.75%
Call Protection	Noncall 3 Years, Par +50% coupon; Par +25%, Par	
Ratings	B1/B	B1/B
Senior Notes		
Ranking	Senior Unsecured	Senior Unsecured
Size (millions)	700	300
Coupon	7.50% to 8.00%	6.25% to 6.75%
Maturity	8 Years	8 Years
Call Protection	Noncall 3 Years, Par +50% coupon, Par +25%, Par	
Ratings	Caa1/CCC	Caa1/CCC

of a "taint" in corporate Europe to being rated below investment grade, while it is largely dissipated in the United States, so if a company has not entered the high-yield bond market for some other reason, management will not be compelled to consider the syndicated leverage loan market.

There is a history of governments encouraging local and national banking relationships in Europe, as there is in Asia. Germany has had a large network of regional savings and cooperative banks that has helped provide finance for its mid-sized and smaller manufacturing firms (often called the *Mittelstand*). The country has appeared somewhat defensive of this network within the broader European banking network. France's large banks have had a history of cooperating closely with the state on national priorities and extending liquidity to long-established relationships and keeping the loans on their books.

This protective system of interrelationships between many regional and national banks has appeared to create a market that is overbanked and has resulted in fewer companies needing to come to the syndicated institutional loan market for financing (this has also probably limited the growth of the corporate bond market). When he was ECB president, Mr. Mario Draghi was quoted as saying the banking sector had outgrown capital markets. He stated that the high number of banks hurt the bank industry's profitability.[15] Furthering this theme, it was stated in *The Economist* that some regions are massively overbanked and that return on capital for European banks is about half of what is seen in the United States, for several reasons, including overbanking and a lack of technology investment.[16] In the past regional politics and regulators have appeared to limit in-country mergers of banks. This has led to an overabundance of banks that have capital needing to be invested. There have been signs that the ECB is now starting to encourage some bank mergers; these signs have included allowing more accounting flexibility in bank mergers; for example, allowing a bank to use negative goodwill in an acquisition valued less than book value to offset restructuring costs. The mechanics are less important than the potential for a reduction in the number of banks in the market. This could lead to mid-capitalization–sized companies looking to access the institutional loan market which could expand the universe of issuers in the market and increase the diversity of financing options for many of these companies.

BUYERS

Nonbank institutional loan investors include pension funds, insurers, as well as some family wealth offices, sovereign wealth funds, and comingled funds. However, some public fund structures, such as Undertakings for the Collective Investment in Transferable Securities (UCITS) funds, have limits on owning bank loans because they are not securities and are deemed to be private placements. By

---

[15] T. Jones, "Mario Draghi: Europe Has Too Many Banks," *Financial Times*, September 22, 2016.
[16] *The Economist*, "Many European Countries Still Have Too Many Banks," September 14, 2020.

far the most dominant segment of buyers in the European institutional leveraged loan market are CLOs.

There are several attractive features of loans for buyers. Most notable are that the investments are typically ranked senior and secured with a floating rate structure. The rate environment in Europe since the GFC has probably been a deterrent for some international fixed income buyers. Since the GFC, much of the region has had extremely low or negative sovereign interest rates. Even with base rate floors on many loans and the low cost of currency hedging, this has limited the attractiveness for non-European buyers. Additionally, the callability of bank loans can make them less attractive for some investors that look to match liabilities.

CLOs have continued to be successfully raised in Europe. Similar to U.S. issuance, they can attract buyers because their tranches are securities that offer floating rate features and some call protection, along with often offering a rating enhancement over buying secured loans directly. One of the major differences between the U.S. and European CLO markets is in the area of risk retention rules. Although risk retention is not required in the United States, for CLOs in Europe it is. Additionally, some European-based buyers of CLO tranches are required to only buy CLOs that are risk retention compliant.

Risk retention can be met by using a number of methods:

1. Retention of at least 5% of the nominal value of each tranche of notes issued.
2. Retention of an interest in revolving assets equal to at least 5% percent of the value of underlying assets.
3. Retention of randomly selected assets equal to at least 5% of the value of the portfolio.
4. Retention of the most subordinated payment obligation in the structure so long as it represents at least 5% of the exposure.
5. Retention of the first loss position in at least 5% of the underlying assets.[17]

The dependence on the CLO market as a buyer in Europe can influence the type of issuance that comes to market. While many

---

[17] C. Sweet, P. Matthews, and T. Kradjian, "Lawflash: Multijurisdictional Securitization in the Age of the New EU Securitization Rules," Morgan Lewis, February 20, 2019.

nonbank buyers of syndicated leveraged loans may be willing to buy loans without a rating, CLOs require ratings for their purchases. This may be a deterrent for some issuers.

Direct lending (or "private debt") has a significant presence in Europe, with many U.S. and non-U.S. firms having raised private funds to invest in the market. Some market participants believe that these funds have taken some product away from the traditional institutional leveraged loan market and offer certain advantages to borrowers.

Direct lenders appear to primarily lend to LBOs of a modest size where those lenders can offer early commitments and unitranche-style financings. They are also more willing to work with nonpublic financials and do not require a credit rating agency process. Direct lending firms have also been more active in project and infrastructure finance projects than has the institutional bank loan market, although both markets tend to avoid construction and staggered drawdown structures, with infrastructure investments tending to be made when the projects are closer to the operational phases.

APPROVED AND NONAPPROVED ASSIGNEE LISTS

With LBOs such a dominant part of issuance in the United States and Europe, it is important to understand how private equity firms work with the underwriters and manage the list of which firms can be shown new financings.

The list of potential buyers that are approved by the sponsor is an *Approved Assignee List* (they are commonly referred to as *whitelists* in Europe). Approved Assignee Lists are a means to control which institutions can buy the loan. Sponsors may want to exclude certain institutions from the loan; these often include investors that are viewed as likely to cause difficulties to the equity in the event of a default or restructuring (though debtholders certainly have the right to pursue repayment in full, even if that is viewed as being "difficult"). The Approved Assignee List is standard in Europe, whereas the standard approach of limiting those entities that can buy a loan in the United States is through the use of a *Disqualified Institution List* ("DQ List"). The DQ List is a list of investors the sponsor wants to exclude from the syndication and allows the underwriting banks to approach entities not on the list.

The U.S. approach has the potential of reaching a broader spectrum of the market's participants than the European approach. These lists are typically utilized in the market for secondary trading as well, because the agent will monitor the list and deny consent to assignments to buyers who are looking to join the syndicate of lenders.

The institutional leveraged loan market and specifically European CLOs are dependent on having investment opportunities in which to invest. In the current environment those opportunities are dominated by LBOs. With this structure there is a risk of actual, or perceived, conflicts arising. This is not the only market where these risks exist; they are high in the U.S. leveraged debt markets and especially in the direct lending market (where secondary trading is rarely an option). The use of both Approved and DQ Lists heightens these concerns. One area of conflict could arise (or appear to arise) when a manager feels pressured to invest in a transaction they do not particularly like because they do not want to be "cut-off" from future opportunities from the sponsor. Another conflict could also appear to occur in a loan that requires restructuring where a lender may not wish to be as adversarial with a sponsor, even if it is to protect their investors' interest, so that they can still have access to the sponsor's new issues. This can appear to be more problematic if the manager has multiple funds or CLOs, some of which own the distressed loan and some that do not.

SECONDARY TRADING

The Loan Market Association (LMA), the European industry association, cites in its literature how important the secondary trading of loans is for the development of the syndicated loan market in Europe. There is secondary activity in both the par and distressed segments of the loan market, with the vast majority of trades being on par documents.[18] However, practitioners that have operated in both the U.S. and European markets note that the level of secondary trading is lower in Europe and is also more controlled by the agent bank than in the United States.

In almost all cases, the consent of the borrower and the agent bank are required for the transfer of a loan, as in the United States. There are cases where consent has not been granted, but there is case

---

[18] Loan Market Association, "A Loan Market Association Guide to Secondary Loan Market Transactions," 2018.

law in the U.K. that supports enforcement of the economic benefits of a trade even if transfer is refused. Similar to the position in the United States, the refusal of any necessary consent will not lead to the transaction being terminated. Instead, the seller and buyer will be required to settle the proposed transaction by a funded participation or by some mutually acceptable alternative means.

As in the United States, there are several different ways to transfer a loan in the European secondary market. The following all fall under English law and include:

- Novation, which is the most common
- Legal assignment
- Equitable assignment
- Subparticipation

In the first two, the new lender has a direct contractual relationship with the borrower. Novation cancels the existing lender's obligations and the new lender is put in privity of contract with the borrower. The agent and the borrower need to consent to this type of transfer. The legal assignment requires the transfer of all the rights of the existing lender to the new lender.

In an equitable assignment the new lender gets a beneficial interest in the debt. In contrast to a legal assignment, the new lender joins the existing lender, as assignor, in any actions. A subparticipation is a funding arrangement between the original lender and the new lender, and the terms of it are covered in a separate contract from the loan agreement. The structure does not transfer to the new lender a beneficial interest in the debt. The borrower consent is not usually required for this last method of transfer.

One of the challenges that is often brought up by practitioners in the European market is the time it takes to close secondary loan transactions. While this is an issue in the United States as well, practitioners that have been in both markets say that the problem is more extreme in Europe. Anecdotally, there also appear to be fewer cases of ticking fees being paid on delayed settlement in Europe than in the United States. There does appear to be significant efforts in Europe on improving settlement times because most parties involved recognize the benefits of greater efficiency and its potential to increase the participation in the market. The different European jurisdictions have their own legal systems and tax codes that can impact the purchases and transfers of loans, and this, too, may contribute to settlement delays. On cross-border transactions the local laws of each relevant jurisdiction need to be considered, and each can have separate rules about assignments and other related transactions.[19]

STRUCTURAL DIFFERENCES

There are some structural differences that are often seen in the loans issued in Europe and in the United States. In Europe, the following terms can vary by jurisdiction:

- For amendments and waivers in Europe, it is typical to require 66.6% of loans, versus a simple majority in the United States. Similar requirements are needed for acceleration of the debt.
- Europe often does not have prepayment premiums in first liens, while it is common to have soft calls in the United States.
- How subsidiaries are set up can vary between the two markets. Unrestricted subsidiaries are typically not a concept in European structures, but are very common in the United States.
- It is also much less common in Europe to have intercreditor agreements, something that is more common in the United States when collateral is shared between classes of creditors.
- In Europe, an equity infusion to cure a default is typically used to repay part of the loan; this is not common in the United States.

Furthermore, in Europe it is much more common to have the loan be "portable" should the company be bought, assuming a certain level of credit quality is maintained. In the United States, there are typically "change of control" terms that require the existing loan to be retired. Many of these common differences in structures are shifting, and the private equity community has been pulling some of the common U.S. features over to Europe. The exception is portability of debt, which the private equity community is trying to

---

[19] Clifford Chance, "Loan Trading Across the Globe," July 2018.

pull the other way and make a more common feature in U.S. credit agreements.

RESTRUCTURING

The varied jurisdictions under which loans are issued in Europe can become a significant factor if a restructuring needs to be pursued; this is different from in the United States where in most respects there is one large, homogenous system. Despite efforts by the EU, there are significant differences in restructuring laws across the different European jurisdictions. Countries still can vary considerably on topics such as automatic stays and cramdowns. In most jurisdictions, senior lenders are not able to get an automatic stay, which can give more junior creditors more standing; thus, there is considerable focus on intercreditor agreements. Management and equity holders also can have significantly stronger positions in some jurisdictions than others. Historically, European restructuring efforts have been viewed as more "value destructive" than in the United States. This has led to many more out-of-court restructuring efforts in Europe. Additionally, some of these features can more commonly lead to a sale of some or all of the company or the issuer's assets.[20]

The European Parliament and the Council of the EU have issued directives that have tried to promote cooperation of different jurisdictions in the area of restructuring laws. These efforts could simplify some of the restructuring process.[21,22] The Asian markets have no common organization to try to develop consistent laws for corporate reorganization. In some countries in Asia, restructuring concepts are nascent and in others they are evolving.

CONCLUSION

The European institutional leveraged loan market is more concentrated in both the types of issuers and the types of buyers than in the United States. Some of the differences by jurisdiction can

---

[20] D. Winick and A. Young, "Across the Pond and Back Again: US and European Leveraged Finance Terms," *Butterworths Journal of International Banking and Financial Law* (November 2015).
[21] Clifford Chance, "Loan Trading Across the Globe," July 2018.
[22] S. Lerner, "How Does the EU Restructuring Directive Compare to Chapter 11?" November 6, 2019, available at https://www.restructuring-globalview.com.

make it quite daunting. However, the market is actively being used for funding buyout transactions and will likely continue to attract more investors.

The EU's recent actions indicate it is now willing to make it easier for bank mergers to occur, and this could reduce the overbanking in the market. This could create a virtuous circle in which more issuers utilize the syndicated institutional loan market for funding, thus diversifying the private sector's access to capital while diversifying the types of issuers in the market and attracting more diversity in the investor base. As private equity firms expand in Asia, we expect this market to see a more developed leveraged loan market as well.

Being able to invest outside the United States is beneficial for investors, even if they are U.S.-based. It can increase an investor's opportunity set, giving an investor access to more diverse companies, industries, and differentiated business and interest rate cycles. Thus, a more diverse global institutional loan market should help investors in all markets.

The Global Syndicated Loan Market–EMEA

Clare Dawson
Loan Market Association (LMA)

INTRODUCTION

Since its origins almost 60 years ago, the syndicated loan market in Europe, the Middle East, and Africa (EMEA) has shown remarkable growth and adaptability. Many new borrowers and investors have come into the market, the size of transaction that can be successfully syndicated has increased markedly, new products have been developed, a wider range of loans are syndicated, and a secondary market for loans has become well established.

Since the GFC, the financial markets have gone through a number of unprecedented events, and the syndicated loan markets have weathered them all successfully, to the extent that they retain their role as a core funding element for the corporate sector and other borrowers and continue to offer both flexibility and speed of execution that make them an invaluable element of borrowers' funding options. The latest of these events has of course been the COVID-19 pandemic, which has caused huge economic disruption, particularly because of lockdowns or other restrictions imposed by governments, in addition to the medical impact. Once again, the syndicated loan market rose to the challenge, and despite the fact that in many countries working from home had become the norm for many staff at banks and other market participants, the market was able to continue to function very efficiently and deliver financing to the corporate sector. Indeed, syndicated loan volumes in EMEA for the period of April 2020 to March 2021 were almost exactly the same as for April 2019 to April 2020, at around $1.2 trillion.[23] It is hard to imagine that this could have been the case even three years earlier, given the very rapid recent improvements to technology that have facilitated remote working.

Following the GFC, a number of striking developments in the loan markets have emerged, some in direct response to the GFC, others as a result of broader changes in the financial markets or even in response to wider societal concerns.

REGULATION

The regulatory response to the GFC differed from previous responses to a financial crisis in several respects. Although the cause of the GFC was largely the consequence of very poor subprime mortgage lending in the United States, it rapidly snowballed into a global credit crisis, affecting nearly all asset classes. It is worth remembering that it was initially a real estate lending crisis, which, because of the way the assets were securitized, turned into a liquidity crisis, which required a considerable level of state intervention and global support of the whole financial system.

There was therefore a political dimension to the solution and the necessity to apply new regulatory tools to regulate liquidity management, as well as the need to strengthen capital requirements.

The consequences of the regulatory response were therefore more wide-ranging and, on occasions, less considered than they should have been, and led to negative unintended consequences

---

[23] Data from Dealogic.

for the loan market, which the LMA endeavored to correct, with some considerable success.

The most obvious examples of this were the hastily drafted European securitization legislation, which was so poorly thought through that it resulted in tarnishing all securitizations by the same brush, so as to be inoperable for CLOs, and the initial proposals for the liquidity coverage ratio (LCR), which would have penalized borrowers as much as lenders.

Fortunately, regulators and legislators listened to most of the suggestions to rectify the initial proposals, so that the final outcome did not overly harm the loan market, which proved yet again its power to adapt. In fact, it can reasonably be said that many of the measures taken were successful in strengthening the financial system and positioning it to be able, a dozen years later, to play a significant supportive role in the current crisis, which as we know is medical, rather than economic or financial, in origin.

After the initial, it could be said, emergency-driven regulatory response to the GFC, another, not always welcome, trend in regulation began to emerge. This was the increasing appetite among regulators to extend the scope of their regulation beyond their own jurisdiction—so-called extraterratoriality. Examples of this include the Foreign Account Tax Compliance Act (FATCA), which in its initial form would have required banks based outside the United States to send information relating to U.S. persons holding accounts with them directly to the U.S. tax authorities or incur a 30% withholding tax on certain payments. The reporting would in many instances have led to a direct conflict with local confidentiality laws, and after considerable lobbying by the industry, including by the LMA, to both United States and local regulators, the scheme was amended to allow for banks to send the information to their own regulators, to be passed on by them to the U.S. authorities, provided those regulators had entered into an agreement with the United States.

Another example of regulators extending their reach beyond their own territory was the EU Benchmarks Regulation, which prohibits those entering into financial instruments from using benchmarks regulated outside the EU unless those benchmarks are deemed by the EU to meet certain requirements. In this case, the potential problem created was for market participants inside the EU, rather than external participants, the opposite effect of the FATCA legislation.

SUSTAINABLE LENDING

Over the last several years sustainable lending products have evolved at a very rapid pace in the syndicated loan market, in response to the growing emphasis being placed on environmental, social, and governance (ESG) issues by lenders, borrowers, regulators, investors, and other key market stakeholders.

As the systemic risks posed by climate change have come into sharp focus and countries across the world have set ambitious net-zero carbon emissions targets, the syndicated loan market has reacted by seeking to channel capital into environmentally sustainable (or "green") projects and activities. This led to the development of the green loan product, which is used exclusively to fund green projects and activities. The Green Loan Principles (GLP), which were first launched by the LMA in March 2018, in collaboration with the Asia Pacific Loan Market Association (APLMA) and the Loan Syndications and Trading Association (LSTA), introduced a high-level framework of market standards and guidelines for use across the wholesale green loan market, allowing the green loan market to grow, while at the same time retaining its flexibility and preserving its integrity. Since the development of the GLP, the green loan market has grown rapidly in EMEA.

The Sustainability-Linked Loan (SLL) product has proved to be a star performer in the syndicated loan market since its inception in 2017. With sustainability and ESG issues moving to center stage, the SLL product has provided lenders with a means of incentivizing borrowers to align their business activities to broader sustainability targets, usually by way of a pricing mechanic built into the facility agreement. Unlike green loans, SLLs can be used for general working capital purposes, and so can be accessed by borrowers across a wide variety of sectors. For this reason, the SLL product has expanded the reach of the sustainable lending market to a broad range of corporates across industry sectors, providing a unique and exciting opportunity for lenders and borrowers to work together to set ambitious and meaningful sustainability performance targets. The launch of the Sustainability-Linked Loan Principles by the LMA, the LSTA, and the APLMA in March 2019 was followed by a striking increase in the volume of SLLs in 2019, to around $114 billion in EMEA alone. The potential for the SLL product to drive the transition toward a more sustainable economy is likely to further accelerate demand for this product in 2021 and beyond. Indeed, in EMEA volumes of SLL in the first quarter of 2021 reached $56 billion.

As SLLs continue to go from strength to strength, there has also been a significant increase in the volume of social loans being originated in the market. This mirrors the broader response to the COVID-19 pandemic and the need for targeted funding to meet the numerous and varied social challenges posed by it. Volumes of loans labeled specifically as Pandemic loans reached a huge $222 billion in EMEA in 2020, although this fell back to only $3.8 billion in the first quarter of 2021. In response to this development, the LMA, LSTA, and APLMA have now published a set of Social Loan Principles.

The regulatory horizon across EMEA and beyond looks set to further catalyze growth in the sustainable lending market. Recent years have seen corporates increasingly reporting on ESG issues in line with voluntary international standards, such as the Task Force on Climate-related Financial Disclosures (TCFD) recommendations. However, regulators are now increasingly stepping in to set mandatory ESG disclosure standards for financial institutions, corporates, and investors. The EU's Sustainable Finance Disclosure Regulation, for example, which took effect in March 2021, requires, among other things, finance market participants to disclose to investors the manner in which sustainability risks are integrated into their investment decisions. The pressure from regulators to ensure that sustainability risks are being properly taken into account is likely to further drive ESG issues into mainstream finance.

INSTITUTIONAL INVESTORS

It is fair to say that in general since the GFC the loan asset class has attracted a much broader range of institutional investors. The initial resurgence of the investor base post-crisis most visibly targeted gaps in the market where banks were, at least temporarily, reticent to extend credit. This, arguably, was the precursor for the growth in direct lending as we know it today. At the same time, institutional investors also began to roll out strategies incorporating real estate debt and infrastructure.

Today's investor will often adopt and adapt strategies to most effectively access risk and yield, both across loan asset classes and the capital structure. Despite asset class diversification, however, it is more often than not the broader leveraged loan market that remains the core focus of the loan fund manager. Leveraged loan volumes in Europe began to recover in earnest after the sovereign crisis and resultant ECB quantitative easing. This, in turn, paved the way for the return of the former bellwether of the institutional market, the CLO, in 2013. From literally a standing start, post-financial crisis European CLO issuance reached €16 billion in 2016, surging to a high of just under €30 billion in 2019. Volume pared back to €22 billion in 2020 in challenging market conditions, nevertheless attracting 66 new European CLO vehicle issues versus 40 some five years earlier.[24]

Although there are no exact data, practitioners often estimate the volume of separately managed account money today at the same ballpark level as outstanding CLO issue, pointing to a European investor base of more than €200 billion, tallying neatly with institutional loan volume outstandings per the S&P European Leveraged Loan Index (ELLI) of approximately €220 billion in 2020. This suggests that, in the mainstream leveraged loan market alone, both the addressable market and the investor base have doubled in a little over five years. It is no surprise then that institutional investor participation is key to the success of any given syndicated leveraged loan transaction, aside perhaps from local bank-led club deals. The pro rata market sold to banks is generally much less than 20% of deal volume today (with the second quarter of 2020 being the exception with significant COVID-related revolving credit facility origination).

It is worth emphasizing that ELLI data does not include institutional volume in real estate or infrastructure, nor indeed does it include volume in the increasingly important direct lending market, despite the latter having at its core the private equity–led small to mid-cap leveraged space. Regarding the latter, research by Deloitte points to over €100 billion being raised by over 60 fund managers for deployment in the European direct lending arena over the last five years.[25] Some 270 transactions were tracked in 2016, and this had risen to 504 in 2019 before a significant decline in 2020. Recent successful fundraising rounds toward the end of last year, however, suggest that this will most certainly remain a key focus

---

[24] See S&P Global Market Intelligence.
[25] Deloitte, "Direct Lenders Poised for Action in Uncertain Market," *Deloitte Alternative Lender Deal Tracker* (Spring 2021). Available at: https://www2.deloitte.com/content/dam/Deloitte/lu/Documents/private-equity/lu-deloitte-alternative-lender-tracker-spring-2021.pdf

for the institutional investor, once dubbed "alternative lenders" in the sector. Much like in the syndicated leveraged market, provision of term debt in the small to midcap market by a nonbank lender is certainly more mainstream now than alternative.

SECONDARY MARKETS

Increased Volatility Post-Financial Crisis

Reported trading volumes in the European market are dominated by leveraged loans (approximately 75%), with the balance made up of investment grade, emerging markets, and distressed loans. Although investment grade and emerging markets have remained relatively insulated, the leveraged loan asset class post-financial crisis has exhibited significantly increased price sensitivity to both technical and fundamental influences. Over the last five years there have been several occasions where external events have led to material price movements, as investors have sought to manage positions. A few examples to illustrate the point: the sell-off in Chinese and Asian stock markets and a tumbling oil price led to heightened volatility in the first quarter of 2016 after a period of relatively sustained recovery following the European sovereign crisis; the market also saw a short-lived sell-off in early summer that year in the wake of the unexpected U.K. referendum result to leave the EU; a mix of rising U.S. rates, potential U.S.–China trade wars, a sharp downturn in European economic sentiment, Brexit uncertainty, and (for once) an oversupply of leveraged loan issuance led to a turbulent 2018 before perhaps more fundamentally driven price fluctuations in 2019 on credit cycle concerns.

The first quarter of 2020 brought a new dimension to post-crisis loan volatility, however. In March 2020, once the reality of pandemic lockdowns had hit, the market saw the most dramatic correction in its history, swifter, though not as deep, as in the GFC. This was matched by an equally astonishing recovery during April and May. The S&P ELLI fell almost 20 points in the two weeks to March 24 from a weighted average of 98c to 78c for senior performing loans, before recovering 15 points by May. LMA settlement data from the period proves that this was not simply a repricing exercise, with record trade settlement volume in the second quarter of 2020, some 50% up on the previous quarter.

Increasing Depth of Liquidity

The depth of liquidity in today's market—together with an ongoing supply and demand imbalance and more tempered COVID-related default projections (than originally forecast) going forward—saw the ELLI index close the year at 97.55, just a point below where it opened. Indeed, the increasing depth of the market and underlying liquidity is backed by reported trading and settlement volumes, particularly the number of individual transactions involved. In overall volume terms, 2016 saw approximately €53 billion in reported nominal volume, rising to €75 billion in 2020, the highest total since 2007. Trade settlement numbers better illustrate depth, as these include all suballocations sitting behind the fund manager. Data collated by the LMA show that three times more individual trades were settled in 2020 than in 2016, pointing to a much wider universe of available liquidity. Time to settlement remains an issue for the market, and greater efficiency could unlock even further liquidity.

It is worthy of note that these trading and settlement data are representative only of reported volumes in the bank-led trading market from volunteer contributors. Actual volumes will be higher and liquidity deeper. Disintermediated trades directly between counterparties and not involving trading houses are not included, nor are bespoke portfolio trades in nonperforming or noncore loans in Europe, which had averaged well in excess of €100 billion per annum from 2016 to 2020 as noted by Deloitte in its market updates.[26] The vast majority of this latter volume has traded from banks into institutional hands.

CONCLUSION

Since the GFC there have been a number of major shocks to the markets—be they political, such as Brexit, or arising from other causes, such as the COVID-19 pandemic. Throughout all of these shocks the syndicated loan market has proved extremely resilient, and has helped borrowers to weather the resulting economic impacts. Moreover, the market has continued to attract new investors, not least encouraged by an active secondary market, particularly in the leveraged space. After some 60 years as a core source of funding for a huge range of borrowers, and for many, acting as their first step into

---

[26] Ibid.

EXHIBIT 15.2

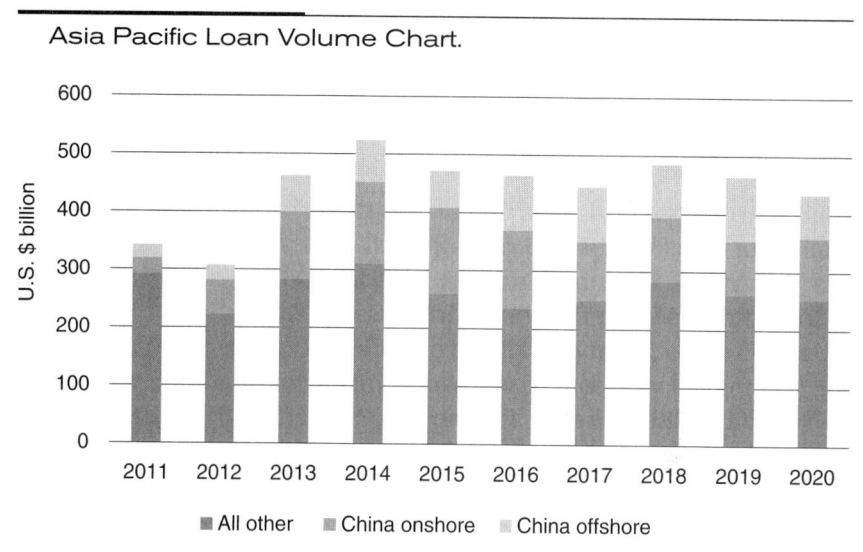

Asia Pacific Loan Volume Chart.

■ All other   ■ China onshore   ■ China offshore

*All international currency and Rmb syndicated and club loans (excluding Japan).
** *Source*: Refinitiv LPC.

international markets, the syndicated loan market shows no sign of losing its importance in the global economy.

The Evolving Asia Pacific Loan Market[27]

Sadaf Khan
Asia Pacific Loan Market Association (APLMA)

Loan activity in Asia Pacific (excluding Japan) has grown significantly over the past decade, propelled by the rise in borrowing by China-related companies. In the early 2000s, the Asia Pacific loan market was still recovering from the 1997 Asian financial crisis, and it was not until 2005 that volumes reached $148.4 billion, crossing the precrisis level of $144.8 billion back in 1997. Moving ahead to the start of the next decade, loan activity had more than doubled to $341.5 billion in 2011 before reaching a high of $523 billion in 2014, as shown in Exhibit 15.2. Since then, declining mergers and acquisitions

---

[27] Volume numbers and rankings are sourced from Refinitiv LPC.

(M&A) activity and increasing geopolitical tensions have dampened loan volumes to $464.2 billion in 2019 and $434 billion in 2020.

RISE OF CHINESE BANK LENDING

The growth in demand for loans from China-related companies has resulted in increased lending by Chinese banks. The pickup in Chinese bank lending can be observed by the Mandated Arranger rankings in the region. Back in 2011, with ANZ grabbing the top spot in the league table rankings, the Bank of China was the sole Chinese bank to be part of the top 10, with a 6% market share. China Development Bank and ICBC came in at numbers 20 and 21.

2020's Mandated Arranger league table (Exhibit 15.3) shows that the Bank of China captured the top spot with a resounding

EXHIBIT 15.3

2020 Asia Pacific Loans Mandated Arranger.

2020 Rank	2021 Rank	Change	Mandated Arranger	2020 Market Share	2021 Market Share
1	4	▲3	Bank of China	15.36%	5.58%
2	10	▲8	DBS Bank	4.07%	2.80%
3	1	▼2	ANZ	3.68%	8.69%
4	21	▲17	Industrial & Commercial Bank of China	3.40%	1.25%
5	72	▲67	China Construction Bank	3.29%	<0.5%
6	7	▲1	Sumitomo Mitsui Banking Corp	3.27%	4.16%
7	115	▲108	China Merchants Bank	2.87%	<0.5%
8	5	▼3	Commonwealth Bank of Australia	2.68%	5.55%
9	27	▲18	Agricultural Bank of China	2.66%	0.95%
10	11	▼1	Mizuho Bank	2.57%	2.69%
11	6	▼5	HSBC	2.55%	4.52%
12	8	▼4	Standard Chartered Bank	2.41%	3.37%
13	63	▲50	Bank of Communications	2.27%	<0.5%
14	39	▲25	China Citic Bank	1.97%	<0.5%
15	9	▼6	MUFG Bank	1.93%	3.13%
16	13	▼3	OCBC Bank	1.93%	2.26%
17	14	▼3	UOB	1.79%	2.00%
18	2	▼16	National Australia Bank	1.76%	6.12%
19	15	▼4	BNP Paribas	1.59%	1.48%
20	23	▲3	Mega International Commercial Bank	1.54%	1.18%

*All international currency and Rmb syndicated and club loans (excluding Japan).
** *Source*: Refinitiv LPC.

lead over other banks by taking 15.4% of the market share. Out of the 1,288 deals closed in 2020, the Bank of China was mandated arranger on 469 of them. And 2020's top 10 ranking included other Chinese banks such as ICBC, China Construction Bank, China Merchant Bank, and Agricultural Bank of China.

Chinese banks have also grown their lending market share beyond China-linked companies. In the Australian loan market, the Bank of China ranked fifth in 2020's Mandated Arranger league tables by arranging 31 deals. This marks a significant increase from the seven deals it arranged in 2011 when it ranked 19 in the Australian Mandated Arranger table.

REFINANCING CONTINUES AS M&A LACKS LUSTRE

Refinancing has been the major driver for loan volume, accounting for 43.3% of total lending in 2020. M&A volume has been lacking in Asia Pacific (excluding Japan) since reaching a high of $80 billion in 2016. Loans backing acquisitions fell to $35 billion in 2019 but picked up pace to reach $52.8 billion in 2020 thanks to some notable transactions such as the $7.2 billion bridge loan backing Thai conglomerate Charoen Pokphand Group's purchase of British supermarket chain Tesco's Asian business. Other significant M&A transactions in the region included the €6.75 billion loan backing China Investment Corp.'s 2017 acquisition of European warehouse firm Logicor from Blackstone for €12.25 billion and the $6.9 billion loan financing the MMG-led (MMG being China Minmental's offshore arm) consortium's purchase of Las Bambas copper mine in Peru from Glencore Xstrata.

Current trade tension between Australia and China has dampened M&A activity in the region. The Australian foreign investment watchdog has recommended blocking jumbo acquisitions, citing national security concerns in the past. In 2018, CK Infrastructure Holdings Ltd.–led consortium's $13 billion AUD bid for energy infrastructure business APA Group Ltd. was rejected. In April 2020, China's Yibin Tianyi Lithium Industry withdrew an investment application in AVZ Minerals based on negative government feedback. In June 2020, a subsidiary of Shangdong Goldsea Group dropped its bid for gold miner Alto Metals after the Foreign Investment Review Board (FIRB) sought more time to review the deal.

The negative sentiment is not limited to China-linked acquisitions in Australia. In August 2020, Hong Kong–listed China Mengniu Dairy Co. Ltd. pulled out of a deal to buy Lion Dairy & Drinks Pty. from Japan's Kirin Holdings Co. Ltd. after Treasurer Josh Frydenburg said the purchase would be "contrary to the national interest."

ESG AND GREEN LENDING

With social and environmental concerns becoming more crucial, almost $47 billion in ESG loans (including green loans and sustainable loans) have been closed in Asia Pacific (excluding Japan) since 2018. A majority of these loans have been raised in Singapore, Australia, and Hong Kong. Singapore has raised close to $14 billion and the Monetary Authority of Singapore has started a green and sustainability-linked loan grant for corporates and banks that will cover part of expenses incurred to engage independent sustainability assessment and advisory service providers. DBS Bank raised its sustainable finance target in early 2020 from $20 billion by 2024 to $50 billion. The Australian market closed $12.9 billion of loans, and Taiwan, with its push toward energy independence, raised the largest ESG/green loan in the region with a NT$87 billion facility for its offshore wind project, Changfang Wind Power.

REGIONAL ACTIVITY

HONG KONG LOAN MARKET GROWS ON BACK OF CHINA-LINKED BORROWING

Hong Kong loan volumes grew to a historic high of $137.5 billion by the end of 2019—a 241% increase from $40.3 billion back in 2010, as displayed in Exhibit 15.4. However, 2020 saw Hong Kong lending fall 25.4% year over year to $102.6 billion with the market's partial shutdown in the first half of 2020 due to the global pandemic. The massive growth in Hong Kong loan volumes can be directly attributed to the rise in China-linked borrowing. Over the past decade, increasing numbers of Chinese borrowers have been raising their loans in the Hong Kong market, including loans issued for Chinese technology giants such as Alibaba, Tencent, Alipay, and Ant Financial. In 2018, $78 billion of the $110.6 billion in loans raised in the Hong Kong market were for China-related

EXHIBIT 15.4

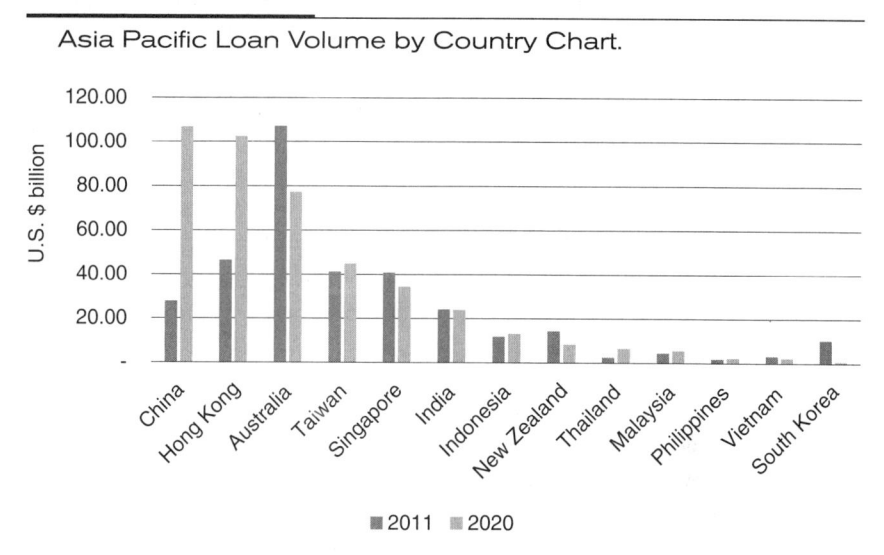

Asia Pacific Loan Volume by Country Chart.

*All international currency and Rmb syndicated and club loans (excluding Japan).
** *Source*: Refinitiv LPC.

borrowers, and that number increased to $96 billion in 2019. In 2020, offshore Chinese borrowings accounted for two-thirds of Hong Kong's total volume.

However, China-linked deals might come under pressure due to the current geopolitical environment. Back in 2019, Trip.com easily raised a $2 billion loan, with seven non-Chinese lenders committing to the deal. In August 2020, the company took six months to close its $1.295 billion loan and saw only five non-Chinese lenders participating in the loan.

Apart from the China angle, the Hong Kong loan market has been driven by real estate borrowing. From 2017 until the end of 2020, nonresidential property lending in Hong Kong has totaled approximately $41 billion. Real estate giant Sung Hung Kai has been a prolific borrower, raising a HK$20 billion loan in 2019, a HK$21 billion loan in 2018, and a HK$22 billion loan in 2017. Real estate lending is expected to grow further given that the Hong Kong Monetary Authority announced on August 2020 that it was raising the loan-to-value ratio cap on nonresidential properties to 50% from 40%. The rule change is expected to boost investment demand for Hong Kong property.

The years 2020 and 2019 had already seen increased M&A activity surrounding the real estate sector. In 2019, Gaw Capital obtained a HK$2.8 billion loan for the acquisition of a commercial building from a joint venture between Swire Properties and China Motor Bus, as well as a HK$8.3 billion loan for the LBO of Cityplaza Three and Cityplaza Four from Swire for HK$15 billion.

At the end of 2020, Gaw Capital Partners and real estate investment manager Schroder Pamfleet were raising a HK$4.9 billion loan for a proposed leveraged buyout of an office building, Cityplaza One, from Swire Properties Ltd. for HK$9.8 billion. The year also saw a HK$25 billion loan backing the privatization of property developer Hopewell Holdings.

U.S.–China political tensions have led several Chinese firms to consider delisting from U.S. stock exchanges and seek secondary listing in Asia or go private. As of May 2021, 248 Chinese companies were listed on the three largest U.S. exchanges, with a total market capitalization of more than $2.1 trillion, according to the U.S.–China Economic and Security Review Commission.[28]

So far, lending opportunities from these delistings have only been availed by Chinese banks. The $3.5 billion debt financing for New York–listed 58.com's buyout of 5 billion was provided by four Chinese banks. Nasdaq-listed Chinese online media conglomerate Sina's buyout has China Minsheng Bank as the sole lead on a $2.08 billion loan. For the proposed China Biologic Product take-private, Ping An Bank is arranging a $1.6 billion loan with a group of other lenders.

Back in 2015, following some accounting scandals and short-seller attacks that pushed down equity valuations, 30 out of 127 U.S.-listed Chinese companies announced take-private deals, which led to $11 billion in loans in 2016.

CHINA SPURRED ON BY CAPITAL EXPENDITURES

After reaching a high of $148.6 billion in 2015, loan volumes in China have been declining, reaching $93.5 billion in 2019. The country has been suffering from prolonged economic weakness

---

[28] U.S.–China Economic and Securities Review Commission. "Chinese Companies Listed on Major U.S. Stock Exchanges" (May 13, 2021). https://www.uscc.gov/research/chinese-companies-listed-major-us-stock-exchanges.

and has struggled with the uncertainty of its trade war with the United States. In 2020, loan volumes picked up pace, thanks to government-introduced stimulus measures, reaching $106.9 billion, making it the most active market in the Asia Pacific (excluding Japan) region.

The pickup in 2020 loan volume can be accredited to an increase in capital expenditure (capex) loans that accounted for 64% of lending and a pickup in event-related financing that resulted in $13.7 billion of M&A-related loans. The onshore RMB-dominated China loan activity is mostly driven by capex, infrastructure, project finance, and real estate loans. The largest loan brought to the market was a RMB 160 billion project financing for Chinese state-owned semiconductor maker Fujian Jinhua Integrated Circuit in 2018.

Given the nature of the market and currency restrictions, the China loan market is primarily dominated by local Chinese banks. Among the biggest lenders in 2020 were the Bank of China, which dominated China's 2020 loan market by capturing 45% of the Mandated Arranger market share, followed by China Construction and Agricultural Bank of China.

AUSTRALIA VOLUME ENDS DECADE ON A LOW NOTE

The Australian loan market began the decade with a resounding $107.2 billion in volume in 2011 thanks to large project finance loans, totaling $14.3 billion, and $16 billion of M&A lending. The market soon encountered liquidity pressures as European banks such as BNP Paribas and Société Générale pulled back and BOS International Australia exited the leveraged market. In 2018, Australian loan volumes reached $95.53 billion, a four-year high, as the market became flush with liquidity with the return of some European banks and the expansion of Asian lenders in the Australian market. In 2020, loan volumes fell to $77.3 billion as the country faced its first recession in almost three decades amid the pandemic.

Refinancing has been the largest contributor to Australian loan volume, accounting for 62% in 2020. The largest loan closed in 2020 was an $8.4 billion loan for the Ichthys Liquefied Natural Gas project in Western Australia for French oil and gas giant Total SA and Japan's Inpex Corp. Apart from refinancing, Infrastructure/project finance have also added significant volumes to the Australian loan market. The largest deal closed in the market was the 2012 $8.5 billion loan backing the Origin Energy and ConocoPhillips-sponsored Australia Pacific LNG Pty. Ltd. project, though only $2.875 billion was provided by banks.

M&A deal flow has been lacking in the market, accounting for 11% of volumes in 2019 and 12% in 2020. Amongst the largest transactions have been an A$8.4 billion loan backing IFM Investor and AustralianSuper's 2016 purchase of AusGrid electricity network and an A$5.25 billion loan to finance the 2020 merger of Vodafone Hutchison Australia and TPG Telecom.

Back in 2011, Australian lending was dominated by the big four Australian banks that controlled 64% of Mandated Arranger market share and maintained the top four rankings. The market dynamics have changed since then, with Asian and Japanese banks challenging the Australian banks. In 2019, the market share of Mandated Arranger league tables controlled by the big four Australian banks fell to 31%. The Bank of China ranked third, and MUFG and HSBC saw their rankings climb to fifth and sixth, respectively.

Nonbank lenders have also been increasingly participating in Australian loans. Metrics Credit Partners and Singapore's Eastspring Investments participated in Woolworths' A$2bn refinancing in October 2019, and Blackrock Capital Investment Corp. and Japan's Meiji Yasuda Life Insurance and Daido Life Insurance participated in Newgen Neerabup Pty. Ltd.'s A$252 million loan. Meiji Yasuda Life, Daido Life Insurance, Dai-ichi Life, as well as Hong Kong Mortgage Corp participated in AusGrid's A$1.6 billion 2019 loan.

TAIWAN PUSHES TENORS ON ECO-FRIENDLY LOANS

The volume of loans in the Taiwanese market has remained steady over the past decade. Loan volume back in 2011 was $41.2 billion. It fell to $33 billion in 2019 but climbed back to $44.9 billion in 2020. Project financing and refinancings made up almost 73% of loan volume in 2020.

Taiwan has seen some large M&A transactions in its technology sector. In 2016, Micron Technology raised the largest acquisition loan in Taiwan, a NT$80 billion loan, to back its $4 billion acquisition of the shares it did not own in Inotera Memories. And in

2018, Advanced Semiconductor Engineering and rival Siliconware Precision raised NT$90 billion to back their merger.

Since 2016, the Taiwanese loan market has seen the start of windfarm project financing loans being raised to back the government's target of installing 5.5GW of offshore wind power capacity to its energy supply mix to reduce its heavy reliance on oil and coal imports.

So far there have been $9.7 billion of loans raised to back windfarm projects in Taiwan, with the NT$2.5 billion five-year loan for Formosa I Offshore Wind Farm (OWF), a joint venture between Swancor, Macquarie, Orsted, and Japan's JERA Co. Inc., the inaugural offshore wind farm–related loan raised back in May 2016. And 2020 saw a NT$87 billion project financing for Changfang Wind Power Co.

Windfarms have a long construction period, ranging from 5 to 10 years, and their financings need to be longer termed than the usual project financing loans. To ease Taiwanese lenders into these longer-termed, nonrecourse financings, the initial deals that came to the market were structured as corporate five-year loans tied to the project sponsor. The financing for Formosa I OWF was broken into a NT$2.5 billion 5-year loan for the first stage of construction in 2016 and NT$18.7 billion 16-year financing for the second stage in 2018. Since then, long-termed loans for these projects have become more frequent, with 2020 alone seeing four windfarm project financing loans arranged with 18-year maturities.

The sector has received a lot of interest from nonlocal banks and investors, but domestic state-owned Taiwanese banks have stayed away. To encourage more local participation, the Taiwanese government is setting up a credit guarantee fund.

SINGAPORE LOAN VOLUME DIPS DESPITE GROWTH IN COMMODITY BORROWING

After its growth spurt in the early 2000s, the Singapore loan market stabilized in the past decade, excluding 2014's record volume of $53 billion. Loan volume reached $45.6 billion in 2019, up 10% from the $40.8 billion closed in 2011, and then fell to an eight-year low of $34.3 billion in 2020.

Commodities borrowing had been the big boom over the past decade with lending representing 20% of Singapore volume in 2019 and 30% in 2020. Global energy companies such as Mercuria, Vitol,

Olam, and Trafigura were repeat visitors, raising $9 billion in 2019 and $10 billion in 2020.

The year 2020 saw defaults and accounting scandals emerge in the Singapore commodity trading sector, which accounts for 4.5% of Singapore's GDP. Singapore-based Hin Leong Trading, one of Asia's largest oil traders, was placed under judicial management in April to restructure billions of dollars of debt after a crash in oil prices revealed a massive, years-long fraud at the firm. There were also large losses with Agritrade International, which collapsed with $1.55 billion of outstanding liabilities. In response, the Association of Banks in Singapore has launched the city state's first set of commodity financing best practices for the industry.

Loans for the real estate sector have also been major contributors to Singapore's loan market volume. In 2019, loan volumes for borrowers from the sector reached $48 billion, and in 2020, thanks to deals like property developer M+S Pte. Ltd.'s S$1.95 billion green loan, loan volume reached $34 billion.

SOUTH AND SOUTHEAST ASIA LOAN VOLUMES CONSISTENT

Loan volumes remained relatively benign in other South and Southeast Asia sectors with a few exceptions thanks to jumbo project financings and M&A transactions.

Malaysia loan volume was $4.6 billion in 2011. It reached $14.4 billion in 2018, thanks to an $8 billion jumbo loan for Petroliam Nasional Berhad's Refinery and Petrochemical Integrated Development (RAPID) project. In 2019, volumes reached $13.6 billion as the country closed the largest deal in the Asia Pacific: Pengerang Refining's $7.1 billion loan, which was part of a broader $9.7 billion project financing package for the RAPID project.

Loan activity in India (non-Indian Rupee) remained static in the past decade, starting 2011 with $22 billion, reaching $18.2 billion in 2019, and ending the decade with $23.8 billion in loans closed. The year 2020 saw a pickup in M&A activity in the Indian market with a $1.75 billion loan for the delisting of Vedanta, a subsidiary of Vedanta Resources, and a $1.1 billion loan for U.S.-based aluminum producer Novelis, a subsidiary of India's Hindalco Industries to finance its acquisition of Aleris.

Indonesia loan volume has also remained flat, reaching $13.6 billion in 2018, $12.7 billion in 2019, and $13.2 billion in 2020.

Some notable deals closed in 2020 were Indofood's return to the loan market after a decade to raise $2.05 billion through a dual-currency loan for the proposed $3 billion acquisition of manufacturing partner Pinehill. And Pertamina is seeking a one-year bridge loan of more than $3 billion to fund its purchase of energy assets from oil and gas producer Occidental Petroleum Corp for $4.5 billion.

INCREASING POOLS OF LIQUIDITY: PRIVATE CREDIT FUNDS

Even though investments by private credit funds in Asia Pacific are dwarfed by their investments in the United States and Western Europe, the number of funds focusing on Asia Pacific has been steadily rising.

Hedge funds and distressed/special situation funds entered the market after the 1997–1998 Asian financial crisis. Fund investments in the performing space really kick-started in 2012 when U.S. TLB structures were introduced for Australian corporates.

The direct lending strategy was first deployed in Australia in 2017 with Hybridge Capital providing a A$650 million unitranche to fund The Carlyle Group and the Pacific Equity Partners' buyout of iNova Pharmaceuticals, quickly followed by a A$250m six-year unitranche backing KKR's acquisition of Laser Clinic Australia.

Meanwhile, the Asian markets saw direct lending deals emerge initially in India in 2018 with a unitranche financing Apax Partners' 2018 buyout of Healthium Medtech, followed by Partners Group's $150 to $200 million 2019 unitranche financing of Baring PE Asia's acquisition of India-based AGS Health. Outside India, 2019 saw a $200 million unitranche loan financing provided by Partners Group backing TA Associates acquisition of Taiwanese bubble tea maker Gong Cha Group.

In 2018, Clifford Capital broke new ground with the first Asian CLO that would primarily invest in project finance borrowings. The $458 million CLO transaction was structured with multiple classes of U.S. dollar–denominated senior secured notes backed by cash flows from a portfolio of 37 project finance loans from across 30 projects across Asia Pacific and the Middle East. The transaction had the encouragement of the Singapore government, which sought to promote the city state as an infrastructure financing hub.

The pandemic has not put a stop to private credit fundraising as shown in the chart provided by Preqin in Exhibit 15.5. The

EXHIBIT 15.5

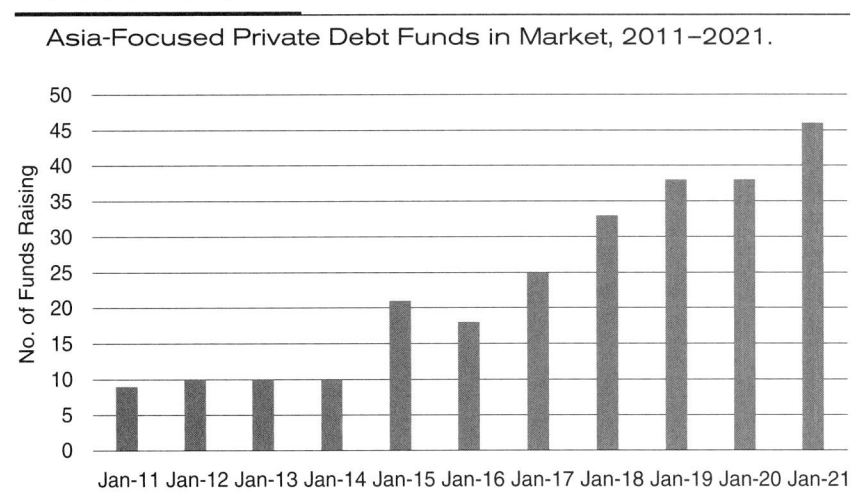

Asia-Focused Private Debt Funds in Market, 2011–2021.

Source: Preqin.

number of funds raised to invest in private debt rose to 46 by the beginning of 2021.

In October 2020, Australia's AMP Capital launched a mezzanine infrastructure debt strategy in Asia Pacific, while Hong Kong–based OCP Asia was raising $500 million for a direct lending fund to provide senior secured loans to family-owned businesses and small to medium-sized enterprises.

In December 2020, Boutique asset manager 360 Capital Group Ltd. was seeking $70 million AUD for units in one of its listed funds to invest in private credit in Australia and New Zealand, and European middle market investment firm Hayfin Capital Management was expanding into the Asia Pacific region with the opening of a new office in Singapore.

SECONDARY LOAN ACTIVITY PICKS UP AS DEMAND OUTSTRIPS SUPPLY

Demand for loans in the secondary market has been on the rise in Asia Pacific (excluding Japan). Unlike the U.S. and Western European markets, limited leveraged transactions have meant that most of the demand has been for solid blue-chip names and infrastructure loans. The growth in the secondary loan market in Asia Pacific has been spurred not only by increasing primary activity over the years, but also by an increasingly larger pool of buyers of these loans. Among the banks contributing to this increased demand are the Taiwanese banks, Japanese regional banks expanding to non-Japanese and non-Yen denominated loans, and the Philippines regional banks actively seeking allocations in foreign loans.

The year 2020 saw some of the demand pressures ease as certain banks and funds retreated from the market. Demand for loans from sectors not impacted by COVID-19 remained high, while other sectors, such as coal-based infrastructure projects, lost their appeal.

DEFAULTS LAY LOW FOR NOW BUT NOT FOR LONG

Defaults and bankruptcies are expected to rise with Moody's APAC high-yield nonfinancial corporate default rate expected to rise from 5.3% (as of June 2020) to as high as 8.1% by the end of 2020. After two consecutive years of record defaults in 2018 and 2019 in China, five of China's state-linked enterprises defaulted for the first time in 2020 in the onshore bond market, with a total of eight state-owned enterprises defaulting as of early December 2020.

Outside China, the rest of the market will also see more defaults emerge as covenant waiver and amendment fatigue sets in. Companies that were struggling with payments toward the end of 2020 included Hong Kong–listed Victory City International, which was expected to miss a 10% loan repayment on its $333 million facility. PT Bali Perkasa Sukses, a unit of Indonesian developer PT Agung Podomoro Land Tbk., is seeking a further extension for its loan installments, and Fitch has downgraded its parent to restricted default. SsangYong Motor, the South Korean subsidiary of India's Mahindra & Mahindra, missed a loan repayment of around W60 billion ($55 million) to three banks. Meanwhile, Singapore Telecommunications' subsidiary Singtel Services Australia entered voluntary liquidation.

AS SOME LENDERS RETREAT, OTHERS APPROACH FRONTIER MARKETS

Toward the end of 2020, the market saw Taiwanese banks, under increased scrutiny from the Ministry of Finance, reviewing their participation in overseas syndicated loans amid growing signs of stress among mainland Chinese borrowers. The focus on overseas loans came after Zhaoheng Hydropower Holdings and luxury car dealer China ZhengTong Auto Services Holdings both missed repayments on loans that were syndicated to Taiwanese lenders and led by investment banks that ended up with no exposure to the borrower.

Dutch bank ABN AMRO Bank was also approaching lenders to offload its loan portfolio in Asia Pacific as it winds down its operations outside of northwest Europe. The bank is selling its corporate loan book in Asia Pacific and is bundling project finance loans in the region into parcels by countries.

While some banks are retreating into more domestic lending, others have been finding opportunities in smaller markets. In July 2020, Reliance Bangladesh LNG & Power raised a $642 million loan for a 718-megawatt natural gas combined cycle power plant in Bangladesh. The financing was provided by Japan Bank for International operation, Asia Development Bank, Mizuho Bank, MUFG, Société Générale, and Sumitomo Mitsui Banking Corp. The Vietnamese market saw volume of loans double from $3.9 billion in 2018 to an all-time high of $7.7 billion in 2019 after Moody's and Fitch upgraded the country's rating in 2018 and S&P followed suit in 2019. In 2020, Vietnam Technological & Commercial Joint-Stock Bank (Techcom Bank) raised a $500 million loan that received an overwhelming response from a syndicate of 19 banks. The lending group includes a diverse group of banks, including several Taiwanese, Chinese, and Singaporean banks.

CONCLUSION

As the Asia Pacific loan market evolves, it is likely to remain a heavily banked, refinancing driven, and China-linked market. The pandemic, an active bond market, and fewer China outbound investments resulted in 2020 loan volumes falling to an eight-year low. The secondary market activity in the region, though limited and driven mainly by market technicals and single names, continues to mature, and we expect it to be increasingly influenced by private debt investors and private equity sponsors in the future.

CHAPTER 16
Middle Market Lending

Fran Beyers
Managing Director
Cliffwater, LLC

INTRODUCTION

Up until about a decade ago, explaining a "middle market loan" to someone not in the lending business took a few tries. Most people easily understand and recognize giant publicly traded companies like Amazon, Microsoft, and Netflix. Additionally, most are equally familiar with the idea of small mom-and-pop businesses such as the local dry cleaners, pizzerias, and bagel stores. That said, in between the "large" and the "small" lies the backbone of the U.S. economy, often affectionately referred to as "the middle market."

There are estimated to be more than 200,000 middle market companies in the United States. These are not startups, but rather viable companies with sustainable business models that demonstrate strong growth and staying power through multiple cycles. These midsized businesses span almost all industries and are responsible for approximately 45 million American jobs and comprise roughly one-third of U.S. private sector gross domestic product (GDP).[1] While some middle market businesses are big enough to warrant being publicly traded entities, such as those companies included in the Russell 2000 Index, the vast majority remain private, family-owned, or sole proprietorship businesses with annual revenues below $100 million.

Small and medium-sized enterprises' access to the capital markets is not as efficient nor as deep as it is for larger companies. But what was once an underserved asset class that relied almost exclusively on bank financing to fuel growth has gained significant popularity and focus from institutional loan investors, asset managers, and pension funds in the last two decades.

CHARACTERISTICS OF A MIDDLE MARKET LOAN

Let us start first with understanding the definitions of the market because (all too often) a "middle market" loan may mean different things to different people because there is no definition that is universally accepted.

The National Center for the Middle Market, an authority on research in the U.S. middle market, pegs middle market businesses

---

[1] National Center for the Middle Market, "Middle Market Indicator Overview," available at https://www.middlemarketcenter.org/middle-market-indicator-overview.

as small as $10 million in annual revenue up to $1.0 billion. Some data providers limit middle market businesses to those that generate up to $500 million in revenues. Meanwhile, other information providers scope the market using different metrics altogether, such as loan commitment deal sizes, market capitalization, or even the number of employees.

But perhaps the most common way lenders size this market is in terms of earnings before interest, taxes, depreciation, and amortization (EBITDA), which is a proxy for cash flow in the loan market. Most market participants place a middle market issuer in the $5 to $50 million EBITDA range, but even as high as $100 million can still be considered middle market.

Definition matters because various segments of middle market lending can look very different in terms of issuance volume, pricing, structure, and terms and conditions.

Often lenders will delineate the middle market into "upper" versus "lower" when structuring and pricing deals. Upper middle market companies tend to have, at a minimum, approximately $25 million of EBITDA and up to as much as $75 to $100 million, whereas lower middle market issuers tend to have EBITDA of between $5 million and $25 million. Interestingly, the "middle" of the middle market has EBITDA of around $25 million.

Although EBITDA stands as the primary data point one considers in middle market lending, it is important to know that it numerically represents another important term—scale. The scale of the borrower plays a very important role in terms of the financing options available, the types of lenders willing to finance the borrower, and the structuring and pricing of the credit.

At the very small end of the lower middle market, at approximately $5 million to $15 million of EBITDA, financing options are quite limited, with only a subset of lenders willing to extend credit to an issuer of this size. That is because the smaller the issuer, the higher the perceived level of credit risk stemming from the company's business profile.

Common characteristics of credit risks found at the extreme lower end of the middle market can include, but are not limited to, high customer concentration, heavy reliance on just a few suppliers, narrow product offerings, lower barriers to entry, lack of geographical diversity, competitive pressures from larger, more-established competitors, and a higher vulnerability and volatility of cash flows due to exogenous events.

Often, lenders that extend credit to very small issuers will ask themselves, "Is there a reason for this company to exist?" given that lower middle market businesses can have a higher risk of failing during periods of economic turmoil due to their reduced scale and weaker market position.

To mitigate the higher level of business profile risk at the very low end of the middle market, lenders will underwrite and structure loan financings for these issuers at a more conservative level versus an upper middle market or large corporate issuer. Lenders will often require lower leverage levels, two to three financial maintenance covenants with tight cushions, greater amortization, very tight negative covenants, borrowing bases on working capital assets, a higher level of information flow from the management team of the borrower, and more frequent and onerous reporting requirements.

The incentive to extend credit to these smaller borrowers is that lenders will often receive a much higher level of compensation in the form of higher spreads, London Interbank Offered Rate (LIBOR) floors, and fees. The main lenders at the extreme lower end of the middle market typically include commercial banks, regional and national banks, mezzanine funds, SBIC Lenders (small business investment company), business development companies (BDCs), and smaller private credit platforms.

As a middle market issuer moves up the EBITDA size spectrum, the borrower-specific credit risks stemming from lack of scale and potentially weaker business profile ease. This affords lenders the ability to loosen up on the criteria governing the structure of the deal.

As a middle market issuer grows larger, the number of lenders willing to extend credit increases, creating a more issuer-friendly environment and more financing options for the borrower. For issuers with EBITDA in the $25 to $40 million range, lenders may only require one or two covenants, looser covenant cushions, and less-frequent reporting requirements. More lenient documentation terms that are often found within large corporate borrowers' credit agreements can also trickle into the credit documents of larger middle market issuers. Upper middle market issuers can also obtain higher leverage levels and tighter pricing, although sector and cash flow profile do matter greatly.

Once an issuer hits the $40 to $50 million EBITDA range and above, it is considered large enough to warrant obtaining a public rating, which unlocks even more financing options, including access to the institutional loan market. However, given that the rating agencies also view scale as one of the most important factors to obtaining a rating, most middle market issuers are generally capped in the level of corporate ratings they can achieve. Most middle market issuers that decide to obtain a public rating receive a corporate rating somewhere in the low- to mid-single-B area. But CCC can often be the outcome if lenders decide to structure the deal too aggressively from a financial leverage standpoint relative to the borrower's cash flow profile. And middle market borrowers have a higher chance of being downgraded to the CCC area if they exhibit subpar financial performance relative to bigger credits.

Given the meaningful degree of risk in receiving a CCC rating, which is an unfavorable outcome by most institutional investors' standards, most middle market issuers choose to stay in non-rated executions, driving over 90% to 95% of middle market loan volume each year. Those middle market issuers that decide to get a public rating and execute a loan financing via the institutional loan market are typically backed by a private equity sponsor and have the intent to scale the business longer term.

The incentive for a middle market borrower to tap the institutional loan market includes more issuer-friendly structures such as higher leverage levels, less onerous covenants, cheaper pricing, and looser documentation terms as opposed to what the typical direct lending executions would offer.

In all, there is a common balance to risk and return in the middle market lending spectrum that investors must be made aware of. Namely, as an issuer starts the early life cycle, investors work to price/protect against the limited scale an obligor has to fend off market downturns.

As the obligor increases in size and scale, the questions then shift—to less of a question on the underlying staying power of the fundamental business, but rather "is the price and structure of the loan" adequate for the risk the lender is taking in the structure (as well as the business)?

MIDDLE MARKET COMMERCIAL AND INDUSTRIAL LENDING

Just as the large corporate market is segmented into investment-grade lending and leveraged lending with very different borrower profiles, the middle market lending arena can be divided a similar way.

The commercial and industrial (C&I) lending market is more akin to investment-grade lending and is dominated by regional and commercial banks who extend credit to middle market businesses to help fuel financing needs such as for working capital, capital expenditures, refinancings, expansions, select mergers and acquisitions (M&A) financings, or other corporate purpose needs. This C&I lending market can also be called the non-sponsored lending market (meaning these management-owned businesses are not backed by a private equity owner) or the middle market corporate lending market.

Non-sponsored C&I lending is highly relationship oriented and can be regionally or nationally focused, but oftentimes smaller borrowers obtain financing with a bank in reasonable proximity to their business. As an example, data shows that banks in the southern part of the country may do a higher share of oil and gas lending compared to banks situated in the northeast. However, as an issuer grows larger, they often seek financing at a more national level, placing less focus on relationships and more focus on obtaining better terms.

Sizing this market can be very challenging given the difficulty in defining a middle market loan and tracking the data on private businesses. But to provide some perspective on the meaningful size of this market, the Federal Reserve looked at the top 30 banks in the United States in 2018 and concluded they held $549 billion in credit facilities to middle market issuers with annual revenue between $10 million and $250 million.[2]

For most smaller issuers, regional and commercial banks will typically hold the entire credit facility on their balance sheet, but as deal sizes grow larger, they often choose to syndicate the credit facility to a group of banks to help manage their credit exposure.

Refinitiv LPC, a loan data provider covering syndicated loan market trends, highlights that, depending on market conditions, anywhere from 500 to over 1,000 non-sponsored credit facilities are syndicated annually. As illustrated in Exhibit 16.1, this equates to annual volume ranging from as low as $60 billion to as high as

---

[2] Available at https://www.federalreserve.gov/econres/notes/feds-notes/are-there-competitive-concerns-in-middle-market-lending-20200810.htm

EXHIBIT 16.1

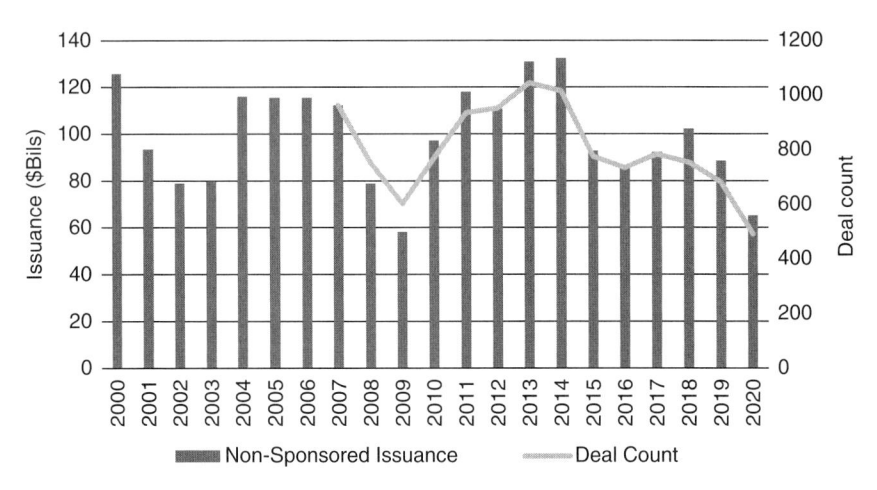

Non-Sponsored Syndicated Loan Issuance.

Source: Refinitiv LPC.

$130 billion per year (for issuers with revenue and a total loan commitment up to $500 million).[3]

Revolving lines of credit are the most common facility type in middle market non-sponsored lending, making up between 60% to 70% of syndicated new issue volumes each year, with term loans comprising a lesser 30% to 35% share of loan volumes.[3] Maturities on these facilities typically range between three and five years, with five years being the most common.

Due to the heavy relationship focus, high-quality non-sponsored issuers can obtain very affordable pricing from banks. The drawn spread over the benchmark rate (typically one- or three-month LIBOR) on non-sponsored loans can range anywhere from 100 basis points up to 400 basis points, with the 20+ year average residing at around 205 basis points, as illustrated in Exhibit 16.2. Because part of these facilities can remain undrawn, issuers typically pay an undrawn fee somewhere in the 12.5 to 50 basis points range on the amount of the commitment that is not being utilized.

When bankers are pricing credit facilities for middle market borrowers, they consider the amount of cross-selling opportunities

---

[3] Refinitiv LPC's "US Middle Market 2Q21 Review" available at: https://www.loanconnector.com/AnalyticDocDisplay/AnalyticDocContent?segmentId=5010&docTypeId=178&regionId=1

EXHIBIT 16.2

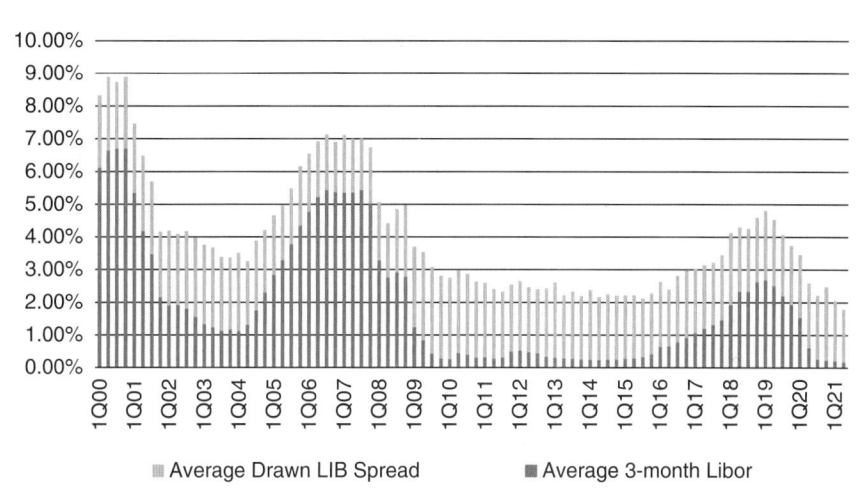

Non-Sponsored Yields (3-Month Libor + Drawn Spread).

■ Average Drawn LIB Spread   ■ Average 3-month Libor

Source: Refinitiv LPC.

an issuer might offer their institution, commonly referred to by bankers as "ancillary business." Ancillary business can include things like deposits, cash and treasury management, interest rate swaps, mortgages, and foreign currency hedging, etc. And for larger issuers, banks aspire to generate fees from capital markets services such as M&A advisory or debt and equity underwritings. However, the smaller the middle market company, typically the fewer ancillary business opportunities they present compared to a bigger company.

While banks have historically been the most common institution type to extend credit to non-sponsored borrowers, the market has seen more direct lenders compete in the space in recent years. Some management-owned businesses may decide to execute transactions that require high levels of leverage and might be a bit too risky for regulated banks' risk appetite, such as dividend recaps or management buyouts.

In those situations, family-owned businesses may seek out financing from direct lenders, business development companies, or mezzanine lenders, and these types of lenders will surely require pricing levels much higher than what a regulated bank would expect with first lien spreads ranging from 500 basis points up to as high as 800 basis points over LIBOR or even higher depending on market conditions and the underlying risks of the transaction.

SPONSORED OR PRIVATE EQUITY–BACKED LENDING

As private equity firms have raised unprecedented sums of capital over the past three decades, many middle market "non-sponsored" or "corporate" borrowers have been acquired and converted to "sponsored" borrowers. This is not in and of itself a bad thing, because (often) high-performing middle market companies and founders seek both capital and operating partners to enhance long-term value. Enter the middle market private equity sponsor . . . seeking a sponsor-backed loan. Middle market sponsor-backed loans look very different in terms of pricing, leverage levels, and structure, and hence overall credit risk relative to a non-sponsored or corporate borrower loan.

Sponsor-backed borrowers are akin to leveraged issuers in the broadly syndicated market, and regional banks have been constrained in their ability to participate in many of these financings due to heightened regulations and capital requirements.

The credit profile of these borrowers is largely unpalatable for most regional and commercial banks due to higher leverage levels, lower levels of amortization, looser documentation, and a more aggressive financial policy by the private equity owner. That said, you will find the other side of the coin is the higher-performing businesses that chose to seek financing outside of the bank ecosystem can offset what is seen to be as "higher leverage" with better business prospective/resilient models.

As a result, the primary buyers of sponsor-backed middle market loans have been yield-focused players such as direct lenders, mezzanine funds, finance companies, pension funds, collateralized loan obligations (CLOs), asset managers, insurance companies, and business development companies (BDCs). At the upper end of the middle market (EBITDA greater than $40 million), investment banks will compete head on with direct lenders for this business. However, few investment banks intend to hold these loans, but rather they employ an underwrite-to-distribute model, with the intention of earning fees on the deal execution and syndicating the loans to CLOs and other institutional loan buyers.

Sponsored lending is typically fueled by leveraged buyouts, tuck-in acquisitions, and dividend recapitalizations. In a leveraged buyout, enterprise or transaction multiples for middle market companies can range anywhere between 5 times EBITDA up to 20 times

EBITDA, but the most common multiple for a middle market company is in the 8 to 11 times area.

Historically (pre–Global Financial Crisis [GFC]), middle market businesses were purchased at lower multiples than larger corporate businesses, but that is just not the case anymore. Many middle market issuers illustrate high-growth and resilient business models, and sponsors can pay just as much or sometimes even more for these businesses relative to a large corporate company, depending on the sector and the level of competition for the asset. Private equity sponsors typically finance 40% to 60% of the purchase price with their own equity capital, and then will seek out debt financing for the remainder of the transaction value.

Unlike non-sponsored capital structures that are predominantly comprised of revolvers, debt financings backed by private equity firms have a much bigger funded term loan component with revolvers making up only a minority share of the M&A financing (somewhere between 5% and 20% of the total loan financing).

Given the popularity of tuck-in acquisitions in recent years, many sponsors will often include an unfunded delay draw term loan (DDTL) component to be utilized at a future date. The inclusion of these DDTLs gives the sponsor flexibility to execute a tuck-in acquisition with additional debt capital, without having to reopen the credit agreement and subject themselves to changing market conditions. Term loans are funded at close and typically have a 5- to 7-year maturity, while delay draw term loans are unfunded at close and are expected to be utilized within the first 3 to 36 months of the life of the deal.

Middle market borrowers backed by private equity sponsors typically have a handful of capital structure options available to them to finance acquisitions ranging from all first lien debt to a combination of senior and junior debt as illustrated in Exhibit 16.3.

Utilizing "first lien debt only" will require sponsors to put in higher levels of their own equity capital to finance a buyout of a middle market business. The interest rate on first lien term loans for private equity–backed issuers is significantly higher than the rates banks charge non-sponsored issuers for two main reasons.

First, the buyer base of middle market private equity–backed loans has a much higher cost of capital relative to banks because these buyers include private debt funds, asset managers, hedge funds, finance companies, pension funds, CLOs, and BDCs.

EXHIBIT 16.3

Capital Structure Options for a Hypothetical LBO at a 10x Valuation Multiple.

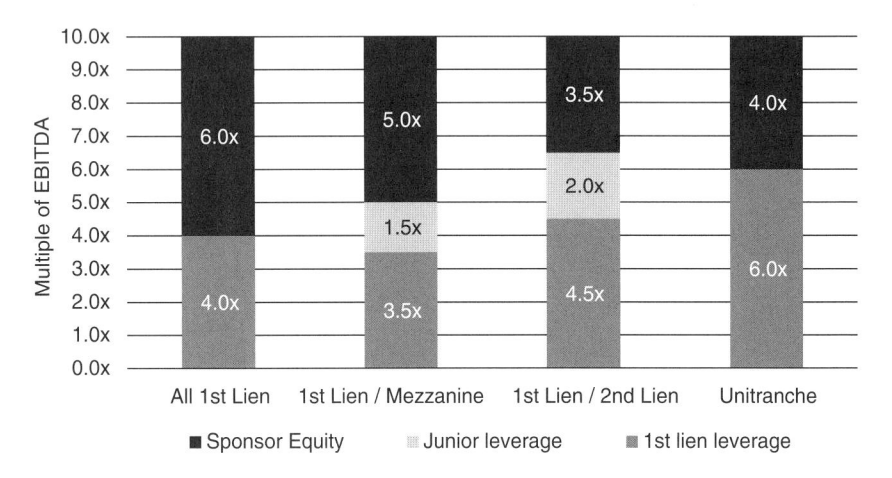

Structure	Sponsor Equity	Junior leverage	1st lien leverage
All 1st Lien	4.0x	—	6.0x
1st Lien / Mezzanine	5.0x	1.5x	3.5x
1st Lien / 2nd Lien	3.5x	2.0x	4.5x
Unitranche	4.0x	—	6.0x

Secondly, the credit risk increases due to the sophistication of the private equity shop owners coupled with a heavy funded debt burden. First lien pricing typically ranges between 400 basis points up to 600 basis points over LIBOR (one month or three months) with issuer size, credit risk, and market conditions playing an important role in how these loans are priced. Upper middle market issuers typically see first lien spreads over a benchmark rate in the 400 to 550 basis points range, whereas lower middle market issuers typically pay a higher spread over LIBOR in the 450 to 700 basis points range.

Sponsors that wish to lower their equity contribution may decide to layer junior capital beneath the first lien debt by incorporating either second lien or mezzanine financing into the mix. A sliver of second lien or mezzanine capital can add an additional one to two turns of leverage into the capital structure. But it will also increase the cost of capital for the sponsor as junior capital is surely more expensive than a first lien only capital structure.

Mezzanine debt is more often structured on lower middle market credits with an average EBITDA in the $20 to $30 million range or below, while second lien tranches are reserved for bigger issuers, with an average EBITDA closer to $40 to $50 million and above.

Mezzanine debt is a fixed rate instrument with all-in yields ranging between 10% and 15%. Often mezzanine facilities are structured with a heavy percentage of the interest paid at a cash rate (typically 10% to 12%) and a minor part of the yield generated from a paid-in-kind (PIK) component (1% to 3%). They are often structured as unsecured loans with no amortization requirements. Mezzanine lenders often ask the sponsor to share some of the equity upside with them to enhance their yield in the form of warrants or equity interests.

Meanwhile, second lien facilities are typically structured as floating rate instruments with average spreads around 750 to 950 basis points over LIBOR depending on market conditions. And second lien facilities often include a LIBOR floor in the 50 to 150 basis points area depending on market conditions, along with upfront fees or original issue discounts (OIDs) in the 50 to 300 basis points range (again depending on market conditions).

One of the newest capital structures to gain meaningful popularity over the last decade is the unitranche structure, which is an all first lien structure, but its leverage and pricing are reflective of a blend between a senior and junior structure. Consequently, the average blended spread on a "one stop" or "unitranche" financing ranges between 550 and 800 basis points.

The benefit of the unitranche is it allows lenders to earn an outsized yield while taking "first lien only" risk. Lenders are compensated with additional spread on this first lien loan not only because they are pushing leverage levels to more aggressive levels relative to a traditional first lien loan, but also because they are eliminating execution risk for the sponsor as these facilities are typically bilateral, clubbed up, or lightly syndicated with little flex built into the structure.

Quantifying the amount of sponsored middle market loan issuance closed each year has been an extremely challenging hurdle for lenders and investors. Unlike for the regulated bank universe, there is no central authority regularly collecting direct lending or private equity–backed loan data; however, some funding vehicles such as BDCs and middle market CLOs are required to follow regular and strict reporting requirements. Exhibit 16.4 highlights middle market–sponsored backed loan volume trends by tranche type collected by Refinitiv LPC. This offers some directional guidance; however, it is important to caveat that the data collection process is imperfect and incomplete in this market.

EXHIBIT 16.4

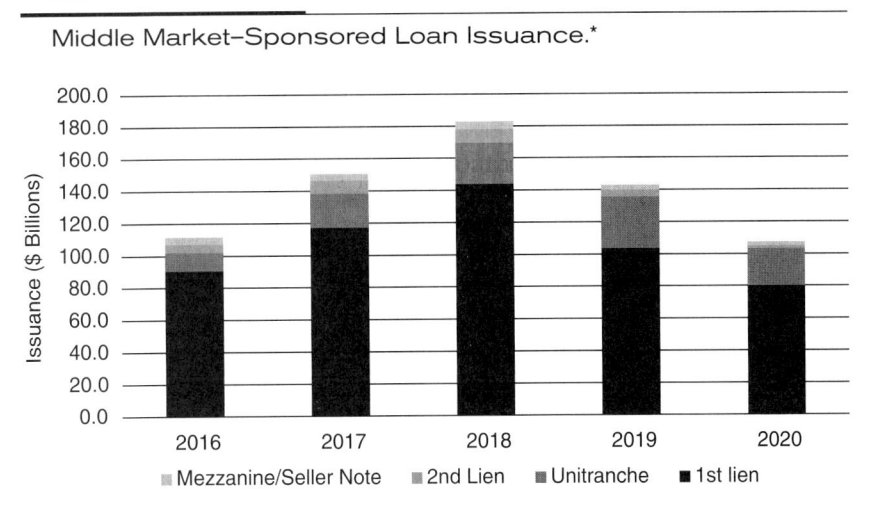

Middle Market–Sponsored Loan Issuance.*

Source: Refinitiv LPC.
*For issuers with revenue and deal sizes up to or equal to $500 million.

At the height the market back in 2018, it is estimated that over $180 billion in middle market–sponsored backed loans were closed.

Meanwhile, in Exhibit 16.5, Cliffwater LLC provides some insight on the different risk premiums and all-in yields earned on loans through time in the various market segments within the U.S. middle market.

BUSINESS DEVELOPMENT COMPANIES

One of the most prominent and visible lenders that were designed to support the growth and financing of middle market companies are business development companies, or BDCs. Congress created the BDC in 1980 through Section 54 of the Investment Company Act of 1940. Their predominant purpose is to lend to domestic small and medium-size businesses to help fuel job and business growth in the United States.

BDCs are closed-end investment vehicles registered with the Securities and Exchange Commission (SEC) and are required to have 70% of their assets invested in private companies or public U.S. firms with a market value of less than $250 million. Beginning in the early 2000s at under $10.0 billion in total assets, the universe has grown tremendously at a compound annual growth rate

EXHIBIT 16.5

Available Risk Premiums in Direct U.S. Middle Market Loans, June 2016 to June 2021.

Current Yield (LTM)	Jun-16	Sep-16	Dec-16	Mar-17	Jun-17	Sep-17	Dec-17	Mar-18	Jun-18	Sep-18	Dec-18	Mar-19	Jun-19	Sep-19	Dec-19	Mar-20	Jun-20	Sep-20	Dec-20	Mar-21	Jun-21
Second Lien, Subordinated Debt	4.2%	4.2%	3.8%	3.5%	3.0%	4.0%	3.3%	2.9%	2.5%	2.4%	1.8%	2.0%	2.1%	2.2%	2.5%	2.3%	2.2%	3.3%	2.5%	3.4%	
Directly Originated, Upper Middle Market	2.9%	2.9%	2.9%	2.4%	2.4%	2.7%	2.4%	1.9%	1.7%	1.6%	2.0%	1.9%	1.7%	1.9%	2.1%	1.8%	2.1%	2.2%	2.1%	2.0%	
Lower Middle Market	2.5%	2.5%	2.6%	2.7%	2.6%	3.0%	2.8%	2.4%	2.3%	2.3%	2.3%	2.4%	2.6%	2.1%	1.9%	2.2%	2.0%	1.9%	2.3%	2.0%	
Non-Sponsor Borrowers	1.5%	1.5%	1.6%	1.9%	2.1%	1.8%	2.4%	2.5%	2.4%	2.6%	2.3%	2.1%	1.8%	1.7%	1.8%	1.5%	1.7%	1.6%	2.0%	2.3%	
Broadly Syndicated Loans	4.8%	4.8%	4.7%	4.6%	4.4%	4.2%	4.0%	3.8%	3.7%	3.7%	3.8%	4.0%	4.1%	4.3%	4.6%	4.6%	4.3%	4.2%			
Risk-free Rate (T-bills)	0.2%	0.3%	0.3%	0.4%	0.5%	0.7%	0.9%	1.1%	1.4%	1.6%	1.9%	2.1%	2.3%	2.2%	2.0%	1.7%	1.2%	0.7%	0.7%	0.1%	0.1%

Source: Cliffwater, LLC.

EXHIBIT 16.6

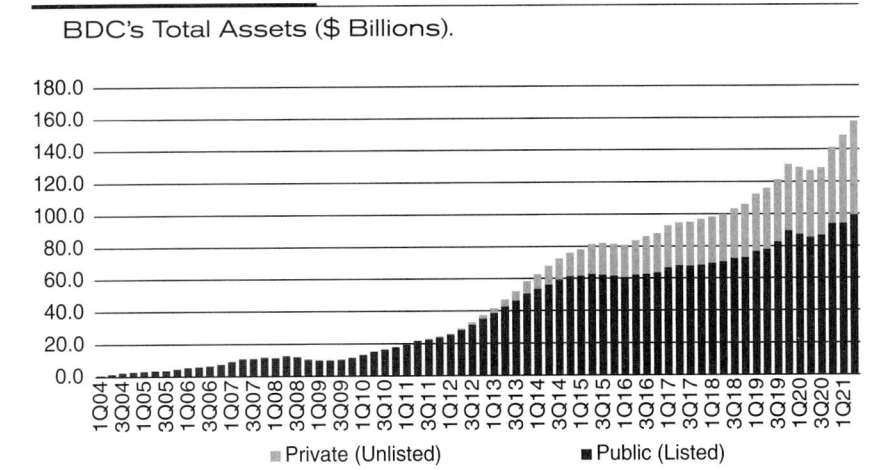

BDC's Total Assets ($ Billions).

■ Private (Unlisted)　■ Public (Listed)

Source: Cliffwater Direct Lending Index.

(CAGR) of 25%, with total assets reaching nearly $160 billion as of June 30, 2021 as illustrated in Exhibit 16.6.[4]

As of June 30, 2021, there were approximately 95 BDCs with active investment portfolios, with 46 being public entities listed on an exchange, offering shareholders daily liquidity, with the balance being unlisted or private (about 49 or so). Because public BDCs are considered permanent capital, the BDC universe typically grows over time. However, the universe of names is in constant flux because new private BDCs are launched every year and some managers may decide to merge their private vehicles into their listed vehicles to enhance size and trading liquidity. Furthermore, consolidation can occur in any given year, particularly after periods of market dislocations, with stronger managers acquiring weaker underperforming vehicles as the space continues to mature and become more efficient.

Public BDCs are popular among income-seeking retail investors because they produce annual dividend yields in the area of 8% to 12% depending on the risk profile of the manager/portfolios. These vehicles are treated as regulated investment companies, or RICs, and they must derive 90% of their income from dividends, interest, or capital gains. BDCs are required to pay out 90%-plus of their taxable

---

[4] Cliffwater, LLC. Cliffwater Direct Lending Index can be accessed via: http://www.cliffwaterdirectlendingindex.com/

income to shareholders, which allows for the benefit of being exempt from corporate income tax. They are similar to a real estate investment trust (REIT) or a master limited partnership (MLP), and the income is passed through to the shareholder, who will be taxed at the individual shareholder level.

BDCs can have anywhere from 25 to 325 different borrowers within their portfolio, depending on the manager's scale and how long the vehicle has been in existence. Some BDC vehicles are as small as a few hundred million in assets under management, while the biggest manager to date, Ares Capital, has as much as $18 billion in assets under management (as of June 30, 2021).

The average portfolio size across the landscape is around 90 to 100 portfolio companies and $1.6 billion in total assets.

According to Cliffwater, LLC, there are an estimated 7,000 unique borrowers being financed by BDCs, with the vast majority being smaller, middle market borrowers, although they can selectively lend to larger borrowers, too.[5]

As the middle market landscape continues to evolve, it is clear that business development companies are an important source of debt and equity funding for middle market companies. Much of their lending is tied to sponsored-backed deals, but some BDCs also elect to have a minority share of their focus on non-sponsored lending.

HISTORY AND EVOLUTION OF MIDDLE MARKET LENDING

While middle market lending gained meaningful visibility in the news and media following the GFC due to the massive growth of private credit, the reality is that middle market lending has been around for a very long time. Long-standing and well-respected life mutual insurance companies began the private lending practice as early as the 1950s as they found the yield premiums well worth the limited increase in obligor risk.

Yet it is without question that banks were the most prominent lenders to small- and medium-size businesses, and it was not until the 1990s that a visible shift began, and banks started to pull back from middle market lending.

An easing of state and federal restrictions on banks in the mid-1990s from regulations such as the Riegle-Neal Act and the

---

[5] Cliffwater's 2021 Q2 Report on U.S. Direct Lending, http://www.bdcs.com/

Financial Services Modernization Act resulted in an unprecedented wave of consolidation in the banking sector.

According to the Federal Deposit Insurance Corporation (FDIC), in 1990 there were 12,351 FDIC-insured commercial banks in the United States, and by the mid-2000s that number had decreased to 7,524. Fast-forwarding to 2020, the number was even lower at 4,430, a 64% drop compared to 30 years ago when consolidation began to accelerate. In fact, the top 10 bank holding companies in the United States account for nearly two-thirds of the $21.1 trillion in total assets held by U.S. banks.

As banks gained scale over the years, much of their lending focus gravitated toward bigger issuers who offered greater amounts of ancillary business, fee generation, and overall return profitability. But with middle market businesses reliant on loan financing for their survival and growth, it created an opportunity in the marketplace for new players to step in and fill the void.

In the early 2000s, the "institutionalization" of the syndicated loan market and rapid growth of the securitization market helped fuel more interest in middle market loans. The rapid growth of institutional players such as CLOs, hedge funds, BDCs, mezzanine lenders, and small direct lending platforms all created incremental interest in middle market borrowers.

Middle market loans offered richer pricing to compensate investors for smaller scale and a lack of liquidity in the secondary loan market. Drawn to the higher yield compared to what was being offered in the broadly syndicated market, investors began to dip down market and add these smaller credits to their portfolios. However, at the time, questions and concerns remained around trading liquidity and credit resiliency because few of these investors had evidence of how smaller loans would perform in a downturn situation. The benefits and drawbacks of adding middle market credits to a typical leveraged loan portfolio can be seen in Exhibit 16.7.

Trends that were more typical for the broadly syndicated market quickly started to become more accepted for middle market borrowers. For example, middle market CLO issuance accelerated, summing up to $73 billion between 2003 and 2007, compared to only $14 billion between 1999 and 2002.[6]

---

[6] Wells Fargo Securities LLC & Refinitiv LPC. "MM Weekly – Middle Market CLOs". (March 12, 2021). www.loanconnector.com

EXHIBIT 16.7

Middle Market Lending vs. Broadly Syndicated Lending	
Benefits to the loan investor	**Drawbacks to the loan investor**
Higher pricing	Business profile risk can be greater
Tighter structures, lower leverage levels	Smaller scale of the issuer
More documentation protections	Less resilient in downturn situations
Tighter financial/maintenance covenants	Limited trading liquidity
More negotiation power over terms/conditions	Weaker ratings, if at all
Direct access to management teams	Harder to access public information
Smaller bank groups	Lenders need origination capability
Higher recoveries/lower losses	Heavier due diligence required

The birth of middle market second liens began in 2003 with $34 billion issued between 2004 and 2007, and a true sign of frothy times was evident when the first "covenant-lite" middle market loan was syndicated in 2006.[7]

Private equity's growing interest in these smaller companies was a key driver to create a supply of middle market assets to feed these institutional investors. Between 2002 and 2008, also known at the time as the "buyout boom," private equity sponsors raised nearly $900 billion dollars in equity capital.[8]

While news headlines were dominated by massive mega-leveraged buyouts (LBOs) for issuers such as Clear Channel Entertainment, Harrah's Entertainment, First Data Corporation, and Energy Future Holdings (aka TXU), most of the private equity firms out raising money at the time were too small to partake in these mega-buyout financings. The reality is that roughly 70% to 80% of LBO financings executed in the syndicated market during the buyout boom years by deal count were for middle market issuers.

Sponsors recognized that middle market businesses were exhibiting faster growth trajectories and clearly required less equity dollars given lower transaction values relative to large-cap businesses, making them extremely enticing targets. Furthermore, sponsors acquired middle market businesses to fuel bolt-on

---

[7] Refinitiv LPC. "Middle Market Historical Data: US MM Second Lien Loan Volume & Covenant-Lite Volume." www.loanconnector.com
[8] Refinitiv LPC. "Historical Data: US Private Equity Fundraising." www.loanconnector.com

EXHIBIT 16.8

U.S. Middle Market Inventory of Currently PE-backed Companies.*

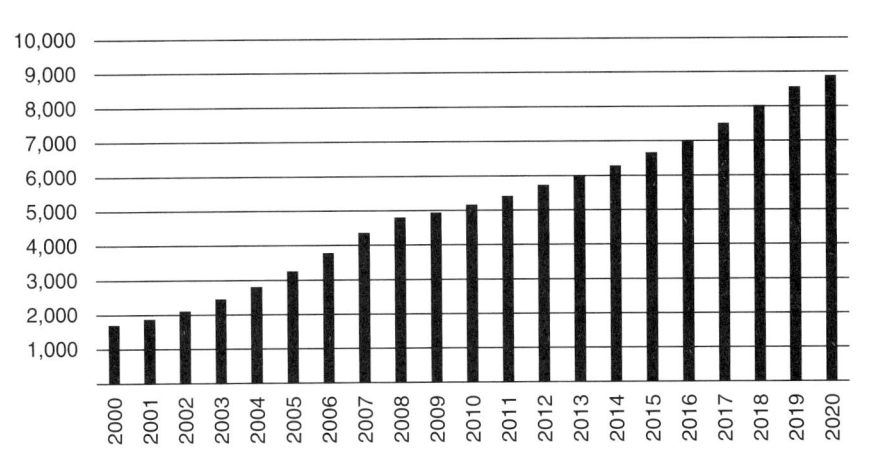

Source: Pitchbook.
*For companies with revenues between $25 million to $1.0 billion.

acquisitions, effectively integrating a smaller business into another portfolio business to create synergies, scale, and ultimately boost exit multiples.

According to data from Pitchbook, the inventory of U.S. middle market companies (with revenues of $25 million up to $1.0 billion) backed by private equity shops grew from roughly 1,700 in the year 2000 to over 4,800 by 2008, a 14% CAGR. And this trend only accelerated in the years following the GFC with the number rising to nearly 8,900 by 2020 as evidenced by Exhibit 16.8.

When the buyout boom came to a screeching halt in the years 2008 through 2009 due to the GFC, middle market issuers were certainly not immune to the volatility felt in the institutional loan market. Many institutional players that dipped down, such as hedge funds and CLOs, learned a valuable lesson that middle market loans certainly were not liquid and should be treated as "buy and hold" assets.

On a positive note, many market participants took notice at how well middle market loans performed from a default and loss perspective, despite their smaller scale. Lower leverage levels, tight covenants, smaller bank groups, and tighter structures all proved to be helpful mitigants in navigating a business through a downturn,

EXHIBIT 16.9

12-Month Default Rate Across Asset Classes.

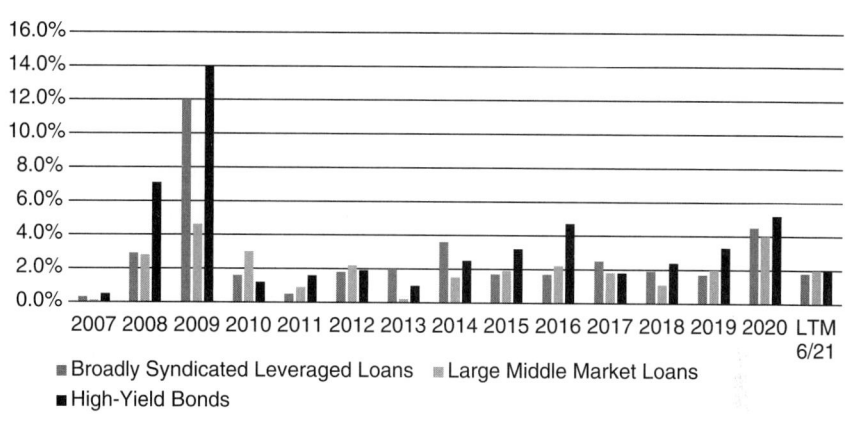

- Broadly Syndicated Leveraged Loans
- Large Middle Market Loans
- High-Yield Bonds

Source: Fitch Ratings.

while many larger deals quickly became over-levered and unruly in workout scenarios due to large banks groups and covenant-lite structures.

Defaults on both broadly syndicated leveraged loans and high-yield bonds skyrocketed to 12% and 14%, respectively, in 2009, while "upper" middle market credits illustrated more subdued default statistics, peaking at under 5%, as illustrated in Exhibit 16.9. However, it is important to caveat that this data was tracked on larger middle market issuers toward the upper end of the EBITDA spectrum.

Following this tumultuous period in the broader financial markets, government agencies responded by passing regulations such as the Dodd-Frank Act to help limit future bailouts, and they refined rules such as Leveraged Lending Guidance to limit excessive risk taking within the banking system.

While the intent of these onerous regulations was never to curtail middle market borrowers' access to bank financing, these tighter lending standards and higher capital requirements placed on the banks did make middle market lending a less-attractive investment, particularly for higher levered transactions such as private equity–backed M&A financings.

Many experienced and talented bankers hamstrung by these new regulations fled banking institutions to start up new direct lending platforms or joined existing ones that had made it through the GFC still intact.

The decade following the GFC, characterized by low interest rates and fewer yield opportunities globally and across markets, incentivized pension funds, insurance companies, endowments, sovereign wealth funds, and high net-worth family offices to look beyond traditional investment strategies to new alternatives. And so begins the birth of a new era and asset class within the loan market called private credit, or direct lending.

CHAPTER 17
Private Credit

KKR & Co. Inc.

INTRODUCTION

Private credit most commonly takes the form of illiquid debt financing entered into via directly negotiated agreements between borrowers and lenders. Private credit managers raise capital from institutional and high net worth investors to source and make direct investments in debt issued by borrowers rather than participating in a broad syndication managed by an agent, such as a bank. As a result, typical private credit deals are closely held by one or several lenders compared to dozens of lenders in a bank-led syndicated deal. As a result, private credit debt is not issued nor traded publicly. Based on the illiquid nature of these investments, private credit instruments are often higher-yielding, generate an illiquidity premium, and can cover a range of risk and return profiles.

Private credit lenders typically retain additional structuring advantages over syndicated deals and are often able to negotiate enhanced protections, including seniority, specified collateralization, preventative or restrictive covenants, early repayment and nonpayment penalties, and board representation. Summary terms across private and public markets are illustrated in Exhibit 17.1.

EVOLUTION OF PRIVATE CREDIT

Prior to the Global Financial Crisis (GFC) of 2008, the primary providers of debt capital to the middle market included national and regional banks, specialty finance companies, collateralized loan obligation (CLO) issuers, investment banks (often through proprietary trading desks), and hedge funds. Concurrently, the securitization boom catered powerfully to nonbanks' "originate-to-distribute" model, allowing these institutions to efficiently access debt investments despite having limited capitalization. More relaxed risk frameworks, including friendly off-balance sheet treatments, meant that banks also took exposure to riskier lending segments, often as the ultimate buyers of repackaged specialty credit.

The GFC and factors that played out in its aftermath marked a dramatic end to this chapter, setting private credit up for transformation and growth over the past decade. The policy response in ensuing years proved relentless, ranging from

EXHIBIT 17.1

	Private Credit			Public Markets			
	Senior	Subordinated	Noncorporate	Bank Loans	High-Yield Bonds	Investment Grade Bonds	Structured Credit
Issuer Overview	Small to mid-sized corporates	Small to mid-sized corporates	Asset-based	Larger corporates	Larger corporates	Larger corporates	Varied
Fixed / Floating Rate	Floating	Fixed or floating	Fixed or floating	Generally floating	Generally fixed	Fixed or floating	Fixed or floating
Public Ratings	Nonrated	Nonrated	Nonrated	Rated	Rated	Rated	Rated
Capital Structure Position	Senior	Junior	Varies	Senior	Senior or Junior	Senior	Varied
Security	Secured (on first- or second-lien basis)	Unsecured	Varies	Secured (on first- or second-lien basis)	Secured (on first- or second-lien basis) or unsecured	Generally unsecured	Varied
Liquidity	Illiquid	Illiquid	Illiquid	Large and liquid market	Large, liquid, and transparent market	Large, liquid, and transparent market	Varied, generally less liquid

full-scale tightening of regulatory rulebooks to higher capital requirements and tighter guidelines on risk-taking and governance (e.g., the Volcker Rule in the United States and Basel III in Europe). The resulting derisking pressure forced banks to focus on narrower, commoditized lending segments underpinned by regimented underwriting, all of which excluded large segments of corporate and noncorporate borrowers. Furthermore, the securitization market's implosion triggered by the credit contagion from subprime U.S. mortgages enabled nonbank capital to take an even greater share of the private asset–based finance markets (i.e., private credit backed by large, diversified pools of hard and financial assets). As illustrated in Exhibit 17.2, the U.S. primary broker-dealer securities inventory has declined over 90% since the end of 2007 to year-end 2020, and bank loan holdings have seen a similar trend.

This reduction in lending capacity has had an impact on the ability and willingness of banks to provide financing, and, as a result, banks have gradually migrated the focus of their lending businesses to sizable, broadly syndicated debt financings of large corporate issuers whose risk can be distributed to the market with more ease. In the middle market, corporate borrowers typically

EXHIBIT 17.2

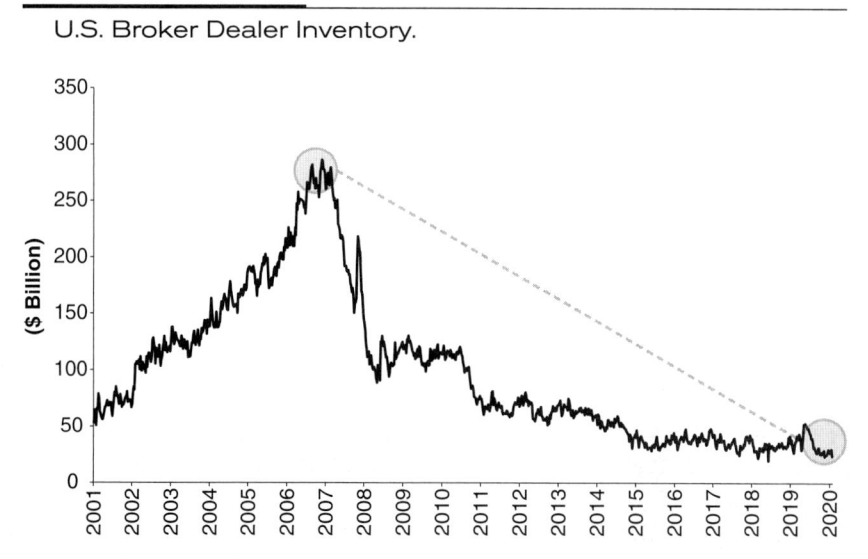

U.S. Broker Dealer Inventory.

Source: Federal Reserve Bank of New York, Haver Analytics. Data December 31, 2020.

are not large enough to warrant the focus of the capital markets desks of large national and regional banks. The smaller size of these corporates, coupled with the fact that they often do not have credit ratings, can require additional time and costs for banks to due diligence, making lending to these borrowers less appealing to banks.

As a result, nonbank lenders have stepped into this lending gap and now represent a significant share of the lending market. Standard and Poor's (S&P) estimates that nonbank lenders provide approximately 86% of leveraged loans in the United States. Furthermore, private credit as an asset class has increased more than 3.5 times since 2008, and as of June 30, 2020 stands at over $880 billion in assets under management globally as illustrated in Exhibits 17.3 and 17.4.[1]

Today, many middle market companies are left with limited financing options, providing an opportunity for private credit. On occasion, even larger-cap corporates face limited public market access—for example, more complex situations such as corporate carve-outs—further increasing the need for private credit. Given the relative illiquidity of these investments, providing private credit capital requires skilled managers who have the capabilities to source, diligence, negotiate, execute, and monitor these transactions.

Although hedge funds have remained active in this space throughout and following the GFC, they typically play a less meaningful role in the smaller and more illiquid segment of the market due to lack of origination capabilities and the liquidity needed for open-ended fund structures and periodic redemption requirements. Furthermore, certain previously active specialty finance companies have either contracted their lending activity or exited their lending businesses completely, which we believe has further exacerbated the lending gap, particularly in the United States and Europe. This, together with the increased depth of resources needed, has driven increased scale and consolidation in the private credit market, as witnessed by the increase in mergers and acquisitions among the business development companies (BDCs).

BDCs have emerged as a significant source of private credit capital in the United States. BDCs are a type of company regulated

---

[1] Data from Preqin as of June 30, 2020, data accessed March 16, 2021.

EXHIBIT 17.3

Leveraged Loan Primary Investor Market.

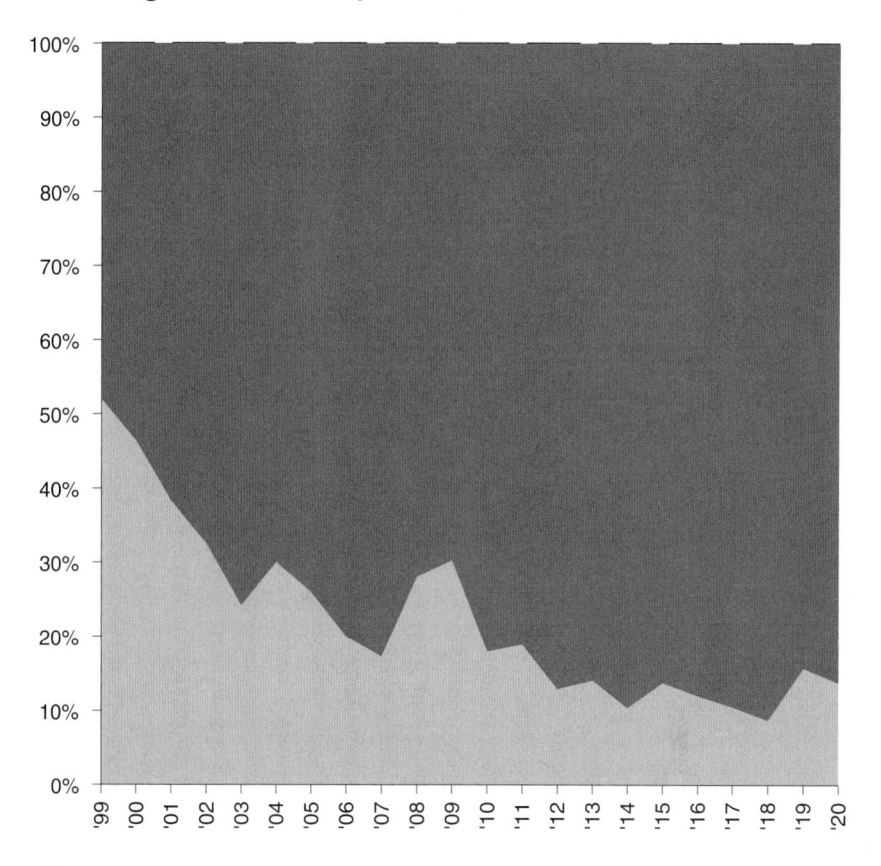

■ Non-Banks (institutional investors and finance companies)
■ Banks & Sec. Firms

Source: S&P Intelligence, as of December 31, 2020.

by the U.S. Securities and Exchange Commission (SEC) that primarily invest in the debt of small and mid-cap companies and frequently are subject to minimum distribution requirements. BDCs are limited in the amount of capital they can provide to noncorporates as well as non-U.S. companies driven by Investment Company Act–mandated investment guidelines. CLOs have also ramped up on loan assets. However, the relatively short investment timeline typical of these vehicles generally requires them to focus on liquid lending opportunities. As such, despite the increase in

EXHIBIT 17.4

Global Private Credit Assets Under Management.

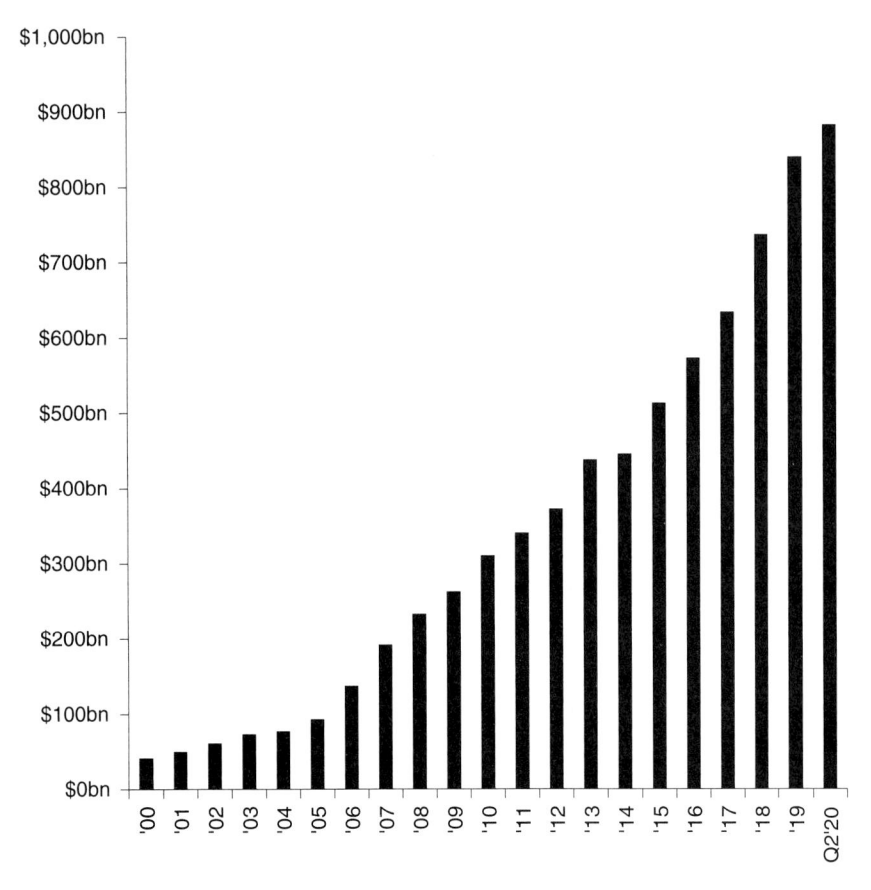

Source: Preqin as of June 30, 2020, data accessed March 16, 2021.

private credit providers over the past 10 years, there continues to be strong demand from corporate and noncorporate borrowers for direct lending solutions. The evolution of middle market lending capital providers is illustrated in Exhibit 17.5.

PRIVATE CREDIT LANDSCAPE

Private credit has grown to be a large, diverse asset class over the last 10 years. Today, private credit is used by a number of borrower types to meet a variety of needs.

EXHIBIT 17.5

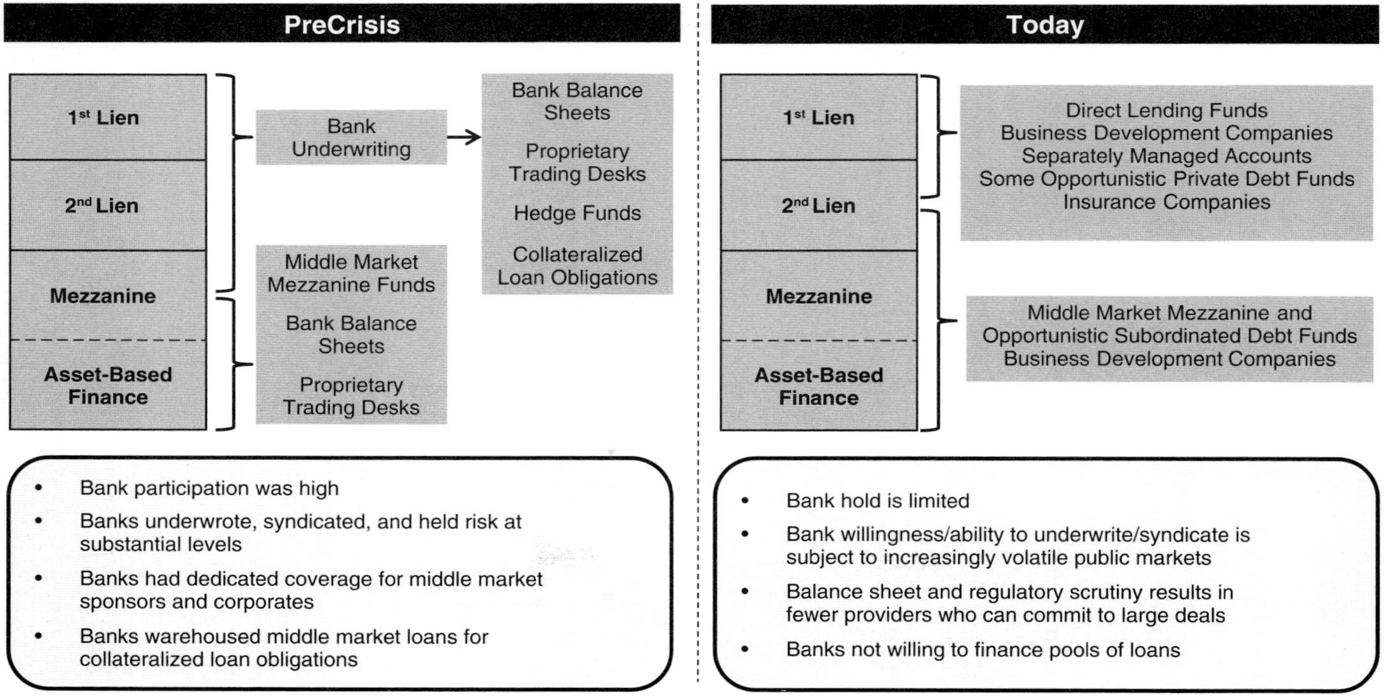

PreCrisis

- 1st Lien
- 2nd Lien
  - Bank Underwriting → Bank Balance Sheets, Proprietary Trading Desks, Hedge Funds, Collateralized Loan Obligations
- Mezzanine
  - Middle Market Mezzanine Funds, Bank Balance Sheets, Proprietary Trading Desks
- Asset-Based Finance

- Bank participation was high
- Banks underwrote, syndicated, and held risk at substantial levels
- Banks had dedicated coverage for middle market sponsors and corporates
- Banks warehoused middle market loans for collateralized loan obligations

Today

- 1st Lien
- 2nd Lien
  - Direct Lending Funds, Business Development Companies, Separately Managed Accounts, Some Opportunistic Private Debt Funds, Insurance Companies
- Mezzanine
  - Middle Market Mezzanine and Opportunistic Subordinated Debt Funds, Business Development Companies
- Asset-Based Finance

- Bank hold is limited
- Bank willingness/ability to underwrite/syndicate is subject to increasingly volatile public markets
- Balance sheet and regulatory scrutiny results in fewer providers who can commit to large deals
- Banks not willing to finance pools of loans

Note: Provided for illustrative purposes only. Summarizes non-syndicated sources of capital.

Although often thought of as middle market lending or SME (small and medium-sized enterprises) lending, the increased scale of direct lenders has allowed them to evolve from working primarily in simple club deals executed on best efforts basis in sub $50 million EBITDA companies into influential market players who can lead committed deals in excess of $1 billion.

From a credit exposure point of view, exposure ranges from corporates to noncorporates. While private credit has historically been associated with directly originated and negotiated senior and subordinated corporate lending (i.e., direct lending and corporate mezzanine debt), the retreat of banks over the past decade has had an equally profound impact on noncorporate activity, a segment that comprises a large portion of the global capital markets and economy. Directly originated, noncorporate lending encompasses a broad range of industries and financing types that some refer to as *asset-based finance*.

Much like leveraged lending is to corporates, asset-based finance is the lifeblood of millions of businesses and consumers globally, financing day-to-day operations and lives through mortgages, credit cards, receivables financing, consumer installment loans, automobile financing, and equipment leasing, to name a few. As a result, private asset–based finance is estimated to be a $4.5 trillion market, approximately one and a half times larger than its estimated size in 2007 of approximately $3.1 trillion.[2] From 2021–2026, private asset–based finance is estimated to grow over 50% from $4.5 trillion today to $6.9 trillion.[3]

In the case of corporates, repayments typically rely on cash flows generated by the operations of the underlying company. In the case of asset-based finance, repayments typically rely on the cash flows generated by the underlying physical or financial asset. These noncorporate financings may include, but are not limited to, aircraft, royalties, renewables, real estate development, and consumer finance sectors such as mortgages and auto loans.

---

[2] Represents the global stock of private financial assets originated and held by nonbanks related to household (including mortgages) and business credit. It excludes loans securitized or sold to agencies and assets acquired in capital markets or via other secondary/syndicated channels. Data are from Integer Advisors and KKR research estimates based on shadow banking data from the Financial Stability Board.
[3] Data from Integer Advisors.

There are many types of transactions for which private credit capital may be used, with the primary types of activities summarized below:

- Private equity/sponsor-driven buyouts
- Refinancings
- Capital expenditures/growth
- Mergers and acquisitions
- General corporate purposes
- Dividend recapitalizations

Furthermore, there are numerous strategies under the private credit umbrella generally categorized as "capital preservation" or "return maximization." Capital preservation strategies, such as sponsor-focused senior debt and mezzanine funds, seek to deliver predictable returns, primarily in the form of current income, while protecting against losses. Return maximizing strategies include distressed corporate credit funds focused on capital appreciation, typically in the form of equity upside potential.

In addition, some strategies straddle a few different categories, such as opportunistic strategies (i.e., investing across the credit spectrum as market opportunities permit), as well as niche and specialty strategies, such as aviation finance, healthcare royalties, and supply chain financing.

PRIVATE CREDIT STRUCTURAL CONSIDERATIONS

Although characterized as bespoke financing specific to each opportunity, there are certain structural features that are common in private credit, including the security package, structural seniority (in the form of a single tranche or first and second secured term loans), floating rate or fixed rate, contractual yield, amortization and call protection, financial covenant protections, company financial reporting requirements, and management access.

Covenant-lite structures have been on the rise in the syndicated market over the last several years as illustrated in Exhibit 17.6; however, direct lenders have largely been able to hold the line on structural protections and negotiate protective covenant packages

Covenants generally fall into two categories: maintenance and incurrence. Maintenance covenants are tested on a recurring

EXHIBIT 17.6

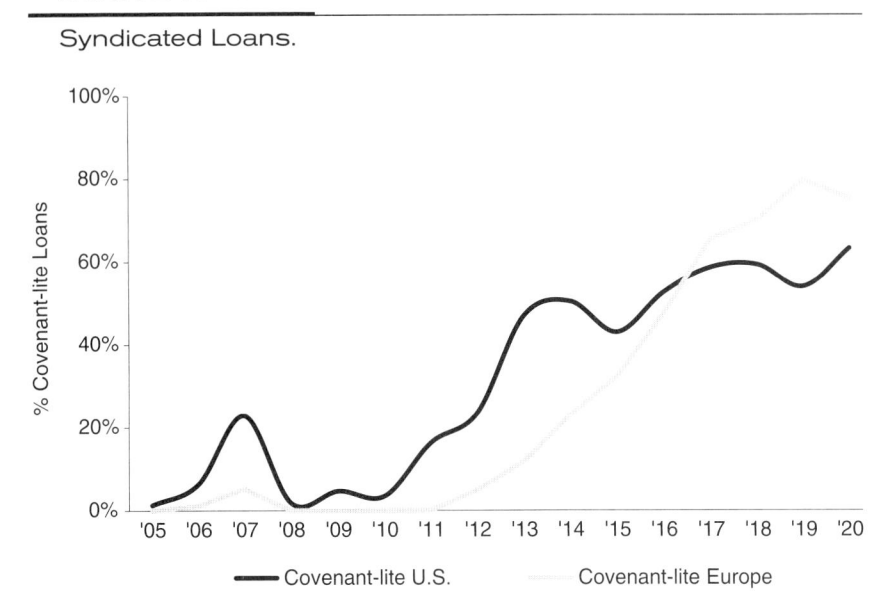

Syndicated Loans.

Source: S&P LCD as of December 31, 2021.

basis, whereas incurrence covenants are tested for a predefined event. For example, leverage maintenance covenants are oftentimes tested quarterly against a determined debt-to-EBITDA ratio. On the other hand, a borrower may not be able to incur additional debt if the debt-to-EBTIDA ratio is above a certain threshold. As such, incurrence covenants are only tested when the borrower considers incurring additional debt. In both cases, covenants provide a way for lenders to proactively monitor the performance of borrowers. Importantly, covenants provide early warning signs to lenders and allow them to quickly get involved with borrowers to help mitigate credit deterioration. Covenant breaches can also act as a way to extract additional value in the form of amendment fees or as a way to reengage with management to tighten documentation.

From a return perspective, although less frequent in senior term loans and more common in subordinated structures, features may include warrants or other equity-linked structures that provide upside potential to alternative lenders should a company or asset outperform. That said, the lion's share of private credit returns is contractual in nature and is structured as a combination of coupon, paid-in-kind (PIK), and upfront transaction fees, as illustrated in Exhibit 17.7.

EXHIBIT 17.7

Illustrative Components of Return.

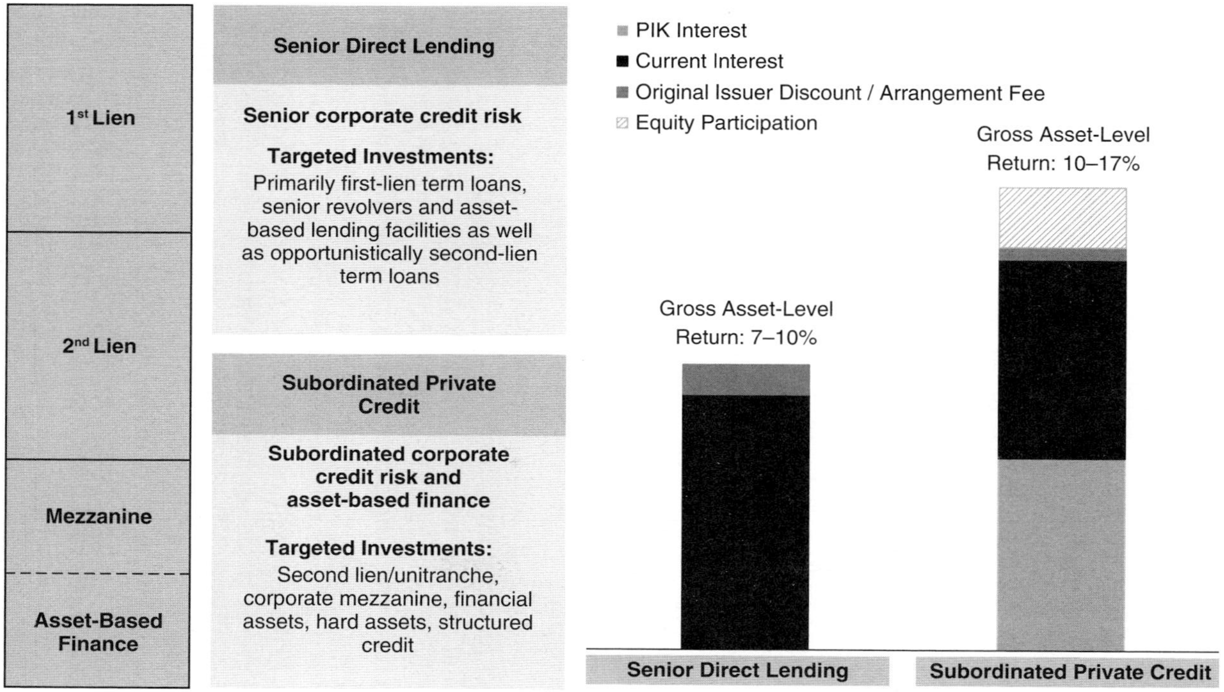

Senior Direct Lending

Senior corporate credit risk

Targeted Investments:
Primarily first-lien term loans, senior revolvers and asset-based lending facilities as well as opportunistically second-lien term loans

Subordinated Private Credit

Subordinated corporate credit risk and asset-based finance

Targeted Investments:
Second lien/unitranche, corporate mezzanine, financial assets, hard assets, structured credit

- 1st Lien
- 2nd Lien
- Mezzanine
- Asset-Based Finance

Legend:
- PIK Interest
- Current Interest
- Original Issuer Discount / Arrangement Fee
- Equity Participation

Gross Asset-Level Return: 7–10% — Senior Direct Lending

Gross Asset-Level Return: 10–17% — Subordinated Private Credit

BENEFITS OF PRIVATE CREDIT

There are many reasons why a sponsor or company may choose an alternative to traditional bank or public market financing. In general, private credit financing is bespoke in nature and can provide borrowers execution ease, speed, and certainty, especially in times of broader market volatility.

Private credit can be customized to meet companies' growth needs. In these instances, delayed-draw term loans can act as a committed solution for future add-on acquisitions. Although the syndicated market has added growth agreement provisions to allow for future acquisitions, the company takes the risk of raising those future funds, relying on uncertain markets for both additional capital and pricing at that time. Therefore, banks typically are limited in their ability to provide growth capital. In these instances, direct lenders have a critical competitive advantage in their ability to provide delayed-draw term loans that are committed upfront and can be drawn subject to certain agreed upon provisions being met. The flexibility in structure has led to large corporates who have access to cheaper syndicated financing to opt into private credit solutions given efficiency and certainty of financing that better suits future growth plans.

As private credit has evolved over the past decade, some large direct lenders have developed in-house capital markets expertise. Capital market teams are able to underwrite a transaction alongside the direct lender to provide holistic financing across the capital structure, including providing a private mezzanine solution coupled with leading a syndicated senior financing, as well as committing to hold and anchor an entire tranche.

Private credit can also offer speedier execution because private credit deals often do not require preparation of confidential information memoranda or other marketing materials. The elimination of the marketing period leads to a more streamlined process. Given the bilateral nature of these transactions, a borrower is able to interface with a small group of direct lenders, which provides certainty of pricing and terms, unlike flex provisions present in the syndicated markets. Although private credit is generally less competitive than indicative pricing on a syndicated solution, the ultimate pricing can be competitive to the fully flexed syndicated provisions.

From an investor point of view, private credit has emerged over the past decade as a core allocation in many investment portfolios. As greater financial regulation, coupled with bank deleveraging and derisking, continues to reshape the global capital markets, we have continued to witness an attractive illiquidity premium emerge in the fixed income markets. Senior and subordinated private lending strategies have delivered a 250 to 450 basis point average spread over the public markets since 2007, as illustrated in Exhibit 17.8. From a structural standpoint, covenant-lite loans have become increasingly more prevalent in the syndicated markets. In comparison, private credit investments are typically characterized by highly negotiated, customized, private transactions with the potential for robust, negotiated covenant packages and, in some instances, carry enhanced governance rights, such as board seats. In addition, because private credit instruments are illiquid and typically held to maturity, they face substantially less price volatility than actively traded public loans and securities. Given the liquid nature of the assets underlying the traded market indices and the numerous market makers, as well as exchanges who supply quotes, the traded market indices tend to be much more volatile, resulting in a higher standard deviation of returns.

CONSIDERATIONS LOOKING AHEAD

There are many considerations looking ahead for private credit, including portfolio monitoring resources; specialized industry expertise; governance and workout resources; and environmental, social, and governance (ESG) factors, to name a few.

As the industry matures, experience levels throughout business cycles, deep industry expertise, and a focus on credit risk management are essential. Seeing early warning signs of underperformance could be the difference between helping a borrower navigate through a difficult time and working through a default scenario. The ability to step in early will be driven by a direct lender's portfolio monitoring resources and, more important, the predetermined triggers in place, such as covenants set at appropriate levels, to drive the borrower and lender back to the table to help a company navigate through a challenging moment in time. This element has proven out through the 2020 COVID-19 pandemic cycle where covenant structures drove constructive discussions, with

EXHIBIT 17.8

Senior Originated Debt Illiquidity Premium and Subordinated Debt Illiquidity Premium.

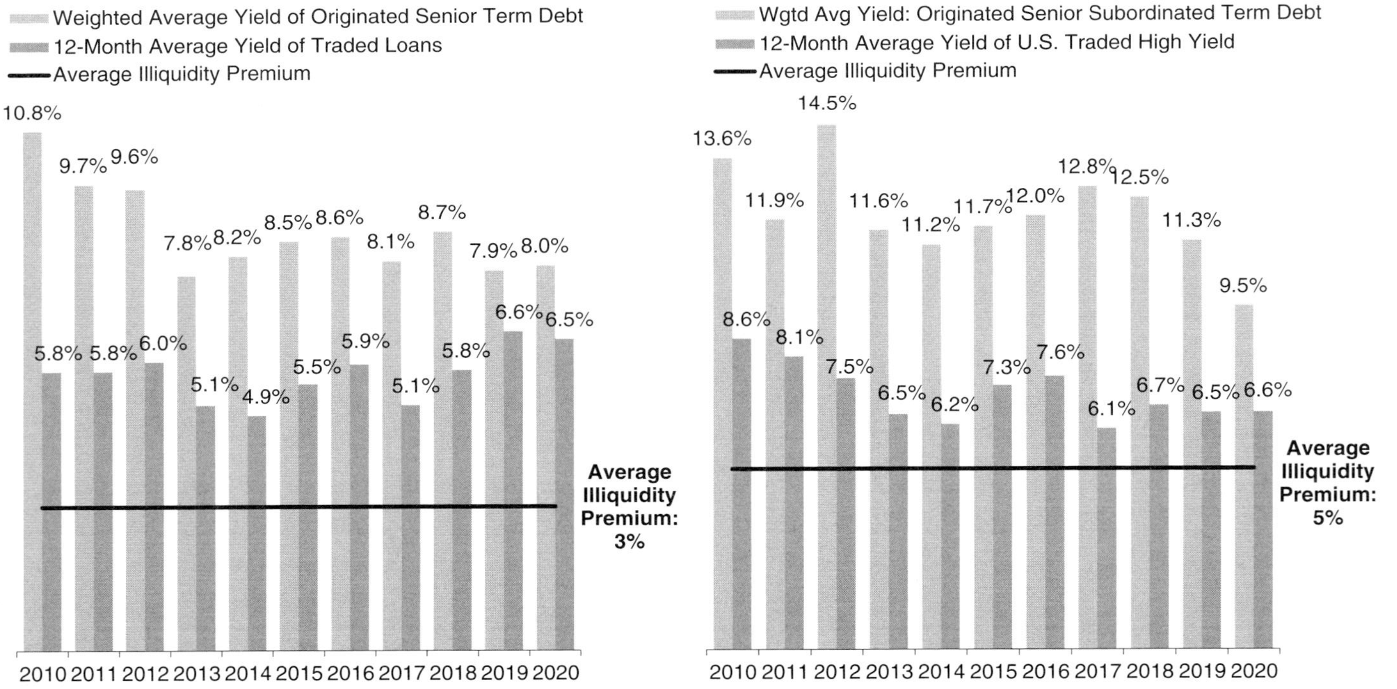

Source: Data as of December 31, 2020. Originated senior and subordinated term debt weighted average yields from ARCC quarterly filings. Traded loans yields from S&P LSTA Loans Index and US traded high yield from BAML High Yield Index.

sponsors contributing additional capital to support businesses. In the event of a stressed situation, a direct lender may find itself owning the underlying asset; in such situations, the build out of workout and governance resources will be crucial.

Importantly, ESG will increasingly be an area of focus for all stakeholders—lenders, borrowers, and investors. While private equity managers historically more prevalently incorporated ESG into their approach, given the different level of influence and control for direct lenders, there is a continued focus from direct lenders to encompass ESG into their investment processes and, in some cases, to build it into credit agreements. Private credit's core focus on capital preservation and fundamental credit quality naturally coincides with ESG considerations to assess risk metrics and thematic issues related to climate change, governance, consumer protection, stakeholder expectations, ethics, and integrity, as well as inclusivity and diversity. That said, the varying subasset classes within private credit require different approaches to ESG, and historically there were no industry best practices to incorporate ESG metrics into private credit investments. Over the last several years in particular, there has been a spotlight on ESG integration and potential ways for direct lenders to work with their borrowers to incorporate credit-relevant ESG issues throughout the life cycle of an investment and even within their own organizations.

CHAPTER 18

ESG in the Loan Market

Introduction

    Tess Virmani
    Associate General Counsel and Executive Vice President,
    Public Policy Group
    Loan Syndications and Trading Association

ESG Considerations in Credit Analysis

    Swami Venkataraman, CFA
    Senior Vice President and Manager–ESG Analytics
    and Integration
    Moody's Investors Service

Sustainable Lending: Where We Stand as We Enter 2021

    Amara Gossin
    Vice President, Legal
    Barclays

    Robert Lewis
    Partner
    Sidley Austin LLP

The Evolution of Sustainability-Linked Lending: Watershed Moments and Expanding Investor Participation

    Maria Christina Dikeos
    Global Head of Loans Contributions
    Refinitiv LPC

Introduction

Tess Virmani
Loan Syndications and Trading Association

What does "ESG" mean? As an umbrella term, ESG refers to the environmental, social, and governance factors that contribute to a company's sustainability profile and overall performance. However, ESG can be adopted in a multitude of ways. As applied to credit risk, ESG is narrowed to refer to those environmental, social, and governance factors that are financially material to a company's performance and risk profile. Some investors, however, see ESG as going beyond what is financially material to also look at a company's environmental and social impacts. While the alacrity in which ESG has swept through the investment world has been remarkable, ESG is perhaps more relevant to corporate practices. In some cases, companies may focus solely on the ESG risks (and opportunities) that directly impact their business model or, in other cases, companies may look to their impact on a broader set of stakeholders.

ESG integration—whether in investment decisions, financial products, or corporate practices—is a fast-evolving, unstoppable trend. At the time of writing, the confluence of growing investor demand and a favorable shift in U.S. policy is paving the way for significant advancement of understanding of and appreciation for ESG. In particular, the crescendo of investors' calls for greater ESG disclosure by companies, together with new regulatory interest in seeing increased ESG disclosure by corporates and investment firms on their ESG offerings, has reached an inflection point. As ESG has become an integral part of how managers and investors approach mainstream investment decisions, ESG has also become embedded in new financial products and offerings. For the corporate loan market, this has translated into new loan structures that are tied to certain green and social projects as well as an explosive rise in loans linked to improvements in a borrower's sustainability profile. Although these are the loan structures that have gained the most traction to date, further innovation is inevitable.

The Loan Syndications and Trading Association (LSTA) has taken an active role in supporting ESG integration in the loan market. Calling upon its years of experience setting industry standards, the LSTA, together with Europe's Loan Market Association (LMA) and the Asia Pacific Loan Market Association (APLMA) in Asia, maintain global frameworks (and related guidance documents) in support of sustainable loan structures. These voluntary frameworks offer guidance and clarity on the core components of each sustainable loan structure and serve as a bulwark against one of the great risks in this space—green-washing. Greenwashing (or ESG-washing) is a term that has been used to describe situations where claims on green or sustainability credentials are misleading, inaccurate, or inflated. Maintaining the integrity of and encouraging transparency in sustainable loan structures will enable continued growth and responsible innovation going forward. The LSTA also leads the industry's ESG disclosure efforts. Because many borrowers in the corporate loan market are private companies, the nature of the market—where information is shared on a confidential, contractual basis—presents a structural challenge to lenders' access to ESG information. Given the prevalence of asset managers having ESG-integrated investment frameworks, having access to ESG information on the borrowers to which they lend is inescapable. Recognizing this growing need for information in light of the disclosure challenge present in the loan market, the LSTA worked with its members to develop and introduce both a disclosure tool and best practice for establishing an ESG disclosure hygiene. In 2020 the LSTA launched its first ESG Due Diligence Questionnaire for borrowers to complete and share with lenders and prospective lenders. The questionnaire is designed to be completed by the borrower at the diligence stage of any loan market transaction. Best practice calls for the completed questionnaire to then be included with a borrower's financial/traditional diligence materials and available to all lenders and prospective lenders. At the time of writing, broad but uneven uptake of the questionnaire had taken hold. Looking forward, we hope the current increased focus on ESG throughout the financial markets will serve as a boon to the establishment of regular ESG disclosure in the loan market.

Given the rapid evolution of ESG, any attempt to offer here a current examination of its influence on the corporate loan market is an exercise in futility. However, the increasing relevance of ESG means that it cannot and should not be overlooked. With that in mind, this chapter seeks to offer readers some historical context to what they are encountering, as well as to address the fundamental ESG challenge facing the corporate loan market—the need for reliable, decision-useful, and consistent corporate disclosure. First, the chapter discusses the connection between ESG and credit risk and the consequent impact on credit ratings. It then describes the key ingredients of sustainable lending, with a detailed look at two key structures—green loans and sustainability (or ESG)-linked loans. The chapter then presents a view into the origins of sustainable finance, a sense of its exponential growth, and predictions of likely future developments.

ESG Considerations in Credit Analysis

Swami Venkataraman, CFA
Moody's Investors Service

ESG IS RAPIDLY GAINING PROMINENCE IN GLOBAL FINANCIAL MARKETS

ESG analysis is rapidly gaining greater prominence within the mainstream investment community. Institutional investors are seeking ways to integrate ESG into their asset allocation and risk management practices as a means to minimize risks and protect the value of their traditional investment portfolios or to pursue stand-alone sustainable investment strategies. Such heightened focus is reflected in the marked rise of global assets managed under sustainable investment strategies to $35.1 trillion in 2020 from $30.7 trillion in 2018 (see Exhibit 18.1).[1]

There is also a burgeoning movement amongst policymakers and institutions to pursue stronger sustainability and climate agendas to foster economic development and safeguard against financial instability. The ratification of the Paris Agreement in 2016 represented a significant milestone in globally orchestrated climate policies. In addition, institutional efforts such as the G20 Green Finance Study Group, the Financial Stability Board's Task Force on Climate-related Financial Disclosures (TCFD),[2] the European Commission's action plan for sustainable finance, and China's ambitious agenda to establish a green financial system provide further evidence that ESG will play a more central role in financial markets going forward.

ESG AND ITS RELEVANCE TO CREDIT ANALYSIS

ESG refers to a broad range of qualitative and quantitative considerations that relate to the sustainability of an organization and to the broader impact on society of its businesses, investments, and activities. Examples include a company's carbon footprint and the accountability of a company's management or a nation's government. Moody's credit ratings focus on the aspects of ESG that can

---

[1] Sustainable investing is an investment approach that considers ESG factors in portfolio selection and management. For the purpose of its global report, the Global Sustainable Investment Alliance (GSIA) uses an inclusive definition of *sustainable investing*, without drawing distinctions between this and related terms such as *responsible investing* and *socially responsible investing*. Sustainable investment encompasses the following activities and strategies:
  1. Negative/exclusionary screening
  2. Positive/best-in-class screening
  3. Norms-based screening
  4. ESG integration
  5. Sustainability-themed investing
  6. Impact/community investing
  7. Corporate engagement and shareholder action

[2] The TCFD is global; its members were selected by the Financial Stability Board and come from various organizations, including large banks, insurance companies, asset managers, pension funds, large nonfinancial companies, accounting and consulting firms, and credit rating agencies. Moody's Investors Service is a member of the TCFD. See "Final Report: Recommendations of the Task Force on Climate-related Financial Disclosures, Financial Stability Board," June 2017. https://assets.bbhub.io/company/sites/60/2020/10/FINAL-2017-TCFD-Report-11052018.pdf.

EXHIBIT 18.1

Global Sustainable Assets under Management by Region ($ trillion).

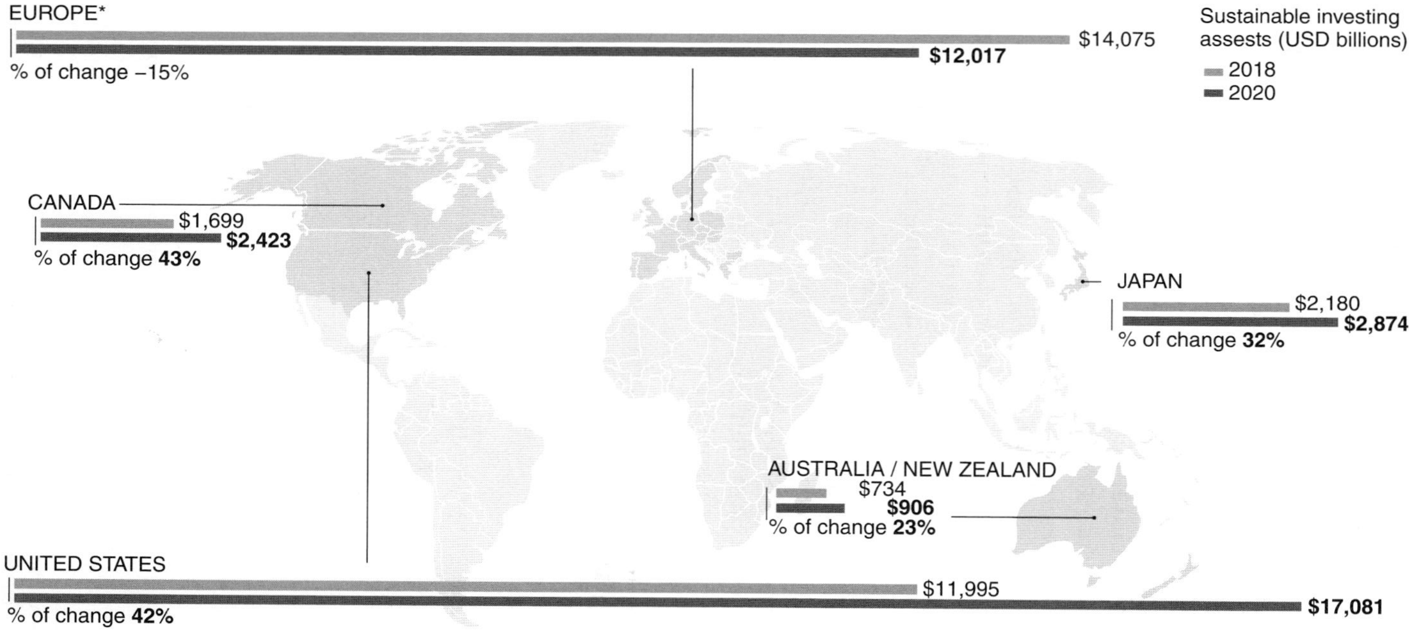

EUROPE*
- 2018: $14,075
- 2020: $12,017
- % of change −15%

CANADA
- 2018: $1,699
- 2020: $2,423
- % of change 43%

JAPAN
- 2018: $2,180
- 2020: $2,874
- % of change 32%

AUSTRALIA / NEW ZEALAND
- 2018: $734
- 2020: $906
- % of change 23%

UNITED STATES
- 2018: $11,995
- 2020: $17,081
- % of change 42%

Sustainable investing assets (USD billions)
- 2018
- 2020

* In 2020, Europe includes Austria, Belgium, Bulgaria, Denmark, France, Germany, Greece, Italy, Spain, Netherlands, Poland, Portugal, Slovenia, Sweden, the UK, Norway, Switzerland, Liechtenstein. Europe and Australasia have enacted significant changes in the way sustainable investment is defined in these regions, so direct comparisons between regions and with previous versions of this report are not easily made.

Source: http://www.gsi-alliance.org/wp-content/uploads/2021/08/GSIR-20201.pdf.

have a material impact on the credit quality of an issuer,[3] but others may have different approaches to ESG analysis based on their specific objectives.

The classification of ESG considerations across financial markets is imprecise, due largely to the multiple and diverse objectives of various stakeholders. Several institutions, notably the Principles for Responsible Investment and the Sustainability Accounting Standards Board, have sought to establish voluntary definitions for ESG, but at the time of writing there is no single set of ESG definitions or metrics that is comprehensive, verifiable, and universally accepted. The definition of ESG issues is also dynamic because what society classifies as acceptable evolves over time, resulting from new information (e.g., the impact of carbon dioxide emissions) or changing perceptions (e.g., what constitutes privacy). As an example, to provide transparency into Moody's assessment of ESG risks and benefits, we have developed an ESG classification nomenclature (see Exhibit 18.2) that includes components (E, S, and G) and, for each component, categories and subcategories of the ESG considerations that we view as most likely to have credit implications across sectors. For the E component, the categories are the same for public and private sector issuers; for the S and G components, there are different categories for public and private sector issuers.

Credit analysis is concerned with the material considerations that may influence the relative risk of default and expected financial loss in the event of default for issuers and debt obligations, regardless of whether they are classified as ESG risks.

In considering ESG in credit analysis, the objective is thus not to capture all considerations that may be labeled green, sustainable, or ethical, but rather those that have a material impact on credit quality. This distinction is important. Individual companies encounter a multitude of ESG-related risks and opportunities, many of which will have little tangible impact on operating or financial performance. For example, a company's volunteer work, charitable activities, and other such initiatives are important to the extent that they produce social value, but they are unlikely to materially affect the issuer's financial health or credit standing. Materiality is also a fluid concept, and will invariably differ from one sector to another,

---

[3] Considerations that are material to credit quality may not include all investment parameters that some market participants would regard as green, sustainable, or ethical.

EXHIBIT 18.2

ESG Classification Captures Credit-Relevant Risk Categories.

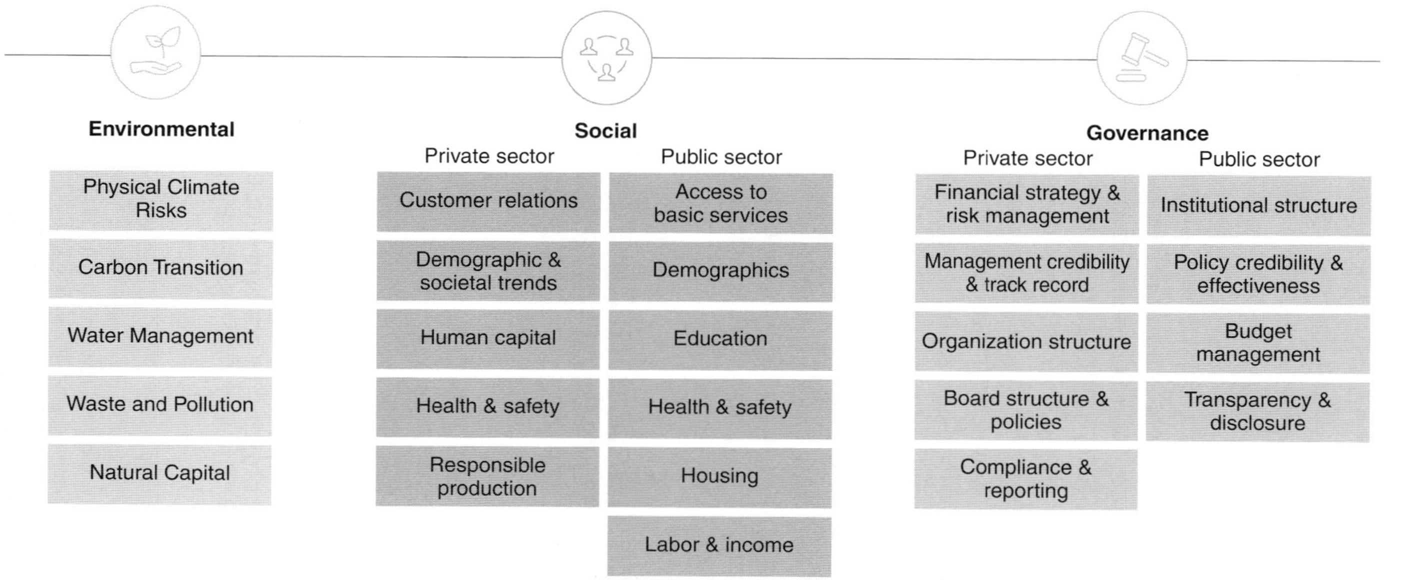

Environmental

- Physical Climate Risks
- Carbon Transition
- Water Management
- Waste and Pollution
- Natural Capital

Social

Private sector
- Customer relations
- Demographic & societal trends
- Human capital
- Health & safety
- Responsible production

Public sector
- Access to basic services
- Demographics
- Education
- Health & safety
- Housing
- Labor & income

Governance

Private sector
- Financial strategy & risk management
- Management credibility & track record
- Organization structure
- Board structure & policies
- Compliance & reporting

Public sector
- Institutional structure
- Policy credibility & effectiveness
- Budget management
- Transparency & disclosure

Source: Moody's Investors Service.

across companies within the same sector or even for a given company over time.

CHARACTERISTICS OF ESG CONSIDERATIONS

As a broad and dynamic group of factors, ESG considerations and their importance to issuers' credit profiles can vary widely across sectors.[4] For example, the ESG issues material to a sovereign are likely to be substantially different from those that are material to a mining company. Some ESG issues can also vary widely across issuers and may be important only under certain circumstances or only for a subset of issuers in an industry.

Credit analysis considers the credit impact of the distinct aspects of ESG for an entity, as well as the combined impact of ESG considerations. For example, a company could have excellent governance and employee relations that do not offset the negative credit impact of a large carbon footprint. There may also be an interplay of ESG considerations. For example, a country's environmental problems or governmental policies may increase the risk of social instability or have a negative impact on the economy.

ESG CONSIDERATIONS, INDIVIDUALLY OR JOINTLY, OFTEN HAVE MORE POTENTIAL CREDIT RISK THAN CREDIT BENEFIT

Some ESG issues may have greater downside risk than upside potential. As an example, a company with a track record of health and safety violations may face litigation risks that pressure its operating income, whereas another company that demonstrates outstanding health and safety practices may not see a comparable credit benefit.

ESG considerations are not always negative; they can be credit strengths. A company or government that has outstandingly

---

[4] Moody's has published environmental and social heat maps that score the relevance of each of the risk categories in the ESG classification above for every rated sector. Available at: https://www.moodys.com/login?ReturnUrl=http%3a%2f%2fwww.moodys.com%2fresearchdocumentcontentpage.aspx%3f%26docid%3dPBC_1280897 and https://www.moodys.com/login?ReturnUrl=http%3a%2f%2fwww.moodys.com%2fresearchdocumentcontentpage.aspx%3f%26docid%3dPBC_1281698.

strong governance is more likely to have a management culture of 360-degree risk assessment and informed decision-making that supports long-term creditworthiness. Also, the business profiles and cash flow stability of renewable energy developers may benefit from supportive government policies.

SECTOR-WIDE EXPOSURE IS COMMON

In some sectors, most issuers have a similar level of exposure to ESG risks, although there may be variations. In some cases, ESG risks that are common to issuers in a sector may be reflected in the overall calibration of the factors and subfactors in the sector methodology. For example, all oil refiners sell a carbon-intensive product, which entails transition risks that are incorporated into a forward-looking view of long-term demand, future cash flows, and appropriate leverage and coverage ratios for all issuers in the sector. Within the sector, carbon transition risks are a discernible ratings differentiator for oil refiners whose exposure is unusually high (e.g., refineries located in a jurisdiction with exceptionally stringent environmental requirements) or whose risks are unusually well mitigated (e.g., a refiner that is successfully diversifying into lower-carbon business activities that are profitable).

ASSESSMENT CHALLENGES

The potential credit impact of many ESG considerations is challenging to assess because it must often be inferred or estimated from multiple sources based on reporting that generally is not standardized or consistent. It is widely acknowledged that current disclosure on ESG matters varies across sectors and issuers, largely because of the differences in reporting standards across jurisdictions as well as different levels of market focus on ESG topics.

Assessing the credit materiality of ESG considerations often entails qualitative judgment, for example in assessing how an issuer's stakeholders may react to an issue or event, which can be difficult to predict and can vary across sectors, countries, and regions. A similar exposure to an ESG risk may be perceived differently by customers, employees, or policymakers depending on their own sociopolitical background, and thus may have different credit implications where there are different circumstances.

CREDIT RATINGS, TIME HORIZONS, AND ESG

Environmental and social issues can often be diffuse, with long or uncertain time horizons (e.g., climate change and demographics), and are subject to the variability of potential policy measures (e.g., carbon regulations and immigration policies) and the performance of the economy. This can result in a wide range of potential credit outcomes for affected issuers.

As with other rating considerations, future ESG trends can be incorporated into ratings when there is visibility into those trends. In most cases, however, the ability to forecast the impact of trends that will only unfold far into the future is necessarily limited. Nearer-term risks generally have a more direct impact on ratings because there is typically far greater certainty of their impact on credit profiles. As a general principle, as the time frame for a source of risk lengthens, the less certain one can be of its impact on an issuer's cash flow–generating ability and other credit metrics, and the less clarity one has regarding the importance of that risk in relation to other risks the issuer faces (see Exhibit 18.3). For example, longer time frames give an issuer more time to adapt by lowering costs, adopting new technologies, or realigning its business model, budgetary spending, or balance sheet to changed circumstances; however, some issuers may not be able to or may fail to take effective mitigating actions.

These characteristics are not unique to ESG. Credit analysis for any sector involves an evaluation of factors with inherent

EXHIBIT 18.3

Uncertainty on the Probability and Timing of Risks Often Increases as Time Frames Lengthen.

Near-term risks are typically more meaningful and have a more direct impact on ratings	As time frame lengthens, probability and impact of risks become less certain, as does importance relative to other risks	A longer time frame provides companies with greater capacity to take mitigating (or self-damaging) actions in response to risks

Source: Moody's Investors Service.

uncertainty or poor visibility. While the future impact of diffuse, uncertain, or very long-term risks cannot always be calibrated, fundamental credit strengths that provide resilience against short-term risks also provide resilience against most long-term risks.

SCENARIO ANALYSIS IS A USEFUL TOOL FOR INCORPORATING UNCERTAIN, LONG-TERM RISKS

Scenario analysis can be a powerful tool in incorporating uncertain, long-term risks such as climate change into credit analysis. Carbon transition and physical risks of climate change have increasing relevance to credit analysis. At the time of this writing, we expect a more pronounced decarbonization trajectory and more frequent and volatile extreme weather in the future. The credit impact of the energy transition and the physical risks of climate change will not be uniform across or within sectors. Consequently, climate scenarios are critical in providing consistent starting points for assessing the implications for rated entities across sectors globally. At Moody's, as an example, we first identify sectors that are most exposed to the risks highlighted by the scenarios and then assess the ways in which the risks indicated by the scenarios could transmit into a credit impact for issuers within those sectors.

At the time of this writing, there is substantial uncertainty and a wide range of possibilities for the precise trajectory of decarbonization that the world will take, including country paths that may differ from one another. From a physical risk perspective, the nature of climate models means that they produce a range of potential outcomes for a certain type of extreme weather event in a given region, but they cannot indicate exactly when and where such events will happen.

In the face of these uncertainties, scenario analysis can be used to better understand the relative positioning and strategic response of companies, governments, and assets with regard to transitioning and the physical risks that are possible. These scenarios describe plausible trajectories for decarbonization and plausible climatic outcomes against which to test the resilience of issuers in the most exposed sectors, including how exposed they are and their ability to adapt business models and policies over time to adjust for the possible outcomes.

Our credit analysis does not look over a specific time horizon and is intended to incorporate relevant credit considerations as far into the future as visibility permits. For climate risk assessment frameworks, we strike a balance between the need to assess a prolonged period during which the effects of climate change can crystallize and the reduced visibility, and hence limited impact, of extremely long time horizons on credit analysis.

FOR CARBON TRANSITION RISK, SCENARIO ANALYSIS AIDS THE ASSESSMENT OF CREDIT IMPLICATIONS

The speed and scale of change in the supply and consumption of energy is hard to predict. However, the direction of travel toward decarbonization is clear, considering emissions targets in major countries, the improving economics of renewables, and technological advances. We use transition scenarios to help us understand a range of future outcomes that may materialize.

The Stated Policies Scenario (STEPS) developed by the International Energy Agency (IEA) incorporates national commitments to limit or reduce greenhouse gas (GHG) emissions enshrined in the Paris Agreement's Nationally Determined Contributions (NDCs). This scenario is estimated to result in a rise in average global temperatures of 2.7 degrees to 3.0 degrees Celsius above preindustrial levels by the end of this century (Exhibit 18.4). STEPS can be used

EXHIBIT 18.4

STEPS Is Broadly Consistent with Existing Paris Agreement Commitments.
International Energy Agency's global emission scenarios.

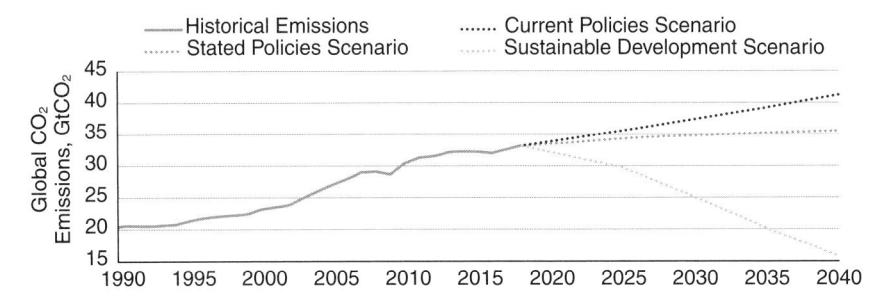

Note: Current Policies Scenario (CPS) assumes no change in policies or technology from today, Stated Policies Scenario (STEPS) includes policies and targets announced by governments, and Sustainable Development Scenario (SDS) assumes an accelerated clean energy transition that puts the world on track to meet goals related to climate change, universal access, and clean air.
Sources: Moody's Investors Service, International Energy Agency.

as a starting point to consider climate policy developments and commitments and what they mean for energy demand and production across the globe.

The global STEPS trajectory conceals significant variations in emissions pathways and underlying assumptions at a national or regional level. In part, this situation reflects the disparate stages of economic development in developed and emerging economies. A range of possible energy mixes can result in the same emissions and warming outcomes. In other words, multiple pathways could deliver the same long-term results. The direction of travel indicated by the scenarios is still informative, given the fact that any particular scenario that is selected is unlikely to be 100% correct.

To provide insight into an issuer's resilience, the IEA's Sustainable Development Scenario (SDS) can also be used to provide a more ambitious low-carbon transition scenario. The SDS is aligned with reaching global "net zero" carbon dioxide (CO_2) emissions in 2070. If net emissions stay at zero after this point, this is estimated to mean that there is a 66% chance of limiting the rise in the global average temperature to 1.8 degrees Celsius above preindustrial levels. Comparing the impact of these long-term scenarios provides the ability to test relative positioning against an assumed direction of travel. At Moody's, for instance, the sector analysts then use this information as an informational input into their assessment of the credit risks facing individual rated entities and the implications for the credit ratings of these entities.

FOR PHYSICAL CLIMATE RISKS, SCENARIO ANALYSIS IS SIMILARLY USEFUL IN CREDIT ASSESSMENTS

In addition to climate transition risk, physical climate risks can also impact credit assessments. Whereas carbon transition risk captures the impact of the transition to a low-carbon economy on an issuer, physical climate risks are those risks to an issuer's operations, workforce, supply chain, and markets caused by the impact of climate change. Examples include the increased frequency of wildfires, flooding, and drought.

Approaches to physical climate risks vary, so as an illustration this chapter focuses on Moody's approach to physical climate risks. Moody's uses a single scenario and primarily focuses on the implications for the next 30 years. Our approach to physical risk analysis and choice of scenarios draws significantly on our affiliate Four Twenty Seven's views on physical climate scenarios, which are characterized by the following key features, as illustrated in Exhibit 18.5:

1. Because of the inertia and time lag involved in how carbon emissions affect the earth's climate, the negative effects of climate change through 2050 are largely already locked-in by emissions to date.
2. Given the historical high emissions pathway observed, and taking into account the risk of tipping points and feedback loops, it is a reasonable approach to apply a representative concentration pathway (RCP)[5] of 8.5 to assess the broad range of possible climate outcomes through to 2050. Even if we significantly reduce emissions in the next 30 years, consistent with other RCP pathways, the divergence in climate outcomes from those of RCP 8.5 will only be felt beyond 2050 because of the time lag effect mentioned above.
3. Until 2050, the range of potential physical climate outcomes may be represented by the variability in RCP 8.5 climate models themselves (i.e., the range of possible outcomes projected because of the climate impact of emissions to date).
4. It is possible to group the climate outcomes of various climate models under RCP 8.5 into high, medium, and low tiers. This is one approach to exploring the range of potential outcomes. These percentile-based tiered scenarios represent lower- to higher-risk climate outcomes that can

---

[5] To analyze physical risk, we refer to representative concentration pathways (RCPs) as adopted by the UN Intergovernmental Panel on Climate Change (IPCC). An RCP is a scenario that incorporates an array of projections, such as through the year 2100 for a wide range of greenhouse gas emissions and concentrations that are based on a different set of assumptions. An RCP uses this data to estimate the warming effect of those greenhouse gases. Climate models predict temperature, rainfall, and other parameters for each RCP scenario. A number of climate models exist, resulting in a range of outcomes for climate parameters. The IPCC has four primary RCPs, of which RCP 8.5 represents the most adverse climate impacts pathway, leading to a likely increase of 3.2 to 5.4 degrees Celsius in global mean surface temperature by 2100 in relation to historical levels. The TCFD and other climate literature point to RCP 8.5 as a high-emissions scenario, and hence a plausible pathway to account for the largest climate outcomes.

EXHIBIT 18.5

Physical Climate Impacts over Different Time Frames.

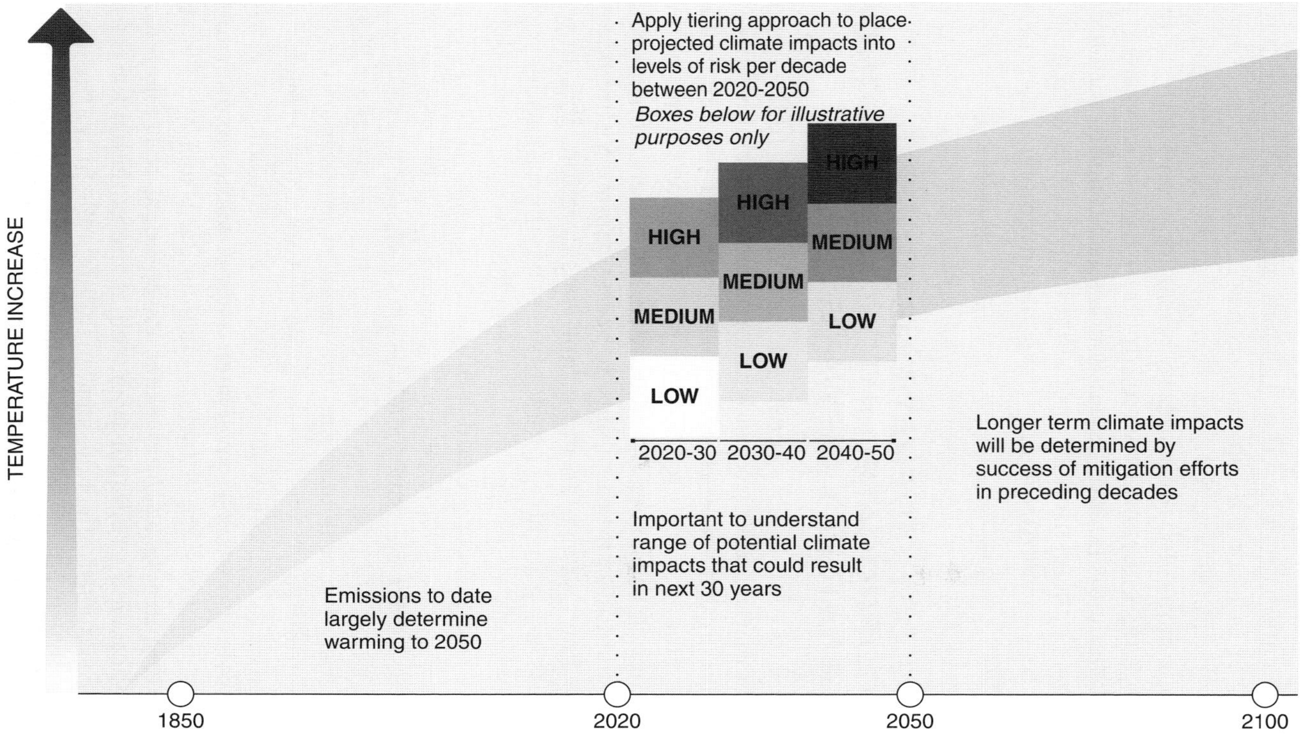

then be used to assess the climate risk faced by individual rated entities in the most exposed sectors.

Climate impacts are "locked in" over the next 30 years and then start to differ based on mitigation pathways post-mid-century.

By adopting a common scenario and risk-based approach to the implications of that scenario for each sector, we can assess the implications globally across sectors from a consistent starting point. Adopting a scenario-based approach that is consistent with our affiliate Four Twenty Seven enables us to apply forward-looking climate data and indicators to highlight entities within sectors that exhibit exposure to climate risks that are greater than others in their sector.

ESG CONSIDERATIONS ARE INCORPORATED INTO CREDIT RATINGS IN A VARIETY OF WAYS

The approach to ESG considerations is similar to the approach for other material credit considerations in that it includes an assessment of the impact on an issuer's cash flows and the value of its assets over time; the sufficiency and stability of cash flows and assets in relation to the issuer's debt burden and other financial obligations; and liquidity and the ability to access capital. Visibility into future cash flows is also an important consideration. It is important to assess any mitigating or adaptive behavior that issuers undertake. In some instances, one might even identify ESG trends that are positive for an issuer's credit profile.

For example, for a nonfinancial corporate, one might seek to assess how ESG issues such as product safety and carbon transition risks influence credit drivers such as demand for its products, the cost of production, and the need for financing to make capital expenditures, as well as the potential for these drivers to change meaningfully over time. For financial institutions, one might seek to assess how ESG issues such as governance and customer relations influence credit factors such as the issuer's ability to access funding in wholesale markets, its liquidity, risk tolerance, capital position, and profitability, as well as the potential for these governance issues to affect the sustainability of the firm's business model. For structured finance transactions, one might assess how ESG considerations may affect underlying asset values, in addition to considering how the special-purpose vehicle's governance affects creditors. For sovereigns, meanwhile, one might seek to assess how ESG considerations such as the economic effects of environmental issues, including climate change, or social and governance-related issues, such as control of corruption and the rule of law, could affect gross domestic product (GDP), the trajectory and stability of the government's revenues and expenditures, and the government's ability to withstand shocks, among other drivers of government creditworthiness.

Credit rating methodologies provide general guidance on how qualitative and quantitative risk characteristics are likely to affect rating outcomes for debt issuers operating in a given sector or industry. In this context, there are a number of channels through which material ESG issues can be considered in rating methodologies. A few practical examples of how ESG is adopted in Moody's rating methodologies are set forth below:

- *ESG considerations are typically captured within scored factors in our rating methodologies.* ESG issues, where material for a particular sector will influence the scored factors in a given rating methodology. For example, our assessment of the business profile of a soft beverage manufacturer includes an analysis of reputation and image, both of which are important to brand value. For global reinsurers, we evaluate exposure to and management of catastrophe risk—from both natural and human-caused events—in the context of the firm's capital resources.
- *In some instances, ESG criteria may be explicitly scored factors in a rating methodology.* For example, "Financial Policy" is an explicitly scored factor in approximately three-quarters of our corporate industry methodologies globally, and scoring is influenced by our view of corporate governance. "Governance," meanwhile, is an explicitly scored factor in our rating methodology for U.S. states that examines the quality of financial decision-making and execution.
- *ESG considerations outside of the rating methodology scorecard may have an impact on ratings.* For example, the expected long-term decline of the thermal coal industry cannot be fully captured in a scorecard unless the financial metrics are projected decades into the future. Such a scenario would raise false-precision issues. So, our long-term

expectations are typically taken into account as qualitative considerations that may result in a rating that differs from the scorecard outcome. This follows the same approach as many other risks that affect credit quality but are not scored individually, such as litigation, changes in technology, and competitor strategies.

Moody's methodology for the automobile manufacturing industry provides an example of how ESG issues are captured via different channels (Exhibit 18.6). We consider the impact of an issuer's emissions-reducing technologies and alternative fuel vehicle product development, as well as its ability to meet future regulatory standards, in our assessment of "Business Profile." "Financial Policy" is an explicitly scored grid factor, which includes an assessment of the perceived tolerance and track record of a company's governing board and management for financial risk. Finally, our expectations for how carbon transition and regulatory considerations will affect a company's market position, product breadth or strength, and future financial ratios are considered qualitatively.

MOODY'S PRODUCES ESG SCORES THAT SUPPORT ESG INTEGRATION IN A TRANSPARENT AND GLOBALLY CONSISTENT MANNER

Moody's ESG methodology describes the framework for establishing issuer profile scores (IPS) that reflect our opinion of an issuer's, obligor's, or transaction's exposure to E, S, and G risks and benefits. We refer to these as E, S, and G IPSs, which are expressed on a five-point scale, from E-1, S-1, or G-1 (Positive) to E-5, S-5, or G-5 (Very Highly Negative). They are inputs into the Moody's credit rating. E, S, and G IPSs illustrate the issuer's exposure to these risks, incorporating related mitigants, or benefits, using a unified scale across all sectors. Mitigants and benefits include actions taken at the issuer's own initiative or actions fostered or required by external parties (e.g., policies, regulations, or international commitments). The ESG credit impact score (CIS) is an output of the rating process that more transparently communicates the impact of ESG considerations on the rating of an issuer or transaction. The CIS is also expressed on a five-point scale, from CIS-1 (Positive) to CIS-5 (Very Highly Negative).

EXHIBIT 18.6

Illustrative Example of How Material ESG Issues Are Reflected in Our Methodology for Automobile Manufacturers.

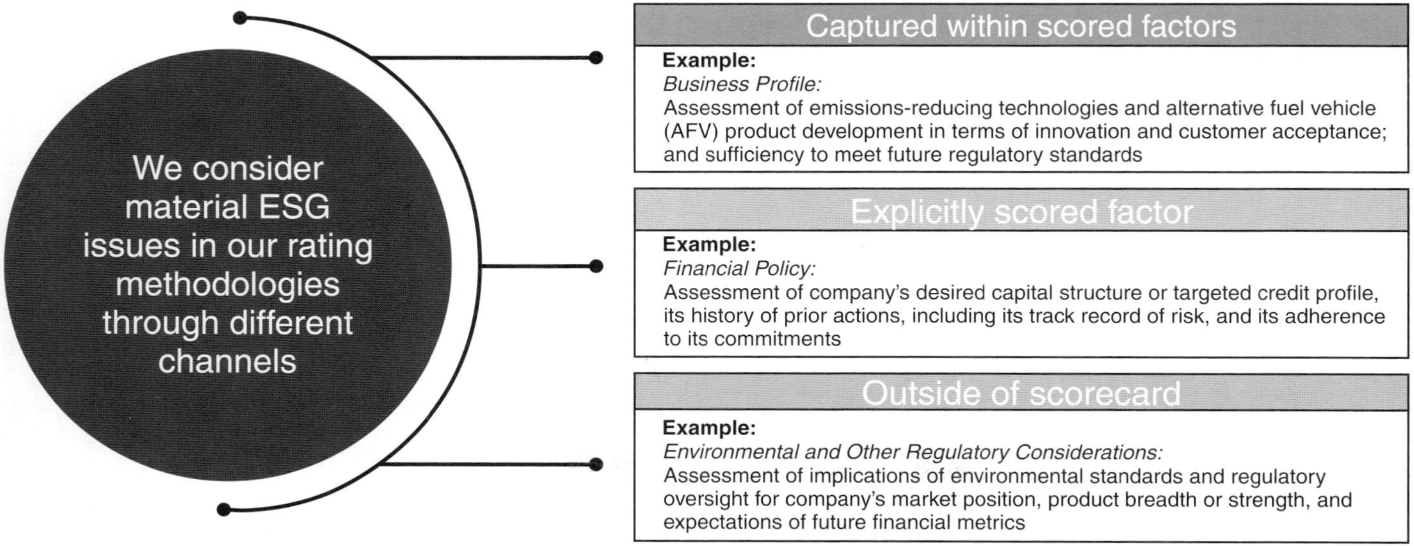

We consider material ESG issues in our rating methodologies through different channels

Captured within scored factors

Example:
Business Profile:
Assessment of emissions-reducing technologies and alternative fuel vehicle (AFV) product development in terms of innovation and customer acceptance; and sufficiency to meet future regulatory standards

Explicitly scored factor

Example:
Financial Policy:
Assessment of company's desired capital structure or targeted credit profile, its history of prior actions, including its track record of risk, and its adherence to its commitments

Outside of scorecard

Example:
Environmental and Other Regulatory Considerations:
Assessment of implications of environmental standards and regulatory oversight for company's market position, product breadth or strength, and expectations of future financial metrics

Source: Moody's Investors Service.

These CIS scoring levels indicate the extent, if any, to which the rating of an issuer or transaction would likely be different if exposure to ESG risks did not exist. Where the score is CIS-4 (Highly Negative) or CIS-5 (Very Highly Negative), it means we think the rating is lower than it would have been if ESG risk exposures did not exist. Where the score is CIS-3, ESG risks have a limited impact on the current rating with potential for greater future negative impact over time. Where the score is CIS-1, we perceive material positive ESG impacts, with a positive rating impact. Where the score is CIS-2 (Neutral-to-Low), the overall influence of ESG attributes on the rating is nonmaterial. These scores, and their relationship to rating methodologies, are illustrated in Exhibit 18.7.

The materiality of ESG considerations is likely to increase in the future. Key environmental and social issues are likely to be of growing importance in the assessment of issuer credit quality, driven by such considerations as stricter environmental regulations, demographic and societal changes, and heightened public awareness of such disparate issues as climate change, sustainability challenges, diversity, data security, and income inequality.

Sustainable Lending: Where We Stand as We Enter 2021[6]

Amara Gossin
Barclays

Robert Lewis
Sidley Austin LLP

The year 2021 promises much progress in the world of sustainable finance. Interest in sustainable finance is exploding, which is stimulating rapid developments while at the same time creating a

---

[6] This article has been prepared for informational purposes only and does not constitute legal advice. This information is not intended to create, and the receipt of it does not constitute, a lawyer–client relationship. Readers should not act upon this without seeking advice from professional advisers. The content therein does not reflect the views of Barclays Bank PLC or any of its affiliates or of Sidley Austin LLP.

EXHIBIT 18.7

Illustration of How ESG Considerations Are Captured in Ratings.

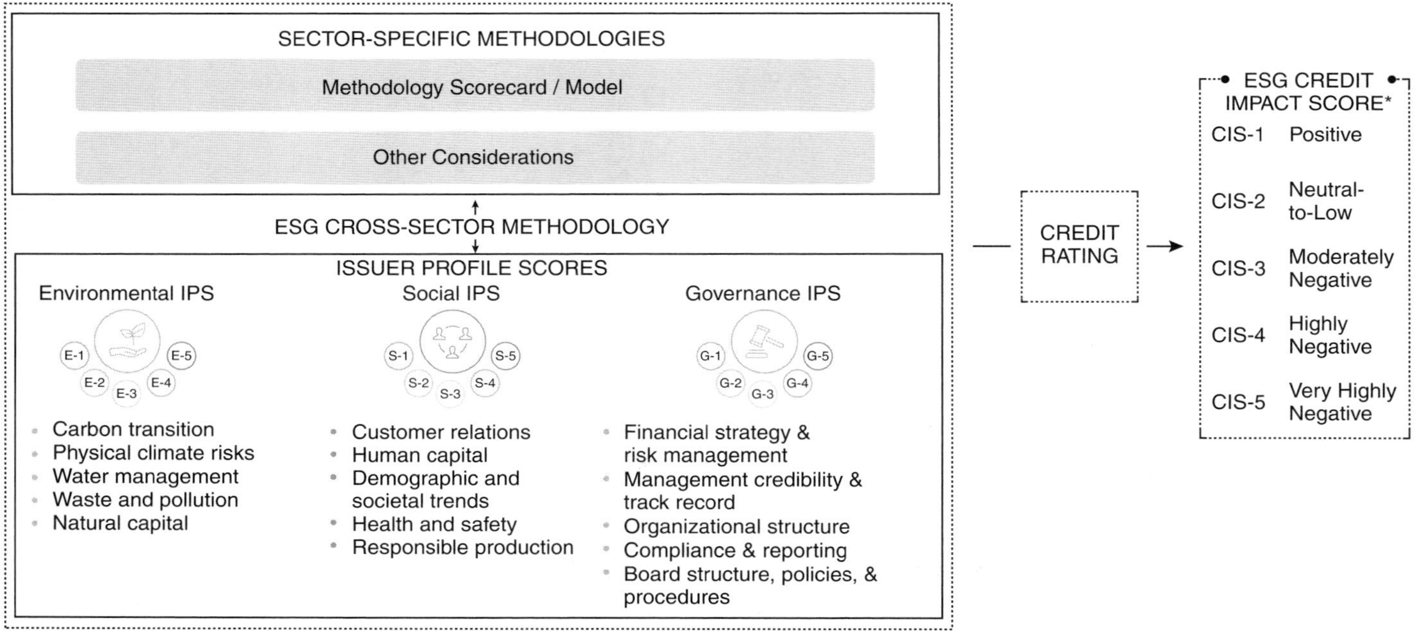

SECTOR-SPECIFIC METHODOLOGIES

- Methodology Scorecard / Model
- Other Considerations

ESG CROSS-SECTOR METHODOLOGY

ISSUER PROFILE SCORES

Environmental IPS (E-1, E-2, E-3, E-4, E-5)
- Carbon transition
- Physical climate risks
- Water management
- Waste and pollution
- Natural capital

Social IPS (S-1, S-2, S-3, S-4, S-5)
- Customer relations
- Human capital
- Demographic and societal trends
- Health and safety
- Responsible production

Governance IPS (G-1, G-2, G-3, G-4, G-5)
- Financial strategy & risk management
- Management credibility & track record
- Organizational structure
- Compliance & reporting
- Board structure, policies, & procedures

→ CREDIT RATING →

ESG CREDIT IMPACT SCORE*

- CIS-1 Positive
- CIS-2 Neutral-to-Low
- CIS-3 Moderately Negative
- CIS-4 Highly Negative
- CIS-5 Very Highly Negative

Source: Moody's Investors Service.

somewhat fragmented and possibly overwhelming landscape to participants.

This article focuses on sustainable lending—a distinct subcategory of sustainable finance that aims to accomplish ESG ends concurrently with more traditional lending purposes.[7] We identify the key drivers and considerations for sustainable lending to allow market participants to successfully navigate the fast-changing topography. In so doing, we hope to inspire the industry to make sustainable loans ambitious, consistent, meaningful, and ubiquitous.

First, we describe the two products in the market as of the time of writing, in December 2020: green loans and sustainability-linked loans. Second, we describe the principal relevant market constituencies and their interest in sustainable finance in general and sustainable lending in particular. Third, we explore the fundamental characteristic of sustainable loans: sustainability. Finally, we look at specific drafting and diligence items that market participants should consider to ensure the integrity of sustainable loans. We use climate change mitigation as our primary example because it is a relatively well-developed and cross-cutting sustainability objective,[8] but the principles are relevant to any sustainability objective.

OVERVIEW OF GREEN LOANS AND SUSTAINABILITY-LINKED LOANS

As of December 2020, the loan market has two dedicated sustainability products: green loans and sustainability-linked loans. While at the time of this writing there is no regulation of sustainability-themed loans as such in the United States, the market has broadly adopted voluntary principles promulgated by the LSTA, LMA, and APLMA for each product: the Green Loan Principles and the Sustainability-Linked Loan Principles.

---

[7] For purposes of this article, the focus is primarily environmental sustainability. However, as noted, a "sustainable" finance product may also or alternatively address objectives related to the social and governance aspects of ESG. Many use *ESG finance* and *sustainable finance* interchangeably. In this article, we use *sustainable* because it is more consistent with the international frameworks cited in this article.

[8] As Justin Worland has eloquently put it, "If a storm destroys a school, students can't learn. If the sugarcane crops are flooded, farmers lose their jobs. If sea levels rise too much, entire communities disappear. . . . That will come one way or another. Every country will be combatting climate change for the foreseeable future." See Justin Worland, "2020 Is Our Last, Best Chance to Save the Planet," *Time Magazine* (July 9, 2020). https://time.com/5864692/climate-change-defining-moment/.

Green loans and sustainability-linked loans both have the characteristics of a standard loan product, but with a sustainable feature added. Specifically, green loans are loans the proceeds of which are expressly designated for a use that is determined to be "sustainable" (to date, the green loan product only contemplates environmental sustainability objectives, but we expect that will soon broaden to include other ESG objectives).[9] Sustainability-linked loans are not determined by their use of proceeds; rather, their sustainability characteristics are determined with reference to specific sustainability-related business ambition(s) incentivized by the debt instrument (usually through a pricing adjustment). Thus, while green loans aim to achieve one or more specific sustainable project objectives, sustainability-linked loans, when crafted in a meaningful manner, aim to incentivize the long-term pursuit of sustainability objectives in borrowers.

In both cases, the loan products have counterparts in the capital markets—namely, green, social, or sustainability bonds and sustainability-linked bonds—and the industry principles are purposely aligned.[10]

Table 18.1 provides a comparison of certain characteristics of these two loan and bond products to better illustrate their use in the market.

The two sets of relevant loan principles as of December 2020 are summarized in Table 18.2.[11]

MARKET CONSTITUENCIES

Sustainable lending is attractive to many constituencies. It combines a shared set of public and private goals: economic risk reduction, opportunity realization, and the mitigation of systemic sustainability challenges. Recognition of the mutuality of corporate and social

---

[9] Readers should note that following the finalization of this article for publication, Social Loan Principles were published. These principles, current as of April 2021, are available here: https://www.lsta.org/content/social-loan-principles-slp/.

[10] See "LSTA Green Loan Principles," LSTA, May 2020, and "Sustainable Finance—FAQs," LSTA, July 2019, Readers should note that updated Green Loan Principles were released following the finalization of this article for publication. The latest versions can be found on the LSTA website at https://www.lsta.org/content/green-loan-principles/.

[11] Readers should note that following the finalization of this article for publication, the SLL Principles were updated. Readers should review the updated SLL Principles, current as of May 2021, available at https://www.lsta.org/content/sustainability-linked-loan-principles-sllp/. The changes emphasize the importance of ambition and transparency, and, among other things, update the external review and verification of SPTs from optional to required.

TABLE 18.1

	Green or Sustainable Loans / Bonds	**Sustainability-Linked Loans (SLLs) / Bonds**
Market debut?	The first green bond was issued by the World Bank in 2008 and was dedicated to financing projects that addressed climate concerns.[1]	The first SLL was issued by Philips in 2017 and was designed to incentivize an improvement in a sustainability score provided by a third-party sustainability ratings agency.[2]
Who provides the credit?	Capital or financial markets participants looking to invest in accordance with specific mandates.	Capital or financial markets participants seeking to improve the sustainability characteristics of their investment portfolios or invest in accordance with specific impact mandates while maintaining a diversified asset base.
What is it for?	Allocation of capital to projects identified as "eligible" in accordance with specified investment principles. Useful for channeling capital to sustainable projects. May not necessarily alter the sustainability profile of a borrower/issuer.	Usually general corporate purposes. Incentivizes improvement in selected "eligible" sustainability-related practices that are core to the borrower/issuer's business through adjustments in lending terms (typically pricing).
What does it measure?	The use of capital for well-selected sustainability-related projects through careful tracking and proceeds management.	A borrower's/issuer's sustainability performance using "performance targets" established via transparent and regular reporting.

1 "From Evolution to Revolution: 10 Years of Green Bonds," The World Bank (November 27, 2018) https://www.worldbank.org/en/news/feature/2018/11/27/from-evolution-to-revolution-10-years-of-green-bonds.
2 "Philips Couples Sustainability Performance to Interest Rate of Its New EUR 1 Billion Revolving Credit Facility," Koninklijke Philips N.V. (April 19, 2017) https://www.philips.com/a-w/about/news/archive/standard/news/press/2017/20170419-philips-couples-sustainability-performance-to-interest-rate-of-its-new-eur-1-billion-revolving-credit-facility.html.

TABLE 18.2

Green Loan Principles	**Sustainability-Linked Loan Principles**
Use of proceeds: Proceeds must be used for eligible "Green Projects" described in the finance documents.	*Relationship to the borrower's overall corporate social responsibility strategy:* Any borrower of an SLL should have sustainability objectives, or key performance indicators (KPI), that are core to its business and align with the performance targets set out in the loan documentation.

Green Loan Principles	Sustainability-Linked Loan Principles
Process for project evaluation and selection: Borrower must clearly communicate (a) its environmental sustainability objectives, (b) how it selects eligible projects for application of loan proceeds, and (c) how it manages material environmental risks related to the Green Project. Borrowers are encouraged to contextualize the project evaluation and selection process within their wider business environmental sustainability objectives.	*Target setting:* The targets for the KPIs chosen should be ambitious and meaningful in relation to the borrower's business.
Management of proceeds: Loan proceeds must be tracked to provide transparency on use in accordance with facility terms.	N/A – proceeds may be used for any purpose.
Reporting: The borrower should be able to provide to credit providers up-to-date information relating to the use of loan proceeds, including where possible a breakdown by project. The borrower should also report on the expected impact of the funded Green Projects, including quantitative performance measures where possible.	*Reporting:* The borrower should be able to provide up-to-date information relating to the selected KPIs and, where possible, should publicly report on the KPIs.
Review: External review is recommended in appropriate cases. Parties can determine the extent and nature of the review—for example, an external party could review the borrower's proposed process for project evaluation and selection against an external standard, or against the borrower's own standards; or an external reviewer could review the borrower's report of expected environmental sustainability impacts of the funded projects. In contrast to the bond market, because loans are traditionally relationship-driven the Green Loan Principles recognize that borrowers can self-certify their green loans if they have appropriate internal expertise (which should be well documented).	*Review:* Where no public review or audit is undertaken, it is strongly recommended that a borrower receive a third-party review of the selected KPIs against the documented targets. If no third-party review is available, the borrower should have the internal expertise necessary to validate its reporting of its performance.

objectives is becoming widespread; for example, in the prominence of "stakeholder capitalism," as expressed in statements like the Business Roundtable's 2019 "Statement on the Purpose of a Corporation," in which several hundred CEOs of America's leading businesses agreed that "all stakeholders" are essential and corporate purpose includes delivery of value "for the future success of our companies, our communities and our country," and the statement by the World Economic Forum's January 2020 Annual Meeting in Davos that stakeholder capitalism is essential "to overcome income inequality, societal division and the climate crisis."

Through sustainable finance, the financial sector shows its commitment to use the capital raising and capital allocation power of finance to enable and accelerate sustainable development; that is, development that "meets the needs of the present without compromising the ability of future generations to meet their own needs."[12]

This signaling is important to communities, customers, employees, and others included within stakeholder capitalism. But it is also critical to more traditional finance constituencies for traditional financial reasons. The market's appetite for sustainable loans is driven by deficiencies in existing products that lead to the following three broad areas of concern or interest:

- Mitigation of specific economic risks to financial returns that arise from inattention to sustainability (e.g., exposures of mortgage loans to flood risk or agricultural investments to drought).
- Development of economic opportunities created by sustainability challenges (e.g., providing for flood protection or increasing drought resilience).
- Avoiding contribution to systemic sustainability challenges (e.g., refraining from investments in activities or sectors that contribute to increasing flood or drought risk).

Done well, sustainable loans respond to each of these concerns by allowing credit providers to shift their portfolios toward lower-risk investments that are positioned for long-term value and by allowing borrowers to shift their business practices to do the same. Every market constituency has clearly stated its appetite for this shift. The following are some examples of actions by key constituencies that demonstrate the appeal of sustainable lending:

- *Investors*. Whether to better understand their risk exposure, to seek better returns,[13] to meet an explicit sustainability impact mandate, or because they cannot invest away from

---

[12] UN World Commission on Environment and Development, "Report of the World Commission on Environment and Development: Our Common Future," March 20, 1987, https://sustainabledevelopment.un.org/content/documents/5987our-common-future.pdf.

[13] Robert G. Eccles and Svetlana Klimenko, "The Investor Revolution," *Harvard Business Review* (May–June 2019), https://hbr.org/2019/05/the-investor-revolution.

the systemic risks that sustainability issues create,[14] investors have long been leaders in developing sustainable finance. Through the Principles for Responsible Investment (PRI), more than 3,000 investors, including many of the world's largest, have committed to integrating sustainability into their decision-making.[15] Similarly, more than 360 investors, including Blackrock, among other significant market actors, with over $34 trillion in assets under management, support Climate Action 100+, an investor engagement initiative with commitments, among other things, "to take action to reduce greenhouse gas emissions across the value chain in line with the overarching goals of the Paris Agreement." Investors' taste for sustainability in their portfolios will continue to grow and refine.

- *Regulators.* Not surprisingly, regulators have also been attentive to the development of sustainable finance. For financial institutions, central banks have made clear that it is essential to understand and reduce climate risk exposure. For example, the Central Banks and Supervisors Network for Greening the Financial System (NGFS) encourages central banks to implement climate stress testing and prudential guidance,[16] which as of the date of this writing many have begun to consider or do.[17] In the United States, the Board of Governors of the Federal Reserve System joined the NGFS in December 2020 after recognizing in its November 2020 Financial Stability Report that climate change "is likely to increase financial stability risks" and that it is likely to be a material risk that banks must monitor.[18] A September 2020 report by the Climate-Related Market Risk Subcommittee of the

---

[14] Ibid.
[15] Principles for Responsible Investment, Annual Report 2020, "Foreword" (2020), https://www.unpri.org/annual-report-2020/foreword
[16] The NGFS is a voluntary coalition of 54 central banks and supervisors, including the regulators of more than three-quarters of the global systemically important banks. See NGFS, "A Call for Action: Climate Change as a Source of Financial Risk," April 2019, https://www.banque-france.fr/sites/default/files/media/2019/04/17/ngfs_first_comprehensive_report_-_17042019_0.pdf.
[17] See Bank for International Settlements, "Climate-Related Financial Risks: A Survey on Current Initiatives," April 2020, https://www.bis.org/bcbs/publ/d502.pdf.
[18] Board of Governors of the Federal Reserve System, "Financial Stability Report," November 2020, https://www.federalreserve.gov/publications/files/financial-stability-report-20201109.pdf.

Commodity Futures and Trading Commission (CFTC) Market Risk Advisory Committee urged "urgent and decisive" regulatory action to address climate risk.[19] For financial institutions regulated by the New York State Department of Financial Services, which is an NGFS member, the regulator sent a letter to "commence a dialogue" on such questions.[20] To date, this regulatory discussion has been aimed at facilitating, rather than restricting, sustainable finance, and we expect such facilitation to continue. In addition, although bank loans are not securities, initiatives in the securities markets will influence the bank loan market, and securities regulators are increasingly emphasizing the importance of robust, consistent, and transparent disclosure of sustainability risks and activities to better inform investment decisions.[21]

- *Credit providers.* Banks around the world have begun to set ambitious climate goals. As of the date of this writing, the Principles for Responsible Banking (PRB), launched in late 2019 as the banking-side counterpart to the PRI, has more than 190 members who have committed to aligning their business activities with society's goals as expressed in, among other places, the Paris Agreement. The world's leading banks are putting more specificity behind those commitments by setting out their plans for aligning their portfolios with the goals of the Paris Agreement and achieving net-zero emissions by 2050.[22]

- *Ratings agencies.* All of the major ratings agencies, including Fitch, S&P Global, and Moody's, have committed to

---

[19] U.S. Commodity Futures Trade Commission, "Managing Climate Risk in the U.S. Financial System: Report of the Climate-Related Market Risk Subcommittee, Market Risk Advisory Committee of the U.S. Commodity Futures Trading Commission," September 9, 2020, https://www.cftc.gov/sites/default/files/2020-09/9-9-20%20Report%20of%20the%20Subcommittee%20on%20Climate-Related%20Market%20Risk%20-%20Managing%20Climate%20Risk%20in%20the%20U.S.%20Financial%20System%20for%20posting.pdf.

[20] New York State Department of Financial Services, "Letter to Chief Executive Officers or Equivalents of New York State Regulated Financial Institutions Re: Climate Change and Financial Risks," October 29, 2020, https://www.dfs.ny.gov/industry_guidance/industry_letters/il20201029_climate_change_financial_risks.

[21] Board of the International Organization of Securities Commissions, "Sustainable Finance and the Role of Securities Regulators and IOSCO: Final Report," Report FR04/2020, April 2020, https://www.iosco.org/library/pubdocs/pdf/IOSCOPD652.pdf.

[22] Major banks in the U.S. market that have committed to such targets in principle include Barclays, JPMorgan Chase, and Morgan Stanley, among others.

incorporating ESG criteria into credit ratings and analysis in a systemic and transparent way.[23] They have also grown their sustainability expertise with acquisitions of specialist sustainability ratings agencies—for example, S&P Global acquired RobecoSAM's ESG ratings business, Moody's owns a majority interest in Vigeo Eiris, and Morningstar owns Sustainalytics. The relevance of these and other specialist sustainability ratings resources will grow as investors increasingly demand third-party ratings and as sustainability-focused financial products increasingly require independent opinions that assess issuer ESG quality, the alignment of an issuance with the relevant themed principles, and the sustainability quality of the projects financed.

- *Companies*. America's business community is similarly focused on sustainable finance. Issuance of sustainable financial instruments—across green/social loans and bonds and sustainable loans and bonds—reached nearly $360 billion for the first nine months of 2020, an almost 100% increase from 2019 totals.[24] In terms of climate change ambition, thousands of such businesses (as well as other U.S. subnational actors, including municipalities and investors) have signed the declaration of We Are Still In, pledging to "support climate action to meet the goals of the Paris Agreement," irrespective of the U.S. federal government's commitment to doing so. Many have already put forward ambitious plans for meeting those commitments. From Microsoft's plan to be carbon negative by 2030, to Walmart's Project Gigaton plan to avoid one gigaton of greenhouse gases from its supply chain by 2030, business leaders have recognized the importance of assessing and mitigating environmental risks in their business.

In this context, borrowers and credit providers are particularly well matched. Because relationship-based credit providers in the loan market bring a deeper understanding and commitment to a borrower's business strategy and development, they are able to

---

[23] See Principles for Responsible Investment, "Statement on ESG in Credit Risk and Ratings." https://www.unpri.org/credit-risk-and-ratings/statement-on-esg-in-credit-risk-and-ratings-available-in-different-languages/77.article.

[24] Refinitiv, "Sustainable Finance Market Continues 2020 Growth," November 11, 2020.

simultaneously promote the borrower's sustainability objectives and their own internal targets. Indeed, sustainable lending should be an intimate financial means to achieve both parties' sustainability objectives. These joint efforts will also promote the development of new sustainable finance products, including sustainable securitization structures (which will require a thoughtful melding of the sustainability mandates of the bond markets and the loan markets) and sustainable derivatives products.[25]

In addition, in a competitive market the benefits of a consistent presentation of a borrower's sustainability profile for comparison against that of competitors will help to ensure successful placement of the borrower's debt issuances, which will benefit both the borrower and its credit providers. This incentive to satisfy their multiple constituencies' sustainability requirements will operate to make borrowers themselves a leading driver for the promotion of consistency and transparency in meaningful sustainability disclosure.

DEFINING SUSTAINABILITY

The primary component of a sustainable loan is sustainability. Because different actors will have different objectives and needs, the adoption of a singular definition of *sustainability* for financial products is unhelpful. Nevertheless, identifying acceptable parameters or themes is fundamental to the success of sustainable finance. In particular, the parties must be clear about (1) the defined sustainability objective, (2) the contribution of the activity being financed or incentivized to achieving such objective, and (3) an evaluation of any significant negative impacts that may undermine the sustainability determination.

The international community has recognized challenges to continuing to meet both the needs of the present and the future and that action must be taken to meet these challenges. This is expressed in the following three international agreements, which offer a robust set of sustainability benchmarks: (1) the 2030 Agenda for Sustainable Development,[26] which sets out 17 Sustainable

---

[25] For example, the market saw a cross-currency swap whose interest payments were tied to parties' achievement of sustainability targets in the underlying instruments. See Anna Hirtenstein, "JPMorgan Currency Deal Highlights Finance's Green Shift," *The Wall Street Journal*, October 26, 2020.

[26] See United Nations General Assembly Resolution A/RES/70/1 at paragraph 53, September 25, 2015, https://www.un.org/ga/search/view_doc.asp?symbol=A/RES/70/1&Lang=E.

Development Goals—a comprehensive set of sustainability objectives; (2) the Paris Agreement,[27] which provides specificity around addressing climate change and low-carbon development; and (3) the Sendai Framework for Disaster Risk Reduction (the UN Agreements).[28] The Paris Agreement in particular also expresses a scientific consensus around mitigating the profound economic costs and disruption that environmental change will, if left unaddressed, bring to the world's economies and societies.

The UN Agreements established sustainability objectives and initiated the inertial movement of national governments toward achieving those objectives. However, the UN Agreements do not include the technical criteria pursuant to which credit providers and borrowers can evaluate the contribution of any particular loan or activity to achieving those objectives nor of any potential harm that such loan or activity may incidentally cause. Extending credit to a wind farm that will more efficiently power fossil fuel extraction may lower greenhouse gas emissions, but can the private sector participants in that transaction designate that credit as sustainable? Similarly, a wind farm that displaces coal-powered supply to a utility may seem an obvious candidate for the label. But what if the wind farm is built in an environmentally sensitive area?

Today's leaders in establishing technical criteria for sustainability designation include supranational bodies, national or subnational governments, and private actors, such as industry groups, independent ESG rating firms, self-initiating issuers, and even credit providers. And although there has been significant effort made to establish classification protocols for financial instruments, the breadth of the participants has ensured that no single system dominates. To give a small sample of these types of technical standards, one long-standing private resource is the Climate Bonds Initiative (CBI) with its Climate Bonds Taxonomy (which, despite the title, applies to loans as well).[29]

---

[27] The Paris Agreement is the latest global agreement reached under the auspices of the UN Framework Convention on Climate Change (UNFCCC), which was agreed in 1992 and committed the world to limiting anthropogenic temperature rise. Among other things, it requires annual meetings of its signatory parties to further its objectives.

[28] Sendai Framework for Disaster Risk Reduction 2015–2030. https://www.unisdr.org/files/43291_sendaiframeworkfordrren.pdf.

[29] CBI provides its taxonomy for use "by any entity looking to identify which assets and activities, and associated financial instruments, are compatible with a 2-degree trajectory." See "Climate Bonds Taxonomy." https://www.climatebonds.net/files/files/CBI_Taxonomy_Tables-Nov19.pdf. CBI also provides a certification scheme that can be used to certify green loans (but not sustainability-linked loans, due to their unspecified use of proceeds).

More recently, in the public sector, the European Union (EU) passed into law the EU Taxonomy Regulation,[30] which outlines six environmental objectives for an economic activity to be environmentally sustainable, and requires that a qualifying activity must make a "substantial contribution" to at least one of these six objectives, and not cause "significant harm" to any of the others.[31] Limited drafts of technical standards for conducting this evaluation have already been proposed, but as of the time of this writing remain subject to discussion. This dual set of objectives—substantial contribution and "do no significant harm"—should become one of the cornerstones of the future development of the sustainable finance market, but market participants should brace themselves for continued competition on technical standard setting.

Although there is therefore currently no single, widely adopted criterion for making sustainability determinations, credit providers and borrowers can use these taxonomies or specialist providers' expertise (as the parties determine is appropriate) to identify the loan's sustainability objective (or set of objectives), together with the loan's contribution toward achieving that objective, and to measure the successful avoidance of significant ancillary harm. The parties should ensure transparency and consistency in the loan process so that the sustainability characteristics that led to the designation of such sustainable loan are readily apparent to the participants and can be explained to third parties. In this way, consistent minimum parameters and themes will apply to sustainable loans, notwithstanding a broad market application of the product.

ADDITIONAL DRAFTING AND DILIGENCE CONSIDERATIONS

The following are some of the central considerations for structuring and key components for drafting any sustainable loan.

---

[30] Regulation (EU) 2020/852 of the European Parliament and of the Council of June 18, 2020, on the establishment of a framework to facilitate sustainable investment, and amending Regulation (EU) 2019/2088 (the "EU Taxonomy Regulation").

[31] The EU Taxonomy Regulation sets out the criteria for "substantial contribution" and "significant harm" for each of the objectives. For example, a loan to a wind farm could be classified as environmentally sustainable under the current proposed screening criteria under the EU Taxonomy Regulation if it meets all of the criteria for Production of Electricity from Wind Power at Annex A, including the screening criteria to ensure that it is not significantly harming the achievement of any other sustainability goals.

- *Identify the purpose.* A first step in the successful crafting of a sustainable finance product is the identification of the meaningful sustainability objectives to be achieved. This determination should be made with reference to the three motivators discussed earlier (economic risk reduction, opportunity recognition, and the avoidance of contribution to systemic sustainability challenges). This determination will often not be straightforward.

  Consider a green loan that finances a wind farm that will contribute to a sustainability objective of increasing renewable power generation. The specifics of that contribution will vary depending upon the broader context. A wind farm that powers increased fossil fuel extraction will have a different profile to one that displaces a large amount of existing fossil fuel–powered generation. Furthermore, if the wind farm represents a small portion of an otherwise fossil fuel–focused portfolio, and does not represent a meaningful transitional movement to sustainably sourced generation, the loan is unlikely to alter either the borrower's or (if they are looking to the borrower's overall credit profile for repayment) the credit providers' exposure to climate related risk.

  Regulatory developments may offer additional rationales for sustainable loans. While still speculative as of the date of this article, a game-changing development for sustainable lending would be a regulatory attribution of reduced capital charges accruing to loans structured to achieve meaningful sustainability objectives (or, conversely, a capital surcharge on loans that are especially exposed to climate risk).[32] Perhaps indicative of such regulatory

---

[32] Action 8 of the EU's "Action Plan: Financing Sustainable Growth in 2018" was to explore this possibility, and since then the European Parliament and Council have mandated the European Banking Authority to "(1) [i]dentify the principles and methodologies for the inclusion of ESG risks in the review and evaluation performed by supervisors, and (2) [e]xplore the prudential soundness of introducing a more risk sensitive treatment of 'green asset' (so-called green supporting factor)." The idea was hinted at in the EU's Green Deal announcement: "Third, climate and environmental risks will be managed and integrated into the financial system. This means better integrating such risks into the EU prudential framework and assessing the suitability of the existing capital requirements for green assets." See European Commission, "Communication from the Commission: The European Green Deal," November 12, 2019.

acceptance in the future, the European Central Bank (ECB) announced in September 2020 that, commencing in January 2021, certain sustainability-linked bonds will be eligible as central bank collateral and also potentially eligible as assets for the purposes of its asset purchase program and pandemic emergency purchase program, subject to compliance with program-specific eligibility criteria. Credit providers who wish to have their loans qualify will need to be familiar with the program requirements.

- *Align with latest best practices.* As described above, the field of sustainable finance is developing quickly, and best practices are continuing to emerge. As such, credit providers and borrowers should be willing to update their sustainable loan documentation as sustainability standards evolve. For example, a sustainability-linked loan may incentivize a sustainable transition objective that initially represents a Paris-aligned best practice. However, if the pace of transition is later determined to be too slow, it may be appropriate for the parties to amend the documentation to incentivize a more ambitious timeline.

    As discussed earlier, a tremendous advantage to sustainable loans as a whole is the intimate relationship between credit providers and borrowers that allows this sort of iterative change. The parties should engage in regular dialogue about the adequacy of the loan to achieving the identified sustainability objectives.

- *Public disclosure of sustainability targets and progress.* Unlike public securities markets, the loan markets are largely nonpublic. Even for public companies, the only documentation related to a sustainable loan that may become public is the credit agreement. Although a publicly filed credit agreement will reveal the metrics and targets chosen, such disclosure will be lacking any context. A borrower that sets meaningful and ambitious targets may require some additional disclosure describing any differences between the aspirational targets established in their loan documents for purposes of more favorable financing terms and any other strategic targets the borrower otherwise may have publicly disclosed. Similarly, companies should carefully consider the level of detail they provide on both the sustainability metrics selected and the targets set

and where those are best disclosed (i.e., in securities filings or elsewhere, such as in self-published sustainability/ESG reports or frameworks on their websites).
- *Elements of a good green loan.* Green loans are designed to finance eligible "green projects." Thus, the sustainability value of a green loan lies in the project's selection and in the rigor applied to ensure that the loan's proceeds are used for that purpose. The following are some key considerations credit providers and borrowers should take into account in making these decisions, in addition to the basic features described above:
  - *Identification.* A project may be pure green or transition focused.[33] In either case, best practice would ensure that the project is identified in accordance with the principles set out above; that is, that it achieves a recognized sustainability objective in accordance with a credible taxonomy and does not cause incidental, significant harm.
  - *Use of proceeds.* There are two ways in which the use of proceeds may be mandated in green loan documentation. The specific project or projects may be identified in the use of proceeds covenant. Alternatively, if proceeds are meant to be used for sustainable projects identified over time, the borrower can instead provide a "framework" that explains how the borrower will identify such projects, and the use of proceeds covenant will require the borrower to select projects in accordance with that framework. In general, the borrower would not seek credit providers' approval for each project as it is entered into. Credit providers should, however, receive updates on project status and use of proceeds with other financial performance reporting (typically monthly or quarterly).
  - *Consequence of breach.* Whereas in the bond market there is currently no covenant default if an issuer fails

---

[33] We note that neither of these categories is entirely clear-cut, but, in general, in the context of climate change "green" projects are those that are already sufficiently low carbon that they do not need to change to be consistent with a future zero-carbon world, and "transition" projects are those that are not yet sufficiently low carbon, but for which there is a clear and credible plan according to which they will lower their carbon within a time frame that can meet the goals of the Paris Agreement.

to use the bond proceeds in accordance with the use of proceeds framework described in the securities offering materials, the loan market is more prescriptive. Thus, although the green loan principles do not require this, a best practice is to tie an event of default to a breach of the "green" use of proceeds covenant. The close relationship between credit providers and borrowers, and the loan market's receptivity to loan document modifications (unlike bond indenture modifications) to meet the changing needs of credit providers and borrowers encourages the inclusion of a specific default tied to use of proceeds. Indeed, changed economic conditions or specific project developments may necessitate amendments. For example, in 2020 COVID-19 may have interfered with a borrower's ability to apply a green loan's proceeds to specified sustainable projects, and we would expect that in such a case credit providers would have provided a temporary amendment or waiver to allow otherwise ineligible uses of proceeds, with the requirement that when circumstances permit, the proceeds would again be used only for eligible projects.

- *Alignment with the borrower's business strategy.* While a borrower's business strategy is not always as directly relevant to green loans as it is for sustainability-linked loans, it brings itself to bear in two ways.
  - For pure green loans, there may be reputational risk to credit providers if the borrower's overall sustainability profile is dubious.
  - For transition-focused green loans, an understanding of how the project fits into and assists with the borrower's broader sustainability strategy is critical to ensuring the appropriate application of the label. For example, if no clear and credible path exists for the borrower's transition to a business model aligned with the Paris Agreement targets, the application of the sustainability label may be inappropriate.
- *Accurate reporting.* Borrowers should provide annual reports to credit providers that cover (1) the use of proceeds, including the green projects financed, a

description on how and why they qualified as eligible projects and the amounts allocated to each project, and (2) if possible, the ongoing and expected environmental impact of the projects. Where the projects financed are transitional, the environmental impact reporting should reflect alignment with the pathway agreed at the initial documentation phase, or, if appropriate, the parties should agree to an update to that pathway. As with the use of proceeds covenant, the loan documentation should reflect a default if the borrower breaches the reporting covenant.

- *Independent review of reporting.* Third parties can provide valuable expertise prior to entering into the loan documentation (e.g., a review of the project selection framework or of the alignment of the loan with the Green Loan Principles), especially in cases where the projects financed are transitional or where the borrower does not have demonstrated internal expertise to confirm that the loan, and in particular the projects that it finances, aligns with the selected taxonomy. Whether ongoing third party is necessary will depend upon the complexity of the project selection process as well as the borrower's expertise.

- *Elements of a good sustainability-linked loan.* The allure of a sustainability-linked loan rests on its ability to incentivize a genuine transition in the borrower's business to improved sustainability practices. To achieve that improvement, credit providers and borrowers must focus on the metrics, or key performance indicators (KPIs), to measure and set meaningful goals for improving those KPIs. The following are some key considerations for credit providers and borrowers in making these decisions:
  - *KPI selection.* Each KPI must be (1) core to the borrower's business and (2) a demonstrable marker of sustainability in that business. For example, renewable energy generated may be a meaningful KPI for a utility but may not be as meaningful for a retailer that generates its own power on site. In general, these KPIs should be identified in connection with sustainability materiality assessments that form part of the borrower's broader risk assessment and strategy development programs.

- In some cases, multiple KPIs may present a more holistic reflection of the borrower's sustainability profile. In such cases, however, each KPI should reflect the qualities set out here. In addition, the parties should be thoughtful about the value of each sustainability objective reflected in the KPIs, and ensure that each KPI is clearly tied to a relevant objective.
- As an alternative to a borrower-generated KPI, third-party sustainability ratings, rather than a business-related metric, may be an appropriate choice for a KPI in certain circumstances. However, the use of third-party ratings may have limitations. Parties should give careful consideration to the independence of the rating provider, the transparency of the rating provider's methodologies, and the rating provider's substantive credentials for providing ratings to similar companies and should address in the loan documentation the protocols if the rating provider's methodology changes or the rating ceases to be available.
- Each KPI should reflect a sustainability indicator that the borrower has reported on in a consistent and measurable manner for some time or can adapt to reflect consistently and measurability over time. Any changes in reporting over time should be clear and accounted for in the documentation to ensure an apples-to-apples comparison. For example, a metric of renewable power generation over time that excludes hydropower in early years but later includes hydropower would not accurately reflect a change in the borrower's sustainability profile over time, even if the parties agree that hydropower qualifies for inclusion.
- No KPI should be a "business as usual" metric. It is not appropriate to apply the sustainability label to something that is a standard business practice. For example, workplace reuse and recycle programs for common office waste may achieve sustainability objectives but are also ubiquitous, and therefore

should not need to be incentivized by special loan features.
- *Establish a clear initial benchmark.* Each initial KPI is a benchmark and must accurately reflect the current state of the borrower's business. The parties should mutually agree to, and expressly state, both the qualitative description of the benchmark KPI and the initial quantitative measurement of that KPI. It must be easily identifiable to all parties. Setting such an initial benchmark KPI may require deciding whether to use an average of that metric over a recent period or a single-year benchmark.
- *Establish and incentivize ambitious targets.* Once the parties select an appropriate KPI, the loan documentation should ensure that the transition being rewarded is sufficiently ambitious and incentivized.
  - *Target improvement over benchmark.* The targeted improvements in performance of the KPI should be aligned with a mutually agreed upon and science-based quantification of meaningful improvement (such as the Paris Agreement). This may require escalating targets over the life of the facility and, as discussed above, may require recalibration over time to remain aligned with scientific best practices.
  - *Pricing incentive.* The carrot-and-stick approach is a best practice. A borrower should be incentivized to both improve on the KPI, but also to avoid any regression in the chosen metric. A bilateral economic incentive would reflect that the achievement of the sustainability performance target gives rise to a pricing or other benefit, while regression results in a pricing or other penalty. Consider also whether a sustainability pricing modification should apply to interest rate margins and facility costs throughout the facility structure or, as has more often been the case in the United States to date, only to drawn amounts under the facility.
  - *Ensure accurate reporting.* Accurate and reliable reporting of a borrower's performance of its sustainability targets is paramount. Creditors must receive borrower-certified

reports at least annually, customarily with the borrower's annual financial compliance certificate. The reliability of such certifications materially improves when the borrower includes information that is either publicly filed and subject to securities laws or verified by third parties (noting again the use of third parties is not without limitations).

- *Reviewing the reports.* Preclosing engagement with a third party to assess the ambitious nature of both the KPI and the targeted improvements (e.g., whether sufficiently aligned with the Paris Agreement) is likely helpful. Ongoing third-party assessment of the sustainability performance metric is particularly helpful when the selected KPI is relatively complicated.
- *Inaccurate reporting.* In the event that a borrower's sustainability reporting is determined to be inaccurate, and as a consequence the borrower improperly obtained the benefit of lower pricing, the loan documentation should provide that the borrower must retroactively repay amounts that would have been payable but for the inaccuracy. Whether such inaccuracy gives rise to an event of default under the agreement has typically been left to an interpretation of the standard reporting representations and covenants.

CONCLUSION

The complaint that sustainable finance is an "alphabet soup" and a confusing morass obscures its crucial and urgent purpose. Indeed, there is more agreement than disagreement in the markets that sustainable finance, and in particular for this article, sustainable loans, are integral to market participants' success. Sustainable lending mitigates economic risk that arises from inattention to sustainability objectives, provides valuable new economic opportunities, and avoids exacerbating systemic sustainability challenges. With an increasing number of global financial institutions committing to the goals of the Paris Agreement, including an increasing number of "net zero by 2050" pledges by leading banks, future lending should embed sustainability in the ordinary course. The market appetite for green loans and sustainability-linked loans is an important step in that direction.

The Evolution of Sustainability-Linked Lending: Watershed Moments and Expanding Investor Participation

Maria Christina Dikeos
Refinitiv LPC

In 2007, the world was introduced to green financing via the first climate awareness bond issued by the European Investment Bank. It would be another five years before the first bank-led benchmark transactions hit the market and another two years beyond that before the inaugural draft of the Green Bond Principles would be published in 2014. By the end of 2018, global green bond volume totaled nearly $132 billion via 351 deals, an increase of 5.5 times since the publication of the principles.

In the loans world, green lending was a bit delayed by comparison. The first corporate loan issued on behalf of U.K. supermarket chain, Sainsbury, with the express purpose of supporting environmental and sustainability initiatives, came to market in 2014. A bilateral credit that did not allow for either a diverse investor base or an upsizing to the original $200 million commitment, the loan was structured consistent with Green Bond Principles.

"There was nothing wrong with the Sainsbury deal but there was nothing right with it either," said one arranger.

It did, however, set a benchmark, a precedent for green and/or ESG lending in the loan market.

In March 2018, the LMA and the APLMA, with the support of the LSTA in the United States, published the first set of Green Loan Principles that laid out the framework for green loan designation based on use of proceeds. Nearly one year later, these same organizations published the first draft of the Sustainability-Linked Loan

Principles that took the concept of green lending one step further by focusing primarily on the issuer of debt that effectively commits to operating in a more environmentally sustainable manner.

The concept of green and ESG lending in the loan space quickly gained traction globally, albeit to different degrees depending on the regional home base of borrowers tapping the market.

METRICS AND OTHER FACTORS

It's not easy being green. In the absence of a clear road map and broadly espoused metrics, it is even less so. For the loan asset class, the crafting and adoption of green and ESG metrics is in its infancy, although sustained momentum and demands for market transparency are building.

In contrast to the drivers that have buoyed the green bond market, including a growing pool of investors and portfolio managers who have set internal goals to meet green objectives, as well as the emergence of dedicated funds that only invest in green instruments, the loan market has less of a committed, green investor base—although this is changing.

Instead, the impetus for growth in the loan space has largely been fueled by corporates themselves. In most cases, the momentum and focus have been against a backdrop of shareholder and employee advocacy efforts as well as government-supported regulations.

"It [has been] a combination of companies becoming more aware of having to do business in an increasingly responsible way and finding a path to aligning this with financial benefits," said one lender. More important, there is growing acknowledgment that there "is not a trade-off between green and P&L goals."

Still, there are inherent complexities. Although green project financings are arguably straightforward given deal purpose and associated monitoring, sustainability-linked financings are largely untested in so far as how they can or will have a measurable, positive impact on corporate behavior.

"We are dissecting something that doesn't have parameters," in the words of one U.S.-based lender. "More specificity is necessary."

And this can only come with a slow but steady build of data history around ESG lending and its impact. Arguably, sustainability-linked loans may be a minor tool in the ESG corporate tool kit. It is still unclear whether ESG lending practices incentivize more responsible corporate behavior or validate existing corporate mandates and mantras.

Time and data history should allow for deeper understanding of the potential benefits to borrowers and their lending partners as well as the larger global ESG community.

"There has to be a balance between the goals that are set for an issuer and how meaningful it is for the company to meet them," said one European lender. "You have to track accountability. Once we have 5 to 10 years' worth of data, you can go to central banks and make a case for loss given default to be lower and then a case for smaller liquidity reserves against green lending."

WHY DO WE CARE?

The adoption of green and sustainability-linked lending has been uneven across regions, with loan volume out of Europe representing over 80% of the global total on the back of broad-based political support. The concept has also gained momentum among borrowers in Asia Pacific, most notably out of China.

In the United States, federal policy under the Trump administration largely ignored climate change, rolling back prior administrations' policies around development, social protections, and hiring practices. The Biden administration signaled a reversal of the Trump administration policies. Despite the contrasts of the two administrations at the federal level, however, over the course of the last few years, messaging and efforts around green and sustainable growth have been picked up at the state level in the wake of several "once in a hundred years" floods and wildfires that have ravaged wide swaths of the country.

"Most major US cities are near bodies of water," said one U.S.-based arranger of loan debt. "How many times do people say something is weather related inferring it is 'different'? When does it stop being different? When does it impact sales? Some of the biggest companies in this country are focused on weather-related impact. Our clients care."

IMPACT OF 2020: PANDEMIC, FIRES, AND SOCIAL UPHEAVAL

Amid the spread of the COVID-19 pandemic across nearly 200 countries, raging wildfires across two continents, melting icecaps, social upheaval, and economic uncertainty, 2020 forced a global reckoning around sustainable corporate operations and personal behavior.

No longer was ESG accountability a localized or regional matter, but one of global stewardship and socioeconomic justice. Broader efforts around sustainability were renewed, although initiatives were neither smooth nor easy. They did, however, build on a growing trend over the last several years, one in which the debt capital markets emerged as increasingly engaged participants.

A record $701.5 billion of green and ESG-linked lending was completed globally in 2020, an 80% jump over 2019 prepandemic levels. More important, in a testament to the market's upward trajectory, between 2017 and the end of 2020, issuance for the combined loan and bond markets increased over 4.5 times since 2017 (Exhibit 18.8).

"ESG is real and it is accelerating," said one arranger of leveraged debt. "People are voting with their feet and, some, with their money."

MANAGING A CREDIT CRISIS AND REINFORCING ESG FRAMEWORK

Despite positive popular sentiment, in practice, the pipeline of green and ESG-linked financings got off to a rocky start in 2020.

EXHIBIT 18.8

2020 Global Green & ESG-linked Volume Jumps 80% to Record US Dollars $701 billion.

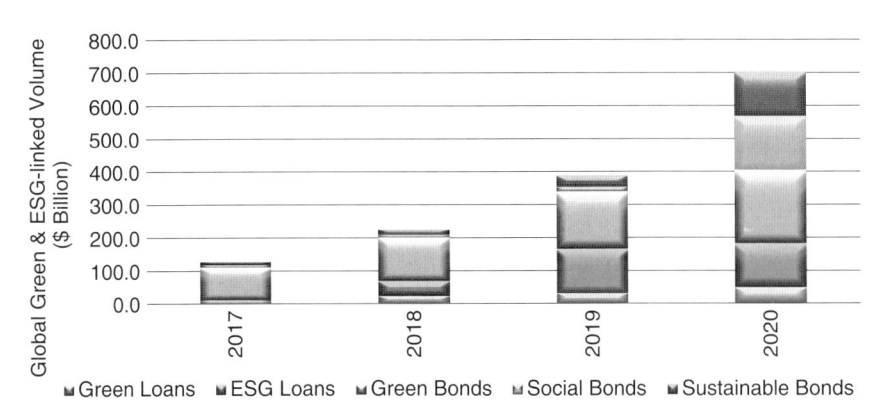

Source: Refinitiv LPC *Includes Schuldschein.

With the sudden and dramatic spread of COVID-19 in the first quarter of 2020, both borrowers and lenders initially set aside environmental, social, and sustainability-linked performance metrics in favor of rapidly placed, pandemic response liquidity.

"The focus was to get companies through the crisis, keep the lights on and protect employees," said one arranger.

At just over $104.3 billion, first-quarter 2020 green and ESG-linked loan and bond issuance was down nearly 25% compared to fourth-quarter 2019 results (Exhibit 18.9).

Nevertheless, the impact of the pandemic—including the economic and operational paralysis that followed, and even the ability of corporates to raise liquidity to manage the fallout—underscored the growing view that the crisis was in no small part due to the culmination of environmentally insensitive behavior and further aggravated by entrenched socioeconomic inequities.

"There is a view that we have to do things differently," said an arranger.

With that, new questions were raised about "what the world looks like after the pandemic and how we take the lessons we have learned into the post-crisis world."

"We had a tremendous emergency response [to the pandemic]," according to another lender. "How do we make companies that benefitted from [the response] more accountable? Do you

EXHIBIT 18.9

Record Global Green & ESG-linked Issuance Tops U.S. $241.5 Billion in Fourth Quarter 2020.

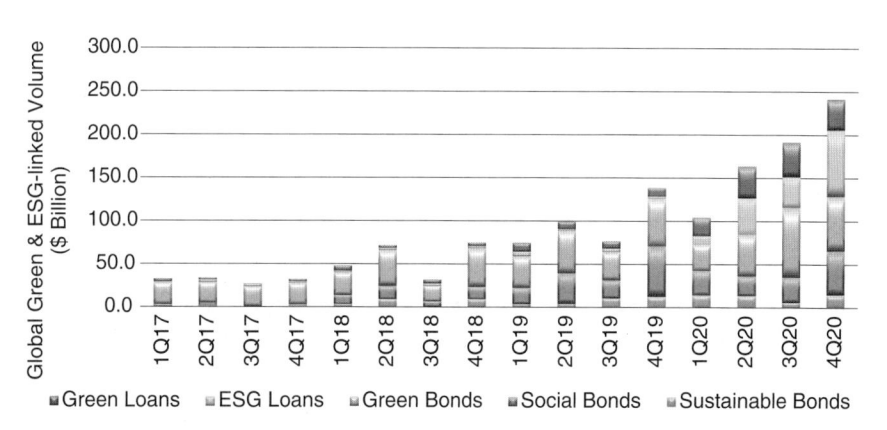

Source: Refinitiv LPC *Includes Schuldschein.

include conditions with respect to carbon footprint? Social governance? How do you not lose momentum?"

ESG corporate financing advocacy did not come together via consistent messaging or even sustained momentum in the wake of a crisis like COVID-19. The sudden drop in oil prices in the second quarter of 2020 made renewable energy alternatives less attractive—and sustainability-linked loan and bond issuance suffered. At the same time, airlines and other brown industries that were slow to put sustainable financing in place at the outset, pulled back amid the rushed need for liquidity as the travel sector suffered in the wake of COVID-19 restrictions.

In February 2020, JetBlue Airways Corp. placed a $550 million revolving credit facility that included a sustainability-linked pricing provision based on the company's ESG score. With the onset of COVID-19, it would be another nine months—in November 2020 when Airbus Group tapped the loan market for a €6 billion three-year revolver—before a second airline would come to market with a sustainability-linked loan financing.

ESG IS INTEGRAL TO CREDIT-RISK DISCUSSIONS

Despite the fitfulness of the ESG pipeline, there has been a deepening market awareness of the broader relevance of ESG-linked metrics in discussions around corporate credit risk.

Efforts around meaningful progress have been two-pronged: (1) increased focus on standardization of practices and disclosures for the market to assess corporate sustainability-linked metrics and performance against the stated metrics and (2) the emergence of social bonds and loans as targeted financing structures in which use of proceeds is for defined social good. The bond market has been the cornerstone of both undertakings.

Over $164 billion in social bond issuance was raised in 2020, more than 12 times 2019 figures, to set a new record. Of this total, 47% was raised in the fourth quarter of 2020 alone. An additional $133.5 billion in sustainability-linked bond volume was also completed during the year, more than 3.75 times greater than 2019 results, to mark a new market high, and green bond issuance was up 27.5% year over year at $222 billion.

In testament to the broader understanding of the need for, and significance of, sustainability-linked financing, in May 2020,

Corporacion Andina de Fomento (CAF), the Development Bank of Latin America, issued a €700 million five-year social bond to support the region's member states with COVID-19–related aid and recovery costs, including health care and emergency economic support. The issue represented one of the first ESG financings for the region.

From an administrative and functional standardization standpoint, the market also made inroads. In February 2020, the loan market saw the launch of the LSTA's ESG Due Diligence Questionnaire, as part of an effort to facilitate market transparency and streamline information sharing between loan market transactors and borrowers. In May the Securities and Exchange Commission (SEC) issued its recommendation that SEC-registered issuers adopt an ESG disclosure framework that provides transparency and consistency to prospective investors. In December, the International Capital Market Association (ICMA) and Climate Transition Finance published their Transition Bond Guidelines, providing the capital markets with a road map and tool kit to work with brown-industry issuers who do not currently meet the strict standards of a green or sustainability-linked financing but who have made a commitment to moving toward green business practices.

The loan market followed the same principles and guidelines as the broader bond market, albeit at a smaller pace. In July 2020, French resource management company Suez signed a €100 million social revolving credit facility with use of proceeds directed to fighting the impact of COVID-19 by supporting charity foundations, frontline employees, and customers who had been impacted by the pandemic or been on the frontline during lockdown.

To date, the growth of ESG lending via the loans space has not been as steep as that of the bond market (Exhibit 18.10). Nevertheless, lenders are recognizing the importance of aligning portfolio commitment with efforts to support clients who are committed to green and socially responsible practices.

"KPIs show there is intention," according to lenders.

Few expect that investors and other lenders will sell out of deals due to ESG concerns in the next few years, but there is consensus that lenders may not increase positions if a borrower's sustainability-linked practices confront negative scrutiny. Future deals may be turned down and incremental investment may be delayed until there is clarity around specific borrower behavior.

EXHIBIT 18.10

Global Green & ESG Loan Volume Grows Over 15 Times in Four Years.

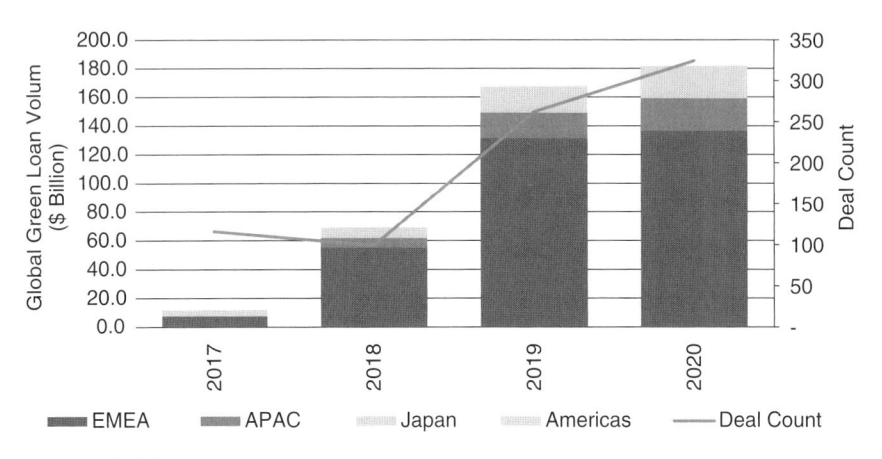

[Bar and line chart showing Global Green Loan Volume ($ Billion) on left axis (0 to 200) and Deal Count on right axis (0 to 350) for years 2017–2020. Categories: EMEA, APAC, Japan, Americas, Deal Count.]

Source: Refinitiv LPC.

In the loan market specifically, the institutional investor community is cautiously lining up behind ESG-linked loan structures, although standardized taxonomy and performance metrics are cited as critical prerequisites for broader market traction. Spanish telecom operator Masmovil was the first leveraged issuer to tap lenders for an ESG-linked facility in May 2019, although the ESG component was linked to a €250 million revolving credit facility. By the end of the same year, Spanish maker of jean manufacturing equipment Jeanologia tapped a club group of bank lenders for its ESG-linked leveraged buyout financing. In 2020, another two issuers—Logoplaste and Kersia—tapped lenders, with Logoplaste's amended €570 million financing marking the first ESG-linked loan to test institutional investor appetite.

ESG POPPING UP IN EVERY FINANCING CONVERSATION

According to arrangers of bank debt, in the wake of COVID-19, ESG themes are regularly coming up in financing conversations among both high-grade and leveraged issuers. The broader messaging around sustainability-linked lending, the legitimacy and specificity of key performance metrics adopted by borrowers who commit to moving toward more sustainable and socially responsible operations, and the correlation between the successful adoption of better practices and the long-term credit quality of an issuer are expected to become more integrated. This will allow for what the market hopes to be the next watershed moment for ESG lending, one that focuses on standardization of market standards and benchmarking.

CHAPTER 19

Accounting for Loans

Cara Brugel
Audit & Assurance Manager
Deloitte & Touche LLP

Chase Hodges
Senior Manager, Audit & Assurance
Deloitte & Touche LLP

Chris Rogers
Partner, Audit & Assurance
Deloitte & Touche LLP

INTRODUCTION

This chapter sets out the highlights of accounting for loans and loan products under U.S. generally accepted accounting principles (GAAP). To apply these rules to any individual set of facts and circumstances will require due diligence and exercise of professional judgment. Adequate loan accounting policies and procedures are essential to sound and effective overall risk management processes in a bank.

LOANS AND INVESTMENTS

As defined by the Financial Accounting Standards Board (FASB) Accounting Standards Codification (ASC) 310-10-20, a *loan* represents the "contractual right to receive money on demand or on fixed or determinable dates that is recognized as an asset in the creditor's statement of financial position."

Loan Classification

Although there are a variety of loan types, such as asset-backed loans, student loans, and others, the accounting treatment and classification of a loan are both largely dependent on and driven by management's holding intent. Therefore, it is important for a bank to have a clear set of policies and procedures in place to determine which positions should be included in, and which should be excluded from, each loan classification. Common loan classifications include the trading book, the banking book, and held for sale.

- *Banking book (held for investment).* Loans that are originated or acquired for the purposes of long-term investment can be designated as *held for investment* (HFI) and recorded in the bank's banking book. ASC 948-310-25-1 states that in order to designate a loan as HFI, a bank must have "both the ability and intent to hold the loan for the foreseeable future or until maturity."
- *Loans held for sale.* Some banks may classify loans in a *held for sale* (HFS) portfolio recorded within its banking book. Loans classified in this way include asset-backed loans or other loans that are held in order to be securitized or sold.

- *Trading book (held for trade).* Loans that are originated or acquired either with a trading intent or to hedge other elements of the trading book can be designated as *held for trade* (HFT) and recorded in the bank's trading book. Examples of loans that are typically recorded as trading loans include loans acquired in the secondary market, including any distressed loans that are acquired and held intentionally for short-term resale, and loans that are held to hedge total return swaps (TRSs) in the trading book. A bank should determine HFT classification on an instrument-by-instrument basis.

Loan Recognition and Measurement

An entity should recognize a loan on its balance sheet on the basis of its accounting policy, typically either using trade date or settlement date accounting. Under trade date accounting, an entity will recognize a loan on the date on which an agreement is entered into. Under settlement date accounting, an entity will recognize a loan when the financial transaction is settled and the consideration for the transaction is received. The measurement of the loan at time of recognition will be dependent on the loan classification, as described above.

- *Measurement of HFI loans—amortized cost basis.* HFI loans originated or acquired should be measured at amortized cost basis, and any interest income should be recognized on an accrual basis. As defined under U.S. GAAP, amortized cost basis is the amount at which a financing receivable or investment is originated or acquired, adjusted for applicable accrued interest, accretion, or amortization of premium, discount, and net deferred fees or costs, collection of cash, write-offs, foreign exchange, and fair value hedge accounting adjustments. Any credit impairment will be recognized as an allowance—or contra-asset—rather than as a direct write-down of a financial asset's amortized cost basis (see further discussion on allowance for credit losses below).
- *Measurement of HFS loans—lower of amortized cost basis or market value.* These loans are measured at the lower of amortized cost basis or market value, as of the balance sheet date.

- *Measurement of HFT loans—fair value.* HFT loans are measured at fair value; that is, they are marked to market with changes in fair value recognized through net income. Fair value is determined based on market value, but when market prices are not readily available, fair value is estimated using pricing models that are based on current market data wherever possible.
- *Measurement of loans transferred between classifications.* The transfer of a loan between trading (HFT) and banking categories (either HFI or HFS) is accounted for at fair value; however, given the short-term nature of a trading asset, transfers into or out of the trading category are rare. Between banking categories, loans should be transferred from the HFI portfolio to the HFS portfolio when a decision is made to sell a loan or portion thereof that was initially originated or acquired for the purposes of long-term investment.

   Loans transferred into the HFS portfolio are recorded at the lower of their amortized cost basis or fair value on a loan-by-loan basis. At the time of transfer, an entity should reverse in net income any allowance for credit losses (discussed below) previously recorded on the HFI loan. The loan should then be transferred to the HFS classification at its amortized cost basis, which will be reduced by any previous write-offs but excludes allowance for credit losses. Further, if an HFI loan has been the hedged item in a fair value hedge, the loan's cost basis used in the lower of amortized cost basis or fair value accounting shall reflect the effect of any adjustments to its carrying amount due to the hedge relationship. If it is determined that the amortized cost basis exceeds fair value, the entity should record the transferred loan at fair value and record the loss as valuation allowance with the change in valuation allowance to be included in net income during the period of the change.

LOAN ORIGINATION FEES AND COSTS

Loan originators will typically incur nonrefundable fees and origination costs associated with lending arrangements. The classification of nonrefundable fees and origination costs drives accounting recognition and measurement. For loans within the scope of ASC 310-20

(HFI loans, HFS loans, and available for sale debt securities), fees paid by borrowers that qualify to be considered loan origination fees and expenses paid by lenders that qualify to be considered direct loan origination costs should be netted against each other, deferred, and recognized as yield adjustments on a straight-line basis over the life of the related loan.

- *Loan origination fees.* As part of typical origination and lending activities, a borrower may be required to pay the lender fees. If a fee meets the definition of a loan origination fee, the lender must net it against any direct loan origination costs, defer the netted amount, and recognize the fees/costs as yield adjustments over the life of the loan as described above. ASC 310-20-20 states that loan origination fees consist of the following:
  - Fees that are being charged to the borrower as prepaid interest or to reduce the loan's nominal interest rate, such as interest buy-downs (explicit yield adjustments, sometimes referred to as an original issuance discount or premium).
  - Fees to reimburse the lender for origination activities.
  - Any other fees charged to the borrower that relate directly to making the loan (e.g., fees that are paid to the lender as compensation for granting a complex loan or agreeing to lend quickly).
  - Fees not conditional on a loan being granted by the lender, but are in substance implicit yield adjustments because a loan is granted at rates that would not be considered without such a fee (e.g., certain syndication fees as discussed below).
  - Fees charged to the borrower in connection with the process of originating, refinancing, or restructuring a loan; this includes, but is not limited to, points, management, arrangement, placement, application, underwriting, and other fees pursuant to a lending or leasing transaction. This also includes syndication and participation fees to the extent they are associated with the portion of the loan retained by the lender.
- *Syndication fees.* A loan syndication is a transaction in which several lenders share in lending to a single borrower. Each

lender loans a specific amount to the borrower and has the right to repayment from the borrower. This is one method by which a loan can be funded when the amount to be borrowed is greater than any one lender is willing to lend. Specific to syndication fees, a loan syndicator should recognize the loan syndication fees when the syndication is complete, except in cases where the syndicator retains a portion of the syndication loan.

When a portion of the syndicated loan is retained by the syndicating bank, if the yield on the portion of the loan retained by the bank is less than the average yield to the other syndication participants after considering the fees passed through by the bank, then the bank should defer a portion of the syndication fee to produce a yield on the portion of the loan retained that is not less than the average yield on the loans held by the other syndication participants. The balance of fees can be recognized as income on completion of the syndication. Further, if the syndicator additionally receives a recurring fee for servicing the loan, it should be recognized in income over the period it is earned.

- *Participation fees.* Loan participation fees are amortized into earnings over the term of the loan. When part of a loan is subsequently sold off, a proportionate amount of unamortized loan participation fees should be recognized at the time of sale. The remaining unamortized fees related to the retained portion of the loan should be included in the net carrying amount of the loan and should be amortized into earnings over the remaining term of the loan. See below for more detail on accounting for loan participations.
- *Direct loan origination/acquisition costs.* Direct loan origination or acquisition costs include costs to originate or acquire a loan that (1) result directly from and are essential to the lending transaction and (2) would not have been incurred by the lender had the lending transaction not occurred. Examples of these are third-party payments for appraisal and legal fees, commissions paid to loan brokers, and employees' compensation costs that are directly related to time spent performing origination activities. As described above, direct loan origination or acquisition costs are to be netted against loan origination fees, deferred, and

recognized as yield adjustments on a straight-line basis over the life of the loan.
- *Incremental lending-related costs.* All other incremental lending-related costs, including costs pertaining to activities performed by the bank for advertising, soliciting potential borrowers, servicing existing loans, and other ancillary activities related to establishing and monitoring credit policies, supervision, and administration, are charged to expense as incurred. Employees' compensation and fringe benefits related to those activities, unsuccessful loan origination efforts, idle time, and other overhead costs are also charged to expense as incurred.

DEBT SECURITIES

Although loan origination is one method by which entities acquire credit exposure, entities may further gain exposure through investments in debt securities of loans that meet the definition of a security. These investments are accounted for under ASC 320, which defines a *security* as a share, participation, or other interest in property or in an entity of the issuer or an obligation of the issuer that is (1) represented by an instrument issued in bearer or registered form, or registered in books maintained to record transfers by the issuer; (2) commonly dealt in on securities exchanges or markets, or commonly recognized in any area in which it is issued or dealt in as a medium for investment; and (3) either one of a class or series, or by its terms is divisible into a class or series of shares, participations, interests, or obligations.

Debt securities are any security representing a creditor relationship with an entity. If an investment meets the conditions to be accounted for as a debt security, the entity should classify and document the debt security as trading, available for sale, or held to maturity, which will drive the measurement of the investment. The term *debt security* includes all of the following:

- Preferred stock that by its terms either must be redeemed by the issuing entity or is redeemable at the option of the investor.
- A collateralized loan obligation (CLO) or other instrument that is issued in equity form but is required to be accounted for as a nonequity instrument regardless of how that

instrument is classified (i.e., whether equity or debt) in the issuer's statement of financial position.
- U.S. Treasury securities, U.S. government agency securities, municipal securities, corporate bonds, convertible debt, commercial paper, and interest-only and principal-only strips.
- All securitized debt instruments, including as CLOs.

Note that the term *debt security* excludes option contracts, financial futures contracts, forward contracts, and lease contracts. Further, receivables that do not meet the definition of *security* and so are not debt securities include trade accounts receivable arising from sales on credit by industrial or commercial entities, as well as loans receivable arising from consumer, commercial, and real estate lending activities of financial institutions.

When determining whether an investment should be accounted for as a debt security, entities should not regard the classification of the instrument from the perspective of the issuer. This is because, although legal form should be considered in classification of a debt security, form does not always determine whether an investment should be accounted for as a debt security.

The accounting treatments for debt securities that are held for trading and held to maturity are basically the same as the treatments for loans that are in the trading book and the banking book, respectively. However, a debt security can be classified as held to maturity only if the bank has the positive intent and ability to hold that security to maturity. A sale of an investment from the held-to-maturity portfolio will most likely bring into question the bank's intent and may taint the classification of the entire remaining portfolio. Debt securities not classified as trading or held-to-maturity securities are classified as available-for-sale securities. Available-for-sale securities are measured at fair value on the balance sheet. Unrealized holding gains and losses on available-for-sale securities are reported in other comprehensive income until realized.

ALLOWANCE FOR CURRENT EXPECTED CREDIT LOSSES

The FASB issued its new standard on the measurement of expected credit losses, Accounting Standard Update (ASU) 2016-13 (codified as ASC 326), in 2016. ASU 2016-13 adds to U.S. GAAP an impairment model, known as the current expected credit loss (CECL) model, that is based on expected losses rather than incurred losses. Under the new guidance, an entity recognizes as an allowance its estimate of expected credit losses, which the FASB believes will result in more timely recognition of such losses. ASU 2016-13 is also intended to reduce the complexity of U.S. GAAP by decreasing the number of credit impairment models that entities use to account for debt instruments.

Initial Recognition

The CECL model does not specify a threshold for the recognition of an impairment allowance. Rather, an entity will recognize its estimate of expected credit losses for financial assets immediately upon either origination or acquisition and will adjust its estimate in each subsequent reporting period. Credit impairment will be recognized as an allowance—or contra-asset—rather than as a direct write-down of a financial asset's amortized cost basis. Financial assets within the scope of the CECL model are generally measured at amortized cost. Such assets are recorded at their amortized cost basis because an entity expects to realize the total value of the financial asset by collecting this basis.

Unit of Account

An entity must evaluate financial assets within the scope of the model on a collective (i.e., pool) basis if they share similar risk characteristics. If a financial asset's risk characteristics are not similar to those of any of the entity's other financial assets, the entity would evaluate that financial asset individually. Although ASC 326-20-55-5 identifies risk characteristics that an entity could consider when segmenting its portfolio of financial assets, ASC 326 does not discuss how the entity should choose such characteristics. Therefore, an entity can determine the segmenting characteristics that will result in its best estimate of current expected credit losses.

Measurement

Under ASU 2016-13, an entity can use various measurement approaches to determine the impairment allowance. Some approaches project future principal and interest cash flows (i.e., a discounted cash flow, or DCF, method), whereas others project only future principal losses. If an entity chooses to estimate credit losses by using a method other than a DCF method, it has the option of estimating such losses on the asset's amortized cost basis in the aggregate or by separately measuring the components of the amortized cost basis (e.g., premiums and discounts). Regardless of the measurement method used, an entity's estimate of expected credit losses should reflect the losses that occur over the contractual life of the financial asset. The entity is not allowed to consider expected extensions of the contractual life unless (1) extensions are a contractual right of the borrower or (2) the entity has a reasonable expectation as of the reporting date that it will execute a troubled debt restructuring (TDR) with the borrower.

An entity is required to consider expected prepayments either as a separate input in the method used to estimate expected credit losses or as an amount embedded in the credit loss experience that it uses to estimate such losses. Prepayment expectations may reduce the term of a financial asset, which is likely to lead to a reduction in the entity's exposure to credit losses. Therefore, prepayments could have a significant effect on the estimate of expected credit losses, and that impact will vary on the basis of whether the entity is estimating such losses by using a DCF method or another measurement method.

To appropriately estimate the collectability of financial assets within the scope of ASC 326-20, an entity should use judgment in developing estimation techniques and apply those techniques consistently over time. ASC 326-20-55-7 emphasizes that an entity should use methods that are "practical and relevant" given the specific facts and circumstances and that "[t]he method(s) used to estimate expected credit losses may vary on the basis of the type of financial asset, the entity's ability to predict the timing of cash flows, and the information available to the entity." Regardless of whether an entity changes its current method(s) of estimating credit losses upon adoption of ASU 2016-13, the method(s) used must be disclosed by portfolio segment and major security type in accordance with ASC 326-20-50-11.

- *Practical expedients.* ASC 326 permits entities to use practical expedients to measure expected credit losses for the following two types of financial assets:
  - *Collateral-dependent financial assets.* In a manner consistent with its practice under existing U.S. GAAP, an entity

is permitted to measure its estimate of expected credit losses for collateral dependent financial assets as the difference between the financial asset's amortized cost and the collateral's fair value (adjusted for selling costs, when applicable).
- *Financial assets for which the borrower must continually adjust the amount of securing collateral (e.g., certain repurchase agreements and securities-lending arrangements).* An entity is permitted to measure its estimate of expected credit losses on these financial assets as the difference between the amortized cost basis of the asset and the collateral's fair value.
- *Credit enhancements.* Among other factors that may affect expected credit losses on a financial asset (or group of similar financial assets), an entity should consider whether the asset includes an embedded credit enhancement provided by a third-party guarantor (e.g., private loan insurance). If the financial asset includes an embedded credit enhancement feature, the entity should consider how the cash flows associated with such a feature should be incorporated into the expectation of cash flows that are recoverable on the financial asset. By contrast, the entity must not consider cash flows associated with a freestanding credit enhancement contract (e.g., credit insurance purchased by the entity, including credit default swaps) even though the objective of obtaining such a contract is the same as if it were embedded in the financial asset (i.e., to mitigate credit exposure).

  To avoid double counting, an entity is prohibited from considering the effects of a freestanding credit enhancement feature when estimating expected credit losses. For example, the cash flows from a credit default swap that is a credit enhancement of a loan asset should not be included in the measurement of expected credit losses because such a swap would be recognized separately as a derivative financial instrument. Even if the freestanding credit insurance is not accounted for as a derivative, cash flows from freestanding credit insurance should not be considered in the estimation of expected losses on the related "covered" assets.
- *Troubled debt restructurings.* ASU 2016-13 does not affect the guidance in ASC 310-40 on identifying whether a modification is a TDR. That is, an entity would still

continue to apply the guidance in ASC 310-40-15-5 that states that "[a] restructuring of a debt constitutes a troubled debt restructuring . . . if the creditor for economic or legal reasons related to the debtor's financial difficulties grants a concession to the debtor that it would not otherwise consider."

Consequently, the CECL model will not affect an entity's (1) process for determining whether a concession has been granted to the borrower as part of a modification, (2) analysis of whether the borrower is experiencing financial difficulty, and (3) accounting for the TDR on an individual loan basis. However, because ASU 2016-13 requires an entity to include all effects of TDRs in its allowance for expected credit losses, the FASB indicated that an entity must use a DCF method or a reconcilable method if the TDR involves a concession that can only be measured by using a DCF method (e.g., an interest rate or term concession).

FINANCIAL ASSET TRANSFERS

ASC 860, Transfers and Servicing, contains accounting and disclosure guidance on transfers of financial assets. With respect to such transfers, ASC 860 addresses the accounting by both the transferor (e.g., the entity that transfers financial assets) and the transferee (e.g., the entity that receives financial assets). A transfer of financial assets or the rights to service financial assets is accounted for as either a sale or a secured borrowing. The accounting conclusion depends on the terms and conditions of the transfer, including the nature of any continuing involvement of the transferor. The complexity of the accounting analysis depends on the complexity of the transaction.

The accounting as a sale or secured borrowing is symmetrical. That is, if the transferor meets the conditions to account for a transfer of financial assets or rights to service financial assets as a sale, and therefore derecognizes the transferred financial assets or rights to service financial assets, the transferee accounts for the transfer as a purchase of financial assets or rights to service financial assets. Similarly, if the transferor does not meet the conditions to account for a transfer of financial assets or rights to service financial assets as a sale and reflects the transfer as a secured borrowing (i.e., it does not derecognize the financial assets or rights to service financial assets), the transferee accounts for the transfer as a receivable from the transferor. ASC 860 provides guidance addressing the initial and subsequent measurement by both transferors and transferees; the measurement guidance an entity applies depends on whether the transfer is accounted for as a sale or a secured borrowing.

Derecognition of Financial Assets Sold

To determine whether a transfer of financial assets should be accounted for as a sale, entities must first evaluate whether the transferee is a consolidated entity; derecognition guidance should only be applied if the transferee is an unconsolidated entity. Following the determination that the transferee is an unconsolidated entity, the transferor should then determine whether control over the transferred financial assets has been surrendered. All arrangements or agreements made between entities at the time of transfer should be included in this consideration, and entities should include in their consideration (1) whether the transferee should be consolidated under the variable interest entity (VIE) accounting model and (2) whether the transferor has a continued involvement in the transferred assets. If the transferor has surrendered control over transferred financial assets, the transfer should only be accounted for as a sale if the following conditions are met:

- Transferred assets have been isolated from the transferor (i.e., put beyond the reach of the transferor and its creditors, even in bankruptcy or other receivership).
- Transferred assets can be pledged or exchanged by each transferee without constraint or provision of benefit to the transferor.
- Transferred assets are not under effective control of the transferor.

Transfers of financial assets take many forms; one common form of transfer is a participation agreement, whereby a single lender makes a large loan to a borrower and subsequently transfers undivided interests in the loan to other entities. In determining whether an asset transfer through participation should be accounted for as a sale, there are additional factors that an entity should consider.

Participation Agreements

In certain industries, a typical customer's borrowing needs often exceed its bank's legal lending limits. To accommodate the customer, the bank may participate the loan to other banks (i.e., transfer under a participation agreement a portion of the customer's loan to one or more participating banks). Transfers by the lender may take the legal form of either assignments or participations. The transfers are usually on a nonrecourse basis, and, in the case of a participation agreement, the transferor continues to own legal title of the loan. The transferee (participating entity) may or may not have the right to sell or transfer its participation during the term of the loan, depending on the terms of the participation agreement.

A loan participation is a transfer within the scope of ASC 860-10 because it represents a transfer of an interest in an existing loan to a third party. To qualify for sale accounting, the interest transferred must meet the definition of a participating interest. This differentiates loan participation from loan syndication, which is not within the scope of ASC 860-10 because it represents an origination of a loan by the participating banks.

If the arrangement does not meet the definition of a participating interest (and is not the transfer of an entire financial asset), the transferor and transferee must account for the transaction as a secured borrowing.[1] If the transfer does meet the definition of a participating interest, sale accounting is appropriate so long as the transferee is not consolidated with the transferor and all other sales conditions under ASC 860-10-40-5 are met. Transfers of portions of entire financial assets that contain unique terms and features are often considered not to qualify as participations.

It is important to continually reassess the appropriate treatment for any given transfer. Transferred interests in portions of entire financial assets that are initially accounted for as secured borrowings may subsequently meet the definition of participating interests. For example, if the passage of time or modification to the agreement results in expiration of (1) recourse to a transferor or (2) priority rights of an interest holder, the transferor should reassess its conclusion on treatment as a participating interest. Alternately, previously transferred participating interests may no

---

[1] See also Seth Grosshandler and Kate Sawyer's article, "FAS 140 as Applied to Assignments and Participations" in the first edition of the Handbook.

longer meet the definition of a participating interest, in which case the entity must rerecognize the previously sold interest and apply secured borrowing accounting.

Trade-Date versus Settlement-Date Accounting

The transferor's accounting for sales of financial assets on a trade-date or settlement-date basis depends on the type of financial asset sold, certain industry practices, and an entity's accounting policies. Except for certain sales of securities and sales of derivative instruments, entities generally recognize sales of financial assets on a settlement-date basis. For example, settlement-date accounting is generally applied to sales of loan receivables by financial services entities. Sales of derivative instruments are generally accounted for on the trade date by all entities.

Measurement of a Sale of Financial Assets

After determining that a transfer of financial assets should be accounted for as a sale, the transferor must derecognize the transferred financial assets and recognize the fair value of all assets obtained or liabilities incurred in the sale. Any difference between the carrying amount of the financial assets derecognized and the net proceeds received in the sale (i.e., the fair value of the assets obtained less the fair value of any liabilities incurred) is recognized in earnings as a gain or loss on sale. In a transfer of an entire financial asset or a group of entire financial assets, the transferor derecognizes the existing carrying amount of the financial asset(s) sold. Special consideration is required when a transfer involves the sale of a participating interest. In such a transfer, the transferor must allocate the previous carrying amount of the entire financial asset between the participating interest sold and the interest that continues to be held by the transferor.

All assets obtained and liabilities incurred in a sale, regardless of nature or form, must be recognized by the transferor as part of the sale and measured at fair value. Common assets received and liabilities incurred in a transfer include, but are not limited to, servicing assets or liabilities, beneficial interests in securitized financial assets, contingent repurchase features, call and put options, forward commitments to transfer additional financial assets, and other derivative assets or liabilities.

CHAPTER 20

The Loan Market, Blockchain, and Smart Contracts: The Potential for Transformative Change

Josias Dewey
Partner
Holland & Knight LLP

Bridget K. Marsh
Executive Vice President & Deputy General Counsel
Loan Syndications and Trading Association

INTRODUCTION[1]

The Loan Syndications and Trading Association (LSTA) is the trade association in the United States for the corporate loan market. We promote a fair, orderly, and efficient loan market and actively seek ways in which we can achieve that. During the past few years, the LSTA has considered how blockchain (or distributed ledger technology, DLT) and related advanced technologies will impact the industry and believes that this new technology can propel the syndicated loan market forward and help address some of its current challenges.

This chapter provides a brief description of the loan market and its participants to put our conversation in context, sets out the basics of blockchain technology, reviews the concept of "smart contracts," and examines how the primary and secondary loan markets can benefit from these new technologies.

U.S. LOAN MARKET AND LOAN MARKET PARTICIPANTS

There is no single regulatory authority charged with the responsibility of regulating the syndicated loan market in the United States. Of course, most loan market participants are regulated institutions that have one or more regulators overseeing their activities, but the loan market itself is not regulated. The LSTA is, therefore, the entity to which loan market participants turn for standard forms, best practices, and general assistance with primary loan market activities and secondary market loan trades.

The LSTA maintains a suite of documents that can be used by market participants in the origination, servicing, and trading of loans. Since its formation 25 years ago, the LSTA has published standard agreements, forms, and best practices for use in the primary loan market that have been widely adopted by market participants. The LSTA's comprehensive suite of secondary trading documents are used by all loan market participants to evidence their loan trades and then settle those transactions.

At its most basic, in the primary loan market there are several interested parties involved in the origination of any large syndicated

---

[1] The original version of this chapter was published in *GLI Blockchain & Cryptocurrency Regulation 2021* by Global Legal Group, Ltd.

loan, the terms of which are documented in a credit agreement. There must be: (1) a borrower to which the loan is made, and which is responsible for principal and interest payments under the terms of the credit agreement; (2) one or more lenders in the syndicate, each of which owns a portion of the outstanding loan; and (3) an administrative agent that is responsible for the ongoing administration of the loan until its maturity date. Although complex deal terms may vary from deal to deal, the basics of each loan will generally operate the same way. In the secondary loan market, each loan trade will, of course, include a selling lender and a legal entity buying the loan, an administrative agent who must acknowledge or consent to the loan assignment, and a borrower whose consent to the loan trade is also typically required. The buyer and seller of the loan execute an LSTA Par/Near Par Trade Confirmation (Par Confirm) to evidence their loan trade, and the relevant form of assignment agreement pursuant to which the loan is then assigned to the buyer. Finally, the administrative agent updates the register of lenders to reflect the loan assignment.

For the trading of performing loans (par trades) where the borrower is making timely loan payments in accordance with the terms of the credit agreement and neither the borrower nor the applicable industry is in any type of financial distress or experiencing any type of turmoil, most of the steps outlined above have become standard practice in the U.S. loan market, and LSTA trading documentation is used uniformly by all participants. After the relevant consents are obtained, those par trades are typically settled on an electronic platform with little or no lawyer involvement and few, if any, modifications. Instead, market participants expect the LSTA to provide the market with trading documents that are periodically updated to reflect current market practices, legal developments, and the latest deal trends.

Because there is no (or very limited) tailoring of documents in the trading of par loans and with practices being quite streamlined and uniform, distinct elements of this market seem ideally suited for the implementation of blockchain technology.

BLOCKCHAIN BASICS

The terms *blockchain* and *DLT* are often used interchangeably by those in financial services, and both terms seem to be used as acceptable nomenclature for this technology. Although there is a technical distinction between a blockchain and a DLT, for the purposes of our discussion, the terms will be used interchangeably, though it seems that the term *blockchain* is the preferred term today by those in financial services.

Perhaps surprising to some is that the technology underlying blockchain is actually a collection of technologies, none of which is new. Blockchain is a decentralized peer-to-peer network that maintains a ledger of transactions (e.g., a transfer of an asset from one party to another party) that uses cryptographic tools to maintain the integrity of transactions and the integrity of the ledger itself, and a protocol-wide consensus mechanism that verifies the data and determines if, when, and how to update the ledger. The decentralized network makes this technology distinct from a traditional centralized database that has one authoritative database maintained by a trusted third party. For example, central banks around the world serve as that trusted third party for a state's banking system; similarly, for a syndicated loan, the administrative agent is the trusted third party that maintains the register of lenders, administers the loan, and keeps a record of all loan positions, including related interest and principal payments. Lenders in the syndicate must reconcile their own records with those of the administrative agent whose entries in the register are conclusive, absent manifest error. Without a trusted party to maintain a ledger, by contrast, in a blockchain, the cryptographic tools (e.g., a public or private encryption key) keep the information secure, because they are used to control the ownership of and/or the right to access the information on the ledger.

A blockchain is often considered to be immutable or tamper-proof because of the technology used to maintain the integrity of the ledger. Although there have been a few examples of hacking of digital currencies that rely on this technology, the unique way in which the information is stored and updated does make it incredibly secure, so it is most definitely tamper resistant. For example, to create each "block" in a blockchain, transactions are aggregated together and, using the appropriate protocol (a protocol can be thought of as software or a set of rules for a particular system), subjected to a special mathematical algorithm. The calculation results in an alphanumeric string that is put on the next block, and those two blocks are now inextricably chained together or "cryptographically linked." The process is then repeated for each bundle of transactions that are aggregated together; the number of blocks will increase, and the chain will continue to grow over time. To tamper or attempt to hack into or change some of the stored information would be nearly impossible and incredibly expensive. Because a new entry on a blockchain ledger is verified by a consensus mechanism at the time of entry and updated across all computers simultaneously, the computers rely on and trust this single source of truth. One of the enormous benefits of this technology is the potential for cost savings because separate reconciliation efforts will no longer be needed. (This alone makes it incredibly attractive technology for the loan market.)

PUBLIC OR PERMISSIONED LEDGER

DLT can be implemented with or without access controls, depending on whether an open, public network is used or a restricted, permissioned network is chosen. The decentralized digital currency, Bitcoin, is likely the most well-known example of an open, public network where anyone can query the ledger and broadcast transactions without any authorization (assuming, of course, the individual has the proper computer equipment and software). In a public blockchain, ledgers are replicated across many computers referred to as *nodes*, which are connected to a common network over the Internet. Those operating the nodes are referred to as *miners*. In contrast, a closed, permissioned network is restricted to certain individuals who have been given permission and the necessary credentials to access the ledger by a trusted third party.

It is not surprising that the financial services industry is currently favoring the implementation of permissioned networks. Because of anti-money laundering (AML), know-your-customer (KYC), and privacy considerations (discussed more in-depth below), public networks are not really feasible in financial services at this time. A Bitcoin miner that is anonymous on a public network should be subject to the requirements of the Bank Secrecy Act and a financial institution's own KYC program as if it were to be involved in a similar function in the financial services industry for a bank. Thus, it is unlikely that financial institutions would rely entirely on public blockchain networks as the infrastructure underlying a loan origination or trading platform. As the technology evolves, however, it is possible that the permissioned networks utilized by financial institutions may be enhanced by the integration or interoperability of certain functionality and/or data with one or more public networks.

Each member of a permissioned network knows the identity of the counterparty on the other side of a transaction. Being able to identify a counterparty is important for many reasons in a transaction, including KYC and AML. For financial transactions, in particular, it provides parties with a way to make formal demands against each other in the event of nonperformance by one of them. Similarly, if the nonperforming party fails to cure a default, the other party may file a lawsuit and exercise its rights and remedies under the transaction documents. By contrast, on public networks, people are often transacting anonymously or with those who have not disclosed their true identity.

SMART CONTRACTS

The term *smart contracts* can be misleading, especially for lawyers who have a definite idea of what must be shown for there to be a binding legal agreement between parties. At a minimum, a contract requires there to be an offer by one party, an acceptance by another party, and some form of consideration to exist. When the term is used by software engineers, it means computer code that is self-executing (the type of code will depend on the protocol on which the code is implemented). We think a more useful structure for the loan market is a hybrid legal contract that has certain parts of it coded and other parts that remain in human prose. The term *smart legal agreements* has been used to describe this type of hybrid legal contract, and this combination of a legal agreement with a smart contract would be most useful for financial instruments. One could envision how the library of LSTA's standard forms and agreements could become smart legal agreements with certain provisions remaining in human prose; for example, the reference to LSTA Arbitration Rules in the Par Confirm could remain as text while provisions relating to the calculation of the loan purchase price for the applicable trade could be coded and thus become self-executing.

There is an aspect of utilizing smart legal agreements that does increase the risk of error or corruption and should therefore be highlighted—the management of information that is drawn from an external source referred to as an *oracle* in the blockchain nomenclature. Because smart contracts are programmed to be self-executing, some information may need to be pulled in from an external source, and therefore it is essential that this information from the oracle be accurate. For example, pursuant to the terms of the Par Confirm, if a trade does not timely settle, then upon settlement the buyer is credited for certain interest payments made by the borrower, but it must also pay the seller the interest that would accrue at the one-month London Interbank Offered Rate (LIBOR) for deposits in the applicable currency as set by the ICE Benchmark Administration on the amount equal to the purchase price. If the LIBOR, an oracle, is corrupted for any reason, then of course there will be repercussions for trades settling on the blockchain, where the Par Confirm has been turned into a smart legal agreement with certain elements of it coded, and thus self-executing.

Smart contracts build on the innovation of blockchain technology and have the potential to allow parties to structure and effectuate transactions in a more efficient and secure manner than traditional contracts; however, there are still challenges and obstacles that must be overcome before smart legal agreements become commonplace. Although we recognize that the technology remains in its infancy and is not a panacea for all our market's present challenges, we remain confident that smart contracts and blockchain technology will ultimately transform our market.

BLOCKCHAIN, SMART CONTRACTS, AND THE LOAN MARKET

There is enormous potential for the marriage of blockchain technology and smart contracts to result in incredible strides forward for the loan market. Although the typical syndicated loan agreement is a complex instrument that cannot be reduced simply to computer code, there are aspects of it that do lend themselves to becoming coded and, where a legal agreement has been standardized for a particular market or asset, then it can be more easily coded and efficiently implemented.

In the context of the loan market, the origination of a syndicated loan—from the time the credit agreement is drafted and the loan funded—could be made using blockchain technology (as has been done in the European loan market). In today's market, a credit agreement is typically drafted by legal counsel based on deal terms that have been emailed to them. The lawyers then prepare the draft credit documentation based on that information. This approach introduces the risk of manual transcription errors, and validation rules will not have been applied to the information included in the credit agreement. By using document-automation tools, together with a distributed ledger, the credit agreement can be generated from data stored on the ledger that has already been validated. Although this can, of course, be accomplished without a blockchain, in the absence of one there is no single source of validated data. Having a single source of truth as to the ownership of a syndicated loan ultimately will eliminate the redundant, time-consuming, and costly exercise of multiple parties manually processing and accounting for primary allocations, payments, and assignments.

In today's loan market, the closing of primary trades is a slow and time-consuming process. After initial funding of the loan by the administrative agent, each party with a primary market allocation must then fund its portion of the loan and execute an assignment agreement to evidence the settlement of their primary trade. With the disparate systems used by loan market participants today, each party is likely still emailed a PDF or another form of the executed agreement, and from those documents it must then extract the relevant information and manually input that information into its own back-office system (with all the human touchpoints, there is a greater risk of error and delay with this type of process).

With a blockchain, the credit agreement and related documents could be digitally signed and delivered electronically at closing, thus allowing the deal terms, including information about loan positions, automatically to populate on the network's ledger—the same ledger accessed by all lenders. Think how a DLT network with the applicable credit agreement, assignment agreement, and Par Confirm, all structured as smart legal agreements, could implement identical functionality in a way similar to today's loan operations—but one where the contracts are self-executing and the database replicated across an entire network of computers. Although the computers in the network (assuming a permissioned network is used) will be controlled by potentially hundreds of lenders in the syndicate, the integrity of the data across the network will be ensured by the integration of a protocol-wide consensus mechanism.

A blockchain platform for a syndicated loan could also track a loan's interest rate, interest and principal payment dates, and any other data fields relevant to the life cycle of the loan. In a typical syndicated loan, many different parties, each storing information about a syndicated loan, have to continually reconcile all information they receive against their own internal databases. A blockchain platform could eliminate the need for, or significantly reduce the time spent on, reconciling data across the market. That alone could save the loan market an enormous amount of time and money. In addition, other aspects of a credit agreement could also be coded. For example, when a borrower submits periodic financial reports to the syndicate, certain data from those reports could be extracted, thus allowing financial covenants in the credit agreement automatically to be tested.

Secondary market trades in the loan market are memorialized by the parties executing a Par Confirm. Settlement of the trade—when the seller's legal ownership of the loan is transferred to the purchaser, and the purchaser pays the purchase price to the seller—typically occurs days or even weeks after the trade is entered into by the parties. It is easy to imagine how the transfer of this asset could be done far more seamlessly and efficiently on a blockchain, with smart legal agreements self-executing and data being updated on the ledger automatically. In this way, one can imagine lenders in the syndicate on a permissioned ledger using private keys digitally to execute the Par Confirm and applicable assignment agreements. When the assigning lender digitally signs the Par Confirm and relevant assignment agreement (and any other consents have been obtained), the register of lenders (assuming existing nomenclature is retained) will be updated automatically to reflect the assignee's account being credited by the amount of the loan transferred to it, and a corresponding debit to the assignor's account. No one will need to reconcile their own positions because they will all have access on the permissioned ledger to the same information.

Although the adoption of blockchain will shorten the settlement times for loan trades, the loan purchaser must still make payment of the loan purchase price. Although it is not currently possible to transfer U.S. dollars across a distributed ledger, there now exist a number of "stable coins," which are designed to maintain a stable relationship with the U.S. dollar (often through reserving liquid assets). These digital assets can be exchanged for U.S. dollars through various virtual currency exchanges. There are even a few U.S. depository institutions that have issued U.S. dollar–equivalent digital assets. Ultimately, central bank–issued digital currency could make settlement on the blockchain seamless. A number of central banks have explored the possibility of issuing digital currency on a blockchain, and some have indicated that a limited-purchase digital token for cross-border settlements may be feasible in the not-so-distant future. The lack of a means for making payment on a blockchain, however, can be overcome by parties continuing to use traditional payment rails to effect payment. Reliance on such external processes may be acceptable on a permissioned blockchain network, where the identities of parties are known to each other and regulated financial institutions are involved.

In 2019, the LSTA completed the automation of the LSTA Revolving Credit Facility form. Working with OpenLaw, a blockchain-based protocol for the creation and execution of legal agreements, we used Solidity, the language native to the Ethereum platform, to code aspects of the credit agreement and create a smart legal agreement. The entire credit agreement was not turned into a smart contract; provisions relating to the mechanical aspects of the credit agreement were coded, including those relating to borrowing requests, interest and principal payments, and loan transfers. The creation of this prototype demonstrated that: (1) the drafting of syndicated credit agreements can be partly automated using legal technology tools with evidence of the parties' agreement and associated electronic signatures stored on a blockchain; (2) smart contracts can be used to automate certain aspects of loan administration, particularly responsibilities performed by the agent; (3) blockchain technology and smart contracts can be used to hard code regulatory compliance, in the form of approved addresses that can help ensure compliance with KYC/AML requirements (see further discussion below); (4) blockchain technology and smart contracts can be used to hard code disqualified lender lists to help streamline the borrower consent process; and (5) blockchain technology can be used to digitally represent a lender's interest in a syndicated loan, creating opportunities to shorten settlement times for syndicated loan trades. The agreement could still be accessed, viewed, and scrolled through. Importantly, the automated contract still looked like the LSTA's credit agreement from cover page to signature page.

Unfortunately, at this time, there remain many practical limitations relating to the implementation of this new technology and smart contracts in the loan market. Because smart contracts can only interact with tokenized assets, digital assets need first to gain broader usage in our industry before blockchain-based applications and services can be widely adopted in our market. Nevertheless, we were greatly encouraged by the results of the creation of this prototype and have begun to work on automating the LSTA's Form of Investment Grade Term Sheet so that the information in that form can seamlessly flow into the LSTA's automated Form of Revolving Credit Facility. We are also pleased to report that vendors focused on developing platforms for the U.S. corporate loan market are making significant progress, and we look forward to their use in the years ahead.

AML AND KYC ISSUES

An appropriately built blockchain solution for the loan market would meet both KYC and AML requirements, and in so doing, would likely improve both the speed of implementation and accuracy of a financial institution's compliance program while satisfying any legal and regulatory requirements. The LSTA's 2018 Know Your Customer Considerations for Syndicated Lending and Loan Trading (LSTA KYC Guidelines) serve as a comprehensive report outlining the specific due diligence and other compliance work required to engage in primary and secondary loan market transactions in the United States. The LSTA KYC Guidelines, which accurately set forth what is required for different primary and secondary loan market transactions and relationships between loan market participants, can be embedded in the smart legal agreement implementing the framework. We are pleased to report that we are currently working with U.S. regulators on "KYC Frequently Asked Questions," which are based on the LSTA's KYC Guidelines, and these FAQs once finalized will set out the KYC diligence required in the market in a straightforward question and answer format.

Because the KYC and AML requirements would be incorporated in this way, there would no longer be any need to have a separate stream of compliance work to satisfy a bank's KYC requirements and AML diligence in any syndicated loan that is processed through the framework. For example, perhaps checking the sanctions lists on the U.S. Department of the Treasury's Office of Foreign Assets Control website to ensure that a counterparty is not on any of the lists, which is typically the only due diligence required under U.S. law by an agent on a new lender, could be like an oracle, with the diligence thereby completed seamlessly and without any delays. This would result in huge cost savings for our market and would likely also lead to much shorter loan trade settlement times.

Regulators would also benefit greatly from the adoption of blockchain in the loan market. Because blockchains contain a complete history of all transactions that have taken place on the network, including a time stamp for all such transactions, internal auditing would be much simpler, and regulators could be granted access to the ledger to confirm that all related transactions are consistent with the stated intentions and information provided by customers. The ability to see transactions in real time would also be beneficial to regulators, who could monitor the transactions and more easily detect and identify illicit activities.

COMPETITION LAW ISSUES AND CORPORATE GOVERNANCE MATTERS

There are, of course, competition law considerations that must be taken into account when considering the implementation of this new technology, and as a trade association, whose members are often competitors of each other, we are acutely aware of these. During the process of selecting the appropriate DLT, there will be collaborative efforts necessary to implement the chosen DLT to the particular use case within the loan market. This collaboration and the development of a technological solution raise intellectual property concerns that the parties should seek to address. Although the task of identifying the correct technology may be challenging, once common ground is reached by market participants on that issue, the focus should then turn to internal governance matters, and the relative rights and obligations of the participants.

These efforts are complicated by the ever-present need to ensure compliance with applicable antitrust law, an issue that requires continuing diligence and vigilance among industry participants. We would caution consortium participants about antitrust issues that may arise in such circumstances, and to seek advice from counsel where appropriate. The exchange of specific data on current and future prices and competitive activities—as opposed to aggregated past information—is likely to attract the greatest antitrust scrutiny. Thus, participants in blockchain consortia should take care to ensure that they are not, or could not be perceived to be, agreeing to eliminate their independent decision making as to any aspect of the prices they charge or markets they serve.

CONCLUSION

The LSTA remains optimistic about the potential for blockchain, or any type of advanced technology, to have a positive effect on the U.S. loan market, and we are pleased that in recent years vendors have been increasing their focus on developing advanced technological solutions for our market. At its simplest, blockchain is an efficient way to transfer any asset, including a loan, and the current systems and practices of the U.S. syndicated loan market could benefit enormously from this technology. The LSTA is well placed to lead the legal, technological, operational, and business efforts to develop a general framework for implementing solutions that address the life cycle of a loan from origination to repayment. Our market participants should understand not only the potential benefits of blockchain but also the challenges to its adoption. This suggests that a sustained educational initiative targeting all loan market participants is necessary, and the LSTA is committed to offering that. The LSTA has been following developments around blockchain and providing educational resources to its members for a few years and will continue to be a resource as its members navigate many of these challenges and, in some cases, take a leading role in helping to craft standards that facilitate the efficient deployment of the technology. Forging consensus within an entire industry about standards, best practices, and other uniform approaches and protocols is challenging, as we know, but the LSTA is well placed to lead these efforts.

Although blockchain technology will not eliminate all inefficiencies in the loan market, it seems very likely that blockchain technology will eventually bring about fundamental change in how syndicated loans are originated, administered, and traded in today's loan market. Yet, there is much work to be done before this can be achieved. Computer software engineers, finance professionals, lawyers, and operational personnel will need to work together to analyze all of the processes used in the loan market, loan administration, and secondary loan trading. Policy, legal, and regulatory issues will need to be addressed thoughtfully, and we must always balance our desire to promote innovation with the need for a strong, stable, and reliable loan market.

GLOSSARY OF TERMS[1]

A

Accordion Feature An accordion commitment increase provision is normally used only for increases in a revolving credit facility. It works by allowing the amount of the commitments to go up (usually up to some specified maximum) if the borrower is able to convince new lenders to provide the increase or existing lenders to increase their current commitments. Because the increase is to an already-outstanding facility, the interest, maturity, and other terms applicable to the increased loans will be identical to those of the existing revolving credit facility.

Adequate Protection Order (APO) Any order of the relevant Bankruptcy Court authorizing or ordering a borrower to make adequate protection payments to the lenders.

Adequate Protection Payment (APP) As used in the LSTA's trading documents, the amount, other than paid-in-kind (PIK) interest, authorized and/or ordered to be paid with respect to the debt by the applicable Bankruptcy Court to lenders as adequate protection for interest and accruing fees on the obligations owed under the credit agreement pursuant to an adequate protection order.

Administrative Agent (Agent) The institution specified in the credit agreement that performs the recordkeeping associated with a loan, handles the interest and principal payments to be made in connection with the loan, and monitors the ongoing administration of the loan.

Administrative Questionnaire A document provided to the agent containing a lender's wire, notice, and signature block information. The LSTA has published a form of Administrative Questionnaire.

---

[1] A version of this glossary was prepared by Tess Virmani of LSTA and Maria Barclay of Practical Law. That "Glossary of Terms" is available at https://www.lsta.org/content/lsta-glossary-of-terms/.

Affiliated Lender   An affiliate of the borrower and, where applicable, the sponsor. Affiliated Lenders are typically subject to a number of restrictions under the credit agreement.

Agreement Among Lenders (AAL)   Pursuant to an AAL, which the borrower is not typically party to, the unitranche lenders will divide the unitranche loans into a first-out tranche and a last-out tranche. The AAL will contain a payment waterfall, under which the first-out tranche will be entitled to be paid before the last-out tranche, and in exchange, the last-out tranche will be entitled to receive a larger share of the interest payments made by the borrower. The AAL will also typically set forth the relative rights of the first-out tranche and the last-out tranche with respect to voting, exercise of remedies, standstills, buyout rights, and bankruptcy matters. The LSTA has published a form of Agreement Among Lenders. (See also "Unitranche Financing.")

Allocation   In the primary market, the distribution of a facility among committed investors by the arranger. It takes place when the sales process has been completed. The primary syndication is considered completed once the allocations have been made. In the secondary market, allocation or suballocation is the process by which a fund manager divides up its purchase of a loan and allocates certain amounts of such loan to specific funds.

Amendment   A revision to the terms (financial or otherwise) of a credit agreement, typically requested by a borrower.

Amendment and Restatement   A revision of a credit agreement that reflects substantial amendments made to the original credit agreement (either in one amendment or in a series of previous amendments).

Applicable Margins   The interest rate on each base rate loan and each London Interbank Offered Rate (LIBOR) loan includes an additional margin, sometimes also referred to as the *spread*. In some cases, the applicable margin is a flat rate fixed for the life of the agreement, but in other instances it increases over time or is dependent on the credit ratings and/or leverage of the borrower.

Approved Fund   As used in the LSTA's form of Investment Grade Revolving Credit Facility, any fund that is administered or managed by (1) a lender, (2) an affiliate of a lender, or (3) an entity or an affiliate of an entity that administers or manages a lender.

Arrangement Fee   The fee paid by a borrower to the arranger for structuring and syndicating the loan.

Arranger   The firm that leads the structuring and syndication of a loan. (See also "Lead Arranger.")

Assignment   A transfer of a loan in which the buyer-assignee comes into privity of contract with the borrower as a lender of record under the applicable credit agreement, obtaining the rights and assuming the obligations of the seller-assignor thereunder. A loan can only be transferred by assignment when the buyer is an "eligible assignee" under the applicable credit agreement and all necessary consents to the transfer have been obtained. (See also "Confirmation" and "Participation.")

Assignment Agreement (A&A)   The agreement that documents the sale and assignment of rights and obligations under a credit agreement by a lender to an assignee. This agreement is typically a form that is attached to each credit agreement. The LSTA has published a form of Assignment Agreement.

Assignment Fee The fee charged by an Administrative Agent and set forth in the applicable credit agreement for the costs associated with causing an A&A to be effected. Such fees are typically split equally between the buyer and the seller and are paid in such amount as specified in the applicable credit agreement. Many institutions waive assignment fees on a reciprocal basis or eliminate them entirely.

B

Bank Loan Nonrestricting Information Information that does not include material nonpublic information (MNPI) and is provided confidentially by or on behalf of a borrower to members and potential members of a lending syndicate. Bank loan nonrestricting information is subject to standard confidentiality undertakings. The most common example of bank loan nonrestricting information is information contained in a confidential information memorandum, or "bank book," that is provided to members and potential members of a lending syndicate and developed specifically for loan market participant (LMP) personnel who do not wish to receive MNPI because they wish to be able both to extend loans to and to trade the loans and securities of the borrower. Although this type of confidential information memorandum does not contain MNPI, it may contain sensitive business information and is therefore subject to a confidentiality undertaking. (See also "Borrower Restricted Information," "Confidential Information," "Material Nonpublic Information," and "Syndicate Information.")

Bankruptcy The situation in which a debtor, upon voluntary petition or one invoked by the debtor's creditors, is judged legally insolvent. The debtor's remaining property is then administered for the creditors or is distributed among them.

Bankruptcy Code The Bankruptcy Reform Act of 1978, 11 U.S.C. §§101 et seq., as amended.

Bankruptcy Rules The Federal Rules of Bankruptcy Procedure and any corresponding or other local rules of the Bankruptcy Court.

Best Efforts Syndication A transaction in which the arranging syndicate (or arranger) does not firmly commit to provide all the funds requested by a borrower; rather, the arranging syndicate (or arranger) commits to using its "best efforts" to raise the money. As a consequence, the related pricing and fees will typically be lower than those of fully underwritten transactions. If other banks elect not to join the deal, then the credit is not closed.

Bid–Ask Spread (Bid–Offer Spread) The difference between the bid and ask (offer) prices.

Bid Price The price at which a potential buyer would agree to purchase an asset.

Big Boy Language Representations attesting to the market sophistication of the parties and to alert a party that there may be information unknown to it that is known by the counterparty. The LSTA's Par Confirm and Distressed Confirm contain "big boy" language.

Bilateral Netting Agreement This agreement provides that transactions evidenced by two trade confirmations between the parties may be netted against each other to determine the "netting amount" to be paid by the party who paid more for the debt than the other party with respect to the two trades. Upon receipt of the netting amount, the rights and obligations of both parties with respect to the two trades will be deemed satisfied and performed. The LSTA has published a form of Bilateral Netting Agreement—Par/Near Trades and form of Bilateral Netting Agreement—Distressed. (See also "Multilateral Netting Agreement.")

Bookrunner See "Lead Arranger."

Borrower Consent The consent of the borrower is typically required for a lender under the applicable credit agreement to transfer the loan via assignment to a buyer, that is, for the buyer of the loan to become a lender of record under the applicable credit agreement. (See also "Assignment.")

Borrower Restricted Information Confidential information, which may include MNPI, that is made available by or on behalf of a borrower to some but not all members and potential members of a lending syndicate. Borrower restricted information might include, for example, information provided privately by a borrower to the Administrative Agent or to a limited number of syndicate members (often referred to as *agent-only information*) or information made available to a steering committee or certain creditors during the course of a restructuring. Borrower restricted information often becomes syndicate information upon its communication to the entire syndicate of lenders. For more information, please refer to the LSTA's Statement of Principles for the Communication and Use of Confidential Information by Loan Market Participants. (See also "Bank Loan Nonrestricting Information," "Confidential Information," "Material Nonpublic Information," and "Syndicate Information.")

Business Development Company (BDC) A type of company regulated by the Securities and Exchange Commission (SEC) that primarily invests in small and mid-cap companies and is frequently subject to minimum distribution requirements. BDCs are limited in the amount of capital they can provide to noncorporates as well as non-U.S. companies driven by the mandated investment guidelines of the Investment Company Act of 1940.

Buy-In/Sell-Out (BISO) A detailed, contractual termination mechanism available under the LSTA's Confirms that permits the terminating party (either the buyer or the seller) to enter a "cover trade" with a third party if its counterparty has not satisfied all of its delivery obligations in a timely fashion.

C

Change of Control A merger or acquisition of an issuer, some substantial purchase of an issuer's equity by a third party, or a change in the majority of the board of directors of an issuer. One of the events of default in a credit agreement is a change of control of the issuer.

Closed-End Fund A fund that has a fixed number of shares outstanding; the shares are generally traded on an exchange. (See also "Open-End Fund.")

Closing Date The date on which a credit agreement closes or takes effect.

Club Deal A loan that is premarketed to a small group of relationship lenders.

Collateral The assets of a borrower that are pledged to secure its loans. Collateral can be specific assets like inventory and receivables or include all of the assets of a borrower. Nearly all leveraged loans are secured by collateral.

Collateral Agent The agent in a syndicated loan who is responsible for monitoring collateral and ensuring that all liens securing the collateral are properly filed.

Collateral Annex Under LSTA documents, unless otherwise agreed at time of trade, the seller may require the buyer to post collateral with the seller for any unfunded portion of a revolving loan/commitment in which the buyer acquires a participation. The LSTA has published a form of Collateral Annex for Par/Near Par Trades and a form of Collateral Annex for Distressed Trades to be used with the applicable form of participation agreement. (See also "Participation.")

Collateralized Loan Obligations (CLOs) A special-purpose investment vehicle established to accumulate a diversified pool of loans as collateral. The accumulation of the collateral is funded by the issuance of a series of rated notes plus equity. The rated notes are sequentially tranched, with the higher-rated tranches having a priority claim on the cash flows generated by the collateral pool and increasingly higher levels of subordinated capital support to protect against collateral losses. Having performed extraordinarily well during the financial crisis, CLOs are the largest single investor type in the loan market.

Commencement Date In connection with a trade, the date when delayed compensation begins to accrue. Under the LSTA's Confirms, the commencement date is 7 business days after the trade date in the case of par loans (T + 7) and 20 business days after the trade date (T + 20) in the case of distressed loans. (See also "Delayed Compensation.")

Commitment The amount of credit that lenders have collectively agreed to provide to a borrower under a credit agreement.

Commitment Fee Compensation for the lenders' contractual commitments to make loans. Typically, they are charged on revolving credit commitments, usually based on the daily average of the unused portion of each lender's outstanding revolving credit commitment. The rate at which commitment fees are payable is generally either flat for the duration of the credit agreement or subject to grid pricing. Accrued commitment fees are generally payable quarterly in arrears. Term loan commitments sometimes accrue a commitment fee known as a *ticking fee*. (See also "Ticking Fees.")

Conditions Precedent The conditions precedent in a credit agreement are in essence a simplified closing list. They specify what the borrower must deliver to the lenders (or the Administrative Agent), what actions it must take, and what other circumstances must exist in order for credit to be available.

Confidential Information All nonpublic written, recorded, electronic, or oral information provided to a party by another party in the course of exchange of such information between those parties and identified by the providing party as confidential information. The LSTA has published a form of Master Confidentiality Agreement for Secondary Trades and a form of Master Confidentiality Agreement for Trade Claims that set forth the terms that will apply to the treatment of confidential information that either party to the agreement may supply to the other party. (See also "Bank Loan Nonrestricting Information," "Borrower Restricted Information," "Material Nonpublic Information," and "Syndicate Information.")

Confidential Information Memorandum (CIM) The information memorandum or "bank book" provided to prospective lenders after the arranger and the borrower have agreed on the basic structure and terms of a proposed loan. The bank book typically has a legend on the cover and contains a letter or memorandum identifying the information as confidential and advising the prospective lender that by accepting the bank book the prospective lender is agreeing to treat the information received as confidential. In today's market, sometimes Lender Presentations are used to market deals instead of CIMs.

Confirmation (Confirm) A trade confirmation evidences the key terms of a trade. In loan trading, the LSTA's form of Par/Near Par Trade Confirmation ("Par Confirm") and form of Distressed Trade Confirmation ("Distressed Confirm"), as applicable, are used to document U.S. loan trades. Each confirm is a two-part document consisting of the face of the confirm, which sets forth the trade-specific information, including the key terms required for a binding trade and any special riders, and standard terms and conditions, which govern the transaction. For par trades, the Par Confirm continues to exist after the trade is settled. For distressed trades, the purchase and sale agreement supersedes the Distressed Confirm. A legally binding contract exists once the material terms of the trade (for most trades, the borrower's name; the name, facility type, and amount of the loan to be sold; and the price to be paid for the loan) are agreed, and the trade is then memorialized by checking the appropriate boxes and filling in other required information on the applicable face of the confirm. The standard terms and conditions contain many important provisions, such as the calculation of the purchase price (Section 4), the applicable interest convention (Section 5), and the calculation of delayed compensation (Section 6). Of particular note, Section 1 of each standard terms and conditions sets forth the "settlement waterfall" that will apply to the trade. Unless "Assignment Only" has been elected on the face of the confirm, if the parties are unable to settle their trade by assignment (e.g., the borrower or agent withholds consent), the parties must then settle by participation. If the trade is "Assignment Only" or a participation is not able to be effected, then the parties must settle by a mutually agreed alternative that affords the parties the economic equivalent of the trade. (See also "Delayed Compensation," "Interest and Accruing Fees," and "Purchase Price.")

Covenants Covenants in a credit agreement can be divided into three categories: financial covenants, affirmative covenants, and negative covenants. As the labels might suggest, affirmative covenants stipulate what borrowers must do, negative covenants describe what borrowers are prohibited from doing (though subject to highly negotiated permissive exceptions), and financial covenants require the borrower to hit certain financial performance targets. (See also "Financial Covenants.")

Covenant-Lite Broadly characterized as syndicated leveraged loan facilities with (1) no financial covenants or financial covenants (usually the leverage ratio) that apply to the revolving loans only and not the term loans and (2) a negative covenant package similar to or based on those used in high-yield bonds, which are usually given on an "incurrence" (met at the time of the specific event) rather than a "maintenance" (met at all times or at periodic intervals) basis.

Credit Agreement Refers to the agreement entered between the borrower, the lenders, the agent, and other financial parties, which describes the terms and conditions of the loan being made to the borrower and the obligations and requirement for the borrower, its related entities (if any), and the lenders.

Glossary of Terms

CUSIP Acronym for Committee on Uniform Securities Identification Procedures, which was created in July 1964. The main goals of the CUSIP were to develop specifications for a uniform security identification system. Now, the acronym is used to refer to the CUSIP system, which is owned by the American Bankers Association and operated by Standard & Poor's (S&P) and which facilitates the clearing and settlement process of financial instruments. A CUSIP number consists of nine digits, the first six of which uniquely identify the issuer and have been assigned to issuers in alphabetic sequence, and two other characters (alphabetic or numeric), which identify the issue. The ninth digit is the check digit.

D

Debtor-in-Possession Loan (DIP Loan) A credit agreement entered by a borrower during the course of its Chapter 11 bankruptcy case that is secured and has priority over existing debt and other claims.

Default A default under a credit agreement means any event or condition that constitutes an event of default (EOD) or that, with the giving of any notice, the passage of time, or both, would be an EOD. Although the loans may be accelerated if any event of default occurs, the lenders are entitled to refuse to increase their exposure if a mere default exists. (See also "Event of Default (EOD).")

Delayed Compensation Under the LSTA's Confirms, delayed compensation is a component of pricing in the settlement of loan trades that is intended to put parties in the approximate economic position on the delayed settlement date that they would have been in if they had timely settled the loan trade. (See also "Commencement Date" and "Settlement Date.")

Direct Lending Direct Lenders are nonbank lenders that make loans to borrowers without an intermediary (e.g., an investment bank). These loans are negotiated directly between a company and a lender or a small group of lenders. Most or all of the loan is typically held by the originating lenders. (See also "Club Deal.")

Disqualified Institution An institution that is prohibited under the credit agreement from acquiring the relevant loan in the secondary market (or in the primary syndication if identified as of the closing date). Under the LSTA's "DQ Structure," (1) (a) an entity designated by the borrower as a "disqualified institution" on or prior to the closing date and (b) any entity that is a "competitor" (to be defined in the applicable credit agreement) of the borrower that has been so designated and (2) lenders are prohibited from transferring these loans to disqualified institutions by assignment or participation. (See also "Closing Date" and "Eligible Assignee.")

Distressed Confirmation See "Confirmation."

Distressed Loan A loan for which the borrower is not expected to make full and/or timely payments to lenders. Because the loan is not expected to be paid at the face value, the loan will typically trade at a discounted rate; however, the price at which a loan trades is just one indicator that a loan may be distressed. Ultimately, the market determines when a loan should commence trading on distressed documentation. For LSTA distressed trades, the loan should be transferred pursuant to the LSTA's form of Purchase and Sale Agreement and the relevant assignment agreement. (See also "Assignment Agreement," "Purchase and Sale Agreement," and "Shift Date.")

Distribution Any payment of interest, principal, notes, securities, proceeds, or other property (including collateral).

Drawdown Typically refers to a borrower making a drawing under a revolving credit facility or a beneficiary of a letter of credit making a drawing under that letter of credit.

Due Diligence An investigation into the business, legal, and financial affairs of a company that may be undertaken in connection with a financing.

E

EBITDA Add-Backs Adjustments a borrower can make to its earnings before interest, taxes, depreciation, and amortization (i.e., EBITDA) for purposes of calculating compliance with its financial covenants. EBITDA add-backs are often heavily negotiated. Examples include gain (or loss) from discontinued operations (or operations disposed of outside of the ordinary course of business); extraordinary, nonrecurring, or unusual items (e.g., gain or loss from the sale of capital assets other than in the ordinary course of business); and noncash items (e.g., noncash stock-based compensation expenses or unrealized foreign currency gains or losses).

Effective Date The date specified in a contract as the date upon which the terms of that contract will take effect.

Elevation With respect to participations, the process whereby the participant becomes a lender of record under the relevant credit agreement. The elevation is effected once an Assignment Agreement (A&A) is submitted to and accepted by the agent. (See also "Participation.")

Eligible Assignee A party that is permitted to enter an assignment with a lender with the consent of any party whose consent is required pursuant to the terms of the applicable credit agreement. (See also "Assignment" and "Disqualified Institution.")

ESG Acronym for environmental, social, and governance. ESG issues are becoming increasingly important for investors.

Event of Default (EOD) A default under a credit agreement that has not been remedied or waived by the lenders after the expiration of any applicable grace period. (See also "Default.")

F

Facility Fee A fee that is computed on the total amount of revolving credit commitments, both used and unused. The fee is either calculated at a flat rate or subject to grid pricing and is generally payable only until the revolving credit commitments terminate. A facility fee generally does not apply to term loan facilities. Commitment fees and facility fees are mutually exclusive—the same revolving credit facility would not provide for both. Facility fees are most often seen either when the usage of a revolving credit facility is expected to be low or when the facility provides for competitive bid loans.

FATCA The Foreign Account Tax Compliance Act. Effective July 2014, FATCA imposes a 30% withholding tax on payments to foreign financial institutions that do not participate in the FATCA scheme as implemented in the United States or their home jurisdiction, as the case may be.

Federal Funds Rate Typically defined in a credit agreement for any day as the average rate on overnight federal funds transactions for the preceding business day, as published by the Federal Reserve Bank of New York.

Fee Letter The letter that identifies the type and amount of fees payable by a company with respect to a syndicated loan, including arrangement and structuring fees or underwriting fees, administrative agency fees, collateral agent fees, and other amounts payable to the arrangers. The letter will also generally reflect flex language, which details certain provisions of the facility that may be subject to change if necessary to complete syndication (e.g., the structure of the facility and its terms or pricing). (See also "Flex Language.")

Filing Date The date of the filing of a petition for relief under Title 11 of the United States Code by or against any obligor(s) under the applicable credit documents.

Financial Covenants A type of covenant set forth in a credit agreement. They can be divided into two categories: those that test the borrower's financial position at a particular date (such as a net worth or current ratio covenant) and those that test performance over one or more fiscal periods (such as the leverage ratio covenant, interest coverage covenant, fixed charges coverage ratio covenant, and capital expenditures covenant). (See also "Covenants.")

Financial Institution A term used in the market to describe different types of loan market participants, including commercial banks, insurance companies, mutual funds, pension funds, structured vehicles, hedge funds, and other institutional investors. (See also "Institutional Investors/Institutional Lenders.")

Financial Sponsor A financial sponsor finances the acquisition of a company through a combination of debt and equity. The equity portion is contributed by the financial sponsor, and the debt portion is raised by the company to be acquired. These transactions—known as *leveraged buyouts* (LBOs)—are a key driver of activity in the leveraged loan market.

First Lien The first attachment on a borrower's asset, which may be a perfected first lien if duly recorded with the relevant government body so that the lender will be able to act on it should the borrower default.

Flex Language A provision in the fee letter (to keep it confidential) that permits the agent banks to change the amount, pricing, structure, yield, tenor, conditions, and other terms of the financing if necessary to successfully syndicate the loan. Typical types of "flex" are pricing flex, structure flex, call premiums, and covenant flex. Conversely, if a loan is "oversubscribed" because more lenders are willing to commit greater amounts to the loan than the borrower needs, the agent bank may change the terms of the loan to make it more favorable to the borrower (*reverse flex*).

Flip Representations A limited set of representations set forth in the LSTA's form of Purchase and Sale Agreement, which are used to shield a "riskless principal" from direct liability.

Fraudulent Conveyance Fraudulent conveyance laws have been enacted in every state and have been incorporated into the Federal Bankruptcy Code. They are intended to capture a transaction in which (1) an entity undertakes an obligation or transfers property without receiving reasonably equivalent value and (2) the entity is insolvent at the time of, or would be rendered insolvent as a result of, the transaction.

Fully Underwritten Syndication A transaction in which the arranging syndicate firmly commits to providing all the funds requested by a borrower. (See also "Best Efforts Syndication.")

Funding Memo A memo that sets forth the calculations, applicable rates, and amounts used to determine the purchase prices of par trades.

G

Global Financial Crisis (GFC) The period from 2007 to 2009 when banking systems and financial markets around the world experienced a period of extreme stress.

Green Loan Any type of loan instrument made available exclusively to finance or refinance, in whole or in part, new and/or existing eligible "green projects" (indicative categories of "green projects" are set forth in Appendix 1 of the Green Loan Principles). Green loans must align with the four core components of the Green Loan Principles: use of proceeds, process for project evaluation and selection, management of proceeds, and reporting. The Green Loan Principles are published by the LSTA, the Loan Market Association (LMA), and the Asia Pacific Loan Market Association (APLMA).

Grid Pricing When the applicable margin in a credit agreement is dependent on the credit rating and/or leverage of the borrower, the various rates are set forth in that credit agreement in the form of a grid that varies by type of loan (by tranche and by pricing option) and the relevant financial measure. When grid pricing is based upon credit ratings, the relevant parameters will include reference debt, the identity of the credit rating agencies to be relied upon, and the treatment of split ratings (i.e., when the rating agencies assign different ratings to such reference debt). When grid pricing is based upon leverage, the relevant date to test leverage is the end of the borrower's most recent fiscal quarter. Regardless of the form of grid pricing, many credit agreements will provide that, during an event of default, the applicable margin will bump up to the highest level on the grid.

Guarantee A guarantee is an undertaking by one party to pay for the debts, or perform the obligations, of another party in the case of a default. Guarantees can be *upstream* (a subsidiary guaranteeing the debt of its parent), *cross-stream* (a subsidiary guaranteeing the debt of a "sister" company, where both are ultimately owned by the same parent), or *downstream* (a parent guaranteeing a subsidiary). An upstream or cross-stream guarantee may be vulnerable to attack under federal and state insolvency laws because, except to the extent that the guarantor has received the proceeds of the guaranteed loans or other "reasonably equivalent value," one of the two requirements for a fraudulent conveyance or fraudulent transfer will have been established. If, after giving effect to the guarantee, the guarantor is insolvent, then both requirements will have been established. Credit agreements deal with this risk in two ways. Some incorporate a so-called solvency cap or savings clause, where the agreement will limit or cap the guarantee at the maximum amount that would allow it to be enforced without resulting in a fraudulent conveyance. Other credit agreements insert a so-called cross-contribution concept, in which the borrower and each of the other guarantors agree that if any guarantor makes payment under a guarantee greater than the excess of its assets over its liabilities, it will be entitled to reimbursement by the borrower and each other guarantor for the amount of the excess. Neither of these solutions may work if an upstream or cross-stream guarantee is being given by an entity organized outside the United States. Many countries have so-called financial assistance rules that carry much more severe consequences than the fraudulent conveyance and fraudulent transfer doctrines in the United States. If a guarantee would render a guarantor insolvent, violation of these rules can result in personal liability for managers or directors and even, in some cases, criminal liability. Often, savings and cross contribution clauses such as those described above will be ineffective.

Guarantor The grantor of a guarantee, an endorsement, a contingent agreement to purchase or otherwise to become contingently liable with respect to the indebtedness or other obligations of any person, or a guarantee of the payment of dividends or other distributions upon the stock or equity interests of any person.

I

Incremental Facility An incremental facility, in comparison to an accordion feature, contemplates the creation of a new tranche of loans or an increase in an existing tranche of term loans, rather than a mere increase in existing revolving commitments. Depending on the flexibility afforded to the borrower, the new tranches may be either revolving credit or term loan facilities. The pricing, payment, and other terms of an incremental facility, unlike those of an increase pursuant to an accordion feature, are not required to be the same as those of any other tranche in the credit agreement. The LSTA has published a form of Incremental Facility Amendment. (See also "Accordion Feature.")

Instinct Loans The name of Bank of America's innovative electronic platform, which is designed to simplify the secondary trading of syndicated corporate loans. For large syndicated loans, the bank's trading desk sets fixed, mid-market prices and then hosts simple matching sessions.

Institutional Investors/Institutional Lenders Nonbank investors seeking longer-term capital deployment and higher yields by investing in term loans with longer tenures and limited amortization. These investors may include collateralized loan obligations (CLOs), pension funds, mutual funds, debt funds, and insurance companies, among others. (See also "Financial Institution.")

Intercreditor Agreement An agreement entered by classes of lenders of an issuer which sets forth the arrangement governing how those lenders will exercise their rights and remedies under the applicable credit agreement. For example, first-lien lenders and second-lien lenders will enter into an intercreditor agreement pursuant to which the second lien lenders forego or restrict their rights. For example, second-lien lenders may agree (1) not to take enforcement actions (or to limit their right to take such actions) with respect to their liens, (2) not to challenge enforcement or foreclosure actions taken by the holders of the first liens, or (3) to limit their right to challenge the validity or priority of the first liens. Second-lien lenders may also acknowledge the first-lien lender's entitlement to the first proceeds of the shared collateral.

Interest and Accruing Fees   Interest, excluding paid-in-kind (PIK) interest, and accruing ordinary course fees payable in connection with the debt pursuant to the applicable credit agreement from and after the trade date. Examples of such fees are commitment, facility, and letter of credit fees. (See also "Commitment Fee," "Confirmation," "Facility Fee," "Letter of Credit Fees," "Paid on Settlement Date," "Settled without Accrued Interest," "Swingline Loan," "Trades Flat," and "Utilization Fees.")

Investment Grade   A rating of BBB or higher by Fitch Ratings or Standard & Poor's and BAA or higher by Moody's.

L

Lead Arranger   The lead arranger is essentially the "middle-man" in the syndication process. One or a small group of banks act as the lead arranger or co-lead arrangers, with responsibility for structuring, syndicating, and administering the loan. In most transactions, the lead arranger drives the deal; sets the terms; interfaces with the client and investors; prepares, negotiates, and closes documents; and manages the syndication process. Consequently, the lead arranger generally receives premium compensation, which increases with the complexity or difficulty of the financing. The title of "Lead Arranger" is the most significant designation for the lender responsible for executing the transaction. The "Bookrunner" title designates the lender managing the syndication process, which is usually one of the co-lead arrangers.

Letter of Credit   A letter of credit is a guarantee by the issuer that a required payment by the account party will be made, subject only to the delivery of specified documents. The letter of credit obligates the issuer unconditionally to honor drawings under the letter of credit upon presentation of the prescribed documents. In the case of commercial letters of credit issued to support the purchase of goods, the drawing under the letter of credit will itself constitute payment by the account party to the beneficiary. When payment is made upon a drawing under the letter of credit (assuming the documents appear on their face to be proper), the account party is obligated to reimburse the issuer for the amount paid.

Letter of Credit Fees   Because letters of credit are issued under a revolving credit facility, all of the revolving credit lenders share in the credit exposure, even if they are not the letter of credit issuer, because each acquires a participation in any letter of credit upon its issuance. Accordingly, borrowers are obligated to pay a letter of credit fee to each revolving credit lender that accrues at an agreed per annum rate on their participation in the undrawn amount of each outstanding letter of credit. In the case of the issuer of each letter of credit, its participation therein for purposes of this calculation is deemed to be its remaining credit exposure after subtracting the participations of the other revolving credit lenders. It is very common for the letter of credit fee rate to be the same as the applicable margin for London Interbank Offered Rate (LIBOR) loans, taking into account the use of any applicable grid pricing. These letter of credit fees are customarily payable quarterly in arrears. (See also "Letter of Credit.")

Leveraged Lending Guidance The Interagency Guidance on Leveraged Lending was published in May 2013 by the three U.S. banking regulators: the Office of the Comptroller of the Currency (OCC), the Federal Reserve, and the FDIC. The guidance influences bank examinations and applies to loans held and/or originated by the bank. Per the Guidance, leveraged borrowers ought to show an ability to repay all of their senior debt or half their total debt from free cash flows within a five- to seven-year period. Additionally, loans exceeding 6 times leverage are concerning in most industries. The Guidance was used by bank examiners to communicate their views on bank safety and soundness. In 2017, the Guidance was scrutinized under the Congressional Review Act, and regulators confirmed that it was simply "guidance."

Leveraged Loan A loan that is made to a company that has less than an investment-grade rating (below BBB–). These loans carry a higher risk profile and are typically made to smaller companies with which investors may not be as familiar. Because of the higher risk profile, leveraged loans carry a higher spread, are usually secured by the borrower's collateral, and contain more restrictive terms and covenants. Leveraged loans comprise nearly all of the loans that are traded in the secondary market.

LIBOR Acronym for the London Interbank Offered Rate. LIBOR is an interest rate benchmark published by ICE Benchmark Administration Limited that is used as a reference rate for a wide range of financial transactions, including loans and derivatives. It is intended to reflect the average current rate at which certain panel banks can obtain unsecured funding in a specific currency and for a specific term in the London interbank market. LIBOR rates are published daily for five currencies (including USD), and for each currency, rates are quoted for deposits with seven different maturities. In July 2017, the Financial Conduct Authority (FCA), the regulatory agency currently responsible for overseeing LIBOR, stated that the lack of active markets on which to base LIBOR quotations has rendered using LIBOR as a benchmark unsustainable and undesirable. The FCA and the panel banks submitting LIBOR quotations have therefore committed to supporting the current LIBOR-setting process only through the end of 2021. The Federal Reserve–sponsored Alternative Reference Rates Committee has already selected the Secured Overnight Financing Rate (SOFR) as the preferred alternative to USD LIBOR for use in derivatives. (See also "Secured Overnight Financing Rate.")

Loan Credit Default Swap (LCDS) A derivative product designed to allow loan market participants to isolate and trade the credit risk underlying a single bank loan or portfolio of loans. Although LCDS no longer trades in the current market, it remains a potential hedging strategy for the future.

Loan Total Return Swap (LTRS) A derivative contract between two parties to exchange the return of one or more bank loans. LTRS have contributed to the growth of the loan market over recent decades and remain widely deployed by market participants today. Also called a *Bank Loan Total Return Swap*.

Loss Given Default (LGD) The loss incurred by a lender in the event that the borrower of the loan defaults.

M

Mandatory Prepayments   Mandatory prepayments mandate that the borrower prepay loans upon the occurrence of specified events. In a credit agreement, the prepayment is usually required to be made immediately, and the lenders (with an exception for B loan tranches) will not be given the opportunity to opt out of a prepayment.

Mark-to-Market   Recording the price or value of an asset (e.g., a loan) to reflect its current market value.

Material Adverse Change (MAC)   A clause often found in a credit agreement that typically includes a representation and warranty by the borrower that, since a specified date, there has been no material adverse change in its business, condition (financial or otherwise), assets, operations, or prospects, or in its subsidiaries, taken as a whole. The continued accuracy of representations will generally be a condition precedent to new loans under a credit agreement. Thus, if a MAC has occurred, the MAC representation cannot be truthfully made, and the lenders' obligations to make new loans will be suspended for so long as the material adverse change continues (or unless the condition is waived).

Material Nonpublic Information (MNPI)   Information that is material to a security or issuer and is not public information. Although there is no bright line rule, under U.S. federal securities law, information generally is deemed to be material when (1) there is a substantial likelihood that a reasonable investor would consider the information important in making an investment decision, (2) there is a substantial likelihood that the disclosure of the information would be viewed by the reasonable investor as having significantly altered the total mix of information made available, or (3) the disclosure of the information is reasonably certain to have a substantial effect on the market price of the security. Syndicate information and borrower restricted information may include MNPI. (See also "Bank Loan Nonrestricting Information," "Borrower Restricted Information," "Confidential Information," "Public Information," and "Syndicate Information.")

Middle Market   Portion of the market characterized by loans to companies whose size limits their access to capital. The definition of middle market continues to fluctuate, but as traditionally defined, middle market lending includes loans of up to $500 million that are made to companies with annual revenues of less than $500 million.

Multilateral Netting Agreement   A typical multilateral netting arrangement arises in a situation where the seller ("Party A") enters a trade confirmation with a buyer ("Party B") and subsequently, Party B enters a trade confirmation to sell to another buyer ("Party C"). Parties A, B, and C may agree, for administrative ease and convenience, that Party A shall transfer the debt directly to Party C. On the settlement date, Party C will pay the purchase price owed to Party B under their trade confirmation and Party B will pay the purchase price owed to Party A under their trade confirmation, thereby maintaining the confidentiality of each trade confirmation, in particular, with respect to the purchase price. The LSTA has published a form of Multilateral Netting Agreement—Par/Near Par and form of Multilateral Netting Agreement—Distressed. (See also "Bilateral Netting Agreement.")

N

Nonperforming Loan See "Performing Loan."

Nonrecurring Fees Any fee other than interest and accruing fees or paid-in-kind (PIK) interest that is paid with respect to the debt pursuant to the credit agreement from and after the trade date, such as a fee payable to lenders for granting a waiver or amendment under the credit agreement or another similar, nonordinary course fee. Unless otherwise agreed, nonrecurring fees are for the account of the buyer under the LSTA's Confirm. (See also "Confirmation.")

O

Open-End Fund A mutual fund with an unlimited number of shares that can be issued, purchased, or redeemed at any time.

Optional Prepayment The general rule under New York law is that a loan may not be prepaid without the consent of the lender. Credit agreements will nearly always expressly override the general rule and allow the borrower to prepay loans at any time at its option. This is subject to certain exceptions, such as with respect to competitive bid loans, and, of course, any payment of a London Interbank Offered Rate (LIBOR) loan prior to the expiration of its interest period will need to be accompanied by a break-funding payment. Voluntary prepayments may usually be made only upon notice given by the borrower to the administrative agent (who then advises the appropriate lenders). Prepayments will be required to be in certain minimum amounts (and sometimes, multiples in excess of those minimums) to ease the administrative burden of dealing with small funds transfers.

Original Issue Discount (OID) A tax-related term that represents the discount from the par amount of a debt instrument at the time it was issued. Credit documentation often refers to OID and upfront fees interchangeably. (See also "Upfront Fee.")

P

Paid on Settlement Date An interest convention available under the LSTA's Confirm that provides that all interest and accruing fees up to but excluding the settlement date are for the account of the seller, and an amount equal to the accrued but unpaid amount of interest and accruing fees up to but excluding the settlement date, are paid by the buyer to the seller on the settlement date. This interest convention is not often used by loan market participants because assignment agreements typically provide that interest accrued up to but excluding the effective date of the assignment agreement is paid to the seller, and interest that has accrued on and after the effective date is paid to the buyer ("paid on settlement date" is an interest convention that is similar to the way bonds are traded under the "settled with accrued" convention). (See also "Interest and Accruing Fees" and "Settlement Date.")

Par Confirmation See "Confirmation."

Par Loan Generally, a loan that is expected to be paid in accordance with the terms of the applicable credit agreement. For par trades, the loan is traded on a Par Confirm and is transferred pursuant to an assignment agreement.

Pari Passu A Latin term meaning "without partiality." A term describing an equal claim by lenders to a borrower's assets. Typically, the term is used in a representation with respect to "pari passu ranking" to the effect that the borrower's obligations under the credit agreement rank at least pari passu with all of the borrower's other obligations. This provides assurance that the laws of the borrower's country do not grant senior status to other claims that might trump the lenders' rights.

Participation A sale of an undivided 100% participation interest in an underlying loan and/or commitment to a borrower by a seller ("grantor") to a buyer ("participant"). Unlike in an assignment, the grantor is and remains a lender of record under the applicable credit agreement, with full obligations thereunder. The grantor maintains the relationship with the borrower in all respects, and a participant has no direct rights against the borrower. Under the LSTA's documentation, lenders have the right to grant participation interests, but there are restrictions on which rights may be granted to a participant (e.g., the right to control the lender's vote on certain issues). The LSTA has published two-part forms, the Participation Agreement for Par/Near Par Trades and the Participation Agreement for Distressed Trades, consisting of transaction-specific terms relating to specifics of the relevant trade and governed by standard terms and conditions. The LSTA's Participation Agreements are drafted so that the transfer of the participation should be afforded sale accounting treatment. (See also "Assignment" and "True Sale.")

Paydown A payment of principal by the borrower, which reduces the overall amount outstanding under a debt facility. (See also "Permanent Reduction.")

Payment-in-Kind or Paid-in-Kind (PIK) Interest A form of payment in which the interest owed by the borrower is added to the principal amount owed to a lender. Under LSTA documents, PIK interest that is capitalized or accreted on or after the trade date is for the benefit of the buyer for no additional consideration.

Performing Loan Generally, a loan in which the borrower is making timely and full payments to the lenders under the credit agreement.

Permanent Reduction Under the LSTA's Confirm, permanent commitment reductions and permanent repayments of principal as of or after the trade date are referred to as *permanent reductions*, and they are taken into account when calculating the purchase price (i.e., the buyer receives the economic benefit of any permanent reductions on or after the trade date).

Portfolio Manager The manager of a fund. A portfolio manager considers investment alternatives and seeks to analyze investments in the portfolio to try to achieve a strong performance.

Prepayment Fee The general rule is that credit agreements do not impose a fee as the price of an early prepayment of the loan but instead will look to cover losses for their cost of funds for any current interest period (a *breakfunding fee*). There are exceptions to this general rule, and in addition to any breakfunding payments, prepayment premiums for Term Loan Bs may be required; in this instance, the borrower may be required to pay an additional fee in a percentage equal to the amount of principal being prepaid. In a credit agreement, this prepayment premium will be in much lower amounts than are typically found in bond indentures (2% descending to 1%) and will only apply to prepayments made in the first or second year following the closing. In addition, some agreements provide that a premium is not payable at all unless the source of the prepayment is a refinancing by the borrower with the proceeds of cheaper debt (a so-called soft-call).

Private-Side Lender A lender that receives and uses syndicate information (which may include material nonpublic information) in loan originating, trading, and/or lending and is therefore subject to trading restrictions if in possession of material nonpublic information.

Proceeds Letter An agreement used to settle a trade after a credit facility has been terminated or restructured, in which a lender receives cash, notes, preferred shares, common shares, warrants, new debt, or other property in lieu of the original debt and must pass these resulting proceeds on to its buyer. The LSTA has published two forms of Proceeds Letters. The LSTA's form of Chapter 11 Plan Proceeds Letter Agreement for Post-Effective Date Settlement of Distressed Trades should be used to settle distressed trades in which the borrower is a debtor in a Chapter 11 bankruptcy case, its plan has been confirmed, and the plan's effective date has occurred. The LSTA's form of Short-Form Proceeds Letter Agreement for Post-Repayment Date Settlement of Distressed Trades should be used only when the loan, although traded on LSTA distressed documents, pertains to a borrower that has not filed for bankruptcy and has made a final cash payout to the lenders for all amounts outstanding, including any accrued interest and fees.

Proof of Claim A document filed by a creditor with the Bankruptcy Court setting forth details of the debtor, the creditor, and the claim (e.g., the basis for the claim, the amount of the claim, and whether it is secured or unsecured). This serves as notice to the debtor that such property is owed and is being claimed against the assets of the debtor.

Pro Rata Tranches These include revolver and term loan A (TLA) loans. These loans are typically held by banks. Revolvers usually have a five- to six-year tenure, whereas TLAs typically amortize over a three- to six-year (majority five- to six-year) period to ensure repayment. (See also "Revolving Credit Facility" and "Term Loan A.")

Public Information Information that has been broadly disseminated to, or is accessible by, the public, for example, via a press release from the company that has been picked up on a national news service, disclosure on the company's website, a news story disseminated by a national news service, or a public filing with the U.S. Securities and Exchange Commission (SEC) or a court.

Public-Side Lender A lender that has elected to conduct loan trading and/or lending solely on the basis of public information; typically, a public-side lender is also involved in securities trading and sales.

Purchase and Sale Agreement (PSA) Agreement than governs the purchase and sale of distressed loans, commitments, and other rights being transferred in connection with those loans and commitments and contains, among other things, representations, warranties, and indemnities made by the seller and the buyer. The LSTA has published a form of Purchase and Sale Agreement for Distressed Trades, which is a two-part document consisting of transaction-specific terms relating to specifics of the relevant trade and governed by standard terms and conditions. Upon execution, the PSA supersedes the Distressed Confirm.

Purchase Price As used in the LSTA's trading documents, the amount to be paid by the buyer to the seller for the amount and type of debt specified in the applicable confirm, as calculated in accordance with the confirm, or, if such calculations produce a negative number, the amount to be paid by the seller to the buyer in respect of such debt. The purchase rate is used to calculate the purchase price. (See also "Purchase Rate.")

Purchase Rate The rate specified as a percentage of the face value of debt that is set forth in the applicable confirm.

R

Recovery Rate The share of defaulted credit that a lender receives after resolution.

Recovery Value The market price of a loan immediately following an event of default. Defaulted loans are generally priced based on the market's perception of the likelihood of repayment.

Register The list maintained by the administrative agent that identifies the name and address of each lender and the amounts of their respective commitments and loan balances. The credit agreement will normally state that the loan register is conclusive and binding, absent manifest error, and thus is the definitive determinant of who must consent to modifications to the agreement and who are the "Required Lenders" for voting purposes.

Regulation FD Securities and Exchange Commission (SEC) regulation that became effective on October 23, 2000; it eliminated the practice of selective disclosure and is designed to promote the full and fair disclosure of information by issuers, and to clarify and enhance existing prohibitions against insider trading. The rules address issues such as the selective disclosure by issuers of material nonpublic information and when insider trading liability arises in connection with a trader's "use" or "knowing possession" of material nonpublic information.

Revolving Credit Facility (Revolver) Loans that "revolve" within "commitments" established by the lenders. The borrower may borrow, repay, and reborrow the loans during the term of the commitments, so long as the applicable lending conditions are satisfied. By contrast, term loans, once borrowed and repaid, may not be reborrowed. The LSTA has published a form of Revolving Credit Facility for investment-grade borrowers.

S

Second-Lien Loans Second lien facilities provide for secured term loans, but the priority of their liens with respect to the collateral is junior to identical liens in favor of the first lien lending syndicate. (See also "First Lien.")

Secured Loans/Security The asset collateral of the borrower pledged to repay the lenders in the event of default on a loan facility. Secured loans are commonly used in the leveraged loan market.

Secured Overnight Financing Rate (SOFR)   SOFR is the combination of three overnight Treasury repo rates and is published daily by the Federal Reserve Bank of New York. It is very liquid and very deep, with more than $800 billion of trading on a daily basis. This means that it will likely be robust, durable, and hard to manipulate—all alleged shortcomings of the London Interbank Offered Rate (LIBOR). In the United States, the Alternative Reference Rates Committee (ARRC) has identified SOFR as the LIBOR replacement for derivatives, and it is likely to become the replacement rate for cash products such as syndicated loans.

Settled Without Accrued (SWOA) Interest   A loan trading interest convention available under LSTA loan trading documents for loan trades that do not timely settle. It provides that the interest and accruing fees on the applicable loan that accrue prior to but excluding the earlier of the settlement date and the commencement date under the LSTA's Confirm belong to the seller, irrespective of which party receives such payment, and after that date, they belong to the buyer. This interest convention is generally the preferred convention for performing loans. Under the LSTA's form of Par Confirm, SWOA shall apply unless the parties agree otherwise at the time of trade. Under the LSTA's form of Distressed Confirm, a credit may "flip to flat," even if SWOA was elected as the interest convention, if the loan is no longer a performing loan. (See also "Commencement Date," "Interest and Accruing Fees," and "Settlement Date.")

Settlement Date   The date on which payment of the purchase price occurs against the transfer of the purchase amount of the debt.

Shift Date   The date on which market convention for transferring the debt has shifted from par documentation to distressed documentation. The shift date is determined by the LSTA in accordance with the LSTA's Shift Date Rules and is generally based on a historical analysis of that credit's trading data. Parties to a distressed trade for which step-up provisions apply are required to use the relevant shift date published by the LSTA. (See also "Step-up Representations.")

Spread   The amount of yield the loan pays above a benchmark market interest rate given a particular price in the secondary market. (See also "Applicable Margins.")

Standard Terms and Conditions   See "Confirmation," "Participation," and "Purchase and Sale Agreement."

Standstill Period   A period during which lenders agree to refrain from taking certain enforcement action in order to allow a borrower time to work with its financial advisor to restructure its debt.

Step-up Representations   Under the LSTA's distressed trading documentation, the buyer may request what are referred to as *step-up representations* or *step-up provisions* when it believes that the seller has not obtained the appropriate definitions, representations, warranties, indemnities, or distribution provisions in the upstreams. This situation arises when any portion or all of the purchase amount of the debt being sold was purchased by the seller or a prior seller on par documents on or after the relevant shift date. In this instance, the seller will be obligated to provide the buyer with customary step-up representations that would typically be found in the LSTA's distressed trading documentation. (See also "Shift Date" and "Upstreams.")

Sterling Overnight Index Average (SONIA) The Bank of England is the administrator for SONIA. SONIA is based on actual transactions and reflects the average of the interest rates that banks pay to borrow sterling overnight from other financial institutions and other institutional investors.

Subordination In traditional debt subordination, the debt claim itself is subordinated; thus, if a subordinated debt holder obtains anything of value in a bankruptcy from any source, it agrees to turn it over to the holders of senior debt until the senior debt is paid in full. In the case of second-lien loans, only the liens are subordinated; the underlying debt claim is not. What this means is that the holder of a second-lien loan only agrees to turn over proceeds from sales of shared collateral to the first-lien lenders. The holder of a second-lien loan claim does not have to turn over funds to the first-lien lenders distributed to it from other sources.

Subparticipation An undivided interest in a participation interest. A participant may be restricted from granting subparticipations of its participation interest. The LSTA form of Participation Agreements permits the buyer of a participation to grant subparticipations without the prior consent of or notice to the grantor, provided that it meets certain requirements, including that it does not violate the law or cause the grantor to violate or be in breach of any provision of the applicable transaction documents and the subparticipant makes to the buyer-participant, for the benefit of the grantor, the same representations, warranties, and confidentiality obligations as the buyer-participant makes to it. No contractual relationship is created between the subparticipant and the seller-grantor, and the buyer-participant remains solely responsible for its obligations under the participation agreement with the seller-grantor. (See also "Participation.")

Sustainability-Linked Loan Any type of loan in which the borrower is incentivized, typically through loan pricing, to meet predetermined sustainability performance target levels. If a borrower meets the predetermined target level, there is a discount in the borrower's cost of borrowing (or a premium if the borrower fails to meet the target level). Unlike green loans, the use of loan proceeds is not a determinant, and many sustainability-linked loans are used for general corporate purposes. The LSTA, the Loan Market Association (LMA), and the Asia Pacific Loan Market Association (APLMA) have published Sustainability-Linked Loan Principles.

Swingline Loan Loans normally made available as an adjunct to the revolving credit facility by one of the revolving lenders, which is designated as the "swingline lender." Swingline loans are designed to give the borrower more rapid access to funds than would otherwise be permitted by the notice periods in the credit agreement, which typically require at least three business days' notice for London Interbank Offered Rate (LIBOR) loans and one business day's notice for base rate loans. Even when same-day availability is allowed for base rate loans, a swingline facility provides greater flexibility by permitting swingline loans to be made later in the day. Swingline loans can be made on such short notice because they are being advanced by only one lender, often (but not always) the lender serving as the Administrative Agent. Some agreements may contemplate more than one swingline lender, but rarely will the number exceed two or three. Revolving lenders may be named as swingline lenders in the agreement or may be designated as such at a later time by the borrower; however, it is typically within a lender's sole discretion whether or not to accept the designation as a swingline lender, and a swingline lender can typically resign from acting in such capacity.

SWOA   See "Settled Without Accrued Interest."

Syndicate Information   Confidential information that a borrower provides or makes available (typically through an Administrative Agent or arranger) to all members and potential members of a lending syndicate. Syndicate information is subject to specific confidentiality undertakings contained in credit agreements, evaluation materials, and standalone confidentiality agreements. Syndicate information can be more extensive than that which is publicly available and in certain circumstances may constitute MNPI. Syndicate information may be provided orally or in writing, including by posting on electronic workspaces. It typically consists of (1) information made available by a borrower in connection with the origination of a loan, (2) information periodically made available by or on behalf of the borrower to the entire syndicate of lenders in accordance with the terms of the applicable credit agreement, and (3) information periodically made available by the borrower to the entire syndicate of lenders regarding developments or other special circumstances, and it may include requests for amendments, waivers, and/or consents. (See also "Confidential Information," "Bank Loan Nonrestricting Information," "Borrower Restricted Information," and "Material Nonpublic Information.")

Syndication Agent   The bank that handles the syndication of the loan. The title of "Syndication Agent" is often awarded in conjunction with large commitments, but the actual responsibilities of such roles may be shared or handled by the administrative agent or the lead arrangers.

T

Tax Gross-Up   A mechanism included in a provision of a credit agreement that is intended to protect the lender against taxes that would reduce its yield on the loan. The primary concern relates to taxes that the borrower would be required to withhold from the stated interest that it would otherwise pay to the lender. The provision will therefore typically require the borrower to "gross-up" the interest payment so that the lender realizes an amount in cash that, after deduction for the withheld taxes (including further withholding taxes on the gross-up payments), is equal to the stated interest on the loan. For example, assume that the interest on a loan made by a bank located in the United States is 6%. Assume also that the borrower is in a jurisdiction that imposes a withholding tax on interest payments made to the United States of 30%. Absent a gross-up, the lender will receive only 4.2% per annum on its loan; that is, (100% minus 30%) times 6%. The taxes clause will accordingly gross-up the interest payment to an amount equal to 8.571% (i.e., 6% divided by .70). When the 30% withholding is then applied to the 8.571%, the lender will receive in cash 6% (8.571% times .70% = 6.0%).

Term Loan   A loan that may be drawn down by a borrower during a given commitment period and is then repaid by the borrower in accordance with a scheduled series of installments; once borrowed and repaid by the borrower, term loans may not be reborrowed. In the loan market, term loans have evolved into two principal types: so-called A loan tranches and B loan tranches. (See also "Term Loan A" and "Term Loan B.")

Term Loan A (TLA)   Term loans that are made by bank lenders (as opposed to other institutional investors) and that have a maturity shorter than that of any B loan tranche and are entitled to the benefit of real amortization (i.e., installments that over the term of the loan will represent sizable paydowns of the facility). Revolvers and Term Loan As are often referred to as the *pro rata tranches*. (See also "Term Loan B.")

Term Loan B (TLB)   Term loans structured to be sold to institutional investors. They typically have a maturity longer than any related term loan A (usually six months to a year further) and will have only nominal amortization until the last year (i.e., typically 1% per year until the last year or the very final installment). They may also be referred to as B Loans. (See also "Institutional Investors/Institutional Lenders" and "Term Loan A.")

Ticking Fees   Commitment fees that accrue on term loan commitments. Ticking fees are most commonly found in commitment letters (or related fee letters) for committed term loan financings for which the commitment period is relatively long. The ticking fee may start to accrue immediately or after some period of time following the effectiveness of the commitment letter and will typically accrue until and be payable on the closing date. The rate of the ticking fee may be fixed or may increase with the passage of time. Ticking fees may be documented in the credit agreement but do not need to be if they are in a commitment or fee letter.

Trade Date   The date listed on the confirm as the date on which the trade between the buyer and the seller took place.

Trades Flat   An interest convention available in the LSTA's Distressed Confirm that provides that all interest and accruing fees and, if applicable, adequate protection payments unpaid as of the trade date, whether accruing before, on, or after the trade date, are for the buyer's account. This interest convention is generally the preferred convention for nonperforming loans. (See also "Performing Loan" and "Settled Without Accrued Interest.")

Tranche   In the context of term loans, tranche refers to either the A loan tranche or B loan tranche.

Transaction-Specific Terms   See "Participation" and "Purchase and Sale Agreement."

Transfer Notice   Any notice and evidence of transfer with respect to transferred rights, filed in a bankruptcy case in accordance with the Bankruptcy Rules.

Transferred Rights   As defined in the LSTA's Purchase and Sale Agreement, the seller's rights, title, and interest in the loans and commitments and all other amounts payable to the seller under the credit documentation and all related claims, guarantees, and collateral that are being acquired by the buyer under the Purchase and Sale Agreement. (See also "Purchase and Sale Agreement.")

True Sale   An accounting treatment under Financial Accounting Standards Board's Accounting Standards Codification (ASC) 860-10 that can recognize a participation as a sale by a grantor to a participant of an undivided interest in an underlying loan, rather than as a financing arrangement between the grantor and the participant. For a participation to be afforded "true sale" treatment, certain legal and accounting conditions must be met. The LSTA form of Participation Agreements was drafted to be used by parties seeking sale treatment. Of particular interest to participants, sale treatment supports the argument that a grantor holds no beneficial interest in the loan participated in, and accordingly, the loan and proceeds thereof are not part of a grantor's bankruptcy estate. For example, in the Lehman Brothers bankruptcy case, the LSTA participation agreements under which Lehman was a grantor were afforded sale accounting treatment. (See also "Participation.")

U

Underwriting Fee A fee paid to the arranging syndicate for underwriting a loan. The fee will be more expensive than the fee paid to the arranging syndicate in a "best efforts syndication," because, in an underwritten deal, the arranging syndicate must provide the funds even if less than the committed amount is sold.

Unfunded Commitment The portion of the total commitment under a revolving credit facility that has not been drawn down by the borrower. Such amount is available to be funded at the request of the borrower.

Unitranche Financing A unitranche credit facility combines into a single credit facility what would otherwise be separate first lien and second lien credit facilities. From a credit agreement perspective, the agreement is the same as with any other loan transaction. Namely, the borrower in a unitranche financing will only have a single set of covenants and reporting obligations to monitor and comply with, will pay a single blended interest rate on the unitranche loans (typically, a cheaper rate than it would pay in aggregate for separate first-lien and second-lien loans), and will grant a single lien on collateral, securing the unitranche loans. However, along with a typical credit agreement, the lenders will also enter a separate intercreditor agreement that is referred to as an *Agreement Among Lenders* (AAL). (See also "Agreement Among Lenders.")

Upfront Fee Upfront fees are compensation to lenders for making a loan. They do not accrue over time but instead are payable on the closing date as a percentage of the lender's term loan amount or revolving commitment amount. Upfront fees are often netted by term loan lenders from the proceeds of the loans they fund at closing. Upfront fees can also be netted by revolving lenders, but only to the extent that they fund their revolving commitments at closing (often, they do not), and otherwise must be paid as a cash fee. Upfront fees are sometimes referenced in the credit agreement but do not need to be if included in a commitment or fee letter. Credit documentation often refers to upfront fees and original issue discount (OID) interchangeably. (See also "Original Issue Discount.")

Upstreams Applicable in distressed trades, this term refers to the predecessor purchase and sale agreements and assignment agreements that evidence the chain of prior ownership of the debt. (See also "Shift Date.")

Utilization Fees For transactions in which the revolving credit commitments are not expected to be heavily utilized, the commitment fee or facility fee may be lower than in other comparable transactions. However, to address the possibility that utilization may turn out to be high, the credit agreement may provide for an additional utilization fee to be payable if utilization exceeds a certain percentage (e.g., 30% or 50%) of the commitments. On each date that this percentage is exceeded, the fee is payable on all utilizations of the revolving credit facility and not merely on the portion in excess of the 30% or 50% threshold. In contrast to the approach used to calculate the commitment fee, utilization for this purpose is more likely to be defined broadly, including more than just outstanding revolving credit loans, letters of credit, and bid loans. Like commitment fees and facility fees, utilization fees are either calculated at a flat rate or subject to grid pricing. The frequency of payment of utilization fees can vary.

V

Volcker Rule   Section 631 of the Dodd-Frank Act is commonly known as the "Volcker Rule" (named after its main proponent, former Fed Chairman Paul Volcker). The Volcker Rule limits proprietary trading by banks and also limits their ability to own or invest in equity-like securities of certain types of funds.

Voting Mechanics   The basic rule with respect to the voting provisions of a credit agreement is that the "majority" or "required" lenders must approve any modification, waiver, or supplement to any provision of the credit agreement. "Majority" or "required" will normally mean lenders holding more than 50% of the aggregate credit exposure (i.e., unused commitments and outstanding loans and letters of credit). Sometimes the credit agreement will break out particular issues and require a so-called supermajority vote for changes. In so-called club deals, the definition of *Required Lenders* may include a concept that a minimum number of lenders, as well as the holders of a minimum percentage of loans, vote in favor of a change. In a multitranche agreement, one issue that will be addressed is whether the lenders vote as a single pool or each tranche votes separately. The near-universal practice that has developed in recent years is that all lenders vote together as a pool; however, an additional clause may also be included that requires a separate majority vote of a tranche if a change would adversely affect that tranche without equally affecting all other tranches.

W

When-Issued Trade   A trade following the allocation of a facility by the arranger to committed investors, but before the loan has closed.

Withholding Tax   Tax that a borrower is required to withhold on an interest payment to a lender. The taxes clause in a credit agreement is intended to protect the lender against taxes that would reduce its yield on the loan. The primary concern relates to taxes that the borrower would be required to withhold from the stated interest that it would otherwise pay to the lender. The typical approach of the tax clause is to require the borrower to "gross-up" the interest payment so that the lender realizes an amount in cash that, after deduction for the withheld taxes (including further withholding taxes on the gross-up payments), is equal to the stated interest on the loan. (See also "Tax Gross-Up.")

INDEX

A

ABR. *See* Alternate Base Rate (ABR)/Prime Loans
Acceleration in events of default, 252–253
Accordion features, commitments, 111–114
Accounting, 861
   allowance for current expected credit losses, 867–868
      initial recognition, 868
      measurement, 868–871
      unit of account, 868
   changes, 227–228
   debt securities, 866–867
   financial asset transfers, 871–872
      derecognition of financial assets sold, 872
      participation agreements, 873–874
      sale of financial assets, 874
      trade-date versus settlement-date accounting, 874
   loans and investments, 861
      classification, 861–862
      recognition and measurement, 862–863
      origination fees and costs, 863–866
Account party, 108
Acquisition covenants, 217, 220
Acquisition debt, 215
Acquisition financings, conditionality in, 172–174
Acquisition liens, 213
Acquisition lines, 340
Acquisitions (M&A) financings, 773
Acting in good faith, 83, 135, 290
Actual fraud, Chapter 11 bankruptcy, 563
Add-backs, 197
Additional public or quasi-public debt, 215
Adequate protection, Chapter 11 bankruptcy, 566–567
Administrative agent, 45
   delegation, 259
   exculpation, 258–259
   fees, 128
   mechanics of funding and, 116–117
   reliance, 259
   successor agents, 260–261

Administrative claims, Chapter 11 bankruptcy, 564
Administrative Procedure Act (APA), 705, 720
Affected lender concept, 262–263
Affiliate transactions covenants, 225–226
Affirmative covenants
   collateral packages, 235–236
   disclosure covenants, 203–205
   maintenance of insurance, 205–206
   in term sheet, 56
   visitation rights, 205
Agency provisions, in credit agreements, 256–261
   appointment, 257–258
   delegation, 259
   exculpation, 258–259
   filing proofs of claim, 260
   no fiduciary duty, 258–259
   reliance, 259
   successor agents, 260–261
   syndication and other agents, 261
Agenda for Sustainable Development, 2030, 838–839
All-In-Rate, 90–91, 94, 97, 98
Allocation, loan settlement, 459
Allocation decision, 643
A loans
   defined, 339
   incremental facilities, 112
   tranche, 106–107
Alternate Base Rate (ABR)/Prime loans, 306
Alternative Reference Rates Committee (ARRC), 297, 299
Amend and extend, 536
Amendments
   loan settlement, 466
   to organic documents and other agreements, 226–227
Amortization and maturity, 142–156
   advancing the maturity date, 144
   application of prepayments among tranches, 153–154
   cover for letter of credit, 154
   multiple borrowers, 155–156

913

Amortization and maturity *(Cont.)*
  payments
    immediately available funds, 142
    provisions, 55
    scheduled repayment, 143–144
    time of, 142–143
  prepayments
    mandatory, 146–153
    voluntary, 145–146
  364-day facilities, 144–145
Amortized cost basis loan, 862
Analytics and performance, 479–525
  quantitative tools, 479–507
    CLO life cycles and management style, 481
    compliance tests, 482–483
    Diversity Score, 494–495, 501–502, 675
    open-source code, 503–507
    portfolio optimization, 492–500
    robust credit research, 479–480, 502–503
  Ultimate Recovery Database, 507–525
Annualized periods, 197–198
Anticipated investor demand, 49–50
Anticorruption regulations, 178
Antifraud liability considerations, 324–327
Anti-money laundering (AML), 880–881, 885, 886–887
APA. *See* Administrative Procedure Act
Applicable margin, 46, 119, 125–126, 127, 130, 474
Appointment, agency provision, 257–258
Appraisals, 168–169
Approved assignee list, 740
ARRC. *See* Alternative Reference Rates Committee
Asian financial crisis, 763
Asia Pacific loan market, 753–754
  Australia volume, 759–760
  China spurred on by capital expenditures, 758–759
  Chinese bank lending, 754–755
  defaults, 765
  ESG and green lending, 756
  Hong Kong loan market, 756–758
  Indian loan market, 762
  Indonesia loan volume, 762–763
  lenders retreat, 765–766
  Malaysia loan volume, 762
  private credit funds, 763–764
  secondary loan activity, 764–765
  Singapore, 761–762
  South and Southeast Asia, 762–763
  Taiwan, 760–761

Asia Pacific Loan Market Association (APLMA), 748, 810, 830
Asset-based finance, 798
Asset-based lending, 340–341
Asset-based revolving facilities, 338
Asset managers, 6, 59, 411, 412, 440, 459, 554, 641, 667, 776
Asset sales, 148–150
  Chapter 11 bankruptcy, 567–568
  collateralized loan obligations (CLOs), 696–697
  covenants, 216–217
  secured creditor right to approve, 350
Assets under management (AUM), CLO, 669–670
Assignment agreement, 83, 85, 86, 88, 89, 96, 271, 391, 457, 466–467, 878, 883–884
Assignments, 267–273
  consent rights, 268–269
  distinguishing assignments and participations, 267–268
  eligible assignees and disqualified lenders, 270
  loan register, 271
  loan trading settlement, 460–461
  minimums, 270–271
  restrictions on second lien loans, 367
  securities laws and, 271–273
  transfer fees, 271
Association of Southeast Asian Nations (ASEAN), 733
Australia loan market, 759–760
Australian foreign investment, 755
Avoidance powers, Chapter 11 bankruptcy, 559–563

B

Balance sheet test, 562
Bank-centric versus market-centric market, 730–733
  regulatory environment, 733–735
Bank Company Holding Act, 333
Bank credit risk, 3–6
Banking Act of 1933, 4
Banking Agencies, 718
Bank-led trading market, 752
Bank loan mutual funds, 40
Bank loans
  default on, 9–10
  historical review of, 3–6

Index   **915**

leveraged loans as asset investment
    class, 6–9
risks and returns with, 11–28
    bankruptcy, 8–9
    current market, 27–28
    default *vs.* recoveries, 9–10
    economic recovery and way forward, 22–24
    first credit test, 20
    Global Financial Crisis (GFC) of 2008 and, 8, 20, 21–22
    historical review of, 11–18
    narrative of, 18–28
    rebound of 2003, 21
    timeline of, 19–20
Bank loan total return swaps (LTRS). *See* Loan total return swaps (LTRS)
Bank meeting, 53, 78
Bankruptcy, 183, 196, 554–574
    acceleration in events of default, 252–253
    adequate protection rights, 349–350
    automatic stay, 231
    as bank loan risk, 10–11
    Bankruptcy Code restrictions, 355
    Chapter 11
        adequate protection, 566–567
        alternative paths, 570–571
        asset sales, 567–568
        assumption and rejection of executory contracts and unexpired leases, 565–566
        avoidance powers, 559–563
            actual fraud, 563
            constructive fraud, 561–562
            fraudulent transfers, 561
            preferential transfer, 560–561
        commencement, first-day orders, and the automatic stay, 557–558
        estate and debtor in possession, 558
        exchanges, 572–573
        goals, 556–557
        plan of reorganization and disclosure, 568–569
        prenegotiated and prepackaged plans, 572
        priority of claims, 563–565
            priority claims and administrative claims, 564
            secured claims, 563–564
            superpriority claims, 565
            unsecured claims and equity claims, 564–565

        use of cash collateral, 566
        U.S. trustee and creditors committee, 558–559
        voting and confirmation, 569–570
    comprehensive restructuring, 544–545
    loan total return swaps (LTRS), 637
    post-petition interest, 349
    priority vis-à-vis trade and other unsecured creditors, 348–349
    reinstatement, 232
    relationships between multiple secured creditors at law absent intercreditor agreement, 352–355
    right to approve asset sales, 350
    right to approve secured DIP financings, 350–351
    right to object to use of cash collateral, 350
    second lien lender restrictions, 356–358
    secured creditors rights in, 348–351
    unsecured creditors rights in, 352
    unsecured creditors rights outside of, 351–352
Bankruptcy Abuse Prevention and Consumer Protection Act of 2005 (BAPCA), 556
Bankruptcy Code, 130, 183, 196, 231, 232, 236, 251, 252, 253, 348, 349–353, 355, 356, 358, 555–574, 721
Banks
    commercial versus investment, 4
    and development of leveraged loans, 6–8
    as dominant funding source, 410–411
Bank Secrecy Act, 880
Base rate, 118–119
BDC. *See* Business development companies
Benchmarks, 100–102
Best evidence rule, 286
Bids Wanted In Competition (BWIC), 423
Bitcoin, 880
B loans
    defined, 339–340
    incremental facilities, 112
    prepayment opt-outs, 154–155
    second lien loans (*see* Second lien loans)
    soft call, 155
    tranche, 106–107
Blockchain, 878–880, 882–886
Bloomberg Barclays Aggregate Bond Index, 644
Blue-sky laws, 327–330

Boilerplate, credit agreement, 275–287
  borrower indemnification consequential damages, 277–279
  captions, 285–286
  counterparts clause, 285
  cumulative remedies, 276
  electronic execution, 286
  enforcement provisions, 280–284
  expenses, 276–277
  governing law, 279–280
  integration clause, 285
  judgment currency, 284
  no deemed waivers, 275–276
  notice provisions, 275
  severability clause, 284–285
  survival clause, 286–287
  USA Patriot Act, 287
  venue and forum non conveniens, 282–283
  waiver of jury trial, 283
  waiver of sovereign immunity, 283
Bonds
  cash and cash equivalents, 219
  sale-leasebacks, 217–218
  trading loans versus bonds, 395–396
  versus loans, 389–390
Book runners, 44
Books and records covenants, 206
Borrowers, 648, 731
  business strategy, 844
  confidentiality, 292–293
  credit risk analysis of, 43
  desire to protect confidential information, 64
  foreign, 156
    events of default, 249–250
    representations for, 188–190
    special conditions applicable to, 167
  insolvency of, 232–233
  loan repayment, 142–156
  multiple, 155–156
  representations and disclosures regarding the business, 184–187
  rights, 288–293
  right to designate additional, 290
  sovereign, 190
  use restrictions, 293
  See also Loans
Borrowing base, 147–148, 341
Brand value, 825
Breach of contract risk, 64
Breach of covenants, 241–242
Breakfunding, 138–139

Broadly syndicated loans (BSLs), 663, 670–671
Business-day conventions, 132–133
Business development companies (BDCs), 342, 771, 775, 776, 780–783, 794–796
Businesses
  lines of business, 220
  mergers, 216–217
  overview, 52
  representations and disclosures regarding, 184–187
Buy-in/sell-out (BISO), 466
Buyout boom, 430, 785, 786

C

CAGR. *See* Compound annual growth rate (CAGR)
Capital adequacy test, 562
Capital allocation, 834
Capital costs and yield protection, 136
Capital expenditures, 773
  in financial covenants, 202
  growth, 799
Capital injection in distressed companies, 541–542
Capitalization, 184–185
Capital markets as alternative to commercial banks, 379–381
Capital preservation, 799, 805
Capital raising, 34, 834
Capital structure trades, 402–403
Carbon dioxide emissions, 814, 821
Carbon emissions, 822
Carbon footprint, 812, 816, 854
Carbon-intensive product, 817
Carbon negative by 2030, 837
Carbon transition risks, 817, 820–821, 824
Cash and cash equivalents, 219
Cash collateral, Chapter 11 bankruptcy
  use of, 566, 574–575
Cash flow
  bank loan total return swaps (LTRS), 629–631
  discounted cash flow (DCF) analysis, 593–595
  excess, 150–151
  in lieu of EBITDA, 196–197
  ratio, 200
  test, 562
Casualty events, 150
Catchall condition, 170

Index

CBOs. *See* Collateralized bond obligations (CBOs)
CDS. *See* Credit default swaps (CDS)
Central banks, 22, 135, 835, 851
CFTC. *See* Commodity Futures and Trading Commission (CFTC)
Change of control, 151–153
   events of default, 248–249
Chapter 11 bankruptcy
   adequate protection, 566–567
   asset sales, 567–568
   assumption and rejection of executory contracts and unexpired leases, 565–566
   avoidance powers, 559–563
      actual fraud, 563
      constructive fraud, 561–562
      fraudulent transfers, 561
      preferential transfer, 560–561
   commencement, first-day orders, and the automatic stay, 557–558
   estate and debtor in possession, 558
   exchanges, 572–573
   goals, 556–557
   plan of reorganization and disclosure, 568–569
   prenegotiated and prepackaged plans, 572
   priority of claims, 563–565
      priority claims and administrative claims, 564
      secured claims, 563–564
      superpriority claims, 565
      unsecured claims and equity claims, 564–565
   use of cash collateral, 566, 574–575
   U.S. trustee and creditors committee, 558–559
   voting and confirmation, 569–570
Chinese bank lending, 754–755
C&I lending market, 773
Circuit Court, 709, 721, 724
CIS. *See* Credit impact score (CIS)
Citibank, 7, 410, 432
Clawback clause, 265–267
Clean-downs, revolving, 147
ClearPar, 391
Climate Bonds Initiative (CBI), 839
Climate Bonds Taxonomy, 839
Climate change, 372–374, 819, 825
Climate risk assessment, 820
Climate stress testing, 835
Climate Transition Finance published their Transition Bond Guidelines, 855

CLOs. *See* Collateralized loan obligations (CLOs)
Club deals, 343, 371
CMBS. *See* Commercial mortgage-backed securities (CMBS)
CNI. *See* Consolidated net income (CNI)
Co-agents, 44, 45
Collateral
   bank loan total return swaps (LTRS) requirements, 629–631
   COVID-19-induced recession and, 18
   deemed dividends, 237–238
   drop-down transactions, 538–541, 602–608
   enterprise value as, 10–11
   guarantees, 221, 230–235
      continuing, 233
      downstream, cross-stream, and upstream, 233–235
      generally, 230–231
      insolvency of borrower, 232–233
      of payment versus guarantee of collection, 231
      reinstatement, 232
      subrogation, 232
      summary procedure, 233
      waivers, 231
   packages, 235–236
   perfection of, 162–163, 188
   restrictions on disposition of, 353–354
   rules governing foreclosure on real property, 354–355
   second lien loans, 360–361
   springing liens, 236
   in term sheet, 55
   true-up mechanism, 237
   use of cash, Chapter 11 bankruptcy, 566, 574–575
   voting securities and guarantees, 236, 263–264
Collateral-dependent financial assets, 869–870
Collateralized bond obligations (CBOs), 20
   Global Financial Crisis (GFC) of 2007–2008 and, 22
Collateralized loan obligations (CLOs), 6, 7, 8, 34, 385–386, 641, 642, 659–701, 707, 729, 739, 776, 791, 866–867
   AAA rated, 677, 679–680
   assets under management (AUM), 669–670
   bank loan total return swaps (LTRS), 628
   benefits of investing in, 661, 666–668

Collateralized loan obligations (CLOs) (Cont.)
  broadly syndicated loans (BSLs), 663, 670–671
  coverage tests, 684
  defined, 670–675
  during the Global Financial Crisis, 422–423
  equity sample return, 677–679
  first credit test, 20
  historical CLO and structured product loss rates, 670
  introduction, 661
  as largest segment of the institutional market, 40
  leading up to the Global Financial Crisis, 416
  life cycle, 671–675
  market background, 661–663
  market growth, 662–663
  mezzanine tranches, 667, 677
  middle market, 663
  new issue, 664
  over-collateralization (OC) ratio, 684–687
  over-collateralization (OC) test, 684, 692–694
  portfolio criteria, 687–690, 698
    collateral quality tests, 687–689
    concentration limitations, 689–690
  primary market, 664
  quantitative tools, 479–507
    portfolio optimization, 492–500
  ratings process, 50–51
  refi, 664
  regulatory impact, 699–700
  reset, 664
  resurgence, 430
  secondary market, 665–666
  structure, 661, 675
  terms construction and negotiation, 691–699
    commonly asked questions and issues for new issue CLOs, 691
    documentation points, 691–699
  tranches, 667, 675–677
  Volcker Rule and, 334
  waterfalls
    cash flow, 681
    interest, 681–684
    principal, 684
  why issue, 669–670
Collateral-stripping transactions, 602–608
Collection, guarantee of, 231
Combination of coupon, 800

Comingled funds, 738
Commercial and industrial (C&I) lending market, 773
Commercial banks, 771
Commercial banks in project finance, 369–381
  competition from capital markets, 379–381
  constraining factors, 374–376
  project finance defined, 369–370
  traditional role, 370–372
Commercial letters of credit, 108, 109
Commercial mortgage-backed securities (CMBS), 22
Commitment fees, 128–129, 338
Commitment letter, 54–55
Commitments
  increasing, 111–114
  reducing, 110–111
  several liability, 110
  terminating, 111
  term-out of revolving, 114
Commodities borrowing, 761
Commodity Futures and Trading Commission (CFTC), 836
Common law duty of confidence, fraud, and unfair dealing, 64–65
Company authorization letter, 69–70
Competitive-bid option (CBO), 338
Compliance
  with laws, 207
  with licenses, 177
Compound annual growth rate (CAGR), 780, 782
Comprehensive restructuring, 533, 543–545
Conditionality in acquisition financings, 172–174
Conditions
  for availability, 55–56
  collateral packages, 235
Conditions precedent, in credit agreements, 156–174
  appraisals, 168–169
  catchall, 170
  conditionality in acquisition financings, 172–174
  conditions relating to perfection of collateral, 162–163
  corporate and organizational matters, 158
  effectiveness, 170–171
  environmental due diligence, 169
  execution, 157–158

Index

government approvals, 159
insurance, 169
legal opinions, 159–161
MAC (material adverse change) clause, 164–167
ongoing conditions, 171–172
other conditions, 168–170
promissory notes, 163
repayment of other debt, 167–168
solvency, 168
special conditions applicable to non-U.S. borrowers, 167
USA PATRIOT Act, 169–170
Confidential information
categories of, 61–68
LSTA guidance and trading documents, 68–75
maintained in the loan market, 68
public- and private-side LMPs and, 62–63
what is "material" and who makes that determination in, 63–64
why it matters, 64–67
Confidentiality, borrower, 292–293
Confidentiality Principles, 63
Confirmation
primary allocation, 87
trade, 457–459
and voting, Chapter 11 bankruptcy, 569–570
Congressional Review Act (CRA), 705, 717
Consent rights, 268–269
Consolidated net income (CNI), 151
Consolidating statements, 204
Consolidation, substantive, 208–209
Constructive fraud, Chapter 11 bankruptcy, 561–562
Contingent liabilities, 221
Continuing guarantee, 233
Controlling agent system, 365
Control positions, loan trading, 401–402
Conversion, loan, 118, 121–122, 171
Conviction, 651
Coronavirus Aid, Relief, and Economic Security Act (CARES Act) of 2020, 26
Corporate borrowers, 776, 793
Corporate governance, distressed companies, 587–588
Corporate loans, 4
Cost-of-carry calculations, 90–94
Costs
right that lenders mitigate, 289
second lien loans, 345

and yield protection
capital, 136
increased, 134–136
Counterparts clause, 285
Covenant-lite structure, 229–230, 387, 448–449, 799
Covenants, 190–230
affirmative, 203–210
collateral packages, 235–236
further assurances, 210
hedging transactions, 209–210
substantive consolidation, 208–209
in term sheet, 56
use of proceeds, 209
benchmarks, 100–102
breach of, 241–242
categorizing, 191–193
restricted and unrestricted subsidiaries, 191–193
subsidiaries generally, 191
collateralized loan obligations (CLOs), 698
covenant-lite, 229–230
definitions, 194–197
key financial, 195–197
financial, 56–57, 197–203
capital expenditures, 202
date-specific, 197–198, 203
debt service coverage ratio, 201
fixed charges coverage ratio, 201–202
interest coverage ratio, 201
lease payments, 202
performance-based, 197–198, 200–202
phase-in and pro forma treatment, 198–200
in term sheet, 56–57
incorporation by reference, 228–229
insurance, 169, 205–206
loan benchmarks, 100–102
negative, 58, 211–228
affiliate transactions, 225–226
amendments to organic documents and other agreements, 226–227
debt, 214–216
derivatives, 220–221
disqualified stock, 216
dividend blockers, 224
dividends and equity repurchases, 222–223
fiscal periods and accounting changes, 227–228
fundamental changes, asset sales, and acquisitions, 216–217

Covenants *(Cont.)*
    guarantees or contingent liabilities, 221
    investments, 218–220
    lien covenant, 211–213
    lines of business, 220
    modification and prepayment of other debt, 224–225
    negative negative pledge, 213–214
    sale-leasebacks, 217–218
    tax-sharing payments and permitted tax distributions, 223–224
    in term sheet, 58
  subsidiaries, 185
    generally, 191
    restricted and unrestricted, 191–193
    significant, 193
    three categories, 190
Cover for letter of credit, 154
  demand for, 253–254
COVID-19 pandemic, 746, 749, 803, 851–852, 853–854
  bank loan total return swaps (LTRS), 628
  default projections, 752
  distressed companies, 583
  impact on commercial banks international opportunities, 372–374
  liability management transactions, 534
  loan market characteristics, 397–399, 601
  recession caused by, 18, 25–26
  secondary loan market sell-off, 428
Crammed down creditors, 351
Credit agreements, 105–293, 842, 878, 883, 885
  agency provisions, 256–261
  amortization and maturity, 142–156
    advancing the maturity date, 144
    application of prepayments among tranches, 153–154
    cover for letter of credit, 154
    multiple borrowers, 155–156
    payments
      immediately available funds, 142
      provisions, 55
      scheduled repayment, 143–144
      time of, 142–143
    prepayments
      mandatory, 146–153
      voluntary, 145–146
    364-day facilities, 144–145
  assignments, 267–273
    consent rights, 268–269
    distinguishing assignments and participations, 267–268
    eligible assignees and disqualified lenders, 270
    loan register, 271
    minimums, 270–271
    securities laws and, 271–273
    transfer fees, 271
  boilerplate understanding, 275–287
    borrower indemnification consequential damages, 277–279
    captions, 285–286
    counterparts clause, 285
    cumulative remedies, 276
    electronic execution, 286
    enforcement provisions, 280–284
    expenses, 276–277
    governing law, 279–280
    integration clause, 285
    judgment currency, 284
    no deemed waivers, 275–276
    notice provisions, 275
    severability clause, 284–285
    survival clause, 286–287
    USA Patriot Act, 287
    venue and forum non conveniens, 282–283
    waiver of jury trial, 283
    waiver of sovereign immunity, 283
  borrower rights, 288–293
  business-day conventions, 132–133
  clawback clause, 265–267
  collateral analysis, 648–649
  commitments, 110–114
    increasing, 111–114
    reducing, 110–111
    several liability, 110
    terminating, 111
    term-out options, 114
  conditions precedent, 156–174
    appraisals, 168–169
    catchall, 170
    conditionality in acquisition financings, 172–174
    conditions relating to perfection of collateral, 162–163
    corporate and organizational matters, 158
    effectiveness, 170–171
    environmental due diligence, 169
    execution, 157–158
    government approvals, 159
    insurance, 169
    legal opinions, 159–161

MAC (material adverse change) clause, 164–167
  ongoing conditions, 171–172
  other conditions, 168–170
  promissory notes, 163
  repayment of other debt, 167–168
  solvency, 168
  special conditions applicable to non-U.S. borrowers, 167
  USA PATRIOT Act, 169–170
confidentiality, 292–293
covenants (see Covenants)
cure rights, 290–292
events of default (see Events of default)
guarantees, 221, 230–235
  continuing, 233
  downstream, cross-stream, and upstream, 233–235
  generally, 230–231
  insolvency of borrower, 232–233
  of payment versus guarantee of collection, 231
  reinstatement, 232
  subrogation, 232
  summary procedure, 233
  waivers, 231
interest, 118–125
  accrual conventions, 132
  applicable margins, 125–126
  base rate, 118–119
  computation, 131
  default, 12–13, 127–128
  fees and, 128–131
  LIBOR rate, 119–123
  other pricing options, 124
  payment dates, 126–127
interest savings clauses, 141–142
introduction to, 105
lender indemnification, 261
lending offices, 133
letters of credit, 108–110
loan pledges, 274–275
loan register access, 267
for loans, 106–108
mechanics of funding, 116–117
minimums, multiples, and frequency, 115–116
multicurrency facilities, 114–115
participations, 268, 273–274
payments generally, 142–143
pricing, 118–132
pro rata treatment, 264
representations, 171–190

completeness of disclosures and, 187–188
and disclosures regarding the business, 184–187
financial condition, 180–184
foreign borrowers, 188–190
legal matters, 175–180
perfection and priority of security, 188
status as senior indebtedness, 188
and warranties, 56
sharing of setoffs and other claims, 264–265
variants, 106–110
  letters of credit, 108–110
  loans, 106–108
voting, 261–264
  affected lender concept, 262–263
  basic rule, 261–262
  collateral security, 236, 263–264
  multitranche agreements, 262
yield protection, 133–141
  breakfunding, 138–139
  capital costs, 136
  Eurodollar market disruption, 136–137
  illegality, 137
  increased costs, 134–136
  taxes, 139–141
Credit analysis, 42–43, 814, 816, 818–819
Credit bidding, 721
Credit default swaps (CDS), 621
  standard LCDS terms and distinctions from, 625–626
Credit drivers, 824
Credit enhancements, 870
Credit events, loan credit default swap (LCDS), 625
Credit impact score (CIS), 826
  scoring levels, 828
Credit impairment, 862, 868
Credit materiality of ESG, 817
Creditors, in distressed situations, 546–547
  protections, 587–588
Creditors committee, 558–559
Credit providers, 836
Credit ratings, 824–826
Credit-relevant risk categories, 815
Credit risk
  bank, 3–6
  with bank loans, 10–11
  default events, 9–10

Credit risk *(Cont.)*
  management of, 5
  standards, 43
    collateralized loan obligations (CLOs), 696
Credit-risk portfolio management, 5
Credit selection, 646–650
  company-specific analysis, 647–648
  credit agreement and collateral analysis, 648–649
  relative value comparison, 649–650
Credit-sensitive rates (CSRs), 300–301
  fallback provisions, 309
Critical portfolio metrics, 652–653
Cross-acceleration, 242–245
Cross-border transactions, 743
Cross-currency LBO funding in bonds and loans, 737
Cross-default, 242–245
  second lien loans to first lien loans, 367–368
Cross-stream guarantees, 233–235
Cumulative remedies, 276
Cure rights, 290–292
Currency judgment, 284
Current expected credit loss (CECL) model, 868

D

Daily Compounded SOFR, 305–308
Daily Simple SOFR, 304–308
Date-specific covenants, 197–198
Deal count, 36
Debt basket, 216
Debt capacity, distressed companies, 584–586
Debt exchange transactions, 552
Debt issuances, 150
Debtor-in-possession (DIP) financing, 342, 547, 549–550, 577–580
  second lien loans advance consent to, 361–362
  secured creditor right to approve, 350–351
Debtors, in distressed situations, 545–546
Debt ratio, 196, 197, 200
Debts
  covenants, 214–216
  defined, 195–196
  disclosure of existing, 184–187
  equitization of, 586–587
  modification and prepayment of other, 224–225
  parent company, 223
  senior indebtedness status, 188
  tag-along, 211–212
  See also Liens
Debt securities, 866–867
Debt service coverage ratio, 201
Debt subordination, 347–348
Debt-to-EBITDA ratio, 719, 800
Decarbonization, 819–820
Decentralized digital currency, 880
Deemed dividends, 237–238
Default
  collateral packages, 236
  events of, 58, 238–250
    breach of covenants, 241–242
    change of control, 248–249
    cross-default, cross-acceleration, 242–245
    environmental, 248
    ERISA events, 247–248
    foreign borrowers, 249–250
    inaccuracy of representations, 240–241
    insolvency, 245–246
    invalidity of guarantees or liens, 249
    judgment, 247
    material adverse change (MAC), 250
    in payment, 240
    specialized, 250
    in term sheet, 58
  in ongoing conditions, 172
  rates, 12–13, 127–128
  Ultimate Recovery Database, 507–525
  unmatured, 239
  versus recoveries, 9–10
Defaulting lender provisions, 288–289
Delayed-draw term loan (DDTL), 340, 777
Delayed compensation
  commencement, 89–90, 96–99
  and cost-of-carry calculations, 90–94
Delayed settlement, 90
Delay Period, 91–92
Delegation, agency provision, 259
Deliverable obligations, loan credit default swap (LCDS), 625
Derivatives, 220–221
  bank loan total return swaps (LTRS), 628, 637–638
  loan credit default swap (LCDS), 621–622, 626–627

Index

Development and Export Finance
    Institutions (DEFIs), 373
Direct lenders, 775, 776
Direct lending, 341–342, 740
Direct leverage comparisons approach,
    649, 650
Direct loan origination/acquisition costs,
    865–866
Disclosure covenants, 203–205
Discounted cash flow (DCF) analysis,
    593–595
Discounted debt repurchases and
    exchanges, 542–543
Discretionary sales, CLO, 698
Disintermediated trades, 752
Disposition of collateral, restrictions on,
    353–354
Dispositions, 217
Disqualified institution list (DQ List), 740
Disqualified lenders, 270
Disqualified stock, 216
Distressed companies, 527–618
    analysis
        comparable company, 595–597
        comparable transaction, 597
        discounted cash flow (DCF), 593–595
        going concern versus liquidation,
            600
        liquidation, 598–599
        valuation, 589–590, 597–598
    Chapter 11 bankruptcy
        adequate protection, 566–567
        asset sales, 567–568
        assumption and rejection of executory
            contracts and unexpired leases,
            565–566
        avoidance powers, 559–563
            actual fraud, 563
            constructive fraud, 561–562
            fraudulent transfers, 561
            preferential transfer, 560–561
        commencement, first-day orders, and
            the automatic stay, 557–558
        estate and debtor in possession, 558
        exchanges, 572–573
        goals, 556–557
        plan of reorganization and disclosure,
            568–569
        prenegotiated and prepackaged
            plans, 572
        priority of claims, 563–565
            priority claims and administrative
                claims, 564
        secured claims, 563–564
        superpriority claims, 565
        unsecured claims and equity claims,
            564–565
        use of cash collateral, 566
        U.S. trustee and creditors committee,
            558–559
        voting and confirmation, 569–570
    comprehensive restructuring, 533,
        543–545
    creditor protections and corporate
        governance, 587–588
    critical financial considerations, 574–600
        liquidity analyses, 575–577
        liquidity is king, 574
        use of cash collateral, 574–575
    debt capacity, 584–586
    debtor-in-possession (DIP) financing, 342,
        547, 549–550, 577–580
        second lien loans advance consent
            to, 361–362
        secured creditor right to approve,
            350–351
    developing a strategy and business
        plan, 580–582
    discounted debt repurchases and
        exchanges, 542–543
    documentation, 467–468
    equitization of debt, 586–587
    executory contracts and leases, 582–583
    factors affecting recovery rates, 553–554
    injection of capital, 541–542
    kick the can transactions, 534–538
    liability management transactions,
        533–534, 601–618
        collateral-stripping (drop-down)
            transactions, 602–608
        concerns around value leakage,
            601–602
        introduction, 601–602
        uptiering transactions, 608–610
            within same credit agreement,
                610–615
            under separate facility, 615–617
    market history, 529–555
    options for, 532–533
    parties in, 545–547
        competing motivations of, 588–589
    projections development, 591–593
    retention of management, 583–584
    types of opportunities, 547–553
    uptier exchanges and drop-down
        transactions, 538–541

Distributed ledger technology (DLT), 877.
  See also Blockchain
Diversification, 651
Diversity Score, 494–495, 501–502, 675
Dividend basket, 223
Dividend blockers, 224
Dividends
  covenants, 222–223
  deemed, 237–238
  recapitalizations, 799
Documentation
  agents, 44, 45
  loan closing, 466–475
    choosing par or distressed documents, 469–470
    delayed settlement compensation calculations for par loans, 474–475
    distressed loans, 467–468
    LSTA Purchase and Sale Agreement (PSA), 468–469
    par loans, 466–467
    par trades, 472
    pricing and payment, 471–472
    settled without accrued interest treatment, 472–473
    step-up representations, 470
    term loans, 472–473
    upstream due diligence, 469
    See also Information distribution
Dodd-Frank Wall Street Reform and Consumer Protection Act of 2010, 24
  derivatives regulation, 626–627, 637–638
Downstream guarantees, 233–235
Drafting and diligence considerations, 840–848
Drop-down transactions, 538–541, 602–608
Due authorization representations, 176
Due execution representations, 176
Due organization representation, 175–176
Due diligence, 54, 76, 160, 161, 169, 178, 318, 319, 320, 321, 324, 325, 327, 331, 332, 340, 469, 647, 691, 723, 794, 861, 886
  ESg Questionnaire, 810, 855

E

Early Day Trade, 95
EBITDA (earnings before interest, taxes, depreciation, and amortization), 57, 113–114, 770
  defined, 196–197
  distressed companies, 585
  excess cash flow, 151
  fixed charges coverage ratio, 201–202
  interest coverage ratio, 201
  phase-in and pro forma treatment, 198–199
  restricted subsidiaries, 192
ECB. *See* European Central Bank
Economic opportunities, 834, 848
Economic risk reduction, 831
Economic Stimulus Act of 2008, 23
EEA. *See* European Economic Area (EEA)
Effective date, 170–171
  notification of, 86–87
Electronic execution, 286
Electronic Settlement Platform (ESP), 83
  delivery of information to, 84–85
  submission of allocation details to, 86
  submission of assignment agreement to, 85–86
Eligible assignees, 270
Emergency Economic Stabilization Act of 2008, 23
Emissions-reducing technologies, 826
Emissions targets, 820
Employee Retirement Income Security Act of 1974 (ERISA), 182–183
  events of default, 247–248
  restricted and unrestricted subsidiaries, 192
Employee stock plans, 222
Energy Future Holdings, 785
Energy transition, 372–374
Enforceability, 159, 176
Enforcement provisions, 280–284
  control over, 353
  submission to jurisdiction and process agents, 280–282
Enterprise value, 10–11
Environmental, social, and governance (ESG) factors, 748, 803, 809–811
  assessment challenges, 817
  carbon transition risk, 820–821
  characteristics, 816
  considerations, 816–817
  credit analysis, relevance to, 812–816
  credit impact score (CIS), 826
  credit ratings, 824–826
  credit ratings, time horizons, 818–819
  credit strengths, 816–817
  Due Diligence Questionnaire, 810
  in global financial markets, 811–812
  and green lending, 756
  integration, 809

Index

linked loans, 811
material ESG issues, 827
materiality of, 828
Moody's ESG methodology, 825–828
physical climate risks, 821–824
in ratings, 829
related risks and opportunities, 814
scenario analysis, 819–820
sector-wide exposure, 817
Environmental due diligence, 169
Environmental events of default, 248
Environmental matters disclosures, 187
Equitization of debt, 586–587
Equity
    claims, Chapter 11 bankruptcy, 564–565
    collateralized loan obligations (CLOs), 677–679
    cure provisions, 291
    infusion, 743
    issuances, 150
    -linked structures, 800
    portfolio management, 641
    repurchases, 222–223
ERISA. *See* Employee Retirement Income Security Act of 1974 (ERISA)
E-Sign Act, 286
Eurodollar
    deposits, 122–123, 131
    market disruption, 136–137
Euro Interbank Offered Rate (EURIBOR), 675
European Central Bank (ECB), 731, 842
European Economic Area (EEA), 733
European secondary market, 742
European securitization legislation, 747
European sovereign crisis, 751
European syndicated loan market, 733–734
European Systemic Risk Board (ESRB), 732
EU Taxonomy Regulation, 840
Evaluation materials, production and distribution of, 79–81
Events of default, 58, 238–250
    breach of covenants, 241–242
    change of control, 248–249
    collateralized loan obligations (CLOs), 694–695
    cross-default, cross-acceleration, 242–245
    environmental, 248
    ERISA events, 247–248
    foreign borrowers, 249–250
    inaccuracy of representations, 240–241
    insolvency, 245–246
    invalidity of guarantees or liens, 249
    judgment, 247
    material adverse change (MAC), 250
    in payment, 240
    remedies, 251–254
        accelerate, 252–253
        demand cover for letters of credit, 253–254
        demand payment from guarantors, 254
        institute suit, 254
        stop lending, 251–252
        terminate commitments, 252
    rescission right, 254–255
    setoff, 255–256
    specialized, 250
    in term sheet, 58
    waterfalls, 255
Evergreen option, 108–109, 339
Excess cash flow, 150–151
Exchanges, Chapter 11 bankruptcy, 572–573
Exchange traded funds (ETFs), 426, 427–428
Exculpation, agency provision, 258–259
Execution, conditions precedent, 157–158
Executive summary, 51
Executory contracts and leases, distressed companies, 582–583
Existence and franchises covenants, 207
Existing debt and liens, 185
Expansions, 773
Expenses provisions
    boilerplate, 276–277
    collateral packages, 236
Extraterritoriality, 747

F

Facility fees, 129
Fallback provisions, 309
    collateralized loan obligations (CLOs), 698–699
Family-owned businesses, 775
Family wealth offices, 738
FATCA. *See* Foreign Account Tax Compliance Act (FATCA)
FCPA. *See* Foreign Corrupt Practices Act of 1977 (FCPA)
Federal Communications Commission (FCC), 186
Federal Deposit Insurance Corporation (FDIC), 699, 784
Federal Rules of Civil Procedure, 563
Fedwire Funds Service, 142

Fees
- accrual conventions, 132
- commitment, 128–129, 338
- computation, 131
- facility, 129
- letter of credit, 130–131
- syndication process, 48
- transfer, assignments, 271
- utilization, 129–130

Fees letter, 55
Finance companies, 41, 776
Finance transactions, 824
Financial assets, measurement of, 874
Financial condition representations, 180–184
- financial statements, 180–181
- pension and welfare plans, 182–183
- projections, 182
- taxes, 182

Financial covenants, 56–57, 197–203
- capital expenditures, 202
- date-specific, 197–198, 203
- debt service coverage ratio, 201
- fixed charges coverage ratio, 201–202
- interest coverage ratio, 201
- lease payments, 202
- performance-based, 197–198, 200–202
- phase-in and pro forma treatment, 198–200

Financial decision-making, 825
Financial Industry Regularity Authority (FINRA), 67
- if loans were securities, 321
- regulation under, 327–330
- Rule 2111, 329
- Rule 2121, 329–330
- Rule 5110, 328–329
- Rule 5121, 329

Financial Institutions Reform, Recovery and Enforcement Act of 1989 (FIRREA), 169
Financial projections, restructuring, 591–593
Financial Services Modernization Act, 784
Financial Stability Board, 812
Financial Stability Report, 2020, 835
Financial statements, 180–181
- annual, 204
- consolidated, 204
- covenants, 194–195

Financing to the corporate sector, 746
Firm's capital resources, 825
First credit test, 20

First lien loans
- limits on amount of future, 366
- second lien lender right to purchase, 363–364
- second lien loans cross-defaulted to, 367–368
- separate set of security documents, 364–365
- voting, 365–366

Fiscal periods, 227–228
Fixed charges coverage ratio, 201–202
Fixing America's Surface Transportation Act of 2015, 318
Flat margin, 125
Flex, pricing, 47–48
Flexible structuring, 31
Flip representations, 465
Floating rate/callable assets, 31–32
Fluid concept, 814
Foreclosure, 354–355
Foreign Account Tax Compliance Act (FATCA), 747
Foreign assets control regulations, 178–179
Foreign borrowers, 156
- events of default, 249–250
- International Financial Reporting Standards (IFRS), 195
- representations for, 188–190
- special conditions applicable to, 167

Foreign Corrupt Practices Act of 1977 (FCPA), 178
Foreign Investment Review Board (FIRB), 755
Foreign state, 283
Form of Credit Agreement, LSTA, 72–73
Formosa I Offshore Wind Farm (OWF), 761
Forms
- LSTA, 72–75
- syndicated loans
  - commitment letter, 54–55
  - fee letter, 55
  - term sheet, 55–58

Forum non conveniens, 282–283
Fossil fuel–powered generation, 841
Franchises and existence covenants, 207
Fraud, Chapter 11 bankruptcy
- actual, 563
- constructive, 561–562

Fraudulent transfers, Chapter 11 bankruptcy, 561
Fronting arrangement, 157–158
Fulcrum security investing, 550–551
Fundamental changes covenants, 216–217

Index 927

Funding
  mechanics of, 116–117
  notification of date of, 86–87
Fund liquidity, 657
Fund structure, 656
Further assurances covenants, 210

G

G20 Green Finance Study Group, 812
GDP. *See* Gross domestic product (GDP)
General Accountability Office (GAO), 717
General corporate purposes, 209, 799
  fiscal periods and accounting changes, 228
General investment basket, 220
General lien basket, 213
Generally accepted accounting principles (GAAP), 180–181
  covenants, 194–195
Glass-Steagall rules, 4
Global credit crisis, 746
Global Financial Crisis (GFC) of 2007–2008, 8, 20, 21–22, 661, 707, 731, 791
  collateralized loan obligations (CLOs) and, 661, 662
  default cycle associated with, 509–510
  economic recovery and way forward after, 22–24
  recovery period, 425–429
  secondary loan market, 415–425
  spread to maturity, 452–455
Globalization
  Asia Pacific loan market, 753–766
  global syndicated loan market–EMEA, 745–752
  non-USD syndicated institutional leveraged loan market, 729–744
Global reinsurers, 825
Global sustainable assets, 813
Global Sustainable Investment Alliance (GSIA), 812
Global syndicated loan market–EMEA, 745–746
  institutional investors, 749–751
  regulation, 746–747
  secondary markets
    increasing depth of liquidity, 752
    volatility post-financial crisis, 751
  sustainable lending, 748–749
Governance, 825
Governing law, 279–280

Government approvals representations, 177
Government-controlled financial system, 735
Grandfathered debt, 214
Grandfathered investments, 218
Grandfathered liens, 212
Green Bond Principles, 849
Greenhouse gas (GHG) emissions reduction, 820, 822, 837, 839
Green loans, 830, 841
  elements of, 843
  principles, 748, 832–833, 845
  and sustainability, 811
  and sustainability-linked loans, 830–831
  transition-focused, 844
Greenwashing, 810
Grid pricing, 125–126
Gross domestic product (GDP), 769, 825
Guarantees, 221, 230–235
  continuing, 233
  downstream, cross-stream, and upstream, 233–235
  generally, 230–231
  insolvency of borrower, 232–233
  invalidity, 249
  of payment versus guarantee of collection, 231
  reinstatement, 232
  subrogation, 232
  summary procedure, 233
  waivers, 231
Guarantor restricted subsidiaries, 602

H

Hard collateral, 10–11
Hart-Scott-Rodino approval, 177
Hedge funds, 386, 422, 763, 791
Hedging transactions, 209–210
  loan trading, 403
Held for investment (HFI) loans, 861, 862
Held for sale (HFS) loans, 862, 863
Held for trade (trading book) (HFT) loans, 862
  measurement, 863
Held-to-maturity portfolio, 867
HIBOR (Hong Kong), 124
Highly leveraged transaction (HLT) regulations, 7, 409
High-yield bonds, as asset class, 4–5
High-yield portfolio management, 641
Historic financial overview, 52

I

IBOR (indeterminate global markets), 124
ICMA. *See* International Capital Market Association (ICMA)
IFRS. *See* International Financial Reporting Standards (IFRS)
Illiquidity, 803
Immediately available funds, 142
Immunity, foreign borrowers, 188–189
Inaccuracy of representations, 240–241
In arrears rates, 306–308
Income-seeking retail investors, 782
Incremental facilities, commitments, 111–114
Indemnification, lender, 261
Indian loan market, 762
Indonesia loan volume, 762–763
Industry overview, 52
Information distribution
    categories of confidential information in the syndicated loan market, 61–68
    confidentiality maintained in the loan market, 68
    introduction and scope, 59–61
    loan market disparities, 394–395
    Loan Syndications and Trading Association (LSTA), 60, 68–75
      agency splash page principles, 70
      Code of Conduct, 68
      formation of, 7–8
      form documents, 72–75
        Form of Credit Agreement, 72–73
        LSTA Trade Confirmation/Purchase and Sale Agreement, 73–75
        Master Confidentiality Agreement, 73
      Guidance Note and Confidentiality Legends for Distribution of Syndicated Loan Marketing Materials, 69–70
      guidance regarding trading loans in the secondary market with confidential information, 71–72
      Statement of Principles for the Communication and Use of Confidential Information by Loan Market Participants, 68–69
    loan total return swaps (LTRS), 636
    risk management, 75–81
      agents and, 77–78
      information barriers, controls, policies, and procedures, 76–79
      lenders and, 76–77
      production and distribution of evaluation materials, 79–81
      use of nonreliance acknowledgments and waivers, 75–76
    Rule 10b-5 disclosure letter, 319–320, 325–326
    Syndicate Information, 331–332
    what is "material" and who makes that determination in, 63–64
    See also Documentation
Information sharing and flow, 730
In-house capital markets, 802
In re Owens Corning, 208–209
Insolvency of borrower, 232–233
    events of default, 245–246
Inspection rights, 205
Institutional investors, 39–40, 749–751
Institutionalization, 784
Institutional leveraged loan market, 744–745
Institutional loan market, 772
Institutional term loan, 39
Insurance companies, 34, 776
    CLO mezzanine issuance, 667
    as investors, 40–41
Insurance covenant, 169, 205–206
Insurers, 738
Integration clause, 285
Intellectual property disclosures, 186–187
Intercompany debt, 215
Intercompany dividends, 222
Intercreditor agreements, 743, 744
Intercreditor arrangements, 347
    enforceability, 362
    relationships between multiple secured creditors at law absent, 352–355
    restrictions in period before bankruptcy filing, 357
Interest, 118–125
    accrual conventions, 132
    applicable margins, 125–126
    base rate, 118–119
    computation, 131
    default, 12–13, 127–128
    fees and, 128–131
    LIBOR rate, 119–123
    loan trading settlement treatment, 462–464
    other pricing options, 124
    payment dates, 126–127
    savings clauses, 141–142
Interest coverage ratio, 201
Interest coverage (IC) tests, CLO, 684

Index   929

Intergovernmental Panel on Climate
    Change (IPCC), 822
Internal rate of return (IRR), 678
Internal Revenue Service (IRS)
    deemed dividends, 237–238
    Employee Retirement Income Security
        Act of 1974 (ERISA), 183
    taxes representations, 182
International Capital Market Association
    (ICMA), 855
International Energy Agency (IEA), 820
International Financial Reporting Standards
    (IFRS), 195
International Monetary Fund (IMF), 190,
    250
International Organization of Securities
    Commissions (IOSCO), 297–298
International Swaps and Derivatives
    Association (ISDA), 621
Invalidity of guarantees or liens, 249
Invesco Senior Loan ETF, 426
Investment Advisors Act of 1940, 67, 707
Investment banks, 791
Investment Company Act of 1940, 177–178,
    482, 795
Investment considerations, 52
Investment covenants, 218–220
Investment grade, 751
Investment-grade lending, 773
Investment portfolios, 811
Investors, 834–835
    anticipated demand by, 49–50
    bank loan mutual funds, 40
    collateralized loan obligations (CLOs), 40
    finance company, 41
    institutional, 39–40
    insurance company, 40–41
    meeting, 53
    niche, 41
    primary market, 37–42
    pro rata, 38–39
Involuntary default, 246
Issuers
    primary market, 37
    profile scores (IPS), 826

J

Judgments
    currency, 284
    default, 247
Jumpstart Our Business Startups Act, 324

Jurisdiction, submission to, 280–282
Jury trial, waiver of, 283

K

Key-man life insurance, 206
Key performance indicators (KPIs), 845–848
Kick the can transactions, 534–538
Kirschner v. JPMorgan, 722–724
Know-your-customer (KYC), 83, 880

L

Labor matters representations, 186
LCDS. *See* Loan credit default swap (LCDS)
LCDX. *See* Loan credit default swap index
    product
Lead arrangers and agents, 44
League tables, 44
Lease payments, 202
Legal characterization of loans, 316–334
    advantages, 320
    legal background, 316–320
    loans as securities, 321–330
    practice under Rule 144A, 319–320
    regulation under federal securities laws,
        316–317
    Rule 144A exemption, 318–319
    Section 4(a)(2) exemption, 317–319
    as securities
        antifraud liability considerations,
            324–327
        compliance with registration
            requirements, 321–324
        origination/syndication process, 331
        practical implications, 331–334
        public-private nature of primary and
            secondary loan market, 331–332
        secondary trading, 332–333
        Volcker Rule, 24, 333–334
Legal form representations, 189
Legal matters representations, 175–180
Legal opinions, 159–161
Lehman Brothers, 427
Lenders
    acting in good faith, 290
    affected, 262–263
    clawback clause, 265–267
    cure rights, 290–292
    debt, 214
    defaulting lender provisions, 288–289

Lenders *(Cont.)*
  eligible assignees and disqualified, 270
  indemnification, 261
  liens, 212
  mitigating costs, 289
  risk management in information
    distribution, 76–77
  swingline, 107–108
  yank-a-bank provision, 289–290
Lending offices, 133
Letters of credit (LOCs), 108–110, 340
  commercial, 108, 109
  cover for, 154
  evergreen, 108–109
  fees, 130–131
  refinance, 109–110
  replacement, 110
  standby or performance, 108
Leverage, bank loan total return swaps
  (LTRS), 631–633
Leveraged buyouts (LBOs), 4, 37, 408, 715,
  729, 733, 734, 740, 785
Leveraged Lending Guidance, 712, 716,
  719, 787
Leveraged Loan Index (LLI), 23, 441–455
  covenant-lite norm, 448–449
  Global Financial Crisis, 427
  loan market performance, 450–452
  single B domination, 446–447
  spread to maturity, 452–455
  tech boom, 444–446
  U.S. $1.2 trillion asset class, 442–444
Leveraged loans
  market size and scope, 35–36
  origins as investment class, 6–8
  overleveraging, 19–20
  quantitative tools, 479–507
Leverage ratio, 200–201
Liability
  antifraud, 324–327
  several, 110
  uptiering within same credit agreement,
    610–615
Liability management transactions,
  533–534, 601–618
  collateral-stripping (drop-down)
    transactions, 602–608
  concerns around value leakage, 601–602
  introduction, 601–602
  uptiering transactions, 608–610
    within same credit agreement,
      610–615
    under separate facility, 615–617

LIBOR. *See* London Interbank Offered
  Rate (LIBOR)
Licenses, compliance with, 177
Liens
  covenant, 211–213
  disclosure of existing, 184–187
  invalidity, 249
  springing, 236
  See also Debts
Limited partners (LPs), 23
Lines of business covenants, 220
Liquidation analysis, 598–599
Liquidity, 731, 752, 763–764
  analyses, 575–577
  coverage ratio (LCR), 747
Liquidity Risk Management Rule,
  433–435
Litigation disclosures, 185–186
Loan asset class, 3–28
  current market, 27–28
  economic recovery and way forward,
    22–24
  first credit test, 20
  historical risk and return in, 11–18
  and history of bank credit risk, 3–6
  leveraged loans as new class, 6–11
  narrative of risk and return in bank
    loans, 18–28
  rebound of 2003, 21
  timeline of, 19–20
  See also specific types of loans
Loan closing documentation, 466–475
  choosing par or distressed documents,
    469–470
  delayed settlement compensation
    calculations for par loans, 474–475
  distressed loans, 467–468
  LSTA Purchase and Sale Agreement (PSA),
    468–469
  par loans, 466–467
  par trades, 472
  pricing and payment, 471–472
  settled without accrued interest
    treatment, 472–473
  step-up representations, 470
  term loans, 472–473
  upstream due diligence, 469
Loan conversion, 118, 121–122, 171
Loan credit default swap (LCDS), 621–627
  in the current market, 627
  as derivative product, 621–622
  derivatives regulation, 626–627
  evolution, 623–624

Index

931

introduction and structure, 622–623
standard terms and distinctions from CDS, 625–626
Loan credit default swap index product (LCDX), 621, 623, 624
Loan Market Association (LMA), 741, 810, 830
Loan market participants (LMPs), 59–60
  borrowers' desire to protect confidential information, 64
  breach of contract risk, 64
  common law duty of confidence, fraud, and unfair dealing, 64–65
  information barriers, controls, policies, and procedures, 76–79
  maintenance of policies and procedures and, 67
  public- and private-side, 62–63
  receipt of MNPI, 66
  regulatory risk and, 65–66
  reputational and relationship risk and, 67
  violation of internal policies and procedures and, 67
  why confidentiality matters to, 64–67
Loan participation funds, 40
Loan pledges, 274–275
Loan Pricing Corporation, 8
Loan register
  access to, 267
  assignments, 271
Loans
  allocations, 642
  bank
    default on, 9–10
    historical review of, 3–6
    leveraged loans as asset investment class, 6–9
    risks and returns with, 11–28
      bankruptcy, 8–9
      current market, 27–28
      default *vs.* recoveries, 9–10
      economic recovery and way forward, 22–24
      first credit test, 20
      Global Financial Crisis (GFC) of 2007–2008 and, 8, 20, 21–22
      historical review of, 11–18
      narrative of, 18–28
      rebound of 2003, 21
      timeline of, 19–20
  classification, 861–862
  conditions precedent, 156–174
  coverage by securities laws, 271–273
  credit agreements for, 106–108
  defined, 861
  investors, 642
  Liquidity Risk Management Rule, 433–435
  market characteristics, 397–399
  monitoring (*see* Covenants)
  as nonTRACE instrument, 387
  pricing, 118–132
  recognition and measurement, 862–863
  securitizations, 710
  single B domination, 446–447
  transferred between classifications, 863
Loan structures, 335–381
  commercial banks in project finance, 369–381
    competition from capital markets, 379–381
    constraining factors, 374–376
    credit buy-side emergence, 5–6
    credit culture, 3–4
    credit offered by, 3–4
    expanded roles, 376–379
    high-yield bond market, 4–5
    impact of COVID-19 pandemic and energy transition on international opportunities for, 372–374
    project finance defined, 369–370
    traditional role, 370–372
  second lien loans, 337–368
    advance consent
      to DIP financing approved by first lien lenders, 361–362
      to sales of collateral, 360–361
      to use of cash collateral, 360
    asset-based lending, 340–341
    background information, 346–355
    cross-defaulted to first lien loans, 367–368
    debtor-in-possession financing, 342
    defined, 342–343
    difference between debt subordination and lien subordination, 347–348
    direct lending, 341–342
    enforceability of intercreditor agreements, 362
    first lien lender permission for, 345–346
    junior credit acceptance of, 346
    lender ending up worse off than unsecured creditor, 362–363
    mandatory prepayments, 367
    pros and cons, 344–345

Loan structures *(Cont.)*
   restrictions
      in bankruptcy proceeding, 358
      with respect to period before bankruptcy filing, 356–357
   restrictions on assignability, 367
   right to purchase first lien loans, 363–364
   secured creditors rights in bankruptcy, 348–351
   separate set of security documents, 364–365
   silent/quiet/well behaved, 345–346, 355–356
   structuring, 355–368
   types of syndicated loan facilities and, 338–340
   voluntary prepayment, 367
   voting, 365–366
   waiver of rights
      to oppose adequate protection for first lien loans, 359
      to seek adequate protection, 358–359
Loan Syndications and Trading Association (LSTA), 60, 68–75, 298, 656, 706, 724–725, 748, 810, 830, 877
   agency splash page principles, 70
   Arbitration Rules, 881
   Code of Conduct, 68
   confidentiality clause, 293
   Distressed Trade Confirmation, 462–464, 465
   expenses provisions, 277
   formation of, 7–8, 411
   form documents, 72–75
      Form of Credit Agreement, 72–73
      LSTA Trade Confirmation/Purchase and Sale Agreement, 73–75
      Master Confidentiality Agreement, 73
   Guidance Note and Confidentiality Legends for Distribution of Syndicated Loan Marketing Materials, 69–70
   guidance regarding trading loans in the secondary market with confidential information, 71–72
   indemnification, 278
   loan credit default swap (LCDS), 621
   loan credit default swap (LCDS) standard terms, 626
   mark-to-market (MTM) process, 411–412, 418
   Model Credit Agreement Provisions, 134, 270
   notification provisions, 275
   Par/Near Par Trade Confirmation, 878
   Proceeds Letter, 468–469
   Purchase and Sale Agreement (PSA), 468–469
   risk management, information distribution, 75–81
      agents and, 77–78
      information barriers, controls, policies, and procedures, 76–79
      lenders and, 76–77
      production and distribution of evaluation materials, 79–81
      use of nonreliance acknowledgments and waivers, 75–76
   Shift Date Rules, 470
   Statement of Principles for the Communication and Use of Confidential Information by Loan Market Participants, 68–69
   waiver of jury trial, 283
Loan total return swaps (LTRS), 627–638
   cash flows and collateral requirements, 629–631
   derivatives regulation, 637–638
   documentation and issues, 635–637
      Information issues, 636
      ISDA Credit Support Annex, 635
      ISDA master agreement, 635
      Master Confirmation Agreement and supplemental confirmations, 635–636
      voting and control, 636–637
   introduction and overview of structure, 628–629
   leverage, return, and yield, 631–633
   primary uses and types, 633–635
   tax and bankruptcy concerns, 637
Loan trading, 6–7, 383–404
   binding contracts, 392
   versus bond trading, 395–396
   capital structure trades, 402–403
   control positions, 401–402
   getting in the information flow, 401
   hedging, 403
   information disparity in loan market, 394–395
   introduction, 385–389
   loan market characteristics, 397–399
   loans versus bonds, 389–390
   macroeconomic factors, 403
   market technicals, 397

Index 933

primary market versus secondary
    market, 400–401
secondary market, 399–401
settlement, 390–392, 455–476
    allocation, 459
    amendments/restructures, 466
    assignment fees, 475
    assignment or participation, 460–461
    background, 456
    buy-in/sell-out (BISO), 466
    closing documentation, 466–475
    confirmation, 457–459
    flip representations, 465
    forms of purchase, 460–466
    interest treatment, 462–464
    loan credit default swap (LCDS), 626
    pretrade issues, 456–457
    principal-agency issue, 459
    purchase amount/type of debt, 461
    purchase rate, 462
    reasonably acceptable documents, 465
    subject to the buy-in, 464
    trade-specific other terms of trade, 464
settlement issues, 390–392
using leverage, 400–401
volatility, 393–394
Local currency tranches, 115
Lock-up agreement, 544, 571
London Interbank Offered Rate (LIBOR),
    19, 31–32, 389, 644, 771, 779, 882
    in advance rates, 308
    in arrears rates, 306–308
    breakfunding, 138–139
    business-day conventions, 132–133
    collateralized loan obligations (CLOs),
        675, 677
        fallback language, 698–699, 700
    computation of interest and fees, 131
    default rates, 128
    Eurodollar deposits, 122–123
    Eurodollar market disruption, 136–137
    illegal loans and, 137
    interest rate pricing, 119–123
    known-in-advance aspect, 299
    lender offices, 133
    loan conversion, 121–122
    minimums, multiples, and frequency
        of loans, 115–116
    rate architecture, 300–302
    as reference rate, 297
    swingline loans, 107
    transition process away from, 124–125,
        297–298

    versus SOFR, 298–300
    voluntary repayments, 145–146
    winding down legacy loans using,
        309–310
    yield protection, 133–141
    See also Secured Overnight Financing
        Rate (SOFR)
Long-only investors, 546
Long-term liquidity projections, 575–577
Lookback, 304
Low-carbon development, 839
Low-carbon economy, 821
Low-carbon transition scenario, 821
Lower-carbon business activities, 817
Low- to mid-single-B area, 772
LSTA. *See* Loan Syndications and Trading
    Association (LSTA)
LSTA's Complete Credit Agreement Guide,
    Second Edition, The, 105

M

M&A. *See* Mergers and acquisitions (M&A)
MAC. *See* Material adverse change (MAC)
Macroeconomic factors, loan trading, 403
Mahindra & Mahindra, 765
Main Street Lending Program (MSLP), 26
Management overview, 52
Managing agents, 44, 45
Mandatory prepayments, 146–153
    application among tranches, 153–154
    asset sales, 148–150
    borrowing base, 147–148
    casualty events, 150
    change of control, 151–153
    cover for letters of credit, 154
    cross-default clause, 245
    currency adjustments in multicurrency
        deals, 153
    debt and equity issuances, 150
    excess cash flow, 150–151
    revolving clean-downs, 147
    second lien loans, 367
Manufacturers Hanover, 7, 8
Margins, 125–126
    regulations, 179–180
Margin stock, 179–180
Market-centric economies, 730–733
Market constituencies, 831–838
Market Entity Identifier (MEI), 83
Market-oriented economy, 730
Mark-to-market (MTM) process, 411–412, 418

Mark-to-market securities, 731
Master Confidentiality Agreement, LSTA, 73
Master limited partnership (MLP), 783
Material adverse change (MAC), 164–167
  events of default, 250
Material adverse effect (MAE), CLO, 692
Material covenants, 241
Materiality, 63–64, 814
Material nonpublic information (MNPI), 60, 66, 69–70, 394–395
Matters Requiring Attention (MRAs), 715
Maturity
  collateralized loan obligations (CLOs), 698
  date advancement, 144
  extension of, 536
Maximum volatility, 644
Meiji Yasuda Life Insurance, 760
Mergers and acquisitions (M&A), 216–217, 408, 444, 799
Merrill Lynch, 8
Metrics Credit Partners, 760
Mezzanine debt, 779
Mezzanine funds, 771, 776, 799
Mezzanine lenders, 775
Mid-capitalization–sized companies, 738
Middle market, 793–794
  borrowers, 777
  businesses, 777
  CLOs, 663
  corporate lending market, 773
Middle market lending, 769
  business development companies, 780–783
  characteristics, 769–772
  commercial and industrial lending, 772–775
  covenant-lite, 785
  history and evolution, 783–788
  sponsored or private equity–backed lending, 776–780
Middle market loans, 37
Miners, 880
Minimums
  assignment, 270–271
  in credit agreements, 115–116, 270–271
Mitigation
  specific economic risks, 834
  systemic sustainability, 831
MNPI. *See* Material nonpublic information (MNPI)
Model Credit Agreement Provisions, 134
Monetary Authority of Singapore, 756

Moody's credit ratings, 812
Moody's ESG methodology, 826–828
Most-favored-nation (MFN) clause, 113
Multicurrency facilities, 114–115, 338
Multiple borrowers, 155–156
Multiples, in credit agreements, 115–116
Multitranche agreements, 262
Mutual funds, 34, 641, 642
  bank loan, 40
  Global Financial Crisis (GFC) of 2007–2008 and, 21–22

N

NAIC Risk-Based Capital Charge Revision, 700
Naked sales, 568
Naked short sales, 395–396
National Center for the Middle Market, 769
Nationally Determined Contributions (NDCs), 820
Nationally Recognized Statistical Rating Organizations (NRSROs), 24
Negative covenants, 58
  affiliate transactions, 225–226
  amendments to organic documents and other agreements, 226–227
  breaches of, 241–242
  debt, 214–216
  derivatives, 220–221
  disqualified stock, 216
  dividend blockers, 224
  dividends and equity repurchases, 222–223
  fiscal periods and accounting changes, 227–228
  fundamental changes, asset sales, and acquisitions, 216–217
  guarantees or contingent liabilities, 221
  investments, 218–220
  lien covenant, 211–213
  lines of business, 220
  modification and prepayment of other debt, 224–225
  negative negative pledge or burdensome agreements, 213–214
  sale-leasebacks, 217–218
  tax-sharing payments and permitted tax distributions, 223–224
Negative negative pledge, 213–214
Negative pledge, 211
Net asset values (NAVs), 412

Index

Network for Greening the Financial System (NGFS), 835
Net-zero emissions by 2050, 821, 836, 848
New York Civil Practice Law and Rules (CPLR), 163, 233
New York Debtor and Creditor Law, 256
New York General Obligations Law, 279–280
Niche investors, 41
No burdensome restrictions representations, 187
No conflict representations, 176–177
No deemed waivers, 275–276
Nodes, 880
No fiduciary duty, agency provision, 258–259
Nonbank institutional loan investors, 738
Nondisclosure agreements (NDA), 331–332
Nonguarantor restricted subsidiaries, 602
Non-LBO corporate issuers, 736
Nonratable committed loans, 114–115
Nonrefundable fees, 863
Non-sponsored borrowers, 776
Non-sponsored C&I lending, 773
Non-sponsored syndicated loan issuance, 774
Non-U.S. borrowers. *See* Foreign borrowers
Non-USD syndicated institutional leveraged loan market, 729
   approved and nonapproved assignee lists, 740–741
   bank-centric versus market-centric, 730–733
      regulatory environment, 733–735
   buyers, 738–740
   categories, 735
   issuance and issuers, 735–738
   restructuring, 744
   secondary trading, 741–743
   structural differences, 743–744
Non-use fee, 48
Notes, 271–272
Notice provisions, 275
Notice to and undertaking by recipients, 69
Nuisance investor, 552–553

O

Offering material and preparation, 51–53
Office of Foreign Assets Control (OFAC), 178
Offshore banks, 34
Offshore Wind Farm (OWF), 761
One Form of Action Rule, 276
OpenLaw, 885
Operating cash flow, 197
Opportunity realization, 831
Opt-outs, prepayment, 154–155
Order of priority, 352–353
Ordinary course items, 219–220
Organisation for Economic Co-operation and Development (OECD), 239, 249
Original issue discounts (OIDs), 48, 779
Originate-to-distribute model, 791
Origination fees and costs, 863–866
Overall performance, 809
Over-collateralization (OC)
   ratio, 684–687
   test, 684, 692–694
Overleveraging, 19–20
Ownership interest, 710

P

Paid-in-kind (PIK), 462, 800
Pamfleet, Schroder, 758
Pandemic loans, 749
Par Confirm, 883–884
Parent company debt, 223
Pari passu ranking, 189
Paris Agreement, 372, 812, 820, 835–837, 839, 847, 848
Par loans documentation, 466–467
Participants, loan market, 877–878
   AML and KYC issues, 886–887
   blockchain basics, 878–880, 882–886
   competition law issues, 887
   corporate governance, 887
   public or permissioned ledger, 880–881
   smart contracts, 881–886
Participation, 268, 273–274
   agreements, 873–874
   fees, 865
   loan settlement, 460–461
Parties to the financing, 55
Par trades, 472
Paycheck Protection Program (PPP), 26
Payments
   dates, interest, 126–127
   default in, 240
   demand for, from guarantors, 254
   dividend, 222
   guarantee of, 231

Payments *(Cont.)*
  immediately available funds, 142
  loan closing documentation, 471–472
  prepayments
    mandatory, 146–154
    opt-outs, 154–155
    premiums, 155
    voluntary, 145–146
  provisions, 55
  repayment
    of other debt in conditions precedent, 167–168
    scheduled, 143–144
  time of, 142–143
Peer-to-peer network, 879
Pension Benefit Guaranty Corporation (PBGC), 182–183, 247
Pension funds, 34, 738, 776
  financial condition representations, 182–183
Perfection of collateral, 162–163, 188
Performance-based financial covenants, 200–202
Performance covenants, 197–198
Performance letters of credit, 108
Permitted acquisitions covenants, 216–217
Permitted encumbrances, 211, 212
Permitted tax distributions, 223–224
Personal jurisdiction, 281–282
Phase II report, 169
Phase I report, 169
Physical climate risks, 821–824
PIK. *See* Paid-in-kind (PIK)
PIK interest, 538
Plan of reorganization, Chapter 11 bankruptcy, 568–569
Pledges, loan, 274–275
Policies and procedures, 67
Popular vote system, 365–366
Portfolio management, 641, 655–656
  credit-risk, 5
  credit selection, 646–650
    company-specific analysis, 647–648
    credit agreement and collateral analysis, 648–649
    relative value comparison, 649–650
  defined, 5
  ESG considerations, 657–658
  first applications of, 5
  investment in loans, 641–643
  loan portfolio, 643–645
  manager, 643
  performance attribution, 654–655
  portfolio construction, 651–653
  return and volatility goals, 643–644
  risk analytics, 653–654
  total portfolio risk, 645–646
Post-crisis loan volatility, 751
Post-downgrade trading restrictions, CLO, 695
Post-petition interest of secured creditors, 349
PRB. *See* Principles for Responsible Banking (PRB)
Preferential transfer, Chapter 11 bankruptcy, 560–561
Preferred dividends, 222–223
Preferred stock, 866
Prefunding agreement, 117
Premiums, prepayment, 155
Prenegotiated and prepackaged plans, Chapter 11 bankruptcy, 572
Prepayments
  expectations, 869
  mandatory, 146–154, 245
    second lien loans, 367
  and modification of other debt, 224–225
  opt-outs, 154–155
  premiums, 155, 743
  voluntary, 145–146
    second lien loans, 367
Pricing, loan, 118–132
  business-day conventions, 132–133
  defined, 45
  flex, 47–48
  interest, 118–125
    accrual conventions, 132
    applicable margins, 125–126
    base rate, 118–119
    computation, 131
    default, 12–13, 127–128
    fees and, 128–131
    LIBOR rate, 119–123
    other pricing options, 124
    payment dates, 126–127
  loan closing documentation, 471–472
  spread, 45–46
Primary allocations
  background, 83–84
  buyer's responsibilities, 88–99
    delayed compensation and cost-of-carry calculations, 90–94
    delayed compensation commencement, 89–90, 96–99
    with respect to allocations under the protocol, 88–89

with respect to pre-trigger and post-trigger trades under the protocol, 95–96
confirmation, 87
introduction to, 82
Post-Trigger, 84
Pre-Trigger, 84
seller's responsibilities, 84–87
   delivery of information to ESP, 84–85
   notification of effective date and funding date, 86–87
   primary allocation confirmation, 87
   submission of allocation details to the ESP, 86
   submission of the assignment agreement to the ESP, 85–86
Trigger Date, 84
Primary broker-dealer securities inventory, 793
Primary market, 31–102
   benchmarks, 100–102
   brief history of loans in, 32–34
   credit analysis, 42–43
   distinguishing attributes of, 31–32
   forms used in, 54–58
      commitment letter, 54–55
      fee letter, 55
      term sheet, 55–58
   funding and breaking into the secondary market, 54
   information distribution
      categories of confidential information in the syndicated loan market, 61–68
      introduction and scope, 59–61
      LSTA guidance and trading documents, 68–75
      methods of managing risk, 75–81
      what is "material" and who makes that determination, 63–64
      why it matters, 64–67
   investors, 37–42
      meeting, 53
   issuers, 37
   offering material and preparation, 51–53
   primary allocations, 82–99
   public-private nature of, 331–332
   ratings process, 50–51
   sales process, 53–54
   secondary market versus, 400–401
   size and scope, 34–37
   syndication process, 43–48
   syndication strategy, 49–50

Prime rate, 19, 118–119
Prime rate funds, 40
Principal-agency settlement issue, 459
Principles for Responsible Banking (PRB), 836
Principles for responsible investment (PRI), 835
Priority claims, Chapter 11 bankruptcy, 564
Private asset–based finance markets, 793
Private credit, 788, 791
   benefits of, 802–803
   considerations, 803–805
   environmental, social, and governance (ESG) factors, 803
   evolution of, 791–796
   funds, 763–764
   lenders, 791
   private credit landscape, 796–799
   and public market, 792
   returns, 800
   structural considerations, 799–801
Private debt funds, 341. *See also* Direct lending
Private equity, 785
   backed issuers, 777
   backed M&A financings, 787
   firms, 776
   sponsor-driven buyouts, 799
   sponsorship, 736, 777, 785
   and firm-wide recoveries, 517–520
Private market, loan market as, 32
Private-side investors, 52
Proceeds covenant, 209
Proceeds Letter, 468–469
Process agents, 280–282
Product safety, 824
Projected financial overview for private side investors, 52
Project finance
   commercial banks traditional role, 370–372
   defined, 369–370
Projections, 182
   restructuring, 591–593
Promissory notes, 163
Proofs of claim, agency provision, 260
Property disclosures, 185–186
Property maintenance covenants, 206–207
Proprietary trading, 333
Pro rata commitment, 39
Pro rata investors, 38–39

Pro rata sharing principle, 610–615
Pro rata tranches, 107
Pro rata treatment
  credit agreements, 264
  secondary loan market, 407
Protection Buyer, loan credit default swap (LCDS), 622–623
Protection Seller, loan credit default swap (LCDS), 622–623
Prudential guidance, 835
Public- and private-side LMPs, 62–63
Public BDCs, 782
Public market, loan market as, 32
Public or permissioned ledger, 880–881
Public policy, 705–706
  history of regulation of syndicated loan market, 706–707
  judicial rulings, 720
    Kirschner v. JPMorgan, 722–724
    RadLAX Gateway Hotel, LLC v. Amalgamated Bank, 720–721
    Stonehill Capital Management v. Bank of the West, 721–722
  laws from Congress, 707–708, 711
    risk retention, 708–709
    Volcker rule, 707, 710–711
  LSTA in, 706, 724–725
  rules and guidance originating from the regulators, 711–712
    Congressional Review Act, 717–719
    leveraged lending guidance, 712–713
    2013 Guidance, 713–716
Public-private nature of primary and secondary loan market, 331–332
Purchase and Sale Agreement (PSA), 468–469
Purchase money debt, 214
Purchase money liens, 212–213

Q

Qualified institutional buyers (QIBs), 322
Quantitative tools, 479–507
  CLO life cycles and management style, 481
  compliance tests, 482–483
  Diversity Score, 494–495, 501–502, 675
  open-source code, 503–507
  portfolio optimization, 492–500
  robust credit research, 479–480, 502–503
Quiet or well-behaved second lien, 345–346, 355–356

R

RadLAX Gateway Hotel, LLC v. Amalgamated Bank, 720–721
Ratable committed loans, 114
Ratings
  bank risk, 8–9
  primary market process, 50–51
Ratings agencies, 836–837
Ratio debt basket, 216
RCP. *See* Representative concentration pathway (RCP)
Real estate investment trust (REIT), 783
Real property
  disclosures, 185
  rules governing foreclosure on, 354–355
Reasonable acceptable documents, 465
Rebound of 2003, 21
Recessions
  COVID-19 and, 18, 25–26
  Global Financial Crisis (GFC) of 2007–2008, 8, 20–24
Recovery
  after the Global Financial Crisis (GFC) of 2007–2008, 22–24
  of bank loans, 9–10
  factors affecting rates of, 553–554
  research on, 8–9
  on revolving versus term loans, 514–515
  Ultimate Recovery Database, 507–525
    firm-wide recoveries varying little based on PE sponsorship, because of tactics, 517–520
    milestone and lessons from, 508–510
    Moody's related publications, 521–525
    recoveries negatively influenced by default rates, regardless of industry, 515–517
    significance of debt structure, 510–515
Recovery Rate, 675
Reducing revolving credit facility, 110–111
Reference entity, loan credit default swap (LCDS), 622–623
Reference rate
  in advance rates, 308
  architectures, 300–302
  in arrears rates, 306–308
  drafting in post-LIBOR world, 306
  future-proofing fallback language, 309
  LIBOR as traditional, 297
  LIBOR versus SOFR as, 298–300
  strengths and weaknesses of alternatives to LIBOR, 302–304

Index 939

transition process, 297–298
winding down legacy LIBOR loans, 309–310
Refinancing, 755–756, 773, 799
  collateralized loan obligations (CLOs), 692
  loan credit default swap (LCDS), 625–626
Refinery and Petrochemical Integrated Development (RAPID) project, 762
Refinitiv LPC, 773
Refinitiv's Sponsored Middle Market League Tables, 716
Regional and national banks, 771
Registration
  Rule 4(a)(7), 322
  Rule 144A, 322
  Section 4(a)(2), 321–322
Regulation, 746–747
  after 1987 stock market crash, 7
  anticorruption laws, 178
  collateralized loan obligations (CLOs) impact on, 699–700
  federal securities laws, 316–317
  foreign assets control, 178–179
  governing law and, 279–280
  highly leveraged transaction (HLT), 7, 409
  loan credit default swap (LCDS), 626–627
  loans covered by securities laws, 271–273
  loan total return swaps (LTRS), 637–638
  margin, 179–180
  state blue-sky laws and FINRA rules, 327–330
  syndicated loan market, 24
  U.S. Risk Retention, 699–700
Regulation U, 179–180
Regulation X, 179–180
Regulators, 835–836
Relationship-oriented banks, 32
Relative value comparison, 649–650
Reliance, agency provision, 259
Remedies for events of default, 251–254
  accelerate, 252–253
  cumulative, 276
  demand cover for letters of credit, 253–254
  demand payment from guarantors, 254
  institute suit, 254
  rescission, 254–255
  stop lending, 251–252
  terminate commitments, 252
Reorganization plan, Chapter 11 bankruptcy, 568–569

Repayment
  of other debt in conditions precedent, 167–168
  scheduled, 143–144
Representations, 171–190
  collateral packages, 235
  completeness of disclosures and, 187–188
  and disclosures regarding the business, 184–187
  financial condition, 180–184
  flip, 465
  foreign borrowers, 188–190
  inaccuracy of, 240–241
  legal matters, 175–180
  perfection and priority of security, 188
  status as senior indebtedness, 188
  step-up, 470
  and warranties, 56
Representative concentration pathway (RCP), 822
Reputational and relationship risk, 67
Request for proposal (RFP) process, 371
Rescission, 254–255
Rescue lending, 549
Residential mortgage-backed securities (RMBS), 22
Restricted lists, 77
Restricted securities, 318–319
Restricted subsidiaries, 191–193
Restructuring, 744
  and bank loan risk, 8–9
  collateralized loan obligations (CLOs), 697–698
  comprehensive, 533, 543–545
  loan settlement, 466
  projections development, 591–593
  retention of management in, 583–584
  valuation in, 589–590, 597–598
Restructuring support agreement (RSA), 544, 571, 572
Retention of management, 583–584
Return and volatility goals, 643
Return maximization, 799
Returns
  with bank loans, 11–28
    bankruptcy, 8–9
    collateral, 9
    default vs. recoveries, 9–10
    Global Financial Crisis (GFC) of 2007–2008 and, 8, 20, 21–22
    historical review of, 11–18
    rebound of 2003 and, 21
    timeline of risk and, 19–20

Returns *(Cont.)*
  bank loan total return swaps (LTRS), 631–633
Revolving credit facilities, 31, 106
  borrowing bases, 147–148
  clean-downs, 147
  defined, 338
  letters of credit, 109
  promissory notes, 163
  recovery rates on, 514–515
  scheduled repayment, 143–144
  swingline loans, 107–108
  term-out options, 114
Revolving Credit Facility form, 885, 886
Riegle-Neal Act, 783
Risk
  with bank loans, 11–28
    bankruptcy, 8–9
    collateral, 9
    default *vs.* recoveries, 9–10
    Global Financial Crisis (GFC) of 2007–2008 and, 8, 20, 21–22
    historical review of, 11–18
    rebound of 2003 and, 21
    timeline of return and, 19–20
  credit
    avoidance of, 5
    bank, 3–9
    with bank loans, 9–10
    default events, 9–10
  for LMPs
    regulatory, 65–66
    reputational and relationship, 67
Risk management
  information distribution, 75–81
    agents and, 77–78
    information barriers, controls, policies, and procedures, 76–79
    lenders and, 76–77
    production and distribution of evaluation materials, 79–81
    use of nonreliance acknowledgments and waivers, 75–76
  loan liquidity, 433–435
Risk retention, 739
  rules, 707, 708
Risk Retention Rule, 24
Risks, uncertainty on probability and timing, 818–819
Rolling periods, 197–198
RSA. *See* Restructuring support agreement (RSA)

Rule 4(a)(7), 322, 324
Rule 10b-5 disclosure letter, 187, 319–320, 325–326
Rule 144A
  antifraud liability considerations, 327
  blue-sky laws and, 328
  capital markets, 379
  exemption, 318–319
  origination/syndication process, 331
  practice under, 319–320
  registration requirements, 322–324
  secondary loan market, 413

S

Sale-leasebacks, 217–218
Sales process, syndicated loans, 53–54
Sanctions, economic, 178–179
SBIC Lenders, 771
Scenario analysis, 819–820, 824
  carbon transition risk, 820–821
  physical climate risks, 821–824
Schedules repayment, 143–144
SDS. *See* Sustainable Development Scenario (SDS)
SEC. *See* Securities and Exchange Commission (SEC)
Secondary loan activity, 764–765
Secondary loan market, 399–400, 405–476
  COVID-19-induced price volatility, 435–441
  leading up to the Global Financial Crisis, 415–419
  loan liquidity risk management, 2018, 433–435
  next phase of market expansion, 429–433
  origins, 408–410
  primary market versus, 400–401
  public-private nature of, 331–332
  recovery period and subsequent liquidity test of 2011, 425–429
  settlement, 455–476
  terminology and background, 407
  through lens of S&P/Leveraged Loan Index (LLI), 23, 441–455
    covenant-lite norm, 448–449
    Global Financial Crisis, 427
    loan market performance, 450–452
    single B domination, 446–447
    spread to maturity, 452–455
    tech boom, 444–446

by the turn of the century, 410–415
2007 and the Global Financial Crisis of 2008, 419–425
Secondary trading, 332–333
Second lien loans, 337–368
   advance consent
      to DIP financing approved by first lien lenders, 361–362
      to sales of collateral, 360–361
      to use of cash collateral, 360
   asset-based lending, 340–341
   background information, 346–355
   cross-defaulted to first lien loans, 367–368
   debtor-in-possession financing, 342
   defined, 342–343
   difference between debt subordination and lien subordination, 347–348
   direct lending, 341–342
   enforceability of intercreditor agreements, 362
   first lien lender permission for, 345–346
   junior credit acceptance of, 346
   limits on amount of future, 366
   limits on amount of future first lien loans, 366
   mandatory prepayments, 367
   pros and cons, 344–345
   restrictions
      in bankruptcy proceeding, 358
      with respect to period before bankruptcy filing, 356–357
   restrictions on assignability, 367
   right to purchase first lien loans, 363–364
   secured creditors rights in bankruptcy, 348–351
   separate set of security documents, 364–365
   silent/quiet/well behaved, 345–346, 355–356
   structuring, 355–368
   types of syndicated loan facilities and, 338–340
   voluntary prepayment, 367
   voting, 365–366
   waiver of rights, 358–359
Section 4(a)(1) exemption, 329
Section 4(a)(2) exemption, 317–319, 329
Section 4(a)(7) exemption, 318–319
Secured claims, Chapter 11 bankruptcy, 563–564
Secured creditors
   ending up worse than unsecured creditors, 362–363

   relationships between multiple, at law absent an intercreditor agreement, 352–355
   rights in bankruptcy, 348–351
Secured Overnight Financing Rate (SOFR), 298
   in advance rates, 308
   in arrears rates, 306–308
   collateralized loan obligations (CLOs), 677
   compounded in advance, 303
   credit-sensitive rates (CSRs), 303–304
   daily compounded, 305–306
   daily simple, 304–305
   future-proofing fallback language, 309
   LIBOR versus, 298–300
   rate architecture, 300–302
   rates known in advance, 302–304, 310–311
   as risk-free rate, 299
   term, 302–303
   See also London Interbank Offered Rate (LIBOR)
Securities (trading instruments)
   federal securities laws, 316–317
   notes as, 271–272
   restricted, 318–319
   Rule 144A
      exemption, 318–319
      practice under, 319–320
   secondary trading, 332–333
   Section 4(a)(1) exemption, 329
   Section 4(a)(2) exemption, 317–319, 329
   Section 4(a)(7) exemption, 318–319
Securities Act of 1933, 316–317
   antifraud liability considerations, 325–326
   blue-sky laws and, 327–328
   registration requirements, 321–323
   Section 4(a)(2) exemption, 317–319
   security defined, 271
Securities and Exchange Act of 1934, 61, 67, 316–317
   antifraud liability considerations, 325–326
   loan credit default swap (LCDS) regulation, 626–627
   public-private nature of primary and secondary loan market and, 332
   reporting companies under, 239
   security defined, 271
   valuation methodology rules, 413
Securities and Exchange Commission (SEC), 482, 709, 780, 795, 855
   Chapter 11 bankruptcy exchanges, 573
Securitization of loans, 316–330

Select mergers, 773
Sendai Framework for Disaster Risk Reduction, 839
Senior indebtedness, 188
Senior managing agents, 45
Separately managed accounts (SMAs), 641, 642
Service of process, 282
Setoffs, 255–256
    sharing of, 264–265
Settlement, loan trading, 390–392, 455–476
    allocation, 459
    amendments/restructures, 466
    assignment fees, 475
    assignment or participation, 460–461
    background, 456
    buy-in/sell-out (BISO), 466
    closing documentation, 466–475
    confirmation, 457–459
    flip representations, 465
    forms of purchase, 460–466
    interest treatment, 462–464
    loan credit default swap (LCDS), 626
    pretrade issues, 456–457
    principal-agency issue, 459
    purchase amount/type of debt, 461
    purchase rate, 462
    reasonably acceptable documents, 465
    subject to the buy-in, 464
    trade-specific other terms of trade, 464
Settlement-date accounting, 874
Settlement issues, loan trading, 390–392
Settlement liquidity, 656
Severability, 284–285
Several liability, 110
Shared National Credit (SNC), 34, 719
Short-selling, 395–396
SIBOR (Singapore), 124
Signatures, electronic, 286
Silent second lien, 345–346
Siliconware Precision, 761
Singapore, 761–762
Single passport, 733
Size of transaction, syndication process and, 49
SLL. *See* Sustainability-linked loan (SLL)
Smaller private credit platforms, 771
Smart contracts, 881–882, 885
Social Loan Principles, 749
SOFR. *See* Secured Overnight Financing Rate (SOFR)
Soft call, 155
Solvency, 168, 183–184

South and Southeast Asia loan market, 762–763
Sovereign borrowers, 190
Sovereign immunity, 283
Sovereign wealth funds, 738
Specialized events of default, 250
Specified Acquisition Agreement Representations, 172–173
S&P/LSTA Leveraged Loan Index (S&P/LSTA LLI), 644
S&P/LSTA LLI. *See* Leveraged Loan Index (LLI)
Sponsored borrowers, 776
Sponsored lending, 776–777
Sponsor-focused senior debt, 799
Spread, 45–46, 125–126
    collateralized loan obligations (CLOs), 698
    Leveraged Loan Index (LLI) and, 452–455
Spread for the rating approach, 649, 650
Spread per unit of leverage approach, 649, 650
Springing liens, 236
Stakeholder capitalism, 833
Stalking-horse bidder, 568
Standard and Poor's (S&P), 794
Standard Terms and Conditions, 73–75, 87, 457–459
Standby letters of credit, 108
Standstill period, 357, 365
State blue-sky laws, 327–330
Stated Policies Scenario (STEPS), 820–821
Step-up representations, 470
Stock dividends, 222
Stonehill Capital Management v. Bank of the West, 721–722
Subinvestment-grade loan market, 641
Subject-matter jurisdiction, 281, 282
Subordination, debt, 347–348
    by majority consent, uptiering, 615–617
Subrogation, 232
Subsidiaries, 185
    covenants, 219
    generally, 191
    restricted and unrestricted, 191–193
    right to designate additional borrowers, 290
    significant, 193
Subsidiary debt, 215
Substantive consolidation, 208–209
Successor agents, agency provision, 260–261
Successor/refinancing events, loan credit default swap (LCDS), 625–626

Suit, institution of, 254
SunGard conditionality, 172–174
Superpriority claims, Chapter 11
    bankruptcy, 565
Survival clause, 286–287
Sustainability, 830, 838–840
  bonds, 831, 832
  finance, 828
  indicator, 846
  investing, 812
  investment strategies, 811
  materiality assessment, 845
  profile, 809
  ratings agencies, 836–837
Sustainability-linked bonds, 842
Sustainability-linked loan (SLL), 748, 830,
    831, 832, 845, 849–850
  COVID-19 pandemic, 851–852
  credit crisis and reinforcing esg
    framework, 852–854
  credit-risk discussions, 854–856
  financing conversation and ESG, 856–857
  metrics and other factors, 850–851
  principles, 832–833
Sustainable Development Goals, 838–839
Sustainable Development Scenario
    (SDS), 821
Sustainable Finance Disclosure
    Regulation, 749
Sustainable lending/loans, 748–749,
    828–830, 834, 841
  additional drafting and diligence
    considerations, 840–848
  companies, 837
  credit providers, 836
  drafting considerations, 840
    accurate reporting, 844–845, 847–848
    consequence of breach, 843–844
    green loan, elements of, 843
    identification, 843
    inaccurate reporting, 848
    independent review of reporting, 845
    initial benchmark, 847
    KPI selection, 845–846
    pricing incentive, 847
    proceeds, use of, 843
    public disclosure of sustainability
      targets and progress, 842–843
    report review, 848
  green loans and sustainability-linked
    loans, 830–831
  investors, 834–835
  market constituencies, 831–838
  ratings agencies, 836–837
  regulators, 835–836
  sustainability, 838–840
Swingline loans, 107–108, 338
Syndicated loans, 4, 6, 408
  agency provisions, 261
  categories of confidential information,
    61–68
  defined, 34
  forms used, 54–58
  funding and breaking into the secondary
    market, 54
  investor meeting, 53
  letters of credit, 108–109
  leverage buyouts, 37
  loan credit default swap (LCDS), 625
  LSTA guidance regarding trading, 71–72
  offering material and preparation,
    51–53
  public-private nature of primary and
    secondary loan market, 331–332
  ratings process, 50–51
  regulation of, 24–25
  sales process, 53–54
  strategy, 49–50
  syndication process, 43–48
  types of facilities, 338–340
  See also Loan Syndications and Trading
    Association (LSTA); Secondary
    loan market
Syndication agents, 44, 45
Syndication fees, 864–865
Syndication process, 43–48
  agent titles, 44–45
  different types of fees, 48
  leader arrangers and agents, 44
  league tables, 44
  pricing, 45–47
  pricing flex, 47–48
Synthetic funds, 34

T

Tag-along debt, 211–212
Taiwan loan market, 760–761
Task Force on Climate-related Financial
    Disclosures (TCFD), 749, 812
Taxes
  loan total return swaps (LTRS), 637
  payment covenants, 207–208
    tax-sharing and permitted tax
      distributions, 223–224

Taxes *(Cont.)*
  representations, 182
    for foreign borrowers, 189
  yield protection, 139–141
Tax-sharing payments, 223–224
Tech sector, 444–446
Terminating commitments, 111
  upon events of default, 252
Term loan B (TLB), 39, 729, 732
Term loans, 106, 339, 777
  delayed-draw, 340
  recovery rates on, 514–515
Term-out options, 114, 338–339
Terms and amounts of the facilities, 55
Terms and conditions, 52
  LSTA standard, 73–75
  Term sheet, 55–58
Thermal coal industry, 825
The Sustainability Accounting Standards Board, 814
Third-party guarantor, 870
13-week liquidity forecasts, 575–577
360-degree risk assessment, 817
364-day facilities, 144–145
Three-statement model, 591–592, 594
Time of payment, 142–143
Timing to close, 49
Tippers and tippees, 66
Title to property disclosures, 186
Total portfolio risk, 645
Total return swaps (TRSs), 422–423, 862
Trade Confirmation/Purchase and Sale Agreement, LSTA, 73–75
Trade date accounting, 874
Trade tension between Australia and China, 755
Trading flexibility, CLO, 695–696
Trading gains, CLO, 695
Trading liquidity, 655–656, 782
Tranches
  application of prepayments among, 153–154
  A and B loan, 106–107
  collateralized loan obligations (CLOs), 667, 675–677
  incremental facilities, 112–113
  local currency, 115
  most-favored-nation (MFN) clause, 113
  multitranche agreements, 262
  pro rata, 107
Trans-European Automated Real-time Gross Settlement Express Transfer [TARGET2] payment system, 142

Transferee, 872
Transfer loan in European secondary market, 742
Transferor, 872
Transfers and servicing, 871
Transition-focused green loans, 844
Troubled Assets Relief Program (TARP), 23
Troubled debt restructurings, 870–871
True-up mechanism, 237

U

U.K. Bribery Act 2010, 178
Ultimate Recovery Database, 507–525
  firm-wide recoveries varying little based on PE sponsorship, because of tactics, 517–520
  milestone and lessons from, 508–510
  Moody's related publications, 521–525
  recoveries negatively influenced by default rates, regardless of industry, 515–517
  significance of debt structure, 510–515
Undertakings for the Collective Investment in Transferable Securities (UCITS) funds, 738
Underwrite-to-distribute model, 776
Underwritten versus best efforts, 49
Unexpired leases, 565–566
Uniform Commercial Code (UCC), 161, 173, 274, 353
  rules governing foreclosure on collateral under, 354
Unmatured default, 239
Unrestricted subsidiaries, 191–193, 602
Unsecured claims, Chapter 11 bankruptcy, 564–565
Unsecured creditors, 351–352
Upfront fees, 48, 112, 113, 128, 141, 288, 779
Upstream due diligence, 469
Upstream guarantees, 233–235
Uptiering
  exchanges, 538–541
  under separate facility, 615–617
  transactions value diminution, 608–610
  withing same credit agreement, 610–615
USA PATRIOT Act, 169–170, 179, 287
U.S. Bankruptcy Code, 707
U.S.–China political tensions, 751, 758
Use restrictions, 293
U.S. Risk Retention regulation, 699–700
U.S. Sovereign Immunity Act of 1976, 189

Index

U.S. Trustee Program, 558–559
Utilization fees, 129–130

V

Valuation, restructuring, 589–590, 597–598
Variable interest entity (VIE) accounting model, 872
Venue requirements, 282–283
Victory City International, 765
Visitation rights, 205
Volatility
   COVID-19-induced price, 435–441
   loan trading, 393–394
   post-financial crisis, 751
Volcker Rule, 24, 333–334, 707, 710–711, 787, 793
   collateralized loan obligations (CLOs), 699
Voluntary default, 246
Voluntary international standards, 749
Voluntary prepayments, 145–146
   second lien loans, 367
Voting, 261–264
   affected lender concept, 262–263
   basic rule, 261–262
   collateral security, 236, 263–264
   and confirmation, Chapter 11 bankruptcy, 569–570
   loan total return swaps (LTRS), 636–637
   multitranche agreements, 262
   popular vote system, 365–366
   by various classes of creditors, 365–366

W

Wachovia, 8
Waivers, 231
   of jury trial, 283

Walmart's Project Gigaton plan, 837
Watch lists, 77
Waterfalls, 255
   collateralized loan obligations (CLOs), 681–684
We Are Still In, 837
Weighted average cost of capital (WACC), 594–595
Weighted Average Life (WAL), 675
Weighted Average Rating Factor (WARF), 483–490, 675
Weighted Average Spread (WAS), 483, 484–490, 675
Welfare plans financial condition representations, 182–183
Wells Fargo, 8
When-issued trading, 54, 82
Who-can-object covenants, 206–208
Wind farm, 839
Working capital, 773
Working capital debt, 214–215
World Economic Forum, 834

Y

Yank-a-bank provision, 289–290
Yield, bank loan total return swaps (LTRS), 631–633
Yield protection, 133–141
   breakfunding, 138–139
   capital costs, 136
   Eurodollar market disruption, 136–137
   illegality, 137
   increased costs, 134–136
   taxes, 139–141

Z

Zhaoheng Hydropower Holdings, 766